Donum Balticum

Donum Balticum

To Professor Christian S. Stang

on the occasion of his seventieth birthday

15 March 1970

Edited by

Velta Rūķe-Draviņa

Almqvist & Wiksell

Stockholm

Printed in Sweden by

Almqvist & Wiksells Boktr. AB, Uppsala 1970

CONTENTS

TABULA GRATULATORIA

ANNA ĀBELE
Latvijas Ūniversitāte

MOSHÉ ALTBAUER
The Hebrew University
Jerusalem

VYTAUTAS AMBRAZAS
Lietuvos TSR Mokslų Akademija
Lietuvių kalbos ir literatūros instirutas

HENNING ANDERSEN
Harvard University
Slavic Department

PAUL ARISTE
Eesti NSV Teaduste Akadeemia

PEETER ARUMAA
Stockholms Universitet

ROBERT AUSTERLITZ
University of California
Department of Linguistics

LUCIA BALDAUF-JURGUTYTĖ
Universität München

BALTISCHES FORSCHUNGS-
INSTITUT
Bonn

THE BALTIC INSTITUTE IN
SCANDINAVIA
Stockholm

ALFRED BAMMESBERGER
Universität Freiburg
Sprachwissenschaftliches Seminar

ÉMILE BENVENISTE
Collège de France
Paris

KNUT BERGSLAND
Universitetet i Oslo

HANS HOLM BIELFELDT
Deutsche Akademie der Wissenschaften zu Berlin

HARALDS BIEZAIS
Donnerska institutet för religionshistorisk och kulturhistorisk forskning
Åbo Akademi

HENRIK BIRNBAUM
University of California, Los Angeles
Department of Slavic Languages

ENDRE BOJTÁR
Institut d'Histoire Littéraire de l'Académie Hongroise des Sciences
Budapest

SPRACHWISSENSCHAFT-
LICHES INSTITUT DER
UNIVERSITÄT BONN

x

CARL HJ. BORGSTRØM
Universitetet i Oslo
Lingvistisk institutt

TAMARA BUCH
The Hebrew University
Jerusalem

WITOLD CIENKOWSKI
Uppsala Universitet
Slaviska institutionen

ÉTIENNE DECAUX
École Nationale des Langues orientales vivantes
Paris

GIACOMO DEVOTO
Unione Accademica Nazionale
Roma

KĀRLIS DRAVIŅŠ
Lund

EDGARS DUNSDORFS
University of Melbourne

IVAN DURIDANOV
Sofijski Universitet

RAINER ECKERT
Karl-Marx-Universität
Leipzig

TREVOR G. FENNELL
The Flinder University of South
Australia, School of Language and
Literature

GORDON B. FORD, Jr.
Northwestern University
Department of Linguistics

INGER FRØYSET
Norsk Målførearkiv
Oslo

ARNE GALLIS
Universitetet i Oslo
Slavisk-baltisk institutt

PAUL GARDE
Aix-en-Provence

ALFRĒDS GĀTERS
Hamburg

JURIS GRĪNBERGS-GREENE
Edinburgh

RASMA GRĪSLE
Riga

DAVID GEORGE GUILD
University of Edinburgh
Department of Russian

SPRACHWISSENSCHAFT-
LICHES SEMINAR
DER UNIVERSITÄT
GÖTTINGEN

SEMINAR FÜR ALLGEMEINE
UND VERGLEICHENDE
SPRACHWISSENSCHAFT
UNIVERSITÄT HAMBURG

ERIC P. HAMP
University of Chicago
Department of Linguistics

MICHAŁ HASIUK
Uniwersytet im. Adama Mickiewicza w Poznaniu

EDITE HAUZENBERGA-
ŠTURMA
Sprachwissenschaftliches Institut
der Universität Bonn

KRISTINE HELTBERG
Odense Universitet

ANNE MARIE HINDERLING-
ELIASSON
Universität Regensburg

ROBERT HINDERLING
Universität Regensburg

ERICH HOFMANN
Universität Kiel

VYACHESLAV VS. IVANOV
Institut russkogo jazyka
Akademii Nauk SSSR

ROMAN JAKOBSON
Harvard University and Massachusetts Institute of Technology

BENJAMIŅŠ JĒGERS
Northern Illinois University
De Kalb

ANDREJS JOHANSONS
Stockholms Universitet
Religionshistoriska institutionen

PETRAS JONIKAS
University of Chicago

SIMAS KARALIŪNAS
Lietuvos TSR Mokslų Akademija
Lietuvių kalbos ir literatūros insti-
tutas

KONSTANTĪNS KARULIS
Riga

JONAS KAZLAUSKAS

Vilniaus Valstybinis V. Kapsuko
universitetas
Lietuvių kalbos katedra

VALENTIN KIPARSKY
Helsingin Yliopisto

ANTANAS KLIMAS
University of Rochester
Department of Languages and Lin-
guistics

JOHANN KNOBLOCH
Sprachwissenschaftliches Institut
der Universität Bonn

STANISŁAW FRANCISZEK
KOLBUSZEWSKI
Uniwersytet im. Adama Mickie-
wicza w Poznaniu

KOSTAS KORSAKAS
Lietuvos TSR Mokslų Akademija
Lietuvių kalbos ir literatūros insti-
tutas

ERIC KRAG
Universitetet i Oslo
Slavisk-baltisk institutt

CZESŁAW KUDZINOWSKI
Uniwersytet im. Adama Mickiewicza w Poznaniu

TERĒZE LAZDIŅA
London

WINFRED PHILIPP LEHMANN
The University of Texas at Austin
College of Arts and Sciences

JULES F. LEVIN
University of California, Riverside
Department of German and Russian

SEMINAR FÜR VERGLEI-
CHENDE SPRACHWISSEN-
SCHAFT DER JUSTUS
LIEBIG-UNIVERSITÄT
Giessen

JUOZAS LINGIS
Uppsala universitet
Slaviska institutionen

JAN PETER LOCHER
Université de Neuchâtel

SIRI SVERDRUP LUNDEN
Universitetet i Oslo
Slavisk-baltisk institutt

IRMGARD MAHNKEN
Sprachwissenschaftliches Seminar
der Universität Göttingen

JIŘÍ MARVAN
University of California, Davis
Department of German and Russian

TERJE MATHIASSEN
Universitetet i Oslo

VYTAUTAS MAŽIULIS
Vilniaus Valstybinis V. Kapsuko
universitetas
Lietuvių kalbos katedra

WERLAND MERLINGEN
Universität Wien

KAZYS MORKŪNAS
Vilniaus Valstybinis V. Kapsuko
universitetas
Lietuvių kalbos katedra

JULIUS MÄGISTE
Lunds Universitet

SLAVISCH-BALTISCHES SE-
MINAR DER UNIVERSITÄT
MÜNSTER

SÉMINAIRE DE LANGUES ET
LITTÉRATURES BALTIQUES
ET SLAVES UNIVERSITÉ
DE NEUCHÂTEL

LINGVISTISK INSTITUTT
UNIVERSITETET I OSLO

JAN OTRĘBSKI
Uniwersytet im. Adama Mickiewicza w Poznaniu

RADEGAST PAROLEK
Filosofická fakulta
University Karlovy
Praha

JÜRGEN PRINZ
West-Berlin

EDUARDS PUTNIŅŠ
Riga

MARTA RASUPE
Roma

G. REDARD
Universität Bern
Institut für Sprachwissenschaft

ERHARD RIEMANN
Universität Kiel

HELGE RINHOLM
Kristiansand

JAROSLAV B. RUDNYĆKYJ
University of Winnipeg
Department of Slavic Languages

MARTA RUDZĪTE
Pētera Stučkas Latvijas Valsts Uni-
versitāte
Latviešu Valodas Katedra

VELTA RŪĶE-DRAVIŅA
Stockholms Universitet

RUHR-UNIVERSITÄT, BOCHUM
SPRACHWISSENSCHAFT-
LICHES INSTITUT

ALGIRDAS SABALIAUSKAS
Lietuvos TSR Mokslų Akademija
Lietuvių kalbos ir literatūros institutas

JAN SAFAREWICZ
Uniwersytet Jagielloński
Kraków

INSTITUT FÜR ALLGEMEINE
UND VERGLEICHENDE
SPRACHWISSENSCHAFT
AN DER UNIVERSITÄT
SALZBURG

HERMANN SCHALL
Berlin-Adlershof

WILLIAM R. SCHMALSTIEG
The Pennsylvania State University
Department of Slavic Languages

WOLFGANG P. SCHMID
Universität Göttingen
Sprachwissenschaftliches Seminar

KARL HORST SCHMIDT
Ruhr-Universität, Bochum
Sprachwissenschaftliches Institut

ALFRED SENN
University of Pennsylvania

GEORGE Y. SHEVELOV
Columbia University in the City of
New York
Department of Slavic Languages

FANNY DE SIVERS
Centre National de la Recherche
Scientifique, Paris

ANDERS SJÖBERG
Stockholms universitet
Slaviska institutionen

SLAVISKA INSTITUTIONEN
VID STOCKHOLMS
UNIVERSITET

SLAVISK-BALTISK INSTITUTT
Universitetet i Oslo

SEPPO SUHONEN
Helsinki

OSWALD SZEMERÉNYI
Universität Freiburg
Sprachwissenschaftliches Seminar

VLADIMIR N. TOPOROV
Institut slavjanovedenija i balkanistiki
Akademii Nauk SSSR

PAVEL TROST
Filosofická fakulta
University Karlovy
Praha

OLEG N. TRUBAČĚV
Institut russkogo jazyka
Akademii Nauk SSSR

VINCAS URBUTIS
Lietuvos TSR Mokslų Akademija
Lietuvių kalbos ir literatūros institutas

ANDRÉ VAILLANT
Collège de France et
L'École des Hautes-Études
Paris

A. VALECKIENĖ
Lietuvos TSR Mokslų Akademija
Lietuvių kalbos ir literatūros institutas

OTTO A. WEBERMANN
Universität Göttingen

SEMINAR FÜR INDOGERMA-
NISCHE UND ALLGEMEINE
SPRACHWISSENSCHAFT AN
DER UNIVERSITÄT WIEN

TEODOLIUS WITKOWSKI
Deutsche Akademie der Wissenschaften zu Berlin

VILMOS VOIGT
Eötvös Loránd Tudományegyetem
Folklore Tanszék
Budapest

D. S. WORTH
University of California, Los Angeles
Department of Slavic Languages

LUDWIK ZABROCKI
Uniwersytet im. Adama Mickiewicza
w Poznaniu

TADEUSZ ZDANCEWICZ
Uniwersytet im. Adama Mickiewicza
w Poznaniu

Z. ZINKEVIČIUS
Vilniaus Valstybinis V. Kapsuko
    universitetas
Lietuvių kalbos katedra

MOSHÉ ALTBAUER

A Previously Unnoticed Slavic and Baltic Dativus Auctoris

In my researches on the East-Slavic Bible translations from Codex #262 (of the Central Library of the Lithuanian Academy in Vilnius)[1] I noted a calque of the Hebrew Biblical construction: *passivum + dativus auctoris* in Ruth III: 10: *blahoslovena ty hospodu dočko moja*, rendering the Hebrew בְּרוּכָה אַתְּ לַיהוָֹה בִּתִּי (*bᵉrûḵā 'att la'dônāj bitti*, literally 'you are blessed to the Lord, my daughter').

Since I have no doubt that the translation from Codex #262 was based on the original Hebrew text of the Bible, I consider *blahoslovena ty hospodu* as a typical (for Jewish translation technique) syntactical calque of the Hebrew Biblical construction, which has been defined by Gesenius[2] as follows: "The efficient cause (or personal agent) is, as a rule, attached to the passive by לְ (thus corresponding to the Greek and Latin dative)".

When I compared the phrase *blahoslovena ty hospodu* in the translation of Codex #262 with the same phrase in earlier and contemporary East-Slavic Bible translations, I found the same construction of *passive participle + dative*, as for instance:

(1) in the so-called "Cyrillic"[3] translation of the book of Ruth: *bl(ago)-s(lo)vena ty g(ospode)vi dšti*;

(2) in the so-called "Glagolitic"[3] version of this book: *blagoslovena ti gospodevě bogu dešti*;

(3) in a translation from the (unpublished) Codex #52 of the Academy Library in Vilnius: *bl(ago)s(lo)vena ty g(ospode)vi dšti*;

(4) also in the first printed Russian Bible (the so-called Ostrog Bible of 1580–1581) we find the same construction: *b(lago)s(lo)vena ty g(ospode)vi b(og)u dšči moja.*

All these translations were based on the Septuagint, which rendered the Hebrew construction by participle and dative; this construction was genuine in Greek,[4] and appeared not only in translated texts. The phrase under consideration (Ruth III: 10) was translated in the Septuagint: Εὐλογημένη σὺ τῷ κυρίῳ θεῷ, θύγατερ.

In addition to the cited phrase there are seven other examples in the Old Testament of the passive participle of the root B–R–Ḳ ('bless'), in singular and plural, and dativus auctoris: Gen. XIV: 19; Jud. XVII: 2; Ruth II: 20; 1 Sam. XV: 13; XXIII: 21; 2 Sam. II: 5 and Psalms CXV: 15 (in the Septuagint-CXIII: 23). In all these examples we find the same Biblical construction in Greek: *passive participle + dative*, and the same construction again in the *older* East-Slavic Bible translations based on the Septuagint (apart from some errors, as for instance in Ruth II: 20, where the dative form was changed into a nominative, as in Codex #52 and in the Ostrog Bible: *bl(ago)-s(lo)venь estъ g(ospod)ь* 'blessed is the Lord').

The Vulgate renders the Biblical construction three times only: Gen. XIV: 19 (*Benedictus Abram Deo excelso*); Jud. XVII: 2 (*Benedictus filius meus Domino*); and 2 Sam. II: 5 (*Benedicti vos Domino*); in the five other examples there is a prepositional construction: *a Domino* (four times) and *in Domino* (once). While Catholic Bible translations render the Vulgate (as for instance the Polish Bible of Jakub Wujek, 1599), the Arian translation of Szymon Budny (1572) renders the original Hebrew construction: *Błogosławionaś ty Jehowie, coro moia*, whereas in Wujek's translation we find: *Błogosławiona jesteś, córko, od Pana* as in the Vulgate: *Benedicta, inquit, es a Domino*.

In my paper "O technice przekładowej Szymona Budnego" I mentioned, perhaps for the first time,[5] this use of *dativus auctoris* in Slavic.

The *later* Slavic Bible translations replaced the borrowed dative construction by a Slavic *instrumental* construction, as for instance in the so-called "Synodical" Church-Russian Bible of 1856: *blagoslovena ty Gospodemъ Bogomъ*, or by a prepositional construction with a genitive form in the newer Russian Bible translation (of the American Bible Society): *blagoslovena ty ot Gospoda*. We find a similar *instrumentalis auctoris* in an Old Polish phrase: *bogiem sławiena*. In the latest Polish Catholic version (the so-called "Millenium Bible"[6]) a preposition with accusative occurs six times: *przez Jahwe* and an *active* phrase twice: *Niech was Jahwe błogosławi* (1 Sam. XXIII: 21). Also, in the new Croatian Bible translation[7] there is no longer a dative construction, but active phrases occur six times and prepositional constructions twice: *Od Boga Svevišnjega* (Gen. XIV: 19) and *Blagoslovljen da si od Jahve!* (1 Sam. XV: 13).

The above-mentioned versions for the *passive* and *dativus auctoris* are reflected also in the *Baltic* Bible translations.

In the (unpublished) *Lithuanian* translation by Bretkunas[8] (1590) we read as follows:

(1) "Perſʒegnotas buk Abrame aúkſchcʒiaúſúam Diewúi" (Gen. l.c.)
(2) "Perſʒegnotas buk mana sunaù PONUI" (Jud. l.c.);

(3) "Perſʒegnotas ... PONUI" (Ruth II: 20);
(4) "Perſʒegnota bùk tu' PONUÍ mana Dùkte" (ibid., III: 10);
(5) "Perſʒegnotas bùk tu PONUI" (1 Sam. XV: 13);
(6) "Perſzegnoti este ius' PONUI" (ibid., XXIII: 21);
(7) "Perſʒegnoti este ius' PONUI" (2 Sam. II: 5);
(8) "Iús este perſzegnoti Wiéſchpaties [genetivus singularis!] (Psalms CXV: 15).

In the two *printed* Lithuanian Bibles, that of the Berlin[9] edition of 1858 and that of the British and Foreign Bible Society[10] (I cite the edition of 1949), there is a similar *dative* construction (in the examples 1–7), with addition of the word *Dievui* after *Ponui* and, as in BRETKUNAS' Bible, a *genitive* in Psalm CXV: 15, which renders the same genitive form in Luther's German Bible (1545):

Jus este peržegnotieji Pono Dievo, as in Luther's version: *Ir seid die gesegneten des HERRN*.[11]

In the only *Latvian* Bible[12] available to me there are further examples of the same type:

Swehtihts laid irr Ahbrams tam
wiſſu=augſtakam STIPRAM DEE=
WAM,

"Swehtihts laid irr Ahbrams tam wiſſu-augſtakam STIPRAM DEEWAM" (Gen. XIV: 19), and the same dative form in Jud. XVII: 2; Ruth II: 20, III: 10; 1 Sam. XV: 13, XXIII: 21; 2 Sam. II: 5: "...*tam KUNGAM*", and again, as in the Lithuanian translation, a *genitive* form in Psalms CXV: 15:

Juhs eſſat ta Kunga ſwehtiti

When we compare the above examples from the Lithuanian and the Latvian Bibles with the Hebrew original and the Septuagint on the one hand, and on the other hand with the German Bible of Luther (which renders the dative form seven times and uses a genitive once), we may presume that Luther's German version was the source of the *passivum + dativus auctoris* construction in the cited Baltic Bible translations.

As in the newer Slavic translations, the new Catholic Lithuanian[13] translation avoids the borrowed syntactical construction: *passivum + dativum*, and uses a more indigenous *genitive* form:

Tebūna Abramas palaimintas augščiausiojo Dievo (Gen. l.c.); *Būk Viešpaties palaimintas, mano sūnau* (Jud. l.c.); *Palaiminta tu Viešpaties, dukte*

4

(Ruth III: 10); *Būkite Viešpaties palaiminti* (1 Sam. XXIII: 21); *Jūs esate palaiminti Viešpaties* (Psalms CXV: 15) or an *active* phrase, as in Ruth II: 20: *Tegul jį Viešpats palaimina.*

Since I have no access to a newer Latvian Bible, I cannot establish whether the traditional Biblical construction has been replaced by a more genuine Latvian construction.

Notes

1. Cf. my paper presented at the VIth International Congress of Slavists, Prague, August 1968: "Some Methodological Problems in Research of the East-Slavic Bible Translations (Vilnius Codex #262)", *Israeli Slavists' Committee*, Jerusalem, 1968; s. note 6.

2. Gesenius' Hebrew Grammar, ed. by E. Kautzsch, Second English Edition by A. E. Cowley, Oxford, 1910 (reprint of 1956), Ch. 121 f, p. 389. Cf. also Г. М. Глускина, „О выражении логического субъекта при помощи предлога л в страдательной конструкции в сирийском языке", *Краткие сообщения Института Народов Азии, АНСССР, 86 История и филология Ближнего Востока. Семитология*, 1965, Москва, 2–24.

3. The so-called "Cyrillic" version of the book of Ruth is that of Undolskij's and Grigorevič's manuscripts from the 15th century. The "Glagolitic" version is that of the Glagolitic Codex of Vit from Omyshl' of 1396 (ed. by J. Vajs in Glagolitica, v. III, 1905). Our quotations come from A. Mikhaylov's „Древне-славянский переводъ кн. Руеь" in *Русский филолог. Вѣстникъ*, LX (1908), 1–36.

4. Cf. for instance: F. Blass–A. Debrunner, *Grammatik des neutestamentlischen Griechisch*, 1949⁸, 88–89, § 191; E. Schwyzer, *Griechische Grammatik* II, 1950, 149–150; J. Humbert, *Syntaxe grecque*, 1960³, Ch. 479, p. 287.

5. In *Studia Językoznawcze poświęcone S. Rospondowi*, Wrocław, 1966. As far as I can establish on the basis of the Slavic literature available to me, this *dativus auctoris* has passed unnoticed; it is mentioned neither by Miklosich and Vondrák, nor by Klemensiewicz (in his "Składnia historyczna języka polskiego" in *Gramatyka historyczna języka polskiego*, with T. Lehr-Spławiński and S. Urbańczyk 1955) although such a construction appears in the extant parts of the oldest Polish Bible, the so-called Queen Sophia's Bible, e.g., in Gen. XIV: 19 *Blogoſlawyon abram bogu nawiſſzemu*, which is based on the Czech Old Testament of Carda: *Blahoſlaueny Abram bohu naywyſſiemu*; the two editors of the new edition of Queen Sophia's Bible (P. I 1965; P. II 1967), S. Urbańczyk and V. Kyas, have failed to explain this *dativus auctoris*. Nor did S. Severyanov in his concordance to the Psalterium Sinaiticum (ed. by him in 1922) explain the OCS phrase *Bl(agoslove)stvenii vy g(ospod)ju* (as in Psalterium Bolon.). Likewise, M. Brodowska did not mention the dativus auctoris construction in Old Polish in her paper "Historyczne procesy przekształceń celownika" in *Studia z filologii polskiej i słowiańskiej*, I (1955). H. Birnbaum cited (in "On Deep Structure and Loan Syntax in Slavic", *Studies in Slavic Linguistics and Poetics in Honor of Boris O. Unbegaun*, 1968, 21–31) the chapter "Naśladowanie konstrukcji biblijnej: *Passivum +*

Dativus" in my paper on Budny's translation technique and other materials on this phenomenon communicated to him by me (cf. note 18, p. 31). It remains to mention that in the comprehensive monograph of H. Bräuer *Der persönliche Agens beim Passiv im Altbulgarischen* (edited by the Akademie der Wissenschaften und der Literatur in Mainz, Jahrgang 1952-Nr. 3, Wiesbaden 1952) there is not a single Slavic example of the *passivum + dativus auctoris* construction.

6. *Pismo Święte Starego i Nowego Testamentu w przekładzie z języków oryginalnych,* Pallotinum, Poznań, 1965.

7. *Biblija, Stari i Novi Zavjet, Stvarnost HKD Sv. Cirila i Metoda,* Zagreb, 1968. In the earlier Croatian Bible translation by Daničić (I cite the edition of BFBS) there are three examples of a dative construction (Gen. XIV: 19); 1 Sam. XV: 13 and 2 Sam. II: 5.

8. *BIBLIA tatai esti Wiſsas Schwentas Raſchtas, Lietúwiſchkai pergŭltitas per Joana Bretkŭnam Lietúwos Plebona Karaliacziúie.* 1590. I cite from the microfilm of the manuscript of Bretkunas' translation kindly delivered to the National and University Library in Jerusalem by the Staatsarchiv in Göttingen.

9. *Bybelēs, Tai esti: Wissas Szwentas Rasztas Seno ir Naujo Testamento, Lietuwiszkay perstattytas,* Berlynè, 1858.

10. *Biblija tai esti visas Šventas Raštas Seno ir Naujo Testamento į Lietuviškają kalbą perstatytas,* BFBS, 1949.

11. Cited from *Biblia Germanica* 1545 (Eine faksimilierte Ausgabe der Lutherbibel von 1545), Württembergische Bibelanstalt, Stuttgart, 1967. This *passivum + dativus auctoris* construction is well known in Modern German: *sei mir gegrüsst* or *seid mir gegrüsst, befreund'te Scharen* (Schiller). Martin Buber in his Bible translation into German (Die Schriftwerke von Martin Buber, Hegener Verlag, Köln, 1963) uses the Hebrew construction: *Gesegnet seiet Ihm* seven times; only in Gen. XIV: 19 is there a different interpretation of the Hebrew text.

12. *BIBLIA, tas irr: Ta Swehta Grahmata, jeb Deewa Swehti Wahrdi ... Tahm Latweeſchahm Deewa Draudſibahm par labbu istaiſita.* Peterburgâ, pee T. Rutta un dehla, 1825.

13. *Šventasis Raštas Senojo Testamento I–II. Vertē ir komentorių pridējo ... Juozapas Jonas Skvireckas,* Roma, 1955–1958.

V. AMBRAZAS

Dėl lietuvių kalbos netiesioginės nuosakos

(modus relativus)

Netiesiogine nuosaka dažnai vadinamos lietuvių kalbos dalyvių vardininko formos, einančios tariniu ir žyminčios netiesiogiai patirtus ar abejojamus veiksmus[1], pvz.: *girdėjau, (kad) jis gyvenąs (gyvenęs, gyvensiąs) mieste; rytoj jie čia būsią.* Šia reikšme jos paliudytos nuo XVI–XVII a., plg.: [Jėzuitai] *mokin | žmogu ... galinti pradeti prisiwertima | kurj potam Dwassia schwen-toij buk padedanti ir pabeigenti* (S. Vaišnoras, „Žemčiūga ...", 69). Panašiai vartojami dalyviai ir latvių kalboje (vad. atstāstamā izteiksme), tiktai joje greta būt. 1. dalyvių vardininko (pvz.: *kâdam tễvam bijuši trîs dễli*) jau randame įsigalėjusias naujesnes es. ir būs. 1. nelinksniuojamų dalyvių formas (pvz.: *aiz priekiem es dzieduot*)[2]. Apie atitinkamų konstrukcijų buvimą prūsų kalboje aiškių duomenų neturime.

Dėl lietuvių ir latvių kalbų netiesioginės nuosakos kilmės yra įvairių nuomonių. B. Delbrückas[3] ir J. Endzelynas[4] manė, kad ji galėjusi išriedėti iš tokių accusativus cum participio konstrukcijų, kaip *girdėjau tėvą atei-sianti*, greta kurių buvę vartojami sinonimiški pasakymai *girdėjau, (kad) tėvas ateis.* E. Tanglis[5], o pastaruoju metu ir I. Marvanas[6] kildina net. nuosaką iš nominativus cum participio konstrukcijos, kuri, jų manymu, atsiradusi iš acc. c. part. taigi: *sako save atėjusį → sakosi atėjęs → sako, (kad) tėvas atėjęs.* Net. nuosakos ryšį su nom. c. part. buvo nurodęs ir A. Potebnia[7]. J. Kazlauskas mano, kad net. nuosaka galėjusi susidaryti iš perifrastinio optatyvo su dalyviais, perkėlus optatyvinės reikšmės krūvį iš dalelytės *bi* į dalyvį[8]. V. Pisanis iš viso abejoja indoeuropietiška net. nuosakos kilme ir, gretindamas su estų kalbos modus obliquus dalyvinėmis formomis (pvz.: *isa tulevat* 'tėvas ateinąs'), įžiūri čia Pabaltijo finų kalbų įtaką arba seną bendrą baltų ir finų izoglosą[9].

Lietuvių kalbos dalyvių sintaksinėje sistemoje net. nuosakos formos išsiskiria dviem svarbiausiais požymiais — predikatyvine funkcija sakinyje, artima verbum finitum, ir netiesiogiai patirto ar abejojamo veiksmo reikšme. Remiantis šia reikšme, net. nuosaka dažniausiai ir kildinama iš acc. ir nom. c. part. konstrukcijų, kur dalyvis daugeliu atvejų taip pat žymi perpasakotą veiksmą. Tačiau dalyvio funkcija tose konstrukcijose, kaip ir pati jų vidinė struktūra, ryškiai skiriasi. Acc. c. part. pagal savo sandarą ir kilmę neatsiejama nuo veiksmažodžių valdomų vardažodinių junginių, vad. dvejybinio galininko (plg.: *mačiau jį važiuojantį* ir *mačiau jį piktą*), o nom. c. part. — nuo konstrukcijų su predikatyviniu atributu einančiais būdvardžiais, plg.: *jis sakėsi (jautėsi) sergąs* ir *jis sakėsi (jautėsi, atrodė) sveikas*. Nors semantinis ryšys tarp acc. bei nom. c. part. ir net. nuosakos neabejotinas, bet sunku įrodyti, kad vien dėl analogijos su sinonimiškais veiksmažodiniais pasakymais iš tokių hipotaktinių konstrukcijų, kaip *sakė jį sergantį* arba *jis sakėsi sergąs*, būtų galėję susidaryti parataktiniai pasakymai, kaip *sakė, jis sergąs*, arba savarankiški sakiniai su dalyviniais tariniais, kaip *tėvas sergąs*. Ieškant net. nuosakos pamato lietuvių kalboje, pravartu atkreipti dėmesį į tas konstrukcijas, kuriose dalyvių vardininkai turi tą pačią funkciją, kaip sudarydami net. nuosaką, ir skiriasi tik tam tikrais reikšmės atspalviais. Keletą tokių atvejų čia ir norime paminėti.

Prie net. nuosakos glaudžiai šliejasi esamojo laiko neveikiamieji dalyviai su afiksu *be-*, vartojami staigiai, netikėtai ar pavėluotai patirtiems, nuostabą bei kitas emocijas keliantiems veiksmams reikšti, pvz.: *Po trijų dienų tėvai žiūri — visas žalčių pulkas bešliaužiąs į jų kiemą* (Lietuvių tautosaka, III, 296); *su nagais besanti motriška — krepšį padirbo* (Kuršėnai)[10]. Šie dalyviai pagal reikšmę dabar koreliuojami ne tiek su būtuoju ar būsimuoju pradėtiniu laiku (plg. *buvo* ar *bus bešliaužiąs*), kiek su būtojo kartinio laiko dalyviais (plg. *atšliaužęs*), kurie, eidami be jungties, turi lygiai tokias pat modalines reikšmes, pvz.: *Žiūrėk, koks didelis lazdynas išaugęs!* (Kupiškis); *koki čia graži brolija susiėjusi!* (Kvėdarna), plg. taip pat atitinkamas neveikiamųjų dalyvių formas: *nueina, žiūri — jo brolis prie kaladės prikaltas* (Griškabūdis). Skirtumas čia yra tas, kad tariniu einantys es. 1. dalyviai su *be-* dabar vartojami tik su minėtais modaliniais atspalviais, o būt. k. 1. dalyviams tie atspalviai yra fakultatyvūs. Tačiau liaudies dainose, kurių ritminė struktūra įgalina išlaikyti daugiau sintaksinių archaizmų, es. 1. veik. dalyviai su *be-* dažnai neturi kokios nors apčiuopiamos modalinės reikšmės ir žymi tiesiog dabartyje trunkantį veiksmą, pvz.: *Ką tas bernužėlis bemislijąs, ką jaunasis bedūmojąs, aukso žiedą, žiedą bekaldinąs ir mano vardužį bemušdinąs* (V. Kalvaičio dainos, 163). Tokios vartosenos senumą patvirtina ir XVI a. raštai, plg.: *Amβina Tewa sunelis / Edzosu nu begulis* (Mažvydas, 181); čia dalyvis su *be-* kartais pavartojamas net su jungtimi, pvz.: *Saka ... Jog est begulis edzosu* (Mažvydas 193) ir tuo būdu visai įeina į sudurtinių laikų sistemą.

Tie būt. k. 1. veik. dalyviai, kurie savo modalinėmis reikšmėmis atitinka es. 1. veik. dalyvius su *be-*, dabartinėje lietuvių kalboje yra taip pat labai susiję su sudurtiniais laikais ir daugeliu atvejų gali būti suprantami kaip esamojo atliktinio laiko formų ekvivalentai, plg.: *aš jau pavargęs ir aš jau esu (buvau, būsiu) pavargęs*; panašiai ir es. bei būt. 1. nev. dalyviai, plg.: *čia bulvės sodinamos (sodintos)* ir *čia bulvės yra (buvo, bus) sodinamos (sodintos)*.

Be platesnio konteksto net neįmanoma pasakyti, ar, pavyzdžiui, pasakyme *brolis į miestą išvažiavęs* dalyvio vardininkas turi staigiai patirto, netikėto, perpasakoto veiksmo reikšmę ir laikytinas net. nuosakos forma, ar čia turime tiesiog tariniu einantį dalyvį, dabartinės kalbos atžvilgiu sietiną su esamuoju atliktiniu laiku (*yra išvažiavęs*): abiem atvejais dalyvio forma ir perfektinė reikšmė yra tokia pat. Kai modaliniai atspalviai silpniau jaučiami, dalyvis esti artimesnis sudurtiniam laikui, kai jie ryškesni — netiesiogine nuosakai, plg.: *Dabar visa prapuolę* (A. Baranauskas); *Ale sriubą, mama, tai gerą išvirus* (Skaisgirys, Joniškio r.); *Ar jai sakęs, ar ne — vis tiek* (Žemaitė). Kokių nors specialių gramatinių rodiklių, skiriančių staigiai patirto, netikėto, pabrėžiamo veiksmo reikšmės dalyvius nuo kitų, nėra. Tiktai perpasakoto ar abejojamo veiksmo reikšmė gali būti išryškinta prie būt. k. 1. veikiamųjų ir visų laikų neveikiamųjų dalyvių pridedamomis es. 1. veik. dalyvio *esąs, -anti* formomis: *jis esąs pavargęs, esąs mušamas, esąs muštas* — tuo būdu sudaromos es. 1. sudurtinės net. nuosakos formos. Mat, es. 1. veik. dalyvis, eidamas tariniu, dabartinėje lietuvių (kaip ir latvių) kalboje visada turi modalinę reikšmę, tad yra nedviprasmiškas ir gali būti net. nuosakos rodikliu. Tačiau tokia jo išskirtinė būklė irgi nėra senoviška — tai rodo senųjų raštų ir tarmių sudurtinės formos *est essąs* (Vaišnoro „Žemčiūga …“, Praef., 13), *sanczios yrá* (Daukšos Postilė, 206), *búwo êssą* (t. p., 164)[11], *bus nēsą* (Kuliai) ir pan., taip pat specialesnę reikšmę gavę es. 1. veik. dalyviai su *be-*.

Latvių kalboje net. nuosakos ryšys su kitais tarinio funkciją atliekančiais dalyviais matyti ir iš formalių požymių: net. nuosakos reikšme vartojami būt. 1. veik. dalyviai, artimi sudurtiniam esamajam laikui (pvz.: *reiz uznācis sausums*), išlaikė linksnio formą, o labiau izoliuotos es. ir būs. 1. dalyvių formos yra praradusios fleksiją, sustabarėjusios.

Pati sudurtinių laikų sistema, prie kurios šliejasi tariniais einantys dalyviai (su modalinėmis reikšmėmis ar be jų), baltų kalbose yra nauja ir galutinai nesusiformavusi. Nėra jokio pamato manyti, kad dalyviai, einantys tariniu be jungties, tą jungtį kada nors būtų turėję ir praradę; priešingai, daugelio giminiškų kalbų istorija rodo, kad tas sakinio tipas, kuriame dalyviai, kaip ir kiti vardažodžiai, yra siejami su veiksniu be jungties, yra ne jaunesnis, o gal ir senesnis už veiksmažodinį tipą.

Reikšdami subordinuotą, antraeilį sakinio veiksmą, dalyvių vardininkai taip pat gali turėti predikatyvinę funkciją ir eiti verbum finitum atitikmenimis. Iš tokių atvejų visų pirma minėtinos dalyvių konstrukcijos su tam tikrais jungiamaisiais žodžiais — *kur, kiek, kada, iki, ligi*, įvardžio *kas* linksniais ir pan., pvz.: *vaikas ... turėjo duonos kiek noris* (M. Valančius); *žiūrėk ką daranti* (Skirsnemunė); *išgirsi ko negirdėjęs* (Žemaitė), taip pat po veiksmažodžio *būti: bus kas valgą, nėra kas darą* ir pan.[12] Šio tipo konstrukcijos, stabarėjančios ir nykstančios dabartinėje kalboje, žymiai plačiau paliudytos senuosiuose raštuose. Vidinė rekonstrukcija ir santykis su atitinkamais kitų, ypač slavų, kalbų faktais (s. sl. *žъnjọ ideže ne sěavъ* Assem. Mat. 25, 26 ir pan.) rodo jas esant sintaksiniais archaizmais, kuriuose išliko dalyvio, kaip antrojo — vardažodinio predikato, funkcija[13]. Kad tokios konstrukcijos susijusios su netiesiogine nuosaka, yra minėjęs jau A. Potebnia[14]. Tačiau netiesioginei nuosakai jos artimos tik tada, kai eina po kalbėjimą, jutimą, patyrimą ar mąstymą reiškiančių veiksmažodžių, pvz.: *ji priėjo prie to jaunikaičio ir ėmė pasakoti, ko ieškanti* (Liet. tautosaka, III, 290); turėdami skirtingą veiksmo subjektą, tokie dalyviai dabar visai nebesiskiria nuo net. nuosakos formų: *ūkininkas to pono paklausė, kurlink jis einąs* (Pakalviai). Tuo tarpu dalyviai, einantys po kitokios reikšmės veiksmažodžių, žymi subordinuotą veiksmą be jokių perpasakotos kalbos ar abejojimo atspalvių. Būt. k. 1. veikiamieji ir es. bei būt. 1. neveikiamieji dalyviai savo reikšme artimi sudurtinių laikų formoms, pvz.: *vaikai veža „diedelį" iš kur paėmę* (M. Katkus), plg.: *iš kur yra (buvo) paėmę; darau ką lieptas* (J. Baltušis), plg.: *ką buvau lieptas;* ypač su skirtingu veiksmo subjektu: *eina, kur budelis įsakęs* (Darbėnai), plg.: *kur yra (buvo) įsakęs.* Es. ir būs. 1. veik. dalyviai tokiose konstrukcijose, kaip *dirbk ką galįs* (M. Valančius), *kad tik ... jie susilauktų prie ko galvą priglausią* (J. Basanavičius, Mit. II 244) šiuo metu yra visai izoliuoti, stabarėja ir užleidžia vietą asmenuojamoms veiksmažodžių formoms, bet dar XVI–XVII a. jų vartojimas po *kas, kur, iki, net* ir kt. jungiamųjų žodžių buvo dėsningas ir įprastas. Iš konstrukcijų su jungiamaisiais žodžiais aiškiai matyti perpasakotą ir apskritai subordinuotą veiksmą žyminčių dalyvių reikšmės santykis. Net. nuosakai būdinga perpasakoto, abejojamo veiksmo reikšmė čia yra antrinė, priklausanti nuo veiksmažodžių leksinės raiškos, o šios reikšmės formos — tik tam tikras subordinuotą veiksmą žyminčių dalyvių pogrupis.

Pažymėtina, kad dalyviai su *kur, kaip, kas* ir kt. kartais pavartojami ir pagrindiniam veiksmui nusakyti su tam tikra emfaze ar emociniais atspalviais, pvz.: *Ką tu belaukęs senatvės? Kur jis geriau ras, ko jis nėjęs? Na, kur nesimeldęs, anoks maldininkas* (M. Katkus), plg. atitinkamus sustabarėjusius pasakymus ir be minėtų prieveiksmių ar įvardžių: *Nebebuvą* [=nebebus], *kad aš ąž jo eič* (Dusetos); *Nebegyvenąs* [=nebegyvensiu] *čia — kad tik šiuo kartu gerai pasibaigtų!* (Sudeikiai); *Versmė ją nematą tos apkiautėlės* (Kupiškis); taip pat reiškiant alternatyvą, pvz.: *šėręs nešėręs, nė kiek* [arklys] *nejuda* (Vabalninkas) ir pan.

Antra vertus, prie predikatyviškai pavartoto dalyvio jungtuku gali būti jungiamos ir asmenuojamosios veiksmažodžio formos; taip susidarė tokios konstrukcijos su *ir*, kaip *muzikantas atsisėdęs ir čyruoja* (Armoniškis), turinčios ryškių atitikmenų slavų kalbose (plg. s. sl. *i prizъvavъ oba na desęte i načętъ ję sъlati* Marc. 6, 7, Zogr. Mar.)[15]; atitinkamos sandaros pasakymai nesvetimi ir kitoms ide. kalboms[16].

Taigi lietuvių kalbos net. nuosaka yra glaudžiai susijusi su kitomis predikatyvinėmis konstrukcijomis, kuriose dalyvis pagal savo funkciją artimas verbum finitum. Tokios dalyvių funkcijos archaiškumą, be s. slavų ir gotų kalbų, rodo labai savarankiškas dalyvių vaidmuo Veduose ir Homero epuose; šiuo atžvilgiu simptoniškas ir kai kurių dalyvinių formų (pvz., slavų k. dalyvių su pries. *-l*) vėlesnis įtraukimas į veiksmažodžio paradigmas. Kas dabar įprasta vadinti netiesiogine nuosaka, iš tikrųjų yra specializuotas dalyvių predikatyvinės vartosenos atvejis, kuris nuo kitų skiriasi tik aiškiai apibrėžta netiesiogiai patirto ar abejojamo veiksmo reikšme.

Šios reikšmės įsigalėjimui svarbų vaidmenį turėjo suvaidinti nom. c. part. konstrukcija, kuria dažnai reiškiamas iš kitų lūpų girdėtas veiksmas, pvz.: *jis sakė(si) dirbęs*. Nom. c. part. ir net. nuosakos intensyviausio vartojimo sritis lietuvių k. tarmėse ryškiai sutampa — ji apima visą žemaičių tarmės plotą, vakarų ir vidurio aukštaičių šiaurinį pakraštį ir rytų aukštaičių šiaurės rytų kampą (maždaug ligi linijos Kupiškis — Anykščiai — Saldutiškis — Ignalina); abi konstrukcijos vartojamos ir vakarinėje bei pietinėje vakarų aukštaičių dalyje, vietomis ir dzūkuose[17]. Gyvojoje kalboje nom. c. part. neatsiejama nuo tokių parataktinių pasakymų, kaip *jis sakė(si)*, *daug dirbęs* (*dirbąs*), kur dalyvis sudaro atskirą predikatyvinį vienetą ir nuo kalbėjimą, jutimą, ar suvokimą žyminčio veiksmažodžio skiriamas intonacija (plg.: *jis sakė(si)*, *daug dirbo* ar *dirbu*). Šitokių pasakymų randame visose tarmėse, kur tik plačiau vartojama nom. c. part., pvz.: *sakės, daug darbo turįs* (Klaipėda); *mama sakė, kuone verkus, kaip karvę išvedė* (Pašvitinys); *girias, matęs Janikę* (Raudėnai) ir pan. Iš jų perpasakoto veiksmo reikšmė galėjo būti perkelta ir į nuo seno vartotus sakinius be asmenuojamųjų veiksmažodžio formų, kaip *jis daug darbo turįs, mama kuone verkus*. Acc. c. part., be abejo, taip pat stimuliavo modalinę predikatyvinių dalyvių vartoseną. Ide. kalbų istorija duoda ir daugiau pavyzdžių, kaip iš veiksmažodžių padarytos vardažodinės formos naujai įprasminamos pakitusioje sakinio sandaroje ir gauna modalinę reikšmę; čia gali prisiminti, pavyzdžiui, jau minėtų slaviškų dalyvių su *-l* virtimą atpasakojamąja nuosaka bei admiratyvu bulgarų kalboje arba supino panaudojimą tariamajai nuosakai liet. kalboje.

Netiesiogiai patirto ar abejojamo veiksmo reikšmė nėra išskirtinė veikiamųjų dalyvių ypatybė. Jau J. Jablonskis[18] gražiai parodė, kad tokią pat reikšmę turi ir predikatyviškai vartojamos nev. dalyvių bev. g. formos, dažnai einančios su subjekto kilmininku, pvz.: *gandai skelbė, kad esama ir užmuštų* (V. Mykolaitis-Putinas); *sako, šiąnakt vilkų būta* (Palūšė). Jos, beje, žymi ir netikėtą, pavėluotai patirtą, nusistebėjimą ar kitas emocijas žadinantį veiksmą, pvz.: *žiūrėk — ir jo čia esama* (J. Jablonskis); *o ten krūme kiškio sėdėta* (Suginčiai). Semantinis paralelumas su veikiamaisiais dalyviais čia akivaizdus, nors konstrukcijų sandara skirtinga. Tie patys veiksmo modaliniai atspalviai, kurie žemaičių tarmėje nusakomi tik veik. dalyvių vardininkais, aukštaičių tarmėse beveik visur (o daugelyje vietų — kartu su pastaraisiais) reiškiami nev. dalyvių bev. g. formomis, kurios tik retkarčiais eina veiksmažodžių valdomose konstrukcijose (pvz.: *parėjus radau ir Antano atvažiuota*, Juknėnai), o nom. c. part. irgi nebūdingos. Tačiau visai neabejotinas šių konstrukcijų artimumas sudurtinėms veiksmažodžių formoms, plg.: *čia, matyt, žmonių yr kada gyventa* (Žagarė); *jo jau buvo išeita* (Seirijai, Alanta).

Dalyvių modalinės reikšmės išsikristalizavimui galėjo būti palanki ir ta aplinkybė, kad, kaip įtikinamai parodė Chr. S. Stangas[19], su dalyvių vardininko formomis lietuvių kalboje nuo seno buvo perifrastiškai sudaromas optatyvas (**-bi negelbąs, *-bi nekėlęs*), t. y. toji nuosaka, kuria daugelyje giminiškų kalbų reiškiama netiesioginė kalba[20].

Čia probėkšmais paminėti net. nuosakos ryšiai su kitais tariniu einančiais dalyviais, mūsų manymu, leidžia spėti, kad šios nuosakos struktūrinį pamatą sudarė predikatyvinė dalyvių vartosena, paremta nominaliniu sakinio tipu. Greta verbalinių *sūnus kalba* tipo sakinių ide. prokalbėje, matyt, nuo seniausių laikų egzistavo tokie nominaliniai sakiniai, kaip *sūnus einąs* (plg. *sūnus geras*). Kintant sakinio sandarai, vieni tarinio funkciją atliekantys dalyviai galėjo būti įtraukti į veiksmažodinio tarinio formų sistemą, kiti — suartėti su antraeilį, dažnai perpasakotą veiksmą žyminčiomis konstrukcijomis ir gauti modalinę reikšmę. Apie finų kalbų vaidmenį šiame procese bus galima aiškiau spręsti tik palyginus vidinės rekonstrukcijos būdu atstatytas dalyvių sintaksines sistemas abiejose kalbų grupėse. Dėl struktūrinių skirtumų (estų k. dalyvių partityvas — liet. ir lat. k. dalyvių vardininko ir bev. g. vardininko–galininko formos) tiesioginis estų k. modus obliquus poveikis, bent jau lietuvių kalbai, atrodo sunkiai įtikimas. Tačiau visai galimas dalykas, kad prie savarankiškos dalyvių funkcijos išlikimo ir specifikos baltų kalbose nemaža prisidėjo senieji kontaktai su Pabaltijo finų kalbomis, pasižyminčiomis labai plačia bei įvairia dalyvinių formų vartosena.

Išnašos

1. Plačiau žr. J. Jablonskis, *Rinktinai raštai*, I, Vilnius, 1957, 522 tt.; E. Fraenkel, „Litauische Beträge", *IF*, XLXV, 44–45 su lit.

2. J. Endzelīns, *Latviešu valodas gramatika*, Rīgā, 1951, 976 tt.

3. B. Delbrück, *Vergleichende Syntax der indogermanischen Sprachen*, II, Strassburg, 1897, 491.

4. J. Endzelīns, *op. cit.*, 976.

5. E. Tangl, *Der Accusativus und Nominativus cum Participio im Altlitauischen*, Weimar, 1928, 47–51.

6. И. Марван, „О некоторых предикативных функциях литовского причастия", *Kalbotyra*, IV, 35–37; „К вопросу о лингво-географическом положении балто-славянских языков", *Baltistica*, V (1), 18.

7. А. А. Потебня, *Из записок по русской грамматике*, I–II, Москва, 1958, 231.

8. J. Kazlauskas, „Iš optatyvo istorijos", *Lietuvių kalbotyros klausimai*, IV, 87.

9. V. Pisani, „Zu einer Baltisch-Estfinnischen Partizipialkonstruktion", *Rakstu krājums veltījums ... Jānim Endzelīnam*, Rīgā, 1959, 215–217. Į latvių ir estų k. net. nuosakos panašumą dar 1935 m. atkreipė dėmesį P. Arumaa, žr. J. Lohmann, "Ist das idg. Perfektum nominalen Ursprungs?" *KZ*, LXIV, 46.

10. Žr. J. Jablonskis, *op. cit.*, 528; N. Sližienė, „Apie sudurtines pradėtines veiksmažodžių formas", *Lietuvių kalbotyros klausimai*, IV, 69 tt. su lit.

11. Daugiau pavyzdžių iš sen. raštų žr. N. Sližienė, „Lietuvių literatūrinės kalbos sudurtinių veiksmažodžių formų struktūra", *Lietuvių kalbotyros klausimai*, IX, 80; J. Palionis, *Lietuvių literatūrinė kalba XVI–XVIIa.*, Vilnius, 1967, 198.

12. Žr. J. Jablonskis, *op. cit.*, 460, 466, 474; E. Fraenkel, „Litauische Beiträge", *IF*, XLVI, 45 tt.; P. Skardžius, „Dėl pusdalyvių raidos", *Archivum Philologicum*, VI, 102 tt.; aut., „Lietuvių kalbos dalyvių konstrukcijos su jungiamaisiais žodžiais", *Lietuvių kalbotyros klausimai*, IX, 43 tt.

13. Aut., *op. cit.*, 58–62.

14. А. А. Потебня, *Из записок по русской грамматике*, I–II, Москва, 1958, 222 tt.

15. Plačiau apie tai žr. aut., *Baltistica*, I (1), 53–56 su lit.

16. Žr. Th. Forssmann, *Die Übertragung der griechischen Partizipialkonstruktionen in dem Ostromirschen Evangelium*, Strassburg, 1877, 15; L. Bednarczuk, „On certain participial constructions in Balto-Slavic, Germanic and Celtic", *Acta Baltico-Slavica*, III, 30–31.

17. Lietuvių k. dialektologinio atlaso medžiaga rodo, kad net. nuosaka kiek plačiau, negu nom. c. part., po verba dicendi vartojama vakarų aukštaičių tarmės vakarinėje dalyje (į pietus nuo Šilutės ir Tauragės, Panemunėje, Dubysos žemupyje); taip pat ir rytų aukštaičių tarmėje ji kiek labiau išplitusi į pietus ir vakarus, negu nom. c. part. Daugiau net. nuosakos atvejų aptikta ir rytinių dzūkų plote (ypač šiaurėje ir Baltarusijos pasienyje). Nei nom. c. part., nei net. nuosakos pavyzdžių neužrašyta vidurio ir rytų aukštaičių tarmių plote tarp Radviliškio — Panevėžio — Ukmergės — Jonavos — Kėdainių.

18. J. Jablonskis, *op. cit.*, 464–466, 530.

19. Chr. S. Stang, „Die litauische Konjunktion *jeib* und der lit.-lett. Optativ",
Norsk Tidsskrift for Sprogvidenskap, XVIII, 348–356; *Vergleichende Grammatik der Baltischen Sprachen*, Oslo–Bergen–Tromsö, 1966, 429 tt.
20. Plg. dar J. Kazlauskas, *Lietuvių kalbos istorinė gramatika*, Vilnius, 1968, 402–403.

On modus relativus in Lithuanian

Syntactical relations of modus relativus (*girdėjau, jis gyvenąs ⟨gyvenęs, gyvensiąs⟩ mieste*) with other predicative participles (*jis jau beeinąs* etc.), constructions with relative pronouns or adverbs (*nežino ko prašąs*) and conjunctions (*stojęs ir sako*) are discussed. It is stated that modus relativus represents the specialized case of predicative usage of participles which is distinguished from other cases by its modal meaning. The same meaning is characteristic of neuter passive participles having a predicative function and connected with genitive of subject (*jo čia gyventa*). The view is held that the structural basis of modus relativus was provided by nominal clauses of such type as *sūnus einąs* (*ėjęs*) which can be reconstructed for the oldest periods of Baltic and other IE. languages. Such clauses could have taken on modal meaning later as a result of the influence of the participial constructions expressing retold action (e.g. accusativus and nominativus cum participio).

HENNING ANDERSEN

On Some Old Balto-Slavic Isoglosses

$IE *s > š$ after $*ĭ$, $*ŭ$, $*r$, $*k$, $*k̂$. There can be no doubt that the development of IE $*s$ and $*k$, $*ĝ(h)$ gave rise to some of the earliest significant divergences between Baltic and Slavic. The merger of IE $*k̂$ with one of the variants of $*s$ (we will write it s_1) in Slavic and with the other variant (s_2) in Baltic (cf. fig. 1) resulted in a striking isogloss between the two groups of dialects, an isogloss which defined not only a different lexical distribution of Proto-slavic s and x and Protobaltic s and $š$, but also a difference in the productive phonological sequential constraints and—very significantly—a difference between the morphophonemic systems of Protoslavic and Protobaltic.

	Protoslavic	Protobaltic
"After i, u, r, k"	$x : s$	$š$
"Elsewhere"	s	$s : š$

Fig. 1. *The partial preservation of the distinction between IE $*s$ and $*k̂$ in Protoslavic and Protobaltic.*

As a result of the merger of one of the variants of $*s$ with $*k̂$, both Proto-slavic and Protobaltic had morphophonemic alternations involving the former positional variants of $*s$. Since in Protoslavic some s (those reflecting $*k̂$) did not alternate with x, the Protoslavic $s \sim x$ alternations could be produced only from basic forms with x. This is the reason why in Slavic x has been generalized in all categories which originally presented such alterna-tions. In Protobaltic, the $s \sim š$ alternations could be produced only from underlying s, for some $š$ (those reflecting $*k̂$) did not alternate with s. In a development completely parallel to the Slavic generalization of x in in-flectional and derivational morphology, Baltic has sharply curtailed the inherited $s \sim š$ alternations, with the effect that s has been reintroduced after *ĭ, *ŭ, *r, *k, thus producing the many apparent exceptions to the change of *s > s$_2$.[1]

A correct understanding of the morphophonemic relations that obtained after the merger of *k̂ with the different variants of *s in Baltic and Slavic makes it possible to understand most of the Baltic exceptions to Pedersen's rule as the result of morphophonemic simplification. The few lexemes in Lithuanian in which s (instead of the expected š) cannot be explained in this way may be attributable to interference from other Baltic dialects in which š, ž had changed to s, z.[2]

To the *ĭ, *ŭ, *r, *k (and *g(h)) traditionally recognized as conditioning the change of *s > s$_2$ we can add *k̂ (and *ĝ(h)). This seems to be the best way of accounting for the fact that sequences of š + s and ž + s in word internal position do not follow the productive regressive assimilation rule which applies at prefix boundaries (where š + s → s, ž + s → s), but, instead, a morphophonemic rule by which š + s → š, ž + s → š; cf. iššemti, užsakyti with [-s-], but {neš-s-Ø} → neš, {vež-s-Ø} → veš. This morphophonemic rule, which at first blush appears to reflect a progressive assimilation, shows that the change of *s > s$_2$ took place after *k̂, *ĝ(h). It constitutes the only evidence offered by Baltic that the change of *s > s$_2$ occurred before the assibilation of *k̂, *ĝ(h).[3]

It may be noted that the reflex of *k̂s and *ĝ(h)s in Baltic is š, i.e. identical to the reflex of *k̂. The same is the case in Slavic (cf. Lith. tašyti, neš, veš and OCS tesati, něsъ, věsъ). There is no need to assume that the development of *k̂s, *ĝ(h)s in pre-Slavic was different from the development we can reconstruct for pre-Baltic.

In position after *ĭ, *ŭ, *r, *k, *k̂ and before an obstruent, *s has yielded Lith. š, Slavic s. Both reflexes are ambiguous: Lith. š can represent s$_2$ and *k̂, whereas Slavic s can represent s$_1$ and *k̂. Traditionally these ambiguous reflexes have arbitrarily been interpreted as evidence that *s changed to s$_2$ in Baltic but not in Slavic in this environment. But it is just as possible to see behind these reflexes two shared innovations, viz the change of *s > s$_2$ and a subsequent merger of s$_2$ with *k̂ in this one environment before *k̂ lost its palatal character in Slavic. This sequence of events exactly parallels the development attested in Sanskrit though the ultimate reflexes are different: the reflex of both *s and *k̂ in this environment is ṣ in Sanskrit, i.e. identical to s$_2$; while in Baltic and Slavic it is identical to *k̂, hence Baltic š and Slavic s.[4]

Thus, if one looks at the development of *s after *ĭ, *ŭ, *r, *k, *k̂ in its relation to that of *k̂ and *ĝ(h), one must conclude that there are no demonstrable differences between Baltic and Slavic in the development of the originally positional variation of s$_1$ and s$_2$ for *s.[5] Only through the subsequent phonemic identifications of *$\hat{k}$ with one or the other of these variants can we define a difference between Baltic and Slavic. In the merger of *$\hat{k}$ with s_2 before obstruent, the Baltic and Slavic developments were still parallel. But the later merger of *$\hat{k}$ in other environments with s_2 in Baltic but with s_1 in Slavic gave rise to tangible differences between the two groups of dialects, differences in phoneme inventory, in phonological sequential constraints, and in morphophonemic rules.

The isogloss that defined these differences is perhaps the oldest ascertainable isogloss between Baltic and Slavic. However, there are some details in the development of IE *s indicating dialectal innovations which possibly preceded the merger of *$\hat{k}$ with the variants of *s. We will briefly examine three pertinent problems below, the development of *$s\hat{k}$, the metathesis of *sk, and the development of initial *$s+g(h)$.

I E *$s\hat{k}$* in Baltic*. The development of *$s\hat{k}$ in Baltic is an unsettled question which has long been discussed on the level of etymology, but still awaits a clarification in terms of the phonological system involved.

The various attempts that have been made to derive the present tense suffix *-sta-* from *$s\hat{k}e/o$- were aptly characterized by Fraenkel as "samt und sonders ... verfehlt", a judgement which must be extended to the most recent such attempt.[6] On the other hand, the opinion advanced by Endzelin and Fraenkel that the regular reflex of *$s\hat{k}$ was $\check{s}$ was not based solely on a soberly inductive analysis of the words which could reasonably be expected to have etyma with *$s\hat{k}$, but was motivated as much by a desire to find some source other than *s for the examples with $\check{s}$ for *s after i and u and abetted by a willingness to posit ad hoc *$s\hat{k}$ sequences in the most unlikely places. Now that the relation between s and $\check{s}$ after *$\check{i}$, *$\check{u}$, *r, *k, *$\hat{k}$ has been clarified, Endzelin's and Fraenkel's strained constructions have at most historical interest.[7]

In the opinion of Būga, $\check{s}k$ was the regular reflex of *$s\hat{k}$, whereas the normal reflex of *sk was sk.[8] In phonological terms, the central point in this conception is that *$\hat{k}$ was identified with *k after sibilant, or, in other words, that the *$\hat{k}$:*k opposition was neutralized in this environment. As to the question of what was the opposition that was neutralized, there seem to be two possibilities with a clear chronological difference: either the tonality opposition acute *vs* grave was neutralized while the *$\hat{k}$ was still a mellow palatal stop, or the strident *vs* mellow opposition was neutralized after *$\hat{k}$ and *$\hat{g}(h)$ had become hushing affricates, phonemically the strident counterparts of *k and *g.

In choosing between these two possibilities, we cannot ignore the fact that Slavic presents sk for both *$s\hat{k}$ and *sk, that is, that also in Slavic the *$\hat{k}$:*k

opposition has been neutralized after sibilant. Since both in Baltic and in Slavic this innovation must have preceded the merger of *$\hat{k}$ with the different variants of *s, it seems a priori likely that this neutralization was a shared Balto-Slavic innovation. If this is the case, then the opposition neutralized must have been the acute *vs* grave opposition, for when *$\hat{k}$ and *$\hat{g}(h)$ became affricates in Slavic, one must assume, they became the strident counterparts not of *k and *g, but of *t and *d.

In Būga's view, the distinction between *$s\hat{k}$ and *sk was preserved in Lithuanian in the quality of the sibilant, as $šk$ *vs* sk. Such a development, which seems to imply a change of *$s > s_2$ before *$\hat{k}$, is not in itself implausible[9] and is compatible with the Slavic reflex sk for both clusters (cf. above, p. 16). Still, there is good reason to doubt the correctness of this view, for in most of the examples of $šk$ for *$s\hat{k}$ which are usually cited, the $š$ may be conditioned by the preceding vowel: *aiškus, ieškoti, laiškas, kiška, raiškas, reiškia, puškas, rūškanas*, which Būga cited, may have their $š$ as a consequence of the change of *$s > s_2$, and may then have preserved $š$ because $š$ in these lexemes did not alternate with s. In the few examples where this is not the case, $šk$ alternates with $kš$ before consonant, and the $š$ may have developed after the Baltic metathesis of -SK- clusters (see below).

In short, now that we have understood that *s changed to s_2 after *$\check{i}$ and *$\check{u}$ as well as after *r, *k, *$\hat{k}$, we can return to the position, held by Kuryłowicz in the thirties, that the regular reflex of *$s\hat{k}$ in Baltic was sk.[10]

The metathesis of -SK- clusters. The metathesis of clusters of the type sibilant + compact stop before consonant has long been recognized as a common Baltic characteristic.[11] The question of how old this metathesis is has never been discussed, but it is obvious that this question must be posed.

It has long been supposed that in Baltic the change of *s after *$\check{i}$, *$\check{u}$, *r, *k, *$\hat{k}$ applied not only to original *ks clusters, but also to metathesized *sk clusters. Thus Endzelin accounted for the occurrence of -$šk$- in *bloškia, broškia, reškia, teškia, troško* by assuming that the $š$ arose "under the influence of forms where after the metathesis before consonant -$kš$- developed from -ks-", e.g. the infinitives *blokšti, brokšti, rėkšti, tėkšti, trokšti*;[12] cf. also Fraenkel, *LEW*, s. vv. This account of the forms in question implies that the metathesis took place before the change of *$s > s_2$.

There is no evidence that would contradict such an early date for the metathesis. Rather on the contrary, it seems reasonable to explain the existence of both -$šk$- ~ -$kš$- and -sk- ~ -ks- type alternations both after i, u, r and after other segments as the result of morphophonemic simplifications and lexical innovations which have obscured from our view an earlier stage of the language in which after i, u, r, -$\check{s}k$- alternated with -$k\check{s}$-, while after other segments, -sk- alternated with -$k\check{s}$-.

If, as has long been supposed, -SK- clusters were metathesized before the change of $*s > s_2$, then the metathesis may have given rise to a Balto-Slavic isogloss of even greater age than the isogloss that defined the different results of the merger of $*\hat{k}$ with the variants of $*s$. For it is clear that a change like the Baltic metathesis did not take place in Slavic. Here the loss of syllable final obstruents has left the distinction between $*$-ksn- and $*$-skn- intact; cf. $luna < *louksn\bar{a}$ and, on the other hand, $t\check{e}sn\check{o} < *toisknos$, $jasn\check{o} < *\bar{o}isknos$. (Before obstruent, the distinction has been obscured, cf. $r\check{e}ste < *r\bar{e}kste$ and $t\check{e}sto < *toisktom$.)

This permits us to conclude that the Baltic metathesis of -SK- clusters gave rise to one of the oldest isoglosses in the bundle of isoglosses which early developed between Baltic and Slavic.

We must ask whether the metathesis of -SK- clusters preceded or followed the change of $*s\hat{k} > sk$. If it preceded, the resulting $*s\hat{k} \sim *\hat{k}s$ alternations would now be represented by $sk \sim \check{s}$ alternations. If it followed, however, original $*s\hat{k}$ clusters would now be indistinguishable from $*sk$ clusters before vowel as well as before consonant. In the absence of any evidence of $sk \sim \check{s}$ alternations, we may tentatively conclude that the change of $*s\hat{k} > sk$ preceded the metathesis of -SK- clusters. This agrees well with the Balto-Slavic character of the former change and the specifically Baltic character of the latter.

Initial $*s + g(h)$. The treatment of initial clusters beginning with $*s$ in Baltic and Slavic poses several problems whose relations to one another remain to be clarified, and which probably have to be clarified before any of these problems can be adequately defined, let alone solved.

The question of the origin of the IE "s mobile" is only one of these, though perhaps a central one. Of the various explanations that have been proposed, the sandhi explanation seems to be the most satisfying one, for, as Edgerton has shown, it finds support in actually attested sequential constraints of Vedic Sanskrit.[13] But whether this explanation is accepted as sufficient, the different distribution of "s mobile" in Baltic and Slavic must be given due attention in the final account.

It seems doubtful that the absence of initial spr-clusters in Slavic—vis-à-vis the existence of str- and skr- clusters—would be due to a regular sound change, as has once been supposed.[14] On the other hand, the absence of skl-clusters may be significant. Illič-Svityč's account of such doublets as $*kloniti < *klon$- and $*sloniti < *sklon$- is tantamount to positing for primitive Slavic a sequential constraint which is unknown to Baltic (cf. Lith. $skleisti$, *sklesti*) but has a parallel in Germanic.[15] The possibility exists that this constraint is a shared Germano-Slavic innovation. Perhaps it is typologically related to the change of IE *$sr > str$, general in Germanic and Slavic, but not in Baltic.[16]

More clearly significant is the difference between the Baltic and Slavic reflexes of initial *$s + g(h)$. Illič-Svityč has shown that while Baltic has *sk*- for both *$s + k$ and *$s + g(h)$, Slavic has *sk*- for the former, but *x*- for the latter; cf. Lith. *skara*—Sl. *$skora$ (and without "*s* mobile", Sl. *$kora$), La. *škepele*—Sl. *$skopiti$, *$ščepa$ (Gr. *kóptō*) and, on the other hand, Lith. *skusti* —Sl. *$xudъ$ (Lith. *gausti*), Lith. *skriaudus*—Sl. *$xrustъ$ (Lith. *graudus*). The correspondence IE *$s + g(h)$—Sl. *x*- is established on the basis of sixteen reliable examples and, like the correspondence *$s + g(h)$—Baltic *sk*- is past dispute.[17]

In evaluating this difference between Baltic and Slavic, one must note first of all that it is the result of innovation both in Baltic and in Slavic. The Baltic reflex of *$s + g(h)$ shows a neutralization of the voiced *vs* voiceless opposition, a neutralization which has applied to all stops after initial *s, not only in Baltic, but in all the Indo-European languages, including Slavic.[18] When, despite this neutralization, *$s + k$ and *$s + g(h)$ have remained distinct in Slavic as *sk*- and *x*-, there can be only one explanation: *$s + g(h)$ must have ceased to be a sequence of $s + $ voiced stop before the neutralization was introduced.

The question must be posed of how this happened. There are evidently several ways in which a cluster of sibilant + compact stop can develop into a compact fricative; e.g. $sk > šk > š$ (as in German), $sk > sx$ (as in Dutch) $> x$, $sg > sγ > sx$ (as in Czech) $> x$, or $sg > ks > kx > x$. But there does not appear to be any internal or external comparative evidence which could help us choose among these several possibilities. Only a more advanced knowledge of phonological typology than we have at present will make it possible to select one of them and assign it to a definite stage of development of the language at which alone the synchronic structure would motivate such a phonetic innovation.

Still, the fact that this innovation must have preceded the common Indo-European neutralization of the voiced *vs* voiceless opposition after initial *s suggests a very early date for this innovation. In view of this, it is not without interest that one of the possibilities we mentioned—the metathesis of initial *$s + g(h)$—implies that the phonetic innovation in question preceded the change of *$s > s_2$. There is, then, adequate reason to regard the isogloss between Baltic *sk*- and Slavic *x*- from *$s + g(h)$ one of the oldest Balto-Slavic isoglosses.

Notes

1. See the author's "IE *s* after *i, u, r, k* in Baltic and Slavic", *Acta Linguistica Hafniensia* XI, 171–190.
2. *Op. cit.*, p. 186 f.
3. *Op. cit.*, pp. 175, 188.
4. E. Fraenkel, *Litauisches etymologisches Wörterbuch* (Heidelberg 1962–1965) (hereinafter *LEW*) cites one prefixal formation in which this morphophonemic rule seems to be reflected: *ūšmalas* 'mitten' < **ūž + smal-*. If this etymology is correct, it shows that originally the **s > s₂* change did take place at prefix boundaries (as one would expect, and as is normally assumed for such Slavic examples as **xoditi*); but after the assibilation of **k̂, *ĝ(h)* the morphophonemic rule which produced *s ∼ š* alternations at prefix boundaries was eliminated, leaving only this lone lexicalized compound as residue. For parallels to such a development, see the author's "A study in diachronic morphophonemics: the Ukrainian prefixes", *Language* 45, 807–830.
4. Cf. "IE **s* after *i, u, r, k ...*", pp. 176, 189 f.
5. It is worth emphasizing also that there are no demonstrable differences in the development of **s* within Baltic. It is true that there is no evidence of the **s > s₂* change in Latvian or Old Prussian, but it is entirely arbitrary to assume, as has sometimes been done, that the change did not take place in all of Baltic (thus, for instance, E. Fraenkel, *Die Baltischen Sprachen* (Heidelberg 1950), p. 113, and more recently V. V. Ivanov, *Obščeindoevropejskaja, praslavjanskaja i anatolijskaja jazykovye sistemy* (Moskva 1965), 36). We know that the assibilation of **k̂, *ĝ(h) > š, ž* was pan-Baltic, for *š, ž* were the reflexes of **k̂, *ĝ(h)* in the easternmost reaches of the Baltic speech area (cf. V. Thomsen, *Berührungen zwischen den finnischen und den baltischen (litauisch-lettischen) Sprachen*, in *Samlede Afhandlinger, IV* (Copenhagen 1931), 134 ff., 243; on the time and place of these Fenno-Baltic contacts, see P. N. Tret'jakov, *Finno-ugry, balty i slavjane na Dnepre i Volge* (Moskva 1966), 63–113; on the recent date of the change of *š, ž > s, z* in Latvian, see K. Būga, *Lietuvių kalbos žodynas* (Kaunas 1924), p. lx = *Rinktiniai raštai, III* (Vilnius 1961), p. 99 f.). To assume that the even earlier change of **s > s₂* was not pan-Baltic is capricious.
6. Cf. E. Fraenkel, *op. cit.*, p. 91; E. P. Hamp, "On IE **s* after *i, u,* in Baltic", *Baltistica*, III(1), 9 ff. On the origin of the *-sta-* presents, see Chr. S. Stang, *Vergleichende Grammatik der baltischen Sprachen* (Oslo 1966), 342 ff. and A. Vaillant, *Grammaire comparée des langues slaves, III* (Paris 1966), 171 ff.
7. Cf. J. Endzelin, *Slavjano-baltijskie ètjudy* (Kharkov 1911), p. 57 ff.; *idem*, "Über den slavisch-baltischen Reflex von idg. *sk̂*", *Zeitschrift für slavische Philologie*, XVI, 107–115; E. Fraenkel, *op. cit.*, 113 f. and *LEW*, s. vv. Endzelin's best examples of the correspondences IE **sk̂*—Baltic *š*—Slavic *s*, Lith. *aušta* and Slavic **pasǫ*, have been put into a new perspective by the clarification of the relation between the Indo-European **-s-* and **-sk̂-* formations; see V. V. Ivanov, *op. cit.*, 139–174.
8. Cf. *Kalba ir senové* (Kaunas 1922), 249 ff. = *Rinktiniai raštai, II* (Vilnius 1959), 284 ff.
9. Cf. Chr. S. Stang, *op. cit.*, 92.
10. J. Kuryłowicz, *Etudes indoeuropéennes, I* (Cracow 1935), 19 ff.
11. See, for instance, J. Endzelin, *Lettische Grammatik* (Heidelberg 1923), 167.
12. Cf. *Slavjano-baltijskie ètjudy*, 56 f.

21

13. Cf. F. Edgerton, "Indo-European 's movable' ", *Language* XXXIV, 445–453.
14. Cf. R. Trautmann, "Über die Behandlung der Anlautsgruppe *spr-* im Urslavischen", *Zeitschrift für vergleichende Sprachforschung*, XXXVII, 66–68.
15. Cf. T. Siebs, "Anlautstudien", *Zeitschrift für vergleichende Sprachforschung*, XXXVII (1901), 279, 285, 297, 314 ff.
16. On the preservation of *sr* in Lithuanian, see Z. Zinkevičius, *Lietuvių dialektologija* (Vilnius 1966), 193.
17. Cf. V. M. Illič-Svityč, "Odin iz istočnikov načal'nogo *x-* v praslavjanskom. (Popravka k 'zakonu Zibsa')", *Voprosy jazykoznanija* 1961, no. 4, 93–98.
18. Cf. T. Siebs, *op. cit.*, 294 ff.

PEETER ARUMAA

Zur Geschichte der baltischen Genera

In der geschichtlichen Überlieferung des Baltischen überrascht jeden
Forscher die äusserst lückenhafte Vertretung der indogermanischen Genera
im Gegensatz zu der erstaunlichen Altertümlichkeit des Deklinations-
systems. Auch die ostsee-finnischen Sprachen mit ihren uralten baltischen
Entlehnungen können zur Chronologie des baltischen Neutrums keinen
wesentlichen Beitrag liefern. Für *o*-Maskulina gibt es wohl Fälle mit be-
wahrtem auslautendem *s* sogar unter Adjektiven (estn. *haljas* gleich lit.
žalias 'grün'), doch sucht man vergebens nach Entsprechungen mit auslautendem *n* oder *s* für alte baltische Neutra. Das einzige Wort unter den im
Altpreussischen bezeugten Neutra, das sich im ostseefinnischen Bereich
findet, ist möglicherweise altpreuss. *kelan* 'Rad', welches man in finn. *kela*
'Haspel', südestn. *kõla* 'Werkzeug zum Weben allerlei bandartiger Textile',
liv. *kẹlà, kilà* 'Biegung, Kreis' wiederzufinden geneigt ist. Wenn diese
Etymologie sich halten lässt[1]), würde es dennoch zu gewagt sein, daraus für
das Fehlen des auslautenden Nasals im baltischen Neutrum irgendwelche
bündige Schlüsse ziehen zu wollen.

Die richtige Beurteilung des Zustandes im baltischen Genussystem wird
besonders dadurch erschwert, dass es über den Ursprung des idg. Genus
keine allgemein anerkannte Theorie gibt und dass es keinem der Forscher
gelungen ist, wenigstens von dem Begriffe 'Genus' eine umfassende Definition zu bieten, vgl. z. B. die wertvolle Arbeit von Götz Wienold, *Genus und
Semantik* (Meisenheim am Glan 1967, mit reicher Bibliographie). Bekanntlich ist das Altpreussische die einzige baltische Sprache, für die die Drei-
teilung des idg. Genus, wenn auch nicht in vollem Umfange, nachweisbar
ist, während dessen Schwestersprachen vom Neutrum nur einige spärliche
Relikte bewahrt haben. Wäre es nun möglich, den Weg zum Verlust des
Neutrums auf einem grossen Gebiet des Baltischen wenigstens in einigen
Etappen nachzuweisen, so würde dies auch für die ganze Ursprungsfrage des
idg. Genus von grundsätzlicher Bedeutung sein.

Die allgemeine Struktur der idg. Nomina führt uns zur Annahme, dass in
der idg. Grundsprache der grösste Teil der Kasusendungen schon bestanden

habe, als das Neutrum im Genussystem aufkam. Für die Motion, d. h. die
Scheidung der Substantiva in männliche und weibliche, wie überhaupt für die
Verteilung des Genus im Suffixsystem lässt sich die relative Chronologie
nicht so einfach bestimmen. Frühzeitig muss jedenfalls die scharf begrenzte
neutrale Gruppe, zu welcher alle Gegenstände, die nicht beseelt waren,
gerechnet wurden, aufgekommen sein. Zu diesem Bild stimmt nun das
Altpreussische, in dem alle Neutra — in der Gesamtzahl etwas mehr als
100 Fälle — nur unbeseelte Gegenstände bezeichnen. Allein eine deutliche
Ausnahme bilden die Bezeichnungen der Tierjungen mit dem neutralen
Diminutivsuffix, aber auch dies ist ja indogermanisch. Das Altpreussische
scheint das Suffix *-stian* (Typus *eristian* 'Lamm' gegenüber lit. *ēras*) mit dem
Illyrisch-Thrakischen zu teilen, vgl. Specht, *KZ* 65, 176 (aufgrund des
Materials von Būga und Pokorny).[2] Auch *k* hat diminutive Bedeutung an-
genommen in *wijrikan* 'Männlein' zu *wijrs*, vgl. noch *madlikan* 'Gebetlein'.
Im Ausdruck für 'wildes Pferd' *paustocaican* spürt man einen gewissen
Gefühlswert, vgl. Fraenkel, *Lit. etym. Wb.*, 202. Das Altpreussische kennt
auch das im Indogermanischen geläufige Suffix für nomina instrumenti in
piuclan 'Sichel' gegenüber lit. *piúklas* 'Säge'.

Die Schaffung des Neutrums war rein äusserlich auch dadurch begünstigt,
dass bei ihm die blosse Wurzel die Grundlage dazu bildete und dass man das
Neutrum folglich nicht besonders zu charakterisieren brauchte. Die vollere
Gestalt der *o*-Stämme zeigt eine deutliche Vorliebe für den *e*-Vokalismus,
wenn der neutrale Begriff zugrunde liegt, vgl. Lohman, *Genus und Sexus*
(1932) 9 ff., z. B. apreuss. *kelan* n., aber gr. πόλος m. Auffällig bleibt dabei
jedoch die Endung *m* der *o*-Stämme, die möglicherweise zunächst im Akkusativ Sg. eingeführt wurde.[3] Sehr beachtenswert ist noch das Schwanken
zwischen *-an* und *-a* (=idg. *-om* und *-o*) bei neutralen Adjektiven des Hethitischen. Vgl. hierzu Friedrich, *Hethitisches Elementarbuch I* (Heidelberg
1960²), S. 42 f. Dazu will Kronasser, *Vergl. Laut- und Formenlehre d. Hethitischen* (Heidelberg 1956) 107 f. die hethitischen Adjektivformen mit *-a*
statt *-an* nicht als endungslose Neutra der *o*-Stämme gelten lassen, da nach
seiner Ansicht hier die singularisch gebrauchte Pluralendung *-a* vorliegen
soll. Doch machen die baltischen akzentologischen Verhältnisse, wo die
neutralen Adjektiva den Iktus vielfach auf dem Stamm aufweisen, vgl.
z. B. lit. *gẽra*, *mãža*, *daũgi*, diese Pluraltheorie wenig wahrscheinlich. Die
reinen Stammformen der litauischen Adjektiva im Neutrum finden jedenfalls ihre natürliche Erklärung in ihrer Funktion. Diese kommen bekanntlich nur in der prädikativen Verwendung vor, wo das Verhältnis zum Genus
des Subjektes nicht markiert zu werden braucht. Die syntaktischen Modelle
dafür sind folgende: *kàd iř prãsta, jeĩ dernù, taĩ iř gražù* 'wenn auch einfach,

doch, wenn es anständig ist, ist es auch schön'; *neĩ daũg, neĩ mãža šiõs dienõs dárbo* 'für heute gibt es weder viel noch wenig Arbeit'. Weitere Beispiele s. *Lietuvių kalbos gramatika* (Vilnius, 1965) § 925. Die Adjektiva auf *-i* sind im Baltischen frühzeitig verloren gegangen, doch sind einige Reste auch beim Neutrum nachweisbar: alit. *daugi* 'viel', altpreuss. *arwi* zu *arwis* m. 'wahr'. Das Litauische lehrt uns also, dass sowohl bei der Entstehung als auch beim Untergang des Neutrums die *syntaktische Funktion* gewisser Formkategorien eine besonders wichtige Rolle gespielt hat.

Auch in einigen adverbialen Bildungen des Litauischen will man Spuren von alten Neutralformen erblicken. Wenn aber ein derartiges Adverb hinsichtlich seiner äusseren Struktur ganz isoliert dasteht, so ist es natürlich schwierig, darnach die Funktion des Neutrums näher zu bestimmen, gerade weil bei einem Adverb die syntaktische Funktion die grammatische stark überwiegt. Im litauischen Illativ *namõn* 'nach Hause', mundartlich noch in vollerer Gestalt *namonà*, will man den Rest eines Neutrums, und zwar im Nominativ-Akk. des Plurals **namã+nã* sehen, vgl. Stang, *Vergl. Grammatik d. balt. Sprachen*, 188. Unbegreiflich bleibt die Wahl des Plurals gerade bei einem Ausdruck wie 'nach Hause'. Ferner darf die Form *namõn* von ihren vielen Varianten[4] nicht getrennt werden, nicht nur von *namõniui*, sondern noch weniger vom Allativ *namópi* in gleicher Bedeutung. Es dürfte klar sein, dass der Illativ *namõn* eine Kontamination mit dem Allativ *namópi* darstellt, wobei die weitverbreitete Alternativform *namõ*, ohne die Postposition *-pi*, den Ausgangspunkt bildet. Eine hybride Bildung wie *namõn* konnte leicht dadurch zustande kommen, dass der Gebrauch der sekundären Kasus auf *-pi* im Litauischen sehr früh in Verfall geraten ist, die Illativbildungen dagegen in einem grossen Teil der litauischen Mundarten noch bis zum heutigen Tage lebendig sind.

Zum besseren Verständnis des Wesens wie auch des Ursprungs des Genus ist es notwendig eine besondere Aufmerksamkeit auch der Frage zu widmen, wie die Verhältnisse zwischen verschiedenen Suffixen sich in der späteren Geschichte des Baltischen abgespielt haben, gerade vom Standpunkt von Genera. Schon bei den sog. Wurzelnomina kann man beobachten, wie die spätere Entwicklung der Genera dahin geführt hat, dass in einzelnen idg. Sprachen an diese nicht selten Suffixe angehängt werden, die mit dem Genus der Wurzel wenig zu tun haben. Man vergleiche z. B. die Erweiterungen von der Wurzel **dhu̯er-*, **dhu̯or-*, **dhur-* 'Tür'. Im Baltischen und im Slavischen erscheinen die Ableitungen teils in femininer Gestalt: lit. *dùrys* pl. (alit. und dial. *dures* pl.), slav. *dverь*, teils als Maskulina: lett. *dvars* 'Art Pforte', slav. *dvorъ* 'Hof', aber im Lateinischen als Neutrum *forum*.

Noch verwickelter erscheint die Funktion des Genus da, wo zwei heterogene Formantia mit einander verwachsen sind und so eine suffixale Doppelheit bilden. Dann steht man vor der Frage, inwiefern das Genus des Vordergliedes die Wahl der folgenden Komponenten beeinflusst hat. Hier liefern auch die baltischen Gewässernamen wichtiges Material, wobei unsere Aufmerksamkeit besonders auf diejenigen mit dem Formans *-es-* gerichtet ist, weil nach der Ansicht vieler Forscher darin die alten idg. Neutra verbaut sind. Einige dieser Fälle müssen direkt zum baltischen Gemeingut gerechnet werden, wie z. B. *Laukesà*, welches als Flussname nicht nur in Litauen und Lettland (*Laucesa*), sondern auch als baltisches Substrat in Westrussland (*Lučesa*), in den früheren Gouv. Vitebsk und Smolensk bezeugt ist. Dieser Typus ist unter den lettischen Gewässernamen spärlich vertreten, hat aber in Litauen eine bedeutende Intensität erreicht, dazu noch mit Varianten, die den idg. Ablaut erkennen lassen, vgl. *Narasà* FN, *Degėsis* FN neben *Degesį̃ upẽlis*. Das Formans *-as-* kann sich mundartlich wohl aus *-es-* entwickelt haben. Auffällige Ablautsabstufungen lassen sich im Flussnamen *Žvelesỹs* neben *Žvelsà* und *Žvelsãlė* belegen. Diese Bildungen bezeichnen nicht nur Flüsse, sondern auch Seen, wobei der zu erwartende Unterschied im Genus — Feminina auf *-a* oder auf *-ė* bei Flussnamen und Maskulina auf *-as* oder auf *-is*, *-ys* bei Seenamen im Einklang mit dem Genus der entsprechenden Appellativa keineswegs folgerecht durchgeführt ist, vgl. *Burbėsis* FN (Kr. Nevarėnai) und *Pelesà* SN (Kr. Rudnia) oder *Rudesà* sowohl Fluss- als auch Seename im Kr. Molėtai. Vgl. *Lietuvos TSR upių ir ežerų vardynas* (Vilnius 1963). Die Vermutung, dass gerade die litauischen Seenamen auf *-es-*, entsprechend dem Neutrum *assaran* des Altpreussischen, unverändert bewahrt seien, findet heftigen Widerspruch im Tatbestand. Die *es*-haltigen Gewässernamen zeigen im Litauischen jetzt eine derartige Produktivität, dass sie auch von nichtneutralen Stämmen gebildet werden, vgl. z. B. *Vilkesà* FN und *Vaikėsas* SN. Noch wichtiger ist die allgemeine Feststellung, dass die idg. *es*-Neutra auf dem baltischen Boden sowohl maskuline als auch feminine Suffixe annehmen können, und zwar nicht nur bei Namen, sondern auch bei gewöhnlichen Gattungsnamen, s. Skardžius, *Lietuvių kalbos žodžių daryba* (Vilnius, 1943) 311 ff.

Die baltischen Gewässernamen liefern noch einen anderen interessanten Fall. Aus dem Zeugnis der verwandten Sprachen weiss man, das die *men-*Nomina ursprünglich nur Maskulina und Neutra umfassten, im Baltischen werden sie jedoch bei Gewässernamen oft in die Kategorie der Feminina überführt. Beispiele aus Litauen: *Akmenà*, auffälligerweise sowohl als Flusswie auch Seename bezeugt, *Ašmenà* FN oder *Graumenà* FN neben zwei maskulinen Flussnamen *Graumuõ*. Nur einen See bezeichnet z. B. *Laumenà* (neben *Laumẽžeris, Laũminas* u. a.). Bei Flussnamen überwiegt wohl das

weibliche Formans -*mena*, aber daneben begegnen nicht selten auch uner-
weiterte Maskulina: *Girmuõ* (neben *Girmuonỹs*), *Jiešmuõ* (*Viešmuõ*), *Lašmuõ*,
Lenkmuõ, *Odmuõ*, *Šelmuõ*, *Žélmenys* pl. (neben *Žélmenà*). Auch hier wiederholt sich derselbe Genuswechsel bei gleichgebildeten Gattungsnamen. Vgl.
z. B. *armenà* 'oberflächlich gepflügte Erdschicht', zu *árti* 'pflügen'; hierher
gehören wohl auch die Flussnamen *Armenà* und *Armonà*. Weitere Beispiele
bei Skardžius, a. a. O., S. 233.[5]

Auch die Vertretung der *i*-Stämme zeigt in der litauischen Hydronymie
eine deutliche Tendenz zur Scheidung der Flussnamen von den Seenamen.
In der stark überwiegenden Mehrzahl werden diese Feminina für Flussnamen
verwendet (Typus: *Nerìs*, Gen. -*iẽs*), doch fehlen nicht Fälle, wo auch den
Seenamen dieselbe Verwendung zukommt, wenn auch in sehr begrenztem
Umfange: *Páltis*, -*ies* f. zwei Seenamen (Kr. Dūkštas und Vabalninkas)
neben vier gleichlautenden Flussnamen; *Glitìs*, -*iẽs* m. (!) neben *Glìtis*, -*čio*
(Kr. Gaurė); *Pušìs*, -*iẽs* f. neben *Apušỹs* (Kr. Tytuvėnai).

Man muss gestehen, dass die weitverbreitete Ansicht, wonach die Flüsse
im Litauischen in der Regel durch feminine Formantia charakterisiert
werden und dass dies durch den Einfluss des weiblichen Appellativums *ùpė*
'Fluss' zu erklären wäre, nicht stichhaltig ist. Einer solchen Auffassung
widerspricht schon der Name des grössten Flusses in Litauen —
Nēmunas. Weiter darf nicht vergessen werden, dass im Litauischen neben
ùpė auch *ùpis* in regem Gebrauch steht. Die Scheidelinie zwischen den
lettischen Genera (Femininum für Flussnamen und Maskulinum für See-
und Sumpfnamen) lässt sich etwas deutlicher ziehen, aber dieser Umstand
steht kaum im Zusammenhang mit der Tatsache, dass die maskuline Entsprechung zu lit. *ùpis* im Lettischen ganz zu fehlen scheint. Man kann sich
vielmehr der Ansicht von Kretschmer in der Festschrift für Holger Pedersen
(*Acta Jutlantica* IX, S. 86) anschliessen, wonach die Flussnamen in der idg.
Grundsprache zweigeschlechtig waren, was dann auch leicht verständlich
macht, warum die arischen Flussnamen nur das weibliche und die griechischen und lateinischen nur das männliche Geschlecht aufweisen. Für die
Zweigeschlechtigkeit würde auch das Keltische sprechen.

Beachtenswert sind auch die weiblichen Ableitungen vom neutralen
Gattungsnamen 'See' — apreuss. *assaran*, slav. *ozero*: in Litauen *Ežērė*,
Seename im Kr. Molėtai, *Ežeruona*, Nebenfluss der Jūra (Kr. Tauragė in
Žemaitija) und *Ežeryščia* FN (Kr. Šiluva). Über den lettischen Fluss- und
Sumpfnamen *Ezere* s. Endzelīns, *Latvijas PSR vietvārdi* (Rīga, 1956), S. 279.
Das slavische Appellativum *ozero* kann auch auf weiten Gebieten sowohl mit
einem femininen als auch mit einem maskulinen Suffix vereinigt werden:
Ozerec als Bezeichnung sowohl eines Sees als auch eines kleines Flusses und

Ozera gleichfalls als See- und Flussname z. B. im Novgoroder Gebiet. Die Verhältnisse im Slavischen werden durch das Femininum *jézera* neben *jezêro* im Slovenischen noch mehr verwickelt. Die slavischen Mundarten, ob im Osten, Westen oder Süden, kennen die männliche Variante *jezerъ* (vgl. schon abulg. *jezerъ*), so dass Sławski und Machek in ihren etymologischen Wörterbüchern die maskuline Nebenform sogar für die slavische Grundsprache voraussetzen.

Der entscheidende Ausgangspunkt für die Entstehung der heutigen Zweigeschlechtigkeit im Baltischen scheint unseres Erachtens vor allem in der Tatsache zu liegen, dass gerade durch die Wortbildung grosse Verschiebungen im Bereiche der Genera eingetreten waren, so dass bei einem Teil der Balten der Sinn für das Neutrum allmählich abgeschwächt wurde. Diese These kann an der Bildung verbaler Abstrakta sehr schön illustriert werden: im Altindischen wird dafür das Suffix -*eno*- im Neutrum verwendet (*vártanam* 'das Drehen'), ebenso im Slavischen im Neutrum, aber konkretisiert (**verteno* 'Spindel') und im Germanischen ist das Neutrum die regelrechte Form für den Infinitiv (got. *wairþan* 'werden'). Im Baltischen dagegen ist diese Bildungsart durch das Femininum vertreten: lit. *gyvenà* 'Leben', *eisenà* 'Gehen, Gang' u. a.

Nach diesen Auseinandersetzungen ist es nicht mehr so schwierig, die obengestellte Frage über das Genus eines zusammengesetzten Formans zu beantworten. In slav. *jezykъ* 'Zunge' zieht man einen verbauten langen *ū*-Stamm und Specht, *KZ* 62, 255 ff. schliesst daraus, mit Hilfe des Awestischen und Litauischen, dass es im Indogermanischen auch maskuline *ū*-Stämme gegeben habe. Er glaubt eine Bekräftigung für seine Theorie gerade in der *k*-Erweiterung maskulinen Geschlechts im Slavischen zu finden. Er beruft sich dabei ferner auf awestisch *hizu-* 'Zunge', das ein Maskulinum ist. Aber schon Lommel, *KZ* 50, 260 ff. hat gezeigt, dass ein langvokalisches *hizū-* fürs Arische unerweislich ist. Das maskuline Geschlecht lässt sich hier aus einem kurzen *u*-Stamm erklären. Auch das litauische Maskulinum *liežùvis* dient nicht zum sicheren Beweis für einen maskulinen *ū*-Stamm. Die idg. Feminina auf -*tū*- sind im Baltischen meistens Feminina geblieben (Suffix -*tuva* od. -*tuvė*: *kaltuvė* 'Handgriff, Stiel des Dreschflegels' zu *kélti* 'aufheben, bewegen'), teils haben sie jedoch auch männliche Gestalt angenommen (Suffix -*tuvis* bzw. -*tuvys*: *muštùvis* neben *muštùvė* 'Butterfass' zu *mùšti* 'schlagen'), s. Skardžius, a. a. O., S. 385. Die Betonung im zweisilbigen *liežùvis* (vgl. die einsilbigen Oxytona und Feminina wie *bruvìs*, Gen. -*iẽs* 'Augenbraue') zeigt, dass hier die Beeinflussung seitens der *tū*-Stämme mitverantvortlich ist. Zum Vergleich kann man etwa *pietùvis* od. *pietuvỹs*, das von einem kurzen *u*-Stamm, lit. *pietùs* 'Süd, Mittag' abgeleitet ist, heranziehen. Vgl. noch *peĩtvis* m. od. *peitvȳs* 'Südwind'. Gerade auf die gleiche Weise kann lit. *liežùvis* zu einem kurzen *u*-Stamm, der noch im Arischen vorliegt, bezogen sein. Bei Rückschlüssen über das Genus eines Konglutinats ist also grösste Zurückhaltung geboten. Aus der slavischen Grundform für 'Sonne' *s̑-*ni*- in *sъlnьce* kann man nicht unbedenklich aus dem angehängten neutralen Suffix -*ce* den Schluss ziehen, dass die slavische Grundsprache einst auch ein neutrales Suffix -*ni*- gekannt hätte. Das Genus eines Stammes kann durch neue Zusätze und Verästelungen derart überwuchert werden, dass es seinen ursprünglichen Charakter leicht einbüsst. In einem zusammengesetzten Suffix erlaubt das Genus des Hintergliedes keinen tieferen Hinblick in die Genusverhältnisse des Vordergliedes.

Die Untersuchung der semantischen Möglichkeiten nominaler Klassen, so wie sie Wienold in der obenerwähnten Arbeit mit der Methode semantischer Korrelationen durchgeführt hat, lässt uns daneben an eine funktionelle Klassifikation der idg. Suffixe denken. Diese funktionellen Korrelationen würden uns vielleicht auch ein neues Verständnis des Neutrums erlauben.

Anmerkungen

1. Vgl. Y. H. Toivonen, *Suomen kielen etymologinen sanakirja* I, Helsinki, 1955, 179.
2. Über den Einfluss von slav. -*išča* s. Skardžius, a. a. O., S. 332.
3. Zur Gleichwertigkeit der neutralen Endungen -*o* neben -*om* vgl. noch Agrell, *Zur Geschichte des idg. Neutrums*, Lund, 1925/26, 17 ff.
4. Reichliches Material jetzt in *Liet. kalbos žodynas* VIII (Vilnius 1970), 534–536.
5. Vgl. auch Vanagas, *Lietuvos hidronimų daryba* (Vilnius 1970), 39, 183, 188.

On the History of Genders in Baltic

Old Prussian is the only Baltic language in which the existence of the three genders of Proto-Indoeuropean is observed, even if not to the full extent, while in its sister languages only a few odd remnants of the neuter are preserved. The more than 100 examples of Old Prussian neuter nouns designate objects without life. The only exceptions are the designations of the offspring of animals with a neuter diminutive suffix, but this, too, is an accepted IE practice. The Old Prussian diminutive suffix -*stian* has its counterpart in the Illyrian-Thracian language. The suffixless forms of Lithuanian adjectives in the neuter (*mãža* 'little', *gražù* 'fine', *daũgi* 'much') find their natural explanation in their function. They occur only in two syntactic patterns with a predicative usage, where the relation to the gender of the subject does not need to be emphasized. Thus they represent the very root of the adjective. The Lithuanian illative *namõn* 'home' cannot be an old neuter form, viz. in nom.-acc. plural *namā + postposition nǎ, but has developed through contamination with the logically related allative namópi 'to the house'. In the heterogeneous formantia (stem-forming elements) of the Baltic languages traces of old neuter nouns are still sought, as for instance of the IE neuter in -es in place names, after the pattern Laukesà. It is not possible to define the gender of the first element of the compound from the gender of the second element of the compound in compound formantia. In the words for 'tongue': Slavic językъ and Lith. liežùvis, it is not possible to prove the existence of a masculine ū-stem.

LUCIA BALDAUF

Über die Pronominalform des Adjektivs im litauischen Prädikat

Während die einfache Form des Adjektivs im Litauischen sowohl prädikativ, wie auch attributiv gebraucht wird, kommt die Pronominalform nur ganz selten in einem litauischen Prädikat vor. Diese, wenn auch ganz selten vorkommenden Pronominalformen des Adjektivs im Prädikat wurden bis jetzt für die Prädikatsnomina gehalten, und man behauptete, daß die Pronominalform, wenn auch ganz selten, doch auch im Litauischen prädikativ gebraucht würde.

Sind diese Formen aber auch wirklich Prädikatsnomina? Es gibt im Litauischen dreierlei Typen der adjektivischen Prädikate:

1) Adjektivische Prädikate, deren Kopula irgendeine Form des Verbums *būti*, sein ist: *Blogas būsi, kad kalbėsi, o netikęs, kad tylėsi.* (S. Daukantas, *Dainos*, 168) 'Schlecht wirst du sein, wenn du reden wirst, ein Taugenichts, wenn du schweigen wirst'.

2) Adjektivische Prädikate, deren Kopula ein Hilfsverbum ist, z. B. *tapti, pasidaryti, rastis* 'werden' u. ähnliche: *brolis tapo (rados) lobingas* (J. Jablonskis, Gr. 55), 'Der Bruder wurde reich.'

3) Adjektivische Prädikate, deren Kopula durch selbständige Verba gebildet werden, u. zwar meistens durch Verba der Bewegung oder Verba, die eine Zustandsveränderung zum Ausdruck bringen: *Graži, šilta išaušo diena* (Žemaitė *Raštai*, II, 3), 'schön und warm brach der Tag an'.

Nur in den Sätzen des ersten und des zweiten Typs, also mit Kopula von *būti*, sein, oder einem Hilfsverbum wie *tapti, pasidaryti, rastis*, werden, — kommen ab und zu, jedoch sehr selten, die Pronominalformen des Adjektivs in solch einem Prädikat vor. Gerade diese Formen wurden bis jetzt als Prädikatsnomina angesehen. So schreibt A. Schleicher in *Handbuch der lit. Sprache* (S. 261): „Das adjectiv als praedikat steht in der bestimten form, wenn im deutschen der bestimte artikel beim adjektiv steht, z. b. *tas kelias tikrasis*, der weg ist der rechte, d. h., bloß dann, wenn beim substantiv das demonstrativ oder eine sonstige nähere bestimmung steht." Auch Fr. Kurschat schreibt in seiner *Grammatik* (S. 365), daß die Pronominalform des

Adjektivs meist attributiv, doch manchmal, wenn auch ganz selten, prädikativ gebraucht wird und führt zum Beweis folgenden Satz an: *Ta sermėga (tai) naujoji* 'dieser Rock ist der neue'. Über den prädikativen Gebrauch des Pronominaladjektivs spricht auch A. Baranauskas in *Kalbamokslis Lietuviškos Kalbos* (S. 71). Genau wie Kurschat und Schleicher bemerkt er, daß das Pronominaladjektiv prädikativ nur selten vorkommt und führt folgendes Beispiel an: *Šitas žodis tikrasai,* 'dieses Wort ist das richtige'. J. Jablonskis äußert sich über diese Frage überhaupt nicht in seiner Grammatik. Am ausführlichsten spricht darüber A. Valeckienė in ihrer Arbeit *Dabartinės lietuvių kalbos įvardžiuotinių būdvardžių vartojimas.* Aber auch sie bleibt bei der traditioneller Behauptung, die Pronominalform des Adjektivs kann, wenn auch ganz selten, prädikativ gebraucht werden. Auch sie hält diese Pronominalformen für Prädikatsnomina.

Sind sie es wirklich? Meiner Meinung nach sind alle diese Pronominalformen keine Prädikatsnomina, sondern nur Attribute zu einem substantivischen Prädikatsnomen, das zwar nicht ausdrücklich erwähnt wird, aber aus dem logischen Zusammenhang des Satzes uns dennoch recht wohl ersichtlich ist. Die Pronominalform des Adjektivs kann im Litauischen als Attribut des Prädikatsnomens auftreten und tritt auch so auf:

Seržentų mėlyna manderužė, dragunų aukštoji kepuružė (*Liet. svotbinės dajnos* užrašytos par A. Juškeviče, 88), 'die Sergeanten haben blaue Röcke, die Dragoner hohe Mützen'.

Um dieser besonderen, spezifisch litauischen, Satzkonstruktion gerecht zu werden (*seržentų* ist hier Gen. Pl., ferner die ausgelassene Kopula *yra* 'ist') müßten wir hier eine umschriebene Übersetzung vornehmen: 'Die Uniform der Sergeanten ist ein blauer Rock, die Uniform der Dragoner ist eine hohe Mütze'. Auch in dem litauischen Satz ist *manderužė* ein Prädikatsnomen, ebenfalls *kepuružė* und *mėlyna* 'blau', ebenfalls *aukštoji* 'hoch' Attribute dieser Prädikatsnomina. Es kann, wie wir aus diesem Satz sehen, sowohl in einfacher (*mėlyna*), wie auch in Pronominalform (*aukštoji*) auftreten.

Wir wollen alle angeführten Beispiele von Schleicher, Kurschat und Valeckienė, die zum Beweis des prädikativen Gebrauchs dienen, näher prüfen. Ich erwähne nur diese drei Namen, weil die anderen zwar behaupten, daß die Pronominalform des Adjektivs im Litauischen, wenn auch ganz selten, Prädikatsnomen sein kann, doch keine Beispiele dafür geben.

So heißt es bei Fr. Kurschat, *Grammatik der littauischen Sprache,* S. 365 § 1339): ,,Das prädikative Adjectiv steht gewöhnlich in der einfachen (Unbestimmtheits-) Form, in der Bestimmtheitsform nur selten und zwar nur dann, wenn dadurch eine Hervorhebung oder eine Identitätsbezeichnung geschehen soll. Bsp.: dieser Rock ist der neue, *ta sermėga (tai) naujoji*. Doch sagt man dafür lieber: *tai naujoji sermėga*, das ist der neue Rock.

Bei Schleicher, *Litauische Grammatik*, 261 heißt es: „Das adjectiv als praedikat steht in der bestimten form, wenn im deutschen der bestimte artikel beim adjectiv steht, d. h. bloß dann, wenn beim substantiv das demonstrativ oder eine sonstige nähere bestimmung steht." Also:

Ta sermėga (tai) naujoji 'dieser Rock ist der neue'; *Tas kelias tikrasis* 'dieser Weg ist der rechte'.

In diesen beiden Sätzen handelt es sich nicht um Prädikatsnomina, sondern um die Attribute logischer Prädikatsnomina; denn wir könnten ohne weiteres sagen:

Ta sermėga tai naujoji sermėga 'dieser Rock ist der neue Rock', und *tas kelias tikrasis kelias* 'dieser Weg ist der rechte Weg'.

In beiden Sätzen sind die Pronominalformen *naujoji* und *tikrasis* ganz einwandfreie Attribute der Prädikatsnomina *sermėga* und *kelias*. Es kann hier aber der Zweifel entstehen, ob man im Litauischen nicht mit jedem attributiven Prädikat so vorgehen könnte. Die Frage ist deshalb gerechtfertigt, weil das Adjektiv als Prädikatsnomen, im Gegensatz zu dem deutschen Sprachgebrauch, immer das Geschlecht und die Zahl des Substantivs hat. Man sagt *sermėga nauja* 'der Rock ist neu', aber *sermėgos naujos*, 'die Röcke sind neu'. So könnte man glauben, daß man auch bei einem einfachen prädikativen Adjektiv das Substantiv im Prädikat immer wiederholen könne, also anstatt *sermėga yra nauja* auch immer *ta sermėga yra nauja sermėga* sagen könne. Dieser Zweifel muß hier behoben werden. Daher wollen wir jetzt diese beiden Sätze näher betrachten: *Ta sermėga yra nauja sermėga* und *Ta sermėga (tai) naujoji sermėga*.

Der erste Satz antwortet auf die Frage: Wie ist der Rock? — *Sermėga nauja* 'der Rock ist neu'.

Beim zweiten Satz müßten wir die Frage stellen: Welcher Rock ist es, der neue oder der alte, welcher von beiden?

Daraus ergibt sich: Wenn wir zu dem attributiven Prädikat das Substantiv des Subjekts wiederholen, bleibt der Satz grammatisch gesehen richtig, doch der Sinn des Gesagten wird ein anderer. Deshalb müssen wir unsere Zweifel aufgeben und eindeutig feststellen: man kann im Litauischen nicht mit jedem attributiven Prädikat so vorgehen. Dasselbe läßt sich natürlich zu den Sätzen von Kurschat und Schleicher sagen. Auf die Frage: Wie ist der Weg? müßten wir antworten: *kelias tikras*. Doch auf die Frage: welcher Weg ist das, der rechte oder der falsche? können wir antworten *tas kelias tikrasis*, aber würden antworten: *tas kelias — tikrasis kelias*, weil das der normale Sprachgebrauch ist.

Nachdem wir die verschiedene Fragestellung bei der einfachen und der Prominalform des prädikativen Adjektivs festgestellt haben, um die Frage, um welchen Satzteil in welchem Fall, um Prädikatsnomen oder um das Attribut, es sich handle, beantworten zu können, müssen wir wissen, auf welche Fragen in einem litauischen zusammengesetzten Prädikat das Prädikatsnomen oder das Prädikat antworten kann, und auch auf welche Fragen ein litauisches Attribut antwortet.

In der litauischen Syntax von J. Jablonskis erfahren wir folgendes über die zusammengesetzten Prädikate in einem litauischen Satz: sowohl die Kopula als auch Prädikatsnomina können in einem zusammengesetzten Prädikat sehr verschieden sein. Er führt eine Menge Beispiele an. Sie antworten auf verschiedene Fragen, meist aber auf *wie ist etwas?* oder *was ist etwas?* Jedoch in allen diesen Sätzen fand ich kein einziges Beispiel, das auf die Frage *welcher, welcher von beiden?* antworten könnte. Bei der näheren Definition des litauischen Attributs führt J. Jablonskis an, daß es auf die Fragen *welcher?, was für ein?, welcher von beiden?, wessen?, der wievielte?* u. s. w. antwortet und daß es, unter anderen Funktionen, die der näheren Bestimmung der Prädikate hat.

Wenn wir auf die Frage „wie ist der Rock?" mit dem litauischen Satz *sermėga nauja* antworten, haben wir es mit einem Prädikat zu tun, dessen Prädikatsnomen die einfache Form des Adjektivs ist. In dem Satz *ta sermėga (tai) naujoji* müssen wir die Frage aber stellen *welcher Rock ist es, der neue oder der alte?* und haben es also mit einem attributiven Adjektiv zu tun, das die Aufgabe hat, das logische Prädikatsnomen, das zwar nicht im Satz steht, doch aus dem logischen Zusammenhang leicht ersichtlich ist, von anderen Gegenständen dieser Art zu unterscheiden. Fügen wir dieses Prädikatsnomen zu dem Attribut hinzu, so verändern wir nicht den Sinn des Satzes. Es ist gleich, ob wir sagen: *tas kelias tikrasis* oder *tas kelias, tikrasis kelias*. Beide Male antworten wir auf die Frage *welcher der beiden Wege ist es?* Wenn wir dagegen diese Änderung in einem adjektivischen Prädikat *tas kelias tikras* vornehmen, das auf die Frage *wie ist der Weg?* antwortet, ändern wir den Sinn des Satzes; denn wenn wir sagen *tas kelias, tai tikras kelias*, so antworten wir auf eine andere Frage, und der Sinn des Satzes hat sich also verändert. In dem zweiten Satz haben wir es wieder mit einem zusammengesetzten Prädikat zu tun, wo *kelias* Prädikatsnomen, *tikrasis* aber nur ein Attribut des Prädikatsnomens ist. Daraus geht hervor, daß wir statt eines nicht attributiv gebrauchten Adjektivs im Prädikatsnomen seine attributive Verbindung mit einem Substantiv einsetzen können.

Es soll hier noch vermerkt werden, daß Jablonskis im § 23 seiner Syntax über einen sehr häufigen Gebrauch des sogenannten logischen, im Satz nicht erscheinenden Prädikatsnomens spricht. Aus dem Gesagten geht hervor, daß die beiden Pronominalformen des Adjektivs, mit denen Kurschat und Schleicher den prädikativen Gebrauch der Pronominalform des litauischen Adjektivs beweisen wollten, keine Prädikatsnomina, sondern Attribute zu diesen Prädikatsnomina sind und also nicht prädikativ, sondern attributiv gebraucht worden sind, da sie auf eine Frage antworten, die einem litauischen Attribut und nicht einem litauischen Prädikat eigen ist.

A. Valeckienė glaubt den prädikativen Gebrauch in den Sätzen zu finden, in denen die Prädikatsnomina allgemeine Begriffe bezüglich der Personen sind, wie z. B. *žmogus,* 'Mensch', *moteris* 'Frau', *mergaitė* 'Mädchen', *vaikinas* 'Jüngling'. Sie sind aus dem logischen Zusammenhang sehr leicht ersichtlich und werden wegen dieser Deutlichkeit ausgelassen. Rein äußerlich gesehen, treten dann im Prädikat nur ihre Attribute, also die Pronominalformen der Adjektiva, an ihrer Stelle hervor.

Dies geschieht in den folgenden Sätzen:

Negi gražasai (berniokas), ale baika (Sudeikiai, Utenos r., Valeckienė), 'er ist kein schöner Bursche, aber das ist nicht wichtig'.

Nepyk, Jurai: tu mūsų kaime pažangusis (žmogus), daugiau ir už mane moki, o mano galva kitaip rodo (P. Cvirka, *Raštai* VIII, 59), 'sei nicht böse, Juras: du bist der fortschrittliche Mensch in unserem Dorf, doch sagt mir mein Verstand was anderes'.

Negi aš čia senoja (moteris), ale nebegaliu, ir gana (Skapiškis, Valeckienė), 'ich bin keine alte Frau, aber ich kann nicht mehr, und das ist so'.

Diese „allgemeinen Begriffe" von A. Valeckienė sind nichts anderes als dieselben logischen Prädikatsnomina, wie sie schon Jablonskis nennt. Die Pronominalformen der Adjektiva sind die Attribute zu diesen logischen Prädikatsnomina. Auch hier ist die Funktion dieser Pronominaladjektiva, nicht auszusagen, *wie* sie sind, sondern sie von den anderen Personen dieses Kreises zu unterscheiden. Sie werden also nicht prädikativ, sondern attributiv gebraucht.

Ferner hält sie die Fälle, in denen die Pronominalform des Adjektivs in Verbindung mit den hinweisenden Pronomina wie *pats, visų, visu, kuo* einen Teil des Prädikats bildet, für den prädikativen Gebrauch der Pronominalform. Sie führt folgende Beispiele an:

Ta dičkė tai pati drąsioji (Vilkaviškis, Valeckienė) 'dieses große Mädchen ist die allermutigste'.

Karūniniai linai buvo patys geriejai (Skuodas, Valeckienė) 'der Kronenflachs war der allerbeste'.

Liepinis medus pats gerasai (Ignalina, Valeckienė), — — — 'Lindenblütenhonig ist der allerbeste'.

Pats gerasai ans man buvo (Dukštas, Valeckienė) 'Jener war zu mir der allerbeste'.

O už kan, o dėl ko tu jai dovanojai? Dovanojai tai mergelei didžias dovanėles. Tai už tai, tai dėl to, kad ji graži buvo: skaistveidelė, geltaplaukė, pati panagioji. (*Lietuviškos svotbinės dainos*, A. Juškevič) 'Und wofür und weshalb hast du sie beschenkt? Du hast diesem Mädchen große Geschenke gemacht. Das habe ich dafür, das habe ich deshalb gemacht, weil sie schön war: leuchtendes Gesichtlein, blondes Haar, und sie war die allergeschickteste'.

Po teisybės, stačiai per jį prapuolė mano rugiai ... Būdavo, iš viso lauko bus čia kuo geriausieji ... (Žemaitė, *Raštai* II, 248),

'Wenn man die Wahrheit sagt, es ist so, daß durch ihn mein Roggen nichts mehr taugt ... Und früher, vom ganzen Feld war er der allerbeste ...'

Šitas arklys bus visų gerasis (J. Jablonskis, *Gramatika*), 'dieses Pferd wird wohl das allerbeste sein'.

Kad druktesnio nebūt, būčiau visu druktasis (Kretingos r., Valeckienė), 'Wenn es keinen Stärkeren gäbe, wäre ich der allerstärkste'.

Wir haben es in diesen Sätzen also mit den folgenden Formen zu tun: *pati drąsioji, patys geriejai, pats gerasai, pati panagioji, kuo geriausieji, visų gerasis* und *visu druktasis.* Doch diese Formverbindung — Pronomen *pats, visų, visu, kuo* + Pronominalform des Adjektivs — ist im Litauischen nicht eine Pronominalform des Adjektivs, sondern ein gewisser Grad der Steigerung, die höchste Form des Superlativs, über welche uns alle Grammatiken der litauischen Sprache berichten: J. Jablonskis (*Lit. Gramm.* § 47) sagt: „Der höchste Grad der Adjektiva wird anders gebildet (als der Superlativ): *Jis visų (visu) geriausias mokinys* 'er ist der allerbeste Schüler, der beste Schüler'; *šitas arklys bus kuo geriausias* 'dieses Pferd ist wohl das allerbeste'; *čia bus pats gerasis, pats tikrasis šautuvas* 'diese Flinte ist die allerbeste, die allersicherste'. Er führt also folgende Formen des Superlativs an:

visų geriausias
kuo geriausias
pats tikrasis
pats gerasis.

Das heißt: Pronomen + Pronominalform des Adjektivs ergeben den Superlativ des Adjektivs.

A. Senn führt in seiner *Kleinen litauischen Sprachlehre* zur Bildung des

Superlativs: *pats gerasis, visų gerasis, visu gerasis* an und übersetzt es mit 'der allerbeste'.

In der Grammatik der litauischen Akademie der Wissenschaften (Vilnius, 1965, § 922) heißt es: „Die Bedeutung des 'visų aukščiausias laipsnis' (des allerhöchsten Steigerungsgrades) haben in der heutigen litauischen Literatursprache auch die umschriebenen Formen, gebildet aus den Pronominalformen des Adjektivs und mit diesen koordinierten Formen des Pronomens *pats* oder, zu einem Partikel gewordenen Gen. Pl. des Pronomens *visas.*" Wir sehen, daß aus der Verbindung des Pronomens *pats* oder *visas* + Pronominalform des Adjektivs eine neue grammatische Form entsteht — ein Superlativ, nämlich der allerhöchste Superlativ.

So tritt in allen diesen vorher zitierten Sätzen von Valeckienė die Pronominalform des Adjektivs nicht in der Funktion des Prädikats, sondern in der Funktion der Steigerung auf.

Aber wir können diese Superlativformen genausowenig für Pronominalformen des Adjektivs halten, wie die Pronominalformen, die heute Substantiva sind, ablehnen. Die Substantivierung ist eine der Funktionen der Pronominalform und als substantivierte Adjektiva treten diese Formen als Prädikatsnomina auch auf. Sie treten hier in der Funktion der Substantivierung auf, also als Substantiva, auch wenn sie die Form eines Pronominaladjektivs bewahren. Auf diese Art können wir die letzte Gruppe des vermeintlichen prädikativischen Gebrauchs der Pronominalform erklären.

Aus dem Gesagten geht hervor, daß die Pronominalformen des Adjektivs in einem Prädikat keine Prädikatsnomina sind. Es handelt sich dabei um:

1) Attribute der logischen Prädikatsnomina
2) Superlative der Adjektiva
3) substantivierte Adjektiva, also Substantiva.

Diesen Sachverhalt finden wir in allen Sätzen, die den prädikativen Gebrauch der Pronominalform des Adjektivs beweisen sollten. (Dabei ist nicht zu vergessen, daß sie sehr selten in der Sprache und im Schrifttum gebraucht werden.) Zwangsläufig geht daraus hervor, daß die Pronominalform des Adjektivs zwar einen Teil eines zusammengesetzten Prädikats bilden kann, daß sie aber nie als selbständiges Prädikat im Litauischen auftreten kann.

On the Definite Forms of the Adjective
in the Lithuanian Predicate

The definite form of the adjective in Lithuanian (seldom used in speech and literature) can never occur as an independent predicate, but only as part of a compound predicate, and the sense is strictly speaking not predicative. This form is in fact either: 1) an attributive of the logical predicative noun; 2) the superlative of the adjective, or 3) a nominalized adjective, i.e. a substantive.

ALFRED BAMMESBERGER

Litauisch *lãpė* und lateinisch *volpēs*[1]

1. Zum Beweis voreinzelsprachlicher *-ē-Stämme werden in der indogermanistischen Fachliteratur oft die Gleichungen lat. *facēs*: lit. *žvãkė* 'Kerze',[2] lat. *volpēs* 'Fuchs': lit. *lãpė* 'Fuchs'[3] angeführt. Vom Standpunkt des Indogermanischen sind Stämme auf *-ē- praktisch nur für die nominale Verwendung einer auf *-ē-* endigenden Wurzel zu postulieren: ai. *śrad-dhā* 'Vertrauen, Glauben' basiert auf einem Stamm idg. *-dhē-,[4] und dieser Stamm *-dhē-[5] dürfte in lat. *crē-dē-s* vorliegen, das seinerseits die Grundlage für die sonst unbegreifliche Bildung *fidēs* 'Treue, Glaubwürdigkeit'[6] war. Es soll hier nun überprüft werden, ob die erwähnten Gleichungen zwischen Lateinisch und Baltisch beweiskräftig sind.

2. Für die erste der beiden Gleichungen muß der Hinweis genügen, daß *facēs* nur als Glossenwort[7] bekannt ist. Strikt beweisen läßt sich nicht, daß diese Form *facēs* der Ausgangspunkt von lat. *fax* 'Fackel' ist. Daher kann man auf die Zusammenstellung lat. *facēs*: lit. *žvãkė*[8] nichts bauen[9].

3. Die Überprüfung der Gleichung lat. *volpēs*: lit. *lãpė*[10] geschieht in zwei Schritten: wenn hier eine beweiskräftige Übereinstimmung vorliegt, müssen sich die beiden Wörter für 'Fuchs' in Wurzel und Stammbildung gleichen.

4. Schon bei der Betrachtung der Wurzel kommen jedoch Zweifel an der Richtigkeit dieser Verknüpfung auf. Während lat. *volp-* wohl mit Recht auf idg. *wl̥p-[11] zurückprojiziert wird, müßte diese Wurzelstufe lit. *vilp-* ergeben und liegt möglicherweise in lit. *vilpišỹs* 'wilde Katze' vor. Völlig unbefangen würde man für lit. *lap-* von idg. *lop-* ausgehen: *wlop-* ist freilich auch denkbar[12] und kann als *o*-Stufe zu *wl̥p-* aufgefaßt werden. Wenn aber Ablautvarianten anzunehmen sind, dann verliert die Gleichung sehr an Durchschlagskraft. Für die *ē*-Stämme würden wir theoretisch entsprechendes Ablautverhalten erwarten wie bei den *ā*-Stämmen: keine Ablautalternationen in der Wurzel, lediglich für das Stammelement *-ē- würde man Ablaut mit der Nullstufe *-ə-* annehmen. Es ist daher unbegreiflich, warum ein ursprünglicher *ē*-Stamm die beiden Ablautvarianten *wl̥p-ē-* (>lat. *volpēs*) und *wlop-ē-* (>lit. *lãpė*) aufweisen sollte.

5. Beim Vergleich der Stammbildung von lat. *volpēs* und lit. *lãpė* fallen sofort zwei Unterschiede auf:[13] lat. *volpēs* hat sigmatischen Nom. Sg. gegenüber dem asigmatischen lit. *lãpė*; das -*ė* von lit. *lãpė* ist geschleift intoniert[14], während man für einen indogermanischen Monophthong *-ē- Stoßton erwarten sollte. Diese beiden Abweichungen könnte man jedoch durchaus als einzelsprachliche Neuerungen begreifen. Bei lat. *volpēs* wäre das -*s*, das fast alle Deklinationen im Nom. Sg. aufweisen, verallgemeinert worden; andererseits könnte die geschleifte Intonation des -*ė* in lit. *lãpė* von denjenigen *ė*-Stämmen herrühren, deren -*ė* als Kontraktionsprodukt regelmäßig Zirkumflex[15] hatte. Trotzdem lassen es die angeführten Diskrepanzen kaum zu, die Gleichung lit. *lãpė*: lat. *volpēs* aufrechtzuerhalten. Wir müssen nun untersuchen, wie sich die beiden Wörter im Lexikon des Litauischen und Lateinischen einordnen lassen.

6. Lit. *lãpė* muß zweifelsohne im Zusammenhang der Tiernamen auf -*ė* gesehen werden. Dafür zunächst einige Beispiele: lit. *blãkė* 'Wanze', *gyvãtė* 'Schlange', *griežė̃* 'Wachtelkönig', *kãlė* (und *kalė̃*) 'Hündin', *kándė* 'Motte', *katẽ* (und *kãtė*) 'Katze', *kiaũlė* 'Schwein', *kiáunė* (und *kiaunẽ*) 'Marder' (vgl. apr. *caune* /Voc. 663/ 'mart'), *kregždẽ* (und *krẽgždė*) 'Schwalbe', *musẽ* (und *mùsė*) 'Fliege', *sráigė* (und *sraigė̃*) 'Schnecke', *stum̃brė* 'Büffelkuh', *vìlkė* 'Wölfin', *žýlė* 'Meise', *žvýnė* 'Ratte'[16], lett. *sniedze* 'Schneevogel'.

7. Bei den meisten der angeführten Tiernamen auf *-ē* ist die etymologische Verknüpfung zu unklar, um Spekulationen über die Entstehung des Stammelements *-ē- zu gestatten; aber bei einigen kann man den Versuch immerhin wagen.

8. Da lit. *vìlkas* 'Wolf' offensichtlich zu ai. *vṛka-* 'Wolf' gehört, wird man auch lit. *vìlkė* mit ai. *vṛkí-* (<idg. *$w\k^{w}í$-) zusammenstellen. Es wäre denkbar, daß bei *$w\k^{w}$-i- im Baltischen noch das typische Femininzeichen -*ā*[17] antrat und *vilk-ī-ā über *vilk-ij-ā zu *vilk-ē wurde. Kuryłowicz leitet *vìlkė* von der *y*-Bildung idg. *$w\k^{w}$-iy-o- ab[18], deren Femininum zu lit. *vìlkė* führt. In beiden Deutungen wird -*ė* als Reflex von *-iyā aufgefaßt.

9. Die Ansicht, daß *-ē* als Reflex von idg. *-iyā gelten kann, läßt sich durch folgende Tiernamen stützen. Apr. *wosee* (Voc. 676) 'czege' = 'Ziege' steht lit. *ožȳs* 'Ziegenbock', lett. *ázis* gegenüber. Da die maskuline Form *āžis (>lit. *ožȳs*, lett. *ázis*) kaum etwas anderes als idg. *aĝ-iyo-s[19] darstellen kann, wird man das in apr. *wosee*[20] vorliegende balt. *āžē als das zugehörige Femininum *āĝ-iyā betrachten.

10. Die durch apr. *wosee*: ostbalt. *āžīs angedeutete Vermutung, daß baltische Tiernamen auf *-iy-Bildungen zurückgehen können, deren Maskulinform *-iyo-s durch *-īs reflektiert wird, während das dazugehörige Femininum *-iyā als *-ē auftritt, läßt sich durch das Wort für 'Pferd' er-

härten. Lit. *arklỹs* muß wohl als 'zum Pflug (*árklas*) gehörig' aufgefaßt werden, d. h. es liegt eine Bildung auf *-iy-o*, nämlich *arkl-ĩs*[21], vor.

11. Obwohl die Alternante *-iy-* des Morphems *-y-* nach dem Gesetz von Sievers und Edgerton[22] ursprünglich nur nach langer Silbe auftrat, finden wir balt. *-ė*, also den Reflex von *-iy-ā*, auch nach kurzer Silbe. So kann etwa trotz der semantischen Schwierigkeiten kaum ein Zweifel bestehen, daß lit. *gyvãtė* 'Schlange' zu *gyvatà* 'Leben' gehört[23]. Aber die Bildung von *gyvãtė* geschah eben zu einer Zeit, da das Gesetz von Sievers und Edgerton nicht wirksam war.

12. Man braucht sicherlich nicht für jeden Tiernamen auf *-ė* eine Grundform auf *-iyā* zu postulieren. Vielmehr hat sich *-ė*, das in einer Anzahl von Fällen regelmäßig entstanden ist, ohne Zweifel über seine ursprünglichen Grenzen hinaus verbreitet. Auch der umgekehrte Vorgang läßt sich beobachten: nach dem Gesagten ist *kándė* 'Motte' regelmäßig von *kand-ijā* zu erwarten, wir finden aber auch *kándžia*, also den Reflex von *kand-jā*[24].

13. Es ist daher willkürlich, wenn man *lãpė* aus dem Zusammenhang der Tiernamen auf balt. *-ė* < *-iyā* herausreißt und einen Stamm auf *-ē* dafür postuliert. Wenn wir jedoch im *-ė* von *lãpė* den Reflex der Femininform *-iyā* des Bildungselements *-iy-o-* erkennen, dann erhebt sich die Frage, wie *lãp-* aufzufassen ist. Eine überzeugende Antwort scheint nicht möglich. Da aber 'Pferd' als 'das zum Pflug gehörige Tier' zu verstehen ist (vgl. § 10), kann man immerhin erwägen, ob 'Fuchs' vielleicht als 'das zum Blatt (*lãpas*), d. h. zum Laub des Waldes, gehörige Tier' aufgefaßt werden kann[25]. Freilich ist das nicht mehr als eine Vermutung. Jedenfalls dürfte kaum ein Grund vorliegen, in lit. *lãpė* einen grundsprachlichen *-ē*-Stamm zu suchen: die wenigen angeführten Beispiele, die sich beliebig vermehren ließen, zeigen, daß *lãpė* in den Kreis der Tiernamen gehört, deren *-ė* auf *-iyā* zurückgeht.

14. Während sich lit. *lãpė* als baltische Bildung gut begreifen läßt, ist es ungleich schwieriger, lat. *volpēs* zu erklären. Von den auf *-ēs* endigenden Tiernamen (z. B. *fēlēs* 'Wildkatze', *mēlēs* 'Marder, Dachs') ist jedenfalls *canēs* 'Hund' als eine Neuerung des in gr. κύων, ai. *śvā́* und lit. *šuõ* vorliegenden *n*-Stammes aufzufassen. Für *verrēs* 'Eber'[26] erwägt Leumann, *Lateinische Grammatik* 232 Entstehung aus Nom. *wr̥s-ē*[27] > *worrē* > *werrē* mit Antritt eines *-s*. Wenn diese Erklärung zutrifft, können sich *canēs*[28] und *volpēs* nach *verrēs* gerichtet haben. Dann besteht auch vom Standpunkt des Lateinischen kein Grund mehr, in *volp-ēs* einen Stamm auf *-ē* zu sehen.

15. Obwohl bei der Beurteilung von lit. *lãpė* und lat. *volpēs* im einzelnen noch zahlreiche Fragen offen bleiben, dürfte doch klar sein, daß die Gleich-

setzung der beiden Wörter ausgeschlossen ist. Mit dem Namen für 'Fuchs' kann man also indogermanische *-$\bar{e}$-Stämme nicht wahrscheinlich machen.

Anmerkungen

1. Warren Cowgill und Oswald Szemerényi haben Entwürfe dieses Artikels gelesen und zahlreiche Verbesserungen vorgeschlagen. Ich bedanke mich dafür aufrichtig. Für verbleibende Mängel bin ich allein verantwortlich.

2. H. Pedersen, *La cinquième déclinaison latine*, Kopenhagen, 1926, 59 f., mit weiteren Hinweisen; E. Hermann, *KZ*, LXIX, 66 (1951); F. Specht, *Stand und Aufgaben der Sprachwissenschaft* 1924, 638.

3. W. Schulze, *KZ*, XLV, 287 f. = *Kleine Schriften* 218 f.; vgl. auch F. Specht, *Der Ursprung der indogermanischen Deklination*, Göttingen, o. J., 41. E. Fraenkel, *KZ*, LXIII, 190: ,,Die Gleichung ἀλώπηξ = *volpēs* (*volpēcula*), lit. *lãpė* ist ebenso evident wie lat. *facēs* = lit. *žvãkė*.''

4. Vgl. J. Kuryłowicz, *BSL*, LXI, 19. Über den ersten Bestandteil **kret-* und die phonologische Entwicklung von **kret-didhēmi* zu lat. *crēdō* s. O. Szemerényi, *Archivum linguisticum*, IV, 49–51.

5. Hierher gehören auch die lit. Bildungen auf -*dė*, z. B. *alù-dė* 'Bierstube'; Pedersen, *La cinquième déclinaison* 74 schreibt: ,,Ce sont là des nomina loci, développés sans doute de nomina actionis.''

6. Vgl. A. Meillet, *MSL*, XXII, 215–218. Leumann, *Lateinische Grammatik*, 232: ,,*fidēs* eine merkwürdige Kontamination aus Wurzelnomen **fid* und **crēdē*.''

7. W. M. Lindsay, *Sexti Pompei Festi de verborum significatu quae supersunt cum Pauli epitome* 77.19: *faces* antiqui dicebant, ut *fides*.

8. Das ähnliche Bedeutung aufweisende Trio lit. *lópė* 'Fackel, Licht, Bündel Leuchtspäne' (vgl. P. Skardžius, *Lietuvių kalbos žodžių daryba*, 74), apr. *lopis* (Voc. 44) 'Flamme (vgl. R. Trautmann, *Die altpreußischen Sprachdenkmäler*, 372), lett. *lãpa* 'Fackel, Kienfackel' (vgl. Mühlenbach–Endzelin, *Lettisch-deutsches Wörterbuch*, II, 439) basiert auf einer Grundlage balt. **lãp-*, deren Ursprung hier nicht von Bedeutung ist (vgl. Fraenkel, *Litauisches etymologisches Wörterbuch*, 386, Holthausen, *IF*, XXXIX, 62 f.): die drei Substantiva lassen sich als Stämme auf *-$\bar{a}$ (lett. *lãpa*), *-iyā* (lit. *lópė*) und *-iyo-s* (apr. *lopis*) verstehen. Unter diesen Umständen wird man nicht ohne weiteres für lit. *žvãkė* einen ursprünglichen *-$\bar{e}$-Stamm postulieren: *žvãkė* kann bildungsmäßig in Parallele zu *lópė* gesetzt werden, nur fehlt bei *žvãkė* das Vergleichsmaterial aus den Schwestersprachen.

9. Vgl. Ernout-Meillet, *Dictionnaire étymologique de la langue latine*[4], Paris, 1959, 222: ,,Il n'y a rien à tirer de la glose P.F. 77,19 ... parce qu'on ne sait ce qu'il faut entendre par *facēs*. ... Le rapprochement de lit. *žvãkė* 'lumière' est en l'air. Mot technique, d'origine inconnue.''

10. Lit. *lãpė* hat eine genaue Entsprechung in apr. *lape* (Voc. 658) 'vochz' = 'Fuchs'. In lett. *lapsa* liegt eine Weiterbildung vor, deren -*s*- an -*š*- in lit. *vilpišỹs* erinnert: ein kurzer Vokal kann im Lettischen zwischen -*p-s*- durchaus synkopiert worden sein.

11. Vgl. etwa J. Pokorny, *Indogermanisches etymologisches Wörterbuch*, 1179.

12. Vgl. Specht, *KZ*, LIX, 118.

13. Vgl. Pedersen, *La cinquième déclinaison*, 60.

14. Ein stoßtoniges -*ė*- hätte nach dem Gesetz von F. de Saussure den Akzent der vorhergehenden zirkumflektierten Silbe *lãp*- angezogen.

15. Siehe Stang, *Vergleichende Grammatik der baltischen Sprachen*, 202, auch 115.

16. Die Akzentuierung der litauischen Beispiele ist aus Niedermann–Senn–Brender– Salys, *Wörterbuch der litauischen Schriftsprache*, I–V, Heidelberg, 1932–1968, übernommen.

17. Professor Szemerényi macht mich aufmerksam auf eine umfassendere Tendenz der *-ī/ij*-Stämme in die *-ī/(i)yā*-Klasse überzugehen; balt. *vilkijā* kann auch auf diesem Weg erklärt werden. Vgl. Skardžius 71 zu lit. *vilkė* gegenüber ai. *vṛkī*-: ,,yra galimas daiktas, kad čia kuriuo nors analoginiu būdu pirmykštis -*ī* yra paverstas į mūsų -*ė*."

18. *Indogermanische Grammatik*, II, 147 (Heidelberg, 1968): statt **u̯ilkii̯'ā* muß es **u̯ilkii̯'ā* heißen. Die Form **wl̥kʷ-iy-o*- wäre nach dem Gesetz von Sievers und Edgerton (*Language*, X, 235–264; IXX, 83–124; XXXVIII, 568) für das Indogermanische nicht zulässig. Durch die Entwicklung **l̥ > *il* wurde jedoch die erste Silbe im Baltischen lang: wenn zu jener Zeit das Gesetz wirksam war, entstanden **vilk-ij-as* m. und **vilk-ij-ā* f. regelmäßig. Über die Bedeutung der Bildungen auf **-yo*- bemerkt J. Kuryłowicz, *BSL*, LXI, 14: ,,Les noms hérités en -*i̯o*-, -*i̯ā*-, ainsi que leurs variantes en -*ii̯o*-, -*ii̯ā*-, étaient en principe, au moins à l'origine, des adjectifs, bien que fréquemment une forme en -*ios*, en -*iom*, ou en -*iā*, sémantiquement détachée et isolée, devenait un substantif."

19. Vermutlich wird man **āĝ-iyo*- als Vṛddhibildung **āĝ*- zu dem in ai. *ajá*- 'Ziegenbock' vorliegenden idg. **āĝ-ó*- mit dem Ableitungssuffix -*y*-, d. h. -*iy*- nach langer Silbe, auffassen.

20. Über balt. **ā* im Preußischen vgl. N. van Wijk, *Altpreußische Studien*, 42–47, wo jedoch *wosee* nicht behandelt wird. S. noch Stang, *Vergleichende Grammatik*, 37–42, Endzelin, *Altpreußische Grammatik*, 38. Zum *w*- in *wosee* vgl. W. R. Schmalstieg, *Studies in Slavic Linguistics and Poetics in Honor of Boris O. Unbegaun* (New York– London, 1968), 191.

21. Zur phonologischen Entwicklung **-iyo-s > *-ijas > -īs* s. Stang, *Vergleichende Grammatik*, 188–192, J. Endzelin, *Lettische Grammatik*, (Heidelberg, 1923), 302. Über das Wort 'Pflug' (idg. **arə-tro*-), das im Baltischen und Slavischen in gleicher Weise umgestaltet wurde, vgl. O. Szemerényi, *Kratylos*, II, 120 f., *Die Welt der Slaven*, XII, 277 f.

22. Vgl. Anm. 17.

23. Vgl. Fraenkel, *Litauisches etymologisches Wörterbuch*, 155, Skardžius, 338, Leskien, *Die Bildung der Nomina im Litauischen* 282.

24. Vgl. auch *musià* und *mùsė* 'Fliege'; s. W. R. Schmalstieg, *Lingua*, IX, 263.

25. Da in Bildungen wie lit. *lapijà* 'Laubwerk' (Skardžius, 81) -*ija* nicht zu -*ė* kontrahiert wurde, müssen wir wohl annehmen, daß diese Formationen einer Epoche nach der Entwicklung **-ijā > *-ē* entstammen; vgl. dazu ausführlich F. Sommer, *Die indogermanischen iā- und io-Stämme im Baltischen*, Leipzig, 1914, 23 ff.

26. Es ist unverständlich, wie V. Pisani, *Baltistica*, IV (1), 16 lat. *verrēs* mit lit. *veřšis* 'Kalb' gleichsetzen kann, nachdem er auf der vorhergehenden Seite lat. *volpēs* mit lit. *lãpė* vereint hat: der Gen. Sg. von lit. *veřšis* lautet *veřšio*, also liegt im Lit. ganz klar eine Bildung auf **-iy-o*- vor, die in keiner Weise mit der Stammbildung von lat. *verr-ēs* vergleichbar ist.

27. Zur Stütze dieses Ansatzes wird etwa bei Walde-Hofmann, *Lateinisches etymologisches Wörterbuch*, II, 761 ,,gr. el. Ϝάρρην 'männlich'" angeführt; vgl. auch A. Ernout, *BSL*, XLI, 112, ders., *Philologica*, I, Paris, 1946, 150, M. Leumann, *Lateinische Grammatik*, 232, V. Pisani, *Baltistica*, IV (1), 16. Diese Angabe beruht jedoch auf einem Irrtum. Bei der Form Ϝαρρεν in der eleischen Inschrift αἴ ζέ τις κατιαραύσειε, Ϝάρρἐν ὂρ Ϝαλεῖὅ handelt es sich um einen imperativisch gebrauchten Infinitiv; s. H. Collitz, *Sammlung der griechischen Dialektinschriften* I, Berlin, 1884, 321, Bechtel, *Die griechischen Dialekte*, II, Berlin, 1923, 864, Schwyzer, *Dialectorum Graecarum exempla*, Leipzig, 1923, 211, C. D. Buck, *The Greek Dialects*, Chicago–London, 1965, 259 f. Buck übersetzt: 'If any one brings a charge (against them), he shall be prosecuted as in the case of (a charge against) a citizen of Elis'. (260). Im Griechischen finden sich nur die Formen ἄρσην, ἄρρην, ἔρσην (vgl. av. *aršan-*); s. E. Benveniste, *BSL*, XLV, 101, H. Frisk, *Griechisches etymologisches Wörterbuch*, I, Heidelberg, 1960, 566, P. Chantraine, *Dictionnaire étymologique de la langue grecque*, Paris, 1968, 116.

28. S. Kuryłowicz, *BSL*, LXI, 20 (1964). Zur Deutung von *can-* vgl. O. Szemerényi, *Studi linguistici in onore di Vittore Pisani*, Brescia, 1969, 979–984.

Lithuanian *lãpė* and Latin *volpēs*

Lith. *lãpė* and Lat. *volpēs* have repeatedly been adduced as evidence for Indo-European stems in *-ē*. The two nouns must, however, be included in the groups of animal names which in Lithuanian appear with the ending *-ė*, in Latin with *-ēs*. It can be shown that Lith. *-ė* here reflects IE *-iyā*; therefore *lãpė* cannot be used as evidence for original *-ē*-stems.

HANS HOLM BIELFELDT

Die baltischen Lehnwörter und Reliktwörter im Deutschen

1. Unmittelbares Einzugsgebiet baltischen Wortschatzes war das Deutsche in „Ostpreußen", wo seit dem 13. Jh. bis zum Ende des Deutschen Reiches i. J. 1945 deutsche Sprache lebte, das Gebiet von der Memel bis zur Weichsel.

1.1. Von den baltischen Sprachen hat das Lettische die geringste unmittelbare Berührung mit dem Deutschen Ostpreußens gehabt. Kurische Fischer sind in mehr oder weniger nomadisierender Lebensweise an der Küste der Ostsee von nördlich Memel (Клайпеда) bis fast nach Danzig (Gdańsk) seit dem 13. Jh. historisch bezeugt, besonders kompakt auf der Kurischen Nehrung, auch an den festländischen Ufern des Kurischen Haffs; Tetzner nannte die Zahl der lettisch sprechenden Fischer in Ostpreußen für das Jahr 1897 mit 3816 Seelen[1]. Hiervon ausgehende lettische Wörter im Deutschen Ostpreußens sind nie festgestellt worden. Das „Baltendeutsche" in Lettland und Estland hat viele lettische Lehnwörter, die aber im folg. nur zum etymologischen Vergleich gelegentlich herangezogen werden[2]. Ob Wörter aus dem Baltendeutschen nach Ostpreußen gelangten, ist im einzelnen Fall schwer nachzuweisen. V. Kiparsky, *Fremdes im Baltendeutsch*, Mém. Soc. Néo-Phil. XI, Helsinki 1936 (weiter: Kip.) S. 118 trennt z. B. baltend. *Witze* 'Rute' (lett. *vice*) von ostpreuß. *Witze, Fitze* gleicher Bed., das er aus lit. *vycas* herleitet.

2. In das Deutsche Ostpreußens sind Wörter aus dem Preußischen und dem Litauischen gelangt. Die neuen Bearbeiter des *Preußischen Wörterbuchs* in Kiel (vgl. E. Riemann, „Wortgeogr. u. Besiedlungsgesch. Altpreussens", Nd. Jahrb. 88 (1965), 72–106 (weiter Rie.) stellen in den Vordergrund, daß die von Westen kommenden deutschen Kolonisatoren auf die preußische Sprache trafen, daß diese in Ostpreußen zum Substrat des Deutschen gehörte. Mit diesem baltischen Preußisch, das nicht über das 17. Jh. hinaus lebte, ist die Bezeichnung des von Deutschen kolonisierten Gebietes als „Preußen" und seiner deutschen Sprache als „preußisch" verbunden; die Unternehmen der Sammlung des Wortschatzes der deutschen Sprache

Ostpreußens werden von Frischbier (1882), Ziesemer (1935 ff.) und auch wieder von den heute in Kiel tätigen Germanisten als ,,Preußisches Wörterbuch'' bezeichnet. Die Bezeichnung einer deutschen Sprache als preußisch braucht nicht mißverständlich zu sein. Auch Germanisten bezeichnen das baltische Preußisch gern als ,,Altpreußisch'', und es bleibt unklar, ob dadurch das deutsche Ostpreußisch unausgesprochen als neupreußisch bezeichnet wird. Wenn in der Baltistik das baltische Preußisch außer preußisch auch als altpreußisch bezeichnet wird, so soll das nur auf das Fehlen des Preußischen in jüngerer Zeit hinweisen. — Aber an den starken Emotionen, die mit dem preußischen Staat, der preußischen Tradition usw. in der deutschen Geschichte verbunden sind, nahmen wohl auch deutsche Linguisten gelegentlich teil. Es ist z. B. charakteristisch, daß nach 1933, als man in Ostpreußen ,,fremde'' alt überlieferte Ortsnamen amtlich durch neue deutsche Bildungen ersetzte, man Ortsnamen litauischer Herkunft beseitigte, nicht aber Namen preußischer Herkunft; was man als preußisch ausgeben konnte, durfte gerettet werden, offenbar auf Grund jener politischen Emotionen. Das Preußische wurde als alt und gewissermaßen heimisch (sogar als germanisch, in offiziellen Schriftstücken) angesehen, das Litauische als fremd. — Rie. sucht im Deutschen Ostpreußens die generelle Unterscheidung alter Reliktwörter aus dem Preußischen gegenüber jungen Lehnwörtern aus dem Litauischen. Aber die Bezeugung des Alters eines baltischen Wortes im Deutschen ist von Zufällen abhängig; die letzte wortgeographische Verbreitung in Ostpreußen, die Rie. für einige Wörter subtil untersucht und auf die er sich stützt, kann durch spätere Wortwanderungen, Aussterben in einigen Gebieten usw. entstanden sein. Falkenhahn wies gegenüber früheren Ansichten nach[3], daß die alte Sprachgrenze zwischen dem Preußischen im Westen und dem östlich von ihm liegenden Litauischen über die Flüsse Alle und Deime hinaus weiter nach Westen lag. Grundlage für Entlehnungen aus dem Litauischen konnte nicht nur die litauische Einwanderung von Osten her seit dem 15. und 16. Jh., sondern auch alteingesessene litauische Bevölkerung in Ostpreußen, und zwar nicht nur in seinem östlichsten Teil, sein. — A. Sabaliauskas, ,,Vokiečių kalbos lituanizmai'', *Lietuvių kalbos leksikos raida*, Vilnius, 1966, S. 96 ff. (weiter:Sab.) erwähnt in seiner Summierung der ,,Litauischen Wörter im Deutschen'' die Alternative preußischer Herkunft gar nicht; von den aus dem Preußischen hergeleiteten deutschen Wörtern läßt er die meisten unerwähnt, andere leitet er aus dem Litauischen her, und für einige wenige Wörter nennt er litauische und preußische Entsprechungen nebeneinander, ohne auf die Alternative einzugehen.

Als Entlehnungen aus baltischen Sprachen gelten im folg. ausschließlich und alle Wörter, die in das Deutsche unmittelbar aus einer baltischen Sprache gelangten, also im Baltischen alt eingesessene Wörter sowie erst aus anderen Sprachen in das Litauische bzw. Preußische gelangte Wörter.

3.1. Aus dem Preußischen stammt mit großer Sicherheit eine Gruppe von Wörtern, die im (deutschen) Schrifttum des Deutschen Ordens (ostwärts des Weichsel) im 14.–16. Jh. bezeugt sind[4]. Die Kontakte des deutschen Ordens mit der preußischen Urbevölkerung liegen auf der Hand. Die im folg. aufgeführten Wörter sind alle zuerst in diesem Schrifttum (Urkunden u. a.) bezeugt und nur wenige außerdem auch noch später in Ostpreußen. Einheitlich erscheint diese Gruppe auch dadurch, daß alle Wörter Bedeutungskreisen des Rechtswesens angehören.

dassumptin 'Zehnte' — preuß. *dessimpts* Trau.[5], lit. *dešimtìs*.

sweike 'Arbeits- u. Dienstpferd', auch nach dem 16. Jh. noch bezeugt. — preuß. *sweike* Trau.

(jor)porlenke, parlenke 'Jahresgebühr', bis ins 18. Jh. bezeugt — preuß. *perlānk(e)i* 'gebührt' Trau., lit. *perleñkis* 'zukommender Anteil' Frä.[6] 356–7, mit d. *Jahr* — zusammengesetzt.

sunde 'Geldstrafe' — preuß. *sūnda* Trau., lit. *saṁdas* 'Miete', slaw. *sǫd* 'Gericht'.

sorgalio 'Wartgeld'.

porrẽpil 'Steuer für Kriegszüge' — vgl. lit. *rẽpti* 'umfassen'.

palleyde 'Hinterlassenschaft des Untertanen' — preuß. *polāikt* 'bleiben' Trau.

waidelotte, waideler, 'Priester der Preußen'. — s. Frä. 1180.

craysewisse 'Hafer' — preuß. *crays* 'Heu' Trau.

slusim 'Abgabe' — s. Frä. 836 s.v. *službà*.

witing 'Ordensdiener preußischer Herkunft' — preuß. *witing*, vgl. russ. витязь, altnord. *vikingr*, s. Vasmer, *Russ. et. Wb.* I, 206.

Dwarnik 'Hofmann'. Das Wort gelangte, wie lit. *dvãras* 'Hof' (Frä. 112), erst aus dem Slawischen ins Baltische; in das Deutsche Ostpreußens kann es aber, im Unterschied zu baltendeutsch *Dwornik* 'Hausknecht' (< russ. дворник, s. Kip. 153), nicht direkt aus einer slaw. Sprache gelangt sein.

3.2. Dieser Gruppe stehen durch ihre alte Bezeugung und ihre Zugehörigkeit zur Rechtsspähre, einige durch beides, folgende Wörter sehr nahe:

Zerm, Zarm 'Begräbnismahl, Leichenfeier, Festlichkeit' — preuß. *sirmen* Trau., lit. *šermens* Frä. 974. *Zerm* ist im D. vom 15.–17. Jh. bezeugt und steht mit diesem Alter und mit seiner Bedeutung jenen Wörtern der Ordenssprache recht nahe.

Kaddig 'Wacholder' — preuß. *kadegis* Trau., lett. *kadegs, kadags,* lit. *kadagỹs* Frä. 201. In *Kattichstrauch* ist das Wort schon bei S. Grunau bezeugt; Grunau (im 16. Jh.) bezeugt auch einige der o. als „ordenssprachlich" zusammengefaßten Wörter, und damit steht auch *Kaddig* in einigem Zusammenhang mit jener Gruppe. Von allen sicher aus dem Baltischen stammenden Wörtern hat *Kaddig* die weiteste Verbreitung im Deutschen erlangt: Es ist in ganz Ostpreußen verbreitet und über Ostpreußen hinaus weit nach Westen in deutsche Mundarten und auch ins neuhochdeutsche Schrifttum gelangt (Bie. 1963[7] S. 156): in Westpreußen, Pommern, Mecklenburg, Brandenburg, in der Altmark, sogar in Hamburg; das Vorkommen in Schlesien wird durch Einwanderung aus Ostpreußen erklärt. Pol. *kadyk* und tschech. *kadík* kommen aus dem Deutschen.[8] Baltendeutsch *Kaddak* ist von dem übrigen deutschen Vorkommen zu trennen; das Wort gelangte auch ins Estnische; lett. *kadiķis* stammt aus dem Nd.

Pawirpen, powirpen 'Tagelöhner, Freimann' seit a. 1604 bezeugt — preuß. *pawirps* 'frei', lit. *pavirpas* Frä. 558.

Talk(e) 'freiwillige Hilfsarbeit; Schmaus' in deutschen Texten Ostpreußens i. d. J. 1450 u. 1525 (wieder auch S. Grunau, der ordenssprachliche Tradition fortsetzt) — preuß. *tallokinikis* 'freier Mann' < **taloko* Trau.; lit. *talkà* 'zusammengebetene Arbeitsgemeinschaft, welche nach der Arbeit mit einem Schmaus bewirtet wird' Frä. Baltendeutsch *Talk, Talkus* ist eine von dem ostpreuß. Wort unabhängige Entlehnung des gleichen Etymons (Kip. 114).

3.3. Für einige Wörter, für die keine älteren Zeugnisse über das 19. Jh. hinaus vorliegen, wird preußische Herkunft ausschließlich aus der wortgeographischen Verbreitung in Ostpreußen geschlossen (Rie.).

Pintsch, Pinsch „Zunder, Feuerschwamm" — preuß. *pintys* Trau., lit. *pìntis* Frä. 504.

Margéll, Marjéll „Mädchen" — preuß. *mergo* Trau., lit. *mergà, marigẽlė,* lett. *mẽrģele* Frä. 439; das Wort ist im Deutschen über Ostpreußen hinaus verbreitet: in Danzig (auch *Mergell*)[9], Posen[10], Schlesien[11]; auch in der allgemeinen deutschen Umgangssprache kommt das Wort gelegentlich vor.

Kujel 'Eber' — preuß. *cuylis* Trau. lit. *kuilỹs* Frä. 305.

Palwe 'Heideland' — lit. *plýnas* 'kahl, baumlos' Frä. 611.

Duck, Dock, Dogg 'Iltis' — preuß. *duckis* 'Hamster' Trau. Baltend. *Ducker* 'Iltis' stammt aus lett. *dukurs* (Kip. 82).

4.1. Im Deutschen Ostpreußens des 19. u. 20. Jh. sind Wörter litauischer Herkunft bedeutend zahlreicher als die preußischer Herkunft. — Die Masse der litauischen Wörter ist erstmalig im 19. Jh., in Frischbiers Wb., bezeugt. Fast alle bereits im 16. Jh. oder noch früher bezeugten Wörter baltischer Herkunft erweisen sich mit größerer oder geringerer Wahrscheinlichkeit als preußischer Herkunft. Viele Studien in anderen Gebieten zeigen, daß in den Einzugsgebieten von Lehnwörtern diese nach ihrem Eindringen auch wieder dem Aussterben ausgesetzt waren; je jünger die Zeit ihres Eindringens, desto weiter reicht ihre Bezeugung oft in die Gegenwart. So könnte in Ostpreußen das erste Eindringen preußischer Wörter im allgemeinen bedeutend älter sein, das Eindringen litauischer Wörter im allgemeinen jünger. — Ziesemer (Anm. 4) und Rie. betonen, daß aus dem Litauischen stammende Wörter meistens nur im äußersten Nordosten Ostpreußens, in der Gegend von Memel, bezeugt seien, so z. B. *Repetschke* „Kröte" — lit. *repèčki* Sab. 100; *Wabbel* 'Käfer' — lit. *vãbalas* Sab. 101; *Burre* 'Schaf' s. u.; *Barbuttke* 'Marienkäfer' s. u.

Frischbier, unsere Hauptquelle für die aus dem Litauischen gekommenen Wörter, macht wenig Angaben über ihre Verbreitung; verhältnismäßig oft nennt er „Litauen" als Verbreitungsgebiet und meint das Gebiet mit starkem Anteil litauischer Sprache im damaligen Deutschen Reich im Nordosten Ostpreußens. — Die obige Beurteilung des quantitativen Verhältnisses von weniger preußischen und viel mehr litauischen Wörtern bedarf einer Einschränkung: Unsere gegenüber dem Litauischen viel geringere Bezeugung des Preußischen und das Fehlen lautlicher Kriterien führen zur Entscheidung für preußische Herkunft nur bei ganz spezifischen Merkmalen; alle merkmallosen Entlehnungen werden dem Litauischen zugeordnet.

4.2. Die kürzlich von Sab. zusammengestellte Liste von 120 aus dem Litauischen stammenden Wörtern, für die Sab. in seinen Formulierungen doch Vollständigkeit beansprucht, läßt sich um vieles verlängern. Im folg. bringe ich nur eine Liste von Ergänzungen, die aber immer noch keineswegs vollständig ist.

balditi 'in der Fischersprache das Klopfen, durch welches die Fische in das Netz gescheucht werden' — lit. *baldyti* Frä. s. v. *belsti*.

Barbutt(ke) 'Marienkäfer' Rie. 106, 92, *Barbusch, Barbuschke* und viele andere Formen Zie[12]. — lit. *barbùtė* Frä. s. v. *barbėti* 'klingen'.

Bluss 'Floh' Zie. — lit. *blusà*.

Burre 'Kiefernapfel', in der Kindersprache 'Schaf' Rie. 106 — lit. *bùre* Interj. zum Anlocken der Schafe; in der Kindersprache 'Schaf'.

Dirschas 'Leibriemen' Zie. Ma. 135 (s. Anm. 4) — lit. *dìržas*.

Fitze 'Rute, Zweig' — lit. *vycas*; s. o. S. 44.

Ganner 'Arbeiter' — lit. *gãnas* '(Pferde)hirt' Frä. s. v. *giñti*.

Krepsch(e) 'kleiner Sack, Brotbeutel'; ein*krepschen* 'heimlich in die Tasche stecken' Zie. 226 — lit. *krepšỹs*.

Marginne 'bunter Frauenrock'' — lit. *margas* 'bunt'.

Meszkere 'Aalangel' — lit. mészkere[13].

Norgel(eisen) 'Pflugschar' — lit. *norãgas*; dieses aus beloruss. нораг.

Padugnis 'Tiefe, Breite'; in die *P.* kommen 'in Bedrängnis kommen' — lit. *bedùgnis* Adj. 'ohne Boden'.

Pakul(k)s, Pokul(k)s, Pikellus 'Teufel' — lit. *pikùlas*, preuß. *pickūls*.

Parêske 'Bastkorb' — lit. *parìšti* 'binden' Wb. (Anm 14) 2, 526, *rìšti*.

Possêkel 'großer Schmiedehammer' — lit. *pasĕkelis, posĕkelis*.

spinken 'poltern, lärmen' — lit. *spiñgti* 'klingen, gellen'.

Stagutt 'Pflug' — lit. *stagùtas*.

Schachtarp 'die Zeit der Überschwemmungen und Unwegsamkeit im Frühjahr und Herbst' — lit. *šãktarpis* Frä. s. v. *šakà*

Scheschke 'Iltis' Rie. 105 — lit. *šẽškas*.

Wuẑen Pl. 'Schuhe aus Stoffresten' (v. Falkenhahn mündlich); Eggen*wuschen* 'dass'. Zie. — lit. *vyžà* 'Bastschuh'.

Diese Wörter, hier nur als Beispiele für die bei Sab. fehlenden Lehnwörter genannt, unterscheiden sich in der Verteilung auf ihre Bedeutungsbereiche nicht von der Gesamtheit der in Sab's Liste stehenden. Auch in diesen Ergänzungen sind z. B. wieder verhältnismäßig viele Bezeichnungen für Teile der Bekleidung und für Tiere enthalten. Der Anteil von Bezeichnungen für Spezifika der litauischen Folklore u. a., die im deutschen Wortschatz evtl. Exotika sein können, ist sogar geringer als in Sab's Liste. Wieviele der von Fri.[15] genannten Wörter so schwach in die deutsche Mundart einverleibt waren, daß sie eher Zitierung litauischer Wörter und weniger „Lehnwort" sind, ist aus Fri.'s Angaben nicht immer zu erkennen; aber auch hierin besteht zwischen Sab's Liste und der o. Ergänzungsliste kein Unterschied. Ob *Karausche* 'ein Fisch' (Bie. 1965[16], S. 37 ff.) ins Deutsche aus dem Litauischen gelangte, ist unsicher. *Karausche* ist außer in Ostpreußen in weiten deutschen Gebieten verbreitet und in die Schriftsprache gelangt. Die älteste Form, zuerst im Nd. a. 1490 *karusse*, ist besser aus lit. *karõsas* (dieses aus beloruss. *karas*) als aus poln. (gemeinslaw.) *karas* herzuleiten; lit. *karũšis* (*Lietuvių kalbos žodynas V* (1959), 32) kann aus dem Deutschen (rück) entlehnt sein, vgl. auch F. Hinze, *Wörterb. u. Lautl. der deutschen Lehnwörter im Pomorawischen* (Berlin 1965), 261.

Kussel, Kuschel 'niedriger Nadelbaum', das ebenfalls außer in Ostpreußen in anderen deutschen Gebieten weit verbreitet ist, ist aus lit. *kuslas* 'verkümmert, von Gewächsen' hergeleitet worden, was ebenfalls unsicher ist[17].

Weite Verbreitung eines Wortes über Ostpreußen hinaus spricht allein nicht gegen Herkunft aus dem Baltischen. Sab.'s Bemerkung (S. 96), in der deutschen Literatursprache gebe es keine litauischen Wörter, es gebe sie nur in den deutschen Mundarten Ostpreußens, muß mindestens durch *Elen* 'Elch' (s. u.), *Daggut* 'Birkenteet' (u. S. 54) und *Kaddig* 'Wacholder' (o. S. 47) korrigiert werden; diese stammen sicher aus dem Litauischen bzw. Preußischen und sind in der d. Literatursprache oder doch in der Umgangssprache bzw. in Mundarten weit nach Westen verbreitet.

5.1. Das Ziel einer historisch-genetisch begründeten Ordnung der Gesamtheit aller aus den verschiedenen slawischen Sprachen in die verschiedenen Bereiche des Deutschen gelangten Wörter verlangt u. a. auch die Aussonderung der aus baltischen Sprachen ins Deutsche gelangten Wörter. — In Ostpreußen, dem Einzugsgebiet baltischer Wörter ins Deutsche, haben Wörter nichtdeutschen Ursprungs häufig Etyma sowohl in slawischen wie in baltischen Sprachen. Die deutschen Mundarten Ostpreußens hatten zum Polnischen und seinen Dialekten mindestens ebenso starke Kontakte wie zum Balti schen; und westlich der Weichsel trafen die deutschen Siedler von vornherein nur auf slawische Bevölkerung. — Die Entscheidung zwischen baltischer oder slawischer Herkunft ist schwierig wegen der starken Gemeinsamkeit des Wortschatzes der baltischen und slawischen Sprachen auf Grund der Urverwandtschaft sowie der mannigfachen Lehnbeziehungen, vor allem der beloruss. Lehnwörter im Litauischen.

Sichere Kriterien für baltische Herkunft, außer dem Vergleich der geographischen Verbreitung in Vergangenheit und Gegenwart, bieten sich nur in den seltensten Fällen. So kann ostpr. *Bluss* 'Floh' (lit. *blusa* — urslaw. *blъcha*) wegen seines Lautstandes nur aus dem Baltischen stammen. — Für das in die d. Schriftsprache gelangte *Elen*tier 'Elch' (vgl. Anm. 16) ist *elint* im deutschen Teil des Elbinger deutsch-preuß. Voc. des 13./14. Jh. (Trau.) das älteste Zeugnis, also im Bereich Ostpreußens, wo der Elch vorkommt; auch im 16. Jh. ist *elendt* in Preußen bezeugt. Wegen der slawischen *j*-Prothese (z. B. poln. *jelen*) erscheint lit. *elnis*, alt *elenis* (preuß. *alne*) als die wahrscheinlichere Quelle; Brückner und Berneker behaupteten dennoch slawische Herkunft; dann müßte der Verlust des *j* bei der Übernahme ins Deutsche geschehen sein. — Für *Kaddig* (preuß. *kadegis*, lit. *kadagỹs* — poln. *kadyk*, s. o. S. 47) ist baltische Herkunft am wahrscheinlichsten, weil das Wort in slawische Sprachen nur durch Lehnbeziehungen gelangte; für poln. *kadyk* sind keine älteren Zeugnisse bekannt. Andererseits kann z. B. *Lodsche* 'Boot' (s. u. S. 54) nur aus einer slaw. Sprache (poln. *to'dz'* usw.), nicht aber aus lit. *aldijà, eldijà* stammen. — *Kissel* 'eine Speise' lautet in Ostpreußen *kisél*, im Baltend. *kisél*, und Kip. leitet das baltend. Wort aus russ. кисель, das ostpr. aus lit. *kisielius* her. — Die gleiche Teilung scheint zu verlangen l. *Pirogge* 'eine Speise' im Baltend., Ostpreußen, in der d. Schriftsprache und in deutschen Reiseberichten seit dem 17. Jh. — russ. пирог 2. *Piragge*, in der gleichen Bedeutung, im Baltend. und in Ostpreußen seit dem 17. Jh. (in Ostpr. in junger Zeit auch *Pirack* und *Pragge*) — lit. *piragas*. *Piroge* im Inseldeutschen der Slowakei — älter slowak. *pirog*[18] steht natürlich abseits; ostpreuß. *Pjerogge* stammt aus poln. *pierog*. Kip. hält für wahrscheinlich, daß die Form *Pirogge* nach Ostpreußen aus dem Baltend. gelangte; aber in die ostpr. Mundarten sind russische Wörter auch auf direktem Wege, durch russische Soldaten, gelangt! (Bie. *Zfsl* XII). Jedenfalls ist *Pirogge* auf verschiedenen Weg in das Deutsche gelangt. Sogar die Form *Piragge* könnte grundsätzlich aus dem Russischen stammen, wenn man den gewöhnlichen Gebrauch des Wortes im Plural und das Akanje (russ. пироги́) berücksichtigt.

Für einige Wörter wird baltische Herkunft behauptet, obwohl keine Argumente gegen ihre Herkunft aus dem Polnischen sichtbar sind. *Bartsch* 'die Pflanze Heracleum sphond.; Getränk daraus; Suppe aus roten Rüben; rote Rübe' (alle diese Bedeutungen bei Fri.), im Deutschen Ostpreußens schon seit dem 17. Jh. bezeugt, steht gegenüber poln. barszcz (russ. борщ usw.) und lit. *bar(k)stis* (Bie. 1963). Als Beweis für die Herkunft aus dem Litauischen nimmt Sab. auschließlich „die Bedeutung des deutschen Wortes" in Anspruch, ohne aber auf den Vergleich der Bedeutungen einzugehen. 'Heracleum', sicher die älteste Bed., ist nur im Deutschen und Poln. bezeugt; 'eine Suppe aus Heracl. im Poln.', ein 'Getränk' daraus im D., nichts derartiges im Lit.; 'die Suppe aus Rüben' in allen drei Sprachen; für das Poln. ist nachgewiesen, in welchen Phasen die Bereitung der Suppe von 'Heracl.' zur 'Rübe' wechselte[19]; die Bed. 'Rübe' ist nur im Lit. und bei Fri. bezeugt, aber diese Bed. konnte aus 'Rübensuppe' entnommen werden. Frischbiers Bemerkung, die Rübensuppe sei „ursprünglich Nationalgericht der Litauer", kann etymologisch nicht entscheiden. Das Wort ist in der Form *Barschtsch* auch im Deutschen Posens (Poznańskie)[20] und Schlesiens[21] bezeugt, in Schlesien (Szlązk) eindeutig aus dem Poln.

Auch ostpr. *Zwickel* 'Runkelrübe' leitet Sab. aus dem Lit. her. Man muß aber die viel weitere Verbreitung im Deutschen berücksichtigen: *Zwickel, Zwichel, Zwischel, Schwickel, Schwichel, Schwechel* — in Ostpr., Westpr., Pommern (Pomorze), Posen, Neumark, Brandenburg, Schlesien und im ungar. Bergland. Dem stehen gegenüber p. *ćwikła*, pomor. *čwikła, čvixla, cvikła* u. a., tschech. *cvikla* usw. — lit. *cviklas, čvikla, sviklas*. Sicher liegen verschiedene Übernahmen ins Deutsche vor. Gegen Entlehnung aus dem Lit. in Ostpreußen spricht auch, daß *Zwickel* schon im 16. Jh. in Westpreußen bezeugt ist[22].

5 – 701648 *Donum Balticum*

Für *Schischke* 'Tannenzapfen' hält Rie. für wahrscheinlich, daß es aus poln. szyszka nicht direkt ins Deutsche gelangte, sondern bereits vor der deutschen Besiedlung Ostpreußens aus dem Poln. in das Preußische entlehnt worden war, also im Deutschen Ostpreußens preußisches Reliktwort sei. Sein Argument ist die weite Verbreitung von *Schischke* in Ostpreußen, nach Westen bis an die Weichsel, die sich mit dem Siedlungsgebiet der Preußen deckt. Aber *Schischke* ist auch über die Weichsel hinaus nach Westen, bis nach Pommern, verbreitet, und Entsprechungen von poln. szyszka (slaw. *šiška*) sind auch in das Deutsche Schlesiens, der Lausitzen, des Vogtlandes, Obersachsens, Thüringens, Oberpfalz, Böhmens (Čechy), Mährens (Morava), Österreichs und noch anderer Gebiete gelangt[23]. Allerdings sind das voneinander unabhängige Entlehnungen aus verschiedenen slawischen Sprachen, die auch noch durch Wortwanderungen weitere Verbreitung erlangten. Slaw. *šiška* könnte, so wie es im Deutschen, Ungarischen und Litauischen (lit. *čečka*, *šyškà* u. a.) bezeugt ist, auch ins Preussische gelangt sein, obwohl es hier nicht bezeugt ist. Die weite Verbreitung der Entlehnungen aus *šiška*, die zum großen Teil durch Ausbreitung in der Zeit nach den Entlehnungen erreicht wurde, läßt aber diesen Weg doch auch für die weite Verbreitung in Ostpreußen zu. Die Herkunft von ostpreuß. *Schischke* aus dem Poln. paßt besser in das Gesamtbild als die aus dem Preußischen, wo das Wort nicht bezeugt ist.

5.2. Für einige ostpreußische Wörter mit der Alternative baltischer oder slawischer Herkunft steht ihrem Vorkommen in Ostpreußen das Vorkommen in der mittelniederdeutschen Schriftsprache des 13.–16. Jh. gegenüber, die Zentren westlich von Ostpreußen, in Lübeck, Wismar, Stralsund u. a. hatte. — In Sab's Liste der Entlehnungen aus dem Lit. stehen auch *Klete* (Fri. 'Nebengebäude; Gefängnis') und *Kausche* (Fri. 'hölzerne Kanne').

Klete ist seit dem 13. Jh. in mnd. Urkunden von Nowgorod bis Lübeck bezeugt, auch im deutschen Teil des Elbinger deutsch-preuß. Voc. des 13./14. Jh. (Trau.), also im Bereich Ostpreußens, und in den deutschen Mundarten Ostpreußens. Als Quelle der Entlehnung kommen vor allem lit. *klētis* und russ. *клеть* in Betracht. In der mnd. Schriftsprache haben wir etwa 50 Entlehnungen aus dem Russischen mit Sicherheit festgestellt, deren historische Grundlage die Handelsbeziehungen der Hanseaten nach Russland waren (Anm. 30); zu dieser Gruppe scheint mnd. *Klete* zu gehören. Andere Entlehnungen sind ostpr. *Klatke*, *Kletke*, hinterpom. *Klottke* aus poln. klatka, pomor. kletka; mhd. *glet* aus slowen. klet. Ob baltend. *Klete* zu jener mnd. Tradition gehört oder eine eigene Entlehnung aus dem Russ. ist, ist nicht sicher. Ostpr. *Klete* kann eine weitere unabhängige Entlehnung aus

dem Lit. sein. Es sind aber auch Beziehungen zwischen dem Deutschen Ostpreußens und dem westlicher liegenden Mittelniederdeutschen möglich. Für
Elen 'Elch' liegt Wanderung von Ostpreußen nach Westen nahe (o. S. 51);
für *Kaddig* 'Wacholder' (s. o. S. 47) ist die Verbreitung von Ostpreußen in
das westliche Niederd. sicher. Andererseits ist zu fragen, ob aus dem Mnd.
Wörter nach Ostpreußen gelangen konnten; die ersten Kolonisten Ostpreußens stammten z. T. aus nd. Gebieten; auch konnten vielleicht über die
hanseatischen Kontore an der Ostsee nd. Wörter nach Ostpreußen gelangen;
Lasten 'Wieselfelle', das zu jener Reihe russischer Entlehnungen im Mnd.
gehört, ist auch in Danzig und Pommern bezeugt.

Für *Kausche* besteht die Alternative seiner Herkunft aus lit. *káušas* oder
russ. ковш; die Reihe der Zeugnisse in allen drei Sprachen wird auch durch
die Bedeutung „Schöpfgefäß — Trinkgefäß" zusammengehalten. Im Mittelpunkt der deutschen Bezeugung steht die lange Reihe nd. Zeugnisse des
16. Jh., von Lübeck bis Stralsund: *kowschen, kowse, kowesken, kouweschen,
kawsch, causeken, kausch*; welche gemeinsame Lautung (welche deutsche
Substitution) — *ow, ou, au* — oder welche Reihenfolge einer evtl. inner-
deutschen Lautentwicklung liegt vor? Einige Formen zeigen die Einverleibung mit dem Dem.-Suffix nd. *-ken* (hd. *-chen*); im Mnd. wechselt *sk* mit
sch. — Auch mit seinem Bedeutungsbereich stellt sich das Wort zu jener
großen Gruppe russischer Lehnwörter im Mnd. (s. o.). Auch in den
Berichten einer hanseatischen Gesandtschaft nach Moskau i. J. 1603 steht
kausch, sicher noch im Zusammenhang jener mnd. — hanseatischen Tradition, und in diesen Berichten stehen etwa 40 eindeutig aus dem Russischen
übernommene Wörter[24], dagegen außer dem in Frage stehenden *kausch*
keine aus dem Lit. übernommenen. In einem nd.-russ. Gesprächsbuch von
ca. 1650 enthalten zwei Satzstücke das Wort ковш (transkribiert *kofs*; in
dieser Hs. russ. ш — ständig *s*)[25]; die Tradition dieser Gesprächsbücher
stammt aus dem 16. Jh., wie die Zeugnisse des Lehnwortes; russ. ковш (seit
dem 14. Jh. bezeugt) war also den nd. Kaufleuten besonders gut bekannt.
Das für das Baltend. a. 1860 aufgezeichnete *Koptschik* liest Kip. (161) als
Kowschik und sieht darin eine Entlehnung aus dem russ. ковшик, Dem. zu
ковш. — *Kausse* 'Schöpflöffel' in Bremen (Wb. a. 1767) kann nicht unmittelbar mit ostpr. *Kausche* verbunden werden, sondern muß jener mnd.
Tradition zugeordnet werden; *Kowse* in dem „Plattdeutschen Wb. nach der
pommerschen u. rügischen Ma." von Dähnert a. 1781 ist von ihm ausdrücklich markiert als veraltet und nur in Urkunden bezeugt. Aus dem Mnd.
hergeleitet werden dän. (Dial.) *kovs*, älter *kouse*, dän. und schwed. Dial.
kaus, schwed. *kausa* schon im 15. Jh.[26] — Fri. verzeichnet für 'hölzerne
Kanne' *Kausche* und *Kauschel*; dem scheinen lit. *káušas, kaušelis* zu ent-

sprechen, wenn *Kauschel* nicht auf deutscher Einverleibung beruht. — Wenn mnd. *kowsche, kausche* ins Mnd. aus dem Lit. kam, dann müßte das Wort von Ostpreußen aus in das (westliche) mnd. Schrifttum gelangt sein, und das ist wenig wahrscheinlich. Es könnten zwei Entlehnungen vorliegen, eine der Hanseaten aus dem Russ. und eine in Ostpreußen aus dem Lit. Ein sicheres und lehrreiches Beispiel (aus einer Reihe gleich gearteter) für Entlehnung des gleichen Etymons in diesen beiden Bereichen und evtl. ihre Begegnung und Kreuzung ist die Bezeichnung eines Bootes bzw. Schiffes: 1) *lodyge* [lodjə] in mnd. hanseat. Urkunden des 13. und 14. Jh. in Nowgorod, Dorpat (Юрьев) und Riga, daraus norweg. *lodje*, schwed. *lodja* — 2) *lodien* Pl. in deutschen Berichten über Rußlandreisen im 17. Jh. — 3) *lodsche* in Preußen seit dem 16. Jh., in Elbing (Elbląg) im 19. Jh., in Danzig im 17. Jh., auf der Weichsel und westlich des Flusses im 19. und 20. Jh. (Fri.; Mitzka[27]), westlich der unteren Oder im 16. Jh.[28] Das ist eine Entlehnung der Hanseaten aus russ. лодья (abgesehen von den Russlandreisenden des 17. Jh.; s. Bie. (Anm. 30) S. 19 ff.) und ein Reliktwort im östlichen Nd. aus pomor. *łoʒ*, poln. *łódź*; die baltische Alternative kommt nicht in Betracht.

Ostpr. *Daggut, Daggot, Daggat, Dagget, Daggert* 'Birkenteer', dazu *daggern* 'schmieren' (Zie.), stammt am wahrscheinlichsten aus lit. *dagùtas*[29], *degùtas* (auch diese Entlehnung fehlt bei Sab.); baltend. *deggut* aus lett. *deguts*. Das Wort ist in junger Zeit über Ostpreußen hinaus weit nach Westen bezeugt (Anm. 30): in Westpreußen und Pommern, *Däg* u. a. Formen bis nach Schleswig-Holstein, auch in Schlesien. Die beiden einzigen alten Zeugnisse — *deiget* im 15. Jh., *däget* im 16. Jh. — sind nd. Herkunft. Diese alten nd. Zeugnisse und das spätere Vorkommen in westnd. Mundarten können von ostpr. *dagut* usw. unabhängig sein, und als Quelle für sie kommt russ. деготь, vielleicht sogar poln. *dziegieć* in Betracht; Kip. (82) erwägt für baltend. Döggut, Deggot Herkunft aus russ. дёготь. Deutsch *Zick* in Hinterpommern ist aus pomor. *zegc* (zu poln. *dziegieć*) entlehnt.

Tolke 'Dolmetscher' stellt neben vielen anderen Fragen (Bie. 1965, 12) außerdem in unserem Gebiet die Frage seiner Herkunft aus russ. толк oder lit. *tùlkas*. *Tolke* ist im mnd. Schrifttum vom 13.–16. Jh. von Reval (Таллинн) bis Lübeck gut bezeugt, deutlich in jener hanseatischen Tradition. *Tolke* ist aber auch in Preußen gut bezeugt: seit dem 14. Jh. im Schrifttum des Deutschen Ordens (s. o. S. 47), und auch im 16. Jh. ist in Preußen starke Verbreitung erkennbar (auch bei S. Grunau, s. o. S. 47); Fri. bemerkt „das Wort ist altpreußischen (also balt.) Ursprungs". Auch für *Tolke* hängt die Entscheidung ab von der Beurteilung des Verhältnisses der Sprache des Deutschen Ordens und Ostpreußens einerseits, in die baltische

Wörter gelangt sind, und der mnd. Schriftsprache der Hanseaten andererseits, in die russische Wörter gelangt sind.

Anmerkungen

1. F. Tetzner, *Die Slaven in Deutschland* (1902) S. 124 ff.

2. Kip. stellt den lettischen Bestand im Baltendeutschen vollständig dar.

3. V. Falkenhahn, *Der Übers. der lit. Bibel Joh. Bretke*, 1941, 13, 17, 20. Außer diesem Buch verdanke ich Herrn Prof. Falkenhahn viele weitere Beratung.

4. Ich folge hier W. Ziesemer, ,,Beob. z. Wortgeogr. Ostpreußens", *ZfdMa.* XVIII, 149–160; *Die ostpreuß. Mundarten*, 1924.

5. R. Trautmann, *Die altpreussischen Sprachdenkmäler*, Göttingen, 1910.

6. E. Fraenkel, *Litauisches etymologisck-s Wörterbuch*, Göttingen, 1955–1965.

7. Bie. 1963 = Bielfeldt, ,,Die slawischen eigentlichen Reliktwörter in den deutschen Mundarten", *ZfSl* VIII (1963), 155–172.

8. Cienkowski in *Poradn. jęz.* 1963, 5/6, 221–6.

9. Förstemann, ,,Slavische Elemente in deutschen, namhaft westpreußischen Volksmundarten", *KZ* I, 414–29.

10. Bernd, Th., *Die deutsche Sprache im Großherzogtum Posen*, 1820.

11. Mitzka, *Schles. Wb.* (1963 ff.).

12. Zie. = Ziesemer, *Preuss. Wb.* (1935 ff).

13. Litauische Wörter ohne Quellenangabe stehen bei Frä.

14. Niedermann, Senn, Brender, *Wörterbuch der lit. Schriftsprache I*, 77.

15. Fri. = Frischbier, *Preussisches Wörterbuch* (1882/83).

16. Bie. 1965 = Bielfeldt, *Die Entlehnungen aus den verschiedenen slavischen Sprachen im Wortschatz der neuhochdeutschen Schriftsprache* (Sitzungsberichte d. Deutschen Akademie d. Wissenschaften zu Berlin, Kl. f. Sprachen, Literatur u. Kunst, Jg. 1965, Nr. 1.)

17. Vgl. Bie. 1965, 50 ff.; Eichler, *Et. Wb. slaw. Elemente im Ostmd.*, 1965.

18. Rudolf, R. L. ,,Die slovak. Lehnwörter im Inseldeutschen der Slovakei", *Acta er. soc. slovacae, Časopis slovanskej uč. spol., I. Linguistica Slovaca* (1939/40) passim.

19. Sławski, *Sl. etym. jęz. polsk.* I, 27.

20. Bernd *Die deutsche Spr. im Groszhe z. Posen* (1820) 14.

21. Mitzka, *Schles. Wb.* I, 93.

22. Marzell, *Wb. d. Pflanzennamen* I, 591.

23. Vgl. die genaue Darstellung von K. Müller in *ZfSl* XI, 657–80.

24. H. Raab, ,,Slav. Studien im Ostseeraum", *Wiss. Zs. E. M. Arndt-Univ. Greifswald* V, *Ges. Reihe* 4/5, 345.

25. Günther, E., *Zwei russ. Gesprächsbücher* ... (Phil. Diss.) Bln. 1964, 121.

26. *Svenska Akad. Ordbok* 16; Rietz, *Ordb. Svenska Allmogespråket.*

27. Mitzka, in Beih. 6 zu *Wörter und Sachen* (1933), 88.

28. Rudolph, W., *Handb. volkstüml. Boote im östl. Nd.*, 1966, 110.

29. So bei Kurschat, *Lit.-d. Wb.* (1883), der besonders das Litauische auf dem Gebiet des ehem. Deutschen Reichs berücksichtigt.

30. Bie. in *Niederl. Jahrb.* 86, S. 17 ff.

Baltic Loan-words in German

This paper attempts for the first time to cover completely all the words taken into German from Baltic languages, and also to differentiate these from the words originating from Slavonic languages. The primary receiver of Lithuanian and Prussian words was the German spoken in "East Prussia" from the 13th Century to the fall of the German Reich in 1945; from it, some words were taken into other German dialects, into colloquial German, and into the written language. For the purpose of deciding whether words of non-Germanic origin in the German of East Prussia derive from Lithuanian, Prussian, Polish, Pomeranian (Kaschubian) or Russian, the classical criteria of etymology, namely linguistic affinity and morphology, are used. But just in this case they reveal themselves as particularly inadequate, for the various possible source languages resemble one another relatively strongly in both vocabulary and phonetics. In addition, therefore, the entire diffusion of the words, in both the past and the present, is investigated and from this further arguments are derived. The starting point of the investigation must be: what sort of contact did the German of East Prussia have at various times with which foreign languages? Another important factor in arriving at etymological decisions is the relationship between East Prussian German and the German of Latvia and Western Low German; in particular, the relationship to the Middle Low German written language is investigated in connection with certain loan-words. In some cases it is shown that the same etymon may have entered German independently from more than one of the Baltic and Slavonic languages.

HARALDS BIEZAIS

Die Bedeutung der Varianten für das Verständnis der Dainas

1.1. Die Dainas der Letten werden als Grundmaterial auf verschiedenen Feldern der Wissenschaft genutzt. Nicht nur die reine Linguistik, sondern auch die Religionsgeschichte, die Kunstgeschichte, die Ethnographie u. a. sind ohne Ausnutzung des Materials der Dainas gar nicht denkbar. Bei solchen Forschungen begegnet man neben anderen Schwierigkeiten besonders der, daß es den Forschern bisher noch nicht gelungen ist, sich darüber zu einigen, in welcher Weise die sehr große Anzahl von Dainas zu verwerten sei, die sich gewöhnlich um ein einziges Thema konzentriert. Dabei entsteht nun die Frage nach der Möglichkeit der Reduzierung dieser Texte unter Beiseitelassung weniger bedeutsamer auf einige bedeutsamere. Dabei erhebt sich aber prinzipiell das Problem der Textbewertung, denn ein Text, der auf dem Gebiet der einen Wissenschaft bedeutsam ist, kann ja in einem anderen Zusammenhang nur geringe Bedeutung haben, oder gar bedeutungslos sein. Solche Überlegungen haben dann zu mancherlei Versuchen geführt, die Texte der Dainas zu systematisieren. Schon seit der Mitte des vorigen Jahrhunderts waren die Sammler und Herausgeber der Dainas von der Notwendigkeit überzeugt, daß ein Klassifizierungssystem notwendig sei. Sie konnten jedoch zu keinem befriedigendem Ergebnis kommen[1].

Der erste, der sich in dieses Problem vertiefte und auch versuchte, seine Prinzipien in der Praxis anzuwenden, war der Herausgeber der Dainas Kr. Barons[2]. Er spricht von Originalliedern oder Grundliedern einerseits[3] und daneben von Varianten oder Wiederholungen[4]. Man erkennt deutlich seine Absicht, rein begrifflich eine feste Grenze zwischen den Liedern zu ziehen, die mit diesen Benennungen bezeichnet sind. Das ist wenigstens in einem Sinne gelungen, nämlich bezüglich der Wiederholungen. Als solche bezeichnet er Texte, die nach Inhalt und Form identisch sind. Derartige Texte gibt es in der Praxi sehr viele und man findet sie sowohl bei den von Kr. Barons so genannten Originalliedern wie bei den von ihm als Varianten bezeichneten. So ist die von uns im weiteren zu behandelnde Daina 6100 in 33 Wiederholungen bekannt, wobei allein die 6. Variante dieses Liedes in 9 Wiederholungen auftritt. Schwierigkeiten entstehen, sobald man versucht, die Grenze zwischen den Texten zu ziehen, die Barons als Originaltexte bzw. als Varianten bezeichnet. Man hat schon mehrfach darauf hingewiesen, daß Kr. Barons keine einzige Eigenschaft erwähnt, die einen Text als Originallied im Unterschied zu einer Variante qualifizierte. Diesen Versuch einer Klassifizierung beurteilt A. Ozols richtig: „Kr. Barons hat keinerlei Prinzip bei der Qualifizierung der Lieder als Originallieder (Grundlieder) oder als Varianten. Fast in der gesamten Liedermenge könnte man ebensogut eine beliebige Variante zum 'Originallied' erwählen und das von Kr. Barons als Originallied qualifizierte unter die Varianten einreihen. Die Aufteilung der Lieder in Originallieder und Varianten hält der Kritik nicht stand. Folkloristisch möglich ist nur die Feststellung der Varianten zu einem Liedtyp, nicht aber die des 'Originalliedes' ... In der Herausstellung der Originallieder spiegelt sich allein die subjektive Anschauung von Kr. Barons selbst. Daher erscheinen dem objektiven Leser die Originallieder (als Grundlieder) willkürlich herausgegriffen."[5]

Das umfangreiche Material der Dainas zwingt dennoch unumgänglich dazu, sich, wenn auch nur aus praktischen Erwägungen, irgendein Klassifizierungssystem zu erwählen.

1.2. Auf die Frage nach der Möglichkeit der Klassifizierung der Texte der Dainas hat seinerseits auch A. Ozols eine Antwort zu finden versucht. Er empfiehlt jede Daina als Variante zu bezeichnen, da in Wahrheit „jede einzelne eine Einheit folkloristischen Materials ist"[6]. Wenn solch eine Einheit bzw. ein solches Erzeugnis sich im Volk verbreitet (Ozols sagt: unter den Massen), dann verändert es sich, ohne seinen ursprünglichen Inhalt zu verlieren. Alle diese abgewandelten Texte, also alle Varianten, die sich um denselben Inhalt konzentrieren, sind dann als Typ zu bezeichnen[7]. Folgerichtig sind dann alle Varianten, also alle Dainas „nach Typen zusammenzufassen, um sich in der Riesenmasse der Varianten orientieren zu können". Gleichzeitig kann man aber feststellen, daß nicht alle Varianten „gleichen Charakters" sind. Deshalb empfiehlt er noch zwei weitere Begriffe zum Aufzeigen dieser Unterschiede, nämlich Version und Variation. Die erste bezeichnet dann eine „im Inhalt (und damit auch formal) unterschiedliche Variante innerhalb eines Typs", die andere ist eine „in der Form unterschiedliche Variante innerhalb eines Typs"[8]. Allein dieser Vorschlag ist rein theoretisch schwer zu begründen und noch schwerer in der Praxis anzuwenden. Er ist nur ein interessanter spekulativer Gedanke. Das deckt schon A. Ozols selbst in den soeben zitierten Formulierungen auf. Bezüglich der Version fügt er in Klammern die Wörter (und damit auch formal) bei. Ganz richtig! Damit ist nämlich gesagt, daß Form und Inhalt bei der Typologisierung der Dainas nicht einwandfrei zu trennen sind[9]. Wenn aber diese Grenze nicht genau zu ziehen ist, dann ist das Ganze kein konsequentes Klassifizierungsprinzip, weil das die Grundforderung eines solchen Prinzips ist.

2.1. Die gegenüber Kr. Barons und A. Ozols gemachten Einwendungen zwingen zur Suche nach einer Lösung dieses Problems, indem man sich noch gründlicher in die Texte vertieft. Zu diesem Zwecke benutzen wir die schon zuvor genannte Daina 6100:

Saule (al. *Saulīt'*) *pina vainadziņu,*	'Saule (al. *dim.*) flocht einen Kranz
Vītolā(i) sēdēdama.	(*dim.*) indem sie im Weidenbaum
Pin, Saulīte[10]*, dod man vienu*	sitzt. Flicht, Saule (*dim.*) gib mir
Man jāiet(i) tautiņās[11]*.*	einen, ich muß ,,unter die Völker
	gehen".'

Diese Daina ist in 170 verschiedenen Texten bekannt[12]. Beim Vergleich dieser Texte erweist es sich, daß allein das in der Terminologie von Kr. Barons ,,Originallied" genannte 35 vollkommen ähnliche, also identische Texte hat, die er Wiederholungen nennt[13]. Sie sind aber an verschiedenen Orten, zu anderen Zeiten aufgeschrieben und sind von verschiedenen Sprechern gesprochen worden. Ebenso ist der von Kr. Barons mit 6 nummerierte Text dieses Liedes (6100,6) in 9 identischen Texten bekannt. Bei der Betrachtung aller Texte erweist es sich, daß auch mehrere weitere identisch sind. Wir erhalten dabei folgende Übersicht:

1. 6100	35	11.	4
2. 6100 (hinzugefügte unnummerierte Texte)	2	12.	4
3.	10	13.	2
4.	2	14.	2
5.	4	15. 6100,1 (V, Beilage zu LD ohne Nr.)	2
6.	21	16. 6100,2	2
7.	4	17. 6100,2 (ohne Nr.)	2
8.	3	18. 6100,4	2
9.	2	19. 6100,6	9
10.	3	20. 6100,6 (ohne Nr.)	3

Alle diese 20 Gruppen mit identischen Texten umfassen insgesamt 118 Texte. Das bedeutet, daß bloß 52 Texte größere oder kleinere Abweichungen aufweisen. Unsere 20 Gruppen gliedern sich nach der Anzahl der zu ihnen gehörenden Lieder wie folgt: 1–35; 1–21; 1–10; 1–9; 4–4; 3–3; 9–2.

Mit Hilfe des oben abgedruckten Textes werden wir mit der 35 Texte

umfassenden Gruppe bekannt. Dieser Text besteht aus 13 Wörtern. Bei der
Prüfung aller Wörter aller dieser Texte stellt man fest, daß sie alle (selbstredend mit Ausnahme der identischen Texte) Veränderungen unter-
worfen sind. Es ist nur die Frage, wie groß die Veränderungen sind und
welche Bedeutung sie haben. Man könnte erst einmal verfolgen, welche
Veränderungen Kr. Barons berücksichtigt hat, als er die Texte in ein „Originallied" mit 35 ähnlichen Texten und 6 Varianten einteilte, die num-
meriert sind und denen ebenso wie dem Originallied unnummerierte Texte
beigefügt sind. Eine solche Untersuchung aber hätte bloß historische Bedeutung. Uns hingegen interessiert die Möglichkeit der Klassifizierung der
Texte selbst und deren Bedeutung für das Verständnis des Inhalts. Richtiger ist es daher, die Texte selbst anzuschauen und zu versuchen, ihre
permanenten und ihre variierenden Elemente festzustellen.

2.2. Zuerst ist hier zu vermerken, daß nur in drei Fällen der Text durch
zwei Zeilen erweitert ist:

Es nogāju tautiņās	'Ich „ging unter die Völker" (*dim.*)
Saules pītu vainadziņu. (186 b[14])	mit einem von Saule geflochtenen
und	Kranz.'
Dod man vienu vainadziņu	'Gib mir ein Kränzchen, ich muß
Man jāiet tautiņās (287, 289 c).	„unter die Völker gehen".'

Wenn es also nur drei solche Erweiterungen gibt, hat man Ursache, von
einer besonderen Stabilität der Strophenform zu reden. Das kann man vom
ganzen Text sagen und insbesondere von der 4. Zeile: „*Man jāiet tautiņās*"
('Ich muß unter die Völker (*dim.*) gehen'). Die Zeile bleibt in allen Texten
so gut wie unverändert. In 159 von insgesamt 170 Texten lautet sie so. Bei
11 weiteren Texten erweisen sich diese Abweichungen als morphologischer
oder fraseologischer Art. So findet sich in einigen Texten statt *jāiet(i)* 'muß
gehen', *jāiete* (ohne Sinnveränderung) (179a), *ko iet* 'mit dem man geht'
(75p), *un es iešu* 'und ich werde gehen' (111d), *es jau eju* 'ich gehe schon'
(280). An Stelle von *tautiņās* (*fem.*) steht auch *tautiņos* (*masc.*) 'unter die
Völker' (241k, 379). Von ein wenig bedeutsameren Abweichungen kann nur
in wenigen Fällen die Rede sein: *man vajag šoruden* 'ich muß in diesem
Herbst' (229[1], 264h). Sämtliche Textabweichungen berühren aber nicht den
semantischen Sinn, an den bei diesen Aussagen gedacht wird. So kann man
sagen, daß wir in allen Texten ein so gut wie unveränderliches stabiles
Element festgestellt haben. Das ist die 4. Zeile. Gleichzeitig haben wir den
Kern des Liedinhaltes aufgedeckt. Man kann ihn so ausdrücken, daß die
Sprecherin des Liedes vor der Verehelichung steht und daß sie einen Kranz

braucht. Um diesen stabilen zentralen Gedanken des Textes gruppieren sich die anderen in den Texten anzutreffenden Vorstellungen. Unter diesen sind folgende zu unterscheiden: a. das Mädchen ist eine Bittende, b. den Kranz fertigt eine Göttin, c. die Göttin befindet sich in einem Baum. Wir wenden uns nun der Art zu, wie diese Momente in den Texten ausgedrückt werden.

2.2.1. Wer ist die Herstellerin des Kranzes? Die Antwort lesen wir in der ersten Zeile — das ist Saule — in 162 Texten. In sehr vielen Fällen ist sie in der Deminutivform benannt[15], oder sie wird *Saules māte*, 'Mutter Saule' (287, 289 c), *Saules meita*, 'Jungfrau Saule' (171 a, 391 Nr. 103, 28 p u. a.) oder *Saules māsa*, 'Schwester Saule' (224 c) genannt. Nur in zwei Texten wird die Biene als Herstellerin des Kranzes genannt und in sechs Laima. So können wir sagen, daß auch in dieser Hinsicht die Stabilität des Textinhaltes sehr groß ist. Das Eindringen der Biene ist in diesen Texten als poetische Metapher zu erklären. Sie konnte entstehen, als der ursprüngliche religiöse Sinn im Bewußtsein der Sprecherin geschwunden war, oder aber auch parallel als Naturpoesie. Ebenso sporadisch und sekundär ist Laima eingedrungen[16]. Auf ein sekundäres Eindringen weist schon gar klar ihr Sitzen im Baum hin. Aber drüber später.

Die inhaltliche Stabilität der ersten Zeile kann den Eindruck entstehen lassen, daß sie auch formal stabil sei, wie wir das bei der 4. Zeile konstatierten. Es gibt hier aber einige Differenzen. So zeigt sich an Stelle des Wortes *pina* 'flocht', *vija* 'wand' (mit ähnlichen Formen) 18 mal (6 c, 75 g, 75 m, 94 u. a.), *šuva* 'nähte' 7 mal (195 a, b, 200 a, 206 u. a.), *rakstīdama* 'stickend' (22 k) einmal, *darīdama* 'machend' (264 p) einmal, *puškodama* 'schmückend' (171 a) einmal. Die drei letzten lassen sich als Zufälligkeiten ansehen. Auch inhaltlich sagen sie äußerst wenig aus — nur gerade die Tatsache des Kranzfertigens. Ebenso haben bei der Bestimmung von Unterschieden die Texte mit *vija* 'wand' geringe Bedeutung, denn die semantische Bedeutung dieses Wortes ist die gleiche wie die von *pina* 'flocht'. Eine geringfügig neue Vorstellung ist mit solchen Bezeichnungen für die Tätigkeit von Saule wie *šuva* 'nähte' und *rakstīdama* 'stickend' (d. i. das Ornament des Kranzes ausnähend) verbunden. Und das deshalb, weil sie an eine andere Fertigungsweise des Kranzes denken läßt, als mit der Tätigkeit, die mit *pīt* 'flechten' und *vīt* 'winden' bezeichnet wird. Daß die lettischen Mädchen ihre Kränze in unterschiedlicher Technik gefertigt haben, ist mehrfach bezeugt[17]. Hier stoßen wir in voller Schärfe auf das Problem von Texten mit ursprünglichen und mit sekundären Vorstellungen. Sind die Texte mit *pina* 'flocht' die ursprünglichen, oder die mit *šuva* 'nähte'? Geht man nach der Quantität, dann wären es die ersten. Aber dieses Prinzip ist nicht immer anwendbar. Zu dieser Frage werden wir zurückkehren, wenn wir mehr solcher Erscheinungen kennengelernt haben.

Wenden wir uns dem dritten Wort der ersten Zeile *vainadziņu* 'Kränzchen' zu, so finden wir, daß mehrere Texte statt dessen (goldene) *kronis* 'Krone' verwenden — 27 (109 b–c, 146 b u. a.). Auch hier kann man genauso fragen: welcher Art sind die genetischen Beziehungen dieser Texte zu jenen, die den Kranz nennen? Hier ist die Frage leichter zu beantworten. Das internationale Wort *kronis* 'Krone' ist in die lettische Sprache durch Vermittlung des Deutschen gelangt[18]. Das kann erst erfolgt sein, nachdem die Letten mit diesem in Berührung gekommen sind, also nach dem 13. Jahrhundert. Das bedeutet aber keinesfalls, daß man folgern dürfte, die Texte mit 'Kranz' seien alle in die Zeit vor dem 13. Jahrhundert zu datieren.

2.2.2. Die 2. Zeile in dem von uns abgedruckten Text umfaßt bloß zwei Wörter. Sie geben eine Erläuterung zur 1. Zeile, nämlich darüber, wo Saule sich beim Fertigen des Kranzes befindet. Wir erfahren dann, daß sie sich 143 mal (unter Einbeziehung der verschiedenen Formen dieses Wortes) im Weidenbaum befindet, 6 mal im Apfelbaum (68 c, 112 b, 181 c u. a.), 11 mal in der Eiche (28 d, 95 a, 95 d u. a.), 3 mal in der Linde (321, 407 a, 185 d), 2 mal im Meer (171 a, 391 Nr. 103), 2 mal am Quellen-(rand, -tal) (11 d, 126 b) 1 mal im Rosengarten (407 c), 1 mal im Morgenschein (93 c); einmal wird kein Ort genannt (18). Die Übersicht zeigt, daß Saule in den weitaus überwiegenden Fällen sich im Weidenbaum befindet und nur sporadisch in anderen Bäumen. Besonders ist auf die fünf Texte hinzuweisen, die aussagen, sie befände sich im Meer, an der Quelle oder im Morgenschein. Diese drei Orte sind in der lettischen Folklore auch in anderen Vorstellungszusammenhängen als Aufenthaltsorte der Saule bekannt. Dabei ist zu beachten, daß das Meer und die Quelle metaphorische Bezeichnungen für den Himmel sind. Hält man sich auch hier an das Quantitätsprinzip, müßte es scheinen, als wäre der ursprüngliche Aufenthaltsort Saules der Weidenbaum. Man kann dagegen auch sagen, daß es keine zwingenden Gründe dafür gibt, daß nicht Linde oder Eiche die ursprünglichen gewesen sein könnten. Die exakt zu datierende Pflanze ist hier nur die Rose, die ebenso auf Beziehungen zur deutschen Kultur nach dem 13. Jahrhundert hinweist[19].

Das zweite Wort derselben Zeile spricht von Saules Stellung. Sie fertigt den Kranz *sēdēdama* 'sitzend'. Hier ist die Einheitlichkeit der Texte noch größer. Wenn man die verschiedenen morphologischen Abweichungen des Wortes *sēdēdama* außer Acht läßt, gibt es nur einen Text, der ein anderes Wort setzt: sie fertigt den Kranz 'auf der Eiche stehend' (345) und in einem

weiteren findet sich eine direkte Naturbeobachtung: 'leuchtend' (268 b).
Außerdem gibt es noch 5 weitere Texte, die nichts über Saules Stellung
aussagen (18, 401, 111 a u. a.). Über den Inhalt der 2. Zeile ist zu sagen, daß
nicht die geringsten Schwierigkeiten bestehen, den Sinn der Metapher 'im
Weidenbaum sitzend' zu verstehen. Das Leuchten der Sonne durch die
Zweige eines Baumes, in unserem Falle einer Weide, hat das Erlebnis mit
der Vorstellung von ihrem Sitzen darin ausgelöst. Das drückt unser Text
mit „im Weidenbaum sitzend" auch schon mit direkten Worten aus (268 b).
Hier erweist ein Text auch schon den früher erwähnten Zusammenhang, daß
nämlich das Leuchten der Sonne durch das Baumgezweig ein dankbarer
Gefühlseindruck war, um die Vorstellung des Windens des Kranzes aus
'Weidenzweiglein' zu schaffen (323 b).

2.2.3. Nun ist noch der Inhalt der 3. Zeile zu betrachten: *Pin, Saulīte, dod
man vienu* 'Flicht, Saule (*dim.*), gib mir einen'. Auch diese Zeile weist wie die
2. und die 4. sehr große Stabilität auf. Selbstredend ist entsprechend der
Aussage der 1. Zeile (*Saule, Laima, bite*) die Anrede in der 3. Zeile an dieses
Wesen gerichtet. Ebenso entspricht der in der 1. Zeile erwähnten Tätigkeit
auch die Tätigkeit in der 3. Zeile. Nur in 6 Fällen ist eine stilistische Abweichung von der gewöhnlichen Ausdrucksweise anzutreffen, z. B. *Man,
Saulīte, vienu dod* 'Mir, Saule (*dim.*), einen gib' (325[1]), *don* 'gib' (181 c, 198 b),
dod manim 'gib mir' (eine andere Form des *dat. sing.*) (159 b), *man viņu* 'mir
ihn' (152), *man to vienu* 'mir den einen' (15 b). Eine echte Abweichung findet
sich nur in 3 Fällen: *Lūgšus lūdzu, dod man vienu,* 'bittend bitte (ich), gib
mir einen' (232) und *Es tev lūdzu, Saules māte,'dod man vienu vainadziņu* 'ich
bitte dich, Mutter Saule, gib mir ein Kränzchen' (287, 289 c).
    Aber auch diese kaum größeren Stil- und Formabweichungen tragen
irgendetwas wesentlich Neues zum Inhalt bei, das etwa die uns bekannte
stereotype Formulierung der 3. Zeile ergänzte. Noch mehr! Diese drei Texte
sind höchst interessant. Sie erschließen den eigentlichen Sinn der ganzen
Liedergruppe mit den Worten: 'gib mir einen'. Das ist Gebet[20]! In diesen
Texten ist das klar und unmißverständlich ausgedrückt. Das ist ein Gebiet
an Saule im Falle der Verehelichung eines Mädchens. Hier wäre fortzu-
fahren und an Saules zentrale Bedeutung in der altlettischen Religion zu
erinnern, an die symbolische Bedeutung des Brautkranzes und an die
Schwierigkeiten, ihn zu beschaffen, wenn man in sozialem Elend lebt. So
wird auch verständlich, wieso Laima, die Schicksalsgöttin und zugleich die
Bestimmerin des Wohlstandes, sich in diese Texte eindrängen und im Weidenbaum sitzen konnte, was im Grunde ihrem Wesen widerspricht. Das aber
sind Fragen, die im Rahmen dieser Schrift nicht zu betrachten sind[21]. Diese

drei Texte bestätigen auch ein übriges Mal, die für die Methoden der Dainas-
Forschung wichtige Erkenntnis, daß das quantitative Prinzip weder für das
richtige Verständnis des Inhalts noch für eine Datierung der Texte bestimmend ist.

3.1. Welche Schlüsse gestatten nun die von uns erörterten Texte? Gehen
wir von dem oben abgedruckten sogenannten „Originallied" (6100) aus und
vergleichen es etwa mit 6100,3 (405):

Saule (al. *Saulīt'*) *sēdēja vītolā(i)*,	'Saule (al. *dim.*) saß im Weidenbaum,
Košus pina vainadziņus.	flocht schöne Kränzchen.
Pin, Saulīte, dod man vienu,	Flicht, Saule (*dim.*), gib mir einen,
Man jāiet(i) tautiņās.	ich muß „unter die Völker gehen".'

Es ist völlig unmöglich anzugeben, welcher von diesen beiden Texten bzw.
Liedern als das Original anzusehen wäre. Das zwingt zur Erkenntnis, daß
Barons' Einteilung nicht aufrechterhalten werden kann[22].

3.2. Wir haben gesehen, daß A. Ozols versucht hat, diese Schwierigkeiten
zu überwinden, indem er empfiehlt, einerseits die Lieder gleicher Thematik
oder mit gleichen Inhalt in einen Typ zusammenzufassen (was Kr. Barons'
metaphorischer Bezeichnung Liederstrauch entspricht). Andererseits empfiehlt er, innerhalb der Grenzen eines solchen Typs die Texte zu unterscheiden, die inhaltlich („und damit auch in der Form") stärker abweichen,
und sie Versionen zu nennen, und solche, die nur in der Form abweichen und
als Variationen zu bezeichnen wären. Wie schon gesagt, ist auch diese
Empfehlung spekulativ und scheint eher künstlich herbeigesucht, als
wirklichkeitsnah zu sein, denn der Inhalt wandelt sich mit der Form. Ein
System, das auf Grund eines so unsicheren Prinzips geschaffen wurde, kann
gerade das nicht bieten, was man von einem System erwartet, nämlich, daß
es ein klares Systematisierungsprinzip bietet. Unsere eingehende Textanalyse zeigt nicht nur die Mängel dieser Versuche auf, sondern weist auch
die Richtung, in der beim Gedanken an eine Klassifizierung der Dainas zu
gehen wäre.

3.3. Es scheint, daß dabei immer zwei Momente bedeutsam sein werden,
die beide aus dem Inhalt der entsprechenden Daina herrühren. Das erste
Moment sind die im Text genannten Gegenstände (Realien). In unserem
konkreten Fall ist das der Baum, der als Aufenthaltsort Saules genannt

wird. Bäume, wie die Weide, die Linde, die Eiche, geben da gar keine An-
haltspunkte, dagegen bieten die Texte mit Rose einen solchen wohl. Mit
großer Sicherheit können wir behaupten, daß derartige Texte Vorstellungen
einer anderen Kulturschicht widerspiegeln. Sie deuten auf die Zeit nach
der Einfuhr der Rose nach Lettland hin, also in die Zeit nach dem 13. Jahrhundert. Diese Feststellung darf aber nicht als Aussage über die Ent-
stehungszeit der Texte angesehen werden. Fast alle Texte von Dainas sind
erst im 19. Jahrhundert aufgezeichnet worden. Damals konnten beide Vorstellungen nebeneinander bestehen. Ihr Auftreten in unterschiedlichen
Texten ist dann aus der individuellen Situation der Sprecherin zu erklären.
Das bedeutet, daß auch eine Klassifizierung der Dainas nach urtümlichen
und späteren Vorstellungen äußerst begrenzt ist. Die große Mehrzahl der
Texte nennt wenig solcher Gegenstände (Realien), die auch nur einiger-
maßen sicher als zu einer Kulturschicht gehörig zu datieren wären. Diese
Schwierigkeit wird gut durch den von uns oben abgedruckten Text (6100)
und 6100,5 (171a) charakterisiert:

Saules meita jūrāi sēdē,	'Jungfrau Saule saß im Meer,
Vainadziņu puškodama.	schmückte ein Kränzchen.
Pin, Saulīte, dod man vienu,	Flicht, Saule (*dim.*), gib mir einen,
Man jāiet tautiņās.	ich muß „unter die Völker gehen".'

In dem einen wie in dem anderen Text ist eine Situation beschrieben, die
nicht zu datieren ist. Hier führt uns, wie mir scheint, ein zweites Moment
weiter. Die Textanalyse hat uns davon überzeugt, daß die in den Texten
ausgedrückten Vorstellungen und Erlebnisse sehr einheitlich sind. Die
Texte dulden kein Mißverständnis. Es sind Gebete eines Mädchens an Saule
um einen Kranz. Erst wenn wir uns diesen zentralen Gedanken vor Augen
halten, erlangen wir die Möglichkeit, die Texte zu beurteilen, in denen nicht
Saule, wohl aber Laima oder die Biene genannt sind. Hier können wir mit
großer Sicherheit sagen, daß diese Texte andere Vorstellungen widerspiegeln
und damit einer anderen Kulturschicht angehören, oder richtiger,
sie haben sich sekundär eingedrängt. Mit anderen Worten, wir gehen
vom gemeinsamen Inhalt der Dainas aus und betrachten in dessen Licht
das einzelne Lied. Dieses zweite Moment könnte man *sensus communis*
nennen.

Ungeachtet der zwei hier aufgezeigten Klassifizierungsprinzipien ist stets
davon auszugehen, daß jeder Text eine selbständige Einheit ist; zum Zwecke
der Forschung ist jeder Text für sich zu analysieren und daraus seine Bedeutung bei der Erforschung eines Problems zu bestimmen. Zur Beleuchtung

dieser Wahrheit können wir uns rein gedanklich vorstellen, von unseren 170 Texten sei bloß ein einziger zugänglich, z. B. 6100,1 (345):

Bite pina zelta kroni,	'Die Biene flocht eine goldene Krone,
Ozolā sēdēdama.	Während sie in der Eiche sass.
Pin, bitīte, dod man vienu,	Flicht, Bienchen, gib mir einen,
Man jāiet tautiņās.	Ich muß „unter die Völker gehen".'

Kennte man bloß diesen Text, müßte gefolgert werden, es handle sich um ein poetisch ausgedrücktes Naturerlebnis mit der fleißigen Biene im Mittelpunkt. Dann käme nie zutage, daß dieser Text zu einer Gruppe mit völlig anderen Hauptgedanken gehört, nämlich zu den Gebeten an Saule. Das zeigt, daß, unabhängig von allen Klassifizierungsversuchen, erst eine große Anzahl von Dainas (in der Terminologie des Kr. Barons — von Varianten), wie schwer auch immer ihr Überschauen in der Praxis sein mag, größere Möglichkeiten zum richtigen Verständnis ihres Inhalts erschließt.

Anmerkungen

1. Zu diesen Versuchen näheres bei A. Ozols, *Raksti folkloristikā*, Riga, 1968, 112 ff.

2. Er hat die lett. Dainas (LD) in 8 Bänden (1894–1917) herausgegeben.

3. So in LD I, VII: „In der Moskauer Sammlung waren nur 16 000 Originallieder ..." Zur Bezeichnung der hier erwähnten „Originallieder" benutzt er in anderem Zusammenhang auch die Bezeichnung „Lieder selbständiger Eigenart" (ib. VII, XX). Ozols, *Raksti folkl.*, 116 behauptet, es gäbe noch den „von Kr. Barons eingeführten Terminus Grundlied". Dafür gibt es in der Dainas-Ausgabe von Kr. Barons keinen Beleg. Unter dem Einfluss von Ozols benutzt K. Arājs, „Par Kr. Barona Latvju Dainās iespiesto tautasdziesmu teksta saskaņu ar oriģināliem", *ZA Valodas un literaturas instituta raksti* XI, 305 f. beide Bezeichnungen: Originallied und Grundlied.

4. S. LD I, XV.

5. Ozols, *Raksti folkl.*, 116 f.; s. auch Arājs, *ZA Val. u. lit. inst. raksti* XI, 307 und Biezais, „Die zweite Sammlung der lettischen Volkslieder von Gustav Bergmann", *Arv* 1967, 21, Anm. 15.

6. Ib. 112.

7. Tatsächlich benutzt Ozols, wie er selbst angibt (*Raksti folkl.*, 118), hier das Wort „Typ" als Synonym für die Bezeichnungen von Kr. Barons „Liederbüschel", „Liederbusch" (LD I, XV) od. „Liederstrauch" (ib. 199).

8. Ozols, *Raksti folkl.*, 112. Vgl. auch *ZAV* 1950, III (XXXII). Ich habe schon darauf hingewiesen, dass solcheine begriffliche Gliederung nur prospektive Bedeutung hätte, wenn man sie als begründet anerkennen würde, und in Zukunft die Dainas nach ihr herausgeben würde (H. Biezais, *Die Gottesgestalt der lettischen Volksreligion*, Uppsala, 1961, 30 f.).

9. Er selbst hat das an einem Beispiel in der Meinung zu zeigen versucht (1968, 118 f.), daß man im Inhalt als Zentrum, um das die Versionen und Variationen sich gruppieren, ein konstantes Motiv auswählen könnte (er benutzt als Synonyme auch „Leitmotiv" und „*caurviju motīvs*" (*caur* 'durch', *viju* 'gen. pl. Ranken'). Er ist sich aber selbst der Schwierigkeiten gewußt gewesen und sogar dessen, daß das besonders in Texten, in denen einem Ablauf in der Natur nach dem Prinzip des *parallelismus membrorum* ein Ablauf im menschlichen Leben entspricht (ib. 120), unmöglich ist.

10. In den Texten ist bisweilen das Wort *Saule* mit kleinem Anfangsbuchstaben geschrieben; dann ist es ein Gattungsname, der Inhalt der Texte aber erweist, daß es sich um ein persönliches Wesen handelt. Wir schreiben es hier konsequent als Eigennamen mit großem Anfangsbuchstaben.

11. Die Phrase *iet tautās* 'unter die Völker gehen' ist als 'verheiratet werden' zu verstehen (A. Ozols, „Paskaidrojošā vārdnīca folkloras leksikai", *Latviešu tautasdziesmas* I, Riga, 1955, 432.

12. In meinem Aufsatz habe ich nur die in den LD abgedruckten Texte benutzt.

13. Diese Anzahl umfaßt auch einen Text, den Kr. Barons in der Ergänzung zu seiner Ausgabe (LD V) abgedruckt und mit 6100,1 bezeichnet hat, der tatsächlich aber eine Wiederholung des „Originalliedes" ist.

14. Um trotzdem einzelne unnummerierte Texte identifizieren zu können, benutze ich hinfort überall, wo ich sie zitiere oder auf sie verweise, die Kennzeichen der Aufzeichnungsorte, z. B. 3 d, 15 a, 26 b u. a.

15. Über die im Lettischen benutzten Deminutiva siehe Grundsätzliches bei V. Rūķe-Draviņa, *Diminutive im Lettischen*, Lund, 1959, bes. 169 ff.; dazu Biezais, *Die Gottesgestalt der lett. Volksreligion*, Uppsala, 1961, 33 und *Mūsdienu latviešu literārās valodas gramatika* I, Riga, 1959, 130; J. Endzelīns, *Latviešu valodas gramatika*, Riga, 1951, 386 f.

16. Über das Eindringen der Schicksalsgöttin *Laima* in die Himmelsmythen habe ich mich genauer geäussert 1955 in *Die Hauptgöttinnen der alten Letten*, 158 ff.

17. Näheres darüber A. Dzērvītis, „Kā latvju zeltene darinājusi un valkājusi vaiņagu", *Latvju tautas daiņas* (LTD) VI, Riga, 1930, 207 f.; auch die farbigen Abbildungen *Latviešu tautas māksla*, Riga, 1961, III, Nr. 564—601.

18. A. Ozols, *Raksti valodniecībā*, Riga, 1967, 466, auch J. Sehwers, *Sprachlich–kulturhistorische Untersuchungen vornehmlich über den deutschen Einfluss im Lettischen*, Berlin, 1953, 59.

19. Ozols, *ibid.*, 468, auch Sehwers, *op. cit.*, 103.

20. Näheres über diese Art der Anrede in unserem Text A. Ozols, „Atonālā uzruna latviešu klasiskajās tautasdziesmās", *ZAV* VI, 20 ff.

21. Das sind Fragen, über die ich mich schon in meinen Arbeiten 1955 und 1961, sowie in im Druck befindlichen „Die himmlische Götterfamilie der alten Letten" geäussert habe.

22. Darauf hat gleich beim Erscheinen des ersten Heftes der Ausgabe von Kr. Barons in seiner Rezension P. Šmits hingewiesen (cf. *Viesis* 1894, Nr. 40). Ungeachtet dessen hat er selbst, als er 1936 begann, die Fortsetzung von Kr. Barons Sammlung herauszugeben, die Texte der Dainas nach dem gleichen System in „Originallieder" und Varianten geordnet. Dasselbe taten auch R. Klaustiņš und J. Endzelīns, als sie 1928 eine neue Ausgabe zu veröffentlichen begannen (LTD). Eine kritische Beurteilung aller dieser Ausgaben findet sich bei Biezais, „Die erste Sammlung der lettischen Volkslieder von Gustav Bergmann", *Arv*, 1961, 1 ff.

The Importance of Variants for Interpreting the Dainas

Two main difficulties arise in using the Dainas (Latvian folksongs) as a source for the study of Latvian culture. Firstly, it is very difficult to date the Dainas. Secondly, there are a great number of variants for each text, which gives rise to difficulties in deciding which of the variants is the original. However, the first difficulty is overcome when objects mentioned in the Dainas can be dated by means of other sources, and the great number of variants can be of advantage in determining the common meaning of the whole group.

HENRIK BIRNBAUM

Four Approaches to Balto-Slavic

Ever since Antoine Meillet's *Les dialectes indo-européens* first appeared (Paris, 1908), shaking the prevailing neogrammarian *Stammbaum* view, the problem of the precise nature of the relationship between the cognate Baltic and Slavic language groups has been one of the most debated issues in Comparative Indo-European Linguistics. Few scholars have contributed so substantially toward a solution of this problem, both in terms of new, revealing observations of relevant data and insightful theoretical conclusions, as Christian S. Stang.[1] If, nonetheless, the Balto-Slavic problem essentially continues to resist a definitive solution, if, in other words, linguists cannot yet find a satisfactory diachronic explanation for the particular degree of structural affinity between the Baltic and Slavic languages, in spite of available comparative data whose specific interpretation has been largely agreed upon, the reason may well lie, at least to some extent, in terminology and approach. The following sketchy remarks, offered here as a tribute to one of the great pioneers of modern Balto-Slavic studies, are primarily aimed at outlining some of the conceivable basic approaches to the problem of Balto-Slavic linguistic relationship, adding a few brief comments on certain of their merits and shortcomings.

If, on the one hand, we are to distinguish between early phases of Proto-Baltic and Proto-Slavic, respectively, and, on the other hand, a separate, preceding Balto-Slavic stage in the development from Late Common Indo-European down to Common Baltic and Common Slavic, the first question that may arise is one of terminology:[2] What exactly is meant when we speak of a possible Balto-Slavic linguistic *unity*? And, when using the term *linguistic* unity, does this imply that we are referring explicitly to a uniform, fully developed, independent *language*, or could we possibly also (or, rather) be referring to a *dialect* within a larger linguistic community, viz., that of Late Common Indo-European or some part thereof? If by linguistic unity we understand a totally undifferentiated, homogeneous linguistic system, as yet unaffected by any regional variation, it is obvious that such a concept is not applicable to any postulated Balto-Slavic protolanguage of post-

Common Indo-European date. For such a protolanguage, no matter how defined, can only be conceived of as a broader unit, dialectally diversified from its very outset. While, to be sure, the evidence of the present-day Slavic languages or, rather, of their earliest attestation (Old Church Slavic, Old Russian, etc.) points to a common, largely uniform protolanguage— Common Slavic and its immediate predecessor, Proto-Slavic—the same can be said of Baltic only with some qualification. As is well known, the recorded history of the Baltic languages is a relatively short one: Old Prussian dates back to the turn of the 14th to the 15th century (the Elbing Vocabulary of ca. 1400); and the literary tradition of Lithuanian and Latvian goes back to the early and late 16th century, respectively (the Dzukovian Prayers of ca. 1515; two Catechisms and a Song Book of the 1580's).[3] However, the marked differences found between the various Baltic languages, especially between West Baltic (represented by Old Prussian) and East Baltic (Lithuanian and Latvian), indicate that many centuries and in all probability more than a millennium must have elapsed since the disintegration of Common Baltic, if indeed such a unified protolanguage ever was a reality. Several of the contrasts and features peculiar to West as opposed to East Baltic, but also to individual Baltic dialects, particularly within Lithuanian, seem ultimately to reflect dialectal characteristics of Late Common Indo-European. As examples one could cite the substitution of the genitive by the ablative in the singular of the -o stems: Lith. *diẽvo*, Latv. *dìeva*, Sl. *boga*, **vъlka* (P *wilka*, R *volka*, etc.) vs. OPr. *deiwas*; cf. Skt. *vŕkasya*, Hom. Gk. λύκοιο < **-os(i̯)o*; abl. Skt. *devāt*, Lat. *deō*. A genitive desinence with -s- is attested also in the Slavic forms *česo*, *čьso*. Further, East Baltic and Slavic -m- in the dative and locative singular where Old Prussian, along with the other Indo-European languages, has -sm-: dat. Lith. *tãmui* > *tám*, Latv. *tam*; loc. Lith. *tamè*; Sl. dat. *tomu*, loc. *tomь* vs. OPr. dat. *stesmu*; cf. also the Old Prussian hapax *schisman* (loc. sing. or, according to Endzelīns, dat. sing., erroneously patterned on the acc.); Skt. *tásmai*, *tásmāt*, *tásmin*, Umbr. *esmei* (=Lat. *huic*), *pusme*, Goth. *þamma*. Of additional agreements between East Baltic and Slavic cf. also the formation of the present passive participle in -mo- (Lith. *nèšamas*, Sl. *nesomъ*) vs. OPr. -man- (*poklausīmanas*, Ench.), Skt. -*mānaḥ*, Gk. -μενος, Tokh. A -*mäṁ*. On the other hand, we find, for example, the same derivational type of possessives in West Baltic and Slavic: OPr. *mais*, *twais*, *swais*, Sl. *mojь*, *tvojь*, *svojь*. East Baltic and other Indo-European languages here prefer other formations, mostly by way of thematization of the stem in the oblique case forms of the personal pronoun. Limited to West Baltic and Slavic are further some agreements in verbal derivation—e.g., OPr. *sind-*, *synd-* = Sl. *sęd-*; OPr. (*po*)*stān-* = Sl.

stan- in the present stem—and inflection; cf., e.g., OPr. *bēi, be,* Sl. *běxъ, bě.*
The positionally conditioned sound change IE *s* > Balt., Indo-Iran. *š* (Skt.
ṣ), Sl. *x* is in Baltic not necessarily limited to Lithuanian (contrary to what
appears to be the case) since *s* and *š* can have merged in Latv. *s* (*š* in Latvian
resulting from palatalization of *s* and from *tj* and thus being secondary) and
the awkward orthography of Old Prussian, adapted to that of Middle Low
German, does not always permit to draw any incontestable conclusions
regarding the underlying phonological system of Old Prussian.

It can be shown that, as a rule, wherever we find sets of features shared
by all Baltic languages, thus pointing to a Common Baltic structure (or to a
particular dialectal Late Common Indo-European structure, which virtually
amounts to the same), this underlying structure—phonological, morphological, or lexical—is of a distinctly archaic nature. The same is not always
true of the Common Slavic sound pattern or form system (either in their
paradigmatic aspect or as regards their presumed syntagmatic utilization);
nor does it necessarily apply to the Common Slavic stock of lexical items.
In this context, however, it should be borne in mind that, in contrast to
Common Baltic, a much larger portion of Common Slavic, or even the more
remote Proto-Slavic, linguistic structure can be recovered with a high degree
of probability by methods of comparative as well as internal reconstruction.[4]
Where linguistic structures of Common Slavic and Common Baltic (or of
locally restricted Late Indo-European, underlying Common Baltic) coincide
or, rather, are related to each other in a one-to-one correspondence, the
Common Slavic sounds and forms are usually derivable from those posited
for Common Baltic (or pre-Baltic Late Indo-European), but not *vice versa*.
With some oversimplification it can therefore be argued that the Common
Baltic or, perhaps rather, Proto-Baltic linguistic model is primary in relation
to its Proto-Slavic counterpart. Consequently, the Baltic evidence is of
greater import for elucidating the prehistory of Slavic than, conversely, the
testimony of Slavic data for the reconstruction of pre-Baltic linguistic
evolution. This view of the nature of the Balto-Slavic linguistic relationship
was explicitly set forth by V. V. Ivanov and V. N. Toporov in their joint
1958 contribution to the IVth (Moscow) International Congress of Slavists.[5]
It follows that, while, by adopting this view, it still remains meaningful—in
spite of some methodological and terminological difficulties—to posit an
intermediate Balto-Slavic stage in the development from Late Common
Indo-European to Early Proto-Slavic (and further on to Common Slavic),
such an intervening evolutionary phase need not actually be postulated for
the prehistory of Baltic. This, of course, does not mean to imply that reference to data of the closely related Slavic branch of the Indo-European

language family would in any way be inappropriate in a comparative treatment of the Baltic languages. Stang's monumental reference work eloquently testifies to the contrary.

As shown even by the few examples quoted above, it is characteristic of the close affinity between Baltic and Slavic that when West and East Baltic differ in that one of the two sub-branches of Baltic may have retained (and further developed) a feature inherited from Common Indo-European while the other one may have replaced it by an innovation Slavic frequently will match one of the two Baltic sub-branches, and more often than not, the one that has introduced the innovation. Thus, we know of a considerable number of exclusive Slavic-(Old) Prussian isoglosses, on the one hand, and of Slavic-East Baltic (as well as merely Slavic-Lithuanian) shared characteristics, on the other. In this context, it should be noted, incidentally, that it is sometimes difficult to determine what exactly should be taken for common Indo-European heritage in Slavic and a part of Baltic and what can be attributed to spreading of secondary, primarily Slavic (especially Polish) influences to Baltic (in particular Old Prussian and Lithuanian). Occasionally also some influence is noted in the opposite direction—Baltic (mostly Lithuanian) on Slavic (particularly Belorussian and, more generally, Early Ruthenian).[6]

How much and how soon the Baltic area (whatever its exact original limits) must have been differentiated in terms of individual languages and idioms is shown by the fairly large number of Baltic loanwords in Finno-Ugric (primarily Baltic Finnic) which largely seem to date back to a very early period. Some of them may have entered Finnic roughly a millennium and a half prior to the appearance of the first Baltic texts, i.e., in the era B. C. As suggested by their phonetic and morphological shape, these early borrowings did not emanate from any Common Baltic protolanguage, but from an already existing individual Baltic language (or dialect). Using phonological criteria, W. Steinitz has cogently demonstrated that three chronological layers of these loans can be identified.[7]

Summing up the preceding considerations, it appears that the positing of an intermediary Balto-Slavic stage, distinct from and preceding the specifically Slavic linguistic evolution, remains methodologically valid. A corresponding postulation as regards the pre-Baltic development, on the other hand, seems less called for since it may be virtually infeasible to draw a sharp line separating Balto-Slavic from Early Proto-Baltic phenomena. It is at least doubtful, however, whether such a pre-Slavic Balto-Slavic phase ought to be thought of as a homogeneous language which actually existed. Rather, it should be perceived as a particular, archaic Late Common Indo-

European dialect (or dialect cluster). In view of the limited possibility of reconstructing anything but a quite fragmentary linguistic structure, it seems more advisable to think in terms of a fairly abstract Balto-Slavic (or Early Proto-Baltic) linguistic model, providing a point of departure for the subsequent preliterary as well as historically recorded development of Baltic and Slavic, respectively, than to conceive of Balto-Slavic as of some concrete protolanguage that potentially can, and ultimately therefore might, be recovered in full detail.

The approach to, Balto-Slavic just outlined could be termed the *modeling* approach. The kind of reconstruction on which it rests is largely that of *internal reconstruction*, at least as regards the inferences concerning Balto-Slavic arrived at on the basis of the data of Common Slavic and Common (or, rather perhaps, generalized) Baltic, respectively. The uniform data of the last phases of preliterary Slavic and Baltic can, in turn, be derived from linguistic reconstruction, both internal and, in particular, comparative.[8]

While this modeling approach (based largely on internal reconstruction) is methodologically different, it appears in substance most closely related to the more traditional assumption of an exclusive Balto-Slavic linguistic unity, i.e., in effect, of a *Common Balto-Slavic protolanguage*, from which both the Baltic and the Slavic language groups subsequently are believed to have developed. The current traditionalist view (at present still held, in one variety or another, by many scholars) represents basically only a slight modification of the earlier, neogrammarian *Stammbaum* approach and is based, primarily, on comparative evidence. In addition to the difference in methods by which these two concepts are reached, the traditionalist view is also at variance with the modeling approach insofar as the latter does not, essentially, distinguish between a separate Balto-Slavic and a hypothetic Proto-Baltic phase in the linguistic evolution. Moreover, the modeling approach conceives of this prehistoric stage as a Late Common Indo-European dialectal development, rather than as a distinctly post-Indo-European, independent language of some status. In this particular respect this approach happens to almost coincide with another interpretation of the relationship between Baltic and Slavic, which, though based on entirely different premises, also views the many agreements between the two language groups as fundamentally reflecting an archaic residue of the Indo-European protolanguage in its last phase.[9] The originator of this interpretation, A. Senn, otherwise belongs to the adherents of yet another approach to Balto-Slavic, viz., that viewing the two language groups as basically *separate*, though *parallel offshoots* of Indo-European. This concept goes back to A. Meillet (1908) but was substantially modified by J. Endzelīns only a few years later.[10] Since then, many experts in the field have, in one cautious formulation or another, adopted this view of the nature of the linguistic relationship between Baltic and Slavic.

Finally, there is still a fourth possibility of accounting for at least a good deal of the many striking conformities between Baltic and Slavic. This fourth view we could label the *Sprachbund* or *convergence* approach to Balto-Slavic. In addition to Baltic and Slavic, some scholars would include in this early linguistic convergence area also Germanic, as did Chr. S. Stang.[11] With the increasing realization of the merely secondary significance of the *centum/ satəm* division as a classificatory criterion of the ancient Indo-European dialects, the grouping together of Baltic, Slavic, and Germanic has become more acceptable. In recent years, the convergence approach has found an advocate particularly in S. B. Bernštejn.[12] However, Bernštejn does not define his convergence or, rather perhaps, *symbiosis* area (*soobščnost', Verkehrsgemeinschaft*) as including, in addition to Baltic and Slavic, also Germanic; rather, he narrows down even the Baltic component to consist primarily only of West Baltic (Prussian and the unrecorded Jatvingian).

The definitions of four basic approaches to the problem of Balto-Slavic linguistic relationship just given should not be interpreted as altogether mutually exclusive. Various combinations of these approaches are, no doubt, conceivable and have in fact been suggested. Nonetheless, an independent evaluation of the chief merits and shortcomings of each of them should be possible. Unfortunately, considerations of space do not allow here for any detailed comparative assessment of these approaches or their possible combinations. Suffice it to state, therefore, that, to the present writer, the concept and method here labeled the modeling approach (which relates to, but also substantially modifies, the traditional view of an assumed Balto-Slavic protolanguage) combined with the interpretation referred to as the *Sprachbund* or convergence approach appears most apt to adequately account for the resemblant, yet in many respects different data of Baltic and Slavic.

Notes

1. Three representative titles may serve here in lieu of any exhaustive or even near-exhaustive list of pertinent references: "Einige Bemerkungen über das Verhältnis zwischen den slavischen und baltischen Sprachen", *NTS*, XI (1939), 85–98; *Das slavische und baltische Verbum*, Oslo, 1942; *Vergleichende Grammatik der Baltischen Sprachen*, Oslo–Bergen–Tromsö, 1966. Some of the illustrative material adduced in this paper is taken from Stang's Comparative Grammar of Baltic.

2. For some additional aspects in particular of the terminological issues at hand, cf.

my forthcoming article "Zur Problematik der zeitlichen Abgrenzung des Urslavischen", *ZfslPh* (1970). The discussion immediately following draws on a section of this article subtitled "Baltoslavisch und/oder Frühurslavisch?"

3. On the Elbing Vocabulary, see J. Endzelin, *Altpreussische Grammatik*, Riga, 1944, 12–13, and *Prūsų kalbos paminklai* (V. Mažiulis,ed.), Vilnius, 1966, 27–29 and 59–75. On the Dzukovian Prayers, discovered in 1962 by O. Matusevičiūtė and first published in 1964 by J. Lebedys and J. Palionis, see A. Senn, *Handbuch der litauischen Sprache*, I: *Grammatik*, Heidelberg, 1966, 50–51, 53–54, and 56. The first more important work in Lithuanian is Mažvydas' Catechism of 1547. Its language was investigated by Chr. S. Stang: *Die Sprache des litauischen Katechismus von Mažvydas*, Oslo, 1929. On the earliest texts published in Latvian, cf. J. Endzelin, *Lettische Grammatik*, Riga, 1922 (and Heidelberg, 1923), 10.

4. For a discussion of internal reconstruction as applicable to Balto-Slavic, see my article "Rekonstrukcja wewnętrzna, kolejność synchronicznych reguł gramatyki syntetycznej i zagadnienie najdawniejszych stosunków między językami bałtyckimi a słowiańskimi", *IJSLP*, XI, 1–24. A revised and expanded English version of this paper is due to appear as a chapter of my book *Problems of Typological and Genetic Linguistics Viewed in a Generative Framework*, The Hague and Paris, 1970.

5. See V. V. Ivanov and V. N. Toporov, "O postanovke voprosa o drevnejšix otnošenijax baltijskix i slavjanskix jazykov", *Issledovanija po slavjanskomu jazykoznaniju*, Moscow, 1961, 273–305, esp. 303–304. Cf. further also, for example, my concurring remarks in *IJSLP*, XI, 18–19, as well as those by C. Watkins in *Ancient Indo-European Dialects* (H. Birnbaum and J. Puhvel, eds.), Berkeley and Los Angeles, 1966, 49–50. Also P. Arumaa's *Urslavische Grammatik* (I, Heidelberg, 1964), extensively adducing Baltic data, is, it seems, implicitly based on a similar assumption.

6. For details, see E. Fraenkel, *Die baltischen Sprachen*, Heidelberg, 1950, 73–123; Chr. S. Stang, *Vgl. Gr. d. Balt. Spr.*, 10–13. On the features which, according to Stang, force us "die balt. Sprachen als eine eigene Sprachgruppe zu betrachten, d. h. als einen Kreis von Sprachen, die in der Vergangenheit eine lange Periode gemeinsamen Lebens durchgemacht haben, ohne dass die Einheit je vollständig gewesen zu sein braucht", see *ibid.*, 2–10. For a partly new interpretation of certain phonological agreements (in accentuation and ablaut) between Baltic and Slavic (as well as, to some extent, Germanic), see J. Kuryłowicz, *Indogermanische Grammatik*, II: *Akzent, Ablaut*, Heidelberg, 1968, 111–190, 235–243, 293–297, 318–326. Particularly difficult to assess, from a methodological point of view, are some syntactic features which may have spread from Baltic to East Slavic or where, rather, Baltic patterns may have reinforced dormant morphological means in Slavic, particularly East Slavic. This applies, for example, to the dative absolute construction (with inflected participle or, especially, corresponding to the Lithuanian construction, with the gerund) found in Early Belorussian (and Ruthenian in general) also outside the strictly literary sphere (more readily susceptible to Church Slavic influence); cf. *Sravnitel'no-istoričeskij sintaksis vostočnoslavjanskix jazykov. Členy predloženija* (V. I. Borkovskij, ed.), Moscow, 1968, 275–286, esp. 278. Also the largely "mechanized" use of the predicative instrumental in (East) Slavic has occasionally been explained as due to Lithuanian influence, with the Lithuanian (or generally Baltic) usage, in turn, said by some linguists to be patterned on the essive and/or translative of a Baltic Finnic substratum. Cf., most recently, V. Kiparsky, "Gibt es ein finno-ugrisches Substrat im Slavischen?", *Annales Acad. Scient. Fenn.* B: 153: 4 (1969), esp. 22–23. On the predicative instrumental in Contemporary Standard

Russian and its historical background, see also *Zwei Studien über den prädikativen Instrumental im Russischen*, Oslo, 1966, by R. Røed, a student of Prof. Stang. Concerning the particular Polish-Old Prussian linguistic relations, cf. esp. T. Milewski, "Stosunki językowe polsko-pruskie", *SlOcc*, XVIII (1947), 21–84. Mr. J. Levin, a student of Prof. Stang and mine, is currently engaged in work on a doctoral dissertation including a critical evaluation of Milewski's findings. The common Balto-Slavic vocabulary, inherited from Indo-European, is treated in R. Trautmann's *Baltisch-Slavisches Wörterbuch*, Göttingen, 1923, whose material is to be supplemented by data from the more recent *Litauisches etymologisches Wörterbuch* I–II, Heidelberg and Göttingen, 1962/5, by E. Fraenkel.

7. The fundamental study of Baltic-Finnic loan relations is still V. Thomsen's *Berøringer mellem de finske og de baltiske (litauisk-lettiske) Sprog*, Copenhagen, 1890; German version: *Berührungen zwischen den finnischen und den baltischen (lit.-lett.) Sprachen*, Copenhagen, 1931 (= *Saml. Afh.* IV). Among more recent work in this field, cf. esp. E. Nieminen, "Über einige Eigenschaften der baltischen Sprache, die sich in den ältesten baltischen Lehnwörtern der ostseefinnischen Sprachen abspiegeln", *Sitz.-ber. d. Finn. Akad. d. Wiss.* 1956 (Helsinki, 1957), 185–206; *id.*, "Beiträge zu den baltisch-ostseefinnischen Berührungen", *Rakstu krājums* (Festschrift Endzelīns), Riga, 1959, 201–210; and W. Steinitz, "Zur Periodisierung der alten baltischen Lehnwörter im Ostsee-Finnischen", *Symbolae linguisticae in honorem Georgii Kuryłowicz*, Wrocław–Warsaw–Cracow, 1965, 297–303 (preprint, under slightly different title, in: *Wiss. Z. d. Humboldt-Univ. zu Berlin*, *GSR* XIII, 1964, 2/3, 335–339), with further references, *i. a.*, to J. Kalima's important 1936 study. See also Chr. S. Stang, *Vgl. Gr. d. Balt. Spr.*, 2.

8. For further discussion, see my article quoted in fn. 4; cf. also V. N. Toporov, "Nekotorye soobraženija otnositel'no izučenija istorii praslavjanskogo jazyka", *Slavjanskoe jazykoznanie. Sbornik statej*, Moscow, 1959, 3–27.

9. Cf. A. Senn's statement: "I could admit the term 'Balto-Slavic' in the sense of 'Baltic and Slavic' and in the meaning of 'Proto-Indo-European of Northeastern Europe in its last phase'. It is the residue of Proto-Indo-European, the remainder left after all adjacent parts had entered into history and developed into independently regulated languages." See *Ancient Indo-European Dialects*, 143, and, taking into consideration also the relationship of these two language groups to Germanic, 150–151 (in his paper "The Relationships of Baltic and Slavic").

10. Cf. I. M. Ėndzelin, *Slavjano-baltijskie ėtjudy*, Kharkov, 1911. For a survey of the differences of opinion on the Balto-Slavic problem, see, e.g., E. Fraenkel, *Die balt. Spr.*, 73–75; B. V. Gornung, "Iz istorii izučenija baltijsko-slavjanskix jazykovyx otnošenij", *Rakstu krājums*, 109–132; and, esp., S. Karaliūnas, "Kai kurie baltų ir slavų kalbų seniausiųjų santykių klausimai", *Lietuvių kalbotyros klausimai*, X, Vilnius, 1968 (= *Baltų ir slavų kalbų ryšiai*, *Lietuvos TSR Mokslų Akademija*), 7–100.

11. See Chr. S. Stang, *Das sl. u. balt. Vb.*, 278. On Germanic–Baltic–Slavic agreements or similarities, cf. further also, e.g., A. Senn, "On the Degree of Kinship between Slavic and Baltic", *SEER*, XX (1941), 251–265; *id.*, "Die Beziehungen des Baltischen zum Slavischen und Germanischen", *KZ*, LXXI (1954), 162–188. Some caution regarding the conclusions reached by Senn seems appropriate, however.

12. Cf. his "Balto-slavjanskaja jazykovaja soobščnost'," *Slavjanskaja filologija*, I, Moscow, 1958, 45–68; *id.*, *Očerk sravnitel'noj grammatiki slavjanskix jazykov*, Moscow, 1961, 27–37. Also S. Karaliūnas, *op. cit.*, assumes a convergent development of Baltic and Slavic dialects ca. 2000–1500 B. C.

TAMARA BUCH

Zur Akzentuierung des Futurums im Litauischen

In der litauischen Schriftsprache, wie auch in den westlitauischen Mundarten, auf die sie fusst, wird eine Neuerung in der Akzentuierung beobachtet, die dem Ostlit. fremd ist: der Iktus ruht auf der Wurzelsilbe dort,
wo er dem de Saussure'schen Gesetz gemäss auf der Endung zu erwarten
wäre, also in der 1. und in der 2. Pers. Sg. der zirkumflektierten und der
kurzvokalischen Verben, vgl. schriftlit. westlit. 1. Pers. Sg. *eĩsiu, sùksiu*,
2. Pers. Sg. *eĩsi, sùksi*: ostlit. 1. Pers. Sg. *eisiù, suksiù*, 2. Pers. *eisì, suksì*
von *eĩti* 'gehen', *sùkti* 'drehen'[1].

Stang bemerkt dazu, dass es sich hier im Schrift- und Westlit. um eine
späte Verallgemeinerung der Betonung der 3. Pers. und des Plurals handele,
ohne näher auf die Ursachen dieser Entwicklung einzugehen[2].

Nun fragt es sich aber, warum der Ausgleich in der Akzentuierung das
Futurum betroffen habe, während die Wirkung des de Saussure'schen Gesetzes im Präsens und im Präteritum aufrechterhalten ist. Eine Antwort auf
diese Frage muss im Aufbau des litauischen Verbalsystems, insbesondere in
seiner Morphonologie gesucht werden. Unten versuche ich an das Problem
von einer rein synchronischen Analyse des schriftsprachlichen Materials
aus heranzutreten.

Das lit. Verbum bildet seine Formen bekanntlich von 3 Stämmen — dem
Präsens-, dem Präterital- und dem Infinitivstamm, wobei sich das Inventar
der finiten und der infiniten Formen ihrer Bildung von den einzelnen Stämmen nach folgendermassen verteilt:

Bei diesen Formen ist ein engeres Verhältnis zwischen den Bildungen vom
Präsens- und von Präteritalstamm bemerklich, während die Bildungen vom
Infinitivstamm abseitsstehen. Dieses betrifft bei den finiten Formen, auf
deren Analyse ich mich hier beschränke, sowohl die Kategorie des Tempus,
als auch den morphonologischen Bau der Formen.

Hinsichtlich der Tempuskategorie kann festgestellt werden, dass das
Präteritum und das Präsens, die notabene die einzigen von ihren Stammen
gebildeten finiten Formen sind, die Opposition Vergangenheit: Nichtvergangenheit eingehen, vgl.

	Präsensstamm	Präteritumstamm	Infinitivstamm
Finite Formen:	Präsens	Präteritum	Imperfektum Futurum Optativus Imperativus Permissivus
Infinite Formen:	Part. Präs. Act. -*ąs*//*is* Part. Präs. Act. -*ant*/*int* Part. Präs. Pass. -*mas*	Part. Prät. Act. -*ęs* Part. Prät. Act. -*us*	Part. Präs. Act. -*damas* Part. Prät. Pass. -*tas* Part. Imperf. Act. -*davęs* Part. Imperf. Act. -*davus* Part. Fut. Act. -*sią̇s* Part. Fut. Act. -*siant* Part. Fut. Pass. -*simas* Part. Necessitatis -*tinas* Infinitiv

Petras skubėjo namo
'Peter eilte nach Hause'

Petras skuba namo
'Peter eilt nach Hause'

Das Präteritum des ersten Satzes bezeichnet ausschliesslich die Vergangenheit und dieser Zeitbezug bleibt auch bei der Erweiterung des Satzes durch eine verallgemeinernde Adverbialbestimmung der Zeit, z. B. *visuomet* 'immer', erhalten[3].

Im zweiten Satz, in dem das Verbum im Präsens steht, wird bei Fehlen anders einstellender Fakta des Kontextes, z. B. entsprechender Adverbialbestimmungen, die Handlung als auf die Gegenwart bezogen aufgefasst, ungefähr *sieh, da eilt Peter gerade nach Hause*. Jedoch im Gegensatz zu dem Präteritum kann das Präsens nicht nur mit Bezug auf die Gegenwart verwendet werden, z. B.

Vakar Petras skuba namo, o Marytė šaukia ... 'Gestern eilt Peter nach Hause, da ruft Marie ...', wo durch das Adverbium *vakar* 'gestern' die Handlung in die Vergangenheit verlegt wird.

Als eines bestimmten Zeitbezuges entbehrend tritt die Handlung bei folgender Erweiterung des Satzes mit dem Verbum im Präsens auf:

Niekuomet po darbo negalima kartu išgerti alaus — Petras skuba namo. 'Man kann nie nach der Arbeit zusammen ein Bier trinken — Peter eilt nach Hause.'

Es ist hier wichtig ein Spezifikum des Lit. zu betonen, nämlich dass der Gebrauch des Präsens mit Bezug auf die Zukunft der Sprache fremd ist. Eine Ausnahme bilden nur solche Grenzfälle, in denen das Präsens zur Bezeichnung einer unmittelbar bevorstehenden Handlung gebraucht wird, z. B. *jau einu* 'ich gehe schon'.

Ob nun die Bezeichnung der Gegenwart oder das Fehlen eines bestimmten Zeitbezuges im Lit. die primäre Funktion des Präsens ausmacht, muss genauer erwogen werden. Wichtig ist in diesem Zusammenhang nur, dass das Präteritum das merkmalhaltige, das Präsens das merkmallose Glied der Opposition Vergangenheit: Nichtvergangenheit ist[4]. Diese hat im Lit. mit dem Bezug der Handlung auf die Zukunft nichts zu tun.

Anders als der Präterital- und der Präsensstamm ist der Infinitivstamm an sich der Tempuskategorie gegenüber neutral. Der Zeitbezug der von ihm gebildeten finiten Formen ist verschiedenartig: das Imperfektum wird ausschliesslich mit Bezug auf die Vergangenheit gebraucht, das Futurum — bei Darstellung einer zukünftigen Handlung, der Optativus kann wie das Präsens sowohl bei der Bezogenheit der Handlung auf die Gegenwart als auch bei Fehlen eines bestimmten Zeitbezuges verwendet werden, ausserdem — und hier unterscheidet er sich vom Präsens — auch bei der Bezeichnung einer zukünftigen Handlung; bei Bezug der Handlung auf die Vergangenheit sind jedoch nur periphrastische Formen des Optativus von *būti* 'sein' mit dem Partizip des entsprechenden Verbs zulässig[5]. Was den Imperativus anbetrifft, so macht die Schriftsprache keinen Unterschied zwischen dem Befehl die Handlung immediat oder in einer weiter abliegenden Zukunft zu vollziehen. Diese Unterscheidung ist in den ostlitauischen Mundarten bekannt[6]. Der Permissivus, der sich seiner Bildung nach vom Imperativus unterscheidet, kann ihm bedeutungsmässig als suppletive Form der 3. Person angegliedert werden.

Bei dieser Sachlage ist es nicht das Tempus, das die vom Infinitivstamm gebildeten Formen untereinander verbindet und sie vom Präteritum und dem Präsens unterscheidet.

Das Gemeinsame für die ersteren ist das Vorhandensein von Kategorien, die ausserhalb der Opposition Vergangenheit: Nichtvergangenheit, die das Präteritum dem Präsens gegenüberstellt, stehen. Diese Kategorien sind für das Imperfektum die Iterativität, das Futurum — die Zukunft, den Optativus — die Irrealität, den Imperativus und den Permissivus — der Befehl (die Aufforderung, die Erlaubnis). Sie sind den Bildungen vom Infinitivstamm als Grundbedeutungen eigen, während sie bei dem Präteritum und dem Präsens eventuell in sekundärer Funktion auftreten, vgl. *jie dažnai eina/ėjo į kavinę* 'sie gehen/gingen oft ins Café', wo das präfixlose Verb im Präsens bzw. im Präteritum in Verbindung mit der Adverbialbestimmung *dažnai* 'oft' eine iterative Handlung bezeichnet. Wenn man jedoch das Adverb fortlässt und andere kontextuelle Fakta, die die iterative Bedeutung aufrechterhalten könnten, fehlen, dann schwindet diese. Bei Gebrauch des Präteritums eines präfigierten Verbums, z. B. *nueiti* 'hingehen', ist die iterative Bedeutung und somit das Adverb *dažnai* ausgeschlossen. Beim Imperfektum ist dagegen die iterative Bedeutung unabhängig vom Kontext vorhanden.

Es scheint, dass in den genannten Kategorien das Spezifikum der Bildungen vom Infinitivstamm dem Präteritum und dem Präsens gegenüber zu suchen ist[7].

Den erwähnten Unterschieden zwischen dem Präteritum und dem Präsens, einerseits, und den Bildungen vom Infinitivstamm, andererseits, entspricht der morphonologische Bau der Formen: die finiten Bildungen vom Infinitivstamm weisen alle im Vergleich mit dem Präteritum und dem Präsens um ein grammatisches Suffix mehr auf, vgl.

1. Pers. Plur. Präs. *suk — a — me*
1. Pers. Plur. Prät. *suk — o — me*
1. Pers. Plur. Imperf. *suk — dav — o — me*
1. Pers. Plur. Fut. *suk — si — ø — me*
1. Pers. Plur. Imperat. *suk — ki — ø — me*
1. Pers. Plur. Optat. *suk — tumė — ø — me*

Im Präsens und im Präteritum folgen hier auf die Wurzel *suk-* zwei Stellen für die eigentliche Verbalflexion: das Tempussuffix Präs. *-a-*, Prät. *-o-*[8] und darauf die Person/Numerusendung der 1. Plur. *-me*.

Bei den Formen vom Infinitivstamm tritt regelmässig eine dritte Stelle auf, die im Imperfektum von *-dav-*, im Futurum von *-si-*, im Imperativ von *-ki-*, im Optativ von *-tumė-* in den angeführten Beispielen besetzt ist. Es sind diese Suffixe, die die Formen voneinander unterscheiden.

Die morphonologische Gestaltung dieser Suffixe — mit Ausnahme von Imperf. *-dav-*, variiert: so weist das Suffix des Futurums ausser der Form *-si-* in der ersten und in der zweiten Pers. Plur. die Form *-ŝ-* in der 1. und 2. Pers. Sg. und die Form *-s-* in der 3. Pers. auf; *-k-* statt *-ki-* ist in der modernen Schriftsprache in der 2. Pers. Sg. Imperat. das Normale[9]; komplizierter liegen die Verhältnisse im Optativus, wo die Analyse der 1. Pers. Sg. auf *-čiau* Schwierigkeiten bereitet. Zweifellos kann man jedoch für den Optativus von einem mit *t/č* anlautenden Suffix sprechen.

Wie ersichtlich, ist die Stelle für das Tempussuffix nur im Imperfektum besetzt, während sie bei den übrigen Formen leer bleibt, was mit ihrem oben erörterten Zeitbezug in Einklang zu stehen scheint.

Der erwähnte Unterschied im Bau zwischen den finiten Formen vom Infinitivstamm, einerseits, und dem Präteritum und dem Präsens, andererseits, wird von einer unterschiedlichen Auswertung des Ablauts und der Akzentuierung begleitet.

Die Ablautsreihen des Verbs in der modernen Sprache müssen gesondert gesichtet werden. Hier sei nur darauf hingewiesen, dass in den meisten Fällen, in denen Ablautserscheinungen auftreten, sie das Präsens vom Präteritum unterscheiden, während der Infinitiv mit einer dieser Formen zusammenfällt[10].

Was nun die Akzentuierung anbetrifft, so sind alle finiten Bildungen vom Infinitivstamm in der Schriftsprache durchgehend barytonisch, während das Präsens und das Präteritum einen Akzentwechsel nach dem de Saussure'-schen Gesetz aufweisen. Dieser kann als morphonologisch relevant angesehen werden, da die erwartete Wirkung des de Saussure'schen Gesetzes im Futurum aufgehoben ist: das de Saussure'sche Gesetz hat aufgehört als „ausnahmsloses Lautgesetz" zu funktionieren. Der unbewegliche Akzent kann hiermit als Kennzeichen der finiten Formen vom Infinitivstamm betrachtet werden, während der bewegliche ein Charakteristikum des Präteritums und des Präsens wäre. Die Akzentzurückziehung im Futurum, die uns hier beschäftigt, wäre als Angleichung an die übrigen vom Infinitivstamm gebildeten finiten Formen zu verstehen.

Die morphonologische Funktion des beweglichen Akzents im Präteritum besteht in der Gegenüberstellung der Numeri bei den zirkumflektierten und den kurzvokalischen Verben: Endbetonung tritt in der 1. und in der 2. Pers. Sg., Anfangsbetonung in diesen Personen des Plurals, zu denen sich auch die 3. Pers. stellt, auf, vgl.

	Präsens		Präteritum	
Singularis	Pluralis	Singularis	Pluralis
1. *einù, sukù*	*eĩname, sùkame*	*ė́jaũ, sukaũ*	*ė̃jome, sùkome*
2. *einì, sukì*	*eĩnate, sùkate*	*ėjaĩ, sukaĩ*	*ė̃jote, sùkote*
3.	*eĩna, sùka*		*ė̃jo, sùko*

Bemerkt sei, dass beim Nomen eine Tendenz zu einer genau entgegengesetzten Entwicklung, und zwar in der städtischen Umgangssprache, bemerklich ist: ein durchgehend barytonischer Singularis wird bei den Substantiven auf -*as* der Akzentuierungstypen *bérnas, vaĩkas* einem durchgehend oxytonischen Pluralis gegenübergestellt[11].

Anmerkungen

1. Vgl. Z. Zinkevičius, *Lietuvių dialektologija*, Vilnius, 1966, 359.
2. *Vergleichende Grammatik der baltischen Sprachen*, Oslo, 1966, 471.

3. J. Jablonskis, *Rinktiniai raštai*, I, sudarė J. Palionis, Vilnius, 1957, 316, führt ein Beispiel mit dem Präteritum an, in dem diese Form ohne Bezug auf die Vergangenheit gebraucht ist, vgl. *Paprašyk padaryti tokius račiukus, kad atsisėdai, pagalvojai — ir, kur nori, be arklio nuvažiavai.* 'Bitte, dass man dir solch ein Wäglein mache, daß du einsteigst (Prät.), nachdenkst (Prät.) — und ohne Pferd reist (Prät.), wohin du wünschst.' Von diesem Gebrauch glaube ich hier absehen zu dürfen.

4. Zum Begriff der primären und der sekundären Funktion vgl. J. Kuryłowicz, *The Inflectional Categories of Indo-European*, Heidelberg, 1964, 14 und die dort angeführte Literatur.

5. Vgl. J. Jablonskis, *op. cit.*, 313, 318 f.

6. Z. Zinkevičius, *op. cit.*, 370.

7. Bei den infiniten Formen nimmt die Stelle der Tempuskategorie die Taxis ein, wobei die Partizipien, die vom Präteritalstamm gebildet sind, die Vorzeitigkeit, die Partizipia vom Präsensstamm die Gleichzeitigkeit bezeichnen. Die letzteren werden ausserdem in sekundärer Funktion in anderen Bedeutungen gebraucht, z. B. *prieš gulant reikia nusiprausti* 'vor dem Schlafengehen (Part. Präs. Act.-*ant.*) muss man sich waschen', wo das Part. Präs. in Verbindung mit der Präposition *prieš* 'vor' eine der Handlung des finiten Verbs folgende Handlung bezeichnet. Es ist vielleicht möglich für die infiniten Formen vom Präterital- und vom Präsensstamm eine Opposition Vorzeitigkeit : Nichtvorzeitigkeit aufzustellen, die der Opposition Vergangenheit: Nichtvergangenheit der finiten Formen entspräche. — Die von Infinitivstamm gebildeten Partizipien besitzen keine einheitliche Taxisbedeutung; so bezeichnet das Part. Präs. Act. auf -*damas* in primärer Funktion die Gleichzeitigkeit, das Part. Prät. Pass. auf -*tas* die Vorzeitigkeit, die Part. Fut. die Folge.

8. Es scheint vom synchronischen Standpunkte aus richtiger, die sog. Suffixe des zweiten Stammes nicht zusammen mit den Tempussuffixen als Einheit zu betrachten, da jene auch dort auftreten, wo diese fehlen, vgl. 1. Pers. Plur. Prät. *sed-ėj-o-me* 'wir sassen' und Part. Prät. Act. *sėd-ėj-ęs*. S. Stang, *op. cit.*, 387, 392, wo ein Präteritalstamm *sėdėjo* angesetzt ist.

9. Den isolierten Permissivus lasse ich hier beiseite.

10. Vgl. Stang, *op. cit.*, 392 f. und *Das slavische und baltische Verbum*, Oslo, 1942, 104 ff.

11. Verfasserin, „Entwicklungstendenzen in der Akzentuierung der Substantive im Litauischen", *IJSlLP* (in Vorbereitung).

On Future-Tense Stress in Lithuanian

An innovation in future-tense stress has come about in West-Lith. dialects and in standard Lithuanian (which is based on these) in which the stress falls on the root syllable: *eĩsiu, eĩsi / eĩti* 'to go', in contrast to the East-Lith. forms *eisiù, eisì* (which are in accordance with Saussure's law).

Fixed stress can be regarded as the sign of the finite forms derived from the infinitive stem, while variable stress is a characteristic of the preterite and present. The displacement of the stress in the future tense may be interpreted as being analogous to the position of the stress in the other finite forms derived from the infinitive stem.

WITOLD CIENKOWSKI

Levels of Analysis in Lexicology:
A Study in Linguistic Methodology

1. The most common levels of analysis used in lexicological research are the form level and the meaning level. This corresponds to the traditional and, roughly speaking, correct view that words are forms+meanings. (By form is to be understood here the acoustic and/or graphic shape and the structural shape of the corresponding words.)

The two-level analysis is applied, for example, by S. Ullmann in his semantic research.[1] This method is not adequate, however, for the analysis of some aspects of word change and of words as units of language. It is, for instance, irrelevant to the analysis of the processes and products of etymological reinterpretation, usually called popular or folk etymology.[2] This is especially the case when the lexical meaning of a word and its form remain unchanged and the only process occurring is its associative (or etymological) interpretation (or reinterpretation).[3] Thus the level in question here is not identical with the lexical meaning level, though very often confused with it.[4]

The introduction of a third level in lexicological research permits also a better explanation of the relevant processes and their projection against the background of the lexical system in question.

In recent years more and more attention has been devoted to the problems of levels of linguistic analysis;[5] this paper seeks to make a contribution to this domain of research.

The new level of lexicological analysis proposed here may be called the level of synchronic etymological meaning; as such the meaning in question is distinct from both the lexical meaning and the etymological or historical meaning. (It may happen of course that the synchronic etymological meaning agrees both with the lexical meaning and with the true etymological meaning of the word in question, but this does not affect the theoretical and methodological aspect of the problem.) This level is called the *synchronic etymological* meaning because we are interested in the—sometimes secondary and as it were artificial—etymological relations to other words used by the same speaking community.

Obviously, there are words with practically no synchronic etymological meaning at all; to these belong some foreign loanwords, or old native words that have undergone changes that have made them structurally intransparent; such words do not suggest any other words of the language in question and their isolation may—in certain favourable conditions—cause them to be interpreted secondarily and thus included in the synchronic etymological (or associative) system of a language.

2. Let us now consider how the new level of analysis is to be employed in presenting some processes of folk etymology in foreign loan words adopted by Lithuanian. In the diagrams below, the following symbols are used:

A_0 — the word undergoing etymological reinterpretation,
Ef — the word influencing A_0, i.e. being associated with A_0,
A_1 — the word resulting from the etymological reinterpretation,
SES — synchronic etymological meaning.

The arrows represent influencing factors and show the directions in which they act.

3. Lith. *beždžiõnė* 'monkey, ape'[6] [Russ. обезьяна 'monkey, ape'].

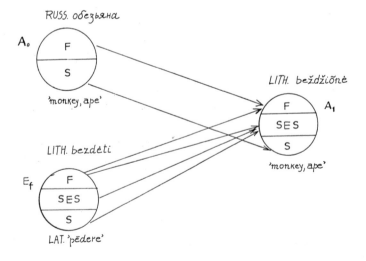

Remarks:

From this diagram we can see that:

(a) the word обезьяна has not been etymologically interpreted by Lithuanians borrowing it; that is why there is no SES level in the (A_0) circle representing it;

(b) the meaning of A_1 (lexical meaning) is precisely that of A_0;

(c) the form of A_1 represents a contamination of the A_0 form by the Ef form;

(d) the appearance of the new relational SES level in A_1 is a result of transferring the associative etymological relations of Ef into A_1; these new relations make the new element (SES) of the lexical unit in question.

4. Lith.[7] *sedlus* 'chair, stool' [Pol. *zedel, zydel* 'chair, stool'].

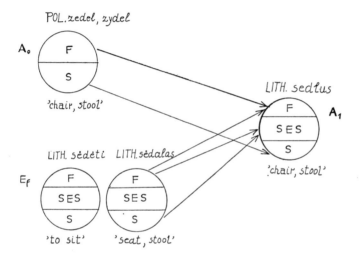

Remarks:

(a) The etymological reinterpretation in this case is easier, as there has been a perfect agreement in meaning between A_0 and Ef;

(b) it is obvious that in this case there has been more than one strong influence (Ef); there are many words in Lithuanian that contain the stem [*sėd-*] or a variant; the two words mentioned here are only examples;

(c) we present here a process of closer assimilation of a loan word [*zedlus*] > [*sedlus*], but this assimilation, i.e. association with the Lithuanian word family, might have already happened by the time the word *zedel, zydel* was being borrowed from Polish; cf. Lith. *slibžakas* (below).

5. Lith. *slibžakas* 'pocket' [Germ. *Schiebsack* ‖ *Schiebesack* 'pocket'.[8]

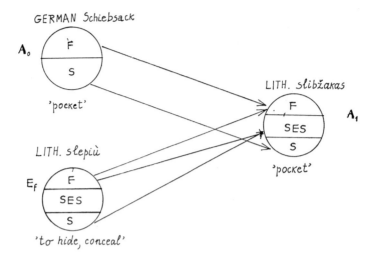

Remarks:

(a) It is possible that Lithuanians borrowing this word knew its primary 'literal' meaning, i.e. 'a bag to put things into', and this may have helped the described association. In addition to this, cf. Remarks for Lith. *beždžiõnė* (a), (b), (c), (d).

Conclusions

(1) All three processes presented here are examples of etymological reinterpretations (of foreign or loan words) of a distinctly contaminational character, as most of the so-called folk etymologies are.

(2) The contamination observed here involves only the form of the words in question; their lexical meaning is left unchanged.

(3) The new synchronic etymological level (etymologically associative level) has been introduced in view of the influence of native paronyms [*bezdėti, sėdėti, slepiù*].

(4) The result of this influence has been a double one: a) change of form, b) association with native words.

(5) Owing to this the corresponding A_1 words are more closely interrelated with the lexical system of the Lithuanian language and are thus more central (less peripheral)[9] than their starting words A_0.

(6) The general and common feature of the processes presented here is that they start with an association (on a graphic or acoustic basis) of A_0

words with some paronyms Ef, to produce the result-words A_1—as shown in the diagrams—, an association between form, lexical meaning and the synchronic etymological meaning being introduced.

(7) The necessity for introducing a third level of analysis in describing processes of etymological reinterpretation (folk etymology) seems clear.

(8) It is noted that synchronic etymological (etymologically associative) meaning has no value in the case of etymologically and structurally obscure words.

(9) The introduction of a third level in lexicological research helps one to understand better the interplay of forces in the use and development of the lexical system of a language.

(10) Finally, the introduction of the third level of lexicological analysis is a means of keeping apart lexical meaning and literal, associative or synchronic etymological meaning.

Notes

1. Cf. his *Principles of Semantics*, New York, 1957, where he uses throughout diagrams representing only two elements: n = name and s = meaning; e.g. on pp. 78, 176, 223, 227, 235, 241, 242 and 243.

2. The term "etymological reinterpretation" has been coined by this writer and used, e.g., in his paper "The Initial Stimuli in the Processes of Etymological Reinterpretation (so-called Folk Etymology)", *Scando-Slavica*, XV, 237–245. For more on terminology in folk etymology research see this writer's "Reinterpretacja w faktach atrakcji paronimicznej czyli tzw. etymologii ludowej (teoria i etymologia)", *Studia Linguistica Slavica Baltica Canuto-Olavo Falk Sexagenario a Collegis Amicis Discipulis Oblata*, Lundae MCMLXVI, 29–42.

3. It is reasonable and useful sometimes to make a distinction between *interpretation* when a word in question has not been interpreted etymologically (synchronically) at all, and *re-interpretation*, when the word has already been interpreted in some way. In the cases treated in this paper it is assumed that the corresponding starting (A_0) words, namely Russ. *обезьяна*, Germ. *Schiebsack* || *Schiebesack* and the Polish loanword *zedel* || *zydel*, have not been primarily interpreted by Lithuanians at all, and thus we can call the process described below 'interpretation', not 're-interpretation'.

4. This mistake has been made by V. Pisani, "Über Volksetymologie", *Studii şi Cercetări Lingvistice*, XI, 633–643, and earlier, e.g. J. Kjederquist, "Lautlich-begriffliche Wortassimilationen ...", *Beiträge zur Geschichte der deutschen Sprache und Literatur*, XXVII, 430. In connection with this problem cf. L. Zawadowski, "O próbie syntezy problemów etymologii (Vittore Pisani, L'Etimologia, Torino, 1947)", Biuletyn Polskiego Towarzystwa Językoznawczego XV, 204.

5. It was one of the main problems treated during the IX International Congress of Linguists in Cambridge, Mass. in 1962, Cf. e.g. E. Benveniste, "Les niveaux de l'analyse

linguistique", *Proceedings of the Ninth International Congress of Linguists* ... 1964, 266–275.

6. Cf. Būga, *Izv.* XVII, 1, 10; *KS* I, 2.

7. "Das aus poln. *zedel* (*zydel*) 'Sitzbock, Pritsche, Sessel' entlehnte lit. *zedlus* erscheint bei Daukantas ausser in dieser Form (Būd. 139) auch als *sedlus* (a. O. 140), natürlich unter Angleichung an *sėdėti* 'sitzen', *sėdalas, sėdynė* 'Sitz, Stuhl', *sóstas* 'Sessel, Thron' usw. (s. auch Būga KS, 1, 140, 280 ff.)", E. Fraenkel, "Kreuzung einheimischer und fremder Synonyma ähnlicher Lautung im Baltischen. Ein Beitrag zur Fremdwortforschung dieser Sprachgruppe", *ZfslPh*, VIII, 413.

8. "*slibžakas* ein Diebsack (nach Ness. [= Nesselmann] zu *slepiù* gehörig"), F. Kurschat, *Littauisch-deutsches Wörterbuch*, Halle, 1883, 338. "*Schiebsack, Schiebesack* 'Kleidertasche etwas hineinzuschieben, Ficke' ", D. Sanders, *Handwörterbuch der deutschen Sprache*, 8. Aufl. von dr J. Ernst Wülfing, Leipzig u. Wien, 1912, 590. Cf. also this writer's "Warmińsko-mazurskie *dybzak* 'kieszeń' ", *Poradnik językowy* 1963, 227–229.

9. Cf. *Travaux Linguistiques de Prague 2. Les problèmes du centre et de la péryphérie du système de la langue*, Prague, 1966.

KĀRLIS DRAVIŅŠ

Die Bezeichnung des ṡ-Lautes in G. Elgers lettischem Manuskript *Evangelia et Epistolae* (um 1640)

1. Das dialektologische Material des lettischen Sprachgebiets weist eine Menge von Variationen auf, was die Qualität und Quantität der Laute, Oppositionen der Phoneme, die Intonationsart, Erweichung der Konsonanten u. a. betrifft. Über die Entstehung und den Entwicklungsgang dieser Fülle der ma. Verschiedenheiten ist der Sprachforscher gezwungen, meistenteils nur theoretische Schlüsse zu ziehen, da sowohl das alte onomastische Material wie auch die ältesten lettischen Schriften in dieser Hinsicht keineswegs aufschlussreich sind. Nur einzelne alte Autoren des 17. Jhs., z. B. G. Manzelius, haben manche karge dialektologische Nachrichten hinterlassen. Verschiedene ma. Wortformen lassen sich auch in Schriften anderer Verfasser jener Zeit (G. Elgers, Chr. Füreckers u. a.) aufspüren. Ein bisher unbeachtetes Zeugnis dieser Art findet man im *handschriftlichen* Material Georg Elgers[1].

2. Von Elgers lettisch geschriebenen *Manuskripten* sind *Evangelia et Epistolæ toto anno ...*, eine Reinschrift für den Druck eines ganzen Buches, und eine Kladde des Liederverzeichnisses (eines alphabetischen Registers) seines Gesangbuchs (nur ein Blatt), beide aus der Zeit um 1640, uns jetzt bekannt[2]. In diesen beiden Handschriften des alten katholischen Autors (gleicherweise wie in anderen seiner lett. Arbeiten) findet man eine Rechtschreibung, die im grossen und ganzen der polnischen Orthographie ähnlich ist[3], wogegen jene altlett. Autoren desselben Zeitalters, die den ev.-luth. Kreisen angehörten, sich an die damalige niederdeutsche orthographische Tradition angelehnt haben.

Den lett. Laut [š] bezeichnet Elger in seinen Manuskripten in der Regel wie im Polnischen, d. h., mit einem Doppelbuchstaben [ſʒ], [ʃʒ], selten auch mit [sʒ]. Gleicherweise selten, ohne Zweifel, als ein Verschreiben, kommt noch eine andere Kombination, nämlich [ſz], vor, z. B. *ſʒurp* (=*šurp* 'her'), Elgers Ms. 6$_{25}$ u. ä.[4], *gaiuſʒi* (=*gājuši* 'gegangen') ib. u. a., aber auch *cêſzan* (=*ciešana* 'Leiden') 1$_{13}$, *celſz* (=*celš* 'Weg') 1$_{18}$ u. ä.

3. Hier und dort in diesem Manuskript der Evangelien und Episteln trifft man noch eine Lautbezeichnung [ṡ], d. h., einen *s*-Buchstaben mit

einem Punkt über demselben. In der Handschrift variiert dieser zwischen einem genauen Punkt und einem kürzeren oder längeren schrägen oder senkrechten Strich (also [ṡ], [s̓] oder [ś], vgl. das Faksimile[5].

Es ist hier anzumerken, dass in der viel später *gedruckten* Ausgabe des Evangelienbuchs Elgers (*Evangelia Toto anno* ..., Vilnae 1672) die entsprechenden Buchstaben ohne einen solchen Punkt bzw. Strich stehen, z. B.:

in Elgers Manuskript:	in Elgers Buche (1672):
7_{21} *ſaccyiṡ*	S. [6] (u. a.) *ſaccyis*
7_{24} *ſtawæiṡ*	[6] *ſtawæis*
7_{26} *bÿiṡ*	[6] *byis* u. v. a.[6]

4. Untersucht man jene Stellen in Elgers Manuskript, wo ein solcher Buchstabe [ṡ] zu treffen ist, so stellt man fest, dass dieses Graphem am öftesten dort steht, wo sonst ein *š*-Buchstabe (nach Elgers Schreibweise also ein [ſʒ])[7] im Schriftlettischen in der Regel zu erwarten wäre (und an manchen anderen Stellen im Manuskript in demselben Wort auch vorkommt!). Einige Beispiele:

$46_{10\ 11}$ und 126_2 *dôṡ* (=duošu) '[ich] werde geben', vgl. 63_{13} *doſʒu* 'dass'; 68_3 u. a. *ſaccÿṡ* (=sacīšu) '[ich] werde sagen', vgl. 87_{20} *ſacciſʒu* 'dass';

29_{19f} *Es êſʒu vnd darriṡ to wæſsel* (=Es iešu un darišu tuo veselu) 'Ich werde gehen und ihn gesund machen', vgl. 21_{2f} *Es êſʒu, vnd darriſʒu to wæſsel* 'dass'.;

31_4 *wæiṡ* (=vējš) 'Wind', vgl. 30_{26} *wæiſʒ* 'dass'.

Es gibt jedoch auch Stellen mit einem [ṡ], wo ein [s] (und nicht einmal ein [š]!) zu erwarten wäre, z. B.:

58_4 *aukſtaiṡ* (=augstais) '[der] hohe [Priester]', vgl. 58_7 *aukſtais* 'dass'. Dasselbe auch in einigen Partizipien, z. B., 130_7 *ſacciṡ* (=sacijis), 130_8 *raddiṡ* (=radījis), 77_8 *vʒmodenaiṡ* (=uzmuodinājis) u. a.

Es lässt sich feststellen, dass *sehr viele* solche Wörter, die auf [ṡ] enden, an anderen Stellen mit einem einfachen [s] geschrieben stehen, s. die Beispiele oben, vgl. noch z. B. 7_{21} 12_{17} 13_{20} und 10_{29} 26_{23} 37_{21} 40_{28} u. a. (*ſaccyiṡ* || *ſaccyis*), 13_{21} und 35_{26} 52_{18} 56_5 u. a. (*rædʒæiṡ* || *rædʒæis*), 66_3 und 66_{16} 67_{23} (*aukſtaiṡ, Aukſtaiṡ* || *aukſtais, Aukſtais*) u. v. a.

5. Es entsteht die Frage, wodurch eine solche Doppelförmigkeit mancher Wörter in Elgers Manuskript sich erklären lässt. Eine nähere Auseinandersetzung mit dem Material erlaubt einige Folgerungen zu ziehen.

Erstens gewinnt man die Überzeugung, dass solch eine Anwendung des

Seite 13 in G. Elgers Manuskript *Evangelia et Epistolae* ... (Bruchstück, die Zeilen 16–27). Die Wörter mit einem [ṡ] am Ende s. in den Zeilen 20, 21 und 27.

Graphems [ṡ] keine Erfindung Elgers selbst sein kann: dieses kommt nur zufällig und unsystematisch hier und da vor. Elgers Manuskript der Evangelien und Episteln ist, wie es sich feststellen lässt, eine Reinschriftversion[8]. Eine solche konnte nur nach einer Kladde geschrieben werden. Das Graphem [ṡ] hat, ohne Zweifel, auch in der letztgenannten gestanden; es mag vielleicht auch in den ersten Büchern Elgers vorgekommen sein. Leider ist sein Gesangbuch *Cantiones Spirituales*, Braunsberg, 1621, nicht bekannt, gleicherweise auch kein Exemplar von seinen *Evangelien* (um 1620), wenn die letzteren überhaupt irgendwann gedruckt gewesen sind[9].

Es ist nicht denkbar, dass Elger, als er seine Arbeiten schrieb[10], keine älteren lettischen Texte als Vorlagen vor sich gehabt hätte. Schon rein theoretisch wäre es ganz unglaubhaft, dass er alle älteren, besonders dazu noch katholischen geistlichen Schriften ohne Beachtung gelassen hätte: einige solche konnten ihm als Übersetzungsgrundlage oder, wenigstens, als Vergleichsmaterial von grossem Nutzen sein.

Dass Elger sich wirklich auf einige ältere Texte gestützt hat, beweist ein Vergleich seines Katechismus[11] mit dem viel früher gedruckten *Catechismus Catholicorum*, Vilnae, 1585[12].

In einigen solchen älteren Vorlagen Elgers muss das besprochene Graphem

[š] gestanden haben. Beim Auswerten derselben während der Übersetzungs-
arbeit oder beim unmittelbaren Abschreiben einiger Textstellen sind diese
Zeichen dann auch in das Elgersche Manuskript sporadisch übergegangen.

6. Selbstverständlich ist es nicht denkbar, dass Elger selbst nicht imstande war, etwas so einfaches wie solche Wortformen wie z. B. $46_{10\ 11}$
dôṡ und 63_{13} *doſʒu* '[ich] werde geben' voneinander unterscheiden zu können.
Wenn er solche angewandt hat, kann man das nur damit erklären, dass
solche ihm selbst gut bekannt waren und als zulässige Parallelformen der
damaligen lettischen Schriftsprache aufgefasst wurden.

Eine Erklärung muss man in der Tatsache suchen, dass die katholischen
Geistlichen bei ihrer Missions- und Rekatholisationsarbeit die Sprache der
von ihnen versorgten Gegenden Lettlands bzw. von Vidzeme angewandt
haben — um von dortigen Letten verstanden zu werden. So kamen verschiedene, nach unserer neuzeitlichen Wertung — ma. Wortformen auch in
von ihnen geschriebenen Aufzeichnungen, kirchlichen Texten, Übersetzungs-
fragmenten usw. vor. Einen guten Beweis hierfür findet man in der bekannten *Agenda Parva*, Braunsberg, 1622, z. B. S. 28 *ſolyſʒ* (= *suoliš* = *suolījis*)
'versprochen', 34 *dom* (= *duomu* = *duodu*) '[ich] gebe', 41 *peſtitayſʒ* (= *pes-
titājš* = *pestitājs*) 'Erlöser' u. a.

7. Im Elgerschen Manuskript der Evangelien und Episteln findet man verschiedene Wortformen, welche an solche erinnern, die noch im 20. Jh. in der
einen oder anderen Ma. von Vidzeme zu hören waren, wie es aus verschiedenen Mundartbeschreibungen zu ersehen ist. So schreibt z. B. Elger einige
Nomina agentis mit der Endung *-taiṡ*, z. B. 36_{22} *reditaiṡ* (= *rēdītājš* = *rēdi-
tājs* 'Rächer, Bezahler'); 103_{25} *pawælætaiṡ* (= *pavēlētājš* = *pavēlētājs* 'prae-
ceptor') u. ä.; vgl. solche ma. Formen wie z. B. *mācĩtaiš* (= *mācītājs* 'Pastor')
in Straupe (Roop) und in der Umgebung[13], *mâᵉcîtâjš* in Ērgļi (Erlaa)[14]
u. a.[15]. Gleicherweise trifft man im Elgerschen Manuskript einige Adjektive
auf *-aiṡ*, z. B. 37_7 *milaiṡ* (= *miļaiš* = *miļais* 'lieber'), 58_4 *aukſtaiṡ* (= *augstaiš*
= *augstais* 'der hohe') u. a.; vgl. die ma. Aufzeichnungen *labaîš* in Straupe[16],
lẹpnàiš in Ērgļi[17] u. a. Dasselbe ist über solche Verbalformen in Elgers
Manuskript zu sagen wie z. B. das Futur: 29_{26} u. a. *nacis* (= *nācĩs* = *nāks*
'wird kommen'), 32_{21} u. a. *tappis* (= *tapĩs* = *taps* 'wird, werden')[18] usw.

8. Die angeführten Exempel können veranlassen zu denken, dass das
Graphem [ṡ] im Elgerschen Manuskript eine parallele graphische Variation,
eine zweite Bezeichnung des *š*-Lautes sein mag, d. h., dass ein z. B. *milaiṡ*
(37_7), *wilciṡ* (132_1), *dôṡ* (126_2) usw. als *miļaiš*, *vilciš*[u], *duoš*[u] usw. zu
lesen wären. Einige Tatsachen sprechen jedoch gegen eine solche Annahme.

Aus dem Elgerschen Manuskript sieht man nämlich, dass das Graphem
[ſʒ] im Anlaut, Inlaut und auch im Auslaut geschrieben wird, wogegen das

Graphem [ṡ] *nur am Ende* der Wörter steht, dazu meistenteils in solchen Wortformen, die man nach unserer neuzeitlichen Auffassung nicht als schriftsprachliche, sondern als mundartliche charakterisieren muss. Eine solche so bestimmt durchgeführte Differenzierung dieser Grapheme kann nicht ohne Grund sein. Es ist zu folgern, dass mit dem Graphem [ṡ] nicht der lettische š-Laut, sondern ein anderer bezeichnet worden ist. So muss man sowohl über die hypothetischen Vorlagen Elgers, wie auch über sein Manuskript der Evangelien und Episteln urteilen.

9. Was für ein Laut wohl mit diesem [ṡ] eigentlich bezeichnet gewesen sein kann?

In der Rechtschreibung des Polnischen bezeichnet man bekanntlich mit [sz] einen š-Laut, mit dem Graphem [ś] dagegen einen anderen, schärferen Zischlaut, einen erweichten s-Laut. Man muss annehmen, dass auch in der Rechtschreibung der katholischen Geistlichen Lettlands im 16. und 17. Jh. dieses Graphem [ś] gleicherweise zu demselben Zweck angewandt wurde.

Wie gut bekannt, wird ein erweichter s-Laut ([s′]), der dem polnischen [ś] ähnlich klingt, noch jetzt, im 20. Jh., in nicht wenigen Mundarten Lettlands gesprochen[19]. Diejenigen katholischen Geistlichen jener Zeit, die des *Polnischen* kundig waren, konnten ein solches erweichtes [s′] von einem š-Laut deutlich unterscheiden und dieses in ihren Aufzeichnungen oder Übersetzungen nach der polnischen Art gleicherweise mit einem [ś] bzw. [ṡ] bezeichnen.

Man muss beachten, dass damals noch keine Stabilität in der lettischen Schriftsprache erreicht war und man manche mundartlichen Varianten als schriftsprachlich korrekte betrachten konnte, wie es auch aus der *Agenda Parva*, 1622, dem Elgerschen Manuskript und auch aus seinen gedruckten Büchern zu ersehen ist, s. o.

Es ist ausserdem sehr möglich, dass ein solcher erweichter s-Laut ([s′]) damals, um die Wende des 16. und 17. Jhs., in einem viel weiteren Gebiet als jetzt zu hören war, d. h., er mag noch viel weiter nach Westen als in unserem Jh. — also auch in den Mundarten um Valmiera und Cēsis (Wenden) gesprochen worden sein, wo jetzt in solchen Wortformen wie z. B. *gāš*, *bîš*, *skuõluotãš* u. dgl. ein reiner š-Laut zu hören ist.

10. An einigen Stellen bei Elger steht, anstatt eines „korrekten" Graphems [ṡ], ein einfaches [s] (ohne Punkt über diesem), z. B. 70_{21} *darris* (anstatt *darriṡ* oder *darriſʒu* 'werde tun', 14_{13} *yʒtauias* (anstatt *yʒtauiaṡ* oder *yʒtauiajis* 'ausgefragt') u. ä. Dass solche Stellen mit einem vergessenen Punkt wie auch viele andere Schreibfehler nicht verbessert worden sind, ist dadurch zu erklären, dass Elgers Manuskript nach dem Abschluss der Reinschrift nicht mehr in seinen Händen verblieb. Es dürfte sehr bald zur

Approbation durch die höhere Geistlichkeit und zum etwaigen späteren Druck in andere Hände übergegangen sein.

Anmerkungen

1. Geboren in Valmiera, Lettland, um 1585, gestorben in Daugavpils, Lettland, am 30. September 1672.

2. Dem Verf. vom Prof. Chr. S. Stang zur Veröffentlichung liebenswürdig übergeben; gedruckt in der Schriftserie *Slaviska Institutionen vid Lunds Universitet. Text- och materialutgåvor* als Nr. 1 mit dem Titel *Evangelien und Episteln. Ins Lettische übersetzt von Georg Elger* (Lund 1961).

3. Vgl. A. Augstkalns, ,,Pirmie latviešu teksti un grāmatas (... 1530–1630 ...)'', im Sammelwerk *Latviešu literātūras vēsture* 2, Rīgā, 1935, 33 (,,Ortografija [Eļģeram] poliska, tikai ar vāciskiem dubultniekiem''); vgl. auch *RKr* XX, 1930 (A. Augstkalns, ,,Veclatviešu rakstu apskats'', S. 113) (,, ... Eļģers nevis *tuvojas* un *pieskaņojas* poļu rakstībai, bet — taisni *pašu šo poļu rakstību lieto*''). Vgl. noch J. Upītis, *Latviešu literātūras vēsture* 1, Rīgā, 1959, 393 f. und auch E. Blese, *Latviešu literātūras vēsture*, Hannau, 1947, 96 (,, ... tikai viņa [= Eļģera] grafikai drusku polisks raksturs''); M. Bukšs, *Latgaļu literaturas vēsture*, München, 1957, 104 (,,Elgers ir lobōjis ortografiju, centīs īvest pūļu raksteibas principus, bet voi jys tūs pōrnese kai pyrmais, voi ari jēme nu vacōkajom ,,agendu'' tradicijom, tys nav eisti nūsokoms'').

4. Ebenso werden Seite und Zeile in Elgers Ms. *Evangelia et Epistolæ* auch im Folgenden bezeichnet, d. h., 6_{25} bedeutet: Seite 6, Zeile 25.

5. In der genannten Ausgabe des Ms. (1961) als ein [ś] (d. h., mit einem *Punkt* über dem Buchstaben) gedruckt.

6. Auf der anderen Seite — im Evangelienbuch vom J. 1672 kommt ein *gedruckter* Buchstabe [ś] (mit einem Akutzeichen über demselben) nur als eine äusserst seltene Ausnahme (d. h., Druckfehler) vor, so S. [13], Zeile 11, iûś (an der entsprechenden Textstelle in Elgers Ms. (13_1) steht iûs).

7. Als eine Ausnahme etwa auch ein [ļz], s. o.

8. Vgl. die Textausgabe (*Evangelien und Episteln* ...), 1961, Einleitung, S. XIV f.

9. Vgl. B. Jēgers, "*Verzeichnis der lettischen Drucke des 16. und 17. Jahrhunderts*", Zeitschr. für Ostforschung IX, 4, 565 f.

10. Elgers frühe Arbeiten mögen um etwa 1615–1620 fertiggeschrieben sein. Schon vor dem waren die katholischen Geistlichen Livoniens (sowohl in Riga selbst wie auch auf dem Lande im ganzen Livland) sehr aktiv, vgl. z. B. M. Bukšs, *Vacōkī rakstnīceibas pīminekli*. München, 1952, 12 ff.; *Latgaļu literaturas vēsture*, München, 1957, 52 ff., 61, 90 f., 101 ff., 108 u. a.

11. *Catechismus sev Brevis Institutio doctrinæ Christianæ* ... Vilnae 1672.

12. Ein vom Verf. angestellter Vergleich der beiden Katechismen erlaubte viele solche Ähnlichkeiten in diesen festzustellen, die keinesfalls ganz zufällig sein können. Vgl. auch J. Upītis, *op. cit.*, S. 391 (,,*Šim 1672. gada katķismam nepārprotama radniecība ar 1585. gadā izdoto Kanīzija katķismu, lai gan Elgers to ievērojami uzlabojis valodas un rakstības ziņā* ...'').

13. R. Grabis, ,,Piezīmes par Straupes draudzes izloksnēm'', *FBR*, XV, 149.

14. J. Zariņš, ,,Ērgļu un Ogres pagasta izloksne'', *FBR*, XI, 11.

15. Vgl. J. Endzelīns, *Lettische Grammatik*, Heidelberg, 1923, 142 f.; *Latviešu valodas gramatika*, Rīgā, 1951, 198 f.

16. R. Grabis, *op. cit.*

17. J. Zariņš, *op. cit.*, 10.

18. Vgl. J. Endzelīns, *Lettische Grammatik*, dass.; über die Futurformen auf -*īs* vgl. S. 661; *Latv. val. gramatika*, 198 ff., 855. Vgl. die Isoglosse über die ma. Futurformen a) *braucīs, mirīs*, b) *brauks, mirīs*, c) *brauks, mirs* im westlichen Teil von Vidzeme bei V. Rūķe, ,,Kurzemes un Vidzemes lībiskais apgabals", *FBR* XX, 125; s. noch M. Rudzīte, *Latviešu dialektoloģija*, Rīgā, 1964, 65, 73, 82, 88 u. a.; *Говоры северной части Видземе*, Riga 1954, 8 ff., 12, 14, 16 f., 22 f.

19. Vgl. z. B. M. Rudzīte, *op. cit.*, 298, 302 ff. u. a.

Denotation of the Sound [ś] in G. Elger's Latvian Manuscript Evangelia et Epistolae (ca 1640)

The author considers the question as to how G. Elger denoted the Latvian sounds, and concludes that the palatalized (soft) *s*-sound [s'] is denoted by the grapheme [š] or [ś], as in Polish.

EDGARS DUNSDORFS

Did Latvians Live in Tribal Societies in the 12th and 13th Centuries?

Linguists,[1] anthropologists, sociologists, archaeologists and historians who have dealt with this region and period have mostly answered this question in the affirmative. In the following I intend to challenge this widely accepted belief.

1. Definitions of the term "tribe"

Authors who use the term "tribe" more often than not fail to define it, and, if the term is defined at all, the so-called definition rarely complies with formal requirements of a proper definition. For instance, the recently (1968) published *Dictionary of Sociology*[2] defines tribe as follows:

"A tribe is a socially cohesive unit associated with a territory, the members of which regard themselves as politically autonomous. Sometimes tribes are split up into sections, especially where the territory is large in relation to the size of population. Very often a tribe will possess a distinctive dialect ..."

According to this definition, the present world consists mostly of tribes. For instance, present-day England, France, Germany and the USA are socially cohesive units. The English, French, Germans and Americans regard themselves as politically autonomous. Their territory is split up into sections and they possess a distinctive dialect (even the Americans as distinct from the English).

With this definition of tribe by a sociologist we can compare another by an anthropologist:[3]

"... a tribe is a grouping of Aborigines who (i) inhabit and own a usually definite area of country; (ii) use a language or dialect peculiar to themselves; (iii) know themselves, or are known, by a distinct name, though sometimes it is difficult to learn what this is, and indeed, it may not exist; (iv) possess customs and laws which often vary in some degree from those of neighbouring tribes; and (v) have their own rites and beliefs which frequently differ from those practised and held respectively by the peoples around."

In the text and the index the author has explicitly called this statement a definition. Regrettably it must be said it is not. The statement contains only an enlarged *genus proximum*, but the *differentia specifica* is completely missing. If all Australian aborigines are grouped into tribes, then it would be sufficient to state that fact, but the term "tribe" had to be defined by pointing out what are the differences between a "tribe" and other groupings belonging to the same category. If we omit from the above statement the word "Aborigines", then this definition resembles the previously quoted one and we can apply to it the same criticism. Nevertheless, the second statement teaches us a lesson. The term tribe is obviously used only to describe a primitive society. The formulation by Kimball Young is couched in such terms: "By 'tribe' we refer simply to a particular primitive society or community which possesses a certain integrated culture".[4] Occasionally in an abusive sense the term "tribe" is applied to societies which by no stretch of the imagination could be called primitive.[5]

A far more satisfactory definition of the concept "tribe" has been provided by the anthropologist A. L. Kroeber:[6] "... folk culture or tribal culture belongs to a small [around five thousand souls], isolated, close-knit society, in which person-to-person relations are prevalent, kinship is a dominant factor, and organization, both social and cultural, is therefore largely on a basis of kinship—sometimes including fictitious kinship ... By contrast, political institutions are weakly developed ... a maximum of equality coexisting with a minimum of authority or control."

The amateur anthropologist L. H. Morgan (still regarded as an authority by Soviet writers) and others classify societies into two groups: (1) *societas*—kinship societies with a primitive culture, and (2) *civitas*—civil or state societies with an advanced culture.[7] The first group, the *societas*, is described as familial, egalitarian, classless, communalistic (no private property etc.). The second group, the *civitas*, is depicted as a non-egalitarian class society with private property, entrepreneurs, markets and a government.[8]

Only quite recently it has been recognized that such a division is too crude. There are obviously societies which have some aspects of *societas* and some others of *civitas*. The first author to point this out is Elman R. Service. He distinguishes five classes or levels of primitive culture: the Band level, the Tribal level, the Chiefdom level, the Primitive State level, the Archaic Civilization or Imperial level.[9]

The main characteristics of Service's classes ("levels") of primitive societies can be summarized as follows:

	Band	Tribe	Chiefdom	Primitive State
Familial integration	present	present	present	present
Supra-familial integration	absent or weak	present (pan-tribal sodalities)	present	dominant
Character of society	segmental, egalitarian, but not excluding some outstanding personalities	segmental, egalitarian,	organismic, non-egalitarian	organismic, non-egalitarian
Classes	absent	absent	social classes present	social, political and economic classes
Leadership	absent (anarchistic society)	charismatic leadership of non-permanent nature (near anarchistic society)	charismatic permanent leadership	true government (legalized monopoly of force)
Economy	self-sufficient; private property absent	self-sufficient; private property absent	largely self-sufficient; reciprocal direct exchange of gifts; private property absent; labour specialization; reward not related to contribution	markets, entrepreneurs; private property present; full economic specialization

2. The source: Heinrici, Chronicon Livoniae

Our main source in answering the question of the headline of this paper is the *Chronicon Livoniae*, completed in 1227.[10] There is no doubt about the author—it was the priest Henry. What is under dispute is whether he was a Latvian or a German.[11] Because of the paucity of information regarding the life of the people, as contrasted to detailed description of warfare and its techniques, knowledge of the ethnic origin of Henry would be of great importance. If he was a Latvian, then it would be understandable that he gives few details about the Latvians and Livonians; in short, they were too familiar to be described. If he was a German, then the conclusion about his silence on these matters could be that mundane affairs in Latvia were not different from those in Germany.

The chronicle mentions the following ethnic groups in Latvia—the Livonians, who were a Finno-Ugrian people; the Letgallians ("Lethi ... qui proprie dicuntur Lethigalli"), Curonians, Semgallians, Selonians—all Baltic people (Indo-Europeans) now commonly described as Latvians. There was also a small colony of Wends (of unknown ethnic origin, possibly Slavs). The chronicle labels these peoples either as *gens, populus* or *natio*. Translators of the chronicle have frequently translated the term *gens* by the term *tribe*,[12] but to avoid contradictions not consistently so.

The language of the chronicle is strongly influenced by the language of the *Vulgata* and, as is well known, the *Vulgata* uses the terms *gens, populus* and *natio* indiscriminately. Consequently, if Henry writes about *gens, gentis*, he more often than not means pagans (H. XI, 6: *de conversione gencium*), although he also uses the term *pagani* (H. VI, 4). Despite this obvious fact, *gens* has often been translated by tribe. For instance, the passage (H. VII, 3): *Quem apostolicus ... de statu gencium circa Lyvoniam existencium multa perquirens pro conversione gentis Lyvonice Deo plurimum congratulatur ...* Brundage translates as follows: [the Pope] "... asked many things about the status of the tribes dwelling about Livonia, and gave many thanks to God for the conversion of the Livonian people". Bauer, on the other hand, translates this passage: "Der Papst ... befragte ihn ausführlich über die um Livland wohnenden Völker und dankte Gott aufs höchste für die Bekehrung des livischen Stammes". The confusion of the translators is nicely illustrated by this passage. What are tribes to Brundage are peoples to Bauer, and vice versa.

Henry does not discriminate between the terms *gentis* and *pagani*, but on the other hand his terminology is consistent in the usage of the title "king" (*rex*). This title is granted by him to Christian rulers only, while non-Christian rulers must do with a less dignifying title (*princeps, maior natu, dux*, even *senior*). Consequently, Christians live in a kingdom (*regnum*), but non-Christians in a province (*provincia*) or territory (*territorium*)[13]. Thus the terminology used by Henry does not help to solve our problem.

3. E. R. Service's scheme adapted to Henry's chronicle

Familial integration

The question whether in the 12th and 13th centuries Latvians lived in a tribal society can be decided by fitting the known data into Service's scheme. Familial integration, as in all types of society, was certainly present during the period under discussion, except that the introduction of the

Christian faith in some instances created loyalties stronger than loyalty to the family (cf., for instance, H. X, 5).

Sodalities

Supra-familial integration was present even before the adoption of Christianity. The whole country was dotted by wooden castles on hills made defensible by excavating ditches and steepening the slopes of the hills[14]. These inhabited castles, with a spacious courtyard to accommodate refugees and their cattle in times of an enemy's invasion, were a formidable obstacle to the German crusaders. The main theme of Henry's chronicle is how siege was laid on these castles and how the crusaders, when successful, burned the castle or converted it into a stronghold of the occupation forces.

Henry's report covers more than a quarter of a century and it is obvious from his story that, during the period of the German conquest, wars among the peoples of different ethnic origins continued as before. Before and during the German conquest the most formidable enemies of the Latvian peoples were the Estonians in the North, the Lithuanians in the South and the Russians in the East. The Scandinavian overseas invasions had stopped centuries before. On the other hand, the Latvian nations retaliated by invading territories of their enemies. The Curonians and Estonians even crossed the Baltic sea and raided Swedish and Danish territory.

The size of the armies called up by the Germans to assist them (matching the size of the German army) varied from 3 000 (H. XVIII, 5) or 4 000 (H. XV, 7) Livonians and Latvians to 20 000 including Latvians, Livonians, Estonians and Germans (H. XXX, 3). The Estonian heathen fleet attacking Sweden on one occasion consisted of 300 sailing vessels (*piraticae naves*— H. XV, 3) with 30 warriors in each (H. VII, 2). Similar information is provided by Henry about the Curonians, who in some naval battles defeated the Germans and on one occasion made a naval attack on the newly established city of Riga.

Supra-familial integration was evident in pagan rites performed by heathen priests and attended by the people in the holy woods scattered through the country. Henry is not very eloquent in reporting this, but there are some glimpses in his chronicle (H. I, 10; about immolation of the captured Germans to pagan gods cf. IX, 12).

Character of society and classes

The character of Latvian society during the period in question is definitely organismic and non-egalitarian. Henry's evidence points to classes. All the peoples mentioned by him have an upper class—the *meliores* (H. II, 2; IV, 4; X, 14; XII, 6) or *seniores et meliores* (H. I, 14; XXX, 5). Only on one occasion does Henry use the term *nobilis* in reference to Osilia (H. XXX, 5); otherwise this term is reserved by him for the Christians. Not realizing the significance of the term *meliores*, Brundage translates this as "better people" or "leaders" instead of using the proper term "nobles".

The ambassadors of the Livonians and Latvians, conferring with the bishop who organized the conquest, were usually nobles (H. II, 2), and they were asked to give their sons as hostages (H. X, 14). They were taken prisoners of war and on one occasion more than a hundred Semgallian noblemen of the 200 who surrendered were massacred by the Germans (H. XXIII, 8). Henry mildly rebukes this as an act by fools frequently to be found (*stulti ... quorum infinitus est numerus ...*).

Although the nobles are mentioned as the active, possibly commanding element, the nucleus of the army was the chief (*senior*) with his "relatives and friends" (*cognati et amici*—H. X, 10; XV, 7; XIX, 3). The nobles, in addition to their function as diplomats and warriors, formed a legislative body deciding about war or peace (H. X, 6). On one occasion, however, an important decision was passed by a meeting of the total population: the Livonians decided (*Lyvonum universitas decernit ...*—H. II, 10) to expel all Christian clerics at a certain date.

A tentative conclusion

From the previous discussion emerges the tentative conclusion that in the 12th and 13th centuries the nations on Latvian territory lived in a non-egalitarian society. The society was not segmental, but organismic. Classes existed. Consequently, the society cannot be labelled as a tribal one. The question then is: were they chiefdoms or primitive states?

The rulers

The rulers had jurisdiction over territories which did not embrace the total ethnic region. The Livonians, Semgallians, Curonians, Selonians and Letgallians lived each in their own territory called by Henry provinces or countries (*terra*). Fragmentation of the Livonians was most pronounced; the Semgallians and Letgallians were split into two territorial units each; and the Selonians were divided among several territorial units which had special names.

The Letgallians lived in Gercike and Tolowa. The ruler of Gercike is given by Henry the title of king (*rex*) because he was a Christian of the Greek orthodox faith, adopted long before the German invasion. Roman catholics are called by Henry *Latini* (H. IX, 10; XI, 7; XIII, 3; XVIII, 3; XX, 3; XXVI, 8; XXVII, 3), but Greek orthodox catholics *Rutheni* (H. XIII, 4 etc.). Henry uses this latter term indiscriminately when he refers not only to Greek orthodox catholics, but also to Russians. Not being aware of this, translators have chosen the easiest way and translated this term only as "Russians". The result of this confusion has been that the two principalities of the Greek orthodox faith—Gercike inhabited by Letgallians (and possibly Selonians), and Kukenoys inhabited by Letgallians, Selonians and Livonians—have been labelled by historians as "Russian principalities". Only Tolowa (inhabited by Letgallians) has escaped this fate because the rulers of it accepted the Greek orthodox faith during Henry's time. Another consequence of the confusion has been that the name of king *Wiscewalde* of Gercike has been Russianized by German and Russian translators as *Vsevolod*. In fact the suffix -walde (-valdis) means in Latvian "ruler", and Henry records several names with this suffix among the members of ruling families. It might well be a name coined under Scandinavian influence, like *Bretwalda* (Ruler of Britain) in ninth century Britain. Clearly there is no justification to Russianize the name of Wiscewalde. One could have some doubts about the king of Kukenoys, *Viesceka*. After the German conquest, he left for Russia and the Russian sources render his name *Vjačko*. Was he a Russian prince who, after ruling over Latvians and Livonians, returned to his homeland, or was he a fugitive seeking refuge in Russia? In the first instance his name rendered by Henry *Viesceka* could be *Vjačko*, and in the other case his name could be *Vecākais* (meaning in Latvian *Elder*)—a question to be decided by linguists.

About Wiscewalde (the Latvian form is *Visvaldis* = Ruler over all and sundry) Henry's chronicle supplies more information. His wife, the queen, was the daughter of the Lithuanian nobleman Daugeruthe (H. XVII, 3). The capital of Gercike with the same name is the only settlement Henry calls *civitas*—city. After occupation of the city the invaders collected booty "from all the corners—clothes, silver, purple, a great number of cattle, and from the churches bells, icons, and other things, money and a large amount of property". The city was burned down and "the king saw the burning from the other side of the Duna (Daugava) river. He heaved a great sigh, bewailed with huge groans, and exclaimed 'O Gerzike, beloved city! O inheritance of my fathers! O unexpected destruction of my people! O woe is me! Why was I born to see the burning of my city and the destruction of my people!' (H. XIII, 4). Although this passage is strongly influenced by expressions used in the Bible (1. Macc., 1, 37 ff.; 15, 33 ff.; 2, 7), there is no doubt that Wiscewalde was a hereditary ruler.

Similarly, Tolowa was ruled by a hereditary prince from the castle of Beverin. When in 1215 the ruler of Tolowa Talibald was tortured to death by the Estonians (H. XIX, 3), his sons Rameko and Drivinalde with the help of their retainers collected an army of Latvians (*colligentes exercitum Lettorum cum amicis et cognatis suis*) to revenge the death of their father. The successor to Talibald seems to have been Rameko. He and his brothers were converted to Roman catholicism from their Greek orthodox faith (H. XVIII, 3—*promittentes se fidem christianam a Ruthenis susceptam in Latinorum consuetudinem commutare*) and Rameko appears to be the leader in 1223 (H. XXVI, 12; XXVII, 1). Certainly, he was not a king because the country had been taken over by the Germans. Nevertheless, the evidence shows that hereditary rule existed in the two kingdoms Gercike and Tolowa and this points to the existence of what Service calls a primitive state and not to a chiefdom. With regard to the ruler of the Semgallians in the realm of Thervetene *Viesthardus* (in Latvian: *Viesturs*), there is not sufficient information to decide whether he was a hereditary ruler or not. No conclusion can be drawn from the fact that, when his sister's son was killed in the battle, he withdrew from the battlefield (H. XXIII, 4). On the other hand, it seems that he ruled as an autocrat without having to ask the advice of the nobles.[15]

The economy

The major branches of the economy were agriculture, animal husbandry, bee-keeping, and fishing. Archaeological evidence reveals crafts and artisanship. Foreign trade flourished. The Livonians asked the bishop in an ironical mood what was the price of salt and cloth in Gothland (H. I, 11). To eliminate competition with Riga, the bishop prohibited foreign merchants from trading in the "harbour of Semgale" (H. IV, 7). Commodities of foreign trade included salt, cloth, metals, weapons, ornaments and the females and boys captured and enslaved after raids in Sweden or neighbouring countries (H. XXX, 1—adult males were usually killed). The Livonian weight (*talentum Livonicum*) was adopted by the Germans and called *Lieszpfund*. Money did exist before the German conquest, for the monetary unit was the osering—equal to half a mark of silver of the German unit of account (H. XVI, 4; XIX, 3). Tribute for the Germans and Russians was sometimes levied in money (H. XVI, 2, 3, 4; XV, 8; XIX, 3).

There is no doubt that private property was an existing institution. Even members of the same family had separate property. When Talibald was tortured by the Estonians he said: "If I were to show you all my money and all my son's money, you would burn me nonetheless" (H. XIX, 3). The most drastic evidence of private property and the existence of a spirit of acquisition (which Werner Sombart regards as a trait of capitalism) is evidenced by the incident of conversion of the Estonian Kyriawanus. He explained that the gods of the Estonians were not satisfactory and requested the Christian priests to provide him with a better God. This was promised by the priests. "So at his urgent request we promised him there that God would be propitious to him and would give him sufficient temporal goods in this life, and also eternal life in the future" (H. XXIII, 7; for further indirect evidence of private property cf. H. X, 15; XVI, 3).

4. Conclusion

The evidence gleaned from Henry's chronicle about the society in Latvia at the end of the 12th century and the first quarter of the 13th century indicates a great many incidents which permit us to establish the existence of what Service calls "primitive states". In fact, in the social structure of society there is no great difference between the German and Danish invaders and the society they found in Latvia and Estonia respectively. The main difference in the initial stages of the conquest was in the technique of warfare; the Germans and Danes had better armaments and better weapons. Just before the invasion they had also acquired the skill to build castles from stone joined by mortar, whereas castles were built from timber and earthwork or loose stones in Latvia and Estonia. Their initial technical superiority proved an ultimate advantage and, allying themselves with the conquered Latvian and Estonian states, they eventually achieved the subjugation of Latvia and Estonia.

It is significant that the conquest lasted for more than a century. The Latvians and Estonians very soon learned the technique of warfare from the Germans (and Danes) and thus conquest became a lengthy and costly affair. Only after killing the kings, absorbing the nobility of the Latvian and Estonian states, and liquidating the pagan and the Greek orthodox faith, was conquest finished. To put the Latvian and Estonian states in the class of tribes would not be compatible with this lengthy struggle for independence. That the states and the various ethnic groups have been called tribes has been the result of a misreading of the sources and the vagueness of the definition of what the term "tribe" means.

It must be noted with satisfaction that Soviet historiography has recently abandoned the tribal myth about the period under discussion. In 1952 the leading textbook of Latvian history published by the Academy of Sciences still featured tribes in the 12th and 13th centuries in Latvia and Lithuania[16].

In 1951 T. Zeids published a book with the title *Feudalism in Livonia* which referred to tribes,[17] but in an article published by the same author in 1962 there is a complete change of face. We now learn that tribes disappeared in the transition from the 9th to the 10th century and that the social structure which followed should be called "feudalism". It is a pity that one myth is supplanted by another, but the explanation is that Soviet historians must by all means cling to the Marxist stage theory. The somersault from tribes to feudalism was not based on investigation of the sources, but on a rereading of the "classics of Marxism-Leninism".[18]

Notes

1. Chr. S. Stang, *Vergleichende Grammatik der baltischen Sprachen*, Oslo, 1966, only once uses the term "tribe" (baltische Stämme), but this is explainable, as he quotes Buga for a period we are not considering in this paper.

2. G. D. Mitchell (ed.), *A Dictionary of Sociology*, London, 1968, 214.

3. A. P. Elkin, *The Australian Aborigines*, London, 1954, 25.

4. K. Young, *Sociology*, New York, 1942, 401.

5. Cf.: C. J. Burkhardt, *Meine Danziger Mission* 1937–1939, München, 1962, 23: "Im europäischen Osten, am Rande des deutschen Reichsgebiets, lebten vor 1914 die verschiedenen Überreste von Volksstämmen, die nach und nach unter der Herrschaft der russischen Zaren gefallen waren. 1918 wurden diese Stämme in kleinen und kleinsten Staaten zusammengefasst ..."

6. A. L. Kroeber, *Anthropology*, New York, 1948, 281.

7. Lewis H. Morgan, *Ancient Society*, Chicago, no date.

8. Some authors see the differences between these two types of society in other dimensions. For instance, J. L. Gillin, *An Introduction to Sociology*, New York, 1945, 287, describes the first type (and specifically a tribe) as a preliterate society.

9. E. R. Service, *Profiles in Ethnology*, New York, 1963; *Primitive Social Organization: An Evolutionary Perspective*, New York, 1962.

10. The edition used is by L. Arbusow and A. Bauer, Würzburg, 1959.

11. The Latvian version is maintained by A. Švābe, "Latviešu Indriķis un viņa chronika", *Straumes un avoti II*, Lincoln, 1963, the German version by P. Johansen, "Die Chronik als Biographie", *Jahrbuch für Geschichte Osteuropas I*, 1953.

12. In the following I refer to two translations only: the English translation by James A. Brundage, *The Chronicle of Henry of Livonia* (sic!), Madison, 1961, and the German translation by Albert Bauer, *Heinrich von Lettland, Livländische Chronik*, Würzburg, 1959. When referring to Henrici, *Chronicon of Livonia*, it is in the usual way by mentioning in brackets H., the chapter in Roman and the section of the chapter in Arabic numerals.

13. V. Biļķins, "Baltu valšķu un valdnieku apzīmējumi viduslaiku tekstos", *Amerikas latviešu humānitāro zinātņu asociācija, Rakstu krājums I*, New York, 1957.

14. For a map showing the location of these castles cf. E. Dunsdorfs, *Latvijas vēstures atlants*, Melbourne, 1969, 24–25.

15. V. Biļķins, *Viestarts kā zemgaliešu valstsvīrs*, New York, 1957.

16. История Латвийской ССР, Riga, 1952, 58.

17. T. Zeids, *Feodalisms Livonijā*, Rīgā, 1951, 51.

18. T. Zeids, "Senākie valstiskie veidojumi Latvijā latviešu buržuāziskās historio grafijas apgaismojumā", *Vēstures problemas V*, Rīgā, 1962.

I. DURIDANOV

Baltico-Bulgarica

1. Bulg. *brúlja* (pf. *brúlna*) 'abschütteln, herunterschütteln, abschlagen, streifen (Früchte, Blätter von den Zweigen); heftig blasen (vom Winde)' ist bisher in bezug auf die Struktur nicht befriedigend erklärt worden. St. Mladenov[1] leitet es von einer Wurzel *bru-* her und führt hierzu als urverwandt an: lit. *braũkti* 'streichen, ziehen', lett. *brukt* 'abbröckeln, knicken, abfallen', lit. *brauklỹs* 'Holzstück zum Verschliessen der Tür; Instrument, um Flachsköpfe abzustreifen', russ. *brosat'* 'werfen' usw. Nach dem neuen Bulgarischen etymologischen Wörterbuch[2] sei *brul'a* wahrscheinlich ein Kontaminationsprodukt von bulg. *brusja* 'abschlagen' und *žulja* 'reiben, einreiben, schlagen'. Doch bietet das Lettische eine genaue Entsprechung zu bulg. *brulja* : *brauļât* 'mit der Hand über das Gesicht streifen', *braulêt* 'in der Brunstzeit sein'. Es handelt sich um eine altertümliche, baltisch-slawische -*l*-Bildung, die bloss im Bulgarischen und Lettischen bis heutzutage erhalten ist.

2. Bulg. *grágor* 'steiniger und sandiger Boden; Kies, Flusskies'[3], zu dem in makedonischen Dialekten Adjektiva *gragorest, gragorliv, gragorovit* 'kiesig' belegt sind[4], wird von St. Mladenov[5] als reduplizierte Bildung der Wurzel *gor-* in slaw. *gora* 'Berg' (verwandt mit alb. *gur* 'Stein') gedeutet. Im zweiten etymologischen Wörterbuch des Bulgarischen[6] wird *gragor* als onomatopoetisches Wort mit Reduplikation (von *gor-*?) aufgefasst und als nahe verwandt mit dem Verb *gъrgorja* (dial.) 'schwatzen' und 'zwitschern' verglichen. Eine bessere Deutungsmöglichkeit ergibt sich aus dem Vergleich mit einigen baltischen Wörtern. So sind im Baltikum in gleicher Bedeutung bekannt: lit. *gar̃gždas* (dial. auch *graždas*) 'Kies(sand), kiesiger Boden, Kiesboden', *gargždýnė* 'mit Kies(sand) bedeckter Platz', lett. *gargzda* 'grauer, sandiger Boden' — Erweiterungen von einer Wurzel *garg-* mit den Suffixen -*ždas* bzw. -*žd-ynė*, -*zda*. Dieselbe Wurzel ist auch in lit. *gargãžė* 'Schlacke', *gárgužės* 'Flockasche, die der Wind bei einer Feuersbrunst umherträgt', *gargĕti* 'sich mit einer Russschicht überziehen', ablautend *girgĕti* 'knarren, knirschen' enthalten[7]. Die baltischen Entsprechungen deuten darauf hin, dass in bulg. *gragor* eher eine Wurzel urslaw. **gъrg-* vorliegt; zum Suffix -*or* <urslaw. -*ărъ*, später -*orъ* vgl. bulg. *grahor* 'Wicke', slowen. *gráhor* 'dass.'

(zu *gràh* 'Erbse'), skr. *kòsor* 'Art Messer Dorn zu schneiden' (zu *kòsa* 'Sense'), skr. *stòbōr* (auch *stòbor*) 'Hof', bulg. *stobór* 'Lattenzaun', lit. *stãbaras* 'trockener Baumast; blattloser, trockener, dürrer (Kraut-)stengel, -strunk' (zu lit. *stãbas* 'Pfosten, Säule', lett. *stabs* 'Pfosten, Pfahl, Säule')[8] u. a.

3. Bulg. dial. *klipav* 'schwach, hinfällig, weichlich, lahm' wird von St. Mladenov[9] als onomatopoetisches Wort angesehen und weiter mit *klépja* 'aufschlagen; klappern (vom Storch)', *klepoúch* 'mit hängendem Ohr, schläfrig' verbunden. Doch ist ein Zusammenhang zwischen *klipav* und *klepja* (russ. *klepat'*, skr. *klepati* usw.) sowohl aus lautlichen als auch aus semasiologischen Gründen abzulehnen. Das bulgarische Adjektiv könnte mit russ. dial. *klypat'* 'hinken' verbunden werden, zu dem baltische Entsprechungen angeführt werden: lit. *klùpti* (*klumpù*) 'stolpern', lett. *klupt* 'dass.', lit. *klaũptis* 'knien' u. a.[10] Denkbar ist auch eine andere Alternative: bulg. *klipav* liesse sich der Bedeutung nach mit lit. *klỹpti* (*klypstù*, -*klypaũ*) 'sich verbiegen, sich verkrümmen', ablautend lett. *klipt* (*klìpu*, Präter. *klipu*) 'verkommen', *sa-klipt* 'dass.' und 'krank, gefühllos werden, erstarren' vergleichen; vgl. auch lit. *kleĩpti* (*kleipiù*) 'verbiegen, verkrümmen, (Schuhwerk) schief treten', intr. 'watscheln, schwanken, torkeln, unsicher gehen'[11]. Da alte Belege für bulg. *klipav* fehlen, ist eine endgültige Entscheidung in diesem Fall kaum möglich.

4. Bulg. dial. *répam* 'zupfen (an den Haaren), auszupfen, ausreissen' hat bereits St. Mladenov[12] mit lit. *ap-rėpti* 'umfassen', *rėplės* 'Zange' verknüpft. Hinzuzufügen ist, dass dem bulgarischen Verb genau lit. *rėpti* (*rėpiu*, -*rėpiau*) mit Parallelform *rėpti* (*rėpiù*, *rėpiaũ*) '(zusammen)raffen, umfassen, umschliessen' entspricht. Die litauische Entsprechung weist auf eine urslawische Form **rěpati* hin. Doch ist auch möglich, dass das bulgarische Wort aus einer Substratsprache (Thrakisch oder Dakisch) übernommen wurde. Von den anderen indoeuropäischen Entsprechungen steht am nächsten alb. *rjep* 'ziehe aus, ab, beraube'.

5. Bulg. *trъšúvam*, *tarašúvam*, *taršúvam* 'herumstöbern, herumwühlen' wird als eine Weiterbildung zu bulg. *tъrsja* 'suchen' gestellt[13]. Wir sind geneigt, es mit lit. *taršýti* (*taršaũ*, *taršiaũ*) 'aufwühlen, aufwiegeln, (zer)-reissen, zupfen, raufen' in Verbindung zu bringen, was semasiologisch recht wohl passt. Auch lautlich liesse sich gegen diese Zusammenstellung nichts einwenden: bulg. *trъšuvam* (mit -*ъ*- aus unbetontem reduziertem -*a*- im Ostbulgarischen) setzt als Grundlage ein verschollenes Verb abulg. **trašiti*, **trašǫ* voraus, letzteres wäre dann auf urslaw. **tăršiti* < **tărchiti* (mit -*rch*- aus älterem -*rs*- gegenüber dem lit. -*rš*-) zurückzuführen. Bulg. *tarašuvam* (für *trašuvam*) könnte man als eine expressive Form erklären, aus der wieder eine Form *taršuvam* durch Synkope des unbetonten zweiten -*a*-

oder durch Umstellung von -ra- zu -ar- (vgl. bulg. dial. *stạrná* aus *straná* 'Land') entstanden wäre.

Anmerkungen

1. St. Mladenov, *Etimologičeski i pravopisen rečnik na bъlgarskija knižoven ezik*, Sofia, 1941, 45.

2. V. Georgiev, Iv. Gălăbov, u. a., *Bъlgarski etimologičen rečnik*, Akademieausgabe, 81 f.

3. N. Gerov, *Rečnik na blъgarskij jazik*, I, Plovdiv, 1895, 243.

4. T. Dimitrovski, Bl. Korubin, Tr. Stamatoski, *Rečnik na makedonskiot jazik, I*, Skopje, 1961, 112.

5. St. Mladenov, *a. a. O.*, 108.

6. V. Georgiev, Iv. Gălăbov u. a., *a. a. O.*, 270.

7. Zur Etymologie dieser Wörter s. E. Fraenkel, *Litauisches etymologisches Wörterbuch*, 137.

8. E. Fraenkel, *a. a. O.*, 891.

9. St. Mladenov, *a. a. O.*, 241.

10. Vgl. R. Trautmann, *Baltisch-Slavisches Wörterbuch*, Göttingen, 1923, 137; M. Vasmer, *Russisches etymologisches Wörterbuch*, I, 574.

11. Zu den baltischen Wörtern vgl. E. Fraenkel, *a. a. O.*, 268.

12. St. Mladenov, *a. a. O.*, 559.

13. St. Mladenov, *a. a. O.*, 641.

Baltico-Bulgarica

The author discusses the etymologies of five Bulgarian words: 1) *brúlja*, 2) *grágor*, 3) (dial.) *klípav*, 4) (dial.) *répam*, 5) *trъšúvam* etc.

R. ECKERT

Zum lexikalischen Bestand der Nomina mit *i*-Stamm im Ostbaltischen

Dank der ersten großen vergleichenden Darstellung der baltischen Sprachen[1] aus der Feder des hochverehrten Jubilars hat auch die Deklination der Substantiva im Baltischen erstmalig eine tiefgründige und umfassende historisch-vergleichende Interpretation erfahren. In ihr ist auch der Geschichte der *i*-Stämme der gebührende Platz eingeräumt. Wenngleich in Einzelfragen der Entwicklung der Endungen, des Vergleiches der baltischen *i*-Stämme mit Entsprechungen aus anderen indoeuropäischen Sprachen und selbst hinsichtlich der prosodischen Charakteristik einzelner Beispiele auch weiterhin Diskussionen unausbleiblich sein werden, zu den grundlegenden Folgerungen Chr. S. Stangs über Stellung und Entwicklung der *i*-Deklination im Baltischen wird in Bälde kaum viel Neues gesagt werden können.

Wir wollen daher ein Teilproblem aus dem genannten größeren Fragenkreis herausgreifen, auf dessen ausführlichere Bearbeitung der Verfasser der „Vergleichenden Grammatik der baltischen Sprachen" angesichts der vorhandenen umfangreichen Arbeiten begründet verzichtete: das Problem des lexikalischen Bestandes der *i*-Deklination. Auch hier möchten wir noch weiter einschränken und uns lediglich dem Ostbaltischen, das im Litauischen und Lettischen seine bis in die Gegenwart reichende lebendige Ausprägung hat, zuwenden.

Unter den ostbaltischen Nomina mit *i*-Stamm gibt es eine kleinere Gruppe von Fällen, die zahlreiche Entsprechungen (auch was den Stamm betrifft) in anderen indoeuropäischen Sprachen aufzuweisen hat, z. B. der maskuline *i*-Stamm[2] lit. *ugnìs, -iẽs*; dial. auch *ugnìs, ùgnies* und *ùgnis, ùgnies* und lett. (z. T. dial.) *uguns, -ns; guns, -s* 'Feuer' und ursl. **ognь* < **ognis*; ai. *agní-ḥ*; sowie lat. *ignis, -is* 'Feuer'. Auch *i*-Stämme, die — soweit uns bekannt — nur in einer der beiden heutigen ostbaltischen Sprachen belegt sind, können exakte Entsprechungen in anderen indoeuropäischen Idiomen besitzen, z. B. lit. *šlitìs, -iẽs* (4) fem. 'Garbenhocke, Heuhaufen, Schober', neben *šlytìs, -iẽs* (4) fem. 'Sich-zur-Seite-neigen; Windschiefwerden; Verlagerung', das sehr gut zu ai. *śriti-ḥ* 'Anlehnung'[3] gr. κλίσις

'Neigung'[4] und aisl. *hlið* 'Seite, Abhang', nhd. *Leite* paßt[5]. Lett. *stātis* nom. pl. 'Wendepunkt' faßt J. Endzelin (Lett. Gr, 279) als *-(s)ti*-Stamm auf und vergleicht es mit russ. стать fem. 'Statur', sowie av. *stā^ti*- 'Stehen, Stand'. Die Beispiele zeigen, daß im Ostbaltischen sowie in den ostbaltischen Einzelsprachen sehr wohl alte indoeuropäische Nomina mit *i*-Stamm bewahrt blieben. Doch nicht diesen ältesten Schichten der *i*-Stämme soll unsere Untersuchung gelten, auch nicht den ostbaltisch-slawischen Entsprechungen, die bereits zahlreicher als die erwähnten Fälle sind, sondern den ausschließlich litauisch-lettischen Gemeinsamkeiten im Bereich der Substantiva mit *i*-Stamm.

Die wohl ausführlichste Materialzusammenstellung dazu finden wir bei J. Endzelin in seiner fundamentalen Beschreibung der lettischen Sprache.[6] Er führt folgende Fälle von Übereinstimmungen im *i*-Stamm bei litauischen und lettischen Substantiva an:

1. Lit. dial. *bitìs, -iẽs* (4, 3) fem.: lett. *bitis*; lett. dial. *b'it's, -s*; *bits, -s* (Lett. Gr., 312);
2. lit. *debesìs, -iẽs* fem. mask. : lett. *debess, -s*; nom. pl. *debesis* fem., selten mask. (Lett. Gr., 275–276)[7];
3. lit. dial. *kandìs, -iẽs* (4), *kándis, -ies* (1) fem. : lett. dial. *kuôds, -s* (Lett. Gr., 312);
4. lit. *kiltìs* (4), *kíltis, -ies* (1) fem. : lett. *cìlts, -s* (Lett. Gr., 279);
5. lit. dial. *krántis, -ies* (1) fem. : lett. *krañts, -s*, das von J. Endzelin (ME, II, 259) als Kuronismus zu lit. *krántis* angesehen wird;
6. lit. *krósnis, -ies* (1) fem. mask. : lett. *krâsns, -s*; auch dial. *kráss, -s*; *krân(t)s, -s*; *krāsts, -s* (?) (Lett. Gr., 212);
7. lit. dial.(žem.) *lingstìs, -iẽs* (4); dial. *linkstìs* (4), *lìnkstis* (1) fem. : lett. *lìksts, -s* (Lett. Gr., 312);
8. lit. *mẽnesis, -ies* (1) mask. : lett. *mẽness, -s* mask. früher z. T. auch fem. (Lett. Gr., 275)[7];
9. lett. *nasts, -s* : lit. *pusiáu naštis* mask., fem. (Leskien, *Bildg Nom*, 539; Lett. Gr., 280);
10. lit. *sagtìs, -iẽs* (4) fem. : lett. *sagts* (das nach Endzelin, Lett. Gr., 280, den Stamm auf *-(s)ti*- besitzt), vgl. ferner lett. *dižsagts, -s* (ME, I, 475)[8];
11. lit. *smiltìs -iẽs* (4, 3), *smìltis, -ies* (1) fem. : lett. *smìlts, -s*, auch *smîlts, -s*, *smîlkts, -s*, *smìlkts, -s*, nom. pl. *smìltis, smîltis, smìlktis* (Lett. Gr., 279);
12. lit. *šalìs, -iẽs* (4) fem. : lett. *sals*, acc. pl. *salis* (Lett. Gr., 312);
13. lit. *tóšis, -ies* (1) fem. : lett. *tãsis*, gen. sg. *tãša* und daneben der *i*-Stamm *tãss, -s* (Lett. Gr., 195), sowie *tãsts, -s, tãrss, -s* (ME, IV, 151);

14. lit. dial. (žem.) *upìs*, gen. sg. *ùpies* (2) fem. : lett. dial. *upśś*, ferner *ups*, -*s* und der gen. sg. des Gewässernamens *Mùolups* (Lett. Gr., 312; ME, IV, 301);

15. lit. *vilnìs*, -*iẽs* (4) mask., fem. : altlett. acc. pl. *vilnis* (Lett. Gr., 212).

Die Anzahl der speziellen litauisch-lettischen Entsprechungen unter den Nomina auf *i*-Stamm können wir gegenüber den von J. Endzelin in seiner „Lettischen Grammatik" festgehaltenen Beispielen um das Zweifache vermehren. Dies war vor allem durch die Heranziehung der mundartlichen Lexik aus den beiden ostbaltischen Sprachen möglich, da verschiedene Dialekte, besonders im Lettischen, die Nomina mit *i*-Stamm weit besser erhalten haben, als die Literatursprachen.

Unserer Untersuchung haben wir, was das Litauische betrifft, die bisher erschienenen Bände des „Wörterbuches der litauischen Sprache" (*Lietuvių kalbos žodynas*, Bd. I–VII, 1. Auflage, Vilnius 1941–1966) zugrundegelegt. Ferner konnten wir im Institut für litauische Sprache und Literatur der Akademie der Wissenschaften der Litauischen SSR in Vilnius durch freundliches Entgegenkommen der Direktion den VIII. Band des LKŽ (im weiteren abgekürzt *LKŽ*, VIII) im Manuskript einsehen; d. h. die restlichen Wörter mit dem Anfangsbuchstaben *m*-, ferner *n*- und *o*-. Für die weiteren Buchstaben (*p*- bis *valdà*) haben wir das *Wörterbuch der litauischen Schriftsprache. Litauisch-Deutsch* von M. Niedermann, A. Senn, F. Brender, A. Salys, Bde II–V, Heidelberg 1951–1966 (abgekürzt *NdŽ*) gründlich ausgewertet, sowie umfangreiche Excerptionen aus der Kartothek des LKŽ Vilnius (abgekürzt *LKŽ*, *K*) vorgenommen. Den Rest (*ž*-) schöpften wir aus B. Sereiskis, *Lietuviškai-rusiškas žodynas*, Kaunas 1932 (abgekürzt *Sereisk*). Außerdem wurde E. Fraenkels *Litauisches etymologisches Wörterbuch* (*LEW*) ständig zu Rate gezogen.

Das lettische Wortmaterial haben wir aus dem fundamentalen *Lettisch-deutschen Wörterbuch* von K. Mühlenbach und J. Endzelin (Bde I–IV, Riga, 1923–1932; abgekürzt als ME) gezogen, ferner aus J. Endzelin, E. Hauzenberg, *Ergänzungen und Berichtigungen zu K. Mühlenbachs Lettisch-deutschem Wörterbuch*, Riga 1934–1946; abgekürzt als EH)[9].

Auf Grund der Tatsache, daß die von uns benutzten Quellen die mundartliche Lexik in breitem Maße erfassen, waren wir in der Lage, eine Anzahl neuer Zusammenstellungen hinsichtlich des *i*-Stammes bei litauischen und lettischen Substantiva zu liefern. Wie geben im folgenden eine Liste der Fälle, die, zu den oben aus Endzelins „Lettischer Grammatik" zitierten Beispielen gerechnet, den ungefähren lexikalischen Gesamtbestand der Substantiva mit *i*-Stamm im Ostbaltischen ausmachen:

1. Lett. dial. *akats, -s* 'eine einschießende, unpassierbare Stelle im Morast, wo nur Moos und Sumpfgras, aber keine Bäume und Sträucher wachsen' (EH, I, 65) : lit. *ãketis, -iẽs* (1); *aketìs* (2b) und *ẽketis, -ties*; *eketìs, -iẽs* (1, 2b) fem. 'aus dem Eis gehauenes Loch, Wuhne; Loch im Sumpf'[10];

2. lit. dial. *bìržis* (1) [E]; *biržìs, -iẽs* fem. 'Birkenhain, Laubwäldchen' (LKŽ, I, 697) : lett. dial. *bìrzs, -s*; *birzs, -s*; *birzts, -s* 'Birkenwald, -hain, -gehege; Laubwäldchen; Waldecke, die irgendwie vom übrigen Walde gleichsam abgeteilt zu sein scheint' (Lett. Gr., 311–312; ME, I, 299–300; EH, I, 221);

3. lit. dial. *biržìs, -iẽs* (4); *bir̃žis* (3), *biržìs* (2), *bìržis* (1) fem. : lett. *birzs, -s* '(Saat-), (Acker)furche; in einem Gang besäter Streifen' usw. (Bielenstein, *Die lett. Sprache*, Berlin 1864, Bd. II, 48; ME, I, 299);

4. lit. *gárankštis* (1) fem. 'Zusammengedrehtes; Knäuel aus Schlingen, Falte; Backenzahn; Zahnwurzel' (LKŽ, III, 111) mit einer Vielzahl mundartlicher Varianten: *garúkštis* (1), *geránkštis* (1) [E], altlit. *gerokštis* fem., *gerúkštis* mask., fem., *gerúokštis* mask., *gerúkštis* [E], *gyránkštis* (1) fem. und *gránkštis* (1) fem. (LKŽ, III, 145, 241, 261, 269, 271, 329, 519) : lett. dial. *dzẽrūksts, -s* 'Backenzahn' (ME, I, 547), *dzẹrùoksts, -s*, *dzẹrûksts, -s* 'Gekroll, Gekräusel (im Garn)', *dzàrûksts, -s* 'die Krolle im Garn' (EH, I, 352, 356);

5. lit. *geležìs, -iẽs* (3b) fem. 'Eisen; Gegenstand aus Eisen (Säge, Messer, Schwert); Schlittschuh; eiserne Ofenplatte; dial. (žem.) auch *gelžìs, -iẽs* [E] fem., mask. (LKŽ, III, 216, 218, 230) : lett. *dzèlzs, -s*; auch *dzẹ̀lzs*, sowie ostlett. *dzelez(i)s* fem. z. T. auch mask. 'Eisen' (ME, I, 543–544; K. Būga, R. R., II, 682). Interessant ist die Nichtübereinstimmung im Stamm mit apr. *gelso*, das eher ursl. **želězo* näher steht.

6. lit. dial. *grį́žtis, -ies* (1), *grįžtìs* (4) fem. (LKŽ, III, 635) : lett. dial. *grizts, -s* 'gedrehtes Bund, Knocke; etwas Zusammengedrehtes' usw. (ME, I, 658–659; 661);

7. lit. *ìltis, -ies* (1) fem. 'Hauer-, Stoß-, Fangzahn, Augenzahn; Riegel an der Wand oder Tür; Teil des Wagens, in den die Deichsel gesteckt wird' (LKŽ, IV, 61) : lett. *ilkss, -s* (nach Endzelin, Lett. Gr., 312 *i*-Stamm), 'Hauzahn des Ebers', *il̂kts, -s* und *ilts, -s* 'Hauer, Hau-, Fangzahn' (ME, I, 706, 707);

8. Etymologisch mit vorigem zusammenhängend zu betrachten sind: lit. dial. *ielakštis* (1) fem. 'Deichsel des Pfluges, die aus einem Baum besteht; Verbindungsteil des Joches; Holzbein' mit den Varianten *ielakstis* (1), *ielekstìs* (3a), *ielekstis* (1), *ielaktis* (1), *ielaktìs* (3a), *ielekštis* (1) [E], *ielektis* (1), *ielektìs* (3a) und *ielekštis* (1) fem. (LKŽ, IV, 13) : lett.

dial. *il̃kss, -s, ìlksts, -s* 'Femerstange am Wagen oder Schlitten; Stollen am Spinnrad, wo das Rad hängt' (ME, I, 706; EH, I, 430);

9. Einem spärlich belegten lit. dial. *kaktis, -ies* 'vorderer Teil des Schlittens' (LKŽ, V, 100) entspricht wahrscheinlich das Zweitglied der folgenden mundartlichen lettischen *i*-Stämme: *kris[t]kakts, -s* 'Ecke des Hauses, wo der Eßtisch steht, weil beim Bau des Hauses hier in der untersten Schwelle ein Kreuz eingeschnitten und, um Brotmangel vorzubeugen, Brotkrümchen darin eingestreut wurden'; 'eine beliebige Ecke'; *kriskapts* (dissimiliert aus *kris(t)kakts*), *-s* 'Stubenecke, wo die Heiligenbilder hängen; Stubenecke' (EH, I, 655–656). Die Wörter gehören sicher zu lit. *kaktas* 'Erker' und lett. *kakts, kakta* 'die von zwei Seiten gebildete Ecke; Winkel';

10. lett. *bìrkstis, biȓkstis* nom. pl. 'glimmende oder auch nur heiße Asche; Funken', sowie *(s)pìrkstis* 'glühende Asche' zählt Endzelin (Lett. Gr., 280) zu den lettischen *-(s)ti*-Stämmen : lit. *kibirkštìs* (3b), *žibirkštìs* [E] fem. 'glühende Flugasche, Funken', auch *kiburkštìs* (3b) fem. (LKŽ, V, 727, 738; LEW, 40–41) : lett. *spìrksts, -s, pìrksts, -s, dzirksts, -s, dzìrkstis* nom pl., *g'ìrksts, -s* (ME, I, 298; 427, 554; III, 223; 1000; EH, II, 236). Der Anlaut in einigen litauischen Bildungen, *ki-* und *ži-*, hängt nach Meinung von E. Fraenkel (op. cit) mit lit. *kibéti* 'herunterhängen' oder *kibiraĩ* 'Reisig' bzw. mit lit. *žibéti* 'glänzen' zusammen. Die verschiedenen Varianten sind z. T. onomatopoetisch beeinflußt.

11. Wenn die folgenden Beispiele *einer* etymologischen Sippe angehören, so liegt auch hier ein ostbaltischer *i*-Stamm vor: Altlett. *liets* 'Sache' (von Endzelin als *i*-Stamm bestimmt, Lett. Gr., 312) und lett. dial. *lĩts, -s*, auch *lĩts* (EH, I, 751) : lit. *lytìs, -iẽs* (4) fem. [E] 'Geschlecht; Gestalt, Figur; Reife; Form; Typ' (LKŽ, VII, 593–594);

12. lett. *maksts, -s*; nom. pl. *makstis* 'Scheide, Futteral', dial. *maksts, -s* 'Netzbeutel', auch *sìrdsmaksts, -s* 'Herzbeutel' (ME, II, 554; III, 844) : lit. *makštìs* (4) fem. [E] 'Scheide; Futteral; Blütenblätter; Hülle, Schale; Kokon; vagina' und *makšnìs* (4) fem. 'Blatteil, der den Stengel oder die Frucht umgibt' (LKŽ, VII, 785–786);

13. lit. *pìlnatis, -ies* (1), *pilnatìs, -iẽs* (3) fem. : lett. dial. *pìlnats, -s* 'Vollmond' (NdŽ, III, 90, 92; EH, II, 232[12])[13];

14. lit. *plókštis, -ies* (1) fem. 'junge (noch flache) Erbsenschote' (NdŽ, III, 149) : lett. dial. *pluoksts* (*i*-Stamm nach EH, II, 305), 'Augenlid'. Zur Semantik vergleiche noch lett. dial. *plêksne* 'dünne, unreife Schote';

15. lett. *riksts* 'Rute' weist nach J. Endzelin (Lett. Gr., 312) den *i*-Stamm auf, vgl. noch lett. dial. *rĩksts, -s* (EH, II, 376) : lit. *rykštìs*, gen. sg.

rykštiẽs (4) 'gerades, glattes, konisches Pflöckchen, das die Kettfäden zu trennen hat, Pflöckchen in der Mitte des Gewebes' (LKŽ, K);

16. lit. dial. *rintìs*, *-iẽs* (4) fem. 'Kerbe, Einschnitt, Falz; Querholz (im Fischerboot); Tür, die von außen die Kühe einsperrt'; lit. dial. *rentìs*, *-iẽs* fem. 'hölzerne Brunnenwandung, die aus einem halben Baumstamm gemacht ist' und wahrscheinlich noch *rañtis*, gen. sg. *rañties*, acc. sg. *rañtį* 'Kerbe, Einschnitt' (LKŽ, K) : lett. dial. *rañts*, *-s* 'Vertiefung, Schramme; Kerbe auf dem Horn von Kühen' (EH, II, 354);

17. lit. *rūdìs*, *-iẽs* (4) mask. teilweise auch fem. 'Eisenrost; Rost (am Getreide)' (Leskien, *Bildg*, 238; Kurschat, I, 365; II, 35 und LKŽ, K) : lett. dial. *rùss*, *-s* 'Rost' (EH, II, 389), wobei *rùss* wohl aus *rūds* entstanden ist, vgl. lit. *rūstas* < *rūdstas*; *rusnùs* < *rudsnus*;

18. lit. *rūgštìs*, *-iẽs* (3) mask. [E] (ist bereits im Altlitauischen als *i*-Stamm bezeugt) 'Sauerteig; Geschmack, Säure (des Brotes); säuerliche Speisen; Gemüse, das zum Kochen der säuerlichen Speisen genommen wird; säuerliche Getränke, Kwas; Gattung; Heimat' (LKŽ, K) : lett. dial. *rûgsts*, *-s* 'Säure, besonders Geschmack und Geruch, der sich beim Gären zeigt' (EH, II, 387);

19. lit. *svìrtis*, *-ies* (1), dial. *svirtìs*, *-iẽs* (4) fem. [E] 'Brunnenschwengel; Schwingbaum; Hebel; Ziehbrunnen; Wagenbalken' und die Varianten lit. dial. *svirstìs*, *-iẽs* (4), *svar̃stis*, *-ies* (2), *svìrbstis*, *-ies* (1), *svirksnìs*, *-iẽs* (4) fem. (NdŽ, IV, 429, 440, 441) : lett. dial. *svìrts*, *-s* 'Brunnenschwengel' ,(ME, III, 1162) und svērts (*i*-Stamm? — so Endzelin, ME, III, 1154), 'Ziehbalken am Brunnen';

20. lit. *šútis*, *-ies* (1) fem. [E] 'Haufen (Steine, Holz u. dgl.)' (Būga, R. R., I, 374, II, 203; NdŽ, IV, 559) : lett. *šûts*, *-s* 'Grube; Gruft, Unebenheit (auf dem Wege); eine Erhöhung' (ME, IV, 111–112), *šùts* (Lett. Gr., 312);

21. lit. dial. (žem.) *utìs*, *-iẽs* (4) fem. [E] 'Laus' (Geitler, Lit. Stud., 118; NdŽ, V, 21; LEW, 1173) : lett. dial. *uts*, *-s*, *vuts*, *-s* 'Laus' (ME, IV, 310, 677). Man vgl. auch die Komposita lit. *lãputis* (1) fem. : lett. *laputs*, *-s* 'Blattlaus' (ME, II, 422), ferner lett. *kùokuts*, *-s* 'Mauerassel' *veļuts*, *-s* 'Filzlaus' (ME, II, 343, IV, 536);

22. lit. dial. *várpstis*, *-ies* (1), *varpstìs*, *-iẽs* (3 oder 4?) fem. 'Spindel, Spule; Spille; dünne Stange; Achse' (LKŽ, K) : lett. dial. *vãrpsts*, *-s* 'Spindel', *vàrpsts*, *-s* 'Spille; Trittstock am Spinnrad; Stäbchen, worauf die Spulen beim Garnwinden aufgereiht werden' (ME, IV, 507);

23. lit. *votìs*, *-iẽs* (3) [E], *vótis*, *-ies* fem. 'bösartiges, offenes Geschwür; Schwäre, Blutgeschwür; Schwulst; Drüse' (LKŽ, K) : lett. dial. *vâts*, *-s*, *vãts*, *-s* '(eiternde) Wunde; Schorf', nom. pl. *vâtis* 'Masern, Pocken' (ME, IV, 511–512);

24. lit. *žebenkštìs, -iẽs* (3b) mask. [E] 'Wiesel' und Varianten: *žẽbenkštis, žìbinkštìs, žabinkštìs, žebrenkštis, -ies* (Sereisk, 1076; Būga, R. R., II, 677) : lett. dial. *zebieksts, -s* 'Wiesel' (ME, IV, 701, EH, II, 803);

25. lit. *žuvìs, -iẽs* (4) mask. [E] 'Fisch', auch *živìs* (E. Fraenkel, Baltoslavica, II, 19) : lett. *zivs, -s*, neben dial. *zuvs*, sowie altlett. *zivis* 'Fisch' (M.-E, IV, 753, 730)[14]. Vgl. noch lit. *didžuvis, -ies* fem. (LKŽ, II, 335) und lett. *valzivs, -s* 'Walfisch' (ME, IV, 463)[15];

26. lit. *usnìs, -iẽs* (4), dial. *usnìs, ùsnies* (2) *ùsnis, ùsnies* (2) fem. '(Kratz)-distel' (NdŽ, V, 20; LEW, 1172) : lett. *usnis* 'Distel', eine Nebenform zu üblicheren *usna, usne*[16];

27. lett. dial. *pâksts, -s* 'Schote; weibliche Scham' (ME, III, 146; EH, II, 195), nom. pl. *pâkstis* weist den *i*-Stamm auf (Endzelin, Lett. Gr., 280). Falls dieses Wort identisch ist mit lit. *puokštis, -ies* [E] 'Blumenstrauß' (wenn mit *uo<o*), was Endzelin mit Bezug auf Leskien (Bildg. Nom., 554) vermutet, haben wir hier ebenfalls einen ostbaltischen *i*-Stamm. Die erheblichen semantischen Unterschiede lassen jedoch diese Zusammenstellung als noch nicht ganz gesichert erscheinen.

28. Im Falle lett. *palts, -s* nom. pl. *paltis* 'Pfütze, Lache, Regenbach' steht ein lettischer appellativischer *i*-Stamm (vgl. Endzelin, Lett. Gr., 312; EH, II, 152) den litauischen Gewässernamen *Páltis, -ies* (1) fem. 1. Nebenfluß des Srautas; 2. rechter Nebenfluß der Nevėžis; 3. rechter Nebenfluß der Amata; 4. Teil des Dysnų-See; 5. Vabalninkas-See und *Paltỹs* (3) — rechter Nebenfluß der Minija (*Lietuvos TSR upių ir ežerų vardynas*, Vilnius, 1963, 117) gegenüber[17].

Die Untersuchung hat gezeigt, daß die mundartliche Lexik der beiden heute gebräuchlichen baltischen Sprachen eine wichtige Ergänzung zu unseren Kenntnissen über die Verbreitung der Nomina mit *i*-Stamm, so wie sie uns aus den baltischen Literatursprachen und dem älteren Schrifttum bekannt sind, darstellt. Das hängt vor allem damit zusammen, daß in der Literatursprache (und z. T. in einigen Dialekten), vor allem im Lettischen, aber auch im Litauischen, die *i*-Deklination im Schwinden begriffen ist und immer weniger lexikalische Einheiten nach diesem Deklinationstyp verändert werden[18]. Für die Beurteilung dieses Deklinationstyps insgesamt jedoch ist die Kenntnis seines lexikalischen Bestandes von Bedeutung, eröffnet sie uns doch die Voraussetzungen für ein umfassenderes Studium der Beziehungen dieser Deklination zu anderen Deklinationen, für die Einschätzung der verschiedenen Stamm- und Suffixalternationen und liefert wahrscheinlich auch wertvolle Aufschlüsse über bestimmte Teilsysteme der Wortbildung und über semantische Gruppierungen (man vgl. z. B. die Bezeichnungen für Insekten und kleine Kerbtiere, die im Ostbaltischen und in den baltischen Einzelsprachen als *i*-Stämme auftreten : lit. *bitìs* – lett. *bits*; lit. *kandìs* – lett. *kuôds*; lit. *utìs* – lett. *uts*; lit. *‚musìs* – ursl. dial. **mъš-i-ca* < **mus-i-ka*; lit. *trandìs, -ies* fem. 'Borkenkäfer; Holzwurm; Motte; Milbe'; lit. *šeršuolìs, -iês* 'Wespe'[19]; lit. dial. *skruzdis, -ies* 'Ameise' und lett. *blakts, -s* 'Wanze'[20]).

In diesem Sinne stellt das oben Dargelegte eher eine Materialsichtung und -vorbereitung dar, die u. E. jedoch notwendig ist, um weitere Forschungen an diesen interessanten Gegenstand knüpfen zu können.

Anmerkungen

1. *Vergleichende Grammatik der baltischen Sprachen* von Chr. S. Stang, Oslo–Bergen–Tromsö, 1966.

2. Vgl. dazu ausdrücklich J. Endzelin, *Lett. Gr.*, 313.

3. Siehe P. Skardžius, *Lietuvių kalbos žodžių daryba*, Vilnius, 1943, 328.

4. Siehe J. Kuryłowicz, *L'accentuation des langues indo-européennes*, Wrocław–Kraków, 1958, 187.

5. Für lett. *slits* 'ein aus Fichtenzweigen geflochtener Zaun' können wir keinen *i*-Stamm, wohl aber einen daneben vorkommenden *ē*-Stamm *slite*, vgl. lit. *šlitė*, ausmachen (ME, III, 933).

6. Wir haben beide Auflagen, sowohl die deutsche (*Lettische Grammatik*, Riga, 1922) als auch die lettische (*Latviešu valodas gramatika*, Rīga, 1951) berücksichtigt.

7. Ursprünglich ein konsonantischer Stamm.

8. Übrigens besteht die Möglichkeit, den ostbaltischen *i*-Stamm mit apr. *sagis* Elb. Voc. 486 'rincke' = 'Schnalle an einem Gürtel, Spange', 544 'Hufnagel' zu vergleichen. Der Unterschied zum apr. Wort besteht aber darin, daß die ostbaltischen Wörter Bildungen auf *-ti* sind. Als unmittelbare Entsprechung zu apr. *sagis* führt Endzelin (*Senpr. val.*, 240) lit. *săgas* 'Schleife zum Befestigen der Leinwand auf der Bleiche' an, sowie lit. *sagà* oder *sagė* 'Schnalle'.

9. Aus den „Ergänzungen ...“ war uns lediglich Heft XVII nicht zugänglich. Heft XVIII erschien bekanntlich 1946 in Riga unter dem lettischen Titel J. Endzelīns, *Papildinājumi un labojumi K. Mülenbacha Latviešu valodas vārdnīcai.* — Die Fälle, in denen J. Endzelīn im Lettisch-deutschen Wörterbuch bei der Registrierung der lettischen *i*-Stämme bereits auf Entsprechungen im Litauischen verweist — ohne daß die Zugehörigkeit des litauischen Wortes zu den *i*-Stämmen im einzelnen erörtert wird — wollen wir besonders kennzeichnen und zwar durch ein [E] hinter dem entsprechenden Wort.

10. Neben den *i*-Stämmen sind *ā*- und *ē*-Stämme vertreten in: lett. *akate, akata* : lit. *aketė, ėketė*. Fast in allen Fällen stehen neben den *i*-Stämmen *ē*-Stämme, so daß wir im weiteren auf Hinweise dieser Art verzichten können.

11. Übrigens enthält auch lit. *pirkšnìs, -iês* (4) fem. 'glühende Ascheflocke, in welcher noch Funken glimmen' den *i*-Stamm.

12. Es handelt sich wohl um elliptische Univerbierung des Ausdruckes *mé'nuo pìlnatis*, vgl. lit. dial. *pilnaties* adv. 'zur Zeit des Vollmonds'.

13. J. Endzelin verweist nur auf lit. *pilnatis, -čio*.

14. Es ist ein altes Wurzelnomen, das Spuren der konsonantischen Deklination bewahrt und bereits im altlitauischen Schrifttum Formen der *i*-Deklination aufweist.

15. Zum *i*-Stamm in lett. *zivs, zuvs* siehe noch V. Rūķe, ,,Tendenser vid de substantiviska stammarnas utveckling i baltiskan", *Språkliga Bidrag*, Lund, IV, 82.

16. Das häufig hierher gezogene aruss. оушь 'Art Distel' gehört nach neueren Untersuchungen (В. А. Меркулова, Очерки по русской народной номенклатуре растений, Moskva 1967, 39) m. E. wohl am ehesten zur Sippe von slaw. *ucho* 'Ohr', vgl. Pflanzennamen vom Typ russ. ушéвник, ушкó, ушня́к треух usw.

17. Auch relativ späte Entlehnungen der ostbaltischen Sprachen aus dem Deutschen zeigen den *i*-Stamm. Man vgl. lit. veralt. dial. *drótis* (1), *drotìs* (4) fem. : lett. *drãts, -s* 'Draht'; lit. *kūtis, -ies* (2) fem. : lett. *kũts, -s* 'Stall' und lit. dial. *rūtis, -iẽs* : lett. dial. *rũts*, auch *rũts, -s* 'Fensterscheibe' bzw. 'Fensterraute'.

18. Vgl. J. Kazlauskas, „Сокращение употребления имён существительных с основой на *-i* в литовском языке", *Вопроты славянского языкознания* V, 71 ff., sowie ders. *Lietuvių kalbos istorinė gramatika*, 200 ff.

19. Vgl. J. Gerullis, Chr. Stang, *Lietuvių žvejų tarmė Prūsuose*, Kaunas, 1933, 91. — Der *i*-Stamm hängt auch hier mit dem konsonantischen Stamm zusammen, vgl. lit. *širšuõ, -eñs* 'Hornisse'.

20. Hier nimmt J. Endzelin (ME, I, 308) sogar an, daß lett. *blakts* das *-ts-* aus *uts* bezogen hat, wegen *blaks* 'eben'.

On the Lexicological Stock of the *i*-Stems in Eastern Baltic Languages

In this paper, an analysis is made of nouns with *i*-stems, which are common to both Eastern Baltic languages, Lithuanian and Latvian. In the first part, the correspondences between Lithuanian and Latvian with regard to *i*-stems from the "Latvian Grammar" of Endzelin have been collected in a list, containing 15 examples. From the study of a number of dictionaries (above all the *Lietuvių kalbos žodynas* I–VIII and the *Lettisch-deutsches Wörterbuch* by Mühlenbach and Endzelin) we were able to draw the conclusion that the number of common Eastern Baltic *i*-stems may be extended by nearly 28 examples. Loan-words with *i*-stem are not considered. In particular, the analysis of dialectological material from Latvian and Lithuanian enlarges our knowledge of the lexicological stock of the *i*-declension in Baltic languages. A certain semantic sub-group of *i*-stems, e.g. nouns denoting insects, can be identified here.

T. G. FENNELL

Open and Closed *e* in Latvian:
A Synchronic Approach

This problem is traditionally dealt with by a diachronically oriented formulation which sees the occurrence of open or closed *e* as depending on the nature of the following vowel or diphthong (closed front or other) or consonant (palatalized or other). From a purely synchronic point of view this formulation is open to a number of objections:

(a) one has frequently to refer to previous stages of phonetic development to determine the earlier nature of a following vowel, e.g. *tēvs* < **tēvas*;

(b) no account is given of vowels in final syllables, e.g., *puķe*;

(c) no account is taken of loan-words, e.g., *bibliotēka*;

(d) the loss of the phoneme [ŗ] partially invalidates the distinction between palatalized and other consonants, e.g., *dzeru*.

It is also misleading to the extent that it suggests a purely environmental explanation, whereas the facts would seem to point more to a combination of environmental and categorial, as far as contemporary usage is concerned. The present formulation attempts to meet objections (a), (b) and (d) above, and to a lesser extent (c) also, although clearly a number of problems remain here.

Nouns and adjectives

The quality of an *e* in the final syllable of the stem is determinable by the environmental rules from the form of the accusative singular:

zęnu, sętu, mežu, ķešu, dęli, mēli,
akmęni, mędu, tęlti, pęlęku, svešu.

The *e* of a non-final stem syllable is similarly determinable:

tęcīlu, cępuri.

In addition, we must specify that any *e* occurring in a noun termination is closed.

Once established from the accusative singular, the quality of an *e* remains unchanged throughout the declension, and in the case of adjectives, throughout the degrees of comparison: hence *bẹrni, bẹrniem,* etc. One exception involves feminine nouns in -*s* (*cf. dẹbẹsi,* acc. sing.) where the expected palatalization of the final stem consonant in the genitive plural does not occur: a stem *e* in such cases is often open, *e.g., dẹbẹsu, Cẹsu,* although an analogical *ẹ* is perhaps more common.

The relation between the accusative singular and the prediction of *e* quality throughout the declension suggests at once that in general terms each type of declension has its prevalent pattern, and that the declensions are groupable into two types: *zēns, sēta, medus* on the one hand, *dēlis, mēle, akmens, telts* on the other. In syllables other than stem finals, *e* behaves appropriately under the influence of what follows. The possibility that the former pattern and the latter may sometimes conflict must be seriously considered on the evidence of such pairs as *vẹsture* and *vẹsture,* etc., *dẹbẹsu* and *dẹbẹsu,* etc. The pair *spilvẹns* and *spilvẹns* further suggests analogy across declensional borders (*cf. akmẹns*), a possibility reinforced by the use of -*tiņš* rather than -*iņš* as diminutive suffix for such nouns as *spilvens* and *deguns.*

Diminutives cause no special problem, and are readily explained by the procedure outlined above. Similarly, most derived nouns: *sẹtnieku, tẹl-niecību,* etc. However, nouns formed with the prefixes *bez, pret* and *ne* are exceptional, and will be considered later.

It should be noted that any noun or adjective in -*erš* (<*erš*) would cause difficulties: we have not found such a type.

As a general rule, we may state that in foreign words *e* is closed in spite of environment: *bibliotēku, šefu, ar(c)hitẹktu,* etc. However, when the *e* is followed by *r* + consonant, *ẹ* is often heard: *latẹrnu, pẹrsonu, ẹrcẹņģeli.* While this may be due to the pronunciation of the language of origin, often German, other processes may be involved, and cannot be ruled out *a priori.* At this stage we can only suggest these as general tendencies: closer study of this aspect of the problem is needed before any definitive answers can be proposed.

Numerals

In cardinals *e* is always closed, in spite of phonetic environment: *čẹtrus, sẹšus, septiņus,* etc. In all other numerals environment is a reliable guide: *cẹturto, sẹsto, septīto, čẹtrējus,* etc.

Pronouns

These exhibit only ẹ: ẹs, mḕs, tẹvi, sẹv, etc.

Prepositions

It appears that all monosyllabic prepositions and postpositions have ẹ: bẹz, zẹm, prẹt, pḕc, dḕļ. When used as noun prefixes, bez and pret are not subject to environmental influence and retain ẹ: bẹzdarbība, prẹtstats. Similar immunity is shown by pret in the verb prẹtoties.

Conjunctions

All monosyllabics seem to have ẹ: bẹt, jẹb, nẹ ... nẹ, nẹdz; so too perhaps for bisyllabics other than those in -mēr: nẹba, nẹkā, but kamḕr.

Adverbs

Monosyllabics seem to have ẹ, e.g., vḕl, šẹ, tẹ, sẹn, although pḕrn is a notable exception.

Derived adverbs retain the e quality of the adjective, noun or preposition on which they are based, e.g., lḕni, lḕnām, vḕlu; piemḕram; pḕcāk. As for conjunctions, the termination -mēr has ḕ: tomḕr, vienmḕr. Diminutives follow environmental rules, e.g., lḕnītiņām.

Particles and interjections

These appear on the whole to have ẹ: jẹl, rẹ, nẹz, nḕ, nẹ. Like bez and pret, ne used as a prefix is not subject to environmental influences, cf. nẹass, nẹlāga, except when immediately followed by ę or ḕ: nẹęsmu, nẹęsam, nẹḕrts.

Verbs

As it was possible to ascribe dominant quality patterns to nouns on the basis of declensional type, so a similar division is useful for verbs, but on the basis of tense rather than of conjugational type.

(a) Infinitive. E is here closed, unless the environment requires ẹ: cf. cẹlt, nẹst, rẹdzēt, mẹklēt, but mẹlot, lẹkāt.

(b) Present. E is open, unless the environment requires ẹ. Concerning the environment, however, it must be noted that r counts as a "closing" consonant for First Conjugation verbs only, that the termination -*ē* (cf. *meklē*) is closed, and that First Conjugation verbs lacking -*i* in the second person singular must be deemed to behave as if an -*i* were present. Thus *rędzu, mę̄loju, nęsu,* but *meklēju, celu, dzęru; rędzi,* (tu) *nęs, meklę̄, cel, dzęr,* but *mę̄lo; rędz, (viņš) nęs,* but *meklę̄, cel, dzęr.* We leave aside here verbs like *pētīt* which are undergoing a change of conjugational type.

(c) Imperatives. The same rule applies (with the same additional notes) as for the present, e.g., *rędzi, rędziet, nęs, celiet,* but *mę̄lo, mę̄lojiet.* Speakers who do not follow the standard -*at*/-*iet* distinction between the indicative and the imperative will have corresponding differences in the quality of *e*.

(d) Imperfect. In the First Conjugation, *e* is always closed; in the other conjugations it is closed unless the environment requires *ę*: *metu, cę̄lu, rędzēju, meklēju,* but *mę̄loju, lę̄kāju.*

(e) Future. *E* is closed unless the environment requires *ę*: *metīs, cels, rędzę̄s, meklę̄s,* but *mę̄los.*

(f) Conditional. *E* is open unless the environment requires *ę*: *męstu, cę̄ltu, rędzę̄tu, meklę̄tu,* but *secinātu.*

(g) Past participle passive. *E* is open, unless the environment (excluding inflections) requires *ę*: *cęlts, rędzę̄ti,* but *medīts.* Cf. the rules for adjectives.

(h) Past participle active. *E* is open unless the environment requires *ę*: *cę̄lusi, dzę̄rušu,* but *rędzējis, skrējusi.*

(i) Present participles in -*ošs* and -*ot*. The quality of *e* is as for the first person singular of the present: *tękošs, rędzot,* but *dzęrot.*

(j) Present participle in -*am(s)*. The quality of *e* is as for the first person plural of the present: *rędzam, mę̄lojam,* but *dzęram.*

(k) Present participle in -*dams*. *E* is open unless the environment requires *ę*: *nęsdams, mę̄zdams, rędzę̄dams,* but *medīdams.*

(l) Conjunctives. The present conjunctive takes its *e* quality from the first person singular of the present indicative; the future conjunctive from the first person singular of the future indicative: *rędzot* but *dzęrot, dzęršot* but *mę̄lošot.*

(m) Debitives. The quality of *e* is as for the third person of the present indicative: *jānęs, jārędz,* but *jādzęr, jāmeklę̄.*

The above considerations hold for reflexive as well as for active forms. The negative particle *ne* (q. v.) has its own rules, independently of the verbal form to which it is attached.

Clearly, the various verbal forms above fall into two major groups: *open unless necessarily closed* and *closed unless necessarily open.* However, the forms of the present and imperfect, with their rather more complex behaviour, prevent such generalizations from being totally valid, although the *ad hoc* adjustments that are required to handle these two tenses can be simply stated, as in (b) and (d) above.

But even though a combination of the environmental and categorial approaches can provide a better synchronic description than can the environmental approach alone, certain difficulties remain. Nothing short of an exhaustive list of adverbs, prepositions, conjunctions and interjections can provide a basis for generalization about these classes. The problems arising from verbs undergoing a change of conjugation represent additional complications. More seriously, there appears to be no non-diachronic way of distinguishing foreign loan-words.

The first of these is, in principle, easily resolved. With the passage of time, the second may well resolve itself, but, unless widespread analogical changes bring foreign loan-words into line with native patterns, the third is likely to represent a very substantial stumbling-block to any description of the Latvian *e* phonemes fully compatible with the exigencies of synchronic method.

GORDON B. FORD, Jr.

The Origin of the Lithuanian First Person Singular Optative

(Conditional or Subjunctive)

In an important article, *"Zur 1. P. Sg. Optativ im Litauischen"*, which appeared in the *Norsk Tidsskrift for Sprogvidenskap*, IX (1938), pp. 298–300, Professor Christian Stang discussed the various forms and origin of the first person singular optative (conditional or subjunctive) in Lithuanian. In this article Stang advances the opinion that -*čio* is a form abstracted from the reflexive form and is historically identical with -*čia*, but he cites the reflexive form *juõkčiasi* from Jablonskis' grammar #107 and admits that this evidence might indicate that -*a* goes back to old -*a*, not to -*ā̃* since -*čia* from *-čiā̃* should have -*čiosi* as its reflexive form. In this case, Stang continues, the ending -*čia* would be distinguished from -*čio*. It is interesting to note that reflexive forms comparable to *juõkčiasi* are also found in Mažvydas' Catechism of 1547 and in the Wolfenbüttel Lithuanian Postilė Manuscript of the year 1573. Mažvydas has *liauczias* (67,2); cf. my forthcoming parallel-text edition and translation of Mažvydas' Catechism, *The Old Lithuanian Catechism of Martynas Mažvydas (1547)*. *makinczias* (203) appears in the Wolfenbüttel Postilė; cf. Wilhelm Gaigalat, *Die Wolfenbütteler litauische Postillenhandschrift aus dem Jahre 1573* in the *Mitteilungen der litauischen literarischen Gesellschaft*, V (1904), p. 233. Thus it seems more likely to assume that we are dealing with two different forms, *-čia* and *-čiā̃*, the former with -*čiasi* as its reflexive form and the latter with -*čiosi* as its reflexive.

The first person singular optative form does not occur at all in the oldest Lithuanian manuscript text discovered in 1962; see my work, *Old Lithuanian Texts of the Sixteenth and Seventeenth Centuries with a Glossary* (The Hague, 1969), p. 11. It does, however, appear in the first Lithuanian book, Martynas Mažvydas' Catechism of 1547. In Mažvydas the ending is -*czia*. The examples are: *negaleczia* (10, 18); reflexive *liauczias* (67,2); cf. Stang, *Die Sprache des litauischen Katechismus von Mažvydas* (Oslo, 1929), p. 150. The Wolfenbüttel Lithuanian Postilė Manuscript of the year 1573 has only forms in -*czia* and -*czias*. Some examples are *garbinczia* (52); *darriczia* (118a); *bucia* (156); and the reflexive form *makinczias* (203); cf. Gaigalat, *Die Wolfenbütteler* *litauische Postillenhandschrift aus dem Jahre 1573*, p. 233. In Vilentas' *Enchiridion* of 1579 the form occurs with the endings *-czią* (3 times) and *-czo* (twice). Here the nasal *ą* does not designate a nasal vowel but is a means of writing a stressed long *ā*, a North Lithuanian equivalent of *o*; cf. my work, *The Old Lithuanian Catechism of Baltramiejus Vilentas (1579): A Phonological, Morphological, and Syntactical Investigation* (The Hague, 1969), p. 103. In Daukša one finds both *-czia* (*-cze*) and *-czio*; cf. Christian S. Stang, *Vergleichende Grammatik der Baltischen Sprachen* (Oslo, 1966), p. 428. In Širvydas' *Punktay Sakimu* of 1629 and 1644 the first singular optative ends in *-ia* 13 times and in *-io* only twice (120,8; II 139,29); cf. Franz Specht, *Šyrwids Punktay Sakimu* (Göttingen, 1929), p. 42*. Specht here expresses the opinion that the normal East Lithuanian optative in *-czią* has nothing to do with that in *-czio*. This is contrary to Stang's view, but I believe that Specht is right. It is possible, as Stang believes, that the form in *-čio* was abstracted from the reflexive form *-čios(i)*, but it is not necessary to accept Stang's view to account for the origin of *-čio*. It is probably better to consider it as the normal development of **-tyā*. Additional forms from older texts cited by Adalbert Bezzenberger in *Beiträge zur Geschichte der litauischen Sprache* (Göttingen, 1877), pp. 212–213, end in *-czią* (equivalent to *-čią*; a Northern Lithuanian form comparable to *-čio*; from **-tyā*); *-cziau* (the Modern Standard Lithuanian form; from **-tya + u* from **ō*); *-czia* (from **-tyă*); and *-cze* (equivalent to *-čia*; from **-tyă*).

Stang is right in asserting that of the four types of first person singular optatives in Lithuanian, *būčiau*, *būčio*, *būčia*, and *būtáu*, the first and fourth are without any doubt of more recent origin; see Stang, *Vergl. Gr.*, 432. I agree with Stang that the theory advanced by J. Kazlauskas in *Lietuvių Kalbos Klausimai*, IV (1961), 84, and again in *Lietuvių Kalbos Istorinė Gramatika* (Vilnius, 1968), 400, according to which *-čia* arose from *-čiau* finds too little support in the other Lithuanian material to be believable. It seems more likely to assume that *-čiau* developed from *-čia* + the first person singular marker *-u*. Stang's theory in *Vergl. Gr.*, 432, that the form *būčiau* is a modification of *būčia* or *būčio* under the influence of the *ē*-preterite seems less probable.

In the dialect of Tverečius one finds two reflexive forms: both *-čăs* and *-č(i)es* (= *-čias*). This fact would seem to indicate that there were two different forms in Proto-Baltic, **-tyāsi* and **-tyăsi*, not merely one as Stang has assumed; cf. Jan Otrębski, *Wschodniolitewskie narzecze twereckie* I (Kraków, 1934), p. 392, and Christian S. Stang, *Das Slavische und Baltische Verbum* (Oslo, 1942), p. 251, and *Vergl. Gr.*, 432. In my opinion, Stang has not sufficiently emphasized the importance of the Tverečius reflexive form in -*ć(i)es*, which is comparable to the form *juõkčiasi* cited by Jablonskis.

I shall now turn to the problem of the origin of the first person singular optative form, which, according to Stang, "gehört zu den schwierigen Fragen der litauischen historischen Grammatik" (*Das Slavische und Baltische Verbum*, Oslo, 1942, p. 252). In his *Vergl. Gr.*, 433–434, Stang refers to the fact that in Daukša there is an example of *buczia* in the meaning 'as' (approximately equivalent to Russian будто). This form seems to be identical to the first person singular optative. I think that we have here an archaic use of the form which betrays its original meaning. Doubtless Stang is right in assuming that the first person singular optative was originally a formation with unreal meaning and without personal meaning. He further maintains that it is his belief that the first person singular optative goes back to a verbal noun of infinitival character, which in the course of time became more and more specialized in its use, and refers to Slavic examples of infinitive forms with a modal meaning. Inasmuch as the other forms of the optative are all formed from the supine, originally a verbal noun, it thus seems natural to assume that the first person singular is also derived from a verbal noun. Although I agree with Stang that the first person singular optative was originally a verbal noun, I do not believe that we are dealing here with an infinitive form but with another type of verbal noun—the gerund. With it may be directly compared the Sanskrit gerund in -*tyă̆*, originally the instrumental singular of an *i*-stem noun; cf. William Dwight Whitney, *Sanskrit Grammar* (Cambridge, Mass., 1889), p. 357, and Karl Brugmann and Berthold Delbrück, *Grundriss der vergleichenden Grammatik der indogermanischen Sprachen*, Vol. II.2 (Strassburg, 1892), pp. 632, 1416–1417. Thus the original meaning of *būčia* (from **bhūtya*) would have been 'being'. It is easy to see how the meaning 'as' could have developed from this and how the gerund could have taken on a modal meaning. In the oldest forms of the first person optative, -*čia* and -*čio*, the first person agent of the gerund would have been implied. Thus Stang's example *jéigu žinóčia, taĩ pasakýčia* 'If I knew, then I would tell' (p. 433) would originally have had a general, impersonal meaning 'If (there is) a knowing (by me), then (there is) a telling (by me).' It is obvious that the first person agent is clearly implied in such expressions. Later, however, it became necessary to characterize the gerund form as belonging exclusively to the first person singular, and then the marker -*u*, characteristic of the first person singular of verbs, was added to the form in -*čia* to make -*čiau*, the form of the literary language. When this form was created, it indicated the fact that the gerund had ceased to be felt as an impersonal form and was restricted solely to the specialized use of expressing the first person singular optative.

References

Bezzenberger, Adalbert, *Beiträge zur Geschichte der litauischen Sprache*, Göttingen, 1877.

Brugmann, Karl, and Berthold Delbrück, *Grundriss der vergleichenden Grammatik der indogermanischen Sprachen*[1], Vol. II.2, Strassburg, 1892.

Ford, Gordon B., Jr., *Old Lithuanian Texts of the Sixteenth and Seventeenth Centuries with a Glossary*, The Hague, 1969.

——, *The Old Lithuanian Catechism of Baltramiejus Vilentas (1579): A Phonological, Morphological, and Syntactical Investigation*. The Hague, 1969.

——, *The Old Lithuanian Catechism of Martynas Mažvydas (1547)*, Assen, 1971.

Gaigalat, Wilhelm, *Die Wolfenbütteler litauische Postillenhandschrift aus dem Jahre 1573. Mitteilungen der litauischen literarischen Gesellschaft*, V (1904).

Kazlauskas, J., "Iš optatyvo istorijos", *Lietuvių Kalbos Klausimai*, IV (1961), 73–91.

——, *Lietuvių Kalbos Istorinė Gramatika*, Vilnius, 1968.

Otrębski, Jan., *Wschodniolitewskie narzecze twereckie I.*, Kraków, 1934.

Specht, Franz, *Šyrwids Punktay Sakimu*, Göttingen, 1929.

Stang, Christian S., *Die Sprache des litauischen Katechismus von Mažvydas*, Oslo, 1929.

——, "Zur 1. P. Sg. Optativ im Litauischen", *Norsk Tidsskrift for Sprogvidenskap*, IX (1938), 298–300.

——, *Das Slavische und Baltische Verbum*, Oslo, 1942.

——, *Vergleichende Grammatik der Baltischen Sprachen*, Oslo, 1966.

Whitney, William Dwight, *Sanskrit Grammar*[2], Cambridge, 1889.

INGER FRØYSET & SIRI SVERDRUP LUNDEN

A "Baltic" Word in a Norwegian Dialect?

In the beginning of the 1950's a 70-year-old man mentioned that old people in Gjerstad, a community in Aust-Agder, used the word *barkomrötar* for 'carrots', Standard Norwegian *gulrötter*. Somewhat later we were asked by the editor of Norsk Ordbok whether we knew the word; Norsk Ordbok had a single record of it, from Gjerstad, and he was in doubt, because this was the only occurrence in any Norwegian dialect. We could confirm its authenticity, and have lately made investigations both in Gjerstad and the neighbouring communities. Only people from Gjerstad know it.

In the summer of 1969 a number of people in Gjerstad were asked whether they knew any synonym of *gulrot* (carrot). Four of these answered without prompting, a) *barkenrot* (two), b) *barkomrot* (two). In all cases the word had intonation I. Three of these people were more than 80 years old, the fourth about 60, and all of them stated that the word was obsolete in their youth. Younger people did not know any other word than *gulrot*, but a man of 60 recognized *barkenrot* as a word his father had mentioned.

The word has no etymological explanation in Norwegian. It seems warranted to compare it to a word which is found in a very restricted area around the Baltic. Kiparsky in his treatise on Baltic German[1] discusses the word, Baltic German *Burkan*, m., *Burkane*, f. 'Daucus carota'. This is recorded as early as 1577 in Riga (*op. cit.* p. 201), i.e., before the Russian influence in the Baltic, so the word cannot be regarded as a loan from Russian.

In Russian the forms are attested as *borkán, barkán, burkán*. The first two forms have been found in modern times in the Leningrad area, as well as in Russian dialects in the Estonian and Latvian Soviet republics as a synonym of 'carrot', *morkov*';[2] in the 16th and 17th cent. there are a few examples of the noun from the Novgorod area (Tikhvin), and in two Russian-German conversation books, which are believed to have had some connection with the Narva–Novgorod area.[3] The word has no Slavic etymology.

La. *buřkãns, buřkanis, buřkants* 'carrot' have been brought into the discussion by Endzelīns and Šmits, but Kiparsky rejects the hypothesis that these forms or Lith. *burkantas* are the source of the Baltic German form, for phonetic reasons.[4] Estonian *porgan(d)*, Finn. *porkkana* 'carrot' are also unexplained. Kiparsky seems to be in favour of Baltic German being the source of the other words, and mentions MLG *brackannige* in a vocabulary from Loccum, 1467 (or *brakannie, brackannye,* 'pastinaca sativa, Mohrrübe, gelbe Wurzel'[5]), "wahrscheinlich die klosterlateinische Wiedergabe des gr. Βράκανα τὰ ἄγρια λάχανα (HESYCH)". Vasmer[6] rejects this as "improbable", but as Kiparsky himself says: "Eine sichere Entscheidung ist nicht möglich."

When this word, with its limited geographical distribution around the Baltic and the Finnish Gulf, appears in one isolated Norwegian dialect, it seems reasonable to presume that it has come to Gjerstad from Denmark. It is known in Old Danish in the form *brackanner*, pl., Mod. Dan. *barkan(i)e-rod*, attested from Bornholm as *barkenaroer*, pl., Jutland *kannirödder*, pl.;[7] in Mod. Danish obsolete. It is known also in Southern Swedish (earlier Danish territory), as *barkanerod, barkenarod* etc.[8]

It is well-known that there was a relatively large influx of Swedish labourers to those parts of Norway in older times, but one should keep in mind also that clergymen and other officials before 1811 studied at the University of Copenhagen, and that above all the clergymen were pioneers in introducing cultivated plants. The fact that *barkenrot* became well known and commonly used in this restricted community, indicates an intensive and conscious connection between "Wort und Sache". The form *barkomrot* is obviously an innovation to suit native vocabulary.

Notes

1. V. Kiparsky, *Fremdes im Baltendeutsch.* (Mémoires de la Société néophilologique 11), Helsinki, 1936.

2. Slovar' russkich narodnych govorov, vyp. III, Leningrad, 1968.

3. Siri Sverdrup Lunden, *The Trondheim Russian-German MS Vocabulary*, Oslo, 1969, 128.

4. [Important for the discussion is the fact that no synonyms of another root are known in Latvian (dialects) for *burkāns* 'carrot' (as E. Šmite, Latviešu valodas un literatūras institūts, Riga, informs us); La. *burkāns* has been loaned also by Lith. dialects (*buřkonas*), cf. *Lietuvių kalbos žodynas*, I, Vilnius, 1968, s. v. — Ed.]

5. Lasch-Borchling, *Mittelniederdeutsches Handwörterbuch* I, Neumünster, 1956.

6. Max Vasmer, *Russisches etymologisches Wörterbuch*, I, Heidelberg, 1953.

7. *Ordbog over det danske Sprog*, bd. I, 1147, Copenhagen, 1919.

8. Sten-Bertel Vide, *Sydsvenska växtnamn*, Lund, 1966.

ALFRĒDS GĀTERS

Die Personennamen in den lettischen Volksmärchen

Hinsichtlich der in Märchen vorkommenden Personennamen macht A. Švābe[1] die folgenden allgemeinen Feststellungen: ,,When ... sometimes the heroes are called by names (e.g. Bearkiller, Pinedrawer, Hillroller etc.) then they cannot be regarded as real proper names but only as those denoting the inherited qualities of the heroes ... On the other hand, a legend (im Gegensatz zu den Märchen, A.G.) is always connected with a fixed place or person (z. B. *Kurbads*, A.G.)."

Bei der Durchsicht der lettischen Märchen begegnet man Personennamen in der Tat häufig. Dabei sind zwei Gruppen zu unterscheiden: 1. die von A. Švābe erwähnte Kategorie der Personennamen, die eine Eigenschaft oder Fähigkeit des Helden bezeichnen (sie wird an einer anderen Stelle näher abgehandelt), 2. die Kategorie der echten Personennamen, deren Vorkommen nur teilweise durch Vermischung der Märchen und Legenden bedingt ist.

Die zweite Gruppe, die mannigfaltig und zahlenmässig stärker vertreten ist als diejenige der oben erwähnten deskriptiven Heldennamen, enthält folgende Personennamen:

1. In einer Märchengruppe tritt als ein schlauer Held *gudrais Ansis* 'der kluge Ansis' (vgl. auch dt. *der gescheite Hans*)[2] auf; XI, 67³ Rūjiena, XI, 96 ibid., XI, 102 ibid., XI, 117 ibid., XI, 121, XI, 131 ibid., XI, 233, 239 ibid., ohne Epitheton XI, 132, 133, 136 ibid.; (nur Ansis) XI, 167 Mujāni; (auch der dritte, dumme Sohn) VII, 434 Riga, XI, 338 Džūkste; *dumais Ancis* 'der dumme A.'[4] XI, 234 Aumeisteṛi; XI, 234 Bilska, XI, 68 Aumeisteṛi; (der dritte Sohn) *Ansis* II, 38 Krūte; (ein starker Sohn) II, 187 Sloka; (ein starker Mann; vgl. dt. *der starke Hans*[5] II, 198 Dursupe; (ein Junge) X, 374 bei Riga, (ein Bruder) V, 253 Slampe; (ein junger Mann) X, 462 Dzirciems; *Ancis* XI, 333 Smiltene, (ohne Determination) XI, 105 Ērgḷi; (ein Sohn) *Ancītis* VII, 99 Krāslava, XI, 49 Blomi; (der einzige Sohn) *Ancītis*, weiter *Anšelis* IV, 267, 268 Kurland; (einer der drei Söhne: der dumme) *Ansītis* X, 63 Džūkste; (der kleinwüchsige Sohn) IX, 147 Skrunda; (ein junger Mann) *pušnieka Ansītis* 'des Nachbarn A.' XI, 335 Džūkste;

Atrastais Ansītis 'der gefundene A.' XI, 429 Pienava, (Anrede durch einen fremden Mann:) V. *Anšu, jaunais brāl!* 'Anšus, jüngster Bruder!' ibid. 431; (ein starker Sohn) *Ansiņš* VIII, 428 Rumbenieki.

Wie ersichtlich, ist der Name *Ansis* und seine Ableitungen über ganz Lettland verstreut und dabei tragen ihn verschiedene junge Märchengestalten. Auffällig ist allerdings, daß 'der kluge Ansis' in den exzerpierten Märchen auf Rūjiena und seine nächste Umgebung beschränkt ist; in der weiteren Umgebung (Mujāni, Smiltene, Aumeisteŗi und Bilska) treten hingegen alterierte Formen auf. Da die Märchen über den klugen Ansis der Sammlung *Gudrais Ansis un velns* I–III (1901–1902) des Schriftstellers Lapas Mārtiņš entnommen sind, sind ihre Authentizität und somit wohl auch die Authentizität des Namens *gudrais Ansis* nicht vollkommen sicher. Lapas Mārtiņš dürfte sein Märchenmaterial auf das einheitliche Thema des klugen Ansis hin mehr oder weniger eigenmächtig abgerundet haben.

2. In Hinblick auf den Stand des Namenträgers weniger einheitlich erscheint *Jānis* und seine Ableitungsformen:

a) Als Pendant zum Ausdruck *gudrais Ansis* kommt sporadisch *gudrais Jānis* vor: (der siebente, jüngste Sohn) V, 11 Kreis Riga, V. *gudro Jāni!* ibid. 13; (ein Sohn) *gudrīs Juonis* VIII, 282 Kapiņi.

b) In einem Fall wird über einen Sohn *stiprais Jānis* 'der starke J.' berichtet, der weiter im Text *Jānis* schlechthin genannt wird (II, 61 Riga).

c) Mehr verbreitet sind dagegen Fälle, in denen der jüngste (oft dritte), dumme Sohn mit dem Namen *Jānis* belegt wird (vgl. lit. *Jonas kvailys* 'J. der Dummkopf'[6]): IX, 42 Kreis Daugavpils, II, 153 Ludza, XI, 122 bei Jelgava; *muļka Jānitis* 'der dumme J.' IX, 87; ohne Attribut 'dumm' (der dritte, jüngste Sohn) *Jānis* IX, 42 Kr. Daugavpils, (der jüngste Sohn) *Jānitis* VIII, 229 Džūkste; *Juoneits* VII, 245 Kr. Rēzekne; (der dritte Sohn) V, 431 Rundāle; (ein dummer Junge) VII, 205 Nereta; (ein Dummkopf) V. *Jāni!* II, 116 Skrunda.

Jānis erscheint fernerhin bei namentlicher Aufzählung mehrerer Söhne ohne abschätzige Nebenbedeutung: II, 115 Riktere; *Juonis* VII, 289 Lettgallen, *Juoņis* VII, 402 Bebrene, *Juoņs* IX, 508 Lettgallen.

c) In einigen Märchen tragen den Namen *Jānis* Könige und Königssöhne: (ein junger König) IX, 217 Litauen, (ein Prinz) II, 152 Ludza, ebenso *Juonis* X, 395 o. O. in Lettgallen; *ķēniņa dāls, saukts Juonis ķeizars* (weiter *Juonis*) 'Königssohn, genannt J. der Kaiser' II, 377 Eglūna; V. *Jāni karaļdēl* 'Jānis, (du) Königssohn' IV, 362 Ludza.

d) Am häufigsten tritt *Jānis* jedoch bei verschiedenen Personen auf: (der Sohn eines Dienstmädchens) II, 380 Dole; (der Sohn eines Schmiedes) V, 17 Kr. Ludza; (ein Soldat) II, 122 Riga; (ein junger, wendiger Mann) II, 518

Smiltene; (der Bruder eines Mädchens Līvija) III, 190 Pustiņas pg.; (ein Diener) III, 76 Jaunroze; VI, 312 Nīca; (ein junger Mann) II, 519 Palsmane, IV, 362 Ludza, V, 48 Ūziņi, V, 449 Lutriņi, V, 104 f. Jaunauce; A. *lielo Jāni* 'den grossen Jānis' V, 104 Jaunauce, N. *liels Jānis* ibid. 105; (ein Sohn) *Juonis* IV, 404 Jāsmuiža; (ein junger Mann) X, 137 Zvirgzdine; (ein Sohn) X, 70 Makašāni; (ein reicher Mann) X, 392 Kapiņi; (ein Knecht) N. *Juonis*, V. *Juoņ* VII, 435 Makašāni; (ein Mann) *Juons* VIII, 51 Kr. Ludza; (ein junger Mann) VIII, 101 Preiļi, X, 272 Viļāni, VII, 433 ibid.; (der Sohn eines armen Mannes) VIII, 400 Baltinava; (ein Ehemann) V, 303 Dagda; (ein Arbeiter) promiscue *Juons* und *Juonis* XI, 58 Sakstagals; (ein Sohn) promiscue N. *Juonis, Juoņs* und *Juons* II, 250 Asūne; (ein Findling) A. *Atrostū Juoni, Atrostū Juoneiti* 'den gefundenen J.', weiter auch N. *Juons*, D. *Juoņam*, A. *Juoņu* X, 433 Ēķengrāve; (ein Arbeiter) *Juoņis* promiscue mit *Juonis*, V. *Juonis, Juoņis* und *Juonīt* XI, 55 f. Sakstagals; (ein Musikant) *Jānītis* V, 232 Vilce; (der Bruder eines Mädchens Zeltīte) IX, 468 Valmiera; (ein hübscher Bräutigam) XI, 339 Mežotne); (ein junger Mann aus der Nachbarschaft) XI, 338 Nereta, V, 181 Misa, X, 14 Jaunroze, V, 458 Smārde; (der liebste Wächter eines Königs) VI, 308 Aumeisteṟi; (ein junger Mann) *Juonīts* X, 272 Viļāni; (ein Vater) G. *Juoneiša* VIII, 51 Kr. Ludza; (ein Junge) promiscue *Juonis* und *Juonīts* VIII, 340 Kr. Ludza; (ein junger Mann) *Janelis* XI, 340 Jaunauce; (der Sohn eines Juden) *Jankelis* VIII, 182 Eglūna.

3. In beschränktem Maße begegnet man in den Märchen anderer Personennamen:

a) (Ein Landwirt: der große) *Pēteris*, (sein Knecht: der kleine) *Pēteris* VII, 384 o. O.; (ein Nachbar) XI, 341 Riga; (ein Sohn) IV, 281 Sāvenieki/ Kurland; (der Putzer eines Soldaten) X, 88 Ērgļi; (der Sohn einer Königstochter) A. *Pēteri* II, 380 Dole; (ein Sohn) *Pīteris* VII, 289 Lettgallen; (ein Bruder) *Piters* IX, 121 Kapiņi, IX, 443 Makašāni, IX, 508 Lettgallen; (der Sohn eines reichen Mannes) VIII, 400 Baltinava; (ein Mann) IX, 510 Makašāni, X, 84 Biržgale, N. *Pīters*, D. *Pīteram* und *Pīterim* XI, 129 Ludza; (ein junger Mann) IV, 284 Kr. Rēzekne; (ein alter Mann) VII, 479 Rēzekne; (ein Schneidergeselle) VII, 364 Lettgallen; *lilais Pīters* und *mozais Pīters* 'der große P.' und 'der kleine P.' VII, 360 Jāsmuiža, ebenso VII, 386 Balvi; (ein Sohn) *Pēteritis* VII, 355 Nīca, *Pītereits* VII, 486 Kr. Rēzekne; (ein schwächlicher Mann) A. *Vārgu Pēterīti* 'das sieche Peterchen' III, 51 Lieģi.

b) (Ein junger Mann) *Jēkabs* X, 276 Kr. Rēzekne; (ein Korndarrenaufseher) XI, 246 Nīca; (einer von drei Brüdern) *Jēkābs* II, 115 Riktere; (einer von zwei Burschen) *Jekabs* X, 462 Dzirciems; (ein sterker Mann) *gaṟais Jēkabs* 'der lange J.' V, 244 Lettgallen; (einer der drei Söhne) *Jākubs* VII, 289

Lettgallen; (ein Knecht) XI, 355 Lettgallen; (ein Bauer) IX, 79 Preiļi; (ein Korndarrenaufseher) *Jekaups* XI, 251 Trikāta; (ein Kranker) *Jēcis* X, 104 Bramberǵi; (ein Hirtenjunge) *Ješka* II, 515 Rūjiena.

c) (Ein junger Mann) *Juris* XI, 66 Brukna; (ein Gärtner) V, 258 Rūjiena; (einer von drei Söhnen) XI, 24 o. O., II, 38 Krūte; (ein Soldat) XI, 63 Vecpiebalga; (ein Bauer) II, 240 Lielvārde; *gaŗais Juris* 'der lange J.' II, 392 Jaunauce; *lelais Jurs* und *mozais Jurs* 'der große J.' und 'der kleine J.' VII, 362 Silajāņi; (ein armer Bauer) *Jurka* X, 4 Asūne.

d) (Der Nachbar) *Miķelis* XI, 345 Ērǵeme; (ein starker Sohn) *Miķēlis* IX, 102 Riga; (vermeintlicher Bruder eines Korndarrenarbeiters) XI, 251 Trikāta; (ein Sohn) *Miķielis* II, 59 Pļaviņas, II, 61 ibid.; (ein Bauer) *Mikels* V, 172 Makašāni; (einer der drei Bauernsöhne) *Mikeļs* VI, 487 Lettgallen; (ein junger Mann) *Mikus*, V. *Mikiņ* XI, 344 Džūkste; (einer von zwei Söhnen) *Miķelītis* VII, 356 Nīca, sonst noch V, 458 Smārde.

e) (Eine Stieftochter) *Anna* V, 451 Riga; (eine Frau) N. *Anna*, V. *Anniņ* X, 507 Nīca; (die einzige Tochter) *Annina* X, 512 Smiltene, IX, 345 Plāņi; (ein Mädchen) *Anite* V, 440 Ozolmuiža; (ein Waisenmädchen) VI, 107 Rēzekne; (eine Tochter) *Ane*, weiter *Anite* X, 70 Makašāni; *Anite* X, 526 Ozolmuiža; *Annele* XI, 431 Kroņa Bērznieki; (ein Zimmermädchen des Königs) *Annuža* II, 32 Mēdzūla.

f) (Ein Mädchen) *Madaļa* IV, 412 o. O., XI, 306 Kapiņi, V, 431 o. O.; (promiscue mit *Madalīte*) X, 525 Malinava; (eine Bauerntochter) *Madaļa* VII, 435 Makašāni; (eine der drei Töchter) VII, 330 Višķi; (eine Ehefrau) XI, 355 Lettgallen, XI, 273 Ozolmuiža/Lettgallen; (die Tochter eines Großfürsten) *Magdalēne* IV, 362 Ludza.

g) (Eine Königstochter) *Helena* IV, 407 Ludza; (die schöne) *Helena* VII, 338 Lettgallen; *Gudrā Helena* 'die kluge H.' IV, 409 Kr. Ludza; (die schöne) *Elina* VII, 326 Kr. Rēzekne; (die schöne) *Gele⁷* VII, 188 Skaista. Der Gedanke, daß hier eine fremde (Märchen)erzählung über die schöne Helena verarbeitet worden ist, liegt nahe. Jedenfalls hat dieser Name kaum die Bedeutung wie in den lit. Märchen *Elenytė*; dazu vgl. A. Šalčiūte, in *Lietuvių tautosakos apybraiža* (Vilnius, 1963, 343).

h) Nur vereinzelt treten auch *Krišus* und seine Varianten auf: (ein starker Sohn) VIII, 68 Džūkste; (einer der drei Söhne) XI, 49 Blomi; (der Sohn einer Frau und eines Wolfes) II, 297 Zaļenieki; (ein alter Mann) XI, 63 Vecpiebalga; (ein Sohn) *Krišelis* VIII, 417 Nīgranda; (ein Bruder) *mazais Kristapiņš* 'der kleine K.' II, 392 Jaunauce.

i) (Ein Mann aus der Nachbarschaft) *Andrejs* XI, 419 Lubāna; (ein junger Mann) XI, 431 o. O.; (einer der drei Brüder) II, 115 Riktere; (ein Sohn) *Andrivs* IX, 415 Sakstagals; (der Freund eines jungen Mannes)

Andrivs X, 272 Viļāni; (ein Ehemann) *Andres* XI, 368 Auce; (einer von zwei Söhnen) *Andriķis* VII, 356 Nīca.

j) (Ein Bauer) *Jezups* V, 170 Ludza; (ein Knecht) VII, 18 Daugavpils; (zwei Männer) VIII, 392 Lettgallen; (ein Sohn) promiscue mit *Jezupiņš* VII, 103 Zaļmuiža, Kr. Ludza.

k) (Einer von drei Söhnen) *Mārtiņš* II, 38 Krūte, XI, 24 o. O.; *bagātais Mārtiņš* 'der̓ reiche ̓M.' X, 419 Dzirciems; (ein Findling) VIII, 407 o. O.; (ein aus Eisen geschmiedeter Sohn) *dzelža Mārtiņš* 'Eisen-Mārtiņš' II, 229 Ēķengrāve; (ein Bauer) *Mārtic*, D. *Mārtinam*, V. *Mārč* XI, 258 f. Smiltene.

l) Nur ganz sporadisch erscheinen andere Namen: (ein Ehemann) *Ādams* V, 216 Baldone; (ein schöner Mann) *Uodums* II, 71 Kapiņi; (eine Frau) *Agata* X, 307 Makašāni; (ein Mädchen) *Agatiņa* IV, 278 Ludza; (ein Königssohn) *Albins* VII, 325 Kr. Rēzekne; (die Tochter des dummen Sohnes) *Adelite* IX, 330 Andrupine; (die schöne Frau eines Gutsherrn) *Amālija* IX Kr. Bauska; (eine Königin) *Anastasija* VII, 291 Lettgallen; (ein Sohn) N. *Aleksandra* XI, 406 Eglūna, N. *Aleksandra*, G. *Aleksandra* und *Aleksandris* IX, 407 Viļāni; (*Antons:*) (einer von mehreren Söhnen) *Ontons* VI, 487 Lettgallen; (Aschenbrödel) V, 369 Rēzekne; (ein Findling, getauft auf den Namen) *Aizmierstais Ontons* 'der vergessene O.', V. *Aizmierstais Onton* X, 416 Bērzgale; (der mittlere Sohn) *Baņuka* VII, 245 Birzgaļi, Kr. Rēzekne; (ein Sohn) A. *Bavu* IX, 354 Mežotne; (der Sohn eines Juden) *Boruks* VIII, 182 Eglūna; (ein Sohn) *Brencis* XI, 421 o. O.; (der jüngste Sohn) VII, 227 Rucava; (eine der drei Töchter) *Ceceleja* VII, 330 Višķi; (die Tochter eines Bauern) *Daiļa* IV, 448 Ūziņi; (eine schöne Königstochter) *Dailīte* II, 168 Sauka; (ein armer Junggeselle) *Dāvits* III, 30 Aumeisteŗi; (zwei Brüder) *Dominiks* und *Donuots* IX, 444 Kapiņi; (die schöne) *Duorta* V, 109 Lettgallen; (eine der Töchter) *Eda* XI, 421 o. O.; (eine faule Frau) *Edaļa* XI, 372 Možeiki; (ein Bauer) *Edgars* V, 170 Makašāni; (die Tochter eines Gutsherrn) *Elfrida* X, 277 Kr. Rēzekne; (ein Mädchen) *Elizābete* IX, 326 Kr. Ludza; (ein Ehemann) *Fricis* VIII, 372 o. O.; (ein kleines Kind) *Gregors* VII, 38 Līksna; (die Tochter eines Nachbarn) *Grieta* V, 145 Brukna; (eine Ehefrau) XI, 377 o. O., X, 123 Skulte; (eine von drei Königstöchtern) *Grita* X, 377 Rēzekne; (ein Sohn) *Gusts* IX, 532 Ūziņi; (ein Königssohn) *Gvida* X, 273 Kr. Ludza[8]; (einer von mehreren Brüdern) *Ignāts* VII, 402 Bebrene, IX, 443 Makašāni; (eine Ehefrau) V. *Ilba* 221 Bērzmuiža; (eine Ehefrau) *gudrā Ilze* 'die kluge I.' XI 368 Riga; (Hexen)[9] *gaŗā Ilze* 'die lange I.' III 47 Višiņķe, *resnā Ilze* 'die dicke I.' III, 44 o. O.; III, 45 Jaunroze, III, 46 Litene, Ūziņi; (einer von zwei Söhnen) *Indriķis* VII, 352 Riga, VII, 355 Nīca, (ein Teufel) VIII, 373 Gaujiena; (ein Mädchen) *Īva* III, 54 Lettgallen; (Juden) *Joska* XI, 297 Rēzekne, *Josks*, *Josels*, V. *Josel* X, 81 Dzirciemnieki; (ein kleiner Teufel) *Jukums* II, 62 Riga; (der ältere Sohn) *Juziks* VII, 245 Kr. Rēzekne; (ein Sohn) *Kārlis* V, 260 Dzirciems, V. *Kārl* I, 366 Riga; (ein Patenkind) VI, 318 Ūziņi; (ein junger Mann) *Karlis*, D. *Karļam* VIII, 353 Lettgallen; *Kārlīts*, A. *Kārlīti* IX, 345 Plāņi; (ein Königssohn) *Kazimirs* V, 41 Daugavpils; (eine der drei Königstöchter) *Katre* X, 377 Rēzekne; (das Kind eines Teufels) *Konstantiņš* V, 464 Udze; (eine Königstochter) *Kristīna*, V. *Kristi* II, 77 Valka; (eine Magd) *Lība* I, 218 Jelgava; (die Tochter einer armen Frau) *Līda* X, 264 Varkava; (eine Tochter) *Lienīte* X, 538 Alūksne; (eine Königstochter) *Līza* II, 377 Eglūna; (eine schöne Frau) *Līze* VII, 103 Kr. Ludza; *vecā Līze* 'die alte L.', V. *Līz* VIII, 372 o. O.; (ein Mädchen) *Līvija* III, 190 Pustiņas pg.; (der Königssohn) *Ludis* VI, 319 Ūziņi; (ein Sohn) *Ļada* VIII, 23 Kr. Ludza; (eine wohlhabende Tochter) *Maija* V, 451 Riga; (eine von zwei Töchtern) XI, 421 o. O.; (ein Nachbarmädchen) IX, 468 Valmiera; (ein altes Mütterchen im Himmel) *Māŗa* IX, 331 Džūkste; (eine Ehefrau) *Muora* V, 303 Dagda; (die Schwester des Königssohnes Jānis) *Marija* IV, 364 Ludza; (ein kleines Mädchen) IX, 348 Nīca; (ein Mädchen) *Mareite* VII, 248 Kr. Rēzekne; (eine Tochter) *Marianna* IX, 333 Lestenieki, *Marjanna* VII, 330 Višķi; (der reiche) *Markus* X, 279 Nīca; *Marks*, G. *Marka* X, 403 Atašiene; (Juden) *Moška* und *Leiba* XI, 297 Rēzekne; (eine Ehefrau) *Od*, G. *Ods*, D. *Ode* XI, 368 Auce; (ein Junge) *Ojars* VIII, 424 Džūkste; (ein Sohn) *Puovuls* X, 393 Kapiņi, (ein Junge) VII, 464 Asūne; (der jüngste Sohn) *Poavils* II, 413 Sauka; (der Sohn eines einfachen Mannes) *Prancis* X, 395 Lettgallen; (eine Tochter) *Praņa* VI, 224 Rēzekne; (eine der drei Königstöchter) *Roza* X, 377 Rēzekne; (ein Sohn) *Salimons* X, 353 Lettgallen; (ein Königssohn) *Salomons* V, 109 Lettgallen; (der Name von hundert Jungen) *Simeons* VII, 38 Līksna; *Sims* (*Sīmanis*) X, 31 Maliena; (eine schöne Königstochter) *Skaistīte* II, 157 o. O., II, 166 Livland, VII, 128 Rūjiena, V. *Skaistīte* II, 166 Veckārķi; *Stepiņš* XI, 290 Prauliena; (eine Tochter) *Tekla* II, 59 Pļaviņas; (der Sohn einer Witwe) *Toms* VII, 444 Stiene; (eine Frau) *Trīna*, A. *Trīni* XI, 418 Jaunauce; (ein Teufel) *Vaņķa* VIII, 341 Kr. Ludza; (ein armer Mann) *Vilis* X, 520 Džūkste; (ein schönes Mädchen) *Virginija* VII, 331 Višķi; (ein Sohn) *Zyberts* VII, 330 Višķi.

4. Es finden sich einige Belege für eine Verbindung der Personennamen mit einem Genetivattribut, das die Herkunft oder die Qualität bezeichnet und funktionell dem im Lett. üblichen vorangestellten Nachnamen im Genetiv gleichkommt: (ein im Unterholz gefundener Junge) *Elkšņu Mārtiņš* 'Erlen-M.' VIII, 407 o. O.; (ein Junge, der sich aus einer Erle entwickelt hat) *Elkšņu Mārtinītis* 'Erlen-M.' II, 468 Sauka; (ein starker Mann) *Elkšņu Pēteris* 'Erlen-P.' II, 205 Riktere; (ein in der Gabelung einer

Esche gefundener Knabe) *Oša Jānis* 'Eschen-J.', V. *Oša Jān*, A. *Oša Jāni* X, 397 f. Lubāna; (ein am See gefundener Knabe) A. *Ezerjāni* 'Jānis vom See' V, 48 Ūziņi, V. 50 Kr. Jelgava; (der Sohn eines Mädchens und eines Bären) *Lāču Krišus* 'Bären-K.' II, 256 Brukna; (ein behaarter Sohn) *Lāču Jānis* 'Bären-J.' II, 259 Bērzaune; (der Sohn einer Stute) *Lāčaustiņu Jānis* 'Bärenohren-J.' II, 314 Gulbene; *Dundurjānis* 'Bremsen-Jānis' VII, 145 Smiltene; (der jüngste Sohn) *Veļu Juons* 'J. der Verstorbenen' II, 133 Rēzekne; *Vjēja-Juoņeits* 'Wind-J.', V. *Vjēja-Juoņeit* VI, 470 f. Viļāni; (der Sohn einer Magd) A. *Pumpuru Miķēli* 'Knospen-Miķēlis' II, 396 Grāvendale; *Kaula Pēteris* 'Knochen-P.' VII, 167 Preiļi; (eine Jungfrau unter wilden Tieren) *Meža Madaļa* 'Wald-M.' VIII, 401 Baltinava; (eine Witwe namens) *Sipolu Mādža* 'Zwiebeln-M.' VIII, 417 Nīgranda; *Kara Pēteris* 'Soldaten-P.' VIII, 80 Smiltene; (der Sohn einer Königstochter) A. *Vasaras Miķēli* 'den Sommer-Miķēlis' II, 396 Grāvendale.

Es handelt sich hierbei also um Prototypen der genetivischen Verwendung des Familien- bzw. Gehöftnamens, die in den Märchen allerdings nur spärlich belegt ist; so *Dēliņu Anna* XI, 408 Bērznieki; A. *Dēņu meitu Anneli* 'die Tochter der Familie bzw. des Hofes Dēņi' XI, 431 Kroņa Birznieki; *Šauceiša Juoneiša dāls* 'der Sohn des Jānis Šauceitis' VIII, 51 Kr. Ludza; (ein Zigeuner) V. *Čipu Tāteli* XI, 314 Džūkste.

An zweigliedrige, aus Vor- und Nachnamen bestehende Gefüge erinnern zuletzt auch folgende Bildungen: *Nūkristjēja jū Juons Palnuruška* 'man taufte ihn auf den Namen Juons Aschenbrödel' II, 50 Viļāni; (ein Herr) *Marks Boguotais* 'Marks der Reiche' X, 394 Lettgallen; *Ievulis Atradenis* (zu *ieva* 'Faulbaum' und *atrast* 'finden') X, 180 o. O.; mit russ. Namensform *Jānis Vetrovičs*, V. *Jāni Vetrovič* II, 156 Kr. Ludza.

5. Aus der vorstehend gebrachten Zusammenstellung geht eindeutig die überragende Rolle des Männernamens *Jānis* hervor; weniger bedeutsam ist *Ansis*, und nur mit erheblichem Abstand folgen *Pēteris, Jēkabs, Juris, Miķelis, Anna, Madaļa, Helena, Krišus, Andrejs, Jāzeps* und *Mārtiņš*[10], während die übrigen im 19. Jhd. oft gebrauchten Namen (*Ilze, Dāvis, Līze, Kārlis, Ieva* u. a.) nur in einigen wenigen Fällen belegt sind.

Die Bevorzugung von *Jānis* dürfte einesteils in der allgemeinen Beliebtheit dieses Männernamens, zum andern darin begründet sein, daß der Name *Jānis* in der lett. Folklore auch sonst eine eminente Bedeutung hat (im Sinne des mythologischen *Jānis* der Dainas ist er in den Märchen allerdings nicht belegt). Darüberhinaus spielen dieser Name bzw. seine Korrelate auch in den entsprechenden Märchen anderer Völker eine bedeutende Rolle (vgl. lit. *Jonas*, russ. *Ivan*), so daß man seine Häufigkeit auch noch unter diesem Aspekt sehen muß. Im Übrigen ist der Gebrauch der echten Personennamen in den lett. Märchen in Bezug zu der Epoche des Traditors zu sehen. So vermutet auch O. Ambainis[11], daß die lett. Märchengestalten unter dem Aspekt, die nahen Beziehungen der Helden zu dem Leben des Volkes zu betonen, mit einem einheimischen Eigennamen belegt sind. Wie aus der namentlichen Zusammenstellung ersichtlich, geht diese Tendenz soweit, daß stellenweise auch fremde Herrschaften mit einem lettischen bzw. volkstümlich umgewandelten Namen bedacht sind (vgl. Juonis der Kaiser, König Jānis, die Tochter eines Großfürsten Madaļa, die Königstöchter Grīta, Katre und Roza u. a.). Andererseits erkennt man an einigen Stellen auch die Neigung, für einheimische Märchengestalten fremde Modenamen des 19. Jhdts einzuführen (vgl. das Mädchen Līvija, Adelīte — die Tochter des dummen Sohnes, der Bauer Edgars, das Mädchen Elizābete, Lida — die Tochter einer armen Frau u. a.) und fremde Herrschaften mit einem wenig alltäglichen Namen zu benennen (vgl. die Königssöhne Albins, Salomons, die Königin Anastasija, die adligen Frauen Amālija, Elfrida u. a.).

Schließlich haben auch die für die Epoche des nationalen Erwachens im 19. Jhd. charakteristischen Bestrebungen, erdachte echt lettische Namen poetischen Gehalts einzuführen[12], in den Märchen vereinzelt ihren Niederschlag gefunden: hierzu gehören die Namen der schönen Frauen *Daiļa*, *Dailīte* und *Skaistīte* (zu *daiļš* bzw. *skaists* 'schön'), die bereits von P. Šmits[13] als Namen echter Volksüberlieferungen angezweifelt worden sind. Der Hang zu einer national betonten Symbolik der Epoche der Märchenaufzeichnung äußert sich in dem folgenden isoliert dastehenden Beispiel: *Šis valsts ķeizaram bija trīs meitas: Kurija, Vidija un Libija. Kurija bija vecākā, Vidija vidējā un Libija jaunākā* 'der Kaiser dieses Reiches hatte drei Töchter: K., V. und L. Kurija (von *Kursa, Kurzeme* 'Kurland') war die älteste, *Vidija* (in Anlehnung an *Vidzeme* 'Livland' und *vidus* 'Mitte') die mittlere und Libija (von *Libija* 'Livenland') die jüngste' VII, 100 Krāslava[14].

Vergleicht man die Personennamen, die innerhalb eines Märchens nebeneinander erscheinen, so fällt auf, daß vor allem in den lettgallischen Märchen mitunter Zusammenstellungen *Jānis* und *Pēteris* sowie *Marija* und *Magdalēna* vorkommen (zwei Brüder *Juoņs* und *Piters* IX, 508 o. O., drei Söhne *Juonis*, *Piters* und *Jākubs* VII, 289, ähnlich VII, 400 Baltinava; die Schwester eines Königssohnes *Marija*, die Tochter eines Fürsten *Magdalēne* IV, 364 Ludza), was den Gedanken an einen biblischen Einfluß in der Namengebung der Märchen nahelegt. Es sei bemerkt, daß das Namenpaar *Jānis* und *Pēteris* z. T. auch in den lit. Märchen auftritt: *Jonas* und *Petruška* in *Lietuvių tautosaka* IV, 178; *Jonukas, Petras* (und *Juozukas*) ibid. IV, 153.

6. Vereinzelt offenbart sich in der Namengebung geradezu eine spielerische Freude zum Abenteuer, wie das der folgende Beleg X, 395 aus Lettgallen veranschaulicht: *Kēneņam* ... *napatyka, kam taids vinkuoršs vuords* [*Prancis*], *jū nūsaucja ķēneņš par Prancivilcijanu* 'dem König gefiel nicht, daß er so einen einfachen Namen [Prancis] hatte; daher benannte ihn der König Prancivilcijans', N. *Prancivilcijans* und *Prancivilcijanus* (ibid.). Fremden Einflüssen und dem Hang, dem bekannten Milieu eine ungewöhnliche Färbung zu verleihen, verdankt man auch den Gebrauch der (z. T. verstümmelten) Namen wie (eine Königstochter) *Milicigrona* X, 395 Lettgallen; (die Tochter des Herrn eines verzauberten Schlosses) *Aidonīte* VIII, 399 Jaunpiebalga; (eine hinter drei Königsreichen lebende, nur namentlich erwähnte Prinzessin) *Bradulbudara* VI, 312 Nīca; (ein Kriegführer) *Kartauzis* X, 274 Kr. Ludza (vielleicht eine Kontamination von *Kartause* 'Mönchskloster' und *Kartusche* 'Pulverladung eines Geschützes; Patronentasche'?); (ein Sohn namens) *Čuinis* IX, 370 Džūkste; (ein Mann namens) *Kvadra*, D. *Kvadrai* X, 140 f. Makašāni; (ein Mann) *Kasmačs* VII, 322 Kr. Ludza (russ. *Kosmáč* 'ein Mensch mit zottigem Haar'). Hier schließen sich weitere russische Namensformen an: (ein starker Sohn) *Ivanuška* VII, 70 Jaunauce; (der Sohn einer Königin) *Ivans-Petrovičs* II, 336 Kr. Ludza; (der Sohn eines Kochs) *Kukarovičs-Semenovičs* II, 336 Kr. Ludza, weiter ibid. 338 auch einfach *Kukarovičs* (im Anschluß an *kuchárka* 'Köchin'?); weiterhin (ein starker Mann) *Kunogins* II, 213 Preiļi; (ein alter Mann) *Sadaks* II, 339 Kr. Ludza; (ein nicht näher charakterisierter Mann) *Guņķens* ibid.; (ein Mann, der eine vom Teufel besessene Königstochter heilt) *Paršus* III, 14 Tirza (zu lit. *paršas* 'verschnittenes Schwein'?).

a) Vielleicht dürfen bei einigen dieser Namen schon Beziehungen zu Familiennamen gesucht werden. Ganz in dieser Richtung liegen: (zwei Bauern) *Lasis* ('Lachs') und *Kalniņš* (Demin. 'Berg') X, 347 Alūksne; (der Freund einer Ehefrau) *Kraukļis* ('Rabe') VII, 103 Kr. Ludza; (ein furchtloser junger Mann) *Miezis* ('Gerste') XI, 157 Džūkste; (ein reicher Kaufmann) *Zurka* VII, 103 Kr. Ludza; (ein alter Soldat) *Lustiņš* (zu *luste* 'Lust'?) X, 86 Blomi; *Rima tāvs* 'Vater Rims', D. *Rimam* X, 121 Varakļāni; (ein Bauer) *Pampis* XI, 143 Blīdiene; vielleicht auch (zwei Verwandte) *Gaitiņiņš* und *Skritulīts* (lett. *skritulis* 'Scheibe') VIII, 342 Lettgallen; D. *Baltzemes* *ķēniņam* 'dem König Baltzemes' VI, 333 f. Lāči, weiter N. *Baltzemnieks* ibid. 335; (ein Kutscher) *Krumultiņš* V, 220 Bērzmuiža; (der Nachname eines Bauern) *Skrabs* XI, 365 Sakstagals; Hofname *Beltes*, dazu der Familienname des Bauern N. *Beltis* VIII, 417, 419 Nīgranda, D. *Beltem* ibid. 418, 419; Hofname *Ikvildas*, Familienname D. *Ikvildam* I, 217 Zaļenieki; (ein alter Mann) *Repis* ('Tabaksbeutel'?) XI, 177 Ābeļi; (ein lahmer Junge, genannt von seinen Brüdern und der Mutter eines Teufels ohne Motiv) *Rimševics* (Schelte?) VII, 64 o. O.; zuletzt auch einige Teufelsnamen[15].

b) Freude am Wortspiel und Witz in der Namengebung äussern sich deutlich in folgenden Belegen: (die Töchter eines Fuchses) *Darija* (volksetymologisch zu *darīt* 'tun'?), *Parija* (zu *parīt* 'verschlingen'?) und *Marija* I, 327 Kroņa Vircava; (ebenso) *Marija, Darija, Lemesnīca* ('Pflugschar') und *Kolps* ('Knecht') I, 329 Kapiņi; (*tris māsām*) *bijuši nesmuki vārdi: Deģe, Nagata* (russ. *nagotá* 'Nacktheit') un *Pūžiņa* '(drei Schwestern) hätten häßliche Namen gehabt: D., N. und P.' XI, 429 Šķibe; (drei Mädchen verkleiden sich als Bettlerinnen und geben an, sie hießen) *Deģe, Ņākaža* und *Piža* XI, 429 Nīca (vgl. drei Jungen *Degis, Nupazas* und *Bizas* in einem lit. Märchen[16]); (ein Mädchen) *Grūša* XI, 434 Ogresgals; (ein Bräutigam namens) *Sprukstiņš* ('Geck') XI, 431 Kroņa Bērznieki.

c) Mit Personennamen sind in den Märchen auch Tiere benannt: (eine Hündin) *Kristīna* IV, 422 Aumeisteŗi; *katrai čūskai esot savs vārds ... Tikai vajagot sieviešu vārdā saukt: Ilziņa, Līzīte, Grietiņa ...* 'jede Schlange habe einen Namen ... Man müsse (sie) nur mit einem Frauennamen rufen: (Dem.) Ilze, Līze, Grieta ...' IX, 71 Rauna; (ein Bär) *Andrievs*, (ein Wolf) *Juris* und (ein Fuchs) *Anna* I, 154 Lubeja; (eine Krähe) *Dārča* I, 172 Lietavas Žeime; (ein Hase) *Kārklu Jēcis* 'J. von den Weidensträuchern' XI, 98 Gulbene; (aus dem Russ. der Name für den Bären) V. *Miška* I, 206 Valgunte, (ein Bär, genannt von einem Russen) XI, 245 Jaunbebŗi.

d) Schliesslich erscheinen noch Personennamen in einigen magischen Beschwörungsformeln: V. *Laurīt* IX, 133 Preiļi; V. *Janeļ* IV, 426 Kr. Rīga; V. *Ziman* (aus *Simeon*?) IV, 433 Lielvārde; V. *Zalaman* (aus *Salomon*) IV, 445 Dzirciems. Der mit großem Buchstaben geschriebene Ruf *Ķitū, Ķitū!* IV, 434 Ķevelnieki ist bei der Aufzeichnung des Märchens dagegen fälschlich als ein Nomen proprium aufgefaßt (vgl. estn. Lockruf für Katzen *kitu, kitu!*).

Um zusammenzufassen: echte Personennamen treten in den Märchen häufig auf, wobei sich besonders *Jānis* und *Ansis* hervorheben. Der letztere Name erscheint in erster Linie bei sich ähnelnden Märchengestalten (der kluge Junge Ansis), während sich bei *Jānis* mehr Anzeichen (z. T. traditionsbedingter) polymorpher Motivstrukturen erkennen lassen (Jānis — der dritte, jüngste Sohn, der einfältige Jānis, der kluge Jānis, Jānis — allgemein ein Märchengestalt u. a.). Die obige Zusammenstellung erhellt auch die Verbreitung von *Jānis* über ganz Lettland, wohingegen andere Namen, die mehrfach belegt sind, eine regionäre Begrenzung aufweisen können (so *Helena, Madaļa* und *Jezups* in Lettgallen, *Krišus* und *Mārtiņš* in Mittel- und West-Lettland). Im Übrigen ist der Gebrauch der echten Personennamen für gewöhnlich rein okkasionell, weitgehend von den Gepflogenheiten der Namengebung im 19. Jhd. abhängig. Nur in beschränktem Ausmaß erscheinen daneben Modenamen bzw. Namen der jüngeren Generation des 19. Jhdts. Isoliert stehen im Volk unbekannte, z. T. expressiv gebrauchte Namen, von denen einige eine erhebliche Verstümmelung erfahren, sowie Familiennamen. Jedenfalls offenbart sich in der besprochenen Namengebung eine ausgeprägte Bezogenheit zum Alltagsleben des Traditors, die nur gelegentlich durch den Hang zum Abenteuer auch in der Benennung und durch den Zwang der fremden Grundlage des Märchens durchbrochen wird.

Anmerkungen

1. *Latvian Folk-Tales*: The New Word, Latvian Monthly Magazine for Literature and Art in Meerbeck, No. 2, 1946, 33; ders., *Latviešu tautas pasakas* : Jaunais Vārds, Latviešu literātūras un mākslas mēnešraksts, No. 2 (Meerbeck 1946), 31.

2. J. Bolte u. G. Polívka, *Anmerkungen zu den Kinder- u. Hausmärchen der Brüder Grimm* I (1913), 311.

3. Nur mit römischen Zahlen werden die hier exzerpierten Bände der Märchensammlung *Latviešu tautas teikas un pasakas*, hrsg. von Pēteris Šmits (Motivverzeichnis von Haralds Biezais), I–XI, Waverly, Iowa, 1962–1968, angegeben (verkürzt LTTP); Kr. = Kreis; pg. = *pagasts* 'Gemeinde, Bezirk'.

4. Vgl. auch dt. *Hans Dumm, der dumme Hans*, Bolte u. Polívka, *op. cit.*, 487.

5. P. Šmits, LTTP I 65; Bolte u. Polívka, *op. cit.*, II (1915) 301.

6. *Lietuvių tautosaka* IV (Vilnius 1967), 177.

7. Von weißruss. Гелена, P. Šmits, *op. cit.*, VII 188.

8. Der heilige Gvīda (Vītus), gestaltet nach poln. Vorlagen, P. Šmits, *op. cit.*, X 276.

9. Über die Namen der Hexen und Teufel vgl. Verf., *Raiņa un Aspazijas Gadagrāmata 1970. gadam* (Västerås 1969), 61 f.

10. In den lit. Märchen bes. *Jonas, Petras, Martynas* sowie die Frauennamen *Elenytė, Sigutė* und *Eglė*, A. Šalčiūtė, in: *Lietuvių tautosakos apybraiža* (Vilnius 1963), 341, 343.

11. In: *Latviešu literatūras vēsture* I (Rīgā 1959), 181.

12. Vgl. Verf., KZ. 82, 308 ff.

13. *Op. cit.* I, 32, IV, 449, VII, 130. *Skaistīte* dürfte nach P. Šmits, *op. cit.* I 32, 128 von T. Zilpaušs — dem Übersetzer der arabischen Märchen *Tūkstoš un viena nakts* II (Jelgava 1867) — im Anschluß an die arabische Vorlage (Zilpaušs, *op. cit.*, 53) erfunden sein.

14. Daß die Namen vom Traditor erdacht sind, erwähnt P. Šmits, *op. cit.* VII, 101.

15. Darüber Verf., *Raiņa un Aspazijas Gadagrāmata 1970. gadam*, 61.

16. *Lietuvių tautosaka* IV, 269.

Personal Names in Latvian Fairy Tales

The heroes of Latvian fairy tales possess, firstly, names which reflect their functions—*nomina appellativa* (Pine Drawer, Hill Roller etc.); secondly, proper Christian names. Heroes of the former category usually possess superhuman attributes; the latter are usually real persons with the qualities of an ordinary human being, though perhaps possessed with a love of adventure. The largest group consists of names familiar in the everyday life of the 19th century, each particular name being mentioned in only a few fairy tales. This leads to the conclusion that the names are only occasionally used in the fairy tales.

Of the names which appear in the fairy tales, the most usual are *Jānis* and *Ansis*, while *Pēteris*, *Jēkabs*, *Juris*, *Krišus*, *Miķēlis* and *Mārtiņš* are used less frequently. Other personal names familiar in the 19th century seldom appear.

In one cycle of fairy tales a particularly clever character is called *Ansis*— 'Clever Ansis', but the name *Jānis*, on the contrary, has been given to various heroes. The bearer of the name *Jānis* may be an average man, a real hero, or a king, but nowhere in the fairy tales does he possess the mythological properties of the *Jānis* mentioned in the folksongs or *dainas*.

The frequent usage of the name *Jānis* in the fairy tales could be explained either by its popularity in real life or by a certain inclination to consider it as a literary image of the polymorphic fairy tales.

JURIS GREENE

The Typology of Anaphorae and Polyptota in Latvian Folksongs

1.

The armory of rhetorical figures contains among others anaphorae and polyptota. Finding a precise and permanently valid dividing line between them has proved particularly elusive; it has its own history, and has persecuted rhetoricians for a few millenia. If a-ae[1] are a repetition of the same word or phrase in several successive clauses (OED 62), not necessarily in the same flexional form, and if p-a are rh.f. consisting of a repetition of a word in *different* flexional forms (OED 1541), we are forced to the conclusion that the p-n is a condensed and specialized variety of an a-a. Thus, a repetition of a word in a different form (:HH)[2], or, although in the same flexion, with a different spelling, or, owing to differing aspects or other reasons, with a different prefix (:WW), or a diminutive ending in one case (:gg) or two different diminutive endings (:DD), constitutes an a-a, even if viewed as a condensed form it is more reminiscent of a p-n. On the other hand, a repetition fulfilling a different grammatical function may be a perfect p-n without necessarily having different endings, as represented in English poetry by Tennyson's: "And did not dream it was a dream".

The a-ae and its condensed and specialized form, the p-n, are unmistakenly psychological phenomena of a very great antiquity and complexity, differing from language to language, depending on the environment and the context in which they appear. They have become an important part of the human rhetorical armory. The amount of variability depends on many factors. Firstly, not all languages have the same rules and possibilities of flexion, secondly, the morphological possibilities of languages are far from equal, and thirdly, languages differ very much in the respect to which word-groups with all their derivatives cluster together and claim descent from a single prototypal form, and in this sense one is able to state that languages are monophyletic (OED 1274) to a greater or smaller degree.

These rh.f. have been consciously applied in literature, and we are able to trace them in the Psalms, in the tragedies of Ancient Greece; we speak about Miltonian and Shakespearian p-a, and in our days Roman Jakobson has tracked down an acrobatic author in this field by the name of V. Xlebnikov.

But much greater ingenuity is shown in that area of their application where one is able to add the element of the unconscious and the unpremeditated. And here appear folklore, and folksongs as a form of folklore, where, one should think, rules of rhythm and poetics added to the normal grammatical system of the language in question would rather limit the possibilities of use of these rh.f.

Applied to the poetic form of Latvian folksongs, the dividing line between a-ae and p-a could perhaps be formulated in the following way: the p-n is a repetition of a word in different flexional form, not necessarily with a different ending (:DQ), it is limited within one dipody, its two or three (:HA, YG) elements may constitute a single line, but may also spread over the dipody, its elements may be the subject and predicate of a sentence (:aP, aR), or the dipody may be a complex sentence (:KK) within which the elements of the p-n have any syntactical value, even form the epithetal part of it alone. But even accepting these rules, one is faced sometimes with the problem whether a dividing comma necessarily directs one towards the conclusion that the rh.f. is rather an a-a, or may be it is still qualifiable as p-n. Sometimes, in the written text of the sources used for this article a comma is obviously mistakenly used at the end of the line, illogically dividing a dipodic sentence (:XF), but more often the written text displays no comma where one ought to expect one: either two sentences are linked together with a common predicate (:RP), or even common subject and predicate (:QQ), or the subject of the first sentence is the object of the second—all within the same dipody (:aB). On the other hand, a dipody may contain without a dividing comma two sentences linked together with a hinge-like p-n, where its first element (the last word of the first line) is complementary to the object, but the second element (the first word of the next line) is the predicate of the second sentence, and we still decide in favour of the p-n, like in W 2/3–4: "Es gaid' irbes iztekot Iztek ciema zeltenit", 'I waited (for the) partridge (to) come forth (And there) came forth (the) maiden (of the) village'.

A dipody may also be a descriptive address without proper subject and predicate (:GK), or two commands with a common addressee, and the p-n having merely an epithetal role in the first line and being the object of the second command (:BD). However, a dipody consisting of a question and an indicative explanatory sentence (:GY) would belong rather to the class of a-ae.

On the other hand, viewing the problem from the point of the p-n, a-ae are similar rh.f. which are either an invariable repetition of a word,[3] or which are linked with a second element in a neighbouring dipody or even further apart (W 244/1+5, B 108/1+5), or which may occur in an area where etymologically similar elements converge, either in the same case (:AA–GG, aa–gg), or e.g. when two adverbial forms constitute an a-a within one dipody (:HH).

There are two main patterns of p-a: the disjected p-n, where there is a break between both elements of the p-n, and the conjected p-n, where the elements follow one after the other (:AR, CO). It may even happen that two conjected p-a of the same type, immediately following each other, constitute one single line of the song (:HO), or occur in both lines of the dipody (B 2089/1, 2, BW 7191/1, 2), or in the corresponding lines of two dipodies of the same song (B 2502/3, 5, BW 3850/2, 4). These three forms of parallelism are equally known with disjected p-a: In one line (:Pa), in two lines of the same dipody (BW 339/1, 2), and in corresponding lines of two dipodies (B 1284/1, 3, BW 251/1, 3).

A p-n consisting of three elements in one stretch within one line is a very rare rh.f. (:GW, HA, YG), but a tripartite rh.f. consisting of a p-n and with a third element radiating outside the polyptotic dipody as an a-a occurs quite often. Tripartite a-ae are also known. At times their central element disrupts a monotonous invariable a-a, thus creating a pair of flexible ones, as e.g. in the case of W 67/2+4 (:HK, KH). Such configuration may cover one line, the first two words are an invariable a-a, but the second with the third form a conjected p-n (:TG, Tb), or with the last word of the line a disjected p-n (:KA, KP). From a pair of invariable a-ae (BW 1207/2) may evolve a pair of flexible a-ae crossing into the second dipody (:KD). A dipody may start with an invariable a-a and end either with a word forming a p-n with any of the anaphoral words of the first line (:PR), or, with a different flexional form of the same word, that only appears to be identical, forms a flexible a-a with the first exclamation (:Ta).

Further, the hinge-like position of an a-a in the centre of a dipody may be even enlivened by the fact that one of its elements forms another, although an invariable, a-a with the first word of the dipody (:WT). A more sophisticated one is the case of W 252 where the first line consists of two p-a of different kinds (:TH and DO), and both radiate a-ae beyond the first dipody: one of them twice (:Dd and OX), which among themselves form a new disjected p-n (:Xd), and the other—once, which with the original first p-n of the first line ("Tec tecini", 'Flow flowingly') form again a pair of flexible a-ae (i.e. imp/pr and adv/pr: "Ietek", '(She) flows (in)'). These radiated a-ae have mostly a downward direction, i.e. one of the elements of p-n is the first element of an a-a (:WT), but there are known cases where the a-a precedes the p-n (:BW, Fe), or even of two identical p-a in neighbouring dipodies (W 86): "Rige! Rige! balta! balta! Kas to baltu balinaj:", 'Riga! Riga! white! white! Who did bleach her white:'. Actually, one can always speak about two preceding a-ae that come down from a common 'apex' to the line of the p-n, i.e., taking the examples just mentioned, besides the vertical (:BW) a-a one could speak about a gen.s/pt a-a, besides the vertical 'end of the line' (:FE) a-a—about a loc.s/gen. pl a-a, and both preceding a-ae of W 86, down from the invariable a-a of line one, would be two adjectival voc.s/acc.s a-ae (W 86/1 + 2, 1 + 4) and two ad/pt vertical a-ae, all from the same 'apex'. Both elements of the preceding a-a (W 121/1 + 2) form in the same order a conjected p-n in the following dipody: "Tās plaviņas plavajiņ!" 'That meadow's mower!', having two anaphoral links from line one to line four, two from line two to line four (:aA), and besides an invariable a-a (W 121/1 + 3).

A special interest may be attributed to the disjective words of a disjected p-n. Sometimes it is only the voc. that follows the imp. in an evocation (:TY), but a similar interjected voc. may form with the preceding imp. a conjected p-n (:GY). In cases where the p-n is represented by predicate and object the disjective words could be the subject and the preposition serving the acc. of the object (:RD), or an epithetal word to the object (:SD). In verbal p-a an adv. or conj. has to serve as a disjective word (:QS, XS) since a pp. or appt. and] a following fut. would somehow be out of place in a conjected position. Pronouns appear as disjective words where subject and predicate form the p-n (:PA). Where the object is in loc. following the predicate, and both constitute the p-n, an epithetal gen. may serve as a disjective word (:XF). The pcl. "ne" may be considered as a disjecting word, and likewise cause the 'disqualification' of an a-a as an invariable one, if one approaches an old source as a purist from a strictly orthographic point of view. It is separated from the following verb in W (:MR, QC), but agglutinated with the verb in B (:QS, VP, VR, XS) or in BW (:PR, ZZ).

A typology of the p-a is notionally possible on an etymological basis only. Somehow it is easier to apply the attitude towards the p-n and the dipodic sentence, as one of the most important factors of the p-n, also to the a-ae, as a variety of a more dispersed or differently developed rh.f., and not to start from the a-ae as the normal case and the p-a as an exception. Whether the pattern and the distribution of the traced types (cf. the second part of this contribution) and their comparison with similar results concerning these rh.f. in other folklores and other languages may lead to some conclusion about the movement of these types from one language to another, is still contestable. However, the antiquity of these rh.f. as such and within the context of the dipodic sentence and the whole folksong does not always reveal the process of their development from time immemorial; we therefore can neither explain it away by some simplifying formulae or generalizingly

Table

Since a-ae and p-a consist of at least two elements, the following Table is arranged according to the etymological value of these elements. It gives a survey of the types hereafter recorded: the capital letters A–G stand for the cases of nouns in sing., and

		SUBSTANTIVES										
		singular						plural				
		NOM A	GEN B	DAT C	ACC D	LOC F	VOC G	nom a	gen b	dat c	acc d	instr e	loc f
pppt.	Z	AZ			DZ			aZ					
pppr.	Y		BY				GY	aY			dY	eY	
appt.	X	AX			DX			aX					
appr.	W	AW	BW		DW		GW	aW	bW		dW	eW	
ap.	V	AV						aV					
cond.	U										dU		
imper.	T		BT		DT						dT		
fut.	S	AS		CS	DS						dS		
pt.	R	AR			DR			aR	bR		dR	eR	
pp.	Q			CQ	DQ		GQ						
pr.	P				DP			aP			dP		
infin.	O		BO	CO	DO								
ad. sup.	N												
ad. comp.	M												
adj.	L				DL								
ad.	K						GK						
adv. sup.	J												
adv. comp.	I												
adv.	H												
voc. pl.	g								bg				
loc. pl.	f	Af	Bf		Df				bf		df	ef	
instr. pl.	e					Fe		ae	be		de		fe
acc. pl.	d				Dd				bd				
gen. pl.	b	Ab	Bb		Db	Fb		ab	bb		db		fb
nom. pl.	a	Aa	Ba		Da	Fa	Ga		ba	ca	da	ea	fa
voc. s.	G	AG			DG	FG	GG	aG	bG		dG		
loc. s.	F	AF	BF		DF	FF	GF	aF	bF			eF	fF
acc. s.	D	AD	BD	CD	DD	FD		aD	bD	cD			
dat. s.	C	AC	BC	CC	DC			aC	bC				
gen. s.	B	AB	BB	CB	DB	FB	GB	aB	bB		dB		
nom. s.	A	AA	BA	CA	DA	FA	GA	aA	bA		dA	eA	

applied magic wand, nor can the development be wound back in order to trace the essentials of such a development which might have acted as agents from one language to another, from folklore to folklore.

2.

Shortage of space made it impossible to differentiate the cases of adjectives and participles. Neither was it possible to expand this survey to conj., nu-

Table

the corresponding cases in plur. are lettered a–g; H–N stand for the various types of adverbs and adjectives, and O–Z for the verbal elements in these rh.f.
The letters inside the Table refer to the types listed later:

ADJECTIVES			VERBS							PARTICIPLES					
ad K	adj L	comp M	infin. O	pr P	pp Q	pt R	fut S	imper T	cond U	ap V	appr W	appt X	pppr Y	pppt Z	
			OZ	PZ	QZ	RZ	SZ	TZ						ZZ	pppt.
KY			OY	PY	QY	RY		TY					YY		pppr.
KX			OX	PX		RX		TX	UX	VX	WX	XX	YX	ZX	appt.
KW			OW	PW		RW		TW			WW	XW	YW	ZW	appr.
				PV		RV		TV		VV	WV				ap.
			OU	PU		RU			UU						cond.
			OT	PT	QT	RT	ST	TT		VT	WT		YT	ZT	imper.
			OS	PS	QS	RS	SS	TS	US		WS	XS		ZS	fut.
KR		MR	OR	PR		RR	SR	TR	UR	VR	WR	XR	YR	ZR	pt.
			OQ		QQ			TQ			WQ				pp.
KP			OP	PP		RP	SP	TP		VP	WP	XP			pr.
KO			OO	PO	QO	RO	SO	TO		VO					infin.
KN															ad. sup.
KM															ad. comp.
KL															adj.
KK	LK					RK									ad.
KI															adv. sup.
KH	LH							TH				XH			adv.comp
								Tg							adv.
															voc. pl.
Ke				Pe	Qe	Re		Te							loc. pl.
				Pd		Rd		Td				Xd			instr. pl.
								Tb							acc. pl.
Ka				Pa			Sa	Ta			Wa				gen. pl.
	LG							TG					YG		nom. pl.
				PF	QF	RF						XF			voc. s.
KD			OD	PD	QD	RD	SD	TD				XD		ZD	loc. s,
					QC										acc. s.
				PB				TB			WB				dat. s.
KA			OA	PA	QA	RA									gen. s.
															nom. s.

merals, prepositions[4] and pronouns. The place of pron. in these rh.f. deserves a special study, as does the question of reflexive v. in p-a. The horizontal scale (top) indicates the first, the vertical scale (left side) the second element, in the order they appear in the folksong. The catalogue itself consists of references to folksongs, which contain a-ae and/or p-a. A reference preceded by an asterisk denotes that the text and its translation has been mentioned in a previous work of the author (CB 184–185, and fn. 188). Other texts have been quoted here concerning most types. These references are only examples, and it is not implied that the type is unknown elsewhere. Neither is it possible to assert that only the types recorded here are known in Latvian folksongs. In two cases are p-a quoted (:HX, XH) which occur in folk-tales. The first figure in the reference is the song-number (in cases of disjected p-a it is in italics). These figures denote, if not preceded in that entry by a special reference, the following sources: 1–411 for W (1807),[5] 412–2854 for B (1844), 2855–35789 for BW (1894–1915).[6]

The second figure (after a diag.stroke) refers to the line or the lines of the printed text quoted. A single number (if not preceded by a +) or two numbers of the same dipody (linked with a dash) indicate a p-n, one or more numbers (preceded or linked with a +, or linked with a tilde) refer to an a-a. A comma is used to separate within one entry examples referred to, or texts quoted. In cases of invariable rh.f., their line-numbers are in italics. Within every entry the references are arranged 'chronologically', i.e. according to the publication of the collection from which they were quoted, not implying that they are arranged according to the antiquity of the song or the rh.f. in question.

AA. 408/19+21, BW 266/+3, 2788/+4: *Kad vējiņš, aizvējiņš.* AB. 317/3+4, 3850/2, 4: *Rads radiņa galiņā,* 4761/1, 10800/5–6: *Kā nevar cilvēks Cilvēka gribēt.* AC. 123/1+3, 3167/1+2, 5996/1, 3: *Virs viram nesasmēja.* AD. 2/1+3, BW *251*/1, 3, 8491/1, 3: *Kā var meita meitu pelt.* AF. 53/2+4, 3285[1]/3+4: *Lieta būšu, māmuliņa, Kad Laimiņa lietā liks,* 5222/1, 1: *Zirgs zirgā, loks lokā.* AG. 192/1+3: *... tautu meita, ... Bēdz meitiņ laimes savas.* Aa. 121/1+2. Ab. 80/1+4: *Dievers ... Caur dieveru pagalmiņ,* Af. *1476*/1. AR. 1868/1: *Sniedziņš sniga,* *15128*/1: *Gribulītis* man' *gribēja.* AS. 863/2+4. AV. 7353/4: *Skan vālīte velejot.* AW. *291*/1, *9213*/1: *Laime* gāja *laimēdana.* AX. 2494/6+7. AZ. *2148*/1: *Smuka pļava* kad *nopļauta,* BW 1048/2: *Tēva dziesma nedziedāta.*

BA. *121*/4, 171/2+4: *No neveikļa kumeļa ... Ne neveiklis kumeliņš.* BB. 3796/+3: *Ne tev kalpa, kalponītes,* 4438/+3: *Ne launaga, palaunaga.* BC. 68/1+3: *... svaiņa māju, ... Svainīšam nikni suņi.* BD. 97/2+3, *289*/1–2: *Ej prom kaŗa* māt Ved prom *kaŗu sav',* 8127, 1/3–4: *Pats aizgāju pie lodziņa* Pa *lodziņu raudzīties.* BF. 149/2+3: *Staļa spāres galiņā Stalī brūni kumeliņ.* Ba. 161/3+4: *Sieniet sila maliņā, Lai trīc sili dancojot.* Bb. 267/2+4: *Rāva pura ... Rāvu puru bridejiņš.* Bf. BW 1859/2: *Zelta šupļa šupolēs.* BO. 6960/2: *Vakariņa vakarēt.* BR. 314/2+3. BT. *1734*/3–4. BW. 314/2+3: *Spēlmamīša* istabā *Spēlēdama nospēlēju.* BY. 1542/2.

CA. 163/1+3: *Mellajam kumeļan ... Zviedz kumeliņ dancodam.* CB. 216/2+4: *Ļauduvinai ... Ļauduviņas asariņ.* CC. 428/+1. CD. 62/1+4: *Mellajam kumeļam ... Tad grožoju kumeliņ.* CO. B 47/1: *Dodi, Dieviņ, lietum līt.* CQ. 1042/3: *Jo es bēdai bēdājos.* CS. 2144/4 + 5.

DA. 294/3 + 4: *Vējiņš nese kļavu lapu Kļavu lapa man atnese.* DB. 246 1 + 2, BW 447/1: *Brauc pa ceļu, ceļa vīrs,* 5795/2, 4: *Zili zīles galiņā.* DC. 152/1 + 3. DD. 408/8 + 9: *Pamet zelta gedzenīt: Gredzeniņu meklēdama.* DF. 352/2 + 3: *Kuŗu ceļu tu aizgāji Ne panāču celiņā.* DG. 246/2 + 3. Da. 55/1 + 4: *Pataisīju eršķu zaķi ... Kādi zaķi Vidzemē,* 224/1 + 3. Db. B 51/4 + 6. Dd. 252/1 + 3: *Tec tecini vārtu vērt ... Atvērusi vara vārtus.* Df. 2558/2 + 4. DL. 1048/3. DO. 40/2 + 4, *252/1 = 279/1, 1762/4: *Ar variti novarēt.* DP. *130/1, 2142/1 + 3, 2 + 4. DQ. 62/2 + 4, 293/1, 2846/1: *Sudrabiņa viju viju.* DR. 916/1: *Dieva dēlis jumtu juma,* 1042/2, 8667/2: *Kam rasiņu rasināji.* DS. 2400/1 + 2, 2551/3–4. DT. 38/1 + 3, 170/3–4: *Es tev došu zelta airi Īries pati maliņā.* DW. 916/2: *Zelta spāru spārodamis.* DX. *280/4, 1764/6 + 7: *Par vaiņaga pinumu. Vēlējos nepinusi.* DZ. 1841/4: *Saldu medu apmedoto.*

FA. 284/1–2: *Lai kaiš tumsā kam kaiš tumsā Man tumsiņa ne kaitei.* FB. 143/2 + 4: *Rīgā jūgts ... Rīgas meitu jūgumiņ.* FD. 232 = 242/2 + 3: *Sila priedes galiņā, Ne drīkstēju galu cirst,* 403/2 + 4, 503/1 + 4. FF. 1675/ + 4: *... ritā parītā.* FG. 3168/1: *Ej druvā druvaliņa.* Fa. 186/2 ~ 4: *Vēl liepā ābelē, Kā liepiņas man' uzaugtu, Kā ābeles noziedēt.* Fb. 261/2 + 4, 281/2 + 4. Fe. 261/2 + 4: *Ozoliņa zariņā ... Pa zariņu zariņiem.*

GA. 5717/1: *Puisīt, šķelmi, tu bij šķelmis.* GB. 78/2 + 4: *Daugaviņ sidrabiņ ... Daudz sidraba valkataj.* GF. 53/1 + 3: *Migla! ... Migliņā to tautu bēgu.* GG. 5217/ + 3: *Ņem, sērdieni, sērdienīti.* Ga. 184/1 + 4: *Ai vainaka vījejin! ... Lai ņem citas vijejinas.* GK. 118/1–2: *Telīt mana ziedaliņ Ziedaiņām kājiņām.* GQ. 17168/1. GW. 15931/1: *Kal, kalēj, ko kaldams.* GY. 489/1 + 2: *Ko rājies, rātulīti, Tev nav tavu rājamo.*

aA. 121/2 + 4: *Zābacaiņi pļāveji ... Tās pļaviņas pļavajiņ.* aB. 202/1 + 2: *Visi areji tīrumā Man araj' vien ne bij.* aC. B 108/1 + 5. aD. 2127/1 + 3. aF. 327/2 + 4, 1517/1: *Bērzi vien bērzājā.* aG. B 149/1. ab. 99/2 + 4, 1040/4: *Bēdas bēdu galiņā.* ae. 2834/2 + 4. aP. 92/2: *Sidrabiņa ziedi zied,* 2311/4, BW 406/4. aR. 211/2: *Balti ziedi noziedej.* aV. 148/1–2: *Čīkstēt čīkst liepas segli Kumelinu seglojot.* aW. 6468/3: *Neredz gani ganīdami.* aX. 7770/3: *Būt tie zari zarojuši.* aY. 2433/1 ~ 3. aZ. BW 1048/1: *Visas dziesmas izdziedātas.*

bA. *103/4, BW 1312/5: *Lielu rakstu rakstītāja.* bB. BW 2012/2: *Ne vārtiņu vērējiņa.* bC. 68/2 + 4: *Gaŗam brāļu rijas dur' ... Brāļam bārga līgaviņ.* bD. 22/1: *Izlociju bērzu birz,* 48/2, 219/1 + 3, 1689/4: *Par vārtiņu vērumiņu.* bF. 392/2 + 4: *Pa liepaju lapiņām ... Aiz ābel's Liepājā.* bG. 90/1: *... bērzu birz!,* 182/1: *Ai vainaku vainadzi'!.* ba. 899/4, 1035/1. bb. 3643/1 + 2: *... es brāļu* *māsa ... brālīšu vidūi.* bd. BW 2763/3: *Griez, meitiņa, zaru zarus.* be. *261/4 (:Fe), 401/2+4, 33557/6: *Likumiņu likumiem.* bf. 400/2+4, 5589/3: *Brāļu* māsa *brālīnos.* bg. 263/1: *Šķiŗieties bērzu birzes.* bR. 2605/1+3. bW. 2193/ 2+3.

cD. 47/2+3: *Uz manām rociņām Kad tu roku nogulēsi.* ca. 224/2+4. dA. 321/2+3: *Muižas manas prasīdam, Muiža mana siliņa.* dB. 345/2+4: *Skuijes nese rociņā ... Pa skuijines birumam.* dG. 5734/1: *Šuv man kurpes, kurpenieki.* da. 244/1+5, 408/1+3, 19+22. db. 2274/2+4. de. BW 2165/ 5+6: *... rozītes sēju, No tām rozītēm kronīti viju.* dP. 2267/2. df. 2145/6+8. dR. 248/1. dS. 4602/4. dT. 1977/1+3. dU. B 384/4: *Tādus zarus izzarotu.* dW. 7770/2: *Zelta zarus zarodama.* dY. 2380/1+2.

eA. B 36/2+3. eF. 408/18+20: *Deviņiem žuburiem ... Devitā žuburā.* ea. 218/2+4: *Aiz ļautiņu valodām ... Auge valodas augamo.* ef. 309/2+4. eR. BW 1030/3: *Ar dziesmām apdziedāju.* eW. 1334/10. eY. 2919/2, 4: *Ar dūrēm dūrējama.*

fF. 277/3+4. fa. B 146/2+3. fb. 361/2+3: *Nāc man līdz tautiņos Šauras tautu klēšu duris.* fe. BW 2165/2+3: *... žagaros braucu No tiem žagariem sētiņu pinu.*

gD. 263/2+4. gd. 28/1+3, 1+3: *Ogas, ogas, rieksti, rieksti ... Lasu ogas, raunu riekstus.* gg. 3643/+1: *Brāļi mani, brālīši.*

HA. 7191/1, 2: *Vērten vēra vērājiņa.* HC. 4099/1: *Labi bija labiešam.* HD. 89/1+2: *Pušu kožu riekstu koļu, Pusit devu ļauduvīn.* He. 6455/2. HH. *51/+3, +4, 58/1+2: *Māte mani mīl auklēja Mīļi kāre šūpulīt, 1318/ 1+2, 6502/+4. HI. 175/2~4. HJ. 2842/1−2. HK. 58/2+4, 67/2+3: *Tur bij labi šupoties Laba mārša bālēliņ.* HO. 9197/1, 1: *Jāšus jāt, braukšus braukt.* HP. *131/4, 357/1: *Gludi glaužu ... HQ. B 360/1: *Lūgšus lūdzu māmiņai.* HR. *10/1, *23/3, *192/1, *307/4, *379/1, 1685/3: *Kam Dieviņi dotiņ devi, 2565/2, 7031/1, 7191/1, 2 (:HA). HS. B 54/1: *Ietin iešu tautiņās.* HT. 192/ 1+3+4. HW. 1154/1+3. HX. LP VI 626: *... zagšus zagti ... HY. 1831/1: *Pūriņš lēti lētināms.* HZ. 23049, 1/1, 2: *Pirktin pirkts arājiņš.*

KA. 116/1: *Zaļa zaļa rudzu zāle.* KD. *129/1, 353/1+3, BW 1207/2+3: *Vieglu vieglu, kuplu kuplu Apenīša vieglumiņu.* Ka. 118/2+4, 163/2+4. Ke. BW 1558, 1/1: *Līk' liku likumien sētiņu daru.* KH. 67/3+4, 175/1~3. KI. 175/1+4. KK. 34/3−4: *Pēc meitām jauni puiši Jāj' jaunus kumeliņus, 46/2+4, BW 832/3, 4, 7045/1+4. KL. 140/1+3, 181/1−2: *Gan man labu ļauž Labajā dieniņā.* KM. 102/1−2, 3−4, 110/2+4. KN. 29/2+3: *Zemu resnu ozoliņ Pie tā visu zemmākā.* KO. 3387/1: *Tās var lielas lielīties.* KP. 5904/1: *Gludu gludu galvu glaudu.* KR. *86/2, 4, *303/1, BW 376/1−2. KW. BW 375/1−2: *Ak tu, manu skaņu balsi, Kur aizgāji skanēdama.* KX. 2581/2+4. KY. 1815/1.

LG. 3148/1: *Ai vecā vecainite.* LH. *1276/1* – 2. LK. B *97/1* – 2.

MR. 172/2 + 3: *Tai miļākai mātes meit, Kuŗa mani ne mīlēja.*

OA. 2506/2 + 4. OD. 1614/1 + 2, 2224/1 + 2. OO. 2227/1 + 3, *9416/1*, 3: *Iet* tautās, *vai neiet.* OP. *18/1, *85/1, *148/1 (:aV), BW 769/2: ... *dārdēt dārd.* OQ. *322/1. OR. *71/1 = 81/3, *300/1, BW *18/2*, 3: *Sacīt* vien *pasaciju.* OS. 1417/1 + 2. OT. 2381/1 + 2. OU. 1298/4 + 6, BW *286/1*: *Dziedāt* vien es *dziedātu.* OW. 2120/1 + 3. OX. 252/1 + 3 (:Dd). OY. 8650/2: *Man būs nest nesamo.* OZ. 1247/3 + 4.

PA. *291/1. PB. *2353/1* – 2: *Piejošos* zelt atslēgu Ceļa *jostas galiņā,* 7014/ 1 + 4. PD. *283/1* – 2: *Es apkaļu* kumelinu Tēraudina *pakaviņ,* 3795/1: *Cērtu cirvi ozolā.* PF. 7175/2: *Paraugos paraugā.* Pa. *2534/1*, 1: *Buŗ* man *buŗi, skauž* man *skaugi.* Pd. 7131/9: *Meitas loka ielociņus.* Pe. *87/1* – 2, *3069,1/2*: *Lapo* zelta *lapiņām.* PO. 123/1 + 3, 1247/1 + 3. PP. 31/1 + 3, 1657/1 + 2. PR. 404/2 + 3, *6659/1* – 2: *Māku, māku, ko es māku,* Vēl es visu *nemācēju.* PS. 148/1 + 3, 357/1 + 3, 2177/3 + 4. PT. 2053/2 + 4, *2122/1* – 2. PU. 325/1 + 3: *Gauži raud* ... *Kaut zinājis tā raudīt.* PV. 113/2 + 4: *Ko tik daudz runājiet* ... *Vis tik daudz runājot.* PW. *291/1, 1076/1*, 3380/1, 2: *Gauži raudu raudādama.* PX. BW 1981/1 + 4, 1 + 4. PY. 75/1 + 3, *155/1, *8650/1*, 35408, 2/1: *Puiši prasa prasāmo.* PZ. 1247/1 + 2, 1763/4 + 5.

QA. 7502/1 + 4. QC. 264/1 + 4 *Tišām lielis es ne augu* ... *Pa savam augumam.* QD. *133/3. QF. B 49/2: *Ko tu vedi vezumā.* Qe. 25/1 – 2: *Viju* savu vainadziņ Deviņām *vijiņām.* QO. 7547/2 + 3: *Pie upītes velējās* Šķita baltu izvelēt. QQ. 3/1 + 2: *Trīs zīdiņas matos pin' Vis' trīs pinu sidrabiņ,* 96/1 + 3, 6060/1. QS. B *353/1*: *Nu es jāju* vairs *nejāšu.* QT. 489/1 + 4. QY. 236/1 + 4, 489/1 + 2 (:GY), 6643/1: *Nebijos biedējama.* QZ. 1632/2 + 4.

RA. 56/1 + 4, 7191/1, 2 (:HA). RD. B 131/2: *Venta aude audekliņu, 1042/1:* *Lai bēdāja* vels par *bēdu,* 2315/1, *3779/1* – 2: *Es nebiju pie bāliņa Aizpērno bijumiņu.* RF. 2291/1: *Es nošāvu šāveni.* Rd. 2050/3: *Vēra vārtus ...,* 2274/ 1 – 2. Re. *2273/3* – 4: *Dieva dēls sastīpoj* Sudrabiņa *stīpiņām.* RK. *390/3* – 4: *Nobālēj* tautiņā Kā *bāla bērzu lapa.* RO. 210/1 ~ 3, *278/2*: *Tev bij* manam *tēva būt.* RP. 10/1 + 2, 52/2 + 3, 146/3 + 4: *Kumeļam sviedri bire Man birst gaudas asariņas,* BW *339/1*, 2. RR. 2/1 + 2: *Irbe svelpe eglainā Es ar svelpu ecedams,* 16/2 + 3, 98/2 + 3, BW 124/2 + 3, 404/ + 1: *Kur palika, nepalika,* 1151/2 + 3, 2044/2 + 3, 6211/ + 1, + 3: *Gāju, gāju, nedagāju.* RS. 180/1 + 3, 1979/1 + 4 + 5, 3591/1 ~ 3: *Pacietīšu, ko darīji, Atdarīšu dzīvodama.* RT. 77/*1 + 3*, 192/1 + 3 + 4, 1977/2 + 3. RU. 335/2 + 3: *Kad tu mīļi ne dzīvoj!* Lai *dzīvotu ta meitiņ,* 370/1 + 4, 4041/1 + 3. RV. 762/1 + 2. RW. 977/2 + 3, 2519/6. RX. 880/3 + 5, 1691/1 + 3, 2468/1 + 3, BW 124/2 + 3: *Drīz dziedāju, drīz raudāju, Noraudājis padziedāju.* RY. 99/2 + 4, *218/4, 2089/1, 2, BW

2324/4, 4993, 1/2, 8025/1, 2: *Vēl man bēŗa beŗamo.* RZ. 1454/1+2, 3+4: *Saderēju to meitiņu, Lai ta auga saderēta,* 2581/1+3.

SD. BW *1048/3: Tad dziedāšu* tēva *dziesmu,* 1824/4: *Došu goves, segšu sagšu.* Sa. 1012/4+6+8. SO. *3/3: Tā būs* arī mā te *būt,* BW 411/2+4, 6398/3: *Tev būs būt, tev nebūt.* SP. 1325/5+6: *Es pārgājis, es nedzeršu Lai dzeŗ mātes bālēliņi.* SR. 1466/4+5, BW 411/2+4. SS. 126/1+2, 127/+2, 254/+1: *Būsi lietā voi ne būs,* B 8/+4: *Iešu pakaļ, voi neieš,* 2246/+1, BW 1123/+3. ST. B 187/3+4, 376/5+7. SZ. 4646/5: *Nu tai pirkšu pirktus svārkus.*

TB. *394/1−2: Guldi* mani māmuliņ Savā *gultas galiņā.* TD. 1620/3, 2502/3, 5: *Cērt cirīt akrimā.* TG. 179/1: *Dziedi dziedi dziedātāja,* B. 170/3, 489/1 (:GY), 2852/1, BW 1030/1, 2482, 1/3, 2860/1: *Listi, līsti, lietutiņi,* 15931/1 (:GW). Ta. 110/*1+2: Ziedi ziedi zemenīt, Ne tev vien balti ziedi.* Tb. 108/1+2, BW 1930, 1/1: *Ziedi, ziedi, ziedu pļava.* Td. *312/1+2, 3+4, 347/1: *Veriet vārtus, laid iekša.* Te. *2538/1−2.* Tg. *1927/1,* BW *797,* 1/1: *Plūciet* linus, *plūcējiņi.* TH. *252/1=279/1, 2585/1, 17409/1, 2: *Ej iešus, māsiņa, Neleci lekšus.* TO. 258/2+3: *Palīdziet man dziedāt, Es būšu jums palīdzēt.* TP. 110/1+3, 252/1+4, 393/1+3. TQ. 124/1+3, 7855/1: *Steidzinies pasteidzos.* TR. 53/1+2, 129/2+3: *Aiztec manu līgaviņ, Līgaviņa aiztecēja,* 2364/1+3. TS. 320/1+2: *Lūdzi lūdzi tautu meit Tu jau manis nepielūgs.* TT. 2502/3+5, 4+6, BW 712/+3: *Mīsim zirgus, atmīsim.* TV. 503/1+4: *Audz godā ... Ar godiņu izaugam.* TW. *229/1, *338/4, *387/1, 930/1: *Nāc nākdama, 4692/1, 2, 15931/1* (:GW). TX. 301/2+4: *Ne peļ savus bālelinus ... Bālelinus izpēlusi,* 4876/1+3. TY. *17414,* 1/1: *Ej,* māsiņa, *ejamā.* TZ. BW 970/1+2: *Saderam, mūs' māsiņas, Mūs' zemīte saderēta.*

UR. BW 1297/2+4: *Kaut man vēsti vesūtītu ... Kumam vēsti atsūtīja.* US. B 103/4+5: *Ne es tevi skaliem cirstu Cirtīšu tev pamatam.* UU. 1015/1+3+4. UX. 988/1+3.

VO. 2452/2+3. VP. 2/3−4, 2283/4∼6: *... attekam, Attek visas sīkas olas Māmulīte neattek,* 31928/4+5: *Gauži raudajam. Ko tu, puķīt, raudi.* VR. 674/2+3: *... uzaugam? Voi uzauge nemalusi.* VT. B 153/2+3. VV. 1492/1+2. VX. 1325/4+5: *No Vāczemes pārejam. Es pārgājis, es nedzeršu.*

WB. 2082/2+4. Wa. 408/21+22: *Sak bāliņš koklēdams, Tās koklītes škaišķi dzied.* WP. 2388/2+4. WQ. 2082/2+3: *Kam nesdama launadziņ? Nesu manam bāliņam.* WR. *314/3. WS. B 374/1+4. WT 229/1+2: *Šūj bitite ko šūdama, Šūj man vasku kamanin.* WV. 1467/1+4, 2289/2+4. WW. 2357/+3: *Nobraukdami atbraukdami.* WX. *57/3−4.

XD. 1014/7+8. XF. *91/3−4: Man māmiņa šūpojus,* Lazdigalas *šūpulī.* Xd. *252/3: Atvērusi* vara *vārtus.* XH. LP III 50: *... nesušas nešus ...* XP. 20/2+3: *Pus vizuli novītuši Lai novīst otra pus',* 1700/2+4. XR. 773/2+3.

XS. *1284/1*, 3: *Nu es metis* vairs *nemešu*. XW. 378/2 +4: *Kur augusi vēriņa,*
... *Kur augdama domājus'*. XX. 2485: *Es piedzēris viriņš biju Man nedzēris*
kumeliņš. *Kā bij man dzērušam Nedzērušu saturēt*.
YG. 8667/1: *List līdamis, lietutiņi*. YR. 1463/2 +3, 2402/2 +4. YT.
268/5 — 6: Ja ir laba vedama Tad *vediet sētiņa*. YW. 4993, 1/2 +3: *Es pabēgu*
bēgamo. *Es bēgdama iztecēju*. YX. 1278/2 +3: *Tautiņu vedama; Tautiņas*
vedušas. YY. 886/2 +4. ZD. 143/2 +4 (:FB), 2377/4: *Māsas slēgtu atslēdziņu*.
ZR. B 326/2 +3. ZS. 1031/2 +4. ZT. 143/2 +3: *Rīgā jūgts kumeliņš, Nojū-*
dzieti man māsiņas, 332/2 +4: *Nepuškoti cepurin*, ... *Puškoj savu cepuri*.
ZW. 611/2 +4. ZX. 2982/2 +4: *Nesukāti tev matiņi!* ... *Izsukājse cekuliņu*.
ZZ. BW *1437/1 — 2: Lūgtas kūmas, lūgtas kūmas*, Jola *lūgta veca māte*,
3242/ +2, +4: *Ij runāta, nerunāta*, 7899/4.

Notes

1. Abbreviations used in this article which are not self-evident, or universally
accepted:
a- = anaphora,
ad = adjective with indefinite ending,
adj = adjective with definite ending,
ap = adverbial participle,
appr. = active participle, present tense,
appt = active participle, past tense,
B = G. F. Büttner, *Latweeſchu ļauſchu dſeeſmas un ſinges* ("*Magazin*, hrsg. von d.
Lettisch-Lit. Ges.", VIII. part 1, Mitau, 1844.
BW = Chr. Baron and H. Wissendorff, *Latwju Dainas*, 6 volumes in 8 parts,
Mitau and St. Petersburg 1894–1915,
CB = *Commentationes Balticae*, XII/XIII, Bonn, 1967.
OED = *The Shorter Oxford English Dictionary*, Oxford–London, ³1964.
p- = polyptoton,
pp = present and past tense, if written form equal,
pppr = passive participle, present tense,
pppt = passive participle, past tense,
pr = present tense,
pt = past tense,
rh.f. = rhetorical figure, -es,
W = (Fr. Daniel Wahr) *Palzmareeſchu Dſeeſmu Krahjums* (Ruien?) 1807.
2. Cross-references to texts quoted at the end of this article have this pattern of two
letters in brackets.
3. Owing to the size of this contribution it was impossible to deal with the problems
of the invariable a-ae unless either the apparently similar forms of the same word
were two different flexional forms (: Da), or if one of the elements took part in a p-n
(W 338/4) or in a flexible a-a. Elements of an invariable adjectival a-a may fulfil dif-

ferent grammatical functions, as in W 223/2 + *4* : (adjectivally:) "Gaṛu caini [Strick-leiter] vīdinaj: ... (adverbially:) Gaṛu vilke audekliṇ", '(the beekeepers) Plaited a long rope-ladder ... (mother) Beamed a length of cloth'.

4. Just to mention the p-a of W *201*/1–2: "Visapkārt *tautas jāje* Apkārt manu rožu dārz", 'Folk rode all about, Around my garden of roses', and of B *29*/3: "Caur *tautām* cauri gāju", 'Going through I crossed the folk'.

5. Orthography according to the modern reprint, ed. by H. Biezais, Uppsala, 1961.

6. Quoting the song-numbers of the BW, a comma, followed by a single number, indicates a reference to a known song-variation. These are quoted from the Copenhagen edition of Latvian folksongs, 12 volumes, Copenhagen 1952–1956.

RASMA GRĪSLE

Latviešu heterotoni

Latviešu vidus dialektā, kas ir literārās valodas pamatā, vēl šķir garās zilbēs trīs intonācijas: stiepto (˜), krītošo (ˋ) un lauzto (ˆ), bet abos pārējos dialektos vairs tikai divas.

Indoeiropiešu akcentoloģijā latviešu intonācijām, kâ zināms, ir patstāvīga vērtība, ko atklājis Jānis Endzelīns; bet arī sazināšanās procesā tām ir savs sēmantisks svars. Intonācijām ir fōnēmatisks raksturs, un ir vārdi, kas, būdami vai nebūdami etimoloģiski saistīti, atšķiras tikai ar intonāciju vienā vai pat vairākās zilbēs. Piem., bieži lietojamie tā [tã] n.s. 'die': tā [tà] 'dessen' : tā [tâ] 'so'; kā [kà] 'wessen' : kā [kâ] 'wie'; jūs [jũs] n. 'ihr' : jūs [jùs] a. 'euch'; auksts [aũksc] 'kalt' : augsts [aûksc] 'hoch'; kopējs [kuõpējs] 'gemeinschaftlich' : kopējs [kùopējs] 'Pfleger'; zāle [zãle] 'Saal' : zāle [zâle] 'Gras'; griezt [grìest] 'wenden' : griezt [griêst] 'schneiden'; grieziens [grìeziêns] 'Wendung' : grieziens [griêziêns] 'Schnitt'; tūkstoš [tũkstuôš] 'tausend' : tūkstošs [tûkstuõš] 'schwellend'. Taču parastā praktiskā rakstībā intonācijas neapzīmē, un pāri par 80 % šādu vārdu ir homografi.

Arī leišiem ir tādi ar (vienas zilbes) intonāciju atšķirīgi vārdi, un dažkārt tie pilnīgi atbilst latviešu piemēriem (lei. sietas [siẽtas], la. siets [sìec] 'gebunden' : lei. sietas [síetas] 'Sieb'). Un senprūšiem 3. katechismā (1561) ar au- resp. āu- rakstītie ausin a. 'Gold' un āusins a.pl. 'Ohr' laikam arī ir atšķīrušies tikai ar intonāciju, vismaz dažos locījumos.

Latviešu gramatiku vēsturē šādus ar intonāciju un leksisko nozīmi atšķirīgus vārdus (un arī pašas intonācijas — stiepto un rietumizlokšņu lauzto) pirmais min Rozenbergers savā *Formenlehre der lettischen Sprache* (Mitau, 1830). Pēc tam vēl daži 19. gs. autori (P. Krumbergs un S. Vēbers) ir snieguši šādu vārdu sarakstus, uzrādīdami ap 80 piemēru. Bet īstenībā tādu ir daudz vairāk. Un ir arī gramatiskas formas, kas visnotaļ atšķiras tikai ar intonāciju. Pat veselas frazes var atšķirties vienīgi ar intonācijām.

Vārdus, kam leksiskā vai gramatiskā nozīme ir dažāda, bet kas fōnētiski atšķiras vienīgi ar intonāciju, īsuma labad saukšu par *heterotoniem*.

Leksisku heterotonu esmu savākusi kādas 400 vienības (to saraksts tiks publicēts), pamatā likdama savu Vidzemes vidienes izrunu ar trim intonācijām (kādu esmu mantojusi, uzaugdama Kauguros pie Valmieras; mani vecāki un vecvecāki runājuši tā paša apvidus Raunas resp. Vecbrenguļu izloksnē). Šās 400 vienības — trijotnes un pāṛi — ietveṛ ap 5 000 heterotonisku formu (literāru); te ieskaitītas arī refleksīvformas gan no pamatvārdu, gan no atvasinājumu (piem., no verbālnōmenu) paradeigmām. Vienību precīzu skaitu pagrūti uzrādīt, jo tas, vārdus lokot, it kâ mainās — kas kāds loceklis vienībā vairs neiederas vai kad kādam pievijas klāt homofōni, piem.: n. *logs* [*luôks*] 'Fenster' : *loks* [*luõks*] 'Lauch' : *loks* [*lùoks*] 'Bogen' a. *logs* [*luôks*] 'Fenster' : *loku* [*luõku*] 'Lauch' : *loku* [*lùoku*] 1) 'Bogen', 2) 'beuge' (inf. *locīt*), 3) 'lecke' (inf. *lakt*). Bez tam dažam loceklim intonācija var būt vai nu svārstīga resp. dažāda (piem., *maisa* [*maĩsa* ‖ *màisa*] 'mischt' : *maisa* [*màisa*] g. 'Sack') vai var atšķirties pa izloksnēm; piem., valmieriešiem heterotoni ir *zīle* [*zĩle*] 'Meise' : *zīle* [*zìle*] 'Eichel', bet turpat kaimiņos brenguliešiem, kauguriešiem, kâ arī tālāk raunēniešiem, abi vārdi ir homofōni: [*zĩle*].

Divu intonāciju sistēmā, kāda ir leišu valodā un latviešu rietumu un austrumu izloksnēs, iespējami tikai heterotonu pāṛi vienā atšķirīgo intonāciju kombinācijā, bet triju intonāciju sistēmā — arī trijotnes un pāṛi trijās kombinācijās. Literārās valodas runātāji vismaz pa daļai patur savas dzimtās izloksnes intonācijas.

Heterotonu trijotņu manā izrunā ir ap 20. Vēl daži piemēri: *raušu* [*raũšu*] g.pl. 'Fladen' : *raušu* [*ràušu*] 'schüre' : *raušu* [*raûšu*] 'werde reißen'; *vāts* [*vãc*] 'Faß' : *vāc* [*vàc*] 'sammel(s)t' : *vāts* [*vâc*] 'Wunde'; *vīli* [*vĩli*] a. 'Feile' : *vīli* [*vìli*] a. 'Naht' : *vīli* [*vîli*] 'trogst'. — Tikai divus no šādu trijotņu locekļiem ar intonāciju šķiṛ arī rietumu un austrumu izloksnēs.

Pāṛi pēc heterotoniskuma var būt —

1) ar stieptu un krītošu intonāciju: *aušu* [*aũšu*] g.pl. 'Alberne' : *aušu* [*àušu*] 'werde (die Füße) ankleiden', *knābis* [*knãbis*] 'Schnabel' : *knābis* [*knàbis*] 'gehackt', *rūsa* [*rũsa*] 'Schutt' : *rūsa* [*rùsa*] 'Rost', *sils* [*sĩls*] 'wird warm werden' : *sils* [*sìls*] 'Nadelholzwald'; *ieplaka* [*iẽplaka*] 'Niederung' : *ieplaka* [*ìeplaka*] 'sank ein', *nogāzi* [*nuõgâzi*] a. 'Berghang' : *nogāzi* [*nùogâzi*] 'stürztest herunter', *(ne)pārdot* [*(ne)pãrduôt*] '(nicht) übergeben' : *(ne)pārdot* [*(ne)pàrduôt*] '(nicht) verkaufen', *pielipi* [*piẽlipi*] a. 'Erhohung am Brotlaib' : *pielipi* [*pìelipi*] 'klebtest an'. — Šādi vārdi nav heterotoni austrumu izloksnēs, kur nešķiṛ stiepto intonāciju no krītošās.

2) ar stieptu un lauztu intonāciju: *apsēšanās* [*apsẽšanâs*] 'das von sich selbst Besäen' : *apsēšanās* [*apsêšanâs*] 'das sich Setzen', *atāls* [*atãls*] 'Grummet' : *attāls* [*atâls*] 'entfernt', *dēt* [*dẽt*] 'machen (Würste)' : *dēt* [*dêt*] 'legen (Eier)', *pods* [*puõc*] 'Liespfund' : *pods* [*puôc*] 'Topf', *slābt* [*slãpt*] 'erschlaffen' : *slāpt* [*slâpt*] 'dursten'; *citāts* [*citãc*] 'Zitat' : *citāds* [*citâc*] 'anders gestaltet',

ceļot [*ceļuõt*] 'hebend' : *ceļot* [*ceļuôt*] 'reisen', *lasīšu* [*lasīšu*] g.pl. dem. 'Lachs' : *lasīšu* [*lasîšu*] 'werde lesen', *sunīt* [*sunīt*] v. 'Hündchen' : *sunīt* [*sunît*] 'hunzen', *virāt* [*virãt*] 'kochtet' : *virāt* [*virât*] 'wiederholt auf- und zumachen'. — Šādi vārdi ir heterotoni visās izloksnēs.

3) ar krītošu un lauztu intonāciju: *aust* [*àust*] 'tagen' : *aust* [*aûst*] 'weben', *iesals* [*ìesàls*] 'Malz' : *iesals* [*ìesaˆls*] 'wird einfrieren', *līst* [*lìst*] 'kriechen' : *līst* [*lîst*] 1) 'roden', 2) 'regnet', *plaucēt* [*plàucêt*] 'brühen' : *plaucēt* [*plaûcêt*] 'sprießen lassen', *sienu* [*sìenu*] 1) a. 'Heu', 2) 'binde' : *sienu* [*siênu*] 'Wand', *zeltu* [*zȩ̀ltu*] a. 'Gold' : *zeltu* [*zȩ̂ltu*] 'würde grünen'. — Šādi vārdi nav heterotoni rietumu izloksnēs, kur nešķiŗ krītošo un lauzto intonāciju.

Uzrādītos heterotonu piemērus apsveŗot, jāņem, protams, vērā, ka dažās saknēs un piedēkļos intonācijām citur var būt citāds sadalījums un arī līdzskaņu izruna beigu zilbēs var būt citāda nekâ Vidzemes vidienē (skat. Kr. Stanga *Vgl. Gramm. d. Balt. Spr.*, 140 skk.).

Leksiskie heterotoni ar stieptu un krītošu intonāciju pārsniedz abas pārējās grupas vienību skaitā, taču ne heterotonisko formu daudzumā.

Kâ no piemēriem jau redzams, atšķirīgā intonācija heterotoniem sastopama gan uzsvērtās (sakņu un priedēkļu) zilbēs, gan neuzsvērtās (piedēkļu, salikteņos arī sakņu un priedēkļu) zilbēs. Trejāda tā ir tikai saknēs, pa daļai arī neuzsvērtās, kādās gan starpība starp stiepto un krītošo intonāciju tiecas zust. Divējāda tā ir priedēkļos (*ie-*, *no-*, *pār-*, *pie-*), proti, stiepta un krītoša (ar lauzumu nav piemēra) un tikai divējāda arī piedēkļos — stiepta un lauzta, jo te, arvien neuzsvērtā pozicijā, kritums ir pielīdzinājies stiepumam.

Ja heterotonu pārī viens loceklis ir saliktenis, tad atšķirīgā intonācija mēdz būt morfoloģiski dažādās zilbēs, piem., vienam pāriniekam saknē, bet otram piedēklī resp. gala zilbē, priedēklī vai tml. Piem.: *apsēs* [*apsēs*] 'wird besäen' : *apsēs* [*apsês*] l.pl. 'Espe', *savāc* [*savàc*] 'sammel(s)t' : *savāds* [*savâc*] 'eigentümlich', *piecīšos* [*pìecìšuôs*] 'strenge mich an' : *piecīšos* [*pìecîšuôs*] l.pl. 'Fünflinge'; *iesit* [*iêsit*] 'werdet gehen' : *iesit* [*ìesit*] 'schläg(s)t ein', *jāsit* [*jâsit*] 'werdet reiten' : *jāsit* [*jàsit*] 'muß schlagen'.

Intonāciju starpība vērojama arī vairākās zilbēs reizē — retumis trijās: *iekārtās* [*iêkàrtâs*] 1. pl. 'Einrichtung' : *iekārtās* [*ìekãrtãs*] g.s., n., a.pl. fem. 'eingehängt', bet biežāk divās zilbēs: *iekurs* [*iêkùrs*] 'Anmacheholz' : *iekurs* [*ìekuˆrs*] 'wird anheizen', *jautāt* [*jaûtât*] 'fragen' : *jautāt* [*jàutãt*] 'ahntet', *norās* [*nuõrâs*] l.pl. 'Brachweide' : *norās* [*nùorãs*] 'wird durchschelten', *raugāties* [*raûgâtiês*] 'schaut zu' : *raugāties* [*raûgâtiês*] 'rülpsen', *solīšu* [*sùolîšu*] 'werde versprechen' : *solīšu* [*suôlîšu*] g.pl. 'Schrittchen'. Daļai šādu piemēru reizē ir leksisku un gramatisku heterotonu daba.

Tīri *gramatiskiem* heterotoniem intonācija šķiŗ deklinācijas un konjugācijas formas. Saknes zilbēs tas vērojams retāk (*brāli* [*brãli*] a. 'Bruder' : *brāli* [*bràli*] v. 'Bruder', *nāc* [*nãc*] 'kommst' : *nāc* [*nàc*] 'komm'), bet dažās piedēkļu resp. gala zilbēs — visnotaļ. Ar intonāciju te atšķiŗas 1) adjektīviem un tiem līdzīgi lokāmiem vārdiem vairāki abu dzimšu noteikto un nenoteikto formu locījumi (*-os* masc., *-ās* fem.), piem.: *stipros* [*stipruõs*] a.pl. 'die starken' : *stipros* [*stipruôs*] l.pl. 'in starken', *stiprās* [*stiprãs*] n., a.pl. fem. 'die starken' (kam pielīdzinājies arī g.s. ar *-às* > *ãs*) : *stiprās* [*stiprâs*] l.pl. 'in starken', 2) verbālo tagadnes *ā*-celmu daudzsk. 2. pers. un infinitīvs ar *-(in)āt*, piem.: *zināt, kustināt* [*zinãt, kustinãt*] 'wißt, bewegt' : *zināt, kustināt* [*zinât, kustinât*] 'wissen, bewegen', 3) adjektīviem līdzīgi lokāmā pagātnes pasīvā divdabja daudzsk. akuzātīvs un refleksīvais kondicionālis (ar ko saskan refl. supīns un minētā divdabja daudzsk. lokātīvs), piem.: *raktos* [*raktuõs*] a.pl. 'die gegrabenen' : *raktos* [*raktuôs*] 'würde sich graben' (sup. 'sich graben', l.pl. 'in gegrabenen').

Bez tam var būt arī *sintaktiski* heterotoni —kad kādas frazes resp. teikuma locekļi ir heterotoniski vārdi vai kad blaku zilbju sēmantiskais grupējums atkarā no intonācijas iespējams dažāds un kad turklāt no šo heterotonisko vārdu abām rindām var veidoties sintaktiski pareizi savienojumi. Šādu iespēju balsta latviešu valodas brīvā vārdu kārta, palīgakcenti un enklize (enklitisks var būt pat verbs). Piemēri: *kā jūs iesit sienā*? [*kà jùs iêsit sìenã*] 'weshalb werdet ihr ins (od. nach) Heu gehen?' : *kā jūs iesit sienā?* [*kâ jùs ìesit siênã*] 'wie schlägt (dringt) man euch in die Wand ein?' Frazes *daudzi nu labo tos* un *daudzinu labotos* izrunā (enklizes un palīgakcenta dēļ) var atšķirties vienīgi ar intonācijām: ['*daŭʒi nu 'labuõ tuõs*] 'viele verbessern nun diese' : [*dàuʒinu labuô.tuõs*] '(ich) nenne oft die Verbesserten'.

Tādējādi dažkārt viena vārda formai heterotoniski atbilst divu vai pat vairāku vārdu fraze ar uzsvērtu pirmo locekli. Piem.: *kārās* [*kãrâs*] l.pl. fem. 'in gierigen' : *kā rās?* ['*kà rãs*] vai ['*kâ rãs*] 'weshalb od. wie wird (man) schelten?' Verba *ieskāt(ies)* '(sich) lausen' formas, īpaši saliktās, var heterotoniski sadalīties padsmitiem frazēs, piem.: *ieskāsiet* [*iêskâsìet*] 'werdet lausen' : ['*iês kà sìet*] 'wird was zu binden gehen', *pārieskāšana* [*pãriêskâšana*] nomen actionis 'nochmaliges Lausen' : *pāries kāšana* ['*pãriês kàšana*] 'Seihen wird vergehen' u.tml.

Transitīvo un pa daļai arī intransitīvo tagadnes *āja-, īja-* un *uoja*-celma verbu divdabji u.c. formas, kuŗu izskaņas sakrīt ar vietniekvārdu formām (*šos, tai, tajā, tajās, tajos, tas, tā, tām, tās, tie, tiem, to, tos, tu*), visnotaļ pārvēršas divu vārdu frazē, ja mainās intonācija — lauztā ar stiepto — celma beigu vokālismā (*-ā-, -ī-, -uo-*), piem.: *pētītie* [*pētîtiê*] n.pl. 'die geforschten' : *pētī tie* ['*pētĩ tiê*] 'diese forschen', *mazgāšos* [*mazgâšuõs*] 'werde mich waschen'

: *mazgā šos* [*'mazgã šuõs*] 'wäsch(s)t od. wasch diese', *celotu* [*celuôtu*] 'würde reisen' : *celo tu* [*'celuõ tu*] 'du reist od. reise du' u.tml.

Latviešu zilbes intonācijām sēmantiskais svars, kâ redzams, ir visai liels. Starp citu, gadās pat, ka it visas funkcijas uzkrauj intonācijai vien: familiārā sarunvalodā ar kailu lauzto intonāciju aizstāj vārdu *nē* [*nê*] 'nein' (ir iespējams katru intonāciju "izrunāt" izolēti, neartikulējot nevienu skaņu).

Intonāciju sēmantiskā slodze lielāka un heterotonu vairāk ir latviešu nekâ leišu valodā, jo latvieši šķiŗ intonācijas ne tikai uzsvērtās zilbēs (kâ leiši), bet arī neuzsvērtās. Bez tam latviešu valodā viegli veselas paradeigmas var būt heterotoniskas vispārinātā pirmās zilbes uzsvara un vienādotās substantīvu un adjektīvu deklinācijas dēļ. Un fōnētisku pārvērtību dēļ latviešiem ir radušies jauni heterotoni (sal. *dzīt* [*zìt* || *zĩt*], lei. *giñti* 'treiben' : *dzīt* [*zĩt*], lei. *gýti* 'heilen').

Precīzi nav izsveŗama intonāciju sēmantiskā slodze. Cik tā saistās ar heterotoniem, tad svarīgs, pirmkārt, ir heterotonu vienību un formu daudzums, bet ne tikai: svarīgs, otrkārt, ir to lietošanas biežums. Cik iespējams spriest pēc Rīgā patlaban iznākošās *Latviešu valodas biežuma vārdnīcas* (I-1 1966, II-1 1969) no pirmā simta visbiežāk lietojamo vārdu kādi 12 ir heterotoni, vismaz dažās formās. Treškārt, svarīgi ir, cik lielā mērā iespējamas heterotoniskās formas līdzīgā kontekstā. Te dažādība liela. Piem., ir grūti pat iedomāties teikumu, kur heterotonus *birzi* [*biřzi*] a. 'Hain' un *birzi* [*biřzi*] 'zerbröckeltest' varētu apmainīt, turpretī *griezt* [*grìest* || *griêst*], lei. *grẽžti* 'wenden' un *griezt* [*griêst*], lei. *griežti* 'schneiden', kas visās paradeigmās un atvasinājumos pilnīgi vienādi lokāmi, gandrīz vai katrā kontekstā ir iespējami viens otra vietā. Un šķiet, ka runātāji it kâ būtu centušies palielināt starp tiem intonējuma atšķirību, aizstādami (piem., ap Valmieru) krītošo, leišu intonācijai atbilstošo, izrunu ar stiepto, jo starpība starp stiepumu un lauzumu ir daudz labāk izdzirdama —arī uzsvērtā pozicijā — nekâ starp kritumu un lauzumu. Vienam vai otram no šiem verbiem intonācija saknē šķiet mainīta arī cituvid (skat. ME, EH s.v. *griêzt, grìezt*).

Heterotonos intonāciju sēmantiskais svars ir vislielāks, un intonāciju sajaukums te rada neizbēgamu pārpratumu, ja neglābj konteksts. Par konteksta glābējspējām var liecināt, piem., J. Jaunsudrabiņa dzejolis "Tumšs rudzupuķu vainadziņš",[2] kur no 39 vārdiem, neieskaitot 8 atkārtotos, vismaz 12 ir heterotoni: *zāles, sienas* I, *tā, aukstumā, siltu, sienas* II, *sārti, ziedu, kā, raugos* (arī *vēl* — literāri neieteiktā izrunā); *mīļās, tumšās*.

Tumšs rudzupuķu vainadziņš
Uz baltas *zāles sienas.*
Pie *tā vēl* ziemas *aukstumā*
Daudz *siltu* stundu *sienas.*

Tumšs rudzupuķu vainadziņš ...
To *sārti* pirksti vija,
Kad rudzu *ziedu* putekļi
Kā migla saulē lija.

Tumšs rudzupuķu vainadziņš
Aizvien man kaut ko sacīs ...
Es *raugos ziedu* zilumā
Kā *mīļās, tumšās* acīs.

Dzejolis ir arī komponēts, un dziedāšanā intonācijas nav izmanāmas. Tomēr dziesmas tekstā leksiskie heterotoni nekādus pārpratumus nesagādā; drusku šaubīties iespējams gan par gramatiskajiem: vai *mīļās, tumšās* ir substantīva nozīmē lietoti ģenitīvi (viens vai pat abi), jeb vai ar apzīmējamo vārdu saskanīgi daudzsk. lokātīvi (kas gan tie īsteni arī būs domāti savienojumā "kā mīļās, tumšās acīs").

Tomēr ne arvien konteksts spēj heterotonu nozīmi noskaidrot. Rakstos daudzkārt traucē, piem., homografi *kā, tā*. Tāpēc Endzelīns ieteica turpināt senu tradiciju un adverbus grafiski atšķirt: *kâ, tâ*.

Tā kā katrā dialektā ir izveidojusies sava intonāciju sistēma, tad arī literārā runā ne visiem latviešiem ir vienādas intonācijas.

Ja intonāciju starpība zustu, heterotoni pārvērstos par homōnimiem resp. homofōniem, kas daudzkārt ir neērti un tiek aizstāti ar citiem vārdiem. Neērtākie tie, kas ir vienas vārdu šķiras un vienādi arī lokāmi. No heterotonu vienībām tādu ir ap 20 %. Intonācijām zūdot, reizē gaistu to sēmantiskais svars un rastos arī leksikā atkal tamlīdzīgas pārmaiņas, par kādām rakstījis Endzelīns *FBR* IX, 8–9 sakarā ar homōnimu vārdu zušanu.

Piezīmes

1. Visu leksisko piemēru tulkojumi salīdzināti ar *ME*, bet ne katrreiz tulkojums ir ņemts no turienes.
2. No krājuma *Zelta tvaiks*. Mīlas lirikas izlase. Izd. "Liesma", Rīgā 1969, 69.

Latvian Heterotones

In the Latvian Middle Dialect three types of intonation in long syllables are still differentiated: the stretched (˜), the falling (ˋ) and the broken intonation (ˆ), which have their own semantic value in the process of communication.

There are words — I name them heterotones — the lexical or grammatical meaning of which is different, but which differ phonetically only in type of intonation. Whole heterotonic phrases and sentences may also occur. (See examples in the Latvian text.) Over 80 % of heterotones are homographs.

The differentiating intonation may be found in stressed as well as in unstressed syllables of the word, and also in more than one syllable at a time.

There are about 400 lexical heterotones (collected by me according to my Middle-Vidzeme pronunciation with three kinds of intonation). These 400 represent approximately 5,000 heterotonic forms of inflexions and derivatives.

As there is a separate system of intonation in every dialect and people confuse them in actual use, it is expected that the intonation types will have a short life. A normative intonation seems to be practically impossible. If the intonation types are lost, the heterotones will become homophones and cause inconvenience and therefore perhaps often be substituted by other words, thus giving rise to changes in the Latvian vocabulary.

DAVID G. GUILD

The Development of the Concept
of Definiteness in Baltic and Slavic

1.1. The term definiteness refers in the present instance to the act of attributing special significance to an object or quality viewed as a class. An object may, for instance, be definite if it has already been mentioned in a previous utterance. Similarly objects which are unique are taken to be definite. In terms of the solar system 'the sun' is unique and in English would have the definite article, which is the overt realisation of this concept in English.

1.2. *The article*

There may however be no systematic means of marking this feature. Or the concept may only be partially realised in overt terms. Turkish for example does not fully realise this concept. In that language the utterances 'A man came' or 'The man came' are usually indifferently rendered 'Adam geldi'. On the other hand in the utterances 'I saw the man' and 'I saw a man' we have 'Ben adam-i gördüm' and 'Ben adam gördüm'. The noun in the first utterance is marked for definiteness while in the second utterance the noun remains unmarked. The suffix -i of the definite object case marks not only definiteness but also the fact that the noun is direct object. This suffix is extensively used and forms part of a well defined system.

1.3. *Definiteness : Indefiniteness*

Conversely definiteness may be expressed in terms of its opposite. Thus in English the use of the article *a/an* would preclude the simultaneous use of *the*. Historically the English forms are reduced forms of the number *one*, and this numeral is one of the commonest means by which non-definiteness may be inferred. Again in Turkish 'Bir adam geldi' may be substituted for 'Adam geldi' where emphasis is laid on non-definiteness of the subject. In the opposition Bir adam geldi : adam geldi the second term of the equation, though grammatically unmarked, would be definite by contrast.

1.31. In Russian too the numeral one may be used to indicate indefiniteness.[1] Alternatively one may substitite some other indefinite word such as какой-то. To emphasize definiteness on the other hand the pronouns этот (this) and тот (that) are used when the author particularly wants to differentiate the word in question.[2] These uses are sporadic and emphatic and have not attained the status of a system.

A Bulgarian scholar, L. Dončeva-Mareva[3], concentrating on predicative usage in Russian and similar usage in French, English, Bulgarian and German (all of which possess articles), has adduced the following contrasts:

1) In negative sentences the Russian accusative may be compared to definite forms in the other languages; conversely the genitive forms in Russian contrast with indefinite forms.

2) A similar contrast exists with partitive usage. Russian partitive genitive is again parallel to indefinite in these languages (often without any article being present). In the last instance French uses the partitive article and English may substitute forms with *some* for those without an article.

This usage in Russian parallels the Turkish usage of the definite object case in that the opposition definite : indefinite is only partially realised. In Turkish however, it is the definite object which is marked (by the suffix -i) while in Russian the indefinite object is marked (by the use of the genitive). In Polish we have a situation similar to Russian in that the partitive genitive is contrasted with the accusative. Cf. Kupiłem herbatę (A)—I bought the tea : Kupiłem herbaty (PG)—I bought (some) tea. In negative sentences exclusive use of the genitive has eliminated this contrast.

1.32. In general East and West Slavic have evolved no clearly expressed system of articles. Where definiteness or indefiniteness is to be stressed this is often by means other than morphological (for instance word order). The morphological oppositions are limited in their distribution and are sporadic in their nature. Nevertheless a system of articles is to be found on the periphery of the Slavic area, namely in Bulgarian and Macedonian. It is also characteristic of the Balkan area as a whole, the only exceptions being Serbo-Croat and Slovene, which in this feature show greater similarities with W. and E. Slavic. That this phenomenon is not restricted to this area is evident from the existence of articles remarkably similar to the Bulgarian and Macedonian forms in N. Russian dialects. Moreover the S. Slavic systems make use of forms whose origin can be traced back to the word stock of Common Slavic.

2.0. *The Origins of the Article in S. Slavic*

2.1. Wherever they occur the definite forms are derived from original deictics. In assuming the function of articles they lose the feature of distancing (with reference to the speaker) in nearly every instance. The position of the article varies from language to language as does its form. Most are clitics (either proclitic or enclitic) while others approximate more closely to affixes.

2.11. Definite forms are a feature of OCS and these must be distinguished from the modern articles of Bulgarian and Macedonian. They possess, however, two common features in diachronic terms: (1) both are derived from deictics; (2) both are postposed. The postpositive article of OCS is formally cognate with the postpositive article of Baltic and their distribution is similar. These forms will therefore be treated in the same section. For the moment we shall consider only those forms which are ancestral to the articles in modern Bulgarian.

2.12. The postposition of deictics in Slavic is by no means a recent phenomenon. In the Повесть Временныхъ лет of the XII c. we find the form Градокосъ[4] (i.e. Градокъ + съ). In that instance the form functions as a deictic; elsewhere there are instances of the use of deictics as articles. The Bulgarian author I. Gălăbov[5] in a paper in the Zeitschrift für Slawistik considers it to be a late proto-Slavic phenomenon. He finds examples of deictics used as articles in the 'osmь čestii slova' (the Eight Parts of Speech) attributed to John, Exarch of Bulgaria. If this attribution is correct the text was written in Preslav in the Xth century, though only later copies of the text have come down to us. I. Gălăbov cites the following examples: blagodatь tou (tǫ), povělenije to, oustrajenije to. The use of the articulated forms may have originated in those masculine and feminine nouns which ended in ъ or ь. In S. Slavic these coalesced early in the back variant [ъ]. The Exarch himself states in the text that the gender of such words may only be determined when the article is present.

2.13. *OCS deictics*

Though the deictics used in OCS are prosodically free forms, none have survived unaltered in the modern languages; it may be that their phonological shape rendered them unstable. In one case Russian has had recourse to reduplication, while Polish and Bulgarian have added suffixes. In Bulgarian this suffix is joined to all forms whereas in Russian and Polish only the nom. sg. masc. is affected: cf.

OCS tъ	R. tot 'that' < tъ + tъ
and OR	P. ten 'this' < tъ + nъ
(this)	B. то-зи (m): та-зи (f): то-ва (n) те-зи (pl.)

The phonetic instability of such forms would not hinder their use as clitics. It is forms such as OR. градокосъ with the vocalisation of the final -ъ- which point to the fact that such forms must have been unaccented in some or all contexts, and this factor facilitated their taking over the functional load of clitics. In Russian only some northern dialects have postpositive articles, and it is to the Balkans that one must look for the most widespread distribution of such forms.

2.2. The Distribution of the Article in the Balkans

Within the Balkan linguistic area Bulgarian, Macedonian, Rumanian, Albanian and Greek all have articles. Moreover in Greek alone is the article proclitic. The adoption of a postpositive article by these other languages points to certain processes taking place concurrently. This is the opinion of Harold L. Klagstad, Jr.:[6] "this would possibly be the result of converging word stress patterns in late Common Slavic and Eastern Primitive Romanic. The characteristics of the results of this convergence would be (1) a high occurrence of word stress on the initial syllable of free groups of morphemes, and (2) the concomitant inadmissability of an utterance-initial definite clitic morpheme stemming from an older (demonstrative) free group of morphemes. In other words two consecutive stressed syllables at the beginning of the utterance were at a given moment no longer compatible, but were separated, e.g. *[tъ vъlkъ] > B [vălkăt], [vălkăt] (the wolf), [illu lúpu] > Ro [lupul] (the wolf)."

2.21. The Bulgarian Definite Article

An analysis of the Bulgarian definite article gives us the following scheme of gender distribution:

	subj. (noun)		non-subj.
MS in C.	ăt		ă
F and M in -a		ta	
N and M in o/e		to	
Plural N (and M in -ta)		ta	
Others		te	

Nouns of the masc. gender ending in -C have in the literary language a separate form for the non-subject case (this is used after all prepositions). In the colloquial language no casual distinctions are made: a form ă corresponds to -ăt/-ă of the literary language.

The following examples should suffice to illustrate these changes:

a) M. in C

> град 'town' : град*ът*
> кон 'horse' : кон*ят*

The iotated form reflects the original softness of this noun class. (cf. R. конь).

> Non-sub.: град*а* [gradă]
> кон*я* [konjă]

b) F. (and M. in -a):

> маса 'table' : маса*та*
> земя 'land' : земя*та*
> нощ 'night' : нощ*та*
> баща 'father' : баща*та*

c) N. (and M. in -o/e):

> село 'village' : село*то*
> поле 'field' : поле*то*
> вуйчо 'uncle' : вуйчо*то*
> куче 'dog' : куче*то*

d) There are additionally a few neuter nouns which end in other vowels in the singular:

> такси 'taxi' : такси*то*
> меню 'menu' : меню*то*

The plural shows an opposition between nouns which are formally neuter (i.e. which end in -a) and other nouns; some of these neuter nouns are animate, others are collective.

e) N.

> села 'villages' : села*та*
> кучета 'dogs' : кучета*та*
> събрания 'gatherings' : събрания*та*

f) Other nouns:

> майки 'mothers' : майки*те*
> синове 'sons' : синове*те*
> войници 'soldiers' : войници*те*

2.22. *Distribution of the Article*

In describing the article as a clitic we are stressing its semi-free nature. In constructions consisting of a single noun or a series of nouns the article is attached to the noun defined: e.g.[7]

градът е голям	'the town is big'
Аз виждам града	'I see the town'
маса*та* и столове*те* са в стаята	'the table and the chairs are in the room'

Should a qualifier or more than one qualifier precede the noun the article is then attached to the first member of the group so formed. e.g.[7]

Хубави*те* градове са в България	'the beautiful cities are in Bulgaria'
Истинско*то* му име	'his real name'
Нова*та* зелена книга стои на маса*та*	'The new green book is standing on the table.'

2.221. In the masc. sg. of the adjectives an opposition has been created between C- and Ci-., the latter appearing before the definite clitic morpheme, e.g.:

$$
\begin{array}{ll}
\text{нов 'new' :} & \text{N. нов-}u\text{-ят} \\
& \text{O. нов-}u\text{-я} \\
\text{наш 'our' :} & \text{N. наш-}u\text{-ят} \\
& \text{O. наш-}u\text{-я}
\end{array}
$$

2.2211. In those adjectives in [-sk-] and certain others 'denominatives' the -i is the normal marker of the nominative, and the contrast between definite and indefinite stems is not realised here, e.g.:

$$
\begin{array}{ll}
\text{български 'Bulgarian' :} & \text{N. български-ят} \\
& \text{O. български-я} \\
\text{божи 'divine' :} & \text{N. божи-ят} \\
& \text{O. божи-я}
\end{array}
$$

2.2212. The origin of the -i- is in all probability the suffix of the long adjective (cf. R. нов : новый).

2.23. *The Article in Macedonian*

The article in Macedonian resembles closely the Bulgarian. Thus we can establish a similar scheme for this language:

M. in C	ot	Pl. N. -ta
F. and M. in -a	ta	Others -te
N. and M. in o/c	to	

The distribution of nouns within the gender classes is determined as in Bulgarian; those in -C of the masc. gender take -ot; animates in -a or -e/o take -ta or -to. All other feminines take -ta and neuters -to. Similarly in the plural nouns in -a require -ta; all others have -te.

2.231. The N/O distinction of literary Bulgarian is not made in Macedonian. The following two examples should illustrate this point. Both are taken from a Macedonian translation of Šolohov's Донские Рассказы.[8] cf.:

Корабо*т* е врзан кон пристанот	'The ship has tied up to the quay'

or,

Откај селски*от* атаман[9]	'to the village headman ...'

2.232. *Distancing in the Article*

Perhaps the most unusual feature of the article in Macedonian is the survival of a feature normally associated with deictics. In addition to the neutral forms there are two distanced forms which may be set out in the following paradigms:

	Neutral	This	That
M.	градо*т*	градо*в*	градо*н*
F.	земја*та*	земја*ва*	земја*на*
N.	село*то*	село*во*	село*но*
N.Pl.	села*та*	села*ва*	села*на*
Others	гради*те*	гради*ве*	гради*не*

The interest of such forms lies in the fact that they have gone full circle. The original deictics pointed to an object in the same way that an article does, but showed the additional feature of distance from the speaker. An association also existed between these deictics and the persons of the verb: i.e. first person: this; second person: that, third person: that over there, not in sight. This article still pointed to an object, distinguished it from others of its class, but it had lost the feature of distance. This feature (of distance) is characteristic of the Macedonian alone in the Slavic group. Though Macedonian possesses a three term system of deictics this has not penetrated fully the article system. The three classes of the article paradigm are allocated as follows:

1. near objects — ов...;
2. distant objects — он...;
3. neutral for distance — от...

The above analysis of the article systems in Bulgarian and Macedonian represents only the first of such systems in Slavic. It is certainly an innovation of the period of historic development (post Common Slavic) and during the OCS period it must have competed with an older system of definition, but one more restricted in its distribution. This second system is of interest not only on account of its antiquity but for the fact that it is very much alive in modern Baltic and is one of the features linking up these two groups.

3.0. *The Definite Adjective in OCS*

Among the deictics inherited by OCS was the form *jь (и). This is nowhere attested as a free morpheme in the nominative, though the other members of its paradigm are the basis of the third person pronoun in all the Slavic languages. Recourse was had to suppletive forms for the nominative, the commonest of these was on ъ. *jь appears as an element in compounds, for instance, in the OCS relative pronoun jiže. For us its most important use is as a clitic (in the early stages) and subsequently as a bound morpheme in the formation of the definite *adjective*. Its distribution is thus more restricted than the corresponding Bulgarian and Macedonian clitics described above. When allowance is made for this restriction to one class of words it does not differ greatly in its functional load from the modern S. Slavic forms. In an opposition of the type OCS slěpa žena (a blind woman): slěpa*ja* žena one could substitute B. сляпа жена : сляпа*та* жена. The difference between the two systems lies in the fact that -ja in OCS is only found with slěpa-. The B. opposition жена : жена*та* would be rendered indifferently in OCS žena.

3.1. *The Fusion of the Adjectival Paradigm with the Forms of *jь*

One of the morphological signs of antiquity in an OCS text is the lack of fusion of the adjectival paradigm with *jъ. Thus GS dobra-jego is older than dobra-go. In all the modern Slavic languages which possess such forms the process of contraction has been continual, if uneven. Together with the process of contraction has gone a change in the functional opposition between the two systems. The opposition is now largely one of attributive: predicative forms of the adjective. The predicative (the uncompounded form) has lost most of its inflections. In Polish only a limited number of true short forms survive. The reason for this decline is a lack of distinction on the grammatical level.

3.2. *The Definite Adjective in Baltic*

In both the surviving Baltic languages there exists an opposition between definite and indefinite adjectival paradigms. Not only does this parallel the OCS system in its basic functions but the pronominal element in it is cognate with OCS *jь. In Lithuanian *jis, ji* is also found as the pronoun of the third person and the association between the two uses of an original deictic is very clear. In Latvian on the other hand no form of *jis* survives as a free morpheme. As a third person pronoun it has been replaced by 'viņš'.

3.21. *Degrees of Fusion in the Definite Adjectival Paradigm*

Latvian is phonologically more advanced than Lithuanian. The reasons for this need not concern us here except in so far as it is reflected in the definite forms of the adjective. A heavy initial stress (certainly the result of substratum) has led to contraction and even loss of endings. Lithuanian, where this feature has not operated, has preserved with great clarity and a minimal degree of fusion the combined paradigms of the adjective and of *jis*. This corresponds to the earliest stages of OCS. The table below shows the differing degrees of fusion in the two languages.

Lithuanian:

NS.	mažas daržas 'a small garden'	: mažas*is* daržas
GS.	mažo daržo	: mažo*jo* daržo
N.Pl.	maži daržai	: mažie*ji* daržai

Latvian:

NS.	mazs dārzs	: maz*ais* dārzs
GS.	maza dārza	: maz*ā* dārza
N.Pl.	mazi dārzi	: maz*ie* dārzi

The commonest marker of contraction in Latvian as in Slavic is an alternation of length. Where such an alternation still exists in individual Slavic languages a direct formal comparison is possible. For instance the Czech *bílá* ruka (white hand, attr.) corresponds to Latvian baltā roka (the white hand). In the Lithuanian examples the degree of fusion is minimal. The form mažasis can still be broken up into mažas jis, with loss of the j- of jis. In the N.Pl. mažieji the separate forms would be maži + jie: -ie < i is secondary, occurring where -i ceases to be word-final: cf. refl. dirbie-s (i) : dirbi 'you work'.

3.22. *The Functional Load of the Baltic Adjective*

Definiteness in Baltic as in OCS is confined to the *adjective* and to that extent is more restricted than in S. Slavic. Nevertheless in constructions containing adjective and noun there will be agreement to mark definiteness even though the means used is different. In utterances of the type *a blind woman : the blind woman* a series of correspondences can be set up (here Bulgarian will stand for the two S. Slavic languages showing this feature):

	Indefinite	*Definite*
OCS	slĕpa žena	slĕpaja žena
B.	сляпа жена	сляпата жена
L.	akla žmona	akloji žmona
La.	akla sieviete	aklā sieviete

3.221. *The Definite Article in Combination in Endocentric Construction*

The definite suffix in Latvian may be found in combination with deictics as šis 'this' or tas 'that'. In 'Latviešu valodas mācība', a school textbook, the following utterance occurs: "šajā brīnišķīgajā pilsētā" 'in this wonderful city'. A parallel construction substitutes a possessive word for the deictic: i.e. mans, tavs ... From the same source: "Tāpēc mūsu lielajā laikmetā ..." 'therefore in our great epoch ...'. The definite lielajā is again conditioned by the presence of mūsu (our).

In Lithuanian this usage has not developed. In Bulgarian the possessive can become definite: i.e. нашият хубав град ... 'our beautiful city ...' but use of a deictic excludes the use of the article. Thus, *тази* маса 'this table' or the *масата* 'the table' are possible constructions, but not *тази* маса*та*.

3.222. *The Article as a Means of Derivation*

The use of the definite article with an adjective where no noun is present makes the adjective into a noun. Such a process may be observed in English: cf. 'the young ones', or 'the whites'. In these two examples we see two stages of this process of substantivisation. Since 'young' has not fully passed over from the category of adjective to that of noun it cannot itself show number (hence 'ones'). However, 'white' in the second example has been fully substantivised.

An adjective may become a noun contextually or it may pass fully into the class of nouns. In either case in Baltic and Bulgarian and Macedonian this process is marked by the definite article. B. пръви*ят* от тях (the first of them …) is an example of the first stage. An example of the second stage is Даните (data) which has been fully substantivised. An example of the first stage of substantivisation in Latvian is *pārējais* "the rest" which is always found in the definite form. *šaujamais* 'fire-arm' is on the other hand fully substantivised. Such forms have been fully developed in Baltic, possibly to an even greater extent than in South Slavic.

Notes

1. Cf. L. Dončeva-Mareva, *ZfSl* XI, 41.
2. In the following examples both *mom* and *это* would be glossed in English by *the* while какой-то is equivalent to *a/an*.

> *Тот* пример, который был в учебнике литературы — не очень удачный.
> Я описал вам *это* явление, которое привлекло мне внимание не так давно.
> Собралось много народа, спрашивают: „Что здесь произошло?“ „*Какой-то* человек попал под машину“.
> Когда я вышел на улице, *какой-то* человек пробежал мимо меня.

3. Cf. L. Dončeva-Mareva, 38.
4. Н. К. Гудзий, Хрестоматия по древней русской литературе XI–XII веков.
5. I. Gălăbov, *ZfSl* XII, 49.
6. Harold L. Klagstad, Jr., *American Contributions to the Vth International Congress of Slavists*, 1963, Sofia, 184.
7. These examples are mainly from A. B. Lord, *Beginning Bulgarian*.
8. Šolohov, *op. cit.*, 42.
9. Ibid., 25.

ERIC P. HAMP

Priemenė 'Entrance (building), Lobby'

B. Forssman, *KZ* 79, 23–5, has given an excellent account of this word, with the inclusion of valuable dialectal material supplied by Zinkevičius. He has shown that the original form must be *priemnẽ*, registered by Būga[1] for Kaĺtanėnai, and confirmed by Zinkevičius also for Zíetala (Zasẽčiai), Varenãvas[2] (Ramaškóniai), Lazū̃nai, and Ródūnia. It is of course to Christian S. Stang that we are indebted, amongst so many other things, for a phonetically exact and systematic record of the phonology and morphology of the isolated and important dialect of Zasẽčiai, *NTS* 18, 171–201. Since Forssman's treatment formed part of a larger argument he did not enter into certain matters of Baltic detail. In view of some residual uncertainties in his argument, an Indo-Europeanist may also feel that Forssman's use of the evidence, and these stray dialect forms, was somewhat eclectic. Two additional aspects may be elaborated which, I believe, serve to strengthen Forssman's persuasive argument.

1. Forssman fails to bring out the important geographic dialect distribution of *priemnẽ*. Not only are the villages mentioned on the very edge of the Lithuanian speech area (a fact that makes their status as relict forms highly possible), but they belong to significantly different dialect groups even in the cases where they are not located many kilometres apart. Zinkevičius makes it clear in his exemplary work on Lithuanian dialectology[3] that Lazū̃nai, like Kaĺtanėnai (though the two are widely distant), belongs to the Vilniškiai Eastern dialect area; that Varenãvas and Ródūnia belong to the Southern Aukštaičiai area; but that Zíetala, though far to the south and somewhat east, goes with Western Aukštaičiai. This is a wide and significant distribution for so few villages, and it adds to the plausibility of ancient status for this form.

It is true that from the point of view of dialectology the Southern Aukštaičiai area appears on several grounds to drive a wedge between the Western (Kaunas) area and the conservative outlier of Zíetala (Zasẽčiai). This could make the separate testimony of Western Aukštaičiai and Zasẽčiai not really as independent as they seem, since they would then be a remnant of a former continuum. Some might then argue that the forms from Varenãvas and Ródūnia are really survivals from an earlier Western type (a substratum). But even if that were so, we still have two widely separate attestations from the Eastern Aukštaičiai. It would be difficult indeed to argue that all these go back to a single recent innovation.

Furthermore the testimony of Kaltanénai as a conservative dialect is valuable in this context. This place, together with nearby Liñkmenys and Rimšẽ, is noteworthy for preserving many traces of the old consonant-stem nouns, eg. gen. sg. *ašès,*[4] *ausès, avietès, dantès, debesès, dieverès, geležès, gramdès,*[4] *iltès,*[4] *kulšès,*[4] *liūtès* ('a long heavy rainfall'), *meškerès, moterès, naktès, obelès, pažintès,*[4] *pirtès,*[4] *pušès, rūgštès, rūšès, skiauturès* (with *-u-* assimilated from the preceding diphthong probably), *šaknès, šerdès, širdès, tulžès,*[4] *ugnès,*[4] *usnès,*[4] *vagès, votès,*[4] *voverès, žąsès, žuvès, žvėrès;* nom. pl. *ánkštes, dañtes, dùres, ìltes,*[4] *kándes, kùlšes,*[4] *ligónes, móteres, pùsnes,*[4] *pùšes, smãgenes, šìrdes, ùgnes,*[4] *ùsnes,*[4] *vãges, võtes,*[4] *vóveres, žąses, žmónes,*[5] *žùves, žvéres.*[6] We also find here archaic nom. pl. toponyms: *Kaltanes* 'Kaltanénai' and *Žeĩmenes*, a lake near there. Nearby Liñkmenys (*Liñkmenes*) also preserves the nom. pl. *túkstantes* 'tūkstančiai'.[7] We are therefore not surprised to find other evidences of archaic noun formation in this area.[8]

2. Forssman has also argued that the forms with intervening vowel, such as *priemenẽ* and *prieminẽ*, reflect anaptyxis after a diphthong in order to lighten a heavy cluster. He notes (fn. 1, p. 25) that Schlerath and Zinke-vičius have reservations about this solution, since Lithuanian does not normally show anaptyxis. I feel that the objections of these Baltic scholars are well taken, although I think we may at the same time rescue Forssman's insight.

Forssman is clearly correct in seeing *priemẽ* and *prienẽ* not as separate suffix formations as Fraenkel does, but as different resolutions of a parallel simplification of the cluster seen in *priemnẽ*. We may perhaps see in this cluster reduction a parallel to that for **nm* seen in such old *n-* stem forms as *wandemi, vandimi* (rebuilt into *vandenimi*), *akmemi, akmemis*. In fact, on these grounds perhaps *prienẽ* might be the more expected form. This then adds another reason for starting from *priemnẽ*. With a pre-form with intervening vowel we would then have no motivation for arriving at these shorter forms, for syncope is just as unexpected in Lithuanian as anaptyxis is. That the Zasẽčiai form is scarcely susceptible of an explanation by syncope is also made virtually certain by the shapes seen in the paradigms given for *piemuõ* and *vanduõ* by Stang, NTS 18, 186.

We must therefore seek a morphological reason for the genesis of forms in *-menẽ* and *-minẽ*. I think there are two possible sources, both of which may have operated simultaneously. Since *priemnẽ* is in origin, as Forssman has shown, a suffixed form *prie-mnẽ* feminized from **prei-mna-*, it is possible that the shape of the word continued for a long time to be viewed as containing a suffix. I have shown elsewhere[9] that Baltic has undergone a degree of productivity in ablaut alternation of suffixes, particularly in the case of *-r-*. One may recall in this context that the Baltic nouns have continued side-by-side *r-* stems and *n-* stems, which have revalued their ablaut by generalizing the full grade. In other words, rather than phonetic anaptyxis, we may regard *priemenẽ* as a neo-guṇa to *priemnẽ*, and *prieminẽ* as a neo-Schwundstufe (e.g. as reflected in verbal preterites), even as a Sievers alternation after a heavy syllable if such conditioning still applied. The relation *-en-/-in-* as a suffixal pair has of course had a long and active, if limited, life up to recent, and even present, times in the *n-* stems, as seen in the paradigm from the older language (particularly Bretkūnas); on this see Kazlauskas LKIG 272. For *piemen-* beside *vándin-* in Zasẽčiai see Stang NTS 18, 186.

On such grounds it would have been possible for a suffixal alternation to have grown up and prospered for some time. But it is not likely in an isolated word that such a fresh alternation would have continued for very long as a pure suffixal function unsupported by other patterns. As it happens, however, a different analysis is, and for a long time has been, simultaneously possible; and it is reasonable to suppose that speakers have intuitively applied that alternative analysis. In this fashion, *prie-m(e)nẽ* may be regarded as a compound derived structure of the form LOCATIONAL + BASE; that is, the adverbial prefix *prie-* plus a form of a nominal. In this fashion the perceived structure would have infused new life and a fresh rôle into the element *-m( )nẽ*. And the semantics would have correspondingly developed as 'pre-/Vor- + the name of something'. That this is in fact what happened is borne out by the fact that a new word *mẽnė* 'Saal' has arisen. Fraenkel LitEW, s.v. *priemenẽ*, correctly recognizes this source for *mẽnė*; but he fails to draw the far more interesting etymological conclusion that the birth of this new word bears witness to the perceived understanding of the make-up of the old word. It is clear from the sequel that *prie-menẽ ~ -minẽ* was understood as containing a noun that could assume the shape in isolation of *mẽnė*.

We may even guess at the "root" of this new noun. If a hall or building, particularly when an entrance, is a place where one steps or walks or treads, this new noun has all the appearances of being a nominalization of the well known verb *mìna, mýnė, mìnti* 'treten', which is clearly related to Slavic *mьnǫ, męti*; on these verbs see Stang VGBS 334, 380. In other words, we may attempt to motivate the vocalisations of the old suffix by claiming to have identified, at least provisionally, the new pseudo-noun which it has become; and the vocalisations found are appropriate for such a noun formation.

It is difficult to choose an absolute priority from among these morphological arguments which turn upon the vocalisms of suffixes and bases. But we find here diachronic regularities that can be specified exactly in a fashion that no phonetic anaptyctic vowel will permit.

There is, moreover, a final confirmation for our hypothesis in the stem-class itself of this noun. Forssman (25) does not motivate the stem-class other than to remark that feminines in *-iā were productive in Lithuanian; but so they were to some degree in many an Indo-European language. The important and confirmatory fact in this case is that nouns formed with a locational prefix quite regularly are moved into the stem-class -is/-ỹs ~ -ė.[10] Thus we find to stãlas 'table' the formations pastalė̃ 'space under the table' and ùžstalė 'space behind the table'; and to angà 'doorway' we find príeangis ~príeangė 'structure in front of the entrance way'. The stem formation of prie-m(e)nė̃ therefore confirms that its surface syntactic structure is LOCATIONAL + BASE with the meaning 'place described by such a locational relation' or 'object filling such a space'.

Instead of having an irregularly inserted vowel, then, we have been led to recognize a well-formed word in its lexical elements, its meaning, its morphological structure, its vocalism (and dialect variations), and its stem class. We may now say with confidence that we have accounted for the transformation of *prei-mno- '± for-ward(s), to-ward(s)' into prie-mnė̃~prie-minė̃~prie-menė̃ etc.

Lithuanian priem(e)nė̃ may therefore take its place, as Forssman has urged, alongside such archaic Indo-European formations as Gk. πρυμνός, Vedic nimná-, Latin antemna (Proto-Romance *antĭnna), and Hittite ša-ra-(a-)am-na. We have seen in the course of our argument, also, how important it is to take proper account of the details of Lithuanian dialects and their distribution, and of the internal historical development of the Baltic languages—topics on which we owe so much to the masterful scholarship of the man whom it is a delight to honour.

Notes

1. *Kalba ir senovė*, 52, as cited by Forssman; now conveniently found in Būga, *Rinktiniai raštai* II, 69. I am indebted to Zinkevičius, the editor of Būga's valuable collected works, for a copy of this indispensable tool.

2. Shown by Forssman as Varanãvas.

3. *Lietuvių dialektologija*, 1966, 446; *Lietuvių kalbos tarmės*, 1968, 44.

4. Forms such as *ašès*, *ugnès*, nom. pl. *pùsnes*, *ùgnes*, etc. show that in these dialects there has been even a slightly productive shift from *i*-stems to the consonant stems. For an analogous observation on the transfer of *i*-stems see Stang, *VGBS*, 206 and 200, and J. Kazlauskas, *Lietuvių kalbos istorinė gramatika* 1968, 215, 216, 254. On the other hand, I see no need to attribute stems in -*i*(-) to Indo-European for the etyma of *akìs* (in the singular) or of *širdìs*, etc., as Kazlauskas, *op. cit.*, 242–3, alludes to. The various developments of the word for 'heart' must be explained in the separate dialect histories of IE. I have already attempted to explain Skt. *ákṣi*, *ásthi*, *dádhi* on different grounds; see *Word*, IX, 135–41, and *KZ* 84, 1970, 140–1. (on Albanian *djathë*).

5. For an extended discussion of this important word, see Stang, *VGBS*, 225–7, esp. 226 in our present context.

6. For a full account of such interesting forms see Zinkevičius, *Lietuvių dialektologija* § 412, pp. 263–6; for these in the context of Old Lithuanian see Stang, *VGBS*, 220, 222, 223. For fuller exemplification of controlled older forms see J. Palionis, *Lietuvių literatūrinė kalba XVI–XVII a.*, 1967, 107–9.

7. Zinkevičius, *LD*, § 570.

8. One may recall that here too we find the old loc. pl. ending -*su*; see Zinkevičius, *LD*, § 362, p. 237, and Stang, *VGBS*, 186–7. This area also furnishes interesting remains of athematic verbs; see Stang, *VGBS*, 317.

9. *Baltistica*, currently appearing.

10. For a clear statement, see A. Senn, *Handbuch der litauischen Sprache* I, § 660.

MICHAŁ HASIUK

Die Ferndissimilation des *k, g* in den litauischen Dialekten

Die Ferndissimilation der Mitlaute in den litausichen Dialekten hat eine ziemlich grosse territoriale Reichweite. Man kann sagen, dass sie für das ganze litauische Sprachgebiet gilt. Derselbe Prozess äussert sich besonders ausdrucksvoll in den Lehnwörtern. Das ist völlig zu verstehen, wenn diese Wörter fremder Gestalt dem Mitlautsystem der litauischen Sprache der Adaptation, die unter neuen Bedingungen funktionieren könnte, unterliegen. Diese Erscheinung beschreibt Z. Zinkevičius in *Lietuvių dialektologija*, 172–174 ff. Die Kraft dieses Prozesses soll das Beispiel bezeugen, in dem die Dissimilation stattgefunden hat, obwohl die Mitlaute [*r* ... *r*] nicht in den Nachbarsilben auftreten, z. B. *kolidorius* Šialiai, Jukiškiai, Biržai, Palėvenė, Alunta oder *kalidorius* Kretinga, Tirkšliai, Šakyna, Eržvilkas, Vilkaviškis, Punskas (Puńsk), Kaniava, Ukmergė, Pandėlys, Adutiškis, *kalidaras* Žasliai, *kalidõras* — ostlit. *kaliduõras* Kuktiškės, Dotinėnai, Palūšė, Salakas, literatursprachlich *koridorius* 'Korridor' ibid., 172. Ein anderes echt litauisches Wort zeigt die Dissimilation des *g* in den Nachbarsilben, z. B. *degùtė/degùlė, degužė̃* Punskas (Puńsk), Rudamina, Leipalingis, Veisiejai, Zietela, Onuškis, Gervėčiai, literatursprachlich *gegùtė* 'Kuckuck' ibid., 174. Hier findet sich auch die Erklärung für den Dorfnamen *Degucie* im Kreis Sejny.

Obengenannte Beispiele illustrieren die Erscheinung der Ferndissimilation von Typ C ... C/Z ... C, wobei Z einen im Ergebnis der Dissimilation entstandene Mitlaut bedeutet. Es gibt gleichfalls Fälle der Veränderungen der zweiten Komponente des Typs C ... C/C ... Z, z. B. *tiknagas : titnagas* 'Kiesel', Zinkevičius, S. 174 (nach *APh* III, S. 65). Auf der S. 172 treffen wir ebenfalls Verben des Typs *bárkštelėti* 'einmal klopfen, kurz klirren' aber *žvilgterėti* 'den Blick auf etwas werfen', wenn der Autor diesen Wörtern auch nicht eine besondere Abhängigkeit der Nachsilbe vom Stammwort verleiht. Nichtsdestoweniger ist zu erwähnen, dass eine solche Abhängigkeit in einigen Gebieten existiert.

Wir sehen also, dass die Restriktion nicht von einem Element, sondern von der Nachbarschaftsberührung herzuleiten ist. So kann sich einmal die erste Komponente, dann die zweite verändern. Die Komponente verändert sich zuerst in ihrer schwächsten Stellung, die sich aus ihrer Relation zur Nachbarschaft ergibt. Darauf beziehen sich unsere Untersuchungen. Die bisher beschriebene Ferndissimilation bezog sich nur auf die Stammwörter. Bei der Betrachtung der Diminutivsuffixe konnten wir feststellen, dass die Ferndissimilation auch in den Wörtern der Art Stamm + Diminutivsuffix auftritt. (Einige Spuren dieser Erscheinung fanden wir in Dialektmaterialien des Instituts für Litauische Sprache und Literatur in Vilnius.)

Besonders deutlich ist die Ferndissimilation bei Diminutivsuffixen der Namen von jungen, unverheirateten Menschen zu sehen. Das Suffix *-ukas*, wird, wie man annehmen kann, im ganzen litauischen Sprachgebiet zur Bezeichnung für obengenannten Namen gebraucht. Die Verwendung des Suffixes ist durch die Linie Kapsukas–Vilkaviškis–Kaišiadorys und weiter nach Süden begrenzt. Die Namen, die durch *k* oder *g* am Themaende gekennzeichnet sind, erhalten nämlich andere Suffixe, z. B. *Senkùtis* (Jung-*Senkus*) Vilkaviškiai, Prienai, Skraiudžiai; *Petrauckėlis* (:Jung-*Petrauckas*), literatursprachlich *Petrauskas* (Nemaniūnai); *Navickùcis* (:Jung-*Navickas*) Nemaniūnai und *Navickýnas* (Jung-*Navickas*) Veisiejai; *Butkùtas* (:Jung-*Butkus?*) Nemaniūnai. Dasselbe betrifft Gattungsnamen, z. B. *langùtis* 'kleines Fenster' [:*lángas* 'Fenster'] Jurbarkas, Vilkaviškis und *langùcis* „dass". Veisiejai, Ramaškonys. Nördlich genannter Linie begegnet man schon *langiùkas* „dass." Radviliškis.

Noch deutlicher ist das zu sehen am Suffix *-utas*, welches man nur bei solchen Wörtern, deren Thema auf *k*, *g* auslautet, trifft, z. B. *bernukùtas*, Koseform von *bernùkas* (:*bérnas* 'Junggeselle, Bedienster', *bernùkas* 'noch junger Junggeselle'); *kaisnukùtas* 'ziemlich kleines Stückchen' (:*káisnis* 'Stück', literatursprachlich *ką̇snis*); *kiškùtas* 'Häschen' (:*kìškis* 'Hase'); *langùtas* 'Fensterchen' (:*lángas* 'Fenster'); *mergutà* 'Mädchen' (:*mergà* 'Mädchen, Magd') alle Beispiele aus der Gegend um Zietela und noch andere wie *takùtas* 'schmaler Pfad' (:*tãkas* 'Pfad') Punia; *vaikùtas* 'Kindlein, Knäblein' (:*vaĩkas* 'Knabe, Kind') Zietela, Punia, Birštonas, Darsūniškis, Kietaviškės und Kruonis.

Wie wir sehen, unterscheiden sich die Suffixe *-ukas* und *-utas* nur durch *t* und *k*, also jeweils ein Element; andere Suffixe wie *-ėlis*, *-utis*/*-ucis*/, *-ynas* weisen stärkere Differenzen auf.

Unsere Beispiele betreffen zwar nur die Ferndissimilation von *k*, *g*, zusammengestellt mit der Dissimilation der anderen Konsonanten lassen sich jedoch Vergleiche mit Erscheinungen solcher Art wie den Auswirkungen des Grassmannschen und des Thurneysenschen Gesetzes anstellen.

Die Wirkung der Ferndissimilation erklären wir auf der Grundlage der phonischen Prozesse, die die Verteilung der phonischen Substanz der Wörter betreffen. Da die Erscheinung der Ferndissimilation so deutlich zum Vorschein kommt und ihre Verbreitung in den litauischen Mundarten bisher nicht erforscht ist, ist es m. E. nötig, sie bei den weiteren Forschungen entsprechend zu berücksichtigen. Es ist möglich, dass eine gegenseitige Abhängigkeit zwischen der Ferndissimilation und der Zahl der Diminutivsuffixe existiert, d. h., dass nicht jedes Stammwort beliebige Diminutivsuffixe annehmen konnte. Historisch gesehen könnte eine solche Situation in der litauischen Sprache existiert haben. Als Beispiel kann hier der Vergleich der Suffixe -*ukas* und -*utas* herangezogen werden. Es ist möglich, dass die Ferndissimilation als eine Ursache für die Erhaltung synthetischer Sprachformen anzusehen ist. Es wäre die Frage zu stellen, warum die Ferndissimilation im Süden stärker und im Norden schwächer ist. Gegenwärtig können wir das noch nicht eindeutig beantworten, doch können wir schon heute einen anderen Sprachprozess zeigen, nämlich die Palatalisierung, die im Norden stärker als im Süden ist. Die Palatalisierung verändert teilweise oder gänzlich die Konsonanten, wobei sie die Dissimilationsprozesse abschwächend beeinflusst.

Incontiguous Dissimilation of k, g in Lithuanian Dialects

The incontiguous dissimilation in Lithuanian dialects occurs in both loan and native words. Either the first or second consonant is subject to a change, e.g. Z ... C or C ... Z, where the Z stands for the changed consonant.

The paper deals with the incontiguous dissimilation of k and g in diminutive words. It applies only to the suffix consonants, i.e. of the C ... Z type.

The author has come to the conclusion that this kind of dissimilation is one of the causes of the great number of suffixes in Lithuanian dialects.

In the northern dialects, where the dissimilation is weaker, another phonetic process, that of palatalization, occurs.

E. HAUZENBERGA-ŠTURMA

Ergänzende Bemerkungen zum baltischen -*sta*-Präsens

Dieser Beitrag sollte lediglich eine Ergänzung sein zu den kurzen Äusserungen des hochverehrten Jubilars über das -*sta*-Präsens im Lettischen (Chr. S. Stang, *Das slavische und baltische Verbum*, 133 und *Vergleichende Grammatik der Baltischen Sprachen*, 344). Es wäre demnach falsch am Platze, hier auf die sehr unterschiedlichen Meinungen über die Entstehung des baltischen präsensbildenden -*st*-Morphems einzugehen. Trotzdem lag es aber nahe, auf einige Fragen der geschichtlichen Entwicklung zurückzugreifen.

Eingangs sei gesagt, dass die Verf. das -*sta*-Präsens für ein ganz eindeutig baltisches Phänomen hält. Die Beweiskraft des von vielen Forschern — allerdings häufiger mit Reserve — hinzugezogenen einzigen slawischen Verbums *rasti*, Präs. *rastǫ* reicht nicht aus für eine „baltisch-slawische Wahrscheinlichkeit" (Otrębski, *Gramatyka języka litewskiego*, II, 326), und zwar, nicht wegen des Vorkommens von -*st*- auch ausserhalb des Präsens des slawischen Verbums (weswegen M. Leumann *IF*, LVIII, 116 die Zusammenstellung für „sicher falsch" hält), sondern weil für das slawische Wort mehr als eine etymologische Deutung in Betracht kommt, s. Vasmer, *Russ. et. Wb.*, II, 494. Es geht nicht an, eine etymologische Entscheidung nur wegen einer im Slawischen ein einziges Mal vorkommenden Ableitung zu treffen. Dieses muss festgehalten werden, denn bei der Beurteilung des -*st*-Suffixes kann auch sein Alter eine Rolle spielen, und für Vertreter konsequent genealogischer Denkweise dürfte dann eine slawische Parallele von Gewicht sein.

Man hatt bekanntlich das baltische -*sta*-Präsens schon für indogermanistische Zwecke missbraucht, so den vereinheitlichten Akut im Präsens mit Wortkern CVR. Wir haben Grund genug, mit Kuryłowicz *BSPL*, XXIII, 181 anzunehmen, dass es sich hier lediglich um eine Vereinheitlichung des Silbentons handelt, deren Resultat den durchgehenden Akut als zusätzliches Kennzeichen dieses Präsens ergibt („surimposée à la suffixation comme un trait redondant"). Dasselbe nimmt Kuryłowicz, l.c., 180 mit gutem Recht für die Verallgemeinerung der Längen *y*, *ū* in diesen Formen an. Es sind ja solche Redundanzerscheinungen für die litauische Wortbildung, könnte man sagen, geradezu charakteristisch: Eine Ableitungsklasse oder ein Wortstand[1] wird zwei- oder dreifach gekennzeichnet — durch das Ableitungssuffix, durch die Vokalabstufung im Wortkern, durch den Silbenton. Vgl. z. B. die Gruppe der Intensiv-Durativa *brýdoti, rýmoti, klū́poti* usw., oder die Verbalabstrakta *dõvis, krỹtis, mū̃šis* usw., oder die Adjektivabstrakta *plõtis, gỹlis, dỹdis, gẽris* usw., u. a. m., nicht zuletzt aber die kleine Gruppe der von Farbadjektiven abgeleiteten *-sta*-Präsentia: *baĩsta : báltas, juõsta : júodas* u. a. (Otrębski, l.c., II, 325). — W. P. Schmid hat ganz bestimmt recht, wenn er *IF*, LXVII, 14 die Nutzung dieses Akuts für indogermanistische Spekulationen ablehnt.

Chr. S. Stang hat fürs Baltische eine formal gekennzeichnete Kategorie des Transitiv/Intransitivs aufgestellt, die einmal in der Opposition von *ē*- und *ā*-Präteritum erscheint, zum andern in der Opposition von *(i̯)o*-Präsens und Präsens mit Nasalinfix, wobei komplementär zu letzterem das *-sta*-Morphem auftritt — demnach also auch dieses, nach Stang, in kategorialer Funktion („Intransitivierungsaffix", *Gramm.* 342), neben der Funktion als Zeichen einer Aktionsart. Es wird auch sonst von „inkohativ-intransitiver Bedeutung" gesprochen (Johansson *KZ*, XXXII, 476) und von „intransitiv-inkohativer Bedeutung" („intranzityvumo-inchoatyvumo reiškimo funkcija" J. Kazlauskas, *Lietuvių kalbos istorinė gramatika*, 318). Präziser drückt sich Kuryłowicz (l.c., 175) aus: „valeur soit intransitive (-passive) soit inchoative".

Denn wir haben, systematisch gesehen, zu unterscheiden zwischen einer lexikalisch-semantischen Kategorie der Aktionsart und einer grammatisch-syntaktischen Kategorie der Transitivität/Intransitivität — letzteres, wenn man transitiv und intransitiv nicht auf das isolierte Verb bezieht, auf dessen Determiniertheit gewisser Art oder Undeterminiertheit, sondern auf das Verb als Prädikat im Satz in seiner Objektbezogenheit oder Subjektbezogenheit.

Es liegt zwar in der Natur der Dinge, dass intransitive Verben u. a. inkohativ sein können, und umgekehrt, dass inkohative Verben intransitiv sind, aber es ist nicht glaubhaft, dass ursprünglich ein Ableitungssuffix geschaffen wurde, um zwei Kategorien zugleich allgemein zu kennzeichnen. Zeichen der Intransitivität war zu einer gewissen Zeit der baltischen Sprachgeschichte das *n*-Infix — einerlei, ob man diese seine Funktion als vorbaltisch verankert, also ursprünglich, betrachtet, wie Stang, *Gramm.* 340, oder ob man sie für sekundär hält, wie z. B. Kuiper, *Die idg. Nasalpräsentia*, 202 f., oder Vaillant, *BSL*, XLIII, 80. Das *-sta*-Suffix umstrittener Entstehung aber ist zur Kennzeichnung einer Aktionsart geschaffen worden. Es ist ein Zeichen, das in verschiedenen chronologischen Schichten der ostbaltischen Sprachen eine Rolle gespielt hat und noch heute spielt, dessen ursprüngliche Funktion wohl der Ausdruck der Inkohativität war, woher es noch heute, teils zu Unrecht, seinen Namen hat. Es ist nun kein Wunder, dass in Fällen, wo die Lautstruktur litauischer Verben ein Nasalinfix nicht zuliess, dieses Inkohativsuffix — seinerseits Morphem intransitiver Verben — an dessen statt genützt wurde. Aber für diesen komplementären Zweck kann es nicht geschaffen worden sein (wie Kazlauskas, l.c., 318, 328 u. a. zu meinen scheint). Es sei hier übrigens an die sehr ansprechende Motivierung des Aufkommens von -sta- bei Kuiper, l.c., 189 erinnert.

Die Kategorie der Transitivität und Intransitivität scheint im litauischen Sprachbewusstsein länger gültig gewesen zu sein als im lettischen, ja vielleicht ist ihre Geltung gar nicht unterbrochen gewesen. Für die hier behandelten Präsentia des Litauischen vgl. das einschlägige Kapitel bei Kazlauskas, l.c. Rein synchronisch gesehen, ist die Verbundenheit der Transitivität und Intransitivität mit gewissen Präsensstämmen bzw. Ableitungsmorphemen im Litauischen viel konsequenter als im Lettischen. Davon kann man sich bei der Durchsicht des Materials bei Otrębski, l.c., einerseits, bei Endzelin andrerseits leicht überzeugen. Im Lettischen gibt es z. B. präsentische -ēja-, -āja-, -uoja-, -dā-, -na-, -a-, sogar -i̯a- Stämme sowohl als Transitiva als auch als Intransitiva; im Litauischen kommt ein solches Nebeneinander viel seltener vor, wenngleich es auch nicht ganz fehlt. — Als formales Mittel zum Ausdruck der Intransitivierung dient im heutigen Lettisch das (mediale) Reflexivmorphem. Vgl. z. B. *cept* tr. und intr. 'backen, braten' : *cepties* intr.[2] 'dass.'; *celt* tr. 'heben' und intr. (dainasprachlich) 'aufstehen' : *celties* 'sich erheben, aufstehen'; *steigt* tr. 'beschleunigen' und intr. 'sich beeilen' : *steigties* 'sich beeilen'.

Bekannt ist in der Baltistik, dass -sta- im Lettischen eine besonders grosse Verbreitung und Produktivität hat, weil eine Ableitung mit Nasalinfix fürs Lettische gar nicht in Betracht kommt, da ja die baltischen Nasaldiphthonge *an, en, in, un* im Lettischen *uo, ie, ī, ū* ergeben haben. Es ist dieses eines der wichtigen Charakteristika, die das Lettische vom Litauischen unterscheiden, und darum ist es geradezu unverständlich, wieso Kazlauskas, l.c., 322 gemeinlettische Verben mit Normalstufe und historischem Nasalinfix, wie 3. Präs. *rùod* = lit. *rañda*, *prùot* = lit. *prañta*, *tùop* = lit. *tañpa* für im Lettischen unabhängig entstanden halten kann („infiksą gali būti gavę savarankiškai, atskirai lietuvių ir latvių kalboje"). Das ist grundfalsch. Auch das Kurische Westkurlands (mit erhaltenem *an, en, in, un*) hat hier, wie das Wortmaterial zeigt, keine Rolle gespielt.

Allgemein kann man sagen, dass die Art der Bildung des -sta-Präsens, wie sie im Litauischen auftritt, gemeinostbaltisch gewesen ist, denn die litauischen Typen, formal und semantisch gesehen, finden sich im Lettischen wieder, wenn auch mit Verallgemeinerungen im Vokalismus und in der prosodischen Struktur. Das Lettische ist weiter produktiv gewesen — und ist es jetzt — im Bilden sowohl „deverbativer" als auch deutlich denominativer -*sta*-Präsentia. Diese letzteren scheinen in der Diskussion um das -*sta*-Präsens zu kurz gekommen zu sein, obschon ihr Alter nicht unerheblich ist, da es eine Anzahl litauisch-lettischer Übereinstimmungen gibt: lit. *sõpsta* = lett. *sāpst*, *baĩsta* = *balst*, *ĩlgsta* = *ilgst*, *skóbsta* = *skābst* u. a.

Hier sei eine semantisch-strukturelle Analyse derjenigen lettischen Verba mit -*sta*-Präsens versucht, die von Adjektiven abgeleitet sind oder heute noch abgeleitet werden, denn sie ergeben einen Ausblick auf den Aufbau des Paradigmas.

Im Lettisch-Deutschen Wörterbuch nebst Ergänzungen (ME und EH) und in einer kleinen persönlichen Sammlung aus der zeitgenössischen Literatur wurden insgesamt 48 solche Verba gezählt. Davon haben aber nur 6 ein vollständiges Averbo: *ilgt* 'dauern, währen' : *ilgs* 'lang (zeitlich)', *sarkt* 'rötlich werden, erröten' : *sarks* 'rötlich', *skābt* 'sauer werden' : *skābs* 'sauer', *slapt*[3] 'feucht werden' : *slapjš* 'nass', *slābt* 'schlaff werden' : *slābs* 'schlaff', -*slimt* 'erkranken' : *slims* 'krank', d. h. nur von diesen sind sämtliche Verbalformen zu bilden. Von den übrigen Verben ist der Infinitiv des Stichworts nur bei etwa der Hälfte faktisch in Beispielsätzen belegt (mit oder ohne Präfix), sonst ist er eine Lexikonform, die grundsätzlich mit dem Asteriskus gezeichnet ist, jedoch nicht immer (besonders zu Beginn des Werkes). Von 14 Verben kommt ausschliesslich das Part. praet. act., und zwar in präfigierter — aktionsartverstärkender oder -modifizierender, oder aber perfektivierender — Form vor, von weiteren 6 ein präfigiertes Part. praet. act. und ein präfigiertes Präteritum. Einmal konnte als einzige Form ein präfigiertes Präteritum festgestellt werden[4]. Ein unpräfigiertes Part. praet. act. kommt gar nicht vor, ein unpräfigiertes Präteritum 4 mal. Das Präsens ist 6 mal mit und ohne Präfix belegt, 10 mal ohne, 3 mal mit Präfix. Es sei ausdrücklich hervorgehoben, dass diese Zahlen nur sehr relativen Wert haben, da das Beispielmaterial im Wörterbuch meist reinem Zufall zu verdanken ist. Trotzdem scheint die Anzahl der präfigierten Part. praet. act.[5] und die Anzahl der belegten unpräfigierten Präsensformen etwas auszusagen.

Alle diese von Adjektiven abgeleiteten Verben drücken ein So-Werden aus, das Werden wie der Inhalt des zugrundeliegenden Adjektivs besagt, das Annehmen der Eigenschaft, die das Adjektiv ausdrückt. Und zwar, nicht nur den Begriff dieses Werdens, sondern zugleich den Vorgang des

Werdens und seine Vollendung. Es ist darum nicht richtig, auch diese De-
nominativa als „inkohativ" zu bezeichnen. Sie haben sich allerdings aus
der inkohativen Bedeutung entwickelt, worauf Spuren im Litauischen hinweisen[6], doch die heutige Struktur ihres Paradigmas widerspricht der inkohativen Einschränkung.

Der Aufbau des Paradigmas lässt sich wie folgt nachvollziehen. 1. Es
wird festgestellt, dass etwas, beispielsweise Milch (*piens*) sauer (*skābs*) geworden ist, oder dass ein Apfel (*ābols*) rötlich (*sārts*) geworden ist: *piens
kļuvis skābs; ābols kļuvis sārts*. 2. Man will etwas aussagen von der Milch
oder dem Apfel, die soeben diese Eigenschaften erlangt haben, zu diesem
Zweck transformiert man das Prädikativsyntagma[7] in ein Determinativ-
syntagma[7], d. h. man fasst die soeben erlangten Eigenschaften attributiv,
und das durch das Part. praet. act., welches durch Präfigierung zugleich
perfektiviert ist und somit den vollendeten Vorgang unterstreicht: *saskābis
piens; apsārtis ābols*. Diese Transformation ist etwas Abgeschlossenes, bei
dem man es bewenden lassen kann, und ihr Resultat, das Partizip — nicht
das Adjektiv — ist der eigentliche Ausgangspunkt für die Bildung des *-sta-*
Präsens. 3. Es liegt nahe, neben dem Part. praet. die entsprechende finite
Form, das Präteritum, zu bilden: *piens saskāba; ābols apsārta*. Dadurch ist
unser Transformationsresultat ins Tempussystem eingetreten. 4. Zum Präteritum kann ein Präsens, zunächst ein präfigiertes, gebildet werden: *piens
saskābst*. Es gibt aber kein *ābols *apsārst*, denn im Grunde genommen ist ein
solches Präsens eine redundante Aussageform neben dem anfänglichen Prädikativsyntagma *'ābols kļūst sārts*. Es gibt eine Reihe von Verben, wo solch
ein Präsens nicht belegt ist, und wenn wir trotzdem gewisse Part. praet. act.
(und dazugehörende Präterita) beim *-sta-*Präsens behandeln, dann nur
darum, weil das lettische Sprachbewusstsein („Sprachgefühl") es einem sagt,
dass hier einzig und allein ein *-sta-*Präsens in Betracht käme. 5. Bis zu einer
Bildung des Infinitivs kommt man, wie gesagt, nicht immer. Der Aufbau
des Paradigmas scheint nach dem Ausweis des (wie bereits erwähnt, zufälligen) Wörterbuchmaterials häufig nicht zu Ende geführt zu sein. Es ergeben sich aber ausserdem auch Fälle, wo die Lautform eines Infinitivs wenn
auch nicht gerade unmöglich, so doch ungewöhnlich und ungefällig wäre,
z. B. -V̄Rt.

Auf Grund eines nur präfigiert vorkommenden Part. praet. act. ist demnach das Paradigma eines präfigierten Verbums entstanden. Präfigierung
aber, die im Lettischen weitgehend Ausdruck unterschiedlicher Aktionsarten ist, ist zugleich auch Ausdruck des sogenannten perfektiven Aspekts.
Damit überschneiden sich in unserem Paradigma die lexikalisch-semantische
Kategorie der Aktionsart mit der grammatischen Kategorie des Aspekts, die

ihrerseits den Ausdruck für den Gegensatz perfektiv/imperfektiv erheischt. Dafür erscheint zunächst im Präsens, und zwar als retrograde Bildung, ein depräfigiertes Paradigma, das einen andauernden Übergang in den neuen Zustand kennzeichnet, während durch ein präfigiertes Präsens im Lettischen der überschaubare Vorgang in seiner Gänze, Anfang und Ende inbegriffen, ausgedrückt wird. Das depräfigierte Präsens kann Ausgangspunkt für ein imperfektives, unpräfigiertes Vollparadigma werden.

Dass auch im Litauischen bei den (denominativen) -sta-Verben der Aspekt mit hereinspielt, zeigt die Tatsache, dass im Averbo unpräfigiertes Präsens neben präfigiertem Präteritum aufgeführt wird, konsequent so bei Otrębski, l.c., 323 ff.

Obige Ausführungen dürften gezeigt haben, dass der Terminus „inkohativ" zumindest für die lettischen denominativen Verben mit -sta-Präsens nicht zu Recht geführt wird. Für semantisch analoge Verbalbildungen von Adjektiven zum Ausdruck des So-Werdens in anderen Sprachen sind der Verf. zwei Termini begegnet: Isačenko, Formenlehre I, 392 spricht von „mutativer" Bedeutung russischer Verben vom Typ краснеть 'rot werden', und Lauri Hakulinen, Handbuch der finnischen Sprache, I, 212, bezeichnet entsprechende finnische Verben als „translativ". Letzterer Terminus wäre für unsere Verben vielleicht nicht unangebracht, denn er würde nicht nur die eigentliche Bedeutung gut charakterisieren, sondern zusätzlich auch den stattgehabten grundlegenden Vorgang der Transformation, den „Transfer" gewissermassen, mit beinhalten — falls die hier vorgenommene Darstellung den Fachgenossen, vor allem aber dem hochverehrten Jubilar, glaubwürdig schiene.

Anmerkungen

1. L. Weisgerbers Terminus für inhaltlich einheitliche Ableitungsgruppen.

2. Die Anmerkung Mühlenbachs, ME, I, 373, *cepties* als Intransitiv sei selten, darf heute als veraltet gelten.

3. *slapt* hat im Präsens ursprünglich ein Nasalinfix: *sluop* = lit. *šlam̃pa*. ME führt auch nur dieses Nasalpräsens auf, was aber dem heutigen Stand der Entwicklung nicht mehr entspricht. Eine Umfrage, die bei insgesamt 28 Personen verschiedenen, auch ziemlich hohen, Alters veranlasst wurde, ergab nur in 7 Fällen den Gebrauch von Präsens *sasluop* 'wird ganz nass', in den übrigen — Präs. *saslapst* (auch die Verf. würde zu den letzteren zählen!). Die Übernahme des bedeutungsmässig klaren Verbs in die entsprechende produktive Ableitungsgruppe ist im Gange. Vgl. auch ein lit. Präsens *pašlāpsta* bei Kazlauskas, l. c., 328.

4. *Laiviņa piere sabarga* (3. Praet.) *kā mākonis pirms negaisa* Velta Spāre, Karogs 1965, 2, 93.

5. Vgl. die entsprechende Beobachtung bei Endzelin § 644 (Lett. Gramm. S. 628 f., Latv. val. gram. S. 814).

6. Vgl. z. B. bei A. Srba, Lietuvių Tauta, II, 1, 52: *tulžtù–tulžti* 'ins Morschwerden kommen'. Oder im Akademie-Wörterbuch, I, 676 zu *barsti* (abgeleitet von *barzdà* 'Bart'): *jau ans apibarzdęs, ir tu barzti, t. y. plaukgauriais želti pradedi*.

7. Trubetzkoys Termini, Mélanges Bally 76.

Further Remarks on the Baltic -*sta*-present

After some criticism of previous views on the Baltic -*sta*-present the author attempts a semantic and structural analysis of those Latvian verbs with -*sta*-present which are derived from adjectives. Examination of the material revealed a prefixed part. pret. act. as starting-point for the constitution of the paradigm. This prefixed participle itself results from the transformation of a predicative syntagma containing an adjective into an (attributive) determinative syntagma. Besides this part. pret. act. there develops a preterite, likewise prefixed; on entering the temporal system the actual constitution of the paradigm begins, i.e. a prefixed one. The prefix, however, which in Latvian to a large extent expresses different modes of action (Aktionsarten), is at the same time the sign of the so-called perfective aspect. Thereby the lexico-semantic category of mode of action overlaps with the grammatical category of aspect, which itself requires differentiation between perfective and imperfective. Then, at first in the present tense, there develops by back-formation a de-prefixed paradigm, which itself becomes the starting-point for an imperfective, unprefixed full paradigm.

These denominative verbs with -*sta*-present are often called 'inchoative'. This is incorrect, since they express the entire process of acquiring the quality of the underlying adjective, including the completion of the action. It is proposed to adopt Lauri Hakulinen's (*Handbuch der finnischen Sprache* I, 212) term „translative" for these Latvian (and Lithuanian) verbs.

ANNE MARIE HINDERLING-ELIASSON

Zur sprachlichen Form der Fragesätze im Altlettischen[1]

I. Die zu behandelnde Kategorie gibt zu folgenden theoretisch-methodischen Überlegungen Anlass:

Aufgrund von Untersuchungen des FS in verschiedenen Sprachen (hauptsächlich Lettisch und Finnisch) bin ich zur Überzeugung gelangt, dass es sich hierbei um eine Kategorie handelt, die man als *grammatisch unbewusst* bezeichnen könnte. Das heisst, dass sie nicht zu den Kategorien gehört, die durch Übersetzungstätigkeit und Sprachpflege von der normierenden Schulgrammatik erfasst wurde, so wie dies z. B. mit dem Tempus- oder Kasussystem der Fall war[2]. Wie unfest und unausgebildet die Vorstellung von einer besonderen Kategorie der Frage ist, sieht man schon aus der Tatsache, dass sie in den Handbüchern oft entweder gar nicht oder dann je nachdem unter recht verschiedenen Überschriften und in verschiedenem Zusammenhang, unter Satzlehre, Wortfolge, unter den Partikeln oder schliesslich unter „Übrigem" behandelt wird.

Auf der anderen Seite steht dem Sprechenden ein ganz klares Fragesatzmodell zur Verfügung, wenn es darum geht, „eine Frage überhaupt" zu formulieren oder einen konkreten FS aus einer fremden Sprache umzusetzen. Das letztere ist in einer zwei- oder mehrsprachigen Sprachgemeinschaft eine sehr häufig auftretende Situation, wenn man die hohe Frequenz und zentrale Stellung der Frage im praktischen Sprachleben überhaupt bedenkt.

Aus dem Gesagten kann man schliessen, dass sich ein fremder Einfluss bei der Ausformung des FS nicht durch schriftliche Übersetzungen (literarische Entlehnungen), sondern im engen Sprechkontakt mit einer anderen Sprache geltend macht. Wie sich dies auswirkt, werden wir im Folgenden fürs Lettische am Beispiel von Elgers Evangelien und Episteln untersuchen.[3]

II. Die FS bei Elger verteilen sich hauptsächlich auf drei Typen, den „intonativen", „inversativen" und „partikulativen" FS. Die Intonation dürfte auch in der Sprache Elgers die Frage überhaupt charakterisiert haben. Den

Namen „intonativ" verwenden wir hier aber nur für diejenigen, bei denen die FS-Intonation das *einzige* Merkmal ist. Der Inversionstyp ist seiner Frequenz nach der häufigste: Es gibt fast 50 Belege, die nur durch die Inversion als Frage gekennzeichnet sind. Ausserdem sind auch die meisten der partikulativen FS zusätzlich noch mit Inversion ausgerüstet.

A. *FS, die ausschliesslich durch Inversion gekennzeichnet sind.*

a) *positiv*: 26 Belege

> Beispiele: *Es tu wens Prophets?* ~ Propheta es tu? Joh 1,21 (7,17)[4]
>
> *Ir šis iuso dæls, kattru iûs sakkat aklu pedzimmušu?* ~ Hic est filius vester, quem vos dicitis caecus natus est? Joh 9,19 (51,25)
>
> *Redzi tu ša sêwa?* ~ Vides hanc mulierem? Lk 7,44 (128,9)[5]

Die lat. Vorlage zeigt hier im allgemeinen den Fragesatztyp ohne Partikel; 3 × steht *numquid*:

> Numquid ego Iudaeus sum? ~ *Esmu es wêns Jôds?* Jh 18,35 (69,4)

auch Mk 14,19 (63,5), Jes. 7,13 (121,13).

An einer Stelle steht auch *si*:

> Domine, si percutimus in gladio? ~ *Kungs, bûs mums ar zôbeni starpa sist?* Lk 22,49 (65,16)

Einmal ist der Sachverhalt im Lat. gar nicht als Frage formuliert: Lk 22,67 (68,2).

Eine besondere Untergruppe bilden die mit *tad* und *gan* verstärkten FS. Sie kommen nur in dieser Gruppe vor:

1. mit *tad*: 6 Fälle

In drei Fällen übersetzt dabei *tad* offensichtlich lat. *ergo*: Lk 22,70 (68,5), Jh 18,37 (69,8), Gal 3,21 (103,17). Interessanter sind die Fälle, wo das *tad* keine direkte Entsprechung im lat. Text hat:

> *Es tu tad wairaks ne ka mûsu tæws Jacobs, katters ...* ~ Numquid tu maior es patre nostro Jacob, qui ... Jh 4,12 (46,7)

Vgl. auch den völlig parallelen Fall Jh 8,53 (55,28). Besonders auffällig ist *tad* 1 Kor 12,29 (131,7), wo es mit *neg* wechselt:

> *Ka? neg wyssi tad Apostuli? wyssi Prophetus? wyssi macetaie? neg wyssi brinumu darritaie? neg wyssems tas dawans wæsseludarrišanas? war tad wyssi wallodas runnat? war tad*

wyssi wallodas tolkæt? ~ Numquid omnes Apostoli? numquid omnes gratiam habent curatorionum? Numquid omnes linguis loquuntur? numquid omnes interpretantur?

2. mit *gan*: 2 Fälle, ebenfalls ohne Entsprechung in der Vorlage:

> *Zin tu gan ka te Pharisæri ši to wardu dzirdæiuši apkaitenaias?* ~ Scis quia Pharisaei audito verbo hoc scandalizati sunt? Mt 15,12 (44,31)
>
> *Rædzæt iûs gan, ka mæs neneku ne spæam?* ~ Videtis quia nihil proficimus? Jh 12,19 (58,26)

b) *negativ*: 24 Belege

> Beispiele: *Kungs, ne es tu labbu sæklu sæis uz tauwu tyrummu?* ~ Domine, nonne bonum semen seminasti in agro tuo? Mt 13,27 (22,26)
>
> *Nerunna tu ar man?* ~ Mihi non loqueris? Jh 19,10 (71,12)

Die lat. Vorlage zeigt hier den partikellosen Typ in 10 Fällen; in weitern 9 Fällen steht *nonne*, dazu einmal *numquam*:

> numquam legistis: ...? ~ *Ne æsset iûs lassijušu: ...?* Mt 21,16 (34,2)[6]

Die Negationspartikel wird manchmal mit dem Verb zusammengeschrieben, bei Elger allerdings nur selten; hier können auch die Fälle mit *newaid* (neulett. *nav* 'ist nicht') eingeordnet werden:

> Beispiel: *Ieb [⟨...⟩] newaid man wallîa darrit ko es gribbu* ~ Aut non licet mihi quod volo, facere? Mt 20,15 (25,15)[7].

B. *Fragesätze mit Fragepartikel*

Für diese Gruppe ist typisch, dass die Partikel oft im Verein mit der Inversion die Frage zum Ausdruck bringt.

a) *positiv:* Partikel *ar*, am Satzbeginn stehend, 16 Fälle[8].

1. Ohne Inversion: 4 Fälle

> Beispiel: *Kungs ar tu šimmems laykems atkal vzcels to walstiba Jsrael?* ~ Domine si in tempore hoc restitues regnum Israel? Apg 1,6 (85,13)

Die lateinische Vorlage zeigt 3 × *numquid*, 1 × *si*[9].

2. Mit Inversion: 11 Fälle

> Beispiele: *Ar zinnat iûs ko es iums æsmu darryis?* ~ Scitis quid fecerim vobis? Jh 13,13 (62,10)
>
> *Ar war akklis akklam cellie râdit?* ~ Numquid potest caecus caecum ducere? Lk 6,39 (90,26)

Die lateinische Vorlage hat 6 × Partikellosigkeit, 3 × *numquid*, 1 × *nonne* und 1 × *si*[10].

3. In einem Fall haben wir einen *Nominalsatz*: Mt 18,21 (44,14)

b) *negativ: Partikel neg*, 15 Fälle

1. *Ohne Inversion:* 7 Fälle

Beispiele: *Neg tas ir kattru te mæklæia nokauwt?* ~ Nonne hic est, quem quaerunt interficere? Jh 7,25 (50,16)

Neg tu wens no ša cilwæku maceklems es? ~ Numquid et tu ex discipulis es hominis istius? Jh 18,17 (66,15)

Die lateinische Vorlage hat 4 + *numquid*, 3 × *nonne*[11].

2. *Mit Inversion:* 6 Fälle

Beispiele: (*Ar war akklis akklam cellie râdit.*) *Neg krit te abbedywwi bæddræ?* ~ Nonne ambo in foveam cadunt? Lk 6,39 (90,26)

Neg ir winš Christus? ~ Numquid ipse est Christus? Jh 4,29 (46,31)

Die Vorlage hat 4 × *numquid* und 3 × *nonne*[12].

3. *Nominalsätze:* 2 Fälle

Belege: Jh 10,34 (57,21), lat. *nonne*; 1 Kor 12,29 (131,8), lat. *numquid*.

C. *Der „rein intonative" Typ:* FS ohne im Text sichtbares Fragecharakteristikum.

Dieser FS-Typ lässt sich negiert nicht belegen.

a) *FS nach 'und':* 5 Fälle

Es handelt sich um eine an eine Feststellung (oder eine Frage) anschliessende, zu ihr im Gegensatz stehende Frage, die im Lateinischen, Griechischen und — was auffälliger ist — z. B. auch im Deutschen genau gleich strukturiert ist.

Beispiel: *Tik ilgu layku es ar iums æsmu vnd iûs man wæl ne æsseti pazinnuši?* ~ Tanto tempore vobiscum sum: et non cognovistis me? Jh 14,9 (122,29)

Ein etwas anders gelegerter Fall ist Mt 15,16 (45,5): *Vnd iûs aridzan esset bes prâtu?* ~ Adhuc et vos sine intellectu estis?[13]

b) Ähnlich ist Joh 9,34 (52,25) zu beurteilen, wo im Lett. allerdings gegen die Vorlage statt der Verbindung mit *et* eine Partizipialkonstruktion erscheint:

Tu wiskim ekšan grækims pedzimmis mûs mâce? ~ In peccatis natus es totus, et tu doces nos?

c) In den folgenden Fällen können wir von einem *emphatischen Typ* sprechen; auch hier hat schon das Griechisch-Lateinische das Modell abgegeben; vier Fälle.

> Beispiel: *Tauwa dwæsel tu par man dôs?* ~ Animam tuam pro me pones? Jh 13,38 (63,26)

Am interessantesten ist der Beleg Jh 1,21 (7,17):

> *Elias es tu? Winš saccya: Es ne æsme. Es tu wens Prophets?* ~ Elias es tu? Et dixit: non sum. Propheta es tu?

Hier entsprechen den zwei völlig parallelen Sätzen des Lateinischen im ersten Fall (wegen des zufälligen gleichen Wortlauts?) FS-Typ C, im zweiten Fall Typ A[14, 15].

Wir haben bei Elger also hauptsächlich zwei FS-Typen, die beide sowohl positiv als negativ vorkommen: 1. FS mit Inversion (Typ A), 2. FS mit Partikel, pos. *ar*, neg. *neg* (Typ B). Bevor wir untersuchen wollen, wie sich die beiden Typen inhaltlich und syntaktisch unterscheiden, erhebt sich die Frage nach den Übereinstimmungen zwischen der Vorlage und Elgers Text, d. h. nach der möglichen Abhängigkeit der lettischen Fragesatzform von der lateinischen.

1. Inversionstyp

Fürs Lateinische entfällt die Frage nach der Inversion meistens aus strukturellen Gründen (vgl. *dormis* gegenüber *gulli tu?*). In den übrigen Fällen herrscht gerade Wortstellung vor.

2. Deutlicher Einfluss der Vorlage liegt dagegen in den kleinen Gruppen Ca und Cc vor.

3. Über die übrigen Entsprechungen gibt zusammenfassend die folgende Tabelle Auskunft:

Lateinisches Original	Wiedergabe im Lettischen durch			
	Inversion		Partikel	
	positiv	negativ	*ar*	*neg*
nonne		10		8
numquid	5		6	8
Partikellosigkeit	11	14	8	
si	1		2	
an	2			
numquam		1		
Keine Frage, sondern Feststellung	1			

Wir können der Tabelle Folgendes entnehmen:

a. Die partikellose Frage der Vorlage erscheint auch bei Elger meist ohne Partikel; besonders auffällig sind die Verhältnisse in der Negation. Dennoch zeigen die 8 *ar* gegenüber lateinischer Partikellosigkeit, dass von einer sklavischen Abhängigkeit keine Rede sein kann.

b. Die Unterschiede zwischen positiver Inversion und *ar* bzw. negativer Inversion und *neg* können nicht aus einer entsprechenden Gruppierung des Lateinischen hergeleitet werden, müssen sich also, sofern sie nicht einfach synonym sind, aus dem Text ergeben. Folgende Beobachtungen können gemacht werden:

1. (Verhältnis positive Inversion: *ar*) Es fällt auf, dass *ar* nur einmal in Verbindung mit dem Verb „sein" vorkommt[16], dagegen 12 × der Inversionstyp. Auch neben der Ausnahme *Meister, ar es æsmu?* (Mt 26,25) steht einige Zeilen früher das parallele *Kungs æsmu es tas?* (Mk 14,19)

2. (Verhältnis negative Inversion: *neg*) Die Tatsache, dass die Fragen mit *numquid* nur mit *neg* wiedergegeben werden, ist auffällig genug. Es scheint sich bei dieser Gruppe teils um rhetorische Fragen, teils um Fragen in der erlebten Rede zu handeln. Beide haben im Griechischen μή (μήτι):[17] im Lateinischen dagegen *numquid*. Bei Elger werden diese *numquid*-Sätze teils positiv, teils negativ gefasst. Die Tatsache, dass allein die *neg*-Sätze zur Wiedergabe dieser speziellen Fragen geeignet erscheinen, hängt offenbar mit einem echten strukturellen Unterschied zwischen den *neg*- und den *ne*-Fragen zusammen, der sich in unserm Text in folgender statischen Beobachtung niederschlägt: die *ne*-Sätze zeigen ein leichtes Übergewicht für die 2. Person (11 von 20 Fällen), die *neg*-Sätze dagegen ein deutliches für die 3. Person (10 von 15 Fällen). Offenbar ist der eine Typ stärker auf die Dialogsituation spezialisiert als der andere, ein Unterschied, den wir deutlich im Neulettischen greifen können, wo der intonative Typ fast ausschliesslich im Dialog vorkommt, während der Partikeltyp diese Beschränkung nicht aufweist.

Wir können das Ergebnis so zusammenfassen: In einem gewissen Grad scheint die Ausformung des FS bei Elger durch die Vorlage bestimmt zu sein. Wir vermuten dahinter das Bestreben, Verschiedenes durch Verschiedenes zu übersetzen, das sich bei jeder treuen Übersetzung beobachten lässt, bei einer Übersetzung der Bibel aber wegen ihrer religiösen Autorität sich besonders stark geltend macht. Dennoch zeigen die erwähnten strukturellen und inhaltlichen Unterschiede zwischen den beiden FS-Gruppen, die die lateinischen Gruppierungen überschneiden, dass die verschiedenen Typen durchaus im lettischen Sprachsystem ihre bestimmten Aufgaben und Grenzen haben.

III. Zufällig ist uns aus derselben Zeit (demselben Jahr?) wie Elgers Übersetzung ein profanes Werk eines andern Verfassers, der „Lettus" von Georg Manzel, überliefert[18]. Die Sätze, die hier in den Wortlisten vorkommen, scheinen uns für einen Vergleich besonders geeignet, da es dem Verfasser hier thematisch um den Wortschatz, nicht die Grammatik geht, so dass wir vermuten können, dass die Verwendung der syntaktischen Strukturen keiner bewussten Normierung unterliegt. Bei Manzel hat der überwiegende Teil der FS Inversion; in einigen Fällen finden wir die enklitische Partikel -g (z. B. *zinnieg tu?*). In zwei Fällen kommt auch die FP *vai* vor. Ob wir es in diesem Falle mit den ersten Anfängen dieser Partikel zu tun haben, die dann zuerst der gehobenen Stilschicht noch nicht angehört hätte, oder ob es sich einfach um dialektale Unterschiede handelt, kann ich nicht entscheiden. Die Partikel *neg* (die ja auch mit dem erwähnten -g gebildet ist) und ihr Gegenstück, *ar*, fehlen auffälligerweise ganz. Dieser merkwürdige Unterschied im Sprachgebrauch der beiden Zeitgenossen dürfte sich mit ziemlicher Gewissheit aus der verschiedenen literarischen Gattung der beiden Werke erklären. Wir vermuten also, dass das Partikelpaar *ar–neg* damals nur noch der religiösen Stilschicht, die bekanntlich Archaismen gerne konserviert, angehörte.

IV. Wir wollen noch kurz einen Blick auf die Verhältnisse des Neulettischen werfen. Auch hier haben wir zwei Haupttypen von FS, den intonativen (mit gerader Wortstellung!) und den partikularen (mit Patrikel *vai*). Die Negation hat keinen besondern Ausdruck mehr. *Ar* und *neg*, aber auch der Inversionstyp sind verschwunden. Eine Fülle von sonstigen Hilfswörtern zeigt uns, dass wir es mit einer sehr lebendigen, viel differenzierteren Kategorie als etwa in den germanischen Sprachen zu tun haben[19].

Diese Lebendigkeit der Kategorie ist offenbar auch der Grund dafür, dass sich ihr Ausdruck immer wieder wandelt. Gleichzeitig spiegelt sich in diesem Wandel die äussere Geschichte der Sprache: in älterer Zeit war die Inversion — offenbar ein Germanismus — üblich, wir können vielleicht sagen: Mode. Heutzutage scheint sich die intonative Frage zu verbreiten — offenbar ein Slavismus. Dazu tritt das ostseefinnische Lehnwort *vai*. Was nun dieses enge *Zusammenleben ostseefinnischer und baltischer Sprachen* betrifft, so lässt es sich überhaupt am Beispiel der Fragekategorie eindrücklich illustrieren: Fürs Baltische muss man von der altererbten Frage mit Fragepartikel (alett., lit. *ar*) in Anfangsstellung ausgehen, fürs Ostseefinnische dagegen von einer enklitischen Partikel (finn. *-ko/-kö*). Das Estnische hat aber diesen Typ ersetzt durch einen FS mit einer selbständigen FP in Anfangsstellung (das etymologisch übrigens unklare *kas*), was an die Verhältnisse im Bal tischen erinnert. Das Lettische seinerseits bewahrt zwar die alte baltische Wortfolge, übernimmt aber die livische Fragepartikel *vai* (während *ar* ausstirbt). Im Estnischen bleibt aber die negative FP *eks* (auch finnisch mundartlich) 'ist nicht?', die aus dem Negationsverb **e-* und den Partikeln *-ko* (FP) und *-s* besteht. Es liegt nahe, das altlettische *ne-g* mit dieser Bildung zu vergleichen[20]. Wie es sich mit der *lautlichen* Übereinstimmung *-ko(-kö)*: *-g* (vgl. auch lit. *-gu*) letzten Endes verhält, ist dabei nicht wesentlich[21].

Anmerkungen

1. Die folgende Untersuchung ist Teil einer im Entstehen begriffenen grösseren Abhandlung über die Fragesätze im Lettischen. Folgende Abkürzungen werden verwendet: FS = Fragesatz, -sätze, FP = Fragepartikel(n).

2. Aus diesem Grunde wurde z. B. das spätgermanische Tempussystem stark von dem des Lateinischen beeinflusst.

3. Zugrunde liegt die Ausgabe von Kārlis Draviņš, *Evangelien und Episteln ins Lettische übersetzt von Georg Elger, nebst einem Register seiner geistlichen Lieder aus der Zeit um 1640. Bd. 1: Texte* (Slaviska Institutionen vid Lunds universitet. Text- och materialutgåvor 1). Lund 1961. Dieses Lektionar ist „eines von den allerältesten bekannten Manuskripten eines lettischen *Buches* überhaupt" (a. a. O., S. VII). Es handelt sich dabei um eine Übersetzung nach der lateinischen Bibel und zwar natürlich nach der Vulgata, die hier in folgender Ausgabe benützt wurde: Novum Testamentum Graece et Latine, Utrumque textum cum apparatu critico imprimemdum curavit Eberhard Nestle. Stuttgart, [22]1963, wo der Clementinus zugrundeliegt. Der kritische Apparat bringt in keinem Falle Abweichungen, die unser Problem berühren. — Nicht berücksichtigt werden im folgenden die indirekten und disjunktiven FS.

4. Die Zahlen in Klammern nach den Bibelstellen beziehen sich auf Seite und Zeile der Elger-Ausgabe. — Aus drucktechnischen und praktischen Gründen wird die Orthographie der kritischen Ausgabe leicht vereinfacht und zwar in Richtung neulettischer Schreibung: *š* statt sz, *č* statt cz u. ä. Auch auf die Wiedergabe von langem *s* wird verzichtet. Vgl. Draviņš, a. a. O., S. XIX.

5. Weitere Belege: Mt 11,3 (6,17), 13,28 (22,28), 20,15 (25,15), 27,11 (69,2);
Mk 14,37 (64,17);
Lk 24,41 (79,14);
Jh 3,10 (123,26), 13,6 (62,1), 18,34 (69,3).

6. Weitere Belege: Mt 6,25 (104,27), 15,16 (45,5), 18,33 (113,1), 20,13 (25,13), 21,16 (34,2);
Mk 14,37 (64,17), 14,60 (67,17);
Lk 2,49 (18,24), 10,40 (130,25), 24,26 (78,6);
Jh 11,9 (53,4), 11,37 (54,4), 11,40 (54,9), 14,10 (123,2), 18,11 (65,21), 18,26 (67,5);
Apg 2,7 (87,6); 1 Kor 9,24 (24,11).

7. Weitere Belege: Lk 17, 17–18 (104, 2–3; 2 Belege); Jh 8,10 (47,31).

8. Mt 5, 46–47 (30,11–12) sieht mit seinem zweimaligen *negierten ar* wie eine Ausnahme aus: ar ne tê mûitneki to darra? ($\sim$ nonne et publicani hoc faciunt?) ... ar ne

darra to te Paggani aridzan? ($\sim$ nonne et ethnici hoc faciunt?). Vermutlich ist aber die Stelle verderbt.

9. Weitere Belege: Mt 26,25 (63,9); Jh 8,22 (37,18); Apg 10,47 (88,8).

10. Weitere Belege: Mt 7,16 (97,26), 20,22 (39,1), 21,16 (34,2), 26,62 (67,17); Lk 14,3 (107,1); Jh 3,4 (123,18), 5,6 (35,27), 9,35 (52,16), 11,27 (53,23).

11. Weitere Belege: Jh 4,33 (47,3), 7,19 (50,7), 7,26 (50,18), 9,8 (51,9), 9,27 (52,7), 18,25 (66,30).

12. Weitere Belege: Lk 24,32 (78,14); Jh 4,35 (47,5), 7,35 (56,14), 8,48 (55,21), 10,34 (57,21).

13. Weitere Belege: Jh 2,20 (49,21), 3,10 (123,26), 11,8 (53,3).

14. Weitere Belege: Lk 22,48 (65,14); Jh 18,22 (66,22).

15. Ein vereinzelter, sonst nicht einzuordnender Fall ist Mt 11, 7–9 (6,24 f.): *Par ko essæti iûs aran gaiuši lûkôt? wena nedra, kattra no to wæiu tôp šurp und turp dzŷta .?.. wenu cilwæku ar mikstems dræbems apterptu? ... wenu Prophetu?* $\sim$ *...* arundinem vento agitatam? ... hominem mollibus vestitum? ... prophetam?

16. Darüber hinaus aber auch in der (hier nicht berücksichtigten) indirekten Frage, z. B. Mt. 26,63 (67,20): *sakka mums, ar tu es Christus Dewa dæls?* $\sim$ ut dicas nobis, si tu es Christus filius Dei.

17. Schwyzer, *Griechische Grammatik* II, 629: ,,Auf Fragen mit οὐ wird im allgemeinen eine *bejahende*, auf solche mit μή eine *verneinende* Antwort erwartet ...''

18. G. Mancelius, *Lettus*. Das ist Wortbuch. 1638. Benutzt nach Günther, Altlett. Sprachdenkmäler II.

19. Zu den Wörtern, die den FS im Neulett. nüancieren können, seien etwa erwähnt: *droši vien* 'sicher', *laikam, jau gan* 'wohl', *taču* 'doch', *tikai* 'nur'. Als eine Art Fragewörter treten auf: *ja* 'wenn', *varbût* 'vielleicht'; nachgestellt: *..., jā? ..., vai ne? ..., ko? ..., vai ne ko?*

20. In den Bereich dieser Übereinstimmungen gehört auch das Paar estn. *pole*/lett. *nav* 'ist nicht'.

21. Eine ähnliche Adstratwirkung hat das Finnische auf das Finnlandschwedische und die nördlichen reichsschwedischen Mundarten ausgeübt, indem die Negation schwed. *inte* (bzw. *int*) dort im FS am Satzanfang erscheint.

The Linguistic Form of Interrogative Sentences in Old Latvian

This paper, part of a longer work on interrogative sentences in Latvian, examines the form of questions in Latvian in the 17th century, on the basis of material from Georg Elger's Gospels and Epistles (K. Draviņš' edition of the first version in manuscript, Lund 1961). In it an attempt is made to determine whether the various structures of questions are dependent on the original (Vulgata). The table on page 192 shows the Latin parallels to the two main types of question in Latvian. An influence is indicated in that the questions without particles in Latin, above all in negatives, mostly show a zero-particle in Latvian, too. A definite influence is also present in a few smaller groups (examples under C). However, the differences between the chief types cannot only be explained by the influence of borrowings. Rather they reflect actual differences in the Latvian language at that time. The sentences contained in the material can be divided into two main groups: 1. Questions with an interrogative particle (positive *ar* negative *neg*); 2. Questions employing inversion. The paper shows in brief that this duality, including the differences in content and structure, has been maintained in Latvian right up to the present day, although in another form (Type 1 with the interrogative particle *vai*, type 2: no particle and no inversion). On the other hand a glance at Georg Manzel's "Lettus", which was written at about the same time, presents another picture. (1. Inversion, 2. Particle type with -*g* and *vai*). This is probably a matter of style but may also be a dialectal form. Finally the origin of the particle *neg* is investigated, and the author refers to the fact that Latvian, in the course of its history, has absorbed foreign elements from neighbouring languages especially as regards question forms. Therefore, as an example of this, one could perhaps compare *neg* with the Estonian *eks* 'is not?'.

ERICH HOFMANN

Das Halbpartizip in Daukšas Postille

Das Halbpartizip (Participium contemporale) auf -*damas* usw. (m-f. sg./plur.,
auch reflexiv) kommt in der Regel nur im Nominativ vor und wird nur
appositionell zum Ausdruck gleichzeitiger Handlung gebraucht, also weder
attributiv noch prädikativ. Es ist eine Neuerung des Ostbaltischen (Lit.,
Lett.); im Westbaltischen (Apreuß.) ist es nicht nachgewiesen.

In dem umfangreichsten Sprachdenkmal des Altlitauischen, in Daukšas
Postille von 1599[1], finden sich 1950 Belege des Halbpartizips, die von 410
Verben gebildet sind. Reiht man die (mit *ap-, at(a)-, į-, iš-, nu-, pa-, par-,
per-, pra-, pri-, su-, už-* und *appri-*) präfigierten Verben bei den Simplicia
ein, so verringert sich die Zahl auf 337. Über die Hälfte (227 von 410) ist
nur einmal belegt. Am häufigsten findet sich *bylodamas* (242), dem *būdamas*
(174), *regėdamas* (97), *turėdamas* (75), *darydamas* (60), *žinodamas* (57),
norėdamas (47), *gyvendamas* (36), *atsakydamas* (32), *tikėdamas* (31), *rody-
damas* (25), *tarydamas* (24), *paliaudamas* (21), *duodamas* (19), *prašydamas*
(19), *sakiodamas* (19), *mokydamas* (18) folgen.

In der auch heute üblichen Weise kann die Gleichzeitigkeit mit einem mo-
dalen Sinn verbunden sein; z. B. 'während, als' *tatai kalbėjau jumus, jusimp
gyvendamas* 235,32: Joh. 14,25 haec locutus sum vobis apud vos manens;
'wenn, obgleich' *kaipog gali žmogus atgimt senas būdamas* 251,41 (= 451,36):
Joh. 3,4 quomodo potest homo nasci, cum sit senex; im Griech. partizipial
γέρων ὤν; 'weil' *o buvo nekuris elgeta vardu Lozorius, kuris gulėjo par vartus
jo, norėdamas priėst iš trupučių, kurie birėjo nuog skomios didžturio* 269,6:
Luk. 16,20 et erat quidam mendicus, nomine Lazarus, qui iacebat ad ianuam
eius, cupiens saturari de micis, quae cadebant de mensa divitis; 'indem'
puolė keliuosemp Jezaus bylodamas 288,4 : Luk. 5,8 procidit ad genua Jesu
dicens; 'ohne zu' *gentis, kaip čia įėjai, neturėdamas rūbo svodbos* : Matth.
22,12 amice, quomodo huc intrasti non habens vestem nuptialem?

Dazu kommen die häufigen biblischen Wendungen, in denen griechische
Übersetzungsaramaismen über das Latein in andere Sprachen übernommen
wurden, wie *ir atsakydamas Simonas bylojo jam* : Luk. 5,5 et respondens
Simon dixit illi, καὶ ἀποκριθεὶς Σίμων εἶπεν αὐτῷ. Die Wiedergabe der

periphrastischen Konstruktion ἦν διδάσκων durch das Halbpartizip muß später erörtert werden.

Ich habe bisher Belege aus der Vulgata angeführt, da es mir leider nicht möglich gewesen ist, Wujeks Postylla Mnieyszey (früher in Breslau und Braunsberg) einzusehen. Doch scheint mir diese Versäumnis nicht sehr schwerwiegend zu sein. Denn die Durchsicht der von Wolter in seiner Chrestomathie Sp. 29–50 abgedruckten Parallelversion (= Daukša S. 68–73) zeigt, daß das litauische Halbpartizip immer ein polnisches Gerundium (Absolutivum) wiedergibt:

68,36	*gadindamas*	*zabiegaiąc*
71,9	*bylodamas*	*mowiąc*
71,19	*deklaravodamas*	*declaruiąc*
71,49; 72,26	*abejodama*	*wątpiąc*
72,16	*ieškodami*	*szukaiąc*
72,27	*mokydama*	*nauczaiąc*

Einmal wird das Gerundium, das sich auf den Plural bezieht, fälschlich durch den Singular wiedergegeben. In demselben Satz findet sich kurz vorher der gleiche Fehler bei der Übersetzung des ebenfalls unveränderlichen Part. prät. des Polnischen auf -wszy: *mes turime ... parodęs ... ne abejodamas*, bei Wujek *my ... mamy ... przełożywszy ... niewątpiąc*.

Während im Märchen und in Erzählungen gewöhnlich nur ein, höchstens zwei Halbpartizipien in einem Satz verwendet werden[2], finden sich im eindringlichen Predigtstil der Postille oft Häufungen des Halbpartizips, sogar acht hintereinander: *nekurie heretikai, klepodami, persakiodami, ištremdinėdami, o kartais ir išmušinėdami, tikruosius krikščionis, kunigus, minikus, ir kitus tarnus Dievo, bažnyčias plešdami, paveikslus kapodami, myniodami š. sakramentus, bliužnydami ne tiktai šventuosius, bet ir patį Dievą, Traiceje vieną, ertes tikis labai gerai darą* 234,31 'manche Ketzer meinen vielleicht sehr gut zu handeln, wenn sie gegen die wahren Christen, Priester, Mönche und andere Gottesdiener streiten, sie verfolgen, verjagen und bisweilen auch erschlagen, Kirchen einreißen, Bilder zerschlagen, die heiligen Sakramente zertreten und nicht nur die Heiligen, sondern auch Gott selbst, den Einen in der Trinität, lästern'. Ich füge noch zwei Beispiele mit je 5 Halbpartizipien an: 174,7 heißt es von Christus *per visą naktį ir dieną neturėjai ne vieno atilsio, o smarkūs budeliai rodė ant tavę visus kunštus savus: mušdami, spiaudydami, mušdami plaštakomis, kumščiomis, plakdami ir karunavodami tave* 'die ganze Nacht und den Tag hindurch hattest du keine Ruhe, sondern die starken Büttel zeigten an dir alle ihre Kunststücke: indem sie schlugen, spukten, mit Handflächen und Fäusten schlugen, mit

Ruten geißelten und dich krönten'. Von christlichem Verhalten bei Todesfällen heißt es 578,25 *kiti vel ant laidojimų užprašytieji daro tūliaropus darbus mielaširdumo: nuliūdusius linksmindami, su verkančiais verkdami, atlankydami našles ir palikūnis jų prilietime, numirusius pakasdami ir už Dievą V. prašydami* 'andere wiederum zum Begräbnis Geladene tun mancherlei Werke der Barmherzigkeit, indem sie die Betrübten aufheitern, mit den Weinenden weinen, die Witwen und ihre Nachkommen in der Not besuchen, die Verstorbenen begraben und den Herrgott anrufen'. Dreimalige Setzung desselben Partizips ist 612,29 belegt, wo es von Maria heißt *ant to ir ing Bethlehem užėjo, kad jau artinos metas jos pagimdimo, nešiodama aną brangiausiąjį lobį savo įsčioj, nešiodama naštą lengvą, nešiodama šitą, kuris ją pačią nešiojo* 'danach ging sie hinauf nach Bethlehem, als die Zeit ihres Gebärens nahte, indem sie jenen teuersten Schatz in ihrem Schoß trug, indem sie eine leichte Last trug, indem sie den trug, der sie selbst trug'[3].

Nicht alle Partizipialformen auf *-damas* stellen ein aktives Participium contemporale dar. Das *-d-* kann auch zum Präsensstamm des Verbs gehören, an den *-amas* getreten ist, die Endung des Part. praes. pass. Eine doppeldeutige Form ist *duodamas*, dem wir uns zunächst zuwenden. Danach müssen wir noch auf das Paar *dėdamas/dėdamas* eingehen. Beide Verben *duoti* und *dėti* werden im Altlitauischen überwiegend athematisch flektiert, also *duost, duome, dėst, dėme*. Aber die heute üblichen thematischen Formen *duoda, duodame, deda, dedame* dringen allmählich vor[4].

I. *duodamas*

Es besteht also die Möglichkeit, *duodamas* abzuleiten entweder < *duo-damas*: Inf. *duo-ti* = Halbpartizip, oder < *duod-amas*: 1. plur. *duod-ame* = Partizip passivi. Wir müssen daher die *-amas*-Partizipia aussondern.

1. Partizip passivi.

a) Verbum simplex

nesa visokiam prašančiam est duodama ir klambenančiam est atadaroma 389,29.31. 'denn jedem Bittenden wird gegeben und dem Anklopfenden aufgetan', vgl. Matth. 7,7; Luk. 11,9.

kurios visiems šventiems est duodamos 439,53 '(alle Gnaden,) die allen Heiligen gegeben werden'.

sila ir vaisius est duodamas 604,27 'Kraft und Frucht wird gegeben (das Partizip nur auf das zweite Subjekt bezogen).

b) präfigiertes Verbum

per kurį sūnus žmogaus išduodamas est 104,33 'durch den des Menschen Sohn verraten wird'.

ypačiai žmogui savas angelas ant sargybės est priduodamas 521,24 'besonders dem Menschen wird sein Engel zur Hut beigegeben'.

Im Akkusativ: *nes toksai ir dūšią turi parduodamą* 155,49 'denn ein solcher hat auch die Seele zum Verkauf'.

2. Halbpartizip

a) Verbum simplex

jei bažnyčia paklydo duodama ta sakramenta 136,39 'wenn die Kirche irrte, indem sie die Sakramente austeilte'.

žinią duodamas 98,13; 224,39; 255,2; 466,31; 480,7 'Kunde gebend'.

duodamas ant pavaizdo Elijošių pranašą 225,6 'indem er als Beispiel den Propheten Elia gab'.

atajo Jezusop motina sūnų Zebedaišo su sūnumis savais, duodama jam garbę puolus knupsčia ir prašydama 482,13: Matth. 20,20 tunc accessit ad eum mater filiorum Zebedaei cum filiis suis, adorans et petens aliquid ab eo. Weitere Belege für das Simplex 202,36; 218,23; 291,4; 292,12; 330,29; 341,16; 430,29; 467,34; 616,32; 626,2.

b) präfigiertes Verbum

atduodamas visa rankosn jo 177,35 'indem er alles in seine Hände gab'; *ataduodamas* 294,49.

induodamas kūną ir dūšią savą ing galingas rankas jo 370,17 'Leib und Seele in seine starken Hände übergebend'.

nusidėjau išduodamas kraują teisų 163,18 : Matth. 27,4 peccavi tradens sanguinem iustum.

vienam Petrui avis savas paduodamas užgyrė visiemus vienybę 611,32 'indem (Christus) dem Petrus seine Schafe übergab, bestätigte er für alle die Einheit';

perduodami ir pirkdami 413,48 'verkaufend und kaufend';

priduodami tuos žodžius 522,15 'diese Worte hinzufügend'.

II. *dédamas, dẽdamas*

Hier liegt das gleiche Verhältnis vor wie bei *duodamas: dédamas* < *dė-damas* : Infinitiv *dė-ti* = Halbpartizip, *dẽdamas* < *dẽd-amas* : 1. plur. *dẽd-ame* = = Partizip passivi. Nur sind in der gesprochenen Sprache beide Formen durch verschiedenen Öffnungsgrad und die Intonation des langen *e* klar unterschieden. In dem Druck der Postille kommt das aber nicht zum Ausdruck, da nur die Länge des *e* bezeichnet wird, aber auch das nicht immer und nicht einheitlich. Man vergleiche

Part. praes. pass.	Halbpartizip
ê	iždédamas 90,36	pridêdamas 345,15
é	sudédamas 580,5	padédamas 203,23
e	—	sudedamá 429,17[5]

1. Partizip passivi (nur präfigiert belegt)

kuriose kalavijas dvasios išdedamas est 90,36 '(die Scheide,) in der das Schwert des Geistes aufbewahrt wird';

est sudedamas 580,5 'wird zusammengelegt'.

2. Halbpartizip

a) Verbum simplex

viename Viešpatije Christuje dvi personi dédamas 257,50 'in dem einen Herrn Christus zwei Personen setzend';

dédamas já lygiai su savimi ir teipajeg su Tévu 261,39 'ihn (den Heiligen Geist) gleich mit sich und ebenso mit dem Vater setzend';

ir dédams rankas ant já palaimino jiemus 500,44 'und indem er die Hände auf sie legte, segnete er sie'.

b) präfigiertes Verbum

teip kaipo karalius pasiuntiniams saviemus duost galybę ištiesa, padédamas ... 203,23 'so wie der König seinen Boten in der Tat Kraft gibt, indem er ihnen hilft ...';

pradédami tad nuog artikulo pirmojo 257,21 'indem wir nun vom ersten Artikel an beginnen'; ferner 503,14; 572,12;

o Viešpatis ne peikdamas já atsakymo, bet pridédamas tatai 345,15 'indem aber der Herr ihre Weigerung nicht tadelte, sondern das hinzufügte'; ferner 613,10;

sudédama draugia visas maldas ir darbus geruosius 429,17 '(die heilige Kirche,) indem sie alle Gebete und guten Werke zusammenlegt'.

Wie die passiven Partizipien auf *-amas* entwickeln sich solche auf *-(d)amas* gelegentlich zu selbständigen Adjektiven oder Substantiven. So ist in der Postille mehrfach (z. B. 4,9; 484,44; 497,13.23.37; 498,2.23.30.46) belegt *veldamas* 'erblich, Erbhöriger' von *veldéti, vélda* 'besitzen', vgl. Skardžius, *Daukš.akc.* 221, Fraenkel, *LEW* 1218. Substantiviert ist auch *kandamas* 'valgomas duonos gabalas' *LKŽ*, V, 201, Skardžius, *Žod.daryba* 207, von *kásti, kánda* 'beißen'.

Bekanntlich darf das Halbpartizip nach strenger Regel nicht prädikativ verwendet werden. Aber in der Postille finden sich mehrfach solche falschen Setzungen des Halbpartizips statt des Partizips der aktiven Gegenwart.

Einmal beim Typus ἦν διδάσκων: *ir buvo mokydamas kiek dienos bažnyčioj* 309,34 : Luk. 19,47 et erat docens quotidie in templo. Dagegen beim Futur mit den normalen Partizip: *nuog to jau busi žmones gaudąs* 288,9 : Luk. 5,10 ex hoc iam homines eris capiens (ἔση ζωγρῶν).

Häufiger steht das Halbpartizip statt des Part. praes. im Konjunktiv (Konditional): *nenoriu numirimo nusidėjusio bet didžiaus, idant sugriżtų ir gyvas liktų. Ir priduost kaip būtų apgiezdamas. Sugrįžkite nuog keliu jūsų pikčiausių, o kodrin mirštate namai Israelo?* Hier ist zwischen die beiden Sätze Ezechiel 33,11 Nolo mortem impii, sed ut convertatur impius a via sua et vivat und Convertimini, convertimini a viis vestris pessimis et quare moriemini, domus Israel? der Verbindungssatz 'und er fügte hinzu, als grollte er' eingeschoben. Die Umschreibung *būtų apgiezdamas* fällt deshalb besonders auf, weil kurz vorher die einfachen Konjunktive *sugriżtų* und *liktų* stehen. Sie finden sich in einem mit *idant* eingeleiteten Absichtssatz. Der zweigliedrige Konjunktiv steht dagegen in einem irrealen Vergleichssatz mit *kaip* 'wie wenn, als ob'. Und so ist es durchgängig in der Postille: der Konjunktiv von *būti* mit dem Halbpartizip findet sich nur in solchen irrealen *kaip*-Sätzen. Der Übersetzer der Postille hätte unschwer den Konjunktiv *apgieżtų* benutzen können, aber er bildete in Anlehnung an den Konjunktiv der Vergangenheit *apgieżęs būtų* eine entsprechende Umschreibung mit dem Halbpartizip zur Bezeichnung des Konjunktivs der Gegenwart. Weitere Belege:

mušė ing krutis savas kuo parodė gailėjimą tikrą išg nuodėmių padarytų, kaip būtų jau karodamas širdį savą 316,13 'er schlug an seine Brust, wodurch er echte Reue wegen der begangenen Sünden zeigte, als ob er schon sein Herz züchtigte';

kaip būtų išpažindama, jog jis buvo ne tiktai karaliumi, bet ir tikruoju Dievu 482,48 'als würde sie bekennen, daß er nicht nur der König, sondern auch der wahre Gott war'. Ferner: *kaip būtų norėdamas* 473,31; *kaip būtų mylėdamies* 575,46; *kaip būtų budavodamas* 576,3. Besonderes Interesse verdient folgende Stelle: *kaip būtų išpažindamas, jog pažeidė nuodėmėmis savomis sunkiomis augščiausią aną majestotą V. Dievo savo danguje, kaip būtų teip taręs su anuo ...* 316,4 'als bekennte er, daß er mit seinen schweren Sünden jene höchste Majestät seines Herrgotts im Himmel verletzte, als hätte er so mit jenem gesprochen'. Während beim Konjunktiv der Gegenwart das Halbpartizip steht, wird beim Konjunktiv der Vergangenheit das reguläre präteritale Partizip gesetzt. Dafür gibt es reichlich Belege, vgl. z. B. *kad bučio tų ženklų nedaręs* 531,33 'wie wenn ich diese Zeichen nicht getan hätte'.

Im heutigen Litauisch wird *kaip* 'wie wenn, als ob' mit dem reinen Halbpartizip verbunden: *jis vaikščiojo kaip ir nenorėdamas* 'er ging wie widerwillig umher'[6]. In der Postille ist mir eine derartige *kaip*-Konstruktion nicht aufgefallen; denn in *nesa kas gal būt neišmintingesnio kaip žinodamas neabejotinai* 552,22 'denn wer kann nicht klüger sein als der, der unzweifelhaft weiß' bezieht sich *kaip* auf den Komparativ, nicht auf das Halbpartizip. Das ostbaltische Halbpartizip ist eine merkwürdig unpraktische Neuerung. Warum ließ man es nicht beim normalen Präsenspartizip bewenden? Warum schuf man nicht eine bequemere, weil unflektierbare Form wie das Adverbialpartizip (Gerundium, Absolutiv) des Russischen vom Typus даря? Vgl. z. B. молча он выходит 'schweigend geht er hinaus', улыбаясь рассказывает 'lächelnd erzählt er'. Denn auch das Litauische besitzt solche Gerundien, sogar für alle Zeitstufen, im Präsens — das uns hier nur interessiert — auf *-nt* endend. Dieses Gerundium wird aber nicht, wie das Halbpartizip, bei gleichem Subjekt der Haupt- und Nebenhandlung verwendet, sondern nur wenn die Nebenhandlung ein anderes Subjekt hat: *temstant važiavo* 'bei Einbruch der Dunkelheit fuhr er', also Umsetzung eines Impersonale. Auf Verwendung beim Objekt oder im Dativus absolutus brauchen wir hier nicht einzugehen[7].

In der Frage nach dem Ursprung des *-damas*-Partizips kommt man z. Z. über das von Stang, *Vergl. Gramm. der Baltischen Sprachen* 444 f. Gesagte nicht hinaus. Da baltische Zustandspräsentien mit *d*-Suffix, die als Vorbild dienen könnten, schwer nachzuweisen sind, möchte ich zur Debatte stellen, ob das *d* von *-damas* nicht etwa mit dem *-d-* des iterativen Imperfekts auf *-davo* zusammenhängen könnte. Denn es ist sicher zu eng formuliert, wenn man die Funktion des litauischen Imperfekts dahin bestimmt, daß es ein gewohnheitsmäßiges Tun in der Vergangeheit bezeichne, das man im Deutschen mit *pflegte* umschreibt. Ich gebe drei Belege aus der Postille, von denen zwei zugleich ein Halbpartizip enthalten. Im 1. Beispiel ist das Iterative deutlich, in den beiden anderen fehlt es: *amžiuose apastalų ir tuo ženklu ženklindavo ir kryžma krikštydami tepdavo* 455,24 'in den Zeiten der Apostel zeichneten sie sowohl mit diesem Zeichen als auch salbten sie, taufend, kreuzförmig'; *kimšdavos ir verždavos spausdamies* 288,36 (vom Volk am See Genezareth Luk. 5,1) 'sie drängten sich und drangen heran, indem sie sich zusammendrängten'. Das ist ein einmaliges Ereignis, keine Gewohnheit, aber durativ. Endlich in *valgė su elgetomis … valgė su muitininkais … valgė su teisininkais … valgydavo ir su Pharizeušais savais priešakiais* 477,21 'er aß mit den Bettlern … er aß mit den Zöllnern … er aß mit den Gerechten … er aß auch mit den Pharisäern, seinen Gegnern' könnte auch an der vierten Stelle *valgė* stehen, ohne den Sinn zu ändern.

Die Verbindung vom *d* des Imperfekts zum *d* des Halbpartizips ist natürlich schwer zu ziehen. Man könnte an Fälle denken, wo das Imperfekt die Nebenhandlung bezeichnet, und ebendas tut auch das Halbpartizip.

Anmerkungen

1. Zitiert nach dem *fotografinis leidimas*, Kaunas 1926. Die Schreibweise ist, wo es nicht auf die Orthographie ankommt, modernisiert wie in dem in Vilnius erscheinenden *Lietuvių Kalbos Žodynas* (= *LKŽ*).

2. z. B. Andersonas *Pasakos* vertė J. Balčikonis, Vilnius 1966, 12 *aš gyvenau, gyvendamas džiaugiausi ir džiaugdamasis žydėjau.*

3. Weitere Belege 307,8 (7 Halbpartizipien); 251,3 (6); 32,1. 316,18. 392,23 (je 5); 383,31 hat ebenfalls 5 im Sing., die Korrektur dazu 631,44 r. bringt 5 im Plural.

4. Specht, *KZ*, LXII, 84 führt *ne duodameś* 135,18, in dem er einen Konjunktiv vermutet, und *pradedameś* 327,14 an. Vgl. auch Otrębski, *Gramatyka języka litewskiego* III, 187.

5. Skardžius, *Daukšos akcentologija*, 220 bucht es irrtümlich als Passivform.

6. Senn, *Grammatik* § 1108; V. Ambrazas, *Lietuvių Kalbotyros Klausimai*, IX, 49 f. (auch mit anderen Fragewörtern wie *ką, ko, kur, kiek, kada*).

7. G. Bense, *Lietuvių Kalbotyros Klausimai*, VI, 1963, 191–211.

The Semi-participle in Daukša's Postille

Statistical data; verbs with frequently attested semi-participle. Modal variants of contemporaneity. Increased frequency of semi-participles in the style of sermons. Twofold use of *duodamas* and *dėdamas*: semi-participle and present passive participle. Incorrect use of the semi-participle (in lieu of the present active participle) of the type ἦν διδάσκων, and in the present subjunctive with *kaip būtų*. The semi-participle is presumed to have developed from a blend of the passive-intransitive participle in *-ama-* with a *-d*-form as found in the iterative imperfect in *-davo*.

VYACHESLAV IVANOV

Suffix *-sk̂-> Baltic -šk- and the Problem of Verbs Denoting Sounds

The phonological development of Indo-European *-sk̂->Baltic -šk- suggested by Prof. Chr. S. Stang[1] may be illustrated by several archaic verbs containing this suffix. The Baltic and Slavic preterite stem in -ā- reflected in Lith. ieškóti 'seek', ieškójau, Slav. iskati, iskaachъ is explained by the original continuative value of the verb[2] identical in its meaning with Vedic icchati (opposed by its semantic function to other verbal derivatives from the root iṣ-[3]). The ā-stem as an innovation of Western dialects appears also in Germanic where the flectional type of Old High German eiscōn (Old Indian icchati, Avestan isaiti) is identical with that of forscōn>forschen (Old Indian pṛechati, Avestan pərəsaiti) reinterpreted as a denominative from forsca 'question'[4]. The same secondary denominative value was acquired by Latv. ēškuôt 'eat often' connected with ēška 'glutton'.[5] The verbal origin of the Baltic stem ēšk- < *ed-sk- (with the long ē conditioned by the absence of -d- after the root vowel,[6] is proved not only by the comparison with Latin esca 'food': vēscor,[7] but also by the similar Hittite azzik- (iterative from ed- 'eat' with the a-grade usual in the Hittite verbs in -šk-) attested already in ceremonial formulae in the texts of the Old Kingdom[8] and in rituals. This archaic Old Hittite verb has the specific augmentative value 'schmaussen, fressen'[9] which coincides exactly with that of Baltic -ēšk-.

The same exact formal equivalence between Hittite and Baltic may be found if one compares Old Hittite taršk- (iterative from tar- 'say') and Lith. tarskéti 'fortgesetzt klappern, rasseln', traškěti, treškěti 'knistern', Latv. tarškēt 'rasseln, klappern, schwatzen', terškêt 'schnarren, schwatzen'[10] derived from the root of Lith. tarti, taryti,[11] Old Prussian tārin 'voice' (cf. also Latv. terêt 'schwatzen'). The cognate Slavic verb trěskati also belongs to the group of *sk̂-verbs denoting sounds.[12]

The same semantic function is characteristic of a special class of Hittite verbs that are usually described as verba dicendi.[13] In these verbs -šk- is used not as the iterative inflexional morpheme (as in almost all other forms in -šk-) but as a statistically predominant mark of the whole semantic group. This unique verbal group might be shown to preserve some traces of the more archaic use of Old Hittite -*šk*- previous to the transformation of this word-formation suffix into an inflexional morpheme. In this group of verbs not only verba dicendi in a stricter sense but also some other denotations of emission of sounds are found, for instance, *wiyaišk*- 'schreien, rufen', *išham(a)išk* 'singen'. The last stem occurs in such archaic contexts as in the mythological poem about Ulikummi[14] and in the Old Hittite tablet (written in the archaic ductus) K Bo III 40 (Bo Tu 14 α), I 13: *nu-uz-za iš-[ḫ]a-ma-i-iš-ki-iz-zi* 'and one sings'.[15] This impersonal construction introduces the oldest known metrical text in an Indo-European language[16] which is followed by (or which includes) another -*šk*-verb of the same type: *punuš-kimi* 'I ask' (with the same meaning as the Old and Modern English cognates of Lith. *ieškóti*). All the macrotext consists of several microtexts each of them beginning with a verb in -*šk*-. Such a scheme is characteristic of a large number of Hittite texts (especially rituals) where verba dicendi which introduce direct speech usually take the *šk*-suffix: thus *tezzi* 'he speaks' without the following direct speech may alternate with *taršizzi* 'he says' with the following words of the speaker.[17]

As in Hittite the suffix -*šk*- and reduplication were synonymous,[18] Luwian Cuneiform *tatar-iịa*- 'condemn' (: tardi 'he speaks'), Hieroglyphic *tatar(i)a*-, Lydian *tatro* 'order' (: *kan-tro*) may be interpreted as formations with the reduplication (of the Indo-European perfect type) parallel to Hittite *taršizzi*.[19] But for the comparative grammar of Baltic and Slavic languages much more important is the intensive reduplication in Hittite *pariparai* 'blows (a wind instrument)' where C. Watkins found the same "intensive in connection with the production of a musical sound"[20] as in Vedic *saniṣvanat* 'sounds' (Old Irish *sennid* 'plays a musical instrument', Latin *sonāre*). Old Indian athematic intensives of the *janghanti* type were compared by Prof. Chr. S. Stang with the type of Russian тараторить[21] derived from the same root as Lith. *tarškèti* 'тараторить'[22] (in Baltic and Slavic from this root both reduplicated forms and *sk̂-stem were formed as in Anatolian[23]). In the *o*-grade of these intensive reduplications Prof. Chr. S. Stang found the origin of the root vocalism of a whole series of verbs denoting the rhythmical emission of sounds: Lith. *tariù*, Slavic *sopǫ* 'spiele Flöte', *pojǫ* 'singe', *gǫdǫ* 'κιθαρίζω', *stonjǫ* (Russian стону).[24] The intensive reduplication in a verb of the same semantic class may be suggested also in *glagol'ǫ*[25] where the apparent denominative character can be secondary as in some other verbs discussed above.[26] If should be stressed that in the Slavic *o*-grade verbs denoting sounds A. Meillet and Chr. S. Stang discovered the value of the continued, rhythmically repeated action which coincides with that of the verbs with the old *ā*-preterite of the *ieškóti* type.[27]

Typological data may be of some interest for the study of morphological, derivational and inflexional pecularities of Baltic, Slavic and Anatolian verbs denoting continued rhythmical emission of sounds. In such a non-Indo-European language as Ket (Jenissej Ostyak) the verbs denoting sounds are set apart from all other verbs by the use of a special terminal stem [-ta] being in complementary distribution with the suffix of the momentary action [g'es'] and by the impersonal construction with nominal possessive prefixes.[28] In many other languages such verbs denoting sounds have either special derivational characterics[29] or peculiar morphonological shape[30] sometimes combined with grammatical differential features.[31] These data seem to support the idea set forth in modern componential semantics according to which the verbal denotations of sound emitted by different objects might constitute a separate semantic category.[32] In Baltic, Slavic and Anatolian languages (and possibly in some other Indo-European dialects) the verbs of this category seem to represent a special class with unique formal characteristics.

Notes

1. Chr. S. Stang, *Vergleichende Grammatik der Baltischen Sprachen*, Oslo, 1966, 92.

2. Herman Kølln, *Oppositions of voice in Greek, Slavic and Baltic*, København, 1969, 38, 42, 47–48.

3. Т.Я.Елизаренкова, Значение основ презенса в Ригведе, — „Языки Индии", Москва, 1961, 156.

4. See on these relations Manu Leumann, *Kleine Schriften*, Zürich, 1959, 328, 358–359.

The diachronic explanation of these facts given by Manu Leumann is to be rejected in the light of discoveries of Chr. S. Stang and H. Kølln.

5. K. Mülenbach–J. Endzelin, *Lettisch-deutsches Wörterbuch* (ME) I, 578; J. Endzelīns, *Baltu valodu skaņas un formas*, Rīgā, 1948, 95, § 142; J. Endzelīns, *Latviešu valodas gramatika*, Rīgā, 1951, 356, § 183 a. Cognate Lithuanian dialectal forms (*ėskà* 'appetite' in Northern Žemait dialects of Skuodas, Kartera, Kretinga, *ėskùs* 'voracious' in the Western Aukštait dialect of Vadžgirys) do not seem to have been borrowed from other dialects where *šk* > *sk* (as in the Southern Aukštait dialect of Ašašninkai where (*j*)*ieškóti* > [*jieskɔ˙c*], Z. Zinkevičius, *Lietuvių dialektologija*, Vilnius, 1966, 147, § 161 a) and so the morphological explanation by the later inclusion into the nominal stems in -*sk*- (P. Skardžius, *Lietuvių kalbos žodžių daryba*, Vilnius, 1943, 124) is plausible.

6. See on the distribution of allomorphs of this root:
В.В.Иванов, „Отражение двух серий индоевропейских глагольных форм в праславянском", *Славянское языкознание. VI Международный съезд славистов*, Москва, 1968.

The *e*-grade is characteristic of some Western Indo-European verbs in *-sk̂-* (such as *eiscōn*).

7. K. Brugmann, *Kurze vergleichende Grammatik der indogermanischen Sprachen,* Strassburg, 1904, 48: K. Brugmann, *Grundriss der vergleichenden Grammatik der indogermanischen Sprachen,* 2 Aufl., II, Teil 1, 478, 357.

8. В.В.Иванов, *Общеиндоевропейская, праславянская и анатолийская языковые системы,* Москва 1965, 63, 139, 159–162.

9. Wolfgang Dressler, *Studien zur verbalen Pluralität,* Wien, 1968, 189–190, 199, 175, 187.

10. ME IV, 133, 150, 167. Parallel Latvian forms in *-kšķēt < -šķēt* seem to speak against the explanation of Lithuanian verbs in *-kšéti* from *-kš-séti* as suggested by A. Senn, *Handbuch der litauischen Sprache,* Heidelberg, 1966, 282.

11. The verb occurs in Old Lithuanian: J. Palionis, *Lietuvių literarinė kalba XVI–XVIIa.,* Vilnius, 1967, 241.

12. V. Machek, "Slavische Verba mit suffixalem *sk*", *Slavistična Revija*" X, 1957, 67–80; В. В. Иванов, *Отражение двух серий,* 248.

13. G. Bechtel, *Hittite verbs in -sk-,* Ann Arbor, 1936, 198; W. Dressler, *Op. cit.,* 198–199, § 60.

14. W. Dressler, *Op. cit.,* 186, § 41.

15. Calvert Watkins, "A Latin-Hittite etymology", *Language,* 45, № 2, pt 1, 240; Г.Г.Гчоргадзе, „Хетты и хурриты по древнехеттским текстам", *Вестник древней истории",* 1969, № 1, 81.

16. В.В.Иванов, „Эаметки по сравнительно-исторической индоевропейской поэтике", *For Roman Jakobson,* The Hague–Paris, 1967, 977.

17. W. Dressler, *op. cit.,* 199.

18. N. van Brock, "Les thèmes verbeaux à redoublement du hittite et le verbe indo-européen", *Revue hittite et esianique,* XXII, fasc. 75, 1964, 127–128, 144, 152; В.В.Иванов, *Общеиндоевропейская ...,* 145–146.

19. В.В.Иванов, *Отражение двух серий,* 248.

20. Calvert Watkins, "A history of Indo-European verb inflexion", "*Indo-European Grammar. Vol. III. Morphology*", pt 1 (English-language version), pre-print, Stanford, California, 1967, chapt. II, § 7.

21. Chr. S. Stang, *Das slavische und baltische Verbum,* Oslo, 1942, 41.

22. This Russian equivalent of the Lithuanian verb was given by B. Sereiskis, *Lietuviškai-rusiškas žodynas,* Kaunas, 1933, 978.

23. The identity of тараторить and Hittite *tar* was discovered by V. Machek, *Etymologický slovník jazyka českého a slovenského,* Praha, 1957, 533; E. Benveniste, *Hittite et indo-européen,* Paris, 1962, 122.

24. Chr. S. Stang, *Das slavische und baltische Verbum,* 41. On the similarity of the type of *gǫdǫ* and *tarškéti* see W. P. Schmid, *Studien zum baltischen und indogermanischen Verbum,* Wiesbaden, 1963, 73, note 306.

25. Chr. S. Stang, *Das slavische und baltische Verbum,* 38.

26. See on the original verbal character of *glagol'ǫ*: A. J. Buning, *Die indogerm. athematische Conjugatie in het Slavisch,* Amsterdam, 1927, 56, but cf. the objections: J. M. Kořinek, "Presentni tvary kořěne *dō* — 'dávati' v jazycích slovanských a baltských", *Listy filologicke* LXV, 446, note 3.

27. Herman Kølln, *op. cit.,* 38–39.

28. Е.А.Крейнович, *Глагол кетского языка,* Ленинград, 1968, 114–121; А.П. Дульзон, *Кетский язык,* Томск, 1968, 345–350.

29. G. J. Ramstedt, *Einführung in die altaische Sprachwissenschaft*, Helsinki, 1952, § 135.

30. See on Semitic and some other languages: А.М.Газов-Гинзберг, *Был ли язык изобразителен в своих истоках*, Москва, 1965 (with literature).

31. See on sound gestures in Japanese:

Е.Д.Поливанов, *Статьи по общему языкознанию*, Москва, 1968, 301–305, 350–351.

32. А.К.Жолковский, И.А.Мельчук, „О семантическом синтезе", *Проблемы кибернетики*, вып. 19, Москва, 1967, 215.

B. JĒGERS

Zur Etymologie von lit. *kaũlyti* 'zudringlich betteln, feilschen' und lett. *kaũlêt* 'ds.'

Da ich die zeitliche Folge der Versuche, lit. *kaũlyti* und lett. *kaũlêt* etymologisch zu erklären, bewahren möchte, nenne ich zuerst das lett. Wort mit seinen Bedeutungen.

Lett. *kaũlêt* I — so wegen des unten angeführten lett. *kaulêt* II zu bezeichnen — bedeutet nach ME[1]: 1) 'dingen, feilschen', 2) 'mit Hörnern kämpfen wie die Böcke' (wozu bei EH noch hinzukommen 3) 'harte Gegenstände aneinanderschlagen' und 4) 'stark blasen (vom Wind)'), Refl. *-tiês* 1) 'feilschen, dingen', 2) 'durch vieles, unaufhörliches Bitten etwas zu erlangen suchen', 3) 'mit den Hörnern kämpfen; spielend mit den Hörnern kämpfen', 4) 'mit Eiern schlagen (zu Ostern)' (wozu bei EH noch hinzukommt 5) "pūlēties" ['sich anstrengen']; "sisties ar darbiem" ['sich mit Arbeiten abplagen']).

Den schon von Mühlenbach zu diesem Wort gebrachten etymologischen Hinweis (ME s.v.): "Zu li. *kaũlyti* 'durch vieles Bitten zu erlangen suchen' " erweitert Endzelin wie folgt: „*kaũlytis* '[russ.] torgovatьsja ['handeln']; ssoritьsja ['sich streiten']', *kaulỹs* '[russ.] kljanča ['Bettler']', woneben bei Būga RFV. LXV, 316 li. *kaũnyti* u. *kaũzyti* 'beharrlich bitten', und nach Berneker Wrtb. I, 642 zu ai. *kōlāhalaḥ* 'Geschrei von Tieren und Menschen', čech. *kulik* 'Regenpfeifer'. In der Bed. 'mit Hörnern kämpfen; mit Eiern schlagen' dagegen wohl zu le. *kaut(ies)* ['(sich) schlagen']".

Wie man sieht, glaubt Endzelin, daß in lett. *kaũlêt* I zwei verschiedene Wortsippen zusammengefallen sind.

Fraenkel Wb. 230 schreibt: „[Lit.] *kaũlyti* (*-iju*) 'zudringlich betteln, feilschen, markten', daneben *kaũnyti*, *kaũzyti* (Būga RFV 65, 316), *kaulỹs*, *-lẽ* 'zudringliche Person, freche(r) Bettler(in)', lett. *kaũlêt* 'dingen, feilschen, mit Hörnern fechten wie die Böcke'. Weder zu russ. *kulik* 'Schnepfe' usw. (Berneker Wb. 1, 642, Vasmer Wb. 1, 688 [...]), noch zu lett. *klĭja* 'roter Milan', *klienis* 'Flußregenpfeifer' (H. Peterson, Et. Mi. 35), sondern zu lit. *káutis*, lett. *kaûtiês* [...]; vgl. dtsch. (volkst.) *Fechter = Bettler*, *fechten* 'betteln (von den Handwerksburschen)'".

Ich glaube, daß Fraenkel recht hat, wenn er an einen einheitlichen Ursprung von lit. *kaũlyti* und lett. *kaũlêt* I — im Gegensatz von Endzelin (vgl. oben) — denkt und den Zusammenhang mit den Vogelnamen zurückweist. Jedoch ist m. E. die Zusammenstellung von lit. *kaũlyti* usw. der Sippe von lit. *káutis* nicht zutreffend, obwohl er auf eine Bedeutungsparallele ('betteln' : 'fechten') hinweisen kann, die jedoch hier nicht in Betracht kommen dürfte[2].

Weiterhin glaube ich, daß Otrębski auf dem richtigen Weg ist, wenn er in seiner Gram. 2, 391 das lit. *kaũlyti* mit der Einschränkung „może ['vielleicht']" von lit. *káulas* 'Knochen' abgeleitet sein läßt, obwohl, wie er zugibt, die Bedeutungsentwicklung nicht klar ist.

Otrębski kommt zu seiner Vermutung, deren Richtigkeit ich im Folgenden zu erweisen suche, wohl deshalb, weil es nach den Regeln der Wortbildung viel besser ist, lit. *kaũlyti* zu lit. *káulas* (und, wie ich hinzufüge, lett. *kaũlêt* I zu lett. *kaũls* 'Knochen') zu stellen als es mit Endzelin und Fraenkel unmittelbar mit lit. *káutis* (und lett. *kaũtiês*) in Beziehung zu setzen.

Für die Richtigkeit der Vermutung von Otrębski spricht schon der Umstand, daß es sowohl im Lit., als auch im Lett. Verba gibt, deren Ableitung von lit. *káulas*, bzw. lett. *kaũls* über jeden Zweifel erhaben ist.

Es handelt sich um lit. *káulėti* „virsti kaulu; kietėti" 'verknöchern; hart werden' und lett. *kaulêt* II 'würfeln'. Genau wie dem lit. Verbum lit. *káulas* 'Knochen' zugrunde liegt, so geht auch das lett. Verbum auf lett. *kaũls* 'Knochen' in der wohl nur zufälligerweise nicht belegten Bed. 'Würfel' zurück, die jedoch in dem Diminutiv *kaũliņš* II 'Würfel', z. B. in dem Ausdruck *kauliņus mest* 'Würfel spielen', vorliegt. Dagegen ist lit. *káulas* in der Bed. 'Würfel' belegt (LKŽ s. v.), obwohl auch im Lit. das Diminutiv *kaulẽlis* 'Würfel' häufiger vorzukommen scheint. Genau so bedeutet auch russ. *kosti* nicht nur 'die Knochen', sondern auch 'Würfel'. Vgl. noch dt. *Knöchel* 'Würfel' (Diminutiv von *Knochen*!): *knöcheln* 'würfeln' und dt. *Knobel* 'Knöchel; (ein aus Knöcheln geschnittener) Würfel': *knobeln* 'würfeln'.

Außerdem kennt das Lett. *kauluoties* II 'verknöchern', woneben ein *kauluoties* I steht, das nach ME = *kaulėties* I ist.

Es ist auch nicht zu bezweifeln, daß lett. *kaũluôt* 'Reisig sammeln' zu lett. *kaũls* gehört, weist doch dieses Wort auch die Bed. 'Stengel' auf. In dem Beleg BW 13611 *niedru kaulu klēti cirta* 'man baute [für die junge Braut] ein Vorratshaus aus den Halmen des Schilfes' weist *kauli* (Pl. von *kauls*) eine Bed. auf, die sich sehr nahe mit dem Begriff 'Reisig' berührt. Es ist zu beachten, daß in BW 13611, 5 var. die Verbindung *niedru kauli* durch *niedru kuoki* 'Hölzer des Schilfes' ersetzt worden ist, was darauf hinweist, daß hier *kauli* die harten (holzigen) Teile des Schilfes bezeichnen. Somit wird lett. *kaũluôt* 'Reisig sammeln' einst etwa '*Knochen, d. h. trocken und dadurch knochenhart gewordene Äste, sammeln' bedeutet haben. Vgl. noch folgende lit. Belege *didžiulės šaknys sukaulėjusios kaip šakos* 'große Wurzeln [die] hart geworden [sind] wie Äste' (LKŽ s. v. *sukáulėti* 2) und *išdžiũvęs klevas kaulu pavirsta* 'ein ausgetrockneter Ahornbaum wird zum Knochen [wird so hart wie Knochen]' (LKŽ s. v. *káulas* 1)[3].

Aus dem Vorhergehenden dürfte es klar geworden sein, daß man lett. *kaũlêt* I 2) 'mit Hörnern fechten wie die Böcke' und *kaũlêtiês* I 3) 'mit Hörnern kämpfen' als Ableitungen von lett. *kaũls* 'Knochen' auffassen kann, da 'mit Hörnern kämpfen' einst wohl 'mit Knochen (knochenharten Hörnern) kämpfen' bedeutet haben wird, zumal die lett. Sprache keinen Unterschied zwischen den Wörtern *kaũls* 'Knochen' und *rags* 'Horn' macht, wenn sie zur Bezeichnung von etwas Hartem gebraucht werden. Der Lette sagt nicht nur *sasalt kaulā* 'steif frieren', eig. 'frierend zu Knochen werden' (ME s. v. *kaũls* 2), sondern auch *sasalt ragā* 'steif frieren', eig. 'frierend zu Horn (*rags*) werden' (ME s. v. *rags* 18).

Ähnlich wie die eben behandelte Bed. des lett. *kaũlêt* I lassen sich m. E. auch lett. *kaũlêt* I 3) 'harte Gegenstände aneinanderschlagen' *kaulēt riekstus* 'Nüsse', *kaulēt uolas* 'Eier' und *kaũlêtiês* I 4) 'mit Eiern schlagen (zu Ostern)' erklären. Es handelt sich bei diesem Aneinanderschlagen von harten Gegenständen eig. um Eier und solche Früchte, die eine harte Schale haben, ist doch lett. *kaũls* 'Knochen' in der Bed. 'Schale' durchaus greifbar, vgl. etwa BW 16564 var *pušu kuodu rieksta kaulu, pušu rieksta kuoduoliņu* 'ich zerbiß die Schale der Nuß, ich zer[biß] den Kern der Nuß'. Somit bedeutet lett. *kaulēt riekstus* eig. '*die Knochen (knochenartige Schale) der Nüsse zerschlagen' oder anders ausgedrückt '*Nüsse schälen'. Für die Bestimmung des ursprünglichen Gebrauches von lett. *kaulēt uolas* ist der Hinweis auf Ostern wichtig, ist doch das Schlagen mit Eiern zu Ostern ein Brauch, der noch heute von Letten ausgeübt wird. Er besteht darin, daß jeder Teilnehmer an einer Osterfeier sich ein hartgekochtes Ei beschafft, dessen Schale [!] möglichst (knochen)hart ist, und dann mit diesem Ei versucht, die Schalen [!] von möglichst vielen anderen Eiern einzuschlagen, die andere Leute sich zu demselben Zweck ausgesucht haben. Wessen Ei dabei am stärksten ist, d. h. am längsten die Schale heil bewahrt, der wird am längsten von allen leben[4]. Also dürfte kein Zweifel daran bestehen, daß lett. *kaulēt uolas* 'mit den Eiern schlagen' eig. '*die Knochen (knochenartige Schale) der Eier zerschlagen' bedeutet. Vielleicht hat einst *kaulēt uolas* im anderen Zusammenhang die Bed. '*Eier schälen' gehabt[5]?

In lett. *kaũlêtiês* I 5) 'sich anstrengen; sich mit Arbeiten abplagen' ist die Beziehung zu lett. *kaũls* 'Knochen' völlig geschwunden und der Begriff 'schlagen' in den Vordergrund getreten, d. h. *kaŭlêtiês* bedeutet hier wohl einfach 'sich (herum)schlagen', vgl. zur Bed. etwa lett. *sistiês* 'sich schlagen': 'sich herumschlagen, sich abmühen'.

Wie sind nun lit. *kaŭlyti* in der Bed. 'zudringlich betteln' und lett. *kaŭlêtiês* I 2) 'durch vieles, unaufhörliches Bitten etwas zu erlangen suchen' zu erklären?

Da lit. *kaŭlyti* einige Bedeutungen aufweist, die bis jetzt noch nicht erwähnt worden sind, so gebe ich zunächst eine Zusammenstellung dieser Bedeutungen, wobei zu beachten ist, daß das LKŽ, dem ich diese Zusammenstellung entnehme, zwei [!] *kaŭlyti* (*-ija -ijo*) nennt, also sie als Homonyme, bzw. als verschiedenen etymologischen Ursprungs, betrachtet, was m. E. nicht notwendig ist.

Lit. *kaŭlyti* I bedeutet: 1) tr., intr. „prisispyrus, nuolat ko prašyti" 'zudringlich, ständig um etwas betteln', 2) tr., intr. „kalbėti be reikalo; apkalbėti; daryti priekaištus, priekaištauti; skatinti" 'ohne Grund sprechen; klatschen; Vorwürfe machen, vorwerfen; anspornen', 3) intr. „lygtis, derėtis (perkant)" 'dingen, feilschen (beim Kaufen)'. Lit. *kaŭlyti* II bedeutet intr. „ginčytis, vaidytis, bartis" 'sich streiten, sich zanken, sich schelten'.

Ich glaube nun, daß zwischen den Begriffen 'zudringlich um etwas betteln' (lit. *kaŭlyti* I 1), 'durch vieles, unaufhörliches Bitten etwas zu erlangen suchen' (lett. *kaŭlêtiês* I 2), 'dingen, feilschen' (lit. *kaŭlyti* I 3, lett. *kaŭlêt* I 1, *kaŭlêtiês* I 1) einerseits und 'Knochen' (lit. *káulas*, lett. *kaŭls*) genauso eine Beziehung besteht, wie wir es schon oben bei der Besprechung der verschiedenen Bedeutungen von lett. *kaŭlêt* gesehen haben. Allerdings wird diese Beziehung von den heutigen Sprechern nicht mehr gefühlt. Vielleicht steckt in einem Satz wie (*šuo*) *iškaulijo kaulą* '(der Hund) bekam durch langes Betteln den Knochen' noch die ursprüngliche Bed. von *kaŭlyti*, die etwa als '*um einen Knochen (betteln)' bestimmt werden könnte. Später verblaßte die ursprüngliche Bed. und man konnte auch um andere Gegenstände (nicht nur um Knochen) betteln.

Hier können die balt. Sprachen außerdem ein Zeugnis aus der Zeit bewahrt haben, wo Knochen wegen ihres Markes nicht nur in der Nahrung des Menschen eine viel größere Rolle als heute spielten, sondern auch zu Angelhaken, Speerspitzen, Schmuckstücken usw. verarbeitet beim Tauschhandel einen großen Wert darstellten. Gab man dabei einen aus Knochen verfertigten Gegenstand weniger oder verlangte man einen solchen Gegenstand mehr, so sank oder stieg der Preis, so feilschte man.

Auch dürften hier die balt. Sprachen eine Erinnerung an jene Knochen zum Vorschein kommen lassen, die beim Rechnen gebraucht wurden und noch werden. Ich verweise in diesem Zusammenhang auf den Abakus, die älteste „Rechenmaschine" der Menschheit[6]. Der Abakus heißt bei den Russen *ščëty*, wobei die heute auf Drähten aufgereihten Lochscheiben (Lochkugeln) den Namen *ščëtnye kosti* 'Knochen zum Rechnen' tragen[7]. Das weist darauf hin, daß diese Lochscheiben einst aus Knochen, z. B. aus Elfenbein, verfertigt waren, wie das ja auch heute noch oft der Fall ist. Im Anschluß an die eben genannten *ščëtnye kosti*, die auch einfach *kosti* 'Knochen' genannt werden, haben sich im Russ. die Ausdrücke *s kostej doloj* 'von der Rechnung herunter' (eig. 'von den Knochen weg') und *na-kosti* 'hinzufügen' (eig. 'zu den Knochen [hinzu]') entwickelt (vgl. Dalь s. v. *kostь*). Ein Beleg mag das zeigen (Slovarь sovremennogo russkogo literaturnogo jazyka s. v. *kostь*): *Chotь by malenko deševle kupitь [tjulenja] u Merkulova, — dumaet on. Opričь obeščannoj grivny ešče by dve, tri, a ne to i četyre s kostej doloj* 'wenn man [die Robbe] bei Merkulov nur ein wenig billiger kaufen könnte, denkt er. Abgesehen von der versprochenen Grivna, vielleicht noch um zwei, drei, oder sogar vier [Grivnas] billiger'.

Es sei noch auf Folgendes hingewiesen.

Die Ägypter haben nach Herodot mit Hilfe von kleinen Steinen gerechnet. Auch die Römer haben mit Steinchen gerechnet, wie das lat. *calculāre* 'mit Rechensteinen rechnen' beweist (vgl. dt. *kalkulieren*), das eine Ableitung von lat. *calculus* 'Steinchen; Rechenstein' ist, welches die Verkleinerungsform zu lat. *calx* 'Spielstein; Kalk[stein]' bildet. Die Römer haben auch Kupferkugeln und Glaskugeln zum Rechnen benutzt, während die Chinesen Bambus- oder Elfenbeinstäbe gebraucht haben[8]. Bei den Russen sind es dann Knochen gewesen, was auch für die übrigen slavischen Völker und die Balten zutreffen dürfte.

Aus dem eben Gesagten mag es klar geworden sein, daß lit. *kaũlyti* und lett. *kaũlêt(iês)* auch in den Bedeutungen 'betteln; feilschen' zu lit. *káulas* 'Knochen', bzw. lett. *kaũls* 'ds.' gehören. Es dürfte sich ursprünglich um das Betteln (eines Hundes) um einen Knochen gehandelt haben. Da beim Tauschhandel auch mit Knochen oder aus Knochen verfertigten Gegenständen gehandelt wurde, so konnte 'um einen Knochen betteln' sehr leicht über '*einen Knochen weniger geben müssen' oder '*einen Knochen mehr verlangen' zu 'feilschen' führen, was um so leichter geschehen konnte, da Knochen (Scheiben aus Knochen) auch beim Rechnen benutzt wurden und noch werden (vgl. den Abakus).

Eine ähnliche Beziehung zwischen den Begriffen 'Knochen' und 'mit Bitten oder Forderungen belästigen' findet sich im Engl., wo neben dem von *bone* 'Knochen' angeleiteten *to bone*, das u. a. die Bed. 'einen Knochen herausnehmen' hat, ein mundartliches *to bone* „to annoy by repeated dunning, or by constant solicitation" 'einen durch mehrfache Bitten um

Zahlung oder durch ständige Aufforderungen zu zahlen belästigen' vorkommt, z. B. in dem Satz (English Dialect Dictionary, ed. by J. Wright, s. v.) *I doan't like to see a lot o' chaps boanin' at wun o'ther shopmaites for a footing* 'ich sehe es nicht gern, wenn eine Menge junger Leute einen von ihren Arbeitskameraden ständig wegen des Einstandsgeldes mit Forderungen belästigt'.

Etwas Ähnliches kommt auch im Amerikanischen vor, wo es ein Verbum *to bone* nicht nur in der Bed. „to drive in to the bone" '[eine Lanze] bis auf die Knochen eindringen lassen', sondern auch in der Bed. „to annoy or pester (a person)" 'jemanden [mit Bitten] belästigen' gibt. Vgl. den Beleg (Dictionary of American English on Historical Principles, ed. by W. A. Craigie and J. R. Hulbert, s. v.) *you had better go to the head-waiter, and he will give you some [raisins] … And if he don't you give some, bone him* 'du solltest besser zu dem Oberkellner gehen, und er wird dir einige [Rosinen] geben … und sollte er dir nicht einige geben, so belästige ihn (mit Bitten)'.

Auch die nun zu behandelnde Bed. 'ohne Grund sprechen; klatschen' (lit. *kaůlyti* I 2 in etwa *kaulijo ir kaulijo visą kelią apie taũ* 'er sprach den ganzen Weg über dich') spricht nicht gegen den von mir angenommenen Zusammenhang des lit. Verbums mit lit. *káulas* 'Knochen', denn etwas Ähnliches weist auch das Russ. auf. Der Russe gebraucht den Ausdruck *peremyvatь kosti* (*kostočki*) in der Bed. „spletničatь, sudačitь o kom-libo" 'über jemanden sprechen, klatschen' (Slovarь sovremmennogo russkogo literaturnogo jazyka 5,1525), obwohl die eig. Bed. 'Knochen (Knöchlein) waschen' ist. Eine ähnliche Bed. hat auch der russ. Ausdruck *razbiratь, perebiratь po kostočkam* „razbiratь čto-libo podrobno, do meločej, spletničatь o kom-libo" 'etwas genau, in Kleinigkeiten besprechen, über jemanden klatschen' (a. a. O. 5,1520), der eig. 'Knochen (Knöchlein) nach der Reihe auseinandernehmen' bedeutet.

Auf Grund der eben angeführten russ. Ausdrücke erklärt Šanskij in seinem Kratkij étimologičeskij slovarь russkogo jazyka (Moskau 1961) das russ. Verbum *kostítь* 'schelten, schmähen, schimpfen' als eine Ableitung von russ. *kostь* 'Knochen'. Er folgt damit der Deutung von Berneker Wb. 1,583, der auch das ukr. *kostýti* 'ds.' und poln. dial. *koškać* 'schwatzen, scherzen', *koškać się* 'sich zanken' u. a. heranzieht und als Bedeutungsparallele anführt poln. *drwić* 'albern reden; sich über jemand lustig machen', das nicht von poln. *drwa gadać* 'leeres Stroh (eig. Holz) sprechen' zu trennen ist.

Es scheint mir, daß russ. *kostítь* 'schelten, schmähen, schimpfen' von Berneker und Šanskij richtig als eine Ableitung von *kostь* 'Knochen' gedeutet wird[9]. Die Glaubwürdigkeit dieser Erklärung wird nicht nur durch den von Šanskij herangezogenen russ. Ausdruck *peremyvatь kostočki* (vgl.

oben), sondern auch durch die Tatsache gestützt, daß das lit. *kaũlyti* in der Bed. 'ohne Grund sprechen; klatschen' nicht nur eine ähnliche Bed. aufweist, sondern ebenfalls als Ableitung von einem Wort für 'Knochen' (lit. *káulas*) gedeutet werden kann.

Es bleibt noch übrig, auf das lit. *kaũlyti* II 'sich streiten, sich zanken, sich schelten' einzugehen[10]. Dieses weist fast dieselbe Bed. wie das eben behandelte russ. *kostítь* 'schelten, schmähen, schimpfen' auf, das, wie wir eben sahen, eine Ableitung von russ. *kostь* 'Knochen' ist. Man darf also m. E. auch für das lit. *kaũlyti* II eine ähnliche Bedeutungsentwicklung annehmen, bzw. es von lit. *káulas* 'Knochen' abgeleitet und mit lit. *kaũlyti* I, das ja auch von lit. *káulas* abgeleitet ist, wie wir ebenfalls oben sahen, identisch sein lassen[11]. Hinzu kommt noch der Umstand, daß man sich sehr leicht vorstellen kann, daß es sich bei diesem *kaũlyti* II, das gewöhnlich als Refl. *kaũlytis* etwa in dem Satz *kaulijosi su juo didei* 'sie stritten sehr mit ihm' (LKŽ s. v.) vorkommt, ursprünglich etwa '*sich um einen Knochen (wie Hunde reißen)' bedeutet haben mag. Man vgl. hierzu das engl. *bone* 'Knochen' in der Verbindung *bone of contention, discord* 'etwas, was Streit hervorruft', eig. 'Knochen des Streites', in dem Beleg *this became such a bone of contention between these deere friends* 'dieses wurde zu einem solchen Gegenstand des Streites (eig. „Zankknochen", vgl. dt. *Zankapfel*) unter diesen lieben Freunden' (Oxford English Dictionary s. v. *bone*). Früher gebrauchte man einfach *a bone* in dem Ausdruck *to cast a bone between* 'einen Knochen dazwischen werfen', d. h. 'zum Streit anreizen', was (von dem Oxford English Dictionary a. a. O.) als eine Anspielung auf den Streit gedeutet wird, der entsteht, wenn man unter Hunde einen Knochen wirft. Vgl. den Beleg *by this Means she ... cast in a Bone betwixt the Wife and the Husband* 'auf diese Weise warf sie einen Knochen zwischen die Frau und den Mann', d. h. 'sie schuf Streit zwischen ihnen'. Vgl. noch die engl. Ausdrücke *to have a bone to pick with one* 'einen Knochen mit einem zu nagen haben', d. h. 'einen Gegenstand zum Streit haben; etwas Unangenehmes oder etwas, was eine Erklärung braucht, mit einer Person in Ordnung bringen' (vgl. das dt. *ein Hühnchen mit jemandem pflücken*) und *a bone to pick (gnaw)* 'etwas, was einen [wie ein Knochen einen Hund] beschäftigt; eine Schwierigkeit, die überwunden werden muß; eine Nuß zu knacken'.

Außerdem ist m. E. noch Folgendes bei der Erklärung des lit. *kaũlyti* II 'sich streiten' zu beachten. Wie wir schon oben gesehen haben, wurden die beim Würfelspiel gebrauchten Würfel oft aus Knochen verfertigt. Wenn man sich daran erinnert, daß das Würfelspiel wohl das älteste Spiel der Menschheit ist und daß die Würfelspielleidenschaft mancher Völker, z. B. der alten Inder und Germanen, außerordentlich groß gewesen ist, entschied doch manchmal das Würfelspiel über Freiheit und Knechtschaft[12], so darf man vielleicht annehmen, daß lit. *kaũlyti* II 'sich streiten' einst nicht nur die von mir oben vorausgesetzte Bed. '*sich um einen Knochen (wie Hunde reißen)', sondern auch die Bed. '*würfeln' aufgewiesen hat. Noch heute werden ja Streitigkeiten um Vorrang sehr oft durch Würfeln oder andere Arten von Glücksspielen (Losen) entschieden (vgl. etwa den Gebrauch von Münzen, um zu entscheiden, wer etwas gewinnt usw.). Somit könnte lit. *kaulijo apie pirmą vietą* 'sie stritten um den ersten Platz' in einem anderen Zusammenhang vielleicht einst '*sie würfelten um den ersten Platz' bedeutet haben.

Aus den obigen Ausführungen dürfte es klar geworden sein, daß lit. *kaũlyti* nebst lit. *káulėti* und lett. *kaũlêt* in allen ihren Bedeutungen Ableitungen von lit. *káulas* 'Knochen' und lett. *kaũls* 'ds.' darstellen und dabei auf eine weit zurückliegende Zeit weisen, wo Knochen nicht nur ein Hauptnahrungsmittel waren, sondern auch beim Rechnen, beim Tauschhandel und beim Spiel in der Form von Rechensteinen, Waffen, Gebrauchsgegenständen und Würfeln viel gebraucht wurden.

Die schon von Otrębski vermutete Ableitung des lit. *kaũlyti* von lit. *káulas* besteht also tatsächlich.

Es besteht demnach keine Beziehung zwischen der Sippe von lit. *kaũlyti* und der von lit. *káutis* 'sich schlagen', wie sie Fraenkel für lit. *kaũlyti* und lett. *kaũlêt* in allen ihren Bedeutungen annimmt, während Endzelin nur für einen Teil des lett. *kaũlêt* an Zusammenhang mit lett. *kaũt(iês)*, bzw. lit. *káuti(s)* denkt. Fern bleiben auch, trotz der Bed. 'betteln; feilschen', die von Būga herangezogenen lit. *kaũnyti* und *kaũzyti*[13].

Trotz des eben Gesagten läßt sich jedoch vielleicht eine Verbindung zwischen der Sippe von lit. *kaũlyti* und der von lit. *káuti(s)* herstellen, allerdings auf eine andere Weise, als Endzelin und Fraenkel es tun.

Man entsinne sich an den Ursprung von dt. *Knochen* (mnd. *knoke*, schwed. mundartl. *knoka*, norw. mundart. *knuka* usw.). Dieses dt. Wort wird allgemein[14] zu mhd. *knochen* 'drücken, pressen; mit den Fäusten kämpfen, knuffen', anord. *knoka* 'klopfen, mit den Knöcheln schlagen', ae. *cnocian* 'schlagen, stoßen', engl. *knock* 'klopfen' usw. gestellt. Auf Grund dieser Zusammenstellung wird dann dt. *Knochen* als 'das, womit man anstößt oder gegenstößt' bestimmt[15]. Neuerdings werden auch dt. *knacken*, mnd. *knaken* 'knacken, krachen', norw. *knaka* usw. herangezogen[16].

Deshalb ist es vielleicht möglich, lit. *káulas* 'Knochen', lett. *kaũls*, apreuss. *caulan* 'Bein' usw.[17] als Ableitungen von lit. *káuti* 'schlagen', bzw. lett. *kaũt* aufzufassen, indem man die balt. Wörter im Anschluß an die Deutung des dt. *Knochen* als '*das, womit man schlägt' erklärt. Vielleicht ist es jedoch besser, von der Bed. '*etwas, was zerschlagen wird' auszugehen, da ja Knochen auch heute noch zerschlagen werden, um an das Mark zu gelangen[18].

Entschließt man sich zu dieser Deutung der balt. Wörter[19], so hat man im Balt. eine geschlossene Reihe von Ableitungen vorliegen: lit. *káuti* 'schlagen', lett. *kaût*→lit. *káulas* 'Knochen', lett. *kaũls*, apreuss. *caulan* 'Bein' →lit. *káulėti* 'verknöchern', lett. *kauluoties* II, *kaulêt* II 'würfeln', denen sich dann lit. *kaũlyti* I und II und lett. *kaũlêt* I in allen ihren Bedeutungen anschließen[20], wie ich in diesem Aufsatz gezeigt zu haben hoffe.

Anmerkungen

1. Die von mir gebrauchten Abkürzungen sind die gleichen wie in Fraenkels *Litauischem etymologischem Wörterbuch*, das hier zu Fraenkel Wb. abgekürzt wird. Statt Fraenkels Abkürzungen M.-Endz., Endz.-Hauz. und Balčikonis LKŽ benutze ich jedoch ME, EH und LKŽ.

2. Zur Entstehung der Bed. 'betteln' in dt. *fechten* vgl. man etwa die Ausführungen in *Trübners Deutschem Wörterbuch* s. v., wo es heißt: ,,Die Handwerker des ausgehenden Mittelalters hatten sich mannigfach zu Fechtgesellschaften zusammengetan, um sich im Gebrauch der Waffen zu üben. Doch zogen sie auch auf das Land und gaben Fechtvorführungen. Da sie dabei auf Zehrung und Gaben der Zuschauer rechneten, nahm *fechten* im Mund der Zünfte die Bedeutung 'betteln' an". Für die uns hier angehenden balt. Wörter läßt sich nichts Ähnliches nachweisen, was darauf schließen läßt, daß der Ursprung der Bed. 'betteln' woanders gesucht werden muß.

3. Ich kann mich nicht des Eindrucks erwehren, daß hier auch lett. *kaũlêt* I 4 'stark blasen (vom Wind)' in dem Beleg *tas laiks kaulēs, kaṃr̄ sakaulēs lietu* anzuschließen ist, d. h. daß auch diese Bed. des lett. Wortes in einer — allerdings nicht ganz klaren — Beziehung zu lett. *kaũls* 'Knochen' steht. Es scheint mir, daß die angegebene Bed. 'blasen (vom Wind)' nicht das Richtige trifft, spricht doch der Beleg nicht vom Wind (lett. *vējš*), sondern vom Wetter (*laiks*). Vielleicht kann man den Beleg wie folgt übersetzen: 'Das Wetter wird [die Erde so lange] trocken [zu Knochen] werden lassen, bis das [lange] Trockensein [endlich] den Regen hervorruft'. Vgl. den etwas anders gewendeten lit. Beleg *žemė susikaulėjo, negal beišakėti* 'die Erde ist [so] hart [trocken] geworden [so verknöchert], daß man nicht eggen kann' (LKŽ s. v. *sukáulėti* 2). Weitere Belege aus dem Lett. dürften vielleicht einst das hier nur Vermutete zur Gewißheit erheben.

4. Vgl. hierzu bei P. Šmits, *Latviešu tautas ticējumi*, Riga, 1940, die Nr. 17369.

5. Heute gebraucht der Lette jedoch für 'Schale' gewöhnlich *čaula*, woneben die als Hypernormalismen aufgefaßten *ķaula*, *ķaule* und *ķauls* stehen (auch ein *čauls* ist belegt, vgl. EH). Von diesen ist dann lett. *ķaũlêtiês* 'sich (ab)lösen, -schälen' abgeleitet, das m. E. dann das lett. *ķaulêt* II 'schlagen' als letzten Endes identisch deuten läßt. Vgl. zur Bed. etwa lett. *lupt* 'schälen' : 'prügeln', *luôbît* 'schälen' : 'mit dem Fuß einen Schlag versetzen', *mizuôt* 'abrinden, abschälen' : 'hauen, schlagen, prügeln'. Von dem lett. *ķaulêt* II ist m. E. lett. *ķaulêt* I '(unästhetisch) essen; eine Arbeit plump verrichten' nicht zu trennen, weisen doch die eben erwähnten lett. *lupt* und *mizuôt* ebenfalls

die Bed. 'essen, fressen' auf. Man sieht also, wie eng sich die Bedeutungen 'Schale' : 'schälen' : 'schlagen' berühren, was alles für meine Deutung des lett. *kaulēt uolas*, *riekstus* spricht. Es sei noch erwähnt, daß lett. *čàula* usw. etymologisch von lett. *kaũls* 'Knochen : Schale' abgerückt wird, was vielleicht nicht richtig ist, scheint doch lett. *čàula* in einem gewissen — wenn auch weiteren Zusammenhang — mit lett. *kaũls* zu stehen. Aus Raumgründen muß ich jedoch verzichten, hier auf diesen m. E. durchaus möglichen Zusammenhang näher einzugehen.

6. Darüber vgl. etwa V. S. Groza, *A Survey of Mathematics*, New York, 1968, 73–74 (wo S. 74 verschiedene Arten des Abakus abgebildet sind) und D. E. Smith, *Mathematics* (New York, 1963), der S. 24–31 die geschichtliche Entwicklung des Abakus andeutet und S. 101–105 den Einfluß des römischen und griechischen Abakus auf die Methoden des Rechnens beschreibt.

7. Die lett. Bezeichnung für den Abakus *skaitāmie kauliņi* eig. 'Knöchlein zum Rechnen' scheint mir eine Lehnübersetzung aus dem Russ. zu sein. Sie kommt also hier nicht in Betracht.

8. Nach Groza a. a. O. 73 und Smith a. a. O. 23–31.

9. Ob jedoch die von Berneker herangezogenen ukr. und poln. Wörter mit dem russ. *kostitb* verwandt sind, ist nicht ganz sicher, rückt sie z. B. Sławski Wb. 2, 556 von dem russ. Wort ab, was jedoch m. E. die Richtigkeit der etymologischen Deutung von russ. *kostitb* nicht beeinträchtigt.

10. Für dieses Wort belegt das LKŽ in einigen Zusammensetzungen die Bed. 'schlagen, verprügeln', z. B. in dem Satz *jis savo broli̧ apkaulijo* 'er verprügelte seinen Bruder'. Zu dieser Bed. vgl. das oben über lett. *kaũlêt* 'schlagen' Gesagte und auch lett. *tad es tavus kaulus samalšu* 'dann werde ich dir deine Knochen zermalmen' (eine Drohung vor einer Prügelei), dt. *jemandem die Knochen entzweischlagen* 'jemanden tüchtig prügeln' und engl. (English Dialect Dictionary s. v.) *boner* 'ein Schlag auf den Rücken' (Ableitung von *bone* 'Knochen').

11. Auch Endzelin glaubt nicht an zwei verschiedene lit. *kaũlyti*, wie es aus seiner etymologischen Notiz zu lett. *kaũlêt* hervorgeht (vgl. oben).

12. Vgl. hierzu etwa den Artikel „Spiele" bei O. Schrader, *Reallexikon der indogermanischen Altertumskunde*, 2. Aufl., Berlin, 1917–1929.

13. Lit. *kaũnyti* ist vielleicht eine volksetymologische Umgestaltung von lit. *kaũlyti* 'betteln; feilschen' auf Grund der sicher zu lit. *káutis* 'sich schlagen, prügeln' gehörenden *kaũnis* 'Handgemenge' und *kaũnius* 'jemand, der schlägt', die ja um so leichter vorgenommen werden konnte, da lit. *kaũlyti* auch die Bed. 'prügeln' aufweist (s. Anm. 10). Ist auch das lit. *kaũzyti* eine ähnliche Umgestaltung von *kaũlyti* (auf Grund von etwa lit. *káustyti* 'mit Eisen beschlagen; prügeln')? Ich glaube also nicht, daß es sich bei lit. *kaũnyti* und *kaũzyti* um Ableitungen von lit. *káutis* handelt, genau wie ich auch nicht daran glaube, daß *kaũlyti* eine Ableitung von *káutis* ist, wie es etwa Fraenkel glaubt (vgl. oben). Allerdings könnte lit. *kaũnyti* 'betteln; feilschen' auch als eine Ableitung von *kaũnis* oder *kaũnius* erklärt werden, wobei man dann annehmen könnte, das für den Sprecher das Feilschen ohne Prügelei nicht denkbar ist.

14. Vgl. etwa F. Kluge, *Etymologisches Wörterbuch der deutschen Sprache*[17], 383; *Trübners Deutsches Wörterbuch* 4, 208; *Der Große Duden*, 7, 340.

15. *Der Große Duden*, a. a. O.

16. Vgl. etwa *Trübners Deutsches Wörterbuch* 4, 191; *Der Große Duden*, 7, 337.

17. Eine Zusammenstellung der Sippe von lit. *káulas* findet sich bei Fraenkel Wb. s. v.

18. Vielleicht kann man auch dt. *Knochen* ähnlich erklären, da dt. *knacken* auch 'aufbrechen, tr.' bedeutet bei Kernen, Nüssen, Mandeln u. ä.? Dt. *knacken* bezieht sich sehr oft auch auf das Geräusch beim Ein- und Ausspringen von Knochengelenken. Vielleicht bedeutete einst *Knochen knacken* 'Knochen mit Knackgeräusch aufbrechen'? Vgl. etwa (*daß er*) *ihm alle Knochen knacken ließ* (*Trübners Deutsches Wörterbuch* 4, 191), wo *knacken* die Bed. 'zerbrechen tr.' zu haben scheint. In diesem Zusammenhang sei auch an lett. *kaulēt riekstus* (vgl. oben) erinnert.

19. Da lit. *káulas* und seine Sippe auf **kau-l, ku-l-* 'hohl; Hohlstengel, Röhrenknochen' (Pokorny Wb. 537) zurückgeführt werden, wobei die Anknüpfung der ai. und germ. Wörter, die auf **ku-l-* 'hohl' weisen, unsicher ist, vgl. Frisk Wb. sv. *kaulós*, so spricht weder lautlich, noch begrifflich nichts, soweit ich sehe, gegen die Vermutung, daß die balt. Wörter als *l*-Erweiterungen zu der Sippe von lit. *káuti* 'schlagen' gehören, die auf **kāu-, kəu-* 'hauen, schlagen' (Pokorny Wb. 535) beruht. Allerdings wird man dann für gr. *kaulós* 'Stengel, Schaft, Federkiel' und lat. *caulis -us* 'Stengel, Stiel an Pflanzen' von der — im Balt. noch bewahrten — Bed. 'Knochen' ausgehen müssen, die ja leicht die Bed. 'Stengel' ergeben kann, vgl. lett. *kaûls* in der bereits oben erwähnten Bed. 'Stengel'.

20. Vgl. etwa die Reihen lit. *siúti* 'nähen' — *siúlas* 'Garn, Faden' — *siūléti* 'besäumen'; lett. *pũt* 'faulen' — *praúls* (< *pļauls, vgl. lit. *piáulas* 'verfaultes Holz') 'morndes Stück Holz' — *praúlêt* 'modern'. Zu diesen und anderen *l*-Erweiterungen im Balt. vgl. etwa Endzelin Lett. Gr. 250 ff., Skardžius LKŽD 162 ff., Otrębski Gram. 2, 101 ff.

Lith. kaũlyti and Latv. kaũlêt 'to haggle'

The author tries to show that it is not necessary to regard, as proposed by Endzelīns, Latv. *kaũlêt* I in the meaning 'to beat together (hard objects, e.g. eggs)' as being etymologically different from Latv. *kaũlêt* I in the meaning 'to haggle'. In addition, the author points out that not only Latv. *kaulêt* II 'to play dice' and Lith. *káulėti* 'to become hard (as a bone)' but also Latv. *kaũlêt* I in all its meanings and Lith. *kaũlyti* 'to haggle' are derivatives of Latv. *kaũls* and Lith. *káulas* 'bone' respectively.

ANDREJS JOHANSONS

Die lettischen Benennungen der Schlange

Der gewöhnliche lettische Gattungsname, mit welchem alle in Lettland vorkommende Arten aus der Familie der Schlangen bezeichnet werden, ist *čūska*. In alltäglichem Sprachgebrauch versteht man darunter nicht nur die *odze* 'Giftotter' und den *zalktis* bzw. *zaltis* 'die Ringelnatter', sondern auch die *glodene* oder *glauma* 'Blindschleiche', obwohl diese zu der Familie der Eidechsen gehört.

In lettischen Zaubersprüchen und überhaupt im folkloristischen Material werden aber die gewöhnlichen Schlangennamen oftmals durch Deckbezeichnungen und euphemistische Beschreibungen ersetzt. Im nachfolgenden führe ich, alle Nebenformen mit eingerechnet, über hundert hierhergehörende Beispiele an. Die Anzahl ist sicher noch grösser, jedoch genügt die vorliegende Reihe vollauf, um eine allgemeine Tendenz festzuhalten. Auf welche Art der Schlangen sich jedes Beispiel bezieht, ist kaum zu bestimmen. Obschon die Maskulina vorzugsweise mit dem *zalktis* zu verbinden sind, kann das nicht auf Grund der oben erwähnten Begriffsverschiebungen als eine Regel gelten.

Bei der Zusammenstellung der Namen sind sämtliche mir zugänglichen Zaubersprüche der Letten verwertet worden. Ein Teil des Materials stammt aus anderen Kategorien der Volksüberlieferung. Ein Verzeichnis der im Text abgekürzt zitierten Quellen sowie der benutzten Literatur findet sich am Ende des Aufsatzes.

1. *aizjūṛu viešṇa* 'weiblicher Gast aus Übersee'. S, 227.

2. *akmiṇčupas ložātājs* 'der im Steinhaufen Umherkriechende'. T, 157, Nr. 394.

3. *bezzobis* 'der Zahnlose'. T, 159, Nr. 414; K, II, 58, Nr. 477.

4. *brūte* 'Braut'. Anstatt dieses Germanismus wird ebenfalls, jedoch selten, das lettische Wort *līgava* gebraucht. T, 156, Nr. 384; S, 226 f.; *LTT*, 5239, 5244, 5355, 5356, 5360–5364.

5. *cirulītis* (Dim.) 'Lerche'. S, 229.

6. *čukstainīte* (Dim.). Zu *čuksts, čuksta purvs* 'Morast'. S, 229.

7. *čusins, čusnis, čustiṇš* (Dim.), *čuža, čužis*. Die Etymologie ist unklar.

Vielleicht zu *čuksts* 'Morast' (vgl. 6 oben) oder zu der Interjektion *čiš*!, mit welcher man die Schlangen wegzujagen pflegt? Über die denkbare Wirkung des Wortanklangs s. unten. *LTT*, 5186, 5299; ME, Erg. 1, 297.

8. *deguna lauzājs* 'Nasenbrecher'. T, 157, Nr. 394.

9. *desa* 'Wurst', auch *tauka desa* 'fette Wurst' und *tauku desa* 'aus Fett gemachte Wurst'. T, 159, Nr. 411; S, 228; *LTT*, 5308.

10. *dzelzu cūka* 'eisernes Schwein'. S, 229.

11. *gaŗā* (fem. Subst. aus Adj.) 'die Lange'. Mit der mask. Form *gaŗais* wird die Ringelnatter bezeichnet. *LTT*, 3230, 5238, 5290, 8865, 33648.

12. *gaŗā ķēve* 'die lange Stute'. S, 227.

13. *gaŗaste* 'der Langschwanz'. *LTT*, 5239.

14. *gaspažiņa* (Dim., Russizismus) 'Frau'. S, 417, 433.

15. *glodenīte* (Dim.) 'Blindschleiche', wahrscheinlich aber auch zu *glodens* 'glatt' und *glodans* 'hinterhältig'. S, 229.

16. *gluma soma* 'schleimiger Quersack'. T, 159, Nr. 411.

17. *godiga lielmāte* 'ehrliche Edelfrau'. T, 159, Nr. 407; S, 417.

18. *jumprava* (Germanismus) 'Jungfrau', auch *jumpraviņa* (Dim.). *LTT*, 5239, 5353, 5367.

19. *kārklu krūmu līdēja* 'die im Weidengebusch Kriechende'. T, 159, Nr. 412; S, 235.

20. *kas pļavā esat* 'ihr, die ihr da auf der Wiese seid'. Der Mann, der als erster das Heu zu mähen anfängt, redet mit diesen Worten die Schlangen an, um sie zu verscheuchen. *LTT*, 5264.

21. *kukainis* 'Käfer', *meža kukainītis* (Dim.) 'Waldkäfer'. In gewissen Gegenden Lettlands hat das Wort *kukainis* jedoch auch die Bedeutung 'Tier'. S, 227, 229; *LTT*, 5243.

22. *kūlainītis, -te, kulainīte, kuolainīte* (in der Ma. von Kalniena; nach einer persönlichen Mitteilung von A. Gāters), *kulenīte, kūlenīte, kulinīte* (sämtliche Dim.), *kūlis*, sowie die Anredeformen *kūlaš, kūlen, kuli, kuliņ*! Auf Grund des Wortanklanges, der im Wortzauber immer eine grosse Rolle gespielt hat (vgl. Bertholet, 1940, 370 f.), sind auch solche Bezeichnungen wie *kaulenīte, kulastīte, kuplainīte* und *pulainīte* (alle Dim.) sicher zu dieser Gruppe zu rechnen. Das Grundwort *kūlainītis* ist etymologisch mit *kūla* 'altes, dürres Gras, Morastgras' zu verbinden. T, 157, Nr. 388–393, 158, Nr. 395; S, 228 f.; *LTT*, 5358, 5371, 33656.

23. *kundziņš* (Dim.) 'Herr'. S, 417, 433.

24. *ķirmens, ķirmins, ķirmiņš* 'Engerling', mancherorts auch 'Schlange', vgl. lit. *kirminas* 'grosser Wurm, Schlange'. *LTT*, 5373, 5374, 5479, 8899, 8900.

25. *lapča* 'Bastschuh'. S, 228.

26. *lingā putns*. Ein seltenes (nur ein Beleg!) und schwererklärliches Kompositum. Über das Vorderglied vgl. ME, II, 471 f., und ME, Erg. 1, 743: *linga* 'Schleuder, Schlinge', *lingāt* 'schleudern, sich wiegen, schweben', *lingu lingām iet* 'wankend, schwerfällig gehen' u. dgl. m. Etymologisch vielleicht auch zu *ligo, ligot*, vgl. ME, II, 484. Das Schlussglied höchstwahrscheinlich nicht in der gewöhnlichen Bedeutung 'Vogel', sondern 'das Wild' (vgl. 53 unten). Über den ungewöhnlichen Schlussvokal -*ā* des Vordergliedes anstatt der zu erwartenden Gen. Sing. Endung -*as* vgl. Endzelīns, 1951, 259. *LTT*, 5240.

27. *lokainīte*, auch *lokanīte, lunkainīte* (alle Dim.). Zu *locīties* 'sich krümmen, sich schlängeln'. S, 229.

28. *ložņātāja* 'die Umherkriechende', vgl. 2 oben, 68, 72 unten. S, 229.

29. *luteklīte* (Dim.) 'die Verwöhnte'. S, 229.

30. *mamzelīte* (Dim.) 'Mademoiselle'. S, 226; *LTT*, 5357, 5366.

31. *marga* 'Mädchen, unverheiratetes Mädchen'. S, 226.

32. *māsiņa* (Dim.) 'Schwesterchen', auch *meža māsiņa* 'Waldschwesterchen'. S, 226; *LTT*, 5248, 5260.

33. *meža kustonītis* (Dim.) 'Waldtier'. S, 227.

34. *meža vagarīte* (Dim.) 'Fronvogt im Walde'. S, 227.

35. *miets* 'Pfahl'. S, 227.

36. *mironis* 'Toter, Leiche'. Auch *mironiņš* (Dim.) und der Germanismus *liķis* 'Leiche'. Vgl. 47 unten. Man glaubte, dass die Macht dieser Wörter und ein Schlag mit einer Rute die Schlange zum Erstarren bringe. T, 156, Nr. 384; S, 227; *LTT*, 5253.

37. *mošķis* 'Gespenst'. S, 227.

38. *mūdzis, smūdzis* 'Reptil, Ungeziefer'. *LTT*, 8865, 8876, 8908, 17118, 22410.

39. *negoda māte* 'schmachbeladene Mutter' (wörtlich 'Mutter der Schmach'). T, 158, Nr. 405.

40. *negoda tēvs* 'schmachbeladener Vater' (wörtlich 'Vater der Schmach'). T, 158, Nr. 405.

41. *nekristītie* (Nom. Pl.) 'die Ungetauften'. S, 228; *LTT*, 5251.

42. *nelabais* 'der Böse, der Teufel'. *LTT*, 5238.

43. *no meža* 'von dem Wald'. Hatte die Ringelnatter jemandem gebissen, war es üblich zu sagen, dass die Bisswunde „von dem Wald" stammte. *LTT*, 33652, vgl. auch 21735.

44. *noskūta ragana* 'abrasierte Hexe'. T, 157, Nr. 394.

45. *pagāni* (Nom. Pl.) 'die Heiden'. T, 160, Nr. 427.

46. *pīkstulis* 'Peitzger' (ein aalartiger Fisch). S, 228.

47. *pineklis* 'Fessel', auch *saules gozes pineklis* 'in der Sonne liegende

Fessel' und *miroņu pineklis* 'Fessel der Toten'. T, 159, Nr. 411; S, 227; *LTT*, 5204, 5366, 5369.

48. *plēne* 'die weiche, weisse Asche auf Kohlen' scheint eine falsche Schreibart anstatt von *plene* 'die Flechte, das Band' zu sein. S, 230. T, 159, Nr. 410, gibt genau denselben Zauberspruch bis auf *pine* 'Flechte' an Stelle von *plēne*.

49. *pliks* 'nackt', substantivisch gebraucht, vgl. Endzelīns, 1922, § 461. S, 226.

50. *pūķis* 'Drache', *nāvigs pūķis* 'totbringender Drache'. K, II, 63, Nr. 507.

51. *pulka palkavniece, pulku pulkavniece* 'die Oberstin des Regiments'. Das ungewöhnliche Femininum *palkavniece* bzw. *pulkavniece* (Vokalassimilation!) zu russ. *polkovnik* 'Oberst'. T, 159, Nr. 409; S, 230.

52. *pušekļi, pužekļi* (Nom. Pl.). Die Bedeutung ist unklar. In russischer Übersetzung bei T, 200, *polzun'i* 'die Kriecher'. Vielleicht aber auch etwa 'Gespenster'?, vgl. ME, III, 444, und ME, Erg. 2, 340. T, 200; *LTT*, 8862.

53. *putns*, hier nicht in der gewöhnlichen Bedeutung 'Vogel', sondern etwa 'das Wild', *putniņš, putineņš* (beide Dim.), auch *gaŗais putns* 'das lange Wild', *zemes putns* 'Erdwild'. S, 227; *LTT*, 5235, 9910.

54. *raiba pine* 'bunte Flechte' (vgl. auch 48 oben). T, 159, Nr. 411.

55. *raibgalvīte* (Dim.) 'Buntköpfchen'. S, 227.

56. *rīkste* 'Rute', auch *sētas rīkste* 'Zaunrute' oder 'Rute auf dem Hofe, — des Hofes'. S, 229; *LTT*, 9914.

57. *ritainīte* (Dim.), vermutlich zu *ritēt* 'rollen' und *ritināties* 'sich rollen'. S, 229.

58. *ruds pelēks* 'rotbraun grau', eigentlich doch substantivisch gebraucht, vgl. hierzu Endzelīns, 1922, § 461. Dasselbe in der Bestimmtheitsform *rudais pelēkais*. Die Schlange und die Ringelnatter werden überhaupt auf Schritt und Tritt mit Wörtern bezeichnet, die sich auf ihre Farbe beziehen. In ähnlicher Weise wie *ruds pelēks* treten z. B. noch folgende Adjektiva auf: *balts* 'weiss', *melns* 'schwarz', *raibs* 'bunt', *rangains* (= *rankains*, vgl. ME, III, 477, und ME, Erg. 2, 353) 'gestreift', *rusls* 'braun, rotbraun', *rūtains* 'gewürfelt', *sarkans* 'rot', *spangains*, auch *spangaiņš* und *spangans* 'fleckig', *spīdošs* 'schimmernd', *spožs* 'glänzend', *strīpains* 'streifig', *zils* 'blau'. T, 156, Nr. 383, 158, Nr. 399, 401, 159, Nr. 408, 415, 416, 160, Nr. 418, 419, 161, Nr. 430 (?); S, 229–231; K, II, 58, Nr. 479, 58 f., Nr. 480.

59. *sātans* 'Satan'. K, II, 59, Nr. 485, 63, Nr. 505; *LTT*, 5238.

60. *skudru ēna* 'Schatten für die Ameisen'. T, 159, Nr. 411.

61. *sloksne* 'Streifen'. S, 230.

62. *smilkšu kalnu bradātājs* 'der durch die Sandhügel Watende'. T, 157, Nr. 394.

63. *stivnāse* 'Steifnase'. *LTT*, 5234.

64. *striķis* (Germanismus) 'Strick'. Hierher gehören auch solche Benennungen wie *striķa gabals* und *striķa gals* 'ein Stück von dem Strick', *vecs, sapuvis striķis* 'alter, verfaulter Strick'. S, 227; *LTT*, 5236, 5237, 5366, 5369, 5370.

65. *sūnainīte* (Dim.) 'im Moos Wohnende'. S, 229.

66. *sūneklīte* (Dim.) 'im Moosmoor Wohnende'. S, 229.

67. *sūnu baļļa* 'im Moos liegende Balge'. Vielleicht aber auch *baļļa = baļva* 'ein korpulenter Mensch, ein dickes Frauenzimmer', vgl. BW, 16737, 1. S, 229.

68. *sūnu lož(ņ)a* 'die im Moos Umherkriechende'. T, 159, Nr. 410, 411; S, 227, 229.

69. *šis, šī* (Nom. Sing.), *šām* (Dat. Pl.), *šos* (Akk. Pl.). Demonstrativpronomina als Ersatz für ein tabuiertes Nomen, d. h. für den eigentlichen Schlangennamen. *LTT*, 5192, 5272, 5273.

70. *tārps* 'Wurm', auch *garais tārps* 'der lange Wurm'. T, 158, Nr. 397; *LTT*, 3229, 5233, 5235, 5238, 5239, 5296, 8893, 22413.

71. *tekainīte* (Dim.), zu *tecēt* 'schnell gehen, laufen'. S, 229.

72. *ūdens jūras ložātājs* 'der im Wassermeer Umherkriechende'. T, 157, Nr. 394.

73. *ūdzīte, ādzīte* (Dim.) 'Giftotter'. Mit tabuistischer Veränderung des ersten Vokales in Zaubersprüchen anstatt von *odzīte* gebraucht. S, 433.

74. *uš, neuš!* Interjektionen, mit welchen das fehlende Bezugswort bzw. der Schlangenname in einem Zauberspruch ersetzt wird. S, 236.

75. *veca vīze* 'alter Bastschuh'. S, 228; *LTT*, 5250.

76. *velns* 'Teufel', *velna zirgs* 'Teufelspferd', *velna zivs* 'Teufelsfisch'. S, 227; *LTT*, 5368.

77. *vepris* 'Eber'. Man schärft das Messer und sagt, das damit Eber geschlachtet werden, aber tatsächlich denkt man an Schlangen. S, 228.

78. *vilks* 'Wolf'. S, 227.

79. *zaļais Dieviņš* (Dim.) 'das grüne Gottchen'. So nennt man die Ringelnatter. *LTT*, 33667.

80. *zutis* 'Aal', auch *zutiņš* — Dim. oder 'Neunauge'? S, 228; *LTT*, 8912.

81. In einer lettischen Volksüberlieferung (*LTT*, 5225) wird erwähnt: „Die Schlangen haben Menschennamen: männliche und weibliche" (vgl. jedoch auch die entgegengesetzte Meinung 41 oben!). Zu dieser Kategorie gehören dann solche den Schlangen beigelegte Taufnamen wie *Grieta* (auch *Grieta māte* 'Mutter Margarete'), *Ilze, Līze, Anna, Andrejs, Jēkabs, Pēteris* u. a. m. Manchmal wurde die Schlange sogar bei dem Namen *Māŗa* (<Marija, hl. Maria) genannt, was vielleicht damit zusammenhängt, dass die

Schlange eine der Offenbarungsformen der synkretistischen *Māṛa* sein konnte. Die Namen *Ieva* 'Eva' und *Ievas meita* 'Evas Tochter' sind auf 1 Mos 3 zurückzuführen. T, 158, Nr. 403, 404; S, 226 ff.; *LTT*, 5227, 5360.

Alle oben angeführten Benennungen lassen sich in mehrere verwandte Gruppen einteilen.

Mehrfach ist die *captatio benevolentiae* festzustellen. Hierher gehören in erster Linie die vielen Diminutive. Durch die Diminuierung, welche eine erheuchelte Zärtlichkeit zum Ausdruck bringt, versuchte man die sonst so gefährliche Schlange zu beschwichtigen und auf ihre geheimnisvolle Macht einzuwirken. Dasselbe wurde mit schmeichlerischen Verwandtschaftsnamen wie *brūte* 'Braut', *māsiṇa* 'Schwesterchen' usw. bezweckt. Auch die grosse Anzahl der Taufnamen, die der Schlange verliehen werden, ist mit diesem simulierten Verwandschaftsgefühl zu verknüpfen. Die Verwandtschaftsnamen können mit dem Diminutivsuffix versehen werden, denn „doppelt genäht hält besser", wie Wilhelm Havers (1946, 149) in einem ähnlichen Zusammenhang hervorgehoben hat.

Um die Schlangen fernzuhalten, darf man sie nach gewöhnlichem Glauben überhaupt nicht nennen. Vereinzelt steht ein Beispiel da (*LTT*, 17123), wo das gerade Entgegengesetzte behauptet wird. Am ehesten soll man auch allzu durchsichtige Tabunamen wie *desa* 'Wurst', *rīkste* 'Rute' u. dgl. m. vermeiden (*LTT*, 5785, 9914). Es ist aber bemerkenswert, dass Wörter wie *velns* 'Teufel', *vilks* 'Wolf' usw., welche unter anderen Umständen selbst tabuiert sind, als Decknamen für die Schlange als unschädlich gelten.

Nach einem weitverbreiteten Brauch wird das tabuierte Nomen durch ein Pronomen ersetzt. So wird auch die Schlange im Lettischen mit Demonstrativpronomina *šī, šis* bezeichnet. Dennoch ist es interessant, dass diese Pronomina auf Grund des häufigen Gebrauches „unangenehm" geworden sind, weshalb man zuweilen in scheinbar unlogischer und sprachwidriger Weise anstatt des Nom. Sing. *šī, šis* den Dat. Pl. *šām* und Akk. Pl. *šos* verwendet.

Die unter 20 und 43 angeführten Redensarten sind typische Beispiele zu den sog. satzhaften Umschreibungen, wo das tabuierte Beziehungswort nur auf eine dunkelhafte Art angedeutet, nie aber genannt wird.

Die Struktur des seltenen Kompositum *lingā putns* (26) mit dem ungewöhnlichen Schlussvokal des Vordergliedes ist wahrscheinlich von der Scheu bedingt, sakrale oder sonst machttragende Wörter den „profanen" Lautgesetzen zu unterwerfen. In der Tabusprache ist überhaupt ein Festhalten an altem Sprachgut zu beobachten, denn „das Archaische entspricht dem Heiligen" (vgl. hierzu Havers, 1946, 26, 128).

Bei der Bildung der unter 7 verzeichneten Wörter hat der Wortanklang mit einer leichten „tabuistischen" Änderung des gewöhnlichen Wortes (*čūska — čusins — čuža* etc.) eine unverkennbare Rolle gespielt. Vgl. hierzu auch eine Kurzgeschichte von J. Jaunsudrabiņš, 1926, 165, wo u. a. erzählt wird, wie ein Knabe über den Sumpf geht, einen gegabelten Stock mit einer eingeklemmten Schlange in die Luft schwingt und aus voller Lunge schreit: „Alouske! Couske! Blouske!" Die Bildungsprinzipien sind hier wie oben dieselben gewesen.

Die Ursache der Tabuierung des Schlangennamen ist in erster Linie religiöse Scheu. Die Schlange bzw. die Ringelnatter gilt bei den Letten als ein Seelentier (die Verkörperung der Toten sowie der sog. Freiseele des lebenden Menschen), sie kann die Offenbarungsform der Hausgeister und anderer übernatürlichen Wesen sein (vgl. besonders 79, wo die Ringelnatter geradewegs als „grünes Gottchen" bezeichnet wird!). Auch die Tatsache, dass die meisten Deckbenennungen in Zaubersprüchen vorkommen, legt das Zeugnis von ihrem religiösen bzw. magischen Charakter ab. Nichtsdestoweniger kann man von Fall zu Fall an eine Tendenz zu poetischer Ausdrucksweise denken, die immer mit seltenen Wörtern und rätselhafter Metaphorik verknüpft gewesen ist. Ein Sprachtabu im engeren Sinne liegt jedenfalls nur da vor, wo eine Berührung der Verhüllungen mit der übersinnlichen Sphäre nachgewiesen werden kann.

Quellen und Literatur

Bertholet, A., *Wortanklang und Volksetymologie in ihrer Wirkung auf religiösen Glauben und Brauch*. Forschungen und Fortschritte, XVI. Berlin 1940.

BW = K. Barons & H. Wissendorffs, *Latwju dainas*, I–VI. Jelgawâ/Peterburgâ 1894–1915.

Endzelīns, J. (Endzelin), *Lettische Grammatik*. Riga 1922.

——, *Latviešu valodas gramatika*. Rīgā 1951.

Havers, W., *Neuere Literatur zum Sprachtabu*. Akademie der Wissenschaften in Wien, Philosophisch-historische Klasse, Sitzungsberichte, 223: 5. Wien 1946.

Jaunsudrabiņš, J., *Baltā grāmata*, II. Rīgā 1926.

K = Edith Kurtz, *Heilzauber der Letten in Wort und Tat*, I–II. Veröffentlichungen der volkskundlichen Forschungsstelle am Herder-Institut zu Riga, V, VII. Riga 1937–38.

LTT = *Latviešu tautas ticējumi*, I–IV. Sakrājis un sakārtojis P. Šmits. Latviešu folkloras krātuves materiāli (LFKM), A: 6–9. Rīgā 1940–41.

ME = *K. Mühlenbachs Lettisch–deutsches Wörterbuch*, I–IV. Redigiert, ergänzt und fortgesetzt von J. Endzelin. Riga 1923–32.

ME, Erg. = J. Endzelin & E. Hausenberg, *Ergänzungen und Berichtigungen zu K. Mühlenbachs Lettisch–deutschem Wörterbuch*, 1–2. Riga 1934–46.

S = K. Straubergs, *Latviešu buramie vārdi*, I–II. LFKM, A: 5, 10. Rīgā 1939–41.

T = *Materialy po étnografii latyšskago plemeni*. Pod redakciej F. Trejland (Brivzemniaks). Izvěstija imp. obščestva ljubitelej estestvoznanija, antropologii i étnografii, XL. Trudy étnografičeskago otděla, VI. Moskva 1881.

Latvian Names for the Snake

A group of about 80 names for the snake—drawn from magic spells and other folkloristic sources—are discussed, most of them taboo-names (e.g. personal names, diminutive derivations, pronominal forms and other metaphorical expressions).

PETRAS JONIKAS

Tarmės ir bendrinė rašyba

Apie tarmių derinimo atspindžius XIX a. antrosios pusės lietuvių rašyboje

XIX a. viduryje lietuvių raštų (spaudinių) kalba Didžiojoje Lietuvoje dar nebuvo nusistojusi bendra visam kraštui nei tarmės, nei rašybos požiūriu. Nusistoti ji tepradeda maždaug nuo *Aušros* (1883–86) laikų. Tuo požiūriu Didž. Lietuva buvo gerokai atsilikusi nuo Mažosios, kur rašomoji kalba buvo daugiau ar mažiau susinorminusi maždaug prieš porą šimtmečių. Mat, šalia skirtingų tų abiejų lietuvių gyvenamų sričių politinių, visuomeninių ir kultūrinių sąlygų, Didž. Lietuvos buvo didesnis plotas, susiskirstęs į daugiau ir skirtingesnių tarmių negu Mažosios, o, be to, Didž. Lietuvoje nebuvo iki tol organizuotesnio centralizuoto rūpinimosi rašto kalbos bendrinimu[1].

Maždaug nuo XIX a. vidurio iki XIX a. pabaigos kai kurie Didž. Lietuvos autoriai mėgina įvairiai spręsti rašomosios kalbos tarmės ir rašybos klausimus. Tačiau tie mėginimai didesnės sėkmės neturėjo, be kitko, ir dėl to, kad tada dar nebuvo Lietuvoje lietuviškos (lietuvių dėstomąja kalba) vidurinės bei aukštesniosios mokyklos ir įtakingesnių geriau pasiruošusių bei gebančių praktiškai šį reikalą aiškinti ir spręsti kalbininkų. Paties J. Jablonskio (1860–1930), vadinamo rašomosios kalbos tėvu, įtaka maždaug tik nuo XX a. pradžios tepradėjo žymiau reikštis.

Žinoma, lengviausias sprendimas būtų buvęs, jei rašto autoriai būtų teturėję prieš akis vienos (pirmiausia, savo pačių) tarmės, arba ir visai artimų savajai kitų, skaitytojus. Pvz. V. Ažukalnis (Zagurskis, † 1874), pats aukštaitis rytietis, savo rankraštinio eilėraščių rinkinio (1838–56) prakalboje sakosi tenorįs šias eiles skirti skaitytojams rytiečiams ir net paskatinti, kad daugiau kas rašytų rytietiškai[2]. Rašymas savo tarmės atstovams turėjo jau ir senesnę tradiciją; štai vad. 1605 m. anoniminis katekizmas (išleistas Vilniuje), skiriamas rytų aukštaičiams, buvo parašytas jų tarmės pagrindu. Ir vėliau kai kurie spaudiniai (o jų absoliutinis daugumas maždaug iki *Aušros* laikų buvo tikybinio turinio) buvo skiriami kurios krašto dalies gyventojams; buvo net elementorių, išleistų vienos parapijos žmonėms, plg. F. W. [ojciechowskis] *Lewentorius Łankiszko-*

Lietuwiszkas. Diel Wejku Olkiniku [=Valkininko] *parapijos* (išleistas Vilniuje 1862).

Bet toks rašomosios kalbos klausimo sprendimas vargu ar galėjo būti patenkinamas ekonominiu, tautiniu, o taip pat ir įvairiatarmių skaitytojų požiūriu. Juk spaudiniai, knygos paprastai skiriamos viso krašto bei visų kurios tautos tarmių atstovams, kuriems stengiamasi ir tarmės bei rašybos atžvilgiu įtikti. Ypač priešaušrio ir *Aušros* laikais, ėmus kilti lietuvių tautinei sąmonei, anoks ,,parapinis'' šio klausimo sprendimas buvo nepakankamas.

Todėl iš pradžių kai kurie autoriai tarėsi galėsią rašyti savo gimtąja tarme, o skaitytojai galėsią jų raštą persiskaityti kiekvienas vėl savąja tarme. Šitoks rašto tarminio skaitymo principas rėmėsi gyvenimo patirtimi; juk ir dabar galime pastebėti, kad kai kurie žmonės, o ypač jau mažai raštingi, raštą skaito labai tarmiškai. Tarmiškai anuo metu turėjo skaityti net ir vidurinį ar aukštąjį mokslą išėję lietuviai, nes tose mokyklose lietuvių kalbos tada nebuvo mokoma, tik vieną kitą vidurinio mokslo instituciją Lietuvoje teišskyrus, kur tačiau tos kalbos buvo kiek pamokoma tik protarpiais ir nesistemingai (Marijampolės gimnazijoje, Veiverių mokytojų kursuose ir kt.; tik Kauno kunigų seminarijoje nuo 1871 m. lietuvių kalba klierikams jau sistemingiau buvo dėstoma). Kurie tą tarminio skaitymo principą palaikė, galėjo remtis čia ir kitų tautų pavyzdžiais. Vienas L. Ivinskio (1811?–1881) rankraščio apie lietuvių kalbos rašybą kritikas pastebi, jog ir prancūzai savo raštus rašą vienaip, bet įvairių Prancūzijos vietų žmonės įvairiaip juos persiskaitą[3].

Šitokio nusistatymo laikydamasis, S. Daukantas (1793–1864), daugelio knygelių ir lotynų kalbos vadovėlio autorius, rėmėsi savo pajūrinių žemaičių (dounininkų) tarme, o skaitytojus kvietė jo raštus persiskaityti vėl savo tarme. *Pasakojimo apej Wejkalus Letuwiû tautos senowie* (1850) rankraščio prakalboje jis dar nurodo ir kultūrinę savo rašto tarmės pasirinkimo priežastį: jis tokia tarme rašąs todėl, kad jam rodėsi, jog šioje tarmėje esą daugiau mokančių skaityti[4].

Nors Daukantas vartojo ir kiek skirtingų nuo to meto tradicinės tikybinių raštų kalbos rašmenų, tačiau jie buvo skiriami pirmiausia jo paties tarmės skirtingiems garsams pavaizduoti, bet ne tarmėms derinti. Tačiau pats rašto tarminio skaitymo principas, nors Daukanto ir bendrai teužsimintas, čia apskritai buvo aiškus: vietoje autoriaus tarmės garsų, kuriems atstovauja jo rašto žodyje atitinkami rašmenys (grafemos), skaitytojas gali tarti savuosius; dar *Paedraus* rankraščio (1824) pastaboje Daukantas rašė, jog jo ů reikią skaitytojui tarti o ar u pagal tai, ar jis kalbąs aukštaitiškai, ar žemaitiškai[5]. Kitaip sakant, Daukanto raštų rašmenys pasidaro nebe paprasti jo tarmės garsmenų (fonemų) atitikmenys (kurių dėsningumą vienai fonemai vienas ir tas pats rašmuo, žinoma, apriboja ir kiti veiksniai), bet tie rašmenys ypač skaitytojams virsta įvairias tarmes atliepiančiais, taigi daugiagarsmėniais (polifoneminiais) simboliais, iš kurių kiekvienos tarmės atstovas, tokį raštą skaitydamas, turi savuosius garsmenis identifikuoti, ,,atsirinkti" pagal savąjį dialektą ir taip Daukanto raštą ,,išsiversti" į savo tarmę[6].

Nors Daukantas tik labai bendrai kalba apie jo rašto ,,išsivertimą" į skaitytojo tarmę, vis dėlto to išsivertimo jis, matyt, nėra apribojęs vien fonologine sritimi. Minėtojo *Pasakojimo apej Wejkalus Letuwiů tautos senowie* rankraščio prakalboje jis pvz. rašo, kad skaitytojas jo lytis *kantri yr narsi karejwej* galįs skaityti savaip — *kantrus ir narsus karejwej*. Iš to matyti, kad Daukantas neišskyrė (bent tam tikrais atvejais) ir žodžių kaitybos (fleksijos) keitimo pagal skaitytojo tarmę, plg. žem. *narsi* ($\sim narsi$) ir kitų tarmių *narsus* ($\sim narsūs$)[7]. Tie pavyzdžiai kartu rodo, kad Daukanto čia ir gryna savo tarme nerašoma.

Panašiai elgėsi ir kai kurie kiti autoriai. Aukštaitis rytietis A. Kitkevičius (Kikutis, 1805–1857) giesmes iš kitų kalbų verčia į rytiečių tarmę, kaip tai jis pasisako savo knygoje *Hymny Ojców Świętych* (1848 m. išleistoje Vilniuje). Jis rašąs *untis, kintet*, o skaitojas galįs tokias bei panašias lytis persiskaityti pagal savo ,,provincializmą". J. Juška (1815–1886) patarė kiekvienam autoriui rašyti savo tarme, tik laikantis vienos visiems rašybos. Tačiau jo konkrečiai nenurodoma, kaip tada įtikti įvairių tarmių skaitytojams. Iš kai kurių jo pasisakymų galima spręsti, kad ir jam būta nesvetimo rašmenų polifonemizacijos principo (žr. jo *Kalbos lėtuviszko lėžuv'o ...* Peterburge, 1861).

Tačiau anaiptol ne visi svarbesnieji laikotarpio autoriai manė, kad lietuvių rašomosios kalbos pagrindu gali eiti bet kuri tarmė — kad kiekvienas autorius gali rašyti savo paties tarme. Kai kurie, priešingai, tarė, kad tuo pagrindu tegali būti imama tam tikra tarmė, tinkama visų tarmių atstovams.

Panašaus nusistatymo buvo ir leidęs eilę metų kalendorius ir išvertęs keletą knygelių, o taip pat rašęs lenkiškai lietuvišką žodyną L. Ivinskis. Pats nebūdamas kalbininkas, siūlomosios rašomosios kalbos pagrindu tarmės jis nemokėjo apibrėžti nei geografiniu, nei kalbinės sistemos požiūriu. Jis tiktai bendrai teigė, kad ta tarmė turinti būti ,,vidurinė tarmė", mažiau tepaveikta svetimųjų įtakų. Jis apskritai norėjo remtis jau anuo metu tolydžio ryškėjančiu raštuose tarminiu mišiniu su vakarų aukštaičių tarmės pagrindu. Tą mišinį jis stengiasi pateisinti įvairiais, kartais tik paties išsigalvotais tariamais motyvais (grafemos nuosakumo, reikšmės atskyrio, tradicinio įsigalėjimo ir kt.)[8]. Tačiau Ivinskio raštuose randame nemaža ir žemaičių dūnininkų tarmės ypatybių.

Tuo laikotarpiu rimčiau teoriškai pagristą rašomosios tarmės ir rašybos klausimo sprendimą mėgino duoti A. Baranauskas (1835–1902). Tam ypač svarbus akstinas jam buvo tas, kad jam XIX a. Didž. Lietuvoje bene pirmam teko pradėti (1871) sistemingai dėstyti klierikams lietuvių kalbos kursą Kauno kunigų seminarijoje, kur jis tiesiai ir susidūrė su lietuvių kalbos gramatikos ir rašybos pagrindų ir normų teoriniu svarstymu bei praktiniu sprendimu. Ir Baranauskas čia prieina tokias išvadas: kadangi kiekvienam tarmės atstovui atrodo jo tarmė geresnė, o faktiškai nė viena tarmė neturi nei visų lietuvių kalbos formų, nei visų žodžių, tai visiems lietuviams skiriamai bendrai rašomajai kalbai tesą galima remtis visomis (faktiškai tik anuometinės Kauno gubernijos, iš kurios jis teturėjo savo mokinių klierikų) tarmėmis. To jis tarėsi pasieksiąs, suvesdamas fonologines tarmių lytis į bendrą etimologinę formą, iš kurios vėliau ir išriedėjo garsinės atskirų tarmių lytys. Kadangi Baranauskas norėjo, kad taip sukurta jo rašomoji kalba būtų gyva, bet ne mirusi, jis, tas bendrąsias lytis atstatydamas, tik tiek tėjo atgal, kiek leido bent vienoje gyvosios kalbos tarmėje išlikusios fonologinės lytys. Taip kurdamas bendrą rašomąją kalbą, Baranauskas apskritai ir priėjo vakarų aukštaičių tarmę, nes, mat, toje tarmėje senasis lietuvių kalbos garsynas apskritai išlikęs sveikesnis negu kitose tarmėse.

Šią atstatytąją bendrąją visiems lietuviams ,,tarmę" Baranauskas paprastai tevadino (reikšmės požiūriu savo paties susikurtu terminu) rašyba, nes ji tebuvo skiriama raštui. Skaitoma ji Baranauskui teturėjo būti kiekvieno tarmės atstovo pagal savo tarmę[9].

Tad ir Baranauskas, savaip derindamas rašyboje tarmes, rašmenis turėjo laikyti daugiagarsmėniais simboliais (žinoma, tais atvejais, kuriais tarmės skyrėsi). Norint tą principą akivaizdžiau praktiškai iškelti bei skaitytojui signalizuoti jo tarmės garsmeninius atitikmenis, Baranauskui būtų reikėję labiau pritaikyti paprastąjį ano meto plačiajai visuomenei skiriamąjį raidyną bei rašybą[10], įvedant tam tikrų pakeitimų — jei ne naujų rašmenų, tai bent tam tikrų diakritinių ženklų ar rašmenų junginių įvairiafonėmiams tarmių garsams simbolinti. Tai Baranauskas suprato, sakydamas, kad, norint tokią ,,rašybą" sudaryti, reikėtų įvariatarmiams skaitytojams kartu ir nurodymo, kaip kurias raides skaityti. Bet tada būtų reikėję nutolti nuo įprastinio raidyno, ir, be kitų praktinių sunkumų, raštas skaitytojams būtų pasidaręs labai painus, anot paties Baranausko, ,,tiesiog kiniškas"[11]. Dėl to Baranauskas tokių naujovių raidyne ir neįsivedė. Jis apskritai priėmė A. Schleicherio gramatikos (*Litauische Grammatik*, Prag, 1856) raidyną bei rašybą su nedideliais pakeitimais, raidyne kiek nusileisdamas plačiajai visuomenei skiriamai tradicinei rašybai. Tik vienas antras rašmuo Baranausko rašyboje tesignalizuoja tarminę skirtybę ar ir iš dalies tarmių derinimą. Pasilaikydamas *l* savo raidyne, Baranauskas mėgino teisintis ir tarminiais sumetimais: nors lietuvių kalboje priebalsiai apskritai esą minkšti prieš priešakinės eilės balsius, bet čia esanti išimtis rytiečių tarmė, kur *l* esąs kietas prieš *e, ė, ei, ę,* su kai kuriomis išimtimis prieš *e, ei,* todėl *l* tam būtinai esąs reikalingas[12]. Žinoma, čia to *l* pagrindas nėra pakankamas visiems lietuviams skiriamame rašte, nes jame Baranauskas grafiškai nežymėjo ir kitokių rytiečių tarmės skirtybių.

Netiesiogiai tarmių derinimui Baranausko rašyboje patarnavo jo įsivestas *-ą, -ę* rašymas *-ā-* ir *-ē-* kamienų vienaskaitos įnagininke (*su ranką, su eglę*), taigi toks pat, kaip ir tų pačių kamienų vienaskaitos galininke. Šis rašymas iš esmės yra etimologinis: abiejų linksnių galūnės čia yra tos pačios kilmės (tik skirtingų priegaidžių), ilgainiui ir palikusios paralelinius savo raidos atspindžius tarmėse.

Kazimieras Jaunius (1849–1908) čia skyrėsi nuo Baranausko. Jis ne tiek rūpinosi, kaip kad Baranauskas, nustatyti bendras vienerias lytis rašomosios kalbos reikalui, kiek tarmes suderinti rašte, specialų dėmesi kreipdamas į raidyno pritaikymą tam derinimui[13].

Anksčiau Jaunius kartais pasisakydavo, kad jo raštas daugiau žemaičių tarmei pritaikytas[14]. Tačiau JGr. nebent tik žodyne ir posakiuose esama daugiau žemaitiškumo. Morfologijoje kai kur jis, neretai skirdamasis nuo aknstyvesnės savo praktikos, tyčia nebevartoja žemaitiškų formų, jas pakeisdamas aukštaitiškomis, pvz. rašydamas JGr. *výrui* (∼*výrui*), *brôlyje* (∼*brólyje*), *sūnųs* (∼*sūnūs*) vietoj atititnkamų žemaitiškųjų galūnių /uo, ėje, ai/. O fonologijoje, kur jis ir derina įvairias tarmes rašte, Jaunius irgi laikosi polifonemizacijos principo, tad, bent teoriškai, tuo pačiu čia jis ir nesiremia viena, taigi nei savo žemaitiškąja tarme.

Šito principo laikantis, Jauniui normaliai teko tarmių derinime apsiriboti žodžiais ir lytimis, kurie tik fonologiškai, bet ne etimologiškai tesiskyrė. Todėl Jaunius nesistengė tarmių derinti ten, kur žodžių formos buvo skirtingos kilmės. Nesą įmanoma suderinti rašytine lytimi tokių skirtingų (skirtingos kilmės) tarminių formų, kaip *ąžuolas*, užnemuniškių *áržuolas*, Prūsų lietuvių *áužuolas* (JGr. 11; dėl išimties žr. žemiau).

Tuo keliu eidamas, Jaunius tesistengė derinti rašyboje tik didžiuosius tarminius išsiskaidymus fonologijoje; į smulkesnius šnektų skirtumus bei garsų dėsnių išimtis jis vargiai ir begalėjo kreipti dėmesį, nenorėdamas dar labiau supainioti savo raidyno. O tie išsiskaidymai jam, plačiai tyrinėjusiam lietuvių kalbos tarmes ir sudariusiam tarmių klasifikaciją, kuri vėliau ir mokykliniuose vadovėliuose vyravo (plg. JGr. 22 tt.; Ryg. Jono *Lietuvių kalbos gramatika*[2], Kaunas 1922, 233 tt.), atrodė paaiškėję. Todėl Jauniui čia teko kreipti dėmesį ne į tuos atitinkamų žodžių bei formų garsus, kurie buvo visoms tarmėms bendri, bet į tuos, kuriais bent didžiosios lietuvių kalbos tarmės išsiskyrė. Tokiais išsiskyrimo atvejais Jauniui pirmiausia ir rūpėjo nustatyti specialius rašmenis, kurie simbolizuotų bei signalizuotų įvairių tarmių skaitytojams jų garsmeninius atitikmenis. Skaitytojo dėmesiui atkreipti teko tam panaudoti specialių, diakritinių rašmenų, daugiau ar mažiau besiskiriančių nuo ano meto tradicinės ar ir kalbininkų bei kalbos mėgėjų vartojamosios rašybos.

Taigi Jaunius, suteikdamas savo rašto morfemoms grafinį vaizdą, ėjo, taip sakant, nuo polifonemos (kurios fonemos išsiskaidymo pagal tarmes) į atitinkamą bendrą rašmenį, kuris jam buvo fonografema, o skaitytojo, turinčio Jauniaus tekstą persiskaityti, kelias buvo priešingas: jam Jauniaus rašmuo jau buvo bendrosios grafofonemos simbolis, kuris skaitytojui turėjo rodyti kelią į savo tarmės fonemos atsirinkimą (identifikavimą) iš įvairių tarminių fonemos atitikmenų[15].

Tuo būdu Jauniui nesunkus atrodė tarmių suderinimas raidyne priebalsių srityje, nes čia tarmių susiskaidymas nėra taip painus. Bk. (=dabartinės bendrinės kalbos, Lietuvoje dabar vad. literatūrine kalba) /č/ vaizdavimui Jaunius rašė tŝ[16] tais atvejais, kai čia sutiko (nesiskyrė) visos tarmės: pétŝjus (~pẽčius); tŝ — kai vienose tarmėse atliepė /č/, o kitose /c/: tŝjá (~čià); pagaliau t̗, kai vienose tarmėse atliepė /t'/, kitose /č'/: jaût̗jó (~jáučio). Paraleliškas buvo ir Jauniaus bk. /dž/ žymėjimas.

Balsių ir dvibalsių srityje tarmių susiskirstymas įvairesnis, ir čia Jauniui teko vartoti daugiau specialių, diakritinių rašmenų.

Jaunius jautėsi labai gerai tarmes suderinąs bk. /ie/ ir /uo/ atvejais. Bk. /ie/ derinimui vaizduoti Jaunius rašė įvairius rašmenis: iẽ, kai visos tarmės čia sutiko: griẽ'kas (~griẽkas), o tarmių išsiskyrimo atvejais í, kuris akivaizdžiai tarminiam skaitytojui parodąs jo garsmenį, taigi: vieni galį dėti pirma i, paskui e, ir taip gauti savo ie (aukštaičiai); antri pirma e, paskui i, ir taip gauti savo ei (žem. dọunininkai); treti, nežiūrėdami į viršuje patupdytą mažą e, tarti savo (ilgą) i (žem. dūnininkai); ir pagaliau ketvirti tarti tik viršutinį (siaurą) e (žem. klaipėdiškiai)[16a]. Panašiai ir /uo/ atveju.

Bk. ą, ę, į, ų rašmenų vietoje Jaunius šaknyje ir kirčiuotoje galūnėje rašė ąn̆, ęn̆, įn̆, ųn̆, tuo būdu vaizduodamas kai kuriose tarmėse tautosilabinio dvibalsio buvimą [n], o kitose jo išnykimą: kąn̆sti (~kąsti), vaikų̆n̆ (~vaikų̃); tačiau nekirčiuotoje absoliutinėje galūnėje rašė ą, ę, į, ų: pó'ną (~põną), pó'nų (~põnų), o prieš -s rašė -ąs, -ęs: súkęs (~sùkęs), súksjąs (~sùksiąs). Bk. /an, en, in, un/ rašė ąn, ęn, įn, ųn: lą̆nká (~lankà).

Iš analogijos su galūniniais ą, ę, kurie bk. dabar žymi ilguosius balsius /ā, ē/, o kartu tarmėse rodo etimologinių tautosilabinių /n/ dvibalsių refleksus, Jaunius, kaip ir Baranauskas, rašo ir *ā* bei *ē* kamienų vienaskaitos įnagininke trumpiesiems balsiams -*ą*, -*ę* (jau, skiriantis nuo anų galininko -*ą*, -*ę*, su vąšeliais, atsuktais į kairę): *sú algą́, sú eglę̃*. Dėl tų pačių priežasčių Jaunius -*ę* rašo ir vardažodžių vienaskaitos ir daugiskaitos bei dviskaitos vietininkuose: *algoję́, algosę́*.

Vis dėlto tas tarmių derinimas raidyne Jauniaus nebuvo griežtai apribotas vien fonologine sritimi: jis perkeliamas ir į žodžių darybą, pvz. tais atvejais, kai priešdėliai ir priesagos yra panašūs, tarmėse besiskirią dažnai tik viena fonema, plg. *prý̃'* (∼*prỹ*, žem.; *priẽ*, aukšt.); priesaga -*ỹnė: lapý̃'nė* (∼*lapỹnė*, žem.; *lapiẽnė*, aukšt.); priesaga -*ůmenė: didůmenė* (∼*didů́menė*, žem.; *didúomenė*, aukšt.); taip pat: *nié'kas* (∼*nẽkas*<*nẽ kàs*, žem.; *niẽkas*, aukšt.).[16b]

Tuo būdu tarmių derinimui Jaunius vartojo eilę rašmenų, besiskiriančių nuo ano meto tradicinės praktinės ir kai kurių kalbininkų lietuviškosios rašybos. Vieni tų rašmenų buvo paimti iš ankstyvesnių Didž. Lietuvos lietuviškų raštų (kaip pvz. Daukšos *ů*, Maž. Lietuvoje ir vėliau vartojamas, kuris į Lietuvą bus parsigavęs iš čekų), kiti ir iš kitur (pvz. *ṅ*, kurį Jaunius sakosi pasiskolinęs iš F. Boppo, žymėjusio juo sanskrito anusvarą)[17], o treti gal paties pasidaryti (kaip *ỉ*, kuriuo Jaunius pakeičia, dėl analogijos su *ů*, anksčiau savo vartotą iš A. Bielensteino pasiskolintą *î*). Kai kurie šių rašmenų Jauniaus buvo įsivesti specialiai tarmių derinimui, kaip *ỹ*[16b], *ůu*, *ṅ* (dvirašmeniuose *ąṅ*, *ęṅ*, *įṅ*, *ųṅ*), *ś* (dvirašmenyje *tś*), *ż* (dvirašmenyje *dż*); iš esmės taip pat ir *ą*, *ę*, *į*, *ų* (dvirašmeniuose *ąn*, *ęn*, *įn*, *ųn*). Tarmių derinimo pasėka buvo ir *u*, kurį Jauniui teko įsivesti ilgajam /ī/ žymėti, *y* Jauniui sunaudojus tarmių išsiskyrimui signalizuoti. Jaunius tarmių derinimui panaudojo ir prieš jį kitam reikalui vartotų lietuvių raštuose diakritinių rašmenų, kaip *ą*, *ę*, *į*, *ų*, kurie turėjo — taip pat ir Jauniui — etimologinę reikšmę; bet, kadangi tais rašmenimis žymimi garsmenys paliko ivairius savo raidos atspindžius tarmėse, tos grafemos Jauniui tiko ir tarmių išsiskirstymui simbolinti bendrinėje rašyboje.

Anksčiau Jaunius yra vartojęs ir daugiau diakritinių ar ir sintetinių skirtingų rašmenų kai kuriems kitiems tarmių derinimo atvejams iškelti, kaip -*å* (kuris galūnėje vienose tarmėse atstoja /a/, kitose /ō/), -*ȧ* (vienose tarmėse galūnėje /a/ randamas, kitose — atkritęs). Nuo jų vėliau jis bus atsisakęs, viena, vengdamas leistis į painų detalesnį tarmių derinimą; antra, nenorėdamas per gausiu diakritinių ženklų vartojimu apsunkinti raštų spausdinimo ir, žinoma, skaitymo[18].

Taip įvairiai susidarę Jauniaus diakritiniai ženklai, vartotieji tarmėms derinti, kokio aiškesnio sistemingumo ir nesudarė, paprastai tebuvo kiekvieno rašmens ar mažesnės jų grupės modifikatoriai. Tuo budu pvz. tašku rašmens viršuje Jaunius žymėjo ó (šalia é), kur taškas turėjo vieną reikšmę (pvz. aukštaičių tarmėje žymėjo čia ilgus siaurus balsius), ś, ź (dvirašmeniuose tś, dž) jau kitą, o ń (dvirašmeniuose ąń, ęń, įń, ųń) — trečią.

Aukščiau aptarti kalbamojo laikotarpio bandymai duoti Didž. Lietuvos lietuviams bendra rašomąją kalbą, tarmes derinant rašyboje, nepavyko. Principas, kad kiekvienos tarmės autorius gali rašyti savo tarme, kartu būtų reiškęs, jog, kaip ir Baranauskas sakė, tada būtų reikėję kiekvienai tarmei tam reikalui atskiros (norminamosios) gramatikos; o antra, toks rašomosios kalbos suskydimas būtų ėjęs prieš tautinės vienybės stiprinimą. Bet ir Baranausko bandymas remti rašomąją kalbą idealine ,,bendrąja tarme" nepavyko, be kitko, dėl to, kad, pačiam Baranauskui neišleidus jai gramatikos, praktikoje autoriams patiems anokias bendrines lytis susirasti būtų buvę labai sunku. O ir pats tarmių derinimas rašyboje, reliatyviai gerokai detalizuotas Jauniaus, padarė tą rašybą sunkią plačiajai visuomenei, kuri anuomet iš pradžių ir norėdama negalėjo su ja arčiau susipažinti, nes jo gramatika (JGr.) su tos rašybos paaiškinimais K. Būgos pastangomis tebuvo išspausdinta XX a. pradžioje. O jos prototipas, 1885–92 m. Kauno kunigų seminarijos klierikų užrašai, kurie 1897 m. buvo Dorpato universiteto lietuvių studentų hektografuoti[19], plačiau nebus buvęs paplitęs. Tad ir nebus nuostabu, kad visą kalbamąjį laikotarpį, o ir anksčiau, Didž. Lietuvoje nebuvo kokios vienodos, sistemingesniu normuotumu pasižyminčios rašomosios kalbos. Kaip ir paprastai esti rašomųjų kalbų istorijose, knygos neretai buvo rašomos ne grynomis tarmėmis, bet tam tikru tarminiu mišiniu, kuriame tolydžio ėmė iškilti vakarų aukštaičių tarmė. Jau anksčiau esame pastebėję, kad į ją linko ir Ivinskis, kuris, versdamas savo žemaitiškąsias lytis į vakariečių tarmę, ir hipernormalizmų prieidavo. Kaip iš dalies jau esame pastebėję, aukštaitiškų lyčių įmaišydavo, ypač vėlesniuose savo raštuose, ir S. Daukantas. Tam tikru tarminiu mišiniu rašė ir vysk. M. Valančius, kilimo žemaitis dọunininkas, rūpinęsis savo vyskupystės tikybine literatūra, ir eilė kitų autorių.

Vakarų aukštaičių tarmės įsigalėjimą rašomosios kalbos pagrindu nulėmė pirmiausia aukštaitinė vakarietinė Maž. Lietuvos raštų tradicija su savo gramatikomis, A. Schleicherio ir kitų įžymesnių juo pasekusių kalbininkų (kaip F. Fortunatovo) vakarų aukštačių tarmės pasirinkimas gramatinio lietuvių kalbos aprašo pagrindu (kur nemaža svėrė ir tos tarmės fonologinė sistema), o taip pat pirmojo tautinio Didž. Lietuvos laikraščio *Aušros* (kurios redaktorių ir svarbesniųjų bendradarbių tarpe vyravo aukštaičiai vakariečiai bei jiems artimų tarmių atstovai), paskui ir kitų lietuviškųjų laikraščių pasukimas vakarų aukštaičių tarmės keliu[20].

Todėl ir J. Jablonskis, kuris kartu su P. Avižoniu (1875–1939) 1901 m.

paskelbė savo *Lietuviškos kalbos gramatiką*, jau nesvyruodamas tą vakariečių tarmę priėmė, pasisakydamas, kad rašomosios kalbos pagrindu paprastai įsigalinti viena kuri tarmė. Taip ilgainiui išsisprendė iš esmės ir rašybos bei raidyno painiava. Vienai, t. y. vakarų aukštaičių, tarmei nuolat stiprėjant raštuose, kitų tarmių skaitytojams iš lengvo prie jos pratinantis ir patį raštą tos tarmės pagrindu imant skaityti, ilgainiui ir gyvo reikalo nebebuvo tarmių bederinti raidyne ir tuo įvairiais diakritiniais ir kitokiais rašmenimis raidyno bepaininti. (O jau galutinai vakariečių tarmė bendrinės rašomosios kalbos pagrindu sutvirtėjo, 1918 m. atkūrus nepriklausomą valstybę ir lietuviškajai visų laipsnių mokyklai paskleidus krašte vakariečių tarmės pažinimą bei mokėjimą[21].)

Tačiau ir iš esmės vienai, vakariečių, tarmei bei bendrinei rašybai, ta tarme besiremiančiai, lietuvių bendrinėje rašomojoje kalboje įsigalėjus, tam tikras tarminis aspektas rašmenų funkcijoje visai neišnyko. Ir J. Jablonskis yra teigęs, jog pvz. ą, ę, į, ų rašmenų vartojimas rašte palengvinąs įvairių tarmių žmonėms raštą skaityti ir suprasti; jis tarpais net sakydavo, kad reikią mokykloje mokinius mokyti vienos rašybos, nors mokinys ir savaip, kaip mokėdamas, tartų žodžius[22]. Mat, šiokie ir panašūs rašmenys vis tiek įvairiatarmiams skaitytojams, ypač kol jie su bendrine kalba geriau dar nesusipažinę, palieka jau aukščiau minėtos grafofonemos, daugiafonėmiai simboliai, jungią tarmių išsiskaidymo atvejais tarminę ir bendrinės kalbos fonologiją.

Išnašos

1. P. Jonikas, „Lietuvių bendrinės rašomosios kalbos idėja priešaušrio metu", *Archivum Philologicum*, VI, 1937, 40 tt.

2. K. Korsakas ir J. Lebedys (red.), *Lietuvių literatūros istorijos chrestomatija, feodalizmo epocha*, Vilnius, 1957, 428–29.

3. LMDr. (= Lietuvių Mokslo Draugijos rankraštis Vilniuje) G$_1$, G$_2$. — Rankraščių signatūras čia ir kitur šiame straipsnyje rašau tokias, kokias esu radęs prieš 30 m., Lietuvoje rinkdamasis medžiagą lietuvių kalbos istorijai.

4. Rš (= Vytauto Didžiojo Universiteto rankraščių saugyklos rankraštis) 171.

5. Rš 34.

6. Taigi tas identifikavimas susijęs su atitinkamų rašmenų polifonemizacijos principu, o pats to rašto skaitymas balsu pagal tarmes — su polifonetizacija. (Pastarąjį terminą esu vartojęs prieš 30 m.)

7. Plg. Z. Zinkevičius, *Lietuvių dialektologija*, Vilnius, 1966, 274.

8. Plg. L. Ivinskio rankraščius: O pisowni i iloczasie Języka Litewskiego (LMDr. 6G$_1$); O pisowni języka Litewskiego (LMDr. 6G$_2$).

9. K. Alminauskis, „Vyskupo Antano Baranausko laiškai Hugo Weberiui", *Archivum Philologicum*, I, 1930, 86.

10. Tos rašybos (besiremiančios lenkų rašyba), kad ir įvairuojančios, apskritai svarbiausios ypatybės buvo neskyrimas raidyne foneminio balsių ilgio, /ė/ nuo /e/, taip pat rašymas *e* vietoje *a* po minkštųjų priebalsių. Kalbamuoju laikotarpiu nevieno kalbininko, kalbos mėgėjo ar ir galvotesnio rašybos vartotojo (kai kurių laikraščių redaktorių ar knygų bei raštų autorių) buvo stengiamasi tą tradiciną rašybą patobulinti, pritaikyti lietuvių kalbos ypatybėms. Apie teorininkų pastangas pagerinti raidynui 1843–83 m. laikotarpiu žr. P. Jonikas, „Iš lietuvių kalbos rašybos istorijos", *Archivum Philologicum*, VIII, 22–30.

11. A. Baranovskij, *O litovskom jazykě i pravopisanii* (Rš F402).

12. A. Baranovskij, ten pat.

13. Čia mums nerūpi Jauniaus rašybos sistema apskritai — jo rašmenų ir garsmenų santykis bendruoju požiūriu ir kiek šis santykis ribojamas paradigminių, sintagminių ir kt. veiksnių. Šiame straipsnyje tekreipiamas dėmesys į Jauniaus rašmenų santykį su tarmėmis, pirmiausia, kiek jis pasireiškia JGr. (= K. Javnis, *Grammatika litovskogo jazyka; litovskij original i russkij perevod*. Petrograd, 1908–16).

14. Pirmas mėginimas Jaunjaus užvesti moksl28kus raštženkljus, visas tarmenis svarbjausjūse dalykūse sutaikantšjus (LMDr.); 1879.II.14 Jauniaus laiškas, iš Petrapilio rašytas Hugo Weberiui (išrašai iš Leipzigo Indogermanistikos Instituto).

15. Dėl fonografemos ir grafofonemos terminų plg. S. Allén, *Grafematisk analys som grundval för texedering*, Gothenburg, 1965.

16. Taip Jaunius žymėjo ne tik bk. /č/, bet ir [č'] prieš priešakinės eilės balsius; prieš užpakalinės eilės balsius pridėjo dar ir *j* (taip pat čia jotu žymėjo ir kitų negalinių priebalsių minkštumą).

16a. Plg. K. Jaunius, „Apie kun. A. Juškos dainų kalbą", *Lietuvių Tauta*, I, 1907, 553 tt.

16b. Vietoj čia spausdinamo *y* Jaunius vartojo lyg *u* su jo dešinės pusės brūkšneliu, pratęstu į apačią.

17. Pirmas mėginimas Jaunjaus užvesti mokslizkus raštženkljus. Žr. F. Bopp, *Vergleichende Grammatik ...*(Berlin, 1833), 11 (o 3. leid., I t., 1868, 19).

18. Ten pat.

19. P. S. [kardžius], „Kazimieras Jaunius", *Lietuvių Enciklopedija*, IX, 1956, 346.

20. P. Jonikas, Lietuvių bendrinės rašomosios kalbos idėja priešaušrio metu 67 tt.

21. Apie vakarų aukštaičių tarmės įsigalėjimą lietuvių bandrinės rašomosios kalbos pagrindu nuo seniausių laikų plg. P. Jonikas, „Kodėl rašome aukštaitiškai", *Aidai*, 1949.

22. *Jablonskio raštai* (red. J. Balčikonis. Kaunas, 1934), III, 14, 64 ir kt.

Dialects and Conventional Orthography

In this article dialect reflexes of the second half of the 19th century in the orthography of Standard Lithuanian of Lithuania Major are discussed. In the beginning of the period, at least, written Lithuanian was neither dialectally nor orthographically stabilized.

Some authors wrote in their own dialect for speakers of the same dialect, using inaccurate orthography which was scarcely adjusted to Lithuanian phonology and morphology. Those writing in their own dialect wanted speakers of other dialects to be able to interpret these writings for themselves, adjusting them (phonologically, at least) to their dialects. Because of that, the graphemes of such writings had to refer not only to the phonemes of the author's dialect but, at the same time, to the phonemes of the readers' dialects (polyphonemicization of the graphemes). However, the majority of authors did not select any special graphemes for such polyphonemicization to signal to readers the different phonemes in different dialects.

A. Baranauskas originated a theory which claimed that a written standard language should be based on the totality of Lithuanian dialects reconciled on the etymological principle. Although the writings of Baranauskas were to be read by representatives of every dialect according to the principle of polyphonemicization, even Baranauskas on the whole used no special graphemes for that purpose, lest he complicate the orthography for practical uses.

The basic feature of the orthography of K. Jaunius, on the other hand, was an orthographic reconciliation of the dialects, using special letters, mostly with diacritics, to indicate the dialectal divergence in phonology of lexemes and morphemes of the same origin.

The reconciliation of the dialects in the conventional orthography of the written language failed to become established because of the impracticability of such a spelling, and the Western Highland (*vakarų aukštaičiai*) dialect, the structure of which was better fitted for the function of a common standard language than that of other dialects, slowly emerged as the basis of Standard Lithuanian. Nevertheless, some traces of such reconciliation survived; J. Jablonskis assumed that, e.g., the graphemes *ą, ę, į, ų* help people speaking different dialects to read and understand the written language.

SIMAS KARALIŪNAS

Baltų šaknis *dēb- 'mušti, smogti, kirsti'

Liet. *duõbia, duõbė, duõbti* (ir *dúobti* K 100, J I 372) 'daryti įdubimą; skobti, skaptuoti; plėšti, drengti; mušti, smogti, trenkti; žudyti, galabyti' LKŽ II²
865 vartojamas aukštaičių tarmėse. Turinio segmentas 'skobti, skaptuoti'
neretai koegzistuoja su tokiais segmentais kaip 'piauti, kirsti, plėšti ir pan.',
tame tarpe ir ,,smogti, trenkti", plg. liet. *ruõbti* 'gremžti, duobti, skaptuoti;
kasti' ir lat. *rùobît* 'kerben, eine Kerbe hauen, höhlen, in Stücke hauen';
liet. *skúobti* 'skinti, raškyti; drožti, duobti, skaptuoti', *skàpti* 'duobti,
skaptuoti' ir lat. *skabît* 'abhauen (be)kappen'. — Liet. *duõbti* latvių kalboje
tiksliai atliepia *dùobju, dùobu, dùobt* 'aushöhlen, schrapen', *dùobties* 'sich
vertiefen' ME I 532. — Vokalizmą *uo* turi ir visa eilė vardažodžių. Liet.
duobė (acc. sing. *dúobę* ir *duõbę*) 'iškasta ar šiaip įdubusi vieta žemėje; dauba,
slėnys, duburys; kūdra; gili vieta upėje; įdubimas (akių, po krūtine, po
kaklu, skruostuose) etc.' LKŽ II² 862–3 vartojamas tiek aukštaičių, tiek
ir žemaičių tarmėse. — Liet. *duobė* atitikmuo latvių kalboje yra lat. *dùobe*
(ir *dúobe*) 'die Höhlung, Gruft, Grube; das Grab; die Tiefe im Flusse' ME I
531, 'das Tal, die Schlucht; ein Teich' EH I 349. — Remiantis šių lietuvių
ir latvių vardažodžių reikšmėmis (plg. specialesnes reikšmes 'tam tyčia
iškasta vieta bulvėms laikyti, rūsys' Leipalingis, Daukšai, 'iškasta tam
tyčia vieta linams džiovinti' Gudeliai, Kapsukas ir kt. lietuvių kalboje ir
'die Grube; das Beet' latvių kalboje), galima manyti, kad pirminė liet. *duobė*,
lat. *dùobe* reikšmė buvo 'iškasta, išduobta vieta'. Ir tik vėliau, matyt, šiuo
žodžiu buvo imta analogijos keliu vadinti ir tokios natūralios gilesnės vietos,
kaip duburiai, įdubimai žemės paviršiuje ar žmogaus kūne, slėniai. Pirminės
reikšmės 'iškasta, išduobta, t. y. dirbtinė (ne natūrali) vieta' atstatymas
leidžia šiuos vardažodžius susieti su liet. *duõbti*, lat. *dùobt*, plg. liet. *duõbti*
reikšmę 'daryti įdubimą' ('skobti, skaptuoti, aushöhlen', t. y. 'daryti
įdubimą medyje', yra aiškiai variantinė). Tą ryšį rodo ir priegaidės: ir
vardažodžiai, ir veiksmažodžiai greta cirkumflekso (plg. liet. acc. sing.
duõbę, lat. *dùobe* ir *duõbti, dùobt*) turi, nors ir retai, ir akūtą (plg. *dúobė,
duobė̃*, acc. sing. *dúobę, duõbe* ir *dúobti*). — Tai, kad liet. *duobė̃* vartojamas
visame lietuvių kalbos plote, o *duõbti* — tik aukštaičių tarmėse, leidžia

spėti, kad liet. *duõbti* yra denominatyvas. Denominatyvas veikiausiai yra ir lat. *dùobt*, nes lat. *dùobe* ir kiti vokalizmą *uo* turintys vardažodžiai vartojami (bent užfiksuoti) žymiai plačiau negu minimasis veiksmažodis. Vėlesnę šių veiksmažodžių kilmę, gal būt, rodo dar ir tai, kad vardažodžių su vokalizmu *uo* yra daug ir jie turi įvairius kamiengalius (žr. žemiau). — Kiek sunkiau su *duobė*, *duõbti* susieti liet. *dúoba* ir *duobà* (acc. sing. *duõbą*) 'drevė; jauja; ūkis, duba, gyvenimas; įdubimas krūtinės apačioje', *dúobas* 'drėvė' (Linkuva) LKŽ II² 862. Identifikuojant šiuos žodžius, svarbu tai, kad turinio segmentą 'įdubimas krūtinės apačioje' turi ir *duobė*. — Toliau *dúoba* turinio segmentą 'drevė' turi pietų Lietuvos tarmėse (Igliauka, Jieznas, A. Panemunė, Skaudvilė ir kt.). Šiose vietose kaip tik paplitęs ir *duõbti* turinio segmentas 'skobti, skaptuoti', ir tai, gal būt, leidžia tarp turinio segmentų 'drevė' ir 'skobti, skaptuoti' ieškoti genetinio ryšio. *dúoba* turinio segmentas 'jauja' paliudytas žemaičių tarmėse (Darbėnai, Kartena, Mosėdis, Skaudvilė, Skuodas, Šatės, Varduva), o segmentas 'ūkis, duba, gyvenimas' — aukštaičių (Pampėnai) ir žemaičių tarmėse (M. Valančiaus raštuose). Nors geografinis šių turinio segmentų išsidėstymas apie jų diachroninius santykius ir nieko nesako, vis dėlto galima prileisti, kad segmentai 'jauja' ir 'ūkis, duba, gyvenimas' yra išriedėję iš segmento 'duobė'. Turinio segmentų 'duobė' ir 'jauja' jungiamoji grandis, kartu rodanti ir tų segmentų giminingumą, gali būti liet. *duobė̃* reikšmė 'iškasta tam tyčia vieta linams džiovinti' Gudeliai, Kapsukas (plg. dar *dobà* 'iškasta duobė (su pastoge) linams džiovinti' LKŽ II² 599). Su tuo derinasi ir K. Būgos RR II 351 liudijimas: ,,Senovės jaujoje krosnis buvusi *duobėje* (Ds)." Jaujoje gali būti laikomi taip pat ir gyvuliai, pvz., avys, plg. *jáuja* 'avių tvartas' LKŽ IV 299, o tai valstiečiui ir yra ūkis, gyvenimas, plg. *gyvenimas* 'sodyba, žemė, ūkis' LKŽ III 372 (plg. dar liet. *dubà* 'drevė, uoksas; jauja, pakura; pirkia, troba; atskiras ūkis, gyvenimas, sodyba' LKŽ II² 779, kuris priklauso, matyt, skirtingai šakniai, plg. *dùbti* 'darytis dubiam, rastis įdubai, linkti; klimpti, smegti, grimzti; plyšti, irti' LKŽ II² 785, bet manifestuoja analogiškus turinio plano segmentus). Vadinasi, semantinė raida 'duobė, drevė'→'jauja'→'pirkia, troba; sodyba, ūkis, gyvenimas' yra visai įmanoma. — Nors tokia turinio segmentų raida ir galima, tačiau iš to negalima daryti kokių nors ekstralingvistinio pobūdžio išvadų (pvz., kad senovės lietuvių gyventa jaujose ar netgi kūrenamose duobėse ar drevėse), juoba kad *dúoba* 'ūkis, duba, gyvenimas' etimologiškai galima ir kitaip interpretuoti, siejant su liet. *dúobas* 'sankertinys, rentinys' LKŽ II² 862. Pastarasis lietuvių kalbos žodis A. Kossarzewskio rankraštyje ,,Litvanica czyli Wiadomość o Litwie" paaiškintas 'zrąb (=statymui, rentimui nukirsti medžiai, rąstai, sijos)' (žr. K. Būga, RR I

359, II 351). Tai leidžia liet. *dúobas* sieti su liet. *dóbti* 'besti, skobti; mušti, smogti, trenkti, skelti etc.', lat. *dâbt* 'schlagen, hauen'[1] (dėl turinio plano segmentų 'rąstai, sijos' ir 'kirsti' plg. liet. *rą̃stas* 'nukirstas ir nugenėtas storas medis, sienojas': *rę̃sti* 'kirsti, piauti rantant'; lenk. *zrąb* 'sienojai': *rąbać* 'kapoti, kirsti') ir su *dė̃bti*, kurio senesnė reikšmė galėjo būti 'kirsti ir pan' (žr. žemiau), kadangi veiksmažodis *duõbti* segmento 'kirsti' neturi. — Liet. *dúobas* morfologiškai tiksliai atliepia lat. *dùobs* 'die Höhlung, Gruft, Grube' EH I 349. Su šaknies vokalizmu *uo* dar yra liet. *duobùs* 'kurs su duoba, dreve' LKŽ II² 866, lat. *duôbs* 'tief, dumpf; hohl' ME I 531–2, 'niedrig gelegen und nass' EH I 349, *duôbjš* (ir *dùobjš*) 'tief, dumpf' ME I 531, *duobrs* 'tief, dumpf; niedrig gelegen' ME I 532, liet. *dúobstis* 'susidėvėjęs, sudubęs daiktas' LKŽ II² 865, *duoburỹs* 'mažesnis ar didesnis įdubimas žemėje, duobė, dauba, slėnys; šaltiniuota ar išmušta kelio, pievos, dirvos vieta' LKŽ II² 866 (pastaroji reikšmė aiškiai rodo ryšį su *dóbti* 'besti, skobti; mušti, smogti, trenkti, skelti etc.'), lat. *duôbulis* 'die Vertiefung, die Grube, Höhlung' ME I 532. — Liet. *dóbia, dóbė, dóbti* (ir *dõbti* Rudamina) 'mušti, smogti, trenkti; žudyti, galabyti; kankinti, varginti, atimti jėgas, sveikatą; *refl.* išdykauti, šėlti; daryti įdubimą, skobti, skaptuoti' LKŽ II² 602 vartojamas daugiausia pietinės Lietuvos tarmėse, tačiau pasitaiko ir rytų aukštaičių (Ramygala, Tauragnai) bei žemaičių (Kvėdarna, Tirkšliai ir S. Daukanto raštuose) tarmėse. Jo senumą rodo ir tikslus atitikmuo latvių kalboje: *dâbju, dâbu, dâbt* 'schlagen, hauen' ME I 446. Be to, vokalizmą *ā* turi ir kiti lietuvių kalbos veiksmažodžiai bei vardažodžiai: *dóbėtis* (praes. *dóbėjasi*) 'peikėtis', *dóbčiotis* 'maitotis, išdykauti' LKŽ II² 599, *dóbtelėti* 'suduoti, tvokstelėti; toptelėti, dingtelėti' LKŽ II² 60, *dobà* (acc. sing. *dõbą*) 'iškasta duobė (su pastoge) linams džiovinti' LKŽ II² 599, *dóbas* 'ūkis, gyvenimas' LKŽ II¹ 408, *dóbsnė, dóbsnis, dóbstė, dóbstis* 'susidėvėjęs, sudubęs daiktas' LKŽ II² 601–2, *dóbtas* 'susidėvėjęs, sudubęs daiktas; susenėlis, perkaršėlis', *dobstus* 'senas, sudubęs' LKŽ II² 602. — Pastarieji vokalizmo *o* vardažodžiai ir veiksmažodžiai neturi atitikmenų latvių kalboje. Todėl galima manyti, kad jie, būdami lietuvių kalbos naujadarai, susidarė veiksmažodžio *dóbti* pamatu. Iš jo jie gavo ir vokalizmą *o*. — Teksto fragmentai *Miške gyvatę nùdėbiau, Nelįsk, tuoj nudėbsiu* Suvainiškis rodo, kad su *dóbti* yra giminingas *dė̃bti*, kuriuo, vadinasi, paliudijamas nagrinėjamosios šaknies vokalizmas *ė*. Liet. *dė̃bia, dė̃bė, dė̃bti* 'remti, smeigti akis, kreivai pažvelgti' LKŽ II² 352, 'mušti, dobti, galabyti' Suvainiškis (dėl turinio segmentų santykio plg. *del̃bti* 'žemyn leisti, narinti (akis, galvą, uodegą); mušti, smogti', *įdel̃bti* 'įsmeigti, įbesti (akis' LKŽ II² 391) vartojamas aukštaičių tarmėse. Liet. *dė̃binti* 'iš paniūrų žiūrėti' LKŽ II² 351, *debčioti* 'dėbsėti, žvairuoti, šnairuoti' LKŽ II² 348, *dė̃blinti* 'iš paniūrų žiūrėti;

galvą, akis panarinus eiti, niūrinti, žioplinti' LKŽ II² 351, *dė̃ba* 'kas dėbsi, dėbčioja' LKŽ II² 349, *dė̃bla* 't. p.' LKŽ II² 351 ir kt. yra sekundariniai vediniai, atsiradę *dė̃bti* pamatu. — Nagrinėjamajai šakniai, gal būt, galima skirti ir liet. *dabstýti* (praes. *dãbsto*) 'mėtyti, drabstyti' LKŽ II² 207, *dãbyti* (praes. *dãbija*) 'mušti' LKŽ II² 204, *daburỹs* 'sūkurys, verpetas' LKŽ II² 207 ir, kadangi segmentas 'stverti, griebti' pasirodo *dóbti* turinio plane, plg. A. Juškos *Nudobti yra nutverti* LKŽ II² 602, lat. *dabût* (praes. *-ûju*), *dabuôt* (*-uonu, -uoju*), *dabît* (praes. *-îju*), *debît* EH I 313 'erhalten, bekommen; finden, erreichen; in seine Gewalt bekommen, erhaschen, fangen' ME I 428, kuriuos J. Endzelīns ME I 429 linkęs laikyti slavizmais. Jei pastarieji žodžiai iš tikrųjų priklausytų nagrinėjamajai šakniai, turėtume paliudytą ir normalųjį vokalizmą *a* bei *e*. — Čia konstatuotas vokalizmų *uo, o(ā)*, *ē* (ir, gal būt, *a, e*) kaitaliojimasis vienos šaknies formose baltų kalbose yra visai reguliarus, plg., pvz., *rúogti* (*ruõgti*) 'smulkiai ir su migla lyti, dulksnoti': *rókti* 'lynoti'; *slúogti* 'slėgti': *slógti* 'slėgti, spausti': *slė́gti* 'apdėti svoriu, spausti'; *tuõkti* (*túokti*) 'numanyti, suprasti, nujausti': *tõkti* (*tókti*) 'prasimanyti ką, nušnekėti, niekus taukšti': *atsi-tekė́ti* 'atgyti, atsitokti, atsipeikėti, atgauti sąmonę', lat. *at-tecêt* 'aufhören, sich bessern'; *sruogaĩ* 'žvynai': *sriógas* 'žvynas; pelekas': *srė́gai* 'žvynai'; lat. *spruogt* 'kräuseln (das Haar); Knospen gewinnen; kraus werden': *sprâgt* 'bersten, platzen, losgehen etc.', liet. *sprógti* 'plyšti, trūkti, skilti; skleisti pumpurus, lapoti; kaltis daigui etc.': lat. *sprêgt* 'platzen, bersten, Risse bekommen' ir kt. — Sisteminis požiūris (plg. gerai žinomą baltų kalbų generatyvinį modelį: *ė́sti → úodas, brė̃žti → brúožas, rė̃žti → rúožas* ir kt.) pirminiu vokalizmu, šiaip ar taip, leidžia laikyti vokalizmą *ē̃*, nepaisant to, kad liet. *dė̃bti* neturi atitikmens latvių kalboje (t. y. lyg ir atrodo, kad vokalizmas *ē̃* yra lietuvių kalbos naujadaras). Teiginį apie vokalizmo *ē̃* pirmumą galima, atrodo, paremti kitų ide. kalbų duomenimis. — J. Endzelīns[2] liet. *dóbti*, lat. *dâbt* yra susiejęs su angl. *dab* 'tyliai mušti', rytų frizų *dafen* 'suduoti, belsti, daužyti' ir kt., kurie turi normaliojo laipsnio vokalizmą *a*. Su šiais germanų kalbų žodžiais dar siejami angl. *dabble* 'taškytis, pliauškintis (vandenyje)', norv. dial. *dabba* 'grūsti; kalti; trenkti, trypti (koja į žemę)', vid. vok. aukšt. *beteben* 'pervažiuoti, slėgti, spausti' (su *e*, kilusiu iš *a* prieš sekančio skiemens *i, ĭ, į̆*), vid. olandų *dabben* "taškytis, pliauškinti (vandenyje)' etc.[3], kuriuos visus, tame tarpe ir liet. *dóbti*, lat. *dâbt*, norima kildinti iš ide. šaknies *dʰā̆bʰ-* 'schlagen' Pokorny 233. — Reikia pasakyti, kad šios germanų kalbų grupės žodžių genetiniai santykiai nėra aiškūs. Angl. *dab* 'to touch or strike lightly', kilusį iš vid. angl. *dabben*, įtariama esant skoliniu iš vid. danų *dabben* 'to pinch, dabble', o pastarasis greičiausiai yra onomatopėjinės kilmės[4] (plg. dar angl. *tap* 'barškinti, taukšėti' iš vid. angl.

tappen, pasisiskolinto iš s. pranc. (ir dab. pranc.) *taper* 'plekštelėti; stuksenti', kuris irgi yra imitacinės kilmės[5]. Angl. *dabble* 'taškytis, pliauškintis (vandenyje)' yra frekventatyvinis priesagos *-le* darinys iš *dab*. Toliau abgl. *dab* etimologiškai siejamas su *dap* 'to fish by allowing the bait to dip into the water', kuris irgi, spėjama, yra onomatopėjinės kilmės[6]. Onomatopėjinis jų charakteris paaiškina ir tai, kodėl jie remiasi germanų šaknimi su skirtintais jos galo priebalsiais: *dabb-, *dab-* ir *dap-*. Be to, šiuos germanų kalbų žodžius galima sieti ir su kita žodžių grupe, kurios pamatinės reikšmės yra 'šlapias, drėgnas, pelkėtas; liūnas, pelkė, klanas etc.': s. skand. *dafla* 'taškytis, pliuškenti', norv. dial. *dave* 'klanas, balutė', šved. dial. *dave, dava* 't. p.', s. šved. *daevin, daever* 'šlapias, drėgnas', isl. *dapi*, norv., šved. dial. *dape* 'klanas, balutė', vid. oland. *dabben, dabbelen* 'purvinti, teršti' etc.[7] Su šiais germanų kalbų žodžiais siejamas[8] liet. *dãpas* 'potvynis, tvanas' LKŽ II 182, kuris isl. *dapi*, norv., šved. dial. *dape* yra artimas semantika ir harmonizuoja šaknies vokalizmu. — Vadinasi, liet. *dóbti*, lat. *dâbt* ryšys su angl. *dab*, kuris veikiausiai yra skolinys iš danų kalbos, atmestinas. Abejotinas baltiškųjų žodžių ryšys ir su frizų *dafen*, norv. dial. *dabba*, vid. olandų *dabben*, vid. vok. aukšt. *beteben*, nes 1) jie gali būti onomatopėjinės kilmės ir 2) juos galima etimologiškai susieti su drėgnumą, pelkėtumą ir pan. žyminčiomis leksemomis, prie kurių priklauso veikiausiai ir liet. *dãpas*. — Kadangi turinio plano segmentas 'stebinti, stulbinti; stebėtis, būti apstulbusiam' yra susijęs su segmentu 'mušti, smogti, trenkti'[9] (plg., pvz., liet. *pritreñkti* 'apstulbinti nustebinti': *treñkti* 'mušti, duoti; krėsti, spirti atgal; kurtinti, užmušti'; lot. *stupeo* 'esu sustingęs, esu nustebęs, stebiuosi', *stupidus* 'apsvaigęs, apkvaišęs, nustebęs': gr. τύπτω 'mušu, smogiu, kertu', τύπος 'smūgis; žymė'; lot. *fatuus* 'mit Dummheit geschlagen': kimrų *bathu* 'schlagen' ir ypač vok. *betroffen sein* 'būti nustebusiam, pritrenktam, sumišusiam': *betreffen* '(pa)liesti'; pagaliau ir pati nagrinėjamoji šaknis tai remia, plg. liet. *dúoba* 'bukaprotis' LKŽ II 607), todėl liet. *dóbti, dė̃bti*, lat. *dâbt*, rodos, galima gretinti su gr. perf. τέ-θηπα 'aš esu apstulbęs ir sužavėtas', aoristo dalyviu ταφών, vardažodžiu τάφος 'nuostaba' ir veiksmažodžiais θώπεω 'meilikauju, pataikauju', θωπεύω 'meilikauju, pataikauju; glamonėju, myluoju, glostau'[10]. Pastarieji du veiksmažodžiai yra denominatyvai[11], ir, vadinasi, šaknies vokalizmą ō jie gavo iš vardažodžių, plg. gr. θώψ, gen. sing. θωπός 'meilikautojas, pataikūnas'. Stebinantis yra liet. *duõbia*, lat. *dùobju* ir gr. θώπτω tipologinis sutapimas: ir baltų, ir graikų žodžiai harmonizuoja ne tik šaknies vokalizmu ō, bet ir kamiengaliu (gr. ππ iš *pj*); ir graikų, ir, atrodo, baltų veiksmažodžiai yra denominatyvai. Be to, iš graikų kalbos faktų matyti, kad pirminis morfonologinis baltų variantas yra *dēb-, genetiškai identifikuotinas su gr. -θηπ- (iš *dhēbh-), kuris yra perfektinė šaknis. Iš jos su šaknies vokalizmu $\bar{o}$ dėsningai galėjo būti daromi vardažodžiai, liet. $d\check{e}bti \rightarrow duob\tilde{e}$, $d\acute{u}ob\dot{e}$, lat. $d\grave{u}obe$, liet. $d\acute{u}oba$, $d\acute{u}obas$; gr. τέ-θηπα→θώψ, θωπός. Nykstamasis laipsnis a (iš *H greta normaliojo $\bar{e} < *eH_1$) atstovaujamas gr. aoriste ἔτᾰφον ir aoristo dalyvyje τᾰφών.

Išnašos

1. Plg.: „Duoba(s)“ в значении „сруб“ есть возможность производить от лит. глагола dóbiu, dóbti [...], — K. Būga, Rinktiniai raštai, I, 359.

2. J. Endzelin, „Germanisch-Baltische Miszellen“, KZ, 51, 290.

3. Falk, H. und Torp, A., Norwegisch-dänisches etymologisches Wörterbuch, I–II, Heidelberg, 1911, 28, 1237.

4. E. Klein, A Comprehensive Etymological Dictionary of the English Language, I, Amsterdam–London–New York, 1966, 395.

5. E. Klein, op. cit., II, 1572.

6. E. Klein, op. cit., I, 401.

7. P. Persson, „Etymologien“, IF, 35, 204 ir ypač išnaša 1.

8. E. Fraenkel, Litauisches etymologisches Wörterbuch, Heidelberg–Göttingen, 1962, 82.

9. Plg.: „[...] 'staunen, betreten, sprachlos sein' [...] vermutlich als 'geschlagen, betroffen sein' aus einer Grundbed. 'schlagen'", — J. Pokorny, Indogermanisches etymologisches Wörterbuch, Bern, 233. Plačiau apie tų sememų ryšį žr. A. Walde, J. B. Hofmann, Lateinisches etymologisches Wörterbuch, II, Heidelberg, 1954, 609 s.v. stupeō.

10. Šiuos graikų kalbos žodžius E. Fraenkel, Lit. etym. Wb., 89 siejo tik su dépčioti, dėpsḗti, dėpsóti.

11. E. Schwyzer, Griechische Grammatik, 705–732.

The Baltic Root *dēb- 'to beat, strike, hit'

Lith. duõbti (and dúobti) 'to make a hollow; to scoop, hollow out; to beat, hit, strike; to slay, kill', Latv. dùobt 'to hollow out, scrape' may be etymologically connected with Lith. duobẽ 'a dug out place or depression in the ground, pit; ravine, valley etc.', Latv. dùobe 'a hollow, vault, pit, mine; bed; grave; valley, ravine etc.'. Lith. dúoba 'a hollow; barn; farm, living things etc.', dúobas 'a hollow; frame etc.' Lith. duõbti, Latv. dùobt probably are denominatives since, for example, Lith. duõbti is in use only in the Aukštaitish dialect, but the nouns duobẽ etc. occur over the whole Lithuanian-speaking area. — $\bar{a}$ vocalism is found in Lith. dóbti 'to make a hollow; to scoop, hollow out; to beat, hit, strike; to slay, kill etc.', Latv. dâbt 'to strike, cut', Lith. dobà 'a dug out hollow (with a cover) for drying flax', dóbsnis, dóbstis etc. 'a worn out, dilapidated thing'. These nouns are new formations in Lith., since there are no correspondances in Latvian. — $\bar{e}$ vocalism is found in Lith. *dẽbti* 'to stare, to look askew, askance'; the semantic connection with *duõbti, dóbti* is easily demonstrated. The vocalisations *a* and *e* should be found in Lith. *dabstýti* 'to throw, splash', perhaps also Latv. *dabût, dabît, debît* 'to receive, get, find, attain etc.' — Correspondances are to be found in Greek: τέθηπα 'I am stunned, charmed', τάφος 'wonder', θώπτω 'I flatter, ingratiate myself', θώψ 'flatterer, toady'.—The preterite form **dēb-* could have served as the basis for generating nouns with root vocalism $\bar{o}$ (*duobẽ, dùobe, dúoba, dúobas* etc.).

KONSTANTĪNS KARULIS

Eine lettische Wortfamilie
in historisch-semasiologischer Sicht

(Das Wort *gars*, seine Herkunft und Ableitungen)

In formeller Hinsicht liegt dem lett. *gars* und dem entsprechenden lit. *gãras* am nächsten asl. горѣти, russ. горѣть 'brennen'. Doch fehlt dem Substantiv im Lettischen wie auch im Litauischen völlig die Bedeutung 'brennen'; nur selten begegnet man ihr bei einigen Verbalformen dergleichen Wurzel; möglicherweise handelt es sich hier um einen Einfluss des Slavischen.

Bekanntlich wird lett. *gars* zu der ide. Wurzel *g^uher- 'heiss, warm' gestellt, von der auch ai. *háras-* 'Glut', gr. θέρος 'Sommerhitze', arm. *jer* 'Wärme' u. a. (Pokorny, I, 493–495; Plāķis, Ide. 94)[1] abgeleitet werden.

In den ältesten lett. Schriftdenkmälern und in der Folklore trifft man *gars* in folgenden Bedeutungen: 1) 'die Hitze', jedoch nur die der Badestube, 2) 'der Geist' — als eine übernatürliche Kraft, ein übernatürliches Wesen, als die personifizierte Kraft einer Naturerscheinung, 3) 'die Seele': *izlaide to garu* '(er) verschied' (Joh. 19:30—Glück 228), nebst *izlaide to dvēseli* 'ds' (Math. 27:50 — Glück 66). Die 2. und die 3. Bedeutung sind eng verbunden: eine übernatürliche Kraft wurde der Seele eines Verstorbenen zugeschrieben, die mit dem letzten Atemzug ausgehaucht wird; sie wird zu einem Geist, einem Gespenst, davon auch *mirušo gari* 'die Geister der Verstorbenen'. Doch konnten diese beiden Bedeutungen sich nicht direkt aus der ersten herleiten. Offensichtlich muss es hier eine weitere semantische Basis gegeben haben. Es könnte dies 'Hitze, Wärme' (z. B. durch Heizen) und damit verbundene 'warme, feuchte Ausdünstung' sein; *gars* 'die Hitze in der Badestube' ist nur als eine spezielle Einengung dieser weiten Semantik aufzufassen. Hiervon übertragen: 'der warme, feuchte Hauch eines Menschen' — später 'der Träger der Seele'. Denn solange der Mensch noch am Leben ist, trägt er den *gars* in sich als die Lebenskraft, die mit der Körperwärme verbunden ist. Durch spätere Personifikation der Naturkräfte und Naturerscheinungen wurden auch diese schliesslich mit einigen Attributen des lebenden Wesens bedacht — wie mit dem Lebensgeist *gars*. Und zwar haben hier Dunst, Dampf und Nebel, von Gewässern aufsteigend, die Phantasie angeregt, jetzt von einem *upesgars* 'Flussgeist', *purvagars* 'Sumpfgeist' u. a. zu sprechen.

Selten trifft man in der Literatur der vorigen Jahrhunderte das Wort *gars* in der Bedeutung (4) 'Geruch'; auch diese Bedeutung kann man mit 'feuchter Ausdünstung (infolge Wärmen, Erhitzen)' in Beziehung bringen. Öfters findet man *gars* in der Bedeutung (5) 'Neigung, Hang, Streben; Brunst', in der Sprache der Gegenwart jedoch nur in einer begrenzten Zahl von Redewendungen, z. B. *viņam ir gars uz mācīšanos* 'er hat den Hang, die Lust zum Lernen'. Gewiss ist diese Bedeutung von der ursprünglichen Bedeutung 'Hitze' abzuleiten (vgl. *kaislība* 'Leidenschaft' und *kaist* 'glühen').

Im Vergleich zu den genannten sind alle anderen jetzt gebräuchlichen Bedeutungen von *gars* nur weitere semantische Ableitungen: 'Vorstellungsvermögen, Erkennnungsvermögen, Verstand' (vgl. *ar možu garu, garā možs* 'klaren Verstandes, munteren Geistes'), 'Gesinnung, Gemüt' (*paciest lēnā garā* 'sanftmütig dulden'), 'Wesen, Eigentümlichkeit' (*tautas gars* 'der Geist des Volkes'), 'das Geistige' (*gara dzīve* 'das geistige Leben') oder die Personifikation; 'ein grosser Geist'. Diese Bedeutungen hat *gars* vorwiegend erst im 18. und 19. Jh. erhalten, grösstenteils durch den Einfluss des deutschen Wortes *Geist*, deshalb entsprechen sich lett. *gars* und dt. *Geist* — von kleinen Abweichungen abgesehen.

Das lit. *gãras* stützt die angeführte semantische Bedeutungsentwicklung von *gars*. Die Grundbedeutung des lit. *gãras* ist '(Wasser)dampf', ferner auch 'Nebel'; dagegen ist 'der Dampf in der Badestube' nur ein Einzelfall innerhalb des Bedeutungskomplexes. Dass auch in der lettischen Sprache das Wort *gars* eine entsprechende weitere Bedeutung gehabt hat, zeigt die Pluralbildung *gari* 'warmer Dunst, Qualm und Dampf' (Stender, I, 69), die heute nur noch in einigen Maa. vorhanden ist (z. B. in der Kurischen Nehrung, Plāķis, Kurs. 89). Von der ehemaligen weiteren Bedeutung spricht auch das von einem Adjektiv gebildete Substantiv *garaiņi*, ma. *garaiņas* 'Dampf (auch ausserhalb der Badestube)'. Nach Stender wurden die beiden Wörter *gari* und *garaiņi* in derselben Bedeutung gebraucht. Die Identität beider Wörter wird auch durch den Gebrauch des letzteren in der Bedeutung 'die Geister' noch zu Beginn des 18. Jh. (nach G. Bergmanns handschriftl. Lexikon Ulmann, I, 72 bestätigt). Die lit. Pluralbildung *garaĩ* hat die Bedeutung 'Ofen- und Kohlendunst', d. h., sie drückt eine Nebenerscheinung des Heizens aus, ebenso wie der lett. Pl. *gari*, nur der Charakter der Nebenerscheinung ist ein anderer.

Die Bedeutung 'Atem, Geist' ist in der Semantik von lit. *gãras* kaum vertreten, weil in diesem Sinn das Wort *dvasià* (von *dvèsti*; vgl. lett. *dvest, dvèst* 'hauchen, atmen' und *dvēsele* 'Seele', früher auch 'Atem') gebraucht wird. Dagegen trifft man öfter *gãras* in der Bedeutung 'leidenschaftlicher Wunsch, heftige Begierde; eifriges Streben', von der auch im lett. *gars* eine Spur zu finden ist. Dieser Bedeutung entspricht das preuss. Adv. *garrewingi* 'brünstig'. Es ist ein Beweis dafür, dass die Urform von *gars* und *gãras* (vermutlich **garos*) zur Zeit des frühen Gemeinschaftslebens der Balten die Bedeutung 'Hitze' gehabt hat, von der die entsprechenden semantischen Übertragungen stammen. Zu dieser Annahme führt auch die veraltete Bedeutung von lit. *gãras* 'die Oberfläche des vorderen Teils eines (Back)ofens'. Diese Bedeutung erinnert an preuss. *goro* 'Vuerstant' (E 42; 'ein Loch auf dem Herde, um das Feuer einzuscharren', Endzelīns, Senpr. v. 179; 'Herd', Būga, II, 210; eher: 'Feuerstätte; Ofenmund'), vgl. aruss. гърнъ, russ. горн 'Schmelzofen' (Vasmer, I, 442) 'Kohlentopf' (Būga, II, 210) und lat. *fornus* 'Ofen', ehem. 'Kohlentopf'. Im Lettischen findet man eine Parallele zu dieser Bedeutung im Subst. *aizguore* 'der Raum hinter dem Ofen, der Raum zwischen der Wand und dem Ofen od. auch die Ofenbank'; 'der Vorderofen, der vordere Teil des grossen Ofens; Ofenröhre' (ME I, 29), von dem das Subst. **guors* od. **guora* 'Ofen; Feuerstätte, Ofenmund' herzuleiten ist. Hierher soll auch das Verb *guôrît* 'recken, strecken', Refl. *guôrîtiês* 'sich recken, strecken' gestellt werden, das gewöhnlich dann gebraucht wird, wenn vom sich Räkeln in der Wärme die Rede ist. (Zum Vokalismus s. weiter.) Diese Wörter und Bedeutungen zeugen von dem ursprünglichen Sinn des lett. *gars* und lit. *gãras*: — eine Stätte zum Heizen. Damit stimmt auch die lett. Ableitung *garme* überein: 'die Wärme (des Ofens); die von glimmenden Kohlen ausstrahlende Glut'; diese Wort entspricht den übrigen Ableitungen der ide. Wurzel mit einer *-m-* Erweiterung **g^uhermo* und **g^uhormo*: skr. *gharmá-ḥ*, pr. *gorme* (E 41) 'Hitze', lat. *formus*, air. *gorm*, gr. θερμός 'warm' u. a. (Pokorny, I, 493; Kluge 838; Stang 25).

Es scheint offensichtlich, dass das Material der baltischen Sprachen und das Vergleichsmaterial die anfängliche Bedeutung der Wurzel *gar-* mit Hitze (Heizen und seinen Nebenerscheinungen) in Zusammenhang bringt; folglich ist die Semantik von russ. гореть 'brennen' und den entsprechenden Wörtern anderer slavischer Sprachen als das Resultat einer gesonderten späteren Entwicklung zu betrachten.

Neben dem lett. Subst. *gars* ist auch ein Verb **gart* 'erhitzen, heizen' anzunehmen. Davon zeugen mehrere Ableitungen, z. B. *garuôza* '(Brot)-rinde, (Brot)kruste'; davon auch eine Ableitung *garuôzêtiês* 'Rinde backen' (Lange, II, 116), weiterhin zu **gart* auch das Adj. *gards* 'schmackhaft, wohlschmeckend, lecker' (zur Bildung vgl. *gurt*; *gurds*), das anfänglich wohl die Bedeutung 'erhitzt; (im Ofen, auf dem Herde) heiss, warm gemacht' gehabt hat; die heiss gemachten (gebratenen, gekochten) Nahrungsmittel wurden angenehmer zu essen, sie schmeckten besser, und von hier konnte man das Wort *gards* auf alle schmackhaften Lebensmittel beziehen. Da auch lit.

gardùs dieselbe Bedeutung hat, lässt sich folgern, dass die gegenwärtige Semantik dieses Wortes recht alt ist.

Es werden auch mehrere Verben gebraucht, die entweder von lett. *gars*, oder von **gart* abgeleitet sind. Es scheint, dass die Bedeutung von lett. *garuôt* 'dampfen, ausdünsten' erst später entstanden ist. Eine ältere Semantik zeigen die Ableitungen *izgaruôt, izgarêtiês*: vgl. *pirts izgarējusies* 'die Badestube ist von Dämpfen frei, so dass man baden kann', *krāsns izgarējusies* 'der Ofen ist fertig zum Brotbacken' (ME I, 736). Das lett. Adj. *garîgs* 'geistig, geistlich' ist wohl eine neuere Bildung, es bezieht sich auf *gars* im religiösen und intellektuellen Sinne.

Nach dem bisher Gesagten darf man schliessen, dass lett. *gars* die folgende semantische Entwicklung durchgemacht hat: 'Hitze, Wärme'; von hieraus in zwei Richtungen: 1) 'Neigung, Hang, Streben; Brunst' (Bd. 5), 2) 'heisse, erhitzte Luft, heisser Dampf'; von hier: 1) 'Hitze in der Badestube' (Bd. 2), 2) 'warmer Dampf, Atem'; von hier: 1) 'Geruch' (Bd. 4), 2) 'Lebenskraft, Seele' (Bd. 3) — 'die Seele eines Verstorbenen, Gespenst' (Bd. 3a) — 'Geist' als eine übernatürliche Kraft (Bd. 1) und weiter die semantischen Bildungen der neueren Zeit, die unter dem Einfluss der deutschen Sprache und der christlichen Religion entstanden sind.

Die angeführten Wörter mit dem Wurzelvokal *a* sind nicht alle Ableitungen von ide. **g^{u}her-* in der lettischen Sprache. Wie bekannt, kann in der *e*-Reihe der Vokal *e* mit *a/* < ide. *o* wechseln; neben Liquida kommt als die Reduktionsstufe für *e* auch *i* vor und manchmal — vielleicht als die Reduktionsstufe für ide. *o* — auch *u* (Endzelīns, Baltu val. 25).

Der Vokal *e* ist in den Ableitungen von **g^{u}her-* im Lettischen nicht mehr zu finden. Im Litauischen kommen das oft gebrauchte Adj. *gẽras* 'gut, tüchtig, trefflich, günstig, geeignet, passend, recht, richtig, erfreulich, angenehm, gütig, wohlwollend, freundlich' und das entsprechende Subst. *gẽras* vor. Zur Semantik vgl. dt. *warm* 'gut, freundlich'.

Den *i*-Reflex findet man in den lettischen Wörtern *dzirksts, dzirkste, dzirkstele* 'der Funken', *dzirkstīt, dzirkstēt* 'funkeln, Funken sprühen' (ME I, 554; Fraenkel 134), ferner in *dzirties* 'sich etwas vornehmen, einen Vorsatz fassen, wollen, nach etwas verlangen, trachten', das mit lett. *dzirt*, li. *gìrti*, pr. *girtwei* 'loben' in Verbindung steht. Über den Zusammenhang von *gìrti* und *gẽras* s. Būga, II, 191.

Den *u*-Reflex findet man in dem lett. Verb. *gurt* 'matt, schwach werden, abnehmen', ma. auch 'sich legen' (vom Winde), und in seinen Ableitungen. Wie bekannt, alterniert das baltische *u* vor *r* zuweilen mit *a, e* und kommt dann infolge einer Abschwachung von unbetontem ide. *o* oder *a* her (vgl. lett. *smaȊks* : lit. *smulkùs* 'fein'), deshalb ist es möglich, die Wurzel *gur-* in Be-

252

ziehung zu *gar-* zu setzen. Dass hier eine Wurzelform mit *o* vorgelegen hat, das in der Dehnstufe eine Dehnung erhalten hat, zeigen pr. *goro* (wo *o* möglicherweise von *ō*, ME I, 29) und lett. *aizguore*, daneben russ. гарь und жар.

Zur Semantik von *gurt*: wenn **gart* 'erhitzen, heizen' bedeutet, ist hier eine Nebenbedeutung 'erschlaffen, matt werden, nachlassen (in der Hitze)' möglich, und gerade damit verband sich *gurt*, als sich der ursprüngliche Inhalt des Verbs zu differenzieren begann. Dazu gehören auch die Ableitungen: *gurdināt* und *gurināt* 'müde machen', *gurds* 'müde, matt', *gurdeļot* 'siech, kränklich sein' u. a.

Anmerkungen

1. Folgende Abkürzungen werden verwendet:

Būga — K. Būga, *Rinktiniai raštai.* I–III. Vilnius, 1958–1961.

Endzelīns, Baltu v. — J. Endzelīns, *Baltu valodu skaņas un formas.* Rīga, 1948.

Endzelīns, Senpr. v. — J. Endzelīns, *Senprūšu valoda.* Rīga, 1943.

Fraenkel — E. Fraenkel, *Litauisches Etymologisches Wörterbuch,* Heidelberg–Göttingen, 1955–1965.

Glück — *Tas jauns testaments.* Übers. von E. Glück u. a. Rīga, 1685.

Kluge — F. Kluge, *Etymologisches Wörterbuch der deutschen Sprache,* 20. Aufl. Berlin, 1967.

Lange — J. Lange, *Vollständiges deutsch-lettisches und lettisch-deutsches Lexikon.* I–II. Oberpalen-Mitau, 1772–1777.

ME — K. Mühlenbach, *Lettisch-deutsches Wörterbuch.* Red., erg. und fortges. von J. Endzelin. I–IV. Riga, 1923–1932.

Plāķis, Ide. — J. Plāķis, *Indoeuropiešu valodu salīdzināmā gramatika,* Rīga, 1938.

Plāķis, Kurs. — J. Plāķis, „Kursenieku valoda". *Latvijas Universitātes Raksti,* XVI, 1927.

Pokorny — J. Pokorny, *Indogermanisches etymologisches Wörterbuch.* I., Bern u. München, 1959.

Stang — Chr. S. Stang, *Vergleichende Grammatik der Baltischen Sprachen,* Oslo u. a., 1966.

Stender — G. F. Stender, *Lettisches Lexikon.* I–II. Mitau, 1789.

Ulmann — C. Ulmann, *Lettisch-deutsches Wörterbuch,* I., Rīga, 1872.

Vasmer — M. Фасмер, *Этимологический словарь русского языка.* I-II. Москва, 1964–1967.

An Historical-Semantic Consideration of a Latvian Word Family

La. *gars* and Lith. *gãras*, both derived from IE **gʷher-* 'hot, warm', do not have related forms with the meaning 'to burn', unlike the Russian word of the same origin гореть. The primary meaning of *gars* was 'heat, warmth' from which came the later meanings: 1) 'heat (in the bathhouse)', 2) 'soul', 3) 'ghost', 4) 'tendency, trend; passion', 5) 'stench' and 6) the more recent senses corresponding to those of Germ. *der Geist*. Besides the subst. *gars* there was a verb **gart* 'to grow hot, to heat', cf. *garuoza* 'crust'.

Apart from the words with a vowel *a* in the root there are some words of the same origin with *i* (e.g. *dzirksts* 'spark'), with *u* (e.g. *gurt* 'to grow weak') and *o* [*uo*] (e.g. *aizguore* 'the space behind the stove').

JONAS KAZLAUSKAS

Liet. *džiaũgtis* ir jo giminaičiai

Liet. *džiaũgtis* 'Freude empfinden, sich freuen' ir jo vedinių etimologija iki šiol nėra aiški. H. Hirto bandymą[1] sieti šį žodį su gr. γηθεῖν, lot. *gaudēre* (< *gāvidēre*) ir fonetinius skirtumus aiškinti metateze galima laikyti tik bet kokios išeities iš keblios padėties ieškojimu. Ne be reikalo E. Frenkelis šį bandymą palydėjo žodžiais: ,,Doch ist dieses äußerst fraglich"[2]. Palikdami čia nuošalyje lat. *ģaugtiês* 'sich freuen, jubeln, hoffen, erwarten, versprechen, im Begriff sien, liebkosen', kurį J. Endzelynas linkęs kildinti iš kuršių ar liet. *dáugtis* (>liet. *džiaugtis*), ir lat. *ģaubt* 'ergötzen', *ģaubties* 'sich freuen, jubeln, hoffen, erwarten, versprechen, im Begriff sein', kurį J. Endzelynas linkęs laikyti *ģaugties* perdirbiniu ar sena gretimine forma su šaknies variacija[3], sustosime čia prie liet. *džiaugtis*.

Fonetiniu atžvilgiu liet. *džiaugtis* galima būtų sieti su liet. *daũg*, lat. *daũdz* 'viel', kadangi *au* žodyje *džiaugtis* yra po minkšto priebalsio ir, vadinasi, kilęs gali būti iš *eu*[4] (*džiaug-* < *deug-*). Jeigu paaiškėtų, kad tokiam siejimui nekliudo semantika, tai *džiaugtis* etimologija taptų aiškesnė.

Dar E. Bernekeris liet. *daug*, lat. *daudz* abejodamas siejo su rus. дужий, дюжий 'kräftig'[5], o E. Frenkelis[6] ir M. Fasmeris[7] tai daro jau neabejodami. K. Būga su liet. *daug* susiejo ir liet. *dùkšlas* 'erdvus (apie drabužį)'[8], o J. Endzelynas čia dar pridėjo lat. *duksns* 'korpulent' ir *padūgt* 'paspėti, pajėgti' (tiesa, pastarąjį su klaustuku)[9]. E. Blesė, remdamasis dar ir lat. *dàudzinât* 'lobpreisen, verherrlichen' rekonstruoja ankstesnį būdvardžio *daugas, *dauga reikšmę 'mächtig, kräftig, groß'[10]. Kad iš tikrųjų šaknies *daug-* giminaičiai anksčiau tokią ar panašią reikšmę yra turėję, be jau kitų tyrinėtojų pateiktų šios šaknies vedinių, rodo dar ir šie: *dùksas* 'kūningas, tvirtas, pilnas'; *dùkslas, -à* ir *dukslùs, -ì* 'drūtas, pilnas, erdvus, palaidas, talpus', *dùksnas, -à* 'vidutinio storumo, stuomens, gražumo ir didumo'; *duksnùs, -ì* 'drūtas, storas, dukslus'; *dùkstas* 'platus, stangus'; *dùksvas* 'erdvus, palaidas, platus, talpus; drūtas, pilnas', *duksvótas* 'storas, riebus, duksvas'; *dùkšlas, -à* 'dukslas', *dukšlùs, -ì* 'erdvus, palaidas, talpus'; *dukšnùs, -ì* 'dukšlus'. Čia galima priminti dar ir žinomus šių žodžių giminaičius slavų kalbose, plg. rus. дужий, дюжий 'sveikas, tvirtas, stiprus', ukr.

дужий 'tvirtas, galingas', bulg. недуг 'negalia, liga', lenk. *dužy* 'stiprus, tvirtas, didelis', *dužo* 'daug', ček. dial. *duži* 'stiprus', *duh* 'Gedeihen'.

Turint galvoje lat. *pa-dūgt* 'paspėti, pajėgti, galėti', kuris tikriausiai yra susijęs su *daug-* 'galingas, stiprus', plg. dėl to kad ir liet. *pajė̃gti* 'vermögen' ir *jė́gà* 'Kraft, Stärke', galima būtų spėti, kad atitinkamas tranzityvusis veiksmažodis **deugti* galėjo reikšti 'daryti, kad pajėgtų' (plg. *kìsti* ir *keĩsti* 'daryti, kad kistų'), vadinasi, 'stiprinti, daryti šaunų, patenkintą'. Tuo būdu ankstesnė *džiaugti* (< **deugti*) reikšmė galėjo būti panaši į veiksmažodžio *drūténti*, išvesto iš *drūtas*, reikšmę, plg. *sūnus drūtena tėvą: kokia čia bėda — išdvėsė viena karvė, tai bus kita; Pratark, sūneli, meilų žodelį, sudrūtenk, sūneli, mano galvelę.* Plg. *jis mane džiaugia, kad gaus vietą* LKŽ II 727 (čia *džiaugia* dabar reiškia 'džiugina' — anksčiau galėjo reikšti 'stiprina, daro patenkintą'). Lietuvių kalboje nesunku rasti tokių atvejų, kai pasitenkinimas, džiaugsmas ar linksmumas siejamas su stiprumu, drūtumu, sveikata, plg. *Ulioja brolis kaip drūtas; sveikas, drūtas — tai ir linksmas; linksmas, sveiks ir drūts į patalą kopia* (K. Donelaitis). Be to, dar plg. s. ind. *mahān* 'groß, ausgedehnt, mächtig, ehrwürdig' ir *maháyati* 'belebt, stärkt, erfreut, feiert, verherrlicht', mahīyatē 'freut sich'; lat. *vesels* 'sveikas, visas, pilnas' ir s. sl. веселъ 'linksmas'. B. Jėgeris yra įtikinamai parodęs, kad net reikšmė 'schwer' per 'gewichtig, wichtig, tüchtig' gali išriedėti į 'angenehm, schön, gut', plg. liet. *smagùs* 'schwer, tüchtig' ir *smagùs* 'angenehm, gut'[11].

Kai tik *džiaugti* įgijo *džiuginti* reikšmę, tai, suprantama, kad sąvokai *džiaugtis* reikšti nesunkiai galėjo būti sudarytas sangražinis veiksmažodis *džiaugtis*, plg. *keĩsti* ir *keĩstis*. Be to, ir pats *džiaugti* galėjo būti pradėtas vartoti ir intranzityvumui reikšti, plg. *randa sesulę džiaugiančią*. Greta *džiaugti, džiaugtis* susikūrus inchoatyviniam veiksmažodžiui *džiùgti* (*nudžiùgti, pradžiùgti*) ir pasidarius iš jo būdvardį *džiugùs* 'geros nuotaikos, kas greit džiaugiasi' iš pastarojo buvo išvestas kauzatyvinis veiksmažodis *džiùginti* 'daryti džiugiu', kuris beveik visuotinai išstūmė iš vartosenos senesnį kauzatyvinį veiksmažodį *džiaugti*, dabar jau labai retai pasitaikantį lietuvių kalbos tarmėse.

Dabar, tiesa, *džiaugti* ar *džiaugtis*, atrodo, visame lietuvių kalbos areale tevartojama tik sąvokai, susijusiai su džiaugsmu, reikšti. Kokia kita tų veiksmažodžių reikšmė jau nepasitaiko. Tačiau juk ir šaknies *daug-* žodžiai lietuvių kalbos areale dabar tevartojami tik kiekybiniam daugumui reikšti, ir ankstesnė jų reikšmė, susijusi su stiprumu, drūtumu, jau nepasitaiko, išskyrus toponomastiką, kur dar tą reikšmę galima įžiūrėti (ją rekonstruoti), plg. pavardes *Daugáitis, Daũgalas, Daũgelas, Daugė̃lė, Daugė̃lis, Daugė̃nis, Daũgertis, Daugė̃là, Daugelas, Daũgilas, Daugìlis, Daugìnas, Daũgininkas,*

Daugìnis, Daugiñtas, Dáugis, Daũgšas, Daugšà, Daugùdis, Daũgulis, Daugvilà, vietovardį *Daũgai* ir pan.

Kad *džiaugti* anksčiau galėjo turėti ir kitokių reikšmių, be aukščiau nurodytų dalykų, dar rodo ir kai kurie šaknies *džiug-* (< *djug-*), tegalėjusios su balsių kaita susiformuoti tik iš *djaug-* (< *deug-*), žodžiai. Tai visų pirma liet. prieveiksmis *džiugais* 'būriais' (*eina žmonės džiugais* LKŽ II 736). Dėl jo ankstesnės reikšmės plg. kad ir s. ind. *bhūri-* 'viel, reichlich, groß, häufig' ir liet. *būrỹs.* Vargu galima atsieti taip pat liet. *džiugėti* 'gausti, žvagėti' (*džiuga dangus ir žemė* Rietavas), *džiugesys* 'gaudimas' nuo *džiugėtis* 'džiaugtis, linksmintis' ir *džiugesỹs* 'džiaugsmas', kadangi gaudimas gali asocijuotis su džiaugsmu, linksmumu, plg. liet. *ū̃žti* 'gausti ošti' ir *ū̃žti* 'siausti, linksmintis, gerti'. Čia tikriausiai priklauso ir lat. *dudzēt* 'dröhnen', turįs senesnę šaknies formą (**dug-*), plg. *zeme dudz.* Reikšmė 'gausti, žvagėti' gali būti išriedėjusi iš reikšmės 'liestis, spaustis, susidurti, pataikyti'. O pastaroji gali būti išlikusi šiuose baltiškos šaknies **deug- / *doug- / *dug-* giminaičiuose; *dáukštelėti* 'suduoti, kaukštelėti', *dùkšterti* 'bastelėti, durstelėti' (*mán šiáudas akiñ dùkšterėjo*), *dùkstelti, dùkstelėti* 'bakstelėti, stumtelėti, kumštelėti' (*su alkūne į pašónę dùkstelėti*), *duksnóti* 'bildenti' (*lazdukè į žẽmę duksnójo*), *dùkt* (*širdìs dùkt dùkt plãka*). Turint galvoje tik ką paminėtus veiksmažodžius, liet. *daug* ir lat. *daudz* siejimas su got. *daug* 'συμφέρει', s. isl. *duga,* s. angl. *dugan,* s. v. a. *tugan* 'nützen, taugen' (greta s. angl. *duguþ,* s. fryz. *dugeth,* s. v. a. *tugund, tuht* 'Tüchtigkeit, Brauchbarkeit'), gr. τυγγάνειν 'pataikyti (į tikslą), gauti, pasiekti, susidurti, atsitiktinai susitikti', gr. τεύχειν 'statyti, kurti', darosi labiau suprantamas[12].

Išnašos

1. BB, XXIV, 280.

2. E. Fraenkel, *Litauisches etymologisches Wörterbuch,* Heidelberg–Göttingen, 1955 tt., 117.

3. K. Mühlenbacha *Latviešu valodas vārdnīca,* Rediģējis, papildinājis, turpinājis J Endzelīns, I, Rīgā, 1923–1925, 694 (toliau — ME). Dėl lat. *žaudzîtiês* 'sich aufdrängen; liebevoll um einen herumsein, liebkosen, umarmen, küssen; einander liebkosen', žr ME IV, 793.

4. Chr. S. Stang, *Vergleichende Grammatik der Baltischen Sprachen,* Oslo–Bergen–Tromsö, 1966, 73 f.

5. E. Berneker, *Slavisches etymologisches Wörterbuch,* I, Heidelberg, 1924, 217.

6. Žr. E. Fraenkel, *op. cit.,* 84.

7. M. Vasmer, *Russisches etymologisches Wörterbuch,* Heidelberg, 1950 ff., 379 (= Э. Фасмер, Этимологический словарь русского языка, I, Москва, 1964, 550).

8. K. Būga, *Rinktiniai raštai,* I, Vilnius, 1958, 274.

9. ME III, 20.

10. E. Blesse, „Zur Etymologie des lett. FLN Dauguva 'Düna' ", *Studi Baltici* IX, 188.

11. B. Jēgers, „Verkannte Bedeutungsverwandtschaften baltischer Wörter", *KZ* LXXX, 114 tt.

12. Dėl siejimo žr. E. Fraenkel, *op. cit.*, 84 (ir ten nurodytą literatūrą).

Lith. *džiaũgtis* 'to be glad, to rejoice at' and its Cognates

Lith. *džiaũgtis* has no satisfactory etymology. In this paper an attempt is made to establish its kinship with Lith. *daũg*, Latv. *daũdz* 'much, many', Lith. *dùksas* 'strong, powerful, corpulent', Latv. *pa-dũgt* 'to be able, to be in time' and other derivatives of the Baltic root *daug-*, formerly denoting 'strong, powerful, great'. The transitive verb **deugti* (>Lith. *džiaũgti*), corresponding to Latv. (*pa*)-*dũgt*, could have the meaning 'to enable', or 'to make strong, to make content, to gladden'. For instance, in the sentence *jis manè džiaũgia, kad gaus vietą* 'he gladdens me by getting a job' the verb *džiaugia*, now used in the same meaning as *džiùgina*, formerly could mean 'he makes somebody strong or content'; cf. the verb *drūtenti* (: *drūtas* 'strong, powerful, corpulent') in the sentence *pratark, sūneli, meilų žodelį, sudrūtenk, sūneli, mano galvelę* 'say a pleasant word, sonny, make my head strong (i.e. comfort me), sonny'. In Lithuanian one can find cases when satisfaction, gladness, joyfulness, gaiety are associated with strength, health, cf. also OI *mahān* 'great, large, extensive, powerful, venerable' and *maháyati* 'animates, strengthens, gladdens, honours, glorifies', *mahīyatē* 'he is glad, he rejoices', etc. In this paper the Baltic root **deug-/*daug-/ *dug-* is considered to be akin to that in Lith. adv. *džiugaĩs* 'in groups, in flocks', Lith. *džiugėti*, Latv. *dudzêt* 'to ring, to sound, to toll', Lith. *dùkšterti*, *dáukštelėti* 'to knock slightly', etc.

VALENTIN KIPARSKY

Altpreußische Miszellen

Eingedenk der vor fünfunddreißig Jahren in Jānis Endzelīns' Seminar gemeinsam verbrachten Stunden möchte ich unserem verehrten Jubilar einen
baltistischen Gruß entbieten und wähle zu diesem Zweck das Altpreußische,
das allen Baltologen als lieber Verstorbener besonders ans Herz gewachsen
ist.

1. Hartknoch und Komenský

In den etwas wehmütigen Darstellungen der Geschichte der preußischen
Sprache, die „wesentlich die Geschichte ihres Unterganges und ihrer Umbildung unter der Einwirkung des Deutschen" ist, werden von Bezzenberger[1]
bis Mažiulis[2] zwei Aussagen des ostpreußischen Historikers Christoph Hartknoch (1644 – 3.1.1687) zitiert: 1) „Deindè non in uno sed in pluribus adhuc
pagis passim reperiuntur hujus lingvae gnari"[3], und 2) „Denn es ist itzt kein
eintziges Dorff mehr übrig in welchem alle Leute die Alt-Preussische Sprache
auch nur verstehen solten: sondern hier und dort sollen noch einige alte
Leute seyn, so dieselbe verstehen."[4] — Die erstere Aussage vom Jahre 1679
klingt, worauf m. W. noch niemand aufmerksam geworden ist, wie eine
Berichtigung einer Behauptung, es gebe nur noch ein einziges Dorf, wo
Preußisch verstanden werde. Diese Berichtigung kann sich jedoch nicht auf
die nächstvorhergehende Nachricht über das Preußische beziehen, denn
diese letztere lautete folgendermaßen: „... die alte Preusche Sprach, welche
noch in Preussen, bey etlichen Leuten, im Fischhausischen, Schackischen
vnd Labiawschen an der Seekant, vnd Curischem Haff gebräuchlich"
(1625)[5]. Zwischen 1625 und 1679 muß es also noch wenigstens eine Nachricht über das Fortleben des Preußischen in einem einzigen Dorf gegeben
haben, die Hartknoch einer Berichtigung für würdig erachtet hatte. Ich
glaube eine solche Nachricht gefunden zu haben. Der bekannte tschechische
protestantische Theologe und Pädagoge Ján Amos Komenský (Comenius)
lebte während seiner abenteuerlichen Emigrantenzeit u. a. vom Herbst 1642
bis zu Anfang des Jahres 1648 in dem damals unter schwedischer Herrschaft

stehenden ostpreußischen Elbing. Das sogenannte Elbinger Vokabular war damals noch nicht gefunden worden, aber Komenský war für Sprachen überhaupt interessiert und hatte über das in Samland noch vegetierende Preußisch erfahren. An einer Stelle seiner Didactica schreibt er über „aussterbende" Sprachen, von denen man nicht wisse, ob man sie zu den toten oder zu den lebenden rechnen soll, und setzt dann fort: „Exemplo sit *Vetus Prutenica*, totô genere ab aliis Europaeis diversa: quae ita nunc usurpari desiit, ut cum ante annos centum complures etiam fuerint eâ utentes (quorum causâ Pastores aliqvammulti in Ducali Borussia fuerunt alendi, extatque Catechismus Lutheri, Ducis Alberti jussu in eam lingvam translatus, et Regiomonti Anno 1545, typis exscriptus) jam non nisi unicus superesse dicitur pagus, in quo vix aliqvot viri senes eam lingvam intelligunt."[6] Hartknochs „non in uno sed in pluribus adhuc pagis" bezieht sich ganz klar auf Komenskýs „jam non nisi unicus superesse dicitur pagus", eine Nachricht, die Komenský wohl vom Hörensagen hatte. Es ist wahrscheinlich, daß er in Elbing ein Exemplar des I. oder des II. Katechismus vom Jahre 1545 gesehen hatte und als gewiegter Kenner der meisten europäischen Sprachen sofort bemerkte, daß die „*Vetus Prutenica* totô genere ab aliis Europaeis diversa" war, aber er ist, soweit bekannt, weder selbst in Samland gewesen noch hat er das Enchiridion vom Jahre 1561 gekannt.

2. Altpr. *powijstin* (Akk.) 'Ding'

Dieses Wort ist im Enchiridion vom J. 1561 gut belegt: *kirscha wissan powijstin* 'vber alle ding' (10 mal); *kai dei pirsdau wissan powijstin* 'das man für allen dingen'; *stas aupallai ainan labban powijstin* 'der findet was guts' (= ein gutes Ding); *en wissans poweistins* 'in allen dingen'. Die Etymologie dieses Wortes ist jedoch völlig unsicher: nach Trautmann ist es „hergeleitet von einem unklaren Verb **po-wîst* (Wz. *wis-* oder *wid-*, *wit-*)"[7]; nach Endzelīns ist es „nezinâmas cilmes vârds; varbūt īsti: 'Erscheinung', sal. la. *pavîdêt* 'flüchtig erscheinen' und lei. *pavîdalas* 'Bild, Gestalt'"[8]. Weitere Erklärungsversuche sind mir nicht bekannt.

Die äußerliche Übereinstimmung des altpr. *powijsti-*, *poweisti-* mit dem gemeinslav. *pověstь* (altbulg. und altruss. повѣсть 'Bericht, Ruf, Erzählung, Gespräch u. a.', russ. повесть 'Novelle, Kurzroman', poln. *powieść* 'Roman', altpoln. 'Erzählung, Rede, Sage; Ruf; Nachricht, Ausspruch', tschech. *povêst* 'Erzählung, Nachricht, Histörchen; Sage, Gerücht', skr. *pòvest* 'Geschichte, Erzählung', bulg. повест 'Erzählung'; die Bedeutung 'Kurzroman' stammt aus dem Russischen) ist jedoch so auffällig, daß ich diese Wörter trotz der verschiedenen Bedeutungen nicht voneinander trennen möchte.

Die konsequente Schreibung mit -ij- (einmal -ei-, was die im Dialekt der Katechismen häufige Diphthongierung des langen -i- bezeichnet[9] deutet mit Sicherheit auf einen langen Vokal, so daß man von einem balt. $*p°/_a$-vĭd-tis ausgehen muß, während im Slavischen ein sekundär nach dem Präsens des Verbums věděti (vgl. altpr. waidimai 'wir wissen') umgestaltetes *po-věd-tь vorliegt[10]. Was den Bedeutungsunterschied anbetrifft, so verweise ich auf die folgenden bekannten Parallelen: altpoln. rzecz 'Rede usw.' → poln. rzecz 'Sache, Angelegenheit, Ding'; lat. causa 'Grund, Ursache, Rechtssache, Prozeß u. a.' > frz. chose 'Ding, Sache'; d. Sache < ahd. sahha 'Rechtshandel, Streit', vgl. ahd. sahhan 'streiten'; d. Ding < ahd. ding 'Volksversammlung', vgl. d. dingen 'jemanden durch Lohn zu seiner Verfügung gewinnen', bedingen; finn. juttu 'Geschichte, Anekdote, Angelegenheit, Sache', ursprünglich 'Gespräch', vgl. finn. jutella 'sprechen', estn. ütelda, mordw. joftams 'sagen'. Ob dagegen lat. rēs ursprünglich auch 'Wort, Rede' bedeutet hatte, wie Prusík glaubte[11], ist keinesfalls sicher. — Die ursprüngliche Bedeutung des altpr. powijsti- war wohl 'Bericht, Erzählung' und es ist nicht ausgeschlossen, daß die poln. Bedeutungsentwicklung das Altpreußische ebenso beeinflußt hat, wie sie im 14.–15. Jh. die westrussische Kanzleisprache zum Gebrauch des russ. печь im Sinne von 'Sache, Ding' veranlaßt hatte[12].

3. Lautwandel oder Lautwechsel tl/kl?

Es gilt als sicher, daß die schwankende Vertretung des idg. tl, (dl) im Altpreußischen bald als tl bald als kl auf mundartlichem Unterschied beruht, und unser Jubilar erklärt diesen im Litauischen und Lettischen regelmäßig, im Altpreußischen sporadisch vorkommenden Übergang tl, dl > kl, gl durch Differentiation[13]. In einem Fall, wo im Altpreußischen anlautendes tl- mit kl- zu wechseln scheint (clokis 'Bär', caltestisklokis 'Zeidelbär' ~ Ortsname Tlokunpelk „Bärensumpf"), ist in den entsprechenden Wörtern lit. lokỹs, lett. lácis 'Bär' das anlautende *t- oder *k- überhaupt geschwunden. Fraenkel nimmt an[14], daß hier ein *tlākis zu *klākis geworden, wonach das erste k „durch Dissimilation" geschwunden sei. Mit recht bemerkt dazu unser Jubilar[15], daß diese Annahme zwar möglich, aber kaum notwendig ist.

Es ist interessant, daß es ähnliche Fälle in anderen, nicht nahe verwandten Sprachen gibt. So geht z. B. rum. clacă 'Frohne, Robott; Feldarbeit an Feiertagen, die nicht bezahlt, sondern durch einen Schmaus quittiert wird, baltend. Talkus' mit Sicherheit auf skr. tlaka 'id.' zurück. Hier liegt also wohl Differentiation tl > kl, aber kein Schwund des anlautenden k- vor, obwohl die Struktur des rum. und des balt. Wortes sehr ähnlich ist. Die merkwürdige Instabilität der anlautenden *tl-*, *dl-* dürfte innersprachliche (organgenetische?) Ursachen haben und ich glaube, einen Hinweis auf diese Ursachen im folgenden Passus gefunden zu haben: „In some varieties of American English the segments [k] and [t] are in free variation with each other when they occur initially before voiceless [L], e.g. in *clear, clean, class*, etc., all pronounced by speakers of these dialects indifferently with [kL-] and with [tL-].“[16] Neigt also das [l] zum Stimmtonverlust, so werden offensichtlich [k] und [t] davor „neutralisiert“ und können dann entweder als [k] oder als [t] aufgefaßt werden, oder auch als überflüssige Varianten („Allophonen“) ganz schwinden.

Anmerkungen

1. A. Bezzenberger, *Göttingische gelehrte Anzeigen* 1874, 1233 f., 1875, 1142.

2. Vytautas Mažiulis, *Prūsų kalbos paminklai*, Vilnius, 1966, 25.

3. *Selectae dissertationes historicae de variis rebus Prussicis, Opera et studio Christophori Hartknoch*, Anno MDCLXXIX, p. 84; Zur richtigen Datierung dieses Werkes vgl. Mažiulis a. a. O., Fußnote 118. Die Datierung 1689 (so z. B. bei Trautmann, vgl. unten, Fußnote 7) ist schon aus dem Grunde unwahrscheinlich, weil Hartknoch am 3. Januar 1687 gestorben war.

4. *Alt- und Neues Preussen ...* Durch M. Christophorum Hartknoch, Franckfurt und Leipzig, Anno MDCLXXXIV, p. 91.

5. Zitiert nach Mažiulis a. a. O., Fußnote 117.

6. *J. A. Comenii Didacticorum operum pars II. Ea comprehendens qvae ab Anno 1642 ad 1650 scripta et edita fuére.* Caput III, 18.

7. Reinhold Trautmann, *Die altpreußischen Sprachdenkmäler*, Göttingen, 1910, 407.

8. J. Endzelīns, *Senprūšu valoda. Ievads, gramatika un leksika*, Rīgā, 1943, 233.

9. Ibid. § 12.

10. Vgl. Reinhold Trautmann, *Baltisch-slavisches Wörterbuch*, Göttingen, 1923, 338 und Max Vasmer, *Russisches etymologisches Wörterbuch, I*, Heidelberg, 1953, 192.

11. Franz Prusík, *KZ*, XXXV, 597.

12. Beispiele bei I. I. Sreznevskij, *Materijaly dlja slovarja drevne-russkago jazyka*, Sanktpeterburg, 1903, III, 225.

13. Chr. S. Stang, *Vergleichende Grammatik der Baltischen Sprachen*, Oslo, 1966, 107.

14. Ernst Fraenkel, *Litauisches etymologisches Wörterbuch*, Heidelberg, 1962, s. v. *lokỹs*.

15. Vgl. Fußnote 13.

16. Bernard Bloch, zitiert von Archibald A. Hill in *Language*, XLIII, 205.

Old Prussian Miscellany

1. Hartknoch and Komenský

Among the sources of the history of Old Prussian and its decline an important place is occupied by the statement of Christoph Hartknoch, of 1679: ,,Deindè non in uno sed in pluribus adhuc pagis passim reperiuntur huius lingvae gnari.`` This passage sounds like a reply to somebody who would have it that there was only one village left where Old Prussian was still spoken. I presume that this person was Ján Amos Komenský (Comenius) who spent the years 1642–48 in Elbing (East Prussia) and wrote that there was ,,non nisi unicus ... pagus`` where Old Prussian was still spoken.

2. Old Prussian *powijstin* (Acc.) 'thing'

Old Prussian *powijsti-* 'thing' ($<*p^\circ/_\mathrm{a}\text{-}vid\text{-}tis$) corresponds to Common Slavic *pověstь* 'story' ($<*po\text{-}věd\text{-}tь$). The semantic development was probably the same as in Polish *rzecz* 'speech' → 'thing, object', in German *Sache* < Old High Germ. *sahha* 'lawsuit', *Ding* 'thing, object' < Old High Germ. *ding* 'meeting', in French *chose* 'thing, object' < Latin *causa* 'lawsuit, etc.'.

3. Sound Change or alteration *tl/kl*?

The reason for the sporadic change of *tl*, *dl* into *kl*, *gl* in Old Prussian might have been the same as that which Bernard Bloch had found in some varieties of American English: the segments [k] and [t] are in free variation with each other when they occur initially before voiceless [L], so that e.g. *clear, clean, class*, etc. are pronounced with [kL-] and with [tL-] indifferently.

ANTANAS KLIMAS

Baltic, Germanic and Slavic

In his recent and excellent monograph on the relationship of the Baltic and Slavic languages,[1] S. Karaliūnas makes a very important statement:

> "Baltic-Germanic, Slavic-Germanic and Baltic-Slavic-Germanic isoglosses permit us, seemingly, to draw the following conclusion: most probably, the Baltic and the Slavic languages originated from different dialects of the Northern dialect area of the Indo-European speech community. Initially, the "Baltic" dialects may have had closer contacts with the "Germanic" dialects. If it had been the case that Baltic and Slavic languages had originated from one dialect of the Northern Indo-European dialect area, then most definitely the Baltic-Germanic isoglosses would not have occurred, since they then would have encompassed the area of the Slavic languages, too."

This is not a completely new statement. Several linguists had hinted at a similar ancient relationship of these three Indo-European language groups. However, the chronological implications in Karaliūnas' statement are very strong, very clear: before the dialect or dialects from which the Baltic languages eventually emerged came into contact with the dialect or dialects from which eventually Slavic languages emerged, these Baltic dialects were in closer contact with the Germanic dialect area. Since in my opinion this is really the case, then several old notions and hypotheses about the structure and the spread of the Proto-Indo-European language or languages—or even dialects—may have to be abandoned, including many notions about the early interrelationship of many Indo-European dialects, such as Germanic and Celtic, Germanic-Celtic-Italic, etc.

The aim of this article is not to go into a discussion of details, i.e., the linguistic data proper, but to outline some fundamental notions concerning this whole knot of problems.

First of all, let us look at the "negative" side of this problem, that is, at the things that should no longer be done, or putting it a different way, at which general notions, tendencies and hypotheses have to be abandoned.

1. First of all, let us examine the non-chronological hierarchy of linguistic data: the very old and still very strong notion that some Indo-European languages are more important for positing and visualizing ancient linguistic changes and relationships. In other words, let us no longer measure almost

everything in all areas of Indo-European linguistics according to the later interrelationships of the South-Eastern Indo-European languages: Greek, Italic, Indo-Iranian, etc. It is quite clear by now that, in spite of the relatively late written documentation of the Indo-European languages of the Northern region, they often show more ancient features.[2] In spite of the general acceptance of this fact, to the present day many publications in linguistics still reflect the dominance of the Greek-Latin-Sanskrit triumvirate.[3]

2. As in the whole Proto-Indo-European area, so even in the Northern Proto-Indo-European region there is now no need in every case to reconstruct one model, let us say, for "Proto-Baltic-Germanic-Slavic". In the past this has been the undoing of some weighty theories, namely the insistence on reconstructing a dialect-free, uniform structure of Proto-Indo-European. For example, this almost caused the proponents of the Baltic and Slavic "unity" hypothesis to invent similarities.[4] It has led some linguists into ridiculous attempts of trying to reconstruct this phantom: the unprovable, untenable and non-existent "Balto-Slavic" proto-language.[5] In my considered opinion, it is untenable to account for the Baltic developments in terms of and in reference to the developments in Slavic, or vice versa.

There is no need, for example, to puzzle about the fate of the three past tenses, assumed for Proto-Indo-European, in Baltic. This has always been a vexing problem: why do the Baltic languages not show any traces of the Proto-Indo-European s-aorist? We know now that the s-aorist never existed in Baltic.[6] Nevertheless, some people still go to great lengths to locate traces of this s-aorist in Baltic.

3. In discussing the prehistoric relationships of this Northern Indo-European area, one should give up the notion of measuring their ancient interrelationships in terms of their present-day geographical, political and cultural situations. Very often, under the impact of these present-day situations, incorrect assumptions and hypotheses have been made. One example from many is given here.

In his otherwise excellent *Geschichte der deutschen Sprache*, A. Bach states: "Die genannten Gemeinsamkeiten werden in der Regel als jüngere Entlehnungen des Balt.-Slaw. aus dem Germ. angesprochen."[7] What reasons did Bach have for assuming the above cited position? I believe his opinion was clearly influenced by his knowledge that: a) the geographic area of the Baltic speakers in his day was very small in comparison with that of the speakers of Germanic languages; b) that in fact in rather recent times the Baltic languages borrowed a great many loanwords from German. For the prehistoric situation then he also considered a similar possibility; c) for decades, it was assumed that there were quite a few borrowings from Proto-Germanic into Baltic but, for some unexplained reason, that Proto-Germanic did not reciprocate by borrowing from Baltic. We now know that the number of borrowings from Proto-Germanic into Baltic was very small indeed, perhaps even non-existent.

Since the epoch-making work of Toporov and Trubačev[8] and other investigators, it is fairly obvious that at a certain point in prehistoric time the Baltic speech area was much larger than it is today. At one time it may easily have been larger than the area occupied by the speakers of the Germanic dialects of the same period. I am also convinced that around 2500–1000 B.C. the Baltic speaking area was much larger than the Slavic dialect area.

Thus, not only were Proto-Finno-Ugric peoples able to borrow Baltic words into their dialects, but it is quite possible that the Germanic and the Slavic tribes too may have borrowed words from the ancient Balts. The story of the word *kvietys* 'wheat' illustrates the case. For years nearly everybody believed it was a borrowing from Germanic. Now it has been proven to be a genuine Baltic word.

The same reasoning would apply to borrowings from Slavic into Baltic. Ever since the beginning of Indo-European linguistics, all linguists were so impressed by the number of rather recent borrowings from Slavic into Baltic that the reverse process—the Baltic borrowings into Slavic—was never seriously considered. Only now has it become possible to think that the Slavs, at that certain time when they were both less numerous and occupied a smaller area than the Balts, also took loanwords from Baltic, just as did the ancestors of the Finno-Ugric peoples.

It is thus fairly certain by now that the Slavic *rǫka* was borrowed from Proto-Baltic *ranka̅* (OPr. *rancko*, Lith. *ranka*, Latv. *ruoka*). In Slavic, the word *rǫka* cannot be connected with any ablaut series; it stands quite isolated. In Baltic, it cannot be separated from the series of: Lith. *rinkti*, *renka*, OPr. *senrinka* 'sammelt',[9] etc. A similar situation may exist with such words as *ragas* 'horn' which cannot be separated from Lith. *regėti*, *riogsoti*, etc. This phenomenon occurs not only in the lexicon, which is definitely the weakest criterion in determining the interrelationships of languages, but also in the areas of phonology, morphology and syntax.

4. Furthermore, comparative Indo-European linguistics should give up the traditional notion that Germanic languages are somehow "members" of the "western" languages, initially somewhat closer to Celtic, Italic, Latin, Greek. On the other hand, one should give up the notion that both Baltic and Slavic are the "Eastern" languages.

If it were possible to visualize Baltic, Germanic and Slavic as they were about 2000–1000 B. C., I am sure that there would be no great leap from Germanic to Baltic, etc.

5. Finally, I would like to mention one more thorny problem. Many a time in the complex of problems an important judgment was pronounced by a scholar who simply did not have enough working knowledge in all three groups; some knew only the Germanic languages first hand, others only Slavic, and so forth. A good knowledge of all the languages involved, and of their historical development, is needed here.[10]

Until now we have been looking at the negative aspect of this complex of problems, *i.e.*, what *not* to do, how *not* to do it, etc. Let us now turn to the positive aspect and take a glance at what should be done in this area.

1. First of all, a new and fundamental investigation of the Proto-Indo-European velar series should be undertaken:

$$k \quad g \quad gh$$
$$\hat{k} \quad \hat{g} \quad \hat{g}h \quad (\text{and } \hat{k}^w \quad \hat{g}^w \quad \hat{g}h^w)$$
$$k^w \quad g^w \quad g^wh$$

should be thoroughly re-investigated and determined as to their status in the various stages of Proto-Indo-European and, subsequently, in Baltic, Germanic and Slavic.[11] Only when a total picture is clear shall we be able to determine the Indo-European prototypes for Baltic, Germanic and Slavic.

2. In trying to determine the ancient relationships of Baltic, Germanic and Slavic, the newest linguistic findings should be applied. The importance of the similarities, or of common innovations, if there were any, and of the differences should be considered in approximately this order of importance: morphological, syntactic, phonological and finally lexical features. These are, of course, very often difficult to separate, especially the first three, but we know one thing: in reference to change, the most tenacious features in any language are morphological-syntactic, perhaps even the syntactic-morphological structures. Only then should the phonological features be considered. Lexical similarities and divergences have to be used with the greatest caution; the lexicon of a language is the most unstable, least reliable system.[12]

In recent years the following differences between Baltic and Slavic languages have been mentioned by various authors:

a) The ancient verbs in Baltic languages were accented differently from in Slavic. Baltic is much closer here to the verbal accentuation system of Indo-Iranian and Greek.

b) In Baltic (just as in Germanic) the *um, un, ul,* and *ur* do not always come from Proto-Indo-European *m̨, n̨, l̨, r̨.* Some of these have developed from Proto-Indo-European *ōm, ōn, ōl, ōr.* E.g., *grumzdas* < **GRŌM-*, etc.

c) The plural inessive in *-su* was not yet fully formed in Proto-Baltic. On the other hand, it was fully formed in Proto-Slavic and in Indo-Iranian.

d) In the genitive plural, the primordial ending *-ōm* was generalized in Baltic. This also occurred in Germanic, Greek and Indo-Iranian, but in Slavic (and in Celtic, Umbrian, etc.) it was the *-om* which was generalized.

e) Baltic had a completely different ending of the instrumental singular in the feminine nouns of the i-stem: *-im(i), -ia, -e, -i.* Here Slavic had *-ьjǫ.*

f) In Baltic (as well as in Germanic, Italic and Greek) there once existed neuter nouns of the consonantal stems which in accusative singular and in nominative singular had the ending *-i.* No traces of such nouns can be found in Slavic.

g) In the ancient river names, Baltic (as well as Illyrian and Celtic) had frequent doublets: *up-/ap-.* No traces of this can be found in Slavic.

h) The deiotation processes occurred completely independently and at different times in Baltic and Slavic. Prof. Henning Andersen states this as follows:

"The chronology of the lenitions unequivocally shows that the Common Slavic Deiotation took place after the Second Palatalization. Thus the theory proposed by Kuryłowicz (1956: 227–43), that the Deiotation is a shared Balto-Slavic innovation, is irreconcilable with the Slavic facts."[13]

3. All dialect studies in these three groups should be carried out as soon as possible. Some relic linguistic features are bound to be discovered this way. One has only to read a few pages of the newest historical grammar of Lithuanian (J. Kazlauskas, *Lietuvių kalbos istorinė gramatika,* Vilnius, 1968), where dialect material is used extensively, to be immensely impressed by the importance of dialect studies.[14]

4. The whole complex problem of the accentuation systems of Baltic, Germanic and Slavic has to be re-investigated from the very beginning with dialect data. This is very important. Even Karaliūnas has not completely gone into this. For example, he suggests:

"In the systems of the Baltic and Slavic dialects of that time such changes may have taken place: ... the opposition in intonations was formed ("the acute" versus "the circumflex")..."[15]

However, one must consider that Germanic dialects too most probably had intonational patterns in their accentuation system, as has been suggested by Eduard Sievers in several of his books and articles.

Maximum extent of the Baltic culture during the Bronze Age

From: Marija Gimbutas, *The Balts*, Frederick A. Praeger, New York, 1963, p. 63.
Reprinted with permission.

5. The immensely difficult problem of laryngeals in Baltic, Germanic and Slavic should be thoroughly explored.

6. Finally, the relationship of these three groups with other Indo-European languages should be extensively investigated. No scholar, for example, has yet taken upon himself the task of looking more deeply into the relationships of Baltic and Greek, Baltic and Italic languages, Baltic and Hittite, etc. Even the newly deciphered Mycenean Greek and the various Anatolian languages should not be forgotten.

I believe then that, with some help from modern methods of archaeology, we will be able to say much more about the three language groups of Baltic, Germanic and Slavic.

Notes

1. Simas Karaliūnas, "Kai kurie baltų ir slavų kalbų seniausiųjų santykių klausimai", *Lietuvių kalbotyros klausimai* X, 94.

2. E.g., all the efforts spent in searching for the remnants of the various Proto-Indo-European past tenses in Baltic. Cf. also J. Kazlauskas, *Lietuvių kalbos istorinė gramatika*, Vilnius, 1968, 287 ff.

3. At many a university, Indo-European studies are actually studies in Greek-Latin-Sanskrit, adding a few other facts from some other languages once in a while ...

4. Cf. Antanas Klimas, "Balto-Slavic, or Baltic and Slavic? (The Relationship of Baltic and Slavic Languages)", *Lituanus* XIV, No. 2, 5–35; also Simas Karaliūnas, *op. cit.*

5. The most extreme example of this, I believe, can be seen in the following book: W. J. Entwistle and W. A. Morison, *Russian and the Slavonic Languages*, London, 1949. Cf. my discussion of this in "Balto-Slavic, or Baltic and Slavic?", *op. cit.*, p. 28.

6. See footnote 2. Cf. further J. Kazlauskas, *op. cit.*, p. 135.

7. A. Bach, *Geschichte der deutschen Sprache*, 5. Aufl., Heidelberg, 1953, p. 34.

8. Cf. V. N. Toporov and O. N. Trubachev, *Lingvisticheskij analiz gidronimov verkhnego podneprov'ja*, Moscow, 1962; also Marija Gimbutas, *The Balts*, New York, 1963.

9. Cf. A. Sabaliauskas, "Lietuvių kalbos leksikos raida", *Lietuvių kalbotyros klausimai* VIII, 10.

10. This does not mean that every linguist who would like to work in this area has to learn to speak all these languages fluently, but he should have a good working first-hand knowledge of their structure and history.

11. All these language groups have, as far as I know, fairly complete etymological dictionaries. These dictionaries could very well be the starting point for a complete investigation.

12. It had been noted recently by several linguists that there are cases when the vocabulary is completely replaced by a vocabulary borrowed from other languages, the morphological patterns, however, remain almost completely intact.

13. Henning Andersen, *Language* XLV, 572.

14. Cf. J. Kazlauskas, *Lietuvių kalbos istorinė gramatika*, *op. cit.*, 154 ff.

15. Simas Karaliūnas, "Kai kurie baltų ir slavų kalbų seniausiųjų santykių klausimai", *op. cit.*, 94–95.

JOHANN KNOBLOCH

Zu apr. *Wissaseydis* 'Dienstag'

Der im Elbinger Vokabular in der Reihe der Wochentagsnamen aufge-
zählte Dienstag (*Wissaseydis*) birgt eine Reihe von Problemen, die hier
wohl kaum gelöst werden können, doch mögen sie wenigstens aufgezeigt
werden.

Von zwei Seiten[1] ist versucht worden, die Schreibung *Wissaseydis* in
wissaweydis zu emendieren, wobei sich die Annahme eines Missverständ-
nisses von poln. *wtorek* als Erklärung anbietet, was 'Dienstag' und 'allesamt'
heißen kann. Es wäre dann also in die Reihe der Wochentagsnamen selt-
samerweise ein Adverb (*wissaweidin* 'eitel; ganz und gar'; *wissawidei*
'allesamt') aufgenommen worden, eine Vermutung, die J. J. Mikkola, *Studi
baltici* 3 (1933) 131–133 ablehnt. J. Endzelin[2] stellt fest, das Wort habe keine
sichere Etymologie, R. Trautmann[3] gibt keine Erklärung an.

Die Zerlegung in *wiss-aseydis*, die Mikkola vornimmt, erlaubt die Verbindung mit lett. *azaîds* 'Mittagsmahl; Zwischenmahlzeit zwischen Frühstück und Mittagsmahl; Frühstück; Vesperbrot; Abendbrot; Mahlzeit
überhaupt; Zukost'. Diese vielen Bedeutungen lassen auf einen Ausgangspunkt 'Imbiss' (russ. *zakuska*) schließen. Die Verbindung mit lett. *àizêst*
'etwas (vor der Hauptmahlzeit) essen' lässt den Sinn der Vorsilbe erkennen,
schwieriger ist (trotz Endzelin in *ME* I, s. v. *azaîds*) die Zerlegung in **aza-
ẹ̃ds*, da die Lautentwicklung in der Wortfuge anders verlaufen wäre, wie
mir Frau Edite Šturma-Hauzenberga freundlicherweise nachwies. Man wird
deshalb versuchen, eine Zerlegung in *az-aids* glaubhaft zu machen.

Eine diphthongische Wurzel **oid(h)-* für 'essen' lässt sich für den baltischen
und slawischen Bereich durchaus annehmen. Für die Erklärung des Anlauts
von aksl. *jadъ* 'Gift' denkt E. Berneker an eine Vermischung der Wurzel
*oid- 'schwellen' mit der Wortsippe von *ĕmь*, *ĕsti* 'essen'. Aber wegen seiner
Bedeutung passt das Wort für Gift schlecht zu gr. οἰδάω 'schwelle'; zusammen mit aksl. *jadъ* 'Speise' (das im Anlaut gleichfalls auf **oi-* zurückweist)
lässt es sich vielmehr zunächst als **oidhos*, **oidhis* 'Speise' mit lett. *az-aids*
(**aĝh-oidhos* 'Zu-speise') und apr. *wissaseydis* (**uik̂-aĝh-oidh-ios*), dann mit
gr. κακ-ιθής· ἄτροφος ἄμπελος 'schlecht genährt' (was ja das Interpretament
eigentlich besagt), κακιθές· χαλεπόν, λιμηρές, beides Hesychglossen, verbin-

den[4]. Bei Annahme einer Dublette *oit-* könnte auch lat. *ūtor* 'gebrauche', gr. ἀναισιμόω 'benütze, verzehre' hergehören[5]. Die Erklärung dafür, dass apr. *wissaseydis* allein die sonst bekannte Reihe der Wochentagsnamen slawischer (und sicher polnischer) Herkunft unterbricht[6], sieht Mikkola darin, dass es in Osteuropa schon vor der Einführung des Christentums eine eigene Woche gegeben habe, die über den Kaukasus möglicherweise aus den Kulturzentren Vorderasiens gekommen sei.

Hier möchte ich aber zu überlegen geben, dass ein solches Reliktwort gegenüber der Gepflogenheit, besonders wichtige Tage späterhin abweichend von der sonstigen Zählung (oder der Planetenwoche) zu benennen, eine geringere Wahrscheinlichkeit für sich hat. Die Bildung *vis-azaidis* heißt wohl (Tag der) *Allmahlzeit. Sie könnte den Tag bezeichnen, wo man unbesorgt seinen Hunger stillen und alle Zwischenmahlzeiten einnehmen durfte. Dies wiese aber auf das christliche Fastengebot hin, das gerade in Polen am strengsten beobachtet wurde: Oprócz postów od kościola nakazanych, pobożni pościli poniedziałki, środy, piątki i soboty[7]. Da blieb in der Tat neben dem Donnerstag nur der Dienstag übrig. Gerade dieser wurde aber besonders für Hochzeiten bevorzugt. In der baltischen Volkskunde tritt dies, wie mir Frau E. Šturma vielfach belegte, zwar nicht in Erscheinung, aber aus dem weit verbreiteten Brauch (vgl. HDA II 252) ließe sich doch ein Rückschluss für das alte Preußen konstruieren, zumal, wenn hier auch wieder das polnische Vorbild wirksam gewesen wäre.

Nachwort

Der freundliche Hinweis von Frau E. Šturms auf den Artikel V. Kiparsky „Vorchristliches im altpreußischen Kalender" in *Baltistica* IV (2), 247–252, erfordert ergänzende Bemerkungen. Der Autor sieht im Dienstag, dem auf den Montag folgenden Tag, den Überrest einer nach dem lunaren Kalender eingerichteten vorchristlichen Woche. Bei der Bedeutung, die er hierzu dem Mond-tag beimisst, wäre zunächst die Bewahrung dieses Namens in der Reihe der Wochentage zu fordern. Auch müsste, etwa aus dem beigezogenen Baschkirischen, Tschuwassischen oder Wotjakischen die Benennung 'Mond-Tag' für den Ausgangspunkt dieser Zählweise nachgewiesen und die Unabhängigkeit von der Planetenwoche dargetan werden. Die semantische Motivation für 'Tag des großen Mittagsmahles' lässt sich nicht mit dem Hinweis darauf stützen, dass die Ostvölker den Dienstag als Tag des Aufbruchs zu Reiterexpeditionen verwandt und ihn danach benannt haben. „Dass vor einer Reiterexpedition Pferde und Mannschaft besonders gut verpflegt werden müssen, weiß jeder gediente Soldat." Aber hat man etwa

am Tage des Aufbruchs noch bis in den Nachmittag hinein den Tafel-
freuden gehuldigt? Der Autor scheint selbst dieser Ausdeutung keine Beweiskraft beizumessen, wenn er anschließend mit der gleichen vorchristlichen Herkunft auch noch die Deutung von sawayte aus $sa + wait(i\bar{a}t) \sim$
altruss. sъvětъ „Ratsversammlung" rechtfertigt. — Die Herleitung der altpreußischen Wochentagsnamen aus dem Altpolnischen gelingt nicht ohne
lautliche und formale Schwierigkeiten. Man sollte nicht ausser Acht lassen,
dass Adalbert von Prag schon vor der Jahrtausendwende bei den Preußen
missioniert hat. Auch bei einem Rückfall ins Heidentum können die übernommenen Wochentagsnamen fortgelebt haben. Man sollte also vielmehr
das Alttschechische zum Vergleich heranziehen.

Anmerkungen

1. E. Benveniste, *Studi baltici* II, 82 f.; A. Brückner, *KZ XLIV*, 332.

2. J. Endzelīns, *Senprūšu valoda*, Rīgā, 1943 s. v.

3. R. Trautmann, *Die altpreussischen Sprachdenkmäler*, Göttingen, 1910, s. v.

4. Die Verbindung des ersten Bestandteils mit got. *hūhrus* 'Hunger' wäre dann unnötig; dass ein ἄτροφος ἄμπελος statt 'schlecht genährt' vielmehr „hunger-brennend"
sein sollte, wie dies nach der Etymologie von A. Bezzenberger *BB IV*, 357, der W.
Schulze *KZ XXIX*, 269 zugestimmt hat, der Fall sein müsste, ist semantisch wenig
überzeugend.

5. Die archaische Rechtsformel *ūsus frūctus* käme dieser Grundbedeutung entgegen, wobei das Hysteron proteron durch Winklers Aleph-Beth-Regel der Aufeinander-
folge in Zwillingsformeln (*tagenbaren* „[in Bremen] erzogen und geboren") bedingt
wäre.

6. *nadele, ponadele, wissaseydis, possissawaite, ketwirtice, pentinx, sabatico.*

7. Rok polski w życiu, tradycyi i pieśni, hrsg. v. Z. Gloger, Warschau, 1900, S. 128.

On Old Prussian *wissaseydis* 'Tuesday'

An explanation is still lacking for the fact that, of the days of the week, only
Tuesday retained a native name in Old Prussian, the others reflecting
borrowing from Old Polish (or perhaps Old Czech?). The reason may be that
a Christian custom gave rise to a designation for this day of the week. Since
one had to fast on Mondays, Wednesdays, Fridays and Saturdays, the
faithful who wished to observe these restrictions had little more than Tuesday on which to eat well. For this reason, *wiss-aseydis* can be explained as
"all meals".

STANISŁAW FRANCISZEK KOLBUSZEWSKI

Einige slawische Wörter in den sog. ostlettischen Mundarten

(Randbemerkungen zum *Litauischen etymologischen Wörterbuch* von E. Fraenkel)

1. *Ostlettisch* (= streng hochlettisch) werden diejenigen hochlettischen Maa. genannt, die den Übergang *ie* > *ī*, *uo* > *ū* kennen; vgl. J. Endzelīns, *Lettische Grammatik* 5 (= *Latviešu valodas gramatika* 14), M. Rudzīte, *Latviešu dialektoloģija*, 259 f. Die Verteilung der sog. ostlettischen Maa. wird auf der beiliegenden Karte gezeigt, wobei die Forschungsergebnisse von V. Rūķe, „Latgales izlokšņu grupējums", *FBR* XIX, 133 ff., J. Kuškis, „Dažas sēļu valodas vokālisma īpatnības pēc mūsdienu latviešu valodas sēlisko izlokšņu materiāliem", *Latviešu valodas apcerējumi*, 9 ff. und M. Rudzīte, Латышская диалектология (Автореф.), 7 ff. berücksichtigt worden sind. Siehe Karte 1.

2. Slawische Wörter, die im Lettischen vorkommen, haben im *Litauischen etymologischen Wörterbuch* von E. Fraenkel, was ihre Verteilung in den lettischen Maa. und lettischen Dialekten anbetrifft, eine nicht immer genaue und nicht immer sichere Bezeichnung: z. B. das als „lett." (= also gemeinlettisch? Verf.) angenommene *karčamnieks* ist nur einmal in dem Volkslied *LD* 21397, 3 aus Tirza in Livland (= Vidzeme) verzeichnet, d. i. also in einer selonischen, nicht ostlettischen Ma. des Hochlettischen[1]; *teslis* (II) hat die Bedeutung 'Knabe, der aus Kurzweil Holz zu behauen pflegt' allein in der infläntischen, ostlettischen Ma. Varakļāni in Lettgallen (= Latgale)[2], und das in einem Rätsellied *LD* 2400, 2 aus „ostlett." (? Verf.) Auļukalns belegte *pāns* entstammt, wie es scheint, der mittellett. Ma. von Drusti (Vidzeme)[3].

3. Die folgenden Bemerkungen stellen den Versuch dar, an Hand einiger dem Verf. z. Z. zugänglichen Werke möglichst genau die geographische Verteilung von *kărmans, kopka* und *klìnis*[2] in den ostlett. Maa. festzustellen. Gemäss E. Fraenkel (*LEW* I, 216) ist *kopka* als lettgallisch anzusehen, während *kărmans, klìnis*[2], von E. Fraenkel (LEW s. v. v.) als „lett." bezeichnet, in Wirklichkeit (fast ?) nur im Ostlettischen erscheinen. Vgl. das beiliegende Wortmaterial und die Wortkarten.

4. Aus den obigen Erörterungen geht hervor, dass es nützlich wäre, das bei Fraenkel vorkommende lett. maa. Wortmaterial slawischen Ursprungs

274

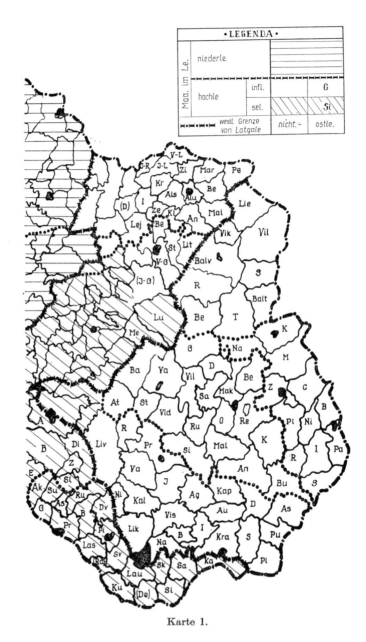

Karte 1.

einer genauen Analyse zu unterziehen, was für die etymologischen und semantischen Forschungen besonders wichtig wäre.

5. *Wortmaterial und Wortkarten*

a) *karmans* 'die Tasche = *kabata*', E. Fraenkel, *LEW* I, 322 und *EH* I,

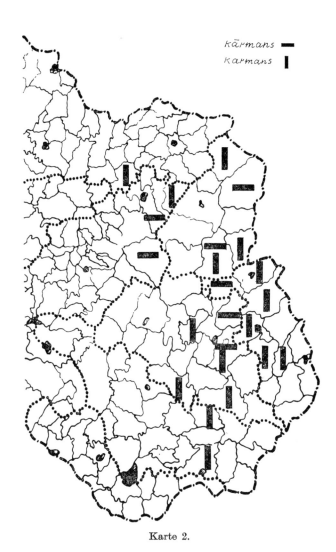

Karte 2.

589, A. Summent, *Unbeachtete slavische Lehnwörter im Lettischen* (Göttingen, 1950), 147, G. Borowsky, *Die slavischen Lehnwörter im Lettischen* (Wien, 1944).

Etymologie: nach *EH* aus russ. *karmán* 'die Tasche' (vgl. Borowsky); nach *LEW* nebst lit. *karmõnas*, aus wruss., poln. *karman, korman* 'ds' (vgl. Summent).

Geographie: die lett. Form *karmanis* (vgl. *EH*) ist nur (?) in einer einzigen Variante (*LD* 26006 Var. aus Mūrmuiža bei Kauguri in Vidzeme) im Mittellettischen belegt (vgl. auch *karmančiks* 'ein Taschendieb' in C. Chr. Ulmann,

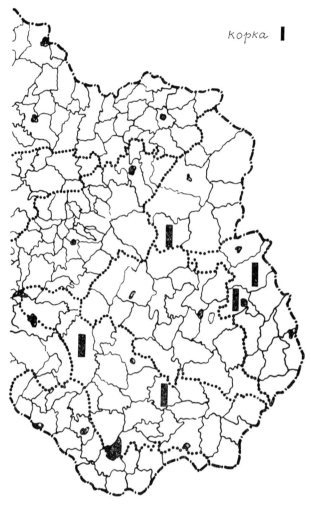

Karte 3.

Lettisch–deutsches Wörterbuch (Riga 1872), 102 und bei A. Upīts aus Skrīveri, nach D. Zemzare, *Latviešu vārdnīcas* (Riga 1961), 534).

Nur im Ostlettischen (genauer: in den infläntischen Maa. von Vidzeme und Latgale) erscheint dagegen das von E. Fraenkel als „lett.“ bezeichnete *karmans* 'die Tasche': *EH:* vgl. *LD* 26006 + Var.; Lettg. ohne Ortsangabe (P. Šmits, „Piezīmes“, *Tautas dziesmas* IV, 214), vgl. *Tdz* 48154; Zvirgzdene (A. Bezzenberger, *Lettische Dialektstudien*, Göttingen 1885, 171); Krāslava (*-ts*) (A. Alksnis, *FBR* XII, 27; *LD* 26006: Litene, Lejasciems; *Tdz* 58425:

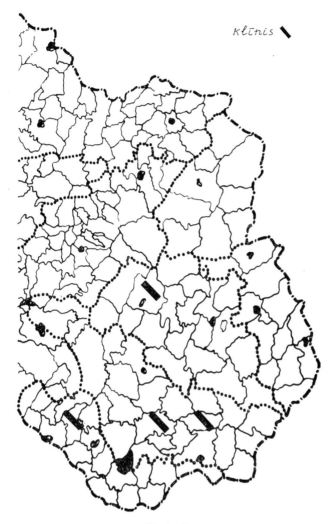

Karte 4.

vgl. Var. 11 (Andrupene), 2 (Baltinava), 3 + 7 + 14 (Kārsava), 10 (Mērdzene),
1 (Sakstagals), 15 (Silajāņi), 6 (Zvirgzdene); *Tdz* 58492: vgl. Var. 1 (Kā-
piņi), 6 (Kārsava), 0 (Liepna), 5 (Ludza [? — 605, 59, 13]), 4 + 9 + 10 (loc.
sg. *-uo*) + 12 + 14 + 18 (loc. sg. *-ņā*) + 19 (Mērdzene), 13 (Nirza), 16 + 25
(Pilda), 15 (Tilža), 7 + 26 (Zvirgzdene); *Tdz* 58503 (Rēzna).

Von den zahlreichen Varianten des Wortes (*kārmans, karmons, karmuns,
karmins, karmyns*), die auch im Ostlett. vorkommen (*Tdz* 58492 usw.)
werden hier nur diejenigen mit *-ā-* untersucht: *kārmans* 'die Tasche' — Lettg.

(*Tdz* IV, 214), Lubāna im 19. Jh. (D. Zemzare, *Latv. vārdn.* 534), Vecgulbene (*Tdz* 58494, 3), Bērzgale (*Tdz* 58492, 23), *Tdz* 58425, Var. 12 (Nautrēni), Var. 9 (Rēzna), Var. 8 (Tilža); Viļaka (*Tdz* 58494,0). Vgl. Karte 2.

b) *kopka* 'Frauenjacke = blūze': [*kapka*] vgl. E. Fraenkel, *LEW* I, 216, A. Summent 145: [*kopka*] vgl. A. Bezzenberger, *Lett. Dial.-St.*, 171, P. Šmits *Tdz* IV, 214.

Etymologie: aus poln. russ. *kapka* 'Kapuze, Kutte' (E. Fraenkel). Geographie: Lettg. (E. Fraenkel, *LEW*, A. Summent u. P. Šmits), Zvirgzdene (A. Bezzenberger, *Lett. Dial.-St.*), Mērdzene (*Tdz* 58327). Vgl. auch (nach dem Verf.): *Tdz* 58327, 3 ebenda + *Tdz* 58602 Līvāni und *Tdz* 58397, 8 (*kopkiņa*: dat. sg.) Bērzpils, *Tdz* 58412, 8 Agluona (= 605, 9, 1 ?). Vgl. Karte 3.

c) *klīnis* 1) 'kleines Stück Zeug, das man als *spēdele* benutzt', 2) 'ein keilförmiger Ausschnitt', 3) (= 1 ?) 'sevišķas iešuves zem paduses, kreklus šujot' = [*kļeini*], vgl. E. Fraenkel, *LEW* I, 272, A. Summent 150 und *EH* I, 619, V. Rūķe, *Ceļi* IX, 404.

Etymologie: nach *EH* aus poln. *klin*. Die Länge des Vokals -*ī*- ebenso der Wortausgang sprechen (nach A. Summent) eher für die Entlehnung aus russ. *klin*, nom. pl. *klin'ja* 'Keil (als Einsatz am Kleide)'. Aus poln. *klin* (E. Fraenkel, *LEW*).

Geographie: E. Fraenkel s. v. bezeichnet das Wort als „lett." Es erscheint aber nach obenerwähnten Quellen nur im Ostlett.: *klīnis*[2] Bebrenes Kaldabruņa, bei A. Sprūdžs (aus Varakļāni, vgl. M. Bukšs, *Latgaļu liter. vēsture* (1957), 590), Auleja (*EH* s. v.), Višķi (*Ceļi* IX, 404). Siehe Karte 4.

Anmerkungen

1. Zur Etymologie von *karčamnieks* vgl. Verf., „Artura Ozola diena", *Acta Baltico-Slavica* VI, 373–374 s. Anm. 6 mit Lit.; zur Geographie — D. Zemzare, *Palīgs apvidu vārdu vācējiem* VI, 4.

2. *teslis* hat im Hochlettischen verschiedene Bedeutungen: (I) = 1) 'ein Instrument zum Behauen' (Alsviķis, Varakļāni), (II) = 2) 'ein Knabe, der aus Kurzweil Holz zu behauen pflegt' (Varakļāni), s. E. Fraenkel, l.c., 3) '?' in der Redewendung *teš kā teslis* Bērzpils, 4) 'ein Säufer' Kalsnava; 'wer viel isst und trinkt' Graši, Lubāna, Jaungulbene, Stāmeriena, s. *ME* s.v.

3. Vgl. *EH* s.v. *pāns* und J. Endzelīns, *Latvijas PSR vietvārdi* I, 53.

A Few Words in the So-Called East-Latvian Vernaculars

1. The upper-Latvian vernaculars which show the changes *ie* to *ī* and *uo* to *ū* are called the East-Latvian vernaculars (= *austrumnieku izloksnes*), cf.

J. Endzelin *Le Gr* 5 (=*La Gr* 14), M. Rudzīte, *Latv dial* 259 n. Their extent is shown on map 1.

2. The Slavic words encountered in Latvian are not always precisely defined in the *Litauisches etymologisches Wörterbuch* by E. Fraenkel, as far as their spread in the Latvian dialects and vernaculars is concerned. Cf. La. *karčamnieks* 'innkeeper' (?) (*LEW* I, 221); Upper-La. *teslis* 'boy who hews wood as pastime' (*LEW* II, 1084); *pāns* 'host' from east-La. Auļukalns *LEW* I, 638); *karčamnieks* has been noted only once, in a Latvian folksong *LD* 21397, 3 of Tirza in Vidzeme, meaning in the Selonic vernacular of the non-eastern group of the Upper-La. dialect and not in Latvian generally; *teslis* in the meaning 'boy who hews wood as pastime', according to *ME* IV, 168 occurs in Varakļāni in Latgale (in the territory of former Polish Livonia), i.e. it occurs in the Inflantic vernacular of the East-Latvian group of the Upper-Latvian dialect (cf. also the footnote 2); finally *pāns* has been noted also only once, in a folk song-riddle *LD* 2400, 2 from the domain (=*muiža*) Auļukalns in the community Drusti in Vidzeme (cf. J. Endzelīns, *Latvijas PSR vietvārdi* I-1, Rīga, 1956, p. 53), i.e. in one of the vernaculars of the central Latvian dialect, and not in the East-Latvian group as such (= 'east-Latvian').

3. This article aims at trying to trace precisely the (geographical) extent of 3 Slavic words encountered in the so-called East-Latvian vernaculars, namely: *kārmans* 'pocket'; *klinis*[2] (=*spēdele*) 'a little piece of fabric, a wedge-shaped cutting'; *kopka* (=blūze) 'a blouse'. Except the last one, the above words (from the semantic group 'clothes') do not have the proper definition in the dictionary of E. Fraenkel, as far as their spread in area (and time) is concerned.

4. Thus it seems useful to investigate the Slavic borrowings noted in the *Litauisches etymologisches Wörterbuch*, both in the Upper and Lower Latvian dialects, primarily as regards their geography rather than their chronology. Often the lack of chronology and geography of a word results in the etymological explanation being only probable but in no case certain.

CZESŁAW KUDZINOWSKI

Aus dem Gebiet der Intonationen im Litauischen

Die Intonation bildet einen integralen Teil der litauischen Prosodie und hängt eng mit der Quantität zusammen. Die Intonation steckt in der atonischen Silbe und wird erst durch den Akzent zum Vorschein gebracht. Der litauische Akzent ist ein Resultant verschiedener Komponenten, die für das litauische Ohr eine Ganzheit bilden.

Über litauische Intonationen hat man schon viele Bände geschrieben und verschiedene Gesetzmässigkeiten festgestellt. Die Hauptprobleme bleiben jedoch bis jetzt ungelöst.

Die erste Beschreibung der Intonationen gibt ein unbekannter Verfasser in Universitas[1]. Dann folgen zahlreiche Arbeiten. Die Vielfalt der Formulierungen ergibt sich aus den verschiedenen Auffassungen von den Stämmen auf -*a*-, wobei die Frage offen steht, ob sie Barytona oder Oxytona sind. Meillet[2] z. B., der diese Stämme für Barytona ansieht, setzt hier die Form *kótu* [Instr.] voraus, während Endzelin sie von **kotù* herleitet.

Die Ursache der Schwierigkeiten ist im Mangel an überliefertem Material zu sehen und daher ist die Möglichkeit, diese Probleme zu lösen, minimal. Man darf nicht vergessen, dass keines dieser Gesetze, einschliesslich des de Saussure'schen, imstande ist, alle Ausnahmen zu erklären.

Die vorliegende Arbeit ist gewissermassen mit Metatonie verbunden. Die Benennung stammt von de Saussure[3]. Er sagt: ,,Il nous sert à désigner tout changement d'intonation dont le principe n'est pas encore clair." ,,Les causes de métatonie sont probablement diverses, et sans aucun rapport entre elles." Hjelmslev[4] stellt fest, dass ,,toute syllabe accentuée revêt l'intonation de la syllable immédiatement suivante". Diese Wirkung wäre also älter als der Schwund der Intonationen in nichtbetonter Silbe, z. B.

$\tilde{e}desis < *\tilde{e}d\tilde{e}s-$: *ránkioti* $< *ra\tilde{n}ki\acute{a}$-

und älter als die Wirkung des Leskienschen Gesetzes[5], z. B.

várna $< *va\tilde{r}n\acute{a}$

Man kann jedoch fragen, woher der Verfasser weiss, dass in *ēdes-* das -*ē*-

eine Zirkumflexintonation hatte, und *var̃nas* ursprünglicher als *várna* sein soll. Am wichtigsten ist jedoch die Tatsache, dass dann, die Entstehung der „Disintonanten" von Typus *áukštas : aũkštas* unverständlich bleibt.

Die Meinungsverschiedenheiten der Forscher auf diesem Gebiet sind gross. Zweifellos sind sie auf die Schwierigkeit und Verwickelheit der Betonungsprobleme zurückzuführen. Der Hauptgrund liegt aber darin, dass man diese Fragen zu früh angeschnitten hat. Auf der ersten Etappe hätte man die Intonationen einzelner Dialekte ausführlich erforschen müssen, unter denen die Unterschiede doch bedeutend sind, und die Schriftsprache, auf die sich die Erforschung hauptsätzlich stützt, stellt keineswegs den ältesten Stand dar.

Der Vergleich eines z. B. litauischen Wortes mit dem ihm entsprechenden slawischen Worte ist sinnlos, solange wir nicht wissen, ob die urbaltische und urslawische Form dieselbe Betonung und auf derselben Stelle hatte.

Eine Reihe von Theorien und zwar sogar aus den letzten Jahren stützt sich auf ein aus verschiedenen Dialekten nach Bedarf der einzelnen Theorien zugepassten Material.

Die vorliegende Arbeit soll ein Beitrag zur Erkennung eines Gesetzes aus dem Gebiet der litauischen Intonationen sein.

Im Litauischen, das ausser der freien Betonung noch Intonationen hat, gibt es drei Möglichkeiten:

1. Dieselbe Intonation — verschiedene Stelle der Betonung,

   kánkinti 'befriedigen' : *kankìnti* 'quälen'

   dãbar 'noch' : *dabar̃* 'jetzt'

2. Verschiedene Intonation — verschiedene Stelle der Betonung,

   baltúoti 'weissen' : *baltuoti* 'weiss schimmern'

   ilsìnti 'ermüden' : *il̃sinti* 'ruhen lassen'

3. Verschiedene Intonation — dieselbe Stelle der Betonung,

   káltas 'Stemmeisen' : *kaltas* 'schuldig'

   lìnkė 'Werkgestell' : *liñkė* 'Biegung'

Es wird nur der letzte Fall behandelt. Die Beispielpaare müssen jedoch aus ein und demselben Dialekt stammen. Dieser Umstand ist sehr wichtig, weil die einzelnen Erscheinungen ihre Begründung nur in der gegebenen Mundart finden, indem sie sich in die Gesamtheit des Systems einbeziehen. Dies ist um so wichtiger, da die dialektischen Schwankungen bedeutend sind, z. B.

   liter. *daĩktas* : Dzisna *dáiktas*

   liter. *čiõn* : Kurschat *čión*

Ausserdem kommen Unterschiede in ein und demselben Dialekt vor.

Für die Wortpaare, die sich lediglich durch die Intonationen (und Bedeutung) unterschieden, schlage ich die Bezeichnung *Disintonanten* vor. Diese Bezeichnung weist gleichzeitig auf die Quelle ihrer Entstehung hin. Wie kam es zur Entstehung der Disintonanten? Um diese Frage zu beantworten, muss man sich die Entlehnungen näher ansehen. Es wird allgemein angenommen, dass die entlehnten Wörter durch den Zirkumflex charakterisiert werden, der manchmal — mangels anderer Argumente — über die Entlehnung entscheidet. Die Bearbeitung des ganzen, die Entlehnungen betreffenden Materials, ist aus zwei Gründen unmöglich: das Fehlen ausführlicher Bearbeitungen einzelner Dialekte und das Fehlen der Intonationen in Denkmälern. Dort, wo die Akzente bezeichnet sind, wie bei Daukša, bleiben sie unklar.

Die grundlegenden Arbeiten über die slawischen Entlehnungen von Brückner[6] und Skardžius[7] fussen nicht nur in grossem Masse auf dem Material aus Denkmälern, also ohne Intonationen, sondern sie enthalten auch noch viel Widersprüche. Diese Unterschiede scheinen dadurch entstanden zu sein, dass das zitierte Material aus verschiedenen Dialekten stammt, z. B.

Skardžius	Brückner
blõznas	*blóznas*
burõkas	*burókas*
põsmas	*pósmas*
rẽtẽžis	*rétẽžis*

Zwangweise muss man sich also auf einen gewählten Dialekt stützen. In dieser Beziehung gibt es leider keine Auswahl. Wir haben umfangreichere Bearbeitungen von nur zwei Dialekten: von Otrębski[8] und Kurschat[9]. Für unsere Zwecke eignet sich jedoch nur die Bearbeitung von Kurschat.

Es hat sich nämlich erwiesen, dass das gegenseitige Verhältnis der slawischen und germanischen Entlehnungen mit dem Zirkumflex, Akut und Gravis — dabei wohlgemerkt, dass viele Wörter keine Intonation besitzen — sich wie folgt dargestellt 6 : 5 : 1. Schon daraus geht hervor, dass die oben erwähnte Meinung über die Zirkumflektierung der Entlehnungen ungenau ist.

Welcher Faktor entscheidet also darüber, dass wir einmal den Zirkumflex, ein anderes Mal den Akut [den Gravis nur bei kurzen Vokalen], haben. Allgemein können wir sagen, dass sich das entlehnte Wort dem System der gegebenen Sprache anpasst. Diese Tendenz sehen wir ausdrücklich im Suffixteil, den man nicht im streng phonetischen Sinne auffassen darf, z. B.

bagõtas, ablõtas   wie *šakõtas, galvõtas*
tramýnas, klýnas wie *beržýnas*
bagõčius   wie *kuprõčius*
balvõnas   wie *žiūrõnas*

oder sogar mit Beibehaltung der Betonungsstelle, z. B.

ãkrutas : pol. *okrę̃t*
rekrútas : germ. *Rekrut*

Solche Fälle stellen jedoch nur einen kleinen Prozentsatz der Entlehnungen dar. Diese Beispiele sind dann sehr belehrend, wenn das entlehnte Wort schon seine lautliche Entsprechung in der Sprache hatte. Soviel ich weiss, ist diese Erscheinung ganz und gar übersehen worden. In diesem Falle beachten wir eine Erscheinung, die wir Intonationsdissimilation nennen können.

1. Das entlehnte Wort hat den Akut, weil eine Entsprechung mit dem Zirkumflex bestanden hat.

dė̃lę 'Diele' [Acc.]   : *dė̃lę* 'Blutegel'
gárdas 'Gardist'   : *gar̃das* 'Burg'
gónką 'Vorschauer am
    Eingange'   : *goñ ką* 'Lehne'
kùrtas 'Windhund'   : *kur̃tas* 'taub'
márkė 'Marke'   : *mar̃kė ~ markýti* 'rösten'
márszas 'Marsch'   : *mar̃šas* 'Vergessen'
síetas 'Sieb'   : *siẽtas* 'Strich'
wérkė 'Werk[statt]'   : *wer̃kė ~ werkti* 'weinen'
wóga 'Waage'   : **wõga* 'Furche'[10]

Das entlehnte Wort hat den Zirkumflex, weil eine Entsprechung mit dem Akut bestanden hat.

mar̃gas 'Morgen'   : *márgas* 'bunt'
rȳmo 'Riemen' [Gen.]   : *rýmo ~ rýmoti* 'aufgestützt dasitzen'
rõdo 'Rath' [Gen.]   : *ródo ~ ródyti* 'zeigen'
stȳro 'Steuer' [Gen.]   : *stýro ~ stýroti* 'steif und lümmelhaft dastehen'
sūdyti 'richten'   : *súdyti* 'salzen'
sūdo 'Gericht' [Gen.]   : *súdo* 'salzt'

Das Material bei Kurschat ist ohne Ausnahme. Aus anderen Gebieten kann man viele Beispiele anführen:

plónis 'snop dożyn-
   kowy, plon'   : *plõnis* 'cienkość'
rĕtis 'rzeszoto'   : *rĕtis* 'rzadkość'
kar̃das 'kord'   : *kárdas* 'Echo'
kar̃tis 'korzec'   : *kártis* 'Stange'
trõtinti 'verlieren'   : *trótinti* 'ein wenig necken' u. a.

Die Lebendigkeit dieser Empfindung geht aus den neuesten Entlehnungen hervor:

áutas 'Auto'   : *aũtas* 'Fusslappen'
ìndas 'der Hindu'   : *iñdas* 'Gefäss'
kalkės 'Pauspapier' : *kálkės* 'Kalk'
kõvą 'Kaffee' [Acc.] : *kóvą* 'Streit'
tránas 'Tran'   : *trãnas* 'truten'

Die ganze Formbildung sich auf die Disintonation stützt. Man zitiert gewöhnlich nur wenige Beispiele dieser Erscheinung, wie

áukštas : *aũkštas*   *gìnti* : *giñti*
kándis : *kañdis*   *mérkti* : *mer̃kti*

Ich habe ungefähr 900 solche Paare gesammelt.

Anmerkungen

1. *Universitas Lingvarum Litvaniae in principali ducatus eiusdem dialecto*, Vilnae, 1737; denuo ed. J. Rozwadowski, Cracoviae 1896.

2. „Sur l'accentuation des noms en indo-européen", *MSL*, XIX, 65.

3. „A propos de l'accentuation lituanienne", *MSL*, VIII, 429. [Rez. J. Zubatý, *IFA*, 272.]

4. *Études baltiques. La métatonie.* Kopenhague, 1932. [Rez. E. Fraenkel. *GGA*, 1938, S. 257]

5. „Die Quantitätsverhältnisse im Auslaut des Litauischen", *AslPh*, V, 188.

6. *Die slawischen Fremdwörter im Litauischen*, Weimar, 1877. [Rez. A. Weber, *AslPh*, III, 185.]

7. *Die slawischen Lehnwörter im Altlitauischen*, Kaunas, 1931.

8. *Wschodniolitewskie narzecze twereckie*, Kraków, 1934. [Rez. P. Skardžius, *APh*, V, 219; A. Vaillant, *RES*, XV, 83.]

9. *Wörterbuch der litauischen Sprache*, I. Halle, 1870. [Rez. A. Schleicher, *BVS*, VI, 107; A. Bezzenberger, *Götting. Anz.* XXIII, 1885.]

10. Bei Kurschat ist die Intonation nicht bezeichnet, aber sie muss Zirkumflex sein.

On Lithuanian Intonation

It is generally agreed that most of the Slavic (and Germanic) borrowings in Lithuanian have a circumflex. Research in this subject has to be limited to material from one dialect because of the intonation variance in different dialects.

On applying this theory to the Kurschat dialect it was found that "disintonants" exist. If the borrowed word had a phonetic equivalent in Lithuanian with acute intonation, then a circumflex was affixed, and if the equivalent had a circumflex, then acute intonation was given. The "disintonation" phenomenon had further influence on the structure of the language (cf. metatony).

W. P. LEHMANN

Definite Adjective Declensions
and Syntactic Types

In the course of syntactic development of many of the Indo-European languages from a Subject Object Verb (SOV) to a Subject Verb Object (SVO) or Verb Subject Object (VSO) type, Baltic and other centrally located languages did not assume the characteristics expected of a consistent type. The modern Indo-Aryan languages, for example, have genitives as well as adjectives preceding nouns, and include postpositions (see Greenberg 1966, pp. 73–113, especially 108–111); in this way they may be characterized as representatives of a consistent SOV type. Modern Armenian is similarly consistent, exhibiting the same characteristics as the Indo-Aryan languages. In the western area of Indo-European languages, Greek, Albanian and the Romance languages exhibit syntactic features of a consistent SVO type, having genitives as well as adjectives following nouns, and prepositions. Celtic also exhibits these characteristics, and is of a VSO type. But the central languages have features of both types. Lithuanian, though SVO, has the genitive noun as well as the adjective noun order of the SOV type, and includes postpositions as well as prepositions. Slavic, also SVO, has prepositions and the genitive following nouns, but it has the adjective noun order of the SOV type. Modern Persian, though of the SOV type, has genitives as well as adjectives following nouns, and prepositions. And in the Germanic languages, which are SVO and prepositional, some may have the genitive noun and adjective noun order as well as the noun genitive. In these languages which are inconsistent in type we find on the one hand a definite (or weak) adjective declension, or on the other hand in Persian a relative construction which has been compared with the definite adjective inflection of Baltic and Slavic. I should like to suggest that these constructions arose because of the indeterminate types of the languages in which they are found.

The data may be consulted in any of the standard handbooks. Senn (1966, pp. 163–169) describes the Lithuanian definite form of the adjective as a construction based on the usual form of the adjective plus the suffixed pronoun jìs, jì. Kiparsky (1967, pp. 164–168) states that the longer adjective

Table of contemporary Indo-European language types
(based on Greenberg, 1966)

			Gen	Adj	Ppn
SOV	Indo-Aryan		GN	AN	Po
	Armenian		GN	AN	Po
Transitional	Persian	SOV	NG	NA	Pr
	Slavic	SVO	NG	AN	Pr
	Baltic	SVO	GN	AN	Pr/Po
	Germanic	SVO	NG/GN	AN	Pr
SVO	Albanian		NG	NA	Pr
	Greek		NG	NA	Pr
	Romance		NG	NA	Pr
VSO	Celtic		NG	NA	Pr

inflection of Old Slavic is constructed from the shorter adjective inflection plus *ji ja je. Senn equated the suffix with the relative pronoun; Kiparsky, with the definite article. Delbrück (Gdr. 5, p. 392) had already discussed various theories on the origin of the formation, and implying a relative construction translated OCS *vino novoje* as 'wine which (is) new' in contrast with *vino novo* 'new wine'. However much we may admire Delbrück for his contributions to our understanding of Indo-European syntax, we regard as secondary in importance the morphological mechanism by means of which the construction is characterized. For inasmuch as we are dealing with a syntactic phenomenon, the essential to clarify is the position of the construction in the syntactic component of the language.

From the point of view of general syntactic theory, adjective plus noun constructions are derived from embedded sentences which may be equated with relative clauses. For the early Indo-European languages we may support this position by noting that in constructions consisting of adjective plus vocative, the adjective is in the nominative case, e.g. φίλος ὦ Μενέλαε 'Menelaos who art dear > dear Menelaos'. The essential phenomenon to explain then is the development of two kinds of adjective constructions, one an indefinite, one a definite.

In the indefinite construction, the adjective may be derived from the verb phrase of a sentence; if derived from an embedded (relative) clause, it has been reduced to its simple form, with no special marker, somewhat comparable to English 'a pattern characteristic of him' < 'a pattern which is characteristic of him'. In the definite construction, the embedded (relative) clause has however retained a marker of the underlying clause. I should like to note briefly the mechanism by which the definite adjective construction was accomplished.

From Hittite we have learned the earlier form of relative constructions in the Indo-European languages. Friedrich (1940, p. 97) gives as pattern: 'whichever man you have seen, he is my father' in contrast with the pattern found in SVO languages 'the man whom you have seen is my father'. For the purposes of my study, the chief point to note is that in Hittite, and in other early Indo-European languages, relative constructions precede the word modified, in accordance with the pattern of SOV languages. With the evidence of Hittite we therefore can extend the discussion of Indo-European relative constructions given by Delbrück (Gdr. 5, pp. 295–406). For if, as Delbrück had concluded, Proto-Indo-European was an SOV language, all relative clauses must have preceded their modifiers. We may posit this relationship for the early dialects as well, though in our attested materials it is maintained more consistently in some constructions than in others. In Vedic, for example, the relative construction precedes especially when the main clause contains a correlative pronoun, e.g. RV 3. 53. 21 *yó no dvéṣṭy ádharaḥ sás padiṣṭa* 'who hates us, may he fall to the ground' (Gdr. 5, p. 299).

If in Proto-Indo-European and the early dialects the relative clause consisted of an adjective, it would have preceded the word modified, as in RV 1. 89. 8 *vy àśema deváhitaṃ yád âyuḥ* 'may we attain the age which is determined by god'. When however the SOV pattern became less consistent, the relative clause might be placed after the antecedent. For example, in Delbrück's first example of a relative followed by *ca* (Gdr. 5, p. 306), the relative clause follows its antecedent; RV 1. 25. 11 *áto víśvāny ádbhutā cikitvâṅ abhí paśyati kṛtâni yá ca kártvā* 'from there the wise man surveys all wonderful things: (those) which (have been) accomplished and (are) to be accomplished'. Rather than a complete shift of the entire relative construction as of *kṛtâni yá* in this sentence, most Vedic relative clauses have the relative pronoun directly after the antecedent, e.g. RV 1. 18.1 *kakṣîvantaṃ yá auśijáḥ* 'K., who is a descendant of Usij'. But if the relative clause had not been remodeled in this way, one would have the pattern: 1. Antecedent; 2. Modifier; 3. Relative pronoun. This is the pattern that was maintained in Baltic and Slavic, beside the pattern: 1. Modifier; 2. Relative pronoun; 3. Antecedent. (See Wissemann 1958, p. 63). The pattern gave rise to the definite adjectives in Slavic and Baltic, for example OCS *dobrъji človekъ* and Lith. *geràsis žmõgus*.

We may support this conclusion by noting that in Old Church Slavic the predicate adjective is always in the indefinite form. A predicate adjective is not embedded in a noun phrase but derived from the verb phrase of the sentence. Accordingly there is no reason for a relative pronoun, or a definite adjective. The simple or indefinite adjective of Baltic and Slavic accordingly continues the Indo-European adjective construction with no further suffix.

Another syntactic pattern of the Baltic and Slavic languages supports this point of view. In Lithuanian, adjectives of the third declension do not make definite forms (Senn 1966, pp. 159–163 et passim). We may account for the lack of definite forms by noting the adjectives which belong to the third declension. Some like *begédis* 'one who has no shame' are possessive compounds. Others are determinative compounds, for example *sąsenis* 'very old'. Others are complex adjectives, made with characteristic suffixes, for example *-áitis*, which was used to form patronymics. Members of the third declension are therefore nominal adjectives, related to other nouns appositionally rather than by means of embedding. Their nounlike characteristics may be demonstrated from the absence of comparatives and superlatives for them (Senn 1966, p. 162, 170). Since adjectives of the third declension become modifiers in this way, and not through relative constructions, it is not remarkable that they lack the definite declension.

The first and second declension adjectives of Baltic however, when inflected according to the definite adjective declension, are derived from relative clause constructions which became frozen when these languages did not remain SOV in type nor develop to consistent SVO types. Since Germanic is similar in this development, we would expect a similar definite adjective syntactic pattern for it, if the derivation proposed here for definite adjective inflections is correct. In Germanic however, reflexes of the yo-relative are not found. Yet as is well-known, Germanic has a definite adjective inflection formed with another marker, the n-inflection. The Germanic n-inflection, or weak adjective inflection as it is known after Grimm, parallels in use the Baltic and Slavic definite adjective forms. (See Prokosch 1939, pp. 259–260.) The strong inflection is found in predicative positions, where it is not derived from a relative clause; the weak inflection in those patterns that may be derived from relative clauses. Moreover, the weak adjective may be found when modifying a vocative, as in the Gothic version of Luke 1: 28: fagino anstai audahafta, frauja miþ þus, þiuþido þu in qinom 'hail, thou filled with grace, the Lord be with you; blessed are you among women'. (See Streitberg 1920, pp. 183–183.) Accordingly we may relate syntactically the Germanic weak adjective inflection and the definite adjective inflections of Baltic and Slavic, though they are marked by different morphological means.

Modern Persian *iżāfa*, that is *-i-*, fulfills a similar function: *pidar-i buzurg* means 'the father who is honorable > the honorable father'; in *pidar-buzurg* 'grandfather', on the other hand, the relationship is appositive. (See Seiler 1960, pp. 118–119.)

Like the Baltic and Slavic languages, Germanic and Persian therefore show definite adjective constructions. All of these languages are central in the Indo-European area, and have developed from the SOV type of Proto-Indo-European towards the SVO type slowly, and as noted above inconsistently. On the basis of this development I have attempted to account for the presence of a distinct syntactic category in these languages of inconsistent type. My primary aim has been to account for a syntactic construction by means of syntactic criteria. The morphological elements in that construction have been analyzed as productively as seems possible. (See Delbrück, Senn, Kiparsky.) We should now like to account for syntactic constructions on the basis of general syntactic principles in somewhat the same way as historical linguists have long accounted for phonological patterns and phonological changes. The means we may develop to account for syntactic patterns may never be as precise as those we use in historical phonology. For syntactic structures are more elusive than are the relatively restricted number of phonological patterns that are possible in speech. As von Raumer, Sievers and other phonologists of the last century showed the way to an accounting for phonological development of language, we now must deal with the complex syntactic structures of language and attempt to account for their historical development.

Notes

Bibliography, which may be consulted for further references:

B. Delbrück, *Vergleichende Syntax der indogermanischen Sprachen*, I–III, Strassburg, 1893–1900.

I. Friedrich, *Hethitisches Elementarbuch. I. Kurzgefasste Grammatik*, Heidelberg, 1940.

J. H. Greenberg, "Some Universals of Grammar with Particular Reference to the Order of Meaningful Elements", *Universals of Language*, ed. by J. S. Greenberg, Cambridge, [2]1966, 73–113.

V. Kiparsky, *Russische historische Grammatik. II*, Heidelberg, 1967.

Ed. Prokosch, *A Comparative Germanic Grammar*, Philadelphia, 1939.

H. Seiler, *Relativsatz, Attribut und Apposition*, Wiesbaden, 1960.

A. Senn, *Handbuch der litauischen Sprache. I. Grammatik*, Heidelberg, 1966.

W. Streitberg, *Gotisches Elementarbuch*, Heidelberg, 5/6 edition, 1920.

A. Vaillant, *Grammaire Comparée des langues Slaves. II. Morphologie. 2. Flexion pronominale*, 1958.

H. Wissemann, "Zur nominalen Determination", *IF*, LXIII, 61–78.

JUOZAS LINGIS

Išnykę ir pasikeitę socialinės reikšmės žodžiai lietuvių kalboje

Didžioje Lietuvos Kunigaikštystėje, apėmusioje netik patį valstybės branduolį — Lietuvą, bet ir plačias slavais apgyventas sritis, rašto kalba neatitiko kasdieninės kalbos. XIV a. pabaigoje, Lietuvai priėmus krikščionybę ir politiniai bei kultūriniai įsitraukus į vakarų Europos veiklos sferą, atsirado reikalas raštu surašyti visus nuosprendžius, pažadus bei privilegijas, kurios įvairiais iškilmingais atsitikimais buvo žodžiu perduotos. Pietinėse ir rytinėse Didžiosios Lietuvos Kunigaikštystės srityse oficialūs aktai jau buvo rašomi Lietuvai krikščionybės dar nepriėmus. Aktai ten buvo rašomi ne ukrainiečių ar baltarusių kalbomis, kaip kad dažnai nepagrįstai sakoma, o surusinta senąja bulgarų kalba su kaikuriomis rusų tarmių priemaišomis. Toji vadinamoji ,,rusiškoji'' kanceliarinė kalba rytų Europoje atstojo vakaruose naudotą lotynų kalbą. Tačiau tos kanceliarinės kalbos ,,rusiška'' pavadinti negalima. Didžioje Lietuvos Kunigaikštystėje toji kalba buvo vadinama ,,rusų'', o Maskva vadino ją ,,lietuvių'' kalba.

Sudarius Didžiosios Lietuvos Kunigaikštystės kanceliariją, į ją buvo pakviesti ir raštininkai, o raštininkai atsinešė su savimi tą kalbą, kurie ją mokėjo. Iš rytų atėję raštininkai rašė kanceliarine ,,rusų'' kalba, o iš vakarų — lotyniškai ir vokiškai. Gauti raštininkų iš vakarų buvo labai sunku. XV a. ir XVI a. pradžioje Didžioje Lietuvos Kunigaikštystėje buvo vartojamos trys kalbos: kanceliarinė ,,rusų'', lotynų ir vokiečių. ,,Rusų'' kalba buvo labiausia paplitusi, nes lengviausia buvo gauti raštininkų tai kalbai. Pvz. XVI a. viduryje Kaune buvo trys raštininkai — lotynų, vokiečių ir ,,rusų'' kalboms. ,,Rusų'' kalbos raštininkas buvo pigiausiai apmokamas.

Laikui bėgant ir Lietuvai po krikšto imant labiau santykiauti su Lenkija, lenkų kalba ima palengva išstumti ,,rusų'' kalbą iš oficialių aktų. Tačiau lenkų kalba ir pačioje Lenkijoje net ligi XVI a. vidurio nebuvo vartota kaip oficiali rašto kalba, ir tik apie XVI a. vidurį ji pradėjo išstumti lotynų kalbą iš oficialių aktų. Tik XVII a. pabaigoje buvo senoji kanceliarinė ,,rusų'' kalba Didžioje Lietuvos Kunigaikštystėje pakeista lenkų kalba (galutinai į teismus lenkų kalba buvo įvesta Coaequatio iurium įstatymu 1697 m.). Tačiau aktuose, rašytuose lenkų kalba specialūs būdingi grynai lietuviški ar „rusiški" terminai nebuvo verčiami į lenkų kalbą, o buvo paliekami tokie, kokie jie buvo "rusų" kalba rašytuose aktuose.

Didžiosios Lietuvos Kunigaikštystės kanceliarijos aktuose, rašytuose tiek „rusų", tiek lenkų kalbomis, yra įsiterpę daugybė grynai lietuviškų žodžių. Vieni iš tų žodžių sutinkami tik dokumentuose, liečiančiuose grynai lietuviškąsias sritis, kiti gi buvo vartojami ir daug plačiau. Tie žodžiai galėjo patekti į kanceliarinę kalbą dėl įvairių priežąsčių. Nemaža žodžių pateko tiesiog dėl raštininko nežinojimo lietuviško žodžio atitikmens negyvoje rašto kalboje, o kanceliarinė kalba buvo ne žmonių kalbamoji, o grynai rašto kalba. Gana dažnai lietuviškus terminus paliko raštininkai sąmoningai dėl pačių sąvokų apimties. Žodžiai, reiškę būdingus lietuvių socialinių, ekonominių, juridinių, fiskalinių santykių, papročių, įrankių, drabužių ir kitus pavadinimus, buvo palikti dėl jų lietuviškos specifikos, nes atitinką žodžiai slavų kalbose reiškė daugiau ar mažiau visai skirtingas realijas ir tam reikalui netiko. Vieni iš tų senuose aktuose sutinkamų žodžių yra dabar visai išnykę iš gyvosios lietuvių kalbos, kiti yra visai pakeitę savo reikšmę. Skaitant ir nagrinėjant senuosius tekstus lietuvių kalba, kur tų kategorijų žodžiai dar panaudojami, svarbu žinoti, ką tie žodžiai tada reiškė.

Chr. Stangas savo vertingoje studijoje apie senąją Lietuvos kanceliarinę kalbą, apžvelgdamas savo darbui panaudotų tekstų leksiką, sumini tik kelis lietuviškuosius skolinius: djaklo (*dúoklė*), mezleva (*mezliava*), dojlid, dojlida (*dailìdė*), stirta (*stìrta*), sviren (*svirnas*), iš kurių *mezliava* plačiau išanalizuojama[1]. Wolteris savo straipsnyje apie lituanizmus rusų-lietuvių teisinėje kalboje atkreipia dėmėsį į jam žinomus 20 žodžių[2]. Tačiau tokių lietuviškų žodžių kanceliariniuose aktuose kur kas daugiau. Jablonskis, peržiūrėjęs visus spausdintus ir jam prieinamus nespausdintus šaltinius, surinko jų 299. Tie žodžiai paskelbti jo kruopščiai paruoštame darbe[3]. Tą savo darbą Jablonskis tęsė ir toliau iki pat savo mirties surasdamas nemaža naujų, anksčiau neužtiktų ir todėl į jo rinkinų nepatekusių. Dėja, tie žodžiai dar nėra paskelbti, tačiau jo rankrašču jau yra pasinaudoję kaikurie kalbininkai bei istorikai.[4] Jablonskis buvo suplanavęs išleisti ir tų žodžių analizą. Kai kurių žodžių prasmės aiškinimus jis yra palietęs savo paskaitoje, skaitytoje pirmoje Pabaltijo istorikų konferencijoje Rygoje 1937.[5] Visus senuosius lietuviškus skolinius senoje kanceliarinėje kalboje ir naujesniuosius lietuviškus skolinius dabartinėje baltarusių kalboje yra mėginęs apžvelgti A. Veržbovskis. Pagrindinis jo darbas dar tebėra rankraštyje, tačiau kaikas iš jo yra jau spaudoje paskelbta.[6] Žodžius, nusakiusius liečiamo laikotarpio agrarines, socialines bei ekonomines sąvokas, yra išanalizavę savo darbuose Z. Ivinskis[7] ir J. Jurginis[8], kur yra nurodyta ir gausi literatūra tais klausimais.

Kaip jau minėta, vieni iš tų lietuviškų žodžių senoje kanceliarinėje kalboje yra visai išnykę iš gyvosios lietuvių kalbos, kiti gi smarkiai pakeitę savo prasmę. Ir vienos ir antros kategorijos žodžiai yra tačiau įdomūs tiek kalbiniu, tiek kultūristoriniu požvilgiu. Pavyzdžiais tokių žodžių kategorijoms gali būti žodžiai *krienas, veldamas* ir *kaimynas*. *Krienas* yra dabar visai išnykęs iš gyvosios lietuvių kalbos net ir giminaičių nepalikdamas. *Veldamas* yra išnykęs gyvoje kalboje, tačiaus tos pačios šaknies ir panašia reikšme žodžių dar pasitaiko kasdieninėje lietuvių kalboje, tuo tarpu *kaimynas* tebevartojamas ir dabar lietuvių kalboje, tačiau jo reikšmė yra visai pakitusi. *Veldamas* ir *kaimynas* savo senąja reikšme sutinkamas ir senuose rašto paminkluose lietuvių kalba (Mažvydo, Vilento, Bretkūno, Daukšos ir kitų raštuose). Nežinant tų žodžių tuolaikinės reikšmės, tekstas kartais gali pasidaryti nesuprantamas ar neaiškus.

Krienas savo reikšme senuose aktuose nieko bendro neturi su slavišku skoliniu krienas (Cochlearia Armoracia), kurio šaknys vartojamas prieskoniui. Kaip gausūs XVI–XVIII a. dokumentai rodo — reikia prisiminti, kad tuo laiku Lietuvoje buvo smarkiai įsigalėjus baudžiava — *krienas* buvo mokestis, kurį, valstietei merginai ištekant, jaunikis per jaunosios tėvus ar globėjus turėjo sumokėti feodalui, jaunosios ponui. Taigi *krienas* buvo feodalizmo laikų vedybinis mokestis. Tačiau *krienas* kaip mokestis nebuvo feodalizmo įvesta naujovė, o paveldėtas iš senesnių laikų, kada jo prasmė buvo kiek kitokia. Aktuose, kur *krienas* minimas, sakoma, kad ,,mergaitės pagal gerus senovinius papročius sumokėjusios savo ponui krieną arba kunicą, gali tekėti ir už kito pono valdinio''[9]. Pastaba ,,pagal gerus senuosius papročius'' čia yra gana svarbi. Baudžiauninkai, paprastai, naujovių nemėgo, o įvedus kokią naujovę, kuri apsunkindavo jų naštą ir buvo priešinga veikiantiems įstatymams ar papročio teisei, tuojau skųsdavosi didžiajam kunigaikščiui, kad įvedama naujovė, kurios per amžius nebuvo. Didysis kunigaikštis, paprastai, tokius skundus išklausydavo ir pabrėždavo, kad jis jokių naujovių savo pavaldiniams neįveda ir jų senovės neliečia. Galimas daiktas, kad senais laikais, kai valstiečiai dar nebuvo baudžiauninkais, *krienas* buvo mokamas šeimos galvai, t. y. nuotakos tėvams. Mykolas Lietuvis (Michalo Lituanus) savo apie 1550 m. parašytoje ir 1615 m. išleistoje knygelėje apie lietuvių, totorių ir maskvėnų papročius rašo: ,,Mercandarum sponsarum morem, qui est apud Tartaros, patet fuisse etiam apud Israelitas, Genes. 29. &:. Reg. 18. quedadmodum & in nostra olim gente soluebatur parentibus pro sponsis pretium, quod Krieno a Samagitis vocatur. Sed nunc mancipamur dotibus vxorum, & serui propter eas efficimur quaerentes magnificas affinitates.''[10] Taigi, anot Mykolo Lietuvio, *krienas* buvo seniai vartotas mokestis už žmoną jaunosios tėvams.

Tatai yra ne kas kita, o tik reminiscencija seno papročio pirkti sau nuotakas. Kad ir lietuviai seniau pirko nuotakas, liūdija kad ir negausūs folkloristiniai duomenys bei istoriniai šaltiniai[11]. Ankstyvesniuose istoriniuose šaltiniuose mokestis už nuotakas neturi savo specialaus pavadinimo. Mykolo Lietuvio minėtoje knygutėje *krienas* (Krieno) sutinkamas faktinai pirmą kartą ligi šiol žinomuose šaltiniuose. Gyvoje lietuvių kalboje *krieno*, mokesčio už nuotaką prasme, jau nebežinoma. Į Juškos lietuvių kalbos žodyną *krienas* (*krena*) pateko iš minėtos Mykolo Lietuvio knygutės. *Krienas*, nors kiek kita prasme, žinomas latviams. Mancelis XVII a. mini krieną kaip pinigus, kurios jaunikis duoda nuotakos tėvams, nuotakos draugams[12]. Elgeris savo latviškai-lenkiškai-lotyniškame žodyne latvišką *krieną* verčia 'posag, wiano, dos'[13]. Lange savo latviškai-vokiškame žodyne *krieną* verčia dovana nuotakai[14]. Iš Langes žodyno *kriens* pateko į Ulmanno žodyną, o paskui jau ir į didįjį latvių kalbos žodyną[15]. Latvių enciklopedijoje ,,*kriens*" aiškinamas nuotakos kaina ar simboliškuoju nuotakos mokesčiu[16]. Latvių žodynuose *kriens* dažnai verčiama pasoga, kraičiu. Tačiau ,,krienas" nei su kraičiu, nei su pasoga nesusijęs[17]. Lietuvių *krienas*, ankščiau kaip išpirktinis mokestis jaunosios tėvams, vėliau senuose aktuose kaip mokestis feodalui, yra išlaikęs pirmykštę, nepakitėjusią jaunosios pirkimo reikšmę, o latvių *kriens* — jaunikio dovanos nuotaikai ir jos draugams — yra vėlesnių laikų paprotys, išsivystęs iš senesnio mokesčio už nuotaką[18].

Senuose Didžiosios Lietuvos Kunigaikštystės aktuose *krienas* rašoma keleriopai: chren, chreny, kreny, kreni, chriny, kryiny, kryny ir pan. Kad *krienas* susijęs su pirkimu, rodo ir paties žodžio etimologija. *Krienas* siejamas su senovės slavų ,,krynuti" — pirkti[19]. ,,Krynuti" prasme pirkti sutinkamas senuose slavų dokumentuose. Pvz. Smolensko kunigaikštis Matislavas savo sutartyje su Ryga 1229 m[20]. ir Kijevo kunigaikštis su graikais 945 m.[21] vartojo žodį ,,krynuti" prasme pirkti. *Krienas* labai primena ir slavų ,,krivna" arba ,,grivna"[22]. Senoje bulgarų kalboje forma ,,ukrijenaago" reiškė ,,pirktojo" (gen. sg. part. pret. pass.)[23]. Šaknis *kri*-siejama su sen. indų *krīnāmi* 'perku'[24], sen. airių *crenim* — 't. p.'[25], sen. rusų *krenuti* 'pirkti' (čia šaknis *kre*- yra kilusi iš senesnės lyties *kri*-)[26]. Bendra indoeur. forma bus buvusi *qurinami* 'perku'[27].

Žodis *veldamas*, išnykęs iš lietuvių kalbos jau XVII a. pabaigoje, yra kilęs iš dar tebevartojamo žodžio *veldėti* 'ką nors valdyti, turėti valdžioje, gauti, įsigyti ką nors valdyti, turėti'. Mažvydas savo 1547 m. katekizme sako: ,,... padotyji alba veldami" (lot. *subditos*)[28]. Tos pačios šaknies ir darybos žodis yra *veldene* (Krauzės žodyne reiškia valsčių, vok. Sprengel oder District)[29]. Bretkūnas savo biblijoje mini kitą tos pačios darybos žodį *veldenija*: ,,... ghis io Tiewikschcziu Lobu (aR: Weldaenija) Szemeie butų ... padawiau ... ant Tievainistes (ar.: Waeladenios)"[30]. *Veldėti* yra giminingas su sen. bulgarų *vlasti (vladǫ)*, *vladěti*; rus. *volodetъ*, sanskr. *vladati*, čėk. *vlásti*, lenk. *wládać, wlodać*, got. ang. saks. *waldan*, sen. anglų *wealdan*, sen. vok. aukšt. *waltan* ir pan[31]. *Veldamas* XV–XVI a. reiškė žmogų esantį kito žmogaus valdžioje, o tokiu žmogumi buvo vadinamas nelaisvas valstietis[32]. Tačiau toks *veldamo* nusakymas toli gražu nenusako jo tikrosios sąvokos to laiko prasme, kada jis buvo kalboje vartotas. Ši nelaisvų valstiečių kategorija nebuvo kiek giliau pagvildenta Lietuvos socialinių santykių tyrinėtojų. Pirmasis juos paminėjo Kamieniecki[33], vėliau Ivinskis[34]. Ryškiausiai *veldamų* klausimu yra pasisakęs Jurginis[35].

Iš šnekamosios ir raštų kalbos *veldamą* išstūmė *paduonis* (lenk. *poddany*), su kuriuo susiduriama jau XVI a. lietuviškuose raštuose. Daukša savo postilėje[36] vartoja ir *veldamą* ir *paduonį*, tačiau iš teksto sunku nustatyti, ar tarp tų abiejų pavadinimų yra koks esminis skirtumas, ar ne. Kiek labiau paaiškėja palyginus su lenkišku Vuiko originalu, iš kurio postilė versta[37]. Daukšos Postilės vertime 499 p. sakoma: „... tur tarnaut' welda-miemus / kaip ir iam weldamieii ...", o Vuiko originale 841 p.: „... služyc poddanym iako y iemu poddani ..." Daukšos 535 p.: „... ne kąkinime nei prispaudime ubagų padônu: bet' mielaszirdume", Vuiko 913 p.: „... ani w vcisnieniu ubagich poddanych ...", Daukšos 86 p.: „... yra sawamė vrede kaip ir padutniu ...", Vuiko 146 p.: „... w swym vrzedzie iako y poddanych ..." Kaip matyti, Daukša lenkiškąjį „poddany" verčia ir į „veldamą", ir į „paduonį" bei „paduotinį", nematydamas jų prasmėje jokio skirtumo. Atrodo, kad XVI a. lietuviškuose raštuose *veldamas* ir *paduonis* buvo sinonimai ir skirtumo tarp jų nebebuvo.

Daug daugiau šviesos į *veldamo* prasmę atskleidžia teisiniai bei ūkiniai Didžiosios Lietuvos Kunigaikštystės aktai, rašyti tiek „rusiškai", tiek lenkiškai. Čia, tačiau, reikia priminti, kad *veldamas* sutinkamas tik tuose tekstuose, kurie liečia Didžiosios Lietuvos Kunigaikštystės lietuviais ap-gyventas žemes. Kaip toji valstiečių kategorija buvo vadinama slavais apgyventose kunigaikštystės apgyventose srityse, sunku pasakyti. Lotynų kalboje nebuvo tinkamo atitikmens *veldamui* nusakyti, ir ši valstiečių kategoria buvo nusakoma net keliais žodžiais. Viename 1538 m. lotyniškai surašytame akte, pvz., sakoma: „... Conscribo ... kmetones villanos vulga-riter weldonych numero sex"[38]. Seniausias ligi šiol žinomas aktas, kuriame minimas *veldamas*, yra iš 1454–1470 m[39]. Iš XVIII a. gana gausių aktų ligi šiol tesurasta tik vienas, kuriame minimas *veldamas* 1719 m[40]. Kas gi, pagaliau, buvo tas *veldamas* per žmogus?

Pirmiausia *veldami* buvo viena iš žemdirbių kategorijų, o tokių kategorijų buvo daug, jų ir teisės bei prievolės buvo nevienodos, jų padėtis priklausė tuo to, kieno žemę jie dirbo — valstybinę t. y. didžiojo kunigaikščio, ar privačią — bajoro ar didiko (pasauliečio ar dvasininko). Kokiai gi žemdirbių kategorijai priklausė *veldamas*? Pagal istorikų, tyrusių Lietuvos socialinius bei agrarinius santykius, naujausias tyrimo davinius[41] *veldamais* buvo vadinami valstiečiai, priklausę didžiajam kunigaikščiui, kuriuos jis paskui už įvairius nuopelnus padovanodavo savo nusipelnusiems pareigūnams — bajorams, bažnyčiai (parapijoms) ar vyskupų valdoms. *Veldamu* buvo atiduodamas ne atskiras asmuo, ne individas, bet kartu ir jo naudojama žemė, jo gyvuliai ir kitoks turtas. Atiduotas bajorui, didikui ar bažnyčiai *veldamu* valstietis iš pradžių dar turėjo kunigaikščiui duoti dėklą (mokestis natūrā: javais, linais, šienu, medumi ir pan.) ir mokėti sidabrinę (mokestis karo reikalams, mokamas visų valstiečių bei miestiečių sidabriniais pinigais). Bet paskui, feodalams reikalaujant iš kunigaikščio daugaiau privilegijų, *veldami* buvo atleisti nuo pajamų valstybei, kurios paskui atiteko feodalams. Tuo *veldamu* padėtis smarkiai pablogėjo. Būdami didžiojo kunigaikščio žemės valstiečiai, *veldami* turėjo savo žemę, ją dirbo, atliko savo prievoles valstybei ir naudojosi taip vadinama išeivystės teise — jie galėjo palikti žemę, išsikelti kitur, kur jiems atrodė geriau ir laisvai pasirinkti sau kitą poną. Atduotas *veldamu* jis tos išeivystės teisės nustodavo. Veldamas, nors ir visiškai atitekęs bajorui, didikui ar bažnyčiai, vistik tvarkydavo savo ūkio ir šeimos reikalus kiek laisviau, negu tai atlikti galėjo kitos valstiečių kategorijos atstovas — kaimynas, kuris naudojosi vien tik bajorui priklausoma žeme. Bajoras negalėjo parduoti veldamo be žemės, tačiau pasielgti jis galėjo su kaimynu. Ir veldamo šeimos nariai buvo laisvesni, negu kaimyno. Veldamas galėjo laisvai išleisti už vyro savo dukterį, sumokėjęs bajorui *krieną*. Tačiau po 1557 m., įvedus taip vadinamą valakų reformą, išmatavus visas žemes ir nustačius feodalines prievoles ne nuo tarnybos, t. y. atliekamo darbo, kaip ligi šiol, o nuo dirbamos žemės ploto, skirtumas tarp veldamo ir kaimyno išnyko.

Savo senąja socialine padėtimi *veldamui* artimas yra *kaimynas* senąja to žodžio prasme. Dabartinėje lietuvių kalboje *kaimynas* reiškia gretimą gyventoją, susijusį su kitais artimais savybės ar gretimumo ryšiais. Lietuvos kaime *kaimynu* yra laikomas netik gretimos sodybos, bet ir kiekvieno kaimelio ar gretimo vienkiemio gyventojas. *Kaimynu* vadinamas ir gretimas žmogus bei to paties krašto žmogus. Šia proga gal reikėtų priminti, kad kaikuriose švedų kalbos tarmės sutinkamas žodis *kaima, kajme* bendravardžio prasme. Šis žodis yra paskolintas iš suomių kalbos *kaima* (gen. *kaiman*) ir reiškia 'vyriškis', kuris savo ruožtu yra paskolintas iš baltų kalbų[42].

Etimologiškai *kaimynas* yra susijęs su *kaimu* bei *kiemu*. *Kaimas*, taip pat ir *kaima*, dabar reiškia gyvenvietę. Kiti žodžiai gyvenvietei pažymėti lietuvių kalboje yra *kiemas*, *sodžius* (soda), *dvaras*. *Kaimas* reiškia taip pat ir visus kaimo gyventojus. *Kaimas* yra priešingybė miestui.

Kiemas dabar reiškia: 1. žemės plotą tarp vienos sodybos pastatų, atšlaimą, aikštelę prie gyvenamo namo, 2. atskirą kaimo sodybą, ūkį, 3. kaimą (sodžių), 4. kaimo gyventojus, 5. viešnagę, svečiavimąsi, vaišes, pokylį (kieminėtis arba eiti kieman reiškė eiti į svečius, vykti į kitą kaimą, 6. patogią, tinkamą vietą[43]. ,,Kaimas-kiemas'' sutinkamas ir kitose baltų kalbose, pvz. latvių *ciems, ciema, ciemuoties* ('eiti į svečius'), sen. prūsų *caymis*[44]. Tos pačios šaknies ir ta pačia prasme yra got. *haims*, vid. viekiečių *haima*, sen. anglų *hām*, isl. *heimr*, sen. švedų *heejm*, sen. aukšt. vok. *heima*, vok. *Heim*, ang. *home*[45]. Plg. sen. sanskr. *kshema* 'jaukus, patogus, smagus, poilsis, malonumas'[46].

Senuose XIII–XIV a. Lietuvą liečiančiuose šaltiniuose sutinkama nemaža ir vietovardžių su *kaimas*, daugiausia senųjų prūsų ir vakarinių lietuvių gyvenvietėse: *Kaym, Kayme, Cayme, Kaymen, Keymal, Aukaimis, Tverkaimis, Kalny Kaym, Vindakaymen* ir pan[47].

Nors *kaimas-kiemas* amžiams bėgant ir išlaikė pavadinimą gyvenvietės prasme, tačiau senovėje tie žodžiai stovėjo kiek aukštesnėje socialinėje gyvenviečių pakopoje. *Kaimas* ir *kiemas* buvo lyg ir sinonimai. *Kaimą* XII–XIV a., sprendžiant iš istorinių šaltinių, sudarė žemvaldžio ir jam priklausančios šeimynos, t. y. žemę dirbančių žmonių, nariai. Žemvaldžio *kaimas* buvo aptvertas, į jį buvo galima patekti tik pro vartus. Žemvaldžio gyvenvietė susidėjo iš daugelio pastatų, o jo žemę dirbančio valstiečio dažniausia iš vieno. Toje žemvaldžio iš daugelio pastatų susidedančioje sodyboje — *kaime* buvo ir *kiemas*, t. y. aikštelė tarp gyvenamojo namo ir ūkinių pastatų. Tat *kiemu* buvo vadinama ne visa sodyba, o tik aptvertoji sodybos dalis. Laikui bėgant tobulėjo ir paprasto valstiečio sodyba, joje atsirado daugiau pastatų ir ji pasidarė panaši į žemvaldžio — ir ji buvo pradėta vadinti *kiemu*, o žemvaldžio sodyba buvo pradėta vadinti *dvaru*, kuris senąja savo prasme lietuvių kalboje buvo *kiemo* sinonimas. Grįžkime prie *kaimyno*. Ką gi seniau reiškė *kaimynas* etimologiškai taip tampriai susijęs su *kaimu-kiemu*? Ką galvojo Daukša savo Ledesmos katekizmo vertime (1595) sakydamas: ,,Kaip turi šeimyna, kaimynai ir tarnai po akim viešpatų savų laikytis ir gyventi!'' arba Vuiko ,,Postilės'' vertime (1599): ,,Kurie turi tarnus, vaikelius arba kaimynus, jog jų nemokė, neplakė, nebarė, nekuopė''[48]. Čia žodis *kaimynas* tikrai nereiškė *kaimyno* dabartine prasme. Lietuviškas žodis *kaimynas* pateko į senąją slavų ir lenkų kalbomis rašytus aktus[49]. Sprendžiant iš tų aktų, *kaimynas* reiškia tam tikrą valstiečių kategoriją. Tačiau kokią? XIX a. Lietuvos visuomeninių santykių tyrinėtojai šiai valstiečių kategorijai tikslaus aptarimo nerado. Vieni iš jų aiškino, kad *kaimynai* buvo valstiečiai, gyvenę savo namuose prie kitų valstiečių, bet ne prie žemvaldžio kiemo[50]. Šis istorinis terminas buvo mėginamas aiškinti dabartinės šnekamosios kalbos prasme. Tačiau *kaimynas* ligi XVI a. vidurio reiškė visai ką kitą, o ne greta gyvenantį valstietį. XVI a. pabaigoje *kaimynas* jau galėjo reikšti kaimyną dabartine žodžio prasme. Kiti gi tvirtino, kad *kaimynai* sudarė tarpinę grupę tarp valstiečių ir nelaisvosios šeimos ar dvaro bernų-tarnų (parobkų). *Kaimynai* netarnauja dvare, kaip nelaisvoji šeima, gyvena savo namuose ir dirba jam dvaro skirtą žemę, tačiau jie neturi asmeninės laisvės, negali pasitraukti iš gyvenamosios vietos. Jie taip pat neduoda dėklų ir nemoka mokesčių, o patarnauja dvare ir net dvaro laukus dirba. Tokiu būdu jie priartėja prie nelaisvos šeimos. Buvo spėjama, kad *kaimynai* atsirado iš nusigyvenusių valstiečių[51]. Daugiau šviesos į *kaimynų* atsiradimo klausimą įnešė K. Jablonskio tyrinėjimai. Peržiūrėjęs naujai surastus aktus, jis konstatavo, kad *kaimynai* yra kilę iš nelaisvos šeimos[52]. Jablonskio nuomonei pritarė ir Ivinskis, laikydamas *kaimynais* tuos baudžiauninkus, kurie iš nelaisvų dvaro bernų (slav. *parobok*) pasidarę valstiečiais gavę žemės iš dvaro[53]. Jurginis, iš naujo peržvelgęs senuosius oficialiuosius aktus ir nustatęs, kokią žmonių kategoriją *kaimynais* vadina tie aktai, kiek suabejojo Jablonskio išvadomis, nes aktuose aiškiai pabrėžiamas esminis skirtumas tarp berno-tarno (*parobko*) ar nelaisvos šeimos ir *kaimyno*. Pagal Jurginį esminis skirtumas tarp *parobko* ir *kaimyno* yra teisinis, kokybinis, susiklostęs iš papročio teisės per gana ilgą laiką — *kaimynas* visai kitokios kategorijos žmogus[54]. *Kaimynas* yra dėl neturto ar kitų priežasčių į baudžiavą patekęs valstietis. XVI a. baigiantis, *kaimynų* institutas išnyksta ir *kaimynai* jau nebebuvo skiriami nuo kitų valstiečių baudžiauninkų. *Kaimynas* galėjo būti paverstas *veldamu*, tat *kaimynas* yra atsiradęs anksčiau už *veldamą*. Kaip ir iš kur *kaimynai* atsirasdavo, sunku pasakyti, nes trūksta šaltinių iš XIII–XV a.

Oficialaus termino *kaimynui* Didžioje Lietuvos Kunigaikštystėje vartota senoji kanceliarinė ,,rusų" kalba neturėjo. *Kaimynas* galėjo būti vadinamas ir *selianin*, ir *kmiec* (lit. *kumetis*), ir dar kitokiais pavadinimais. *Selianin* yra ne kas kita, o tik etimologinis *kaimyno* vertimas iš slav. *selo* 'kaimas', kas aiškiai matyti senuose aktuose. Pvz. viename akte pieva vadinama lietuvišku vardu *kaimyniške*, o kitame toji pati pieva *selianskaja*[55].

Kaimyno terminą ne dabartinės lietuvių kalbos žodžio prasme yra pavartojęs Daukša iš lenkų kalbos verstuose Ledesmos katekizme 1595 m[56]. ir Vuiko ,,Postilėje" 1599 m.[57] Katekizme lenkišką tekstą ,,A iakož się ma sluga albo poddany zachovac przeciw Panu swemu?" Daukša išvertė: ,,Kaip turi šeimyna, kaimynai ir tarnai po akim viešpatų savų laikytis ir gyventi." Kaip matome, tas žmonių kategorijas, kurios lenkiškai buvo nusakytos *sluga* ir *poddany*, Daukša išvertė trimis žodžiais, todėl neaišku, kurį iš tų žodžius jis išvertė *kaimynu*. Kitoje gi vietoje katekizme Daukša *sluga* verčia ne *tarnu*, o *šeimyna*: ,,A panowie iako przeciw slugom?" (Daukšos vertime: ,,O viešpates kaip turi su šeimyna laikytis?"). Postiljė lenkiškąjį tekstą: ,,Lakoś sprawował dziatki y czeladke swoie; iakoś rządził y opatrował poddane swoie?" Daukša išverčia: ,,Kaip rėdei vaikelius ir šeimyną savą? Kaip rėdei ir apveiszdėjai kaimynus savus?" Čia Daukša *kaimynu* verčia lenkiškąjį *poddany*. Daukšos vienalaikiai Mažvydas[58] ir Vilentas[59], rašę kiek anksčiau, lenkiškajam *poddany* nusakyti vartojo *padonis* ir *veldamas* (lot. *subditus*). Čia reikėtų įsidėmėti ir tai, kad anoniminio autoriaus 1605 pataisytame Daukšos katekizme žodis *kaimynas* pakeistas valstininku[60]. Anoniminis taisytojas *kaimyno* pakeitimą *valstininku* motyvuoja tuo, girdi, *kaimynas* esąs žemaitiškas žodis ir todėl kitiems lietuviams sunkiai suprantamas, o tuo tarpu, sprendžiant iš senųjų aktų, *kaimynas* kaip tik buvo vartojamas Aukštaitijoje, o ne Žemaitijoje, kur ši baudžiauninkų kategorija greičiausia buvo kitaip vadinama. Daukša lenkiškąjį *poddany* verčia ir *padoniu* ir *veldamu*[61], tačiau pagal senuosius oficialiuosius aktus *kaimynas* neatitiko nei *padonio*, nei *valstininko* terminui. Tą nevienodumą būtų galima paaiškinti gal tuo, kad, kai Daukša rašė, *kaimyno* institutas jau buvo beveik išnykęs, todėl nyko ir jo senoji prasmė. Didelio skirtumo tada tarp tų pavadinimų jau nebebuvo.

Kodėl gi dabar tam tikra į baudžiavą patekusių valstiečių kategorija buvo vadinama *kaimynais*, t. y. gretimai gyvenančiais dabartine to žodžio prasme? Žemvaldžio sodyba, kaip jau minėta, buvo vadinama *kaimu-kiemu*, o tarp *kaimo-kiemo* ir *kaimyno* yra aiškus etimologinis ryšis. Priesaga *-yna-* yra susidariusi jau priešistoriniais laikais, todėl jos kilmė dabar nebevisai aiški. Lietuvių kalboje ši priesaga yra plačiai vartojama ir dariniai su ja yra gana įvairūs[62]. Kai kurie iš tų darinių yra veikiausiai sudaiktavardėję būdvardžiai. Kad taip būta, rodo iš dalies ir tai, kad lytys yra lygiagretės, t. y. ir vyriškos ir moteriškos giminės, pvz. *arklynas/arklyna* 'paprastas, menskas arklys', *kaimynas/kaimyna* 'gretimai gyvenąs'. Tą patvirtina ir kitų indoeuropiečių kalbų duomenys, pvz. lot. *vicinus* ir *vicus* (*kaimas*). Remiantis tais daviniais, atrodo, kad seniau galėjo būti buvęs ir būdvardis *kaimynas 'kaimiris, kaime gyvenąs, kaimui priklausąs, iš kaimo kilęs'. Tat senuose aktuose sutinkami *kaimynai* buvo ta baudžiauninkų kategorija, kuri gyveno kaime, buvo kilusi iš kaimo ar priklausiusi kaimui. Tačiau tiek kalbiniai duomenys, tiek teisinio pobūdžio aktai paaiškina tik socialinę senovinę *kaimyno* prasmę, jo atsiradimo išaiškinti ji negali.

300

Išnašos

1. Chr. S. Stang, *Die westrussische Kanzleisprache des Grossfürstentum Litauen*, Oslo, 1935, 145–146.

2. E. Wolter, „Lituanismen der russisch-litauischen Rechtsprache", *Mitteilungen der litauischen literarischen Gesellschaft* IV, Heidelberg, 1899.

3. K. Jablonskis, *Lietuviški žodžiai Lietuvos raštinių kalboje*. I, Kaunas, 1941.

4. V. Žukas, „Prof. K. Jablonskio bibliografija", *Bibliotekininkystės ir bibliografijos klausimai* IV, Vilnius, 1965.

5. K. Jablonskis, „Die offizielle Urkundensprache des litauischen Grossfürstentums als kulturgeschichtliche Quelle", *Pirmā vēsturnieku konference Rīgā 1937*, Riga 1938, 269–75.

6. V. Urbutis, „Dabartinės baltarusių kalbos lituanizmai", *Baltistica* V (1), 45.

7. Z. Ivinskis, „Geschichte des Bauernstandes in Litauen", *Historische Studien*, Heft 236, Berlin 1933.

8. J. Jurginis, *Baudžiavos įsigalėjimas Lietuvoje*, Vilnius 1962.

9. K. Jablonskis, *Lietuviški žodžiai Lietuvos raštinių kalboje*. I, Kaunas, 1941, 92, nr 1.

10. Michalonis Litvani, *De moribus tartarorum, litvanorum et moscorum*, Basileae 1615, 28.

11. J. Baldauskas, „Pirktinės vestuvės", *Mūsų tautosaka* X, Kaunas, 1935.

12. J. Mancelius, *Phraseologia Lettica*, Riga 1638, sp. XXXII.

13. G. Elger, *Dictionarium polono-latino-lottauicum*, Vilnae, 1683, 581.

14. J. Lange, *Vollständiges deutsch-lettisches und lettisch-deutsches Lexicon*, Mitau 1777, 157.

15. C. Ch. Ulmann, *Lettisches Wörterbuch*, Riga, 1872, 120; K. Mühlenbach–J. Endzelin, *Lettisch-deutsches Wörterbuch* I–IV, Riga 1923–25, 284.

16. *Latviešu konversācijas vārdnīca* I–XXI, Riga, 1927–1940, 18237.

17. K. Būga, *Rinktinai raštai* III, Vilnius, 1961, 651–652.

18. P. Skardžius, „Lietuvių kalba ir jos senovinė kultūra", *Aidai* 1947, nr 8, 347.

19. E. Berneker, *Slavisches etymologisches Wörterbuch* I, 635.

20. K. E. Nopierskie (red.), *Russko-Livonskije akty*, Petersburg, 1868, 405–447.

21. = 11.

22. J. Jurginis, *op. c.*, 95.

23. F. Miklosich, *Etymologisches Wörterbuch der slavischen Sprachen*, Wien, 1886, 144.

24. C. Uhlenbeck, *Kurzgefasstes etymologisches Wörterbuch der altindischen Sprache*, Amsterdam, 1898–1899, 68.

25. H. Pedersen, *Vergleichende Grammatik der keltischen Sprachen* 1, Göttingen, 1909, 128.

26. P. Skardžius, „Lietuvių kalba ir jos senovinė kultūra", *Aidai* 1947, nr 8, 347.

27. A. Walde, *Vergleichendes Wörterbuch der indogermanischen Sprachen* I, 1930, 523.

28. *Mažvydo Katekizmas* — Catechismvsa prasty Szadei, Makslas skaitima raschta yr giesmes del kriksczianistes dei del berneliu naujey suguldytas. Karaliauczui VIII. dina Meneses sausia, Metu vszgimima Diewa M. D. XLVII (fotografuotinis leidimas: Mosvid. Die ältesten litauischen Sprachdenkmäler bis zum Jahre 1570, ed. Gerullis J., Heidelberg, 1923.

29. J. Jurginis, *op. c.*, 203.

30. P. Skardžius, „Die slavischen Lehnwörter im Altlitauischen", *Tauta ir Žodis* VII, Kaunas, 1931, 234.

31. E. Fraenkel, *Litauisches etymologisches Wörterbuch*, Göttingen, 1955–1965.

32. J. Jurginis, *op. c.*, 203.

33. W. Kamieniecki, *Rozwój własności na Litwie w dobie przed I Statutem*, Kraków, 1914.

34. Z. Ivinskis, „Geschichte des Bauernstandes in Litauen", *Historische Studien*, Heft 236, Berlin, 1933.

35. J. Jurginis, *op. c.*

36. *Daukšos Postilė* — Postila katolicka, tai esti Izguldimas Ewangeliu kiekwienos nedelios ir szwentes per wisus metus, per Kuniga Mikaloiu Dauksza, Kanaunika Medniku, iž lękiszka perguldita, su walu ir dalajdimu wiresiuju. Wilniui, drukarnioi Akademios Soc. Jesu. A. Dni 1599 (fotografuotinis leidinys, Kaunas, 1926).

37. J. Jurginis, *op. c.*, 204.

38. K. Jablonskis, *Lietuviški žodžiai Lietuvos raštinių kalboje*, 1, Kaunas, 1941, 250.

39. ibid. 249.

40. J. Jurginis, *op. c.*, 205.

41. J. Jurginis, *op. c.*, 203–215.

42. *Ordbok över svenska språket XIII*, Lund, 1935.

43. *Lietuvių kalbos žodynas V*, Vilnius, 1959.

44. E. Fraenkel, *Litauisches etymologisches Wörterbuch*, Göttingen, 1955–1965.

45. = 42.

46. A. Frich, *Vergleichendes Wörterbuch der indogermanischen Sprachen* I, Göttingen, 1874.

47. *Scriptores rerum Prussicarum*, red. T. Hirsch, M. Töppen, E. Strehlke, I, 91, 419, 685; II, 518, 519; *Preussisches Urkundenbuch*, red. Philippi, Seraphim, I: 2, 145, 173, 322, 718.

48. J. Jurginis, *op. c.*, 147.

49. K. Jablonskis, *Lietuviški žodžiai Lietuvos raštinių kalboje* I, Kaunas, 1941.

50. H. Gorbačevski, *Slovar' drevnego aktovogo Severo-zapadnogo kraja i Carstva Polskago*, Wilna, 1874, 182.

51. M. Vladimirski-Budanov, *Krestjanskoe zemlevladenie v zapadnoj Rossii do polovni v.*, Kiev, 1893, 22.

52. K. Jablonskis, „XVI amžiaus belaisviai kaimynai Lietuvoje", *Praeitis* I, Kaunas, 1930, 166–213.

53. Z. Ivinskis, „Kaimynas", *Lietuvių Enciklopedija* X, Boston, 1957.

54. J. Jurginis, *op. c.*, 156–157.

55. J. Jurginis, *op. c.*, 153.

56. J. Jurginis, *op. c.*, 147.

57. = 36.

58. *Mažvydo Katekizmas*, 32.

59. Gordon B. Ford, Jr., *The Lithuanian Catechism of Baltramiejus Vilentas*, Louisville, Kentucky, 1965, 41.

60. E. Sittig, *Der polnische Katechismus des Ledesma und die litauischen Katechismen des Daugsza und des Anonymus*, Göttingen, 1929, 80.

61. *Daukšos Postilė*, 449, 535.

62. P. Skardžius, *Lietuvių kalbos žodžių daryba*, Vilnius, 1943, 266–272.

Old Lithuanian Social Terms which have Disappeared or Changed Meaning

Three old Lith. words used in the official documents of the Grand Duchy of Lithuania, written in ,,Russian", are discussed in detail, namely, *krienas* 'payment for the wife to the father-in-law', *veldamas* 'enslaved citizen, subordinate subject', and *kaimynas* 'member of a certain category of citizens, earlier serfs'. *Krienas* and *veldamas* have disappeared in modern Lithuanian, whereas *kaimynas* is still in use but only with another meaning.

JAN PETER LOCHER

Lettisch *tauta*, plur. *tauti* usw.: Varianten des Stammauslautes in ihrer Beziehung zur Wortbedeutung

1. In dem neben der lettischen Bibelübersetzung wohl bedeutendsten alt-lettischen Schriftwerk, der Postille des Mancelis (1593–1654) vom Jahre 1654[1], treten auf rund 1200 Druckseiten den weit über 700 Belegen für *Łaudis* (maskulines Pluraletantum, analytisches Kollektivum, der Bedeutung nach dem deutschen „Leute, Volk" zu vergleichen) nur 32 Stellen mit *Tauta* entgegen.

Der Bedeutungsbereich dieses Wortes ist, verglichen mit jenem von *Łaudis* — trotz einiger Berührungsflächen[2] — in der Vorstellungswelt des Mancelis offensichtlich eher marginal. Dies bestätigen die spezifischen Charakteristika seiner Verwendung: Im Plural (15 Belege) erscheinen die *Tauti* (sic) ausnahmslos als fremde Kollektive oder „Völker". Sie stehen einem näheren, „eigenen Bereich" gegenüber[3] (gekennzeichnet z. B. durch *mehs* „wir" [Postille 1.172], *fawus Łaudis* „die eigenen Leute" [1.7] u. ä.), in welchen sie — die Beispiele sind fast stereotyp — eindringen können: 1.375 *Weens Konigs palieds und pefti fawus Łaudis no fweffcheem Tauteem* „Ein König hilft und erlöst seine Leute von fremden *Tauti*." 2. 75 *Zeekahds taggad par fcho Semm wafajahß ... no fweffcheem Tauteem no fawas Tåhwa-Semmes?* „Wie mancher wurde auf dieser Erde von fremden *Tauti* aus seinem Vaterland verschleppt?" Vgl. 2.195 usw.

Im Singular (17 Belege) ist *Tauta* entsprechend verwendet, d. h. generell gesetzt, z. B. in 1.184 Kaum hatte das Jahr 1602 begonnen, *tad fweffcha Tauta usklieda no wiffeem Mala-Maleem, tee ißpohftija wiffu fcho Semm* „... da tauchte fremde *Tauta* von allen Seiten her auf, die (Plural) ver-heerten dies ganze Land." Vgl. 2.150 usw. In mindestens 7 Fällen dagegen erscheinen auch die Juden, wenn sie neben fremden oder Heiden-Tauti auftreten, ihrerseits als *Tauta*[4]: Vom Blickpunkt des Mancelis und der Letten ist offensichtlich zur *Tauta* der Juden ebenso Distanz gegeben, wie zwischen den Fremden und dem jeweilen nahen oder eigenen Lebenskreis innerhalb des biblischen Kontextes: 1.304 *Es åßmu Proweets unnd Paliedfå-tais teems Ifraelitereems dohtz, tee gir manna Tauta, manni Łaudis* „Ich bin den Israeliten als Prophet und Helfer gegeben; diese sind meine *Tauta*,

meine Leute." 3.88 Die Hohepriester müssen „Recht suchen" *Teeſſu meck-
leht py Rômero-Łaudeem, tee by to Juddo-Tautu und Semm usjåhmuſchi und
nowahrejuſchi* „bei den Römern, welche die *Tauta* der Juden und ihr Land
übernommen und bezwungen hatten" usw.

2.1. Die Tatsache, dass Mancelis *Tauta* nie auf den lettischen Bereich
bezieht[5], lässt sich bestimmten Beobachtungen hinsichtlich der Morphologie
des Wortes zuordnen: Der Reichtum verschieden zu beurteilender Flexions-
endungen ist selbst bei Mancelis auffallend. Wir finden nebeneinander:
Singular Nom. *-a*, Gen. *-as*, Akk. *-u*, so auch gewöhnlich in Verbindung
    mit der Präp. *no*; die hybride Endung *-us*[6];
Plural Nom. *-i*, Gen. *-o*[7], Dat.-Instr. *-eem(s)*, Akk. *-us*.
Den femininen Formen im Singular stehen, zunächst überraschend, im
Plural ausschliesslich maskuline gegenüber[8]. Da nichts die Annahme eines
alten *-o-* bzw. *-io-* Stammes nahelegt — auch nicht die mit *taut-* gebildeten
baltischen Eigennamen[9] — müssen wir von den femininen Endungen als
den primären ausgehen. Der maskuline Plural lässt sich in der Folge bequem
als Analogiebildung verstehen: Besonders der geläufige Dativ-Instrumental
auf *-eem(s)*, für den unter insgesamt 15 Stellen im Plural 9 Belege zur Verfügung stehen[10], findet seine Stütze in den sehr zahlreichen Parallelbildungen
desselben Bedeutungsbereiches[11]. Am stärksten dürfte *Łaudis* als Muster
gewirkt haben, sowohl von seiner Bedeutung her, als auch weil dieser so
häufige maskuline *i*-Stamm selbst anstelle des erwarteten **-ihm* den Dat.-
Instr. plur. ausnahmslos auf *-eem(s)* bildet[12].

Der besonders auffallende Nominativ des Plurals auf *-i* in 3.49 (*Deewam*)
wiſſi Tauti, Łaudis, Mehles kallpaht buhß „Gott werden alle Völker, Leute,
Zungen dienen" erklärt sich unter solchen Umständen unschwer als retrograde Bildung — ebenso wie der Akkusativ in 1.548 *wiſſus Zillwåkus,
wiſſus Tautus, Juddus und Paggaŋus* „alle Menschen, alle Völker, Juden und
Heiden". Diesen zwei Belegen stehen vier hinsichtlich des Geschlechts
„neutrale" Genetive (1.172 *Karra- und Tauto-Laikohß* „in diesen Kriegs-
und *Tauti*-Zeiten", analog 2.201 und 2.38: hier neben *Tauto-Laikà* auch
fweſſchà Tauto-Semmeh) und die oben genannten neun Belege mit dem
Dativ-Instrumental auf *-eem(s)* gegenüber[13].

2.2. Darüber hinweg ordnet sich *Tauteem(s)* sogar einer im Ansatz er-
kennbaren, übergreifenden Tendenz ein, der zufolge seltenere Feminina auf
-a den Dativ-Instrumental des Plurals auf *-eem(s)* anstatt *-ahm* bilden.
Vgl. beispielsweise: *Mala* „Rand, Seite" 2.209 *Und taß* (i. e. Christus)
jehme to no teem Łaudeem fawißke py mallas „... nahm ihn für sich beiseite",

2.186 *wiſſahß mallahß ſpaidieß* „werden auf allen Seiten bedrängen", vgl.
2.226 usw. und andererseits, im Dativ-Instrumental der Mehrzahl: 1.151
ar Aſſareems lieds Mala-Mahleems „mit Tränen (angefüllt), bis ganz an den
Rand", 1.184 *no wiſſeem Mala-Maleem* „von allen Seiten", vgl. 1.193
tahß Willnas kaukdami (sic) *no wiſſeem Maleem* „Wellen, die von allen Seiten brausen".

Dahwana „Gabe, Geschenk" 2.127 *Deewa Dahwana* „die Gabe Gottes"
(vom Brot), dagegen 2.131 (von der Hand Gottes) *Winja wiſſas Leetas ap-
pufchko ar faweem Dahwaneem* „Sie verschönt alle Dinge mit ihren Gaben"[14].

Diese Tendenz zur Bevorzugung maskuliner Formen werden wir schwer-
lich direkt mit der bekannten Vorliebe des Livonischen für Maskulina verbinden können: Mancelis hielt sich in Lettland nie im Bereich der livonischen
Mundarten[15] auf[16]. Auch ist wenig wahrscheinlich, dass Beeinflussung durchs
Estnische vorliegt, wo ein Genusunterschied ebenso unbekannt ist wie im
Livischen[17], dem die livonischen Dialekte des Lettischen ihre teilweise
Substituierung des Femininums durch entsprechende Maskulinformen ver-
danken[18] — Mancelis war zwar 1625 bis 1632 „Oberpastor" in Tartu, aber
doch für die deutsche Gemeinde an der Johanneskirche[19]. Im Gegenteil,
auffallend ist vielmehr, dass bei Mancelis der Neigung, im Plural bisweilen
maskuline Flexionsformen vorzuziehen, im Singular — wenn auch bloss im
Ansatz erkennbar — eine gegenläufige Tendenz zu entsprechen scheint:
Anstelle des sonst geläufigen *i*-Stammes *Zilts* (vgl. Bibel 1689 Ex. 31.2 *no
Juda Zilts*, Nu. 31.4 *ſtarp wiſſahm Iſraëla Ziltim* usw.[20]) bietet Mancelis nur
Zillta und entsprechende Formen[21]. 1.83 *Wanuels no to ʒilltu* (vgl. unten)
Aſer, kattra ʒillta nhe lohte auxta by „Phanuel aus dem Stamme Aser, welcher
Stamm nicht sehr hoch(-gestellt, d. h. angesehen) war". 2.191 ... *tee nu no
Abrahama Zilltas und Ṣlackas by* „die nun waren aus Abrahams Stamm und
Geschlecht", vgl. 3.183 usw. Ähnlich findet sich *vilta* neben dem *u*-Stamm
vîltus; siehe ME s. v., 4.596 f. Vergleichbare Stellen der Bibelübersetzung
von 1685/89 sind genusindifferent[22]. Bei Mancelis dagegen: 1.499 *nhekahda
Willta*[23] „kein Betrug", oder 2.154 *beß Willtas* „ohne Tücke".

Wenn *Tauta* im Singular nur feminine Formen aufweist, so muss hier
offen bleiben, ob die eben aufgewiesene Tendenz dafür mitverantwortlich
zu machen ist, dass die Maskulinformen des Plurals nicht auch auf den
Singular übergegriffen haben[24]. Unter solchen Umständen hätten wir damit
zu rechnen, dass im Falle von *Tauta* primär eventuell nur Tendenzen phonetisch motivierter, vereinheitlichender Analogiebildungen wirksam sind.

2.3. Von der Morphologie der Singularformen zu *Tauta* lässt sich tatsächlich eine Brücke zum maskulinen Plural nur indirekt schlagen: Unter

den 17 Belegstellen im Singular sind immerhin 7 genusindifferent, d. h. auslautend auf -*u* in der Funktion des Akkusativs oder Instrumentals, siehe etwa 1.304 *ka Mofes tawu Raddu und Tautu nolahdejis* „dass Moses deine Verwandschaft und *Tauta* verflucht hat"; vgl. 3.88 oder 1.322 *weenu tautu, kattra* „eine *tauta*, welche": Das unmittelbar anschliessende relative *kattra* verrät auch hier das Femininum. Die übrigen Belege erscheinen alle in Verbindung mit *no* und dem Akkusativ-Instrumental[25]. Siehe 1.88 *no to Juddo-Tautu by nahkt* „aus der Juden-*Tauta* kommen sollte", 1.224 dito, 3.206 *no Paggaṇo Tautu bijufchi* „aus Heiden-*Tauta* stammend". Vergleichbare Syntagmata finden sich passim[26] — doch ist auch der Genetiv mit *no* belegt[27]. Mancelis hat sich, so scheint es, von phonetischen Anklängen leiten lassen: die Bildung auf -*as* kann sich an vorangehendes -*as* in *Bafnizas* (1.40) bzw. *Ewas* (3.149) „anlehnen"[28].

2.4. Wir stellen daher fest: Es gibt einen Bruch, der quer durch die Gesamtheit der Belege für *Tauta* bei Mancelis verläuft und einen maskulinen Plural von einem femininen Singular trennt — wobei allerdings nicht ausser Acht zu lassen ist, dass hier wie dort genusindifferente Kasus eine Art „morphologischer Brücke" bilden[29]. Dahinter erscheint eine Unsicherheit im Wortgebrauch wirksam, die uns in Mancelis' Schriften gewöhnlich bloss bei seltener vorkommenden Wörtern begegnet, z. B. *Dahwana* „Gabe" oder *Willna* „Welle" (Anm. 14).

Sie hat einen möglichen Grund wohl mit darin, dass Mancelis *Tauta* nie auf die Letten bezieht, sondern ausschliesslich im Hinblick auf andere, fremde Kollektive setzt: Dem nahen, bekannten, eigenen Kreis (wir, unser Land o. ä.) stehen „draussen", im Plural die *Tauti* — so wohl unter dem Einfluss anderer Maskulinbildungen (S. 304) — gegenüber, vor denen man sich zu schützen hat. Diese Situation erscheint bei insgesamt 15 Belegen im Plural immerhin 7mal[30] in einen eindeutig lettischen weiteren Sachzusammenhang gestellt — unter den 17 Stellen im Singular dagegen bloss 3mal[31]; immer ist dabei das kollektive *Tauta* feminin: Ein System- oder Analogiezwang, der über *Tauti* hinaus hätte *Tauts* bilden lassen wie *Nabbs* für geläufiges *naba* „Nabel"[32], war offenbar nicht stark genug, im Gegenteil: Die drei genannten Belege ordnen sich vielmehr den übrigen 14 Stellen im Singular ein. *Tauta*, so im Singular, gehört dabei überall einer andern Sphäre an, jener der biblischen Welt — bis auf 1.304 *Paggaṇo-Tauta* „Heiden-Tauta", 3.206 *no Paggaṇo-Tautu* und 1.360 *Rômero-Tauta* „Römer-Tauta" wird *Tauta* überall nur von den Juden ausgesagt. Kurz: Einem in seiner Verwendung viel breiter gestreuten, maskulinen Plural *Tauti*, der ebensogut biblische wie lettische Sachzusammenhänge voraussetzt, steht ein femininer Singular *Tauta* gegenüber, der nicht richtig in einen lettischen Kontext eindringen kann — wahrscheinlich, weil eine dann naheliegende Identifikation: Letten = eine *Tauta* in der Sicht des Mancelis nicht möglich ist[33]. Die semantische Charakterisierung, die es erlaubt, einem „biblischen" Singular einen allgemeiner verwendeten Plural entgegenzustellen, scheint also eine Widerspiegelung in morphologischen Besonderheiten zu finden, nämlich der Opposition zwischen femininem Stammauslaut im Singular und maskulinem Stamm im Plural.

3.1. Im Altlettischen erscheint *tauta* mit verschiedenem Stammauslaut auch im Werke des Juris Eļǵers (1585–1672). Dabei sind folgende Übereinstimmungen und Unterschiede zum Sprachgebrauch des Mancelis feststellbar:

Schon das jetzt in der Ausgabe Draviņš 1961[33a] zugängliche Manuskript der Evangelia et epistolae vom Jahre 1640 bietet — wie die Druckfassung von 1672[33b] — auf 138 Seiten *tauta* nur als hapax legomenon: 58 Draviņš (zu Ev. Jo. 11.47 ff.): Hohepriester und Pharisäer beratschlagen; wenn sie Jesus gewähren lassen ... *nåks tautas no Romu pylli, vnd atiems mums muſo ʒemme vnd liâudis.* „... werden *tautas* aus der Stadt Rom kommen und uns unser Land und unsere Leute wegnehmen." Der Beleg passt ausgezeichnet in das für Mancelis ermittelte Begriffsbild: Den fremden *tautas* aus Rom sind unser Land (*muſo ʒemme*) und unsere Leute (*liâudis*) entgegengesetzt.

3.2. Das Dictionarium Polono-Latino-Lottavicum von 1683[34] erlaubt eine Reihe aufschlussreicher Ergänzungen: *Tauta* bzw. Ableitungen davon finden sich unter den Lemmata *Cudʒy* (S. 45): *Alienus, externus, exter(eri: m)* — *Sweßis* (sic), *tauts* (sic) / *Cudʒoʒiemiec* (45): *Extraneus, peregrinus, alienigena* — *Swæßis* (sic), *tauts, tautwets, ſweßneks* / *Cudʒoʒiemski* (45): *Barbarus, exoticus, externus* — *Swæß* (sic), *tauts*[35]. Daneben: *Niewlaſny* (283): *Improprius, alienus* — *Sweßis, tauts, ſweßneks* / *Obcy* (292): *Externus, extraneus* — *Swæß, ſwaeſneks* (sic), *tauts, tautwets* / *Niebywaly* (257): *Hospes, peregrinus* — *Swæß tauts* / *Przychodʒień* (440): *Advena(æ m)* — *Sweßis tauts* / Auch: *Wygnaniec* (590): *Exul* — *Tautos dʒiwotåys*. Aber umgekehrt: *Wygnany* (590): *Pulsus* etc. — *No tæwe ʒem iʒdʒits* — also ebensowenig unter Beizug von *tauts* o. ä. ausgedrückt wie *Tuteczny* (sic, 552): *Indigena huius loci* — *Sʒas ʒemmes cylwæks*. Ableitungen finden sich unter den Stichwörtern *Poganin, pohaniec* (397): *Paganus, gentilis, ethnicus* — *Pagans, nækriſtits cylwæks, Tauts* (sic) und *Pogański* (397): *Ethnicus* — *Tautigs* (zu erwarten: *Tautisks*) / *Pogańskie* (sic), *po pogáńsku* (397): *Ethnico more* — *Tautig* (für erwartetes *Tautigi*) / *Pogaństwo* (397): *Gentilitas* — *Tautums*.

Dagegen erscheint der Wortstamm weder unter den Stichwörtern *Lud/Populus* (202) oder *Národ/Natio* (250) oder gar *Pokolenie/Stirps, progenies* (401), wo lettisch überall *Liâudis, Cilta* u. ä. eintreten.

3.3. Ohne auf Einzelheiten einzugehen, bleibt doch festzuhalten, dass für Eļģers *taut-* offenbar soviel wie „fremdes Volk" bedeuten muss — anders wären die Ableitungen *tautwets* und *tautigs* mit den angegebenen Bedeutungen und ebenso die singuläre, als Substantiv wie als Adjektiv deutbare Maskulinform *tauts* kaum denkbar. Eļģers' Angaben erwecken den Eindruck, als ob der katholische, von Mancelis sicher weitgehend unabhängige, Autor eine auffallend präzise Vorstellung von den *tautas* hätte — ohne Gelegenheit zu finden, diese auszudrücken, da er nicht nur in seinen Predigten, sondern auch im Wörterbuch von polnischen bzw. lateinischen Begriffskategorien herkommt. Was indessen an Bedeutungskonturen ersichtlich ist, deckt sich auffallend gut mit Mancelis' Wortgebrauch. Für poln. *plemie* (sic) bzw. *pokolenie* ist Eļģers eher bereit, *cilta* (sonst Übersetzung von *rod*) oder *plenni*[36] (sic: so auch für *potomek* und *rod*) einzusetzen, anstatt das gleichsam „freie" *tauta* zur Wiedergabe zu benützen. Er bringt dafür einen substantivisch wie adjektivisch deutbaren maskulinen Nominativ des Singulars *tauts* „cudzy, alienus" bei — oder bildet diesen sogar selbst: Ein Gegenstück mit femininem Stammauslaut, also *tauta*, dürfte Eļģers kaum recht geläufig gewesen sein. Dies wenigstens legen die Angaben s. v. *Pochodʒenie* (382) nahe, die sich mit den übrigen kaum zusammenbringen lassen: *Ortus, derivatio — Eſakums, cylta* (sic), *tauta* — weder der Sprachgebrauch des Mancelis noch jener von Eļģers selbst in den Evangelien und Episteln (1640) bekräftigen eine solche Gleichung.

Trotz des wenig umfangreichen Belegmaterials lässt sich hinter dem Nebeneinander im Stammauslaut — *tauts* neben *tauta* (einmal im Wörterbuch) und *tautos* (Lok. plur., mask., einmal im Wörterbuch) neben *tautas* (Nom. plur., fem., einmal im Evangelientext) — auch bei Eļģers eine Unsicherheit besonders im Gebrauch des Singulars erkennen. Sie wäre erklärt, wenn wir annehmen, dass ein Singular Eļģers im Grunde gar nicht geläufig war, ebensowenig wie Mancelis, der *Tauta* im Singular nur auf Israel, dagegen nicht auf die Letten bezieht. Bildungen wie *tauts* bei Eļģers oder *Tauti* bei Mancelis erscheinen von hier aus eher als isolierte „Wucherungen" zu einem im Plural geläufigen *tautas* mit der Bedeutung „fremde Sippen- oder Volksgemeinschaften". Ein mindestens von den entsprechenden baltischen Eigennamen her (vgl. z. B. *By-tautas* usw. bis *Žu-tautas*, als Vorderglied etwa *Tauta-gina(s)* usw.[37]) zu postulierender alter, lettischer

Singular *tauta* war offensichtlich nicht in lebendigem Gebrauch. Diese Folgerung legen auch die Verhältnisse in den Dainas nahe.

4. A. Gāters stellt Orbis (Louvain) 14, 1965, 479 einander gegenüber: **tauts* [poetische Bildung?] „Freier": *tauta*, pl. *tautas*. Den maskulinen Nominativ des Singulars gewinnt er aus dem Dainabeleg 21 637 var[38]. [Zlēkas, Kreis Ventspils] *Izkūst tauta ledus svārki* „Es zerschmilzt der aus Eis gemachte Rock des Freiers" (übers. Gāters). *Tauta* (Gen. sing.) nimmt direkt den voraushegenden Singular in *Tautīšam ledus svārki* „Der Freier (eig. Angehörige der *tautas*) hat einen Rock aus Eis" wieder auf, steht aber nach Ausweis von Barons im Wechsel mit ebenfalls überliefertem *tautu* (Gen. plur.) [Kuldīga].

Das von Gāters für die Dainas angesetzte **tauts* ist allerdings völlig isoliert — auch das entsprechende feminine Gegenstück *tauta* ist so im Singular kaum vertreten: Der Verfasser dieses Beitrages hat auf 1000 Liednummern der Sammlung Barons, die alle der Brautwerbung gewidmet sind, in der allein unser Wort geläufig ist[39], 297 Belege gezählt für den Plural *tautas* (Nom. plur., fem.) mit der „Doppelbedeutung" „die Freiersleute" bzw. „die Leute, zu denen sich der junge Mann auf Freite begibt". Beide Bedeutungen erweisen sich dabei als verschiedene Aspekte desselben Sachverhaltes: Sowohl der Bursche, der *tautās iet*, d. h. „Leute und Gegend aufsucht, wo eine Braut zu finden ist" wie das Mädchen, „das auf den Hof des Bräutigams zieht", begeben sich über ihren gewohnten Lebensbereich hinaus — jenen der archaischen, im Grunde vorfeudalen, eigenen Sippschaft[40] — zu anderen, fremden, Sippschaften, den *tautas*[41]. Eine Selbstidentifikation der eigenen Gruppe als *tauta* findet nicht statt. Der Verfasser hat bloss drei eindeutig überlieferte Stellen gezählt, an denen ein Singular *tauta* offensichtlich einen einzelnen Freiersmann bezeichnet[42]. Ein maskuliner Singular ist dagegen voraussetzbar in einer weiteren Stelle: *Nei redzēju pašu tautu, Nei tautieša kumeliņa* „Weder den Freier selbst, (*pašu tautu*) hab' ich gesehen, noch sein Ross (Dim. — *tautieša kumeliņa*)" 13515: Mārciena.

Umgekehrt zeigt ein Beleg wie der nachfolgende, dass sich ein Singular *tauta* selbst in der Bedeutung „Freiersmann" auch dann nicht aufdrängt, wenn mit aller Wahrscheinlichkeit einer einzigen Nuss ein Freiersbursche gegenüber gestellt wird: *Būs man viena rieksta* (Gen. sing.) *dēļ Līdz zemīti lagzdu liekt? Būs man vienu tautu* (Gen. plur.) *dēļ Rūdināt māmuliņu?* 14706.3: Ance „Soll ich wegen einer einz'gen Nuss den Haselstrauch bis auf den Boden (Dim.) biegen, einer *tautas* (Plur.) wegen das Mütterchen betrüben?" Die Parallelsetzung im Vergleich lässt erwarten — trotzdem das *viens* auch zu Pluraliatantum treten kann[43] — dass *vienu tautu* (Gen. plur.) soviel wie „eines Freiers wegen" zu bedeuten hat.

Damit drängt sich der Schluss auf, die von uns beleuchteten Dubletten im Stammauslaut — d. h. *tauta* neben *tauts*, *tautas* neben *tauti*[44] — seien nicht zuletzt darauf zurückzuführen, dass in unsern Quellen (Mancelis, Eļģers; Dainas) ein mit dem eigenen nahen Lebenskreis in direkte Verbindung zu bringender Singular *tauta* überhaupt nicht auftaucht. Damit fehlt eine selbstverständliche Bezugseinheit.

Anmerkungen

1. Mancelius Georgius, *Lettifche Lang-gewúnfchte Poſtill* ... Rīga, 1654.

2. So gibt es Stellen, in denen *Ļaudis* und *Tauta* einander wechselweise ablösen: In 1.88 sind die Juden zunächst *Deewa-Ļaudis* genannt und erscheinen unmittelbar nachher, im Gegensatz zu fremden und Heiden-Völkern oder *Tautas*, selber als *Tauta*. Vgl. 3.49, 3.88 usw.

3. Im Sinne der typologischen Kulturbeschreibung von Ju. M. Lotman: vgl. z. B. "O metajazyce typologických popisů kultur", *Orientace*, Praha, IV, 1969; II, 67–80.

4. 1.88, 224, 304, 3.88, 90, 134, 149.

5. Obschon er in der deutschen *Dedicatio* zur Postille (S. a iv) von der *Gemeine Lettifcher Nation* spricht.

6. 1.356 *no ... Dawida Zilltas, unnd no Juda Tautus*. Vgl. Anm. 28.

7. Zum Lautwert A. Ozols, *Veclatviešu rakstu valoda*, Rīga, 1965, 181.

8. Keine Parallelen verzeichnet bei J. Endzelīns, *Lettische Grammatik*, Rīga, 1922, oder Шмидт, П., „Особенности языка латышскаго писателя Г. Манцеліа", Живая старина СПб 5, 1895, 162–170 — auch nicht bei Ozols 1965, 180 ff.

9. Zusammenstellung K. Būga, *Rinktiniai raštai*, Vilnius, 1958–62, Index 197 und 283.

10. Belege für Dat.-Instr. plur.: 1.7, 88, 173, 375, 2.75, 191, 195, 3.130, 153.

11. Z. B. *Zillwâkeem(s)* "Menschen": 1.4, 25, 33 usw., passim; *Juddeem(s)* „Juden": 1.89, 106, 130 usw.; *Bâhrneem(s)* "Kindern": 1.93, 128, 132 usw.

12. Z. B. 1.12, 14, 17 usw.

13. Anm. 10.

14. Doch 2.375 *ar leelahm Dahwanahm*. — Nicht direkt vergleichbar, aber der phonetischen Tendenz nach auffallend ähnlich ist eine analoge „Verengung" bei *Willna* „Welle" (für heute schriftsprachliches *vilnis*): 1.189 *Tahß Willnas gir tha ghajuſchi, ka ta Laiwa gir ar Willneem ka klahtin apklahta*. Sogar: 1.191 *leelas Willnes* (Akk. plur.), 1.186 *ar Willnehm*.

15. Zum Begriff: Endzelīns, 1922,3; zuletzt V. J. Zeps, *Latvian and Finnic Convergences*, Bloomington/'s-Gravenhage, 1962, 55 f., M. Rudzīte, *Latviešu dialektoloģija*, Rīga, 1964, 147–257.

16. Lebensdaten: Zuletzt A. Johansons, *Latviešu literātūra no viduslaikiem līdz 1940. gadiem*, Stockholm, 1953, 18 f. und K. Draviņš, „Georg Manzels und Paul Einhorns Briefe" ..., *Svio-Estonica*, Stockholm, XVIII, 1967, 141–152.

17. Über das Livische L. Kettunen, *Livisches Wörterbuch*, Helsinki, 1938 und ders., *Hauptzüge der livischen Laut- und Formengeschichte*, Helsinki, 1947.

18. Endzelīns 1922, 342 f.

19. Schmidt 1895, 162.

20. Doch vgl. Mülenbachs, K.–Endzelīns, J., Latviešu valodas vārdnīca, Bde. 1–4, Rīga, 1923–1932 (Abkürzung: ME); s.v. *cìlts, -s*, 1.382: ... **cilta* „das Geschlecht, der Stamm". *ne ciltām, ne ciltīm* u. ä. „nicht im geringsten".

21. Eine Ausnahme in 1.49. Ozols 1965, 181: *Zillta* als Femininum ev. fehlerhaft?

22. Nu. 25.18 *ar Wiltu*; Jos. 9.3 *arridſan Willtu*.

23. Nach ME s.v. *vilta*, 4.596, wo versehentlich als Belegort 1.483 steht. Die dortige 2. Belegstelle 2.384 zu *blēņi ir un vilta* bleibt noch zu identifizieren.

24. Vgl. *Nabbs* in 2.330 für sonst geläufiges *naba*, ME s.v. *naba*, 2.685 und Būga, 1958–62, 3.263.

25. ME s.v. *nùo* 2.755.

26. Z. B. 1.359 *no Deewu*, 3.149 *wiſſi, kaß no Adamu Zilltas*.

27. 1.40 *no Baſniʒas-Kungho Tautas*, 3.149 *no ... Ewas Zilltas*.

28. Doch ist Schlüssigkeit nicht möglich: Mancelis zeigt bisweilen Schwanken oder Unsicherheit hinsichtlich der Form. In 1.356 folgen aufeinander *no Dawida Zilltas*, *unnd no Juda Tautus*. Die letzte Form wirkt wie eine Kontamination von *Tautu* und *Tautas* — so in Anlehnung an das vorangehende *Zilltas*. Vgl. 1.157 *no Wackara puſſus* neben 1.114 *no Rieta = puſſes*.

29. S. 304 f.

30. 1.172, 173, 548, 2.38 (2x), 75, 195.

31. 1.184, 2.150, 2.240².

32. Anm. 24.

33. Mit einer Setzung wie 1.304 *Iſraelitereems ... tee gir manna Tauta* "den Israeliten, die sind meine *Tauta*" hat Mancelis den modernen Sprachgebrauch des Wortes, in dem *Tauta* absolut gesetzt erscheint, zwar nicht vorweggenommen — der entscheidende Schritt einer Identifikation mit dem Begriff der Dedicatio (S. a iv der Postille) *Lettiſche Nation* fehlt — aber doch vorbereitet. Der Bezug auf die Juden des biblischen Sprachgebrauchs dient dabei als eine Art „Brücke".

33a. Georg Elger, Evangelien und Episteln ... Herausgegeben von K. Draviņš, Lund, Slaviska Institutionen vid Lunds Universitet, 1961, (Text- och materialutgavor 1).

33b. Zugänglich bei A. Günther, *Altlettische Sprachdenkmäler in Faksimiledrucken*, 1, Heidelberg, 1929.

34. G. Elger, *Dictionarium Polono-Latino-Lottavicum*, Vilnius, 1683 (Benützt: Exemplar des Stifts- och Lärovennsbiblioteket, Skara).

35. Offensichtlich adjektivisch aufzufassen, wie mir Herr K. Draviņš, Lund, bestätigt.

36. Bei ME und den zugehörigen Ergänzungsbänden (Endzelīns, J.–Hauzenberga, E., Papildinājumi un labojumi K. Mülenbacha Latviešu valodas vārdnīcai, Rīga 1934–46, Nachdruck Chicago 1956) nicht verzeichnet.

37. Anm. 9.

38. Zählung nach der Ausgabe K. Barons–H. Visendorfs, *Latwju Dainas*, I–VI, 1894–1915, Nachdruck Rīga 1922.

39. Liednummern 14150–15150; die Auswahl erfolgte unter dem Gesichtspunkt, möglichst ergiebige Motivzusammenhänge anzuschneiden.

40. A. Švābe spricht von der *Brāļu lielǵimene* (in Endzelīns, J.–Klaustiņš, R.,

Latvju tautas daiņas, I–XII, Rīga, 1928–32, 5, 171–191). Sie ist in den Dainas nach aussen durch die *b(r)āliņi* vertreten.

41. Belege für *iet tautās* — vom Burschen her gesehen: ... *es jāju tautiņās Līgaviņu lūkoties* 13 874: Irji/Kreis Kuldīga „ich bin zu den *tautas* gefahren, nach einer Braut mich umzuschauen"; (Zu *līgaviņa* jetzt: E. Hauzenberga–Šturma, Lett. „*līgava, ļaudava*" „(künftige) junge Ehefrau > Verlobte, Braut" in *In honorem Endzelini*, Chicago, 1960, 52–63) Vgl. 13 958 usw.; vom Mädchen aus: *Laiks man iet tautiņās* ... 14 034: Jaun-muiža/Kreis Kuldīga „Zeit ist es, zu den *tautas* (Dim.) zu gehen — der Boden der Vor-ratskammer ist, wo die Aussteuer steht, schon durchgebogen." Vgl. 14 048 usw.

42. *Nedod, māte, sav' meitiņu Pirmā tautas jājumā! Lai segloja tautas dēlis Trīsreiz savu kumeliņu* 14 966: Engure „Mutter, gib dein Mägdelein nicht beim ersten *tauta*-Ritt! Satteln soll der *tautas dēlis* drei Mal sein Ross (Dim.)". Der Genetiv *tautas* ist also gleich durch eine der festen Bezeichnungen für den einzelnen Freiersburschen erläutert; *Tas saņēma, nosegloja Pirmo tautas kumeliņu* 14 581.1: ohne Ortsangabe „Der hat abge-nommen, abgesattelt das erste *tauta*-Ross (Dim.)", d. h. das erste Pferd des Freiers; *Lai nāk tauta nakamo* 15 014: Birzgale; Mutter, bleib unter den Mädchen, „dass *tauta* (d. i. ein Freier) komme, ja komme".

43. Endzelīns 1922, 371.

44. Endzelīns 1922, 193 f. zitiert auch ostlettisches *tauty* als maskuline Variante im Plural.

Latvian *tauta*, plur. *tauti* etc.: Variants of the Final Sound in the Stem as Related to Word Meaning

The alternative variants of the stem found in Latvian *tauta* '(the) people' (fem. sing.) vs. *tauts* (masc. sing.) and *tautas* (fem. plur.) vs. *tauti* (masc. plur.) can be traced back to the fact, that in the sources in question (Man-celis [1593–1654], Eļģers [1585–1672]; Dainas [folksongs]) there does not exist a singular *tauta* which could be brought into direct connection with the speaker's own, close Latvian environment. A self-evident unity of re-ference is missing—although an *older* Baltic feminine singular remains to be postulated (proper names; Old Prussian evidence).

JIŘÍ MARVAN

Inflectional Structure of the Lithuanian Noun[1]

1. Stem and ending

The contemporary concept of the principal inflectional structure of the noun[2] (henceforth SW, i.e. "substantival word") is given in the following definition: "Since, from the point of view of modern Lithuanian, that part of the word which changes with inflection is considered to be the ending (galūnė), the stem (kamienas) of the words *akìs, akiẽs, ãkiai, ãkį* (i.e. 'eye' Sg. N, G, D, A) etc. is thus not *aki-* but *ak-*,[3] i.e. that part of the word, which remains after the ending had been dropped.[4]"

This formulation is obviously strongly directed against the use or rather misuse of historical criteria in the description of modern, synchronic structure. Nevertheless, even such a formulation could appear misleading. The following three arguments prove this.

Argument 1. A) It is apparent that each of the segments 1. [*i*], 2. [*ie*], 3. [*į*], 4. [*y*] (of the forms 1. *ak[i]s, ak[i]ai;* 2. *ak[ie]s;* 3. *ak[į]* 4. *ak[y]s, ak[y]se* Pl. N, L) obligatorily includes the element *i*, henceforth [i]. Since one of these segments is obligatory in each form of SW *akis*, the stem is equivalent not to *ak-* but to *ak[i]-*, and it is *"vocalic"*.

B) SW *ausis* 'ear' has the same forms as SW *akis*. There is only one different form, Pl. G: *akių : ausų*. But the consequence of this difference is that [i] is not obligatory in SW *ausis*, i.e. the stem of this SW is equivalent to *aus-*, and it is "consonantal".

C) Moreover, if we construct the limit (symbol /) between the stem and the remaining part of SW we obtain the opposition

ak[i]/ ... : aus/[i] ...

for all cases except Pl. G.

These theoretically acceptable conclusions absolutely contradict both the definition (cf. A) and its real meaning (cf. B, C).[5] The paradox of two empirical observations is evident.

Argument 2. Let us consider two SW, [1] *viršus* 'top' : [2] *paviršus* 'surface', having certain analogous features with SW *ausis, akis* (cf. Pl. G *viršų* : *paviršių*). The element *i* in SW [2] is not only constant, as in SW *akis*, but also unchangeable, unlike SW *akis* (cf. Arg. 1), e.g. Sg. G *paviršiaus*, D *paviršiui*, A *paviršių* etc. If we apply the initial definition, there is no doubt that the constant element *i* must belong to the stem. In spite of this conclusion, this element is inflectionally relevant because it is the only criterion of the special Plural paradigm, cf.

Pl.	SW *viršus*	SW *paviršius*	SW *kelias* 'road', *brolis* 'brother'	
N	*viršūs*	*paviršias*	*keliai*	*broliai*
D	*viršums*	*paviršiams*	*keliams*	*broliams*
I	*viršumis*	*paviršiais*	*keliais*	*broliais*

Table 1.

The Lithuanian grammars (including AcadGram) do not follow this definition and yet they respect the opposition represented in [1] : [2]. The definition differs from the reality, at least from the reality described in AcadGram.

Argument 3. Let us consider the following SW: 1. *mėnuo* 'moon, month', 2. *akmuo* 'stone', 3. *duktė* 'daughter' (normative forms of Sg. N, G, D, A will be discussed):

Sg.	SW *mėnuo*	SW *akmuo*	SW *duktė*
N	*mėnuo*	*akmuo*	*duktė*
G	*mėnesio*	*akmens*	*dukters*
D	*mėnesiui*	*akmeniui*	*dukteriai*
A	*mėnesį*	*akmenį*	*dukterį*

Table 2.

As we see, the constant parts of these SW are 1. *mėn-*, 2. *akm-*, 3. *dukt-* or *dukt[e]*, however the stems, in spite of the definition, are traditionally interpreted as 1. *mėnes-*, 2. *akmen-*, 3. *dukter-*. Only in the last case the endings such as (*mėnes-*) *-io, -iui, -į* are identifiable with those in SW *brolis* 'brother' (*brol-*) *-io, -iui, -į* etc.

Therefore, there is no doubt that a new definition is needed.

2. Base and formant, methods of their delimitation

The concept of inflectional duality in SW is the positive portion of the cited definition. However, in order to avoid misunderstandings which the traditional terms "stem" and "ending" cause we will use the terms *base* (symbol

B) and *formant* (symbol F). In the initial stage of the investigation the *base* is defined as the *non-formal part* of the word and indicated by the symbol Bel (i.e. "B elementar") and the *formant* as the *formal part* of the word, recorded as Fel. Hence, every SW can be expressed as

$$SW = Bel + Fel \qquad (0)$$

in this obligatory order.

The initial problem—the limit between Bel and Fel—cannot be solved only by observation of the formant, cf. 1. On the contrary, the formant shall be the subject of further research. Thus the base must be used for the delimitation of Bel and Fel. Of course, the inverse definition, "the base (i.e. stem) is an invariable part", would lead to similar or, more exactly, similarly vague results. This circle cannot be broken unless the inflectional criteria are dropped, i.e. as far as the elementary concepts of inflection are interpreted by means of inflection itself. This is why the *external*, i.e. *derivational* and not the *internal*, i.e. *inflectional* formal criteria must be applied for delimitation.

3. Main problems of derivational delimitation

In the "denominative" (i.e. postsubstantival) derivation, only marginal cases show alternations in the base, e.g. *dievas→deivė* 'god, goddess', *sniegas→snaigė* 'snow, snow-flake', *vagis→vogti* 'thief, steal'. If these easily identifiable cases are ignored, the following is applicable: every derivative includes 1. the formal (derivational) part (affixes, another component of a compound), Dr, 2. the constant, obligatory part of the fundamental SW, the base of SW, Bel. This base bears the semantic meaning of SW and is obligatorily present. Thus every derivative (symbol dr) can be expressed as:

$$dr = Bel + Dr \qquad (0')$$

Let us consider SW *akis* (with additional meanings 'bud, stitch, mesh') and its derivatives *akinis* 'eye, adj.', *akylas* 'sharp-sighted', *akytas* 'meshed, porous', *akišveitė* 'eye-bright, bot.' (*šveisti, šveitė* 'to polish, shine') etc. All these derivatives contain [i]. Is the formation *ak[i]*- the stem?

4. Minimal base, Bmin; maximal formant, Fmax

However, the dr-set[6] of SW *akis* contains the following dr: *akutė* 'bud, stitch, mesh', *akti, ako* 'grow blind, lose eyesight' etc. Since these dr no not include [i], the element [i] cannot be considered an obligatory part of B. Therefore, the following definition must be given: The obligatory part of B is the minimal number of graphemes that are present in an ideal dr-set of the given SW.[7] Technically, in order to obtain the obligatory part, B must be minimized to the lowest limit (absolutely minimized).

Definition 4.1. Minimal base (symbol Bmin) is the absolutely minimized B formation.

Now, if we apply the expression Bmin in (0), the following formula will be obtained:

$$SW = Bmin + F^o \qquad (1')$$

where $F^o = Fel$.

Let us analyze F^o. As is obvious from (1'), F^o is the formal part of SW. According to the definition 4.1., F^o is F maximized to the highest limit. This maximized F formation will be designated as *maximal formant* and symbolized Fmax. Thus the formula (1') yields the following definitive form:

$$SW = Bmin + Fmax \qquad (1)$$

The formula (1) expresses the principal inflectional structure of any SW. The expression Fmax represents the formation which is to be the main subject of the inflectional analysis.

5. P-subsets

Let us consider all SW as a set. The set of all SW consists of a certain number of paradigmatical subsets, henceforth P-subsets. The concept P-subset corresponds in the Lithuanian grammars to "paradigm" or "declension" (Lith. linksniuotė). The traditional paradigms accept a certain number of irregularities.

The strictly formal approach must exclude some irregularities from our initial investigation. First of all, only the morphological SW will be treated, i.e. no *indeclinabilia*, no substantivized adjectives and participles, no reflexive verbal nouns. There is also no reason to consider *singularia* and *pluralia tantum* nor the heterobasic cases (*žmogus : žmonės* 'homo, homines') and heteroclites.

6. Definitions of P-stand and its constituents

This elimination of irregularities was necessary for the formulation of the *standard P-subset*, henceforth *Pstand*.

1. Every *Pstand* consists merely of those SW that have the identical sum of formants (i.e. "exactly the same endings").

2. This sum will be denoted $(P)Fmax$ and called the property of Pstand.

3. The set of all Pstand constitutes the standard SW-set. The number of all Pstand in standard SW-set will be denoted by n.

Note: the number n will be considerably higher than the number of traditional paradigms since any group of SW or even one SW with one single different ending must be according to 6.2. regarded as a separate Pstand. This also has practical reasons: the higher number can be easily eliminated while the lower one would necessitate construction and definition of a new Pstand.

4. Any Pstand as a subset of standard SW-set will be denoted $P_m$stand where $1 \leqslant m \leqslant n$. The standard SW-set, i.e. the set which will be the subject of the subsequent investigation, can be expressed as the following sum:

$$P_1\text{stand} + P_2\text{stand} + \ldots + P_n\text{stand} \qquad (2)$$

5. (P)Fmax of $P_m$stand is (P_m)Fmax.

6. Any element of $P_m$stand (i.e. "any noun, SW, the endings of which are identical with (P_m)Fmax") is denoted by (P_m)SW.

Thus sumarily:

I. $P_m$stand, a subset in the standard SW-set,

II. is the sum of all (P_m)SW

III. possessing the property (P_m)Fmax.

This statement may be generally expressed in the following table:

A. Subset	P_1 stand	P_2 stand	P_n stand
B. Any noun belonging to the given subset	(P_1) SW	(P_2) SW	(P_n) SW
C. Sum of the typical formants of the set to the given subset	(P_1) F_{max}	(P_2) F_{max}	(P_n) F_{max}

Table 3.

Each row of the table represents certain objects of the investigation:

Row A according to (2) contains the sets of all SW for which the initial investigation is immediately applicable, i.e. all SW, theoretically considered.

Row B represents the minimal sum of SW which must be directly investigated.

Row C represents the sum of formants which will be the main subject of the inflectional investigation itself.

7. The relations of standard P-subsets and their constituents

(P_m)Fmax is the constituent property of $P_m$stand, i.e. it is universally compulsory for all elements of $P_m$stand and is representable.

The compulsoriness of any (P_m)Fmax will be expressed as

$$P_m\text{stand} \sim (P_m)\text{Fmax} \rightarrow (P_m)\text{SW} \sim (P_m)\text{Fmax} \tag{3a}$$

(where $\sim$ ... "has property", $\rightarrow$ ... necessitates)
and formulated as follows: If any $P_m$stand possesses the property (P_m)Fmax, then this property is possessed by every (P_m)SW.

The representability of any (P_m)Fmax will be expressed as

$$(P_m)\text{SW} \qquad (P_m)\text{Fmax}—P_m\text{stand} \qquad (P_m)\text{Fmax} \tag{3b}$$

and formulated as follows: If any element of $P_m$stand, i.e. any (P_m)SW, possesses the property (P_m)Fmax, then the entire $P_m$stand possesses this property. Thus any (P_m)SW may represent the whole $P_m$stand (comparable but not identical with the traditional: "any noun of a given paradigm may be declined to obtain the paradigm").

The principle of representability is of primary importance in the delimitation of Fmax. There is no need to determine a Bmin in all SW, since (P_m)Fmax of any $P_m$stand is proved if it is proved in any single (P_m)SW.

8. Main rules for grapheme identification

In this way, it is possible to select for our investigation such SW so that the identification of the graphemes in the morphological suture will be most effective and provide the most complete information. Nevertheless, the following provable rules (though not proved here) must be observed:

1. The grapheme *i* is not realized before *i*- and *e*-graphemes (*i, y, į; e, ė, ę*) except in case of the diphthong *ie*; e.g. for SW *velnias* 'devil', *i* appears in Sg. N, G *veln/i/as, veln/i/o* but not in Sg. L, V *veln/yje, veln/e*. Then, for instance, it cannot be decided, whether the grapheme *i* is present before Dr ("overlapped" by the following *i*) or not in the case of dr *veln/iškas* 'devilish', Dr -*iškas*.

2. The groups a) *či*, b) *dži* before *a*- and *u*-graphemes (*a, o, ą; u, ū, ų*) have the morphological value of the pairs a) *ti*, b) *di*, e.g. a) SW *marti* 'daughter-in-law': Sg. N, G *marti, marčios* → morph. *marti, martios*, (cf. dr *mart/auti* 'to be d.'); b) SW *gaidys* 'rooster': Sg. N, G *gaidys, gaidžio* → morph. *gaidys, gaidio* (cf. *gaid/ukas* dim.).

Table 4.

1. P_m stand	2. (P_m) SW	3. Number of SW	4. dr	5. Dr	6. B_{min}	7. F_{max}
i	*ragas, rago* 'horn'	many	*ragiukas* dim.	*-iukas*	*rag-*	*-as, -o*
ii	*svečias, svečio,* V *svety* 'guest'	few	*svetainė* 'drawing-room'	*-ainė*	*svet-*	*-ias, -io* *-y*
iii	*velnias, velnio* V *velne* 'devil'	1	∅			
iv	*mokytojas, mokytojo* 'teacher'	many	∅			
v	*brolis, brolio,* V *broli* 'brother'	many	*brolužis* dim.	*-užis*	*brol-*	*-is, -io* *-i*
vi	*mėnuo, mėnesio* V *mėnesi* 'moon'	1	∅			
vii	*gaidys, gaidžio* V *gaidy* 'rooster'	many	*gaidukas* dim.	*-ukas*	*gaid-*	*-ys, -io* *-y*
viii	*liepa, liepos* 'lime-tree'	many	*liepukai* 'lime-blossom'	*-ukai*	*liep-*	*-a, -os*
ix	*giria, girios* 'forest'	rather many	*giraitė* 'grove'	*-aitė*	*gir-*	*-ia, -ios*
x	*marti, marčios* 'daughter-in-law'	2	*martauti* 'to be d.'	*-auti*	*mart-*	*-i, -ios*
xi	*upė, upės* Pl. G. *upių* 'river'	many	*upokšnis* 'creek'	*-okšnis*	*up-*	*-ė, -ės* *-ių*
xii	*viršus, viršaus* Pl. N. *viršūs* 'top'	rather many	*viršelis* 'lid'	*-elis*	*virš-*	*-us, -aus* *-ūs*
xiii	*paviršius, paviršiaus,* Pl. N. *paviršiai* 'surface'	rather many	*paviršutinis* 'superficial'	*-utinis*	*pavirš-*	*ius* *-iaus* *-iai*
xiv	*ausis, ausies;* D *ausiai,* Pl. G. *ausų* 'ear'	rather many	*ausuoti,* Past *ausavo* 'box one's ears'	*-uoti* *-avo*	*aus-*	*-is, -ies* *-iai* *-ų*
xv	*akis, akies,* D *akiai* Pl. G *akių* 'eye'	many	*akutė* 'bud, stitch'	*-utė*	*ak-*	*-is, -ies* *-iai, -ių*
xvi	*dantis, danties;* D *dančiui;* Pl. G *dantų* 'tooth'	few	*dantuotas* 'toothed'	*-uotas*	*dant-*	*-is, -ies* *-iui* *-ų*
xvii	*žvėris, žvėries,* D *žvėriui;* Pl. G *žvėrių* 'animal'	2	∅			
xviii	*akmuo, akmens;* D *akmeniui;* Pl. G *akmenu* 'stone'	many	*akmenuotas* 'stony'	*-uotas*	*akmen-*	*-∅, -s* *-iui* *-u*
xix	*duktė, dukters* D *dukteriai;* Pl. G *dukterų* 'daughter'	2	∅			

3. The grapheme *j* always has the morphological (inflectional) value of the pair *ji*, e.g. in SW *žvejys* 'fisherman' Sg. N, G *žvejys, žvejo*→morph. *žvejys, žvejio*, cf. corresponding forms *gaidys, gaidio; genys, genio* (SW *genys* 'woodpecker'). The practical consequence is that *i* is not here identifiable by means of the derivational criteria and that other methods must be used in this case.

9. Constructing the concrete minimal bases (Bmin)

Table 4 contains all $P_m$stand. According to Table 3, these are represented by (P_m)SW. The number of $P_m$stand exceeds the number of the traditional paradigms (cf. 6., 3. Note). In column 2. Sg. N, G will be shown in all cases. All cases are in the Sg. unless Pl. is indicated.

10. Modeling the limit between Bmin/Fmax

As we see in Table 4, the limit between Bmin/Fmax is defined for (P_m)SW and consequently (cf. (3b)) for $P_m$stand which represent the number of SW which considerably exceeds 90 % of the elements in the standard SW-set. This is a satisfactorily representative corpus of SW for modeling a general limit between Bmin/Fmax. According to the data for positive cases in table 4:

(*Model 1*.) The last grapheme of Bmin is the last consonantal grapheme of B. The limit between Bmin/Fmax immediately follows. The following vocalic grapheme is the first grapheme of Fmax.

The cases like *mėnuo; akmuo, akmens; duktė, dukters* (cf. $P_m$stand vi; xviii; xix) are not suitable for the application of this model at this stage of investigation.

Further investigation for the negative cases (iii, iv, vi, xvii, xix) proves Model 1 as a universal model of the limit between Bmin and Fmax for any Lithuanian noun.

Notes

1. This article develops the ideas presented in my article "K základum současné litevské deklinace", *Slovo a slovesnost* XXVIII, 401–405 and is dedicated to the memory of my unforgettable meeting with Professor Ch. S. Stang in May 1969 in Uppsala.

2. i.e. delimitation of the formal and non-formal parts (stem and ending) of the noun.

3. These words reject the traditional conception of "vocalic stem".

4. See *Lietuvių kalbos gramatika, I Fonetika ir morfologija*, Vilnius 1965, 210. Henceforth AcadGram (the explanations in brackets are my own).

5. AcadGram, according to tradition, combines the nouns *akis, ausis* in one common paradigm. Some briefer descriptions simply ignore the type SW *ausis*, e.g. for one of the latest cf. *Jazyki narodov SSSR, I. Indojevropejskije jazyki*, Moscow 1966; (Litovskij jazyk, 500–527) p. 508 f.

6. The expression "dr-set" denotes "set of all derivatives".

7. Not every real dr-set is able to provide derivatives which would prove Bmin exactly. But this is a matter of the chance conditions, i.e. due to neutralization of certain features (weak cases), accidental absence of strong cases, etc. Thus, "ideal" means "lacking these conditions". The practical solution of the problem is suggested in the conception of standard P-subsets in 6. and is applied in the subsequent investigation.

TERJE MATHIASSEN

Baltisch und Slawisch.
Zur Chronologie und Bedeutung
der Kürzung langer Diphthonge

Die genaue Bestimmung des Charakters der Beziehungen zwischen den
baltischen und den slawischen Sprachen stellt ein schwieriges Problem dar,
das keine endgültige Lösung gefunden hat. Es dürfte wohl niemand bestrei-
ten, dass hier nahe Berührungen bestehen — wenn auch diese nicht derart
eng sind wie etwa diejenigen zwischen dem Indischen und dem Iranischen,
welche ja ziemlich eindeutig auf eine arische „Ursprache" weisen. Was die
Frage nach einer baltisch-slawischen Gemeinschaft und der zeitlichen Bestimmung dieser eventuellen Einheit betrifft, so gibt es darüber schon eine
fast unabsehbare Literatur, die unter Berücksichtigung bald der einen, bald
der anderen Kriterien von höchst variierenden Stellungnahmen zeugt. Im
Rahmen dieses Aufsatzes ist es selbstverständlich nicht möglich, auf die
gesamte Frage einzugehen. Ich will bloss betonen, dass zwischen den beiden
extremen Punkten, der Annahme einer baltisch-slawischen Einheitsperiode,
welche Ansicht unter Forschern wie z. B. J. Endzelin, R. Trautmann, A.
Vaillant und, wie es scheint, J. Kuryłowicz ihre Anhänger zählt, und dem
vornehmlich von A. Meillet, *Études sur l'étymologie et le vocabulaire du vieux
slave*, Paris, 1902, 201–2, *Les dialectes indo-européens*, Paris, 1908, 40 ff.,
vertretenen Standpunkt, welcher die ausgesprochene Ablehnung einer besonders nahen Verwandtschaft dieser Sprachen in nachieur. Zeit bedeutet,
eine erhebliche Anzahl von nuancierten und untereinander z. T. stark
abweichenden Ansichten besteht. In diesem „nebelhaften Niemandsland"
befindet sich auch der Verfasser der vorliegenden Studien. — In *einem*
Punkte möchte ich aber hier meine Auffassung von den baltisch-slawischen
Beziehungen etwas näher präzisieren; es betrifft dies die Frage nach den
langen Diphthongen (Typus (-)$\bar{E}RT$, wobei E ein beliebiger Vokal, R ein
Sonant und T ein beliebiger Konsonant ist) sowie der Chronologie und
den Folgen ihrer Kürzung.

In mehreren Arbeiten ("Le degré long en balto-slave", *Rocznik Slawistyczny*
(abgk. *RS*) XVI, 1948, 1–14; *L'apophonie en indo-européen* [abgk. *Ap.*],
Wrocław 1956, 286 ff. u. passim; *Indogermanische Grammatik* [abgk. *IG*] II,
Heidelberg, 1968, 318 ff. u. passim) hat J. Kuryłowicz die Bedeutung der

Kürzung der langen Diphthonge für den (sekundären) quantitativen Ablaut, Typus (-)ER, (-)ET : (-)$\bar{E}RE$, (-)$\bar{E}TE$, (besonders) im Baltischen und Slawischen betont. Hat in diesen Sprachen die Quantität der tautosyllabischen Langdiphthonge im Akut eine direkte Spur hinterlassen, so scheint in der Verbindung (-)$ERHT$- infolge des Wegfalls des *Schwa* (konsonantischer oder schon vokalischer Geltung?) eine *Dehnung* des Vokals stattgefunden zu haben. Die so entstandene Länge wurde dann — welche Annahme in Betracht einer gewissen Diskrepanz zwischen der phonologischen und der morphologischen Ebene übrigens nicht unproblematisch ist — nach der Ansicht Kuryłowiczs zunächst auf deren heterosyllabische Entsprechung übertragen, insofern es um eine *deverbative Ableitung* geht (NB. diese Begrenzung hat Kuryłowicz, *IG* II, 319, begründet). *Nach* der lautgesetzlichen Abkürzung der tautosyllabischen Länge musste die prävokalische Form als ,,Dehnstufe'' (ein unadäquater Ausdruck!) erscheinen, was die allmähliche Übertragung der Länge auf Wurzeln *aniṭ*, (-)ER-E, und schliesslich noch die Struktur (-)ET-E nach sich zog. Grundsätzlich finde ich diesen Mechanismus, wo es um das Baltische und das Slawische geht, ansprechend. Das Wirkungsgebiet dieser ,,Formel'' bedarf aber m. E. einer schärferen Umgrenzung, welche Frage ich in einer hoffentlich bald erscheinenden Arbeit ausführlich behandelt habe.

In der *Ap.*, 286, hat Kuryłowicz das folgende chronologische Tableau aufgestellt:

1) $ERH > \bar{E}R$, $\underset{\circ}{R}H > \bar{R}$ (oder $iRH > iR$)
2) Entstehung der Intonationen
3) Kürzung der langen Diphthonge

Diese schematische Darstellung, deren relative Chronologie nach meinem Dafürhalten zwingend ist, wird sogleich vom Verfasser in folgender Weise kommentiert: "Les diphtongues longues *sont nées et ont disparu* (Hervorhebung Kuryłowiczs) à une époque préhistorique très reculée.'' In der *IG* II, 115, macht aber Kuryłowicz diese lakonische aber interessante Bemerkung: ,,Es ist nicht ausgeschlossen, dass die Kürzung der Langdiphthonge unabhängig im Balt. und Slaw. stattgefunden hat.'' (Vergleiche jedoch noch *op. cit.*, S. 296, § 377, Anm. 23, worauf Kuryłowicz selber hinweist.) Schlüsse aus dieser Eventualität hat Kuryłowicz eigentlich keine gezogen.

Auf den Gedanken einer unabhängigen Kürzung im Baltischen und Slawischen bin ich vor dem Erscheinen des Kuryłowicz'schen Buches gekommen, werde aber durch seinen kleinen Hinweis zu weiteren Überlegungen angeregt. Dabei möchten wir zunächst fragen, was für Folgen einer derart späten Kürzung entspringen würden, falls wir sonst an dem obigen System festhalten und ihm beharrlich dieselbe Bedeutung zusprechen möchten. Die Antwort lautet wohl: 1) Der Ausbau des von Kuryłowicz in den obengenannten Werken veranschaulichten Quantitätswechsels, was zu der Benennung *Ablaut* berechtigt, müsste *unabhängig* im Baltischen und Slawischen durchgeführt worden sein. 2) Man müsste die Ansicht über die sog. *métatonie rude* (siehe Chr. S. Stang, *International Journal of Slavic Linguistics and Poetics* X, 111–2) modifizieren, indem sie ja als analogische Erscheinung (ihr eigentliches Gebiet!) *nur* sonderbaltisch, bzw. sonderslawisch hätte wirken können. Beide Vorgänge setzen die besprochene Kürzung voraus, und es wäre dementsprechend höchstens mit blossem auf gemeinsamen Voraussetzungen beruhendem Parallelismus zu rechnen. 3) Man erhielte ein wertvolles Werkzeug zur Bestimmung des Umfangs der dem Schema $(-)(E)RT : (-)\bar{E}RT$ folgenden (reellen) *Vṛddhi* (in der technischen Bedeutung als nominalen Ableitungsmittels), die m. E. auch im Baltischen und Slawischen — unabhängig von der „Formel" Kuryłowiczs — eine beträchtliche, wenn auch nicht derart tiefgreifende Rolle wie im Arischen und wohl noch im Germanischen gespielt hat.

Wie liesse sich aber nun diese unsere Hypothese von *einer* verhältnismässig späten, unabhängigen Kürzung beglaubigen? Es sprechen dafür der m. E. tatsächlich bestehende, erhebliche Unterschied in dem Ausbau des quantitativen Ablauts im Baltischen und Slawischen, worauf ich hier, abgesehen von dem blossen Hinweis auf die Iterativa, bzw. sek. Imperfektiva des Slawischen, die Zustandsverba auf *-ėti* im Litauisch-lettischen samt einigen deverbativen Nominaltypen, nicht näher eingehen kann, sowie gewisse lautliche Entwicklungen innerhalb des Ostbaltischen, welche mich zu der Schlussfolgerung bewegen, dass die besprochene Kürzung unabhängig im Ostbaltischen und Westbaltischen vor sich gegangen ist. Scheint hier das Baltische bezüglich der uns interessierenden Frage in zwei Gebiete gespalten werden zu müssen, was ich unten sofort näher begründen werde, so liegt es auch sehr nahe, das Slawische als die naturgemäss entferntere Gliederungsgrösse zugleich als selbständiges Gebiet abzusondern. *Vielleicht* gibt es auch für das Slawische eine unmittelbare Indikation (wozu siehe weiter unten). In dieser Weise gelangte man zu der Schlussfolgerung, *dass sich die Kürzung im Ostbaltischen (Litauisch-lettischen), im Preussischen und im Slawischen unabhängig vollzogen hätte*, wobei ich bloss bemerken möchte, dass das Preussische hinsichtlich der konkreten Folgen einer Sonderkürzung künftiger und erneuter Analyse bedarf.

Wenden wir uns jetzt an die möglichen inneren Kriterien des Ostbaltischen:

A) Ie. *ō scheint ostbalt. *uo* und *ā ergeben zu haben, wobei die letztere Vertretung durch eine Art Ausgleich bei lebendigem Ablautswechsel entstanden sein wird. Wenn es uns nun gelingen würde, einem *isolierten* auf ie. (-)ōRT zurückweisenden Fall nachzuspüren, so erhielten wir je nach dem Reflex (*-aRT* oder *-uRT*) wertvolle Information über das relative Alter der Kürzung, denn wo nämlich die Lautung -*uRT* vorläge, müsste sich *ō schon zu *uo* entwickelt haben, wonach die Kürzung erst ostbaltischen Alters sein könnte; bei -*aRT* wäre sie älter als der Übergang von *ō zu *uo*.

Sicherer Beispiele (ie. *ōRT bezeugender Fälle) gibt es (im Baltischen) nicht viele. Einen brauchbaren Beleg bietet aber m. E. der Akk. Pl. der ŏ-Stämme, denn: ,,Lit. -*us*, best. Adjektivform -*úosius*, žem. (auch N.-W. žem.) -*úśus*, -*ų́śus*; lett. -*us*, best. Adj.form -*uõs* (vgl. lit. *tuõs*, lett. *tuõs*) beweisen, dass die Endung auf ur-lit.-lett. *-*uons* < *-*ōns* zurückgeht. Hierzu stimmt skt. *deván*." (Chr. S. Stang, *Vergleichende Grammatik der Baltischen Sprachen* [abgk. *VGB*], Oslo 1966, 186. Vgl. jedoch abweichend J. Endzelin, *Slavjano-baltijskie ètjudy*, Char'kov 1911, 169. ,,Schwankend" sind A. Vaillant, *Grammaire comparée des langues slaves* [abgk. *GCS*] II[1], Paris 1950, 34, und J. Otrębski, *Lingua Posnaniensis* III, 1951, 356.)

Soweit ich darüber zu urteilen vermag, besteht die Schlussfolgerung Stangs zu Recht. Hat aber hier tatsächlich, wie ich glaube, *-*uons* vorgelegen, spricht nach meinem Dafürhalten dieser Umstand ziemlich eindeutig dafür, dass die Kürzung bei der Abtrennung des Ostbaltischen noch nicht eingetreten war, denn eben auf den Nachweis der Lautung *-*uons* kommt es hier an. Dass wir es mit einer auslautenden Silbe und darüber hinaus etwas spezieller lautlicher Struktur zu tun haben, tut m. E. wenig zur Sache.

Gegen diesen Hintergrund könnte man sich über die Lautung des lit. Instr. Pl. der ŏ-Stämme -*aĩs* gegenüber skt. -*aiḥ* etwas verwundern. Warum erscheint in diesem Falle *a*, was auf frühe Kürzung deuten könnte? Zu vermuten wäre etwa, dass dieser Kasus früh von dem Lok. Pl. beeinflusst worden sei. In der späteren Entwicklung wäre dann dieser letztere umgebildet. (Hiervon abweichender Ansichten bin ich mir bewusst; hier sei bloss auf *eine* denkbare Lösung hingewiesen.)

Was das Preussische anbelangt, so sind im Akk. Pl. der ŏ-Stämme keine Spuren eines langvokalischen Ausgangs mehr vorhanden; dieser Ausgang wird wahrscheinlich frühe Kürzung erfahren haben (Stang, *VGB*, 186). — Eine Analyse der entsprechenden slawischen Form vorzunehmen, ist zwecklos.

In *einem* Punkte fällt es mir aber schwer, Stang beizupflichten. *VGB*, 18 (Fussnote) wird nämlich folgendes behauptet:

„Die Langdiphthonge scheinen zwar zum Teil bis ins Urbalt. erhalten worden zu sein [...]. Balto-slavisch war aber wohl die Kürzung von altererbten oder auf ieur. Tradition beruhenden Langdiphthongen auf *r, l, m, n*, vgl. die Vr̥ddhi-Bildung *várna – vrãna* < balt.-sl. **vắrnā<* **uárnā* zu **u̯ornos*. Wäre die Verkürzung erst urbaltisch, hätte man im Lit. **ùrna* < **vúornā* erwartet."

Es kommt mir hier methodisch und realiter als wenig ansprechend vor, mit zwei verschiedenen Kürzungsschichten, wie es Stang andeutet, zu rechnen: *methodisch*, weil m. E. die Logik für einheitliche Behandlung spräche, *realiter*, weil uns der obengenannte Ausgang des Akk. Pl. — falls richtig beurteilt — eine ie. Länge (NB. die ältere Schicht Stangs) zeigen würde, die erst ostbaltischer Kürzung unterlag. Man würde damit einverstanden sein, dass die neu entstandenen langen Diphthonge (siehe oben) zu derselben Zeit gekürzt wurden wie die altererbten, und dass die ganze Entwicklung eine lautgesetzliche gewesen ist. (Es ist aber möglich, dass meine Kritik in diesem Punkte nicht ganz genau getroffen hat, vgl. weiter unten.)

Die Schlussfolgerung Stangs, dass bei später Kürzung lit. **ùrna* zu erwarten wäre, ist unter bestimmten Voraussetzungen — nämlich den von Stang angenommenen — logisch richtig. Zu bemerken ist aber, wenn man auf diesen Bildungstypus und dieses wichtige Beispiel eingehen soll, dass weder das Vorliegen von ie. **o* (**u̯ornos* = „Rabe") noch **ō* für bewiesen gelten kann, indem diese Worte für „corax, corvus" auf das Baltische und das Slawische begrenzt sind, wenn man von dem Vorkommen ähnlicher, dieselben Vögel symbolisierender Worte in den finno-ugrischen Sprachen (siehe M. Vasmer, *Russisches etymologisches Wörterbuch* I, Heidelberg 1953, 228–9) absieht, wozu man in diesem Zusammenhang wohl berechtigt wäre. Akademiemitglied E. Itkonen, Helsingfors, der für die Redaktion einer neuen Auflage des finnischen etymologischen Wörterbuches verantwortlich ist, fasst — wie ich durch die freundliche Vermittlung V. Kiparskys erfahren habe — die finno-ugrischen Worte als onomatopoetisch auf. Eine ähnliche Lösung könnte für das Baltische und das Slawische angedeutet werden, wobei man gar nicht an den Reflex eines ie. ŏ-Lautes zu denken braucht. Es könnte ebenso gut etwa ă (: ā) vorliegen. Bei onomatopoetischer Herkunft würde ich die finno-ugrischen Bildungen auf ein und dasselbe Schema zurückführen, wie ich auf der anderen Seite *mutatis mutandis* parallel die baltisch-slawischen Belege für einheitlich hielte. Derartige Worte können zu jeder beliebigen Zeit irgendwo spontan entstanden sein. — Und selbst wenn die betreffenden Worte eine indoeuropäische Etymologie besässen, was übrigens durchaus möglich wäre (siehe J. Pokorny, *Indogermanisches etymologisches Wörterbuch*, Bern 1959, 1166, s. v. $\sqrt{u̯er}$-'brennen'), so könnte man sich denken, dass die in diesem Falle zu rekonstruierende *o*-Stufe schon durch balt. und *slaw. a* (A. Vaillant, V. Georgiev, G. Y. Shevelov u. a.) vertreten wäre. (Man beachte hier noch die von J. Pokorny, *a. a. O.*, und J. Kuryłowicz, *IG* II, 304 — übrigens mit alternativen Deutungen — gegebenen Rekonstruktionen, worauf aber nicht zu viel Gewicht gelegt werden sollte; vgl. schliesslich *Ap.*, 159.) — M. a. W., derjenige Vokal, der dem Prinzip der *Vṛddhi* gemäss verlängert wurde, war m. E. nicht ein [*o*], sondern ein [*a*], dessen Längenpendant ein [*ā*] war. Die scheinbaren Fluktuationen zwischen *ă* und *ŏ* auf baltischem Boden brauchen nicht in entscheidender Weise gegen unsere Annahme zu sprechen. Als wahrscheinliche Folge des beschriebenen Zustandes käme die Vermutung, man habe es mit baltisch-slawischer Produktivität der nominalen *Vṛddhi* zu tun, was *in casu* noch durch *den* Umstand gefördert wird, dass ja unsere Worte auf das Baltische und das Slawische beschränkt sind. Ich bin wegen des genauen Parallelismus dieser Bildungen im Baltischen und Slawischen überzeugt, dass hier echte *Vṛddhi* und nicht etwa blosse Metatonie (wie wir diesen Begriff oben S. 324 bestimmt haben) vorliegt. Für allgemeine, auf dieses Beispiel bezügliche semasiologische Betrachtungen sei auf M. Leumann, *IF LXI*, 10 u. 11, verwiesen.

Falls das genannte Beispiel trotzdem ie. *Vṛddhi* bezeugen sollte, wäre dennoch denkbar, dass hier (-)*āRT* nach dem Schema balt. *a* : *ā* statt früh. *o* : *ō* realisiert worden wäre, indem ja jenes produktiv wurde, für welches Ergebnis mehrere Momente wirksam gewesen sein können. Die Voraussetzung dafür war aber, dass das Prinzip der nominalen *Vṛddhi* bis in die Periode der Entstehung eines *baltisch-slawischen Dialektgebiets* (siehe weiter unten) lebendig war, was m. E. auf Grund noch anderer Kriterien und zusätzlicher Beispiele, worauf hier nicht näher eingegangen werden kann, mit ziemlich grosser Wahrscheinlichkeit erschlossen werden darf.

(In dem von H. Pedersen, *Études lituaniennes*, Kopenhagen 1933, 58, genannten Beispiel lit. *várpa* 'Ähre' : *vaȓpas* 'Glocke' sehe ich aber keine *Vṛddhi*.)

Ich setze mich entschieden dafür ein, dass bei *várna, vräna* etc. echte „baltisch-slawische" *Vṛddhi* vorliegt — wenn wir auch keine erschöpfende Darstellung dieses Problems in dem knappen Rahmen der vorliegenden Studien liefern können — und nehme zugleich eine im Baltischen und Slawischen auf gemeinsamen Voraussetzungen beruhende unabhängige Durchführung von deverbativen Längen nach der „Formel" Kuryłowiczs und dem (sich daraus ergebenden) Schema *a→ā* an. Dabei scheiden Beispiele mit ostbalt. *uo* als zu einer anderen chronologischen Schicht gehörig aus; andererseits kann aber keineswegs behauptet werden, dass Belege mit *ā* (: *a* : *e*) sämtlich in der baltischen und slawischen Periode entstanden sind. Somit scheint die von uns angenommene einheitliche, späte und in den betreffenden Sprachen unabhängig durchgeführte Kürzung zu keinem Widerspruch führen zu müssen.

Bei den Verba vom Typus lit. *kálti* 'schmieden, hämmern', die, etwas erstaunlich, keine Länge im Präteritum aufweisen (= *kãlė*), könnte man sich zunächst denken, dass zur Zeit des eigentlichen Produktivseins des langvokalischen Präteritums im Baltischen (welche Entwicklung m. E. grössenteils der „Formel" gemäss erklärt werden könnte) der Infinitivstamm und der Präteritalstamm noch nicht identisch waren, vgl. etwa *kùlti* 'dreschen', das ein neues (tiefstufiges) Präteritum hat entwickeln können. Zu beachten ist aber der Umstand, dass die *a*-stufigen Verba im Lettischen ein *ā*-Präteritum bilden (siehe z. B. J. Kuryłowicz, *RS* XVI, 14, und Chr. S. Stang, *VGB*, 390). — Nach den Forschungen P. Gärtchens, Chr. S. Stangs u. a. scheint mir wahrscheinlich, dass wir es bei den „Verba des Schlagens" etc. jedenfalls z. T. mit ins Ie. zurückgreifender *o*-Stufe im Präsensstamm zu tun haben. Falls der trotz E. G. Pulleyblank, *Word* XXI, 1965, anzunehmende Übergang ie. $*o > $ balt. (und slaw.) *a* und Einführung dieses Vokalismus (*a*) in den Infinitiv älter sind als der Wegfall des *Schwa* im Wortinneren, so wäre mit der Entwicklung $(-)aRT > (-)āRT > (-)áRT$ zu rechnen; sonst wäre analogische Übertragung des Akuts — NB. *nach* der Kürzung — auf das *a* anzunehmen ($*kúlti \rightarrow kálti$), was der direkten Verwendung der „Formel" nicht günstig wäre (vgl. slaw. *-kalati*). Es sollte noch betont werden, dass von dem Akut (in lit. *kálti* u. ähnl.) nicht in sämtlichen Fällen mit absoluter Sicherheit ein postsonantisches *H* erschlossen werden darf. Auch hebe ich hervor, dass die Frage nach der Lautung des balt. und slaw. Infinitivs hier in etwas vereinfachter Gestalt behandelt worden ist.

In diesem Zusammenhang sollte übrigens betont werden, dass auf den ersten Blick „vielversprechende" Belege wie lit. *aštuñtas* (die Ordnungszahl zu *aštuonì* 'acht') oder lit. Inf. *pùlti* 'fallen' (Präsens *púola*, Präteritum *púolė*) kaum als Beweismaterial für die Annahme einer späten einheitlichen Kürzung der langen Diphthonge benutzt werden dürfen, da hier junge Analogiebildung nach den betreffenden -*ḖRE*-Formen vorliegen kann, was selbstverständlich in [*u*] ausmünden musste, da ja *uo* in dieser Stellung nicht geduldet wird. (Bei *pùlti* wäre wohl nicht ganz ausgeschlossen, dass das *u* eine alte Tiefstufe direkt widerspiegelte.) Wie dem auch sei, so liessen sich m. E. diese und ähnliche Fälle am bequemsten im Lichte unserer Chronologie rechtfertigen. — Bei der Beurteilung etwaiger Fälle, die gegen die von uns befürwortete Chronologie zu reden schienen, muss im Auge behalten werden, dass das historisch zu erwartende Ablautsschema durch analogisch bedingte Verschiebung gestört sein kann.

Somit halte ich es — die bisher genannten Fälle durchmustert und interpretiert — für durchaus möglich und sogar wahrscheinlich, dass wir es mit einer einheitlichen Kürzung ostbaltischen Alters zu tun haben. — In ähnliche Richtung deuten allem Anschein nach B): gewisse Fälle mit lit.-lett. *uo* (vornehmlich bei Nomina), die wohl in *u*-diphthongischen Belegen ihre Verwandten haben. Da aber solche Fälle an sich schwierig sind — wobei z. B. auf *Evidence for Laryngeals*, The Hague, 1965, 121, hingewiesen werden soll — so wage ich es nicht, mich auf ein bestimmtes Beispiel zu berufen, zumal man hier in den Details leicht irre gehen kann (ich verweise aber auf mögliche Fälle bei Stang, *VGB*, 75 ff.). — Es kommt mir als wahrscheinlich vor, dass wenigstens ein Teil der in Frage kommenden Fälle auf ererbtes *$\bar{o}u$ weist, das sich zu ostbalt. *uou* mit darauffolgender Vereinfachung des Triphthongs zu *uo* hätte entwickeln können. An Beseitigung der zweiten Komponente eines Langdiphthongs im Wortinneren fällt mir schwer zu glauben; auch verbieten uns, wie es scheint, entscheidende Argumente, eine der Abwandlung bei *i*-Diphthongen (=*ie*) parallele Entwicklung oder ähnl. anzunehmen. Ich nehme deshalb, wenn auch zurückhaltend, an, dass wir auch hier ein Zeugnis für eine späte Kürzung der langen *in casu* abermals auf *ie*. Tradition beruhenden Diphthonge besitzen. Es machte somit B) eigentlich nur eine Abart von A) — vgl. oben — aus.

C) In seiner *IG* II, 296 (§ 377, Anm. 23) weist Kuryłowicz auf eine Indikation, die seiner Ansicht nach die Annahme einer späten Kürzung nahelegen könnte. Dies betrifft übrigens die obengenannte Entwicklung von *ei, ai* zu *ie* im Ostbaltischen, deren Bedingungen umstritten sind. Mich überzeugt aber die teils auf typologischem Vergleich, teils auf inneren Kriterien beruhende Beweisführung Kuryłowiczs eigentlich nicht (wie wäre z. B. danach etwa lit. *liepa* 'Linde' neben skr. *lĭpa* dass. zu beurteilen?). Ich verweise besser den Leser auf die erwähnte Stelle.

Fügten wir das Kriterium Kuryłowiczs noch hinzu, stünde unsere Sache um so stärker. Ich bin aber hier etwas zurückhaltend, wie sich diese Skepsis noch bei der Frage nach einem *positiven* „Beweis" der späten Kürzung der Langdiphthonge auch im Slawischen geltend macht. Wenn auch zunächst ansprechend, so scheint jedoch der Wert einer Indikation fraglich zu sein, die uns zusätzlich zu dem oben S. 324 erwähnten übrigens unzuverlässigen (indirekten) Kriterium ein unmittelbares Kriterium verleihen könnte. Ich denke an die Vertretung der Liquidametathese im Anlaut in allen slawischen Sprachen bei gestossener Betonung durch *ra, la*. Es wäre auf den ersten

Blick eine sehr ansprechende Annahme, dass hier *a* deswegen erscheine, weil es ganz einfach eine in die präslawische Zeit zurückgreifende Länge, die durch den Akut gekennzeichnet wird, direkt fortsetze. Es würde dies offenbar dem Standpunkt Vaillants, *GCS* I, 245, entsprechen. — Meine Bedenken kommen vor allem darin zum Ausdruck, dass, wenn eine alte tautosyllabische Länge in der umgestellten Form direkt fortleben sollte, so müssten die tautosyllabischen Langdiphthonge bis in die Zeit der einzelnen Slawinen beibehalten worden sein, da die Metathese im Anlaut nicht urslawisches Alter beanspruchen darf, a) wegen tatsächlich begegnender Fälle wie asl. *alŭkati* (neben *lakati* : lit. *álkti*) — siehe z. B. P. Diels, *Altkirchenslavische Grammatik* I, Heidelberg 1932, 60 — und b) wegen der uneinheitlichen Vertretung des Umstellungsprodukts bei geschleift betonten anlautenden Liquidaverbindungen in den slawischen Sprachen; man muss ja die Umstellung sowohl von akutierten als auch zirkumflektierten Liquidaverbindungen des besprochenen Typus prinzipiell und reell auf dieselbe chronologische Schicht zurückführen. Falls sich aber das erwähnte Kriterium (= Bewahrung präslawischer Quantität) als stichhaltig erweisen würde, so hätte dies für die Beurteilung der „Formel" im Slawischen weitgehende Folgen, da sich ja der von Kuryłowicz beschriebene Dehnungsprozess nur innerhalb der einzelnen Slawinen hätte vollziehen können, was betreffs seiner Wahrscheinlichkeit ungünstig wäre, nicht zumindest darum, weil die Belege der neuen „Dehnstufe" im Slawischen auf ein System deuten, das nicht jünger als die urslawische Gemeinschaft sein kann. Da aber m. E. die „Formel" Kuryłowiczs bei einer Reihe slawischer Dehnungskategorien eine ansprechende Erklärungsgrundlage bietet, ziehe ich es vor, den direkten Reflex ehemaliger tautosyllabischer Langdiphthonge in den Umstellungsprodukten *ra*, *la* anzuzweifeln, zumal es eine brauchbare Erklärungsalternative gibt, die aus den Handbüchern der Slawistik (e.g. G. Y. Shevelov, *A Prehistory of Slavic*, Heidelberg, 1964, 391 ff. — und noch H. Schelesniker, *Resumé* [VI. Mezinárodní Sjezd Slavistů v Praze 1968], Prag 1968, 469) bekannt ist. Es ist aber wichtig, darüber klar zu sein, dass die zunächst als genial hervortretende Theorie Kuryłowiczs — wo es um die genauere Analyse ihrer Voraussetzungen geht — auf erhebliche Schwierigkeiten stösst und nicht für sicher gelten kann.

Für die Chronologie der Kürzung der langen Diphthonge im Slawischen sollte also der Wert der unmittelbaren Kriterien nicht überschätzt werden. Dementsprechend ist man auch nicht gezwungen, auf die Annahme einer „gemeinslawischen" Kürzung zu verzichten.

Ist die Kürzung, wie ich vermute, in den drei Sprachen, dem Ostbaltischen, dem Preussischen und dem Slawischen, eine einmalige und unabhängige gewesen, so ergibt sich, dass die sog. *métatonie rude* als analogische

Erscheinung (siehe oben S. 324) nur bei deutlich lebendigen Ableitungskate-
gorien des aktuellen Sprachzweiges möglich ist (*sc.lic.* Typus lit. *várpa*
'Ähre' [*ā*-Stamm], in welchem Falle nicht ausgeschlossen ist, dass reelle
Länge vorgelegen haben wird; hier geht es aber um die notwendigen *Voraussetzungen* der *métatonie rude*). — Falls aber der Akut bei „isoliert(er)en"
(nicht mehr lebendigen) Bildungen begegnet, so ist vielmehr mit echter
Länge zu rechnen (die *métatonie rude* ist ja eigentlich *theoretisch*). Als Illustration kann das obengenannte baltisch-slawische Wort für „Krähe"
trotz des *ā*-Stammes und der Erwägungen N. v. Wijks, *Die baltischen und
slavischen Akzent- und Intonationssysteme*, Amsterdam, 1923, 89 ff., und
L. Hjelmslev, *Études baltiques*, Kopenhagen 1932, 25, gewählt werden. —
Schwierig zu deuten sind Fälle wie etwa lit. *lándžioti* (vgl. *leñda*, *lį̃sti*) : skr.
vrãćati, russ. *voróčat'* (gegenüber lit. *ver̃čia*). Bei lit. *bráidžioti* (*brēda*, *brìsti*)
spricht die Wahrscheinlichkeit für blosse *métatonie rude*.

Die Bestimmung der Chronologie der Kürzung der langen Diphthonge ist
darum von grossem Belang, weil dadurch eine präzisere Beschreibung von
Erscheinungen wie der *métatonie rude* und der *nominalen Vṛddhi* ermöglicht
wird. Von allergrösster Bedeutung wäre aber die besprochene Chronologie
in Bezug auf den Dehnungsmechanismus in den Flexions- und Wortbil-
dungssystemen des Baltischen und des Slawischen: Hat hier, wie ich zu
glauben geneigt bin, die „Formel" Kuryłowiczs gewirkt, und ist ferner die
Kürzung spät und unabhängig im Ostbaltischen, (im Preussischen) und
im Slawischen eingetreten, was ich also ebenfalls für wahrscheinlich halte,
so muss die Durchführung der betreffenden Längen sonderostbaltisch,
sonderslawisch (etc.) sein. Es bildete m. E. dies zugleich ein wichtiges Kor-
rektiv einer verbreiteten Auffassung von dem Verhältnis zwischen dem
Baltischen und dem Slawischen: Zu einer Zurrückführung der aktuellen
Erscheinungen auf ein und dasselbe Schema unter der mechanischen Annahme einer baltisch-slawischen Einheitsperiode ist man nach meinem
Dafürhalten nicht berechtigt; es bestehen hier für die genaue Betrachtung
erhebliche Unterschiede. Man hat vielfach mit divergierender, wenn auch
auf gemeinsamen Grundlagen beruhender Entwicklung zu tun, und wo
dennoch Berührungen vorliegen, wäre entweder mit Parallelismus (bzw.
Entlehnung) zu rechnen, was eine durchaus mögliche Annahme ist, oder
man müsste (*in casu*) die Wirkung der „Formel" in Abrede stellen und statt
dessen „ererbte" Länge (bzw. Entlehnung) annehmen, die ihrerseits entweder von einem früheren baltisch-slawischen *Dialektgebiet* (dessen Existenz
ich voraussetze), bzw. irgendeiner (sehr hypothetischen) nachindoeuro-
päischen sprachlichen Gruppierung oder dem diffusen Gefüge der „Grundsprache" selbst, herrühren könnte.

In dieser Weise weicht, wenn ich auch an der Grundlage der „Formel" festhalte — oder wenigstens keine zwingenden Gründe gefunden habe, sie zu verwerfen — meine Auffassung von der Entstehungsgeschichte der langvokalischen Bildungen im Baltischen und Slawischen von derjenigen Kuryłowiczs prinzipiell und reell wesentlich ab: Gerade im Spielraum der „ererbten" Längen (siehe den vorigen Abschnitt), woran sich neue, in den beiden Sprachen unabhängig voneinander entstandene „Dehnungsprodukte" gesellen, sehe ich die Eigenart des besprochenen Ablauts und zugleich dessen Motivierung.

Somit scheint mein Beitrag, die Konzeption des Charakters der baltischslawischen Beziehungen in *einem* wichtigen Punkte modifizieren zu können; will man sich ein klareres Bild von diesen Beziehungen im ganzen verschaffen, geht m. E. der Weg zu dieser Kenntnis nach der genauen Problemstellung durch das Spektrum der kritischen Analyse dieser beiden Sprachsysteme in ihrer Totalität, d. h. der Summe der auf dem Gebiete der Phonologie, der Morphologie, des Wortschatzes und der Syntax vorliegenden Erscheinungen. Eine solche Analyse ist aber noch nicht genügend vorgenommen worden. Dringend erforderlich ist auch ein erneutes Studium des Preussischen im Lichte dieser Problematik.

Baltic and Slavic. On the Chronology and Significance of the Shortening of Long Diphthongs

On the basis of the study of certain *isolated* cases, such as the acc. pl. of ŏ-stems, the author is inclined to conclude that the inherited (IE) long diphthongs were preserved until after the establishment of East Baltic as a separate dialect area. In other terms, it might be plausible to posit *one late* layer of shortenings, comprising all types of long diphthongs, old and new. Hence there should be sufficient evidence to question the correctness of the apparently current assumption of a *Balto-Slavic* shortening.

If it has been carried through in East Baltic, Old Prussian and Slavic independently, the attractive well-known mechanism accounted for by Kuryłowicz as to the spread of "lengthened grade" formations of the -*ĒKE* type could not possibly relate back to a postulated period of Balto-Slavic community, but must be of purely Baltic *and/*or Slavic date. It should be emphasized here that the ablaut patterns of Old Prussian are in strong need of renewed investigation. Furthermore, there could be no question of a Balto-Slavic *métatonie rude*, only Baltic and Slavic. The latter finding would supply us with a useful criterion, when dealing with the problem of real length : metatony in certain cases with acuted -*ERT*.

Here, it is essential whether the category (formation) in question is productive or not.

The author is aware that his concept meets with considerable difficulties; still, he regards the evidence in favour of his hypothesis as more substantial than the arguments against it and hopes to have succeeded in defining the much debated interrelationship between Baltic and Slavic on one central point.

V. MAŽIULIS

Dėl balt. *u̯ nykimo

Tiek rytų, tiek ir vakarų baltų sonantą *u̯ randame tam tikrose pozicijose išnykusį[1]. Iš tų pozicijų čia paliesiu tik tą, kai sonantas balt. *u̯ buvo prieš balt. *ō (>lie.-la. uo); šiam reikalui ryškesnės medžiagos randame rytų baltuose[2], dėl to prie jų plačiau ir sustosiu.

Pirmiausia prisiminsime, kad ryt. balt. *u̯ prieš (ryt. balt.) *ō[3] išnyko[4] nevisur: jis išliko tais atvejais, kai jam nykti *trukdė* morfologinės ,,sistemos prievarta"[5], kitaip sakant, kai jis buvo morfologiškai stiprus (=M-stiprus). Pvz., formos ryt. balt. *tēu̯ó ,,tėvas" (nom.–acc. du.) sonantas ryt. balt. *u̯ prieš *ō buvo aiškiai M-stiprus[6] ir, vadinasi, negalėjo išnykti.

Sonantas ryt. balt. *u̯ prieš *ō išnyko tais atvejais, kai jam nykti *netrukdė* morfologinės ,,sistemos prievarta"[7], kitaip sakant, kai jis buvo morfologiškai silpnas (=M-silpnas). Iki šiol aiškiai atsekti yra tik du M-silpnojo (=išnykusio) ryt. balt. *u̯ prieš *ō atvejai — dvi deklinacinės formos:

1. Lie. *šuõ* (nom. sg.)<ryt. balt. *š(u)u̯ō [< *š(u)u̯ōn]; čia sonantą ryt. balt. *u̯ prieš *ō buvus M-silpną rodo tas, kad forma ryt. balt. *š(u)u̯ō (nom. sg.), oponuojama kitoms paradigmos formoms [plg. lie. *šun-į* (acc. sg.), *šun-es* (gen. sg.) ir t. t.], buvo aiškiai supletyvi[8].

2. Lie.-la. (dial.) *duo* 'du' (nom.–acc. du masc.)<ryt. balt. *d(u)u̯ō; čia sonantas ryt. balt. *u̯ prieš *ō buvo M-silpnas, kadangi čia turime nepilnos paradigmos, kuri, be to, nebuvo nesupletyvi, skaitvardį[9].

Jau ir iš to, kas pasakyta, matyti, kad atvejų su M-silpnuoju ryt. balt. *u̯ prieš *ō yra buvę kur kas mažiau, negu su M-stipriuoju ryt. balt. *u̯ prieš *ō[10]. Toliau, nesunku suprasti, kad M-silpnasis (=vėliau išnykęs) ryt. balt. *u̯ prieš *ō ieškotinas bent jau tais formų darybos atvejais[11], kai paradigma buvo vienaip ar kitaip *supletyvi*[12]. Visiems yra aišku, kad rytų baltų supletyvios paradigmos žodžiai buvo ne vien *š(u)u̯ō 'šuo' ar *d(u)u̯ō 'du', bet ir kai kurie kiti. Čia turiu galvoje, pirmiausia, asmeninius įvardžius, kurių paradigmos aiškiai turėjo būti labiau supletyvios, negu, pvz., žodžio ryt. balt. *š(u)u̯ō paradigma[13]. Vadinasi, jeigu galima asmeninių įvardžių paradigmose atsekti sonantą ryt. balt. *u̯ prieš *ō, tai jis turėjo būti M-silpnas, vadinasi, jis vėliau turėjo išnykti. Manau, kad asmeninių įvardžių paradigmose atvejų su ryt. balt. *u̯ prieš *ō atsekti galima ir, būtent, — štai dėl ko.

Kildinant pr. acc. pl. *wans* 'jus' iš vak. balt. acc. pl. *u̯āns* < *u̯óns* (= s. sl. *vy* 'jus')[14], galima laukti ryt. balt. acc. pl. *u̯óns* > *u̯ós*[15], kuri, turėdama M-silpnąjį ryt. balt. *u̯* prieš *ō*, privalėjo išvirsti į ryt. balt. acc. pl. *ós* 'jus'. Pastaroji, esant visos *o*-kamienės deklinacijos fleksijai ryt. balt. acc. pl. (*-ōns* >) *-ós*, pasidarė *plika* *o*-kamiene acc. pl. fleksija[16], ir ji — ryt. balt. acc. pl. *ós* 'jus' — ėmė nykti[17]. Dabar forma ryt. balt. nom. pl. *i̯ús* 'jūs', veikiama *u*-kamienės ryt. balt. acc. pl. (*-ūns* >) *-ús*, pasidarė ryt. balt. nom.–acc. pl. *i̯ús*[18]. Vadinasi, nėra kliūčių manyti, kad iš pradžių visi baltai greta balt. nom. pl. *i̯ús* (>pr. *ioūs* =la. *jūs* =lie. dial. *jŭs*) turėjo balt. acc. pl. *u̯óns* 'jus'. Jeigu pastaroji rytų baltuose, netekdama šakninio *u̯-* (ryt. balt. *u̯óns* > *u̯ós* > *ós*), išnyko, tai vakarų baltuose ji neturėjo išnykti, nes ji negalėjo prarasti šakninio *u̯-*: dar neprasidėjus M-silpnojo *u̯* prieš *ō* nykimui vakarų baltuose[19], forma vak. balt. acc. plg. *u̯óns* 'jus' spėjo išvirsti į vak. balt. *u̯áns* 'jus' (> *u̯ăns* >pr. *wans*)[20], kurioje M-silpnasis vak. balt. *u̯* atsidūrė ne prieš *ō*. Slavai sonanto *u̯* niekur neprarado, todėl ir šiuo atveju jis (kaip M-silpnasis) išliko: s. sl. acc. pl. *vy* 'jus' <sl. *vy(s)* < *u̯ús* < *u̯ós* < *u̯óns* (=balt. *u̯óns*)[21]. Tačiau sl. nom. pl. *i̯ús* (=balt. *i̯ús*)[22] vėliau negalėjo išlikti: ji išvirto į sl. (*i̯ús* > *i̯y* >) *i̯i*, t. y. sutapo su įvardžio 'jis' forma sl. nom. pl. *i̯i* 'jie'[23]; iš to nebesunku suprasti, kodėl atsirado sl. nom.–acc. pl. *vy* 'jūs, jus'[24].

Panašiai galima suponuoti ir formą ryt. balt. acc. du. *u̯ó* 'judu' (=s. sl. *va*), egzistavusią šalia ryt. balt. nom. du. *i̯ú*[25] (žr. toliau). Ryt. balt. acc. du. *u̯ó*, netekdama šakninio *u̯-*, išvirto į ryt. balt. acc. du. *ó* ir ėmė nykti[26] (plg. tai, kas pasakyta apie ryt. balt. acc. pl. *u̯ós* > *ós* nykimą). Dabar forma ryt. balt. nom. du. *i̯ú*, veikiama *u*-kamienės ryt. balt. nom.–acc. du. *-ú*, pasidarė ryt. balt. nom.–acc. du. *i̯ú* >lie. *jù(du)*[27]. Panašiai[28] ir iš vak. balt. nom. du. *i̯ú* resp. acc. du. *u̯ó* galėjo atsirasti vak. balt. nom.–acc. du. *i̯ú* (žr. toliau). Slavuose forma sl. acc. du. *u̯ó* (=balt. *u̯ó*) > *u̯ā*, kaip kad baltuose, išnykti negalėjo (sonantas sl. *u̯* niekur nenyko). Bet čia negalėjo išlikti sl. nom. du. *i̯ú* (=balt. *i̯ú*), nes ji, virsdama į sl. nom. du. (*i̯ú* > *i̯y* >) *i̯i*, sutapo su sl. nom. pl. (*i̯ús* > *i̯y* >) *i̯i* : tuo metu, kai vietoj sl. nom. pl. *i̯i* atsirado sl. nom.–acc. pl. *vy* (žr. aukščiau), pagal tai vietoj sl. nom. du. *i̯i* lengvai galėjo atsirasti ir sl. nom.–acc. du *vy*; dėl to ir pati sl. acc. du. (*u̯ō* >) *u̯ā* turėjo pasidaryti sl. nom.–acc. du. *u̯ā*. Šitaip, man rodos, aiškintinas tas faktas, kad senovės slavų raštai turi ne tik nom.–acc. du. *va*, bet ir nom.–acc. du. *vy*[29]. Visa tai, savo ruožtu rodo, kad slavai iš pradžių bus turėję sl. nom. du. *i̯ú* resp. acc. du. *u̯ō* ir sl. nom. pl. *i̯ús* resp. acc. pl. *u̯ōns*.

Jeigu slavai įvardžio 'jūs' šakninį *u̯- (M-silpnąjį) išlaikė, tai baltai, kaip sakyta, jo neteko. Šitaip turėjo atsitikti, suprantama, ne vien formoje balt. acc. du. *u̯ṓ > *ṓ ar ryt. balt. acc. pl. (*u̯ṓns >) *u̯ṓs > *ṓs, bet ir visose kitose šio įvardžio formose, turėjusiose kamieną balt. *u̯ṓ- (= s. sl. va-) > *ṓ-. Tačiau šis balt. *u̯ṓ-, netekdamas M-silpnojo *u̯-, iš tikrųjų, neteko šaknies (vienafoneminės *u̯-), ir jis, t. y. balt. (*u̯ṓ- >) *ṓ- pasidarė plikas kamiengalis, asocijuojamas su balt. acc. du. (*u̯ṓ >) *ṓ. Dabar kartu su balt. acc. du. (*u̯ṓ >) *ṓ pakeitimu į balt. nom.–acc. du. *į̯ú (žr. aukščiau) lengvai galėjo ir dualinis bei pluralinis balt. (*u̯ṓ- >) *ṓ- pasikeisti į balt. *į̯ú-. Tokiu būdu iš formų, pvz., balt. dat. du. bei pl. [*u̯ṓ-m- (= s. sl. va-m-) >] *ṓ-m- atsirado balt. dat. du. bei pl. *į̯ú-m- > pr. ioū-m- = lie. ju-m- (čia -u- sutrumpėjęs[30]); arba, iš balt. gen. pl. [*u̯ṓ-sōn (= s. sl. va-sъ) >] *ṓ-sōn atsirado balt. *į̯ú-sōn > pr. ioū-san = lie. jú-sų̨. Šitas balt. *į̯ ú-išstūmė senąjį balt. (*u̯ṓ- >) *ṓ- visoje šio įvardžio paradigmoje, išskyrus vak. balt. acc. pl. (*u̯ṓns >) *u̯āns (kadangi čia *u̯- negalėjo išnykti, žr. aukščiau). Be to, perdirbant balt. (*u̯ṓ- >) *ṓ- į balt. *į̯ú-, buvo perdirbtas ir balt. *nṓ- (= s. sl. na-sъ 'mūsų' ir pan.) į balt. *nú-, plg., pvz., pr. noū-son = lie. *nū-son (> mú-sų̨)[31]; čia išimtį sudaro vak. balt. acc. pl. (*nōns >) *nāns, nes ją veikė vak. balt. acc. pl. (*u̯ṓns >) *u̯āns. Vadinasi, net ir pats kamieno balt. *nō- į balt. *nū- pakitimas tam tikru būdu remia išvadą, darytiną iš to, kas aukščiau pasakyta: 1) dualinėmis bei pluralinėmis asmeninių įvardžių formomis visi baltai ir slavai iš pradžių buvo labai panašūs[32], 2) baltai ir slavai šiuo atžvilgiu gerokai išsiskyrė tuomet, kai baltai (o ne ir slavai) ėmė prarasti sonantą (= M-silpnąjį) balt. *u̯ prieš *ō (suprantama, ir prieš *ū).

Be (ryt.) balt. nom. sg. *š́(u)u̯ṓ(n) ir nom.–acc. du. *d(u)u̯ṓ ir be ką tik minėtų įvardžio 'jūs' du. resp. pl. formų, M-silpnąjį (= išnykusį) balt. *u̯ prieš *ō randu dar dviem atvejais, iš kurių čia paminėsiu tik vieną[33].

Kaip jau esu rašęs[34], baltų prokalbėje u-kamienas buvo dvejopas: apofoninio kamiengalio (u₁-kamienas) ir neapofoninio (u₂-kamienas); u₁-kamieniai vardažodžiai buvo generis masc.–fem., o u₂-kamieniai — generis neutr[35]. U₁-kamienė balt. gen. pl. forma buvo *-au̯ōn ir u₂-kamienė — *-(u)u̯ōn[36]. Čia sonantas balt. *u̯ prieš *ō buvo M-silpnas[37], ir jis vėliau išlikti negalėjo: dėl to u₁-kamiene balt. gen. pl. *-au̯ōn (= s. sl. -ovъ) resp. u₂-kamiene balt. gen. pl. *-(u)u̯ōn išvirto į *-a[u̯]ōn > (kontrakcija) *-ōn (> lie. sū́n-ų̨) resp. *-[(u)u̯]ōn > *-ōn[38].

Išnašos

1. J. Endzelīns, *Baltu valodu skaņas un formas* (= *BVSF*), Rīgā, 1948, 49–50; Chr. S. Stang, *Vergleichende Grammatik der Baltischen Sprachen* (= *Vergl. Gr.*), Oslo, 1966, 101.

2. Jau vien dėl to, kad vakarų baltai (prūsai) turi nedaug rašto paminklų.

3. Čia ir kitur toliau žymiu ryt. balt. **ō* vietoj įprastai rašomo ryt. balt. **uo*. Taip darau ne vien dėl tam tikro rašybos patogumo, bet ir dėl kitų priežasčių (apie jas žr. J. Kazlauskas, — *Baltistica*, IV, 129).

4. Visiems žinomas faktas, kad nuo tam tikrų epochų sonantas balt. **u̯* prieš **ō* ėmė fonetiškai nykti (ir išnyko), šiame straipsnyje bus nagrinėjamas ne visais aspektais, o tik vienu: ar galima atsekti daugiau (be jau žinomų) atvejų, kuriais šitokios pozicijos sonantas balt. **u̯* išnyko?

5. J. Endzelīns, *BVSF*, 49, plg. 7 išn.

6. Žodis ryt. balt. **tēu̯as* buvo nesupletyvios ir pilnos (visų trijų skaičių) paradigmos, daugely savo (pirmiausia, tiesioginių linksnių) formų turėjo ryt. balt. **u̯* ne prieš **ō* [plg. lie. *tėvas* (nom. sg.), *tėvą* (acc. sg.), *tėvai* (nom. pl.) ir kt.]; pastarosios pozicijos [t. y. ne prieš **ō* (ar **ū*)] sonantas ryt. balt. **u̯* nenyko, dėl to jis morfologiškai atsistatinėjo ir tose šio žodžio formose, kuriose jis (ryt. balt. **u̯*) buvo prieš **ō*.

7. J. Endzelīns, *BVSF*, 49.

8. Šiame straipsnyje formų supletyvumą suprantu plačiausia prasme: kai formos skiriasi ne tik šaknimis, bet ir kamiengaliais (tiksliau sakant, kamiengalių struktūra).

9. Šis žodis neturi sg. ir pl. formų (nepilna paradigma), — jis turi dualines formas, o ne skaičiaus kategoriją. Po to, kai ryt. balt. **d(u)u̯ei-m-* išvirto į **d(u)u̯ē̦-m-* (> lie. *dvie-m*), atsirado visgi nemažas kamiengalių skirtumas (supletyvumas), — **d(u)u̯-ō: *d(u)u̯ē̦-m-: *d(u)u̯ei̯-ōn* (vėliau perdirbta į **-ē̦i̯-* > lie. *dv-iej-u̯*). Pagaliau, šis žodis buvo skaitvardis, o skaitvardžių fonetinei raidai kartais turi įtakos ir pati jų vartosena, plg. kad ir lie. liter. *du* (nom.–acc.) vietoj laukiamos lie. liter. *duo* 'du' (nom.–acc.).

10. Juk vien tik, pvz., žodis ryt. balt. **tēu̯as* turėjo keletą atvejų — keletą formų su M-stipriuoju ryt. balt. **u̯* prieš **ō: *tēu̯ō̃* (dat. sg.), **tēu̯ǫ́* (instr. sg.), **tēu̯ǫ́* (nom.-acc. du.), **tē̦-u̯óns* > **tēu̯ós* (acc. pl.) ir kt.

11. Šiam reikalui negalėčiau pateikti nė vieno patikimesnio pavyzdžio iš žodžių darybos.

12. Žr. 8 išn.

13. Žr. 8 išn.

14. Vak. balt. **u̯-óns* (acc. pl.) išvirto į **u̯-āns* tada (ir dėl to), kai vak. balt. **(deiu̯)-óns* (Chr. S. Stang, *Vergl. Gr.*, 186) išvirto į **(deiu̯)-āns* (> pr. *deiw-ans* apie tai plačiau žr. aut(orius), *Baltų ir kitų indoeuropiečių kalbų santykiai, Deklinacija* (= aut., *Deklinacija*), Vilnius, 1969, 186 tt.

15. Lietuviuose žemaičiuose atsirado, gal būt, (ryt. balt. **u̯óns* >) **u̯ás* (plg. lie. žem. *vilk-us* < **-ás*, žr. aut., *Deklinacija*, 185). Žr. 16 išn.

16. Forma lie. žem. (**u̯óns* >) **u̯ás* > **ás* (ir čia M-silpnasis **u̯* turėjo išnykti) dėl *o-* = *u*-kamienės lie. žem. acc. pl. **-ás* irgi būtų pasidariusi plika fleksija.

17. Šiai ryt. balt. acc. pl. **ōs* 'jus' (plikai fleksijai), praradusiai šakninį **u̯-*, sunku buvo pasiskolinti šakninį **i̯-* iš nom. pl. **i̯-ūs*: šitokia (**i̯- + **ōs* >) **i̯ós* būtų sutapusi su įvardžio 'jis' acc. pl. forma. Ji (t. y. **i̯- + acc. pl. **ōs* > **i̯ōs*) gal kur tarmėse „nuėjo"

į nom. pl. (čia ji nesutapo su įvardžio 'jis' nom. pl. forma), plg. raštų formą nom. pl. *juos* 'jūs' (Chr. S. Stang, *Vergl. Gr.* 256.).

18. Plg. J. Endzelīns, *BVSF*, 164.

19. Ir be tolimesnių (žr. tekste) samprotavimų galima spėti, kad M-silpnasis vak. balt. *ų̃* prieš *ō̃ nuo tam tikros epochos irgi išnyko: plg. vėlyvųjų prūsų (XVI a.) ir lietuvių bei latvių tarmes, kurios sonanto v (prieš atitinkamus balsius) nykimo tendencijomis yra gana panašios, žr. J. Endzelīns, *BVSF*, 49–50.

20. Žr. 14 išn.

21. Dėl šios sl. *(ų̃)-ōns* (= balt. *ų̃-ōns*) plg. sl. acc. pl. *(ų̃ilk)-ōns* (= balt. *-ōns*), apie kurią žr. aut., *Deklinacija*, 192 tt.

22. Tokią formą slavams suponuoti galima, plg. sl. nom. du. *įū̃* 'judu' (žr. toliau tekste).

23. Plg. 17 išn.

24. Formos sl. nom. pl. (*įū̃s > *įy >) *įi a) šakninis *į-, veikiamas kitų formų šakninio *v-, nesunkiai galėjo būti pakeistas į *v-, o b) jos balsis *-i, atsidūręs prieš nejotacinį *v-, galėjo išvirsti į sl. *-y (be to, vienu ir kitu atveju veikė ir sl. acc. pl. *vy). Šitaip sl. nom. pl. (*įū̃s > *įy >) *įi galėjo būti perdirbta į sl. nom. pl. *vy.

25. Vadinasi, (pra)baltų įvardžio 'jūs' nom. du. ir pl. formos turėjo vienodą kamieną [*įū̃ (nom. du.) = *įū̃- (nom. pl.)], tačiau tos pačios įvardžio 'mes' formos skyrėsi net savo šaknimis: balt. nom. du. *ų̃ė 'mudu' [lie. žem. *vė-du*, tur būt, vietoj *vè-du < *ų̃ē (= s. sl. *vě*), plg. lie. *jù-du < *įã* (Chr. S. Stang, *Vergl. Gr.*, 257)] ir balt. nom. pl. *mes* 'mes'. Plg. tą faktą, kad sen. indų kalboje įvardžio 'jūs' du. ir pl. formos turi irgi tą patį kamieną (s. ind. *yŭ-*), bet įvardžio 'mes' du. ir pl. formos savo kamienais skiriasi.

26. Šitokiai balt. acc. du. *ã́ nelengva buvo gauti šakninį *į- iš balt. nom. du *įã́, nes ji (t. y. *į- + *ã́ > *įã́) būtų sutapusi su įvardžio 'jis' nom.–acc. du. forma, plg. 17 išn.

27. Plg. Chr. S. Stang, *Vergl. Gr.*, 257.

28. Tačiau, matyt, ne kartu su rytų baltais.

29. Dėl pavyzdžių žr. N. van Wijk, *Geschichte der altkirchenslavischen Sprache*, Berlin–Leipzig, 1931, § 49.

30. Žr. J. Endzelīns, *BVSF*, 163.

31. Apie formos balt.-sl. gen. pl. *ų̃ōsōn kamieno *ų̃ōs- kilmę teks kitur pakalbėti. Lietuvių raštuose sutinkama gen. pl. *juosų̃* 'jūsų' galėtų būti iš ryt. balt. (*ų̃ōsōn >) *ōsōn su *į- iš nom. pl. *į-ūs: ji (t. y. *į- + *ōs-ōn > *įōs-ōn) nesutapo su įvardžio 'jis' gen. pl. forma (plg. 17 išn.). Plg. dar Chr. S. Stang, *Vergl. Gr.*, 256.

32. Čia turiu galvoje ir tas formas, kurių dėl vietos stokos nesu šiame straipsnyje plačiau nagrinėjęs.

33. Apie kitą atvejį (sudėtingesnį!), kurį randu tik rytų baltuose, — apie s. sl. (*syn*)-*ovu* (gen.-loc. du.) tipo formą (formas) ryt. balt. [balt. *-ãų̃au resp. *-(u)ų̃au >] *-aų̃ō resp. *-(u)ų̃ō [ir apie patį diftongo balt. *au virtimą į ryt. balt. *ō (žr. 3 išn.) > lie. liter. *uo*] žr. aut., *Deklinacija*, 304–305.

34. *Baltistica*, III, 39; aut., *Deklinacija*, 262 tt.

35. Aut., *Deklinacija*, 263 tt.

36. Op. cit., 298–304.

37. Juk forma balt. gen. pl. *-aų̃-ōn (u_1-kam.) resp. *-(u)ų̃-ōn (u_2-kam.), oponuojama daugumai kitų u_1- resp. u_2-kamienės paradigmos (pirmiausia, tiesioginių linksnių) formų (u_1-kamienių nom. sg. *-u-s, acc. sg. *-u-n, acc. pl. *-ã́-ns > *-ã́-s, nom.–acc. du. *-ū ir kt., u_2-kamienių nom.–acc. sg. *-u, nom.–acc. pl. *-ū ir kt., žr. aut., *Deklinacija*, 263–306), buvo aiškiai supletyvi (žr. 8 išn.). Plg. 6 išn.

38. Tuomet, kai iš balt. gen. pl. *-auōn resp. *-(u)uōn (dviskiemenių) atsirado balt. gen. pl. *-ōn (vienskiemenė), ir balt. nom. pl. (u₁-kam.) *-aues (masc.–fem.) išvirto į *-aus > lie. dial. sãn-aus (nom. pl.), žr. aut., Deklinacija, 298 [lie. sãn-ūs (nom. pl.) nėra iš *-uues, žr. op. cit., 297–301].

On the Disappearance of the Baltic *u̯

This article deals with one position of the loss of the Balt. *u̯, i.e. when the *u̯ was followed by *ō (> Lith., Latv. uo). So far only two cases of such forms have been clearly determined: (1) Lith. Nom. Sg. šuõ 'dog' < Balt. *š(u)u̯ō(n) and (2) Lith., Latv. (dial.) duo 'two' < Balt. *d(u)u̯ō. The conclusion is drawn that the Balt. *u̯, lost before *ō, should also be sought in some other instances, which may have existed in Baltic (and Slavic), viz.: (a) in the forms of personal pronouns of the 2nd person—Balt. *u̯ō- (= Slav. *u̯ō- > O. Slav. va-), Acc. Pl. *u̯ōns (= Slav. *u̯ōns > O. Slav. vy), Acc. Du. *u̯ō (= Slav. *u̯ō > O. Slav. va) parallel with Balt. Nom. Pl. *i̯ūs (= Slav. *i̯ūs > O. Slav. vy) and Nom. Du. *i̯ū (= Slav. *i̯ū > O. Slav. vy); (b) in the u-stem forms (see Baltistica, III, 39–42)—Balt. Gen. Pl. *au̯ōn (= Slav. *-ou̯ōn > O. Slav. -ovъ) resp. *-(u)u̯ōn [= Slav. *-(u)u̯ōn, lost later] > *-a[u̯]ōn > *-ōn resp. *-[(u)u̯]ōn > *-ōn (cf. Lith. Gen. Pl. sūn-ų̃).

W. MERLINGEN

Phonematik und Orthographie: Baltische Probleme

Das Phonem ist etwas anderes als der Laut — dies ist Fundament und raison d'être aller Phonematik (Phonologie), soweit sie sich mit den Sprachlauten als Elementen der Verständigung befasst[1]. Das Wesen des Phonems im Gegensatz zum Laut ergibt sich aus der Natur der Sprache als Verständigungsmittel. So wie hinter den verschiedenen möglichen Formen eines Buchstabens ein „Graphem" steckt, das in der Vorstellung des Schreibenden und Lesenden nur aus dem besteht, woran es wiedererkannt wird, so steckt hinter dem (gesprochenen und gehörten) Laut sein Phonem, das in der Vorstellung des Sprachträgers ebenfalls nur aus dem besteht, woran er wiedererkannt wird, in der Summe dessen, was wiedererkannt wird. Beim Sprechenden selbst handelt es sich natürlich nicht eigentlich um ein Wiedererkennen, sondern um das Äquivalent auf seiner Seite, die „Lautabsicht"; was für Sprecher und Hörer gemeinsam vorliegt, wäre etwa doch mit „Lautvorstellung" oder „Lautbild" zu bezeichnen[2]. Was darüber hinaus artikuliert bzw. wahrgenommen wird, liegt außerhalb der Sprache in ihrer Funktion als Verständigungsmittel. Es liegt in der Natur der Verständigung, dass als beabsichtigt bzw. wiedererkennbar vom ganzen Laut nur das gilt, was — zunächst — mit *Wortbedeutung* verbunden ist; also zwar indirekt, über ganze Wortgestalten hinweg (die gewöhnlich aus mehreren Phonemen bestehen), aber doch auf jeden Fall mit Bedeutung in Beziehung stehend.

Das Phonem ist nun also nicht nur wirklich etwas anderes als der Laut, sondern auch das, worauf es in der funktionierenden Sprache ankommt. In der eigenen Sprache meint der Sprechende *nur* das Phonem und nimmt der Hörende *nur* das Phonem wahr. Und eine der Natur der Sprache adäquate *Orthographie* kann daher ihre Aufgabe nur dann voll erfüllen, wenn sie die Phoneme wiedergibt — nicht einfach die Laute.

Hier liegen aber auch die größten Schwierigkeiten. Bei der Schaffung einer Orthographie — gewöhnlich mit der Übernahme der Schrift einer andersgearteten Sprache verbunden — und bei der Regelung oder Reform einer Orthographie kommt der von außen Beobachtende dazu, dem es ohne besondere Hilfsmittel meist unmöglich ist, hinter den phonetischen Erscheinungen die Phoneme selbst zu erkennen[3]. Statt der Phoneme dringen die äußeren Erscheinungen der Laute durch, auch in der erweiterten Form, dass die Interpretation von Lauten oder lautlichen Erscheinungen aus einer fremden Sprache unrichtig in die eigene übernommen wird. Beispiele dafür bieten alle Kultursprachen der Welt, im heutigen oder in einem früheren Stadium; Beispiele, die bei genauerer Analyse erkennen lassen, wie weit Phonem und äußerer Anschein auseinandergehen können. Die phonematische Analyse darf sich nur nicht darauf beschränken, einfach die phonetisch beschriebenen oder orthographisch fixierten Laute einander gegenüberzustellen.

Zu den ergiebigsten Fällen, an denen wir auch Phonematik und Orthographie des *Litauischen* und *Lettischen* vergleichen wollen, gehören die der *Ein- und Zweiphonemigkeit*; Probleme übrigens, die vorläufig zu denen gehören, in denen die Phonologie am meisten ausrichten kann:

Es gibt bekanntlich zweideutige Lautverbindungen, die in den einen Sprachen — entsprechend der Norm, dass hinter jedem Laut auch ein Phonem steht — tatsächlich auf zwei Phonemen beruhen, in anderen Sprachen jedoch, abweichend von dieser Norm, zusammen nur éin Phonem bilden. Am bekanntesten sind die Gebilde [tš], [ts] usw., die nur selten tatsächlich /t+š/, /t+s/ sind, sondern meistens einphonemig, d. h. als /č/, /c/ usw. zu bezeichnen. Der zweite „Laut" in diesem Verbindungen ist dann nur eine zwangsläufige Begleiterscheinung der besonderen Artikulation (gehobene Vorderzunge mit Längsrille), bei der die Explosion von selbst ein starkes Nachschleifgeräusch erzeugt. Ähnlich steht es mit den sog. mouillierten (und auch den palatalisierten) Konsonanten: zwischen diesen Konsonanten und Kons. +j (z. B. zwischen [ň], [ń] und [nj] ist von Sprache zu Sprache keine strikte Grenze zu ziehen. In allen diesen Fällen entscheidet erst die phonematische Analyse. Ausführlich über diese Probleme zuletzt Verf., *Über Ein- und Zweiphonemigkeit* (ZfPhon., XIII, 98–176; im folgenden mit *Ü* bezeichnet)[4]. Für Einphonemigkeit kann etwa diese allgemeinste Formel gelten: Die Lautverbindung verhält sich — aktiv oder passiv — wie die Einzelphoneme bzw. nicht wie die Phonemverbindungen der betreffenden Sprache; entweder wegen eines Bestandteils oder wegen der ganzen Verbindung (*Ü*, 121). Es gibt verschiedene Arten und Grade der Einphonemigkeit (oder umgekehrt der Zweiphonemigkeit), wobei sich aus den Graden besondere Probleme ergeben[5]; und es gibt verschiedene Kriterien und Proben (Vertauschprobe, Selbständigkeitsprobe[6], Zerlegsprobe). Am häufigsten ist die Einphonemigkeit, die auf Beziehungen zur lautlichen Umgebung beruht, also die „kombinatorische" Einphonemigkeit[7]. Sie „gehört zwar zu den schwächeren Graden, bildet aber anscheinend die häufigsten Typen.

Auf diese Weise ist z. B. die Einphonemigkeit der *c* und *č* der meisten slavischen Sprachen begründet: es fehlen parallele Verbindungen von Konsonanten (Explosiven) mit Spiranten, wie *kx tx px, kf tf pf, ks ps, kš pš*"[8] (*Ü*, 134), sie sind untypisch, vor allem im Anlaut.

Für die *baltischen* Sprachen ergeben sich hierin folgende Abweichungen von Orthographie und herkömmlicher Auffassung[9]:

1. Dem *Litauischen* werden „palatalisierte" Konsonanten zugeschrieben[10], die ähnlich den poln. oder russ. pal. Konsonanten klingen und — wie im Polnischen — in der Regel mit nachgestelltem *i* bezeichnet werden: *liaukà* gegenüber *laũkas* usw. Einphonemigkeit könnte nur dann nachgewiesen werden, wenn es die „weichen" Lautgebilde auch in Stellungen gäbe, wo sie normalerweise nicht /Kons. + j/ sein können, also vor Konsonanten und im Auslaut (/j/ existiert an sich nur relativ und ist zunächst nur vor oder nach Vokal möglich, vgl. *Ü*, 129 ff.). Nun gibt es aber in der litauischen Schriftsprache Konsonanten mit selbständiger „Weichheit" nur vor Vokalen, nie vor Kons. oder im Auslaut[11], und nach der Formel: „Zweideutige Lautgebilde sind nur dann einphonemig, wenn sie auch in *der* Umgebung auftreten, in der sie nichts anderes als einphonemig sein *können*", ist die bedeutungsbildende Funktion des vermuteten Merkmals — Palatalisierung — eben nicht nachweisbar (*Ü*, 130). „Man müsste also z. B. nicht *kiautas* ('Schale') oder *siunčiù* ('ich schicke') schreiben ..., sondern *kjautas, sjunčju*, so wie man *jaunas* ('jung'), *koja* ('Fuß') schreibt"[12]; man schreibt ja auch *pjedestãlas, pjèsė* (statt *pie* ..., worin *ie* den Diphthong bedeuten würde), gegenüber Schreibungen in anderen Fremdwörtern, wie *biùras, plagiãtas* (mit *i*).

2. Auch die sog. *palatalen* Konsonanten des *Lettischen* (geschrieben *ŗ, ļ, ņ, ģ, ķ*) lösen sich phonematisch in /Kons. + j/ auf. Ihre Einphonemigkeit ist nicht nachweisbar. Zunächst stehen *ģ* und *ķ* nur vor Vokalen, nie vor Konsonant oder im Auslaut (man dürfte nur *gj* und *kj* schreiben). Bei *ŗ, ļ, ņ* spielt ein /j/ mit, „das nicht auf der Nachbarschaft zu einem Vokal beruht, sondern dessen Existenz durch ein Formenparadigma gleichsam erzwungen ist" (*Ü* 132 f.), wie es bei einem Adjektiv wie /dzilj .../ 'tief' vorliegt, das zahlreiche Formen mit /-j + Vokal/ hat (/dzilja, dziljam, dzilju/ usw.), denen sich eine einzige mit /-j + Kons./ notgedrungen anschließt: /dzil-j-š/ (hier kann das [j] in einer fast gleichzeitigen Artikulation mit [l] untergebracht werden, daher die Schreibung *dziļš*; in Fällen wie *rupjš, dumjš* ist das nicht möglich, aber immerhin wird ein *j* geschrieben). Also „*ŗ, ļ, ņ* sind zweiphonemig, d. h. sie bestehen aus /r, l, n + j/, weil sie entweder nur vor Vokal stehen oder ihre Mouillierung nur morphologischer Natur ist. In dieser Eigenschaft geraten sie auch in den Auslaut: *-iņ* = /-inj/ ..., *dēļ* = /dēlj/

... *celgals* = /celjgals/ 'Ende des Weges' usw.''; phonematisch wäre also auch /vinjš/ 'er', Gen. /vinja/, /karjš/ 'Krieg', Gen. /karja/, usw. zu schreiben (statt *viņš*, *viņa* usw.); wie man ja auch *rupjš* usw. schreibt. — Dass die lett. /rj, lj, nj, gj, kj/ bei der Einführung der Schrift als Einzelphoneme aufgefasst werden konnten, ist natürlich dadurch begünstigt worden, dass die Artikulation des [j] viel stärker vorausgenommen (mit der von [r, l, n, g, k] „verschmolzen'') wird, als es die deutsche Zunge zustandebrächte; es handelt sich um eine Wiedergabe des akustischen Eindrucks vom Deutschen aus. Wäre die Schrift aus dem Polnischen oder Russischen übernommen worden, so hätte sich auch die Schreibung anders gestaltet; allerdings auch nicht dem Lettischen selbst gemäß.

3. Lit. [tš] wird nach dem Muster slavischer Sprachen *č* geschrieben, aber diese Lautverbindung hat im Lit. so wenig Unfreiheit, dass sie nicht gut als einphonemig nachzuweisen ist. Das Kriterium in den slavischen Sprachen, dass nämlich Spiranten mit vorhergehenden Explosiven keine regelmäßigen Verbindungen eingehen, fällt weg; Verbindungen wie *-kš-*, *-ks-*, *-gž-* usw. sind ja gerade für die baltischen Sprachen charakteristisch. Eine einzige kleine Unfreiheit besteht im Lit. darin, dass (außer in [tš, dž, ts]) Kons. + Spirans (*kš-*, *ps-* usw.) im *Anlaut* nicht vorkommt[13]. Dieser kleinen Unfreiheit steht aber entgegen, dass im Lit. die meisten [tš] im Inlaut *morphologisch* („etymologisch'') zerlegt werden: sie entstehen aus /t + j/, wie in *jáučio*, Gen. von *jáutis*, oder *verčiù* (1. P. Sg.) — *vertì* (2. P.). Schreibt man *jautšjo*, *vertšju*, so ist leichter ersichtlich, dass sowohl das *-t-* als auch das *-j-* (s. Punkt 1) verblieben ist, nur dass sich zwischen ihnen ein [š] entwickelt hat, ein Vorgang, der sich ja auch sonst leicht einstellt (z. B. in der romanischen oder englischen Lautgeschichte). Ebenso verhält sich [dž], das immer ein /j/ nach sich hat (sogar in einem neuen Fremdwort wie *džiazas* 'Jazz'). Den Massen von morphologisch zerlegbaren /-t-š-j-, -d-ž-j-/ steht nur eine verhältnismäßig geringe Anzahl von (heute) unzerlegbaren [tš-, dž-] gegenüber[14], vor allem im Anlaut, wo es sich z. T. um ursprünglich **tj-* (< **tēu-*) handelt, meist aber um onomatopoetische und Fremdwörter; die meisten wieder mit nachfolgendem /-j-/ (*čia-*, *džia-* usw. geschrieben). Die Zerlegbarkeit ist jedenfalls so stark, dass dem Lit. nicht /č, ǯ/ (bzw. /č', ǯ'/), sondern nur /tš, dž/ (/tšj, džj/) zuzuschreiben sind; auch in Bildungen wie *plãč-kelnės* 'Pluderhosen' = /platš-/ (zu *platùs*; vgl. Fraenkel, *Lit. etym. Wb.* unter *pìčpilnis*) oder *repečkà* 'auf allen Vieren kriechend' = /repetška/. Die phonematisch-orthographische Regel würde im Lit. lauten: Zwischen *t* und *j* wird immer ein š, zwischen *d* und j ein ž eingeschoben. — *c* ([ts]) kommt im Lit. nur in Fremdwörtern und onomatopoetischen Wörtern vor; Einphonemigkeit wieder nicht nachweisbar, also phonematisch ebenfalls

/ts/. — Anders die *lettischen* c und *dz*: sie nehmen so häufig die Plätze ein, an denen nur Einzelphoneme möglich sind bzw. an denen /t+s, d+z/ nicht möglich sind, dass sie nur als Einzelphoneme gelten können, also als /c, ʒ/. Lett. *č*, *dž* (in ererbten Wörtern aus *cj, *dzj, wie in *lāču*=Gen. Pl. von *lācis*, *jūdžu*=Gen. Pl. von *jūdze*): Einphonemigkeit *nicht* erweisbar, also /tš, dž/ (oder Parallelismus mit /c, ʒ/, also doch /č, ǯ/).

4. Die meisten lit. und lett. *Diphthonge* sind auf einfachste Weise zerlegbar, d. h. zweiphonemig: /ai, au, ei, ui/; *ie, uo* haben jedoch Anspruch auf Einphonemigkeit, und zwar durch „natürliche" Bedingungen (vgl. oben S. 341 f. mit Fn. 6 und 7). Am klarsten bei lett. „*o*" (Endzelin u. a.: *uo*): von den Lauten des [uɔa] existiert wenigstens das [ɔ] in reinlett. Wörtern nicht als eigenes Phonem außerhalb dieser Gruppe, daher ist [uɔa] nicht in /uɔa/ zerlegbar und das ganze bildet ein Einzelphonem. Auch der zweite Bestandteil von lit. *uo* kommt als selbständiges Phonem in reinlit. Wörtern nicht vor. Bei lit. und lett. *ie* könnte man das *e* als selbständigen Vertreter des selbständigen e ([ε]) betrachten; jedoch darf man hier den immerhin recht deutlichen „Parallelismus" mit *uo* gelten lassen, vgl. *Ü*, 120 f. — Es zeigt sich, dass hier die früheren lit. Schreibungen *ů* und *ë* phonematisch richtiger waren als die jetzigen, da sie die Einphonemigkeit deutlich machten (nur hätte konsequenterweise statt *ë* etwa *ï* stehen müssen). Auch lett. *o* ist im Rahmen des Lettischen phonematisch richtig, *uo* nur phonetisch, und auch nur annähernd.

Insgesamt stellt sich für die beiden baltischen Sprachen heraus, dass in einigen auffallenden Punkten phonematischer Status und Orthographie nicht übereinstimmen: die sog. palatalisierten Konsonanten des Lit. und die sog. mouillierten Konsonanten des Lett. zerfallen in /Kons.+j/, lit. *č* in /t+š/, und zwar im Gegensatz zu anderen Sprachen, wo diese selben Lautverbindungen einphonemig sind; *c* ist lit. /ts/, lett. /c/; *ie, uo* sind einphonemig, im Gegensatz zu *ai* usw.

Diskrepanzen zwischen Orthographie und Phonematik aufzuzeigen, kann für fest eingeführte Orthographien selbst natürlich kaum von Nutzen sein. Wohl aber für die Phonematik: Es zeigt sich, wie weit das bloße Beobachten von außen von der inneren Ordnung der Dinge entfernt sein kann.

Anmerkungen

1. Diese Auffassung ist den folgenden Ausführungen zugrundegelegt. Die Phonemtheorien sind im Laufe der Jahrzehnte oft recht verschiedene, z. T. mehr philosophische Wege gegangen.

2. Eigentlich Begriffe aus der Anfangszeit der Phonologie, von denen man dann u. a. wegen des Vorwurfs des Psychologismus wieder abgerückt ist; sehr zum Schaden der Phonologie, die damit immer mehr die Sprache vom Menschen getrennt hat.

3. Für unsere Ausführungen ist von Bedeutung, „wie schwer man die phonologischen Zustände einer Sprache 'fühlen' kann, wiesehr auch das 'Sprachgefühl' in der eigenen Muttersprache versagen kann. Man darf nicht vergessen, dass man die 'Phonologie' seiner Muttersprache am frühesten erlernt und damit am tiefsten ins Unterbewusstsein versenkt. Dieses vermeintliche Sprachgefühl in Dingen des Phonemsystems wird zunächst von der *Orthographie* überdeckt, ja von der Orthographie erst gebildet, die man ja später erlernt und die dem Bewusstsein schon unvergleichlich nähersteht. Wenn ungeschulte Leute phonetische Angaben über ihre Muttersprache oder überhaupt über irgendeine Sprache machen, so nehmen sie immer die Schreibung zur Grundlage ... Wenn nun dazu die *phonetische Schulung* kommt, so lenkt sie durch ihren rein äußerlichen Aspekt noch mehr vom Erfassen der phonologischen Zustände ab. — Wir können also vieles nicht mit dem 'Sprachgefühl' erfassen; in der Phonologie muss vielmehr alles erst *errechnet* werden ..." (Verf. in *Acta Linguistica*, VI, 93).

4. Einzelnes z. B. noch von M. Adamus, „Sur la théorie des affriquées" (*Studia językoznawcze pośw. ... St. Rospondowi*, Wrocław 1966, 43 ff.); I. Futaky, „Trubetzkoys Regeln für monophonematische Wertung", *Phonetica*, XVI, 14 ff.); N. Morciniec, "Phonologische und morphologische Identifikation", *Biuletyn fonogr.* IX, 81 ff.).

5. Verschiedene *Grade* von Ein- und Zweiphonemigkeit: „Das scheint zunächst absurd: entweder *ist* ein Laut ein Phonem oder er ist es nicht, ein Zwischending ... dürfte es, so meint man, doch wohl nicht geben. Wir behelfen und vorläufig mit der Formulierung, dass die Ein- und Zweiphonemigkeit fraglicher Lautgebilde in verschiedenen Graden leicht oder schwer *erkennbar* ist" (*Ú*, 133; über die Art der Entscheidung innerhalb eines Phonemsystems s. ebenda 137 f. Allerdings gibt es gewiss Grenzfälle, die für den von außen Beobachtenden nicht genügend errechenbar bleiben. Es sei aber jedenfalls darauf hingewiesen, dass die meisten der Lautverbindungen, die allgemein als einphonemig gelten ([ts, tš] usw., s. u.), in ihren Graden hart an der Grenze liegen. — Über solche Grade vgl. Fn. 6, 7, 8.

6. d. h. wenn ein Glied der Lautverbindung außerhalb dieser Verbindung selbständig nicht oder nur stark beschränkt auftritt, so ist die Lautverbindung einphonemig. Es entspricht dies allgemeinen Regeln von Freiheit und Unfreiheit: Eine unfreie Lautverbindung ist keine Phonemverbindung, sondern ein Einzelphonem; ein unfreier Laut ist kein Phonem, sondern entweder ein Phonemmerkmal oder Phonem + Phonem; s. *Ú*, 121 ff.

7. Bei den sog. Affrikaten [tš, ts], auch [pf] usw. gibt es eine „natürliche" Einphonemigkeit, deren höchster Grad darauf beruht, dass die betreffende Sprache sonst gar keine Spiranten kennt (in exotischen Sprachen, vgl. *Ú*, 113; 133 f.); hier tritt ein bestimmter „Laut" außerhalb dieser Verbindung überhaupt nicht auf. So verhalten sich übrigens auch gewisse Diphthonge des Lit. und Lett., s. u.

8. Stärker begründet z. B. im Ungarischen, das im Anlaut [Kons. + Kons.] nicht kennt, wohl aber [ts, tš] (= /c, č/).

9. Zumeist schon früher begründet. Zu den pal. Konsonanten vgl. Verf. in *Ezikovedski izsledvanija ... St. Mladenov* (Sofija 1957), 499, und *Ú*, 130; zu lett. *ŗ* usw. *Ú*, 129, 132, 151; zu *ie, uo*: *Ú*, 102, 113, 121, 141, 144 ff.

10. Verschiedene Äußerungen über Einzelheiten bei A. Senn ,*Kleine lit. Sprachlehre* Heidelberg, 1929, 7, J. Otrębski, *Gramatyka języka litewskiego*, I, Warszawa, 1958, 309,

D. Augustaitis, *Das lit. Phonationssystem*, München, 1964, 3, 45 ff., 63 ff. (mit weiteren Zitaten).

11. Nach Senn a. a. O. ist das *l* von *del*, *dél*, *daugel* u. ä. „weich" (dazu vgl. *Ü*, 133); nach Otrębski a. a. O., 261, 263, kommt das nur in Dialekten vor; nach Augustaitis, 91 f., nicht in der Schriftsprache.

12. Nach Augustaitis, 38, 47, wäre auch ostlit. *mjatas*, *gjaras* usw. statt westlit. *metas*, *geras* zu schreiben.

13. Was immerhin z. T. die Einphonemigkeit der (süd)deutschen [kh], [ts], [pf] begründet, *Ü*, 118.

14. Z. B. im Russ. sind umgekehrt die morphologisch zerlegbaren *č* (*metát'–mečú*) weitaus in der Minderheit. Außerdem ist russ. *č* noch aus anderen Gründen einphonemig (*Ü*, 108, 120).

Phonemics and Orthography: Some Baltic Problems

Phonemics, as the theory of speech sounds working as elements of communication, is the natural basis of an adequate orthography: in one's own language one only distinguishes the phonemes, from which the phonetic realization differs to a greater or lesser extent. In this respect, the question of the monophonematic or biphonematic status of sound clusters is most instructive. In Lithuanian and Latvian, orthography and phonemic status prove to disagree in some striking points: the Lith. „palatalized" consonants (written *liau* ..., *pio* ... etc.) and the Latv. *ŗ*, *ļ*, *ņ*, *ķ*, *ģ* ("mouillé") divide into /C+*j*/, Lith. *č* divides into /t+š/, in contradistinction to the monophonematic status of the same clusters in other languages (*c* is /ts/ in Lith., /c/ in Latv.); on the other hand, *ie* and *uo* are monophonematic, in contradistinction to *ai*, *ei*, *au*, *ui*. Discrepancies like these reflect the extent to which mere external observation may disagree with the internal arrangement and structure of phonemes.

K. MORKŪNAS

Kelios M. Daukšos raštų kalbos ypatybės

Lietuvių kalbos istorinei gramatikai ir dialektologijai vertingų duomenų atskleidžia M. Daukšos raštuose — Katekizme[1] ir Postilėje[2] — vartotos rašybos analizė. Remiantis virš raidžių esančių diakritinių ženklų reikšmės tyrinėjimais, plačiai aprašytà M. Daukšos kirčiavimo sistema[3]. Nemaža šviesos tam tikrų fonetinių ir morfologinių ypatybių aiškinimui teikia ir "nosinių" raidžių vartojimo tyrimas. Į šių raidžių vartojimą vienas pirmųjų yra atkreipęs didesnį dėmesį F. Špechtas[4].

M. Daukšos ortografijoje diakritiniais ženklais, kuriais žymima balsių nazalizacija (nosinis rezonansas), kalbininkai paprastai laiko: a) apatinę raidės dalį įkypai kertantį tiesų brūkšnelį ($=ą$, $ę$, $į$, $ų$[5]) ir b) vąšelio formos ženklelį, rašomą raidės apačioje (panašiai kaip ir dabartinės lietuvių literatūrinės kalbos rašyboje). Tačiau, reikia pridurti, pastarąjį diakritinį ženklą M. Daukšos raštuose turi tiktai rašmuo (e ($=ę$).

Iki šiol buvo manoma, kad abiem šiais diakritiniais ženklais be skirtumo žymėtas nosinis balsis e. Tai, kad „nosiniais" rašmenimis, ypač ženklu $ę$, neretai žymėtas ir paprastas (be nazalizacijos) balsis e, aiškinta M. Daukšos rašybos nenuoseklumu bei ribotomis spaustuvės galimybėmis[6] (tiems patiems garsams žymėti neturėta didesnės vienodų raidžių atsargos). Paskutiniųjų metų tyrinėjimai[7] šias nuomones patikslina: nosinį rezonansą turėjęs e M. Daukšos raštuose žymėtas tik ženklu e (kaip ir nosinį rezonansą turėję balsiai a, i, u daugiausia žymėti ženklais $ą$, $į$, $ų$), o ženklu $ę$ žymėtas (neištisai) paprastas platusis e, norint jį atskirti nuo siaurojo e ($=ė$). Plačiajam balsiui e žymėti dar vartojami rašmenys $(i)e$, $(i)\overset{a}{e}$ (Postilėje tik pirmosiose keliose dešimtyse puslapių) ir ia, plg. (Postilės pavyzdžius): gen. sg. kelo 1_{19}, $k\overset{a}{e}lo$ $4_{42, 43}$, $ki\overset{a}{e}lo$ 1_{20}, acc. sg. kęlą 4_{28}, nom. sg. $ki\acute{a}li\overset{a}{e}s$ 7_{45}, pakiélt 8_{17}, téisus 3_{34}, $t\overset{a}{e}i\int us$ 2_{47}, nutęifinimo 1_{34}.

Žinodami minėtas M. Daukšos rašybos taisykles, galime tiksliau nustatyti: a) kur buvo tariamas e su nosiniu rezonansu ir kur paprastas (be nosinio rezonanso) e, b) kur buvo tariamas platusis e ir kur siaurasis e ($=ė$). Pateiksime tik kelias jo raštų kalbos ypatybes, kurių ligšiolinius aiškinimus mūsų iškeltos rašybos detalės verčia koreguoti arba į kurias kalbininkų dėmesys apskritai nebuvo atkreiptas.

348

a. *Su nosiniu rezonansu e ar paprastas (be nosinio rezonanso) e?*

1. Daugelio nuomone, M. Daukšos inesyvo (lokatyvo) postpozicijos -e buvo tariama su nosiniu rezonansu. Kaip šis -e rašomas?

Geriausiai postpozicijos -e yra išlaikęs daugiskaitos inesyvas: Katekizme jį turi visos (63) formos, o Postilėje iš beveik 1440 formų su -e yra apie 1 425 formos[8]. Tas -e žymimas: rašmeniu e Katekizme 16, Postilėje apie 890 formų (*darbůſe* P 21_{12}, *piktůſe* K 6); rašmeniu ę Katekizme 22 formos, Postilėje apie 210 (*darbůſſę* K 93, *darbůſę* P 298_{46}); rašmeniu $\overset{a}{e}$ Katekizme 24, Postilėje 37 formos (*darbůſễ* K 67, P 19_{50-51}; Postilėje 35 formos yra p. 2–25 ir po vieną formą p. 41, 44); rašmenimis *ia* tik Postilėje — apie 290 formų (*darbůſia* 493_9). Tiktai kelios formos, turinčios rašmenį ę (*mêtůſę* K 117, *kuriosę* P 52_{34}, *baʒniczioſę* P 268_{34}), greičiausiai yra korektūros klaidos (vietoj *mêtůſę, kuriosę baʒniczioſę*), kurių, kaip žinoma, M. Daukšos raštuose pasitaiko nemaža.

Vienaskaitos inesyvo formų postpozicijos -e po *j* gana dažnai nukritęs: *anói dienói* P 7_{10}, *dągui, ʒ́emei*[9] K 46. Po kitų priebalsių ir po *j* išlikęs postpozicijos balsis žymimas tais pačiais rašmenimis, kaip ir daugiskaitos inesyvo formų, pvz.: *dąguié* P 7_{39}, *tikéiime* P 18_{34}; *anoię* P 10_{26}, *tikéiimę* P 18_{34}, *widuię* P 16_{27}; *anoię̃* P 11_4, *dąguié* K 37, *raβtê* P 2_{16}; *dąguia* K 33, P 5_{53} (Katekizme su -e 44 formos, su -ę — 24, su $\overset{a}{e}$ — 68 ir su -ia — 21 forma).

Vadinasi, rašyba nerodo, kad M. Daukšos vienaskaitos ir daugiskaitos inesyvo formų postpozicijos balsie -e buvo tartas su nosiniu rezonansu. Tačiau tą rezonansą, matyt, dar buvo išlaikiusi įvardžiuotinių formų pirmojo dėmens postpozicija, kurios -e- daugiausia žymėtas su nosiniu diakritiniu ženklu (=ę), plg. Postilėje kiek dažniau pasitaikančias šios rūšies formas: pl. *grinůſęiůſę* 485_{43-44}, *piktůſęiůse* 599_{28}, *ſenoſęiůſe* 547_{30}, *ſenůſęiůse* 551_{10-11}, *βwętůſę́iůſe* 190_{20} (su -ę- 5 formos), *ſianůſéiůſe* 304_{40}, *βwęntůſe iůſe* 238_{10} (su -e- 2 formos); sg. m. *didimę́iime* 139_{37}, *mažamęiime* 456_5, *nauiamę́iime* 463_{36}, *paſkirtumę́iime* (=*paſkirtamę́iime*) 203_{18}, *pirmamę́iime* 43_{12}, 169_{47}, 554_5, *Pirmamę́iime* 407_{22}, *pirmamęiime* 407_{35}, 526_7, *pirmamę́iimę* 394_7, 411_{43}, *pirmamęiimę* 452_{38}, *tikramę́iimę* 450_{23} (su -ę- 14 formų ir 1 forma Katekizme: *tamę́iég* 121), *ne pirmaméiime* 195_{20}, *sawámeiime* 196_{32}, *tamę́ieg tikraméiime* 195_{35} (su -e- 3 formos[10]); sg. f. *βwęntoiąieia* (=*βwęntoiąioia*) 494_{25}, *βwentoięioi'* 245_{30-31}, *βwęntoięioi'* 457_{37}, *tikróięioie* 265_{13}, *tikroięioie* 417_{34-35}, *tikroięioi'* 375_{35-36}.

Rašyba rodo, kad su nosiniu rezonansu greičiausiai buvo tariamas ir tos pačios kilmės -e-, esantis iš daiktavardžių vienaskaitos inesyvo padarytose įvardžiuotinių būdvardžių formose, plg. Postilės pavyzdžius: nom. sg. m. *dąguięiis* 33_{14}, f. *dąguięii* 616_{13}, nom. pl. m. *ʒ́emeięiie* 616_{33}, gen. sg. m.

widuriįeio 239₆, f. *dąguięios* 34₁₄, gen. pl. *dąguięių* 411₄₀, *dienoięių* 268₃₂₋₃₃, acc. sg. f. *daguîęią* (=*dąguîęią*) 90₁₁, acc. pl. m. *dûbéięius* 520₄₄, f. *dąguięies* 520₄₃, instr. sg. m. *widuriięiu* 122₄₃, f. *dąguięie* 104₁₈, pl. m. *dąguięieis* 542₁₆, f. *βirdiięiomis* 626₃₁, ines. sg. m. *dąguięieme* 596₄₇, f. *wiriięioie* 613₄₉, pl. m. *dąguięiûſę* 440₁₉, f. *Dąguięioſſe* 542₁₇, ill. sg. f. *dąguięion'* 93₃₂, all. sg. m. *dąguięiop̃* 229₃₇, f. *dąguięioſp̃* 200₄₅. Šio tipo formos, kurių -e- neturi nosinio diakritinio ženklo, palyginti retos, pvz. (Postilėje): gen. sg. m. *dąguiéio* 8₁₄, f. *dąguiéios* 7₂₀₋₂₁, pl. *pragaréių* 411₄₁, ades. sg. *dąguieiep* 32₁₇, all. pl. *kalneiùmp̃* 619₃₀.

2. Darbatinėse lietuvių kalbos tarmėse (daugiausia rytų ir vidurio aukštaičių šnektose) vartojamas asmeninių įvardžių acc. sg. formas *manĩ*, *tavĩ*, *savĩ* (‖*manì*, *tavì*, *savì*) kalbininkai neretai tapatina su M. Daukšos raštų formomis *manę*, *tavę*, *savę*. Iš tikrųjų absoliuti jo raštuose randamų formų dauguma rodo, kad jų galūnėje žymėtas paprastas platusis (be nosinio rezonanso) balsis *e*, plg.: *mané* K 112, *tawe* K 168, *tawé* P 8₄₆, *ſawé* K 112, P 7₄₈; *maně̊* K 65, P 10₄₆₋₄₇, *tawe̊* K 167, P 11₁₂, ₂₈, ₂₉, *ſawẽ* K 70, P 18₁₃; *manę* K 137₍₂ₓ₎, P 7₄₆, *tawę* K 132, P 8₄₈, *ſawę* K 88, P 13₃₄ (Katekizme tik 1 forma *manę* 133). Šios M. Daukšos formos atitinka dabartinės lietuvių literatūrinės kalbos (ir kai kurių tarmių) formas *manè*, *tavè*, *savè*. Kartu jos skiriasi nuo to paties autoriaus gen. sg. formų, kurių -e paprastai žymimas su nosiniu diakritiniu ženklu, pvz.: *manę̃* K 154, *tawę̃* P 157₃₄, *ſawę̃* K 4, *ſawę* P 488₁₅ (retai *ſawé* P 432₃₇; dažniausiai M. Daukša vartoja gen. sg. *manęs*, *tawęs*, *sawęs*).

b. *Platusis e ar siaurasis e*(=*ė*)?

1. Dabartinės lietuvių literatūrinės kalbos rašmenį *ė*, kuriuo žymimas siaurasis *e*, M. Daukšos ortografijoje atitinka rašmuo e. Juo žymimas tiek kirčiuotas, tiek ir nekirčiuotas siaurasis *e* (kirčiuotas dažnai turi diakritinius kirčio ženklus: *é*, *ê*, *ė*), pvz.: *gerétis* P 4₃₄, *sedédamas* P 3₄₉, nom. sg. *garbe* P 5₅₂, gen. sg. *garbés* P 3₂₈, 3. praet. *dawe* P 5₁₅, nom. sg. *ʒ̇ęme*, gen. sg. *ʒ̇ęmes* P 4₆. Tai rodo, jog abiejose pozicijose šis balsis greičiausiai buvo tariamas vienodai ir skyrėsi nuo plačiojo *e*. Tiesa, iš kai kurių formų, pvz., 3. praet. *gimę* K 23, nom. sg. *karaliſtė* P 2₃₂, instr. pl. *ſkreiſtęmis* P 4₅, rašybos galėtume spręsti, kad dabartinės lietuvių literatūrinės kalbos nekirčiuotą *ė* M. Daukšos raštuose atitinka platus (ar nežymiai susiaurėjęs) *e* (resp. *ę*). Tačiau tokios formos yra labai retos, ir rašmenys *e̊*, *ę* jose gali būti korektūros klaidos vietoj *e* (kaip ir, sakysim, formoje *nę pridęgętė* P 16₂₂ antrasis *ę* korektūros klaida vietoj *e*[11]).

2. Lietuvių dabartinėse tarmėse labai įvairuoja 1. asmens įvardžio nom. pl. formos vokalizmas: *mès*, *mēs* (literatūrinės kalbos norma), *mẽs*, *màs*, *mãs*, *meñs* (*męs*), *meĩs*, *maĩs*, *mũs*, *mũs*[12]. Aiškinant kiekvieno tų

variantų atsiradimą, svarbu žinoti tikslius senųjų raštų duomenis. M. Daukšos Katekizme šis įvardis rašomas m$\overset{a}{e}$s (iš viso 15 kartų), Postilėje — dažniausiai pagrečiui mês (knygos pradžioje), męs, mes, plg. po 1 kartą mês ir męs p. 6, 10, 13, męs 63, 116$_{(3\times)}$, 117$_{(6\times)}$, 119$_{(2\times)}$, 129, 131$_{(2\times)}$ greta mes 63$_{(3\times)}$), 116, 117$_{(3\times)}$, 119, 129, 131$_{(2\times)}$. Tai rodo, kad M. Daukša šioje įvardžio formoje žymėjęs balsį e (ilgumas?). Korektūros klaida greičiausiai reikėtų laikyti vienoje kitoje Postilės vietoje (63$_{13}$, 62$_{38}$) randamą męs (ę labai neryškus, gali būti ir ę).

3. Rašyba rodo, kad M. Daukša vartojęs su senesniuoju šaknies balsiu e- veiksmažodžio eiti būtąjį laiką[13]. Šio laiko ir iš jo padarytų formų šaknies balsis gana dažnai žymimas pagrečiui rašmenimis e, $\overset{a}{e}$, ę, pvz. (Postilėje): êio 1$_{21}$, eio 63$_{21}$, atêio 39$_1$, ateiimo 128$_{13}$, iêio 73$_{17}$, iβêio 78$_8$, iβêiote 17$_{14}$, notêio 72$_6$, nuêio 82$_{34}$, prieio 79$_{26}$; at$\overset{a}{e}$iimas 6$_{27}$, iβ$\overset{a}{e}$iote 17$_{11}$, iβ$\overset{a}{e}$iot' 17$_{12}$, Nu$\overset{a}{e}$ię 1$_{16}$, pra$\overset{a}{e}$io 13$_{14}$; ęio 39$_{14}$, $_{27}$, atęjo 45$_{16}$, įęio 47$_{24}$, iβęio 117$_1$, iβęiimas 94$_{10}$, notęio 72$_{23}$, prięies 74$_{20}$ (priĝięs 73$_{10}$ korektūros klaida vietoj prięięs).

Išnašos

1. Kathechismas arba mokslas kiekvienam krikszczionii priwalvs ... Iżgulditas iż lieżuwio łąnkiβko ing lietuwiβka per kuniga Mikałoiu Daugβa ... Wilniuie ... 1595 (toliau sutrumpintai — K).

2. Postilla catholicka tái est: iżguldimas ewangeliu kiekwienos nedelos ir ſzwętes per wiſſús metús per kúniga Mikałoiv Davksza kanonîka Médniku iż łękiβko pergúldita ... Wilniui ... 1599 (toliau sutrumpintai — P).

3. P. Skardžius, Daukšos akcentologija, Kaunas, 1935.

4. F. Specht, „Zur Bedeutung des Nasalvokals bei Daukša", Tauta ir žodis, IV, 85–100.

5. D. Kleinas šiuos rašmenis, vartojęs 1653 m. gramatikoje („Grammatica Litvanica") nosiniams balsiams žymėti, vadino „su skersinėmis šakelėmis" („cum virgula transversali"), žr. Pirmoji lietuvių kalbos gramatika, Vilnius, 1957, 97–106, 418–424.

6. Dėl to lingvistinėje literatūroje cituojamų M. Daukšos kalbos pavyzdžių skirtingi „nosiniai" diakritiniai ženklai paprastai suvienodinami (ę ir ę dažniausiai perteikiami dabartinės lietuvių literatūrinės kalbos ortografijoje vartojamu ženklu ę), o atskirais atvejais ir visai nežymimi.

7. Žr. Aut., Iš rytų aukštaičių tarmių daugiskaitos inesyvo formų istorijos, "Lietuvių kalbos morfologinė sandara ir jos raida", Lietuvių kalbotyros klausimai, VII, 150–151; J. Palionis, Lietuvių literatūrinė kalba XVI–XVII a., Vilnius, 1967, 33 tt.

8. Su kitu balsiu daugiskaitos inesyvo formų Postilėje yra keliolika: akiſa 613$_{30}$, iſcioſa 441$_{18}$, nůdzioſa 441$_{43}$, paczioſa 27$_{50}$, ritûſa 58$_{12}$, βirdiſsa 30$_{34}$, βwęteſſa 33$_{35}$, tamſibeſa 510$_7$, wáloſa 30$_{34}$; dienoſú 372$_8$, wiſtikłûſú 35$_{10}$; dienoſi 58$_{38}$.

9. Katekizme sutrumpėjusios vienaskaitos inesyvo formos sudaro apie 38,8 % visų šio tipo formų: sutrumpėjusių yra 45 formos, nesutrumpėjusių — 71. Tiesa, ne visų kamienų sutrumpėjusios formos yra vienodai dažnos, pvz., (i)ā-kamieno iš 55 formų

galinio balsio neturi 27 formos, ė-kamieno iš 27 formų — 12, (i)u-kamieno iš 24 formų — 6, o i- bei priebalsinių kamienų visos 6 ir io-kamieno 4 formos yra su galiniu balsiu (dar plg. J. Kazlauskas, *Lietuvių kalbos istorinė gramatika*, Vilnius, 1968, 150–157). Panašiai yra ir Postilėje, plg. Z. Zinkevičius, *Lietuvių kalbos įvardžiuotinių būdvardžių istorijos bruožai*, Vilnius, 1957, 34–35.

10. Dar viena šios rūšies forma yra su korektūros klaida: *ſenamóiime* (= *ſenamêiime*?) 253_{27}.

11. Plg. Postilės formas *turėtų* 13_{28}, *tęwai* 13_{44}, *turėtus* 66_{24} klaidų atitaisyme ištaisytas į *turėtų, tewai, turėtus*.

12. Plg. Z. Zinkevičius, *Lietuvių dialektologija*, Vilnius, 1966, 296, 302.

13. Šį e- yra išlaikiusios kai kurios tarmės, plg.: *ėjo* Akmenė, Laipalingis, Palanga, Plungė, Skuodas, *apėjo* Eržvilkas, Kelmė, Kretinga, Laukuva, Raseiniai, Telšiai, Utena, *išėjo* Dusetos, Ignalina, Mažeikiai, *nuėjo* Alytus, Zietela ir kt. Kitose tarmėse ir literatūrinėje kalboje vartojamos formos su ė (*ėjaũ, ėjaĩ, ėjo* ...).

Some Peculiarities of the Language
of M. Daukša's Writings

It was supposed that a nasalized vowel e was marked with graphemes ę and ę in M. Daukša's writings—,,Katechismas" and ,,Postilla catholicka". An analysis of the orthography of these writings shows that nasalized e was marked only by means of the first grapheme, whereas the second grapheme, as well as several other graphemes, was used to mark open vowel e. This detail allows a more precise determination of: a) in what cases nasalized e was uttered and in what cases simple one (unnasalized or denasalized), b) where open e was pronounced and where closed e (= ė). On the grounds of statistical evidence some other more similar cases from the language of M. Daukša's writings are pointed out:

a. 1. Nasal resonance must have been lost in a postposition -e in the forms of inessive (locative) singular and plural, but it was still preserved in the first component of the forms of pronominal adjectives, where it occurred in the middle of a word, e.g. iness. sg. m. *pirmamęiime*, iness. pl. m. *piktůſęiůſe*; nom. sg. m. *dąguięiis*.

2. The accusative singular forms of personal pronouns in ,,Katechismas" and ,,Postilla catholicka" correspond to the forms *manè, tavè, savè* (-e without nasalization) of contemporary standard Lithuanian.

b. 1. There must have been no distinction in pronunciation of a closed vowel e (= ė of contemporary standard Lithuanian) in stressed and unstressed position, and it must have been distinguished from an open vowel e.

2. The form *mes* ,,we" (-e- open) of personal pronouns.

3. The preterite of the verb *eiti* ,,to go" preserved the older (open) e-.

JULIUS MÄGISTE

Estn. *(h)õis* 'Blüte' und seine Sippe
— ein balt. Lehnwort?

Estn. *õis*, Gen. *õie* 'Blüthe' (Wiedemann) weist, wie später ausgeführt wird,
nur abgeleitete Stammverwandte in den ostseefi. Sprachen und keine
sicheren etymologischen Anknüpfungen in den übrigen fi.-ugr. Sprachen
auf. Wie u. a. der Pühalepa-Dialekt von Hiiumaa (Dagö) zeigt, hat dieses
Wort ursprünglich ein *h*- im Anlaut gehabt, s. Pühalepa nach P. Ariste,
Acta et Commentationes Universitatis Tartuensis B XLVII, 1 *hõĭjèz* '*õis*',
Plur. *hõĭDəD* '*õied*' (ein sekundäres -*es*-Wort, wie *pilves*=*pilv* 'Wolke' u. a.
in den westestn. Mundarten[1]), vgl. auch das Verb *hõĭttsəmv* '*õitsema*',
'blühen'. Die Herkunft von estn. *(h)õis* bedarf der Klärung. Mit Rücksicht
auf das anlautende *h*- und auch darauf, dass der velare Diphthong *õi* (*ei*)
in diesem Fall aus dem palatalen *ei* hervorgegangen sein kann (s. z. B.
Verf. Suomi V Serie, X, 244–252 und Erkki Itkonen, *Virittäjä* 1945, 179–
180), darf man wohl für estn. *(h)õis* die frühostseefi. Ausgangsform (*õis* /
hõis < *heisi* <) *šeiti < *šeite rekonstruieren und es als ein baltisches Lehnwort im Urfi. ansehen, und zwar von dem balt. Wort, das im Lit. und Lett.
folgendermassen vertreten ist: lit. *žiedas* 'Blüte; Ring', lett. *zièds* 'Blüte,
Blume', vgl. auch das von demselben Stamm gebildete Verb lit. *žiedėti*
'blühen', lett. *ziêdêt* 'blühen, Blüten treiben'. Zu diesen balt. Wörtern s. ME,
wo auch ihre idg. Etymologie behandelt worden ist. Zur Etymologie der
balt. Sippe s. auch Kluge-Götz *Etym. Wb.* s. v. *Keil* und *Keim* und Walde,
Etym. Wb. I, 544: balt. *žied*-, *ziêd*- (< *žeid-) dürfte den idg. Stamm *ĝei-
'keimen, aufbersten, aufblühen' enthalten, der (nach Walde) in den balt.
Sprachen durch *d* erweitert worden ist. S. auch Ernst Fraenkel, *Litauisches
etymologisches Wb.* II, 1305 s. v. *žydėti*. Zu balt. *ž*- =ostseefi. *h*- (< *š*- < *ž*-) s.
Kalima, *Itämerensuomalaisten kielten balttilaiset lainasanat* 59 (z. B. lit.
žirnis=fi.-estn. *herne*, *hernes* 'Erbse' u. a.), zu der Repräsentation von balt.
ei (>*ie* im Lit. und Lett.) durch *ei* im Urostseefi. s. daselbst S. 73 (z.B. lit.
siena, lett. *siêna*=fi.-estn. *seinä*, *sein*, *sain* 'Wand' u. a.), zu der Vertretung
einiger balt. *as*- Wörter mit ostseefi. *e*-Stämmen s. daselbst S. 79 (z. B. lit.
rietas=fi.-estn. *reisi*, *reis*, *rais* 'Schenkel' [St. *reite*-] u. a.). Urostseefi.

*šeite (≫*heiti, St. heite-) und balt. źiedas, ziêds stimmen also miteinander Laut für Laut überein.

Estn. õis bzw. (h)õies steht aber in den ostseefi. Sprachen nicht ganz isoliert da. Zur endgültigen Klärung der Etymologie müssen wir versuchen aufzuzeigen, dass estn. (Wiedemann) õis-puu, koera-õis-puu 'Wasserholunder (Viburnum opulus)', saksamaa-õis-puu 'Flieder (Sambucus nigra)', fi. (Lönnrot) heisi-pensas, -puu 'olvon (Viburnum opulus); fläderhyll (Sambucus nigra)' von dem Stamme heite- abgeleitet sind. Diese Baumnamen verbindet man gewöhnlich mit estn. õis. Wollen wir deshalb zuerst die zahlreichen ostseefi. Verbal- und Nominalableitungen von õis 'Blüte' näher betrachten.

Das estn. Verb (Wiedemann) hõitsema bzw. õitsema, heitsemä, südestn. häitsema 'blühen', Dagö höitsema ist deutlich als eine Ableitung von (h)õis, wahrscheinlich aus urspr. < *heiðitse- ~ südestn. *häiðitse- (zum Wechsel von ei ~ äi vgl. nordestn. veits ~ südestn. väits 'Messer', nordestn. seitse ~ südestn. säidse 'sieben') zu erklären. Es ist offenbar durch das Suffix -itse- abgeleitet, wobei also die Entwicklungsreihe *heiðitse- > *heijitse- > heitse- > (h)õitse- bzw. südestn. *häiðitse ≫ häitse- vorauszusetzen ist.

Zum Schwund von j vor i im Estn. vgl. z. B. äikene 'Donner' < *äijikene < *äijükkeinen und (nach Wiedemann, Wb.) leis 'Finderlohn; Fund' < *leijis < *leüðüs; s. auch Tauli, Phonological Tendencies in Estonian S. 53–54, 57. Die Annahme von *heiðitse- im Estn. wird auch dadurch gestützt, dass diese Verbalableitung auch im Wot. und Weps. noch vorkommt, vgl. Setälä, Yhteissuomalainen äännehistoria, 469, MSFOu. 135,3 S. 57 und Kettunen, Vatjan kielen äännehistoria², 43 (72,1) edðitså (Infin.), edðitsäв 'hetiä (rukiista)', edjitsäв 'heilimöi', 'blüht', Kettunen, MSFOu. 86 S. 135: 26 südweps. ī hän heiḑitsȩ 'ei se kuki', 'es blüht nicht', 248: 34 rughet heiḑitas 'ruis heilimöi', 389: 28 koñz vezi heiḑiˌtšob 'kun vesi kukkii', 442: 20 mittelweps. rugiž heińitˏšȩb 'ruis heilimöi' (-ń- volksetymologisch, vgl. heiń 'Heu'!), 333: 1 südweps. heiḑitšȩškandob 'alkaa kukkia', 'fängt an zu blühen (Lein)'.

Eine andere Ableitungsweise vom Nominalstamm heite-, und zwar mit dem ostseefi. Verbalsuffix -i-, dürfte sich im fi. (Lönnrot, Wb.) V. heitiä 'blühen (insbesondere vom Roggen und von der Gerste)' wiederspiegeln, wovon fi. heide, Gen. heiteen 'Blühen' offenbar ein Deverbalnomen (< *heiðek) ist.

Das von Wiedemann angegebene estn. Substantiv õierm resp. hõierm, Gen. õierma bzw. hõierma = õis 'Blüthe' ist sicherlich durch das ostseefi. Suffix -rma (-rmä) (vgl. solche denominale Nominalableitungen wie z. B. estn. vabarm, fi. vadelma 'Himbeere', fi. sinermä 'Strieme', südestn. oarmu 'Schneetrift' u. a.) von unserem Nominalstamm heite- abgeleitet, also

*heiδe-rmä > *heijermä > (h)õierm. Südestn. (Wiedemann). *häiermü* 'Blüthe'
ist dagegen von dem Stamm *häite-* gebildet, also *häiermü* ≪ *häiδe-rmü* bzw.
-rmoi. Liv. *ēdrȝm* 'Blüte', das von Kettunen in seinem *Livischen Wörterbuch* als *heiderma* rekonstruiert und mit dem aus einem estn. Dialekt
herangezogenen *eiermud* 'die Blüten' (welches übrigens im Wb. von Wiedemann fehlt) und mit fi. *hedelmä* 'Obst' (gewöhnlich 'Frucht usw.', s. unten)
verglichen wird, ist offenbar mit estn. *(h)õierm* identisch und also gleichfalls
eine Ableitung von dem ostseefi. St. *heite-*. Das liv. Verb *ēdrikš̀ȝ* 'blühen',
das von Kettunen l.c. als *heideri/kse-* erschlossen und natürlich mit
ēdrȝm etymologisch zusammengestellt wird, gehört auch sicherlich hierzu,
vgl. auch Setälä, *Yhteiss. äh.,* S. 181 *ēdrikš̀ȝb* 'kukkii'. Man darf vielleicht für
dieses liv. Verb eine Ausgangsform auf *-rm-* ansetzen, also etwa *heiδer-
mikse-* (? *heidermikse-*), welche > *ēdrmikš-* und letzten Endes nach dem
durch die Konsonantenhäufung bedingten Schwund von *m* > *ēdrikš-*
ergeben konnte. Aber es ist jedoch auch möglich, dass in dem Nomen
ēdrȝm das auslautende *-m* als ein sogen. Instrumentalsuffix (vgl. liv. *jelȝm,*
kiⱦkìm, sidȝm, sidìm u. a. Posti, *MSFOu.* 85, S. 282 § 164,2) und *ēdrȝ-* als
Stamm aufgefasst wurden, von dem dann das V. *ēdrikš̀ȝ* mit dem Suffix *-ikš-*
bzw. *-ks-* deriviert worden ist. Auch im Fi. ist das ostseefi. *heiδermä (-rma)*
belegt, vgl. (nach dem Supplementheft von Lönnrots Wb.) *heiderma = hede*
'Roggenblüte', wie schon Ojansuu, *Virittäjä* 1903, S. 119, wo diese estn.-
liv.-fi. Sippe auf *-rmä (-rma)* behandelt wird (s. unten), festgestellt hat.

Ernstere Schwierigkeiten tauchen bei der Erklärung von gewissen estn.
Synonymen auf *-lm-* bzw. *-l-* dieser *-rmä- (-rma-)* Sippe auf, vgl. zwar estn.
(nach Wiedemann) *õile* 'Blüthe', *õilema* 'blühen', *õilis* 'Blüthe'[2], *õilitsema,*
õelitsema, õiluma, õilmeldama, õilmendama, õilmetsema, (?) *elitsema* 'blühen'.
Das zuletzt erwähnte *elitsema* lautet in der Volkssprache wohl gewöhnlich
eelitse/ma, -mä, denn der Verf. kennt es aus dem nördlichen Tartumaa
(nördlich von Dorpat, in Maarja-Magdaleena) als *ēlitsema* und auch Kettunen, *MSFOu.* XXXIII, 107 führt aus Kodavere *ḗlitsemä* 'blühen' (*ḗ-*
anstatt *ē-* ein Versehen?) an und vergleicht es etymologisch mit fi. *hedelmä.*
Alle diese estn. *-l(m)-* Wörter dürften auf urfi. *heiδelmä* (> *hõiδelma* estn.)
zurückgehen, das von dem Stamm *heite-* mit dem Suffix *-lmä* (resp. *-lma,*
vgl. fi. *odelma* 'Grummet, Nachwuchs', fi. *sinelmä = sinermä,* fi. *vadelma =*
vaderma, estn. *oalmu = oarmu* usw.) gebildet worden ist. Aus *heiδelmä*
bzw. *hõiδelma* würde man im Estn. > *(h)eielm* bzw. *(h)õielm* erwarten,
wir finden aber statt dessen *õile,* Gen. *õilme* bzw. *õile.* Estn. *õile* ist wohl als
analog anzusehen: die seltsame Bildung *(h)õielm* hat sich vermutlich der
reichhaltigen Kategorie der estn. Instrumentalnomina (vgl. das oben über
liv. *ēdrȝm* Gesagte) wie z. B. *koole,* Gen. *koolme, kuule,* Gen. *kuulme, sõõre,*

Gen. *sõõrme, lade,* Gen. *lademe* u. dgl. (s. Wiedemanns Wb.) angeschlossen und dabei im St. *õilme-* sein *e* der 2. Silbe eingebüsst. Von diesem *õile* bzw. (Gen.) *õilme* sind die gesamten estn. Wörter auf *õil-* die eben erwähnt worden sind (*õilema, õilitsema, õilmendama* u. a.) abgeleitet. Aus dem nördl. Tartumaa kenne ich auch die (von Wiedemann nicht erwähnte) entsprechende vordervokalische Analogieform *eile* (*eele*) 'Blüte', Plur. *eilmed* (urspr. **heiδelm-*), wovon dort das eben erwähnte Verb *élitsämä, élitsema* gebildet ist. Südestn. *häilmü* 'Blüte' (nach Wiedemann) < **häijelmü* < **häiδelmü* bzw. **-lmoi* hat dagegen die ursprünglichere Gestalt bewahrt, wobei das *e* der 2. Silbe jedoch verloren gegangen ist (vgl. dazu estn. *raiesmik, raiestik ∼ raismik, raistik* nach Wiedemann, dial. *õite* 'gar, sehr' ∼ *õiete, õieti* u. dgl.). Von diesem **heiδelmä* (bzw. *-lma*) bzw. **hõiδelma* wurde mit dem Suffix *-itse-* im Estn. das V. **heiδelmitse-* bzw. **hõiδelmitse-* gebildet, das in der estn. Volks- und Schriftsprache jetzt als (**hõijelmitse-* >) *õilmitsema* 'blühen' (nicht belegt im Wb. von Wiedemann) belegt ist. Auf urostseefi. **heiδelmoi* geht auch das von Kettunen *Vatjan kielen äännehistoria*[2] S. 106 angegebene wot. *edjᴇʌᴍᴏ* '(rukiin) siitepöly' zurück, aber die Frage von fi. *hedelmä* ist etwas komplizierter, und wir müssen sie ausführlicher behandeln.

Toivonen hat in seinem *Suomen kielen etymologinen sanakirja* I das bereits oben erläuterte fi. Verb *heitiä* 'kukkia (ruis, ohra)' und die damit etymologisch zusammenhängenden fi. Wörter *heide, heiderma* '(vilja- ja heinäkasvien) kukka, kukinta' u. a. behandelt und auch die meisten oben analysierten ostseefi. Wörter (weps. *heiδita,* wot. *edjïtsäʙ, edjᴇʌᴍᴏ,* estn. *õis,* [*h*]*õierm,* [*h*]*õies, õitseda, heitse-, häitseda* 'kukkia, kukoistaa', *õitse, õits, heitse, häitse, õilitseda, elitseda, õilme, häilmü, häiermü* usw., liv. *ēdrikš̂, ēdrᴅm* usw.) herangezogen, ohne jedoch ihre Zusammengehörigkeit zu begründen (in seinem kurzgefassten *Et. Wb.*). Er verbindet ohne Vorbehalt mit unserer Sippe auch gewisse lautlich unklare fi. Wörter, die statt *ei* ein *e* in der 1. Silbe haben: fi. *hetiä* = *heitiä, hede, hedin, hetu* = *heide, -rma,* auch *hedelmä* (aus dem Fi. ins Norwegisch- und Inari-lappische entlehnt), (nach Ganander) *hedelmänaika* 'kukinta-aika', *hedelmöi/tä, -dä,* dial. *heilimä, heilmä, hielma, heilimöi/tä, -dä, hielimöitä* usw. 'kukkia (etenkin ruis)' u. a. Der sonst so kritische Toivonen hat diesmal, vielleicht um sich kurz zu fassen, dem Wechsel von *ei* (*õi*) ∼ *e* in der Stammsilbe keine Bedeutung beigemessen. Wie wir schon oben gesehen haben, hat auch Kettunen die Wörter auf *ei* (*õi*) und fi. *hedelmä* miteinander verbunden. Derselben Ansicht ist aber schon Setälä, *Yhteissuomalainen äännehistoria,* 469 gewesen, vgl. auch Airila, *Johdatusta kielen teoriaan* I, 70 u. a. Ojansuu hat *Vir.* 1903 S. 118–119 die Zusammengehörigkeit der Stämme auf *ei* und *e* auch lautgeschichtlich zu begründen versucht, indem er die zur Zeit

verworfene Theorie des Stufenwechsels der Vokale herangezogen hat und
etwa von dem urspr. Wechsel *heδek : *heiteγen ausging, wobei also heitiä,
heide, heidin u. dgl. die starke und die (beinahe) synomischen Pendants
hedelmä 'ax- l. sädesblomma; frukt, produkt, afkomma', hede 'blomning',
hedin = heidin 'blomningsorgan' die schwache Stufe repräsentieren sollten.
Sogar mehrere estn. Wörter, die wir oben alle auf ei (õi) zurückführten,
wollte Ojansuu mit dem kurzen Vokal der 1. Silbe erklären (õilme < *heδelm-,
õitsema < *heδitse- usw.). Nach dem Wegfall dieser Stufenwechselerklärung
von Ojansuu ist die vorbehaltlose Heranziehung der i-losen fi. Varianten
(hedelmä, hede, hedin u. a.) in diesem Zusammenhang riskant, weil der
Wechsel von ei und e in der 1. Silbe des Fi. so ungewöhnlich ist, dass man
die Wörter mit dem Stamme het- und heit- voneinander trennen sollte. Auch
solche vereinzelten dialektischen Schwundfälle der zweiten Komponente
von Diphthongen wie z. B. die im Estn. von Tauli, op. cit., 86–89 behandelten (estn. dial. leiva ~ leva 'des Brotes' usw.) können hier kaum als Parallelen dienen. Will man in unserem Falle der alten guten (oder schlechten)
lautgeschichtlichen Betrachtungsweise treu bleiben, so scheint es ratsam
zu sein den Standpunkt einzunehmen, dass im Wort hedelmä neben *hei-
delmä und möglicherweise auch in hetiä neben heitiä, hede neben heide u. dgl.
zwei urspr. verschiedene Wortstämme, der eine heit- (von balt. Ursprung)
und der andere het- (einheimisch, vielleicht urspr. von deskriptiver Art)
sich kontaminiert haben. Der letztere dürfte mit dem Deskriptivstamm identisch sein, welcher (nach Lönnrots Wb.) z. B. in den fi. Deskriptivwörtern
auftritt: hetajaa 'slarfva (t. ex. en trasig klädning), hänga slarfvigt, dingla,
fladdra, svaja', helpeet hetajavat tuulessa, Subst. hetale 'fladdrande l. svängande
ting; slarfva, trasa' = heitale, hetule (hetkale), hetalehtaa 'röras trasigt l.
slarfvigt', hetelehtää 'vara lättrörlig, ostadig; vara sprättaktig'. Die Staubfäden der Blüten, besonders beim blühenden Roggen und bei der Gerste,
sind ja eigentlich wie herabhängende, flatternde Franzen, Fasern, vgl. auch
estn. (Wiedemanns Wb.) tolmu-narmas 'Staubfäden (in der Blüthe)',
eigentl. 'Staubfranze, -faser'. Die Kontamination der urspr. einander fremden Stämme dürfte deshalb im Fi. leicht vorstellbar sein. Im Estn. und in
den anderen ostseefi. Sprachen, wo es keinen Deskriptivstamm auf het-
(hed-) gibt, ist kein Anlass zur Kontamination vorhanden gewesen, und dort
hat man die ursprüngliche diphthongische Lautgestalt unseres Stammes
bewahrt. Von dem sekundären het- Stamm muss man in ostfi. Dialekten
auch in der Stammvariante heil- ausgehen, obwohl sie bisweilen in der Literatur direkt mit den estn. õil- (< *heiδel-) Stämmen zusammengebracht
worden ist (s. Kettunen, Liv. Wb., 53 fi. heilimoida = estn. õelitsema =
õilitseda, õõlitsema). So sind zwar die ostfi. Lönnrots Wb. und Supplem.

Dialektvarianten *heilmä = heelmä = hedelmä, heilimä* 'axblom', das Verb *heilmoa* 'blomma, stå i blomning', Freqv. *heilmoilla*, Faktit. *heilmottaa, heilim/öitä, -iöitä* 'blomma' u. dgl. alle irgendwie von Stamme **heδelm-* herzuleiten (wobei *δ > O* in den ostfi. Mundarten).

Und nun noch zur Frage des Ursprungs von estn. *õis-puu* und fi. *heisi-pensas, -puu*, die am Anfang unseres Aufsatzes schon gestreift wurden. Schon Ojansuu a. a. O. hat ostseefi. *õis-, heisi-puu* mit estn. *õis* und seiner Sippe etymologisch verbunden. Andererseits hat man mehrere Male in der Literatur diesen Baumnamen als ein uraltes fi.-ugr. Erbe in den ostseefi. Sprachen gedeutet und für ihn Entsprechungen aus Mordw., Tscher., Syrjä-nischen und Wotjakischen vorgelegt, s. Setälä, *Yhteissuomalainen äänne-historia*, 469–470 und *Nyelvtudományi Közlemények* XXVI, 396, Wichmann, *FUF* IX, 119, Beke, *FUF* XXII, 121, Uotila, *MSFOu.*, 65, 252, I. Sebestyén-Németh, *Nyelvtud. Közlem.*, LII, 331 und (etwas zweifelnd) auch Toivonen a. a. O. Nach Toivonen gehören zu fi. *heisipuu (hõisi-hõysi-, höys-, helsi-, hersi-, hörsk-* usw.) und estn. *õis-, iispuu* evtl. aus dem Mordw. *čęύģeí, čavdire, čeύģä* usw. 'heisipuun marja'(?), tscher. *šaršə̂, šoršo* usw. 'id.'(?), wotj. *šu, šuu* 'heisipuu, heisipuun marja', *šu-pu* 'heisipuu', syrj. *žo, žol, žov, žovpu* usw. 'id.'. Die mordw. und tscher. Beispiele hat Toi-vonen berechtigterweise mit Fragezeichen versehen, denn ihre Zusammen-gehörigkeit mit *õis-, heisipuu* ist lautlich wirklich sehr zweifelhaft. Aber auch die angenommenen perm. Entsprechungen von *õis-, heisipuu*, die bisher gewöhnlich gebilligt worden sind, scheinen nicht so unantastbar zu sein. Erkki Itkonen hat in seiner Abhandlung Zur Geschichte des Vokalismus der ersten Silbe im Tscheremissischen und in den permischen Sprachen, *FUF* XXXI, 149–343, wo er alle sicheren ostseefi.-tscher.-permischen Wortver-gleichungen herangezogen hat, den in Frage stehenden Baumnamen nicht erwähnt, wohl weil er seine bisherige Etymologie nicht billigt. Wenn die perm. Wörter mit dem ostseefi. Stamm **heite-* etymologisch verwandt wären, müsste man in der 1. Silbe der perm. Entsprechungen statt *o, u, uu* etc. etwas anderes erwarten, m. E. möglicherweise *i* (vgl. perm. *bi*[?], und *pi, pi-pu* Itkonen *op. cit.*, S. 316). Wie man aus den von Toivonen erbrach-ten fi. Beispielen ersieht (man beachte *hersi-, hers-, hörsk-*), ist unser Baum-name im Fi. volksetymologischen Deutungen (lautlich zu gewissen deskrip-tiv-onomatopoetischen Wortsippen) ausgesetzt worden (vgl. fi. Lönnrot *hersua, hersyä* 'frasa, svaja, vaja, svänga sig, fladdra ...', *hörskyä* 'frasa, knarra, fräsa', *hörskä, hörskyttää* usw.). Fi. *hõisi-, höys(i)puu*, olon. *höüdöi* und lüd. *höüdüöi = heisipuu*, die Toivonen a. a. Ort ebenfalls angeführt hat, können nicht direkt mit dem Stamm *heite-* verbunden werden, sondern deuten wahrscheinlich auf einen etymologischen Zusammenhang mit dem deskriptiven fi. Wort (Lönnrot) *höytö* 'fjun, fan (på fjäder), fnas, flinga' = *höyty*, *höytäle* 'fjun, fnas, flinga; flocka' = *heitale* ~ *hetale* (Lönnrot, Ergänzungsheft) *höyty* 'sädesblomma', *höytä*, *lumen h.* 'snöflinga', hin, vgl. auch kar. Ojansuu, *Karjala-aunuksen äännehistoria*, 104 *höütäleh*, *lumen h.* 'kepeä lumi', *lumihöüdelö* 'lumihiude' usw. Es ist unmöglich zu sagen, ob diese Varianten mit *öü* in der ersten Silbe auch vom Stamm *heite-(heisi)* ausgehen und man an die volksetymologische Einwirkung seitens der deskriptiven Sippe auf *höüt-* denken muss oder ob man es hier von Anfang an mit einem andersstammigen Synonym (vom Stamm **heüte-*) zu tun hat. Zu dem fi.-kar.-lüd. deskriptiven Stamme **heüte-*, *heite-* gehört auch estn. *heie*, Gen. *heide*, *heies*, *häie*, südestn. *häüe* 'Faden . . ., Vorgespinnst, Flocken, Fasern, die sich vom Zeuge abschaben' und die Ableitungen dieses Wortes (s. Wiedemann, < **heitehe-*,? **heütehe-*, **häütehe-*), die Toivonen a. a. O. bei der Behandlung des Wortes fi. *heisi*, *höisi*, *höysi* usw. 'Bandwurm usw.', olon. *höüdǯi* '(kleiner) Springwurm', lüd. *heižmado*, *höudïäińe* usw. 'Spring-, Bandwurm', weps. *hīže*, *heiže̬* 'id.' herangezogen hat. Diese Sippe hängt etymologisch nach Toivonen mit fi. *heisi(puu)*, *höysipuu* zusammen. Wir sehen also in den zuletzt behandelten fi.-olon. Baumnamenvarianten und in der Benennung des Band- bzw. Springwurmes in Fi., Olon., Lyd. und Weps. und in dem mit ihnen zusammengehörenden estn. Wort (*heie* usw.) in der 1. Silbe eine so reichliche Variation des Vokalismus (*ei* ~ *öi* ~ **eü* [>estn. *ei*, fi.-olon. *öü*], *äü*), dass man die ganze Sippe als urspr. deskriptiv ansehen muss, was auch zu ihrer wahrscheinlich ursprünglichen Bedeutung 'Faser, Franze, Flocken u. dgl.' gut passt. Ausserdem haben wir oben schon eine synonyme und beinahe homonyme diphthonglose Variante dieser Sippe, (vgl. fi. *hede*, *hetiä*, *hedelmä*) kennengelernt. In diesem Zusammenhang dürfte man vielleicht auch annehmen, dass die Bezeichnung für 'Wasserholunder' auch in den östlichen fi.-ugr. Sprachen (mordw., tscher., perm., s. oben) deskriptive Elemente enthält (man beachte das unerwartete *ž-* im syrj. *žo-pu* usw., s. auch Uotila, *op. cit.*, 65, 43), so dass man auf ihrer Basis schwerlich uralte fi.-ugr. Etymologien aufstellen kann. Erkki Itkonen hat wiederholt darauf hingewiesen (besonders *op. cit.* und *FUF* XXIX), dass die fi.-ugr. Baumnamen öfters lautlich „unkorrekt" sind, und dies dürfte gewöhnlich auf Volksetymologien, Anwendung der deskriptiv-affektiven Elemente u. dgl. beruhen.

Schlussfolgerungen: Das im Anfang vorgeführte ostseefi. Material zeigt, dass der ostseefi. Stamm **heite-* 'Blüte', der durch das Estn., Liv., Wot., Fi. und Weps. belegt ist, also urostseefinnisch ist und auch deshalb wohl als ein frühurostseefi. balt. Lehnwort angesehen werden darf. Die aufgestellte fi.-ugr. Etymologie von estn. *õispuu*, fi. *heisipuu* 'Wasserholunder', die im ersten Kompositionsglied diesen balt. Lehnstamm enthalten, scheint (nicht nur für mich, sondern offenbar auch für E. Itkonen) höchst unsicher zu sein und wir dürfen wohl vorschlagen diese zu streichen. Die Etymologie von *õis* wird aber dadurch kompliziert, dass im Fi. der genuine Deskriptiv stamm *het(e)-* (auch *heite-*!) die lautliche Struktur einiger Ableitungen von **heite-* 'Blüte' volksetymologisch und lautlich beeinflusst hat (vgl. fi. *hedelmä, hetiä* u. a.). Noch weitere Komplikationen erscheinen bei der lautlichen Analyse der ostseefi. Bezeichnungen für 'Wasserholunder' (urspr. **heisi-pū*) und für 'Bandwurm; Springwurm' (fi. *höysi, höisi, heisi,* olon. *höüdöi* u. a.), die urspr. denselben entlehnten balt. Stamm *heite-* enthalten dürften, aber später volksetymologisch mit dem genuinen, lautlich wechselnden (mit *het[e]-* synonymen) Deskriptivstamm *heite-* (**heitä-*), **heüte-* (**heütä-*), *häüte-* (**häütä-*) vermengt worden sind. Der deskriptive Einschlag in der von uns behandelten ostseefi. Sippe ist so stark, dass man alternativ sogar auf den Gedanken kommen könnte, dass die ganze Sippe, der zu Anfang behandelte *heite-* 'Blüte' Stamm einbegriffen (man beachte z. B. fi. *höyty* 'sädesblomma' oben!), ursprünglich genuin sei und demselben mit den Diphthongwechseln in der 1. Silbe variierten Deskriptivstamm gehöre und dass es also der oben vorgeschlagenen Erklärung über den balt. Stamm von *heite-* nicht bedarf. Die sowohl lautliche als semasiologische Einstimmigkeit zwischen dem balt. Wort für 'Blüte, Blume' und der im Anfang dieses Aufsatzes behandelten ostseefi. **heite-* Sippe ist jedoch so klar und die vom ostseefi. Stamm **heite-* gebildeten ('Blüte, blühen') Wörter so einheitlich, weitverbreitet und altertümlich, dass man sie nicht einfach einer Deskriptivsippe einreihen darf; vielmehr ist die Erklärung ihres Stammwortes als baltisch vorzuziehen.

Anmerkungen

1. Estn. dial. *höïjèz*, WIEDEMANN *õies*, Gen. *õide*, könnte auch eine direkte Entsprechung des unten zu behandelnden fi. *heide*, Gen. *heiteen*, sein. Dies ist jedoch wenig wahrscheinlich, weil es im Estn. den Verbalstamm *heiti-* (vgl. fi. *heitiä*, wovon fi. *heide* wohl abgeleitet ist) nicht gibt.

2. Dieses Dialektwort hat in der estn. Schriftsprache vor etwa dreissig Jahren die Bedeutung 'edel' erhalten (vgl. auch *õilistama* 'veredeln' usw.), s. Verf. *Sõna* 1949 (Stockholm), 52–53.

Estonian *(h)õis* 'blossom' — a Baltic Loan Word?

The author discusses the etymology of the Estonian word *õis*, gen. *õie* 'blossom', and examines in detail all traceable derivatives of this word and words in other Balto-Finnic languages which are more or less likely to be related. He reaches the conclusion that the parent word of this family, **heisi*, root **heite-*, must be among the oldest Baltic loan words in (Proto-) Balto-Finnic and come from the Baltic original represented by Lith. *žiedas* 'blossom' and Latv. *zièds* 'blossom, flower'. Thus, Baltic **žaida-* > Proto-Balto-Finnic roots **šeite-/*šaite-* > Balto-Finnic **heite- ~ *häite-* (> *heisi*, *hõis* > *õis*, etc.).

JAN OTRĘBSKI

Lit. *šakà* und Verwandtes

Es handelt sich in diesem Aufsatz vor allem um eine Reihe von etymologisch
zusammengehörigen litauischen Wörtern: *šakà, -õs* f. 'Ast, Zweig'; *šãkė*,
meist pl. *šãkės* f. 'Gabel, Forke'; *šaknìs, -iẽs*, gen. pl. *šaknų̃* f. 'Wurzel (des
Baumes, Zahnes usw.); *šakar̃nis, -ė* 'ästig, zackig'. Diese Wörter warten
noch immer genau untersucht zu werden.

Zugrunde liegt wohl der Stamm **šak-ar/n-*. Davon sind abgeleitet:
einerseits das Adjektiv *šakar̃nis*, anderseits das Substantiv *šaknìs*. Was
nun das Wort *šakà* anbetrifft, so ist es, wie ich annehme, ein altes von
*šak-ern- abgeleitetes Kollektiv auf *-ā-*. Das Wort *šãkė(s)* beruht auf Umbildung von *šakà* mittels des Kollektivsuffixes *-i̯ā-*; dieses Wort kam zustande in einer Periode, als *šakà* semantisch schon singularisiert wurde.

Der Stamm **šakar/n-* ist der Herkunft nach eine Reduplikationsbildung,
enthaltend die Wurzel **ker/n-* bzw. **kar/n-* und die Reduplikationssilbe
ša-. Die Wurzel **ker/n-* ist identisch mit der von lit. *kèras* m. 'Strauch,
Baumstumpf' und slaw. (aksl.) *korenь* m. 'Wurzel'.

Die Reduplikationssilbe *ša-* von **ša-kar(n)-* verdient eine besondere
Aufmerksamkeit. Es ist nun nicht der einzige Fall, wo dem anlautenden *k-*
in der Reduplikationssilbe das palatale *k-* (>lit. *š-*) entspricht. Es genügt
hier anzuführen aind. *śákr̥t, śaknáḥ* n. 'Mist, stercus' = **ša-k(e)r/n-* neben
gr. σκῶρ, σκατός n. 'Kot' aus **s-kōr, *s-kṇ-t*. In diesen Zusammenhang gehören die Wörter wie lit. *šaũkti, šaũkia* 'laut rufen, schreien; jmd. nennen'
neben *kaũkti, kaũkia* 'heulen; winseln'; *šaũkti* ist semantisch die mildere
Variante von *kaũkti*.

Der Vokal *a* der Reduplikationssilbe in lit. **ša-karn-* ist auffällig. Da er
sich von demjenigen der Wurzelsilbe nicht unterscheidet, ist wohl eine
Vokalharmonie vorauszusetzen.

Lit. *šakà* ist ein altes, schon baltisches Wort. In den lettischen Mundarten findet sich *saka* 'eine Verästelung beim Baum', auch 'Verästelung
eines Stromes oder Flusses', pl. u. a. 'Kummethölzer'. Aus dem Baltischen
stammt finn. *hako* 'abgehauener Baum' und estn. *hagu* 'Reisig; Wipfel
eines Baumes'.

Als verwandt mit balt. *šakā wird allgemein aind. śấkhā f. 'Ast, Zweig' (mit vielen übertragenen Bedeutungsnuancen, z. B. 'vedische Schule') betrachtet. Doch ist die Lautform dieses Wortes nicht klar. Das lange ā in der ersten Silbe ließe sich irgendwie erklären. Schwierig ist aber die Aspirate kh: ist sie in der Tat schon indogermanisch (wie von einigen Indogermanisten angenommen wird[1]), oder stellt sie ein Erzeugnis der phonetischen Entwicklung des Altindischen, etwa der sekundären Aspiration dar?

Niemals zweifelte man daran, daß balt. (lit.) šakà 'Ast, Zweig' und slaw. socha 'Hakenpflug' das gleiche Wort sind. Unüberwindliche Schwierigkeiten bereitet aber dabei das ch von socha. Der Versuch dieses ch direkt auf idg. kh zurückzuführen muß als verfehlt betrachtet werden, wie immer man auch das kh von aind. kh beurteilen will: schon in der ursprünglichen baltisch-slawischen Sprache gab es keine Aspiraten mehr. Die Lautform von socha bildet also eine interne Frage der Slawistik.

Unter den Ableitungen von slaw. *soka (=lit. šakà) bzw. socha ist für unsere Frage besonders wichtig das gemeinslawische Wort rosocha aus *roz-soka, mit dem Präfix roz- aus *orz-. Im Polnischen bedeutet rosocha, geschrieben auch rozsocha (mit wiederhergestelltem Präfix roz-) — nach Linde[2] — 'der Zacken an einem Geweihe, ein gabelförmiger Ast an einem Baume, ein Gabelstock, Gabelast mit zwei Enden'. Die gleichen oder ähnlichen Bedeutungen weist rosocha auch in den übrigen slawischen Sprachen auf.

Dem Wort *ro(z)soka (>rosocha) messe ich eine besondere Bedeutung in der Entstehung der Lautform socha bei. Im Sprachbewußtsein der Slawen erschien es als eine Ableitung mit dem Suffix -oka. Da die Funktion dieses vermeintlichen Suffixes nicht klar war, neigte man dazu, es zu ändern. Bestimmend für die Richtung der Änderung war natürlich das semantische Moment: *rosoka stellte ein charakteristisches Augmentativum dar. Es gibt nun Beispiele dafür, daß die Slawen in derartigen Wörtern das k durch den expressiven Hauchlaut (ch) ersetzten:

Slaw. chobotъ m. in r.-ksl. chobotъ 'Schwanz', russ. chobot 'Elephantenrüssel', apoln. chobot u. a. 'Schwanz' gehört zusammen mit lit. kabė́ti, kába 'herab-, herunterhängen'[3]. Die etymologische Bedeutung von chobotъ war also aller Wahrscheinlichkeit nach 'etwas Herabhängendes'; diese Bedeutung besitzt auch lit. kabùklas.

Poln. alt und dial. cholebać 'wiegen, schaukeln', cholebka f. 'Wiege' sind Nebenformen von kolebać, kolebka 'dss', aksl. kolěbati, kolěblʹǫ 'σαλεύειν, agitare' usw.

Slaw. *chъrkati in ukr. chorkaty 'kreischen; mit heiserer Stimme sprechen', skr. *hŕkati* 'schnarchen' haben das *ch-* für *k-*, worauf slaw. *kъrkati* z. B. in čech. *krkati* 'rülpsen, grölzen; krächzen' hinweist.

Dem expressiven *ch* für *k* (und andere Konsonanten) widmete ich einen besonderen Aufsatz[4].

Das Wort *rosocha* spielte eine wichtige Rolle nicht nur in der Umbildung der Grundform *soka* (> *socha*), sondern auch in der Entstehung des bedeutungsverwandten Wortes *leměchъ*. — Man verstand *rosocha* ohne Zweifel als eine Bildung mit dem augmentativen bzw. pejorativen Suffix -*ocha*, wie z. B. in russ. *sumatocha* f. 'Durcheinander, Wirrwarr' (= *su-mat-ocha* — von der Wurzel *mat-*, wie in poln. *matać* 'wickeln, verdrehen' und *matnia* f. 'Strickgarn; Schlinge'). Das Wort *rosoka* fand also in der neuen Form *rosocha* eine Stütze an den Bildungen vom Typus *sumat-ocha*.

Wie *ros-ocha* zerlegte sich im Sprachbewußtsein der Slawen auch *pos-ocha* (aksl. 'Stock, Stab') sowie *pos-och(ъ)* (russ. 'Krückstock, Stock, langer Stab'). Dies ermöglichte die analogische Entstehung des slawischen Wortes *leměchъ*, das eben in dieser Form und mit der Bedeutung 'eine Spitze bei Hakenpflug und Pflug (welche den Erdboden schneidet)' in den russischen Mundarten vorkommt. Es war ein gemeinslawisches Wort. In den historischen slawischen Sprachen erscheint es aber meist mit dem Suffix -*jь*: *leměšь* aus *leměch-jь*. Lett. *lemesis* dss. ist ein Lehnwort aus dem Russischen.

Die Etymologie von *leměchъ* ist im Grundlegenden seit langer Zeit bekannt[5]. Dieses Wort ist nämlich eine Ableitung von der Wurzel *lem-* : *lom-* 'brechen' in russ. *lom* m. 'Brecheisen' und *lomitь* 'brechen'; die schwundstufige Form dieser Wurzel tritt im Preussischen auf: *limtwei* 'brechen'. Unerklärt blieb bisher das Morphem -*echъ*, eigtl. -'*ochъ*. Es entpuppte sich jetzt als ein von *pos-ochъ* abstrahiertes „Suffix". Man verwendete es zur Erweiterung des alten von der Wurzel *lem-* abgeleiteten Substantivs *lem-jo-*.

Eine besondere Behandlung erfordert die Wurzel des Morphems *šakar/n-* in lit. *šakar̃nis* usw. Wahrscheinlich ist sie nicht verschieden von *(s)ker/n-*, die u. a. den folgenden Wörtern zugrunde liegt: gr. κείρω (aus *κεριω) 'abschneiden; scheren'; ahd. *sceran* 'scheren; abschneiden' : lit. *skìrti, skìria* 'trennen, scheiden'; — lit. *skìnti, skìna* 'pflücken; abreißen, aushauen, (Wald) roden, lichten' — in diesen Zusammenhang gehört u. a. noch lit. *karnà* f. 'Bast', ein ursprüngliches Heteroklitum.

Ableitungen von der in Rede stehenden Wurzel *(s)ker-* erscheinen mitunter auch in der augmentativen bzw. pejorativen, also stimmhaften Form: lit. pl. *žagaraĩ* 'dürres Strauchwerk, Reiser, Gestrüpp'; *žãgrė* f.

'Pflug(schar)'. — Es wird hier nicht unangebracht sein daran zu erinnern, daß dem litauischen Substantiv *šaknìs* im Preussischen die Variante mit stimmhaftem *g* entspricht: *sagnis* f. 'Wurzel'.

Anmerkungen

1. Vgl. H. Pedersen, *KZ* XXXVIII, 391.
2. *Słownik języka polskiego* V, 118.
3. Brückner, *Słownik etymologiczny języka polskiego*, 505 f.
4. Der Aufsatz wird in der Zeitschrift *Die Welt der Slaven* 1970 erscheinen.
5. Vgl. Berneker, *Slav. etymolog. Wtb.* I, 700 f.

Lith. *šakà* and Related Words

Lith. *šakà* 'branch' represents an old collective noun in -*ā*-. It was derived from the heteroclitic root in **ker/n* (*kar/n) which is still preserved in Lithuanian: *šaknìs* 'root' and *šakar̃nis* 'branched stock; stub'. *šakern- is here regarded as reduplication *ša-kern- and related to Lith *kěras* 'bush', OCS *korenь* 'root'. Slav *socha* 'wooden plough' is considered to be the same word. The 'ch' owes its origin to the later expressive aspiration, particularly evident in the compound *orz-socha. Polish *ro(z)-socha* 'fork-shaped branch or stub'. The assumption that the *ch* sound goes back to the IE *kh* is rejected by the author. Further examples of expressive *ch* for *k* are mentioned. Skt. *śắkhā* 'branch, twig' deserves separate discussion treatment.

Р. ПАРОЛЕК

К переводу Гейдуком латышских дайн на чешский

Наступление эпохи романтизма открыло миру возможность познакомиться с рядом национальных литератур, которые были до того времени мало известны. Это были прежде всего литературы германские и скандинавские, а затем — благодаря Гердеру и Гёте — также литературы славянские и прибалтийские, в которых романтики находили что-то экзотическое.

Деятели чешского национального возрождения считали тогда, что балтийские народы, в языке которых находили отдаленное родство с языками славянскими, принадлежат к широкому контексту славянских культур. Этим объясняется факт, что во 2-ом томе «Славянских народных песен» Челаковского помещено несколько образцов литовских песен. В 1827 году выходит в свет сделанный Челаковским перевод сборника литовских дайн (*Litevské národní písně z původního jazyka dle sebrání Dra J. L. Rhesy přiložené*, Praha 1827). Заинтересованность была, очевидно, взаимной. В прибалтийских странах уделяется некоторое внимание чешской словесности, особенно в Латвии. Например, хорошо известная латышская песня «Nevis slinkojot un pūstot ...» (1864), автором которой считают Ю. Алунана, является переводом одного из стихотворений Челаковского. Позже поэт Райнис пишет статью о Врхлицком и переписывается с чешским поэтом Петром Безручем.

Однако хорошего перевода латышских дайн чешскому читателю пришлось ждать долго, вплоть до начала XX века. Только в 1901 году выходит в Праге в свет в издательстве Й. Отто как 23-ий том Сочинений Адольфа Гейдука прекрасно оформленная книга Латышские мотивы, 1898–1899. Её появление нашло уже подготовленную почву в чешской культурной и литературной общественности благодаря профессору д-р Иосифу Зубатому, который уже в 1894 году опубликовал в журнале Вестник чешского королевского общества наук (*Věstník Královské české společnosti nauk*) обширную статью «Об аллитерации в латышских и литовских дайнах» («O alliteraci v písních lotyšských a litevských» — около 40 страниц) и вплоть до первой мировой войны регулярно печатал в чешских научных журналах рефераты о новостях балтославянской филологии[1].

Латышские мотивы А. Гейдука переносят чешский интерес к балтийским литературам за границы научных кругов, так как Сочинения издававшиеся в издательстве Й. Отто принадлежали к наиболее популярным чешским изданиям начала XX века. Возникновению «Латышских мотивов», несомненно, содействовали также горячие симпатии Гейдука к маленьким угнетенным нациям Прибалтики, в стремлениях и культуре которых можно было найти много параллелей к чешскому национальному возрождению.

На 120 страницах своей книги Гейдук напечатал всего 93 стихотворения, которые распределены по четырем не одинаковым по объему разделам: «Песня и природа» (16), «Любовь и жизнь» (53), «Сиротство и смерть» (11), наконец «Разные истины» (13). Только в немногих случаях соответствует одно стихотворение одной дайне, например, «Смерть» (стр. 114) или «Опоздавший» (стр. 51); в большинстве же стихотворений перед нами объединение нескольких тематически родственных дайн в новое целое, которому поэт дает свое название.

Об источниках можно сегодня только догадываться. В музее Гейдука (в городе Писек, в Южной Чехии) не сохранилось никаких документов на этот счет ни в остатках его личной библиотеке, ни в его переписке. Главным ключом к решению этой загадки остается, по-видимому, предисловие поэта, в котором говорится: «Из нерифмованных латышских песенок в две или четыре строчки, которых пастор Ульман собрал около 500 и которых новейшие исследователи Барон и Виссендорф в их большом произведении Chansons nationales latviennes — Latvju Dainas и с вариантами насчитывают более 153 000, я свил свой собственный букет небольших песен в духе народной поэзии для тех, кому простые цветы лугов иногда также милы, как дивные орхидеи тропиков ...»

Так как Гейдук, согласно свидетельству всех известных документов, латышским языком не владел, а свой «букет» свил в 1898–1899 годах, приходится принимать во внимание некоторые известные тогда в Чехии сборники с русским или немецким переводом дайн. По информациям г. Вильмы Гребле (Академия наук Латвийской ССР) это следующие сборники:

1) Памятники латышского народного творчества. Собраны и изданы Иваном Спрогисом. Вильна 1868.

2) (Составитель Фр. Бривземниакс.) Сборник антропологических и этнографических статей о России и странах ей прилежащих, издаваемый В. А. Дашковым (...), книга II, Москва 1873. Некоторые разделы

этого сборника: I. Песни о пѣніи (...), III. Созерцаніе природы, IV. Любовныя песни, V. Свадебныя песни (...).

3) *Lettische Volkslieder übertragen im Versmass der Originale.* Von Karl Ulmann, Riga, 1874.

Кроме того, с помощью консультанта Гейдук мог использовать первые тетради латышских дайн, изданных Бароном, т. е. первый том *Latvju Dainas.* Об этой возможности свидетельствует приведенное Гейдуком французское название произведения, которое можно прочитать в заглавии, далее фамилия Барона (без Кр.) и фамилия издателя Виссендорфа (без Г.). Убедительным доказательством можно считать также количество дайн, приведенное Гейдуком. В указателях бароновского издания дайн (*Vietu un Krājēju un skaitu reģistrs*) отмечается на 153 431 дайн — у Гейдука в соответствии с бароновским изданием приводится «более 153 000». Однако Гейдук мог использовать только первых десять тетрадей *Latvju dainas,* так как до 1901 года, когда появились Латышские мотивы Гейдука, в свет вышел только их первый том в десяти тетрадях (I. — 1894, X. — 1898).

Из всего сказанного следует, что Гейдук в своем распоряжении имел минимум два источника — Барона и Ульманна. Оба источника были известны чешским научным кругам. Уже до Гейдука на Ульманна обращает внимание профессор д-р. Зубатый, который ссылается на составленные Бривземниаком и Спрогисом сборники, и также приводит цитаты из книг: *Rakstu krājums izdots no Rīgas Latviešu Biedrības Zinību Komisijas* (Riga 1890) и Материалы для этнографии латышского племени витебской губернии. Собр. Э. А. Больтер, I. Санктпетербург 1890[2].

Общий характер книги Гейдука позволяет предположить, что наиболее вероятным образцом перевода дайн на чешский язык был сборник Ульманна. Такой вывод подсказывается прежде всего отбором дайн, в котором чувствуется слегка сентиментальная, а местами даже морализаторская тенденция, столь характерная для Ульманна, особенно в разделе «Разные истины». С Ульманном связывает Гейдука также введение заглавий к отдельным стихотворениям. У Ульманна этот принцип применяется последовательно только в единственном цикле (*Längere Lieder verschiedenen Inhalts*), т. е. в 20 случаях из 512. В противовес Ульманну Гейдук дает заглавия всем своим стихотворениям, даже коротеньким четверостишиям. Его заглавия не всегда соответствуют основному мотиву дайны. Например, известная дайна с мотивом хмеля, который, только сочетаясь с ячменем, может стать пивом, получила название «Гордец» (Hrdopýšek).

С Ульманном Гейдука роднит использование рифмы. Но и здесь

чешский поэт последовательнее. В сборнике Ульманна рифма используется сдержанно, прежде всего опять же в цикле *Längere Lieder verschiedenen Inhalts*, чаще всего по схеме abcb, реже abbc, abcc итд. Например в стихотворении «Soldatenabschied» (*Nu ardievu, Vidzemīte*):

> Lebe wol, mein theueres Livland,
> Länger bleib’ ich nicht allhier,
> Nicht mehr klopf’ in dunklen Nächten
> ich an meines Mädchens Thür ...

Гейдук рифмует всюду, чаще всего по схеме abab, но также по всем остальным в четверостишиях возможным схемам. Его рифмы почти всегда двухслоговые (мужские), в отличие от преимущественно однослоговых (женских) рифм Ульманна. Слишком частая рифмовка заставляет Гейдука переводить вольнее и приводит к увеличению количества слогов в стихе.

В большинстве латышских дайн (четырехстиший и шестистиший) используется хореический стих, который состоит из двух диподий. Большое значение в таком стихе имеют промежутки между словами, которые соответствуют границам диподий. Диподия имеет четыре слога — в таком случае последний слог — краткий, или три слога — в таком случае третий бывает долгим. Значит, в прозодической системе дайн силлаботонический принцип сочетается с принципом количественным[3]. Эту систему Ульманн упростил в своих переводах введением традиционного силлаботоноческого хорея, без переносов, иногда с паузой в середине стиха или рифмой в его конце. Уменьшительные слова он не всегда сохраняет в переводе, так как знает, что они в латышском оригинале выполняют скорее ритмическую чем деминутивную функцию. В смысле содержания Ульманн очень близок атмосфере оригинального текста. Его поэтический перевод дайн стоял в свое время на хорошем уровне.

По сравнению с Ульманном Гейдук более самостоятелен, но не всегда в своих переводах удачен. Его силлаботонический хореический стих стоит ближе к профессиональной чем к народной поэзии. Его поэтическая переработка дайн в чешские стихи представляет в типологическом отношении что-то среднее между поэтическим переводом и поэтическим отголоском, т. е. почти самостоятельным творчеством, имитирующим какой-нибудь национальный образец, например «Подражания корану» Пушкина или «Персидские мотивы» Есенина.

В чешской поэтической традиции имеют такие «отголоски» большое значение, начиная с «Отголосков русских песен» Челяковского (*Ohlasy písní ruských*, 1829), вплоть до замечательных «Песен старого Китая» Богумила Матезиуса (*Zpěvy staré Číny*, 1939). Развивая основные мотивы, сюжеты и поэтику русских былин, Челяковский создал совершенно самостоятельное произведение; некоторые его новые былины, например Чурила Пленкович, превосходят оригиналы. Стих русских былин он мастерски имитирует в чешском иктовом стихе, т. е. в стихе с определенным объязательным количеством ударяемых слогов — иктов; количество неударяемых слогов и их размещение в стихе при этом не регламентируется. Где-то в середине между такими произведениями — отголосками, ставшими в наше время уже классическими, стоят Латышские мотивы Гейдука. Обратите внимание на самое название книги: не дайны, не песни, а именно мотивы! Автор действительно отбирал характерные мотивы латышских дайн и слагал из них, несмотря на их происхождение и циклическое закрепление в оригинале, свои собственные новые песни в духе народной традиции, близкой чешскому читателю. Это решающий принцип его отбора, который однако приводит к чему-то весьма далекому от первоначального настроения характерного для латышского контекста.

Одинаково свободно поступает Гейдук и в вопросах формы стиха. Четырехстопный стих оригинала с двумя диподиями и без переносов он заменяет чаще всего пятистопным хореем, который в чем-то напоминает сербский десятислоговый стих (*desatarac*). Для ритма его стиха характерна монотонная правильность, которую подчеркивают не менее правильные регулярные рифмы. Если добавить еще частые переносы, то станет ясно, что поэтику дайн Гейдук сближает с поэтикой профессиональной чешской поэзии второй половины XIX века. О фольклорной основе напоминают здесь только некоторые мотивы и устойчивые словосочетания.

Гейдук принадлежал к группе поэтов «Májovci» (от поэмы «Май», автором которой был К. Г. Маха). Эта группа вместе с Яном Нерудой и Витезславом Галеком вступила на литературное поприще в 50–60-ые гг. XIX века. В начале XX века, когда появились «Латышские мотивы», чешская стихотворная техника стояла уже несравненно выше, чем во времена «Маевцев». Поэтому поэзия Гейдука производит в начале XX века уже несколько архаическое впечатление, особенно ее поэтический язык. Это отразилось в какой-то мере также в языке и стихе «Латышских мотивов».

Наиболее удачным из переводов Гейдуком латышских дайн можно считать цикл «Сиротство и смерть», несомненно, под влиянием оригиналов, так как все специалисты сходятся в том, что латышские песни о сиротах (*bāru dziesmas*) вместе с колыбельными песнями (*šūpļu dziesmas*) и песнями — лиго (*Jāṇu dziesmas*) принадлежат к самым красивым народным песням в мире. Однако для отбора мотивов у Гейдука весьма характерно, что как раз песни этих циклов — за исключением сиротского цикла — представлены в его книге довольно слабо.

Разницу между оригиналом, Ульманном и Гейдуком, лучше всего можно демонстрировать на переводах одной из лучших дайн сиротского цикла. По всей вероятности речь идет о вариантах известной дайны:

> *Ai zemīte, ai saulīte,*
> *Manas laimes naidnieciṇi:*
> *Tēvs neredz saules gaismas,*
> *Māti sedza velēniṇas.*

Ulmann:

> 'Ach die Erde! Ach die Sonne.'
> Feinde sind sie meiner Ruh':
> Sonne scheint nicht meinem Vater,
> Erde deckt die Mutter zu.'

Heyduk:

> Neúprosní
> Černá země, slunce zlatoskvélé
> největší jsou moji nepřátelé:
> Otci slunce v tvář se neusmívá,
> černá země matičku mi skrývá.'

Гейдук добавляет еще вторую строфу: Marně dech můj zlaté slunce prosí, / marně slza černou zemi rosí: / slunce nechce otci v líce shlédnout, / zem ě nechce s matičky se zvednout. Во второй строфе — свободно связанной с первой — использован частый мотив латышских дайн: просьба сироты к мертвой матери встать из могилы. И чтобы помочь матери, сирота хочет приподнять дерн на могиле (*pacelt velēniṇu*).

Сразу видно, насколько Гейдук далек от покоряющей простоты латышского оригинала, которая определяется интонацией сдержанного горя. Высокопарный гомеровский эпитет «zlatoskvělý» звучит в скорбной песне сироты слишком патетически. Враги тут злейшие (největší), т. е. снова излишний пафос; земля «черная» — в оригинале простой дерн. Перевод Ульманна звучит в этих случаях менее искусственно. Увеличение количества слов и расширение схемы стиха на 10 слогов исключает, конечно, возможность имитировать ритмическую симметричность дайн (две диподии в каждом стихе). Поэтому перевод Гейдука теряет иногда легкость и подвижность песенного ритма. Исключение составляют дактилические стихотворения «Изменник» (*Nevěrný milý*, 22) и «Крушина» (*Krušinka*, 46–47). Особенно последнее стихотворение без рифмы и в стихах по диподиям принадлежит к наиболее удачным в книге.

К сожалению, ни Ульманн, ни Гейдук не смогли воссоздать изумительную звуковую красоту латышских оригиналов, их аллитерационное богатство, которым восхищался уже в 1894 году в своей статье проф. Зубатый. Однако несмотря на частные неудачи, которые можно в какой-то мере оправдать неустойчивым положением в развитии чешского стиха и чешской стилистике конца 19 века, «Латышские мотивы» Гейдука заслуживают, несомненно, высокой оценки как первая серьезная попытка познакомить чешскую общественность с поэзией латышских народных песен и тогдашней словесной культурой. Вместе с тем это интересный факт межнациональных литературных взаимоотношений, заслуживающий научного внимания в более широком европейском контексте.

Примечания

1. *MNHMA. Sborník vydaný na paměť čtyřicetiletého učitelského působení prof. Josefa Zubatého na Universitě Karlově* 1885–1925, Praha, 1926, 478–496 (Список трудов Иос. Зубатого 1884–1925).

2. Josef Zubatý, *Studie a články*, II., Praha 1954, 235–236.

3. Подробней см. исследование Арт. Озольс, «Par latviešu tautasdziesmām» в книге *Latviešu tautasdziesmas, Izlase I.* Rīgā 1955, 6–12. (Также в книге *Raksti folkloristikā*, Rīgā, 1968).

On Adolf Heyduk's Czech Translations of Latvian Folk-Songs

"Latvian Motives" (Prague, 1901) by Adolf Heyduk (1835–1925) stand half-way between a poetical translation and imitation, as shown in detail in this article. Heyduk selected typical motives from Latvian "dainas" and used them to compose original poems reminiscent of folk-poetry and its traditions. Unlike the German translator Ulmann, whose "Lettische Volkslieder im Versmass der Originale" (Riga, 1874) preserve to the utmost the original poetic forms, Heyduk has changed the number of syllables in a line, introducing rhyme throughout, giving his imitations new titles and bringing the forms of the "dainas" close to those of classical literature. Heyduk's "Latvian Motives" were the first important introduction of Latvian lyrics to the Czech reader.

JÜRGEN PRINZ

Zur Isoglosse *z/ž* in Namen
des baltischen Substrats

Die historische Entwicklung der baltischen Sprachen, ihre Stellung innerhalb der indogermanischen Sprachfamilie und ihr Verhältnis zur slavischen
Sprachgruppe bildeten stets einen Schwerpunkt in den Forschungen
Ch. Stangs. Schon in den ersten Kapiteln seiner *Vergleichenden Grammatik
der Baltischen Sprachen*[1] kommt deutlich zum Ausdruck, wie sehr die Lösung
der genannten Aufgaben durch das Fehlen zuverlässiger Informationen
über die Besonderheiten der schon früh erloschenen Dialekte des baltischen
Substratraumes Westrußlands erschwert ist. Mit Recht betont er S. 2, daß
der gegenwärtige Stand der Erforschung der baltischen Substratnamen ihre
Heranziehung in seiner Arbeit noch nicht gestattet. Wie dringend notwendig
es aber ist, diese Namen für die von ihm verfolgten Ziele verwertbar zu
machen, zeigen z. B. seine Darlegungen S. 24 zu finnischen Lehnworten
aus dem Baltischen, die auf ein altes baltisches dialektisches *ō* für idg. *ā* an
Stelle des erwarteten urbalt. *ā* hinweisen, wie finn. *vuohi* zu lit. *ožys* 'Ziege'
mit anlautendem etymologischem *ā*.

In den Arbeiten des Verfassers dieses Beitrages spielt die Bestimmung
des Alters und der ursprünglichen Verbreitung baltischer dialektischer
Merkmale, die sich in lebenden baltischen Dialektgruppen reflektieren,
unter Heranziehung von baltischen Substratnamen eine wichtige Rolle. In
einer Untersuchung bemühte er sich festzustellen, daß die Slavisierung
baltischer Namen einer großen, aber überschaubaren Zahl definierbarer
Faktoren unterliegt, sodaß sich die baltischen Grundformen slavisierter
Namen mit einer für sprachgeschichtliche Schlüsse ausreichender Genauig-
keit bestimmen lassen. Dabei wurde ein grundlegender Unterschied in der
Verwertbarkeit von Lehnworten und Lehnnamen, hier slavisierten baltischen Ortsnamen, für die Sprachgeschichte negiert, da auch die innerhalb
einer Spracheinheit lebendigen Ortsnamen integrierende Bestandteile des
sprachlichen Systems dieser Einheit darstellen[2]. Von den alten baltischen
Isoglossen, deren Verfolgung anhand der Substratnamen Aufschlüsse ver-
spricht, wurde für diesen Beitrag die Isoglosse *z/ž* gewählt, die das heutige
Schriftlitauische vom heutigen Schriftlettischen und vom überlieferten

Altpreußischen trennt, während Reliktwörter, Ortsnamen und für den litauischen Bereich ganze Dialekte ursprüngliche z-Areale im heutigen litauischen[3] und ursprüngliche ž-Areale[4] im heutigen lettischen Sprachgebiet noch deutlich erkennen lassen[5].

Es genügt jedoch nicht, einfach Substratnamen mit z und ž gebietsweise einander gegenüberzustellen. Der Grad der Sicherheit, mit der die einzelnen Namenbelege dem baltischen Substrat zuzuordnen sind und mit dem ihr z oder ž tatsächlich dieselben Laute der baltischen Grundform reflektiert, ist von Fall zu Fall verschieden. Dasselbe gilt für die Beurteilung der Frequenz von z- und ž-Formen und überhaupt von balt. Substratnamen in bestimmten Gebieten. Da es schon aus Raumgründen unzweckmäßig ist, bei jedem der Namenbelege umfangreiche Kommentare zu geben, sind zunächst eine Reihe von Vorbemerkungen notwendig.

1. Seit der Lubliner Union zwischen Polen und Großlitauen verstärkten sich der polnische Einfluß und die polnische Siedlungstätigkeit im westrussischen Gebiet[6]. Im Norden (ehem. Gouvernements Suwałki, Wilna, Kaunas und der Norden der Gouv. Grodno und Minsk) spielten dabei Träger masurierender Dialekte mit der Aussprache c, s, z für poln. cz, sz, ž eine entscheidende Rolle[7]. Ihr Einfluß blieb bis in unsere Zeit unter anderem in Namensformen dieses Bereichs mit einem z anstatt des zu erwartenden ž sichtbar. Ein solches z hielt sich naturgemäß besonders in solchen Namen, denen kein schriftpolnisches oder schriftrussisches Wort mit ž gegenüberstand. Daher ist ein durch polnisches Masurieren bedingtes z für ž vor allem in Namen baltischen Gepräges erhalten[8]. In diesem Gebiet läßt sich daher oft nicht mit Sicherheit feststellen, ob ein z statt ž in Namensformen bereits durch den Dialekt der baltischen Grundformen[9] oder erst durch das polnische Masurieren zu begründen ist.

2. Ein großer Teil der baltischen Namenstämme ist slavischen Namenstämmen so ähnlich, daß der baltische Namenstamm bei der Slavisierung oft einfach durch den ähnlichen slavischen Namenstamm ersetzt wird (Deutung)[10], sodaß Schlüsse auf die Gestalt des Stammes der Grundform unmöglich werden. Vgl. hierzu z. B. Бржезишки, lit. *Biržiškių* km., Kr. Svencjany, und Бржозовишки, lit. *Beržiškių* km., Kr. Wilna[11], von lit. *biržė* 'Kahlschlag' bzw. *beržas* 'Birke', gedeutet nach poln. *brzoza* 'Birke', *brzozowy* 'Birken-', vor vorderem Vokal *brzez-* (Бржезишки), polnische Formen in kyrillischer Schreibung. In solchen Fällen gestatten die slavisierten Formen keinen Schluß darüber, ob in der baltischen Grundform ein z oder ein ž vorlag.

3. Das baltische Substrat kann je nach dem Gebiet erstens gewaltsam aus seinen Sitzen verdrängt, zweitens durch slavische Übersiedlung oder drittens nur durch den überlegenen slavischen Einfluß allmählich slavisiert worden sein[12]. Im zweiten Fall ergaben sich immer kleiner werdende baltische Reliktgebiete, deren lokale Dialekte durch den abnehmenden sprachlichen Kontakt immer mehr divergierten, bis sie schließlich erloschen. Vgl. hierzu die weit verstreuten Reste ostseefinnischer Bevölkerung (Ingrer/Ižora, Woten, Wepsen) im einstigen Großnovgoroder Gebiet, die sich hier trotz z. T. sehr früher slavischer Siedlungstätigkeit bis heute erhalten haben[13].

4. Die gebietsweise wechselnde Dichte der baltischen Substratnamen weist lediglich auf die Art der Slavisierung hin, s. oben 3. Sie ist naturgemäß bei Typ 1 (Verdrängung) am geringsten und bei Typ 3 am größten[14].

5. Der Verfasser hat bereits mehrfach auf die auf Grund der Substratnamendichte, besonders bei Typ 1 (oben 3), möglichen Schlüsse für das frühe Schicksal des baltischen Substrats hingewiesen. Ein großes Gebiet geringer Substratnamendichte, abgesehen von einigen Substratnamennestern, beginnt bei Smolensk und verbreitert sich zunehmend den Dnepr abwärts, besonders nach Westen. Es ist von Nordwesten bis Osten von Räumen großer Substratnamendichte umgeben, die an ihrem Außenrande z. T. ein ostseefinnisches bzw. wolgafinnisches Vorsubstrat überdecken[15]. Offensichtlich ist mit einem slavischen Vorstoß in dieses baltische Kerngebiet zu rechnen, wobei die ansässige baltische Bevölkerung nach Westen, Norden und Osten abgedrängt wurde und nicht nur die benachbarten baltischen Räume, sondern auch darüber hinaus die angrenzenden ostsee- und wolgafinnischen Gebiete überflutete[16]. Außerhalb des obigen Verdrängungsgebietes ist daher eine gebietsweise Überlagerung zweier verschiedener baltischer Namenschichten denkbar[17].

6. Namenstämme können über den Umweg von aus ihnen abgeleiteten Personennamen in entfernte Gebiete verschleppt werden. Dies ist besonders bei Siedlungsnamen zu berücksichtigen, die mit den in Personennamen häufigen Suffixen *-ev-*, *-ov-*, *-in-* gebildet sind.

7. Als Kriterium eines wahrscheinlichen baltischen Ursprungs dienten bei der Belegwahl besonders:

a) Das Vorliegen vergleichbarer Namen, die im noch heute baltischen Gebiet gleichzeitig in der baltischen und einer slavisierten Form belegt sind; nach Möglichkeit auch das Vorliegen vergleichbarer baltischer Appellative.

b) Das gleichzeitige Vorliegen von Ableitungen desselben Namenstammes mit *z* und *ž*, sofern nicht ein Faktor der slavischen Seite (Masurieren) in Betracht kommt.

c) Die Beschränkung des Vorkommens auf das baltische Substratgebiet, sofern nicht zufälliger Gleichklang von Namenstämmen verschiedenen Substrats vorliegt, vgl. unten Aufstellung I, balt. *varž-*; vgl. auch oben 6.

Aus Raumgründen konnten Namenstämme, die sehr schwach belegt sind oder bei denen der Reflex der Slavisierung weitgehend mit echt slavischen Namensformen zusammenfällt, nicht berücksichtigt werden.

8. Aus demselben Grunde wurde folgende Art der Darstellung gewählt:

(1) Aufstellung I enthält die baltischen Etyma in alphabetischer Folge mit Parallelen aus dem heute noch baltischen Gebiet, die slavisierten Vertretungen (nur Namenstamm) nach RGN und RGW und gegebenenfalls ähnlich lautende slav. Wortstämme, die bei der Beurteilung der Namenbelege zu berücksichtigen sind.

(2) Aufstellung II ist eine räumlich gegliederte Aufstellung der in Betracht kommenden Namensformen.

(3) Eine Aufstellung am Schluß dieses Beitrags stellt die in Betracht kommenden slavisierten Namenstämme mit allen belegbaren Varianten in alphabetischer Folge den anzunehmenden baltischen Namenstämmen gegenüber und bildet so das Bindeglied zwischen Aufstellung I und II.

9. Zur Lokalisierung der Belege wurde die auch in RGN und RGW benützte administrative Einteilung der Zarenzeit gewählt[18]. Belege ohne Quellenzitat sind in den alphabetisch geordneten Namensammlungen RGN (Siedlungsnamen) und RGW (Gewässernamen) s.v. zu finden.

I. Die baltischen Etyma und ihre slavisierten Vertretungen[19]

darž-, nicht immer sicher zu trennen von *derž-*, *dirž-*, auch gelegentliche Einmischung von *dirg-*, *dreg-* 'feucht' (FLEW 96 *dirgti*, 103 *dregti*) bei *g* vor vorderem Vokal nicht ausgeschlossen; bedeutungsmäßig für die Ortsnamenbildung in Betracht kommende Appellative nur lit. *daržas*, lett. *dārzs* 'Garten' für *darž-*; lit. GWN wie *Daržapievis*, *Daržupys* (LUV 27), *Dergintas* (LUV 29); lit. ON wie *Daržalių* km., *Dirgaičių* km., *Diržių* km. (L. 59, Reg. S. 668, 676, 677); slavisierte Formen s. RGN u. RGW

s.v., und zwar für *darž-* unter Дарж-, Дорж-, Дырж-, Дорз-; Дорож-
ist slavisch sehr häufig und baltische Namenreste lassen sich hier nur
sehr schwer aussondern; balt. *darž-* kann auch sekundär für *derž-* sein
(*e-a-*Dialekte)[20], vgl. z. B. Держелис (lit. *Daržalių* km., p. *Dzierželis,
Derželis*), slavisiert wird es zu Держ-, Дерз-, Дерез-; balt. *dirž-* zeigt
dieselben Reflexe, im noch baltischen Gebiet auch Дзирж-, Дырж-.

driež-, drīž-: kein unmittelbar für die Ortsnamenbildung in Betracht kom-
mendes balt. Appellativ; lit. GWN *Driežupis, Dryža* (LUV 32); zu balt.
ON vgl. RGN Дрейзи (lett. *Dreizi*)[21], Дрижа (lit. *Dryžių* km.), slavisiert
Дрейз-, Дрез-, Дриж-, Дриз-; bei Дрижак-/Дрыжак- ist mit westruss.
*дриж- für großruss. дрож(ать usw.), Vermittlung durch PN, zu rechnen; Дрызлово erinnert in seiner Bildung an lit. *driežlė* 'Eidechse, Wachtelkönig', zu *dryžis* 'Streifen auf Tuch'.

gaiž-, giž-: Die beiden Stämme gehen bei der Slavisierung leicht ineinander
über, besonders wenn man die Ablautstufe *giež-* mit berücksichtigt;
Appellative: lit. *gaižus*, lett. *gaizs*, lit. *gižus* 'bitter, herb, sauer u. ä.'; lit.
Gwn *Gaižupis* (LUV 42), *Gyžežeris* (LUV 50); zu lit. ON RGN Гайжуны
(lit. *Gaižiūnai*, p. *Gojžuny*) u. Гейжуны (lit. *Gaižiūnai*, p. *Giejžuny*) bzw.
Гижи (lit. *Gižai, p. Giže*). Slavisierte Formen s. RGN unter Гайж-,
Гейж-, Гойж-, Гез-, Гиж-, Гиз-. Die Einmischung von PN-Stämmen ist
nicht ausgeschlossen, vgl. Гижгайлово. Das Appellativ lit. *gęžė, gęšė*, lett.
dzēse, apr. *geeyse* 'Reiher' paßt zwar bedeutungsmäßig gut, kommt aber
wegen seines Vokalismus weniger in Betracht[22].

ged-, gied- s. unter *žad-*.

gel-, geld- s. unter *žal-*.

gil- s. unter *žil-*.

graiž- s. unter *griež-, gryž-*.

grauž-, griauž-: lit. *graužas* 'grober Sand, Kies'; lit. Gwn *Grauža, Graužė*
usw., *Griaužukas* usw. (LUV 51 f.); lit. ON z. B. RGN s.v. Грауже (lit.
Graužių km., *Graužai*); slavisiert als Гравж-, Грауж-, Гроуж-, durch
balt. u. slav. (Akańje) dialektische Tendenzen auch Грывж-, Грывз-,
mit Regression zur Schriftsprache[23], wo im Gegensatz zum Weißrussi-
schen *r* nicht praktisch durchgehend verhärtet ist, auch Гривж-, Гривз-;
Reflex eines weichen *r* (*griauž-*) nur in Гревженица, Sumpf; die Selten-
heit von *z*-Formen stimmt zu dem Fehlen einer für die Ortsnamenbildung
geeigneten Entsprechung im Lettischen.

graž-, gruož-, gruž-: lit. *gražus* 'schön', *gruož-* als Appellativ nicht belegt,
vgl. aber lit. *grąž-* 'drehen, wenden', lit. *gružas* 'gestutzt, kurz'; zu lit.
Gwn vgl. *Graželenka, Gražupis* (LUV 52), *Gruožaitis, Gruožė* (LUV 53),
Gruožo upelis, Gružupis (LUV 53) und schließlich *Grąžalas* (LUV 52).

Eindeutig für das balt. Substrat lassen sich nur die Formen der Stufen Гряж-, evtl. auch Грож-, in Anspruch nehmen; die z-Stufen Граз- und Гроз- fallen mit slav. Appellativen zusammen, vgl. wr. гразь auch 'Morast' zu r. грязь; dasselbe gilt für Груж-, Груз-; eine durch Akańje bedingte Stufe Грыж-, Грыз-, hyperkorrekt auch Гриж-, Гриз- aus *graž*- läßt sich nicht von entsprechenden Reflexen von *griež*-, *gryž*- trennen; die Vollautstufe Горож- fällt lautlich mit slavischen Bildungen zusammen.

griež-, *graiž*- und *grīž*- gehen in den Reflexen ihrer Slavisierung ineinander über. Eine breitere appellativische Grundlage bietet nur das Lettische, vgl. *grieza* 'Stoppelfeld', *grieze* 'Wachtelkönig', *grīzulis* 'Strudel (im Wasser)'; im Lit. ist *griežlė* 'Wachtelkönig' in Betracht zu ziehen. Zu den lit. Gwn vgl. *Graižė*, *Graižēlis*; *Greižēlis*, *Greižina*; *Gryžupė*, *Gryžuva*; *Grieža*, *Griežupė* usw. (LUV 51 f.), die sämtlich in einem Ablautverhältnis zueinander stehen können; zu lett. ON vgl. RGN s.v. Гризаны (lett. *Griezeni*)[24]. Zu den slavisierten Formen vgl. RGN und RGW unter Грайз-, Грейж-, Грейз-, Гриж-, Гриз- und Грыж-, Грыз-. Die Formen mit *i* und *y* sind praktisch gleichwertig, da im westrussischen Gebiet größtenteils nur ein hartes *r* existiert und eine Schreibung -*ri*- rein graphischen Charakter hat. Грыж-, Грыз- kann auch die Endstufe der Slavisierung von *graž*- unter Einfluß des Akańje sein.

varž-: lit. *varža* 'Fischreuse, Fischwehr u. ä.'; lett. *varza* u. a. ebenfalls 'Fischwehr'. In lit. Gwn trotz guter semantischer Voraussetzungen auffallend schwach vertreten: *Varžavietė* (LUV 188), ebenso in lit. ON (*Varžgalių* km. u. zweimal *Varžų* km. L. 59, Reg. S. 993). Die slavisierten Stufen Варж- und Варз- fehlen ganz; die im RGN belegten Namen dieser Stufe gehören ausschließlich dem ostseefinnischen und permjakischen Bereich an; die normale Vertretung ist Ворж-, Ворз-, diese beiden Stufen treten ebenfalls als Vertretungen eines im ostseefinnischen, permjakischen und auch wolgafinnischen Bereich belegten Etymons auf. Eine Vollautstufe Ворож- läßt sich angesichts des echt ostslav. Wortstammes ворож-, etwa ворожить 'wahrsagen', nur in wenigen Fällen mit einiger Wahrscheinlichkeit für das baltische Substrat in Anspruch nehmen[25].

verg- s. unter *virž*-.

vēž-: lit. *vėžys*, lett. *vēzis* 'Krebs'. Dieses besonders in balt. Gwn naturgemäß sehr stark vertretene Etymon — vgl. lit. *Vėželupis*, *Vėžežeris* usw. (LUV 192) läßt sich für die Lösung der gestellten Aufgabe wegen der Konkurrenz von r. вежа 'Wachtturm', вяз 'Ulme', вязь 'Morast' leider nicht verwenden.

virž- zu lit. *viržis*, lett. *virzis* 'Heidekraut'; gelegentlich Konkurrenz von lit. *vergas* 'Leibeigener, Sklave' möglich, falls das Namenformans mit einem vorderen Vokal beginnt (slav. *g > ž*). Vgl. die lit. Gwn *Verža* (LUV 192) u. *Viržintėlė, Viržuona* u. *Viržuva* (LUV 199) neben *Virgė* (LUV 198). Slavisierte Formen sind Верж-, Верз- (beachte die vielfach mögliche Konkurrenz von slav. верз-, vor allem von верзила 'großer, plumper Mensch'), Вирж-, Вырз-, mit Vollaut Вереж-, Верез-.

žad-, žod-, oft nicht zu trennen von *žied-*: Für *žad-* fehlen balt. Appellative passender Bedeutung; für *žied-* kommen lit. *žiedas, žaidas*, lett. *zieds* 'Blüte' und lit. *žiedžius* 'Töpfer' in Betracht, befriedigen aber aus semantischen und morphologischen Gründen als Grundwort von ON meist nicht. Zu lit. Gwn vgl. *Žadalis, Žadikė, Žadupė* usw. (LUV 201), *Žiedelis, Žiedupė, Žiedupys* (LUV 204); zu ON vgl. vor allem RGN s.v. Жадишки, z. B. 1. (lit. *Žadiškių* km.), 4. (lit. *Žiediškių* km.), 5. (lit. *Žodiškių* km.), zum Übergang von einem Etymon zum anderen Жадовейни 1. (lit. *Žadavainiai*, p. *Žadawejnie*) u. Жидовейни 1. (lit. *Židovainių* km., p. *Žadowiejnia*) u. 2. (p. *Žedowejnie*), von PN[26]? Die slavisierten Formen zeigen Жад-, Жед-, Жод-, Зад-, Зед-, Зод-. In Gebieten, die früh, und zwar vor dem Abschluß der zweiten Palatalisation slavisiert wurden, ist auch mit einem balt. Wortstamm *ged-* bzw. *gied-* zu rechnen, vgl. lit. Gwn, wie *Gedika, Gedupis* (LUV 44), *Giedulis* (LUV 47).

žagar-, zu lit. *žagaras*, lett. *žagars*! 'Gestrüpp', in ON oft *žegar-*; in Gwn naturgemäß recht selten, vgl. lit. *Žagarynė, Žagaris* (LUV 201 f.), in ON häufig, vgl. z. B. RGN s.v. Жагарино (lit. *Žagarinė*), Жагоры 2. (lett. *Žagari*), 3. (lit. *Žagariai*, p. *Žagory*), Жегаришки (lit. *Žegariškiai, Žagariškiai*, p. *Žegaryszki, Zagaryszki*); Жигоринка (lit. *Žagarinka*), mit Reflex des Akańje (Жиг-, sprich *Žyh-*) in der slavisierten Form. In slavisierten Namen tritt es auf als Жагар-, Жагер-, Жагор-, Жегар-, Жегор-, Жигар-, Жигор-, Жигур-, Жогор-, Жугор-[27], dabei ist für die Schwankung des ersten Vokals die durch das Akańje in unbetonten Silben hervorgerufene Unsicherheit in der graphischen Wiedergabe zu berücksichtigen; die Vertretungen der *z*-Stufe bieten durch den häufigen Zusammenfall mit slav. Wortstämmen Schwierigkeiten: Загар- kann auf за + гарь 'Art Brandrodung' zurückgehen, Загор- läßt an за + гора 'hinter dem Berge, jenseits des Berges' denken, während Зегар- sicher baltisch ist. Das *g* ist westrussisch wie *h* zu sprechen, das bei großrussischer Schreibung auch mit х (*ch*) wiedergegeben werden könnte; die häufig belegten Захар-, Жихар-, Жихор- gehören aber mit Sicherheit nicht hierher, sondern zum PN r. Захар- bzw. zu einem Appellativ r. жихарь (Dal' ²I, S. 545).

žal-, vor allem in lit. *žalias*, lett. *zaļš* 'grün, stark', daneben auch *žel-* zu dem ablautenden *želti* 'grünen usw.', gelegentlich kommt auch Einmischung von lit. *gėlė* 'Blüte' und der Ablautstufe *gel-* zu lit. *gilus* 'tief' in Betracht. Zu den Gwn vgl. lit. *Žalelis, Žalesa, Žaliupis* usw. (LUV 202), zu den ON vgl. z. B. RGN Жалишки 1. (lit. *Žališkių* km.), 2. (lit. *Žališkė*), Желенишки (Гирайце, lit. *Želoniškė*), Зальмежники 1. u. 4. (lett. *Zaļmežnieki*). Die slavisierten Formen fallen vielfach mit echt slavischen Wortstämmen zusammen: so Жал- z. B. gegenüber Жалоб́-, Akańje für Жолоб-; Жел- und Ableitungen von alten slav. PN mit dem Erstglied Жели-, wie Желибор; Ableitungen von r. dial. желн, жолн, жолон, dim. желонка (Dal' ²I, 530) 'großer Futter- bzw. Tränktrog' oder von r. желна 'Schwarzspecht', mit dem lautlichen und graphischen Varianten Жевн-, Жовн-, Жолн-, s. RGN III, 276; Зал-, weil slav. за 'hinter' + ein mit *l* beginnendes Appellativ oder ein mit *l* beginnender Ortsname, vor allem Flußname, vorliegen kann, Зел- wegen r. зеленый 'grün', Зол- wegen r. зола 'Asche' usw. Dennoch lassen sich eine Reihe von Namen wegen ihrer Bildungsart für das balt. Substrat aussondern, besonders deutlich z. B. Зальсажья, Kr. Pskov, vgl. lett. *zaļš* 'grün' und *sadža* 'Siedlung, Dorf'. In früh slavisierten Gebieten ist unter Umständen das Vorliegen der balt. Grundworte lit. *geležis* 'Eisen' und *Geld-*, vgl. lit. Gwn, wie *Gelda, Geldupis, Geldupė* (LUV 45), in Betracht zu ziehen, vgl. TopTrub 187 Жалдыбка. Nach FLEW 144 ist lit. *gelda*, lett. *ģelda*, apr. *galdo* 'Mulde' ein Lehnwort aus dem Deutschen.

žalt-, nicht immer zu trennen von *želt-*, zu lit. *žaltys*, lett. *zaltis* 'Ringelnatter' bzw. lit. *želtas* 'golden, goldgelb', lett. *zelts* 'Gold'. Es wird slavisiert zu Жалт-, Желт-, Жолт-, wobei die beiden letzten mit r. желтый 'gelb' zusammenfallen und nur gelegentlich durch morphologische Besonderheiten abgetrennt werden können, und zu Зелт-, Зельт-, Золт-. Zu lit. Gwn vgl. *Žaltinys, Žaltys, Žaltupis, Želtupė, Želtupys* (LUV 202 f.), zu balt. ON vgl. Желтуны (lit. *Žalteinų* km.), Жолтишки (lit. *Želtiškių* km.), Жолтышки (lit. *Želtiškis*). Es wird slavisiert zu Жалт-, Желт-, Жолт-, wobei die beiden letzten mit r. желтый 'gelb' zusammenfallen und nur gelegentlich durch morphologische Besonderheiten abgetrennt werden können, und zu Зелт-, Зельт-, Золт-.

žąs- in lit. *žąsis*, dial. auch *žosis, žūsis*, vgl. FLEW 1292, also mit den zu erwartenden dial. Vertretungen, lett. *zuoss, zoss* 'Gans', vgl. die lit. Gwn *Žąsa, Žąsė, Žąselė* usw., häufig (LUV 203) und die balt. ON im RGN Жосли (lit. *Žasliai*), Жусино (lit. *Žąsiniai*), Зусины 1. (lett. *Zuosini*). Es wird slavisiert zu Жос-, Жус-, Зас-, Зос-, Зус-. Trotz gelegentlicher Überschneidungen mit slav. Wortstämmen lassen sich die hierher gehörenden Bildungen balt. Ursprungs durch ihre Bildungsart gewöhnlich gut erkennen, mit Ausnahme des seltenen Falles einer möglichen Überschneidung mit *Zosin-*, zu poln. *Zosia*, Diminutiv des Namens *Sophie*. Es ist möglich, daß auch der Name des Flusses Зуша (Kr. Čerń u. Novosil'/Tula u. Mcensk/Orel) hierhergehört, falls eine ein halbvokalisches *i̯* enthaltende Endung, etwa *-i̯a*, vorlag.

žeim-, *žiem-*, zu lit. *žiema*, lett. *ziema* 'Winter', als Plural oder mit Suffixen 'Norden', vgl. die lit. Gwn *Žeimena*, *Žeimenys*, *Žeimikė* und die balt. ON Жейме (lit. *Žaimiai* (dial.), *Žeimiai*), Жеймы 2. u. 3. (lit. *Žeimiai*), Зеймули (lett. *Ziemuļi*). Wegen der balt. Stufe *-ei-* ist Einmischung eines PN nicht ausgeschlossen, vgl. PN *Žeimys* (FLEW 1306). Bei den slavisierten Formen sind die Stufen Жейм- und Зейм- gesichert, bei der Stufe Зим-, die nur in günstigen Fällen die Annahme baltischen Ursprungs erlaubt, kann *z* statt *ž* stets durch Deutung nach r. зима verursacht, d. h. sekundär sein. Zu *žiem-* vgl. auch *žem-*.

želmen-, zu lit. *želmuo*, lett. *zelme* 'grünendes Gras u. ä.', läßt sich durch die lit. Gwn *Želmena* u. *Želmenys* belegen, zu den ON vgl. Зельманишки (lit. *Želmeniškių* km., p. *Zelmaniszki*); allerdings kann das lit. *ž* hier auf nachträglicher Deutung eines von dem PN *Seelman* abgeleiteten Ortsnamens beruhen, sowie *Želmenų* km. (2 ×, L. 59, Reg. S. 1017). Slavisiert tritt es neben obigem Зельман- noch auf als Залман- und in den unsicheren Fällen Заламан-, Зелемен-. Die Stufe Желем- dürfte slavisch sein und zu Kurzformen von PN mit dem Erstglied Жели- gehören.

želv- s. *žilv-*, *želv-*.

žemait-, zu *žemaitis* 'Niederlitauer', seiner Bedeutung entsprechend nur in Siedlungsnamen belegt, vgl. Жемайдюки (lit. *Žemaitiškių* vk., p. *Žemojdziuki*), Жемайтишки (lit. *Žemaitiškis*), slavisiert als *Žamajd-*, *Žamojd-*, Жемайд-, Жемайт-, Жемейт-, Жемойд-, Жемойт-, Жомойд-, *Zamojd-*, Земейд-, daneben Deutungen nach dem aus demselben Grundwort entlehnten p. *Žmudź*, r. Жмудь 'Niederlitau/en, -er (pl.)'.

žem-, meist nur durch semantische und morphologische Kriterien zu trennen von *žiem-*, zu lit. *žemas*, lett. *zems* 'niedrig, Unter-', und lit. *žiema*, lett. *ziema* 'Winter', pl. bzw. suffigiert 'Norden'. Vgl. lit. Gwn, wie *Žemalė*, *Žemalupis* usw., *Žiemiškis*, *Žiemragis* und balt. ON, wie Жемагулы (lit. *Žemagaliai*, p. *Žemaguly*, *Žemagule*), Земезголс (lett. *Zemesgals*), Зимели (lett. *Ziemeļi*)[28]. Slavisiert tritt es auf als Жем-, Зем-, Зям-; *žiem-* auch als Зим-. Vgl. auch *žeim-*.

žiaur-: Vgl. lit. *žiaurus* 'grausam, wild, rauh u. ä.', in den lit. Gwn *Žiaurys* u. *Žiaurupis*; als slavisierte Vertretungen kommen Жавр-, Жаур- u. Зевр- in Betracht.

žied- s. unter *žad-*.

žiegždra, žieždra, žiezdra, žizdras 'grober Sand', vgl. die lit. Gwn *Žiegždrelis, Žiegždris, Žiegždupis* (LUV 204 f.), *Žiezdras, Žiezdrelis* (LUV 205), *Žyzdrė* (LUV 206), *Zizdra* (LUV 201): ähnlich in lit. ON; slavisiert vertreten als Жездр-, Жиздр-, Зездр-, Зыздр-.

žiežm- s. unter *žižm-*.

žil- zu lit. *žilas* 'grauhaarig', lett. *zils, ziļš* 'blau' und lit. *žylė*, lett. *zīle* '(auch =) Meise'; vgl. lit. Gwn, wie *Žilė, Žylė* usw. (LUV 205), und balt. ON, wie Жили 1. (lit. *Žilių* km.), Жилины 3. (lit. *Žilinai*), Зили 3. (lett. *Ziļi*). Die slavisierten Vertretungen sind Жил-, Зил-, Зыл-, Зейл-; Жил- steht in Konkurrenz mit den zahlreichen *l*-Ableitungen von r. жить 'leben'. Зейл- läßt sich am besten als Reflex dialektischer, nicht schriftlich überlieferter Varianten erklären[29]. In früh slavisierten Gebieten kommt darüber hinaus ein Reflex von lit. *gilus* 'tief' in Betracht, vgl. lit. Gwn, wie *Gilija, Gilinė, Gilupis, Gilutis* (LUV 47 f.).

žilv-, želv-, wohl zu lit. *žilvitis* 'Uferweide' oder zu lit. *želvas* 'grünlich, gelblich', vgl. die lit. Gwn *Žalvė, Želva, Želvos* (LUV 202 f.), *Žilvia* (LUV 205), *Žilvičiupis, Žilvitynė* (LUV 205) und die z-Formen *Zalvas, Zalvė, Zalvelis, Zalvys, Zelva, Zelvė* (LUV 200), wo die mehrfache Kombination von *a* für *e* und *z* für *ž* interessant ist. Zu den balt. ON vgl. etwa Жельвы (lett. *Želvji*), Жильва (lit. *Žilvė, Žilvia*), Жильвичке (lit. *Žilvičių* km.), Жолвы (lit. *Želvų* km.), Зельва 8. (lit. *Želvė*). In den slavisierten Formen erscheinen Жельв-, lautlich mit r. желвь 'Schildkröte' zusammenfallend, Жильв-, Жолв-, Зальв-, Зельв-, Золв-, Зольв-.[30]

žirg-, zu lit. *žirgas*, lett. *zirgs* 'Roß, Reitpferd', vgl. lit. Gwn wie *Žirginės, Žirgupė* (LUV 206) und balt. ON, wie Зырги (lett. *Zirgi*); slavisiert als Жерг-, Жирг-, Зирг-, Зырг-.

žižm-, žiežm-, vgl. die lit. Gwn *Žiežmojus, Žiežmuo, Žižma* (1 × mit Variante *Žiužma*) (LUV 205 f.), und den lit. ON Жижма 3. u. 4. (lit. *Žižmių* km.), slavisiert Жижм-, Зизман-.

žižmar-, žiežmar-, vgl. *žiežmara* 'Hexe u. ä.', die lit. Gwn *Žiežmara, Žiežmarė* u. *Žiežmarėlė* (LUV 205) und den ON Жижморка 1. (lit. *Žižmorka*, Relituanisierung einer slavisierten Form!); slavisiert Жижмор-, vielleicht auch Жижимор-.

žlaugt-, žlugt-, zu lit. *žlaugti* 'naß machen', *žliaugti* 'auch: stark regnen, fließen', *žlugti* 'einweichen', *žliugti* 'naß werden', lett. *žļugt* 'tauen', vgl. den ON Жлоукта (lit. *Žlaugtų* km., p. *Žłoukty*), slavisiert als Жлоукт-, Жлукт-, Жлут-, *Žłoukszt-*.

žuik-, wohl zu westlit. dial. *zuikis* 'Hase' (FLEW 1281), dazu die lit. Gwn *Zuikinė, Zuikravis, Zuikupis* (LUV 201) und lit. ON, wie RGN unter

Зуйки 4. (lit. *Zuikų* km.), Зуйкишки (lit. *Zuikiškė*, p. *Zajkiszki*), slavisiert als Жуйк-, Зуйк-, Зык-[31].

žuk-, žiuk-, zu apr. *suckis* 'Fisch', vgl. FLEW 1323, mit *l*-Suffix zu lit. *žūklys, žuklys* 'Fischer', vgl. FLEW 1322, mit *r*-Suffix vgl. lett. *žūkuris, dūkuris* 'Taucher (Mensch)', in lit. Gwn nicht belegt, zu balt. ON vgl. z. B. RGN Жуканцы (lit. *Žukonių* km.), Жукелишки (lit. *Žiukeliškių* km., p. *Žukieliszki*), Жукланцы (lit. *Žuklonių* km.), Жукли (lit. *Žuklių* km.), Зуколы (lett. *Zukuli*). Slavisiert als Жук-, Зук-, Зык-, Зюк-. Obwohl die Stufe Жук- mit zahlreichen Ableitungen von r. жук 'Käfer' konkurriert, lassen sich die Formen baltischen Ursprungs dank häufiger lautlicher und morphologischer Besonderheiten meist gut aussondern, vgl. auch Жукин- neben dem slavisch zu erwartenden Жуков-.

žul-, žiul-, vgl. lit. *žuolis* 'dickes Stück Holz, Baumstamm, jetzt Eisenbahnschwelle'; lit. *žolė* 'Gras, Kraut, Blume', lett. *zāle* 'Gras, Unkraut' kommen mit ihrem Reflex eines urbalt. *ā* wegen des konstanten *u*-Lautes der slavisierten Formen kaum in Betracht. An lit. Gwn ist nur *Žulna* (LUV 207), an balt. ON Зулово 3. (lit. *Zulovas*, relituanisierte Form?) zu nennen. Die Slavisierungsstufe Жул-, vgl. r. жулан 'eine Würgerart, vor allem Neuntöter', жулить 'mogeln u. ä.', läßt sich nur ausnahmesweise sicher von slav. Bildungen trennen; daneben treten die Stufen Зул- und Зюл- auf.

žvīr-, vgl. dazu lit. *žvyras* 'Sand, Kies', lt. FLEW 1328 entlehnt aus poln. *žwir* 'Kies', und *žvyrė* 'Moorhuhn, auch Schneehuhn genannt', lt. FLEW 1329 zu *žvyruoti* 'schimmern u. ä.'. Einer Entlehnung von *žvyras* aus *žwir,* vgl. a. FLEW 137 s.v. *gargždas,* Brückner PEW 668[32], widersprechen folgende Umstände: Die poln. Lautverbindung *žw-* läßt sich nur aus etymologisch nicht motivierbarem **ǥьv-* erklären, altes *gv-* müßte erhalten bleiben; der Wortstamm *Žwir-* hat seinen Schwerpunkt in der Ortsnamengebung im Bereich relativ späten Erlöschens des baltischen Substrats, lediglich *Žwir* und *Žwirówka,* die in SG. fehlen, liegen in recht altem polnischem Gebiet (Kr. Okuniew, unweit Warschau); die kleine Siedlung *Žwirowy Kąt* bei Batiatycze, Kr. Żółkiew, später Kr. Kamionka Strumiłowa/Galizien, ist offensichtlich jung; vgl. dazu die Belege Sk. S. 2042. Deshalb liegt es näher, eine Entlehnung von poln. *žwir* aus lit. *žvyras* anzunehmen. — An lit. Gwn sind zu nennen *Žvyrynas, Žvirinčius, Žvyrupis* (LUV 208), zu den balt. ON vgl. RGN Жвирини 2. (lit. *Žvyriniškė*), Жвирница (lett. *Žvirine*) oder Жвиры 4. (lit. *Žvyrių* km.). Die slavisierten Formen zeigen Жвир- und Жвыр-[33].

žvirblis (lit.), lett. *zvirbulis* 'Sperling': Vgl. die lit. Gwn *Žvirblis* und *Žvirblupis* und für die balt. ON Belege des RGN, wie Жвирбли 4., 5. u. 9 (lit.

Žvirbliai) oder Звербули (lett. *Zvirbuļi*). Die slavisierten Formen zeigen vor allem Жвирбл-, daneben auch *Żwerbl-*, Жвирб-, Жирбл-, Звербул-, Звирбл-[33].

žvirgžd-, žviržd-, zu lit. *žvirgždas, žvioiddas* 'grober Sand, Kies', lett. *zvirgzds* 'Kieselstein', in balt. Gwn sehr häufig, vgl. *Žvirgždas, Žvirgždė, Žvirzdė* (LUV 208), ebenso in balt. ON, vgl. RGN Жвиргжда (lit. *Žvirgždė*, p. *Żwirgżda, Zwirgzdy, Żwirgzda*), Звергжа (lett. *Zvirgža*), Звирздино (lett. *Zvirgzdine*, p. *Zwirdzin, Żwirdzino*); slavisiert als Жвиргжд-, Жвиржд-, Звергж-, Зверж-, Звeрзд-, Звиргзд- Звирзд-, Зворгзд-. Dieses im noch heute baltischen Gebiet in Ortsnamen so häufige Etymon ist zwar außerhalb dieses Gebiets nicht belegt, wurde aber aufgenommen, weil es die Vielfalt der möglichen slavischen Reflexe baltischer Namenstämme besonders anschaulich illustriert.

II. Räumlich gegliederte Darstellung der in Betracht kommenden Namenbelege

Die Gliederung geht von der in den Vorbemerkungen unter 5 dargelegten Vorstellung aus, daß eine von den Slaven aus der Mitte des baltischen Substratgebiets verdrängte baltische Bevölkerung die angrenzenden baltischen Gebiete überlagerte und bis in angrenzendes ostsee- und wolgafinnisches Gebiet vordrang. Da eine genaue Abgrenzung von Räumen vorerst nicht möglich ist, wurde eine für den vorliegenden Zweck ausreichende schematisierende Darstellung gewählt, wobei sich folgende Räume ergaben[34]:

1. Das an die litauisch-slavische Sprachgrenze anschließende Gebiet mit z. T. sehr später Slavisierung und Überdeckung baltischer *z-* und *ž-*Areale durch den Einfluß des polnischen Masurierens (*z* für *ž*)[35].

2. Das an die lettisch-slavische Sprachgrenze anschließende Gebiet mit erheblicher Substratnamendichte, relativ später Slavisierung und Nebeneinander von *z-* und *ž-*Formen. Eine vergleichbare dialektische Erscheinung auf slavischer Seite ist sehr früh geschwunden und dürfte keine merkliche Rolle spielen[36]. Es ist mit einem ausgedehnten baltischen Vorsubstrat zu rechnen[37].

3. Der wesentlich früher slavisierte Nordosten des baltischen Substrats mit dem ehem. Gouv. Tveŕ, mit erheblich geringerer Substratnamendichte und Schwerpunkt bei den Gewässernamen. z. T. mit ostseefinnischem Vorsubstrat[37].

4. Der Südosten des baltischen Substrats (Teile der ehem. GG. Černigov, Kaluga, Kursk, Moskau und Orel) mit Schwerpunkt im G. Kaluga, im übrigen wohl größtenteils Verdrängungsgebiet, im Osten mit wolga-finnischem Vorsubstrat[38].

5. Die Mitte des baltischen Substratraums mit den ehem. GG. Minsk, Mogilev und Smolensk. Dieser Raum schließt einen großen Teil des in Vorbemerkungen, 5 besprochenen Verdrängungsgebiets ein und ent-hält im Gebiet von Roslavl', Čerikov und Sluck Inseln erheblicher Substratnamendichte.

Die Namenbelege sind innerhalb dieser Gebiete nach Gouvernementen und Kreisen zusammengefaßt, die ihrerseits nach ihrer geographischen Lage aufgeführt sind. Die in Betracht kommenden baltischen Grundworte sind über die Aufstellung am Schluß dieses Beitrags aus Aufstellung I zu ersehen.

1. Das an die litauisch-slavische Sprachgrenze anschließende Gebiet

Ž

G. Grodno — Kr. Bel'sk: *Žale*; Kr. Pružany: Жадены (p. *Žadzień, Žadzienie, Žadeny*), *Žedyki (Žedziki)*; Kr. Slonim: *Žadejki* 2., Жедейки (p. *Žadejki, Žodejki*); Kr. Białystok: Жедня (p. *Žednia*), *Žodzie*; Kr. Volkovysk: Жодейки (p. *Žadejki, Zadejki*); Kr. Grodno: *Žadejki* 1., *Žamojdzie (Žamajdzie)*.

G. Suwałki — Kr. Augustów: Жалкое (p. *Žałkie, Žałkoje*), Жилины 1. (p. *Žyliny*); Kr. Suwałki: Граже Нове u. Старе (p. *Grauže Nowe* u. *Stare*).

G. Wilna — Kr. Lida: Доржи 1. (p. *Dorže*), Жусины 1. (p. *Žusiny, Zusiny*), Жемойтишки 1. (p. *Žamojtyszki, Žamojciszki*), Жемойтишки 2., Жо-мойдзь 2. (p. *Žamojdź, Žomajdzie, Žomojdzie*), Жомойдзь-Заброды; Жельвидоры (p. *Želwidory, Žylwidory*), Жижма 1. u. 2. (p. *Žyżma*), Жвирбли 6. (p. *Žwirble*); Kr. Ošmjany: Доржи 2., 3. (p. *Dorže*) u. 4., Доржни (p. *Dorżnie*, SG. *Dorožnie, Dorożne*), Граужи 2. (p. *Grauže*), Граужишки (p. *Graužyszki*) 3. u. 4., Граужанка (Fl.), Жемойдзи (p. *Žamojdź, Žamojdzie*), Жемойтуки (p. *Žemojtuki, Žamojtuki*), Жилянка (Fl.), Жижма 5. (p. *Žyżma*) (a. See), Жвирблишки 6. (p. *Žwir-bliszki, Zwirbliszki*); Kr. Wilna: Жвирблишки 13. (p. *Žwirbliszki*); Kr. Vilejka: Вержголувка, Виржи (p. *Wirže*), Жосна Старая u. Новая, Жемолино, Жилинские (p. *Žylińskie, Žymińskie!*); Kr. Svencjany: Держиново, Жодзишки (p. *Žodziszki*); Kr. Disna: Даржели 1., Граужи

1. (p. *Grauže*), Жадо (p. *Žada, Žaba!*) (Ort u. See), Жоде (See), Жви-
ранка, Жвиры.
G. Kaunas — Kr. Novo-Aleksandrovsk: Жеймяны.

Z

G. Grodno — Kr. Pružany: Зулин 1. (p. *Zulin, Zulinek*); Kr. Slonim:
Земейдяки (p. *Žamojdziaki, Žmojdziaki, Zamojdziaki*), Зельва 1.
(Зельвянка) (Fl., a. Kr. Volkovysk); Kr. Volkovysk: Зельва 1. u. 2.
(p. *Zelwa, Zielwa*), Зельвяны (p. *Zelwiany*); Kr. Grodno: *Zalaman-
Pićwoloka, Zaniemeńsk-Zelwiany*.
G. Suwałki — Kr. Suwałki: Зусно (p. *Zuśno*).
G. Wilna — Kr. Lida: Гезгалы (p. *Giezgaly*), Зюки (p. *Ziuki*); Kr. Ošmjany:
Загоришки 1. (p. *Zagórniki*), Залгидзимы; Kr. Vilejka: *Zospoja* (Fl.),
Зуйка 2. (Fl.); Kr. Svencjany: Зуста–Клавсуци–Закрочино; Kr.
Disna: Гизовщина (p. *Gizowszczyzna*) 1., Гизуны, *Zadyca* (*Zadica*) (Fl.),
Земяни (p. *Zamianie, Zimianie*), Замеке (See), Зальвица (p. *Zolwica*).

2. Das an die lettisch-slavische Sprachgrenze anschließende Gebiet

Ž

G. Vitebsk — Kr. Lepel': Жодунь (See); Kr. Drissa: Дрижичино, Гейжа-
ново (p. *Giejzynów*), Гейжиново (p. *Hejżeniewo, Hejzynowo*); Kr.
Polock: Ворожня (Ort u. See), Жагоры 1., Жалдыги; Kr. Gorodok:
Жедон (See), Жигары Новые u. Старые, Жельцы 2. (SG.: *Želcy*) (auch
See), Жельчанка (Ort u. Fl.), Жергалино; Kr. Nevel': Вережье (See),
Ворожейки (Ort u. See), Жигарино.
G. Pskov — Kr. Ostrov: Жегарево, Жегоры, Жугорево, Жаврино,
Жавры 2.; Kr. Oročka: Жагорево (Жагирево), Жигарево, Жавры 1.,
Жукино (Жуково); Kr. Novoržev: Ворожейкино 1., Вержа (Fl.),
Вержица (Fl.)[39], Жегариха, Желонки (Жалоники), Жилино (See),
Жукопино (Жекопино); Kr. Porchov: Желыни, Жалнырь (Fl.); Kr.
Cholm: Держанка (Fl.), Жемаи, Жукрово; Kr. Velikije Luki: Вережье
am See Užo, vgl. den lit. Gwn *Ūžys* (LUV 181), Жегорино; Kr. Toropec:
Вережуни (Ort u. See), Жельно (Жильно) (See), Желянка (Fl.).
G. Petersburg — Kr. Luga: Жельцы 1. (Жильцы).

Z

G. Vitebsk — Kr. Drissa: Ворзово 1. u. 2., Заситино 1., Зулово (p. *Zulowo*)
1. u. 2.; Kr. Sebež: Залосемье (p. *Zaloziemie, Zalosiemie*) (Ort u. See),
Заситино 2. u. 3. (p. *Zasityń, Zasitino, Zasiecin*) (auch See); Kr. Polock:

Зосино (Sumpf); Kr. Gorodok: Заситница (Ort u. Bach), Зюли; Kr. Nevel': Зуйки 2. am See Зубонец; Kr. Vitebsk: Зедани, Зездрино, Зыколино 2.; Kr. Veliž: Зимяни.

G. Pskov — Kr. Pskov: Зальсажья; Kr. Ostrov: Дризели, Ворзы, Ворзовка (Fl.), Зельцы 3., Зилева Гора, Зили, Зилино; Kr. Оročka: Ворзовка (Березовка), Зельцы 1. u. 2., Зили 1., Зуйково 1. am See Зуйково, 2. am Fl. Зуйково; Kr. Porchov: Залеменье, Зуйково 3. (Зыково); Kr. Cholm: Ворза, Засково (See); Kr. Toropec: Зимец 1. See nahe der Зовля.

G. Petersburg — Kr. Gdov: Зальца (Надозерье), Зуйка 1. (Fl.).

3. Der nordöstliche Grenzraum des baltischen Substrats

Ž

G. Tveŕ — Kr. Ostaškov: Воржино, Воржинка (Fl.), Жилинка 2. (Fl.), Жукопа (Ort u. Fl.); Kr. Vyšnij Voloček: Жальцы; Kr. Toržok: Жалинка (Жалина, Жаленка) (Fl.); Kr. Ržev: Жагорин, Жагорина 2., Жалыма; Kr. Zubcov: Держа 2. (Fl.); Kr. Tveŕ: Воржа (Fl.); Kr. Veśjegonsk: Жигариха; Kr. Vežeck: Желдыбино 1.; Kr. Kašin: Жалоновка (Fl.); Kr. Kaljazin: Желдыбино 2.

Z

G. Tveŕ — Kr. Ostaškov: Зальцо am See Селигер (Name ostseefinnischer Herkunft!)[39a]; Kr. Veśjegonsk: Залезинка; Kr. Kašin: Верезино 2.; Kr. Kaljazin: Верезино 1.

4. Der südöstliche Grenzraum des baltischen Substrats

Ž

G. Moskau — Kr. Vereja: Жедочи; Kr. Podol'sk: Жилетовка (Fl.).

G. Kaluga — Kr. Malojaroslavec: Жилинка 1.; Kr. Medyń: Желанейка (Fl.), Желонья (Fl.); Kr. Tarusa: Желоковка (Fl.); Kr. Kaluga: Жалка (Жала) (Fl.); Kr. Mosal'sk: Желонка 1. (Fl.), Жолтяки; Kr. Meščovsk: Жиздринка (Fl.); Kr. Lichvin: Жилень (Fl.), Желова (Жалова, Желовля, Желовь) (Fl., auch Kr. Peremyšl'); Kr. Žizdra: Жиздра (Stadt, Fl. a. andere Kreise), Жуляпова (Вязовна).

G. Orel — Kr. Brjansk: Вержейка (Fl.)[40].

G. Kursk — Kr. Fatež: Желень (Жилень, Желинь) (Fl.)[41]; Kr. Ryl'k: Жадинка, Nebenfluß des Клевень(!, vgl. lit. *klevas* 'Ahorn' und lit. Gwn, wie LUV 76 *Kleva, Klevinė*).

G. Černigov — Kr. Kozelec: Дрижава (Fl.)[42]; Kr. Oster: Жукин; Kr. Černigov: Жолвинка (Жоввинка); Kr. Sosnica: Жукля am Fl. Сестра; Доржавец (Fl., Iput'-Bassin)[43].

Z

G. Moskau — Kr. Volokolamsk: Дрызлово (Дрызловое).

G. Kaluga — Kr. Malojaroslavec: Дерзна (Fl.); Kr. Mosal'sk: Зилинка, (Fl.); Kr. Meščovsk: Верзнево; Kr. Žizdra: Загоричи am Fl. Загорич, Заламанка (Fl.), Зименка (Зиминка), zur Болва (Fl.) (!, vgl. TopTrub 177: zum lit. Gwn *Balvis*).

G. Orel — Kr. Mcensk: Зуша (Fl., a. Kr. Čern u. Novosil'/G. Tula); Kr. Dmitrovsk: Дрезва (Fl., zur Неруса !, balt. Ursprungs, vgl. lit. Gwn, wie *Neris* u. TopTrub 198); Kr. Sevsk: Зевра (Зебра) (Fl., zur Зерская).

G. Kursk — Kr. Putivl': Верзапь (Sumpf).

G. Černigov — Kr. Novgorod-Seversk: Зедиков (Чмарин).

5. Die Mitte des baltischen Substrats

Ž

G. Minsk — Kr. Pinsk: Żoducz (See); Kr. Sluck: Żawrodowszczyzna, Жомойдзь 1. (p. *Žamojdž, Žamowicze, Žamojdy*), Жилинка 2. (p. *Žylinka*); Kr. Novogrudok: Жвири; Kr. Minsk: Гойжево; Kr. Borisov: Жодин (p. *Žodzin, Zodzino, Žodyno*), Жамойск (p. *Zamojsk, Žomajsk*), Жирблевичи (p. *Žyrblewicze, Žyrbajewicze!*); Kr. Igumen: Доржище, Гижгайлово (p. *Gieżgajłowo, Kieżgajłowo, Gażyłów*): Kr. Bobrujsk: Жалый (p. *Żało*), Жолвинец (p. *Želwiniec, Żołwaniec*); Kr. Mozyŕ: Жадень (p. *Žadeń, Žadzień*) (See); Kr. Rečica: Желонка 2. (Желонь) (Fl.), Желонь (ukr. Жолонь, p. *Żołoń*) (Fl., a. Kr. Ovruč/Wolhynien).

G. Mogilev — Kr. Rogačev: Жукочье (Fl.); Kr. Čerikov: Гиженка 1. u. 2.[44], Гижня, Жадунка (Жадунька, p. *Žadunka, Zadunka, Zadumka*) (Fl., a. Kr. Klimoviči), Жилим (Fl.); Kr. Klimoviči: Жадынь (Жадунь, p. *Žadyń*); Kr. Čausy: Дрижеполье (Чертов Перевоз), Желивье (p. *Želiwie*); Kr. Orša: Жолно (Fl.), Жукнево; Kr. Senno: Жаурполье (p. *Žaurpole*), Жауры.

G. Smolensk — Kr. Roslavl': Воржанские, Воржанка (Fl.)[45], Желынец, Жалынец (See)[46], Жилинки; Kr. Smolensk: Жалдыбы, Жалдыбка (Fl.)[47]; Kr. Jel'nja: Жлутовка (Жлутковка, Жлуктовка) (Fl.); Kr. Dorogobuž: Дорожанка (Fl.)[48], Вержа Крутая, Вержино am Fl. Вержа; Kr. Vjaźma: Жемулькино, Жуйково; Kr. Juchnov: Желтибина; Kr. Poreč'je: Жалида (Fl.), Жемоховка 2. (Fl.); Kr. Duchovščina:

Вороженка (Fl.)[49]; Kr. Beloj: Вержа am Fl. Вержица (a. Малая Вержа)[50], Жагорина 1. (Жигорина), Жигарева, Жемоховка 1. (Желиховка) (Fl., a. Kr. Dorogobuž); Kr. Gžatsk: Жилинка 1. (Fl.), Жулевка (Fl.); Kr. Syčevka: Держа 1. (Fl.).

Z

G. Minsk — Kr. Sluck: Гезовщина; Kr. Novogrudok: Зулин (p. *Zulin*) 2.; Kr. Minsk: *Zasula* (*Zasulka*) (Fl.); Kr. Bobrujsk: Березовичи.

G. Mogilev — Kr. Rogačev: Загорище (Sumpf); Kr. Čerikov: Засуское (See); Kr. Mstislavl': Верезубы (p. Werezuby); Kr. Mogilev: Зыли (p. Zyle).

G. Smolensk — Kr. Roslavl': Зодня (Fl.); Kr. Smolensk: Зыколино 1. (Зыколина); Kr. Krasnyj: Зимина (Fl.); Kr. Dorogobuž: Землица (Fl.), zur Велетовка (!, vgl. LUV 189, 190 die lit. Gwn Velétupis u. Veltupys); Kr. Vjaźma: Зимоловка (Fl.); Kr. Duchovščina: Дризменка (Fl.), Зединовка (Гусиня), Fl., Зимец 2. (Земц) (Fl.); Kr. Beloj: Задейка (Задейкова), Зуйки 1.; Kr. Gžatsk: Верзинка (Fl.).

Schluß

Betrachtet man die obigen Namenbelege, so ergibt sich folgendes Bild:

— Im gesamten baltischen Substratgebiet treten sowohl Formen auf, die mit Sicherheit ein *z*, als auch Formen, die mit Sicherheit ein *ž* der baltischen Grundform reflektieren. Die *ž*-Formen sind in der Überzahl, auch wenn man die Belege berücksichtigt, in denen ein *ž* auch aus einem baltischen *g* vor vorderem Vokal erklärt werden könnte.

— Die *z*-Formen zeigen deutliche Schwerpunkte in den Kreisen Ošmjany und Disna (Gebiet 1), am nördlichen Dünauer und in einem sehr breiten Streifen längs der heutigen lettischen Sprachgrenze (Gebiet 2) und im Bereich der oberen Desna und des oberen Dnepr, besonders in den Kreisen Roslavl' und Duchovščina (Gebiet 5).

Dieses Bild bleibt auch unverändert, wenn man den Umfang der Belege nach dem Grad ihrer Zuverlässigkeit für die Lösung der gestellten Aufgabe einengt oder sich auf die Gewässernamen beschränkt.

Die Vertretung *z* oder *ž* in baltischen Substratnamen für idg. *ĝ*, *ĝh* kann nicht Zufall sein. Folgende Erklärungen kommen in Betracht:

1. Auf baltischer Seite lag ein Zwischenlaut vor, der bei der Slavisierung bald durch *z*, bald durch *ž* wiedergegeben wurde. Es fehlen jedoch Variantenpaare mit *z* bzw. *ž* für die Bezeichnung desselben geographischen Objekts.

2. Im baltischen Substratgebiet wurde *ž* erst im Laufe der Slavisierung zu
z, sodaß früher slavisierte Namen ein *ž*, später slavisierte Namen ein *z*
zeigen. Hierfür könnte man das gehäufte Auftreten von *z*-Formen neben
ž-Formen in dem an das lettische Gebiet mit seinem *z* für urbalt. *ž* angrenzenden Gebiet 2 anführen.

3. Der Unterschied zwischen den baltischen *z*- und *ž*-Dialekten ist alt[51].
Im Laufe der slavischen Expansion wurden Gebiete alter *z*-Dialekte von
aus ihren Sitzen verdrängten Angehörigen alter *ž*-Dialektgruppen über-
siedelt. Der umgekehrte Vorgang ist wenig wahrscheinlich, weil die
ž-Formen überwiegen und damit die progressive Erscheinung darstellen.

Ein Nebeneinander von baltischen *z*- und *ž*-Formen auf engem Raum
findet sich noch heute vor allem im Bereich des ehem. G. Suwałki und des
Kr. Novo-Aleksandrovsk/Kaunas (Zarasai) sowie im infläntischen Gebiet
(Kr. Illukst/Kurland und Kr. Dvinsk, Ljucin und Režica/Vitebsk) und
läßt sich hier ebenfalls durch Überschichtung baltischer Dialekte erklären.
Vgl. hierzu das Auftreten des Suffixes *-išk-*, das den lettischen Ortsnamen
sonst fehlt, im infläntischen Bereich[52]. Das gebietsweise Überwiegen von
ž- oder *z*-Formen kann man auf Dialektausgleich zugunsten eines die Herrschaft antretenden Dialekts, etwa des Aukštaitischen ($z \rightarrow ž$) oder des Niederlettischen ($ž \rightarrow z$) zurückführen[53].
Zum Dialektausgleich vgl. auch das Zurückweichen alter dialektischer *a*-
Formen zugunsten von *e*-Formen in infläntischen Gebiet[54]. Für die Entscheidung, ob Lösung 2 oder 3 vorzuziehen ist, reichen die *z*- und *ž*-Formen
jedoch für sich allein nicht aus.
Dialektgebiete unterscheiden sich im allgemeinen auch durch Unterschiede im Wortschatz, die sich auch in den Ortsnamen reflektieren. Wenn
Lösung 3 richtig ist, dann müßten sich im Substrat gegenüberstehen:

a) ein *ž*-Dialektgebiet mit dem Wortschatzbestand A;
b) ein *z*-Dialektgebiet mit dem Wortschatzbestand B, weitgehend über-
   lagert durch *ž*-Dialekte mit dem Wortschatzbestand A, also mit B + A.

Das baltische Verdrängungsgebiet, das durch die Schicht A vertreten
ist, ist leider seiner Natur nach arm an Substratnamen. Hier ist das Namengut des aukštaitischen und žemaitischen Kerngebiets, das jedenfalls alte
ž-Dialekte reflektiert, von besonderem Wert[55]. Vgl. hierzu die aus Aufstellung II ersichtliche begrenzte Verbreitung bestimmter Namenstämme
mit deutlichen Schwerpunkten, etwa von balt. *žuik-*, zudem fast nur als
zuik- belegt, sodaß das sporadische *ž* Folge eines Dialektausgleichs B nach
A sein kann, oder das Fehlen des in Litauen so häufigen *žvirgžd-* im balti-

schen Substratraum. Zur Verbreitung der hier besprochenen baltischen Namenstämme vgl. auch RGN und RGW unter den in Aufstellung I genannten slavisierten Vertretungen.

Register der slavischen Namenstämme

Im folgenden werden die in diesem Beitrag herangezogenen slavischen bzw. slavisierten Namenstämme nach ihrem Phänotyp, d. h. nach der Form, in der sie im RGN oder RGW erscheinen, alphabetisch zusammengestellt. Für jede slavische Form wird das Stichwort angeführt, unter dem Angaben in Aufstellung I über in Betracht kommende baltische Grundworte sowie ähnlich oder gleichlautende slavische Bildungen zu finden sind. Diese Stichworte stellen also nicht eine Deutung der betr. slavischen Formen dar.

Вереж-, Верез-,		Дорж-, Дорз-,	
Верж-, Верз-,		Дорож-	darž-/dirž-
Вирж-	virž-	Дрез-, Дрейз-,	
Ворж-, Ворз-,		Дриж-, Дриз-,	
Вороз-	varž-	Дрыз-	drież-
Вырз-	virž-	Дырж-	darž-/dirž-
Гайж-, Гез-,		Жавр-	žiaur-
Гейж-, Гиж-, Гиз-		Жагар-, Жагер-,	
Гойж-	gaiž-/giž-	Жагор-	žagar-
Горож-	graž-	Жад-	žad-/žied-
Гравж-	grauž-	Жал-	žal-
Граж-, Граз-	graž-	Жалт-	žalt-
Грайз-	grież-	Žamajd-, Žamojd-	žemait-
Грауж-, Гревж-	grauž-	Жаур-	žiaur-
Грейж-, Грейз-	grież-	Żwerbł-	žvirblis
Гривж-, Гривз-	grauž-	Жвир-	žvīr-
Гриж-, Гриз-	grież-	Жвирб-, Жвирбл-	žvirblis
Грож-, Гроз-	graž-	Жвиргжд-,	
Гроуж-	grauž-	Жвиржд-	žvirgžd-
Груж-, Груз-	graž-	Жвыр-	žvīr-
Грывж-, Грывз-	grauž-	Жегар-, Жегор-	žagar-
Грыж-, Грыз-	graž-, grież-	Жед-	žad-/žied-
Дарж-	darž-/dirž-	Жездр-	žiegždra
Дерез-, Держ-,		Жейм-	žeim-
Дерз-, Дзирж-	darž-/dirž-	Жел-	žal-

Желем-	želmen-	Звирбл-	žvirbl-
Желт-	žalt-	Звиргзд-, Звирзд-	
Жельв-	žilv-/želv-	Зворгзд-	žvirgžd-
Жем-	žem-/žiem-	Зевр-	žiaur-
Жемайд-,Жемайт-,		Зед-	žad-/žied-
Жемейт-, Жемойд-,		Зездр-	žiegždra
Жемойт-	žemait-	Зейл-	žil-
Жерг-	žirg-	Зейм-	žeim-
Жигар-, Жигор-,		Зел-	žal-
Жигур-	žagar-	Зелемен-	želmen-
Жижимор-	žižmar-	Зелт-	žalt-
Жижм-	žižm-	Зельв-	žilv-/želv-
Жижмор-	žižmar-	Зельман-	želmen-
Жиздр-	žiegždra	Зельт-	žalt-
Жил-	žil-	Зем-	žem-
Жильв-	žilv-/želv-	Земейд-	žemait-
Жирбл-	žvirblis	Зизман-	žižm-
Жирг-	žirg-	Зил-	žil-
Жлоукт-, Жлукт-,		Зим-	žeim-, žim-
Жлут-	žlaugt-	Зирг-	žirg-
Жогор-	žagar-	Złoukszt-	žlaugt-
Жод-	žad-/žied-	Зод-	žad-/žied-
Жолв-	žilv-/želv-	Зол-	žal-
Жолт-	žalt-	Золв-	žilv-/želv-
Жомойд-	žemait-	Золт-	žalt-
Жос-	žąs-	Зольв-	žilv-/želv-
Жугор-	žagar-	Зос-	žąs-
Жуйк-	žuik-	Зуйк-	žuik-
Жук-	žuk-	Зук-	žuk-
Жул-	žul-	Зул-	žul-
Жус-	žąs-	Зус-	žąs-
Загар-, Загор-	žagar-	Зуш-	žąs-
Зад-	žad-/žied-	Зыздр-	žiegždra
Заламан-, Залман-	želmen-	Зык-	žuk-, žuik-
Зальв-	žilv-/želv-	Зыл-	žil-
Zamojd-	žemait-	Зырг-	žirg-
Зас-	žąs-	Зюк-	žuk-
Звербул-	žvirblis	Зюл-	žul-
Звергж-, Зверж-,		Зям-	žem-
Зверзд-	žvirgžd-		

Anmerkungen

1. Chr. Stang, *Vergleichende Grammatik der Baltischen Sprachen*, Oslo–Bergen–Tromsö, 1966.

2. J. Prinz, *Die Slavisierung baltischer und die Baltisierung slavischer Ortsnamen im Gebiet des ehemaligen Gouvernements Suwałki — Versuch der Entwicklung einer Theorie der Umsetzung von Ortsnamen am praktischen Beispiel*, Wiesbaden, 1968, vgl. z. B. 294 f., vor allem 301.

3. Vgl. Z. Zinkevičius, *Lietuvių dialektologija*, Vilnius, 1966, 147 f., J. Otrębski, *Gramatyka języka litewskiego*, I, Warschau, 1958, 353; K. Būga, z. B. *Rinktiniai Raštai*, III, Vilnius, 1961, 278 f.; J. Prinz, *op. cit.* Anm. 2, S. 256 f., 262; V. Grinaveckis in *Problemy evropejskogo jazykoznanija*, Moskau, 1964, S. 71, 72 u. a. Das Auftreten von *z* wird meist auf nichtlitauische baltische Substrate zurückgeführt, und zwar für den Südwesten gewöhnlich auf westbaltisches (Otrębski, Prinz, Grinaveckis), für den Südosten auf selisches (Būga) Substrat.

4. Ein *ž* ist im lettischen Bereich in einer Reihe infläntischer Ortsnamen (vor allem Kr. Illukst des ehem. G. Kurland und die Kreise Dvinsk, Režica und Ljucin des ehem. G. Vitebsk), sowie in einigen Appellativen belegt, die für Entlehnungen aus dem Litauischen gehalten werden. Zu den Ortsnamen vgl. z. B. RGN Жабеники (lett. *Žabenieki*), Жагоры 2. (lett. *Žagari*), Жагуни (lett. *Žęguni*); Жартмуйжа (lett. *Zārtmuiža*, d. h. die lett. Form ist bereits der schriftlettischen Norm angepaßt) u. a. K. Būga rechnet hier mit einem starken litauischen, auf jeden Fall aber nichtlettischen Einfluß, vgl. seinen Aufsatz „Die Vorgeschichte der aistischen (baltischen) Stämme im Lichte der Ortsnamenforschung" in *Streitberg-Festgabe*, Leipzig, 1924, 32 oder ders. *Rinktiniai Raštai*, Vilnius, 1958 f., III, 564 f. (Suffix *-išk-*). Zu den lettischen Appellativen mit *ž* als Entlehnungen aus dem Litauischen vgl. FLEW 1284 zu lit. u. lett. *žagata* 'Elster', lit. *žagaras*, lett. *žagars* 'dürrer Zweig usw.'.

5. Toporov und Trubačev (TopTrub 238) rechnen mit einem so späten Übergang von balt. *ž* aus idg. *ĝ, ĝh* zu *z* in den betreffenden baltischen Sprachen und Dialekten, daß er sich in den baltischen Substratnamen des oberen Dnepr-Beckens nicht mehr reflektieren konnte. Auch K. Būga rechnet mit einem sehr späten Übergang von *ž* zu *z* im Lettischen, Semgallischen, Kurischen und Selischen, vgl. seinen Aufsatz in der *Streitberg-Festgabe*, op. cit. Anm. 4, S. 27. Umso wichtiger ist es, nach Namen baltischen Ursprungs in relativ früh slavisierten Substratgebieten zu suchen, die ein *z* anstatt des urbaltisch vorauszusetzenden *ž* zeigen.

6. Vgl. dazu die zahlreichen Belege für *Niedźwiad-*, *Niedźwied-* in SG. VII, 66 f. für das westrussische Gebiet, die einen realen polnischen Einfluß wiederspiegeln und gelegentlich sogar die ostslavischen Formen verdrängt haben, wie bei *Niedźwiedzin*, ehem. Kr. Minsk.

7. Zum Masurieren vgl. z. B. St. Urbańczyk, *Zarys dialektologii polskiej*, 3. Aufl., Warschau, 1968, 31 f.

8. Vgl. hierzu z. B. *Zegarynka* (Sk. 1999), zu balt. *žagar-*, *Zwirble* und *Zwirbliszki* (Sk. 2090) zu lit. *žvirblis*, *Zwirynie*, *Zwiryniszki* u. *Zwirynka* (Sk. 2019) zu lit. *žvyras*, sowie die entsprechenden lit. und slavischen Formen im RGN s.v. Жагар-, Жагор-, Жегар-, Жвирбл-, Жвир-.

9. Vgl. Anm. 3 u. 4.

10. Zum Begriff der Deutung s. J. Prinz, *op. cit.* Anm. 2, bes. 41 f.

11. Soweit nichts anderes angegeben ist, sind Siedlungsnamen im RGN, Gewässernamen im RGW sub voce zu finden.

12. Zu den Typen der Slavisierung von Substraten vgl. J. Prinz, *Versuch einer
orientierenden Bestimmung von Namenräumen im frühostslavischen Bereich*, Heidelberg,
1969, 28 f.

13. Vgl. P. von Köppen, *Über die Deutschen im St. Petersburger Gouvernement. Mit
einem Vorwort über die ethnographische Karte des genannten Gouvernements und einem
Anhang über die auf derselben vorkommenden Ortsnamen, nebst Karte*, Petersburg, 1850,
eine Arbeit, die trotz ihrem Titel die Siedlungen der ostseefinnischen Völkerschaften
des behandelten Gebiets sehr genau berücksichtigt; die Karte bei L. Niederle, *Obozrenije
sovremennogo slavjanstva*, Petersburg, 1909; die Verteilung der slavisierten Formen
Кайв-, Койв-, Куйв- zu finn. *koivu* 'Birke' im RGN oder J. Prinz, op. cit. Anm. 12,
S. 78 f. u. Fußnote 118.

14. Vgl. Anm. 12.

15. Das genannte Verdrängungsgebiet und die angrenzenden Räume erheblicher
Dichte der baltischen Substratnamen sind auf der Kartenbeilage 3 der Arbeit von
Toporov und Trubačev (TopTrub) gut zu erkennen. Ein ähnliches Bild ergibt die Karte
der Grabfunde des westrussischen Raumes, die einem lange erhaltenen baltischen
Substrat zuzurechnen sind, in dem Aufsatz von V. V. Sedov, *Sledy vostočnobaltijskogo
pogrebal'nogo obrjada v kurganach drevnej Rusi* in *Sovetskaja Archeologija* V, 2, S. 103–
121. Vgl. auch Anm. 16.

16. Vgl. J. Prinz, Besprechung zweier Aufsätze des sowjetischen Archäologen V. V.
Sedov in *Beiträge zur Namenforschung* XV, bes. 118; ders., ,,Der Reflex des baltischen
Substrats in von **berž-* 'Birke' abgeleiteten russischen Orts- und Gewässernamen'',
Beiträge zur Namenforschung, bes. S. 261 f., 279. Die dort vorgenommene Unterteilung
des baltischen Substratgebiets mußte hier aus Raumgründen schematisierend ver-
einfacht werden.

17. Eine solche Schichtung spielte besonders in den Forschungen K. Būgas eine
Rolle, vgl. z. B. seine Theorie über den Einfluß des selischen Substrats im südöstlichen
Litauen etwa in *Rinktiniai Raštai*, III, 278 f.: sie zeigt sich besonders deutlich in
Karte 1 und 2 seines Aufsatzes in der *Streitberg-Festgabe* (op. cit. Anm. 4); die aus
Karte 1 ersichtlichen, von ihm angenommenen alten Sitze der Kuren, Semgallen,
Selen, Letten und die Ausdehnung des altpreußischen Gebiets bis zur Memel (Nemunas)
beruhen auf einer Trennung des baltischen Namenmaterials dieser Gebiete nach sich
überlagernden baltischen Namenschichten.

18. Zur Wahl dieser Einteilung vgl. J. Prinz, *op. cit.* Anm. 12, S. 33, Fußnote 47.

19. Die Basis für die Gegenüberstellung bestimmter balt. Wortstämme und slavisierter Formen bilden in der Arbeit von J. Prinz, s. Anm. 2, an entsprechendem
Namenmaterial aus noch heute baltischem Gebiet mit altem und intensivem slavi-
schem Einfluß gemachten Beobachtungen über die Slavisierung baltischer Namensformen, auf die hier verwiesen wird.

In der Zusammenstellung werden folgende Abkürzungen gebraucht:

PN = Personenname, ON = Ortsname, Siedlungsname, Gwn = Gewässername, Reg. =
Register.

Brückner PEW = A. Brückner, *Słownik etymologiczny języka polskiego*, 2. Aufl., Warschau, 1957.

Dal' = Vl. Dal', *Tolkovyj slovař živogo velikorusskogo jazyka*, Nachdruck der 2. Aufl., Moskau, 1956.

FLEW = E. Fraenkel, *Litauisches etymologisches Wörterbuch*, Heidelberg u. Göttingen, I, 1962, II, 1965.

L. 59 = *Lietuvos TSR administracinis-teritorinis suskirstymas*, 2. Aufl., Wilna, 1959.

LUV = *Lietuvių upių ir ežerų vardynas*, Vilnius, 1963.

Popović = *Rečnik srpskoga i nemačkoga jezika, II Srpsko-nemački deo*, zusammengest. v. Đ. Popović, Belgrad, 1926.

RGN = *Russisches Geographisches Namenbuch*, Mitarbeiterkollektiv, begr. v. M. Vasmer, hrsg. v. H. Bräuer, Wiesbaden, 1962 ff.

RGW = M. Vasmer, *Wörterbuch der russischen Gewässernamen*, Berlin u. Wiesbaden, 1961 f.

Ristić-Kangrga = *Rečnik srpskohrvatskog i nemačkog jezika, II, Srpskohrvatsko-nemački*, bearb. v. S. Ristić u. J. Kangrga, Belgrad, 1928.

SG. = *Slownik geograficzny królestwa polskiego i innych krajów slowiańskich*, I–XV, Warschau, 1880–1902.

Sk. = *Skorowidz miejscowości Rzeczypospolitej Polskiej z oznaczeniem terytorjalnie im właściwych wladz i urzędów oraz urządzeń komunikacyjnych*, Przemyśl u. Warschau, 1934.

TopTrub = V. N. Toporov und O. N. Trubačev, *Lingvistićeskij analiz gidronimov verchnego Podneprovja*, Moskau, 1962.

20. Zur Tendenz $e \to a$ in lit. Dialekten vgl. J. Otrębski, *op. cit.* Anm. 3, S. 19 f.; Z. Zinkevičius, *op. cit.* Anm. 3, S. 54 f.; im infläntischen Bereich des Lettischen vgl. J. Endzelin, *Lettische Grammatik*, Heidelberg, 1923, 4; zu dem Auftreten dieser Tendenz in Ortsnamen s. unten, Anm. 53.

21. Zu Дрейзи vgl. auch den infläntischen Übergang von $\bar{\imath}$ zu *ei*, s. J. Endzelin, *op. cit.* Anm. 20, S. 4 zum Hochlettischen.

22. Zu diesem balt. Wortstamm vgl. V. Urbutis in *Baltistica* II, S. 173 f.

23. S. Anm. 24.

24. Lett. *Griezeni* kann gegenüber r. Гризаны sekundär sein und eine Regression von der lettischen dial. Form ($\bar{\imath}$) zur lettischen schriftsprachlichen Norm (*ie*) darstellen, vgl. den infläntischen Übergang von *ie* zu $\bar{\imath}$ u. Endzelin, *op. cit.* Anm. 20, S. 4; zum Begriff der Regression vgl. J. Prinz, *op. cit.* Anm. 2, S. 280; die dort angeführten zahlreichen Beispiele für diese Erscheinung lassen sich nach dem Stichwort Regression des Sachregisters dieser Arbeit ermitteln.

25. Zu diesem Namenstamm vgl. auch P. Arumaa, ,,Sur les principes et méthodes d'hydronomie russe : Les noms en -гость'', in *Scando-Slavica* VI, 144–174. Von den S. 147 angeführten Belegen für diesen Namenstamm lassen sich einige auch mit einem baltischen Substrat in Verbindung bringen, z. B. Вороженка als Nebenfluß des Вопь (zu lit. *upė* 'Fluß'), Ворожуй, Raum Jakobstadt, vgl. J. Prinz zum Typ Березуй in *op. cit.* Anm. 16, S. 268; Ворожейкино, vgl. K. Būga zum balt. Ursprung des Personennamensuffixes *-ejk-* in *Rinktiniai Raštai*, I, S. 140 f., zu Вороженка < *varž-* ebda III, S. 548. Den Flußnamen Вороженка bringen Toporov und Trubačev (TopTrub 181) mit balt. *virž-* in Verbindung.

26. Zu lit. PN mit dem Element *žad-* vgl. z. B. O. Skardžius, ,,Die Bindevokale in den lit. zweistämmigen Personennamen'', *Festschrift für Max Vasmer zum 70. Geburtstag*, zusammengestellt von M. Woltner und H. Bräuer, Berlin und Wiesbaden,

1965, 508 *Gaudžadas, Geržadas*, oder K. Būga, *Rinktiniai Raštai*, I, 247 *Žadgaila*, 261 *Žadvainai, Žadvainiai*, 263 Жадовейне.

27. Für die Slavisierungsstufen mit *o* und *u* in der ersten Silbe kommt auch lit. veraltet u. dial. *žugara*, alt 'Reiher' dial. ʿpejorative Personenbezeichnung', in Betracht. Zu diesem Etymon vgl. V. Urbutis, ,,Baltų kalbų garnio pavadinimai", *Baltistica*, II, 2, s. S. 185.

28. Auch hier zeigt die slavisierte Form den am Ort zu erwartenden infläntischen Vokalismus (lett. *ie* = dial. *ī*), während die lett. Parallele nach der Schriftsprache gedeutet ist. Vgl. Anm. 24.

29. Zu Зейл- s. Anm. 21.

30. Die Stufe *želv-* spielt bei Būga wegen der häufigen Schwankung des Anlautes (*ž* × *z*) und des schwankenden Vokalismus eine erhebliche Rolle, besonders für die Bestimmung einer selischen Substratschicht im heute lit. Gebiet. Vgl. vor allem *Rinktiniai Raštai*, II, 134, 278 f., 549.

31. K. Būga nimmt diesen Wortstamm für ein kurisches Substrat im heute litauischen Gebiet in Anspruch, vgl. *Rinktiniai Raštai*, III, 203.

32. Brückner motiviert die etymologische Priorität von poln. *żwir* mit dem Hinweis auf r. dial. гверста 'Kies' (Dal' ²I, 346), skr. dial. зврст (Ristić-Kangrga), зврста (Popović) 'Art Kalkstein, Quarz'. гверста entspricht mit der Erhaltung von *gv-* älteren Besonderheiten des pskover Dialektgebiets, während *zvrst-* die lautgesetzliche skr. Entwicklung reflektiert. Гверст- kommt jedoch laut RGN auch in ON typisch baltischer Prägung vor, vgl. Гверстель, Гверстонь, und geht nur durch Belege im ehem. G. Novgorod über das altpskover Gebiet hinaus. Die Stufe Зверст- fehlt in russ. Ortsnamen. Es ist deshalb damit zu rechnen, daß es sich hier unabhängig von *żwir/žvyras* um ein dem Baltischen und Slavischen gemeinsames Etymon handelt, das in beiden Sprachgruppen nur noch in Relikten erfaßt werden kann.

33. Zu den poln. Varianten mit *z* statt *ž* s. Anm. 8.

34. Vgl. hierzu Anm. 15, 16. Zum Verdrängungsgebiet vgl. auch P. N. Tret'jakov, *Finno-ugry, balty i slavjane na Dnepre i Volge*, Moskau u. Leningrad, 1966. Nach S. 282 ergibt es sich auf Grund archäologischer Beobachtungen, daß in der Mitte des 8. Jhd. im Smolensker Raum auf der linken Seite des oberen Dnepr und am Sož die baltischen Siedlungen von den Krivitschen in weiten Gebieten niedergebrannt wurden und dieser russische Stamm sich in den auf diese Weise neu gewonnenen Gebieten niederließ.

35. Vgl. Anm. 3, 8.

36. Vgl. Chr. Stang, *Die westrussische Kanzleisprache des Großfürstentums Litauen*, Oslo, 1935, 5.

37. Zum ostseefinnischen Vorsubstrat in diesem Gebiet vgl. Karte 1 in K. Būgas Aufsatz in der *Streitberg-Festschrift*, s. Anm. 4. Vgl. weiter M. Vasmer, *Die alten Bevölkerungsverhältnisse Rußlands im Lichte der Sprachforschung*, Berlin, 1941, 20 f.

38. Vgl. hierzu M. Vasmer, *op. cit.* Anm. 37, S. 30; ders., *Beiträge zur historischen Völkerkunde Osteuropas III, Merja und Tscheremissen* = SBPrAkW, Phil.-hist. Kl., 1935, Bd. XIX, Sonderdruck S. 49 f.

39. Vgl. TopTrub 179: zu balt. *virž-*.

39 a. M. Vasmer, *op. cit.* Anm. 37, S. 22 erklärt diesen Namen wegen altruss. *Seregěrь* aus finn. *Särkijär(v)i* wegen finn. *särki* 'Plötze, Rotfeder'; wegen der Form des Sees und des dortigen ON Селижаровка kommt aber auch Ableitung aus finn. *selkä*, gen. *selän* 'плес, d. h. eine langgestreckte, dem Wind ausgesetzte Wasserfläche' in Betracht. Dieser Begriff spielt in der slavischen Namengebung eine große Rolle.

40. Vgl. TopTrub 179: zu balt. *virž-*.

41. TopTrub 188 hält den Namen für unklar und Reflex von balt. *gil-* für möglich.

42. TopTrub 185: unklar. Slavische Herkunft möglich.

43. TopTrub 184: zu lit. *diržus* 'zäh'?, auch slav. Herkunft möglich.

44. TopTrub 182: zu apr. *geeyse* 'Reiher'.

45. TopTrub 181: zu balt. *virž-*.

46. TopTrub 187: zu balt. *gelūn-*?

47. TopTrub 187: Жалдыбка, zu balt. *Geld-*.

48. TopTrub 185: zu balt. *Dargēn-*.

49. Vgl. Anm. 25.

50. TopTrub 179: zu balt. *virž-*.

51. Vgl. Anm. 3, 4.

52. Vgl. K. Būga, *Rinktiniai Raštai*, III, 565 f.

53. Vgl. Anm. 3, 4. Zum Dialektausgleich vgl. J. Prinz, *op. cit.* Anm. 12, S. 38 f., Fußnote 57 und S. 53; *op. cit.* Anm. 2, S. 300; zum notwendig heterogenen Charakter eines jeden Sprachstandes *op. cit.* Anm. 12, S. 22. Diese beiden Auffassungen fanden in jüngster Zeit einen besonderen Ausdruck bei V. K. Žuravlev, ,,K probleme balto-slavjanskich jazykovych otnošenij'', *Baltistica* IV, 2, S. 167–177.

54. Zum Zurückweichen der dial. *a*-Formen zugunsten von Formen mit schrift-sprachlichem *e* vgl. J. Prinz, *op. cit.* Anm. 2, S. 273 und ders. in BNF 1 (1966) S. 167 f. oder RGN Жагуны (lett. *Žęguni*), zum Zurückweichen von *ž* zugunsten von schrift-sprachlichem *z* in infläntischen Ortsnamen Formen des RGN, wie Жартмуйжа (lett. *Zārtmuiža*), Жидо-Пура (lett. *Zieda-Purvs*), wobei die slavisierten Formen gewöhn-lich den älteren, dialektischen Lautstand der baltischen Grundform reflektieren.

55. Es ist in diesem Zusammenhang nicht ohne Interesse, daß bei K. Būga in seinem Aufsatz in der *Streitberg-Festgabe* auf Karte 1 die Urheimat der urlitauischen Dialekt-gruppe mit dem oben genannten Verdrängungsgebiet weitgehend zusammenfällt.

The Distribution of *z* and *ž* in the Toponymy
of the Baltic Substratum

The probable Baltic stems of West Russian place and river names containing *z* or *ž* are recorded together with their Slavic correspondences. A second list shows the distribution of the *z*- and *ž*-forms within the Baltic substratum area. *ž*-forms prevail, but they widely occur together with *z*-names, which show, however, marked centers of frequency. As the *z* of these *z*-forms can hardly be explained otherwise, an early transition of Proto-Baltic *ž* to *z* in certain dialects of the substratum must be supposed. For the simultaneous existence of *z*- and *ž*-forms in the same region, one of three explanations is preferentially adopted. As a large area in the center of the Baltic substratum shows very few substratum names, it is supposed that an early Slavic in-vasion caused the Baltic population of this area probably belonging to a ž-dialect (A) to retreat in all directions except the south, overlaying the Baltic population of the surrounding areas. As far as z-areas (B) were concerned, mixed z-ž-areas (A + B) resulted. Relating name stems of restricted occurrence to A or B will help to verify the above solution.

EDUARDS PUTNIŅŠ

Interjektionen und Schallwörter
in der Mundart von Svētciems im Lettischen

Die Mundart von Svētciems gehört zum niederlettischen Dialekt und ist eine von den sog. „livischen" Mundarten. Die Gemeinde Svētciems, wo diese Mundart gesprochen wird, liegt im nordwestlichen Livland und grenzt an die Rigaer Bucht südlich von Salacgrīva. Diese Mundart ist ziemlich reich an verschiedenen Interjektionen und Schallwörtern, die für einen Sprachwissenschaftler von wichtiger Bedeutung sein können. Da aber hier wegen des vorbegrenzten Raumes eine allseitig ausführliche Darstellung dieses sprachlichen Materials nicht gegeben werden kann, so muss man bei seiner kurzen Skizzierung in alphabetischer Reihenfolge bleiben. Die Stichwörter werden in mundartlicher Form gegeben, doch sind sie alphabetisch so gereiht, wie sie schriftsprachlich transkribiert stehen würden.

Es sei noch kurz darauf hingewiesen, dass neben den meisten Interjektionen ein mit *-š-is* abgeleitetes Substantiv als Schallwort steht, von dem dann weiter ein entsprechendes Schallverbum mit *-ēt* gebildet werden kann, z. B. *bloŭkt!* — *bloŭkš* — *bloŭkšet* 'paff! — der Knall — knallen'. Zusammensetzungen mit Präfixen wie z. B. *oŭret* — *sa-oŭret* oder Ableitungen auf *-ināt* wie *kloûzet* — *kloûzinat* werden nur selten gegeben.

Mit wenigen Ausnahmen werden hier nur die in dem fixierten zur Verfügung stehenden mundartlichen Material vorkommenden Wörter genannt[1]. Damit ist aber nicht gesagt, dass auf diese Weise unbedingt schon alle in der Mundart bestehenden Interjektionen und Schallwörter erwähnt worden wären. Die doppelte Zahl kann davon vermutet werden und vielleicht sogar noch mehr.

ačk, ačkaš, ačks Ausruf des Erstaunens. *kaz jo ačk i pa·visam traks uz kâpšan.* 'die Ziege, Mensch, ist ja aufs Klettern ganz versessen!'

ak 'ach' als Ausruf des Erstaunens gewöhnlich in Verbindung mit *tu* 'du'. *ak tu avetens, kas tur bî!* 'ach, was es da Himbeeren gab!'

oŭret 'schreien; heulen'; derselbe Begriff wird auch durch *kliêkt* 'schreien' ausgedrückt, aber *aŭret* bedeutet eine grössere Intensität. *kliêʒ, oŭre, nakti jâroû špick* — *ja nãk vilks* 'kommt der Wolf, so schreit man, grölt man, in der Nacht muss man ein Streichholz anzünden'. *vẽš oũre ap pakšim un svilpe skuȓstena ka traks* 'der Wind heult um die Hausecken und pfeift im Schornstein wie toll!'

sa-oũret '(schreiend) zusammenrufen'. *jȃsa-oũre visi kuõpa, un ta var iẽt mãja* 'man muss alle zusammenrufen, und da kann man nach Hause gehen'. *baȓkšet* 'prasseln' wie z. B. Regen od. Hagel auf das Dach od. gegen die Fensterscheiben. *pret tuõ luȏg baȓkšei viên, baȓkšei!* 'es prasselte nur so gegen das Fenster!' Erbsen und Bohnen können *baȓkšet*, wenn sie auf die Tenne ausgeschüttet werden.

boũ-oũ! Interj., die das Brüllen (des Ochsen) darstellt.

boũkšet 'dumpf schallen, knallen' z. B. wie ein Schuss, ein kräftiger Schlag. *ka tik nȃk uz desmitim, ta joũ sȃk duñduri boũkšet luõpim apaȓti* 'kommt es nur gegen zehn Uhr, so fangen die Bremsen schon an, um das Vieh zu baukschet!' *kas tur boũkš uz bĕniņim?* 'was poltert dort auf dem Dachboden?'

boũkš onomatopoetisches Schallwort vom Schlagen, Fallen und desgl., z. B. von einem Schuss, dem Donner. *ziȓks salęcas gan nuȏ pȇrkon, var·bût nuȏ tuõ boũkš* 'das Pferd springt wohl auf vom Donner, vielleicht von dem Dröhnen'.

boũret 'brüllen'. Der Ochse *boũre* 'brüllt'. *buļļi jo, ka iȇsȃk, ta boũre ka traki* 'Bullen ja, wenn sie anfangen (oder wenn sie sich angewöhnen), brüllen wie toll!'

nuȏboũret 'eine Zeitlang brüllen'. *buļls tȃ uz mum̃s nuȏboũreį* 'der Bulle hat auf uns so gebrüllt'.

bẽ! Interj., Nachahmung des Blökens der Schafe. *aȋtiņč jo sak tȃ: bẽ! bẽ!* 'das Schäflein sagt ja so: bäh! bäh!'

bẽjiņč das Schaf in der Ammensprache.

biŋkt! boŋkt! Interj. zur Nachahmung des Läutens mit einer grossen Glocke. *a tiẽm mazejim* [zvaniem] *viên* [zvana] *ķiļ! ķiļ! ķiļ! tuõ liẽla* [zvanu] *tik sit biŋkt! boŋkt!* 'mit dem kleinen [Glocken] allein [läutet man] tjill! tjill! tjill! die grosse [Glocke] schlägt man nur binkt! bonkt!' (erzählt vom Läuten in der orthodoxen Kirche).

blaȓkšet dröhnend schallen, wenn gewisse Gegenstände beben od. gegeneinander schlagen. *luȏgi visi tik briẽsmigi blaȓkš — cepelinc mętat bum̃bs briẽsmigi* 'alle Fenster dröhnen so entsetzlich — der Zeppelin werfe schrecklich Bomben ab' (von einem Ereignis aus dem ersten Weltkrieg). *rȃu slũžs vaļa, un gãị ũdenc un maļk leja, ka blaȓkš viên* 'die Schleuse wurde aufgerissen, und [aufgestautes] Wasser und Holz gingen hinunter, dass es nur so polterte.'

bloũkšet 'knallen'

bloũkš das Geräusch eines Schlages, eines Falles; der Knall

bloũkt! Interj., die einen Knall nachahmt.

blĭkšet Nachahmung des Schalls, das beim Schlagen, Stürzen entsteht. *pa'priêkš iêt a zuôbim viřsa, ta liêk diřš kuõpa un speras, ka blĭkš viên.* 'zuerst gehen [sie] mit Zähnen gegeneinander, nachher stecken [sie] die Hinteren zusammen und schlagen aus, dass es nur so kracht' (von Pferden erzählt). *ûdenc blĭkš, nãk ka blĭkš viên* 'das Wasser „blieksch", stürzt, dass es nur so „blieksch" geht'. *lĭst ka blĭkš* 'es regnet in Strömen'. *agrak visi velejas, ka blĭkšei̯ viên* 'früher schlugen alle mit dem Waschbleuel, dass es nur so knallte'. *lâcs loûz guôu̯s nuôsta, ka blĭkšei̯ viên* 'der Bär bewältigte Kühe, dass es nur so krachte'

bliŭkšet 'knallen'

bliŭkš 'der Knall (eines Schusses)'

bliûkt (bliŭkt) Interj. den Knall eines plötzlichen Schlages nachahmend. *lik a kãi̯ pret tuõ siên ka bliûkt* 'man versetzte eins mit dem Fuss puff! gegen die Wand'

bloûkšet, blĭkšet und *bliûkšet* bezeichnen alle drei denselben Knall, z. B. beim Schiessen, aber mit dem Unterschied in der Färbung des Schalls. Bei *bloûkšet* erscheint der Schall dumpfer, *blĭkšet* und *bliûkšet* bezeichnen einen höhern Ton. Also kann man schiessen, dass es „blauksch", „blieksch" od „bliuksch" klingt. Und so wirken auch die entsprechenden Interjektionen, während *bliûkt* (also mit ˆ) die Kürze des Schalles ausdrückt.

blořstiḵs ein Mensch, der viel und allerlei dummes Zeug redet. *blořstiḵs i tâc, kas pasoûlig puĺk aplam runa un plorkš, kur nevajag* 'blorstiks ist so einer, der ungemein viel Unsinniges redet und unangebracht schwatzt'

bḷořrat 'sprechen, reden' (im verächtlichen, zornigen Sinn). *bḷořra bež seu̯ abduõm, ka tiêk kuõpa* 'man plappert ohne Überlegung, wenn man zusammentrifft'. *vai ta tu kuô var paturet, tu joû vis izbḷořra.* 'du kannst ja nichts bei dir behalten, du plapperst ja alles aus'

bobinat (bubinat) leise wiehern bu! bu! *ka ziřks ręӡ seu̯ ȩ̂dinatai̯, ta viņč bobina, tas i tâ lȩnam bobina* 'sieht das Pferd seinen Fütterer, so wiehert es leise' (d. h. bringt leise bu! bu! hervor)

bokšet dumpf schallen, wenn man z. B. mit der Faust gegen die Wand schlägt od. mit dem Fuss gegen die Diele stampft. *ӡiřd, ka viênc [zirgs] koûč kur ȩ̂d un sit pret zem, ka bokš viên* 'man hört, dass ein [Pferd] irgendwo frisst und gegen den Boden stampft, dass es nur so boksch'

bokš das Geräusch von einem weichen dumpfen Schlag

brakšet 'krachen' z. B. wenn trockene Äste od. Zweige brechen

brakš der Schall, der beim Brechen entsteht

brĭkšet 'knackern, krachen'. Im Vergleich mit *brakšet* bezeichnet *brĭkšet* einen mit einem Bruch verbundenen länger andauernden Schall. *Miřtuž tâ krìm̃t sil, ka brĩkš viên* 'Myrte (Kuhname) nagte an der Krippe, dass es nur so knackerte'

briũkšet 'krachen, knackern' *tâ ka briũkš, ka krakš* 'es kracht, knackert etwa'.

bur̃kšet 'ununterbrochen rasseln, rollen'; der Wagen rasselt; auch: 'undeutlich sprechen, schwatzen'

cui! Interj., mit der man Hunde hetzt

čabet 'rascheln'; Blätter (am Baume), auch Stroh *čab* 'rascheln'

čakstet 'rascheln, knistern' *aît tâ guļ, ka ne·maz nečakst* 'das Schaf schläft so, dass es gar nicht *čakst*' (d. h. ganz geräuschlos)

čoũkstet 'rascheln, rauschen, knistern' *putr rûkst, ka čoũkst viên* 'die Grütze gärt, dass es nur so rauscht'; gefallene Blätter, Papier, Heu, Stroh *čaukst*.

es ʒir̃d, ka man aîz mugar kas iêčoũkstas 'ich höre, dass etwas hinter mir kurz raschelt'

čęr̃kstet || čęr̃kšet 'die Stimme *čer̃kst* knarrt rauh'

či! li! li! Interj. zur Nachahmung der Stimme eines Feldhuhns

čilinat Schallverbum, das die Laute eines Feldhuhns bezeichnet. *Tĩrum ir̃b tik tâ čilina: či! li! li! či! li! li!* 'das Feldhuhn singt nur so: tschi! li! li!'

čìkstet || čìkšet 'knarren'; die Tür, der Wagen, das Tor, die Stiefel, der Baum *čìkst* 'knarrt'; *krûti čìkst* 'es schnarcht in der Brust'; 'bittend plagen, sich sträuben'

čir̃kšet 'knirschen' z. B. der Sand unter den Füssen od. zwischen die Zähne geraten, die Feder beim Schreiben und desgl. *čir̃kst* 'knirschen; zwitschern' (z. B. Spatzen, Vogeljungen im Nest)

čir̃kšinat 'anhaltend zirpen'. *sisenc un siênâzs, tiê laĩkam vis viênc ir. ka viņi zeme čir̃kšina, ta i soûs laĩks, laps siên laĩks* 'Heuschrecke und Grashüpfer, das sind wahrscheinlich eins. Wenn sie am Boden zirpen, ist das Wetter trocken, gute Heuerntezeit'

čiš! Interj. zur Bezeichnung des Zischens, wenn man z. B. Wasser ins Gras giesst od. wenn der Schaum zusammenfällt, s. unter *kokš*

čũkstet || čũkšet 'zischen'; auf glühende Kohlen od. erhitzte Gegenstände gegossenes Wasser *čũkst*; nasses schlecht brennendes Holz *čũkst*

čur̃kšet || čurkstet 'mit geringem Geräusch fliessen, rieseln'; das Bächlein fliesst und *čurkst*; das Fleisch, das Fett auf der Pfanne *čurkst*; *vę̂dars čur̃kš* 'der Bauch kollert'

čuš! 'pisch' Interj. zur Bezeichnung eines zischenden Geräusches od. eines misslungenen Versuchs. *nu i čuš* 'jetzt ist es futsch'. *čuš un bę̃* 'futsch und dumm'

dim̃det 'dröhnen'; die Erde, Kanonen *dimd*, vgl. *rîbet. dim̃det* und *rîbet* bezeichnen beide das gleiche Gedröhn, aber mit dem Unterschied, dass *dim̃det* die Dumpfheit des Gedröhns hervorhebt, während *rĩbet* das Vibrieren unterstreicht, z. B. der Wagen *dim̃d* niemals, sondern nur *rĩb*

žĩŋkšet 'summen'. *man vecen sak, ka viņč nevarat isturet, ka viņč* (= ods) *tur žiŋkš* 'meine Alte sagt, dass sie nicht ertragen könne, wenn sie (= eine Mücke) dort summt'

êj! Interj., die zur Aufmerksamkeit auffordert. Davon gibt es auch eine imperativähnliche Form für die 2. Pers. Plur. *êjat!*

çr̃ra! Interj., mit der man Hunde hetzt und reizt

grabet 'rascheln, rasseln', z. B. der Regen auf dem Dach, solange es noch nicht stark und ununterbrochen regnet

ĩi! Interj., die das Muhen der Kuh nachahmt

ĩdet 'leise muhen'. *Jum̃praṷs vel pec gad, ka mani reʒeị, ĩdeị* 'Jumprava (= Kuhname) muhte leise noch nach einem Jahre, wenn sie mich sah'

iûkšet 'wütend kurz wiehern (vom Pferde)'. *viņč tâ iûkš un kuôdele tuõ sil* 'es wiehert so wütend und beisst in die Krippe'

kâ, kâ, kâ, koṹ'liņ! Nachahmung des Geschreis eines Vogels (= eine Art Möwe?), der danach *kâkoṹliņč* heisst. *kâkoṹliņi tâ brẹc: kâ, kâ, kâ, koṹ'liņ!* '... schreien so ...'

koûcet 'heulen; brausen, sausen'. Der Wind, der Sturm *kauc* 'heult'. *ka suņi sâk koûcet, ta tas nau uz lab* 'wenn Hunde zu heulen anfangen, bedeutet das nichts Gutes'. *teṷ jo tiẽ vãǵi tĩri koûc* 'dein Wagen heult geradezu'. *jũr koûc, ka i tâc mež vẽš rudeni* 'das Meer braust, wenn es im Herbst so vom Walde her weht' (d. h. der Wind von der Küste ins Meer bläst).

kič! Interj., mit der man Schafe scheucht. *kič ganas, kič!* 'kietsch zur Weide, kietsch!'

kla! Interj. zur Nachahmung des Schwanengesangs, s. *klaŋkšinat*

klabet 'klappern'. Der Wagen, die Zähne *klab* 'klappern'. *es i ʒir̃deš, ka viņam* (= zirgam) *klab zuôbi iêkš tuõ pãrtik* 'ich habe gehört, dass ihm (= dem Pferde) beim Fressen Zähne klappern'

klabinat 'klappern lassen'. Der Wind *klabina* die Tür, die Fensterladen. Der Storch *klabina*.

klaʒinat 'gackeln, gackern, kakeln'. *gaîls jo klaʒina a, ka viņ kâc nuôbaîd* 'der Hahn gackert ja auch, wenn einer ihn erschreckt'

klak! Interj., mit der man Hühner und Kücken ruft und die hervorgebracht wird, indem man rasch mit der Zunge den Gaumen berührt

klakšinat 'mit der Zunge schnalzen'. *mazs cãḷs klakšina* 'kleine Kücken werden schnalzend gerufen'. *gaîls ka soûc viscs, ta ari klakšina* 'wenn der Hahn Hühner ruft, so schnalzt er auch'

klaŋkš eine Art Schelle. *tâdi klaŋkši bi, kuô liêk zir̃gam kakla* 'es gab so eine Art Schellen, die dem Pferde um den Hals gehängt wurden' *klaŋkšinat* 'schellende Töne von sich geben od. schallen lassen' *gulbi tâ klaŋkšina kla! kla! kla! ka muzikañti iĕt pa gaîs tâ spēledams* 'die Schwäne singen so kla! kla! kla! ziehen wie Musikanten so spielend in der Höhe'

kloûzet 'klopfen, klappern, poltern'. Dreschflegel, Absätze, Wagen *kloûz kloûzinat* 'klopfen', z. B. an der Tür

klizinat 'im Wagen langsam fahren, wobei es klappert'. *es a seu vęc zir̃g tã·pat lę̃nam tik klizina uz mã̧i̧* 'ich schleppe mich [im Wagen] so langsam klappernd mit meinem alten Klepper nach Hause'

kliêkt 'schreien', vgl. *oûret*

klīr klẹ̃r (od. *klã̃r*!) Interj., das Geschrei der Kraniche nachahmend

klukšet 'glucken'. *ka viņč* (= vista) *viên laik dêi, ta grib peret akal, ta klukš tikai klukt! klukt!* 'wenn es (= das Huhn) eine Zeitlang Eier gelegt hat, so will es wieder brüten, so gluckt es nur: klukt! klukt!'

klukt! Interj. zur Nachahmung des Gluckens der Henne

kluŋkšet 'glucksen, klunkern'. Der Bauch *klunkš* 'klunkert'. *viņi paliêk vañckuḷas un kluŋ̂kš* 'sie (= Eier) werden Windeier und glucksen'

kluŋ̂kt! Interj. zur Bezeichnung des Glucksens

knakšet 'knacken'

knakt! Interj. zur Nachahmung des Geräusches, das bei einem kurzen Aufschlag entsteht

knikšet 'knacken'

knikt! gleichbedeutend mit *knakt!*

kniŭkšet 'knacken'. *viņi* (= gnīdas) *ir zîvi, kniŭkš viên, ka koû* 'sie (= Nissen) sind lebend, es knackt nur so, wenn sie zerdrückt werden'

kniŭkt! gleichbedeutend mit *knikt!* Durch *knakt, knikt, kniŭkt* nachgeahmtes Geräusch wird mit den drei sprachlichen Formen in seiner Höhe nuanciert. Mit *kniŭkt* z. B. kann man nicht brechen, sondern nur schlagen, während bei *knakt* und *knikt* kein Unterschied in der Beziehung besteht.

knokšet 'knacken'. *ka iĕt pa gaîs* [slokas], *ta knokš ari* 'wenn [Schnepfen] fliegen, so knackt es auch'

knokšinat 'knacken machen'. *viņč* (= dzenis) *tur a tuô knãb knokšina* 'er (= der Specht) knopft (knackend) dort mit seinem Schnabel'

knukšet 'schnucken'. *knukš ka vęc vist, roûstas un žẹgojas* 'man schnuckt wie ein altes Huhn, wenn man Schlucken hat'. Ein Kind *knukš*, bevor das Weinen losgeht.

ko! ko! Interj. zur Bezeichnung der Töne, die ein Birkhuhn von sich gibt. *tiĕ mãtiši iĕt tâ: ko! ko! ko!* 'die Weibchen gehen so (d. h. geben solche Töne von sich): ko! ko! ko!'

kokš! Zuruf zu den Kühen. *kokš, Kruõnit, kokš!* 'komm, Krone (= Kuhname), komm!'

kokšinat 'Kühe rufen od. begütigen, wobei man *kokš* sagt'. *agrak ganiṇ gar ežmalim, mãtiši nuômîz un soûc: kokš! ciš! ciš! un guôvi nãc un krimt ka traki mẹll zem* 'früher wurde an den Feldrainen gehütet, die Weiber pinkelten dort und riefen koksch! tschisch! tschisch! und Kühe kamen und nagten wie versessen, bis der Boden schwarz wurde'.

kořkšet 'quaken, quarren'. *luk, ka kořkš koñn, tas ir uz liêt. viṇč tâ milzigi kořkš ari, tâli var ziřdet* 'sieh, wenn der Frosch quakt, so gibt's Regen; er quarrt auch so gewaltig, man kann weit hören'. *bi beîkc, un ta tas rîkḷ kořkšeṛ iĺgi vel* 'er war tot, und die Kehle röchelte [ihm] da noch lange'. Ein schlummerndes Huhn, der Bauch kann *kořkšet*.

kra! Interj., welche die Kräh- od. Rabenstimme darstellt. *viṇam tâ kra! kra! kra! i tas krakšinašan.* 'ihr (=einer Krähe) Krächzen ist so krah! krah! krah!'

krakšinat 'krächzen'

krâcet (krâkt) 'schnarchen'. *iêgãš tani gulta un uz'reĩz krâceš un beîkc* 'man hat sich ins Bett gelegt und sofort geröchelt und ist gestorben'. Das Meer, der Sturm *krãc* 'braust'.

krakšet 'krachen', s. *briũkšet*

krakt! Interj., die den Schall des Brechens od. Zerbrechens nachahmt. *drusciṇ paloûz, un šis krakt! nuôst* 'man brach ein wenig, und so krach! war das Stück ab'

krapt! 'happ' Interj. zur Bezeichnung eines plötzlichen Greifens od. Angriffs. *ta viṇč* (=vilks) *lũreš, ka ziřks ệd, un uz'reĩz krapt! piê rîkḷ ciêt* 'so hat er (=der Wolf) gelauert, wo das Pferd frisst, und im Nu happ! es an der Kehle gepackt'

krekšet 'hüsteln, sich räuspern'. *cic joû krekš tik tâli, ka asins spḷoũd âra* 'mancher hüstelt ja so lange, bis er Blut herausspuckt'

ku'dî! Interj. zur Verstärkung od. Hervorhebung eines Begriffs, hauptsächlich der Länge, Höhe und Weite. *viṇč i plac ku'dî!* 'er ist ungemein breit'

kuĩ'lit! Nachahmung der Stimme eines Meervogels, der danach auch *kuilis* genannt wird. *uz tâd muõd viṇi brệc ari: ta viṇi iẽt pa gaîs kuĩ'lit! kuĩ'lit! ka bûs as ziẽmelvẽš* 'auf solche Weise schreien sie auch: so schreien sie in der Höhe kuilit! kuilit!, wenn scharfer Nordwind zu erwarten ist'

kukũ! der Ruf des Kuckucks

kukat 'rufen (vom Kuckuck)'

kuɲkstet 'stöhnen, ächzen, wimmern'

kuš! Interj. mit der Bedeutung 'still! ruhig!' *kuš! kuš! kas tas bi.* 'still! still! was war das'

kušinat 'zum Schweigen bringen, beruhigen (gewöhnlich ein Kind, einen Säugling)'

ķệûkšet 'wie eine Dohle schreien'. *vãlozs ka sviĺp viên sviĺpejat, ta ẹsat smuks laĩks, bet, ka viņi sâk tâ kaķ muõda ķęûkšet, ta neęsat labi* 'wenn Pirole nur so pfeifen, so sei das Wetter schön, wenn sie aber so auf Katzenweise zu schreien (*ķęûkšet*) anfangen, so sei es nicht gut'

ķęûkšinat, Iterativum zu *ķęûkšet. tiē kuõvãrniņi ķęûkšina* 'die Dohlen *ķęûkšina* schreien auf ihre Art'

ķika! ķika! Interj. zur Nachahmung der Stimme der Bekassine. *viņč tâ juõcigi brę̂c, pavasar tâ iēt ķika! ķika!* 'sie schreit so drollig, im Frühling macht so *ķika ķika*'

lor̂kšet 'sprechen' (sehr verächtlich)

lor̂kšet 'laut durcheinander sprechen'. *viņi tur loȓkšeį̃ vis nakt* 'sie schwatzten dort laut die ganze Nacht'

Aus den zwei obigen Beispielen ist zu ersehen, dass die verschiedene Bedeutung einer Form oft durch die Intonation ausgedrückt wird; desgl. weiter *lęȓkšet – lęȓkšet; ploȓkšet – ploȓkšet* u. a.

luk, luku! 'sieh, schau!' (< *lũkojies!*). *męๅlaล̂kšņi derigaki, tiē luk oûg gar teîčim, var baๅķs cir̂st un dēๅs zãģet* 'Schwarzerlen sind mehr nutzbar, sie wachsen, pass mal auf! an den Morasten, man kann sie als Rundhölzer fällen und Bretter daraus schneiden'. *cic akmenc tik nebriēsmig liēls, luku tur˙pat piê Lagast* 'mancher Stein ist so ungeheuer gross, weisst du! dort bei Gesinde Lagasti'.

luȓkš! das Kollern des Birkhahns. *teters ka taĩs tuõ luȓkš, ta viņam laĩkam aci ciêt* 'wenn der Birkhahn kollert, so hat er wahrscheinlich die Augen zu'

lęȓkšet 'viel unsinnig sprechen'

lęȓkšet 'plärren, kläffen, laut lärmen'. *suņi ka satiêkas, ta pleîšas, tũ˙litas nagas, ņęm ka lęȓkš viên* 'wenn Hunde sich treffen, so raufen sie sich, liegen sich sofort in den Haaren, dass es nur so plärrt'

lęr, lęr̂, lęr̂! Nachahmung des Gelärms, das sich erhebt, wenn Hunde od. Kinder sich raufen

ļira ļęra! Interj. zur Bezeichnung eines lauten Durcheinanders. *ję̃ri danca un lęc, brę̂c ļira ļęra! iēt pa ciniš galim tik lustigi ka baîl* 'die Lämmer springen und hüpfen, schreien *ļira ļęra!* tollen von Hümpel auf Hümpel so übermässig lustig'

ļir̂kšet 'laut lachen' (verächtlich), 'grinsen'. *piêgrûž viênc uõtram pe sãnim un ta tig ļir̂kš* 'man stösst einander an die Seite, und dann feixt man nur'

moũret 'muhen, brüllen'. *cic moũre, cic boûre* 'mancher muht, mancher brüllt'

moût 'muhen, brüllen'

mę̃! Nachahmung der Schafsstimme; *aîtiņč sak mę̃! vai ari bę̃!* 'das Schäfchen sagt *mäh!* oder auch *bäh!*'

mę̃ι̃, Dim. *mę̃jiņč* das Schaf (Schäfchen) in der Ammensprache *mẽkš* Bezeichnung für das Blöken von Schafen und Ziegen. *tuô mẽkš viņi* (=pērkoņkazas) *istais a spârnim* 'das Blöken machen sie (=Bekassinen) mit Flügeln'

mũ! Interj. zur Nachahmung des Rindergebrülls. *guôsniņč sak mũ!* 'das Kühlein sagt muh!'

mũjiņč die Kuh in der Ammensprache

na˙ču! (<*nãc šurpu!*) 'komm her!'

noũž ‖ *nũž!* Interj. zur Beruhigung der Kühe. *noũž eîd! noũž eîd!* (auch: *nũž ẽd!*) 'friss Kuh! friss Kuh!'

nũž, Subst. 'die Kuh' (in der Ammensprache)

na! ‖ *nẹ!* ‖ *nu!* ‖ *nû!* Interjektionen, mit denen man Pferde antreibt, *na, nẹ* und *nu* werden unterschiedlos gebraucht, während *nû* schon Ungeduld od. sogar Zorn in sich enthält.

ņẽrkšet 'im Zorn od. Hass knurren'. *suņi plêšas un ņẽrkš* 'Hunde raufen sich und knurren'. Kinder *ņẽrkš*, wenn sie ihre Unzufriedenheit äussern und weinerlich sind.

ņẹũ! Interj., die das Miauen der Katze nachahmt

ņẹũdet und *ņẹũkšet* 'miauen'. *nãk tiê svešaji kaķi un ta ņẹũd pa naktim* '[da] kommen die fremden Katzen und miauen während der Nächte'

ņẹũkš ein dem Katzenschrei ähnliches Geschrei

ņiũkšet zornige Laute von sich geben (von Pferden), vgl. *iũkšet. ta joũ lẽrums ir ari, ka tiêk kuõpa, ta ņiũkš, tad nau zviêkšan vaî* 'wenn Pferde sich treffen, so entsteht ein Tumult, sie *ņiukš* so, da gibt's kein Wiehern mehr'

ņorkšet 'knurren' od. 'weinen' (von Tierjungen, z. B. von Ferkeln). *cũk iľgi ņorkš* [ja nepareizi kauj] 'das Schwein knurrt lange [wenn es nicht richtig geschlachtet wird]'

ņurdet 'knurren'. *viņč i dumš suñc, viņč ņurd uz mãį ciľvek* 'er ist ein dummer Hund, er knurrt auf Hausgenossen'

ņurkšet 'knurren', vgl. *ņorkšet*

iêņurkšetas 'einen knurrenden Laut von sich geben'. *cic cũk, ka ʒird, ka sivenc iêņurkšas, tũˑlit lẹc oũkša* 'manche Sau fährt sofort auf, sobald sie hört, dass das Ferkel knurrt'

paˑšvukt! paˑžvukt! Interj. zur Darstellung eines plötzlichen Verschwindens. *siêu paˑšvukt! pazuds* 'husch! sei das Weib verschwunden'

pẽˑ! 'pfui, bäh!'

pẽk! Interj. für das Entengeschnatter

pẽkšet 'schnabbern'

pẽkšet 'wie eine Kinderschnarre plärren'

pẽkš 'eine Art kleine Pfeife (Schnarre), die im Frühjahr aus Roggenhalmen od. später aus einer nicht ausgereiften Schote verfertigt wird und einen plärrenden Ton gibt'

pi! Interj. zum Aufhetzen der Hunde, vgl. *cui! puc(s)!*

pìkšet 'pfeifen (wie eine Maus)'

piŋkš 'Greiner, Flenner, Tränenbeutel, ein Weinerlicher'

piŋkšet 'laut weinen, flennen' (mit verächtlicher Färbung). *kapec teu̯ ta viê·nâd vajag piŋkšet?* 'wozu brauchst du immer so zu flennen?'

piûkšet 'piep(s)en'. *cãḷi piûkš!* 'die Kücken piep(s)en'. *viên piûkšešan viṇim ir, bet es nevar aku·rãt isteîkt, kâ* 'sie (= gewisse Vögel) piepen auf eine Weise, aber ich kann nicht gerade sagen, wie'

piũkš '(wahrscheinlich) der Regenpfeifer'

plaȓkšet 'schnarren', vgl. *stiȓkšet. ve̦l̂k pêc tuô oûdekḷ un ta viṇč nãk ka plaȓkš viên* 'man zieht an der Leinwand, und da kommt sie [vom Webstuhl], dass es nur so schnarrt'

ploûkšet 'einen klatschenden, laut schallenden Ton von sich geben'. *cũki êd jũrs sûds, ka ploûkšei̯ viên* 'Schweine frassen den Seetang, dass es nur so klatschte!' *guôvim ve̦dari sprâg tâ ka ploûkšei̯ viên puš* 'die Bäuche der Kühe platzten, dass es nur so klatschte'. Man kann schwimmen, dass es nur so klatscht (*ploûkš*)

ploûkšinat '(in die Hände) klatschen'. *un vĩri sâk skriêt un ploûkšinat ruôks* 'und Männer fingen an zu laufen und in die Hände zu klatschen'

plaûkt! Interj. zur Bezeichnung eines klatschenden Schalles. Man fällt zu Boden *plaukt!*

plĩkšet 'einen plätschernden Laut von sich geben; unnötig viel sprechen'. *liêts lĩst, ka plĩkš viên* 'es regnet plätschernd'. *kuô tu plĩkš tik dou̯ʒ* 'was schwatzst du so viel!'

pliŋkšinat 'klimpern'

pliũkšinat 'einen klatschenden Schall erzeugen z. B. mit einer Peitsche'

pliũkt! oft auch in Verbindung *pliũkt! ploûkt!* Nachahmung eines klatschenden Schalles, der beim Schlagen mit einem flachen Gegenstand z. B. mit flacher Hand, einem Riemen, Brett od. aber auch mit einer Peitsche entsteht. *a plân dêlit lik pliũkt! pa ve̦dar* [zirgam] 'mit einem dünnen Brett schlug man pliukt! [dem Pferde] gegen den Bauch'

ploct! Interj. zur Bezeichnung eines weichen Falles. *viṇč joû pa-iêt, pa-iêt — ploct! zeme* 'es (=ein Kind, das zu gehen anfängt) geht ein wenig — dann plotzt! zu Boden'

ploȓkšet 'viel schwatzen, plappern'. *pul̂k aplam runa un ploȓkš, kur nevajag* 'man spricht viel unsinnig und plappert unangebracht'

ploȓkšet wie oben und ein Schallverb, das das Geräusch beim Schlürfen einer Flüssigkeit bezeichnet, z. B. *streb, ka ploȓkš viên* 'man schlürft, dass es nur so *plorkš* geht'

ploȓzat 'unaufhörlich leeres Stroh dreschen'

plukt! Interj. zur Bezeichnung des Zergehens. *nuôpuvuši miêḷas ... baȋti miêḷi — ka viṇ piêņ̣ęm, viṇč iziêt plukt!* '[die Kartoffeln] sind ganz verfault ... wie weisser Bodensatz — rührt man sie an, so zergehen sie plukt!'

pluŋkšet 'plätschern' *kas tur pluŋkš iêkš tuõ ûdenc spain, laȋkam koñn i iêlecs iêkša* 'was plätschert dort im Eimer im Wasser? wahrscheinlich ist ein Frosch hineingehüpft'

pluŋkt! od. *pḷuŋkt!* Interj. zur Bezeichnung des Schalles, der beim Fallen eines Gegenstandes ins Wasser entsteht

pḷękš 'die Plappertasche' und eine Art Wetzstein. *tas i gan pḷękš ciȋveks, doũȥ pḷãpa un runa aplam* 'er ist wohl ein geschwätziger Mensch, er plappert und redet viel Unnötiges'. *tuõs strȋ̧ks soûc pḷękši, gãi̧ pḷik! pḷęk!* 'diese Wetzsteine (zum Wetzen der Sensen) wurden *pḷękš* genannt, sie gaben den Laut *pḷik! pḷęk!*'

pḷękšet 'einen klatschernden Laut von sich geben' z. B. wenn man durch Schmutz, Kot watet oder etwas Breiartiges zu Boden fällt; leeres Zeug schwatzen, plappern. *aplam pḷãpat, tas i pḷękšet* 'albern plappern d. h. *pḷękšet*'. *pḷękš, ka slapš krękḷs gar diȓs* 'man *pḷękš* wie ein nasses Hemd am Arsch'

pḷękšinat 'einen klatschernden Laut machen'. *viṇč* (=melnis) *tâ klusam pḷękšinajat* 'er (=der Auerhahn) singe (*pḷękšina*) so leise'

pḷękt! Interj. zur Bezeichnung des Schalles, der beim Fallen eines weichen od. schweren Gegenstandes entsteht, z. B. einer Schüssel mit Brei od. von etwas Breiartigem allein

pḷę̂r! Interj. zur Nachahmung eines schnarrenden Lautes. *tiẽ griêȥṇi pḷę̂r! pḷę̂r tâ viên sit* 'die Schnarrwachteln schlagen nur so pljähr, pljähr!'

pḷę̂rkšet 'schlabbern, quatschen'

pḷę̂rkšet 'plärrend schallen' wie z. B. eine spielzeugartige „Windmühle", mit der man Maulwürfe zu verscheuchen glaubt

pḷę̂rzat 'dummes Zeug reden', vgl. *ploȓzat*

pḷik! pḷęk! Interj. zur Bezeichnung eines klatschenden Lautes, der entsteht, wenn man z. B. mit flacher Hand gegen die Wange schlägt, s. *pḷękš*

pḷiȓkšinat 'einen schnarrenden Laut machen'. *viṇč tâ pḷiȓkšina uz tuõ muõd ka tas zems vêzs* 'er (=der Ziegenmelker) macht einen *pḷiȓr* auf die Weise eines Erdkrebses'

pḷiȓr! Interj., die einen längeren stimmhaft schnarrenden Schall nachahmt. *leȓps, nakc visc kuô soûc, i tâc pęlaks, ȥęguž liêlum; pa diên maz laȋzas, tâ pḷiȓr iệt un akal tâ pḷęk! pḷęk! laȋzas* 'der Ziegenmelker, der Nachthuhn genannt wird, ist grau [und] von der Grösse eines Kuckucks; am Tage fliegt er wenig, so *pļirr!* gibt er einen Laut von sich und wieder fliegt er so *pļęk pļęk'*. *lakstigals uscēlas piŕmaš un dabuš viŝ ʒiêsm̨s ruôka, bet leŕps, ka guôvi iēt âra un miêz un diŕs pļiŕr! pļęk! pļęk!* 'die Nachtigall sei zuerst aufgestanden und habe alle Lieder beisammen bekommen, aber der Ziegenmelker — erst wenn die Kühe zur Weide getrieben werden und pissen und scheissen *pļiŕr! pļęk! pļęk!'* (aus dem Volksmärchen von der Wette beider genannten Vögel)

pļoŕrat 'viel und schnell sprechen' (verächtlich)

pļoŕzat wie oben und vgl. *pļęŕzat, ploŕzat*

pļuŕkt! Interj., die gebraucht wird, wenn etwas misslingt

pokšet 'leise und weich schallen wie z.B. wenn man gegen ein Kissen schlägt'. *izrak deviņ as ʒiļ* [aku], *un nebi ûdenc, bet, ka nâc tâc ʒiļaks, viêna viêta sâk pokšet* 'ein neun Faden tiefer [Brunnen] wurde gegraben, und es gab kein Wasser, aber als er noch tiefer wurde, so begann es an einer Stelle zu brodeln (*pokšet*)'

poŕkšet 'schwatzen'. *poŕkš ŕita, poŕkš vakara* 'man schwatzt am Morgen, man schwatzt am Abend'

ptrū! Interj., die das Pferd zum Stehen bringt

ptru! Interj., mit der man Kälber ruft

ptruš || ptruž, Dim. *ptružiņč* 'ein Kalb, Kälbchen'

puc(s)! Interj. zum Fort- od. Aufhetzen von Hunden auf jemand, vgl. *cui!* und *pi!*

pucinat 'einen Hund fort-, aufhetzen'

ribet 'dröhnen'; die Erde, der Wagen, der Donner dröhnen (*rib*). Vgl. *dimdet*

rokšet || rukšet 'grunzen', *rokšeį ka vęsals cũk* 'es grunzte wie ein gesundes Schwein'

rubinat 'kollern, falzen' (von Birkhähnen). *tiẽ i tiẽ gaîļi, kas rubina, ascs iz'laîduši tâ ka tītari* 'das sind Hähne, die kollern, die Sterze wie Puter ein Rad schlagend'

rûcet (rûkt) 'brausen; brüllen; kollern; donnern; brummen, knurren'. der Donner, der Bauch, der Hund, der Löwe, die Mühle, das Spinnrad, der Birkhahn *rûc. Bobs rûc uz kaķ* 'Bobis (=Hundename) knurrt auf die Katze'. *eî paskates, kas tur rûc!* 'geh und schau nach, was da knurrt!' *vęcaš jo rûceį gan* 'der Alte brummte ja' (scheltend)

sę! || sę̂! Interj. zum Vertreiben eines Hundes; mit ˆ, wenn man mit Nachdruck und schon erzürnt, den Hund beschwichtigen will. *Bobi, sę maîz!* 'Bobi, ruhig, da hast du Brot!'

si! si! Lockruf für Hunde

sisinat 'Hunde heranrufen'; 'zirpen' — der Grashüpfer zirpt (*sisina*).

skañdinat (auch *skañdinat*) 'erschallen lassen, klingeln; oft nennen', *a tru-meļim un paññim skañdinaį* 'man schlug Teekesseln und Pfannen'

skanet 'tönen, klingen, schallen'. *puĺkstenc nu skan un skan* 'die Glocke klingt ununterbrochen'

sliȓkšet 'rasselnd schallen'. *grâbleķs tâ veĺkas, ka sliȓkš viên* 'die Harke schleift (am Boden über gewisse Ranken), dass es nur so *slirkš*'

sliȓkt un sloȓkt ‖ *slaȓkt!* Interj., die den Laut nachahmt, der beim Entzweireissen von etwas, z. B. von Stoff, entsteht

sproũšļat 'schnauben'

spuȓkšet 'schwirren'; Vögel *spurkš* 'schwirren'

spuȓkt! Interj. zur Bezeichnung des Schwirrens, des schnellen Auffliegens

stenet 'stöhnen'. *man vęcaš jo vaĩrak ne˙kuô ka sten un vaĩd* 'mein Alter [kann] ja nichts mehr als stöhnen und ächzen'

stiȓkšet ein Schallverb zur Nachahmung des Lautes, der beim Reissen von Stoff entsteht, auch beim Mähen von trockenen Pflanzen od. beim Harken über beranktem Boden. *pļūti ka stiȓkš* 'man hat den Durchfall, dass es *stirkš*'.

šmurkšet ein Schallverb, das die Geschwindigkeit einer Bewegung bezeichnet, wobei das Geräusch *šmurkš* zu hören od. zu vermuten ist. *siveni skriên ka šmurkš* 'die Ferkel laufen, dass es *šmurkš*'

šmuȓkš die Schnurre, ein aus dem Schienbein des Schweines und einer Schnur verfertigtes Spielzeug; das Geräusch, das ein rollender od. kreisender Körper erzeugt; der Lärm beim Auffliegen von Vögeln

šņikt! šņakt! šņękt! Interj. zur Bezeichnung des Geräusches, das beim Schneiden entsteht

šņiȓkt! šņęȓkt! wie oben. Der Unterschied zwischen den Formen ohne *r* und mit *r* besteht darin, dass diese das Schneiden z. B. mit einer Schere darstellen, während jene das Schneiden mit einem Messer nachahmen

sviȓkšet 'schwirren'. *dęg ka sviȓkš viên* 'es brennt schwirrend'

sviȓkt (auch *sviȓkt*)! Interj. zur Bezeichnung eines schnellen schwirrenden Schalls. *veči paņēm un râu gar bikšdiȓs oûkša — sviȓkt!* 'die Alten nahmen [Streichhölzer] und zogen sie am Hosenspiegel entlang — schwirkt!' (erzählt wird von den alten Streichhölzern wie sie es früher gab)

ti! ti! Interj., mit der man Hühner ruft

tikšet 'ticken' (von einer Uhr)

tiŋkšet 'klirren'

tiŋkšinat 'klimpern'

tiȓkšet 'rasseln, klirren' (von einer Weckuhr)

tiȓkšinat '*tiȓkšet* machen'

tiš! Interj. zum Wegscheuchen und Eintreiben von Hühnern. *tiš! uz Vãc-*

zem! 'tisch! nach Deutschland!' (sagt man zu Grillen-Heimchen, wenn man sie bei einer Vernichtungsaktion loswerden will)

tišinat 'mit einem *tiš!* Hühner scheuchen'

tutũ! Interj., die bezeichnet, dass etwas verschwunden und nicht mehr da ist (gewöhnlich in der Ammen- und Kindersprache)

û-u! Interj., die das Gurren einer Taube nachahmt. *viêni akal ir tâdi zili pęlaki; tiẽ iẽt: û-u! û-u!* 'die einen sind so blaugrau; sie geben so einen Laut uh-u! uh-u! von sich'

ũũ! Interj. zur Bezeichnung eines rufenden Schreies

ujinat 'rufend schreien'

uřkšet 'knurren und murren'. *cŭkim a jânęs ę̂st, tiẽ jo tâ uřkšeį* 'man muss ja die Schweine füttern, sie haben schon so geknurrt'. *tas vęcaš gan i nejoûks cîlveks, viņč tok coŭr diên uřkš uõtram riņķi* 'der Alte ist ja ein garstiger Mensch, den Tag hindruch brummt er einem auf'

uřkšinat Iterativ zu *uřkšet. tas mašiņč uřkšinaį coŭr ziêm* 'die (Dresch)-maschine surrte den ganzen Winter hindurch'

uřkš knurrendes, murrendes Geräusch od. ein Tumult solcher Art. *uřkš taĩsit* 'einen Tumult erheben'

uš! ‖ *ûš!* Interj., mit der man Schweine vertreibt. *uš bŭda, uš! uš! ganas! uš mâja!* 'usch in den Verschlag, usch! usch zur Weide! usch nach Hause!'

vaĩ! vaĩ! vài! 'wehe! ach!' Laut jammernd ruft man *vaĩ!*, man stöhnt und ächzt *vaî*, beim plötzlichen Schmerz od. bei Verwunderung und Überraschung ruft man aus *vài!*

vaĩdet 'stöhnen, ächzen'. *sten un vaĩd* 'man stöhnt und ächzt'

vaĩmanat 'jammern'

voû! Interj., Nachahmung des Hundegebells

voûkšet '(ohne Grund) bellen'

vę̂č! Interj. zur Bezeichnung eines plärrenden Lautes. *agrak pavasaras bi tâdi zems vêži, ʒîřdeį brękt vę̂č! vę̂č! apuž zem* 'früher gab es im Frühling eine Art Erdkrebse, man hörte sie unter der Erde schreien wätsch! wätsch!'

vęûkšet 'blärren, plärren'. *viņč* (=lapsa) *reį tâ ka sunc — tâ vęûkš, tikai smaļkak* 'er (=der Fuchs) bellt so wie ein Hund, plärrt so, aber dünner!'

viņ̃ķ! Interj. die Stimme des Finks nachahmend. *viņ̃ķiši a raîbim spârnim tâ iẽt: viņ̃ķ! viņ̃ķ!* 'Finke haben bunte Flügel, sie schreien so: *viņķ, viņķ!*'

vořkšet 'quaken, quarren'. *krupem nau kuřkuļi, tas tik vořkš tâˑpatas un lęc; viņč tâ bļoû, tâ vořkš* 'die Kröte hat keinen Froschlaich, sie quarrt einfach so und hüpft, sie schreit so, quakt so!'

vořkšet 'einen quiekend quarrenden Lärm machen, z. B. Schweine, wenn sie ihre Unzufriedenheit äussern, Kinder und auch Erwachsene laut durcheinander sprechend *zlakšet* 'dumpf schallen'

zlakt! Interj. den Schall eines kurzen Schlages nachahmend

zloŭkšet ein Schallverb, das den Lärm beim Fallen der Gegenstände od. des Schlagens darstellt; z. B. kann man die Tür zuschlagen, dass sie slauksch *zloŭkt!* Interj., die beim Fallen od. Schlagen gebraucht wird; man fällt zu Boden *zloŭkt!*

zliŭkšet ist gleich *zloŭkšet*

zliŭkt ist gleich *zloŭkt*, oft in Verbindung *zliŭkt un zloŭkt* gebraucht

zliŭkt Interj., die den Schall eines kurzen Schlages bezeichnet

zloĭkt gleicht *zloŭkt* od. *zliŭkt. zloĭkt! zloĭkt! sit ka nelabaš 'zloikt! zloikt!* schlägt man wie der Böse selbst'

zviêkt 'wiehern'. *êrzeļi viê zviêz ka broŭc* 'Hengste allein wiehern beim Fahren'. *zviêz viêna zviêkšana* 'man lacht ununterbrochen' (sehr verächtlich)

žaʒinat 'schreien' (von der Elster). *ka žagat žaʒinajat, ta tas ȩsat uz pasakim vaî joŭnim ziņim* 'wenn die Elster schreit, so bedeutet es Klatsch od. Neuigkeiten'

žip! Interj., mit der man zu einer Bewegung auffordert od. eine blitzschnelle Bewegung bezeichnet. *cic* [zirgs] *joŭ nu i briẽsmig ãtŗs! žip! uz·reĩz* 'manches [Pferd] ist ja schrecklich flink, *žip!* (fängt es) augenblicklich (an zu ziehen, gehen)'

žņikt! Interj. zur Bezeichnung eines blitzschnellen Schlages. *ta tik a viên kã̦ žņikt! uz·reĩz pa sãn iêgâz* 'so gab man auf einmal *žņikt!* einen Fusstritt an die Seite'

žvaʒet 'klappern, klirren'. Ketten, Waffen, Geld klirren (*žvaʒ*)

žvaʒinat Kausativ zu *žvaʒet. iêliêk puõgs topsita un ta duô* [bērnam], *laî žvaʒina* 'man wirft Knöpfe in eine Büchse und gibt sie dann [dem Kinde], damit es ein Geklirr macht'. *žagac jo žvaʒina uz joŭnim ziņim* 'die Elster *žvaʒina* 'berichten' ja Neuigkeiten'

žvãkšet 'dumpf rauschen'. *liêts nak ka žvãkš viên* 'es regnet so rauschend'. Das Korn rieselt und *žvãkš*.

žvãks dumpfes Geräusch, das entsteht, wenn z. B. das Korn massenweise rieselt od. Wasser über eine Schleuse stürzt. *ka laîzas* [mednis], *ta i tâc truôksņc, žvãkš* 'wenn [der Auerhahn] fliegt, so entsteht so ein Geräusch, ein *žvãkš*'

žvãkt! Interj., die das Geräusch *žvãkš* darstellt

žvaŋkstet 'dumpf klirrend schallen'. *viņč sâceš brȩ̂kt, un noŭd kasc žvaŋkstedams aîzgãš zeme iekša* 'er habe angefangen zu schreien, und die Geldkiste sei klirrend in den Boden versunken'

žvoŭkt! Interj. zur Bezeichnung einer schnellen mit einem gewissen Schall

verbundenen Bewegung. *asc griẽžas žvoũkt nuô viên pus uz uõtŗ* 'der Schwanz
dreht sich *žvoũkt!* von einer Seite auf die andere!'

žvikt un žvakt! Interj., die eine schnelle Tätigkeit darstellt.

Nebenbei sei noch bemerkt, dass die Anzahl solcher Schallwörter verächtlichen Sinnes, die sich auf verwerfliches Sprechen beziehen, prozentual
auffallend hoch ist, was einerseits von der durch aus negativen Einstellung
des Volkes gegenüber dem nichtsnutzigen Gebrauch des Mundwerks zeugt,
andererseits aber beweist, dass diese Unart trotzdem verbreitet ist.

Anmerkung

1. Die mundartlichen Verschiedenheiten auf diesem Gebiet des Wortschatzes sind
gross, vgl. die vorkommenden Ausdrücke in der nordkurländischen Mundart von Stende
in K. Draviņš & V. Rūķe, *Interjektionen und Onomatopöie in der Mundart von Stenden*,
Lund, 1962.

Interjections and Onomatopoeic words in the Latvian Dialect of Svetciems

Primary material gathered by the author in his native dialect is presented
in alphabetical order.

J. B. RUDNYĆKYJ

Lithuanian žąsìs — Ukrainian dzuś

Unlike the laryngeal problem, the question of development of Indo-European *k̑*, *ǵ*-phonemes into *kentum* and *satem*-types remains indisputable in comparative and historical linguistics. Even Tokharian (and, perhaps, Hittite) discovered as belonging to *kentum*-languages, did not change this traditional principle of grouping of Indo-European dialects; the new linguistic discovery eliminated the 'geographical factor from consideration: division of Indo-European languages into "Western" and "Eastern" branches.

It was, however, generally agreed that as far as the Slavic languages are concerned some discrepancies in the regular correspondences are to be found between Slavic and Baltic on the one hand and between Slavic and Indo-Iranian on the other. Although the innovational character of those Slavic "satem-deviations" was assumed, no definite theory of their existence has been so far advanced.

One of the most plausible approaches to this problem belongs to Antoine Meillet. In his book *Les dialectes indoeuropéens* (Paris, 1908; ²1922) he explains the non-satemized phenomena as follows: "In Slavic, when a word has *s* in medial position, the prepalatal through dissimilation, becomes a guttural, e.g. OSl., *gǫsь* in contrast to Lith. *žąsìs*."[1]

This explanation was accepted in later years as one of the "alpha-omegan" teachings of Slavic phonology, and even most recently was repeated with due reverence: George Y. Shevelov in his book *A Prehistory of Slavic*, New York, 1965 formulated Meillet's viewpoint as follows:

"The theory which may be termed of a prohibitive dissimilation seems quite plausible: when spirants *s* or *z* occurred in the same root (or word), by virtue of a dissimilation *k̑*, *ǵ*, would lose their palatalization and yield *k*, *g*, instead of changing into *s*, *z*" (p. 144).

Both Meillet and his followers disregard the possibility of archaic character of both phonemes, namely, the original non-palatal *k*, *g*. Yet, in view of some recent reconstructions of the primitive Indo-European consonant inventory,[2] no presence of the palatal gutturals in the early development of Indo-European is admitted. In other words, the original state of things in cases of Slavic *centum*-forms is theoretically possible. Thus Proto-Slavic *gǫsь despite Lith. žąsìs could be considered as a form lacking palatalization due to the following sibilant *s*. This eventuality has not been taken into consideration either by Meillet or by his followers. Dispalatalization as a restitutive innovation not an archaic retention of *k, g*, in Slavic was a dominant opinion for decades without any linguistic motivation and denial of the other possibility.

In the whole problem one feature has remained unnoticed by scholars. This feature helps us to come closer to the solution of the above question.

According to the linguistic evidence all the Slavic languages have *gǫsь*, however, the Indo-European **ǵhaṇsa- should be reflected not as *gǫsь but as *zǫsь like *zolto — German *Gold*, etc. And here an unnoticed word escaped the attention of comparatists, namely, Ukrainian *dzuś* dialectally known also as *džuś, dzus*, etc., with its basic meaning of an interjection to chase animals or people. Roman Smal'-Stočkyj in his exhaustive work *Prymityvnyj slovotvir*, Warsaw, 1929 mentions this interjection along with *džus* and declares it to be "not clear" (p. 155). Categorizing it (without naming any variantization) as an "affective word" Shevelov does not make it clearer either.[2] *Dzuoss* (instead of standard Latvian *zoss* [*zuoss*]) is known also in several Latvian dialects, see K. Mülenbach's *Latviešu valodas vārdnīca*, I, s.v. and J. Endzelīns and E. Hauzenberga, *Papildinājumi un labojumi K. Mülenbacha Latviešu valodas vārdnīcai*, I. s.v.

Meanwhile, there is no doubt that Ukrainian *dzus'* from the original *zuś < *zǫsь with its later variants: *džus*, etc., reflects the Indo-European **ghaṇsis with semantic reference to 'goose'. Narrowed in its meaning to an interjection expressing shooing of geese and (later) the chasing of all animals, this word has been retained in its original Slavic form without change of the initial consonant to *h-* < *g-*. Today it survives as a parallel formation to *hus', huska* from PS *gǫsь.

All the above considerations led me to the conclusion that the hitherto unnoticed Ukrainian *satem*-remnant *dzusь* < *zǫsь should be considered in etymological research and comparative historical linguistics. Consequently, I introduced the following entry in my etymological dictionary:[4]

гусь 'goose', MUk. гус (XVII c.), гусь (XVIII c.), OUk. гоусь (XIII c.), OES. гоуси (XII c.); BRu., Ru. *гусь*, Bu. *гъска*, Ma. *гуска*, SC. *gȕska*, Sln. *gộs*, Cz. *husa*, Slk. *hus*, Po. *gęś*, LoSo. *gus*, UpSo. *hus*, Plb. *gộs*. — Deriv. *гус[ен]я́, гусеня́т[оч]ко, гуса́к, гусачо́к, гу́с[онь]ка, гуся́, гу́сочка, гусівні́к. -ні́цтво, гусні́к, гуся́р, гу́сятина, гуся́тник, -иня, гуся́тка, гуся́чка, гусакóвий, гусі́ний, гу́сій, гу́ся́чий*, interj. *гусъ!, гусю-гусю!, гуш!, гуша́!*- MUk. по гусяти (1590), гусеня́тъ Gpl. (1574), гусакъ (1753), гуси (XVI с.), гуску Asg. (1666), надъ гусятками (1593), гусятникъ (1693), гусиного Gsg. (1752), гусковбю Isg. (XVIII с.), husiatoie (1552), гусяче (XVIII с.), гускоѣдъ (XVI с.), FN. *Гусаковсъкий, Гýска, Гуснай, Гусятин*, MUk. Гусаковъ (1648 Тупиков 528), Гусевъ (1675 Тупиков l. с.), GN. *Гусъ, Гýськово, Гусятин, Гусаковецъ, Гусаково, Гусарка, Гусачевка, Гусачкин, Гýси, Гусина, -пка, Гуснік, Гýска, Гуски.* — Syn. *(гýска:) рід птáхів родúни качáчих*, УРЕ. 3, 536.

PS. *gǫsь* 'ts'; one of the few names of birds to be ascribed to primitive IE. origin, since it recurs in most of the languages of this group, cf. Skt. *hansá-* 'goose', ModPers. *ghaz*, Lith. *žąsìs*, Gk. *xēn*, OHG. *gans*, ModHG. *Gans*, E. *goose*, etc., IE. root **ǵhans-* should have developed into Sl. *zǫsь*; Uk. interj. *дзус[ь]! (< *зусь!*, like *дсленúй < сленúй, дзвін < *zvonъ, дзéркало < зéркало, etc.)* might be considered the only remnant of *zǫsь* which, under the influence of the imitative interj. *ге-ге, [-ге]!*, was changed to *gǫsь*; initial *g-* instead of *z-* in Sl. was previously explained by G. influence. Kluge 105, Trautmann 365, Kiparsky 1, 103, 108, a. o., the more that according to Pliny large flocks of geese were kept in Germania and the birds (or their feathers) were sent even to Rome (Hist. Nat. 10, 53), cf. Kluge, l. c., Vasmer[2] 1, 478, РССтоцький 4, 28, a. o.; some scholars considered *g-* a result of dissimilation of *z-s* in *zǫsь*, cf. Meillet Ét. 178, MSL. 9, 374; 13, 243, a. o.; see also Machek 151 (:**ǵh-before *o >g!*), Sławski 1, 273–274, Moszyński JP. 35, 115–116, Fraenkel 1929, a. o.

гусь! interj. in calling or chasing geese, ModUk. only. — Deriv. *гусю!-гусю!. гýся!. гусь-гусь-гусь!* (Климчук ЛексI Iо. 29). — Syn. *гиль!, гилá!* Derived from гусь, see the preceding entry, РССтоцький 3, 153.

On the basis of the above considerations, the following conclusions may be drawn:

1) The Indo-European word **ghaṇsis* 'goose', despite its "kentumization" in all the Slavic languages, is preserved in its *satem*-form in Ukrainian *dzuš*;

2) This word confirms the general acceptance of the original Slavic, Baltic, etc. change of *k̂-*, *ǵ-* to *satem*-type consonants leaving no doubts as to their changes into sibilants.

Notes

1. Quoted after Meillet's English translation by Samuel N. Rosenberg, *The indo-European Dialects* (Alabama Linguistic and Philological Series No. 15), University of Alabama Press, 1967, 69–70.

2. W. P. Lehman, *Proto-Indoeuropean Phonology*, Austin, 1952, 1–21; 109–114.

3. George Y. Shevelov, "A latent Phoneme in Making: the Affricate *dz* in Slavic". *Miscelanea Homenaje à Andre Martinet I*, Universidad de la Laguna, Canarias, 261.

4. J. B. Rudnyćkyj, *An Etymological Dictionary of the Ukrainian Language*, Winnipeg, VIII, 773–774.

M. RUDZĪTE

Verba *iet* atematiskās formas mūsdienu latviešu izloksnēs

1. Prof. Kr. S. Stangs grāmatā *Das slavische und baltische Verbum*, Oslo, 1942, 99. lpp. raksta: ,,In den modernen balt. Sprachen sind die athem. Verba fast völlig geschwunden. (Spuren finden sich in lett. Formen wie *iemu* : *iet, esmu* und einigen lit. Dialektformen.)''

Pašreizējā literārās valodas un daudzu izlokšņu paradigma — *eju, ej, iet, ejam, ejat,* tāpat izlokšņu *ęsu, esi, ir, ęsam, ęsat* rāda tendenci aizstāt atematisko formu atliekas ar jauninājumiem 1. un 2. personas formā. Lai noskaidrotu, cik plaši minētā tendence ir skārusi latviešu izloksnes, pārlūkoju materiālus, kas Latvijas PSR Zinātņu akadēmijas Valodas un literatūras institūtā un Pētera Stučkas Latvijas Valsts universitātes Latviešu valodas katedrā savākti pēc 1945. gada. Atematiskas formas visbiežāk vēl ir verbiem *iet* un *būt*, retāk jau *dot, ēst,* taču te pievērsīsimies tikai verba *iet* atematisko formu saglabājumam. (Par atematiskām sauksim te atematisko formu atliekas, t. i., formas, kas ir atematiski veidotas, bet parasti ir ar jauninātām personu galotnēm, piem., *eimu, iemu* u. c.)

2. Visnotaļ saglabājusies ir *3. pers. forma — iet.* Tikai dažās dziļo augšzemnieku izloksnēs šai personā sastop jauninājumus, parasti tomēr saglabājot arī *iet > īt. ît || în* ir Mērdzenē, *ît || iņņa || iņļa || id'ļa || îmļa* Nirzā, *ît || îdļa* Makašēnos, Pildā, Zvirgzdenē, *îdļa* Rundēnos. Viļakas *ît* varētu būt radies arī no *îd,* spriežot pēc visas paradigmas — *îdu, îdi, ît, îdam, îdat.*

Tepat der aizrādīt, ka lībiskajās izloksnēs 3. pers. formu lieto abu skaitļu visās personās. Tāmnieku apgabalā un Vidzemes lībiskajās izloksnēs Duntē, Lādē, Liepupē, Nabē, Salacā, Stienē, Svētciemā, Tūjā, Umurgā, Viļķenē un Vitrupē runā *iẽt,* bet Alojā, Rozēnos, Vainižos — *iẽt[2].* Ainažos, Katvaros, Limbažos, Pociemā un Puikulē ir *iẽt || iẽt[2].*

Arī pārejas izloksnēs — Allažos, Bīriņos, Gudeniekos, Lēdurgā, Pabažos, Pūrē, Ropažos, Sējā, Turaidā, Turlavā visās personās mēdz lietot *iẽt,* bet Idū, Ipiķos — *iẽt[2].* Sevišķi visās viensk. personās *iet* var dzirdēt arī citās lībiskā dialekta kaimiņizloksnēs, piem., Mazsalacā, Ozolos, Skaņkalnē, Ternejā, Vecatē.

3. Samērā labi atematiskā forma ir paglābusies *viensk. 1. personā — eimu*

vai *iemu* (dažādos fonētiskos variantos). Ir izloksnes, kur tā joprojām ir tipiskā šās personas forma. Izlokšņu materiālos vienīgi *eĩmu* šai personā ir pierakstīts Apriķos, Embūtē, Gaiķos, Grenčos, Kazdangā, Lažā, Lutriņos, Nīgrandā, Penkulē, Saldū, Skrundā, Strutelē, Vārmā un Zvārdē, *èimu*² — Aizkrauklē, Andrupenē, Barkavā, Bērzpilī, Dricēnos, Lielvārdē, Lubānā, Nautrēnos, Ozolainē, Sakstagalā, Saukā, Stirnienē, Tilžā, Tirzā, Varakļānos, Viļānos, Viskāļos, *eîmu* — Dūrē, Krapē, *eîmu*² — Purmsātos, Siguldā, *eĩmu* — Atašienē, Daudzesē, Liepkalnē, Ogrē, Sēlpilī, *eĩmu* ‖ *ę̃imu* Vārnavā, *ę̃imu* — Bebrenē, *ę̀imu*² — Koknesē, Kurcumā, Raudā, Ritē; *iẽmu* — Dzērbenē, Ērģemē, Jērcēnos, Kārļos, Kauguros, Lugažos, Valkā, Valmierā, Vijciemā, *iému* — Krustpilī; *eĩmu* ‖ *iẽmu* Valgundē, *eĩmu* ‖ *iému* Vecpiebalgā, *iẽmu* ‖ *eĩmu* Īlē; *ĩmu* — Aglonā, Asūnē, Aulejā, Ciblā, Ezerniekos, Jaunlaicenē, Karvā, Kapiņos, Kaunatā, Krāslavā, Maltā, Rēznā, Skaistā, Veclaicenē, *ímu* — Lašos, Pilskalnē.

Tā ir apmēram viena piektdaļa no tām izloksnēm, par kurām šai jautājumā bija iegūtas ziņas (ziņas ir no apm. 400 izloksnēm.)

Blakus kādai jauninātai formai lieto *eimu* resp. *iemu* vēl citās izloksnēs. *eĩmu* ‖ *eju* reģistrēts Gramzdā, Jaunaucē, Rankā, Tāšos, Tumē, Vecpilī, Ziemupē, *eĩmu* ‖ *eĩmu*² ‖ *eju* — Dobelē, Vilcē, *èimu*² ‖ *eju* Dagdā, Mārcienā, *eĩmu* ‖ *eĩmi* ‖ *ęju* ‖ *ęji* Zalvā, *ę̀imu*² ‖ *ęju* Dignājā, *ę̀imu*² ‖ *ęju* Secē, *eĩm* ‖ *iẽt* Gudeniekos, *èimu*² ‖ *èiņļu*² ‖ *ĩmu* ‖ *ĩņļu* ‖ *ĩd'ļu* Bērzgalē, *àimu*² ‖ *ĩmu* ‖ *aju* Lejasciemā, *iému* ‖ *eĩmu* ‖ *eju* Blīdienē, *iému* ‖ *eju* Bilskā, Jaunraunā, Raunā, *iému*² ‖ *eju* Līvbērzē, *iẽmu* ‖ *eju* Sēmē, Vecmokās, *ĩmu* ‖ *eju* Jaunrozē, *ĩmu* ‖ *aju* Višķos, *ĩmu* ‖ *eju* ‖ *èimu*² Rugājos, *iému* ‖ *eju* ‖ *iẽtu* Liepā, Smiltenē, *iému* ‖ *iẽtu* ‖ *eju* Burtniekos, Jaunburtniekos, *iému*² ‖ *iẽtu*² ‖ *eju* Braslavā, Vilzēnos, *iému*² ‖ *iẽtu*² ‖ *eju* ‖ *eĩmu* Bauņos, *iému*² ‖ *iẽtu*² ‖ *iẽt*² Mazsalacā, Sēļos, Skaņkalnē, Vecatē, *ĩmu* ‖ *ĩtu* Alūksnē, *ĩmu* ‖ *ĩtu* ‖ *àimu*² Litenē, *ĩmu* ‖ *ĩņņu* ‖ *ĩņļu* ‖ *ĩd'ļu* ‖ *ĩmļu* Nirzā, *ĩmu* ‖ *ĩdļu* ‖ *ĩmļu* Pildā, *ĩmu* ‖ *ĩnu* Izvaltā; *eju* ‖ *eĩmu* ir Aizvīķos, Babītē, Bārtā, Bauskā, Bukaišos, Dunalkā, Kabilē, Mārupē, Salā, Sieksātē, Zantē, *eju* ‖ *eĩmu*² Auros, Kalētos, *eju* ‖ *èimu*² Demenē, Ikšķilē, Lizumā, Mēdzūlā, Plāterē, Ružinā, Sinolē, *eju* ‖ *eĩmu* Kastrānē, Kraukļos, Meirānos, *eju* ‖ *èimu* ‖ *eĩmu* Gārsenē, *eju* ‖ *èimu*² Biržos, *eju* ‖ *ę̃imu* Asarē, Pļaviņās, *ęju* ‖ *ę̀imu*² Līvānos, Zasā, *eju* ‖ *iému* ‖ *eĩmu* Drustos, Taurenē, *eju* ‖ *iému*² ‖ *eĩmu* Lestenē, *eju* ‖ *iemu* ‖ *eimu* Jaunvālē, *eju* ‖ *iẽmu* Bēnē, *eju* ‖ *iému* Brenguļos, Gatartā, Launkalnē, Plāņos, Veļķos, *eju* ‖ *iemu* ‖ *èimu*² Jaungulbenē, *aju* ‖ *ĩmu* Kalupē, Līksnā, Vārkavā, Ziemerī, *eju* ‖ *iému* ‖ *iẽtu* Blomē, *eju* ‖ *iému*² ‖ *iẽtu* Līgatnē, *eju* ‖ *ĩmu* ‖ *ĩmļu* ‖ *ĩdļu* ‖ *èimu*² Makašēnos, *iẽtu*² ‖ *iẽtu* ‖ *iému*² Dauguļos, *iẽtu* ‖ *iému* ‖ *iẽnu* Mārsnēnos, *ĩtu* ‖ *ĩmu* Zeltiņos, *ĩdu* ‖ *ĩmu* (vecās paaudzes runā arī *ĩdo* ‖ *ĩmo*) Baltinavā, Šķilbēnos, *ĩdļu* ‖ *ĩmu* ‖ *ĩmļu* Zvirgzdenē.

420

No kopējā izpētīto izlokšņu skaita izloksnes, kur *eimu* resp. *iemu* ir tikai paralēlforma kādam jauninājumam, veido mazliet vairāk par vienu piektdaļu. Tâtad ne mazāk par 40 % izlokšņu vēl mūsu dienās viensk. 1. personā dažādos fonētiskos variantos lieto formu *eimu* resp. *iemu*.

4. *Daudzsk. 1. personā* atematiskās formas tikpat kâ nav vairs sastopamas. Tikai Ritē *ę̀ima²* ir vienīgā šās personas forma. Ir vēl *èimam²* ‖ *ę̀imę̄²* ‖ *ęjam* Dignājā, Zasā, *eīma* ‖ *ejam* Nīgrandā, *ęjam* ‖ *ę̀imam²* ‖ *ę́ima* Līvānos. No dažām izloksnēm ir zināmas atematiskas *imperatīva* daudzsk. 1. pers. formas: *ę̀imę̄²!* Barkavā, *àima²!* Līksnā, *aṁ̇ę!* Bērzgalē, Pildā, Zvirgzdenē, *aṁ̇ę!* ‖ *îmam!* Izvaltā, *aṁ̇ę!* ‖ *îśim!* Nirzā, *aṁ̇ę!* ‖ *èimom²!* Makašēnos.

5. *Daudzsk. 2. personā* atematiskās formas bez kādām paralēlformām vai ar tām ir sastopamas plašākos apmēros nekâ daudzsk. 1. personā. *èit²* runā Plāterē, *eīta* Nīgrandā, Saldū, Sieksātē, *ę̀ita²* Kurcumā, Maltā, Mēmelē, *ę̀ite²* Ritē, *ę́itę̄* Raudā, *ę̀it'ę̄²* Bērzpilī, Rēznā, Stirnienē, Viļānos, *àit'ę̄²* Skaistā, Viškos, *ę̀it'²* ‖ *ę̀it'ę̄²* ‖ *ę̀ita²* ‖ *ę́it'ę̄* ‖ *ęjit'* Līvānos, *eīta* ‖ *ejat* Blīdienē, *eīta* ‖ *ejiêt²* Līvbērzē, *eīta* ‖ *eîta²* ‖ *ejiêt²* Dobelē, *èita²* ‖ *ejat* Zalvā, *eîta* ‖ *ejat* Virānē, *eîta* ‖ *ejèet²* Kraukļos, *èite²* ‖ *ejet* Sinolē, *ę́itę̄²* ‖ *ę̀ita²* ‖ *ęjit* Dignājā, *ę̀it'ę̄²* ‖ *ęjit'* Izvaltā, *àita²* ‖ *ajit'* Līksnā; *ejat* ‖ *eīta* Gaiķos, Rankā, Skrundā, *ejiêt²* ‖ *eīta* Vilcē, *ejat* ‖ *eīta* ‖ *ejaīt* Bilskā, Smiltenē, *ejat* ‖ *eīta* ‖ *eītait* ‖ *eītat* Lestenē, *ejat* ‖ *eîta²* Bikstos, *ęjat* ‖ *ę́ita* Bebrenē, *ejet* ‖ *èite²* Lizumā, *ęjit* ‖ *ę̀itę̄²* Slatē, *ęjit* ‖ *ę̀itę̄²* ‖ *ę̀ita²* ‖ *àita²* Zasā, *ajit'* ‖ *àit'ę̄²* Aizkalnē, Kalupē, Krāslavā, *ęjit'* ‖ *ę̀ita²* Varakļānos, *iêtat²* ‖ *ejiêt* ‖ *eīta* Bauņos, *iêtat²* ‖ *iêt²* ‖ *eīta* Vecatē, *iêtat* ‖ *eīta* Mārsnēnos, *iêtat²* ‖ *ejat* ‖ *ejiêt²* ‖ *iêt²* ‖ *eīta* Braslavā, Vilzēnos, *eîmat* ‖ *ejat* ‖ *eîta* Atašienē, *èimot²* ‖ *ejot* ‖ *ę̀it'ę̄²* Sakstagalā.

Par *imperatīva* daudzsk. 2. personu ziņu ir maz. Liekas, ka šai izteiksmē atematiskās formas paglābušās labāk nekâ indikatīvā, jo nereti indikatīvā ir kāda jauvdīnāta forma, turpretī imperatīvā senā atematiskā forma, piem., imp. *eîta!* : ind. *ejèet²* Lubānā, Meirānos, *èita²!* : *îtet* Vīksnā, *ę̀ite²!* : *ejat* Rubeņos, *ę̀it'ę̄²!* : *èimot²* Dricēnos, *ę̀it'ę̄²!* : *îmat* Kaunatā, *ę̀it'ę̄²!* : *ejot* ‖ *îdḷot* ‖ *îmḷot* Makašēnos, *ę̀it'ę̄²!* : *èimot²* ‖ *èiṁḷot²* ‖ *îmot* ‖ *îṁḷot* ‖ *îd'ḷot* Bērzgalē, *ę̀it'ę̄²!* : *îmḷat* Rundēnos, *àit'ę̄²!* : *îṁḷot* Brigos, *àit'ę̄²!* : *îmat* Ciblā, Rēznā, *àit'ę̄²!* : *îmot* ‖ *iṇṇot* ‖ *îṇḷot* ‖ *îd'ḷot* ‖ *îmḷot* Nirzā, *àit'ę̄²!* : *îmot* ‖ *ajit'* Dagdā, *àit'ę̄²!* : *èimot²* Nautrēnos.

Ir izloksnes, kur indikatīvā paralēli lieto seno atematisko formu un kādu jauvdīnājumu, bet imperatīvā tikai seno formu, piem., imp. *ę̀itę̄²!* : ind. *ę̀itę̄²* ‖ *ę̀ita²* ‖ *ęjit* Dignājā, *àit'ę̄²!* : *ajit'* ‖ *àit'ę̄²* Kalupē, Krāslavā. Daļā izlokšņu blakus atematiskajai formai arī imperatīvā ir jau ieviesies kāds jauvdīnājums, tâ ka imperatīva formas no indikatīva vairs neatšķiras, piem., *ejit'!* ‖ *ę̀it'ę̄²!* : *ejit'* ‖ *ę̀it'ę̄²* Izvaltā, *ajit'!* ‖ *àit'ę̄²!* : *ajit'* ‖ *àit'ę̄²* Aizkalnē.

Arī dažās lejzemnieku izloksnēs imperatīvā vēl ir atematiskā forma, bet indikatīvā kāds jauninājums, piem., *eît²!* : *ejat* Bārtā, *eît!* : *ejaît* Kauguros. Tas liek domāt, ka jauninājumi seno atematisko formu vietā vispirms ir radušies indikatīvā. Šai sakarā der ievērot arī viensk. 2. pers. ind. un imp. formas dažās dziļo augšzemnieku izloksnēs.

Latviešu izloksnēs, izņemot lībiskās un daļu to kaimiņizlokšņu, viensk. 2. personā lieto formu *ej*, retāk *eji* (dažādos fonētiskos variantos). (Par *ej* resp. *ej!* vēsturi J. Endzelīns, *Latviešu valodas gramatikā*, 722–723.) Paradigmas nolīdzināšanas tendences rezultātā šās personas forma indikatīvā ir *èiṁi²* Andrupenē, Dricēnos, Ozolainē, Tilžā, *îṁi* Ciblā, Kaunatā, Rēznā, *îṁĺ'i* Brigos, Rundēnos, *îdĺ'i* Kārsavā, Zvirgzdenē, *èiṁi²* || *èiṁĺ'i* || *îṁi* || *îṁĺ'i* || *îd'ĺ'i* Bērzgalē, *îmi* || *îdi* (vecās paaudzes runā arī *îme* || *îde*) Baltinavā, Šķilbēnos, *îmy* || *îṅ́ṅ́i* || *îṇĺ'i* || *îd'ĺ'i* || *îmĺ'i* Nirzā, *îṇĺ'i* || *îṅ́i* Mērdzenē, *îdi* Viļakā. Taču imperatīvā, cik zināms, ir senā forma, proti, *èi²!* Baltinavā, Šķilbēnos, Viļakā, *è̦i²!* Izvaltā, *ài²!* Bērzgalē, Nirzā, Zvirgzdenē. Pildā, kur indikatīvā ir *îd'ĺ'i* || *ài²*, imperatīvā ir tikai *ài²!*

6. Salīdzinot verba *iet* pašreizējās tagadnes formas ar J. Endzelīna *Latviešu valodas gramatikā* minētajām (720–723), vērojams, ka atematisko formu areāls stipri sarucis. Joprojām stingri turas vienīgi 3. pers. forma *iet*. Viensk. 1. personā gandrīz 60 % izlokšņu formu *eimu* resp. *iemu* vairs nelieto. Vēl mazākos apmēros atematiskās formas ir saglabājušās daudzsk. 2. personā, un daudzsk. 1. personā atematisko formu mūsu izloksnēs tikpat kâ vairs nav.

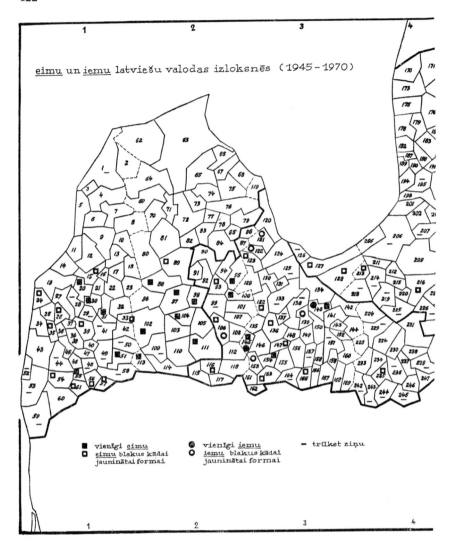

eimu un iemu latviešu valodas izloksnēs (1945-1970)

■ vienīgi eimu
□ eimu blakus kādai jauninātai formai

◉ vienīgi iemu
○ iemu blakus kādai jauninātai formai

— trūkst ziņu

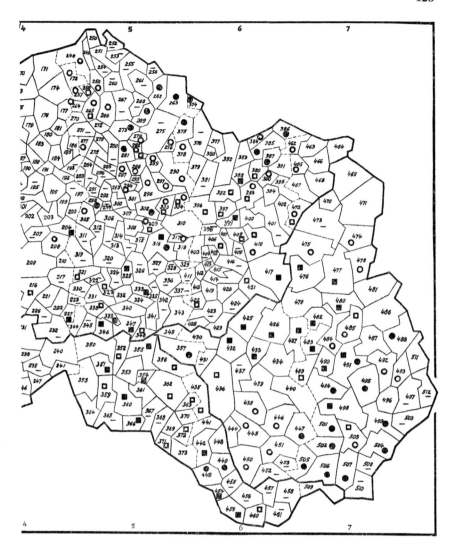

The Athematic Forms of the Verb *iet* in the Contemporary Latvian Dialects

This paper presents dialectal data concerning the use of athematic forms of the verb *iet* 'to go'. The data have been compiled from about 400 Latvian dialects in the period 1945–1970 by the Academy of Sciences of the Latvian S.S.R. and by the Chair of Latvian Language of the Pēteris Stučka Latvian State University.

The analysis of the material shows that the athematic form has been fully preserved only in the 3rd person—*iet*. In the 1st person singular the athematic forms *eimu* or *iemu* is still used in about 40 % of dialects. However, in the majority of dialects this form is now used parallel with a new form. The athematic forms *eime* and *eima* in the 1st person plural has been traced only in some dialects, where they are used parallel with newer forms. It is only in some dialects of Latgale that the imperative *aṁę* has been retained without newer parallel forms. The forms *eite* and *eita* in the 2nd person plural, used as an imperative in particular, enjoy wider usage than the athematic forms of the 1st person plural, but also in this person newer creations have been noted in the bulk of dialects.

When comparing the extent of the athematic forms of the verb *iet* in contemporary dialects with the evidence given in *Latviešu valodas gramatika* by J. Endzelīns, it is obvious that the area has been substantially reduced. Various kinds of newer forms are ousting the ancient form of the 1st and 2nd person.

Izlokšņu apzīmējumi kartē

1 Venta	46 Virga	92 Aizupe
2 Pope	47 Bunka	93 Zante
3 Vārve	48 Priekule	94 Zemīte
4 Zūras	49 Asīte	95 Grenči
5 Užava	50 Nīkrāce	96 Raņķi
6 Ziras	51 Embūte	97 Lutriņi
(Dziras)	52 Pērkone	98 Gaiķi
7 Piltene	53 Nīca	99 Remte
8 Zlēkas	54 Bārta	100 Strutele
9 Ēdole	55 Purmsāti	101 Jaunpils
10 Padure	56 Gramzda	102 Skrunda
11 Jūrkalne	57 Aizvīķi	103 Sātiņi
12 Alsunga	58 Vaiņode	104 Saldus
13 Īvande	59 Rucava	105 Ciecere
14 Ulmale	60 Dunika	106 Blīdiene
15 Gudenieki	61 Kalēti	107 Biksti
16 Basi	62 Ance	108 Zebrene
17 Planīca	63 Dundaga (Dundanga)	109 Pampāļi
18 Kurmāle	64 Puze	110 Kursīši
19 Saka	65 Ārlava	111 Zvārde
20 Apriķi	66 Lubezere	112 Lielauce
21 Klostere	67 Nogale	113 Nīgranda
22 Turlava	68 Upesgrīva	114 Ezere
23 Snēpele	69 Ugāle	115 Ruba
24 Ziemupe	70 Usma	116 Jaunauce
25 Vērgale	71 Spāre (Spārne)	117 Vadakste
26 Dunalka	72 Stende	118 Vecauce
27 Cīrava	73 Pastende	119 Mērsrags
28 Dzērve	74 Laidze	120 Engure
29 Aizpute	75 Vandzene	121 Sēme
30 Laža	76 Lauciene	122 Vecmokas
31 Kazdanga	77 Lībagi	123 Tume
32 Valtaiķi	78 Strazde	124 Milzkalne
33 Sieksāte	79 Zentene	125 Smārde
34 Medze	80 Kuldīga	126 Sloka
35 Tāši	81 Renda	127 Sala
36 Aistere	82 Valgāle	128 Babīte
37 Rāva	83 Virbi	129 Irlava
38 Durbe	84 Kandava	130 Praviņi
39 Vecpils	85 Cēre	131 Slampe
40 Krote	86 Dzirciems	132 Lestene
41 Kalvene	87 Pūre	133 Džūkste
42 Rudbārži	88 Vārma	134 Kalnciems
43 Grobiņa	89 Kabile	135 Annenieki
44 Gavieze	90 Matkule	136 Dobele
45 Tadaiķi	91 Vāne	137 Sīpele

138 Bērze	186 Augstroze	234 Code
139 Līvbērze	187 Liepupe	235 Bauska
140 Valgunde	188 Lāde	236 Vecsaule
141 Ozolnieki	189 Dunte	237 Brukna
142 Pēternieki	190 Stiene	238 Stelpe
143 Tetele	191 Nabe	239 Bārbele
144 Garoze	192 Mazstraupe	240 Taurkalne
145 Īle	193 Rozula	241 Kurmene
146 Naudīte	194 Skulte	242 Rundāle
147 Auri	195 Vidriži	243 Īslīce
148 Šķibe	196 Lēdurga	244 Ceraukste
149 Glūda	197 Lielstraupe	245 Panemune
150 Svēte	198 Bīriņi	246 Jaunsaule
151 Vircava	199 Turaida	247 Skaistkalne
152 Vecsvirlauka	200 Vildoga	248 Mazsalaca
153 Bēne	201 Pabaži	249 Idus
154 Penkule	202 Sēja	250 Ipiķi
155 Tērvete	203 Krimulda	251 Terneja
156 Zaļenieki	204 Sigulda	252 Lode
157 Jēkabnieki	205 Mangaļi	253 Koņi
158 Platone	206 Ādaži	254 Rūjiena
159 Lielvircava	207 Inčukalns	255 Naukšēni
160 Jaunsvir lauka	208 Allaži	256 Omuļi
161 Sniķere	209 Ropaži	257 Braslava
162 Ukri	210 Sidgunda	258 Vecate
163 Bukaiši	211 Dreiliņi	259 Sēļi
164 Augstkalne	212 Stopiņi	260 Jeri (Ģeri)
165 Vilce	213 Mārupe	261 Kārķi
166 Lielplatone	214 Katlakalns	262 Ērģeme
167 Elēja	215 Salaspils	263 Lugaži
168 Sesava	216 Ikšķile	264 Vilzēni
169 Svitene	217 Suntaži	265 Bauņi
170 Ainaži	218 Olaine	266 Burtnieki
171 Rozēni	219 Dole	267 Rencēni
172 Skaņkalne	220 Daugmale	268 Ēvele
173 Salaca	221 Ogresgals	269 Jērcēni
174 Aloja	222 Rembate	270 Ozoli
175 Svētciems	223 Lēdmane	271 Dikļi
176 Pāle	224 Iecava	272 Jaunburtnieki
177 Puikule	225 Baldone	273 Valmiera
178 Vitrupe	226 Tome	274 Brenguļi
179 Viļķene	227 Lielvārde	275 Trikāta
180 Katvari	228 Salgale	276 Plāņi
181 Pociems	229 Zālīte	277 Dauguļi
182 Tūja	230 Misa	278 Ķieģeļi
183 Limbaži	231 Vecumnieki	279 Mujēni
184 Umurga	232 Birzgale	(Mujāni)
185 Vainiži	233 Mežotne	280 Kocēni

281 Kauguri	329 Lubeja	377 Zvārtava
282 Jaunvāle	330 Laubēre	378 Bilska
283 Stalbe	331 Madliena	379 Birzuļi
284 Kūdums	332 Meņģele	380 Grundzāle
285 Vaidava	333 Liepkalne	381 Palsmane
286 Lenči	334 Irši	382 Gaujiena
287 Liepa	335 Sausnēja	383 Trapene
288 Mārsnēni	336 Vestiena	384 Jaunroze
289 Blome	337 Bērzaune	385 Jaunlaicene
290 Smiltene	338 Krape	386 Veclaicene
291 Raiskums	339 Viskāļi	387 Karva
292 Cēsis	340 Bebri	388 Dūre
293 Priekuļi	341 Odziena	389 Ilzene
294 Jaunrauna	342 Vietalva	390 Zeltiņi
295 Baižkalns	343 Kalsnava	391 Alsviķis
296 Rauna	344 Jumprava	392 Sinole
297 Launkalne	345 Skrīveri	393 Lejasciems
298 Kārļi	346 Aizkraukle	394 Beļava
299 Līvi	347 Koknese	395 Kalncempji
300 Vaive	348 Pļaviņas	396 Ranka
301 Veselava	349 Aiviekste	397 Lizums
302 Dzērbene	350 Sērene	398 Druviena
303 Drusti	351 Daudzese	399 Tirza
304 Gatarta	352 Sece	400 Galgauska
305 Līgatne	353 Sunākste	401 Vecgulbene
306 Drabeši	354 Vārnava	402 Stāmeriene
307 Rāmuļi	355 Sēlpils	403 Liezēre
308 Sērmūkši	356 Ābeļi	404 Kārzdaba
309 Taurene	357 Krustpils	405 Graši
310 Jaunpiebalga	358 Mazzalva	406 Kraukļi
311 More	359 Zalva	407 Virāne
312 Nītaure	360 Sauka	408 Aduliena
313 Ķēči	361 Viesīte	409 Dzelzava
314 Kosa	362 Birži	410 Jaungulbene
315 Skujene	363 Zasa	411 Viesiena
316 Vecpiebalga	364 Mēmele	412 Kusa
317 Veļķi	365 Nereta	413 Oļi
318 Mēdzūla	366 Rite	414 Sarkaņi
319 Mālpils	367 Elkšņi	415 Patkule
320 Zaube	368 Aknīste	416 Cesvaine
321 Kastrāne	369 Susēja	417 Lubāna
322 Ķeipene	370 Slate	418 Grostona
323 Plātere	371 Gārsene	419 Lazdona
324 Taurupe	372 Asare	420 Prauliena
325 Ogre	373 Prode	421 Meirāni
326 Ērgļi	374 Valka	422 Mārciena
327 Jumurda	375 Vijciems	423 Ļaudona
328 Vējava	376 Cirgaļi	424 Saikava

425 Barkava	455 Svente	486 Mērdzene
426 Varakļāni	456 Laucesa	(Mērdzine)
427 Viļāni	457 Skrudaliena	487 Zvirgzdene
428 Sāviena	458 Saliena	(Zvirgzdine)
429 Mētriena	459 Kurcums	488 Cibla
430 Medņi	460 Demene	489 Ružina
431 Vīpe	461 Silene	490 Ozolaine
432 Atašiene	462 Ziemeris	491 Rēzna
433 Stirniene	463 Mārkalne	492 Pilda
434 Galēni	464 Pededze	493 Nirza
435 Dignāja	465 Alūksne	494 Malta
436 Līvāni	466 Beja	495 Kaunata
437 Rudzēti	467 Anna	496 Rundēni
438 Vārkava	468 Mālupe	497 Istra
439 Preiļi	469 Liepna	498 Andrupene
440 Silajāņi	470 Vīksna	(Andrupine)
441 Rubeņi	471 Viļaka	499 Ezernieki
442 Bebrene	472 Litene	500 Šķaune
443 Dviete	473 Balvi	501 Kapiņi
444 Nīcgale	474 Šķilbēni	502 Auleja
445 Kalupe	475 Rugāji	503 Dagda
446 Aizkalne	476 Bērzpils	504 Asūne
447 Aglona	477 Tilža	505 Izvalta
(Eglūna)	478 Baltinava	506 Krāslava
448 Laši	479 Gaigalava	507 Skaista
449 Pilskalne	480 Nautrēni	508 Robežnieki
450 Līksna	481 Kārsava	509 Kaplava
451 Višķi	482 Dricēni	510 Indra
452 Naujene	483 Sakstagals	511 Brigi
453 Biķernieki	484 Makašēni	512 Pasiene
454 Rauda	485 Bērzgale	

VELTA RŪĶE-DRAVIŅA

Initial Consonant Combinations
in Lithuanian and Latvian

01. The study deals with word-initial consonant combinations in standard
Lithuanian and standard Latvian, in order to compare both Baltic languages
in this respect.

As is well known, the permitted phoneme sequences vary greatly between
languages, even between those which are genetically or typologically
related. In general, word-initial syllables contain most information in the
communication process. Since no initial consonant clusters are accepted in
Finnish in genuine Finnish words, and since Latvian has been strongly
influenced by Finno-Ugric languages, interest was focused on the beginnings
of words. It is significant to note that, among approximately 400 presumed
Finnic loans in Latvian discussed by V. Zeps in *Latvian and Finnic Linguistic Convergences*, no more than 10 examples contain initial 2-member
clusters.

My investigation concerns four main aspects:

1) the set of consonants which occur before the first vowel in a word,
2) the different ways of combining these consonantal phonemes, i.e. the
   order of these consonants in clusters,
3) the maximum number of consonants which combine in the initial position,
4) the frequency of the permitted consonant combinations.

02. The word is taken as the basic unit. Phoneme (not grapheme) combinations are discussed. Examples are generally given in ordinary spelling. Word
stress in Latvian words is not indicated as it is usually on the first syllable
of the word, even in compounds. In Lithuanian words, both stressed and
unstressed first syllables occur, and the intonation signs function as stress
marks. The morphological structure of the analyzed forms plays a part only
with respect to prefixed words as opposed to simple words, since no Baltic
prefix consists of a 3-member cluster. Proper names are not treated in this
study. On the other hand, foreign words have not been excluded from the
material, as some of them are quite common in both literary and colloquial
styles; nevertheless, it has always been noted when a sequence is only found

LATVIAN

Set of consonants	Single consonants in initial position	Initial 2-member clusters C_1C_2-		Initial 3-member clusters $C_1C_2C_3$-		
		C_1	C_2	C_1	C_2	C_3
p	p-	p	p-		p	
b	b-	b				
t	t-	t			t	
d	d-	d				
k	k-	k	k-		k	
g	g-	g				
ķ	ķ-		ķ-			
ģ	ģ-					
c	c-					
č	č-					
ʒ	ʒ-					
ǯ	(ǯ-)					
m	m-	(m)	m-			
n	n-		n-			
ņ	ņ-		ņ-			
s	s-	s	(s-)	s		
š	š-	š		(š)		
z	z-	z				
ž	ž-	ž				
f	f-	f	(f-)			
v	v-		v-			
x	x-	x				
h	h-					
l	l-	l-				l-
ļ	ļ-		ļ-		ļ-	ļ-
r	r-		r-		r-	r-
j	j-					

in rarely used scientific terms of foreign origin. Interjections and onomatopoeic words show typical differences between Lithuanian and Latvian as concerns the initial and—to a much greater extent—the final clusters, and are of special interest for a description of phoneme distribution in Baltic. The study is based on:

LITHUANIAN material published in Lietuvos TSR Mokslų Akademija, *Lietuvių kalbos žodynas* I–VII, Vilnius, 1968–; Niedermann–Senn–Brender, *Wörterbuch der litauischen Schriftsprache*, Heidelberg, 1932–1968; Alexander Kurschat, *Litauisch-deutsches Wörterbuch* I–II, Göttingen, 1968–; Lietuvos TSR Mokslų Akademija, *Dabartinės lietuvių kalbos žodynas*, Vilnius, 1954; A. Buojatė & V. Subatnieks, *Lietuvių-latvių kalbų žodynas*, Ryga, 1964; and

LATVIAN material published in K. Mūlenbacha *Latviešu valodas vārdnīca* I–IV, Chicago, ²1953–1955; J. Endzelīns & E. Hauzenberga, *Papildinājumi un labojumi K. Mūlenbacha Latviešu valodas vārdnīcai* I–II, Chicago, ²1956;

LITHUANIAN

Set of consonants	Single consonants in initial position	Initial 2-member clusters C_1C_2-		Initial 3-member clusters $C_1C_2C_3$-		
		C_1	C_2	C_1	C_2	C_3
p	*p-*	*p*	*p-*		*p*	
p′						
b	*b-*	*b*				
b′						
t	*t-*	*t*	*t-*		*t*	
d	*d-*	*d*				
k	*k-*	*k*	*k-*		*k*	
k′	*k′-*					
g	*g-*	*g*				
g′	*(g′-)*					
c	*c-*	*(c)*				
ć						
č	*č-*	*(č)*				
č′	*č′-*		*(č′-)*			
ʒ	*(ʒ-)*	*ʒ*				
ʒ́	*(ʒ́-)*					
ǯ	*(ǯ′-)*					
m	*m-*	*(m)*	*m-*			
n	*n-*		*n-*			
ń	*ń-*		*ń-*			
s	*s-*	*s*	*(s-)*	*s*		
s′	*ś-*					
š	*š-*	*š*		*š*		
z	*z-*	*z*	*(z-)*			
ź						
ž	*ž-*	*ž*				
ž′	*ž′-*					
f	*f-*	*f*	*(f-)*			
v	*v-*		*v-*			*v-*
v′	*(v′-)*					
x	*x-*	*x*				
h	*h-*					
l	*l-*		*l-*			*l-*
ļ	*ļ-*		*ļ-*			*ļ-*
r	*r-*		*r-*			*r-*
ŗ	*ŗ-*		*ŗ-*			*ŗ-*
j	*j-*		*j-*			*j-*

E. Turkina, *Latvian-English Dictionary*, Riga, 1962; *Latviešu-vācu vārdnīca*, Rīgā, 1963; *Latviešu-krievu vārdnīca*, Rīgā, 1963; *Svešvārdu vārdnīca*, Rīgā, 1969.

1.0. In comparing the initial sequences in Lithuanian and Latvian we find that the two languages have several common features but in some respects behave in opposite ways. The number of permitted initial consonant combinations in Baltic words is much smaller than the number of permitted medial or final combinations. For example, stops *-kt, -pt* as well as *-lt, -rt* combine in Latvian words finally but not initially. The results of my investigation can be brought together into four sections corresponding to the four aspects mentioned in 01.

1) The number of consonant phonemes in Lithuanian is much larger than in Latvian. The Lithuanian phonemes have been discussed by several authors and (in detail) different solutions have been found. The following consonant phonemes have been assumed: p $\acute{p}$ b $\acute{b}$ t d k $\acute{k}$ g $\acute{g}$ c $\acute{c}$ $\check{c}$ $\check{c}'$ $\mathfrak{z}$ $\acute{\mathfrak{z}}$ $\check{\mathfrak{z}}$ $\check{\mathfrak{z}}'$ m $\acute{m}$ n η s $\acute{s}$ $\check{s}$ $\check{s}'$ z $\acute{z}$ $\check{z}$ $\check{z}'$ f v $\acute{v}$ x h l $\underset{.}{l}$ r $\underset{.}{r}$ j.

Not all of these consonants appear initially. There are Lithuanian words in the standard language beginning with p, b, t, d, k, $\acute{k}$, g, (c),[2] $(\check{c})$, $\check{c}'$, $(\mathfrak{z})$, $(\acute{\mathfrak{z}})$, $(\check{\mathfrak{z}})$, $(\check{\mathfrak{z}}')$, m, $\acute{m}$, s, $\acute{s}$, $\check{s}$, $\check{s}'$, z, $\check{z}$, $(\check{z}')$, f, x, h, v, $(\acute{v})$, l, $\underset{.}{l}$, r, $\underset{.}{r}$, j, e.g. $p\tilde{a}das$, $bal\grave{a}$, $t\tilde{a}kas$, $dant\grave{i}s$, $k\acute{a}lnas$, $kiaũlė$,[3] $g\tilde{a}balas$, $c\grave{a}ptelėti$, $\check{c}\acute{a}i\check{z}yti$, $\check{c}i\grave{a}$, $dz\bar{u}kas$, $dzióbinti$, $d\check{z}\acute{a}ulis$, $d\check{z}iaũgsmas$, $m\tilde{a}\check{z}as$, $miaũkti$, $sul\grave{a}$, $si\acute{u}lyti$, $\check{s}aln\grave{a}$, $\check{s}i\acute{a}udas$, $z\acute{y}lė$, $\check{z}arn\grave{a}$, $\check{z}i\grave{u}rkė$, $f\acute{a}brikas$, $char\tilde{a}kteris$, $v\tilde{a}karas$, $viauksėti$, $laũkas$, $liauk\grave{a}$, $naud\grave{a}$, $ni\acute{a}uti$, $r\tilde{a}tas$, $ri\acute{a}u\check{s}ės$, $j\acute{a}unas$, but some phonemes, i.e., $\mathfrak{z}$, $\acute{\mathfrak{z}}$, $\check{\mathfrak{z}}$, $\check{\mathfrak{z}}'$, $\acute{v}$, c, $\check{c}$, $\check{z}'$, occur initially in only one or a few Lithuanian words.

The following Lithuanian single consonants were not found initially: $\acute{p}$ (in standard pronunciation the words begin with pj-), $\acute{b}$, $\acute{g}$, $\acute{c}$, $\acute{z}$.

Thus, although Lithuanian has both palatalized (soft) and unpalatalized (hard) consonant phonemes, the distribution of the palatalized type is strongly restricted in word-initial position. The situation in Latvian is less complicated. The number of phonemes in the Latvian consonant system is smaller, but Latvian words can begin with every single consonant, namely: p b t d k $\underset{.}{k}$ g $(\acute{g})$ c $\check{c}$ $\mathfrak{z}$ $(\check{\mathfrak{z}})$ m n η s $\check{s}$ z $\check{z}$ f v x h l $\underset{.}{l}$ r j, e.g. $pasaka$, $balts$, $tāls$, $daba$, $kalns$, $\underset{.}{k}epa$, $gabals$, $\acute{g}imene$, $caurs$, $\check{c}aula$, $dzelme$, $d\check{z}ungļi$, $mala$, $nauda$, $\eta audēt$, $sala$, $\check{s}aubas$, $zāle$, $\check{z}agars$, $fabrika$, $vasara$, $harta$, $halle$, $lauks$, $ļauns$, $raksts$, $jauns$. Thus, although the full set of consonants in standard Lithuanian is much larger than that in Latvian, the number of single consonants appearing in the initial position is almost the same in both languages.

2) We can compare the initial 2-member consonant clusters in Lithuanian with those in Latvian with the help of the following tables. Consonants appearing as the first member in the group C_1C_2- are less numerous than the single initial consonants but most of them in this position are the same in both languages, the difference being only that the (infrequent) c, $\check{c}$ and $\mathfrak{z}$ which occur in some Lithuanian words are totally absent in standard Latvian. Similarly, there is no striking difference between both languages as concerns the second component in C_1C_2-: a distinguishing characteristic is that j is lacking in this position in Latvian words (apart from $fjords$ and $fjelli$); Lith. $\check{c}'$ and z, absent in Latvian, occur in Lithuanian only in one or

two rarely used words. Nevertheless, the possibilities of combining these consonants in C_1 and C_2 in initial 2-member groups vary in both languages. The following list shows the possible ways of beginning Lithuanian and Latvian words. One example followed by "*etc*" is quoted in all cases where at least five words were found in the respective standard language. When two, three or four words are quoted, it means that no more examples containing a certain sequence were found. These examples illustrate also the special category (foreign words, onomatopoeic forms) in which the consonant combination occurs.

	Lith.	La.
pj-	*piáuti etc*	*pjedestāls*
pl-	*platùs etc*	*plats etc*
pļ-	*pliópa etc*	*pļãpa etc*
pn-	*pneum(o)-*	*pneum(o)-*
pr-	*pradé'ti etc*	*prasĩt etc*
ps-	*psálmė, pseudo-, psich(o)-*	*psalmi, pseudo-, psich(o)-*
bj-	*biaurùs etc*	—
bl-	*blusà etc*	*blusa etc*
bļ-	*bliáuti etc*	*bļaut etc*
br-	*brangùs etc*	*brangs etc*
bŗ-	*briaunà, briaunaĩnis, briaunótas, briaũkšti*	—
bz-	*bziñkt! bzìkt! bziñ! bzìngelioti*	—
tr-	*traukinỹs etc*	*traukties etc*
tŗ-	*triùkšmas etc*	—
tv-	*tvãnas etc*	*tvans etc*
dr-	*draũgas etc*	*draugs etc*
dŗ-	*drióksėti etc*	—
dv-	*dvasià etc*	*dvaša*
kl-	*klausýti etc*	*klausĩt etc*
kļ-	*kliáti etc*	*kļũt etc*
km-	*kmỹnas (and derivatives)*	—
kn-	*knaibýti etc*	*knaibĩt etc*
kņ-	*kniáubtis etc*	*kņada, kņudēt, kņupus, kņazs*
kr-	*krãštas etc*	*krasts etc*
kŗ-	*kriáušė etc*	—
ks-	*ksilo-, ksero-, ksenònas*	*ksendzs, ksilo-, ksero-, ksenons*
kv-	*kvãpas etc*	*kvēpi etc*
gl-	*glaũsti etc*	*glaust etc*
gļ-	*gliáudyti, gliaudùs, gliaumà*	*gļotas, gļotains, gļēvs*
gn-	*gnáibyti etc*	*gnĩda, gnēze, gneiss, gnozeoloģija*
gņ-	*gniùžti etc*	—
gr-	*gražùs etc*	*grauds etc*
gŗ-	*griáuti etc*	—
gv-	*gvaldùs etc*	*gvelzt, gvarde, gvardists*
cv-	*cvàkt! cvakséti*	—
čv-	*čvánkšt! čvánkšteléti*	—
ʒv-	*dzvàkteléti, dzvìmbti*	—
mn-	*mnemo-*	*mnemo-*
sf-	*sferà, sfìnksas*	*sfēra, sfinksa*

sk-	skaĩčius etc	skaits etc
sl-	slidùs etc	slidens etc
sḷ-	sliaũkti etc	—
sm-	smiltìs etc	smilts etc
sn-	sniẽgas etc	sniegs etc
sṇ-	—	—
sp-	spalvà etc	spalva etc
sr-	srovẽ etc	—
sṛ-	sriubà etc	—
st-	stãlas etc	stabs etc
sv-	sveĩkas etc	sveiks etc
šč-	ščiũti etc	—
šk-	škac! škec! škic!, škotas, škìcas	—
šḳ-	—	šḳaudīt etc
šl-	šlãpias etc	—
šḷ-	šliaũžti etc	šḷakata etc
šm-	šmùlis etc	šmaugs etc
šn-	šnekė'ti etc	—
šṇ-	šniõkšti etc	šṇākt etc
šp-	šparãgas etc	špināti, špaleras, špats, špetns
šr-	šrapnèlis, šrãtas, šriftas	šrapnelis
št-	štai, štiš! štãtas, štãbas, štur-múoti	štats, štābs, šturmēt
šv-	šviesà etc	švīkāt etc
zl-	zlòtas, zliẽkti, zliẽbti	zlots
zḷ-	zliaũkti, zliaũkos	
zm-	zmèkti, zmēkinti	—
zn-	—	znots
zv-	zviñbti etc	zvaigzne etc
žl-	žlaũgti etc	
žm-	žmogùs etc	—
žn-	žnýbti etc	
žṇ-	žniáugas, žniáugti	žṇaugs, žṇaugt, žṇaudzīt
žv-	žvãkė etc	žvadzēt, žvingulis, žvargstēt
fj-	fiòrdas	fjords, fjells
fl-	fleità etc	flauta etc
fḷ-	fliòksas	—
fr-	frãkas etc	fraka etc
xl-	chlor(o)-	hlor(o)-
xr-	chrom(o)-, chrizantemà	hrom-, hrizantēma

Since the phoneme ṛ does not occur in modern standard Latvian, no initial clusters corresponding to Lith. bṛ-, dṛ-, gṛ-, kṛ- are possible in Latvian words. Dialectally these consonant combinations are restricted to the "Curonic" dialect in West Latvia where r and ṛ appear as independent phonemes.

It is a striking fact that s and r do not combine in Latvian but combine in Lithuanian. The lack of initial La. sr- may be associated with the Latvian (and Germanic) introduction of t between s and r, cf. La. straume, Sw. ström, Eng. stream: Lith. srovẽ. Typical for Lithuanian is the cluster sṛ-.

Other initial consonant groups existing in Lithuanian but absent from the basic system of Latvian are: pj-, bj-, km-, gṇ-, (cv-), (čv-), (ʒv-), sḷ-, sṇ-, šč'-, (šk-), šn-, zḷ-, zm-, žl-, žm-, žn-, fḷ-. The clusters permitted in Latvian but absent from standard Lithuanian are few: šḳ- and (zn-).

Thus, *common* to both Baltic languages are the following 37 frequent + 12 infrequent = 49 combinations:

```
        pl-     pl̦-         (pn-)                pr-     (ps-)
        bl-     bl̦-                              br-
                                                 tr-                         tv-
                                                 dr-                         dv-
        kl-     kl̦-         kn-     kn̦-          kr-     (ks-)               kv-
        gl-     gl̦-         gn-                  gr-                         gv-
                                     (mn-)
sk-     sl-                 sm-     sn-          sp-               st-  (sf-) sv-
                šl̦-         šm-             šn̦-  (šp-)  (šr-)      (št-)      šv-
                (zl-)                                                        zv-
                                             žn̦-                             žv-
(fj-)   fl-                                     fr-
        (xl-)                                   (xr-)
```

The initial cluster systems of Lithuanian and Latvian are thus basically very similar. In both of them stops *p b t d k g* occur freely before *r* and all but the dentals occur freely before *l* and *l̦*. Analysis of the various combinations possible and comparison with neighbouring languages help us to find the features typical for Baltic. Characteristic for East Baltic seems to be the total absence of groups of *t* and *d* with *l* initially, whereas *tl-* is found in some Old Prussian forms (cf. *Tlokowe, Tlokumpelk, tlāku* (=*tālku?* 'Germ. tritt') and is a common cluster in the neighbouring Polish (both *tl-* and *dl-* are permitted in Polish).

Baltic permits both sibilants and velar stops to occur before *n*, but the cluster type *vr-* is totally absent in Baltic, unlike Swedish, Russian and some other languages.

Clusters of *š* plus stop, which are normal in German but abnormal in English, do appear in Baltic words but only in a restricted number of words, most of them loan words from German.

The only initial combinations between *s* and *p, t, k* are *sp-, st-* and *sk-*. Nevertheless, *ps-, ks-* and *pt-* occur in a very few rarely used terms of foreign origin and are not avoided by the common substitution of the second component (as in the case of *ps-* among educated speakers of Swedish[4]). The criterion used by B. Sigurd for Swedish in order to mark off the basic system from the marginal one on the basis of varying pronunciation can help us here only in the case of *xl-* and *xr-*, as Lithuanian and Latvian native speakers have a tendency to avoid them by substituting *kl-* and *kr-*. But this may emphasize the uncommonness of the phoneme *x* rather than its low combinability.

Obviously, not all clusters are equally frequent and not all consonants have the same distribution capacity. The commonest groups in both languages seem to be *pr-, kr-, tr-, sk-, sp-, st-*. Initial *s* can combine in the largest number of different ways (8) with consonants following as the second member in a 2-member cluster: *sk-*, *sl-*, *sm-*, *sn-*, *sp-*, *st-*, (*sf-*), *sv-*; initial *k* combines with seven consonants (one of these combinations is infrequent), *š* with seven (three combinations infrequent), *g* with five and *p* with five (one combination infrequent).

r, *l* and *v* are by far the most frequent second components in 2-member clusters in Lithuanian/Latvian. Initial consonant-groups consisting of stops and *r* are more frequent than those with *l* or *ļ*. There are only five consonants which can stand as C_1 or C_2 in C_1C_2-, namely *p*, *k*, *t*, (*s*), (*m*). Among them, *t*, *p* and *k* show the greatest combinability.

A general rule in Baltic is that the voiceless consonant has at least the same but usually a greater distribution capacity (i.e. the possibility of combining with other consonants initially) in relation to the corresponding voiced consonant. Thus *s* has a dominating position in 2-member clusters, whereas the voiced sibilant is of infrequent occurrence; *p* as C_1 combines

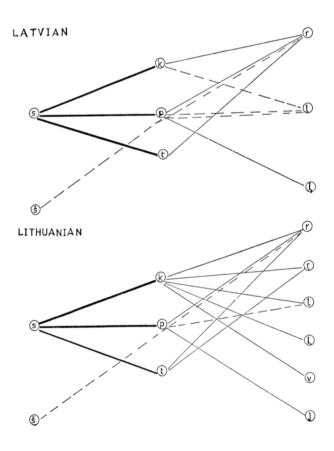

LATVIAN

LITHUANIAN

with l, $ļ$, (n), r, (s) as C_2, but b combines exclusively with l, $ļ$ and r; k combines with l, $ļ$, n, $ņ$, r, (s), v, whereas g combines only with l, $ļ$, n, r, v.

3) The maximum number of members in an initial cluster in Baltic words is clearly three. In prefixed verbs and nouns the number is restricted to two. Examples of *un*stressed first syllables with 3-member clusters are found only in Lithuanian, e.g. *sklaistýti, skruzdẽ, skvarbùs* etc.

The permitted initial 3-member clusters are less numerous than the medial or final ones, at least in Latvian.

All initial 3-member sequences are combinations with:

I s or ($š$) as the first component in $C_1C_2C_3$-,

II p, t or k as the second member and

III v, l, $ļ$, r (in Latvian) and v, l, $ļ$, r, $ŗ$ and j (in Lithuanian) as the last consonant in this consonant group.

Thus, the essential difference between Lithuanian and Latvian lies in $ŗ$ and j as the third member, which is permitted in Lithuanian but not in Latvian words. The difference is more striking when we analyze a) the different ways of combining s with consonants from rows II and III above, and b) the number of words beginning with these combinations in Lithuanian and Latvian:

	Lith.	La.
skl-	sklidùs etc	skleroze, sklandu rauši
skļ-	skliaũstas, skliaũtas	—
skr-	skraidýti etc	skraidīt etc
skŗ-	skriaudà etc	—
skv-	skvarbùs etc	skvērs
spj-	spiáuti etc	—
spl-	—	splīns 'spleen'
spļ-	—	spļaut etc
spr-	spráusti etc	spraust etc
str-	strãzdas etc	strazds etc
stŗ-	striábauti etc	—
stv-	stvárstymas, stvérimas, stvérti	—
špl-	špliñtas	—
špr-	šprìcas, šprotas	šprote

Thus, all initial 3-member sequences in standard Lithuanian and Latvian are made up of sk, sp, st, $+l$, $ļ$, r, $ŗ$, j, v (in Lithuanian) and l, $ļ$, r (v) (in Latvian),

plus the infrequent *špr*- and *špl*- which appear in a few words, generally of foreign origin.

Comparison with Old Prussian (it is difficult to get a complete picture from the restricted material available for such purposes) shows that Old

Prussian had (at least) the triple consonant groups *skr-, str-, stv-, skl-* and *škl-*. This means that West Baltic was richer in 3-member clusters than East Baltic is to-day: *škl-* is totally lacking in standard Lithuanian and Latvian, *stv-* occurs in only three infrequent Lithuanian words and is absent in Latvian, and *skl-* is permitted in Lithuanian but scarcely occurs in Latvian (apart from *skleroze*).

4) Concerning the *frequency* of the permitted consonant combinations, two facts are important: a) a certain initial cluster may be found in many examples or only in a few; b) the cluster may be found in only one or two words of high frequency or in a larger number of words which are used rarely and only by an exclusive speaker-group. One can theoretically imagine a case with a consonantal combination occurring only in ten or more special terms and their derivatives all of which have a very low frequency and are used exclusively by specialists in a narrow field. The appearance of clusters in a certain number of words is illustrated in the above lists.

It is evident that the difference between Lithuanian and Latvian often lies only in the different degree of frequency for certain clusters, i.e. both languages sometimes use the same initial consonant combinations but these combinations are not equally common in both languages. The same situation was observed in comparing word-derivation elements in Baltic languages.[5] In general, Lithuanian permits a greater freedom of combination, and offers a larger number of examples. The question of varying frequencies can be answered more exactly only after a special investigation concerning the number of words beginning with a certain cluster and the frequency of these words. A positive correlation has been found between the frequency of consonant phonemes in a given language and the frequency of consonant groups containing these phonemes, cf. the dominating position of *s* in both respects in Latvian, and the higher frequency of voiceless consonants than the corresponding voiced consonants.[6]

2.0. Conclusions:

1) Lithuanian possesses a richer set of consonant phonemes than Latvian, and combines them more freely in initial 2 and 3-member clusters. Most of the consonant combinations common to both languages have a greater frequency in Lithuanian than in Latvian.

2) Consonants seem to have a greater combinability in West Baltic than they have in East Baltic, and in the East Baltic group there are more possibilities for the Lithuanian consonants than for the Latvian consonants to combine in 2 and 3-member initial clusters.

3) Characteristic Lithuanian initial consonant combinations lacking in standard Latvian (namely *pj-*, *bj-*, *km-*, *gṇ-*, *cv-*, *čv-*, *ʒv-*, *sl̦-*, *sṇ-*, *šč-*, *šk-*, *šn-*, *zl̦-*, *zm-*, *žl-*, *žm-*, *žn-*, *fl̦-*) are often to be found in Polish (cf. such examples as *piątek, biały, kmin, gniazdo, cwał, czwartek, dzwon, szczątek, szkoda, sznur, zlep, zmanić, żleb, żminda, żniwa, flota*). On the other hand, most of the dominant word-initial clusters in Latvian (such as *pr-*, *kr-*, *tr-*, *sp-*, *st-*, *str-*) occur also in Estonian words. All the evidence, manifested in the more restricted possibilities of combining consonants and using the clusters initially in Latvian, strongly supports the hypothesis about Finnic influence on Latvian word structure as concerns the beginning of words.

4) The facts discussed above illustrate the situation in standard Baltic languages. The conditions for consonant distribution differ in the dialects; some of them permit a greater freedom in combining the consonants initially than standard Lithuanian or Latvian. Linguistic geographical data confirm the fact that the tendency to use frequently words with initial 2- and 3-member clusters of various types weakens as one goes from south-west to north-east in the Baltic area. In this respect, the Latvian "Curonic" dialect, especially in some districts in south-western Kurzeme, forms a link between Latvian and Lithuanian, and Old Prussian in possessing a larger number of combination types e.g. *br̦-*, *tr̦-*, *kr̦-*, *gr̦-*, *gṇ-* (*gṇauzt* etc.), *skl-* (*sklidēt, sklidens* etc.), *skn-* (*sknabars* etc.), *škl̦-* (*škl̦aubeniski* etc.) and in using them more frequently than the speakers of dialects in Eastern Latvia do.

5) Thus, consonant combinability, especially in word-initial syllables, seems to be an appropriate criterion for the typological description and comparison of languages and dialects.

6) In discussion of phonetic and phonematic changes involving the disappearance of some phonemes in consonant groups, as Old Prussian **tlokis* (*Tlokumpelk*), in contrast to *clocis*, Lith. *lok̃s* and La. *lācis*,[7] an analysis of the combinations possible in the languages concerned may add a new and fruitful aspect also to historical grammar.

Notes

1. The topic was first discussed at the Phonetic Seminar (under the leadership of Prof. Anna Ābele) of Latvia University in Riga in 1937/38, i.e. during the period when Prof. Chr. S. Stang was visiting Riga and participating in the Baltic seminars of Prof.

440

J. Endzelīns. It is now taken up again here and discussed in detail as an expression of gratitude for all the stimulus which the author, as a very young student of J. Endzelīns, received through personal contact at that time with Prof. Chr. S. Stang and other eminent personalities representing various European linguistic schools.

2. Uncommon initial phonemes are put into ( ) brackets. Baltic *c*, *ʒ*, *č*, *ǯ* have been treated as single phonemes.

3. In Lithuanian ordinary spelling *i* is used to denote palatalization of the preceding consonants (before the vowels *a*, *ą*, *o*, *u*, *ų* and *ū*), thus *kliūti* = [*kļūti*], cf. La. *kļūt*.

4. Cf. Bengt Sigurd, *Phonotactic Structures in Swedish*, Lund, 1965, 64.

5. Cf. V. Rūķe-Draviņa, "Dialektgeographische Unterschiede auf dem Gebiet der Wortbildung im Baltischen", *Communications et Rapports du Premier Congrès International de Dialectologie Générale* II, 151–159.

6. V. Rūķe, "Lauthäufigkeit in der lettischen Schriftsprache", *Slaviska Institutets vid Lunds Universitet Årsbok* 1948/49, Lund 1951, 153–164; A. Lorencs, Z. Nesaule, "Статистические свойства латышского языка", *ZA Vēstis* 195, pp. 41–48.

7. Chr. S. Stang, *Vergleichende Grammatik der Baltischen Sprachen*, Oslo, 1966, 107.

ALG. SABALIAUSKAS

Dėl liet. tvarklas 'piemuo' kilmės

Lingvistinėje literatūroje aptinkamas lietuvių kalbos žodis *tvarklas* 'piemuo'. Pirmasis jį, rodos, mini A. Becenbergeris. Jis nurodo, jog toks žodis 'aptvaro' ir 'piemens' reikšmėmis yra randamas J. Bretkūno biblijos vertime[1]. Šiomis reikšmėmis liet. *tvarklas* nurodomas ir E. Frenkelio etimologiniame lietuvių kalbos žodyne[2].

Be minėtojo J. Bretkūno biblijos vertimo, liet. *tvarklas* 'piemens' reikšme jokiuose kituose lietuvių kalbos paminkluose neaptinkamas. Vėlesniuose Rytų Prūsijos lietuvių biblijos vertimuose J. Bretkūno vartojamą *tvarklas* atitinka liet. *kerdžius* (... *ir kaip kaimenė be kerdžiaus*, Iz. 13, 14)[3]. Vadinasi, galima būtų spėti, kad ir J. Bretkūno biblijoje žodis *tvarklas* vartojamas kerdžiaus — vyresniojo piemens — reikšme. Deja, minėtas žodis į lingvistinę literatūrą 'piemens' reikšme pateko per apsirikimą.

Nurodėme, jog naujesnių laikų Rytų Prūsijos lietuvių biblijos vertimuose J. Bretkūno žodį *tvarklas* anoje frazėje atitinka *kerdžius*. Naujesniuose vokiškuose biblijos vertimuose toji frazė verčiama: „... *und wie eine Herde ohne Hirten*" (Iz., 13, 14)[4]. Tačiau M. Liuterio 1549 metų biblijos vertime ši frazė atrodo štai kaip: „... *und wie ein Herd on hůrten.*"[5] Kad šioje frazėje vok. *hůrten* reiškia ne 'kerdžių' ar 'piemenį', bet 'aptvarą', be kito ko, aiškiai rodo kita iš to paties biblijos skyrelio frazė: „... *die Hirten keine hurten da auffschlahen*" (Iz., 13, 20), kurią J. Bretkūnas ir verčia: „... *Piemens ... Twarklu ne taisis*".

Vadinasi, tiek pirmoje frazėje (ją J. Bretkūnas verčia: „... *ir kaip Gůtas be Twarklů*"), tiek ir antroje J. Bretkūno *tvarklas* reiškia 'aptvarą' (=vok. *Hürde*, vid. vok. aukšt. *hurt*, dgs. *hürte*)', o ne 'piemenį'.

Tokiu būdu liet. *tvarklas* 'piemuo' yra ne tikras lietuvių kalbos faktas, bet kalbininkų „išradimas".

Išnašos

1. A. Bezzenberger, *Beiträge zur Geschichte der litauischen Sprache*, Göttingen, 1877, 333.

2. E. Fraenkel, *Litauisches etymologisches Wörterbuch*, Heidelberg–Göttingen, 1955–1966, 1150.

3. *Biblia, tai esti: Wissas Szwentas Raßtas* ... Karalauczuje, 1816; *Biblija, tai esti Visas Šventas Raštas*, Berlynas, 1931.

4. *Die Bibel oder die ganze Heilige Schrift*, Berlin, 1907.

5. *Biblia: Das ist: die gantze heilige Schrift: Deudsch. Auffs new zugericht. D. Mart. Luth.*, Wittemberg, 1549.

On the Origin of Lith. *tvarklas* 'shepherd'

Lith. *tvarklas* 'shepherd' cannot be considered as a genuine word of Lithuanian. This word appeared in the linguistic literature as an erroneous interpretation of the Biblical text.

JAN SAFAREWICZ

A Latin Parallel to Balto-Slavic Recessive Accent

The essence of the opposition of syllables with circumflex and acute intonation in Balto-Slavic languages is the opposition of a two-mora member with the *first* mora reinforced (circumflex) and a two-mora member with the *second* mora reinforced (acutus), i.e. $\simeq = \breve{\cup}\cup$ opposed to $\perp = \cup\breve{\cup}$, as Chr. S. Stang states in his work *Vergleichende Grammatik der baltischen Sprachen*, p. 125; cf. also J. Kuryłowicz, *Indogermanische Grammatik*, II, 114, § 129. The recessive character of circumflex in morphology is related to such differentiation in intonation; the initial ictus, i. e. the ictus on the first mora of the word, is established in cases of circumflex intonation or when the first syllable is short, i.e. consists of one mora, with the possibility of a shift of stress, as for example, in phrases: **na rǭkǫ>n'a rǫkǫ, *na v'odǫ>n'a vodǫ* (Kuryłowicz, l.c.).

The particular phenomenon which I would like to discuss in this paper is the retraction of stress to the *adjoining* (preceding) mora. In case of a long syllable (i.e. consisting of two morae) secondary acutus occurs: $\cup\cup\breve{\cup}\times >$ $\perp\cup\times$ (i.e. $\cup\breve{\cup}\cup\times$), cf. acc. *móteri̯* besides *dùkteri̯* (where $\cup\breve{\cup}\times > \breve{\cup}\cup\times$).

In Latin, the change occurred in similar prosodic circumstances; it is based on the same tendencies but works in the opposite direction: accentuation of an initial two-mora member, with reinforcement of the *second* mora, resulted in the shift of stress forward, thus bringing about a change in the initial accentuation to the state which is considered characteristic of the classical epoch, i.e. accentuation of the type $\breve{\cup}\cup\cup\times$ ended in the establishment of accentuation of the type $\cup\cup\breve{\cup}\times$: thus, for example, besides *cédimus* we also find *ămámus*.

Prosodical relationships in Latin have been described in detail and genetically explained by J. Kuryłowicz (l.c., p. 193). On the grounds of the formulation of the Latin system of accentuation in the classical epoch offered by R. Jakobson,[1] Kuryłowicz rightly assumes that Latin prosody is based on the opposition between one-mora members and two-mora members, the latter consisting either of a single syllable or of a group of two short syllables (*initial* two-mora group).

The thesis postulating equivalence between one long and two short syllables in the development of Latin had been suggested previously, first by M. Niedermann, then by A. Burger; finally, the problem has also been dealt with by the present author.[2] According to Kuryłowicz, the initial stressed member of polysyllabic words consisted of the first two morae; if the first syllable was short, the two-mora member extended also over the *second* syllable, which also had to be short. If it was long, it became shortened: the phenomenon is known as iambic shortening. Thus, $\_\acute{}$ ..., or $\cup\acute\cup$ ..., or finally: $\cup\underset{\smile}{} $ ...

Iambic shortening at the beginning of polysyllabic words did not occur, according to the opinion of some earlier philologists, in trisyllabic words with a long central syllable, i.e. in words of the type *pŭdīcus, ămīcus, uĕrēbar*.[3] Kuryłowicz explains the transfer from the initial accentuation to the system regulated by the paenultima-law as being due precisely to iambic shortening. In words of the type *stămus* or *lĕgĭmus* the stressed member was the two-mora member *stā-* or *lĕgĭ-*; in words of the type *ămīcus*, where iambic shortening did not occur, the central syllable had to function as the stressed member, i.e. **ắmīcus > ămīcus*. In this way, the feeling might arise that the place of the stress depends not on the initial boundary of the word (initial stress) but on its final boundary (stress regulated by the paenultima-law).

Such reasoning, however, is based on a premise which cannot today be considered as satisfactory: the ample material on iambic shortening collected by A. Brenot[4] shows that the phenomenon occurs in words of the type *ămīcus, dĕdisse*, etc., and especially in groups of three syllables of the type *quod illa, id esse* (Ter. *Haut.* 18), *hom(o) aurum* (Plaut. *Aul.* 185), etc., as frequently as it occurs in words of the type *ămīcitia.* (This problem is discussed by the present author in *Biuletyn Polskiego Towarzystwa Językoznawczego*, XXVIII). Thus the question of how initial stress has been transferred into stress regulated by the paenultima-law remains to be answered.

To explain this change, the distribution of accentuation on particular morae of the word must be considered. Words of two syllables of the type *stămus* have an ictus on the *first* mora of the stressed member ($\cup\cup\times$), which results from the accentuation of words of the type *lĕgĭmus*, the latter being the rhythmical equivalent of words of the type *stămus*.[5] But in the word *cĕdĭmus* the stress can agree with that in words of the type *lĕgĭmus* only if the *second* mora of the first syllable is stressed, i.e. $\cup\acute\cup\cup\times$. Examples of this kind make it possible to state that words of two syllables of the type *stămus* have a stress on the *first* mora of the initial syllable while in words of three syllables of the type *cēdimus*, i.e. with a long first syllable, the stress falls on the *second* mora of the initial syllable. Differentiation between two-mora members with a stress on the first or second mora has no phonological value in Latin as it is strictly conditioned by the prosodical structure of the word; in words of the type *stāmus* a stress on the second mora of the syllable *stā-* is impossible, while in words of the type *cēdimus* the first mora cannot be stressed. In these circumstances, the differentiation between rhythmic structures ◡̆◡ and ◡◡̆ cannot result in the development of a system of intonations, which indeed does not exist in Latin.

There are grounds for assuming that phenomena which occurred in words of the type *amāmus* or *amīcus* were similar to those observed for words of the type *cēdimus*. It is the opinion of the present author that the differences discussed here between the structures of the second two-mora syllable (counting from the end of the word) and the third two-mora syllable (counting again from the end of the word) might explain the transfer from initial accentuation to accentuation in accordance with the paenultima-law. Since in the third syllable (counting from the end of the word) the stress fell on the second mora (i.e. ◡◡̆◡×), in words of the type *amīcus* the stress must have been shifted from the first syllable to the first mora of the second syllable, i.e. ◡̆◡◡× > ◡◡̆◡×, according to the principle that the stressed member must be a prosodic member with the value of two morae. Hence the type *ắmīcus* had to pass into the type *ămícus*. The second possibility was the use of iambic shortening, i.e. changing the type *ắmīcus* into *ămĭcus*, which in fact happened optionally, cf. *ămĭcō* (Plaut. *Mil.* 660). This shortening being optional, however, it did not preclude the possibility of a stress shift from the first short syllable to the second two-mora syllable, with the stress on the first mora (*ămícus*, i.e. ◡◡̆◡×).

This change probably began with words (or groups of words) of four syllables, with the structure ◡◡◡×, where the stress, initial but based on a two-mora member, had to fall upon the second mora, i.e. actually upon the second syllable (the third syllable, counting from the end). Thus, instead of the earlier state ◡̆◡◡× (absolute initial stress), there must have occurred the structure ◡◡̆◡× (initial stress on an initial two-mora member, i.e. ◡◡̆◡× = ─̆◡×).

Some traces of the transfer from absolute initial stress to initial stress on the second mora have perhaps been left in Plautus' versification, in such phrases as *quid igitur* (◡◡◡×). In Plautus' text, such phrases either have an ictus on the first syllable, i.e. *quíd igitúr* (e.g. *Amph.* 382 sept. troch.):

446

quíd igitúr? qui núnc uocáre? ||,

similarly, *Amph.* 492, 603, 719 etc.; or else the ictus on the second syllable occurs, i.e. *quid ígitur,* e.g. *Amph.* 62 (sen. iamb.):

quid ígitur? quóniam hic séruos quóque partís habét,

also, *Curc.* 316; *Mil.* 532; *Most.* 668.

The above examples are quoted not as proof of the coincidence of ictus and stress in Plautus' verse (this has not been proved), but to disprove the argument that words of such rhythmical structure could not have, in Plautus' time, the ictus on the second syllable; such cases do occur. If one wanted to relate the use of ictus to the position of word stress, one would find out, on the basis of the above examples, that in Plautus' time the absolute initial accentuation of the type $\stackrel{\shortmid}{\smile}\smile\smile\times$ still existed, though there certainly occurred also the more recent type $\smile\stackrel{\shortmid}{\smile}\smile\times$, with stress on the *second* mora of an initial two-mora member.

As far as the change of the position of stress in Balto-Slavic languages (the recessive character of circumflex) is concerned, the parallel can be easily seen. In both cases, stress is shifted to the adjoining mora: backwards in the type *n'a vodǫ,* and forwards in the type *ămícus.*

Besides some significant differences, there exist some important similarities between the development of Latin and of the Balto-Slavic languages. One similarity concerns the *prosodic base,* i.e. the significance of the mora for establishing the rhythmic value of a word's particular members, which consist of one mora (short) or of two morae (long). In the latter case, the first or the second mora may be stressed. However, the reasons for change, as well as the actual processes, differ in the two systems, and so do their phonological conditions.

In Latin, the development is due to two factors: 1) In the penultimate syllable, if it is long, the stress falls on the *first* mora, while in the previous syllable (i.e. the third syllable, counting from the end of the word) the *second* mora is stressed; and 2) The initial short syllable (the third syllable from the end of the word) cannot be the only one to carry the stress, which therefore extends over the next syllable (that is, its first mora). Thus, in Latin, the penultimate long syllable always has the stress on the *first* mora (... $\stackrel{\shortmid}{\smile}\smile\times$, e.g. *stámus, ămámus,* etc.). If the stress falls on the long syllable, the third syllable from the end of the word, it is always the *second* mora that is stressed ($\smile\stackrel{\shortmid}{\smile}\smile\times$, e.g. *cédimus,* etc.). In such circumstances, the intonation difference $\stackrel{\shortmid}{\smile}\smile : \smile\stackrel{\shortmid}{\smile}$ never causes the opposition in Latin; and hence, no phonological opposition between acute and circumflex intonations has occurred. It is not so in Balto-Slavic languages. Thus in Lithuanian, for example, every non-final long syllable, irrespective of the length of the word, can be either acute or circumflex; hence, the opposition of intonation has become a significant factor of the phonological system.

Notes

1. Roman Jakobson, "Z zagadnień prozodii starogreckiej", *Prace ofiarowane Kazimierzowi Wóycickiemu*, Wilno, 1937, 73–88.

2. M. Niedermann, "Une loi rythmique proéthnique en latin", *Mélanges de Saussure*, 43–57; A. Burger, *Études de phonétique et de morphologie latines*, Neuchâtel, 1928; J. Safarewicz, *Études de phonétique et de métrique latines*, Wilno, 1936.

3. F. Sommer, *Handbuch d. lat. Laut- u. Formenlehre*², 1914, 127 sq.

4 Alice Brenot, *Les mots et les groupes iambiques réduits dans le théâtre latin*, Paris, 1923.

5. For a similar presentation of the system of accentuation in Latin, see Servius, *Comm. in Don.*, Gramm. IV, 426, 31 sq.

HERMANN SCHALL

Preußische Namen längs der Weichsel

(nach Lucas David, ca. 1580)

Die erst im 18. saec. vergangene[1] Sprache der *Preußen* ist noch ein Stiefkind der Forschung. Bei der Erforschung der Ethnogenese der Balten und Slawen, — Brennpunkt gerade jetzt — darf sie aber nie fehlen. Nach dem Rückschlag des 2. Weltkrieges mehren sich erst seit ca. 1955 weiterführende Publikationen[2]. Wir nennen neuere Sammelarbeiten: 1. G. Leyding bereichert uns mit preuß. Naturnamen, weit über G. Gerullis, R. Trautmann hinaus[3]. 2. V. Mažiulis machte 1966 die bekannten Sprachdenkmäler ('Paminklai') Allen zugänglich[4]. Eine Bibliographie der bis 1965 publizierten Prussica verfaßte W. Kubicka, mit Wörter-Verzeichnis[5]. Kritisch, ergänzend wertete 1968 M. Pollakówna alle bekannten „Chroniken"[6].

Lucas David: „Preußische Chronik" (1576–83).

Trotzdem bleibt viel zu tun: Ein riesiger Vorrat an preuß. Natur- wie Personennamen ist nicht ausgewertet. Zu den kaum ausgewerteten Quellen zählt Lucas Davids „Preußische Chronik"[7]. In Allenstein (Olsztyn) 1503 geboren, studierte er ab 1522 beide Rechte zu Leipzig, wo er heiratete. Zurückgekehrt, war er Historiograph des Tidemann Gise, Bischof zu Kulm. (Chełmno), 1541–49. Ab 1550 war er Hofgerichtsrat des Mgr. Albrecht, in Königsberg Pr. Dort starb er 1583. Im Alter schrieb er die „Chronik", als Landeskind vertraut mit der Natur und Geschichte seiner Heimat. Nur ca. 300 Jahre trennen ihn von der Zeit des letzten Preußenaufstandes. Ihm waren viele Urkunden zugänglich, die seither vernichtet, verschollen sind. Bei allen Mängeln seiner Zeit bleibt sein Werk wertvoll. Für uns enthält es viele sonst nirgends bewahrte Namen, samt den Ereignissen der Zeit. Im Folgenden verweisen wir daher öfter auf Stellen der Chronik.

Alphabetische Liste preußischer Namen

1. *Alg-a* f.: „Algo" (PC V, 80). Name des Preußendorfes an jener Stelle, wo die „*Marienburg*" (DO) erbaut wurde. Stadt poln. „Malbork". — Vergleichsnamen: 1. LaN pr. 1250 Alyem, 1326 *Algem („Algent"), ~ 1350

Algemin, -meyn: = „Gegend um Marienburg, Stuhm, Christburg" (PON 8).
— 2. FlN *Algetos*, Furt b. Schreite/Skrojty (Leyd I 14), Kr. Braunsberg/
Braniewo (PON 8). — 3. FlN 1338 *Algasis*, Wald im Samland (ib.). — In
Litauen: 1. GN *Algė* f. = „Alg", E von Karklė/Karkeln, sowj. „Mysovka"
(Senn Wb 518), ins Kurische Haff (Rozwad 153).

2. *Alg-upỹs* m., Nfl. der Striūnà, b. Bãbtai, Rajon 32, Kaũnas.

3. GN *Alg-uvà* f., bei Mósėdis, R. 1, Skuõdas (UEV 4). — 4. ON *Alg-upio*
k(aimas), R. 32, Kaunas (LAS 570). — Unklar: ON 1540 Algaw = Algaw-
ischken, Memelgebiet, bei Kiparsky (Kur 75). Ob = kur. GN *Alg-ava* f.?
In Lettland: GN 1404 „Weg entlang, gen Algonas, auf die Alghenas'sche
beke" (BGS.451, Nr.103, Grenzbeschr. — Betrifft Gegend in Livland „Roden-
poys/Segewald" = Ropaži/Sigulda, R. 9, Vidzemē). Ob lett. GN *Algone* f.?
Die GN gehören zum Pflanzen lit. *algė* f. = berùtis m. = [Teucrium], „Ga-
mander". Das Lit. Akadem. Wb. (LAW I², 97; 775) unterscheidet: a) váisti-
nis berùtis [T. chamaedrys] von b) raudon-žiẽdis b. [T. scordium]. — Verwandt ist latein. *alga*, -ae f. „Seegras, -tang" (WH I, 28). — Viele verwandte *germ.* Wörter gehören zur Tiefstufe idg. *lgā, vom „Wasserwort" idg.
*ol-: *el- plus g-Formans. Ihre Grundbedeutung ist „klebrig, schleimig,
schlüpfrig" (Rozwad., „Studia" 149–175; 162!) Im Baltischen vgl. lit. *al-
mės* f. pl., GN *Almė* f. (LEW 8; UEV 5). — Zur Bildung der bei „Algo" vermuteten preuß. (Sumpf-) Landschaft *Alg-aminā f. (s. o.) vgl. den lit. GN/
ON Rud-aminà f., am Nfl. der Vókė, R. 39, Vilnius (UEV 213; LAS 231).

2 *As-ā* f.: Im SW Preußens ist bei Historikern als „Grenzfluß" gegen
Masowien (im S) die „Os(s)a."; jedoch sprachlich reichen preuß. Namen süd-
licher (s. den Schluß!). — Belege: 1243 Osze, 1294 Ozza (PON 111); Gerullis
schwankt, unter Hinweis auf 1 lit. GN „Osa = Wosse", ob unser GN preußischer oder polnischer Herkunft sei. Die histor. Formen sind gewiß pol-
nisch beeinflußt. Für baltische Herkunft aber sprechen jetzt lit. GN, die
(dialektal) ein Nebeneinander 2er Ablaut-Stufen zeigen: 1. GN lit. *Vas*-intà
f., dial. *Vuos*-intà, Nfl. der Jarà, b. Svėdasaĩ, R. 19, Anykščiaĩ (nahe Sēlen-
Gebiet!), Abfluß des Sees *Vas*-int-ẽlis m., b. Kunigiškiai, ib. — Ähnlich:
2. GN dial. *ọ̄s*-intà = *Vuos*-intà = *Uos*-intà, Nfl. der Dubýsa, b. Čẽkiškė,
R. 32, Kaũnas. — Vgl. weiter: 3. GN *Óš*-upis m. = a.) zur Ostsee b. Palangà,
b) R Nfl. der Ramýtė, b. Smìlgiai, R. 16, Radvìliškis. — In weiteren lit.
GN wechseln langes ō- mit -uo-. Vgl. auch *Úos*-is m., *Úos*-upis m., -upė f.
(UEV 178; 188). Das V- (dial.) ist prothetisch. Man erkennt 2 Ablaut-St.:
(v-) ōs, -uos: as-; aus idg. *ōs-: *ọ̆s- (Bsl. 203). — Dial. lit. (v-) as- ist viel-

leicht auf „Wahl" von idg. *ŏs- statt sonst idg. *ōs- zurückzuführen, u. U. auf lit. „Überlagerung" (Superstrat)? Jedenfalls ist lit. as- neben ōs- nun belegt. Beide Varianten konnten auch im Preußischen leben; auch die v-Prothese ist dort belegt: Appellativ pr. [vōsis] „woasis" ~ lett. uôsis ~ lit. úosis m. 'Esche' [Fráxinus] (SPV 276). — Leider konkurriert, soweit n-Erweiterungen in Namen vorliegen, eine mit lit. usnìs m.; usna, ūsne, ušņa f. im Lett. belegte (s. LEW 1172), als Appellativ dem Preuß. fehlende, in Namen aber mögliche Entsprechung. In den Wbb. unauffindbar ist „lit. ušis" (sic PON 209) = usnìs 'Distel'. Immerhin können hierzu etliche preuß. NN gehören, wie „Wusn-, Wusen", allenfalls auch „Wosn-, Wosen" (graphisch!). Diese Sachlage gestattet vorerst, mehrere von Gerullis sub „Wosen" (PON 209) verzeichnete NN eher zu pr. *as-ā f. 'Esche' zu stellen; z. B. den GN 1420 Wosen See, nhd. „Wusen-See" b. Kaliningrad (Königsberg). Auch dürfte 2. (GN) 1302 „Wusiniz", b. Thiergart, Kr. Rosenberg (PON 211), poln. „Grodziec", pow. Susz (Rospond 723) besser zu deuten sein, mit poln. Suffix sekundär versehen, als *Wós-(e)nica f. „Eschenbach". — Ähnliche urspr. preuß. Namen wären dann auch:

1. FlN Wusi-waio, Wiese im KA Liebstadt, poln. „Miłakowo", pow. Morąg (Mohrungen, Rosp 595). — 2. GN 1289 Wuskewi-salus, Bach b. Borchertsdorf, Kr. Pr. Holland = poln. „Dębiny", pow. Pasłęk (Rosp 445). Brauchbar ist außerdem nur „Woskawy-salus". Hier scheint sekundär ein poln. Suffix, -awy, -owy?, eingefügt. Wosk- erinnert an: 1305 Wusigkewaye, für den WiesenN (1.). — Es lassen sich erschließen: 1. FlN pr. *Vosike-vajos f. pl. ('Wiesen am Eschenbächlein', s. SPV 270) und

2. GN *Vosike-salus m. 'kl. Eschenbach'. Somit wären belegt: a) pr. *Asā f. samt Diminutiv *Vos-ike f. zu dial. *Vosa f., aus *Vasā f. Neben pr. vōs-is m. (s. o.) liegt also pr. *asis, vosis m. als Appellativ. Für i-St. sprechen: „woassis" wie auch 1305 Wusi-, im Flurnamen.

3. Gard-eja f.: LD nennt ad 1231 „Pipin's Burg", an 1 See „der Pipin'sche Sehe" (PC II, 60 mit Anm. 2). Der eigentliche ON/GN fehlt. Die Beschreibung paßt am besten auf: I. ON/GN „Garnsee", poln. „Gardeja", pow. Kwidzyn (Marienwerder). See mit Abfluß „Gardeja", Mündung zur „Ossa" (2) b. Rogożno–Zamek (Schl. Roggenhausen). II. S Stadt „Garnsee" liegt Dorf poln. „Szlemno" (Rosp 492), bei LD „Schlomno" genannt (PC II, 73). Die Lokalität paßt: „Burgk, so Pippinus in eine enge, da zwene Sehe fast zusammen stoßen, geleget" (ib.). — Der poln. ON 1) Gard-eja f. gehört zu

pr. *gard* m. 'Burg'; Suffix -*eja* f. ist in balt. GN typisch. — ON 2) „Szlemno"
kann beruhen auf a) pr. *salme* f. 'Stroh' (SPV 241), oder eher *b*) auf GN, wie
jatwing. *Selment* m. „Gr. Sellment See", E Lyck (Ełk), mit „masurischem"
S-, gegenüber dem poln. GN „Szelment, Mały i Wielki", W Szypliszki
(Šipliškiai), pow. Sejny (Seinaĩ), s. Leyding (II, 25). Vgl. die lit. GN *Šelmuõ*
m. und *Šelmentà* nahe „Jatwingien" (UEV 162), zu lit. *šelmuõ, -meñs* m.
'Dachfirst'; dial. 'Strohbündel' (Senn IV, 471). — Verwandt ist slaw. **selmę*
poln. ślemię neben szlemię 'Querbalken' (LEW 971, Bsl. 301 f.).

4. *Kab-al-a* f.: *1254* „... duas aquas; nomen uni „Cabal maior", alteri
„Chabal minor", que de Wizla sumentes originem, in Mari recenti finem
sortiuntur; cum *insula*, que eedem aque circumcingunt" (PC III A S. 32
=Sambors Urk. 16, Or); — 1273 Cabula, 1285 Cabala „auf dem Werder"
(PON 52). — Gehört zum vb. intr. lit. *kàbal*-uoti 'wackeln' (LEW 200). Die
GN sind abgeleitet vom FlN der *Insel*, die ein 'Wackelmoor' ('Quebbe') war.
— Entfernt verwandt ist das Part. pf. pass. pr. *kabiūns* 'gehangen' (SPV
186). — In Litauen vgl.: GN *Kablẽlis* m.; *Kabli-upỹs* m. (UEV 65) und
kablis m. 'Haken'; krumm gewachsener Baum' (LEW 200). — In Lettland
vgl.: FlN wie *Kabele* f., *Kabļi* m. pl. u. a. m. (LPSR Vv II 1).

5. *Graudi-andis* m.: StadtN „Graudenz", poln. Grudziądz, am preuß. (E)
Ufer der Weichsel, oberhalb der „Ossa" (1). — Wegen paralleler Bildungen,
wie poln. Goniądz, Raciąż (s. Schluß) am ehesten aus pr. **Graudi-andis* m.
'rauschende Stelle', vom vb. lit. *graud-ýti* =-ĩnti =*grùd*-inti, *grũs*-ti, in der
intr. Bedeutung 'rauschen' (Wasser, LEW 173); vgl. auch lit. *graũd-molis*
m. 'sandig-bröckliger Lehm' (LAW III, 525) usw. — Preußische Namen:
FlN 1284 Graude; 1347 Graudelawke, nemus; ON 1419 *Graudi*-kaym (PON
45) und PN *Grawdio* (PPN 36). — In Litauen vgl.: PN *Graudžius* m. mit
GN *Graudži*-ùpis m., neben GN Gráud-upis m.; Grau(d)-menà f. u. a.
(UEV 51).

6. *Karg-ej* m.: „Cargey", Burg des Pomezanen „Macko" (Matto, s. Pollak
99, 168) Sohn des „Pippin" (PC IV, 18). — Vermutlich vom vb. lit. *karg-
ýti*:*ker̃g*-ti tr. 'leicht befestigen', vgl. *kar̃g*-oti intens. 'Zaun aus Flechtwerk
herstellen' (Senn I, 463). — In Litauen vgl. den Hügel *Kar̃g-antas* m. bei
Kelmė (ŽD 374). Zur Bildung mit -*ej* vgl. Skardžius (ŽD 83 ff.). — In Lettland vgl. den ON (GN?) *Karg-ava* f. bei Viļaka, R. 12, Balvi (LPSR Vv II
51). — Fraglich, ob zugehörig: 2 Güter, lett. *Kar̃ģi*, b. Tirza, R. 11, Gulbene; *Kàrg-āni*, b. Saikava, R. 18, Madona. Da beide nahe Estland liegen,
zweifelt Endzelīns (ib.), ob sie livisch sind. Für den bd. ON „Kargadden",

Gut b. Talsi, Kurzemē verweist auch Bielenstein (BG 259) auf liv. *kargiji* 'Eichhörnchen' (vāvere f.) samt vb. kārg 'springen'. — Nahe der Weichsel sind liv. Namen nicht ganz ausgeschlossen: Der Oberlauf der ,,*Nogat*" heißt 1250 *Lywa* = nhd. ,,Liebe", poln. ,,Liwna". Genauso hieß der Fluß Kurlands 1291 *Lywa*, samt Dorf: *1253* villa ... *Lyva* = h. Seestadt ,,Liepāja/Libau". Ob zu estn. *liiva* 'Sand, Kies'? Näheres s. H. Schall: ,,Ostseefinnische Spuren in Nordwestslawien", S. 154. Wien 1969.

7. *Kvēd-ine* f.: 1233 ,,Lodewicus *in* Quedin", Zeuge der lat. Urschrift der ,,Kulmer Handfeste" (PC III, 144). Demnach war ,,Quedin" bereits 1233 vom DO besetzt. 1228 saßen noch die ,,Schwertbrüder" Livlands mit Willen Konrads v. Masowien am L. Weichselufer. Nach deren Niederlage erschien dort zur Verstärkung DO-Bruder Konrad v. Landsberg. In Kujawien, am W Ufer, erbaute er die 1. DO-Burg, ,,Vogelgesang", gebaut ,,von groben runden Holzern oder Ronen" (PC II, 38). Als 2. DO-Burg baute Br. Hermann Balk(o) ,,Nessau", vordem pr. **Vizna* genannt (s. u.) (PC II, 44). Als Wachstumsspitze auf dem pr. Ufer errichtete man 3. ,,Alt Thorn" (Torún) 1231, etwa 1 Meile stromab. *1233* baute man in Th. eine 4. Holzburg und flößte sie stromab: ,,auf einen Hügel ins *Werder*, 'Quidzin' genannt" (PC II, 68/9). — Diese Inselburg wurde vom DO ,,Marienwerder" genannt und bald verlegt: ,,*auß* dem Werder und *uber* das Flies, ins gebiet *Resen* (s. Riesenburg, -kirch) des Pomesanischen landes" (ib.). — Die bis heute gültigen poln. Formen Kwiedzin, *Kwidzyn* bewahren den Inselnamen pr. **Kvēdine* f. — Verwandte ON in Preußen: 1. 1258 Quedenow, 1302 Quidenowe = nhd. ,,Quedenau", h. Gebiet Kaliningrad (PON 78). — 2. 1419 Queden, ,,Queden" = poln. ,,Kwedzina", pow. Kętrzyn (Rastenburg; Leyd I S. 34 Nr. 188). — Zum InselN gehören bei Gerullis (78) die Belege: 1235 Quedina, 1236 Quedin, 1243 Quidino, ,,Insel". Erst ein Beleg *1470* Que*dz*yn zeigt poln. -dz-. Er beweist, daß ein pr. -i- folgte. Dem Deutschen fehlt solche ,,Erweichung"; daher werden die ON 1, 2 auf pr. **Kvēd-ine* f. bzw. *-in-ove* f. fußen. Zum 2. Suffix, pr. *-ove* f., ~ lett. lit. *-ava* f., vgl. Būga's Beispiele (RR I 168). — Der LaN **Kvēdine* f. gehört zum lit. vb. *kvėd-úoti* tr. 'umwehen, auslüften', intr. 'Wind machen' (LAW VI, 1063). — Das lit. Suffix *-inė* f. bedeutet oft 'Stelle, wo X ist oder hinkommt'; vgl. GN Purv-inė, Saus-inė f. Es wird auch von Verben gebildet: *sėt-inė* = 'sėta girià'; augt-inė = 'augtoji vieta' (ŽD 264 ff.). — Pr. **Kvēdine* f. bedeutete wohl 'Stelle, wo es weht, zugig ist' (Sandinsel: umgebendem Strom). — In Litauen vgl.: 1. ON *Kvēd-arna* f., R. 14, Šilālė. Suffixe *-ar -na* sind sekundär; neben *-ar*-liegt *-al*-, wie neben *-ir*- auch *-il*- (ŽD 291). — 2. GN lit. Kvēd-ar-iškė f., See b. Kùrtuvėnai, R. 11, Šiauliaī. — 3. GN *Kvēd-er-daubė* f., Nfl. der Armenà,

b. Vėliuonà, R. 25, Jùrbarkas (UEV 85). — In Lettland: 2 Wiesen im Rajon 21, Jēkabpils: 1. FlN lett. *Kved-ila* f., b. Maz-zalva (Ērberǵe); 2. FlN *Kved-il-ka* f., bei Mēmele (LPSR Vv II 196). — Das -e- ist beidemal kurz.

8. *Pa-mez-ān-ai* m. pl.: Die westlichste geogr.-polit. Einheit der Preußen, das ‚Hockerland" (PC IV 153), hieß ‚‚Pomesanien", poln. *Pomiedzanie, lat. ‚‚*Pomesan(i)*". Sie erstreckte sich längs der Weichsel, Ostufer. Vom Grenz-flusse ‚‚Ossa" (2) im S nordwärts, zur Gabelung beim ‚‚*Santīr(s)*"; dann den R Arm ‚‚Nogat" abwärts bis zum Frischen Haff (s. PC II, 106) = poln. ‚‚Zalew Wiślany", lit. ‚‚*Ais(t)marės*". Landein, ostwärts grenzte P. (~) längs der pr. *Zirg-une f. = ‚‚Sirge, Sorge" = poln. Dzierzgoń (Leyd II, 152) mit den pr. *Pagezānai, ‚‚Pogezenen". — Die besten neuen Namen-Er-klärungen gibt V. Mažiulis (Paminklai 16, m. Anm. 46). Er bezweifelt, daß P. zu pr. *media*(n) 'Wald' gehöre, erwähnt den ON illyr. *Medi-one* (lt. Krahe). Besser lege man einen pr. *GN Med*- zugrunde. Er vergleicht *lit*. GN, wie *Med-ujà* f., Nfl. Alšià, b. Stãkliškės, R. 37, Príenai (UEV 100). — Dieser wiederholt sich in Pommern: GN *1304 Med-uia*, 1248 stagnum Medui (EO II 88, dort zu *medъ* 'Honig' gestellt) = der ‚‚Madü-See", poln. ‚‚Miedwie" samt ON ‚‚Miedwiecko", b. Stargard (Szczeciński, Rosp 709). — Solche GN gehören eher zu idg. **med(i)*- ‚‚mitten". Vielleicht verwandte pr. FlN/GN stellt Gerullis alle zu pr. *media*(n) 'Wald': 1. FlN 1289 Medio-laucks, Wald b. Borchertsdorf (s. o.); 2. GN 1289 Medyon-azara, See, ib. (PON 96). Man kann ihn als pr. *Mediun azaras m. 'See in Wäldern' deuten; formal entspricht -*iun*, gen. plur., dem -*un* im GN pr. 1343 *Tlōkun-pelk*- 'Bären-Sumpf' (PON 183; SPV 266; 195).

9. *Pastal-ine* f.: 1234 wurde die Preußen-Burg ‚‚Postelen" vom Mgr. Heinrich v. Meißen verbrannt (PC II 82). Belege: 1236 Pastoline, 1249 Pastelina, 1284 Postelin. Ein von Gerullis erwähnter PN: ‚‚Postelyn, Deutscher?" (PON 117) fehlt Trautmann (PPN 79). — Vorzuziehen ist Urform pr. *Pastal-ine f. Am besten zu lett. *pastala* f. 'lederne Sandale' = bd. ‚‚Pastel". Bedeutung des ON: ‚‚Werkplatz f. Sandalen". — Dafür spricht ein ähnlicher ON in *Böhmen: 1125* Postolo-pirt = čech. Postolo-prty pl. ‚‚Postel-berg". Profous (III, 443) erklärt: ‚‚kteři *postoly prt*-ali = škorně opracovali", als ON für ‚‚Gerber, Sandalenmacher". Machek irrt wohl, wenn er *postol* m. als '*Bast*-Schuh' bezeichnet (Et 385): Čech.-prty, prt-ali aber gehört zum lit. vb. *peř-ti* = 4. 'schlagen, prügeln' (Senn III, 62); deutlich in: a) ką *išperti* = 'jemandem das Leder/Fell gerben'; b) kam gerai kailį iš-p. = ‚‚jdn. schlagen, was das *Leder* hält" (VLŽ 576). Lit. *káilis*, io m. ist = 'Tierhaut, Fell, Balg', und *kailã-dirbis* m. der 'Weißgerber' (Senn I, 423).

Informationen zur *Sache* bietet Lettland: Es heißt ~ *1300*: „... III paria *postelen, in corio* adhuc existencia" — ... V paria *postelen* — ... V paria *postelen, cutis elendiensis* ..." (LUB I Nr. 603, s. BG S. 443). Die Urk. betrifft Raub-Übergriffe des DO-Ldms. in Livland wider Kurlands Bischof. Unter den geraubten Sachen sind „*Pasteln*". Ausdrücklich wird gesagt: a) „im Fell", *un*-bearbeitet, bzw. b) „aus *Elch*-Haut", kostbar! — Anderwärts geben August bzw. Tochter Martha Bielenstein beste Auskünfte, mit Abbildungen(!) über die ~ 1850 in *ganz* Lettland noch getragenen „Pasteln": *A.* AB untersucht (BG 276) die Herkunft dieses *Wortes*: „Es bezeichnete *nur Leder*-Sandalen (~ Opanken; Mokassins. H. S.). In Litauen/Preußen *fehle*(?) das Wort! Es entsprechen: Liv. *pastāl*, estn. *pasel*, -sli (lt. Hupel). Die P. werden meist aus *Rinds*-Leder fußgerecht zugeschnitten, selten aus *Elch*-haut. *Geschnürt* wurden sie mit *2 Bast*-Schnüren, lett. *aukla* f., vb. *au*-t(i) 'Schuhe/Strümpfe *anziehen*'.

Etwas *Anderes* sind die aus *Bast geflochtenen* (vgl. 15 *Vizna*!), kurz haltbaren lett. *vīz*-es f. pl., ~ lit. *vyž*-à f. sg., mit *vyž*-pinỹs m. = '*Flechter* von *Bast*-Schuhen' (Senn V, 359). — *Diese* hießen in Preußen *pa-rēsken* pl. Das Etymon ist gut preußisch: vb. pr. per-*rēist* 'verbinden' vgl. aengl. wrī-ōn 'einhüllen' (SPV 224); Ptz. pf. pass. san-*rists* 'verbunden' (SPV 246, sen-). — *B.* MB beschreibt genau die *Leder*-Zubereitung, den Zuschnitt der „Pasteln". Sie gibt Beispiele aus Volksliedern (BH 683 f.).

Trotzdem bleibt das *Problem: Woher* kamen Sache und Wort? Neben lett. *pastala* f. tritt nun preuß. **Pastal-ine* f. Böhmisch *Postolo-prty* ist *früher* Beleg! — Lokotsch (133) weist auf *türkisch postal* 'Janitscharen-Schuh', „hieraus"(?) bulg. *postal*, serb. *posto*(*la*), doch auch russ. *dial. postoly*! — Die „Janitscharen" waren meist gefangene Europäer, auch *Slawen*. In Böhmen sind P. um *1125* belegt, lange *vor* dem Türkeneinfall! — Lett. *pastala* kann ein bsl. Wort sein; eher ist Herkunft von Ugro-*Finnen* denkbar. — Zum Suffix pr. *-ine* f.: Es widerstrebt der Gruppierung (ŽD 253); z. B. *silk-inė* = 'Faß für/voll Heringe', aber auch: *grand-inė* f. 'Eisen, *zum* Schmieden von Ketten' (ŽD 249). — **Pastal-ine* lebt fort im ON nhd. „Pestlin" = „Postolin", pow. Sztum (Stuhm), S davon.

10. *San-tīrs* m.: Sumpfniederung zw. Weichsel/Nogat, später als „Großes Werder" entwässert, besiedelt, bzw. die S Spitze, Abzweigung der Nogat(E). *1245* legte hier H. Svantopolk die Burg S. an, um dem DO den Wasserweg zu sperren (PC III, 83). *1280* vom DO zerstört; stromab geführt Baustoff für „Marienburg" (Algo). — Belege: *1248* in Santir (PC III A, S. 13, Urk. VI Svant's, Or); *1251* de Insula *in* Santhir — pro eadem *parte* Insule (ib. S. 22, XI, Sambors, Or). — *1252* Zeuge: „Wasmudus *in* Zanthyr", DO-Br.

(ib. XII). — Preuß. *San-tīr*(as) m. = 'Sumpf am Zusammenfluß'. Zum GW s.
lit. *týras* m. 'Sumpf, Morast'; pl. týrai = 'Wüstenei, Wildnis' (Senn IV, 673);
Adj. týras 'kahl, baumlos'; *tỹrė* f. 'Brei' zeigen das Landschaftsbild. — Lett.
vgl. *tĩrelis* m. 'Moor'; *tīr-ulis* 'großer, tiefer Morast' (Kiparsky 174). Dazu
GN „*Tĩreḷa Purvs*" m., riesiger Sumpf S Rīga und dem See „Babitis". —
BW ist Nominal-Präfix pr. *san-* 'mit, zusammen' (LEW 753). In pr. Kompo-
sitis: 1. GN/ON 1319 Sam-brad, 1333 Sambrade = See u. Dorf poln. Sam-
bród, pow-Morąg (Samrodt, Mohrungen: Leyd II 150; I 46,48), vgl. lit.
bradà f. 'Schlamm'; vb. lett. *brad-ât* 'waten', *brasls* m. 'Furt' (LEW 58);
FlN lett. *Brasla*, ON *Brasl-ava* f. = „Aiviekste" (LPSR Vv I, 125) u. a. Lit.
GN *Brãdas* m.; *Brastà* f. (UEV 21). — Als GW oft in ON pr.-*brast*: Kukun-,
Stabo-brast (SPV 153). — 2. GN pr. 1388 Sam-plat = See u. Dorf masur.
Sómplat „Samplatter See", pow. Szczytno (Ortelsburg: Leyd II, 348; I, 114),
vgl. lit. *sam-platà* adv. 'ufer-gleich, bis zum Uferrand' (PON 150). — 3. GN
pr. 1487 San-stangen, *1538* Sonstag = masur. „Sǫnstak, San-" = „Szonstag
See" (1921/28: Leyd II 34) b. Juchy, pow. Ełk (Lyck); vgl. vb. lit. *su-stìngti*
'dickflüssig, zäh, steif werden' (Senn IV, 366). — Häufig ist lit. *sántaka*(s)
f. m. 'Zusammenfluß' (confluentes!), s. Senn u. Savukynas (UEV 142). In
West-*Pommern*: GN/ON *1286* Santogk = nhd. „Zantoch", p. Santok, pow.
Gorzów Wkp. (Landsberg: EO II, 113; Rosp 284), einst Pommern-Grenzburg
am Zusammenfluß Netze/Warthe (Noteć/Warta).

11. *Skarp-ava* f.: Poln. „Szkarpawa", nhd. „Scharpau" (GN): R Weichsel-
arm, verbindet sie kurz vor der Mündung mit dem „Frischen Haff". Zweigt
ab unterhalb Stróża (Rothebude, Rosp 673), nach NE, E über „Tujsk"
(Tiegenort; dort pr. GN *Tūja*, ib. 724) und „Graniczna Wieś" (Grenzdorf,
ib. 502). Mündung ins Haff SE „Dubashaken" (Doły, ib. 469). Den früheren
Verlauf der Fr. *Nehrung* (pr. *ner-ija?) schildert LD (PC II, 102 ff.). — GN
pr. *Skarp-ava* f. hat „breites" pr. *-a-* für bsl. *-e-*; ebenso im pr. GN 1651/2
„Scharppe", nhd. Skarpasch, „Skarpe See" (1925) = masur. Skjar'ś (1927),
poln. Skarp: See in den „Krutyńskie Lasy", S vom See „Dusia" (= lit. GN,
2x), im pow. Mrągowo (Sensburg: Leyd II, 174). — Vom PflanzN lit. *skérpės, -ių* f. pl. 'Blasentang' [Fucus vesiculosus] bei Senn (III, 681); vgl. vb.
lett. *šḳērp-êt* 'schneiden, mit d. Rasenpflug', verwandt mit aengl. *scearf*-ian
'kratzen', ablautend mit *scurf* m. 'Schorf, Grind' (LEW 258), wie in ahd.
scorf-wurz 'Grindwurz': vb. *scurf*-en mhd. (Kluge[17] S. 676, 684). — Vgl. lit.
šiur̃p-as m. 'rauh, nicht glatt' (LEW 974, 994) und den jatwing. ON *Šiurp*-
pilis m. = poln. „Szurpiły" N Jeleniewskie, pow. Sejny. — Entfernter verwandt: PflanzN pr. *skerp-tus* m. 'Rüster' [Ulmus campestris]; lit. *skir̃p-stas*
m. 'idem' u. a. (SPV 249; LEW 807).

12. *Spang-ava* f.: Zur „Mottlau" (poln. Motława) W „Dirschau" (Tczew). Dort ON „Spangau" (Szpęgawa); weiter S ON „Szpęgawsk" (NE Star(o)- gard Gd.). Der Bach fließt hart W parallel zur Weichsel. — Belege: 1256 Spangau, aqua (PC III A, S. 33, Sambors Urk. XVII), 1289 Spangawa, 1317 molendinum Spangov (EO II, 26). — Vgl. den pr. GN 1345 Spongio, 1355, 1358 Sponge, 1372 *Spange*, 1376 Spongi (PON 170) = poln. Szpągi, nhd. „*Spangen* See" (1928), W Ustnik, pow. Reszel (Lichtenhagen, Rössel: Leyd II, 309; I, 97). — Beide GN gehören zum PflanzN lit. *spañg-ė* f. ≅ lett. spęng-uoge f. 'Krans-, Moosbeere' [Oxycóccus quadripetalus] (Senn IV, 44). Vgl. das vb. lit. *spang-al-oti* 'glänzen, leuchten, schimmern', ablautd.: *sping*-ėti 'flimmern, glitzern, *schwach* leuchten' (LEW 860; 871); vgl. vb. lett. *spuog*-ât 'glänzen' usw. Dazu preuß. *spang-sti („soanxti", E 35) 'Funke' (SPV 252). In Litauen vgl. GN wie: *Spañg*-upis m.; *Speng*-là f. 4x, 1 See), Speñg-las m. (See; UEV 153). — Unsere „Spang-*ava*" fließt in Alt-Pomoranien.

13. *Stūma* m.: *1234* zerstörte Mgr. Heinrich v. Meißen die Preußenburg „da das Dorf 'Postelen' (s. 9 Pastaline), nicht weit *vom Stume* angelegt ist" (PC II, 82). Die Stadt „Stuhm", poln. „Sztum" trennt der Forst „Ryjewo" (Rehhof, Rosp 665) von der „Nogat" im NW. Nesselmann: „*stumo* locus" (n. Dusburg III, 14), „uw *dem stume*" (n. Vossberg, Münzen 32) (Thes 178). — Der ON fehlt PON/PPN. — Belegt ist ein *PN* „*stumo*" (ib. n. Dusburg III, 138): Der *Preuße* „Stumo" nahm mit „Stutze" (PN) am Aufstand winters 1261/2 teil, er fiel vor Balga (PC V, 41). — Der pr. PN *Stūmo* m. stimmt zu lit. dial. *stūm-u* m. in Kvėdarna = *stuom-uõ*, -*meñs* m. 'Statur, Wuchs, Leibeslänge', neben dial. stúom-*as* m., in Šakiaĩ, jüngrer o-St. aus urspr. -men-St. (wie mén-*as*:mén-*uo*, ŽD 36, 232, 295/6). — Lit. stúomas ist = 1. *stõ-tas* m. 'Gestalt, Statur, Wuchs' und 2. 'Mensch, der *träge* herumsteht' (Senn IV, 110, 127). Sie gehören zu idg. *stō*-, ablautend mit *stā- „stehen". Zu *dieser* gehören auch: lit. sto-muõ m. 'idem' und vb. stó-ti, wie lett. stā-men 'Rumpf', und, mit andren Formantien: lett. *stà-vs* m., russ. sta-*n* 'Wuchs'; vgl. lat. *stā*-men, -minis n., tochar. B stā-*m* 'Baum' (LEW 912; WH II 586). Ablautend, mit kurzem -a-, vgl. ahd. *stam* m. 'Stamm', asächs. stamn n. 'Steven' (Kluge[17] 737). — Der pr. PN *Stūma* bedeutete wohl 'hochgewachsen, stattlich; stämmig'. — Möglich ist Kontamination; vgl. lit. *stūm-a* f. m. 'träge Person, die man *stoßen* muß', vom vb. *stùm*-ti (Senn IV, 125), das sonst fern bleibt.

14. *Tūja* f.: Nfl. der „Scharpau" (s. 11 Skarpava) im „Großen Werder" von S. — Belege: 1248 Tuia, 1345 Thuya (PON 187; Thes 192). Nhd. die

„Tiege" [tīje]. Nach der „Tiege" sind benannt ON: Tiege, Tieger-felde, Tiegen-hof, -hagen, Tieger-*ort* (Mündung!). Die *pr.* Grundlage ist besser bewahrt in den *poln.* Formen: GN Tuja f.; ON Tuj-sk = -ort, Tuj-ec = -hagen, Tuj-skie pole = -felde. Nur „Nowy Dwor Gdański" für „Tiegen-hof" ist anders gebildet (Rosp 724). — Der GN gehört zu bsl. *tū̆i̯-ō* 'werde fett'. Trautmann vergleicht u. a. aind. *tū́ya* 'kräftig, schnell'; griech. *taýs* 'mégas, polýs' (Bsl. 331). — Von idg. *teu-: *tū̆: *tu-* 'schwellen' (LEW 1136/7). Mit *l*-Formans verwandt: russ. *tyl(ъ)* m. 'Nacken; Nachhut'; bair. *doll*-fuß m. 'geschwollener Fuß'; u. U. auch lat. *tull*ius, -ī m. 'Guß, Schwall' (WH II, 714). — Daher bedeutet der GN pr. *Tūja* f. 'zeitweise anschwellender Fluß'. Vgl. damit den lit. GN *Tilžė* f., vom vb. *tilž*-ti 'sich mit Wasser füllen' (LEW 1095). — Parallelen in Litauen: a) GN/ON *Tuj*-aīniu ẽžeras m. (UEV 176) mit Dorf, apyl. Poška, R. 24, Skaudvìlė/Tauragẽ (LAS 394); b) von idg. *teu-*: 1. GN *Tauj*-ẽnis m., See b. Sãlakas, R. 21, Zarasaī (UEV 171). — 2. Mehrere ON: a) Tauj-*ẽnai* m. pl., Stadt, R. 19, Kovarskas, mit 2 Einzelhöfen (1: apyl. Laviškis) und ON Tauj-*an-ẽliai* m. pl. (LAS 208). — b) Taujẽnai m. pl. und Tauj-*ankai* m. pl., apyl. Okainiai, R. 27, Kėdáiniai (LAS 349). — Der ON Tauj-*ūnai* m. pl., apyl. Nauj. Daugèlìškis. R. 22, Ignalinà (LAS 83) mag zu 1 PN gehören? (vgl. PN *Tau*-jotas m., lt. Būga, RR I 136/8, aus *Tava-?). — In West-*Pommern* vgl. u. U. den pom. GN *1253* Tyua, 1305 fluv. Tywa = nhd. die „*Thue*", mit SeeN *1254* stagn. Thiwitz = „Dewitz-See", S Gryfino (Greifenhagen), zur Oder (EO I, 38; II 26). Urform: ?*Tū-va* f., mit *v*-Formans? bzw. *Tūv-ica* f., später: *Tyv-ica*?

15. *Vīz-na* f.: ~ *1230* schenkt Konrad v. Masowien die „Feste" *Visna* samt 4 Dörfern dem DO. Nach Ankunft des H. Balk(o) im „Vogelgesang" errichtet dieser auf 1 Hügel, der ganz von *Weichsel*wasser umgeben ist, unweit V. eine *Feste* wider die Preußen (PC II, 44). Sie ward „*Nessau*" genannt, weil ganz vom „nassen" Bruch umgeben (II, 45). N. lag noch in Kujawien (ib. 48). Auf dem pr. *Ost*-Ufer, ~ 1 Meile stromab wurde Feste „Alt-Thorn" (abwärts Toruń) erbaut, von „Nessau, Vogelgesang" aus versorgt (ib. 46). — *Dorf* poln. „Nieszaw*ka*" liegt W Podgórz in der Weichsel-Niederung. — Namen*gleich* ist: II. *Wizna*, pow. Łomża, unterhalb d. Mündung der „Biebrza" in den „Narew". Die frühe Burg, später „Kastellanie" W. war Zentrum der Expansion Masowiens in „*Jatwingien*". *Wizna II* ist gut belegt: *1230* castri *uisne* (gen. sg.), *1253* (kńaz Danił) „pride *ko Wizńe* (dat.) i preide rěkou *Narov*" (wruss!), *1294* (Bolesta) in castro suo *Wizna* (A. Kamiński: 'Jaćwież' [1953], S. 48 Anm. 55; S. 114). Zur Lage vgl. die *Karte* im Aufsatz von A. K.: 'Pogranicze Polsko-Rusko-Jaćwieskie', S. 12 (ABS I, Białystok

1961). — Preuß. *Vīzna ist sonst schwach belegt: GN 1326 Wisne = 1312 Wysde (!), Bach b. Henrykowo „Heinrikau", pow. Braniewo (Braunsberg: Rosp 527; PON 203). Ob Suffix-Wechsel pr. -da: -na? Zu -da vgl. u. U. den GN lit. Vizd-ijà f., b. Bìrštonas? (UEV 199). — Da preuß. vīz- ~ lit. vyž-, sind an lit. GN zu vergleichen: 1. Vȳž-balė f.; Vȳž-upis m.; sowie 2. ON Vyžu-kalnis m., Hof, apyl. Sužionys, R. 40, Nemenčìnė, N Vilnius (LAS 275); vgl. mit diesem den lat. FlN „Vīminālis collis", in Rom, von vī-men, -minis m. 'Geflecht' (WH II, 786); dazu pr. vī-mino 'Ulme' (SPV 274). — An PflanzN vgl. weiter: Lett. vîksna f. 'idem': lit. vìnkšna f. mit poln. wiąz [vonz]. Bsl. Urform: *vinž-snā f. (Bsl. 360). Das hierin auftretende -n- ist nicht „infigiert", sondern „verbauter" idg. n-Stamm (Specht, Dekl. 58–60). Er liegt, erweitert, auch vor im vb. slaw. *vęz-ati, in Kompositis (vgl. Sadnik-Aitz. Nr. 1077, S. 330). Daß bsl. *vinž- auf vingi- zurückgeht, zeigt lit. dial. vyž-ū̃nas m. = žaltȳs m. „Natter", im Beispiel: „kẽlias žalčių vingi-ãvo" = 'der Weg schlängelte, wand sich' (Senn V, 359, 389); vgl. lit. vìngis m. 'Bogen, Krümmung, Umweg, Windung', dazu Adj. vingi-úotas m. 'gebogen, gekrümmt' und ving-ùlis m. 'Aal', ~ vyž-ū̃nas m. „Natter" (LEW 1256). Das Verhältnis von lit. vyž-: *vinž- möchte Būga „dialektal" erklären, etwa wie bei į̃: iñ 'in', oder bei grȳž-tis: grį́nž-tis (RR II, 654). Im Falle *Vinž-na: Vīz-na würde schon dissimilatorischer Schwund des 1. -n- die Sachlage erklären können. Zu den Baum-Namen s. auch Specht (S. 59 f.). Jedenfalls liegt idg. *vei-: vī-: *vi- „winden, drehen, flechten" vor, woran unterschiedliche Formantien treten. Hierher gehören auch, mit vyž-: viž-, lit. GN/ON: 1. GN Vyž-uonà f. = dial. Vyž-ùnka f., b. Rõkiškis; 2. dimin. GN Vyž-uon-áitis m., See b. Utenà, mit Abfluß Vyž-uon-ẽlė f. — 3. GN Vȳž-intas m., See, mit Abfluß: Vyž-intà f., z. See „Galuonìs" m. mit ON Pa-galuonė f., b. Kuktiškės, R. 20, Utenà (LAS 513). — 4. GN Vìž-ė f., mit ON Už-vižiai, b. Pakapė, R. 11, Šiauliaĩ (LAS 434), alle UEV (199 f.) — Außerhalb der LTSR: In NE Polen die lit. GN/ON: a) Dorf Vìž-ainis m. am E Ufer des „Wischainer Sees" = GN Vìž-ainȳs m. = „Vìžainio ẽžeras", pow. Suwałki (Suvalkaĩ), bei Senn (V, 557). — Ferner 2 ON: 1. Vȳžiai m. p. „Wieschen", apyl. Juknaičiai, R. 23, Šilùtė (Heydekrug, LAS 445); 2. Vyžiai, apyl. Seimatis, R. 20, Utenà (LAS 518). — Alle Namen gehören zum vb. lit. vyž-ti „biegen, flechten, winden", vgl. vy-ti 2 (LEW 1270; 1267). Im Bsl. ist Formans -g, k- angetreten, in anderen Sprachzweigen -d, t-.

Trotz reicher bsl. Vorkommen bleibt noch offen, ob preuß. *Vīzna f. nun eine ‚Flußkrümmung" (in Weichsel, Narew) bezeichnete, eine „Stelle, wo Rüstern wachsen" oder aber eine „mit Flechtwerk befestigte Burg".

Ausblick: Die vorgeführte Auswahl, nur 15 preußische Namen, erlaubte nur einen Streifblick auf riesige, unausgewertete Sprachmaterialien. Doch läßt er erkennen, daß das Ostufer der Unteren Weichsel wie auch ihr Delta, mit der „Nogat", preußisch besiedelt war. Das Beispiel *Vīzna* (15) hat eine Parallele in „Jatwingien". Von dort nach Westen zur „Ossa" (2 *Asā*) bestand eine breite Zone *west*baltischer Namen, quer durch den Norden Masowiens. Ohne nähere Angaben erwähne ich hieraus folgende balt. Namen:

1 GN *Vund-ele* f.: poln. „Wundała"; vgl. pr. ON „Po-wunden" (PON 133) mit 2 GN N von Berlin: a) „Wundel-See", b. Lychen, Kr. Templin; b) „Wandlitz-See", vermutlich GN *Vand-ele* f., plus ON-Suffix -*ici* m. pl. — 2 GN *Rati-andis* m.: im ON poln. „Raciąż" + GN „Raciąż-nica" f. — 3 GN *Sald-ava* f. = ON „Soldau", poln. ON/GN „Działdowo n., -ówka" f. — 4 GN *Vikrā* f.: poln. „Wkra". — 5 GN *Gald-ape* f.: „Gołdap"; vgl. GN pr. Po-gald-us m. (PON 127), mit GN/ON lit. Stãl-up-ėnai m. pl. — 6 GN *Jieskrā* f.: poln. „Jeskra". — 7 GN *Saus-aldā* f. „Suchołda". — 8 GN/ON *Gani-andis* m.: ON „Goniądz". — 9 GN *Sprand-slis* m. „Supraśl". — 10 GN *Veis-ā* f.: „Wissa". — GN *Daugì-spūda* f. = älter poln. Dowspuda, h. „Rospuda" ist vielleicht späteren *lit.* Ursprungs (nach 1500).

Unser Ausblick nach Süden zeigt, daß auch dort viel zu klären ist. Dringend notwendige Einzelforschung kann unserem Bild von „Preußen" und dessen Nachbarstämmen bald tiefere Konturen verleihen.

Anmerkungen

1. Einzelheiten über das langsame Verlöschen des Preußischen jetzt gesammelt bei V. Mažiulis: 'Paminklai' S. 23–26; zuletzt in Anm. 121.

2. An Zeitschriften besonders: a) „Acta Baltico-Slavica", ed. Jerzy Antoniewicz. Białystok 1964 ff. — b) „Baltistica", ed. Jonas Kazlauskas, Vilnius 1965 ff.

3. Gustaw Leyding (-Mielecki): Słownik nazw miejscowych okręgu Mazurskiego. I (ON). Olsztyn 1947 – II (FIN/GN). Poznań 1959.

4. Vytautas Mažiulis: Prūsų kalbos paminklai. Vilnius 1966.

5. Weronika Kubicka: Bibliografia języka Staro-pruskiego. In: „Acta Baltico-Slavica" (ABS), tomus V, p. 257–311. Białystok 1967.

6. Marzena Pollakówna: Kronika Piotra z Dusburga. Wrocław–Warszawa–Kraków 1968. PAN.

7. Preussische Chronik von M. Lucas David, etc., nach der Handschrift des Verfassers, mit Beifügung historischer und etymologischer Anmerkungen, herausgegeben von D. Ernst *Hennig*, Band I–VIII. Königsberg Pr. 1812–1817 (Bd. I–II bei G. K. Haberland; ab Bd. III bei Hartung). — Kürzel: *LD* = Lucas David. — *PC* = Preuß. Chronik. Die *Rein*schrift durch Schreiber des LD erfolgte 1576–1583.

460

Literatur–Abkürzungen

ABS	*Acta Baltico-Slavica.* Białystok 1964 ff. — Siehe *Anm. 2.*
BG	*Bielenstein,* August: Die *G*renzen des lett. Volksstammes und der lett. Sprache in der Gegenwart und im *13.* Jahrhundert. St. Petersburg *1892.*
BH	derselbe: Die *H*olzbauten und *H*olzgeräte der Letten. I: St. Petersburg *1907.* — II: Petrograd *1918.*
Bsl	siehe: Trautmann Bsl.
Būga RR	Būga, Kazys: Rinktiniai Raštai I–III. Vilnius *1958–1961.* RR Indices: Rodyklės, ed. Zigmas Zinkevičius. Ib. *1962.*
Dusburg	Dusburg, Petrus de: Chronicon Prussiae. In ,,Scriptores Rerum Prussicarum", Bd. I. Leipzig *1861.* — Siehe *Pollak* 8 f.
Endzelīns SPV	Endzelīns, Jānis: Senprūšu valoda. Rīgā *1943.*
EO I–III	siehe: Trautmann EO I–III
Jaćwież	siehe: Kamiński.
Kamiński	Kamiński, Aleksander: ,,Jaćwież". Terytorium, ludność, stosunki gospodarzce i społeczne. Łódź *1953.* 2 Karten.
Kiparsky Kur	Kiparsky, Valentin: Die Kurenfrage. Helsinki *1939.*
Kluge[17]	Kluge, Friedrich: Etymologisches Wörterbuch der Deutschen Sprache. 17. Aufl. ed. *Mitzka,* Walther, Berlin *1957.*
LAS	*Lietuvos* TSR *A*dministracinis-Teritorinis *S*uskirstymas (1.II.1959). Vilnius *1959.*
LAW	= ,,*L*itauisches *A*kademisches *W*örterbuch": Lietuvių kalbos žodynas. Bd. I–VII (A-Mėlti). Vilnius *1968* ff.
LD	*Lucas David:* ,,Preußische Chronik" (1576–83). — Siehe: *PC.*
LEW	Fraenkel, Ernst: Litauisches Etymologisches Wörterbuch I, II. Heidelberg *1962, 1965.*
Leyd(ing) I, II	Leyding, Gustav: Słownik nazw miejscowych okręgu Mazurskiego: I. Olsztyn *1947.* II. Nazwy fizjograficzne(zlokalizowane). Poznań *1959.*
Lokotsch	Lokotsch, Karl: Etymologisches Wörterbuch der europäischen Wörter orientalischen Ursprungs. Heidelberg *1927.*
LPSR Vv I, II	Endzelīns, Jānis – Dambe, Vallija: Latvijas *PSR vietvārdi* I, II: A–J. Rīgā *1956;* K–O. Rīgā *1961.*
LUB I	von Bunge, Friedrich G.: Liv-, Esth- und Curländisches Urkundenbuch, nebst Regesten. Bd. I: Reval *1853.*
Machek Et	Machek, Václav: Etymologický slovník jazyka Českého a Slovenského. Praha *1957.*
Mažiulis	Mažiulis, Vytautas: Prūsų kalbos Paminklai. Vilnius *1966.*
Nesselmann Thes	Nesselmann, G. H. F.: Thesaurus Linguae Prussicae. Berlin *1873.*
Paminklai	siehe: Mažiulis. — = ,,Preußische Sprachdenkmäler".
PC	= ,,Preußische Chronik" des M. Lucas *David* (LD). Ed. Ernst *Hennig.* Bd. I–VIII. Königsberg Pr. *1812–17.* — Siehe *Anm. 7.*
Pollak	Pollakówna, Marzena: Kronika Piotra z Duzburga. Wrocław–Warszawa–Kraków *1968.* — Siehe *Anm. 6* und Dusburg.
PON	Gerullis, Georg: Die altpreußischen Ortsnamen. Berlin–Leipzig *1922.*
Profous	Profous, Antonín: Místní jména v Čechách. Díl I–V. Praha 1954–*1960.*

Rosp(ond)	Rospond, Stanisław: Słownik nazw geograficznych Polski Zachodniej i Północnej. I, II. Wrocław–Warszawa *1951*.
Rozwad(owski)	Rozwadowski, Jan: Studia nad nazwami wód Słowianskich. Kraków *1948*.
RR	siehe: Būga RR.
Sadnik-Aitz.	Sadnik, L. und Aitzetmüller, R.: Handwörterbuch zu den altkirchenslawischen Texten. 's Gravenhage *1955*.
Savukynas UEV	Savukynas, Bronys u. A.: Lietuvos TSR *upių* ir *ežerų* *v*ardynas. Vilnius *1963*.
Schall Finn	Schall, Hermann: Ostseefinnische Spuren in Nordwestslawien. In: ,,Disputationes ad Montium vocabula etc." ed. H. H. *Hornung*, Tomus II, p. 153–160. Wien *1969*.
Senn Wb I–V	Wörterbuch der litauischen Schriftsprache: Litauisch-Deutsch. Bearbeitet von *Senn*, Alfred und *Salys*, Antanas. Bd. I–V. Heidelberg *1932–1968*.
Skardžius ŽD	Skardžius, Pranas: Lietuvių kalbos žodžių *daryba* / Die Wortbildung im Litauischen. Vilnius *1941*.
Specht Dekl	Specht, Franz: Der Ursprung der indogermanischen Deklination. Neudruck. Göttingen *1947*.
SPV	siehe: Endzelīns SPV
Thes	siehe: Nesselmann Thes
Trautmann Bsl	Trautmann, Reinhold: Baltisch-slavisches Wörterbuch. Göttingen *1923*.
EO I–III	derselbe: Die *e*lb- und *o*stseeslavischen Ortsnamen. Bd. I, II: Berlin *1948/9*. Bd. III Register (H. Schall). *1956*.
MH	derselbe: Die slav. Ortsnamen *M*ecklenburgs u. *H*olsteins. (Register: in EO III). Berlin *1950²*.
PPN	derselbe: Die altpreußischen Personennamen. Göttingen *1925*.
UEV	siehe: Savukynas UEV
VLŽ	Šlapoberskis, D.: *V*okiečių-Lietuvių kalbų žodynas. Vilnius *1963*.
WH	*W*alde, A. und *H*offmann, J. B.: Lateinisches etymologisches Wörterbuch I, II. Heidelberg 1938, *1954*.
ŽD	siehe: Skardžius ŽD

Sonstige Abkürzungen

aengl.	altenglisch
ahd.	althochdeutsch
aind.	altindisch
Anm.	Anmerkung
apyl(inkė)	Rajon-Abschnitt, in Litauen
asächs.	altsächsisch
bair.	bairisch dial.
Bd.	Band (eines Werkes)
Br.	Bruder (DO-Mitglied)
dial.	dialektal, mundartlich

462

dimin.	diminutiv, verkleinernd
DO	Deutscher Ritterorden = kryžeĩviai; krzyżacy pl.
E	Ost(en), -wärts
ed.	editor, Herausgeber
FlN	Flurname(n)
germ.	altgermanisch
griech.	altgriechisch
GW	Grundwort, Zweitglied
Grenzbeschr.	Grenzbeschreibung, determinatio
GN	Gewässername(n)
ib.	ibidem, ebenda
idg.	indogermanisch
illyr.	altillyrisch
intrans.	verb, intransitiv
jatwing.	jatwingisch (balt.dial.)
káimas	Dorf, in Litauen
kur.	kurisch, lett. dial.
Kr.	Kreis, dt. Verwaltungseinheit
LaN	Landschaftname, regio
lat.	lateinisch
Ldm.	Landmeister des DO
lett.	lettisch
lit.	litauisch
LPSR	Latvijas Padomju Sociālistiskā Republika
LTSR	Lietuvos Tarybų Socialistinė Respùblika
Mgr.	Markgraf, marchio
masur.	masurisch, poln. dial.
mhd.	mittelhochdeutsch
n.	nach, gemäß
N	Norden, nördlich
NE	Nordost, -östlich
Nfl.	Nebenfluß, tributar.
NN	mehrere Namen
NW	Nordwest, -lich
ON	Orts-, Siedlungsname
Or	Original-Urkunde
poln.	polnisch
pom.	pomoranisch (nwslaw.)
pr(euß).	altpreußisch
pow(iat)	poln. Verwaltungseinheit (~ Kreis)
PN	Personenname(n)
R	Nfl. von Rechts
russ.	russisch (groß-)
R(ajon)	sowjet. Verwaltungseinheit (~ Kreis)
saec.	saeculum, Jahrhundert
sowj.	sowjetische Benennung
s.	siehe, vide, confer
S.	Seite(n), pagina(e)

S	Süden, -lich
s. o.	siehe oben
s. u.	siehe unten
tochar.	tocharisch
u. U.	unter Umständen
Vidzeme	Livland LaN
W	West, -lich
Wb(b).	Wörterbuch, -bücher
z. B.	zum Beispiel

Prussian Names along the Vistula (after Lucas David, ca. 1580)

Research on Prussian, sole representative of Western Baltic, which died out during the 18th century, being of high importance for current studies on Slavo-Baltic ethnogenesis, should be advanced more vigorously. There is an immense stock of Prussian names not (previously) evaluated. Attention is drawn to *Lucas David's* "Preußische Chronik", containing much onomastic material scarcely found elsewhere. Here we give only 15 examples, with our interpretations, as well as parallel or similar names or words known in Latvian and/or in Lithuanian:

Alphabetic list of Prussian Names	Quotation: PC
1 *Alg-a* f. RN: bot. algė f. [Teucrium]	lith. Algo V, 80
2 *As-ā* f. RN: dial. Vas-intà f. RN bot. uôsis m. [Fraxinus]	lith. Ossa, passim latv.
3 *Gard-eja* f. RN: cult.-gard- =pilìs m. 'castle'	lith. Pippins Burg II, 60
4 *Kab-ala* f. RN: vb. kàbal-uoti, ~'totter(ing)'	lith. Cabal III A, 32
5 *Graudi-andis* m.: vb. graud-ýti 'rush(ing)' RN	lith. Graudentz, passim
6 *Karg-ej* m. LN: vb. karg-ýti 'fasten(ed)', 'plaited'	lith. Cargey IV 18
7 *Kvēd-ine* f. NN: vb. kvėd-úoti 'draught'	lith. Quedin III, 144
8 *Pamez-ānai* m. pl.: RN Med-ujà f. 'amidst' TN	lith. Pomesan, passim
9 Pastal-ine f.: pastala f. 'leather sandal' LN	latv. Postelen II, 82

10 *San-tīrs* m. LN: san- 'together' +   balt. Santir etc.
    RN týras m. 'bog, morass'   lith. III A, 13, 22
11 *Skarp-ava* f. RN: bot. skérpės f. pl.   lith. ~ Skarpe: Leyding
    [Fucus]
    vb. šķerpêt 'scrape, scurf'   latv. II, 174
12 *Spang-ava* f. RN: bot. spañgė f. [oxy-   lith. Spangau, aqua:
    coccus quadripetalus] 'berry'   III A, 33
13 *Stūm-a* m. PN: dial. stūmū m. 'shape'   lith. Stumo V, 41
14 *Tū-ja* f. RN: RN, LN Tūjaĩniai m. pl.   lith. Stume II, 82
    RN Tau-jĕnis m. 'swell'   lith. ~ Gerullis 187
15 *Vīz-na* f. LN: RN Vȳž-balė f.   lith. Visna II, 44
    bot. vîksna f. [Ulmus]   latv.

(Abbreviations: LN = local   NN = nature   PN = personal   RN = river   TN = tribal *name*.) — Prussian names continue southward, in Mazovia (examples given at end of paper).

WILLIAM R. SCHMALSTIEG

Notes on the Baltic Verb

In earlier articles (Schmalstieg, 1964[1] and 1966[2]) I have explained the Baltic generalization of -a- in the etymological *e/o- verbs as a result of the neutralization of the front/back vocalic contrast following a palatalized consonant (arising in the etymological sequence *[Cj] plus non-front vowel).[3] Watkins (p. 168) objects that this explanation "remains hypothetical because of the question of the chronology of palatalization in Balto-Slavic, the divergent results in Baltic and Slavic, and the unmotivated generalization from the yod-presents".

In the first place the chronology of palatalization in Balto-Slavic really has nothing to do with the general principle which I propose. My theory will work for Baltic even if, for the sake of argument, we suppose that the Baltic palatalization took place *after* the unification of the verbal thematic vowel. Now it is generally accepted that in the history of the Baltic languages the phonemic sequences *[Cjĕ] and *[Cĕ] merged as *[Cĕ] in prehistoric times. As Kazlauskas has pointed out (1968,[4] p. 356) at one time in the history of the Baltic languages it became impossible for front vowels to exist after [j]. Now once this happened there was no possibility of a contrast between front and back vowels following the phonemic sequence *[Cj]; only back vowels were possible in this position (in Proto-Baltic *[ĕ] vs. *[ẵ] functioned as front and back counterparts respectively). Thus one can imagine the following Proto-Baltic conjugational patterns:

	*je/o	*e/o
1 Sg	-C-jō	-C-ō
3 Sg	-C-e	-C-e
1 Pl	-C-jame	-C-ame
2 Pl	-C-ete	-C-ete

Since at this point it is impossible to distinguish the 3 Sg and the 2 Pl of the *e/o- and the *je/o-stems the [j] is again generalized throughout the *je/o-stems. But when this generalization takes place it requires that the etymological [e] be replaced by [a] (the back counterpart of [e]), since in this position (i.e. following a [j]) there can be no [e]. Thus we are confronted with the second step given below:

	*je/o	*e/o
	-C-jō	-C-ō
1 Sg	-C-jō	-C-ō
3 Sg	-C-ja	-C-e
1 Pl	-C-jame	-C-ame
2 Pl	-C-jate	-C-ete

But even when this change was completed the sequence [Ce] was ambiguous in the surface structure of the language, since it could stand either for underlying *[Ce] or *[Cje]. In order to remove the ambiguity the 3 Sg -C-a and 2 Pl -C-ate replaced earlier *-C-e and *-C-ete respectively. Thus the motivation for the morphological changes in question is the retention of a contrast between the *je/o- and *e/o-stems, a contrast which was jeopardized by the merger of *[Cje] and *[Ce], a merger which had abolished the front/back vocalic contrast following the etymological sequence *[Cj].

In my opinion it is not at all clear that the phenomenon of the unification of the thematic vowel took place in exactly the same way in Slavic as in Baltic, although I would suggest that it had something to do with the abolition of the front/back contrast after *[j] which fronted an etymological *[o]>[e]. Thus when Watkins talks of the divergent results of the unification of the thematic vowel in Slavic, I assume that he is referring to the etymological *e/o-stems since, of course, as a result of the fronting by *[j] a form such as *[pišomŭ] 'we write' would be phonologically impossible. In other words, as is well known, in the etymological *je/o-stems the verbal thematic vowel was unified by the fronting of *[o] by [j]. Essentially then the only morphological substitution we are talking about in Slavic is the substitution of [e] for [o] in the 1 Dual and 1 Pl of the etymological *e/o-stems. This substitution is merely a straightening out of the paradigm on the model of the *je/o- and the ī-stems. But in the Slavic case, differently from the Baltic, the distinction between the etymological *e/o- and *je/o-paradigms was never threatened. Thus there is no need to wonder at the divergent results of the unification of the thematic vowel. As I have pointed out before, in both Baltic and Slavic the unification of the verbal thematic vowel is a result of the neutralization of the front/back contrast under certain conditions, but this unification took place in different ways in the two language families.

The previous paragraphs do not signify that I have given up the ideas expressed in other articles about the Baltic thematic vowel. I merely wish to show that the creation of palatalized consonants in Baltic or Balto-Slavic has nothing to do with the loss of the contrast between [e] and [a] in position following [j] in Proto-Baltic. This neutralization arose the minute that earlier *[Cjĕ] and *[Cĕ] merged.

Watkins also objects to my theory (Schmalstieg, 1961)[5] that the Lith. 2 Sg. ending -*i* has its origin in the athematic ending -*si*. Actually I am not the only one to hold this opinion.

Thus Kazlauskas (1968, p. 299) writes, "The element -*i* in Latvian and Lithuanian could have been taken from the 2nd Sg. of the athematic verbs, because in some athematic verbs the ending -*si* coalesced with the verbal root a long time ago and the element -*i* could have been felt to be the ending, cf., e.g., *es* + *si* > *esi*. The element -*i* could have been felt to be the ending also in those athematic verbs, the root of which ends in *d* or *t*, cf. the 2nd Sg. *duosi, desi, ėsi, giesi, rausi, kliesi* and the 3rd Sg. *duosti, desti, ėsti*, and so forth."

As far as the linguistic motivation is concerned, probably all that one can say is that when the athematic and the thematic verbs merged the athematic ending was chosen for the 2 Sg ending and the thematic endings were chosen for the other forms. The phenomenon may be compared to that of the Slavic *o*- and *ŭ*-stem noun classes which merged in principle in Russian, the relatively smaller *ŭ*-stem class furnishing the genitive plural -*ov* for all the old *o*- and *ŭ*-stems. Or in Slovenian, although there was no phonological necessity for this, all the verbs have adopted the etymologically athematic 1 Sg ending -*m*. This is in spite of the fact that in prehistoric Slovenian (to judge by the evidence of Old Church Slavic) it seems likely that the number of thematic verbs far outweighed the number of athematic verbs.

Thus in Slovenian, according to my colleague, Professor Joseph Paternost, there is no phonological reason why a form *dēlaju* 'I make' could not exist, but with the merger of the athematic and thematic conjugations the form *dēlam* was created.

As far as the structural motivation is concerned, my theory of the East Baltic 2 Sg allows us to establish a very neat set of correspondences for the reflexive and non-reflexive endings of Proto-East Baltic. The reflexive has then two allomorphs, one of which is *-As(i)* and the other of which is *-s(i)*. The allomorph *-As(i)* is used in all present tense forms except the 3rd person. We find then:

	non-reflexive	reflexive
1 Sg	-u	-uos(i) = [u-As(i)]
2 Sg	-i	-ies(i) = [i-As(i)]

1 Dual	-va	-vās(i) = [a-As(i)]
2 Dual	-ta	-tās(i) = [ta-As(i)]
1 Pl	-me	-mēs(i) = [me-As(i)]
2 Pl	-te	-tēs(i) = [te-As(i)]

The chief advantage to this approach is that it is unnecessary to go beyond a Baltic development in order to explain the 2 Sg ending -*i*. The theory also explains forms such as Lith. *duomies*(*i*) and *duomiet* 'I give to you' as merely containing the athematic ending -*mi* plus the allmorph -*As*(*i*) and -*At* respectively. Essentially the same explanation is given by Kazlauskas (1968, pp. 292–3). As Kazlauskas says (p. 294), "Thus in Lithuanian there are no data which show that the 1 Sg and 2 Sg of the athematic verbs inherited from the Common Baltic epoch the endings *-mei* and *-sei*."

Both Kazlauskas (p. 294) and Watkins (p. 167) are worried about the Old Prussian 1 Sg ending -*mai*. The main problem stems from the transcription of the old Prussian language. For the 1 Sg of the verb 'to be' we find the variants *asmai, asmau, asmu* and interestingly enough we find the form *asmai* for a 1 Pl also. My guess is that orthographic -*mu*, -*mau* and -*mai* all stand for a 1 Sg ending [mā]. It is perhaps instructive to note that in the three Old Prussian Catechisms we also find the variants (2 Pl ending) -*ti*, -*tei, -tai, -te* and (2 Sg ending) -*si, -sei, -sai, -se*. It doesn't seem likely that very much weight should be given to what were merely orthographic variants for a German scribe. Thus the frequently cited equation of Lith. -*mie*(*si*) = Old Prussian -*mai* is in all probability quite illusory.

Notes

1. William R. Schmalstieg, "A Balto-Slavic Structural Parallelism", *Word* XX, 35–39.

2. William R. Schmalstieg, "Neutralization of [*a*] and [*e*] in Hittite and Baltic", *Annali*, Istituto orientale di Napoli VII, 53–59.

3. Calvert Watkins, "Remarks on Baltic Verb Inflexion", *Baltic Linguistics*, ed. Thomas F. Magner and William R. Schmalstieg, Pennsylvania State University Press.

Essentially the same explanation is given now by Jerzy Kuryłowicz, Indogermanische Grammatik, II, Heidelberg, p. 295. Perhaps Kuryłowicz had already published this explanation earlier elsewhere, but I have been unable to determine this. In any case, it would seem probable that if Kuryłowicz had published such an explanation earlier, his own student, Calvert Watkins, would have seen fit to mention it in the paper quoted here. (This paper was read in April of 1968.)

For my own earlier views which I no longer consider correct, see Schmalstieg, "The Thematic Vowel in Baltic", *Lingua* VII, 428–432 and "The Baltic Thematic Vowel Reconsidered", *Lingua* XII, 217–219.

4. Jonas Kazlauskas, *Lietuvių kalbos istorinė gramatika*, Vilnius, 1968.

5. William R. Schmalstieg, "Primitive East Baltic *-uo-*, *-ie-* and the 2nd sg. ending", *Linga* X, 369–374.

WOLFGANG P. SCHMID

Zur primären -u̯-Ableitung in einigen baltischen Gewässernamen

1.0. In *IF*, (1969), 126–138 wurde der Ableitungstyp idg. *-ā̯u̯os* (lit. *-ovas, -ovė*) behandelt und als voreinzelsprachliche Suffixbildung *-ā- + *-u̯os* gedeutet. Wenn das richtig ist, wird man dem primären Formans *-u̯os*, das also nicht an ā-Stämme, sondern direkt an das bedeutungstragende Element angefügt wird, erst recht voreinzelsprachlichen Charakter zuschreiben dürfen, da es ja durch den *-ā̯u̯os*-Typ schon vorausgesetzt wird.

1.1. Es ist nun allgemein anerkannt, dass sich eine solche -u̯o-Ableitung in alten Farbadjektiven erhalten hat[1].

Man vergleiche z. B.:

ahd. *blāo* 'blau' < *bhlēu̯o- : lat. *flāvus* < *bhl̥u̯o-,

ahd. *falo* 'fahl' < *polu̯o- : lit. *palvas* 'blaugelb', ksl. *plavъ* < *polu̯o-,

ahd. *gelo* 'gelb' < *ǵhelu̯o- : lat. *helvus*, lit. *želvas* 'grünlich',

ahd. *grāo* 'grau' < *ghrēu̯o- : lat. *rāvus* 'grau(gelb)'.

(Über *salu̯os* s. u. § 3.3.)

1.2. In den Einzelsprachen gibt es jedoch Hinweise genug, die den Schluss erlauben, dass die Beschränkung auf die Farbadjektiva sekundärer Natur ist, d. h. dass man auch ausserhalb der eigentlichen Farbbezeichnungen mit alten -u̯o-Bildungen rechnen darf. Erinnert sei z. B. an lit. *gyvas*, ksl. *živъ*, altind. *jīva-*, lat. *vīvus* oder an altind. *devá-*, lat. *dīvus*, lit. *dievas* < *dei-u̯ó-, das zunächst einmal Adjektiv war. Diese alten und ältesten Bildungen stehen oft in einer paradigmatischen Relation zu anderen Suffixbildungen:

*-u̯o-	*-no-	*-ko-	
avest. *aēva-*	alat. *oinos*	altind. *eka-*	'1'
lat. *rīvus*	FIN. *Rhenus*	slav. *rěka*	'Fluss'
lit. *kel-eivis*	altind. *ená-*	lit. FIN. *Raséika*[2], : *ei- 'gehen'	
		Šalteikė etc.	

1.3. Betrachtet man sich das Material in seiner Gesamtheit, so lässt sich feststellen, dass das *-u̯o-Suffix mit keiner bestimmten Ablautstufe verbunden werden kann, — Vollstufe, abgetönte Vollstufe und Schwundstufe liegen vor (vgl. aber unten § 3.4.). Innerhalb des Litauischen könnte man z. B. an *žalsvas* neben *želsvas* 'grünlich' (*$*e/o$) oder an *širvas* neben *šarvas* 'grau' (*$*\mathcal{O}/o$), *rusvas* 'rotbraun' neben *raudà* 'Röte' denken. Über das Baltische hinaus weist das Ablautverhältnis zwischen lit. *šyvas* 'weiss', ksl. sivъ 'grau' gegen altind. *śyāva-* 'dunkel'. Auch unter den substantivischen *v*-Bildungen bietet das Litauische sämtliche Ablautstufen: *gervė* 'Kranich', *galva* 'Kopf', *virvė* 'Seil'.

1.4. Vom morphologischen Standpunkt aus betrachtet fällt auf, dass vor dem Suffix normalerweise Halbvokale, in erster Linie $H = \underset{\sim}{i}, \underset{\sim}{r}, \underset{\sim}{l}, \partial$, seltener Konsonanten (K) zu finden sind.[3] Wir wollen uns deshalb hier auf folgende Wurzelstrukturen beschränken und Namen wie *Ašva*, *Ditva*, *Vadva* von vornherein ausschliessen:

	-e-	-o-	-∅-
I	$KeH_1\text{-}\underset{\sim}{u}o\text{-}$	$KoH_1\text{-}\underset{\sim}{u}o\text{-}$	$KH_1\text{-}\underset{\sim}{u}o\text{-}$
II a	$KeH_1eH_2\text{-}\underset{\sim}{u}o\text{-}$	$KoH_1eH_2\text{-}\underset{\sim}{u}o\text{-}$	$KH_1eH_2\text{-}\underset{\sim}{u}o\text{-}$
II b	$KeH_1H_2\text{-}\underset{\sim}{u}o\text{-}$	$KoH_1H_2\text{-}\underset{\sim}{u}o\text{-}$	$KH_1H_2\text{-}\underset{\sim}{u}o\text{-}$

Da aber der Unterschied zwischen $KoH_1\text{-}\underset{\sim}{u}o\text{-}$ und $KoH_1H_2\text{-}\underset{\sim}{u}o\text{-}$ im Baltischen nur im Akzent zum Ausdruck kommt, dieser aber als alleiniges Indiz nicht ausreicht (vgl. IF. 67, 1962, 7), werden wir im Einzelfall (s. u. § 3.4.) auf diese Unterscheidung verzichten können. Immerhin legt die Tabelle die Vermutung nahe, dass der in IF. 74 (1969), 126 ff. behandelte Typ *Sarāvus*, *Morava*, der auch im Folgenden noch mehrfach eine Rolle spielen wird, zunächst von zweisilbigen Wurzeln seinen Ausgang nahm. Weiter zeigt sich, dass das oben § 1.1. erwähnte Ablautverhältnis von dt. *blau* und lat. *flāvus* genau dem von altind. *śyāva-* : lit. *šyvas* entspricht. Es fragt sich nun, ob sich erkennen lässt, in welcher Weise von den verschiedenen hier aufgezählten Möglichkeiten voreinzelsprachlich und einzelsprachlich Gebrauch gemacht wird.

2.0. Die Berechtigung, die vorangegangenen Erörterungen auf die alteuropäische Hydronymie[4] im allgemeinen und auf die baltische Gewässernamengebung im besonderen zu übertragen, liegt auf der Hand. Einerseits ist bereits — wie eingangs erwähnt — die Existenz sekundärer -$\underset{\sim}{u}o$-Ableitungen in der Hydronymie festgestellt und damit das primäre -$\underset{\sim}{u}o$-Suffix vorausgesetzt. Zum andern aber gibt es seit ältester Zeit bis in die Gegenwart Gewässernamen, deren Grundlage ein Farbwort darstellt[5], so dass auch von dieser Seite her $\underset{\sim}{u}o$-Bildungen erwartet werden dürfen. Zum dritten sind die ältesten Schichten der Hydronymie Alteuropas altertümlich genug, um auch mit Namen vom Typ altind. *pakva-* < *$pek^{u}u̯o$-* rechnen zu können (s. Anm. 4).

2.1. Im Bereich der Gewässernamengebung ergibt sich noch eine zusätzliche Schwierigkeit: Das hier in Rede stehende Suffix ist nicht eindeutig. Es kann sich einerseits tatsächlich um das gesuchte *u̯o*-Formans handeln, es können aber auch thematisierte *u*-Stämme vorliegen. Mit der zweiten Möglichkeit ist immer dann zu rechnen, wenn einzelsprachlich oder voreinzelsprachlich ein *u*-Stamm nachgewiesen werden kann. Zwei Beispiele seien genannt:

1) Apr. *Gilwe* (1294, jetzt: Gilbing-See, Kr. Allenstein) gehört zu apr. *gillin* „tief"[6] in: *Stwi dai deiws ainan gillin maiggun krūt no stan smunentinan* (E. 63.20 f.) „Da liess Gott einen tiefen Schlaf fallen auf den Menschen" (1. Mos. 2.21). Das Adjektiv *gillin* kann hier als Acc. Sing. fem. aufgefasst werden[7] und gehört damit zu lit. *gilùs*, fem. *gilì*. Das Verhältnis von *gilì* zu *Gilwe* wird zusammen mit dem litauischen Beispiel erörtert werden.

2) Die litauische *Pietvė* (→ Babrungas, Kr. Plungė) ist sicher zu *pietus* „Süden" zu stellen. Bezeichnungen für Himmelsrichtungen sind auch sonst in baltischen Gewässernamen zu finden. Man vergleiche etwa lit. *Rytupis*: lit. *rytai* „Osten", lett. *Austrene* (See): lett. *austrumi* „Osten"; lit. *Vakarinis*: lit. *vakarai* „Westen"; lett. *Ziemelene*: lett. *ziemelis* „Norden"[8]. Auffälligerweise fehlen in den vorhandenen Materialsammlungen im Lettischen die Südbäche und im Litauischen die Nordbäche!

Die Beurteilung von apr. *Gilwe* und lit. *Pietvė* hängt ganz davon ab, wie man die Feminin-Bildung *u*-stämmiger Adjektiva im Baltischen ansieht. Zwei gegenseitig sich ausschliessende Meinungen sind bisher vertreten worden: a) Altind. *pṛthu-*, fem. *pṛthvī* ist als indogermanisch zu betrachten, d. h. das fem. Motionssuffix *ī/yā* tritt an den *u*-Stamm an. In diesem Falle muss lit. *gilì* auf phonologischer Ebene aus *gilvī* erklärt werden[9]. b) Die baltische Femininbildung hat mit der altindischen nichts zu tun, das fem. Suffix ist direkt an die Wurzel getreten[10]. — Die Altertümlichkeit der indoiranischen Bildungsweise kann aber noch durch got. *magus* 'Knabe' — *mawi*, gen. *maujos* 'Mädchen', *þius* 'Knecht' — *þiwi* 'Magd' bestätigt werden. Die Erklärung von lat. *mollis* < *$mḷdvi$-* setzt bereits eine Hypothese über die Feminin-Bildung voraus, kann also selbst nicht als Stütze dienen. Immerhin zeigt der Übertritt ehemaliger *u*-stämmiger Adjektiva in die III. Deklination in *gravis*, *brevis*, *svāvis* stets die Bewahrung des *-u-*, was wohl nicht geschehen wäre, wenn man eine Feminin-Bildung nach Art des Litauischen für das Lateinische voraussetzen dürfte. Wir möchten daher annehmen, dass man auch im Baltischen von einem *gilvī*, Gen. *gilvi̯ās* auszugehen hat. In den obliquen Kasus mussten dann in einer Reihe von Fällen phonologisch unzulässige Lautverbindungen entstehen (z. B. *aštrvjās, *stiprvjās), die dann entweder durch den Schwund des -v- oder durch jā > ē vereinfacht wurden. Wenn also in Gilwe, Pietvė nicht schon ein fertiges Suffix vorliegt, können Namen dieser Art als Stütze der Ansicht dienen, dass auch im Baltischen von einem *gilvī auszugehen ist und gilì und Gilwe nur zwei verschiedene Ausgleichsprodukte eines Paradigmas darstellen.

3.0. Die Zahl der aus baltischen u-Stämmen hervorgegangenen Gewässernamen ist jedoch im Baltischen verschwindend gering. Wir wollen deshalb die Aufmerksamkeit auf einen Typ lenken, der unter den Namen, die mit einer v-Ableitung (*-u̯os > -vas, *-u̯ā > -va, *-u̯i̯os > -vis, -vys, *-u̯i̯ā > -vė) versehen sind, besonders hervorsticht, d. i. jener mit o-Stufe des bedeutungstragenden Elementes. Die Kriterien für seine Altertümlichkeit sind folgende:

(1) Die Anknüpfung an ein homonymes Appellativum ist nicht möglich oder führt zu in alter und neuer Gewässernamengebung ungewöhnlichen Bedeutungsansätzen.

(2) Das Grundwort der v-Ableitung ist selbst Gewässername oder Gewässerbezeichnung, sei es im Baltischen, sei es in der alteuropäischen Hydronymie.

(3) Die v-Ableitung steht in einem paradigmatischen Zusammenhang mit anderen Morphemen, etwa derart, wie oben in § 1.2. skizziert.

3.1. Begonnen sei mit einem ebenso einfachen wie klaren Beispiel. Südlich von Tryškiai gibt es einen See Bálvis mit dem dazugehörigen Ortsnamen Pabalvė[11]. In Ostlettland kommt dazu ein ON. Bolwa mit dem Gewässer Bolv-upe[12], in Ostpreussen ein ON. Balweniken[13]. Die Grundform *Balvā wird niemand an das lit., lett. balva „Geschenk" anknüpfen wollen. Damit ist Kriterium 3.0.(1) erfüllt. — Vielmehr wird man es zu der im Litauischen und Lettischen gebräuchlichen Sumpf- und Gewässerbezeichnung bala stellen. In diesem Falle gilt Kriterium 3.0.(2). — Nach Kriterium 3.0.(3) sollte die Ableitung Balva auch n-Bildungen neben sich haben. Auch dies ist der Fall. Der lit. Seename Balnys (mit ON. Pabalnė) gehört zu russ. bolon', wruss. bołóna 'offener Platz vor dem Dorf', čech. blana 'Aue'[14] etc. < *bholnā. Fügt man noch den apr. ON. Balowe hinzu, kann man auch die Reihe

bala — *Balva — *Balna — *Balāvi̯ā
Ala — ? — *Alna — Aloë[15]

aufstellen. Die Altertümlichkeit des Seenamens Bálvis und seiner Verwandten darf damit als gesichert angesehen werden.

3.2. Nach dem in 3.1. gegebenen Muster kann nun noch eine Reihe weiterer Namen behandelt und erklärt werden. Die lit. *Sárva* (→ Šušvė)[16] kann natürlich nicht direkt zu lit. *sarvalai* 'Jauche, Eiter' gestellt werden, sondern ähnlich wie die deutschen Eiterbäche[17] nur auf dem Umwege über die Wurzel, die beiden Wörtern zugrunde liegt.

Mit der Wz. **ser-* 'fliessen' befinden wir uns mitten in der alteuropäischen Hydronymie, sodass es keine Schwierigkeiten macht, eine Suffixkette aufzustellen, deren Glieder innerhalb und ausserhalb des Baltischen bezeugt sind[18].

*Sorā	**Sorvā*	**Sornā*	**Sorāvus*
engl. *Soar* (Leicestershire)	lit. *Sárva*	dt. *Sorna*	*Sarāvus*
frz. *Saire* (→ Manche)		(→Rhein)	(=Saar)
		lat. *Sarnus*	

3.3. In ähnlich günstiger Lage befände man sich bei der Analyse des lit. Moornamens *Sálvis*[19] und des Flussnamens *Sálva* (→Liaudė→Nevėžis→ Nemunas)[20], wenn nicht gerade die *v*-Ableitung mehrdeutig wäre. Diese könnte einerseits mit lit. *salvėti* 'langsam rinnen' zu lit. *salti, selėti* 'fliessen' und damit zu den bei H. Krahe (Unsere ältesten Flussnamen 49 f.) zusammengestellten Namen (*Sala* auch lit., *Salma*, lit. *Salantas* etc.) gehören, andererseits führt aber gerade der Ansatz **sal-u̯o-* zu ahd. *salo* „schmutziggrau, trübe", aisl. *sǫlr* „schmutzig", russ. *solovój* „gelblich-grau", russ.-ksl. *slavo-očije* 'Blau-äugigkeit'[21], also zu einem Farbadjektiv, das in die Reihe der oben 1.1. aufgezählten Beispiele zu stellen ist. In BzN. 16 (1965) 208 habe ich mich für die erste Möglichkeit entschieden. Da nun aber die Sumpfbezeichnungen gern auf Farbwörtern beruhen (*bala:balas, baltas* „weiss", *palios, pelkė:palvas* 'weiss, grau', *purvas*: griech. πυρρός 'rötlich')[22] und *Sálvis* Name eines Moores ist, darüber hinaus mit dem Anschluss an die Farbbezeichnung einerseits eine Wurzeletymologie vermieden, andererseits das fehlende Zwischenglied zwischen Germanisch und Slavisch mit diesem Namen geboten wird, scheint eine Zusammenstellung mit dem Farbwort doch vorzuziehen zu sein. Unter der Voraussetzung, dass das Salz-Wort (Pokorny 1. *sal-*) und das Farbwort (Pokorny 2. *sal-*) nicht voneinander zu trennen sind[23], ergibt sich, dass eine Reihe, die denen in 3.1. und 3.2. entspricht, nun auch für *Sálva, Salvis* aufgestellt werden kann:

lit. *Salà*[24] — lit. *Sálva* — ksl. *slanъ* 'salzig' — apr. *salowis* Nachtigall'[25].

3.4. Die lettische *Palva* (Vietalva, Kr. Wenden)[26] und die weissrussische *Polova* < balt. *Palva*[27] führen in ihrem Verhältnis zu lit. *Palà* (1. → Mūša, 2. → Minija)[28] zu ähnlichen Problemen wie in 3.3. Man wird den Namen der *Palva* nicht von lit. *palvas* 'fahl, bleich', russ. *polovyj* 'fahl', ahd. *falo* (s. oben 1.1.) trennen wollen, zumal auch *pálšas* 'fahl' in dem lettischen Gewässernamen *Palsa* vertreten ist. Damit tritt dieser Name zugleich wieder in einen paradigmatischen Zusammenhang mit den Gewässer- und Sumpfnamen lit. *Palà*[29] und *Palnė*[30] u. a. Wir können hier diesen Zusammenhang nach Ablautstufen (Zeilen) und Ableitungen (Spalten) tabellarisch ordnen. In der Tabelle geben wir die rekonstruierten Formen, wobei die Suffixe der Kürze wegen als *o*-Stämme angegeben, aber stets -*i̯o*- und -(*i̯*)*ā*-Stämme mitverstanden werden:

Wz.- Ablaut	Stammbildung:				
	-o-	*-u̯o-*	*-ko-/-k̑o-*	*-to-*	*-no-*
-o-	**polo-*	**pol-u̯o-*	**pol-ko-*	**pol-to-*	**pol-no-*
-e-	**pelo-*	**pel-u̯o-*	**pel-ko-*	**pel-to-*	**pel-no-*
-Ø-	**pl̥lo-*	**pl̥-u̯o-*	**pl̥-ko-*	**pl̥-to-*	**pl̥-no-*

Diese Tabelle kann mit Hilfe der Gewässernamen und des appellativischen Wortschatzes vollständig ausgefüllt werden, wobei hinsichtlich des Wurzelablauts in thematischen Bildungen auch an lit. *vardas* 'Name', lat. *verbum*, dt. *Wort* (< **u̯r̥dhom*) erinnert sei. Es folgen die Belege:

**polo-*:lit. FlN. *Palà* (s. o.), russ. FlN. *Pola* (s. Anm. 29), slav. *pole* 'Feld' (s. auch **pel-to-*), russ. *pólyj* 'hohl, offen', *polovódьe* 'Hochwasser', *vodopolьe* 'offenes Wasser', lett. *paļi* 'Überschwemmung', lit. *ampalas* 'Aufwasser', lit. *palios* 'grosser Sumpf, Moor', FlN. *Palia* (*Paglia*) (→Tiber).

**pelo-*:lit. FlN. *Pelà* (→Ančia→Šešuvis).

**pl̥lo-*:lit. FlN. *Pylà* (1.→Meer; 2.→Minija)[31], *Pilelė* (→Gelžė), lett. *pile* 'Tropfen' (*pilti* 'giessen').

**pol-u̯o-*:lett. FlN. *Palva* (s. o.), weissruss. *Polova*; lit. *palvas* 'fahl', russ. *polovyj*, ahd. *falo* 'fahl', griech. πολιός 'grau' — preuss. *palwe* 'wüste baumlose Moosfläche, unbeackertes Heideland, ausgerodete Waldfläche' (G. Gerullis, ON. 113).

**pel-u̯o-*:westfäl. *fel* 'falb'[32].

**pl̥-u̯o-*:lit. FlN. *Pilvė* (→Šešupė), *pilvė* 'Schlick, Schlamm'[33], apreuss. *Pilwin* FlN., *Pilwe* SeeN[33].

*pol-k̂o-:lit. FIN. *Pálšis* (→Noruta), lett. FIN. *Palsa*, lit. *palšas*, lett. *palss* 'fahl'; russ. *polosá* 'Landstrich, Flur', gall.-lat. *olca* 'zum Pflügen taugliches Land'.

*pel-ko-:lit. *pelkė* 'Moorbruch' (mit -*k*-), russ. *pelësyj* 'bunt, gefleckt', ksl. *pelesъ* 'φαιός, pullus' (mit -k̂-).

*pl̥-ko-:lit. FIN. *Pilkė*; *pìlkas* 'grau', griech. πάλκος·πηλός (Hesych) 'Lehm, Schlamm, Morast'.

*pol-to-:lett. *palts, palte* 'Pfütze, Lache', russ. FIN. *Polota* (→Düna) mit ON. *Polock*, lit. *Paltìs* Wiesenname[34].

*pel-to-:ahd. *feld* 'Feld', FIN. *Felda* (→Werra), 786 *trans fluvium Feldaha*[35].

*pl̥-to-:as. *folda* 'Boden', FIN. *Fulda* (→Weser). Die ältesten Belege *Fuldae*, *Uulta* (743 ff.) zeigen noch keine -*aha*- Erweiterung, die erst zu Beginn des 9. Jh.'s antritt (823 *Vultaha*)[36]. Damit wird die Fulda < *pl̥-tā eine Ablautvariante von *Polota* < *pol-tā[37].

*pol-no-:lit. *Palnė* (Moosbruch), *palnė* 'Art Sumpfmoor'.

*pel-no-:griech. πελλός < *pel-no- 'grau'.

*pl̥-no-:lat. *pullus* 'schwarzgrau'.

Diese Liste ist hinsichtlich der Belege zwar repräsentativ, aber nicht vollständig. Ferner berücksichtigt sie nicht (gemäss § 1.4.) den Zusammenhang zwischen *pel-* (=Pokorny 6. *pel-*) und *pelə-* 'breit, flach' (Pokorny S. 805 f.). Sie soll lediglich verdeutlichen, wie die Merkmale ,,fahl'' und ,,offene Fläche'' bald auf ,,Wasser'', bald auf ,,Sumpf'', bald auf ,,Erde'' angewandt sind. So sind die Gewässernamen geeignet, das Gesamtbild zu vervollständigen. Die Tabelle kann weiter zeigen, dass die Ableitungen von der *o*-Stufe die grösste Verbreitung haben (vgl. *polo-, pol-u̯o-, pol-k̂o-*), während die schwundstufigen Bildungen eine einzelsprachliche Beschränkung aufweisen. Endlich zeigt sich, dass die Ablautstufe der *u̯o*-Ableitung die Ablautstufe des Grundwortes widerspiegelt, sodass man eben *Palva* auf *Pala* und *Pilve* auf *Pile* beziehen muss. Namen und Appellativa fügen sich in das 1.2. gebrachte Schema ein und erweitern es um die *to*-Bildung.

3.5. Lit. *Marvelė* (→Nemunas) ist sicherlich keine Diminutivform von *marvà* 'Bremse', sondern muss auf den FIN. *Marà* (→Juodoji Ančia) bezogen werden (vgl. auch apreuss. Marunge [See], lett. *Mare*, 1338 *die beke Marra*). Das anzusetzende *Marva ist damit das noch fehlende Glied in der Reihe *Marà — Marva — Marna*[38] — *Morava*[39].

In ähnlicher Weise möchten wir den Flussnamen *Skalvys, Skalvė* (Šiauliai) auf *Skalà* (Žasliai) beziehen und mit lit. *skalauti* 'spülen' verbinden. Ebenso kann man den Seenamen *Gálvė*, falls auf die Form Verlass ist[40], in eine Reihe mit *Galà, Gálnis* u. a. stellen und mit dt. „Quelle" etymologisieren. Mit *galvà* 'Haupt' hat der Name sicher nichts zu tun[41].

4.0. Die vorangegangenen Ausführungen zeigen deutlich, dass zumindest der Typ von *v*-Ableitungen, auf den wir uns hier im wesentlichen beschränkt haben, in vorhistorische Zeit zurückreicht. Dafür sprechen morphologische Gesichtspunkte (§ 2.1.), altertümliche Suffix-Paradigmen (§ 1.2.; 3.1.; 2.; 3.; 4.), Ablautvarianten (§ 3.4.) und semantische Entwicklungen (*Sárva — sarvalai* § 3.2.). Der Formenbestand wird durch die Gewässernamen ergänzt. Die Morphologie der Gewässernamen ist so vollständig in das aus den einzelnen indogermanischen ˙ Sprachen bekannte Morpheminventar integriert, dass gelegentliche Behauptungen, die Hydronymie sei nicht-indogermanisch, geradezu absurd erscheinen. — Betrachtet man sich das von H. Krahe gesammelte Material, dann zeigt sich, dass **u̯o*-Ableitungen besonders in Osteuropa produktiv waren. Der auch in Westeuropa verbreiteten **Arva* stehen sämtliche hier behandelten Namen gegenüber, die vorerst im Westen noch keine Entsprechungen gefunden haben. Dieses an sich gefährliche argumentum e silentio findet aber eine Stütze in der Tatsache, dass auch der *-ā- + -u̯o*-Typ im Osten am stärksten vertreten ist. Der Name der *Saar* < *Sarāvus* ist eine im Westen vereinzelt dastehende Bildung.

Gerade das in § 3.4. behandelte Beispiel *Palva* hat deutlich gezeigt, dass der *-u̯o*-Ableitung keine eigene Ablautstufe zukommt, sondern diese von der des Grundwortes abhängt. So kann man *Palva* eben nur auf *Palà* beziehen, *Pilve* nur auf **Pila, pile*. Dabei ist es wichtig festzuhalten, dass die Reihen, die sich mit der *o*-Stufe aufstellen lassen, in alteuropäische Verhältnisse hineinreichen, während die schwundstufigen Bildungen auf den einzelnen Sprachkreis beschränkt bleiben.

Abschliessend noch eine allgemeine Bemerkung: Die Tatsache, dass die Namen teilweise älter sind als das heutige Litauische, in dem sie eben als Namen vorkommen, hat zur Folge, dass eine synchrone Analyse diese Namen einem falschen Bezugssystem zuordnet, d. h. eine Volksetymologie auslöst. Die Interpretation von *Sárva* durch *sarvalai* 'Jauche', von *Marvelė* durch *marva* 'Bremse', von *Galvė* durch *galva* 'Kopf', von *Karvė* durch *karvė* 'Kuh' berücksichtigt nicht, dass es sich ja um Namen handelt, die auf Grund ihres Alters in ganz andere Zusammenhänge eingeordnet werden müssen. Nur bei jungen Namen ist die synchrone Betrachtung möglich, dann gelten die in 3.0. aufgestellten Kriterien nicht.

Anmerkungen

1. Vgl. A. Leskien, *Die Bildung der Nomina im Litauischen* (Abh. d. Königl. Sächs. Ges. d. Wiss., phil.-hist. Kl. 12,3), Leipzig 1891, S. 345 f.; F. Kluge, *Nominale Stammbildungslehre der altgermanischen Dialekte* (Halle 1926) § 187; F. Kluge – W. Mitzka, *Etymologisches Wörterbuch der deutschen Sprache*, 19. Aufl. (Berlin 1963), S. 243 (s. v. *gelb*); J. Wackernagel – A. Debrunner, *Altindische Grammatik* II, 2 (Göttingen 1954) S. 870.

2. Zu diesem Suffix vgl. auch J. Otrębski, *Gramatyka języka litewskiego* II (Warszawa 1965) § 473.

3. Das mag wenigstens z. T. darin begründet sein, dass die Verbindung Verschlusslaut + *-ɥo-* vielfach Sonderentwicklungen unterlag. Sicher gilt das für das Lateinische, wahrscheinlich auch für das Baltische.

4. Im Sinne meiner Ausführungen in *Alteuropäisch und Indogermanisch* (Abh. d. Mainzer Akad. d. Wiss. u. d. Lit., Geistes- u. Sozialwiss. Kl. 1968, 6), Wiesbaden, 1968.

5. Zu den ältesten Namen mit **albh-*, **arg-* und **bhel-* s. H. Krahe, *Unsere ältesten Flussnamen* (Wiesbaden 1964) S. 52–54. Für das Baltische vgl. lit. *Baltupė, Juodupė, Raudonupė, Sartupis, Širvintà, Želtupė* u. a. — Der lettische FlN. *Blêve* (→Ogre) könnte das für dt. *blau* vorauszusetzende **bhlēvo-* repräsentieren. Vgl. wahrscheinlich auch dt. *Blögge* = 1266 *Blewe* (→ Soest-Bach), D. Schmidt, *Hydr. Germ.* A 6, S. 8.

6. G. Gerullis, *Die altpreussischen Ortsnamen* (Berlin–Leipzig 1922) S. 41.

7. J. Endzelin, *Altpreussische Grammatik* (Rīga, 1944) S. 104, § 151.

8. Vgl. auch *Osterbach, Westernach, Westerbach* bei A. Schmid, *Das Flussgebiet des Neckar* (Hydr. Germ., A 1, Wiesbaden 1962) s. vv.

9. J. Endzelīns, *Latviešu valodas gramatika* (Rīgā 1951) S. 215 f., § 101 g.; *Baltų kalbų garsai ir formos* (Vilnius 1957) § 66 f. E. Fraenkel, *Lit. etym. Wb.* I (Heidelberg 1962) S. 587 s. v. *piêtūs*.

10. Chr. S. Stang, *Vergleichende Grammatik der baltischen Sprachen* (Oslo 1966) S. 262.

11. *Lietuvos TSR upių ir ežerų vardynas* (Vilnius 1963), S. 14.

12. K. Būga, *Rinktiniai Raštai* III (Vilnius 1961) S. 520; J. Endzelīns, *Latvijas PSR vietvārdi* I₁ (Rīgā 1956) S. 83; E. Fraenkel, *Die baltischen Sprachen* (Heidelberg 1950) S. 69 f.

13. G. Gerullis, a. a. O., S. 15.

14. Vgl. K. Būga, a. a. O., S. 520.

15. Zu dieser Reihe vgl. IF. 74 (1969) 135.

16. J. Otrębski, Ling. Posn. 1 (1949) 233; *Vardynas* 143.

17. Dazu H. Krahe, BzN. 7 (1956) 105–116; *Unsere ältesten Flussnamen* S. 29 f.

18. H. Krahe, a. a. O., S. 40 f.; zu **Sorna* A. Greule, *Ältere und älteste Flussnamen am Oberrhein*, maschinenschriftl. Staatsexamensarbeit (Freiburg i. Br. 1968) S. 93 ff. — Zu *Sarāvus* vgl. W. P. Schmid, IF. 74 (1969) 134.

19. G. Gerullis, a. a. O., S. 149; *Vardynas* 141.

20. *Vardynas* 141. Die Zugehörigkeit von apr. ON. *Salwen* ist wegen der Mehrdeutigkeit des *s* (< **s, š, *z, ž*) nicht sicher.

21. J. Pokorny, *Idg. etym. Wb.* 879; M. Vasmer, *Russ. etym. Wb.* II 691.

22. Weiteres s. W. Schulze, *Kleine Schriften* (Göttingen 1933) S. 111–121; E. Fraenkel, *Lit. etym. Wb.* s. vv.

23. P. Thieme, *Die Heimat der idg. Gemeinsprache* (Abh. d. Mainzer Akad. d. Wiss. u. d. Lit., Geistes- u. Sozialwiss. Kl. 1953, 11) S. 28².

24. *Sala* bleibt mehrdeutig: < *Solā* oder *Salā*.

25. Elb. Vok. 727: russ. *solovej* „Nachtigall", apr. ON. *Saloweiten*, Gerullis, a. a. O., S. 149.

26. J. Endzelin, ZslPh. 11 (1934) 148; H. Krahe, *Unsere ältesten Flussnamen* S. 49.

27. K. Būga, *Rinktiniai Raštai* III S. 538.

28. P. Jonikas, *BzN* 2 (1950/51) 13; H. Krahe, *BzN* 3 (1951/52) 232, 233[15]; 9 (1958) 6. J. Otrębski, *Ling. Posn.* 7 (1959) 249; *Vardynas* 116.

29. Vgl. auch *Pola*→Lovot' (Novgorod), Vasmer, *Russ. etym. Wb.* II 390.

30. P. Jonikas, BzN. 2 (1950/51) 13; H. Krahe, BzN. 9 (1958) 7.

31. Falls nicht zu *pyla* „Ente"; beachte auch lit. *pylà* „Regenguss".

32. Vgl. J. Pokorny, *Idg. etym. Wb.* 805.

33. Vgl. E. Fraenkel, *Lit. etym. Wb.* 593; Gerullis, *Ortsnamen* S. 123, 239.

34. Vgl. M. Vasmer, *Russ. etym. Wb.* II, 397; E. Fraenkel, *Lit. etym. Wb.* 533 (s. v. *palios*).

35. R. Sperber, *Die Nebenflüsse von Werra und Fulda bis zum Zusammenfluss* (Hydr. Germ. A 5, Wiesbaden 1966) S. 25.

36. R. Sperber, a. a. O., S. 29 ff.

37. Vgl. J. Rozwadowski, *Studia nad nazwami wód słowianskich* (Kraków 1948), S. 182 ff.

38. *Marna* > *Mare* bei Leiden, Holland, *Marna* > *Meern* (Zuidholland, Utrecht), s. H. Krahe, *Flussnamen* S. 47. Vgl. auch lit. *mernas* „feucht, klamm".

39. Dazu zuletzt W. P. Schmid, IF. 74 (1969) 132.

40. *Vardynas* 42 durch ein * als „unsicher" bezeichnet.

41. Weitere Fälle, für die sich jedoch nicht alle in 3.0 aufgestellten Kriterien geltend machen lassen, könnten etwa sein: *Karvė, Karvys* nicht zu *kárvė* „Kuh", sondern zu einem Farbadjektiv, das auch in *karvelis* „Taube" vorliegt, oder zu *Karupis* (dazu *Gedenkschrift Brandenstein*, Innsbruck 1968, S. 391); *Kálvė* (See), apr. *Kalve*, nicht direkt zu *kalvà* „Hügel", sondern zu got. *hallus*, an. *hallr* „Stein" < *kolno-* (vgl. *Kalupė*, *Gedenkschrift Brandenstein* S. 390); *Kulvė* : *Kulė* (dazu *Henning Memorial Volume* S. 379 f.); *Rausvė* : *Rauda* (dazu *Henning Memorial Volume* S. 383). Zu *Kálvė* würde sich auch die *Hälver* (→ Volme) mit ON. 11. Jh. *Halvara* (D. Schmidt, *Hydr. Germ.* A 6, S. 27) stellen, mit *kulvė* vergleiche man ahd. *huliwa* „Lache, Sumpf", mhd. *hulwe* „Pfüt*e, Pfuhl".

Primary u̯o-Derivations in some Baltic River-Names

The well-known primary suffix *u̯o- (forming adjectives which often but not exclusively denote colours) can also be met with among Baltic river-names. Since it has been shown elsewhere that the secondary suffix *-ā-u̯o- belongs to the oldest layers of the Central-European hydronymy, the assumption seems to be justified that at least some of the Baltic names formed by a primary u̯o-suffix ought to be traceable to a similar period. This paper is mainly concerned with names of the structure *K_1oK_2-u̯o- and suggests three criteria for dating them to prehistoric times:

(1) A semantic relationship between the river-name in question and a homonymous noun does not exist or is at least most unlikely.

(2) The base of the derivation is an old river-name or a common Baltic or even Indo-European noun denoting river, water etc.

(3) The derivation is paradigmatically related to other morphemes which are of prehistoric age (e.g. *-u̯o-, *-no-, *-ko-, *-to-).

According to these criteria Lithuanian names like *Bálvis*, *Sárva*, *Sálva*, Latvian *Palva*, Byelo-russian *Polova* etc. belong—together with their cognates (s. §§ 3.1–3.4)—to the oldest layer of the Baltic hydronymy.

Morphological considerations, ablaut and also the semantic features of this layer integrate the u̯o-derivations into the Indo-European morphemic inventory (see list § 3.4) to such a degree, that occasional statements about the non-Indo-European character of the European hydronymy seem to be rather absurd. Judging by the material available at present the primary -u̯o-derivation seems to have been especially productive in the Baltic area of the Old European hydronymy.

KARL HORST SCHMIDT

Zum Typus der baltischen Personalflexion

Jede indogermanische Sprache kann man unter wenigstens zwei Gesichts-
punkten betrachten: 1. sprachgeschichtlich, 2. sprachtypologisch. Sprachgeschichtlich sind die den relativ-chronologischen Stand der Sprache wieder-
gebenden Fakten in das Modell der zu rekonstruierenden Grundsprache
einzubauen und tragen zu deren Erschließung bei. Sprachtypologisch wird
das Modell der Einzelsprache selbst zum Gegenstand der Betrachtung gemacht. Markante (vom idg. Typus abweichende) Züge lassen sich auch mit
nichtidg. Sprachen vergleichen. Die typologische Konfrontierung hat vornehmlich zwei Ziele: sie kann

a) Mittel zum Zweck,
b) Selbstzweck sein.

Fall a) liegt dann vor, wenn die sprachtypologischen Erscheinungen als
Beweis für linguistische Interferenzen (Ad-, Sub-, Superstrate) gewertet
werden; Fall b) begnügt sich mit der bloßen Feststellung von Übereinstimmungen und Ähnlichkeiten. Festzuhalten ist, daß sich der idg. Typus
ändern kann. Als Beispiele hierfür seien angeführt: der Übergang von flek-
tierender in agglutinierende Nominalflexion im Tocharischen[1] und die
Erhebung der in andern idg. Sprachen bei Aussagesätzen als signifikante
Variante auftretenden Anfangsstellung des Verbums zur merkmallosen
Basisform in den inselkeltischen Sprachen[2]. Die baltischen Sprachen sind
relativ-chronologisch durch konservatives Kasus- und entwickelteres
Verbalsystem charakterisiert (Perfekt und Aorist > Präteritum; Imperfekt
durch besondere Stammbildung markiert; Schwund des Medio-Passivs;
Zerstörung des ererbten Modussystems mit Übergang von Optativ in
Imperativ; Neubestimmung bzw. Aufgabe des Verhältnisses von Primär-
zu Sekundärendungen). Sprachtypologisch bedeutsam ist für sie jedoch die
Neutralisierung des Numerus in der 3. Person: „Die 3. Person hat nur eine
Form, die als Singular, Plural und Dual gebraucht wird und auf die ieur.
Singularform zurückgeht"[3]. Die 3. Person wird in der baltischen Sprache
bei athematischen Verben durch die idg. Primärendung -ti (lit. ẽsti, alit.

est(*i*), *eit*(*i*), lett. *iêt*; preuss. *ast, ēit* u. a.[4], bei thematischen Verbalstimmen durch den Stammvokal markiert (lit. *sùka, sēdi, sãko, sùko, vĕdė́*), hinter dem vorhistorisch die idg. Sekundärendung *-t* ausgefallen zu sein scheint. Die Differenzierung von Primär- und Sekundärendungen erfolgt nach einem von Stang so genannten „Gleichgewichtsprinzip": „Im Baltischen ist eine sekundäre Unterscheidung zweier Typen eingetreten, indem alle Verben mit zwei- oder mehrsilbigem Stamme, d. h. alle thematischen und halbthematischen Verben, in der 3. P. endungslos sind. Andererseits wird die Primärendung *-ti* in der lit. Präteritalform *bit*(*i*) gebraucht, weil der Stamm einsilbig ist." Bei den die Masse des Materials ausmachenden nichtathemat. Verbalstimmen ergibt sich eine Ableitung von Plural und Dual durch Agglutination der diese Numeri in den ersten beiden Personen anzeigenden Morpheme an die Verbalform der 3. Person. (lit. Präs. Sg. 1 *-u*, 2 *-i*, 3 *-a*; Pl. 1 *-a-me*, 2 *-a-te*; Dl. 1 *-a-va*, 2 *-a-ta*; vgl. entsprechend 3. Sg. *-i*: Pl. 1 *-i-me* usw. u. s. das gleiche Prinzip beim Präteritum: 3. Sg. *-o*: Pl. 1 *-o-me* usw., 3. Sg. *-ė*: Pl. 1 *-ė-me* usw. und Futurum: 3. Sg. *-s*(*i*): Pl. 1 *-si-me* usw.). Auf das hier vorliegende unidg. Prinzip hatten u. a. bereits Lohmann l.c. und E. Benveniste[5] hingewiesen: „La '3. personne' n'est pas une 'personne'; c'est même la forme verbale qui a pour fonction d'exprimer la *non-personne*. A cette définition répondent: l'absence de tout pronom de la 3ᵉ personne ..." (Benveniste, l.c. 4).

Am Rande vermerkt sei, daß diese Regelung für das Baltische bei thematischen Verben die hier vorliegende Verallgemeinerung der *o*-Stufe (Stang, Grammatik 420) voraussetzt, möglicherweise auch dazu beigetragen hat, indem sich das Flexionsmuster thematischen Präsens nach den Schemata mit einheitlichem Themavokal (z. B. Präterita) ausgerichtet haben mag.

Der Mechanismus der baltischen Verbalflexion im Plural und Dual macht die idg. ererbte Opposition von Primär- und Sekundärendungen überflüssig. Der Tempuscharakter wird durch die Stammbildung ausgedrückt: lit. Präsens [*a, i, o*]: Präteritum [*o, ė*]: Futurum [*si*], die Personalendungen sind vereinheitlicht worden: lit. Plural [*me, te*]: Dual [*va, ta*]. Die bei starken Verben begegnende historisch ererbte Differenzierung von Präsens- und Präterialstamm durch Ablaut (lit. *liekù* 'ich lasse': *likaũ*) oder Nasalinfigierung (lit. *krintù* 'falle herunter': *kritaũ*) wird zur redudanten Erscheinung.

Die eben besprochene Regelung: 3. Person als Grundlage für die davon abgeleiteten ersten beiden Personen ist in nichtidg. Sprachen sehr häufig. Lohmann (l.c. 91 f.) und Benveniste l.c. weisen u. a. auf den ural-altaischen Sprachbau hin. Der idg. Typus unterscheidet sich davon wesentlich: „Im Idg. stehen alle Personalformen des Verbums gleichberechtigt nebeneinander" (Lohmann l.c. 91). Ausnahmen wie das periphrastische Futurum des Altindischen (1. *kartásmi*, 2. *kartási*, 3. *kartá*) werden von Benveniste behandelt[6], der in diesem Zusammenhang feststellt (l.c. 6): „Il faut réfléchir à tous ces faits concordants pour discerner la singularité de la flexion „normale" en indo-européen, celle par exemple du présent athématique *es-mi*, *es-si*, *es-ti* à trois personnes symétriques : loin de représenter un type constant et nécessaire elle est, au sein des langues, une anomalie."

Wir wollen im zweiten Teil unserer Ausführungen a) das ostkaukasische Tabassaranische zum typologischen Vergleich mit dem Baltischen heranziehen, um daraus b) Einsichten für die schärfere Bestimmung der baltischen Personalflexion zu gewinnen. Alle ostkaukasischen Sprachen kennen ursprünglich weder Personalpräfixe noch Personalendungen. Das Tabassaranische hat jedoch durch enklitische Anfügung von Pronomina der 1. und 2. Person eine Personalflexion entwickelt, mit der endungslosen 3. Person als merkmalloser Basisform: z. B. chivischer Dialekt im Präsens[7]:

Sg. 1. P. *uzu wu-za* 'ich bin' Pl. 1. P. (inkl.) *uxu wu-xa*

　　　　　　　　　　　　　　　 1. P. (exkl.) *uču wu-ča*

　 2. P. *uwu wu-wa*　　　　　　 2. P. *uč°u wu-č°a*

　 3. P. *dumu wu*　　　　　　　 3. P. *durar wu*

Ipf. Sg. 1. P. *uzu wu-j-za* 'ich war' Pl. 1. P. *uxu wu-j-xa*

　　　　 2. P. *uwu wu-j-wa*　　　　　 2. P. *uč°u wu-j-č°a*

　　　　 3. P. *dumu wu-ji*　　　　　　 3. P. *durar wu-ji*

Die beiden Paradigmata beweisen Isomorphismus zwischen den baltischen und tabassaranischen Flexionsschemata: Basis (in beiden Sprachen): Verbalwurzel; Order[8] 1: Tempusindikator = 3. Person: lit. Präs. [*a*, *i*, *o*]:Prät. [*o*, *é*] gegenüber tabass. Präs [*ø*]:Ipf. [*j(i)*]; Order 2: Personalsuffixe für die ersten beiden Personen: lit. (Plural und Dual) [*me*, *te*; *va*, *ta*] gegenüber tabass. (Singular und Plural) [*za*, *wa*; *xa*, *ča*, *č°a*].

Dem Isomorphismus auf synchroner Ebene stehen wesentliche Unterschiede gegenüber, wenn man die beiden Systeme diachronisch betrachtet: 1. die baltischen Sprachen haben das hier vorliegende Modell einer partiellen Personalflexion, wenn man den Typus so nennen soll, aus der Umgestaltung eines vollständigen Personalparadigmas (mit Morphemen für jeweils 3 Personen in den verschiedenen Numeri) entwickelt. Hierfür zeugen noch: a) die von der 3. Person unabhängigen Personalsuffixe in der 1. 2. Person Singular; b) die Formen athematischer Verbalflexion; c) die Tatsache, daß die (die beiden ersten Personen im Dual und Plural anzeigenden) Morpheme der Order 2 historisch auf ältere Personalendungen zurückgehen; d) die

Tatsache, daß sich das Morphem für die 3. Person historisch offenbar auf die Personalendung der 3. Person Singular zurückführen läßt. 2. dem Tabassaranischen (wie allen ostkaukasischen Sprachen) fehlen alte Personalsuffixe vollständig[9]; die neuentwickelte „Personalflexion" ist aus enklitisch angefügten Personalpronomina entstanden: vgl. *uzu* 'ich': *-za, uwu* 'du': *-wa, uxu* 'wir' (inkl.): *-xa, uču* 'wir' (exkl.): *-ča, uč°u* 'ihr': *-č°a*.

Der typologische Vergleich zwischen dem Balt. und Tabass. zeigt zwei Sprachen, die ihren Ausgangspunkt von zwei extrem unterschiedenen Modellen genommen haben: fehlende Personendifferenzierung im Ostkaukasischen gegenüber vollständig ausgebauter Personalflexion im Indogermanischen. Durch Neutralisierung des Numerus in der 3. Person einerseits und Vereinheitlichung der Primär- und Sekundärendungen für die an die 3. Person anfügbaren ersten beiden Personen Pl. und Dl. andererseits kommt im Baltischen ein neuer Typus „partieller Personalflexion" auf. Dieser ist dem Tabass. isomorph, nachdem hier durch der (damit zur 3. Person werdenden) 'non-personne' enklitisch angefügte Personalpronomina für die ersten beiden Personen eine „partielle Personalflexion" ausgebildet worden ist.

Anmerkungen

1. Verf., *MSS* XXV, 105–112.

2. Verf., *Folia Linguistica*, Gedenkschrift Sommerfelt (im Druck).

3. Chr. S. Stang, *Vergleichende Grammatik der Baltischen Sprachen*, 1966, 405; vgl. auch Stang, *Das Slavische und Baltische Verbum*, 1942, 224; in beiden Arbeiten werden die Gründe für die Neutralisierung diskutiert; vgl. dazu außerdem J. Lohmann, *Lexis* IV, 91 f., der an nichtidg. Einfluß denkt.

4. Stang, *Verbum*, 409 f.

5. *BSL*, XLIII, 1–12, bes. 5.

6. Vgl. auch C. Watkins, *Indo-European Origins of the Celtic Verb. 1. The Sigmatic Aorist*, Dublin, 1962, 90 ff.

7. Vgl. die Paradigmata nach A. A. Magometov, *Tabasaranskij jazyk*, Tbilisi, 1965, 227; zum tabass. Verbalsystem vgl. auch Verf., *Revue de Kartvélologie Bedi Kartlisa*, Paris, 1968, 208–213.

8. Terminus nach H. A. Gleason, *An Introduction to Descriptive Linguistics*. Revised Edition, New York, 1966, 112, der darunter „mutually exclusive classes of morphemes forming a word" versteht; vgl. auch Verf. *MSS* XXV, 105 ff.

9. Vgl. G. Deeters, *Die Kaukasischen Sprachen*, Leiden/Köln, 1963, 54.

On the Baltic Type of Verb Inflexion for Person

For the Baltic languages, which are characterized by a conservative case system and a more developed verbal system, the neutralization of number in the third person is of typological importance. The differentiation of primary and secondary endings is based on a "Gleichgewichtsprinzip". With regard to the non-athematic verbal stems, the derivation of the first two persons in plural and dual from the third person (= "non-personne") has become a principle.

Tabassaranian, one of the East Caucasian languages, has developed a secondary "partielle Personalflexion" by the enclitical addition of personal pronouns for the first two persons. In this way we get isomorphism with the Baltic languages, although in this aspect the two languages have widely different starting positions, the one being East Caucasian and lacking differentiation of person, the other Indo-European, with completely developed personal inflexion.

ALFRED SENN

Slavic and Baltic Linguistic Relations

There are basically two types of linguistic relationship: 1) a cultural relationship and 2) a genetic or genealogical relationship.

We stipulate at the outset that of all the Indo-European languages Baltic
(i.e. Lithuanian, Lettish, Old Prussian, and Curonian) is closest to Slavic,
both culturally and genetically. However, in the present paper we are
primarily interested in the problem of genetic relationship and, in this
connection, the theory of an original separate Balto-Slavic unity must be
discussed. The advocates of that theory believe that at one time the Slavic
and Baltic languages had formed a separate unity of undivided speech
within the Indo-European family, a unity of speech not shared by other
branches. That would mean that after the disintegration of the Proto-IE
parent language there existed for a period of time a common Balto-Slavic
language which only later split up into the two branches of Proto-Baltic
and Proto-Slavic. In the discussion of this theory, a thick layer of cultural
Slavic influence covering Lithuanian must be recognized and laid open.

The earliest Lithuanian texts, i.e. those of the 16th century, show such a
strong Slavic influence in vocabulary and syntax that to the layman the
language may actually look like Slavic. This spurious Slavic character was
due not to a close genetic relationship (consanguinity) but rather to a powerful (political and cultural) Slavic influence exerted in an intimate Slavic-
Lithuanian symbiosis which started in the third century and increased
especially in the sixth century. This influence (first White Russian, then
Polish, and finally Great Russian) continued for over 1400 years. No wonder,
therefore, that at the beginning of the 19th century foreign scholars studying
the Lithuanian language for the purpose of comparative Indo-European
linguistics found in it many elements which were outright Slavic or at least
reminded them of Slavic. We have here a striking parallel with the Modern
English language which has accepted an enormous number of French and
Latin expressions and yet is still considered a Germanic language. The
theory of a Balto-Slavic unity owes its origin largely to the prominence
attributed by the above-mentioned linguists to the *literary* Lithuanian

language of the 16th–18th centuries which was replete with Polish loan-words. It should also be remembered that before 1918 Lithuanian had at no time enjoyed the protection offered by the status of an officially established state (administrative) or school language. And yet in spite of all these inequities of history, the Lithuanian people kept their *spoken* language, in the main, pure and unadulterated. What Slavic lexical elements had entered it in the course of time were eliminated during the 19th century and replaced by native forms. Numerous neologisms were coined in this process. As a result, the present-day standard language is more Lithuanian than the literary jargon of the 16th and 17th centuries. But even at that time Slavic influence upon Lithuanian was less significant for the linguistic structure than the foreign influence evident in English. It would be a hard job to eliminate now from the English vocabulary all non-Germanic elements without impairing the expressiveness of the language. In Lithuanian this operation was successful. However, the purge was very much limited to the vocabulary. Syntax was hardly touched.

The term *linguistic unity* in its traditional usage means: "original sameness of language based on blood relationship (consanguinity) with innovations limited to its own area". Many scholars have occasionally lost awareness of this definition. They were looking for common innovations but forgot to establish the exact period of the historical development in which these innovations showed up. Such innovations cannot be used in support of a common proto-language if they appear during the separate historical existence of the two languages or language groups as new creations in one of them and were then taken over by the other. Sameness of language brought about by assimilation (on the basis of political, economic, cultural forces) is not genetic or consanguineous sameness. If expressions like "close mutual relations" or "community" are used in attempts to characterize the situation, this can only mean that no genetic unity is visualized, that the scholar using such expressions, at least unconsciously, rejects the theory of unity.

What criteria can be reliably used in an attempt to establish genetic kinship of languages? Apparently, syntax and vocabulary must be omitted. Syntax is one of the most vulnerable parts of language, always open to outside influences. This is so because syntax, much more than the speech sounds and the inflectional forms, is in close contact with the mental processes of the speaker. It is a more direct expression of the human mind than mere words which may even be involuntary expressions of emotions. Syntax and literary style are *supraracial elements* of language. They can be more easily transplanted from one genetic type of speech community to one of absolutely different character and origin. Therefore, they cannot be used in a genealogical classification of languages.

The following *syntactical features* which have in the past been advanced in support of the theory of a Balto-Slavic unity must be eliminated once for all.

1) *Use of the genitive in negative sentences.* It has been made clear that this use is not limited to Baltic and Slavic. On the other hand, this rule is not all-inclusive either in Russian nor in Lithuanian.[1]

2) *The genitive after the comparative (genitivus comparationis* corresponding to the Latin *ablativus comparationis)* is now regarded by the Lithuanians as a Slavicism (and properly so) and therefore avoided.[2]

3) The use of the *predicative instrumental* in the two groups. Ernst Fraenkel has irrefutably shown that this construction cannot be of Balto-Slavic origin because it was unknown to Proto-Slavic. Even the Old Church Slavic gospel translations yield no examples. The earliest forms are to be found in the younger *Codex Suprasliensis.* Today the predicative instrumental is most widely used in Polish and to a somewhat lesser degree in Russian and Czech.[3] The use of the predicative instrumental in Lithuanian is an imitation of the corresponding Polish and Russian construction.

A more concrete constituent element of language is its *vocabulary.* However, like syntax, the vocabulary is also a very vulnerable element, even more so, very unstable because it is directly connected with the ever changing living conditions of the speakers, with their political, economic, religious, cultural history. Therefore, it cannot be used in a genealogical classification of languages. Attempts to do it anyhow have been shown up as failures.

The primary and most promising criteria in determining the degree of kinship must be sought in *phonology* and *morphology*, that is in the structural development. However, even here we discover areas of borrowing from Slavic to Baltic. Two such phenomena shall be singled out here.

1) The Lithuanian and Lettish diphthong *ie* is the Slavic sound *ě* transferred to the Lithuanian and Lettish cognates of Slavic words,[4] e.g., Old Church Slavic *sněgŭ* (<Proto-Slavic **snoigŭ*) 'snow', Russian *sn'eg*, Polish *śnieg*, Lith. *sniēgas*, Lettish. *sniegs*, but Old Prussian *snaygis*, Gothic *snáiws*. On the other hand, Russian *d'en'* (<Proto-Slavic **dĭnĭ*) 'day', Polish *dzień*, Lith. *dienà*, Lettish *diena*, Old Prussian *deina*. Once this sound was established in the phonetic system of Lithuanian and Lettish, it spread easily to other words by analogy. This spreading received a strong impetus from the ablaut system which it provided with a new grade of the -*i*-series. The introduction of the diphthong *ie* may also have been furthered by the previous existence in Lithuanian and Lettish of the diphthong *uo* (<Proto-IE *ō*) against *ō* in Old Prussian. There is a strong tendency in Lithuanian to have

things arranged in pairs of opposites. As a result of this tendency we find in Lithuanian and Lettish only masculine and feminine nouns and no neuters. In the phonetic system the diphthongs *ie* and *uo* represent opposites and as such belong together. As long as there was only one of the two, a basic tendency of the language remained unrealized. On the other hand, the fact that *ie* goes back to a Proto-IE diphtong and *uo* to a monophthong, would suggest that the two diphthongs did not come into existence simultaneously.

2) *Verbal aspects.* The possibility of making a perfective verb out of a single-occurrence imperfective verb by providing it with a prefix is not limited to Baltic and Slavic and therefore cannot be considered as a Balto-Slavic innovation. It is a well-known fact that we find the same arrangement also in the Old Germanic dialects, e.g., Gothic, Old High German, and Middle High German. In these Old Germanic dialects a perfective present-tense form occurring in a main clause has future meaning just as in Old Church Slavic, Russian, and Polish. Thus we see verbal aspect substituting for a non-existent tense both in Germanic and in Slavic, but not in Baltic. In Lithuanian, there is a distinction between perfective and imperfective aspects, but this contrast is far less significant than in Russian and Polish. In Lithuanian, the perfective present-tense forms cannot serve as sub-stitutes for the future tense, and there is no need for such substitution be-cause there is a regular future tense extant.[5] Whether a verb is perfective or imperfective is determined by its meaning and not by any formative element. The question of verbal aspect in Lithuanian is a matter of exclusively semantic-lexical nature and almost of no grammatical significance. Different tense forms of one and the same verb may express different aspect. Thus, the present-tense form *ateĩna* 'he (she) comes, they come, he (she) is coming, they are coming' is imperfective, while the preterit form *atẽjo* and the future-tense form *ateĩs* are perfective. The infinitive *pažìnti* is imperfective in the meaning 'to know, to be acquainted with', but perfective in the meanings 'to recognize' and 'to get to know, to get acquainted with'. Concerning verbal aspect, three groups can be distinguished in Lithuanian: a) imperfective verbs, b) perfective verbs, c) aspectless or neutral verbs, that is verbs which are neither imperfective nor perfective, or both.

The incomplete system of verbal aspects as used in Lithuanian was taken over from Slavic (White Russian, Polish, Great Russian). It has all the ear-marks of the fifth wheel on a wagon. With both the inherited future tense and the partial differentiation of verbal aspects, the Lithuanian language shows an overabundance of forms which seems not justified by actual needs. In addition, the most widely used perfectivizing prefix in Baltic is *pa-*, the same as Slavic *po-*, and there is complete agreement in the use of *pa-* in

Lithuanian and *po-* in Russian as can be verified by looking at any Lithua-nian-Russian or Russian-Lithuanian dictionary.

It is interesting that also Georgian, a non-Indo-European Caucasian language, possesses a system of verbal aspects and that there, too, the perfective present has future meaning. According to Kita Tschenkéli,[6] the Georgian system of verbal aspects is very much the same as the Russian. It must be assumed that Georgian obtained this system from Russian.

While in studies searching for the degree of genetic relationship the vocabulary can only be of limited usefulness, it is the outstanding tool for investigations in cultural relationship since language, like a mirror, reflects the cultural achievements of those who spoke that language in the past. In such endeavors historical linguistics becomes a very important auxiliary branch of the study of the history of culture and civilization. The cultural image of prehistoric language communities is to a large extent pieced to-gether from lexical material. However, the linguistic material itself can attain a certain degree of relative reliability only after being submitted to a thorough historical illumination, a kind of X-ray treatment as it were, a confrontation with *known facts* of political, economic, cultural, religious history. Unfortunately, only too often, in the absence of known facts, we must be satisfied with working hypotheses. It is in this sense that I shall proceed now.

I see the following *chronological order* of events and conditions in the development of the Proto-Slavic and Proto-Baltic languages and people.

1) Pre-Slavs and Pre-Balts as an undistinguishable part of the Proto-Indo-European mass of population.

2) Existence (in the second millenium B.C.) of a separate community, still speaking Proto-Indo-European but consisting only of the ancestors of the later Proto-Slavs, Proto-Balts, and Proto-Germanic people. During this pre-Slavic-Baltic-Germanic epoch, the sort of cereal called *rye* was introduced into the agriculture and its designation into the vocabulary of the three branches of this community; likewise the numbers *eleven, twelve* (Gothic *áinlif, twalif*, Lith. *vienúolika, dvýlika*) and *thousand* (Gothic *þúsundi*, Russian *týsjača*, Lith. *túkstantis*) were introduced into the numerical system; also a shorter form **dhuktér* (< **dhughtér*) 'daughter' developed out of the longer form **dhughǝtér* (represented by Greek θυγάτηρ and Sanskrit *duhitá*): Gothic *daúhtar*, English *daughter*, German *Tochter*; Lith. *dukté̃* (gen. *duktẽrs*), Old Church Slavic *dŭšti*, Russian *doči* (gen. *dóčeri*).

Innovations of a morphological nature, effected during the period and common only to the three branches of Slavic, Baltic, and Germanic, are:

a) *m* instead of *bh* in the case endings, e.g., in the dative plural.

b) The adjectival formative suffix *-isko-*. However, *-isko-* appears also in Greek, Latin, and Celtic. Characteristic of our group is the fact that this suffix is used as a very frequent and productive means for the formation of adjectives.

c) The use of a nasal suffix or infix for the formation of the present tense with inchoative or passive-intransitive meaning. Present-tense formations by means of a nasal formative element are very frequent also in other IE languages. The innovation in our case lies in the specific narrowing of the meaning.

d) The ending *-mus* in the dative plural. Limited to Slavic and Baltic.

e) *mun-* in the pronoun of the first person singular. Limited to Slavic and Baltic.

f) The genitive $*n\bar{o}s(s)\bar{o}m$ of the pronoun of the first person plural. Limited to Slavic and Baltic.

g) Probably transfer of the *-nt-* participles into the *-i̯o-* declension. For the question arises whether the same change occurring in OHG, OS, and OE, which is generally considered an exclusively West Germanic innovation, is really completely independent of the innovation in Slavic and Baltic.

3) This pre-Slavic-Baltic-Germanic community was destroyed by a Persian invasion sometime between 1000 B.C. and 500 B.C. The Pre-Balts were driven off to the north of the Pripet Marshes into absolute isolation, out of touch with any other Indo-Europeans, even the Slavs. The Pre-Slavs were conquered, occupied, and ruled for a while by the Persians, and became Proto-Slavs. Religious influence was exerted on the Proto-Slavs by the Iranian civilization, that is Zoroastrianism. I am inclined to believe that the Proto-Slavs were Zoroastrians. In their language, the Proto-IE god name *deiwos* was replaced by the Iranian loanword *bogŭ*. Of Iranian origin is also the Slavic numeral *sto* '100'. Neither the Pre-Germanic people nor the Pre-Balts were touched by Zoroastrianism and they preserved, therefore, the inherited word *deiwos* which survived in Lith. *diēvas* 'God' and in English in the word *Tuesday*.

Zoroastrianism had been imposed on the Proto-Slavs by the Persians through military force, by the same Persians whose military expansion and conquests were stopped by the Greeks at Marathon and Salamis in 490 and 480 B.C. respectively. The setback of Persian expansion at the hands of the Greeks in the fifth century B.C. ended the Persian domination of or suzerainty over the Proto-Slavs.

Zoroastrianism originated in northwest Persia, a country inhabited by the so-called *Medes* who were ethnically closely related to the Persians proper. Actually, beginning at about 550 B.C. the two nations are spoken of as one people.

The Greek historian Herodotus (who lived in the 5th century B.C.) mentions the *Scythians* and *Sarmatians* as inhabitants of the area now known as Ukraine. According to the archeologist Max Ebert, in Max Ebert, *Reallexikon der Vorgeschichte*, XIII, 52–114, archeological findings in that area ascribed to the Scythians start to show up around 600 B.C. On the other hand, the linguist Max Vasmer, in the same *Reallexikon der Vorgeschichte*, XII, 236–251, speaks of the Scythians as having replaced the Kimmerians in southern Russia around 700 B.C. Vasmer makes it quite clear that the Scythians and Sarmatians were Iranians. The Scythians and Sarmatians mentioned by ancient authors as neighbors of the Slavs were Persian outposts left behind, the abandoned frontier of the Persian Empire.

4) The *Slavic-Baltic contacts*. In the first millenium B.C., the ancestors of the Balts lived on the northeastern border of the Indo-European language area. They touched in the east on the Mordvines (a Finno-Ugrian tribe), in the north and west on Finnish tribes, in the southwest on Proto-Slavs (ancestors of the West Slavs). In the south, the Proto-Balts were separated from the Proto-Slavs by a large lake (which is now dried up) and a vast impenetrable marshy country, the present-day Pripet Marshes. The former presence of Proto-Baltic tribes in the region north, northeast, and east of the Pripet River is demonstrated by at least 500 hydronyms (names of bodies of water).[7] It is interesting to note that the wide area of the Pripet Marshes (that is the expanse of land formerly separating at least the eastern section of the Proto-Balts from the Proto-Slavs) contains no archeological excavation sites, that is to say that it was not inhabited because it was not inhabitable and formed an impassable barrier.[8] The first to discover that in ancient times the Lithuanians lived much farther east than today, far inland between Vilna and Moscow, was the Russian A. I. Sobolevskij in 1911.[9] K. Buga and Max Vasmer then contributed significantly to the elucidation of the problem. However, when I followed their tracks, Oswald Szemerényi[10] tried to ridicule me by speaking of my "geological" theory. He did this without taking the trouble of checking my evidence which, unfortunately for him, was mostly written in the Lithuanian language. The above-mentioned Russian publication on the river names in the upper Dnepr basin should set the facts straight. Ptolemy's (around A.D. 140) Γαλίνδαι (var.: Γαλίδαναι) and Σουδινοί (var.: Σουδηνοί) clearly refer to these eastern Balts. Thus we see that in pre-Christian times and during the first millenium of the Christian era, the homes of at least the Eastern Balts (the Lithuanians

and the Letts) were very far to the east, while at the beginning of the Christian era, the westernmost Baltic tribe, the Old Prussians, had already reached the shores of the Baltic Sea, in their westward push replacing or absorbing a Finnish population. On the basis of Tacitus' information, the homeland of the Slavs, during the first Christian century, was the area east of the middle part of the Vistula River, south of the Pripet River, west of the Dnepr River, north of the Carpathian Mountains.

The Slavic-Baltic contacts started

1) in the southwest toward (i.e. before) the beginning of the Christian era, as a result of the westward drive of the Balts, and

2) in the east as late as the sixth Christian century, as a result of the Slavic expansion.

The Polish scholar Jan Rozwadowski, who believed in a Balto-Slavic unity, was the first (more than half a century ago) to postulate a long rupture between Proto-Slavs and Proto-Balts, a rupture that followed the original unity and preceded the historical contacts. He placed the period of the original unity in the third millenium B.C., and the period of separation in the second and first pre-Christian millenia.

I cannot recognize any exclusively Slavic–Baltic contacts, limited to these two branches only, prior to the withdrawal of the Pre-Balts to the northeast. All pre-Slavic and pre-Baltic contacts occurred prior to the first pre-Christian millenium, at a time when the ancestors of the Proto-Balts and of the Proto-Slavs were in mutual relations not only with each other but also with the ancestors of the Proto-Germanic people.

By the time the Proto-Slavs and the Proto-Balts came in touch with each other, the Proto-Baltic language, because of its conservatism (the result of its complete isolation), was still very close to Proto-Indo-European, while Proto-Slavic had already become a separate language and was progressing rapidly toward a new form. If we consider as *Proto-Slavic* the thousand years from the sixth century B.C. to the sixth Christian century, we must assume that the language underwent a series of successive changes during that period. Consequently we have to deal with several phases of Proto-Slavic. The loss of the -*s*- future occurred during the earliest phase. A fragmentary future participle of the verb *byti* 'to be' appears in Old Church Slavic. The loss of final -*s* occurred somewhat later[11] and monophthongization of *ou* > *u* still later, as shown by Finnish *rauta* 'iron' < Proto-Slavic **rouda* (> Old Church Slavic, Russian, etc. *ruda* 'ore' > Lith. *rūdà*).[12] On the other hand, Proto-Baltic shows no change for a long time. In the sixth Christian century it is still very much the same as in the sixth pre-Christian century. Proto-Baltic is identical with the earliest form of Proto-Slavic in its first phase;

however, not on the basis of common exclusive innovations, but rather on the basis of inherited Proto-IE material. At the beginning of the Proto-Slavic epoch, that is at the time when the Pre-Balts broke away and withdrew to the northeast, Proto-Slavic and Proto-Baltic were nothing but simple Proto-Indo-European spoken by the Proto-Slavs and the Proto-Balts respectively.

Inherited was the change of Proto-IE palatals to Lith. $\acute{s}$ and $\check{z}$ on the one hand, and Slavic s and z on the other. Examples: IE *$de\hat{k}m(t)$ '10' > Latin *decem*, Greek δέχα, Gothic *taihun*, Lith. *dešimtìs*, Old Church Slavic *desętĭ*; IE *$bhe r\hat{g}$- > English *birch*, German *Birke*, Lith. *béržas*, Russian *berëza*. This places both Slavic and Baltic in the *satem* group, in contrast to Germanic which belongs in the *kentum* group. However, the Proto-Baltic phonetic state is only preserved in Lithuanian, since the other Baltic languages have s and z (Lettish *desimt*, *bērzs*), just as Slavic. On the other hand, Baltic loanwords in Finnish show that Proto-Baltic had only $\acute{s}$ and $\check{z}$ in all these cases. Former $\check{z}$ became h in Finnish (Lith. *žãlias* 'green' > Finn. *hallas*) and the pertinent loanwords in Finnish have all h. This indicates that the partial (i.e. territorially limited) Baltic development of IE palatals to s and z did not occur until after the separation of Baltic and Slavic and represents therefore a later Slavic influence. This influence must have come from West Slavic in the southwest before the beginning of the Christian era and affected first of all Old Prussian and spread then to Curonian and Lettish. Lithuanian, then geographically the easternmost Baltic language, was not reached.

There are quite a number of agreements limited to Slavic and Baltic. Inasmuch as they refer only to Russian and Lithuanian, Russian and Lettish, or Polish and Lithuanian, they may be considered later innovations (Lithuanian or Lettish borrowings).[13]

Notes

1. Cf. my discussion in *The Slavonic and East European Review* XX, 259 with references to other literature.

2. For the proper construction in Lithuanian cf. my *Handbuch der litauischen Sprache*. I. *Grammatik*, Heidelberg, 1966, § 738.

3. Cf. Ernst Fraenkel, *Syntax der litauischen Kasus*, Kaunas, 1928, 47 and Nullo Minissi, "Lo strumentale predicativo nelle lingue slave", *Annali, Sezione slava VII*, 27–70 and VIII, 97–107; also my above-mentioned *Handbuch* I, § 947–972.

4. Cf. my *Handbuch* I, § 75.

5. A description of the Lithuanian practice is given in my *Handbuch* I, § 996–1023.

6. Kita Tschenkéli, *Einführung in die georgische Sprache* I, Zürich, 1958, 82 f.

494

7. Cf. the publication *Lingvističeskij analiz gidronimov verchnego Podneprov'ja* of V. N. Toporov and O. N. Trubačev, Moscow, 1962.

8. Cf. figure 1 (map showing localities mentioned in the text) of Marija Gimbutas' book, *The Prehistory of Eastern Europe*, Cambridge, 1956.

9. In his article "Gde žila Litva?", *Izvestija Akademii Nauk*, VI ser., Nos. 12–18, p. 1051 ff.

10. "The Problem of Balto-Slav Unity—A Critical Survey", *Kratylos* II, 97–123.

11. A. Vaillant, *Grammaire comparée des langues slaves*, 201.

12. A. Senn, *Die Sprache* III, 63.

13. The very interesting book *Balts and Aryans in their Indo-European Background* by S. K. Chatterji, 1968, (Indian Institute of Advanced Study, Simla), while full of valuable information, does not touch on our problem.

FANNY DE SIVERS

Le datif en live

Le datif apparaît assez rarement dans la littérature finno-ougrienne. On en parle en général quand il faut trouver un cas équivalent au datif indo-européen.

Pour l'ouralien on admet six cas : nominatif, accusatif, génitif, latif, locatif, séparatif (ablatif).[1] Le datif indo-européen, lui-même très proche du locatif,[2] peut être rendu par le latif — dans les langues samoyèdes, il y a encore un cas appelé « latif-datif »[3] — ou par le locatif, représenté dans plusieurs langues finnoises par les cas locaux externes (allatif — adessif — ablatif) ou internes (illatif — inessif — élatif).

Les discussions autour du datif en finno-ougrien se situent donc le plus souvent sur le plan sémantique. Le « datif » est un cas répondant à la question « à qui? »

Toutefois, une forme identifiée comme datif s'est développée en mordve (*ava/neń* « à la mère »), en tchérémisse (*imńõ/lan* « au cheval »), en zyriène (*mõs/ly* « à la vache »), en hongrois (*ember/nek* « à l'homme »).[4]

Par contre, le datif en finnois que l'on appelle officiellement « datif-génitif » ne se distingue formellement en rien du génitif :[5] *pojan tulee nälkä* « le garçon aura faim (= au garçon viendra la faim) », *pojan kirja* « le livre du garçon (= du garçon le livre) ». Mais cette forme génitivale exprime souvent le « datif », et, dans certaines expressions, elle peut remplacer l'adessif[6], par exemple, dans les constructions possessives de type *mihi est* : *minulla on* (adess.) ou *minun on* (gén.) « j'ai (= à moi est) »[7].

Dans les langues finnoises de la Baltique, le « datif » (à qui?) se traduit par l'allatif, en lapon on emploie ici l'illatif[8]. Mais dans le parler courant et dans les dialectes, l'allatif et l'adessif se confondent souvent, par exemple en carélien, en vepse[9] — de même l'inessif et l'élatif dans quelques dialectes du lapon. D'autre part, les séries externes et internes sont intimement liées et peuvent se remplacer mutuellement[10]. Il est donc, dans certains cas, difficile de préciser quelles sont les formes destinées à exprimer le « datif ».

Le live a un datif formellement identifiable. Lauri Kettunen[11] l'explique à partir de l'ancien locatif en *-na* qui donnerait en live la terminaison *-n*. Le

« locatif » se rencontre encore dans des adverbes comme *kougə̑n* « loin » (est. *kaugel*, fi. *kaukana*), *tagàn* « derrière, après » (est. *taga*, fi. *takana*), *ə̑də̑n* « le soir, au soir » (fi. *ehtoona*), etc. Mais dans la plupart des cas, il s'agirait du vrai « datif » correspondant au datif-génitif du finnois (live : *mi'nnə̑n um'*, fi. *minun on* « j'ai (=à moi est) ». Or, si le datif et le génitif se ressemblent en finnois, le live emploie ici deux formes bien distinctes. La terminaison *-n* du génitif est supprimée, comme en estonien, mais le nominatif et le génitif, même s'ils coïncident formellement dans beaucoup de paradigmes, se distinguent aussi par des procédés comme le fameux « Umlaut » *(läpš* « enfant », gén. *laps*, cf. fi. *lapsi, lapsen*). A priori, il n'y a donc pas de confusion possible entre le génitif et le datif.

Mais quels sont les rapports entre ce datif et les cas locaux externes des langues finnoises voisines?

Kettunen note que le datif en live correspond à l'allatif, à l'adessif et quelquefois aussi à l'ablatif des autres langues esto-finnoises.

Il est à noter que les cas locaux externes existent aussi en live. On distingue, par exemple, entre *sizàl* « dedans, à l'intérieur » (adess.), *sizàlD* « de l'intérieur » (abl.), *si'zzə̑l* « vers l'intérieur » (allat.). Dans beaucoup de paradigmes, l'adessif et l'allatif sont formellement identiques. Kettunen indique pour l'ablatif la désinence *-lD*, pour l'adessif et l'allatif *-l(ə̑)* : *ta jelāb mōl* ou *mōlə̑* « il vit à la campagne », *ta tu'l' mōlD* ou *mōlDə̑* « il est venu de la campagne », *ta lä'b mōlə̑* « il va à la campagne » (cf. est. *maal, maalt, maale*, fi. *maalla, maalta, maalle*)[12].

L'adessif-allatif apparaît le plus souvent dans des expressions de caractère adverbial comme par exemple *uondžə̑l* « au matin, le matin » (*uomə̑g* « le matin ») et la fréquence même de ces formes a tendance à les rendre inanalysables pour le locuteur qui les traite quelquefois comme des mots simples auxquels on peut ajouter les désinences casuelles. Ainsi, on rencontre dans les textes lives de Setälä[13] un translatif de *uondžə̑l* : *miŋgist tiedə̑ ta sin'nə̑n āndiz uondžə̑ləks?* (p. 325) « Quel travail t'a-t-il donné *pour le matin?* » (Trad. finnoise de Setälä : *aamuksi.*) Sur la même page, nous trouvons des expressions courantes *uondžə̑l* « le matin » (fi. *aamulla*), *uomdə̑ uondžə̑l* « demain matin » (fi. *huomenaamulla*).

Pour la plupart des paradigmes, l'allatif-adessif est remplacé par le datif[14]. Ce datif se rencontre dans les textes[15] couramment avec les verbes qui aussi dans d'autres langues se combinent avec le datif, comme *āndə̑* « donner », *mīdə̑* « vendre », *maksə̑* « payer », *nä'ktə̑* « montrer », *kītə̑* « dire », etc.?

iz ānda mi'nnə̑n (Kett. p. 61) « Il ne *me* l'a pas donné ».

Māmi'ed mä'ddə̑n iz mīttə̑ (Kett. p. 59) « Les paysans ne nous en vendaient pas ».

mis sa min'nən maksād? (Set. p. 156) « Combien *me* payeras-tu ? »
nä'gtəb täm'mən (Set. p. 263) « Il *lui* montre ».
kīttəb poissən (Kett. p. 108) « Il dit *au garçon* ». — *se kīttəp pettərən* (Kett. p. 46) « Celui-ci dit *à Peter* ».

Le datif est aussi de règle dans les syntagmes possessifs où l'estonien et le finnois emploient l'adessif :

i'd izān um' vend ikš tidār (Set. p. 94) « Un père avait une fille (=*à un pere* était une fille) ». (Cf. est. *ühel isal,* fi. *eräällä isällä.*)

sel'l'ist kuorad ne ku sigān (Set. p. 92) « des oreilles comme (celles) d'un cochon (=à un chochon) » (est. *seal,* fi. *sialla*).

sel'l'i ruĩa tä'm tidàrən u'm (Kett. p. 67) « sa fille a cette maladie-là (=à cette fille) ».

mä'ddən äb uo ibistə (Kett. p. 63) « Nous n'avons pas de cheval ».

iemā izā mi'nnən um kúolən (Kett. p. 52) « le père de la mère *à moi* est mort ».

Au sujet de *kītə* « dire », il faut noter que le datif peut être remplacé par un adessif-allatif exprimé dans la postposition *pāl* « sur », comme c'est attesté aussi en estonien parlé, et surtout dans des textes archaïques.

ni tam kītən eńtš naiz pāl (Set. p. 170) « Il a donc dit *à sa femme* » (au lieu de *naizən*) — *sem' kītən täm' pāl* (Set. p. 66) « il *lui* a dit » (au lieu de *täm'mən*). Cf. est. *naise pääle, tema pääle.*

Nous avons donc ici une situation qui admet la variation Datif — Adessif-allatif et confirme ainsi la parenté de ces deux cas.

La remarque de Kettunen que le datif peut aussi remplacer « quelquefois » l'ablatif des autres langues esto-finnoises » nous paraît discutable. En effet, dans les traductions de Setälä on trouve quelques ablatifs, par exemple, p. 124 : *ne lapst seitə täm'mən ve'zzə* … (*Ne lapset söivat häneltä lihaa* …) Mais Setälä lui-même hésite au sujet de la traduction et note entre parenthèses (*hänen lihansa?*). Dans les deux versions nous traduirions en français « les enfants mangeaient *sa* viande ». La première variante permet de dégager une nuance : « la viande *à lui,* qui lui était destinée », la seconde indique seulement la possession : « *sa* viande ».

A cet endroit, on peut se demander, si le datif n'est pas quelquefois destiné à remplacer la forme génitivale disparue dans la plupart des paradigmes comme nous l'avons déjà signalé ci-dessus.

En regardant de près les textes de Setälä, nous y trouvons de nombreux datifs lives traduits par le génitif finnois :

un astən sie karnən sälgə … (p. 71) (ja astunut sen *korpin* selkään) « et il se mit sur le dos *du corbeau* ».

minā panāb ra'i sie jālgan alā (p. 112) « je mets la chaise *sous ce pied* » (fi. *sen jalan alle*).

se vẹnd sie jẹmāndǝn sịzār (p. 96) « c'était la sœur *de cette dame* » (fi. *sen rouvan sisar*).

Dans les exemples cités, Setälä traduit le datif du texte live par le génitif. Mais les parlers dialectaux et l'estonien admettent ici quelquefois l'allatif ou l'adessif. En estonien on pourrait dire *kaarnale selga* « au corbeau sur le dos », *sellele jalale alla* « à ce pied dessous », *sel emandal õde* « à cette dame la sœur ». (Cf. les traductions estoniennes de Kettunen.)

Il est intéressant de comparer ici les traductions finnoises et les traductions estoniennes :

Set. p. 115 : *ta ai'liz sie mi'en tagān* (sen *miehen* perään) « elle courut après cet homme » (fi. génitif) — Kett. p. 82 : *sie sūr ibìzǝn tagàn* (*sellele suurele hobusele* järele) « après, derrière ce grand cheval » (est. allatif).

Set. p. 169 : *un täm' nai um' vẹnd kurēn kilgs* (hänen vaimonsa on ollut paholaisen rinnalla) « Sa femme était à côté du diable ». — Kett. p. 78 : *ta um tō'nd istǝ se kut's̄ǝrǝn kilgǝ* (*sellele kutsarile kõrvale*) « il voulait s'asseoir à côté de ce cocher ».

Bien plus troublant est l'emploi du datif dans les expressions où le finnois et l'estonien ne connaissent que le génitif. Dans les composés comme *pänoùk* (< **pänaukko*) « trou de la tête, encolure », *sìemnàiga* « repas », Kettunen explique la forme en -*n* par l'ancien génitif qui se serait conservé ici pour des raisons phonétiques. Partout ailleurs, même dans les énoncés comme *sie rō' um izàn* « cet argent appartient au père » (all. *dieses Geld ist des Vaters, gehört dem Vater*, fi. *se raha on isän*), Kettunen veut voir des datifs.

En effet, il s'agit ici d'une variante du syntagme possessif qui emploie le datif.

Mais plusieurs expressions ne semblent pas respecter ces « satzphonetischen Verbindungen », évoquées par Kettunen. On trouve des combinaisons où le « génitif en -*n* » varie avec le génitif actuel, par exemple : *jǎranaigās* « sur le bord du lac » (Set. p. 149 *järven rannassa*) et *jǎra ai'gǝ* « sur le bord du lac », illat. (Set. p. 150 : *järven rantaa*); *āma āman izā* « le père de grand'-mère (= père de la mère de la mère) » (Mäg. p. 25) et *izā izā* « le père du père » (Mäg. p. 29). Un génitif indiscutable figure dans *kalān tabār* « queue de poisson » (Mäg. pp. 27 et 31), cf. est. *kala saba*, fi. *kalan pyrstö*.

D'autre part, les pronoms personnels, extrêmement fréquents dans les textes, sont couramment employés sous deux formes : à côté du datif régulier, on rencontre une forme réduite que l'on peut identifier comme « génitif ». L'esquisse grammaticale de Kettunen note pour les 1ère, 2e et 3e personnes sg. les génitifs suivants : *mi'n, si'n, tä'm,* et les datifs : *mi'nnən, si'nnən, tä'mmən.* Or, dans les textes, les deux formes se confondent souvent : *vịta mis sin'nən pi'edrab un li jẹra!* (Set. p. 206) « Prends ce qui t'appartient et va t'en! » — *vịta mis sin pi'edrab un li je'dspēd'ən.* (Id. p. 207) « Prends ce qui t'appartient et vas-y. »

... *täm'mən tutkām ti'edə* et *täm' tutkām ti'edə* (Set. p. 209) « le tuer (=*lui* faire la fin) ».

Ces observations permettent de conclure que le datif live correspond non seulement à l'adessif et à l'allatif de l'estonien et du finnois, mais aussi au génitif[16]. Le fait que la marque du datif actuel coïncide avec la marque de l'ancien génitif favorise sans doute la variété fonctionelle de cette forme[17].

Il faudrait encore étudier les fonctions du datif live par rapport au datif letton. Kettunen pense que l'influence du letton a pu se faire sentir sur le plan fonctionnel, mais à peine dans le domaine phonique. (Il s'agit ici, bien entendu, du datif letton en -*am*.)

On peut, toutefois, constater que les datifs pronominaux lettons, la 1ère personne *man* et la 3ᵉ personne *viņam* sont extrêmement fréquents dans la conversation courante, et que, par leurs nasales, ils se rapprochent des formes correspondantes en live : *min' — min'nən, täm' — täm'mən.* Le letton aussi emploie le datif dans les constructions possessives : *man ir, tēvam ir māja* « j'ai (=à moi est), le père a (=au père est) une maison ». Très important pour le live est sans doute aussi la construction débitive du letton avec le datif : *man jāraksta vēstule* « il faut que j'écrive une lettre (=à moi il faut écrire) », cf. la grammaire de Stender[18], p. 57; *man irr ja raksta* « mihi scribendum est », en live *min'nən um kēratəməst.*

D'autre part, il faudrait aussi revoir le problème des datifs-locatifs en -*n.* Kettunen cite d'après Endzelin *tan rītan, tan vakaran* « ce matin, ce soir » (cf. live *tä'mę̄'dən,* fi. *tänä ehtoona*). De plus, le lithuanien connaît un illatif en -*n* qui peut être employé comme « locatif »[19].

Comme on le voit, il existe une foule de formes semblables qui se groupent autour de la notion du « datif », et une étude approfondie de ces « datifs », « datif-locatif », « datif-génitif » et des cas locaux en général, pourrait jeter une nouvelle lumière sur les rapports entre les langues baltes et les idiomes finnois des régions voisines.

Notes

1. E. Itkonen, *Kieli ja sen tutkimus,* Helsinki, 1966, 261.

2. J. Kuryłowicz, *The Inflectional Categories of Indo-European,* Heidelberg, 1964, 190 parle de « genetic affinity between the dat. and the locat. »

3. B. Collinder, *Introduktion till de uraliska språken*, Stockholm, 1962, 160.

4. E. Itkonen, *op. cit.*, 268.

5. Id. *ibid* : ce cas est probablement le reste de l'ancien latif -*n*.

6. Voir P. Pulkkinen, « Havaintoja adessiivin käytöstä », *Virittäjä*, 1963, 318–337.

7. Pour comparer les emplois du datif indo-européen, voir J. Haudry, « Les emplois doubles du datif et la fonction du datif indo-européen », *Bulletin de la Société de Linguistique de Paris*, 1968, 141–159.

8. E. Itkonen, *op. cit.*, 268. Cf. A. Alhoniemi, *Über die Funktionen der Wohinkasus im Tscheremissischen* (Mémoires de la Société Finno-ougrienne 142), Helsinki, 1967, 46 : les « Wohin-Kasus-formen » (latif, illatif) sont souvent remplacées par le datif.

9. V. Tauli, *Structural Tendencies in Uralic Languages*, The Hague, 1966, 26.

10. P. Pulkkinen, *art. cit.* note que l'adessif apparaît en finnois souvent à la place de l'inessif. Cf. pour l'estonien, F. de Sivers, *Analyse grammaticale de l'estonien parlé*, Clermont-Ferrand, 1969, 134.

11. *Livisches Wörterbuch mit grammatischer Einleitung*, Helsinki, 1938.

12. Voir Kettunen, *op. cit.*, p. LI. L'adessif et l'allatif ne se distinguent plus dans quelques dialects estoniens (J. Mägiste).

13. E. N. Setälä, *Näytteitä liivin kielestä*, Helsinki, 1953, 530 p.

14. Il est intéressant de noter que le grammairien A. W. Hupel, *Ehstnische Sprachlehre für beide Hauptdialekte, den revalschen und den dörptschen; nebst einem vollständigen Wörterbuch*, 2. éd. 1818, p. 10 indique pour le « datif » (Gebefall) estonien la désinence « *le* oder *l* ».

15. A côté des textes de Setälä, il faut tenir compte de deux autres recueils : L. Kettunen, *Untersuchung über die livische Sprache*, I, Tartu, 1925, 160 p; J. Mägiste, *Liiviläisiä tekstejä*, Suomalaisen Kirjallisuuden Seuran Toimituksia 276, Helsinki, 1964, 74 p.

16. Quelques datifs en tchérémisse peuvent aussi être interprétés comme « génitifs ». Voir E. Minn-Kangasmaa, *The Syntactical distribution of the Cheremis genitive*, I, (Mémoires de la Société Finno-ougrienne 139), Helsinki, 1966, 130.

17. Le live aurait donc un « datif-génitif » comme le finnois. On a déjà constaté que, par certains traits, le live est plus proche du finnois que de l'estonien. Voir G. Décsy, *Einführung in die Finnisch-ugrische Sprachwissenschaft*, Wiesbaden, 1965, 209.

18. G. F. Stender, *Neue vollständigere Lettische Grammatik, Nebst einem hinlänglichen Lexico, wie auch einigen Gedichten*, Braunschweig, 1761.

19. J. Endzelin, *Lettische Grammatik*, Riga, 1922, 339.

The Livonian Dative

The dative is not a frequent case in Finno-Ugric grammar. Livonian is the only Balto-Finnic language which has developed a real dative case. But this form resembles the ancient genitive and locative and is often used to replace several other case forms. A comparison with the dative in Latvian and Lithuanian should explain some formal and semantic variations in Livonian and shed light on Baltic-Finnic contacts.

FRANCISZEK SŁAWSKI

Lexikalische Neuerungen
im Baltisch-Slavischen

1. Um lexikalische Neuerungen der baltischen und slavischen Sprachen zu untersuchen, habe ich das Baltisch-Slavische Wörterbuch von R. Trautmann[1] exakt durchgesehen. Es bildet die maßgebendste Grundlage für derartige Untersuchungen, obschon im Verlauf von fast 50 Jahren seit seinem Erscheinen zahlreiche Werke veröffentlicht wurden, die Trautmanns Forschungsergebnisse stellenweise wesentlich verändern. In unserer Untersuchung handelt es sich vorwiegend um das neue baltische Wortmaterial, das vor allem durch die Wörterbücher von K. Mühlenbach[2] und E. Fraenkel[3] geliefert wird. Deshalb revidiere ich die einzelnen Schlagwörter von R. Trautmanns Wörterbuch in Hinsicht auf die neuesten Forschungsergebnisse der sowohl baltischen als auch slavischen Sprachen [im Falle der slavischen Sprachen gehe ich vor allem auf mein Wörterbuch[4] und das von M. Vasmer[5] zurück].

Ich habe das gesamte baltisch-slavische Sprachgut untersucht. An dieser Stelle bespreche ich wegen Platzmangel nur die Untersuchungsergebnisse im Bereich des Substantivs[6]. Es ist zunächst erwähnenswert, daß bereits im Jahre 1911 J. Endzelin[7] ein reiches Material von den nur den baltischen und slavischen Sprachen eigenen Worten veröffentlicht hatte.

Der substantivische Wortschatz von R. Trautmanns Wörterbuch besteht aus ungefähr 888 Schlagwörtern[8], davon wurden etwa 610 Substantive in den Hauptschlagwörtern besprochen, rund 278 bilden Derivate. Die zuletzt genannte Zahl umfaßt eine übrigens recht geringe Anzahl von Schlagwörtern, die von Trautmann nicht abgesondert wurden, jedoch in seinem Wortmaterial enthalten sind, z. B. s. v. *selpi̯ō* 'springe': baltisch-slav. *salpa-*, urslav. *solpъ*, sloven. *slâp* 'Wasserfall, Kaskade; Schwall, Woge' : lit. *saĺpas* 'Bucht, Busen'.

Das Wortmaterial Trautmanns umfaßt drei klar und proportionell voneinander abgesonderte Hauptgruppen:

I. Das indogermanische Erbe,
II. Die Gruppe von Substantiven, die nur in den slavischen Sprachen oder
nur in den baltischen Sprachen bezeugt sind,
III. Baltisch-slavische Neuerungen.

I. Das indogermanische Worterbe bildet etwa 265 Substantive [also
ungefähr 30 % des Ganzen], davon sind 201 Wörter — Grundwörter, etwa
64 — Derivate.

II. Gruppe von Substantiven, die nur in den slavischen oder nur in den
baltischen Sprachen bezeugt sind, ist durch die 334 Schlagwörter [unge-
fähr 37,5 %] vertreten, davon sind 214 Grundwörter und 120 Derivate enthalten. Die Mehrheit bilden die nur baltischen Substantive: 181 [davon
111 Grundwörter, 70 Derivate]. Es gibt 153 nur slavische Substantive [103
Grundwörter und 50 Derivate].

III. 289 Substantive bilden baltisch-slavische Neuerungen [32,5 %], davon
195 Grundwörter und 94 Derivate.

2. Größtenteils [124 Substantive, davon 92 Grundwörter] kommen Termini
vor, die mit der Natur zusammenhängen. Dazu gehören vor allem zahlreiche Namen aus dem Pflanzen- oder Tierreich, so die Pflanzen-, Baum-,
Tier-, Vogel-, Fisch- und Insektennamen. Darüber hinaus zahlreiche Namen,
die mit Bodengestaltung, Wetter, Tageszeit zusammenhängen.

Nachstehend führen wir das dazugehörige Wortmaterial an[9]:

Das Pflanzenreich: *ābalni-* 'Apfelbaum', *ašuta-* 'Distel', *aksti-* 'Spitze, Stachel',
amēlā 'Mistel', *budią-* : *budula-* 'Schwamm', *bumbula-* 'Knollen, Knoten', *degut-*
'Birkenteer', *derua-* 'Baum', *edlā-* : *edli-* 'Tanne', *garṣa-* 'Giersch', *gumba-*
'Auswuchs', *kera-* 'Wurzel, Strauch', *kermuṣa-* 'Faulbaum', *kimena-* 'eine
Pflanze', *kōukšta-* 'Busch', *krāušią-* 'Birne, Birnbaum', *laiska-* : *leista-*
'Blatt', *lēipā-* 'Linde', *lukna-* 'Seerose', *lūnka-* 'Bast', *maurā-* 'Gras, Rasen',
nāti- 'Kräutich', *ōgā-* 'Beere', *papartią-* : *pāparti-* 'Farnkraut', *plēuā-* 'feine
Haut', *reiṣa-* : *-rōiṣa-* 'Nuß', *trušią-* 'Rohr', *ualkti-* 'Rispe, Ähre', *uirba-*
'Reis, Gerte', *uiržią-* 'Heidekraut'.

Das Tierreich: *asila-* 'Esel', *auina-* 'Widder', *āžią-* 'Ziegenbock', *babra-*
'Biber', *kārua-* 'Kuh', *katā-* 'Katze', *kaunā-* 'Marder', *kaunā-* : *kunā-* 'Hündin', *krutu-* 'rührig, Maulwurf', *sirnā-* 'Reh', *telią-* 'Kalb', *ūdrā-* 'Fischotter',
ueprią- 'Eber', *ueuer-* 'Eichhörnchen', *uilkītią-* 'junger Wolf', *auikeinā-*
'Schaffleisch', *āžina-* 'Haut', *ēreinā-* 'Lammfleisch; Lammwolle', *iaunika-*
'Junges', *kārkā-* 'Schweinefuß', *karueinā-* 'Kuhfleisch', *klišią-* 'Krebsschere',
raga- 'Horn', *šukā-* 'Borste, Bürste', *uilkeinā-* 'Wolfsfell';
ānt- 'Ente', *āntukā-* Demin., *arila-* 'Adler', *gegala-* 'ein Wasservogel',

geguž̇ịā- 'Kuckuck', *gēruịā*-:*gerōu̯ịa*- 'Kranich', *gilnā*- 'Specht', *gulbịa*-:*kul-pịa*- 'Schwan', *kāu̯ā*- 'Dohle', *keketa*- 'Finkenart', *kōu̯arna*-:*kōu̯ārnā*- 'Rabe; Dohle', *kōu̯lingā*- 'ein Vogel', *lelịa*- 'Ziegenmelker', *nara*- 'wilde Entenart', *pīlịā*- 'Ente', *slănkā*- 'Schnepfe', *u̯arbịịa*- 'Sperling', *u̯arna*- 'Rabe', *u̯arnītịa*- 'junger Rabe', *u̯ārnā*- 'Krähe', *žansītịa*- 'Gänschen', *putā*- 'Vogel', *putītịa*- 'der kleine Vogel', *žanseinā*- 'Gänsefleisch';

angurịa- 'Aal', *angurītịa*- Demin., *auklēịā*- 'Ukelei [Cyprinus alburnus]', *ešetra*- 'Stör', *ēžgịa*- 'Barsch', *lašašịa*- 'Lachs', *līna*-:*līnịa*- 'Schlei', *šama*- 'Wels', *narša*:*naršta*- 'Laich';

gēbā- 'Kröte', *gnīdā*- 'Niß [Lausei]', *kamāra*- 'Mücke', *šīršen*- 'Hornisse', *trana*- 'Drohne', *uṣi*- 'Laus'.

Termini, die mit Gestaltung des Bodens, Wetter, Tageszeiten zusammenhängen: *baugura*-' Hügel', *brada*- 'Furt', *dănga*- 'Krümmung', *daubā*-:*daupā*- 'Höhlung', *gramata*- 'Haufen', *grumbā*- 'Unebenheiten auf dem Wege', *kama*- 'Klumpen', *kaupra*- 'Hügel', *kapa*- 'Graben', *klana*- 'Neigung', *kōupa*-:*kōupā*- 'Haufen', *lankā*- 'Krümmung', *lankịa*- 'Biegung', *pamariịa*- 'Meeresgegend', *rau̯a*- 'Graben', *salpa*- 'Wasserfall, Kaskade', *slaida*- 'Geleise, Spur', *sraugā*- 'Flut', *srau̯ịā*- 'Strömung', *u̯ilnā*- 'Welle', *u̯iršu*- 'das Oberste einer Sache', *ž̇u̯irsta*- 'Kies';

blaiška- 'Glanz', *brēška*- 'Morgendämmerung', *rīta*- 'Morgen', *u̯ekera*- 'Abend', *u̯ēisula*-:*u̯ēisura*- 'Wirbelwind', *u̯ētrā*-:*u̯ētra*- 'Wind', *žarịā*- 'Glanz', *ž̇u̯aigzdā*- 'Stern';

leda-:*ledu*- 'Eis', *īnịa*-:*īniịa*- 'Reif', *šalnā*- 'Reif'.

3. Nun folgt die zweite Gruppe von 81 Substantiven, die thematisch mit der Menschenarbeit zusammenhängen. Beispielsweise gebe ich eine interessante Gruppe von Termini an, die mit Weben und Nähen zusammenhängen, darüber hinaus die Namen von Gefäßen, Mineralien, Stoffen usw.:

aigulā-:*igulā*- 'Nadel', *bírda*- 'Weberkamm', *nīti*- 'Faden', *mergā*- 'Geflecht, Netz', *pānta*- 'Fessel', *pīntla*-:*pīndla*- 'Band', *pōsma*- 'bestimmte Anzahl von Fäden auf der Haspel', *sịu̯u̯a*- 'Naht', *sịu̯u̯ēịa*- 'wer näht', *sịu̯u̯ika*- 'Schneider, Schuster', *šeịu̯ā*-:*kaịu̯ā*- 'Spule', *u̯iru̯ịā*-:*u̯iru̯i*- 'Seil', *u̯ītula*- 'Garnhaspel';

dalbta- 'Durchschlag, Meißel', *gīrnū*- 'Handmühle', *karba*-:*karbiịā*- 'Korb', *karūta*- 'Mulde, Trog', *katila*- 'Kessel', *kiru̯i*- 'Axt', *kibā*- 'Gefäß', *klumpi*- 'Bank, Stuhl', *krēsla*- 'Stuhl', *lāu̯ā*- 'Bank, Stuhl', *paistā*-:*paista*- 'Mörser', *peilā*- 'Säge', *sēita*- 'Sieb', *skirbā*- 'Ritze', *su̯īda*- 'Hartriegel';

ālu̯a- 'Blei', *angli*- 'Kohle', *gelēža*- 'Eisen', *kremen*- 'Feuerstein', *stikla*- 'Glas', *u̯āpa*- 'Farbe', *u̯aska*- 'Wachs'.

504

4. Im Bereich des physischen Lebens des Menschen habe ich 51 Termini abgesondert [davon 12 Derivate]. Auffallend ist vor allem die große Zahl der Namen von Körperteilen:

bŭrnā- 'Mund', *dēlnā-*:*dōlni-* 'Handfläche', *-dusā-*:*-dausā-* 'Arm', *gālu̯ā-* 'Kopf', *gursti-* 'Handvoll', *gurtla-*:*gurdla-* 'Kropf, Kehle', *ikră-* 'Wade', *inžū-* 'Zunge', *kasā-* 'Zopf', *keli̯a-* 'Knie', *kulkā-* 'Hüfte', *naga-* 'Nagel', *nagut-* 'Nagel', *ōlekt-* 'Ellenbogen', *pentā-* 'Ferse', *pirṣta-* 'Finger', *pirši-* 'Brust', *plesmenā-*:*plesnā-* 'Fußsohle', *pleuti̯ā-*:*plauti̯ā-* 'Lunge', *plutā-*:*pluti-* 'Haut', *rankā-* 'Hand', Demin. *rankikā-*, *rēita-* 'Oberschenkel', *tēla-* 'Gestalt', *u̯ansā-* 'Barthaar', *u̯ēka-*:*u̯āka-* 'Deckel, Augenlid'.

Beachtenswert sind ebenfalls einige interessanten Termini aus dem Bereich der Bekleidung:

drōba- 'Fetzen, Kleider', *kūrpi̯a-* 'Schuh', *lāpa-*:*lāput-* 'Lappen', *laskanā-* 'Lappen', *makas-* 'Beutel', *šarka-* 'Rock'.

5. Nur 5 Termini beziehen sich auf das geistige Leben [davon 3 Derivate]: *u̯aisti-* 'das Wissen', *peišima-* 'das Ziehen mit Kohle, Malen, Schreiben', *auma-* 'Verstand, Vernunft', *lāskā-* 'Liebkosung', *dabā-* 'Eigenschaft, Art'.

6. Im Bereich des gesellschaftlichen Lebens habe ich 28 baltisch-slavische Neuerungen festgestellt [davon 11 Derivate]. Hierin gehören z. B. die Substantive: *mēira-* 'Friede', *šlōu̯ā-* 'Ruf, Ruhm', *u̯einā-* 'Ursache, Schuld', *u̯ada-*:*u̯adā-* 'Führer, Führung', *drauga-* 'Gefährte', *u̯arga-* 'Feind', *šu̯entika-* 'der Heilige', *dausi̯ā-*:*du̯asi̯ā-* 'Atem, Seele', *aldii̯ā-* 'Kahn, Schiff', *maina-*: *mainā-* 'Tausch', *bruni̯ās* 'Brünne', *barni-* 'Zank, Streit', *gintla-*:*gindla-* 'Waffe', *lanka-* 'Bogen', *kalkala-* 'Schelle', *daudā-* 'Pfeife', *gerba-* 'Stück, Los', *u̯ainika-* 'Kranz', *dali̯a-* 'Teil'.

Dazu gehören auch die Verwandtschaftsbezeichnungen: *bābā-* 'altes Weib', *brāli-* Koseform zu *brāter-*, *maldeni̯ka-* 'Kind', *seserēna-*:*sesrēna-* 'Schwestersohn', *strūi̯u-* 'Alter', *šeimā-*:*šaimi̯ā-*:*šaimii̯ā-* 'Familie', *u̯aika-* 'Knabe, Knecht', *ženta* : *ženti-* 'Schwiegersohn'.

7. Ein Großteil des untersuchten Materials, d. h. rund 85 Substantive, sind außerhalb der baltisch-slavischen Sprachgruppe nicht bekannt. Hierin gehören z. B.: *bīrda* 'Weberkamm', *gālu̯ā-* 'Kopf', *gelēža-* 'Eisen', *gegu̯ži̯ā-* 'Kuckuck', *gulbi̯a-*:*kulpi̯a-* 'Schwan', *gumba-* 'Auswuchs', *ikră-* 'Wade', *kāru̯ā-* 'Kuh', *kaunā-* 'Marder', *klumpi-* 'Bank, Stuhl', *kremen-* 'Feuerstein', *krēsla-* 'Stuhl', *leda-*:*ledu-* 'Eis', *lēipā-* 'Linde', *lūnka-* 'Bast', *maură-* 'Gras, Rasen', *mēira-* 'Friede', *nāti-* 'Kräutich', *paistā-*:*paista-* 'Mörser', *pentā-* 'Ferse', *pirṣta-* 'Finger', *rada-* 'Geburt', *raga-* 'Horn', *rankā-* 'Hand', *sēilā-*

'Kraft', ṷarna- 'Rabe', ṷārnā- 'Krähe', ṷeprịa- 'Eber', žarịā- 'Glanz',
žṷaigzdā- 'Stern'.

8. Der überwiegende Teil des untersuchten Wortmaterials geht selbstverständlich auf die ererbten indogermanischen Wurzeln zurück, die auf dem
Grund des Baltisch-Slavischen oder durch spezielle Suffixe, oder aber auch
durch andere morphologische Mittel [der spezifische Ablaut, Reduplika-
tion], zuletzt durch spezielle semantische Veränderungen modifiziert
wurden. So fällt das balto-slavische putā- durch seine Bedeutung 'Vogel'
auf, währenddessen das indogermanische pōu-:pəu-:pŭ- überhaupt 'junges
Tier, kleines Tier, Junges' bedeutete[10].
Besonders beachtenswert sind die auf dem Grunde des Baltisch-Slavischen entwickelten Wortbildungsformante, z. B. -ika- [sịuṷika- 'Schneider,
Schuster', minika- 'Treter'], -ēịa- [sịuṷēịa- 'wer näht'], -ītịa- [ṷarnītịa-
'junger Rabe', putītịa- 'junger Vogel'].

9. Wie aus dem Obigen ersichtlich wird, bilden die baltisch-slavischen
Neuerungen einen bedeutenden Teil des substantivischen Materials, das im
Wörterbuch von R. Trautmann enthalten ist, der sogar das indogermanische Worterbe zahlenmäßig ein wenig übertrifft [32,5 % : 30 %]. Der allgemeine Prozentsatz gegenüber dem Ganzen des baltisch-slavischen substantivischen Sprachguts wäre bedeutend größer, hätten wir nur baltische bzw.
nur slavische Elemente von Trautmanns Wörterbuch außer Acht gelassen,
die ja einen bedeutenden Teil dieses Werkes ausmachen [ungefähr 37,5 %].

Anmerkungen

1. R. Trautmann, *Baltisch-Slavisches Wörterbuch*, Göttingen 1923.
2. K. Mühlenbach, *Lettisch-deutsches Wörterbuch, redigiert, ergänzt und fortgesetzt
von J. Endzelin*, I–IV, Riga, 1923–1932.
3. E. Fraenkel, *Litauisches etymologisches Wörterbuch*, Heidelberg, 1955–1965.
4. F. Sławski, *Słownik etymologiczny języka polskiego*, I–III [*A-kysz*], Kraków,
1952–1969.
5. M. Vasmer, *Russisches etymologisches Wörterbuch*, I–III, Heidelberg, 1953–1958.
6. Vgl. die Abhandlung von J. Safarewicz, „Ze słownictwa bałto-słowiańskiego
(innowacje czasownikowe)", *Slavia Antiqua* VIII, 11–24.
7. J. Endzelin, *Slavjano-baltijskije etjudy*, Char'kov, 1911, 192–200.
8. Eine Anzahl von Substantiven wurde dabei außer acht gelassen, wo im Wörterbuch R. Trautmanns den Substantiven aus einer Gruppe andere Wortarten, meistens
die Verben der zweiten Gruppe entsprechen, so z. B. *šlauža-* 'Schleim' : slav. *sluzъ* : lit.
šliaũžti 'kriechen'.
9. Die Schlagwörter gehen auf das R. Trautmanns Wörterbuch zurück.
10. J. Pokorny, *Indogermanisches etymologisches Wörterbuch*, Bern, 1959, 842–843.

Balto-Slavic Lexical Innovations

The author has analysed the nouns included in a Balto-Slavic Dictionary by R. Trautmann. The total number of 888 nouns has been divided into the following three groups: Group I, comprising the Indo-European inheritance (265 words, approx. 30 %); Group II, comprising either Baltic words only, or Slavic words only (334 words, approx. 37.5 %); Group III, comprising Balto-Slavic innovations (289 words, 32.5 %, out of which 195 words are basic and 94 words are derivatives).

In the third Group the greatest number of words, as many as 124 (92 of them being basic), are terms connected with nature (e.g. the plant or animal world), topographical features, weather, times of the day, etc. Balto-Slavic innovations constitute an essential part of the Balto-Slavic lexical material, exceeding even the Indo-European inheritance.

SEPPO SUHONEN

Zur Mouillierung der späten lettischen Lehnwörter im Livischen

Das Lettisch der Gegenwart kennt allgemein die folgenden mouillierten Konsonantenphoneme: [ķ], [ģ], [ņ] und [ļ]. Im gesprochenen Lettisch kann auch das Allophon [ŗ] verwendet werden, das in der Schrift im jetzigen Lettland nicht besonders bezeichnet wird (vgl MLLVG I, 21)[1]. In den sog. livischen Mundarten des Lettischen werden im Stammauslaut vor *i* und *e*, die selbst geschwunden sein können, die Konsonanten [t], [d], [c], [ʒ] (=dz), [s], [z], [n], [l] und [r] mouilliert — wie Endzelins (LVG S. 188) vermutet (vgl. auch Rudzīte LD S. 186), durch den Einfluss des Livischen. Zu diesen livischen Dialekten gehören u. a. die Mundarten von Dondangen (lett. Dundaga, Dundanga; i. f. = Dn.) und Popen (lett. Pope; i. f. = Po.), die in nächster Nähe des livischen Sprachraums gesprochen werden.

Im Livischen begegnet man den mouillierten Konsonanten [t′], [d′], [ń], [ļ′], [ŕ], [š́] und [ž́] (vgl. Posti GLL S. 284). Diese mouillierten Konsonanten treten auch in vielen späten lettischen Lehnwörtern des Livischen auf[2]. Im folgenden werden die verschiedenen Beleggruppen untersucht[3] und die Ursache der Palatalisation wird erörtert[4].

liv. [ļ′]

Stellung im Inlaut

Substantive

Lett. -*a* (=IV. Dekl.): liv. *dal′à* 'Teil, Anteil' <lett. daļa, Dn. (FBR V S. 140) dàļ | lett. -*e* (=V. Dekl.): liv. *ul′à* (dialektweise *u′l*) 'Radnabe' <lett. ule (auch ula), Dn. (LW) ûļ.

Adjektive

Lett. -*igs*: liv. *mīl′iG* 'lieb; freundlich' < lett. *mīlīgs*.

Verben

Lett. I. Konjugation: liv. *smel′l′ə̑*: Pr. *smel′ùB* 'schöpfen' <lett. smelt: smeļu: smêlu, Dn. (LW) smä'lt; vgl. BFB 129[IV] | lett. II. Konj.: *kīl′ə̑*: Pr. -*B* 'Keil

508

eintreiben', vgl. lett. ķīlêt: -ēju: -ēju | dril'l'ə̀ (~ drillə̀): Pr. drìllə̀B 'bohren' <lett. drill/êt: -ēju: -ēju, Dn. (LW) drilt <mnd. | dīvil'tt'ə̀: Pr. -B 'abtreiben, drillen' <lett. dīvelêt | lett. III. Konj.: liv. mu'ld'ə̀: Pr. -B 'irren, irre werden; irre reden' <lett. muîdêtiês, Dn. (LW) mu'lttə̧s: äs mu'ldə̧s | mīlińttə̀: Pr. -B 'lieben, liebeln' <lett. mîlin/ât: -u (Ulm. Wb. auch -āju = II. Konj.), Dn. (LW) mīlant; vgl. BFB 131ₓ.

Stellung im Wortauslaut
Substantive

Lett. Suff. -ĕl- (mask. -ĕlis = Dn. -el's; Po. -ę̧ls; fem. -ēle = Dn. und Po. -ę̧l); lett. -elis: liv. dappìl' 'junges Rind, Sterke; Spätlamm' <lett. dapelis, Gen. Sg. dapeḷa, Po. (LW) dappę̧ls; lett. -ele: liv. kibìl' 'Unannehmlichkeit, Schwierigkeit; Hindernis', vgl. lett. ķibele <as.; vgl. SKES sub kiipeli: wahrsch. lett. >liv. | lett. -ŭl- (mask. -ŭlis = Dn. -el(i)s oder -als, Po. -ę̧ls; fem. -ŭle = Dn. -el(e), Po. -el); lett. -ŭlis: liv. bobìl' 'Popanz' < lett. bubulis, Dn. (FBR V S. 126) bobę̧l's; lett. -ŭle: liv. vabìl' 'Marienkäfer (Coccinella)' <lett. vabule (vgl. auch vabulis, vabale), Dn. (LW) vàbal | lett. -uol- (mask. -uols, -uolis = Dn. -als, Po. -als): liv. pūppil' 'Kätzchen an der Weide' lett. pùpuõls², pūpuols, pùpuõls usw., Dn. (FBR V S. 134) pûpals, Po. (FBR XVI S. 121) pûpals | lett. -gl- (mask. -glis = Dn. gę̧ls, Po. -*gę̧ls): liv. oùgə̀l' (livW oùglə̀Z) [wahrsch. jedoch mit Stossintonation] 'Frucht' <lett. aûglis, Dn. (FBR III S. 105) oûgę̧ls (Gem. Sg. oûgę̧ḷ, Dat. aûgḷam, Nom. Pl. oûgę̧ḷ) | lett. -is (II Dekl.): liv. lē'l' 'Nachtschwalbe, Ziegenmelker' <lett. lêlis, Gen. Sg. lêḷa, Dn. (LW) lē'ls | lett. -a (= IV. Dekl.): liv. gril 'Karusell' <lett. griḷḷa, Dn. (LW) gril' | lett. -e (= V. Dekl.): liv. škē'l' 'Schnitte (Brot, Fleisch)' < lett. šķèle, Dn. (FBR V S. 130) šķêel's (in Dn. mit is-Suff.!)

Adjektive

Lett. -īgs: liv. pǭrgil' 'unartig' <lett. pãrgalvîgs, Dn. (LW) pãrgā'Inīks | lett. ein anderes Ableitungssuffix: livW trul' 'stumpf' <lett. truls, Dn. (LW) tru'ls | du'bbil'ľ 'doppelt', vgl. lett. dubults, Dn. dùbalt <kas.

liv. [ŕ]
Stellung im Inlaut
Adjektive

Lett. -īgs: liv. kōŕiG 'lustern, begierig' <lett. kãrîgs.

Verben

Lett. I. Konj.: liv. bu'ŕŕə̀: Pr. buŕùB 'zaubern' <lett. buŕt: buŗu: būru, Dn. (FBR III S. 103) buãrt, (S. 101) 3. P. buŗ, Po. (FBR XVI S. 109)

3. P. Pr. bûŕ | lett. II. Konj.: liv. ừǫŕ∂: Pr. ừǫŕ∂B 'treiben, kutschieren; zwingen irgendetwas zu tun', vgl. lett. uõrêt, Dn. (LW) ừǫŕt: äs ừǫŕe <mnd. | ba'ŕĭt∂: Pr. -B 'mästen' <lett. bar/ot: -oju, Dn. (LW) bàŕt, (FBR III S. 101) 3. P. Pr. baŗ | lett. III. Konj.: liv. gừǫŕ∂ 'faulenzen' <lett. guôrît | puŕìŕŕt∂: Pr. -B 'schütteln' <lett. purinât, Dn. (LW) pừŕant.

Stellung im Auslaut

Substantive

Lett. -eris (mask.; = Dn. (LW) -ers, mitunter aufgezeichnet als -ãrs, -ars, Po. -ers): liv. mēldaŕ (∼mēldar) 'Müller', vgl. lett. melderis, Dn. meldęrs < mnd. Möglicherweise wurden die Wörter dieses Typs direkt von germanischer Seite ins Livische entlehnt. | lett. I. Dekl.: liv. dumb∂ŕ '(rätliche) Sumpferde, Moorerde' <lett. dumbrs (vgl. auch dumbris, dumbras), Dn. (LW) dumbars | lett. -is (=II. Dekl.): livW tū'ŕ (∼livO tū'r) 'Winkel' <lett. stùris, stùris² usw., Dn. (LW) stū'ŕs | stō'ŕk̩, Kl. stō'ŕt̩ 'Storch' <lett. stãrk̩is. Dn. (LW) sto'ŕk's <mnd.

liv. [ŕ]

Anlaut

Verben

Liv. ŕuŕd∂ 'knurren' < lett. ņuŕdêt, ņùrdêt², ņuŕdêt, Dn. (LW) ŕuŕt̩ | pľǫp̆p∂ 'schwatzen, plappern' >lett. p̦ļãpât, p̦ļãpêt, p̦ļãpuot, Dn. (LW) pľãpt.

Inlaut

Substantive

Lett. -is (=II. Dekl.): liv. līŕ∂Z, li'n∂Z 'Schleie (Cyprinus tinca)' | lett. -a (=IV. Dekl.): liv. bruŕ∂: Prt. Sg. bru'ŕŕ∂ 'Panzer, Rüstung' <lett. bruņas, Dn. brū'ns | lett. -e (=V. Dekl.): liv. bēŕd̩a 'Henker' <lett. beñde, Dn. (LW) beñD.

Adjektive

Lett. -îgs: liv. bäs̄-ko'uŕiG 'unverschämt' <lett. bezkàunîgs.

Verben

Lett. II. Konj.: liv. is̄-tsē'ŕ∂: -B 'bewirten' <lett. izcìenît | lett. III Konj.: liv. plu'iŕ∂ 'zupfen, zerren' <lett. pluinît, Dn. (LW) plu'int̩ | dǫviŕt̩t̩∂ 'schenken' <lett. dãvinât; dieser auf -inĭt't'∂-endende Verbtypus erscheint im Livischen häufig.

Auslaut

Substantive

Lett. *-in-* (mask. *-iņš* = Dn. und Po. *-iš*: in Dn. begegnet *-iń* in allen Kasus ausser im Nom. Sg.; fem. *-iņa* = Dn. und Po. *-iņ*); lett. *-iņš*: liv. *daКstiń* 'Dachpfanne, Dachziegel' < lett. dakstiņš, daktiņš, Dn. (LW) daКstiš, Nom. Pl. dakstiņ; lett. *-iņa*: liv. *ma'ŕtsiń* 'Pfund' < lett. mãrciņa, Dn. (LW) mã'rt-siš. Lett. *-ĕn-* (mask. *-ĕnis* = Dn. *-en*(*i*)*s*, Po. *-ens*; fem. *-ene* = Dn. und Po. *-ęn*); lett. *-enis*: liv. *kup̀piń* 'zusammengewehter Schneehaufen' < lett. kupenis (vgl. auch kupene), Dn. (FBR V S. 132) kupęn's, Po. (FBR XVI S. 121) kupęns (Dat. Sg. kupiņam ∼ kuppnęm); lett. *-ĕne*: liv. *su͞striń, zu͞striń* 'schwarze Johannisbeere (ribes nigrum)', offenbar < lett. sustarenes, Dn. (FBR V S. 128, 132) sustriņ(i); lett. < estn. | lett. *-uonis* (Dn. *-ens*, Po. *-ens*): liv. *mirìń*(*ƏZ*) 'Leiche, der Tote' < lett. mironis, Dn. (FBR V S. 133) miręn's | lett. I. Dekl.: liv. *trȭ'ń*, Kl. *trȭ'ń* 'Tran' < lett. trãns, Dn. (LW) trã'ns; vgl. BFB 84₁₉ | lett. II. Dekl.: liv. *du͞ntš* 'Messer' < lett. duñcis, Dn. du'nts | lett. *-e* (= V. Dekl.): liv. *re͞ń* 'Rinne' < lett. rene (vgl. auch reñnis).

liv. [*d'*]

Inlaut

Substantive

Lett. *-is* (= II. Dekl.): liv. *kna'dgƏD* (∼ *kna'igƏD*) 'Haken, Pflock', vgl. lett. knaģis, Dn. (LW) knãk's < mnd.

Adjektive

Lett. *-igs*: liv. *strȭdiG* (∼ *strȭdƏG, strȭ'dƏG*) 'arbeitsam' < lett. strãdîgs, Dn. (LW) strã'diks.

Verben

Lett. I. Konj.: liv. *klī'd'Ə*: Pr. *-B* 'herumschweifen' < lett. klîst: klīstu: klīdu, Dn. (FBR VI S. 66) klît: klîst: klîid | *bre'dd'Ə*: Pr. *bred'ùB* (auch *brē'dƏ*) 'waten' < lett. brist: brìedu oder brìenu: bridu, Dn. (LW) brišt: äz bri'ęD 'ich wate' | lett. II. Konj.: liv. *lȭd'Ə* (∼ *lȭt'tƏ*, livW *lā̊d'Ə*) 'laden', vgl. lett. lãdêt, Dn. (LW) lãt' < nd. | lett. III. Konj.: liv. *spī'd'Ə*: Pr. *-êB*, livW *-uB* 'glänzen' < lett. spîdêt, Dn. spī't | *ga'dd'Ə*: Pr. *gad'ùB* 'sich ereignen, sich zu-tragen, Gelegenheit haben' < lett. gadîtiês: gaduôs: gadîjuôs, Dn. (LW) gā̊'ttęs.

Auslaut

Substantive

Lett. I. Dekl.: liv. *su'oĎ* 'Strafe' < lett. sùods, Dn. (LW) su'ǫts | lett. *-a* (= IV. Dekl.): liv. *krä̆p̀pil'Ď*, livW *krä̆p̀pil'Ď* 'Rotz, Schleim aus der Nase'

<lett. krẽpala, Dn. (LW) krãp̆p̧el̦ | lett. -e (=V. Dekl.): liv. sko̦Ď, livW
skãĎ 'Schaden', vgl. lett. skãde, Dn. (LW) skāD<mnd.

liv. [t']

Inlaut

Substantive

Lett. -a (=IV. Dekl.): liv. *mat̆škà, smat̆škà* (auch *mat̆šk*) 'Hure' <lett. mačka,
Dn. mat̄'šk<russ. | lett. -is (II. Dekl.): liv. *tat̆škə̑D* 'Versperrung; Schub-
karren' <lett. tacis (auch tace), Dn. (LW) tat̄s, Nom. Pl. tat̄'s̀; vgl. BFB 226.

Verben

Lett. II. Konj.: liv. *spĭt̆'t'ə̑* : -*B* 'trotzen' <lett. spĩtêt, Dn. spĩt; vgl. BFB
130$_{IX}$ | *sut̆t'ə̑*: *sut̆'t̀uB* 'heiss werden, schmoren' <lett. sutêt, Dn. sut̄ | lett. III
Konj.: liv. *kavĭn̆t̆'t'ə̑* 'verweilen, aufhalten' <lett. kavinât.

Auslaut

Substantive

Lett. I Dekl.: liv. *krĭt̀'* 'Kreide', vgl. lett. krĩts, Dn. (LW) krĩt <mnd.; vgl.
BFB 126$_{67}$ | lett. -is (=II. Dekl.): liv. *sut̆k*, livW *sut̆kə̑Z* 'halberwachsenes
Schwein' <lett. suk̦is, Dn. (LW) suk̦'s | lett. -e (=V. Dekl.): liv. $_2$*rŭt̆* 'Laufzeit
der Hunde' <lett. rũte.

Adjektive

Liv. *du'bbil'i*, s. S. 3.

Über die Ursachen der Palatalisation

Anlautstellung

In den wenigen hierher gehörenden Belegen hat die Palatalisation ihren
unmittelbaren Ausgang im Lettischen (liv. *n̆ur̃də̑, pl'o̦p̆pə̑*).

Inlautstellung

Die Mouillierung im Inlaut in livischen Adjektiven lettischen Ursprungs ist
wahrscheinlich sekundären Charakters und bewirkt durch das nachfolgende
i, vgl. liv. *ko̦n̆riG, stro̦d'iG*.

In der I. Konjugation der lettischen Verben begegnet man einem ähnlichen Konsonantenwechsel wie in den Nomina der II. und V. Deklination,
auch in der Palatalisationskorrelation. In den ins Livische entlehnten
Wörtern spiegelt sich dieser Wechsel häufig wider.

1. Wechsel *l* — *ļ*, z. B. liv. *sme'll'ə̂*.

2. Wechsel *r* — *ŗ*, z. B. liv. *bu'ŕŕə̂*. Obgleich die Palatalisation von *r* in der Mundart Dn. schwächer ist als anderwärts in Kurland, wird das *r* u. a. in der 3. P. des Verbs mouilliert ausgesprochen.

3. Für die Palatalisierungserscheinung im Typus *klī'd'ə̂* und *bro'utšə̂* findet sich kein so unmittelbarer Ausgangspunkt wie in den Fällen 1 und 2. Es ist jedoch nicht zu übersehen, dass in Dn. jene Konsonanten in den Formen des Partiz. Perf. Akt. dieser Verben mouilliert sind, wenn das nachfolgende *i* geschwunden ist, in der diesbezüglichen Form *klīid's* des Verbums *klīt* in Dn. (FBR VI S. 66).

Die Verben der II. und III. Konjugation sind zahlreicher vertreten in der Gruppe der livischen Verben lettischer Herkunft mit Palatalisation als die zur I. Konjugation gehörenden Verben. Ausser dass erstere relativ häufiger sind in der Sprache, ist hier ferner von Bedeutung, dass in der II. und III. Konjugation vielfach ein Palatalisation bewirkender Laut *i* und *j* in einer anderen — nicht in der ersten Silbe steht. In der II. Konjugation kommt *j* sowohl im Suffix des Präsens- als auch des Präteritumstammes vor. Obgleich *j* in der III. Konjugation nicht so oft erscheint, steht im Auslaut der zahlreichen Verben, die lettische Originale vom Typ -*inât*- vertreten, ein -*iňîə̂*.

Auslautstellung

In den zur II. und V. Deklination gehörenden Substantiven des Lettischen begegnet man einem paradigmatischen Konsonantenwechsel. In der II. Deklination sind bestimmte Konsonanten im Gen. Sg. und in der ganzen Pluralflexion palatalisiert, in der V. dagegen nur im Gen. Pl. Die meisten der oben aufgezählten livischen Mouillierungsgruppen gehören hinsichtlich ihrer Originale zur II. Deklination; der demgemässe Wechsel zeigt sich im Livischen folgendermassen:

1. Der Wechsel *l* — *ļ* spiegelt sich in den livischen Wörtern wider, in deren lettischen Original als Ableitungssuffix -*el*-, -*ul*-, *uol*-, -*gl*-, -(*l*)*is* steht.

2. Der Wechsel *n* — *ņ* kommt in den livischen Wörtern zum Ausdruck, deren lettisches Original das Ableitungssuffix -*en*- oder -*uon*- hatte.

3. Der Wechsel *r* — *ŗ* kommt möglicherweise in den livischen Wörtern zum Ausdruck, deren lettisches Original das Ableitungssuffix -*eris* hatte.

Ein entsprechender Wechsel kommt auch in den lettischen Dialekten vor, die in der Nachbarschaft des Livischen gesprochen werden, wo in der II. Deklination etwas mehr Palatalisation erscheint als in der lettischen Gemeinsprache, weil *i* vor *s* ausfällt und der vorangehende Konsonant gleichzeitig etwas mouilliert (koronalisiert) wird. Eine derartige schwache Palata-

lisierung wird von Adamovičs und Krautmane durch einen Strich (') bezeichnet. Ausserdem kann vor einem Konsonanten, der vor *i* steht, ein
epenthetisches *i* erscheinen. Z. B. in dem Wort liv. *taĺškəD* stammt die
Palatalisation offenbar gerade aus dem Dialekt von Dn. Die im selben
Dialekt vorhandene Diphthongisierung *ē>ei* spiegelt sich vielleicht als
Palatalisation wider im liv. Wort *blē'D* 'Betrüger, Gauner' (also nicht liv.
*blē'Ž, vgl. lett. *blèdis: blèža*).

In den livischen Lehnwörtern, die die fünfte lettische Deklination vertreten, lässt sich eine Widerspiegelung des Konsonantenwechsels nicht in
gleichem Masse feststellen wie in den Wörtern der II. Deklination, da es
nicht wahrscheinlich ist, dass ein einziger Kasus des Paradigmas (= Gen. Pl.)
die Lautgestalt des Lehnworts bedeutend beeinflusst hätte. So weisen
Wörter vom Typus *škē'ĺ, skǭD* und *rūĺ* auf eine Angleichung an die *i*-stäm-
migen Substantive hin. Die mit *-ele* und *-ule* abgeleiteten Substantive
glichen sich vielleicht den entsprechenden maskulinen Typen auf *-iĺ, -iĺ* an.

Bei den Substantiven, deren Original zur I. Deklination gehörte, handelt
es sich mit Ausnahme der auf *-iņš-* abgeleiteten offenbar in erster Linie um
eine Angleichung an die livischen *i*-Stämme.

Bei den von Originalen der vierten Deklination herstammenden Wörtern
handelt es sich in der Gruppe der *daļa*-Typen und der mit *-iņa-* abgeleiteten
Originale um einen im lettischen Original vorhandenen mouillierten Konsonanten, und die Mouillierung des Wortes *maĺškà* geht offensichtlich auf den
Dialekt von Dundaga zurück.

Es gibt im Livischen auch Wörter, die als lettische Entlehnungen zu
gelten haben und deren Palatalisierung vermutlich durch das Estnische
verursacht worden ist, z. B. liv. *krańtš* (Hundename), vgl. lett. *Krancis*,
Gen. Sg. *Kranča*, Dn. (LW) *krańts*, estn. *Krańts*.

Mitunter tritt in einem lettischen Lehnwort die Palatalisation im West-
livischen, nicht aber im Ostlivischen, z. B. livW *tū'ŕ*, livO *tū'r* 'Winkel' oder
livW *daĺt'*, livO *daĺt* 'Docht'.

Anmerkungen

1. Folgende Abkürzungen werden gebraucht:

BFB = Beröringer mellem de finske og de baltiske (litauisk-lettiske) Sprog. En
sproghistorisk Undersøgelse af *Vilh. Thomsen.* København 1890.

FBR = Filologu biedrības raksti. Rīgā 1921–.

LW = *Lauri Kettunen,* Livisches Wörterbuch mit grammatischer Einleitung. Lexica
Societatis Fenno-Ugricae V. Helsinki 1938.

LVG = *J. Endzelīns,* Latviešu valodas gramatika. Rīgā 1951.

514

MLLVG = Mūsdienu latviešu literārās valodas gramatika I–II. Rīgā 1959–62.
Posti GLL = *Lauri Posti*, Grundzüge der livischen Lautgeschichte. MSFOu. 85. Helsinki 1942.
Rudzīte LD = *Marta Rudzīte*, Latviešu dialektoloģija, Rīgā 1964.
SKES = Suomen kielen etymologinen sanakirja (Finnisches etymologisches Wörterbuch) I–IV. Helsinki 1955–69.
Ulm. Wb = Lettisches Wörterbuch. Erster Theil. Lettisch–deutsches Wörterbuch von Bischof Dr. Carl Christian Ulmann. Riga, 1872.

2. Unter spätem Lehnwort verstehen wir hier solche Entlehnungen, deren Lautgestalt in leicht feststellbarem Mass dem fremden Original ähnelt.

3. Aus jeder Gruppe wird nur jeweils ein Beleg angeführt.

4. Zum phonetischen Charakter der livischen Palatalisation und zu ihrem Verhältnis zur lettischen Palatalisation s. z. B. Paul Ariste, *Liivi keele palatalisatsiooni olemusest*. (Emakeele Seltsi Aastaraamat IV, 256–61, Tallinn 1959); Mikko Korhonen, *Pääpainottoman tavun vokaalin ja j:n regressiivisestä vaikutuksesta liivissä*. (Publications of the Phonetics Department of the University of Turku. November 1969).

Palatalization of Latvian Loan Words in Livonian

It is well known that Latvian has had a strong influence on Livonian, which has more than 3 000 relatively recent loan words of Latvian origin. The writer examines the phenomenon of palatalization in these loan words, as illustrated by some typical examples. The types are grouped according to the palatalized consonant phonemes, which are [*l', ń, ŕ, d', t'*]. The article then goes on to examine the occurrence of each of the phonemes in the initial, medial and final position. The examples are also divided into substantives, adjectives and verbs. Initial palatalized consonants rarely appear in a loan word. The palatalized consonants appearing in medial and final positions usually derive from the consonant changes (*l–ļ, n–ņ, r–ŗ*) found in the noun and verb declensions and conjugations characteristic of Latvian. Standard Latvian does not, however, have [*d'*] or [*t'*], which are found in Livonian loan words from Latvian for the following reasons:

1) the palatalization effect of an *i* directly following a consonant;
2) the palatalization effect of *i* or *j* later in the word (particularly in those verbs originating in Latvian conjugations II and III);
3) adaptation to Livonian *i*-stem substantives;
4) the influence of Latvian dialects geographically close to Livonian;
5) a phonetic similarity between [*t' d'*] and Latvian [*ķ ģ*].

OSWALD SZEMERÉNYI

The Indo-European Name of the "Heart"

I

1. The traditional material is well known, a neuter root-noun *kerd, with lengthened-grade and nil-grade forms, is attested by practically all IE languages[1]. Note in particular:

(a) Greek κῆρ, κηρός; Att. καρδία, Ion. κραδίη;
(b) Lat. cor cordis;
(c) Old Irish cride (from *kridian, IE *kṛdyom);
(d) Gothic hairto, gen. hairtins;
(e) Old Prussian seyr ntr.; siran acc., siras gen.;
(f) Lithu. širdìs, acc. šìrdį fem. (Old Lithu. masc.), gen. pl. šird-ų̃; East Lithu. (dial.) šerdìs, acc. šérdį;
(g) Old Church Slavonic srъдьce from *sirdiko-, cf. milo-srъdъ; srěda 'middle' from *serdā;
(h) Armen. sirt, instr. srtiv from *kērd-i-;
(i) Hitt. gen. kardas, dat. kardi, etc.

On the strength of this evidence it is assumed that the nom.-acc. sg. was *kērd, while in the oblique cases the nil-grade form *kṛd- appeared in, e.g., gen. *kṛd-ós, dat. *kṛd-éi, etc. In the nom.-acc. sg. an enlargement with i, i.e. *kērdi, is also assumed which would appear in Arm. sirt but also in Skt. hā́rdi which replaces an expected *šā́rdi.

2. Progress is now possible on several essential points. First, additional material can be adduced from several languages. Secondly, the IE paradigm must be reconstructed with greater precision. Thirdly, the ultimate origin of the noun becomes clearer.

II

The Hittite language, as we shall see, presents the IE noun with a very archaic inflexion. According to Friedrich, the full paradigm is as follows[2]:

	singular	plural
nom.-acc.	kēr	kēr
gen.	kardiyas	
dat.-loc.	kardi	
dat. (archaic)	karda	
abl.	kardats	
instr.	kardit	

This paradigm is rather surprising. All cases are based on the IE stem *kerd- — except the gen. sg. which is said to be an -i-stem form. But the paradigm must be corrected. First of all, the expected gen. sg. kard-as exists[3]. Secondly, the gen. sg. kardiyas would be the only trace of an -i-stem (or, possibly, of an -iya-stem), which in itself speaks against the interpretation. There is every reason to believe that this single[4] aberrant case-form is based on a form, or some forms, of the paradigm which could be interpreted as -i-stem forms. Thus the dat. Halki (beside Halkiya) and instr. Halkit were matched by kardi and kardit; this type was therefore able to produce a gen. kardiyas to match the genitive-type Halkiyas[5]. This isolated case-form, which owes its existence to the principle of Gelenkheteroklisie so beautifully worked out by Egli for Greek[6], does not justify the assumption of a stem *kardiya which could then be equated with Greek καρδία.[7]

Nor is there any justification for the inclusion in the paradigm of karats 'intestines', either as a nom. sg. *kard-s or as a fantastic plural form *krāts from IE *krōd[8]. It is quite clear, semantically[9], that the noun karad- has nothing to do with 'heart', and, etymologically, we must now take account of the suggestion that karad- derives from an earlier *ghorod- to be connected with Greek χορδή 'guts, tripe, sausage; gut'[10].

It can then be regarded as established that the Hittite paradigm opposed the nom.-acc. sg. and pl. kēr to a stem-form kard- which supplied all the other cases. The gen. sg. kardiyas, which is an internal innovation, can be ignored for the purposes of IE reconstruction. On the other hand, great importance attaches to the question what IE forms are represented by kēr and kard-.

As to kēr, the general opinion seems to be that it reflects an IE *kērd, with loss of the final dental as in the neuter human 'all' from the pure stem humant-.[11] The vocalism of kard- can be traced to that of IE *kerd since IE e often changes to a before r + consonant[12]. Such an explanation is unavoidable indeed for those who assume that IE ṛ developed into ur in Hittite. But for those who assume that IE ṛ normally developed into Hitt. ar[13] it is not quite logical to derive kard- from IE *kerd-[14] since the IE paradigm undoubtedly had many case-forms with krd-, e.g. the gen.-abl. *krd-*ós*, the dat. *krd-*éi*, etc.[15] One other form, of considerable interest for Indo-European, is the locative *ki-ir-ti* 'in the heart' which will reflect an original *kerd-i*, and not the better known *kardi* reshaped after *kēr*[16].

III

Before continuing our investigation of the morphological problems of the 'heart', it will be of interest to examine certain areas which promise to enrich the material amassed so far.

1. Hittite possesses a number of formations based on a morpheme *kartim-* which has the basic meaning 'anger':

kartimmiya- (act. and deponent) 'zürnen, grollen', e.g. pres. 3. sg.
    kartimmiyattari, 3. pl. *-yantari*, pret. 1. sg. *-yanun*, etc.
kartimmiyanu- (causative) 'zornig machen, erzürnen';
kartimmiyah- (ditto);
kartimmiyatt- (noun) 'Zorn';
kartimmiyawant- (adj.) 'zornig'[17].

Referring to OCS *srъditi sę* 'be angry' : *srъdьce* 'heart' (and for the semantics also to Albanian *zëmëronem* 'I am angry' : *zëmërë* 'heart'), Pedersen suggested that this group was derived from *kard-* in the following way: from *kard-* an -*i*-verb was formed (cf. *srъditi*), from this with -*ma-* a participle, and with -*iya-* its variant *kartimiya-*, the basis both of the verb *kartimiya-* and of the abstract *kartimiyat-*[18].
It has been argued against this analysis that a connection between heart and anger is not evidenced in Hittite[19] but this objection has been disposed of[20]. The formal analysis can, however, be improved. After Laroche's study in the nouns formed with -*ma-*[21] it is clear that *kartima-* is to be analyzed as formed with the abstract suffix -*ma-* (= Greek -*mós*) from a verb *kardiya-*, based on *kard-*.

2. The derivation of *kartimmiya-* from *kard-* can, as we have seen, directly be supported from Slavic. In addition to *srъditi* it is perhaps worth mentioning the Russian phrase *v serdcáx* 'böse, im Zorne' and the Lithu. *širdai* 'Zank, Streit' since they probably show the direction of the semantic development[22]. As correspondences to the verbal formations discussed above we may also mention Lithu. *širdinti* 'to make angry' and *širsti* (*širsta, širdo*) 'to grow angry, indignant', *širdytis* 'be angry, rage', though some of these may be modelled on Slav prototypes.

518

3. A further parallel is supplied by Armenian:

srtnim 'I grow indignant, become angry',
srtmtem or *srtmtim* (from *sirti-mit-*) 'id.'

4. As is known, the original word for 'heart' is replaced in Indo-Iranian by a form which differs in the initial consonant only: instead of *kēr/kṛdos* Sanskrit presents *hārdi/hṛdas* etc. But since the IE word was indubitably **kerd-*, the question arises whether it was completely lost in Aryan, or whether it survives in some specialized usage. The latter seems to be the case.

A Middle Persian present stem *sīr-* is known from two Turfan texts. The first is M 731 which contains quotations from Mani's letters[23]; the relevant passage (R 5 f.) with Müller's translation is:

mrdwḥm pnz 'z	Fünf Menschen von
šḥryg'n n'yd 'b'g 'wyš'n	den Weltlichen führt er mit ihnen
gwyd kw syryšn ny bw'd	spricht er: ... möge nicht sein.

The second text is in the Krotkov-collection in St. Petersburg/Leningrad and was first published 1912 by Salemann[24]; the relevant passage is:

syryd 'n'd "z.

As can be seen, the infinitive (or verbal noun) *syryšn* was left untranslated by Müller; Salemann tentatively suggested 'Sättigung' and for *syrydn* 'satt werden', identifying *sīr-* with the modern *sīr* 'sated', which satisfies neither the context nor the known facts of linguistic history (s. further on). 1925 Bartholomae suggested '*superbire*, Hoffart' for *syryšn* and traced *sīr-* to Aryan *śṛdhyati*, comparing Gāthic *saradanā* 'Verachtung, Verhöhnung' and Vedic *śardhati* 'sich überstark fühlen, übermütig, vermessen, gewalttätig sein', *śṛdhyā* 'Übermacht, Übermut'; but *syryd* eluded him[25]. The meaning of the verb was finally established by Henning who pointed out that *syryd 'n'd "z* was paralleled by another Turfan-text (T III 260 e IR II 34–V I 2): 'Darauf wurde jene betrogene Āz von schwerem Zorn erfüllt', and concluded that *syrydn* meant 'zornig werden', a meaning that suited *syryšn* as well, while Salemann's 'satt' was ruled out by the fact that the early form of this word, still to be expected in the Turfan texts, was *sagr*[26].

The new interpretation was irreconcilable with Bartholomae's etymological suggestion[27] but Henning was inclined to retain the basic form **sṛdya-*, although he felt unable to establish the etymon of the word and consequently did not regard even a reading *sēr-* as impossible.[28] But since the two theoretically possible readings *sīr-* and *sēr-* both presuppose a suffix *-ya-*[29], the choice between various etymological possibilities is severely limited. We know that *sr̥-ya- and *sr̥b-ya-, *sr̥w-ya- would have resulted in sīr- (cf. mīrēd 'dies' from *mr̥-ya-tai, gīrēd 'seizes' from *gr̥b-ya-, pīr 'old' from *pr̥wya-) but there is no root *sar-, *sarb- or *sarw- that could account for the meaning 'grow angry, rage'. We further know that -r̥dy- and -r̥gy- would also have resulted in -ry- and in the end in -īr-; to be sure, examples for these sequences are wanting but the fact that -dy- was assimilated to -yy- (madyāna- gave mayyān, miyān) and -argy- gave -ary- (*darg-yah- 'longer' gave daryah, dēr 'long') guarantee that *sr̥dya- and *sr̥gya- would also have resulted in sīr-[30]. Of these two possibilities *sr̥g- leads nowhere, there is no root of this shape that could have the meaning 'anger, grow angry'. By simple elimination we are thus left with *sr̥d-ya-: we have seen that this root, i.e. the word for 'heart', led in several languages to the meaning in question.

5. If then Iranian at least can be shown to have possessed at one time the general IE form of 'heart', the question arises whether the Aryan deviation from the IE norm, namely the replacement of *kerd by *gherd (or *ghord), can be explained. The late Renou showed in one of his meticulous discussions that in the 9th book of the Rigveda hā́rdi, in contrast to hr̥d, means 'Indra's belly', the receptacle of the soma-drink, while elsewhere hā́rdi, like hr̥d, is the heart as the seat of inspiration[31]. This observation lends support to the old suggestion[32] that IE *kerd got blended with the word represented, i.a., by Greek χορδή[10]. A further factor favouring the blend was no doubt the fact that *kerd- 'grow angry' had a rival in *gher- attested by Skt. hr̥ṇite 'is angry'[33] and Avest. zar-.[34] The shifting relations were:

	a	b	c
I	*kerd- 'heart'	*gherd- 'intestines'	*gher- 'get excited'
II	*śard- 'heart, anger'	*jhard- 'intestines, heart'	*jhar- 'get angry'
III	(sr̥dyati 'gets angry')	*jhard- 'heart'	*jhar- 'angry'

The IE term Ia survives only peripherally in IIIa, while its proper functions were taken over by Ib.

IV

In our efforts to reconstruct the IE paradigm we are faced with two problems: one concerns the vocalism, the other the end of the word.

1. The paradigm certainly contained a long-vowel form (-ēr-) in the nom.-acc. sg. and some Lithuanian forms present an acute intonation. Both facts could be interpreted as pointing to an original long vowel, or, in laryngealist terminology, to a sequence eH. The message of the new gospel was sent forth with blaring trumpets by Whatmough: "Since Pokorny [in the new Idg. etym. Wb.] will have none of the newer theory, he will not write *keHrd, as most of us now do, with Greek κῆρ and the Baltic accentuation in mind"[35]. One can but marvel at the self-assurance with which this impossible doctrine is promulgated. Assuming that a sequence *keHrd was possible in IE, its nil-grade form would have been *kḤrd- (or *kṛHd-?) which would have developed into European *kard- and Aryan *kird- (or IE *kṝd-?), forms that are incompatible with the actually attested *kṛd-; it hardly needs to be stressed that the latter in its turn postulates a full-grade form *kerd- (or *kred-) and, possibly, a lengthened-grade form *kērd (or *krēd). But the reference to the Baltic accentuation is also based on a rather limited acquaintance with Baltic, namely the assumption that acute intonation in itself suffices to guarantee a Proto-IE laryngeal[36]. Guided by this creed one would be compelled to look for a laryngeal even in such innocent cases as Lithu. vanduõ 'water', acc. vándeni, surely a preposterous undertaking. I pointed out many years ago that the Baltic forms simply reflected the old contrast between IE -ēr- and -ṛ-, i.e. Baltic -ér- and -iř-,[37] and the scholar to whom this paper is dedicated has recently summed up the situation almost identically[38]: "Die urbaltische Flexion war gewiss *šēr(d/t): širdès, im Lit.-Lett. vielleicht *šér:*širdès. Der Akut muss vom Nom.-Akk. Sg. herstammen". Not surprisingly, this view is shared by another leading Balto-Slavist[39].

2. The nom.-acc. sg. had ē which, as we have just seen and as we should have expected in any case, was lengthened from ĕ and was not an original ē (laryngealist eH). Since the stem ends in d, it is tempting to add the two features together, i.e. to reconstruct the IE nom.-acc. sg. as *kērd. This reconstruction can be regarded as almost generally accepted today, and it has been current for several generations now[40]. There are, however, several difficulties which make it imperative to revise this reconstruction.

3. The Hittite records present a nom.-acc. sg. (and pl.) kēr. The general view is that the inherited form *kērd lost its final dental (s. fn. 11 above). This is obviously an ad hoc assumption.

4. Greek κῆρ is likewise said to have lost the final dental of IE *kērd, and here the explanation plainly does not work at all. As is known, Osthoff

showed that before semivowel/nasal/liquid + consonant a long vowel was shortened, cp. ἔγνον ἔμιγεν from εγνω-ντ εμιγη-ντ[41]. Accordingly, an IE *kērd should have been shortened to *χερδ and with subsequent loss of the dental developed into *χερ. That the last form should have been lengthened secondarily to χῆρ[42] is quite impossible. But it is just as indefensible to allege that Osthoff's law operated after the loss of final dentals[43]: φέρων does not continue -ōnt, nor is μιάνθην the regular form in contrast to ἔμιγεν. The suggestion that a final group -rd might have lost -d before the operation of Osthoff's law, but -nt its -t only after[44], is a counsel of despair which should be firmly resisted. There is in fact no need for such discrimination between the essentially similar groups -rd and -nt. Instead, we must draw the obvious conclusion: χῆρ has a regular long vowel because it does not continue an IE *kērd but simply *kēr. We can now apply this result to the Hittite form, too: Hitt. kēr has not lost a final d, it is the IE form.

5. This conclusion must now be confronted with the data of the Baltic languages. In Old Prussian, our word appears as seyr in the Elbing Vocabulary while the later sources give the -a-stem forms acc. siran (syran), gen. siras, dat. siru, acc. pl. sirans. Saussure saw that sēr, sīra- continued *kēr, and even threw out the suggestion that IE *kērd might have lost its final d in IE times, "which would resolve the conflict between χῆρ and a well-known Greek phonetic law"[45]—meaning Osthoff's law, of course. From the Baltic point of view, the suggestion that sēr continues IE *kēr rather than *kērd is made probable by the fact that final dentals were kept fairly late— witness the Lithu. tat-aĩ 'that', tačiau 'but' (<tat-jau) which agree with OCS tožde from *tod-je[46]. To assume that an IE *kērd lost its dental earlier is just as unwarranted as the similar assumption for Greek discussed above. And if *kērd developed into Proto-Prussian *sērd, its vowel should have been shortened just as ō was shortened to ŏ (and later became ă) in *wōrnā, the antecedent of Lithu. várna 'crow', whereas OPr. sēr, sīr- show that ē was kept long[47]. This tends to support the suggestion that sēr continues *kēr, not *kērd, and the argument is clinched, I think, by the following consideration. The -a-stem sīra- must be based on some form of the old paradigm which could be interpreted as an -a-stem form (the principle of Gelenk-heteroklisie mentioned above). The only form that met this requirement was the original plural which is thereby shown to have been *sērā, not *sērdā (or *serdā, *sirdā) as it should have been according to the IE pattern[48]; it naturally presupposes a singular without the final d.

6. Summing up, we can say that Greek χῆρ is incompatible with an antecedent *kērd, it must represent an IE kēr. This is also the form presented by

Hittite and Old Prussian; it would be a curious application of the comparative method to obtrude a final *d* which they do not have.

7. This result is corroborated by the fact that structural considerations also demand **kēr* as the nom.-acc. sg. For where does the lengthened grade come from? Streitberg's now almost defunct theory of the origin of the lengthened grade at least had the merit of accounting for it in a rational manner: the two neuters ending in the nom.-acc. sg. in *-d* and exhibiting the lengthened grade, i.e. **kērd* and **sāld* 'salt', were traced by him to the primitive forms **kerod* and **salod* which compensated the loss of the second vowel by the lengthening of the root-vowel[49]. That M. Bloomfield almost immediately, and rightly, objected that such disyllabic forms never existed and therefore the theory was unacceptable[50], does not alter the fact that the phenomenon must be explained. The purely taxonomic statement that neuters of this kind often have the lengthened grade[51] would not help much even if it were true; but it so happens that the lengthened grade appears in Aryan only (e.g. *dāru, jānu, āyu*), and obviously calls for a special Aryan explanation. I cannot go here into more recent theories with which I have dealt elsewhere[52]. Suffice it to say that the only explanation that can hope to account for all the facts is one based on a phonetic process. As I have shown (l.c.), a nominative like **mātēr* continues an earlier **māter-s* with assimilated **māterr* as its immediate antecedent. Similarly, **pod-s* gave **poss* and this became **pōs*, later sometimes restored to **pōds*. It is therefore obvious that an early **kerd* was assimilated to **kerr* and later became **kēr*, i.e. the lengthened grade is (originally at least) incompatible with the presence of the stem-final *d* since its loss (by assimilation) is the precondition of the vowel-lengthening.

8. Thus we can regard as established that the old nom.-acc. sg. of our noun was IE **kēr*. Equally certain is the fact that most of the oblique cases showed the nil-grade form **kr̥d-*; the gen.-abl. sg. was **kr̥d-ós*, the dat. sg. **kr̥d-éi*. But there must also have been a case-form or some case-forms in which the full-grade form **kerd* was in use. This is necessary for certain derivatives, in particular for Germanic **hert-en-* 'heart' and Slavic **serdā* 'the heart, the centre of something'. To be sure, these forms have sometimes been traced to **kērd*—on the assumption that Osthoff's law generally operated in IE[53]. But irrespective of the general validity or otherwise of this phonetic change, we know that **kērd* cannot be the basis of a derivative for the simple reason that derivatives are formed from the stem, not from the nominative. Our evidence presents one such form in the paradigm, the

Hittite loc. *kerdi*, and here again, on structural grounds alone, we would have picked the locative as the only likely candidate since it alone shows the full grade in several declensional classes; cf. Skt. *ah-an-i* 'day' (loc.), but gen. *ah-n-as*, dat. *ah-n-e*, or loc. *pit-ar-i*, but dat. *pit-r-e*. On the strength of the Sanskrit declensional patterns, in which the neuter nom.-acc. pl. of ablauting stems always have the full-grade form, we can perhaps assume that the nom.-acc. pl. was **kerd-ə*, dialectally also **kerd-ā*.

9. Accordingly, the IE inflexion of the word for 'heart' can be reconstructed as follows:

	sg.	pl.
nom.-acc.	*kēr	kerd-ə
gen.	kr̥d-ós	kr̥d-óm
dat.	kr̥d-éi	kr̥d-bh-
loc.	kérd-i	kr̥d-su

V

1. With the reconstruction of **kēr* as the nom.-acc. sg. the question arises how Skt. *hārdi*, and possibly also Armen. *sirt*, fit into the paradigm just presented. For the Sanskrit form is traditionally regarded as representing an inherited **kērdi*, i.e. **kērd* with an enlargement *i*, and the same enlargement is seen not only in Skt. *asthi* 'bone', *akṣi* 'eye', *sakthi* 'thigh', *dadhi* 'sour milk', but also in, e.g., Lithu. *šird-i-s* and other forms[54].

That the *-i* of *hārdi* cannot be a morphological element is nevertheless clear from the fact that its compound presents the masc. nom. sg. *suhārd* (s. also further on). For if the nom. of the basic word had been *hārdi* from the start, the nom. masc. could not have taken any other shape but *-hārdis*. Much the same can be said of *akṣi* where the secondary character of the final *-i* is demonstrated by the compound *anak* 'blind', literally 'eye-less' (masc. nom. sg. from **an-akṣ*), and of *asthi* which is based on a consonantal stem **ost(h)-* as is shown by Avest. acc. sg. *asča* from *ast-ča*. The noun *dadhi* is erroneously grouped with these words since its *i* is certainly not an expansion of a base *dadh-*; *dadhi* is in all probability a reduplicated formation from **dhē(i)-* 'suckle', either as **dhe-dh(ə)i* with the nil-grade of the root, or as **dhe-dh(ə)-i* with a suffix *-i-*[55]. On the other hand, *sakthi* must be left with this group since it has close ties with *asthi*.

The enigmatic *i* which, as is rightly emphasized by Wackernagel, is not found in this function anywhere outside Sanskrit, not even in Avestan (!), can hardly be regarded as of IE origin. It is enough to compare the very peculiar *r*-heteroclisy which finds exact correspondences in Hittite, Greek, Latin, Germanic, etc., to realize that this remarkable absence in other languages can only mean that this -*i* is a purely Indian, not even Aryan, innovation. Its true origin and function is revealed by those anomalous words which do *not* show it, namely *doṣ, doṣ-an-* 'arm' and *yūṣ, yūṣ-an-* 'broth'[56]. For whereas in these nouns there is only one consonant at the end of the stem, in our nouns there are two: *hārd-, asth-, akṣ-, sakth-*. The consequence of this structural peculiarity is that, since at the end of a word only the first consonant of a cluster could survive, in the nom. acc. sg. we would find the forms **hār* (i.e. *hāḥ*), **as, *ak, *sak*.

That this was the linguistic reality is shown by the masc. nom. sg. *anak* 'blind' quoted above and by the nom. of the noun *suhard-* 'friend'. This was given above as *suhārd*, a hapax found at Atharvaveda II 7, 5 b in the segment *suhārttena*. But with *suhārt* the editors deviate from the padapāṭha authorities, of whom 7 give *suhāt*, and one *suhāḥ*, a reading confirmed by *suhār* of the Maitrāyaṇī Saṁhitā[57]. It is quite clear that the true form was *suhār*, and that the text *suhārttena* means *suhārtena*, retaining the final *r* according to the old rules of sandhi, not changing it to *s* before *t*[58].

Now whereas with longer, at least disyllabic, forms the reduction of the volume of the word by the sandhi-rules did not necessarily lead to difficulties in the process of communication, with monosyllables the same kind of reduction (in the present case to **hār, *ak*, etc.) could lead to serious misunderstandings. It was therefore imperative to try to retain the full consonantism. As far as I can see, this could be accomplished in one of two ways, or even by a combination of both.

(a) In the case of 'eye', the dual was the 'normal' number so to speak; in the Rigveda the word occurs eight times, only once in the singular. But the nom.-acc. dual *akṣī*, formed with the case-ending -*ī* from the consonantal stem *akṣ-*, could also be interpreted as the dual of an *akṣi* which was, descriptively speaking, formed with lengthening of the stem-final vowel. When, on account of the emerging sandhi restrictions, *akṣ* was threatened with reduction to **ak* (as in *an-ak*), the simplest way out of this predicament was to produce the singular *akṣi*. As I have pointed out already (s. fn. 48), this was the process by which Lithu. *akìs* 'eye', *ausìs* 'ear', *nósis* 'nose' as well as Latin *auris* arose[59].

An obvious candidate for this kind of solution was also *sakthi* 'thigh' (again, naturally, often found in the dual)—*if* originally it had a consonantal stem **sakth-*. According to Sommer's attractive derivation[60] it had the shape *sakthi* already in Aryan times[61], and in that case it would not belong with our group but would go with *dadhi*[62]. Since, however, the suffix -*ti*- is irreconcilable with the neuter gender[63], it still seems most likely that *sakthi* is transformed from an Aryan **sakt* which may represent an IE **s(k)ṇg-t*.

(b) In the case of *ast(h)-* and *hṛd-* this principle cannot have been at work since there is no reason for assuming that either noun was used with any frequency in the dual. What is more, whereas in the case of *akṣi* and *sakthi* Iranian shows the same process as Indian (*aši – ašibyā, haxti – haxtiyā*)[64], with these two nouns there is no trace of an *-i-*stem.

The alleged Avestan *-i-*stem *asti-* has been shown to be nonexistent[65]. Sommer's confidence in an Aryan **asthi-* is no more warranted than his belief in an IE **osthi*[66]. It is difficult to see how Hitt. *hastai*, gen. *hastiyas* could prove the existence in IE of the nom.-acc. **osthi*. Do we really know how *hastai* is to be interpreted? Pedersen says: "Nimmt man einen Übergang *e > a* vor *j* an, kann hitt. *hastai* dem griech. ὀστέον genau entsprechen; der *-jo-*Stamm wäre in die *i-*Deklination übertragen, aber neutr. geblieben"[67]; in other words, we are asked to believe that a primitive **Hosteyom* became **Hostei*—but even this is not identical with **Hosti*! Kuiper thinks that, in order to combine Vedic *asthi* and Greek ὀστέ(*y*)ον "we may assume a [proterodynamic] inflexion **Hósthi/Hsthéis* ... An unexpected complication however arises from Hittite which has a neuter nom.-acc. *hastai* ... It belongs to the hysterodynamic class of *zahhais* ... but even as such it defies all rules" since it should end in *-i*. "It is unlikely therefore that the nom. *hastai* dates back to the prim. IE period."[68] One could adduce further interpretations[69] but they would not alter the fact that the structure of *hastai* is far from being clear but that it certainly does not represent an IE **Host(H)i*. Of great interest would be the recently unearthed ᵁᶻᵁ*da(n)hasti* which allegedly means 'Doppelknochen', although its first part is supposed to be *dān* 'second'—*if* its end-part could safely be interpreted as 'bone'. Unfortunately, the meaning of the word is anything but certain[70], and it cannot be ruled out that the word is an abstract in *-asti* like *dalugasti* 'length', *lu(m)pasti* 'annoyance', etc.[71] The Luwian plurale tantum *hassa* 'ossa' would in any case rule out Anatolian as presenting evidence for an IE **osthi*; for it most likely continues IE **Host-ā*, i.e. the consonantal stem **ost-*[72].

Skt. *hārdi* has no direct correspondence (i.e. **zārdi*) in Avestan, there is only the instr. sg. *zṛd-ā* and the nom. sg. *zərəδaēm* (i.e. *zṛd-ayam*), attested once each. But the latter no more proves an *-i-*stem for Iranian than does ὀστέον for Greek: both represent derivatives with *-eyo-* from consonantal stems which took over the functions of the basic words in much the same way as *cupreum* replaced *cuprum, fageus* the noun *fagus*, etc., in the Romance languages.

Since *asthi* and *hārdi* cannot represent inherited *-i*-formations we must conclude that the final vowel is a prop-vowel, the function of which was to make the two-consonant cluster at the end of the word possible. As an indistinct murmured vowel it coincided with the inherited shwa and with it developed into *i*: **asthə > asthi, *hārdə > hārdi*[73].

Striking parallels for this kind of development are plentiful, I shall mention just a few. A North Eastern Czech dialect keeps voiced consonants in word-final position (in contrast to the neutralization customary in Czech) but in order to achieve this uses a voiced off-glide: the pronunciation of words like *dub* 'oak', *vid* 'see' is "almost 'disyllabic'", i.e. *dubə vid'ə*[74]. Supporting vowels also appear in, e.g., Italian *sempre* from *semper*, *quattro* from *quattor*, French *ensemble* from *insimul*, etc.[75] In the Norwegian dialect of Bergen a shwa appears after monosyllables (e.g. *fār, mūr*); its function is "de donner à la voix un support et à l'énoncé de l'insistance et un volume qui le fasse mieux entendre". The same author also quotes Portuguese *siñorə amorə* as emphatic forms of *senhor amor*.[76] In Sardinian, Lat. *cras cor sunt* appear as *krasa koro suntu*[77].

2. Armen. *sirt*, instr. *srtiv*, is often traced to an IE **kērdi*[78]. What would seem to be the most consistent attempt to trace the prehistory of the Armenian paradigm[79], regards *sirt* as being parallel to Lithu. nom. *širdis*, acc. *širdį*, and voc. *širdie*, which is quite impossible seeing that the Lithuanian *-i*-stem (masc., today fem.!) is a late innovation. Nor is it safe to regard the Armenian *-i*-stem forms of the singular (gen.-dat.-loc. *srti*, instr. *srtiv*) as direct continuations of an IE *-i*-stem, i.e. of IE *-iyos, -iyi, i-bhi*. On the one hand, the nom. pl. *sirtkh* does not correspond to an IE *-eyes*, nor the acc.-loc. *sirts* to an IE **kērdins* and **kērdisu*. On the other hand, Armenian presents forms which look as if they were from *-i*-stems even when it is quite certain that the IE antecedent was not an *-i*-stem; note, e.g., gen.-dat.-abl. pl. *otich*, instr. pl. *otivkh* from *otn* 'foot' where the IE stem is known to have been **pod-*, not **podi-*. We must therefore take it for granted—even if we can offer no explanation today—that an IE consonantal stem could become an *-i*-stem in Armenian, and so *srtiv* can be transformed from IE **kr̥d-bhi*, in which the stem would have been obscured in any case. The nom.-acc. from IE **kēr* should appear as **sir*. The fact that Armenian presents throughout the paradigm a stem *sirt-* is obviously due to secondary unification: the ablaut-alternants **sir : *sart* were levelled out in favour of uniform *sirt : sirt-*.

VI

Our word is one of the few names of parts of the body which seem amenable to etymological analysis. Quoting such Homeric expressions as πάλλεται ἦτορ 'the heart is being tossed, quivers' (esp. for fear), Schulze thought that a parallel could be detected to κραδαίνω 'swing, brandish', and asked: "enthüllt sich uns hier die Etymologie des idg. Wortes für Herz, das 'Zuck-ende'?"[80] Although for this explanation nowadays usually Schulze is men-tioned,[81] it was found long before him. Muller submitted that *cor* was named after the *pulsus*, "nach der auf- und abschwingenden Bewegung", and be-longed with κραδάω 'schwinge', Old Irish *fo-ceird* 'throws', etc.[82], but the suggestion is found as far back as 1879 (and could perhaps be traced further back still) in Curtius' Grundzüge der griechischen Etymologie (p. 143).

According to this analysis, the heart would be described as (Schulze:) 'das Zuckende', 'the quivering (organ)'. It is interesting, however, that κραδαίνω is never used of the heart. There are on the other hand two verbs which seem regularly to be used to describe the beat of the heart. First, ἅλμα 'spring, leap' is used by "Hippocrates" of the "pulsation, palpitation" of the heart, and seems to have been an established medical term. For its use of the heart we may note the similar use of ἅλλομαι 'I spring, leap' of other parts of] the body, e.g. of the eye: ἅλλεται ὀφθαλμός μευ δεξιός (Theocritus 3,37) 'my right eye jumps = twitches' (indicating that "something wished for was about to happen"). Secondly, the verb πηδᾶν 'spring, leap' is almost habitually used of the movements of the heart, esp. in excitement and fear. The phrase ἡ καρδία πηδᾷ is frequently met with in Classical Attic literature. At Aristophanes, Clouds 1391, it is used to describe the suspense and ex-pectation of young men who can hardly await to hear what Phidippides, the rebel student, is going to say; cf. also Euripides, Bacchae 1288: καρδία πήδημ' ἔχει = πηδᾷ = φοβοῦμαι. In Plato's Symposium (215e) Alcibiades uses it to describe the effect Socrates' words have on him: whenever I listen to him, my heart beats faster (πολὺ μᾶλλον ... ἥ τε καρδία πηδᾷ), and the same words are put by Plato in the mouth of the rhapsode (Ion 535c) who de-scribes his empathy: when he portrays a dangerous situation, his hair stands on end for fear καὶ ἡ καρδία πηδᾷ. The Latin equivalent *salire* is used by Juvenal (VII 159f.) of the normal functioning of the heart (as the seat of intellect, cf. Ennius' and Plautus' use of *cordatus* = wise, prudent):

> laevae parte mamillae
>
> *nil salit Arcadico iuveni*

'in the left part of his breast nothing stirs in the bucolic youth' while Persius says (III 111): at the sight of money or a pretty girl does your heart keep its normal beat?

cor tibi rite salit?

These facts suggest that the heart was thought to be and described as the 'jumper, leaper, springer' and this explanation can be supported etymologically. A basic root meaning 'jump, leap' is attested with the variants *ker(d)-/*sker(d)-[83] in Greek σκαίρω (*skr̥yō) 'skip, frisk, dance', σκιρτάω 'spring, leap, bound'; MHGerm. *scheren* 'hurry' (NHG *sich scheren* 'sich fortmachen'), *scharz, schurz* masc. 'jump, leap'; OCS *skorъ* 'fast'. If Egyptian *'ib* 'heart' is correctly interpreted as the 'dancer'[84], it is interesting to recall Greek κόρδαξ, the name of a lively dance in Old Comedy.

VII

To sum up. 'Heart' was described in Early IE as the 'jumper, springer, leaper' with a root *(s)ker-d-. Its IE inflexion was nom.-acc. *kēr, gen. *kr̥d-ós, loc. *kérd-i. Although this noun is one of the best preserved elements of the IE lexicon, no language (except Hittite?) preserves the old inflexion in its entirety and especially with all ablaut variants. Some have generalized one ablaut-grade, cf. Greek κῆρ (and OPr *sīr-*) on the one hand, Lat. *cor, cordis,* on the other. Old Indian avoided the threatening reduction of volume by an increased use of a prop-vowel which eventually led to a fullfledged *-i*: *hā́rdi.* Most languages sooner or later replaced the monosyllable by more voluminous and therefore clearer and more durable derivatives; *-eyo-/-iyo-* appear in Skt. *hr̥daya-,* Avest. *zr̥daya-,* Greek (Att.) καρδία, "diminutive" *-iko-* in OCS *srъdьce,* the ubiquitous nasal enlargement *-en-* in Germanic *herten-,* etc. But in whatever disguise—after a history of four or five thousand or even more years—the old noun still survives in the surviving IE languages.

Semantically, and from the point of view of linguistic geography, it is interesting that a verbal derivative of this noun acquired the meaning 'get angry' in a compact area: in Balto-Slavic, Armenian, and Iranian.

Notes

1. Cf. Walde–Pokorny I 423 f.; Muller, *Altitalisches Wb.* 72; Walde–Hofmann I 271 f.; Ernout–Meillet[4] 142.

2. Friedrich, *Hethitisches Elementarbuch* I[2], 1960, 58; also *Hethitisches Wb.,* 1952, 103 A.

3. See Kronasser, *Etymologie der heth. Sprache,* Lfg. 2, 1963, 161.

4. Is *kardiyantsa* an abl. based on this form (Sommer–Falkenstein, *Die hethitisch-akkadische Bilingue des Hattusilis* I (= *HAB*), 1938, 94; Kronasser, *Vergleichende Laut- und Formenlehre des Hethitischen,* 1956, 52) or an "ergative" in *-ant-* (Laroche, BSL 57, 1962, 37)?

5. This is essentially Kronasser's argument put forward as early as 1956, see his

Laut- und Formenlehre 52. On the use of this genitive see Kronasser, *Etymologie* 123 f., 332; N. v. Brock, *Revue hittite et asianique* (= RHA) 67, 1960, 144.

6. J. Egli, *Heteroklisie im Griechischen, mit besonderer Berücksichtigung der Fälle von Gelenkheteroklisie*, Zürich, 1954.

7. This is rightly stressed by Kronasser, *Laut- und Formenlehre* 52, in contrast to *Etymologie* 161. A "secondary stem" *kardiya-* (Kronasser, *Etymologie* 161, 340) lacks all support.

8. Pedersen, *Hittitisch und die anderen indoeuropäischen Sprachen*, 1938, 41, 195.

9. See Sommer–Falkenstein, *HAB* 95 f., but especially Kammenhuber, *Zeitschrift für Assyriologie* 56 (N.F. 22), 1964, 150, 155–57, 160, 164–68.

10. Laroche, *Revue de Philologie* 42, 1969, 244–45. This does not mean, however, that we have to separate **ghorod* from IE **gher-*, **ghornā* 'Darm' since **ghorod* is simply **ghor-od-* . See also further on, III 5.

11. Cf. Sommer–Falkenstein, *HAB* 96, and Kronasser, *Laut- und Formenlehre* 52.

12. This explanation is offered by Kronasser, *Etymologie* 161.

13. This was Kronasser's view, see his *Laut- und Formenlehre* 52. On morphological expansions see Kuryłowicz, *Proceedings of the 8th Congress of Linguists*, 1958, 227 f.

14. As is done by Kronasser, *Etymologie* 161.

15. The equation of *kard-* with IE **kr̥d-* is presented by Sturtevant–Hahn, *A comparative grammar of the Hittite language* I², 1951, 42; Kuryłowicz, o.c., 231.

16. This is Sommer's view, see *HAB* 96.

17. See Friedrich, Wb. 103, and Supplement 3, 1966, 18 B. On the much disputed *kartimmes-* see N. v. Brock, o.c., 145 f., who denies its existence and posits a simple **kartes-*, and Kronasser, *Etymologie* 406 (cf. also 497), who is inclined to see in *kartimmesta* a scribal venture, not a real spoken form.

18. Pedersen, *Hittitisch* 40, 148.

19. N. v. Brock, o.c., 144.

20. Kammenhuber, o.c., 204 fn. 100. Note also that N. v. Brock admits that her objection does not really rule out a connection and especially the high price to be paid: she posits an intransitive **karta/i-* 'être en colère' for which there is no evidence in Hittite, only in Indo-Iranian (e.g. Skt. *hr̥-*).

21. Cf. Laroche, BSL 52, 1957, 72–82, on the formation especially p. 79. — Neu, *Interpretation der hethitischen mediopassiven Verbalformen*, 1968, 84–85, lists the forms of *kartimmiya-* but offers no morphological analysis.

22. Cf. Vasmer, *Russisches etym. Wb.* (= REW) II, 1955, 612.

23. First published 1904 by F. W. K. Müller in *Handschriftenreste in Estrangelo-Schrift aus Turfan, Chinesisch-Turkistan*, II, 32 f.; republished 1908 by C. Salemann in his *Manichaeische Studien* I (Mémoires de l'Acad. Impériale de St.-Pétersbourg VIII/VIII/10), 30.

24. Salemann, *Manichaica III* (Bulletin de l'Acad. Impériale 1912, 1–32) 18, number S 13 a; the Glossary was published as Manichaica IV, ibid. 33–50.

25. Bartholomae, *Zur Kenntnis der mitteliranischen Mundarten VI*, 1925, 36 f.

26. Henning, *Ein manichäischer kosmogonischer Hymnus* (Göttinger Gelehrte Nachrichten 1932, 214–228) 215 with fn. 3.; "Das Verbum des Mittelpersischen der Turfan-fragmente" (= *Zeitschrift für Indologie und Iranistik* 9, 1933, 158–253) 205. For the passage of T III 260 see Andreas–Henning, *Mitteliranische Manichaica* I, 1932, 193.

27. I am puzzled by Wikander's statement (*Der arische Männerbund*, 1938, 52) that

"der Verbalstamm *sṛdya-* ist jetzt im Mitteliranischen gut belegt, und zwar in ganz derselben Bedeutung wie ai. *śardhati*", esp. as he quotes Henning's paper in the GGN.

28. See *Verbum* 205 and GGN 1932, 226.

29. The possibility of *sagr-* as an antecedent can be ruled out.

30. On these phonological points see Bartholomae, *Mitteliranische Mundarten* VI 14 with fn. 4, 36, 52¹, and twenty years earlier *Zum altiranischen Wb.*, 1906, 25¹, 102. — Of great interest would be Old Persian *Bṛdya-* if it had survived into Middle Iranian and if it could be depended on. As is known, Gershevitch has argued (*Transactions of the Philological Society*, 1964, 22) that *this* was the name of Kambyses' brother, not, as has always been assumed, *Bardiya*; but see the objections raised by Mayrhofer, "Die Rekonstruktion des Medischen" (*Anzeiger der Österr. Akad.*, 1968, 1–22) 18 with fn. 78 (as also R. Schmitt, *ZDMG* 117, 1967, 122 fn. 22). — As to -*gy*-, it should be noted that it could only be a secondary cluster (as in *darg-yah*-), since an original cluster would have resulted in -*ǰy*- .

31. See Renou, *Études sur le vocabulaire du Rigveda*, 1958, 60 f., but especially *Études védiques et paninéennes* 8, 1961, 56.

32. See Bezzenberger, *BB* II, 1878, 191; Hirt, *IF* XXXII, 1913, 260; Frisk, *GHÅ* 1951(4), 3¹.

33. On some basic problems of this verb see now Insler's masterly paper in *JAOS* 88, 1968, 219–223.

34. Skt. *hṛṇīte* and its group is not listed in Pokorny, *IEW*, but see Walde–Hofmann I 658.

35. Whatmough, *Language* XXIX, 481, and already at the 7th Congress of Linguists (1952), see the *Proceedings*, 1956, 463. I do not know who else may be included in Whatmough's "us" but Lehmann certainly belongs to this group, see his Proto-IE Phonology, 1952, 31, and, alas, even his recent treatment of Vedic *hṛdiya-* 'dear', Studies presented to F. B. J. Kuiper, 1968, 42.

36. Lehmann also allows himself to be guided by the Baltic intonation (1952) although he notes further on that "the acute intonation spread to verbs with circumflex intonation". Unfortunately, even this does not exhaust the categories of secondary acute intonation.

37. Szemerényi, *KZ* 75, 1958, 179¹, with references to previous treatments.

38. Stang, *Vergl. Gram. der baltischen Sprachen*, 1966, 158.

39. Vaillant, *Grammaire comparée des langues slaves* II, 1958, 167. See also Pedersen, *Études lituaniennes*, 1933, 57 f.

40. Cf. e.g., Schmidt, *Pluralbildungen der idg. Neutra*, 1889, 224; Brugmann, *Grundriss* II/1, 1889, 450; Saussure, *MSL* 7, 1892, 79 (= Recueil 443); Bechtel, *Die Hauptprobleme der idg. Lautlehre seit Schleicher*, 1892, 171; Hirt, *Der idg. Ablaut*, 1900, 176; and in more recent years, Benveniste, *Origines de la formation des noms en indo-européen*, 1935, 77; Pokorny, *IEW* 580; Frisk, *GEW* I 787; Gusmani, *I nomi radicali del greco* (Rendiconti dell'Istituto Lombardo 98, 1964, 213–248) 227.

41. Osthoff, *Philologische Rundschau* 1, 1881, 1593 f.; cp. Thumb, in: *Die Erforschung der idg. Sprachen* (ed. Streitberg) I, 1916, 48; Schwyzer, *Griechische Grammatik* (= GG) I, 1934–39, 279.

42. Hatzidakis, *Glotta* 18, 1930, 5¹.

43. See Brugmann, *Griechische Grammatik*³, 1900, 71; Schwyzer, *GG* I 279. It is also assumed by these scholars that Osthoff's law was preceded by the development of intervocalic *s* to *h* — as is shown by Hom. ἠώς from *āusōs and Doric ὤϝατα from

*ōusata; in order to be quite precise, one would of course have to say that Osthoff's law was preceded by the loss of *h*, too, since *auhōs would still have presented the necessary cluster. But I have shown that ὤϝατα never existed as a genuine Doric form (Studi micenei ed egeo-anatolici 3, 1967, 51 f.) and that IE *ausōs likewise never had a long diphthong (KZ 73, 1956, 187[2]); cf. now also (for a rather different view) Kiparsky's paper "Sonorant clusters in Greek", *Language* XLIII, 619–635, esp. 624.

44. Hermann, *Silbenbildung im Griechischen und in den andern idg. Sprachen*, 1923, 76; Lejeune, *Traité de phonétique grecque*, 1955[2], 190[3].

45. Saussure, MSL 7, 1892, 79 (= Recueil 443). Cf. also Stang, *Vergl. Gram. der baltischen Sprachen*, 1966, 45 f.

46. See Stang, o.c., 158[3].

47. See Stang, *l.c.* — Quite impossible is Ivanov's inference (*Voprosy Slavjanskogo Jazykoznanija* II, 13) that *seyr* and κῆρ represent an early root *ker- which was later expanded to *kerd. The word for heart may have been derived from a primitive root *ker- (see the text further on) but for heart only the "expanded" form *kerd was in use, never the original *ker-.

48. It is interesting that *sērā did not lead to a fem. singular as was the case with the word for 'meat': *menso* is a ntr. pl. in the Elbing Vocabulary but a fem.sg. *mensā* appears in the Catechisms as in Latv. *mìesa* and Žemait. *meisa* (Fränkel, Die baltischen Sprachen, 1950, 28). In East Baltic, on the other hand, the gender of heart is feminine but the word belongs to the *i*-class, and this presents a problem. A transfer to this class is "logical" where there was an old acc. in -*in* (and plural -*ins*), e.g. *žūs* 'fish', acc. *žuvin*→nom. *žuvis*—the case with animate nouns—or an old dual in -*ī*, the case with, e.g., *ausis* 'ear', *akis* 'eye', *nósis* 'nose', cf. Szemerényi, *Studi micenei ed egeo-anatolici 3*, 1967, 66 f. But *šird-* was neither animate, nor did it call for a frequent use of the dual. So it is most likely that at first a feminine singular *širdā was built on the neuter plural in -*ā*, and this was later transferred to the *i*-class because many words for parts of the body belonged to that class already. But the fact that in Old Lithuanian (and Old Latvian) the word is masculine (Specht, *OLZ* 1931, 513) and the existence of the masculine plural *širdai* 'row, quarrel' show that the original neuter was also first transferred to the masc. -*a*-class.

49. See Streitberg, *IF* 3, 1892, 346–47.

50. M. Bloomfield, *Transactions of the American Philological Association* 26, 1895, 9. Cf. also Blankenstein, *Untersuchungen zu den langen Vokalen in der e-Reihe*, 1911, *passim*; Persson, *Beiträge zur idg. Wortforschung*, 1912, 625 f.

51. See, e.g., Benveniste, *Origines* 178 f.

52. Cf., for the present, my *Trends and Tasks in Comparative Philology*, London 1962, 12 f.

53. E.g. Hirt, *Der idg. Ablaut*, 1900, 124; Trautmann, *Baltisch-Slavisches Wb.*, 1923, 302; Benveniste, *Origines* 7 (all derive *hert-en- from *kērd-en-).

54. See, e.g. Wackernagel–Debrunner, *Altindische Grammatik* III, 1931, 34.237.305; Pisani, *Ricerche Linguistische* 2, 1951, 48–49.

55. That *dadhi* is wrongly classed is admitted by Wackernagel–Debrunner, o.c., 306. Erroneous is also the assertion (ibid. 305) that OPr. *dadan* 'milk' shows the same *n* as *dadhn-*, since *dadan* is an -*a*-stem nom.-acc. sg., i.e. its -*an* represents IE -*om*, see Szemerényi, KZ 75, 1958, 181[5]. On the reduplicated formation see Benveniste, Origines 184, and, slightly differently, Cuny, Litteris 2, 1925, 51[1] and 54, who rightly points out that the gen. should be *dadhinas, dadhnas* is analogical. This difficulty is avoided by

Hamp (*Word* IX, 140) for whom all these words have *i* from a laryngeal so that, e.g., Skt. *asthi* is from **Host-H* while Avest. *ast* is from **Host*.

56. The usually quoted *ās, ās-an-* 'mouth' cannot be used since *ās* is not attested, see Debrunner, *Kratylos* I, 37.

57. See on this textual point Macdonell, *Vedic Grammar*, 1910, 198[1]; Wackernagel–Debrunner III 237, but especially the detailed note in the Atharva-veda translation by Whitney & Lanman, II 970.

58. On these rules see Macdonell, o.c., 72 (also 73 § 81c!); Renou, *Grammaire de la langue védique*, 1952, 101; W. S. Allen, *Sandhi*, 1962, 74. — The form *suhār* continues, in principle, an IE **su-kōr* from **su-kords*, with compositional *o*-grade.

59. For *akṣi* this explanation was first advanced by me at Studi micenei 3, 1967, 68 fn. 82.

60. The derivation of *sakthi* from a dissimilated **skakthi* in which *skak-* represented IE **skn̥g-* (Sommer, *Festschrift Debrunner*, 1954, 426.428) naturally rules out any connection between Avest. *haxti* 'thigh' and *haxa-* (a-stem) 'sole between heel and toes' (advocated by Gershevitch, *BSOAS* 14, 1952, 488[2]; The Avestan Hymn to Mithra, 1959, 281 fn., and apparently still favoured by Hiersche, *Untersuchungen zur Frage der Tenues Aspiratae im Indogermanischen*, 1964, 135 fn. 66) but even without it, the semantic discrepancy should have given pause. — On the other hand, IE **skeng-* offers a possible explanation for Slavic **stegno* 'Hüfte, Lende, Oberschenkel' (cf. Vasmer, REW 3,8): it could be dissimilated from **skeng-no-* (cf. Italian *stinco* 'shin, shin-bone' from Langobard **skinko*, and especially ON *tyggua* 'chew' from **kyggua*), and this be based on the heteroclitic plural **skeng-na* (interpreted as an -*o*-stem form, s. fn. 48) from **skeng-t* (or **skn̥g-t*), gen. **skn̥g-nos*.

61. Hiersche, o.c., 136, thinks that *sakthi* is a specifically Indian innovation because its *th* is modelled on *asthi* which arose in Indian history. I agree that **asth-* does not point to an IE or PIE **HostH-* (as suggested, after Sturtevant, by Schmitt–Brandt, *Die Entwicklung des idg. Vokalsystems*, 1967, 107[32]) but prefer to regard *th* not as due to the preceding *s* but to metathesis in **Host-*, the form that can be reconstructed with certainty for IE; cf. Scardigli (*Atti e Memorie dell'Accademia Toscana* 22, 1957, 105.114) who thinks of assimilation, i.e. *H—t > H—th*, which seems to me less likely.

62. I should mention here that Fowkes (*Lingua Posnaniensis* VI, 106) connects *sakthi* with Welsh *hegl* 'leg, shank' but this **sek-l-* cannot be accommondated within the IE vocabulary. It was perhaps for this reason that J. Morris Jones (*A Welsh Grammar historical and comparative*, 1913, 141), anticipating Sommer's solution, as it were, derived *hegl* from **skek-l-*, finding this **skek-* in Welsh *ysgogi* 'stir, shake', Lithu. *šókti* 'leap, dance', and the variant **skeg-* both in Engl. *shake* and, nasalized, in *shank*.

63. While Sommer, *l.c.*, 428, does not venture to go beyond an Aryan *sakthi*, Pokorny (*IEW* 930) posits an IE **skn̥g-ti*. This seems to me ruled out by the fact that -*ti-* could not be neuter, see Wackernagel–Debrunner II/2, 1954, 642, § 475.

64. See Bartholomae, *Ai. Wb.* s.v. *haxt-*.

65. See Mayrhofer–Schmitt, *Orientalia* 31, 1962, 313 f., esp. 316 f. and 317[1]; Schmitt, *Beiträge zur Namenforschung* III, 1966, 66 with fn. 10.

66. Sommer, *l.c.*, 426.428.

67. Pedersen, Hittitisch 37. Kuiper comments (Notes on Vedic noun-inflexion, 1942, 63[2]): "this is however highly improbable".

68. Kuiper, o.c., 63.

69. Note, e.g., Kronasser, *Etymologie* 206 (seems to see in *hastai* IE -*ōi* or -*ēi*);

Georgiev, *Symbolae Kurylowicz*, 1965, 87 (*hastai* was a collective with *-eHy*, Greek represents **ost-āy-om*, Aryan has an *-i*-stem *asthi*).

70. See Friedrich, *Heth. Wb.*, Suppl. 3, 1966, 31, but especially Goetze, *Journal of Cuneiform Studies* 22, 1968, 21.

71. See Kronasser, *Etymologie* 208.

72. Cf. Laroche, BSL 53, 1958, 197; Ivanov, *Symbolae Kurylowicz*, 1965, 134; Kronasser, *Etymologie* 550 with fn. — N. v. Brock (*Glotta* 46, 1968, 119) would trace *hassa* to **hastya* but in Luwian even the *-i*-stems form the neuter plural with *-a* (cf. *tuliyassi-* : *tuliyassa*, see Laroche, *Dictionnaire de la langue louvite*, 1959, 138) so that only **hasta* can be expected.

73. This solution was first suggested in my Studies in the IE system of numerals, 1960, 133 fn. 64. Since then I have noticed Saussure's suggestion in the *Mémoire* (Recueil 209) that *i* was not a suffix but a euphonic addition necessitated by multiconsonantal clusters in the plural in such forms as *asth-i-bhis*.

74. See J. Vachek, Some less familiar aspects of the analytical trend of English (*Brno Studies in English* III, 1961) 59.

75. Cf. Meyer–Lübke, *Hist. Gram. der französ. Sprache* I, 1913, 145.

76. L. Flydal, *Travaux de l'Institut de Linguistique de Paris* IV, 1959, 15f., esp. 17 and 20.

77. See Wagner, *Historische Lautlehre des Sardischen*, 1941, § 357 f.

78. See, e.g., Pokorny, IEW 579; Frisk, GEW I 787.

79. Meillet, *Esquisse d'une grammaire comparée de l'arménien classique*, 1936², 196 f., and the references there given.

80. Schulze, *KZ* 57, 1930, 75 = *Kleine Schriften*, 1933, 217.

81. Cf., e.g., Walde–Hofmann I 272; Frisk, *GEW* II 2.

82. Muller, *Altitalisches Wb.*, 1927, 72.

83. See Pokorny, *IEW* 933 f. Pokorny's material needs expansion on the Iranian side which is only represented by an Ossetic form, although there are many cognates of this root. I should also add perhaps that palatal(ized) *k* in **kerd*, non-palatal(ized) *k* after *s-* in **sker-*, and from it *s*-less **ker-* with non-palatal *k* are frequently encountered alternations in the "guttural" series.

84. Cf. R. B. Onians, *The origins of European thought*, 1951, 28.

В. Н. ТОПОРОВ

К балто-скандинавским мифологическим связям

Интенсивный обмен культурными и материальными ценностями между территориями, прилегающими к Балтийскому морю, засвидетельствован уже с давних пор. Результаты археологических разысканий, как и языковые, фольклорные, мифологические данные, помогают уточнить характер культурно-исторического взаимодействия, выделить локальные центры, основные зоны и пути передачи культурных ценностей, определить хронологические рамки и т. п. Такие языковые сходства, как наличие политонии (при безраздельной монотонии на соседних территориях), ряд общих явлений в лексике и фразеологии, связанной с морем (в самом широком смысле слова), в моделях построения сложных имен и прозвищ и т. п., — достаточно основательны, чтобы думать о «языковом союзе», специфическая черта которого — нахождение в середине рассматриваемого ареала моря. Через него, собственно, и осуществляются основные связи (ср. проблему средиземноморского языкового союза), подкрепляемые более специальными связями любых двух смежных языков (ср. шведский–финский, эстонский–латышский, литовский–польский, кашубский–немецкий ит. д.). Среди общих фольклорных и мифологических мотивов и соответствующих им текстов особое место, — как в количественном отношении, так и по своему значению, — занимают те, которые связаны с богом грома и преследованием им его противника[1].

В этой заметке коснемся одного частного вопроса внутри общей темы поединка громовника и его противника. Речь идет о мифологическом персонаже литовского (возможно, и ятвяжского) пантеона, засвидетельствованном западнорусскими источниками, — о *Телявеле*. Происхождение этого названия, как и сведения о функциях Телявеля, остаются темными[2]. Собственно говоря, Телявель упоминается лишь дважды. Во-первых, в Волынской летописи под 1252 г. (в составе Ипатьевской летописи) в сообщении о Миндовге — *крещеніе же его льстиво бысть: жряше богомъ своимъ втаинъ, первому Нънадьеви, и Телявели и Диверикъзу, заеячему богу, и Мьидьину ... и богомъ своимъ жряше, и мертвыхъ телеса сожигаше, и поганьство свое явъ творяше*[3]. Во-вторых, в известной вставке западнорусского переписчика (1261 г.) перевода «Хроники» Иоанна Малалы. После рассказа о погребении Совия, проанализированного в другом месте, следует: *Сію прелесть Совии въведе внъ иж приносити жрътвоу сквернымъ богам Андаеви и Перкоунови рекше громоу и Жвороунъ рекше соуцъ и Телдвели ісгкоузнецю сковавше емоу слнце дко свътити по земли и ввергшю емоу на нбо слнце....*

Из сопоставления этих трех отрывков следует одно весьма важное заключение: там, где упоминается *Дивирикс*, не упоминается Перкун. Значение последнего в литовском пантеоне и его известность за пределами балтийских территорий слишком велики, чтобы считать такой пропуск оправданным. Учитывая вместе с тем положение Перкуна и Дивирикса в списках (после *Нънадея* и *Андая* и в соседстве с Телявелем), напрашивается предположение об их тождестве. Имя *Дивирикс* обычно объясняется из *Dievo* (или *Dievų*) *rikys* (*-is*) как обозначение 'господина богов'. Принимая во внимание отсутствие в литовском слова *rikys* (*-is*), ср. зато пр. *rikijs*, и перифрастического обозначения Перкуна по указанному принципу, приходится предложить другое, новое объяснение вопроса. Оно исходит из хорошо известного наименования Перкуна как *Dievo rykštė* «Божий бич», ср. *Perkūną vadina: «Dundulis»*, «*Dievo rykštė*»; *Kitaip Perkūnas vadinamas* «*Dievo rykštė*» и т. д. и соответствующего объяснения: *Apie Perkūną bijodavo ir išsižioti ... Žaibas-blogadarių rykštė*[4]. Таким образом, Дивирикс из **Dievo-rykš(tė)*; при этом предположении удачно объясняется и конечно -*с* (*Дивирикс*), необычное при иных решениях.

Поскольку, как будет показано в другом месте, *Нънадей* и *Андай* или тождественны (они не встречаются одновременно в перечнях) или весьма сходны (ср. излюбленный у пруссов префиксальный способ образования теофорных имен: *An-trimpus – Na trimpe* и под.), получается последовательность: Нънадей–Андай — Перкун — Телявель или Нънадей–Андай — Телявель — Перкун. Повидимому, первая последовательность отражает более древнюю картину. Предполагая (вслед за традицией), что в *Нънадей* скрывается название бога (лит. *dievas*, лтш. *dievs*, пр. *deiws*), присутствующее и в Андай, можно гипотетически реконструировать (не вдаваясь пока в детали) **Nō-(an)-deiv-* (**Nu-/an/-deiv-?*) и **An(t)-deiv-*, причем семантика префиксов оправдывала бы сообщение *жрѧше богомъ своимъ ... первому Нънадъеви*, ср. как параллель прусское перифрастическое обозначение первого божества *Ocko-pirmus* (ср. *uska –* 'всех' и *pirmas –* 'первый'[5]), иногда глоссируемое как

Juppiter, ср. также в «Der vnglaubigen Sudauen ...»: *Deywoty Zudwity; Ockopirmus der erste Gott Himmelsvnd Gestirnes* ... и др. Если наше предположение верно, то *Нънадей-Андай*, глава богов, относится к Перкуну, его слуге, помощнику, воплощению его воли, 'божьему бичу', так же, как относится *Dievas* современных архаичных представлений литовцев к Перкуну, выступающему в той же самой роли[6]. Ср. такие характеристики, как: *Perkūnas tai Dievo tarnas, a velnias tas jo priešas; Perkūną leidžia Dievas; Dievas liepia ir parodo Perkūnui, kur reikia trenkt; Perkūnas yra Dievo pasiuntinys; Dievas yra Perkūno viršininkas. Jis Perkūną siunčia ten, kur nori; Perkūnas priklauso nuo Dievo valios* и другие[7]. Вообще говоря, отношения господина–слуги (хозяина–работника) в большей степени свойственны мифологическим системам северных народов (ср. скандинавские, финские, лапландские примеры). В таких системах Бог как таковой часто оказывается слишком абстрактным и пассивным началом (при этом он обычно не включен в сеть сюжетных связей), что влечет за собой утрату им актуальности. Он как бы переходит в долговременную пассивную память, а в пределах сферы актуальных представлений его функции исполняются слугой Бога. Заняв место *Dievas*'а, Перкун перенимает ряд его атрибутов, между прочим — и наличие помощника, не успев утратить сюжетных связей. В литовском фольклоре не раз упоминаются помощники Перкуна, как правило, безымянные. Возможно, что такая картина существовала уже в XIII в., к которому относятся вышеприведенные свидетельства. Суть нашего предложения сводится к тому, чтобы увидеть в Телявеле, упоминаемом исключительно в связи с Перкуном, именно такого помощника. Основания для этого — в указании на то, что Телявель сковал солнце и укрепил его на небе, видимо, для Перкуна (*сковавше емоу сл͠нце ... и въвергшю емоу на н͠бо сл͠нце* ...)[8]. Поучительно, что помощник бога грома часто выступает именно как к у з н е ц. Телявель-кузнец, как и Перкун в его отношении к *Dievas*'у, ср. *Perkūnas-tai senas kalvis.* TD, III, № 351 (стр. 170); *Kai griaudžia, tai kalvis Bruzgulis iš patrankų šaudo velnius.* Там же, № 454 (стр. 175)[9] и др. Очевидно, что солнце было выковано и укреплено на небе по з а к а з у Перкуна. В этой функции Телявель аналогичен небесному кузнецу латышских песен космологического содержания, ср.: *Kalējs kala debesīs, | Dzirkstas sprāga Daugavā: | Tai māsai kroni kala, | Kam deviņi bāleliņi* BW. 33722 или: *Kalējs kala debesīs, | Ogles bira Daugavā: | Saules meita saktu kala, | Dieva dēla zobentiņu.* BW. 33728 и др.[10] Дальнейшие аналогии связывают Телявеля с Ильмариненом «Калевалы», сковавшим солнце и луну (ср. сходный мотив в «Калевипоэг») или с тремя братьями-исполинами белорусской сказки, укрепившими на дубе месяц[11]. Учитывая весьма большую распространненность сказочных мотивов, связывающих безымянного кузнеца с громовником и нечистой силой, в Прибалтике и в Белоруссии, можно полагать, что образ, подобный Телявелю, один из остатков старой мифологемы, которая могла некогда отражаться и в недошедших до нас эпических сказаниях[12] (одним из звеньев их мог быть мотив № 753)[13]. Разумеется, нельзя переносить все мотивы, связанные с кузнецом в этом ареале, в мифологему с участием Телявеля. И, тем не менее, весьма вероятно, что с Телявелем некогда связывались хотя бы основные и наиболее достоверные и архаичные мотивы, отнесенные позже к безымянному кузнецу: 1) кузнец на службе у громовника, 2) кузнец выковывает чудесное оружие, 3) кузнец (так или иначе) участвует в схватке с чудовищем, змеем, великаном и т. п.

Вот, пожалуй, и всё, что можно пока извлечь из скудных сведений о Телявеле и что можно восстановить, опираясь на косвенные данные, относящиеся к этой (или смежной) территории. На этом этапе уместно задаться вопросом об этимологии имени *Телявель*. Предлагавшиеся объяснения (от лит. *tēvēlis* или *kalvēlis*, уменьш. от *kálvis* 'кузнец')[14] или далеки от достоверности и требуют неоправданных допущений, или едва ли могут быть проверены. Кажется, однако, что есть возможность указать реальное соответствие имени Телявель (= *Televelis* < *Telvelis?*) в другой традиции. Речь идет о др.-сев. *Þjálfi* 'Тьяльви', имени помощника и слуги бога грома Тора (*Þórr*), и едва ли отделимом от него *Þjelvar*, имени персонажа из «Guta-saga»[15]. Помимо весьма значительной формальной близости балтийского и древнесеверных имен, предполагающей, разумеется, не генетическое соответствие, а заимствование, существуют и аргументы содержательного характера. Прежде всего следует подчеркнуть, что восстановленному мотиву Телявеля как помощника Перкуна, исполнителя его поручений, соответствует роль Тьяльви, выступающего в аналогичной функции[16] в целом ряде мифологических мотивов, связанных с Тором, мать которого носит имя *Fjǫrgyn*, сопоставляемое с *Perkūnas*[17]. Можно думать, что в этой роли Тьяльви (или ближайшее его соответствие) отражен на лапландских шаманских бубнах, где наряду с *Horagalles*’ом, держащим два молота (*Horagalles* — лапландский эквивалент Тора, само его имя — калька с др.-сев. *Þórr karl*), изображена маленькая фигура его помощника[18]. Как известно, в древнесеверной мифологии слугой Тора выступал не только Тьяльви, но и (еще чаще) Локи (*Loki*), причем иногда они выступают вместе[19]. Несмотря на основательную критику старых выводов А. Olrik’а[20], можно все-таки предполагать, что в большинстве случаев Тьяльви и

Локи являются чередующимися воплощениями слуги Тора и что им соответствуют несколько различные ареалы. Во всяком случае после ряда исследований есть основания думать, что Тьяльви тяготеет к восточноскандинавскому ареалу (начиная с Швеции), а Локи — к западноскандинавскому. Если это так, то связь Тьяльви с Телявелем, принадлежащим также к восточнобалтийской зоне, получила бы дополнительную поддержку[21].

Другие схождения еще более специфичны, особенно если попытаться компенсировать скудость балтийских данных о Телявеле результатами реконструкции. Среди этих схождений особое значение приобретает мотив *воровства* противником бога грома его оружия, к приготовлению которого причастен помощник, особенно когда он выступает как кузнец[22]. Ср. этот мотив в «Þrymskviða» (ср. также и «Hymiskviða») в сопоставлении с аналогичными версиями финских и эстонских сказок[23], а также в связи с распространенными объяснениями причины вражды Перкуна к чорту в балтийской традиции, ср.: *Perkūnas velnius tranko dėlto, kad velniai pavogė jo kirvį; Velnias nuo Perkūno pavogė peilį; Perkūnas su velniu pyktasi dėlto kad velnias iš po jo pavogė krūvą akmenų.* TD, III, №№ 84–86 (стр. 154); вырождение мотива — воровство жены, дочери, козла Перкуна, см. там же. Любопытно, что в «Калевале» (руна 49) также представлен мотив воровства в связи с кузнецом Ильмариненом. Но украдены и спрятаны в скалу — солнце и луна. У Ильмаринена не оказывается под рукой нужного оружия и он отправляется домой, чтобы выковать его (эта версия во многом аналогична древне-индийскому мотиву поединка Индры с чудовищем). Показательно, что Тор приходит к *Geirrøðr*'у без молота, без пояса силы, без железных рукавиц (ср. сходные предметы, выкованные небесным кузнецом латышского фольклора), хотя и поражает его именно молотом. Правдоподобно предположение (J. de Vries, — FFC, № 110, стр. 65) о том, что в исходном мифе Тор и Локи пришли к великану с тем, чтобы вернуть молот, который был украден. При этом следует напомнить, что типологически Локи принадлежит к кругу персонажей с функцией культурного героя, связанного с огнем и/или кузнечным делом (Прометей, Гефест, кельт. *Lug* и под.)[24]. И хотя мы не можем отождествлять Локи с Тьяльви, много шансов, что указанная функция (у Локи) в той или иной степени некогда была присуща и Тьяльви. В пользу этой точки зрения могут говорить некоторые общие соображения, например, необходимость найти германское соответствие лат. *Vulcanus*'у из известной цитаты из Цезаря (*Deorum numero eos solos ducunt, quos cernunt et quorum aperte opibus iuvantur, Solem et Vulcanum et Lunam, reliquos ne fama quidem acceperunt*. De bello Gall. VI, 21), видимо, неоправданно подвергавшейся сомнению[25]; или прямые указания на поклонение огню в старых источниках (ср. а.-сакс. *þæt man do weordige hæðne godas ond sunnan odðe monan, fyr odðe flod, wæter* ...)[26] и т. д. Наряду с этим существуют и некоторые более специальные указания на связь Тьяльви с огнем и — более косвенно — с кузнечным делом. Так, судя по вполне вероятному объяснению, имя *Þjálfi* связано с др.-сев. *þialfi, þialmi* 'оковы', 'узы', 'путы'; следовательно *Þjelvar* означает 'Fesselkämpfer'[27]. В свою очередь этот мотив может быть сопоставлен с мотивом небесного кузнеца, выковавшего для божьего сына оружье и шпоры, а для божьей дочери — пояс и корону (см. выше)[28]. Возможно, что небесный кузнец связан с божеством по имени *Tavvals* (видимо, испорченный вариант Телявеля), выступающем в известном сочинении Я. Ласицкого «De Diis Samagitarum...»: *Tavvals Deus auctor facultatum* вскоре после: *Percunos Deus tonitrus illis est ... Percuna tete mater est fulminis atque tonitrui* ... LPG, стр. 356, ср. также: 54, 67–68, 371. Косвенно связь с огнем для Тьяльви может быть обнаружена при анализе эпизода из «Guta-saga», где рассказывается о том, как *Þjelvar* спас остров Готланд, который раньше ежедневно погружался в море, и еженощно всплывал, тем, что обошел его вокруг с огнем[29] (ср. сходный обычай в Исландии при освоении земельного надела).

Еще одно нетривиальное совпадение относится к мотиву укрепления на небе светил. Ср. *и въвергшю емоу на н͠бо с͠лнце* (о Телявеле) в связи с эпизодом из «Снорри–Эдды» (100–104), где рассказывается о заключительной стадии поединка Тора и Тьяльви с *Hrungnir*'ом и *Mǫkkurkáfi*. Здесь передается рассказ Тора *vǫlva*'е *Gróa* о том, как он перебирался через покрытые льдом сверные реки, неся на спине в корзине мужа *vǫlva*'ы *Aurvandil*'я; как один из пальцев последнего замерз и Тор забросил его на небо, сделав созвездием[30]. Возможно, что некоторые новые аргументы в пользу предлагаемого сравнения можно извлечь (учитывая обмен атрибутами между Телявелем и Перкуном, Тьяльви и Тором) из мотива бога грома и козла, особенно в связи с жертвоприношением козла и более поздними переживаниями. Ср., например, известный эпизод посещения Тором *Egill*'я, устройство к нему слугами Тьяльви и его сестры *Rǫskva*'ы[31] как компенсацию за ущерб, нанесенный одному из козлов Тора и т. д.[32] при постоянном мотиве Перкуна и козлов (ср.: *Perkūnas — senis, pasikinkęs į dviratį ožį ir su juo važinėja po debesis. Jis rankose turi kirvį, ir jei kas prasikalsta, tai jis kirvį paleidžia. Kai kirvis krinta žemyn, sužiba ir vėl grįžta atgal* ... TD, III, № 317 (стр. 167), ср. № 316) и старых сообщениях о жертвоприношении козла, отраженных в исторических текстах[33] и в фольклоре[34]. Некоторые другие аналогии еще более косвенны и, главное, гипотетичны (связь с вепрем, рябиной, ср. нем. *Eberesche* и под.); кроме того, их труднее локализировать внутри всего комплекса представлений, связанных с громовником. Несмотря на это, приведенные выше соображения, кажется, позволяют предполагать связь между Телявелем и Тьяльви (и *Þjelvar*)[35] и соотносимыми с ними мотивами.

Примечания

1. Ср. прежде всего *J. Balys*, «Griaustinis ir velnias Baltoskandijos kraštų tautosakoje. Lyginamoji pasakojamosios tautosakos studija», *Tautosakos darbai*, VI, 3–236 (далее — TD). Скандинавско-славянский аспект этого вопроса был подчеркнут еще раньше. См. S. Rоźniecki, «Perun und Thor», *AfslPh*, *XXIII*, 462–520. Реконструкция соответствующей мифологемы по белорусским данным и ее индоевропейские основы представлены в ряде работ Вяч. В. Иванова и автора этих строк.

2. Сводку мнений см.: W. Mannhardt, *Letto-Preußische Götterlehre*, Riga, 1936, 51 и след. (далее — LPG).

3. Ср. пропуск Телявеля в той же летописи (1258 г.): *Романови же пришедшу ко граду и Литвѣ, потекши на градъ Литвѣ, ни вѣдѣша нишь то же, токмо и головнѣ ти, псы течюще по городищу; тужаху же и плеваху, посвоиски рекуще: янда, взывающе богы своя Андая и Дивирикса, и вся богы своя поминающе, рекомыя бѣси.*

4. См. *J. Balys*, «Perkūnas lietuvių liaudies tikėjimuose», TD, III, №№ 167, 192, 201 (стр. 160, 161).

5. См. K. Būga, «Panikas ir Ukapirmas», *Rinktiniai raštai* II, 156 (далее — RR). Ср. имя финского громовника *Ukko?*

6. См. P. Skardžius, *Dievas ir Perkūnas*, Brooklynas, 1964; J. Balys. — TD, III; аналогичная картина отмечена и в латышской мифологии, см. P. Šmits, *Latviešu tautas ticējumi*, III, Rīgā, 1940, 1400 и след. (далее — LTT); его же, *Latviešu mitoloģija*, Maskavā, 1918, 11 и след.; ср. K. Straubergs, *Latviešu buŗamie vārdi*, I, Rīgā, 1939, 383–386; H. Biezais, *Die Gottesgestalt der lettischen Volksreligion*, Uppsala, 1961.

7. См. J. Balys, TD, III, №№ 30, 31, 34, 41, 45, 46 (стр. 151, 152); для латышских текстов более характерны такие сочетания, как: *Pērkons ceļas tad, kad velns strīdas ar Dievu*; *Kad pērkons rūcot, tad Dievs braucot pa debesīm* ...; *Pērkona laikā velns slēpjas no Dieva zem kokiem* ... и т. д. См. *LTT*. III, 1401–1402.

8. Ранее мы ошибочно относили *емоу* к Совию, хотя по смыслу текста перечисленные боги и их деяния предшествуют во времени введению их почитания Совием. За *dativus absolutus* в этом отрывке легко предположить иную конструкцию, где *емоу* не связано с Телявелем.

9. Ср.: *Perkūnas vadinasi Bruzguliu*, *TD*, III, № 172 (стр. 160).

10. Подборку сходных текстов см.: M. Jonval, *Les chansons mythologiques*

lettonnes, Paris, 1929, №№ 454–463; ср. также E. Wolter, *AfslPh*, IX, 641; *BW*, 33721–33731. К *девяти братьям* латышской песни ср. лит.: *Kiti sako esą devyni Perkūnai* ...; *Devyni Perkūnai yra*; *Perkūnas turi devynis sūnus*; *Trauk tave devyni Perkūnai*; *Perkūnas buvo pasaulyje iš eilės devintas sutvertas* и др. Ср. *TD*. III, №№ 2, 256–257, 267, 282, 382–386, 562 и др.; ср. также 9 врат в рассказе о Совии (там же о 9 селезенках) перед упоминанием Теля-веля и тот же мотив в описании Ретры Адамом Бременским (*civitas ipsa novem portas habet*. II, 18) при том, что с этим городом связана легенда о вепре, носящая характер солярного мифа (Титмар).

11. См. М. Federowski, *Lud białoruski na Rusi litewskiej*, I–II, Kraków, 1897–1902, а также Л. Г. Бараг, «Асілкі» белорусских сказок и преданий, — «Русский фольклор» VIII. М.–Л., 1963, стр. 34. К числовой символике космологического значения в связи с вышеуказанными мотивами ср.: ... *jedź dalej u lese, znajdziesz tam dwanaście dube agromnych, a na ich hniezdo, a u tuom hnieździe zmiej budzie z adnajeju haławoju*. М. Federowski. Op. cit. II, 83 (сказка о кузнеце «Pogromca smoków».

12. Предположение высказано в кн.: Теобальд, *Литовско-языческие очерки*, Вильна, 1890. Ср. правдоподобную попытку А. Н. Веселовского связать белорусских *волотов* — *велятней* с персонажами «Тидрексаги» (XIII в.) — *Вельтином* и его сыном, чудесным кузнецом *Велундом* (см. «Уголок русского эпоса в саге о Тидреке Бернском», «Русские и вельтины в саге о Тидреке Бернском»).

13. J. Balys, «Lietuvių pasakojamosios tautosakos motyvų katalogas», *TD*, II, 75 («Kalvis atnaujintojas»).

14. См. *LPG*, стр. 67–68; К. Būga, *RR*, I, 188 (из *Kal-ev-elis* > *Kel-ev-elis* 'Volcanus' = Телавелисъ, эст. *kal-ev* 'faber ferrarius' из пралит. *kal-ev-ys* 'kalvis'); В. Н. Топоров, «Об одной 'ятвяжской' мифологеме в связи со славянской параллелью», *Acta Baltico-Slavica*, III, 149 (с указанием на ю.-лит. или ятв. *k'* > *t*) и др. Также, конечно, не относятся к делу фонетически близкие лит. *teliavėšis, teliavėžis* и под., см. К. Būga, *RR*, II, 625.

15. *Þjálfi* < герм. *Þjelƀan-*; *Þjelvar* < герм. *Þjelƀa-harja*. S. Gutenbrunner, «Zur Gutasaga», *ZfdA*, LXXIII, 159; J. de Vries, *Altgermanische Religionsgeschichte*, II, Berlin, 1957, стр. 129–130 (далее -*AGR*).

16. К отношению Тора и Тьяльви см. F. R. Schröder, *Germanische Urmythen*, *AfRW*, XXXV, 201–221.

17. Учитывая некоторые критические замечания в адрес этого сопоставления, правильнее сравнивать др.-исл. *Fjǫrgyn* с лит. *perkūnė* (*perkūnĭ-*). См. F. R. Schröder, «Erce und Fjǫrgyn», *Erbe und Vergangenheit. Festgabe für K. Helm*, Tübingen. 1951, 25–36; Вяч. В. Иванов, «К этимологии балтийского и славянского названий бога грома», *Вопросы славянского языкознания* III, 105.

18. См. A. Olrik, «Nordisk og Lappisk gudsdyrkelse», *Danske Studier* 1905, стр. 49 (далее *DS*); *AGR*. II, 115; Friis, *Lappisk Mythologi* (изображения 1, 10, 11. 2, 7 и 9); ср. также: E. Manker, *Die lappische Zaubertrommel*, Stockholm, 1950.

19. Таков один из существенных выводов из анализа разных версий истории *Geirrøðr*'a (особенно на материале «Þórsdrápa» и Eilifr'a Goðrúnarson'a). См. J. de Vries, «The problem of Loki», *FFC* N 110. Helsinki, 1933,

стр. 56 и след., особенно 60–61; ср. также E. Mogk, «Die Überlieferung von Thors Kampf mit dem Riesen Geirröðz», *Festskrift tillägnad Hugo Pipping.* Svenska Litteratursällskapet i Finland, CLXXV, 1924, стр. 379–388. В юмористическом рассказе о посещении Тором великана-повелителя Utgarðaloki, сообщенном Снорри в «Gylfaginning»'е (гл. 43–46), Локи и Тьяльви также выступают как спутники Тора, см. *FFC*, № 110, стр. 82.

20. См. J. de Vries, *FFC*, № 110, стр. 18 и след., 99 и след.; H. Celander, «Lokes mytiska ursprung», *Språkvetenskapliga Sällskapets i Uppsala förhandlingar*, 1906–1909, Uppsala, 1911, стр. 18–140: O. Loorits (см. ниже).

21. Ср. дополнительный материал о Локи — A. Olrik, «Loki i nyere folkeoverlevering», *DS*, 1908, стр. 193–207; 1909, стр. 69–84.

22. Ср. вырожденный белорусский вариант: *Бацько ужо дагадаўся, што яны асілкі і патаму ён вялеў кавалю, каб ён зделав ім па страле па зялезнай, Романов.* III, стр. 93, № 13.

23. См. A. Olrik, «Tordenguden og hans dreng», *DS*, 1905, стр. 129–146; его же, «Tordenguden og hans dreng i Lappernes myteverden», *DS*, 1906, стр. 65–69; O. Loorits, «Das Märchen vom gestohlenen Donnerinstrument bei den Esten», *Sitzungsberichte der Gelehrten Estnischen Gesellschaft* 1930, Tartu, 1932.

24. См. подробнее H. Krappe, *The Science of Folklore*, London, 1930; J. de Vries, *FFC*, № 110, стр. 258 и след., 272 и след.

25. См., однако, удачное объяснение этого сообщения — A. G. van Hammel, «IJslands Odinsgeloof», *Verlagen en Mededelingen van de Akademie van Wetenschappen te Amsterdam* 82 B3, 1936, стр. 22–23 (в связи с клятвенными формулами); *AGR* I, 355. Ср. также южногерманское сообщение о кузнеце *Mime*, выковавшем знаменитый меч *Mimming*, см. H. Schneider. *Germanische Heldensage*, I, 311.

26. Ср. пережитки ритуального возжигания огня у германцев (*Osterfeuer*).

27. Семантика наименования, возможно, разъясняется Тацитом («Germ». 31): о железном кольце, носимом хаттами до убийства врага. См. S. Gutenbrunner, *Op. cit.*, 160.

28. См. также W. Mannhardt, «Lettische Sonnenmythen», *ZfEthn.* VII, 1875, 319 и след.

29. Ср.: *þa war Gultland so eluist, at þet daghum sanc oc natum war uppi. En þann maþr quam fyrsti eldi a land, oc siþan sanc þet aldri.* Guta-saga (изд. Pipping'a, стр. 62). Ср. *AGR* I, 295–296; II, 129–130 (в частности, ср. хождение «посолонь» при похоронных и аграрных обрядах). Уже указывались древнеиндийские аналогии этой мифологеме, ср.: V. Rydberg, *Undersökningar i germanisk Mythologi.* II. Stockholm, 1889, 125; O. Huth, *Vesta. Untersuchungen zum indogermanischen Feuerkult*, Leipzig–Berlin, 1943, 146–147. К культу огня у балтов см. *LPG*, 120 и др.; ср. также: ... *Perkuno ignem in sylvis sacrum* ... *perpetuum alebant* (XVIII в.), см. P. Skardžius, *Op. cit.*, 23.

30. См. J. de Vries, *AGR*. II, 133–134; см. также H. Schneider, «Die Geschichte vom Riesen Hrungnir», *Festschrift F. Genzmer*, Heidelberg, 1952, 200–210.

31. Др.-сев. *Rǫskva* (более старое *Vrǫskva*) сопоставляют с гот. *ga-wrisqan* (только 3. Pl. Praes. *ga-wrisqand*. Luc. 8, 14) 'τελεσφορεῖυ' (о последнем см. S. Feist, *Vgl. Wb. d. got. Spr.*, Leiden, 1939, 213). Учитывая последователь-

ность имен Перкун — Жворуна — Телявель во вставке о Совии и сравнивая ее с эпизодом, в котором участвуют Тор (сын *Fjǫrgyn*), *Rǫskva* и Тьяльви, можно прийти к вопросу об отношении *Rǫskva*'ы и Жворуны (последнее название, несомненно, испорчено и подверглось переосмыслению): **Vros-*. ... : **Svor-*. ... (> **Žvor-*. ...), где согласные элементы приведенных частей слова находятся в анаграмматическом отношении. Разумеется, гипотетично.

32. Ср. мотив убийства и оживления Тором своего козла («Снорри — Эдда»).

33. Ср. «Der vnglaubigen Sudauen ihrer bockheiligung mit sambt andern Ceremonien, so sie tzu brauchen gepflegeth», особенно «Wie sie den Bock heiligen».

34. Ср. балтийские аналогии к: ... *леса стоят дремучие, во тех огни горят, огни горят великие, ... он точит свой булатный нож, котел кипит горючий, возле котла козел стоит; хочет козла зарезати...*

35. Предлагаемое отождествление никак не предрешает вопроса об отношении к финск. и эст. *Kalev*, лит. *kalvis* (ср. лтш. *kalve*, но *kalẽjs*; и анаграмматически — белор. каваль).

On Balto-Scandinavian Connections in Mythology

On the basis of internal analysis, supported by some external parallels, the author reconstructs the Baltic mythologeme about the assistant of the thunder-god Perkūnas, the smith *Teljavelj*, who forged the sun and fixed it in the sky. The name *Teljavelj* (< **Telv-el-*) is then compared with that of the assistant of the Scandinavian thunder-god Þórr, *Þjálfi* (cp. the name of Þórrs mother *Fjǫrgyn*, which is compared with Perkūnas). Not only formal similarity but also a number of semantic features give grounds for regarding *Teljavelj* and *Þjálfi* as mythological personages identical in their principal characteristics (such as their being in the service of the thunder-god and their participation in the battle with his adversary; the motif of stolen arms and of creation of the heavenly bodies and their fixing in the sky; the relation of these gods to fire, the smithy, sacrifice, the goat etc.). The motifs connected with *Teljavelj* and *Þjálfi* can be more or less supported and even enlarged by reference to the Latvian, Estonian, Finnish and Byelorussian traditions. However, it is only the Scandinavian and Lithuanian mythological systems that have retained the old name of the principal personage. This similarity must be explained as not genetic, but from borrowing, which is quite natural under conditions of intensive exchange of cultural and material values between the areas surrounding the Baltic.

О. Н. ТРУБАЧЕВ

Этимологические заметки

1. Лит. *iki̇̀*

В Этимологическом словаре литовского языка Э. Френкеля литовское слово *iki̇̀*, выступающее в функции предлога с родительным падежом имени в значении 'до, вплоть до', этимологически возводится к индоевропейской местоименной основе *i̯o*.[1]. Там же автор повторяет свои прежние толкования случаев возможных контаминаций *li̇̀g* и *iki̇̀*, изложенные в специальной монографии[2]. Результатом означенной контаминации явилось, как полагает Френкель, новое *liki̇̀* в той же функции. Этому содействовало, по мнению ученого, естественное оглушение конечного звонкого в *li̇̀g* перед словами на начальный глухой. Впрочем, мысль о смешении литовского *li̇́g* (оглушенный вариант — *li̇́k*) и *iki̇̀* во всем существенном изложена еще в классическом труде Эндзелина[3].

Казалось бы, ничто не препятствует тому, чтобы эта точка зрения считалась единственно возможной, и это, повидимому, имеет место в современной балтистике (по крайней мере, мне пока неизвестны другие этимологии названного литовского предлога). Однако есть факты, ранее как будто не привлекавшиеся в связи с этими балтийскими образованиями и, тем не менее, способные поколебать традиционные воззрения на литовский предлог и на возможность предполагавшихся контаминаций. Я имею в виду кашубско-словинский предлог *lïk'i̇̀* (с родительным падежом) 'до, вплоть до'[4]. Ясно, что ни этот предлог весьма изолированного диалекта прибалтийских славян, ни примыкающее к нему кашубско-словинское наречие *lïk* 'всегда' (там же), удивительно похожие на якобы контаминационное литовское *li̇́k*, *li̇̀k* 'до', не допускают того тонкого объяснения, которое применялось вышеназванными учеными для литовского слова, по той простой причине, что ни основы *li̇̀g-* 'равный, прямой', ни сколько-нибудь подходящей формы от и.-е. *i̯o-* не знали ни прибалтийские, ни какие-либо другие славяне.

Существует другая реальная возможность толкования кашубско-словинского предлога *lïk'i̇̀* 'до', которая перспективна еще и потому, что подходит, как мне кажется, и для литовского предлога *iki̇̀* 'до' и *liki̇̀* в том же значении. Следует оговорить, что проникновение из литовского языка в кашубско-словинский, по всей видимости, исключено. Остается налицо разительная близость формы и значения литовского слова и кашубско-словинского слова, которую надлежит объяснить. Наиболее вероятным кажется мне заимствование из немецкого, где есть богатая значениями группа слов с общим корнем: нижненемецкие формы *licken* и подобные 'быть похожим, походить'[5], ср. далее приставочные др.-сакс. *gilik(o)*, нидерл. *gelijk* (при нововерхненемецком литературном *gleich* 'равный, одинаковый'[6]), наконец шведское *lik*, датское *lig*, др.-исл. *likr* 'равный, одинаковый, вероятный, хороший, полезный'[7]. Интересно отметить, вслед за названными известными словарями, дальнейшее родство этого германского **lika-* и литовского *lýgus* 'равный, ровный'. В формальном отношении наиболее близко кашубско-словинскому *lïk'ï* 'до' нижненемецкое диалектное (прусское) *licken* (см. выше), особенно, если иметь в виду краткость корневого гласного и наличие глухого взрывноко *k*. Можно сказать, что оно же близко нашему слову и семантически и, хотя мы не можем пока указать абсолютно точного немецкого прототипа данного прибалтийско-славянского диалектизма, все же основное значение немецкой лексики — 'равный, одинаковый, быть похожим' — настолько емко и прежде всего — столь близко к идее сравнения, приближения (вспомним хотя бы оттенки англ. anything *like* ... 'что-то *около*'), что предположение о заимствовании из соответствующей немецкой диалектной служебной формы представляется вполне реальным. Вероятно оно и в географическом плане: достаточно вспомнить положение словинского реликтового диалекта накануне его ассимиляции среди местных немецких диалектов.

Итак, есть основания думать, что кашубско-словинское *lïk'ï* (предлог с родительным падежом) 'до' произошло в результате заимствования близкого по форме немецкого диалектного (plattdeutsch) служебного слова со значением приближения. Из того же или аналогичного нижненемецкого источника произошла, видимо, и часть называвшихся выше литовских форм, прежде всего — лит. *likì*, которое, как наиболее полную форму, я считаю, вопреки известной точке зрения, первоначальным, в то время как более краткое *ikì* обязано этой своей краткостью как раз своей роли проклитики. Обратное умозаключение, мне кажется, было бы трудно доказать. Семантические и фонетические особенности этих литовских форм могут быть объяснены точно так же, как и в случае с кашубско-словинским (выше).

Наряду с этим не подлежит сомнению исконность литовского *lýg* и латышского *lidz* (в синонимичном значении 'до'), родственных лит. *lýgus* 'равный', о котором уже приходилось упоминать. Наблюдаемое при этом в данной группе предлогов своеобразное столкновение двух разнородных продолжений индоевропейского *lĭg- — исконнобалтийского lýg и относительно поздно заимствованного, по-видимому, из нижненемецкого в литовский likì — не такой уж редкий случай, как можно было бы подумать на первых порах. Достаточно сослаться на общеизвестный в сравнительном языкознании пример сосуществования исконноиндоевропейского -medùs — и заимствованного германского -mìdus — названия меда в литовском языке.

2. Лит. pliẽnas

Литовское название стали, родственное однозначным латышскому и древнепрусскому словам (лтш. pliens, др.-прусск. playnis), до сих пор как будто не имеет этимологии[8]. Правда, Френкель в своем названном словаре цитирует сближение Траутмана с др.-исл. fleinn 'крюк, острие', др.-англ. flán 'багор, острие, копье', но его собственное отношение к этому сравнению можно охарактеризовать как молчаливо сдержанное. Специальные работы последних лет на самом различном языковом материале показали, что этимологизация такой специфической лексики как названия стали может быть успешной лишь при условии учёта технологических особенностей процесса изготовления стали, которые имели важнейшее культурное значение и не могли, хотя бы косвенно, не отразиться на формировании соответствующей лексики. Между прочим, это первое условие (внимание к моментам материальной культуры при исследовании терминов материальной культуры) важно также в плане лингвистической методологии, так как логически подводит нас к необходимости учитывать второе, уже чисто лингвистическое условие — не приступать к иноязычным, отдаленнородственным сближениям, прежде чем не обследована ситуация внутри данного языка и его соответствующей лексики с требуемой полнотой.

Лит. pliẽnas 'сталь', по моему мнению, самым ближайшим образом родственно таким литовским словам как plėnis, мн. plėnys, pléinė 'пепел, пленка на тлеющих углях', plėnėti, pléinėti 'покрываться пленкой пепла, золы (о тлеющих углях)', лтш. plēne 'белая пленка пепла на угольях', plienis 'пепел', др.-прусск. plieynis 'пепел, зола'. Все это семейство разнообразных слов с основой pl-/pel- и разными расширителями включает также названия пленки, плевы, шелухи, мякины и прочие близкие[9]. Как видно, среди этих форм можно без труда указать практически полностью тождественные, вплоть до апофонической ступени огласовки корня, нашему названию стали — pliẽnas. Что же касается реальной стороны, то достаточно сослаться на то, что среди старинных, традиционных способов получения стали видное место занимал способ получения из окалины, путем последовательного нагревания, охлаждения и *отделения чешуек окалины*[10].

Notes

1. E. Fraenkel, *Litauisches etymologisches Wörterbuch* I, 183.
2. E. Fraenkel, *Syntax der litauischen Postpositionen und Präpositionen*, Heidelberg, 1920, 232–.
3. И. Эндзелин, Латышские предлоги, I. Юрьев, 1905, 77.
4. F. Lorentz, *Pomoranisches Wörterbuch* I, 459.
5. H. Frischbier, *Preussisches Wörterbuch. Ost- und westpreussische Provinzialismen in alphabetischer Folge*, II, Berlin, 1883, 26.
6. Kluge–Götze[15] 270.
7. H. S. Falk und A. Torp, *Norw.-dänisches etym. Wb.* I[2], 642–643.
8. E. Fraenkel, *Litauisches etymologisches Wörterbuch* I, 623: «Etymologie nicht sicher».
9. E. Fraenkel I, 615, 616; K. Būga, *Rinktiniai raštai* I, Vilnius, 1958, 288.
10. Ср. работу: И. Г. Денисов. Уклад 'сталь', Этимология, 1966. М., 1968, 159 и след., особенно стр. 163; там же прочая литература.

Etymological Notes

Lith. *iki* 'till, to' is considered to be an allegro abbreviation of a fuller form *liki* that is a loanword of Low German origin; the same origin is obvious for Slavic (Pomeranian) preposition *lik'i* 'till, to').

Lith. *pliēnas* 'steel' (previously lacking a probable etymology) is held to be connected with the lexical data signifying 'ashes, scale'.

VINCAS URBUTIS

LA. *lasmenis*

Žodis *lasmenis* 'praperša, prasravas, atavaras (neužšąlanti vieta upėje ar ežere)', nors ir nebūdamas labai dažnas ir visiems įprastas (tai daugiausia pareina nuo jo specialios reikšmės), pasitaiko ne vienoje latvių tarmėje ir kartu įeina į literatūrinės kalbos leksiką : jį pateikia daugelis dabartinių latvių kalbos žodynų, ir be jokių nuorodų, kad jis turėtų tarminį ar šiaip kokį stilistinį atspalvį. Dėl šio žodžio kilmės dabar visuotinai laikomasi nuomonės, jog tai skolinys iš suomių kalbų. Bene pirmasis jį įtarė esant paskolintą iš estų *lasme* A. Leskynas[1]. Tik šis A. Leskyno (ir žymiai vėliau taip pat galvojusio H. Ojansū) aiškinimas duotas J. Endzelyno–K. Miūlenbacho žodyne (ME, II, 424). Po to šitoks aiškinimas jau kartojamas kaip visiškai tikras, nekeliantis abejonių[2]. Ir vis dėlto, geriau įsigilinus į žodžio bylą, nesunku įsitikinti, kad jis nėra joks skolinys.

Jau minėtame žodyne (ME, II, 424, 454) ir jo papildymuose (EH, I, 721, 735) pateikti tokie lokalizuoti rūpimo žodžio variantai: *lasmenis* (Zālīte, Lazduona, Birzgale — jei čia reikia ieškoti „Linden in Kurl.", Bauska — jei žodyne cituojamam V. Plūduoniui tas variantas buvo žinomas iš jo gimtinės), *lāsmenis* (Pilskalne), *lasminis* (Līksna; toks variantas jau randamas J. Langės 1773 m. žodyne, iš kur jį su reikšmės atliepiniu v. 'Wasserkolk' įsidėjo į savo 1789 m. žodyną ir G. F. Stenderis), *lasmanis* (Ādaži), *lesmenis* (Zasa, Augškurzeme — vadinasi, kurioje nors iš žiemgališkų šnektų), *lesmins* (Zasa). Pastarųjų dviejų variantų šaknies -e- yra antrinis, atsiradęs tikriausiai dėl regresyvinės distancinės asimiliacijos: *lasmenis* > *lesmenis* (dar toliau morfologiškai perdirbta į *lesmins*), tad dėl žodžio kilmės mažai ką sako. Panašiai yra su *nuolasmenis, nuolasmanis* 'ledo ruožas palei krantą, kai upės vidurys dar neužšalęs', žinomais iš naujesnių raštų (ME, II, 808): juodu veikiausiai bus vėlesni priešdėlio *nuo-* dariniai iš rūpimo žodžio.

Žodynas registruoja tik du ryškesnio nukrypimo nuo įprastinės reikšmės 'praperša' atvejus: apytikriai lokalizuotasis *lesmenis* (Augškurzeme) duotas reikšme (gal irgi apytikre?) 'upės giluma', o *lasmenis* iš Lazduonos pateiktas ir 'praperšos', ir 'aketės (žvejoti)' reikšme. Pastarąją reikšmę tiek dėl jos retumo, tiek ir dėl to, kad reikšmės raida 'praperša (natūrali kiaurymė lede)' > 'aketė (iškirsta skylė lede)' lengviau suprantama, negu priešinga kryptimi (plg. ir r. полынья 'praperša' > trm. 'aketė'), reikia laikyti antrine. Vadinasi, jau vien dėl reikšmės skirtumo la. *lasmenis* 'praperša' kildinimas iš e. *lasme*, reiškiančio 'didelė keturkampė skylė lede (tinklams įleisti)'[3], yra abejotinas.

Kita kliūtis tokiam kildinimui yra žodžių geografija. Grupuojant skolinius iš suomių kalbų pagal geografiją, la. *lasmenis* skiriamas prie netipiško išplitimo žodžių[4]. Reikia pridurti, kad ir toje grupėje jis yra vienišas (kiek panašiau paplitęs la. *āmrija* irgi vargu ar laikytinas skoliniu iš suomių kalbų): šiaipjau būdamas pažįstamas iš įvairių šnektų, ypač pietinių, jis visai neaptiktas šiaurėje, šnektose arčiau Estijos. Savo ruožtu tariamasis prototipas e. *lasme* tėra, matyt, neplačiai žinomas tarminis darinys (plg. e. *laskma* 'leisti'): F. J. Vydemano žodyne jis nurodytas iš Pärnu šnektos (šiaurinių estų dialektų vakarinė tarmė).

Tradiciniam aiškinimui prieštarauja ir formos skirtumas: sunku suprasti, kodėl e. *lasme*, savo sandara gražiai sutikdamas su fonologinėmis bei morfologinėmis pačių latvių žodžių ypatybėmis (plg. la. *druosme, prasme, versme* ir pan.), skolinant turėtų būti perdirbtas (išplėstas priesaga). Skolinio išplėtimas kuria nors produktyvia savo priesaga, leidžiantis atsirasti priesaginiams skolinio variantams, šiaipjau, žinoma, nėra visai neįmanomas, bet tam reikalingos palankios sąlygos. Svarbiausia iš jų — kad skolinys dėl savo reikšmės įeitų į griežtai apibrėžtą semantinę žodžių grupę, kurios nariams kartu būdinga vis ta pati priesaga, plg. latvių kalbos vėjų pavadinimus *àustrenis, rîtenis, sãmenis, sàusenis, tãrpenis* ... ir pagal juos *ĩdenis* šalia *ĩds, ide, idis, idus* (< lyb. ar e. *ida*), uogų pavadinimus *avenes, cũcenes, kazenes, mẽllenes, upenes* ... ir *zust(e)renes, sust(a)renes* šalia *zusteres, zustaras, susteres, sustęri* (< e. *sõstar*). Šitaip atsirasti priesagai žodyje *lasmenis* panašių palankių sąlygų lyg ir nematyti; čia šalimais nėra pažįstamas nė laukiamasis pirminis priesaga neišplėstas variantas, kuris tokiais atvejais tarmėse paprastai dar pasitaiko.

Lengva pastebėti, kad la. *lasmenis* (*lãsmenis, lesmenis*) : *lasminis* (*lesmins*) : *lasmanis* savo morfologine sandara ir jos įvairavimu nesiskiria nuo priesagos -men- (buv. priebalsinio kamieno) daiktavardžių dabartinių atstovų latvių kalboje, dažnokai turinčių atliepinių lietuvių kalboje su -muõ (gen. sg. -meñs), kartais jau irgi įvairiai perdirbtų, pvz.: la. *ēdmenis, ēdminis* (*ēdmiņš*), *ẽdmanis* 'masalas, prievilas, jaukas', lie. *ėdmė̃nė* (-*enė̃*), *ė̃dmenys* (gen. -*nų̃*, -*nių̃*) pl. 'maistas, valgis, ėdesys'; la. *juosmenis, juosminis* 'pusiaujas, apjuostas', lie. *juosmuõ, juosmenỹs* (*juosmenis*), *juosmẽnė* 't. p.'; la. *lekmenis, lekminis* 'liūnas, klampynė', lie. *lekmẽnė* 't. p.', *lakmenà* 'purvynas' (plg. lie. *lēkausis, lekaũsis* = la. *Įękàusis* 'nulėpausis', la. *nùoļekt* 'nuleipti, nulepti'); la. *liêkmaņi* (*lìekmaņas*) 'kogaliai; atlaikai', lie. *liekmuo, liekmenys* (pl.), *liekmena* 'atlaikas, liekana'; la. *šķiêmenis*[2], *šķìemene*[2], *šķìeminis*[2] (ir kt.) 'toks tarpas šaudyklei praeiti audžiant, žiotys; ant riestuvo dedama skala (ir kt.)', lie. *skiemuõ* 't. p.; audeklo gijų pluoštelis'; la. *tesmenis* (*tesmens*), *tesminis* = lie. *tešmuõ* (plg. lie. *tēšia, tēšti* 'tvinkti prieš apsiveršiuojant'); la. *zeľmenis* (*zelmenis, zèlmenis*[2]), *zeľminis* (*zèlminis*[2]) = lie. *žélmuõ* (pl. *žélmenys, žeľmenys* ir *žeľmens*); ir kt. Su *lasmenis* bei jo variantais dėl žymimų realijų kaimynystės dar verta sugretinti la. *līksmenis* (*līksmenis*[2]), *līksminis, līksmanis* 'klampus, linguojantis ežero krantas, liūnas' (siejama su la. *līguôt* = lie. *lingúoti*) ir (tas pats žodis, tik su iškritusiu -k-?) *līsmenis* (*līsmęns*), *līsmins* 't. p.'; skirtingai nuo ankstesnių pavyzdžių su grynu *-men-*, čia turim kontaminacinį sufiksą *-smen-*, dėl kurio dar plg. la. *męsmęns* (ar *mesmenis?*) šalia tos pat reikšmės lie. *metmuõ*, ppr. pl. *mẽtmen(y)s*.

La. *lasmenis*, kaip ir kiti minėti žodžiai su *-men-*, pasirodo, irgi turi savo tikslų atliepinį lietuvių kalboje. Tai lie. trm. *lašmuõ* (acc. *lãšmenį*) 'vieta ežere, kur įteka ar išteka upelis'. Didysis lietuvių kalbos žodynas (LKŽ, VII, 170) duoda tik šį variantą. P. Skardžius, remdamasis to žodyno kartoteka, yra jų pateikęs daugiau[5]. Pagal išgales patikrinus bei papildžius ankstesnę informaciją, galima teigti tikrai esant šiuos variantus (jų visų reikšmė maždaug ta pati): *lašmuõ* (gen. *lašmeñs*, nom. pl. *lãšmens*) (Palūšė), (gen. *lãšmenio*, nom. pl. *lãšmenys*) (Ignalina, Palūšė, Kaltanėnai, ret. Linkmenys), *lašmenỹs* (Strazdai — 8 km. į vakarus nuo Ignalinos, Kirdeikiai, Linkmenys, Kuktiškės); plg. dar *palašmenỹs* 'vieta, kur iš ežero išteka upelis' (Labanoras). Nepatikimas, nepatvirtintos formos ir reikšmės, lieka *lašmēnė* 'aketė' iš Kaltanėnų, LKŽ redakcijai užrašytas neva iš dainos, tačiau, kaip rodo lapelyje pateiktos pora eilučių: „Kad lašmenėn nenuļistum, Su vaikeliu nenuskįstum", ta „daina" — tai tik kiek iškreiptas iš Kirdeikių kilusio poeto bei švietėjo S. Gimžausko prieš šimtą metų atskira knygele paskelbtas eiliuotas kūrinėlis, kuriame tos dvi eilutės atrodo taip: „Kad laszmenin nė inlisti, Su wajkėlu nėnuskisti."[6]

Lie. *lašmuõ* (su variantais), nors dabar pažįstamas tiktai nedideliame rytų aukštaičių plote (Ignalinos ežerų rajone), negali būti paskolintas iš latvių — tam prieštarauja fonetika (lie. *-š-*), morfologija ir iš dalies geografija (arčiau Latvijos — ežeringame Zarasų krašte ir kitur — jis neaptiktas). Tad nėra abejonės, kad lie. *lašmuõ* ir la. *lasmenis* — sena tų kalbų bendrybė. Anksčiau minėti bendrieji dar aiškios darybos *-men-* žodžiai visi yra veiksmažodžių vediniai, tad iš veiksmažodžio tikriausiai bus padarytas ir šis. Tas veiksmažodis — tai lie. *lašéti*, la. *làsêt* (*lasêt*). Kad toks siejimas būtų galimas, jau yra nurodęs A. Leskynas, nors jis, neturėdamas vien tik la. *lasmenis* (*lasminis*), pirmenybę teikė, kaip sakyta, skolinimui. La. *lasmenis* kartu su lie. *lašéti* dar yra užsiminęs, ankstesnio aiškinimo, matyt, nepastebėjęs, J. Gerulis[7], tik ta jo užuomina irgi nesusilaukė vėlesnių la. *lasmenis* etimologizuotojų dėmesio. Semantiškai šalia reikšmės 'varvėti, sunktis' (gal iš dalies seniau ir 'sroventi') veiksmažodžio vedinys reikšme 'vieta ežere (ar upėje), kur nuolat sunkiasi, srovena ir todėl neužšąla vanduo' gana įmanomas. Be to, lie. *lašéti*, la. *lāsuôt* dar yra pažįstami reikšme 'blizgėti, spindėti, tviskėti, mirguliuoti' (dėl jos plg. lie. *láistyti*, r. переливáться), tad nėra visai negalima, kad, sudarant daiktavardį, turėtas prieš akis ledo praperšoje spindinčio (mirguliuojančio) vandens vaizdas, plg. v. (rytpr.) *Blänke* 'praperša, prasravas' (iš kur lie. trm. *bleňkis* 't. p.') šalia *blank* 'spindintis'. Formos atžvilgiu lie. *lašmuõ*, la. *lasmenis* (ir kt.) vedimas iš veiksmažodžio lie. *lašéti*, la. *làsêt* (*lasêt*) abejonių nekelia. Kaip papildomą patvirtinimą čia galima nurodyti paralelinį (matyt, žymiai vėlesnį) vedinį la. trm. *lasminis* 'laštakas; nuo stogo varvantis vanduo, lašinys' (EH, I, 721), kurio darybos ryšys su la. *làsêt* (*lasêt*) bei *làsuôt* (*lâsuôt*[2]) 'lašėti, varvėti' tebėra aiškiai matomas.

Geografiniai apeliatyvai, kaip žinia, neretai virsta tikriniais vietų vardais. Šiuo atveju iš tokių ypač svarbus yra dešiniojo Mūšos intako tarp Pakruojo ir Joniškėlio vardas *Lašmuõ* (ten esanti ir to paties vardo bala)[8] — jis rodo, kad bendrinis *lašmuõ* kadaise yra buvęs kur kas plačiau pažįstamas žodis.

Išnašos

1. A. Leskien, *Die Bildung der Nomina im Litauischen*, Leipzig, 1891, 419.

2. K. Aben, „Eesti ja liivi laene läti sõnavaras", *Emakeele seltsi aastaraamat*, III, Tallinn, 1957, 203; *Mūsdienu latviešu literārās valodas gramatika*, I, Rīgā, 1959, 105; V. J. Zeps, *Latvian and Finnic Linguistic Convergences*, Bloomington, 1962, 142.

3. F. J. Wiedemann, *Estnisch-deutsches Wörterbuch*[3], Dorpat, 1923, 461.

4. V. J. Zeps, *op. cit.*, 90.

5. P. Skardžius, *Lietuvių kalbos žodžių daryba*, Vilnius, 1943, 233 t., 237, 295.

6. [S. Gimžauskas], *Linkmenës*, [Leipcigas], 1870, 16.

7. G. Gerullis, *Die altpreußischen Ortsnamen*, Berlin u. Leipzig, 1922, 83.

8. A. Vanagas, „Ašmena, Lašmuo ir kiti panašios darybos upėvardžiai", *Lietuvių kalbotyros klausimai*, IV, 230.

LATV. *lasmenis*

Latvian *lasmenis* 'unfrozen patch in the midst of ice on a river or lake' is attested in various dialects except the North. It is also used in literary Latvian. According to the generally accepted interpretation, suggested by

A. Leskien, it is a loan-word, going back to dialectal Estonian *lasme* 'a big square hole in the ice for a net'. Such an explanation is not confirmed by the meaning, geographical distribution and morphological structure of *lasmenis*. The strongest objection arises from the fact that this Latvian word has a cognate in Lithuanian dialects in the form *lašmuõ* (acc. sing. *lãšmeni̧*) 'a place in a lake, where a brook flows in or out and where in winter the water is usually not frozen'. Lith. *lašmuõ* is now a rarely used dialecticism, known only around Ignalina in Upper Lithuania. Earlier the word must have been used in a wider area, as is indicated by the river-name *Lašmuõ* in north central Lithuania. Latv. *lasmenis*, dialectal Lith. *lašmuõ* (both existing also in later morphological variants) can be easily explained as East Baltic consonantal *-men-* stem derivatives of Latv. *làsêt* (*lasêt*) 'to trickle, to fall in drops', Lith. *lašéti* 'id.; to glitter'.

ANDRÉ VAILLANT

Le suffixe baltique -*ingas*

Ce suffixe est rapproché (Vondrák, *Vergl. slav. Gramm.*, I², 628) du suffixe russe -*jága*, dont l'histoire n'est pas claire et qui est à côté de -(*j*)*úga* et -*ýga*. Mais il n'est rien dit, ni chez Leskien, *Bildung der Nomina*, 520–530, ni chez Endzelin, *Lett. Gramm.*, 271–274, de sa curieuse ressemblance avec le suffixe -*ing*- si important en germanique, qui a donné au slave un bon nombre de mots d'emprunt en -*ę(d)zĭ*, et qui est une des origines du suffixe r. -*jága*, puisque *rabotjága* 'homme laborieux' est le vieux-russe *robotjaz*- 'esclave', v. pol. *robociądz* (*RÉS*, XVIII, 78).

Sans doute il y a une différence entre les suffixes du germanique et du baltique : le germanique -*ing*- forme des substantifs, et le baltique -*ingas* des adjectifs. Mais la séparation n'est pas telle entre l'adjectif et le substantif : 'pauvre' est les deux à la fois en français, et ailleurs. En vieux haut allemand, *arm* est adjectif et *arming* est le substantif qui en est le dérivé, mais une autre langue qui emprunterait les mots ne serait pas forcée de faire la distinction : le slave *voinikŭ* 'un guerrier', nettement substantif dans le système du slave, a donné en roumain l'adjectif *voinic* 'brave'. Et ce qui montre que le baltique répond à l'opposition germanique de *arm*, adj., et *arming*, subst., mais en confondant adjectif et substantif, c'est que le suffixe -*ingas* lui sert surtout à former des élargissements d'adjectifs : lit. *teisìngas* 'juste' de *teisùs*, *vertìngas* 'digne' de *veŕtas*. Le vieux-prussien *naunīngs* 'novice', sur *nauns* 'nouveau', est substantif comme *Neuling* qu'il traduit, avec -*ling*, sur *neu*, qui est la forme sous laquelle v. h. a. -*ing* est resté productif en allemand.

Ainsi il paraît clair que le baltique a emprunté -*ing*- au germanique en en faisant un suffixe d'adjectifs, tandis que le slave lui empruntait des substantifs, et un suffixe de substantifs, sur base slave, qui n'est attesté sûrement que par v. r. *robotjazĭ*, mais parce qu'il appartenait à la langue expressive, et qui s'est continué dans r. -*jága* de la langue familière ou vulgaire. Le suffixe sl. -*ĭskŭ*, lit. -*iškas*, est également pris au germanique *-iska-*, qui l'a donné d'autre part au roman, ital. -*esco*, etc.

The Suffix -*ingas* in Baltic

The function of -*ing*- in adjectives and substantives is discussed in Baltic, Slavic and Germanic.

A. VALECKIENĖ

Dėl lietuvių kalbos bevardės giminės būdvardžiu

Lietuvių kalboje nėra bevardės giminės daiktavardžių, bet vartojami bevardės giminės būdvardžiai. Jie sudaro šalia vyriškosios bei moteriškosios giminės būdvardžių reguliarų tipą, nors jų daryba tam tikrais atvejais yra ribota[1], plg.: *gĕras, gerà, gĕra, žãlias, žalià, žãlia, gražùs, gražì, gražù.* Iš kilmės šios formos yra (*i*)*a*-, *u*- kam. sustabarėję vn. vard.-gal. linksniai[2], kurių galinis balsis, kaip pastaruoju laiku manoma, yra grynas kamienas[3]. Atitinkamas formas turi kai kurie įvardžiai bei skaitvardžiai, neveikiamieji esamojo ir būtojo laiko dalyviai ir vadinamasis reikiamybės dalyvis, pvz.: *vìsa, šìta, kìta, víena, pìrma, dìrbama, sakýta, rašýtina,* plg. kitokios darybos bevardės giminės įvardžių formas *taĩ, šìtai*[4].

Bevardės giminės būdvardžiams būdingiausia predikatyvinė vartosena, bet visiškai kitokia, negu vyriškosios bei moteriškosios giminės formų. Pastarosios predikatyviškai vartojamos asmeniniame sakinyje, pvz.: *Namas gražus.* Atributyvinė jų vartosena yra šios predikatyvinės vartosenos transformacija, plg.: *Gražus namas*[5]. Tuo tarpu bev. g. formos predikatyviškai paprastai vartojamos beasmeniuose arba tokiuose asmeniniuose sakiniuose, iš kurių atitinkamos transformacijos negalimos. Čia jos reiškia ne pačią daikto ypatybę, bet su fizinėmis, psichinėmis bei kitomis ypatybėmis susijusią būseną. Išskirtini tokie pagrindiniai šios vartosenos modeliai.

1) Nimp (yra) (+Adv, Sap)[6], pvz.:
Tamsu, nors į akį durk. ŽemR I 208. *Kur ten nebus šlãpia!* Pg. *Dabar jau kìta.* Krn. *Negimus neskaudu, nemirus negraudu.* B. *Tarp kalnų, miške skardù.* Jabl.

2) Nimp (yra)+Sd, pvz.:
Neturiu matušės, kaip ma liūdna. JD 93. *Bėda biednam, šalta nuogam.* LTR (Šmk). *Pasidarė vienai klaikù.* Rk. *Gilù* (=skaudu) *širdžiai, kad negauni geistino.* J.

Būsenos subjektą (paprastai asmenį ar asmens dalį) reiškiantis naudininkas[7] į vardininką netransformuojamas, t. y. beasmenio sakinio negalima pakeisti asmeniniu, pvz.: *tėvui klaiku* (nepakeičiama) *tėvas klaikus.* Šių tipų sakiniai gali sutapti tik dėl tam tikros būdvardžių leksinės reikšmės, pvz.: *Man liūdna* yra beveik lygu *Aš liūdnas*, nors pastarasis nelabai vartojamas.

3) Nimp (yra)+Vinf, pvz.:

Senam sunkù gyvent. Skp. *Geru arkliu ramù važiuot.* Plš. *Čia vargù gulėti.* Pc. *Lijo, tai gardù miegot buvo.* Gs. *Gēra tau kalbėt, kai pačiai nereikia.* Skp. *Šie sakiniai taip pat yra beasmeniai.* Bev. g. forma ir bendratis predikatyvinio junginio nesudaro, jos abi sudaro tik tarinį. Tai mums patvirtina ta aplinkybė, kad šių formų junginį dažnai galima pakeisti atributyviniu junginiu su veiksmažodiniu daiktavardžiu, kur būdvardžio vyr. g. forma eina pastarojo daiktavardžio atributu, pvz.: *Senam sunku gyventi* = *Senam sunkus gyvenimas* ir pan. Toks bev. g. formų vartosenos tipas yra labai darus. Tik retais atvejais bevardės giminės ir bendraties formų junginį, pasakytą tam tikra intonacija, galima laikyti predikatyviniu, kur veiksnys yra bendratis, pvz.: *Negražu smaližauti.* Kair. Čia bendratį galima pakeisti vardininku, pvz.: *Negražu smaližauti* = *Negražu smaližavimas* (junginiai predikatyviniai), bet tokiu atveju bevardės giminės negalima pakeisti derinama forma, t. y. pasakymas *Negražus smaližavimas* ≠ (nelygus) *Negražu smaližauti.*

4) Nimp (yra)+Sn, pvz.:

Malonu žentas, gaila varškės. Erž. *Man baisiai neskanù žalias kiaušinis.* Skp. *Galva galvai nelýgu.* Skp. *Barščiai vienu vardu, bet ne visi gardù.* Vl. *Nieks nemíela.* Kpč.

Šie sakiniai asmeniniai. Tačiau veiksniu einantis vardininkas nesuderintas su predikato forma ir jis nėra būsenos subjektas. Tai matyti iš to, kad tokiuose sakiniuose bev. g. formą ne visada galima pakeisti suderinta vyr. ar mot. g. forma, pvz.: *Malonu žentas* nepakeičiama *Malonus žentas*, nes jis pats gali būti visai nemalonus, jis malonus tik kitam asmeniui. Tik dėl tam tikrų būdvardžių leksinės reikšmės abiejų formų vartosena gali sutapti, pvz.: *Galva galvai nelygu* = *Galva galvai nelygi.*

Kad tokiose konstrukcijose vardininkas reiškia (ar bent iš pradžių reiškė) ne būsenos subjektą, bet objektą, rodo retais atvejais pasitaikančios atitinkamos konstrukcijos su netiesioginiu linksniu — kilmininku (žr. 5-ąjį modelį). Objekto reikšmę taip pat turi vardininkas atitinkamose konstrukcijose su neveikiamųjų dalyvių bev. g. formomis, pvz.: *Senų miškai mylėta.* Baran AŠ 31[8]. *Darželis atitverta.* Vrnv. Pakeitus šias konstrukcijas veikiamosiomis, vardininkas virsta galininku, plg.: *Seni miškus mylėjo. Darželį atitvėrė.*

Be objekto reikšmės, tam tikros leksinės reikšmės vardininkas minėtojo tipo konstrukcijose turi aplinkybinio linksnio reikšmę, jis pakeičiamas galininku, reiškiančiu būsenos aplinkybę, plg.: *Nelinksma man šitas vakarėlis*. Krėv D 191 = *Nelinksma man šitą vakarėlį*.

5) Nimp (yra) + Sg.

Paprastai šį modelį sudaro bev. g. formos, reikalaujančios objekto kilmininko pagal savo leksinę reikšmę (dažniausiai reiškiančios kiekį, kartais ir kitų leksinių reikšmių), pvz.: *Gyveniamas pilnas, turto apstù!* Lkš. *Čia gilù* (*v*)*andenio.* Rš. *Dienos jau dabar ilga.* Kp. *Vilkui parako negaila, o kiškiui neverta.* Myk-Put S I 19 (plg. (*ne*)*vertas garbės*). *Nieko nenumanu* (plg. *nieko nenumano*).

Tačiau kartais pasitaiko šio modelio konstrukcijų, kuriose objekto kilmininko negalima paaiškinti būdvardžio valdymo ypatybe, pvz.: *Per gėra vaiko — išmiega pernakt, nei nesurėkia.* Ds. *Negi lýgu žmogaus!* Ds. Šį kilmininką galima laikyti relevantišku bev. g. formų sintaksiniam kontekstui nustatyti. Jis lygus vardininkui 4-ajame modelyje, plg. *Negi lygu žmogus.* Tuo tarpu pirmasis kilmininkas, lemiamas bev. g. formų leksinių valdymo ypatybių, čia nėra relevantiškas[9]. Konstrukcijos su relevantišku kilmininku retos ir gana senoviškos. Jos atitinka bev. g. formoms būdingą beasmenę vartoseną.

Visais minėtaisiais atvejais predikatyvinės bev. g. formos, skirtingai nuo vyr. bei mot. g. predikatyviškai vartojamų formų, negali būti susietos su atributyviniais būdvardžiais ir dėl to taip pat su bevardės giminės daiktavardžiais (jeigu jie buvo, kaip prūsų, ir lietuvių kalboje, žr. toliau). Šios formos pagal savo sintaksinę vartoseną greičiau atitinka beasmenius veiksmažodžius, juo labiau, kad jungtis prie bev. g. formų nebūtina. Beasmeniai veiksmažodžiai vartojami visais minėtais atvejais, kaip bev. g. formos, plg.:

Temsta. Lauke šąla. Niekad jam neganėjo. Nusibodo laukti. Skauda koja (*ir koją*). *Užteko duonos*[10].

Dėl savo sintaksinės struktūros tapatumo beasmeniai veiksmažodžiai ir bev. g. būdvardžiai dažnai pasitaiko toje pat sintaksinėje pozicijoje pagrečiui, plg.: *Kur meilu, ten akys, kur sopa, ten pirštai.* LTR (Slk). *Kur tik klausai, vis linksma: šlama, ūžia siaudžia!* Baran AŠ 4.

Visa tai, kas aukščiau pasakyta, leidžia sieti minėtąsias predikatyviškai vartojamas lietuvių bev. g. formas su kitų ide. kalbų predikatyvais arba vadinamosios būsenos kategorijos[11] atitinkamais žodžiais, plg. rus. *мне скучно, весело, стыдно,* vok. *Es ist kalt, Mir ist warm* ir kt.[12] Rusų kalboje iš kilmės šios formos su -*o* taip pat dažniausiai bevardės giminės. Nuo pastarųjų formų lietuvių bev. g. minėtosios formos skiriasi nebent didesniu produktyvumu. Jų vartosenos modeliai iš esmės sutampa. Pvz., slavų, kaip ir lietuvių kalboje, prie atitinkamų bev. g. būdvardžių, be subjekto naudininko, labai būdingas infinityvas (plg. s. sl. *Нѣсть добро отѧти хлѣба чѧдомъ и поврѣщи и пьсомъ*)[13], taip pat žinomos konstrukcijos su vardininku (plg. rus.: *Ум хорошо, а два лучше того*)[14]. Atitinkamų pastarosios rūšies pavyzdžių, kur predikatyvinė bev. g. forma nesuderinta su veiksnio forma, randama ir sen. graikų bei lotynų kalbose[15].

Rusų kalboje, kur yra bev. g. daiktavardžių, šalia minėtųjų būseną reiškiančių bev. g. būdvardžio formų taip pat vartojamos su bev. g. daiktavardžiais suderintos trumposios (neįvardžiuotinės) bev. g. būdvardžių formos, morfologiškai tapačios su pirmosiomis būdvardžių formomis. Tačiau tarp šių abiejų būdvardžio formų, kaip nurodo V. Vinogradovas, dažnai nėra nei gramatinio, nei semantinio-leksinio paralelizmo. Plg. *Хорошо на душе* ir *Мое здоровье хорошо*. Čia *хорошо* abiejuose sakiniuose yra homoniminės formos[16]. Tai dar kartą patvirtina, kad nederinamų predikatyvinių bev. g. formų ir derinamų būdvardžio formų sintaksinė prigimtis skirtinga; pirmosios neturi jokio sintaksinio ryšio su bev. g. daiktavardžiais.

Nederinamų bev. g. formų vieta lietuvių kalbos sistemoje ir jų santykis si kitų ide. kalbų atitinkamomis formomis leidžia manyti, kad nurodytoji predikatyvinė bev. g. formų vartosena yra labai sena: šios formos siekia tokį ide. nominalinio sakinio tipą, kai predikato forma nebuvo derinama su subjekto forma (pastaroji buvo netiesioginis linksnis), panašiai kaip beasmenių veiksmažodžių, dabar turinčių 3 asm. formą, pirminė nominalinė vartosena[17]. Kad minėtosiose konstrukcijose būsenos objektas iš pradžių, be vardininko, taip pat buvo reiškiamas ir netiesioginiu linksniu, liudytų liet. *per gera vaiko*, nors objekto vardininkas taip pat yra labai senas[18].

Be minėtųjų predikatyvinės vartosenos atvejų, bev. g. formos lietuvių kalboje gana dažnai vartojamos daiktavardiškai vietoj subjekto ir objekto linksnių, pvz.: *Ir platu su kraštu, ir gilu su dugnu*. B. *Iš sena gimsta jauna*. (Kp) Jabls 35. *Iš blogo žmogaus dōra nelauk*. Jnš (LKŽ II 610).

Su substatyvinėmis bev. g. formomis sudaromi predikatyviniai junginiai, pvz.: *Gēra meñka, blōga daug*. Vvs. *Vìsa buvo pigù*. Šr. *Dvinýta nestìpra*. Slm. *Áugalota nebréndalota*. Lkm. Čia tarp abiejų bevardės giminės formų yra lygiai toks pat derinimas, kaip tarp atitinkamų vyr. bei mot. g. formų. Suderintų bev. g. formų predikatyviniai junginiai, taip pat kaip vyr. bei mot. g. formų, gali būti transformuojami į atributyvinius, plg.: *Visa yra gera* ir *Visa gera, visa kita*. Šios rūšies atributyviniai junginiai gana dažni senuosiuose raštuose, plg.: *Neś kas turi Wießpati Diewa, taffái turi wiffa giara*. DP 24. *Vis pikt eft pergaleghis*. Mž 271. *norint kita wifsa turetu ir ftebuklingu dowanu pilnas butu*. SP I 119, plg. dar: *Wifa nauda aba giera / ku ažudirba*. SP I 322[19].

Iš kitų bevardės giminės formų darybos atžvilgiu išsiskiriančios *taĩ,* *tataĩ, ŝìtai* vartojamos tik substantyviškai. Plg. su šiomis formomis predikatyvinius junginius ir jų transformas — atributyvinius junginius: *tay ira* *viſa ir Diewo žodiy.* SP I 354 ir *tatái wiſsa ape mame* (=mane) *pildzias.* DP 19, *ąnt kurio tái wiſa vzgriús.* DP 8. Turėdamas predikato funkciją, *taĩ* antrinis, plg. *kaſǵ tatai butú.* DP 7[20].

Gana plačiai vartojamos substantyvinės bev. g. formos, dėl kurių galima derinamųjų bev. g. formų vartosena, yra specifiškos lietuvių kalbai, nors jos taip pat nėra visiškai naujos. Iš kai kurių samplaikų su šios rūšies bev. g. formomis jau yra susidariusių įvardžių, plg.: *visa kas > viskas.*

Reikia pasakyti, kad substantyvinių bev. g. būdvardžių vartosena atitinka substantyvinių vyr. g. būdvardžių vartoseną. Dabar daugelis junginių su šiomis formomis vartojami lygiagrečiai, plg.: *kas nauja* ir *kas naujo,* *ką gera* ir *ką gero* (reč. *ką gerą*)*, visa ko* ir *viso ko, niekas kitas* (ir *niekas kito* DP 8) ir *niekas kita* ir pan.[21] Plg. dar: *Beda tiemus / kurie wadina pikta* *gieru / á giera piktu.* SP I 115. *adunt pikto łynk tumes o giera daritume.* SP I 6[22].

Substantyvinių bei su jomis suderintų bev. g. formų nei sintaksiškai, nei reikšmiškai negalima susieti su aukščiau minėtomis nederinamomis predikatyvinėmis bev. g. formomis[23], plg. dar: *Čia man gera* (būsenos reikšmė) ir *Visa yra gera, Čia nėra nieko gera* (apibendrinta kokybės reikšmė, būsenos reikšmės čia nėra).

Visa tai rodo, kad šios rūšies bev. g. formos gali būti kongruencijos su bev. g. daiktavardžiais liekana. (Kad baltų kalbose buvo bev. g. daiktavardžiai, liudija ir prūsų kalbos medžiaga, plg. 4-ąją išnašą).

Čia dar reikia pridurti, kad negausiai vartojamos ir linkusios stabarėti bev. g. formos atributyvinėje pozicijoje nėra visiškai tapačios su derinamomis vyr. bei mot. g. būdvardžių formomis atitinkamoje pozicijoje. Tai lengvai įrodoma substitucijos būdu. Atributyviškai vartojami vyr. ir mot. g. būdvardžiai yra priklausomi nuo daiktavardžių ir neturėdami substantyvinės funkcijos, negali sakinyje eiti daiktavardžio substitutais, t. y. *Gražus* *namas stovi* negalima išskaidyti **Gražus stovi* ir *Namas stovi.* Tuo tarpu būdvardžių bevardės giminės bei atitinkamos įvardžių formos, nors ir atributyvinėje pozicijoje, išlieka daiktavardžio substitutais, t. y. *Visa gera* *turi* sintaksiškai galima išskaidyti į *Visa turi* ir *Gera turi.* Dėl to atributyvinius bev. g. formų junginius greičiau galima lyginti su apozityviniais dviejų daiktavardžių junginiais, pvz.: *Sūnus Petras* (*atėjo*), tarp kurių taip pat yra derinimas, bet jie ne priklauso vienas nuo kito (kaip būdvardis nuo daiktavardžio), o koreliuojami vienas su kitu kaip savarankiški vienetai, plg.: *Sūnus atėjo* ir *Petras atėjo.* Tai rodo, kad bev. g. formos atributyvinėje pozicijoje yra antrinės, atsiradusios jau substantyvinių bev. g. formų vartosenos pagrindu.

Tuo būdu bev. g. formos lietuvių kalboje dabar tik periferiškai susisieja su vyr. bei mot. g. formomis. Jų pagrindinės funkcijos yra skirtingos. Vyr. ir mot. g. formų pagrindinė yra priklausoma vartosena atributyvinėje pozicijoje (predikatyvinėje pozicijoje jie yra veiksmažodžių pavaduotojai)[24], o. bev. g. formoms yra būdinga savarankiška vartosena. Kaip nederinamos formos dažniausiai jos eina predikatyvinėje pozicijoje, kuri jiems yra pagrindinė. Taip pat savarankiškos šios formos yra atributyvinėje pozicijoje, kuri joms yra antrinė.

Išnašos

1. Žr. *Lietuvių kalbos gramatika*, I, Vilnius, 1965, 525.

2. Senuosiuose raštuose yra dar *i-* kamieno formų, pvz.: *daugigu* DP 580, plg. pr. *arwi*, žr. P. Arumaa, *Mélanges linguistiques offerts à M. Holger Pedersen*, 433 tt.; to paties kamieno bev. g. galūnė gali būti aukštesniojo laipsnio formose *daugeſni* Mž 481, *giereſni* SP I 232, žr. Ch. S. Stang, *Vergleichende Grammatik der baltischen Sprachen*, Oslo, 1966, 260.

3. J. Kazlauskas, *Lietuvių kalbos istorinė gramatika*, Vilnius, 1968, 124, plg. R. Trautmann, *Die altpreussischen Sprachdenkmäler*, Göttingen, 1910, 244, J. Endzelin, *Lettische Grammatik*, Riga, 1922, 464, E. Nieminen, *Der urindogermanische Ausgang -ǎi des Nominativ–Akkusativ Pluralis des Neutrums im Baltischen*, Helsinki, 1922, 2.

4. Latvių kalboje bevardės giminės formos kaip reguliarus tipas neišlikusios, čia jos dažniausiai pasitaiko kaip sustabarėję prieveiksmiai, žr. J. Endzelin, *op. cit.*, 464–465, 471. Prūsų kalboje šalia bevardės giminės būdvardžių su atitinkamomis galūnėmis, kaip lietuvių kalboje, (*salta, debica*), yra formų su vardažodine galūne (*kirsnan, sywan, labban*), žr. J. Endzelin, *Altpreussische Grammatik*, Riga, 1944, 99–100. Pastarosios derinamos su prūsų kalboje išlikusiais bevardės giminės daiktavardžiais ir vartojamos, kaip vyriškosios bei moteriškosios giminės formos, atributyviškai, plg.: *neuwenen testamenten*, žr. R. Trautmann, *op. cit.*, 214–216, 247.

5. Plg. W. Motsch, „Syntax des deutschen Adjektivs", *Studia Grammatica*, III, Berlin, 1964, 20–21.

6. Nimp — bev. g. forma, *yra* — bet kokia jungtis, Adv — prieveiksmis bei jo funkciją turintis padalyvis, Sap — aplinkybinis linksnis arba linksnis su prielinksniu. Skliaustuose nebūtini nariai. Toliau — Sd — daiktavardžio bei jo funkciją turinčio žodžio naudininkas, Sn — daiktavardžio vardininkas, Sg — daiktavardžio kilmininkas, Vinf — veiksmažodžio bendratis. Į žodžių tvarką schemose neatsižvelgiama. Šaltinių santrumpos kaip Lietuvių kalbos gramatikoje, *op. cit.*

7. Kartais pavartojami du naudininkai, kurių vienas reiškia asmenį, o kitas asmens dalį, pvz.: *Šálta kojoms mums stovėti.* JD 311.

8. Kaip visose neveikiamosios rūšies konstrukcijose, veiksmo subjektas čia reiškiamas kilmininku, plg.: *Tėvo skaitoma knyga → Tėvas skaito knygą.* Tačiau su reikiamybės dalyvių, kaip ir su būdvardžių, bev. g. formomis veiksmo subjektas reiškiamas naudininku, plg.: *Jau man eĩtina.* Kv.

9. Dėl sintaksinio konteksto kategorijų nustatymo plg. N. Chomsky, *Aspects of the Theory of Syntax*, Cambridge, 1965, 79 etc.; R. Růžička, *Studien zur Theorie der russischen Syntax*, Berlin, 1966, 64.

10. Tam tikri beasmeniai veiksmažodžiai eina ne tik su kilmininku, bet ir su galininku bei įnagininku, pvz.: *gelia galvą, kvepia šienu*. Tai priklauso ne nuo jų sintaksinės struktūros, bet nuo leksinių valdymo ypatybių.

11. Žr. В. В. Виноградов, *Русский язык*, Москва-Ленинград, 1947, 399; А. В. Исаченко, *Грамматический строй русского языка в сопоставлении с словацким*, I, Гратислава, 1954, 358.

12. Tai nereiškia, kad lietuvių kalboje galima išskirti atskirą būsenos kategoriją, nes šios formos ir kitaip vartojamos (žr. toliau). (Plg. K. Ulvydas, „Vienaskaitos vardininko kilmės prieveiksmiai“, *Lietuvių kalbotyros klausimai*, XI, 12.) Lietuvių kalbos bevardės giminės formos gali būti gretinamos su prieveiksmiais (žr. J. Kazlauskas, *Baltistica*, IV (2), 324), bet tai atskiras klausimas, šiame straipsnyje jis neliečiamas.

13. В. Л. Георгиева, „Безличные предложения по материалам древнейших славянских памятников“, *Slavia*, XXXVIII, 84 tt.

14. Ф. И. Буслаев, *Историческая грамматика*, Москва, 1959, 446.

15. B. Delbrück, *Vergleichende Syntax der idg. Sprachen*, *III*, Strassburg, 1900, 247, E. Fraenkel, *Baltoslavica*, Göttingen, 1921, 37 ff.

16. Žr. В. В. Виноградов, *op. cit.*, 406.

17. Th. Siebs, „Die sogenannten subjektlosen Sätze“, KZ, XLIII, 267, В. Н. Топоров, „К вопросу об эволюции славянского и балтийского глагола“, *ВСЯ*, V, 64, 70, J. Kazlauskas, *op. cit.*, 304. Dėl šių konstrukcijų santykio su ergatyvine konstrukcija žr. М. М. Гухман, „Конструкции с дательным / винительным лица и проблема эргативного прошлого инд. языков“, *Эргативная конструкция предложения в языках различных типов*, Ленинград, 1967, 58–73 ir nurodytą literatūrą.

18. Plg. V. Kiparsky, „Über das Nominativobjekt des Infinitivs“, *ZfsPh.*, XXVIII, 341

19. Plg. Chr. S. Stang, *op. cit.*, 261 (2 išnaša).

20. Žr. J. Schmidt, *Die Pluralbildungen der idg. Neutra*. Weimar, 1889, 229–230.

21. Latvių dabartinėje literatūrinėje kalboje šiais atvejais vartojamos tik vyr. g. formos, žr. pavyzdžius: *Mūsdienu latviešu literārās valodas gramatika*, I, Rīgā, 1959, 476.

22. Substantyvinės bev. g. formos čia vartojamos vard. ir gal. pozicijoje, o su veiksmažodžiais, reikalaujančiais kitų linksnių (kilm., įn.), eina vyr. g. substantyvinių būdvardžių atitinkami linksniai.

23. Rusų kalboje atitinkamais atvejais paprastai vartojamos įvardžiuotinės (ilgosios) bev. g. substantyvinės būdvardžių formos, pvz.: *Это — главное. Сейте разумное, доброе, вечное. В его улыбке было что-то детское* (žr. Грамматика русского языка, I, Москва, 1953, 314; II, 1960, 336), kurių, kaip derinamų, juo labiau negalima susieti su vadinamosios būsenos kategorijos žodžiais (*Мне скучно*).

24. Dėl to žr. J. Kuryłowicz, *Esquisses linguistiques*, Wrocław, Kraków, 1960, 43 tt.

Concerning Neuter Forms of Lithuanian Adjectives

Neuter forms of Lith. adjectives are usually used independently in contrast to the masculine and feminine forms. In predicative use they generally are not in concord. Attributive transformations of such predicatives (cf., *Malonu svečias*) are impossible (= *Malonus svečias*). Genetically these neuter forms should be associated with such a type of IE nominal sentence, in which the predicative was not in agreement with the form of the subject. These neuter forms are not related to specific Lith. neuter substantive forms either syntactically or semantically. The neuter substantive forms can be in agreement with the other neuter forms both predicatively and attributively (cf., *Visa yra gera. Visa gera turi*). This usage of the neuter forms may be a relic of the congruence with the neuter nouns, which have disappeared from the language. In attributive usage, however, the adjective neuter forms are not quite equal to the masculine and feminine forms. As they can function as noun substitutes (cf., *Visa gera turi* = *Visa turi* and *Gera turi*), they can be treated as secondary.

TEODOLIUS WITKOWSKI

Baltische Ortsnamen westlich der Oder?

0.1. Die in der Überschrift ausgedrückte Frage ist in den letzten Jahren aktuell geworden. In mehreren Publikationen haben Herrmann Schall und V. N. Toporov altes Namenmaterial westlich der Oder baltisch erklärt und zum Teil wichtige Schlüsse aus diesen Erklärungen abgeleitet. Es ist daher zu fragen:

1. Gibt es im Gebiet westlich der Oder Ortsnamen[1], die aus dem Baltischen (bzw. einer baltischen Sprache) erklärt werden müssen? Die Frage könnte auch so gestellt werden: Sind die als baltisch bezeichneten Namen nicht auch und besser aus dem Slawischen oder anderen Sprachen erklärbar?
2. Welche Konsequenzen ergäben sich, wenn es Namen gäbe, die sich nur mit Hilfe des Baltischen erklären ließen?
3. Gibt es historische oder andere Zeugnisse für die Anwesenheit von Balten in den Gebieten westlich der Oder?

Aus methodischen Gründen dürfte es angebracht sein, erst die dritte, und dann die erste und zweite Frage zu beantworten.

1.0. Es gibt keinerlei historische Zeugnisse für die Anwesenheit von Balten in den Gebieten westlich der Oder. Dies gilt mindestens für die Zeit um 1000 oder 1200 p. C. n. und sämtliche früheren Epochen.

1.1. Dagegen waren die Gebiete westlich der Oder entsprechend den historischen und archäologischen Quellen um die Zeitenwende von Germanen (z. T. auch von Kelten) besiedelt.

1.2. In der zweiten Hälfte des 6. Jahrhunderts u. Z. setzte die slawische Landnahme im Raum zwischen Elbe/Saale und Oder/Neiße ein. Sie erfolgte in verschiedenen Etappen und aus verschiedenen Richtungen (etwa aus dem böhmischen, kleinpolnischen und großpolnischen Raum)[2]. Weitergehende Schlußfolgerungen läßt der bisherige Forschungsstand der Archäologie und der Geschichte nicht zu.

1.2.1. Im archäologischen Fundmaterial spiegelt sich die slawische Besiedlung der Gebiete westlich Oder und Neiße wie folgt wider: Bislang sind ca.

4 000 slawische Fundstellen (Siedlungen, Burgen, Gräber, Gräberfelder, Einzelfunde etc.) bekannt[3]. Dem stehen zwei „baltische" Funde gegenüber: eine aus dem 7. oder 8. Jh. unserer Zeitrechnung stammende Armbrustfibel, die nach Ostpreußen weist und bei Prützke im Kreis Brandenburg gefunden wurde, und ein aus dem 12. Jh. unserer Zeitrechnung stammender und bei Pritzerbe im Kreis Brandenburg gefundener Steigbügel, dessen Werkstatt im Küstengebiet östlich des Weichselmündungsgebietes gelegen haben dürfte (vgl. Unverzagt–Herrmann 1958 und Knorr 1958). Baltische Siedlungen, Gräber etc. fehlen gänzlich. Die beiden Funde kommen daher nur als Zeugnisse für den Handel (auch Sklavenhandel!) oder andere lose Kontakte zwischen Balten und Slawen in unserem Raum in Betracht. Gestützt wird diese Interpretation durch die Tatsache, daß Prützke nahe und Pritzerbe direkt an einer bereits im 6. und 7. Jahrhundert unserer Zeitrechnung bestehenden Handelsstraße liegen, die vom Rheinland über Magdeburg ins Baltikum führte.

1.3. Der Name *Prützke* kann (sic!) mit dem Volksnamen der *Preußen* im Zusammenhang stehen[4]. Was aber wurde im konkreten Fall unter einem Preußen verstanden: ein Balte allgemein, ein aus Preußen zugewanderter Slawe oder Deutscher oder einfach ein Mensch, der Preußen kannte? Der Name könnte auf irgendeine Begebenheit mit einem Händler zurückgehen. Wir wissen nichts über das Motiv der Namengebung. Wohl aber wissen wir, daß die übrigen bei Prützke gemachten Funde dem slawischen Prager Typus angehören.

1.4. In diesem Zusammenhang ist die Frage nach der Urheimat oder nach den früheren Wohnsitzen der Balten zu stellen. Hierüber besteht unter den Forschern keine Einigkeit. Aber selbst diejenigen Archäologen (Jażdżewski 1961, Gimbutas 1963), die gewisse Kulturen des zweiten Jahrtausends vor unserer Zeitrechnung mit dem Urbaltischen verbinden, gehen nicht über die Pasłęka (Jażdżewski) oder die Weichsel nach dem Westen hinaus[5]. Es hat unter diesen Umständen keinen Zweck, wenn man sogar Namenmaterial westlich der Oder ohne Not als baltisch deklariert oder gar darauf Hypothesen von einer baltoslawischen Sprachgemeinschaft bis zur Elbe und über diese hinaus, von der Abstammung der Slawen von den Balten u. ä. konstruiert. Diese Hypothesen stehen in keinem logischen Verhältnis zu dem angeblich baltischen Material; denn es ist nicht zu begründen, warum beispielsweise die Slawen von den Balten abstammen sollten, wenn es westlich der Oder baltische Namen gäbe. Mit dem gleichen Recht könnte man behaupten, die Germanen stammten von den Römern ab, weil es in Westdeutschland viele Namen lateinischer (römischer) Herkunft gibt.

2.0. Es ist also zu fragen, ob die Namen, die als baltisch bezeichnet werden, sich nicht auch deutsch oder slawisch oder germanisch etc. erklären lassen, d. h. ob diese Namen wirklich als baltische Namen aufgefaßt werden *müssen*. Die Antwort auf diese Frage erfolgt in erster Linie unter dem Gesichtspunkt, daß eine baltische Erklärung nur dann zu erwägen sei, wenn ein Name sich aus den im Raum westlich der Oder archäologisch und historisch bezeugten bzw. nachweis- und erschließbaren Sprachen nicht erklären läßt und wenn darüber hinaus massive sprachliche Kriterien die baltische Erklärung nahelegen. Daß ein Vergleich vor allem der slawischen Namen mit den baltischen durchaus sinnvoll und nützlich sein kann, bedarf keiner besonderen Begründung.

2.1.0. Der Name *Berlin* ist nach Schall (1963, S. 144 f.) aus kurisch **Burlīni* entstanden, das sich im Westslawischen „lautgesetzlich weiter zu slaw. **Bъrliń*, dann **Berliń*" entwickelt habe. Demgegenüber konnte bereits an anderer Stelle[6] darauf hingewiesen werden, daß die von Krogmann (1937) stammende Erklärung des Namens als Bildung zu einem slawischen Stamm **bъrl-/bъrl-*[7] keinerlei Schwierigkeiten begegnet[8], wenngleich wegen der zahlreichen Vergleichsnamen im ost-, west- und südeuropäischen Bereich (vgl. J. Schmidt 1961) die Erklärung aus dem Slawischen (hier: Polabischen) nicht die einzige Möglichkeit darstellt. Zudem ist darauf hinzuweisen, daß eine Form „**Bъrl-*" im Altpolabischen zu **Barl-* und nicht zu **Berl-* geführt hätte. Es besteht also keine Notwendigkeit, das Baltische zu bemühen, um den Namen *Berlin* zu erklären.

2.1.1. *Alkun*, Wüstung bei Barth Kr. Ribnitz-Damgarten, 1306 *Alkun* (PUB IV, Nr. 2295 Original). Schall (1964, S. 137 f.) rekonstruiert eine baltische Grundform **Alkūne*, die er mit lit. *ùpės alkúne* 'Windung eines Flusses' etc. vergleicht. Zugleich verweist er darauf, daß die Wüstung an einem früheren Lauf des Baches Barthe gelegen habe. Es verwundert, daß Schall nicht versucht, den Namen slawisch zu erklären, obgleich er offensichtlich nicht einmal baltische Vergleichsnamen gefunden hat. Auch ist zu beachten, daß lit. *alkúne* nicht *allein* schon 'Windung eines Flusses', sondern 'Ellbogen' bedeutet. Schließlich erliegt man einer Suggestion, wenn man glaubt, ein an einem Gewässer gelegener Ort *müsse* mit seinem Namen irgendwie auf diese Lage Bezug nehmen. Namengebung erfolgt letzten Endes arbiträr, wenngleich sie durch verschiedene äußere und innere Faktoren determiniert ist. Alkun muß also nicht nach dem Bach benannt sein, an dem es lag. Der Name läßt sich auch als aplb. **Alkunj(-)* 'Ort des Alkun' erklären. Der vorauszusetzende Personenname dürfte zu ursl. **olkati*, enthalten in poln. *łaknąć* 'begierig sein', tsch. *lákati* 'verlangen', russ. лакать, лакнуть 'lechzen' u. a. gehören. In **Alkun* läge das Verb in der nicht umgestellten Form vor. Derartige Formen sind aus dem Altkirchenslawischen wie aus dem Russischen bekannt: aksl. *alkati* 'hungern' u. a. russ. алкать 'dürsten, begehren', алчный 'gierig, heißhungrig', russ. dial. (Gebiet Jaroslavlь) алкид 'gieriger, geiziger Mensch' (SRNG I, 239), aruss. ал(ъ)кати 'hungern' u. a. Die genannten Beispiele zeigen, daß die Liquidametathese bei **olk-* nicht überall durchgeführt ist und daß daher auch eine entsprechende Form im Polabischen durchaus keine alleinstehende Ausnahme bilden würde. — Der PN **Alkun* ist als Bildung mit dem Suffix *-un* für Nomina agentis und Übername für einen gierigen oder hungrigen Menschen aufzufassen. Auch der russische Personenname 1495 Алкачь (Tupikov 1903, S. 88) dürfte das gleiche Stammorphem enthalten.

2.1.2. *Arkona*, Kreis und Insel Rügen, 1136 und 1145 *Arkun*, 1150 *Arcune* etc.[9] Schall (1964, S. 140–142) setzt eine Grundform **Arkūne* 'Wehrburg' an, die er zu lett. *ercêt* 'reißen, nagenden Schmerz verursachen', *ercietis* 'wilder Rosenstrauch', lit. *arkýtis* 'sich ungebärdig stellen', *arktà* 'Rauferei' u. a. stellt. Einen Parallelnamen aus dem Baltischen kennt Schall offensichtlich wieder nicht. Vasmer (1947, S. 320) hatte den Namen mit altnordisch *orku, erku* 'Art Seehund' in Verbindung gebracht und ihn als 'Seehundslandzunge' gedeutet. Diese Erklärung verschweigt Schall. Auch hier ist zu fragen, warum eine baltische Etymologie konstruiert werden muß, wenn sich gleichzeitig eine skandinavische Erklärung anbietet und starke skandinavische Einflüsse sowohl archäologisch als auch historisch und onomastisch nachweisbar sind.

2.1.3. *Calbe* Kr. Schönebeck, 936 *Calvo* (Wauer 1963, S. 15). Schall (1966, S. 452–454) deutet diesen Namen sowie *Kalbe* an der Milde, Bezirk Magdeburg (1121 *Calvo*, nach Schall) baltisch, indem er ihn mit baltischen Ortsnamen (z. B. 1254 *Calve* im „Lande der Selen") und lett. *kalva* 'Anhöhe, Hügel; Insel' vergleicht. Der Vergleich mag auf den ersten Blick bestechen, doch ist er weit hergeholt, wenn man bedenkt, daß sich der Name ohne Schwierigkeiten deutsch (oder auch germanisch) erklären läßt: mhd. *kalve* 'kahle Stelle', mnd. *kale(we)* 'Kahlheit', ahd. *cal(a)wa* 'Kahlheit, kahle Stelle' u. a. zu germ. **kalwa* 'kahle Stelle'. Diese von Wauer 1963, S. 15 gegebene überzeugende Deutung des Namens war Schall bekannt. Er verschweigt sie.

2.1.4. *Dargow* Kr. Herzogtum Lauenburg (Bundesrepublik), 1230 *Dargowe* (MUB I, Nr. 375, S. 363 Original) ist, wie bereits Trautmann (MH 46, EO I,

61) ausführte, einwandfrei slawisch (aplb.) *Dargov-, possessivische Ableitung von einem Kurznamen *Darg (zu aplb. *darg, ursl. *dorgъ 'lieb, teuer'). Der Vergleich dieses Namens mit dem Baltischen (Schall 1963a, S. 387; 1966a, S. 12) ist irreführend und banal. Wenn, dann müßte man sämtliche Namen der tort-Gruppe mit dem Baltischen vergleichen, da ursl. *tort zu plb. tart führte.

2.1.5. 1421 Lynow, Wüstung in Schönberg Kr. Plön (Bundesrepublik), von Trautmann (MH 93 und EO II, 60) mit zahlreichen anderen Ortsnamen (Linow Kr. Neuruppin, Linau Kr. Herzogtum Lauenburg, Bundesrepublik u. a.) zurecht von *lin 'Schleie' (gemeinslawisch) abgeleitet, stellt Schall (1963a, S. 387; 1966a, S. 12) offensichtlich wegen der Schreibung mit y neben den altpreußischen Ortsnamen 1388 Lynow. Abgesehen davon, daß der in Rede stehende Ortsname zu 1460 als Linouwe mit i überliefert ist (MH 93), braucht nur daran erinnert zu werden, daß y in den mittelalterlichen Quellen grundsätzlich i wiedergibt.

2.1.6. Peene, Fluß in Vorpommern. Seit 786 ist dieser Name in zahlreichen Belegen als Peanis, Panis, Penis, Pene (so meist) u. ä. belegt[10]. Es besteht keinerlei Schwierigkeit, diesen Namen zu einem aplb. Appellativum *pěna (so auch ursl.) 'Schaum' zu stellen. In diesem Sinne hat auch Trautmann (EO II, 17; MH 20, 30, 115) den Namen gedeutet. Es stimmt also nicht, daß Trautmann nur Verwandtschaft mit slaw. *pěna gesehen habe (so Schall 1962, S. 58). Näheres vgl. Witkowski 1969, S. 482.

2.1.7. Plane, Nebenfluß der Havel, südwestlich von Berlin. Der Name wird von Schall (1964, S. 131 f.) ohne Zitieren alter Belege und der von Trautmann gegebenen Erklärung mit dem lettischen Flußnamen Plāne und litauisch Plónė, den Appellativen lit. plónė viksva 'haarfeine, -stengelige Segge', lit. plónė 'Art Lebermoos' u. a. verglichen und als Bildung zu einer dieser Pflanzen erklärt.

Der Flußname Plane ist wie folgt belegt: 1205 ad riuum plane (CDB A X, 189 Kopie 14. Jh.), 1208 ad riuum plane (ebd. S. 191 Kopie 14. Jh.), 1234 in riuum planam (ebd. S. 198 Kopie), 1251 aquam que plana vulgariter appellatur (ebd. S. 206 Original). Als Grundform ist *Plona anzusetzen[11]. Der Name gehört zu ursl. *polnъ, enthalten in oso., nso. plony 'eben, flach', p. plonny 'unfruchtbar, dürr', tsch. planý 'unfruchtbar'[12]. Der Fluß fließt durch ein bis ca. 8 km breites, ebenes Urstromtal und hat wahrscheinlich daher seinen Namen (vgl. Herrmann 1968, S. 32). „Die Schreibungen mit a erklären sich aus der mnd. Tondehnung, dem Zusammenfall von tonlangem *o* and *a*[13] ... Außerdem kann diese Schreibung von mnd. *plān* m. 'freier, ebener Platz (in der Stadt), überhaupt Ebene und jeder ebene Platz' beeinflußt sein" (R. E. Fischer 1967, S. 97). Zu beachten ist auch, daß die Plane bei Raben Kr. Belzig entspringt. Dieser Ort liegt im ehemaligen slawischen „Gau" *Ploni*[14]. Gau- und Flußnamen gehören sicher zusammen[15]. Die Schreibungen des um drei Jahrhunderte früher bezeugten Gaues bestätigen die angesetzten Grundform **Plona* (mit *o*) für den Flußnamen. Weitere Vergleichsnamen bei Trautmann (EO II, 27 f.).

2.1.8. *Alt Rehse* Kr. Waren, 1182 *Reze* (MUB I, 135 S. 130 Original). Der Name gehört ebenso wie etwa *Riesa* in Sachsen und *Rhäsa* Kr. Meißen zu einer Entsprechung von ursl. **rězati* 'schneiden, sägen', das in allen slawischen Sprachen belegt ist[16]. Als Grundform wird man plb. **Rěz* oder (mit größerer Wahrscheinlichkeit wegen des erhaltenen *e*-Lautes) **Rěža*[17], etwa in der Bedeutung 'Einschnitt (im Gelände)' oder 'Spalte, Rinne', ansetzen dürfen. Die Ableitung des Namens von gleichbedeutenden baltischen Wörtern (Schall 1964, S. 144 f.) ist unnötig, die Behauptung, im Slawischen seien aksl. *rězati* 'schlagen'[18] und *razъ* 'Schlag, Mal, Kerbe' mit den entsprechenden baltischen Wörtern verwandt (Schall ebd. S. 145) eine Unwahrheit. *Alle* slawischen Sprachen besitzen Kontinuanten von **rězati* und Ableitungen davon.

2.1.9. 1289 *Warne*, Landschaft in Mecklenburg (MH 160) gehört ebenso wie zahlreiche andere ON (*Waren*, *Fahren*, *Warnow* u. a., vgl. MH 160 f.) zu plb. **varn-*, ursl. **vorna* 'Krähe', **vornъ* 'Rabe' oder adjektivisch 'rabenschwarz', also zu einem Wort der *tort*-Gruppe, weshalb das oben zu *Dargow* Gesagte auch hier gilt. Der Vergleich mit oder die Herleitung aus dem Baltischen (Schall 1963a, S. 387; 1966a, S. 12) ist daher völlig irreführend.

2.2. Das oben vorgeführte Namenmaterial stellt nur eine Auswahl der in den letzten Jahren baltisch erklärten Ortsnamen aus dem Raum westlich der Oder dar. Gewiß handelt es sich um besonders krasse Fälle der Fehlinterpretation, die die Anfechtbarkeit der Hypothese von einer baltischen Ortsnamenschicht im genannten Gebiet sehr klar vor Augen führen. Umso unverständlicher ist es, daß V. N. Toporov (1966, 1966a) den Ansichten Schalls beipflichtet, indem er die baltische Interpretation solcher Namen wie *Dargow, Lynow, Peene, Plane, Spandin*[19] übernimmt und andere Namen wie *Baberow* (zu plb. **bobr* 'Biber'), *Briesenick* (zu plb. **breza* 'Birke'), *Plawe* (zu plb. **plaw* 'Vieh- oder Holzschwemme'), *Stolp(e)* (zu plb. **stolp* 'Pfosten; Vorrichtung zum Fischfang' u. a.) hinzufügt.

2.3. Es wäre vielleicht interessant, sämtliche von Schall und Toporov für baltisch ausgegebenen Namen zu durchleuchten, doch kann mit Sicherheit angenommen werden, daß das Ergebnis die dafür gesondert aufgewandte Zeit nicht rechtfertigen würde. Man kann daher die Klärung jeder einzelnen „baltischen" Etymologie Schalls und Toporovs der weiteren Arbeit an den Namenbüchern der betroffenen Gebiete überlassen. Mit Fug darf daran gezweifelt werden, daß sich viele Namen finden werden, die nur unter Zuhilfenahme des Baltischen erklärt werden können. Bisher wurde jedenfalls kein einziger derartiger Name gefunden.

3.0. Damit soll aber nicht geleugnet werden, daß es tatsächlich solche Namen geben *kann*. Als wichtiges Kriterium für die Eruierung derartiger Namen müßte in erster Linie gelten, daß sie Wortmaterial enthalten, das nur dem Baltischen bekannt ist. Stang (1966, S. 7–9) hat eine Liste solcher Wörter zusammengestellt, die nur im Baltischen belegt sind. Diese Liste[20] könnte bei der weiteren Erforschung des Namenmaterials sehr gute Dienste leisten. Es verdient im übrigen Beachtung, daß Stang ausdrücklich annimmt, daß „nicht alle Wörter, um die es sich hier handelt, von Anfang an auf das Baltische beschränkt gewesen sind" (S. 7). Damit wird ein Kernproblem unserer Frage nach eventuellen baltischen Ortsnamen westlich der Oder berührt. Es kann nämlich durchaus sein, daß einzelne slawische Namen Wortmaterial enthalten, das im appellativischen Bereich des Slawischen ausgestorben und nicht mehr nachweisbar, im Baltischen jedoch erhalten ist[21]. Bei der engen Verwandtschaft von Baltisch und Slawisch wäre dies durchaus keine verwunderliche Tatsache, und die betreffenden Namen würden die Verwandtschaft einmal mehr unterstreichen.

3.1. Im übrigen wäre zu klären, ob zwischen Baltisch und Polabisch (evtl. auch Sorbisch) engere sprachliche Beziehungen bestehen bzw. bestanden als zwischen Baltisch und anderen Slawinen. Beim jetzigen Forschungsstand (mangelnde Materialbasis) ist die Klärung dieser Frage allerdings noch nicht möglich. Auch deshalb wäre es verfrüht, aus dem Vorhandensein einzelner „baltisch" aussehender Namen weitgehende Schlußfolgerungen zu ziehen. Es sollte auch darauf geachtet werden, daß es manche baltischen Namen gibt, die sich nur erklären lassen, wenn man das Slawische hinzuzieht. So führt z. B. Otrębski (1964, S. 80 f.) 25 altpreußische Wörter auf, für die er keine Parallelen im Litauischen, wohl aber im Slawischen findet. Ferner nennt er (S. 78 f.) die jatwingischen Seenamen *Baĺtajis Bìlsas* und *Juõdajis Bìlsas*, die das im Baltischen sonst nicht bezeugte *bìlsas* 'weiß oder weißlich' enthalten, das zu russ. белесый 'weißlich, schmutzigweiß' gehört. Völlig zurecht leitet Otrębski daraus nicht ab, daß das Altpreußische oder

Jatwingische vom Slawischen abstamme, sich aus diesem entwickelt habe. Umgekehrt glaubt aber Schall (in allen Publikationen seit 1962) auf Grund der von ihm als baltisch deklarierten Namen behaupten zu können, diese Namen bewiesen das Vorhandensein einer baltoslawischen Sprachgemeinschaft im Raum westlich der Oder und die Abstammung der Slawen von den Balten. Daß die letzte Behauptung jeglicher logischen Grundlage entbehrt, selbst wenn alle von Schall und Toporov für baltisch gehaltenen Namen wirklich baltisch wären, liegt auf der Hand.

4.0. Es ist nicht möglich, hier auf alle Aspekte der in der Überschrift dieser Arbeit formulierten Frage einzugehen. So viel läßt sich jedenfalls schon heute sagen: Die meisten der in den letzten Jahren für baltisch ausgegebenen Namen lassen sich slawisch oder germanisch oder auch indogermanisch bzw. alteuropäisch[22] erklären. Sofern das in einigen Fällen nicht möglich sein sollte, könnte das Baltische gute Dienste zur Erhellung der Etymologie leisten. Denkbar wäre in Einzelfällen die Entstehung von Namen, die mit dem Handel zwischen Balten einerseits und Slawen, Germanen usw. andererseits im Zusammenhang stehen (z. B. *Prützke*). Archäologische Befunde und historische Quellen gestatten es jedoch nicht, solche evtl. vorhandenen Namen als Namen einer baltischen Schicht oder baltischen Substratsprache zu deklarieren oder irgendwelche Schlüsse zur Genese der Slawen zu ziehen. Nicht auszuschließen wären Namenentlehnungen und Namenübertragungen sowie in ganz seltenen Fällen von einzelnen Balten (Sklaven?) gebildete Namen.

4.1. In seiner verdienstvollen vergleichenden Grammatik der baltischen Sprachen hat Stang (1966, S. V) das schöne Wort gesprochen, daß „die Wissenschaft ... ein Dialog" sei. In diesem Sinne hat die Äußerung extrem falscher Ansichten bestimmt oft die Diskussion angeregt und die Klärung mancher Fragen erleichtert. Die Beschäftigung mit den Hypothesen von Schall und Toporov hat gezeigt, daß der Substanzgehalt dieser Hypothesen minimal, wenn nicht gleich null ist. Andererseits sind wir uns jetzt mehr als früher dessen bewußt, daß die baltischen Sprachen (und damit ihre Namen) viel zur Erhellung des Slawischen und der slawischen Namen beitragen können. Das sollte die Slawistik nicht aus dem Auge verlieren.

Anmerkungen

1. Daß es baltische *Personennamen* gibt, liegt auf der Hand, da ja ein in Deutschland lebender Litauer oder Lette seinen Familiennamen in der Regel nicht aufgeben wird. — Zu den baltischen Lehnwörtern vgl. den Beitrag von H. H. Bielfeldt in diesem Buch.

2. Vgl. Coblenz 1960; Herrmann 1968, S. 68 f. und 73 f; Herrmann 1968 a, S. 21 f.; Brachmann 1969, S. 19 f.

3. Für freundlich erteilte Auskünfte sei auch an dieser Stelle Herrn Prof. Dr. Joachim Herrmann (Berlin) gedankt. Zur Zeit erfolgt eine Bestandsaufnahme sämtlicher slawischer Funde in der DDR. Die genannte Zahl (4 000 Fundstellen) könnte sich nach Abschluß der Bestandsaufnahme noch erhöhen.

4. Vgl. zuletzt R. E. Fischer 1967, S. 100 f., wo auch eine andere (slawische) Erklärung des Namens erwogen wird.

5. Vgl. auch die Karten in SSS 1, 74 f. Man wird freilich derartige Grenzen nicht allzu eng auslegen dürfen, so als hätten sie ein unverrückbares und unüberbrückbares Hindernis dargestellt. Aber einen gewissen Anhalt bieten sie doch. Von seiten der Namenforschung konnten, wenn auch in kleinem Rahmen (Lorentz 1966) baltische Namen auch westlich der Weichsel nachgewiesen werden, ja Krahe (1943) ging sogar bis an die Persante.

6. Witkowski 1965, S. 586; 1966; 1969, S. 479 f.

7. Enthalten in poln. barlóg 'Lager von Wirrstrah, Unrat', nso. barlog 'Bucht, Streu', skr. bŕljati 'verwirren, beschmutzen' u. a.

8. Vgl. auch Mikołaj Rudnicki in: SSS I, 107 f.; NdS. 84 f.

9. Belege nach Schall 1964, S. 140.

10. Vgl. die zahlreichen Formen bei Schall 1962, S. 58.

11. So bereits Trautmann (EO I, 31), ferner R. E. Fischer 1967, S. 97.

12. Zur Etymologie vgl. Machek 1957, S. 371.

13. In ǭa. Der Name der an der Plane gelegenen Wüstung Planow wird mundartlich plǭanō ausgesprochen. Vgl. R. E. Fischer 1967, S. 97 und 148.

14. So in Belegen zu 948 (Original) und 973 (nach R. E. Fischer 1967, S. 97).

15. Vgl. hierzu auch Herrmann 1968, S. 32.

16. Zu Rhäsa und Riesa vgl. Eichler–Walther Daleminze I, 277–279 und (zu Riesa) DNS 122 f.

17. Vgl. slowen. Reža 'Spalte, Rinne, Schlitz etc.'.

18. Die Bedeutung stimmt nicht, sondern 'schneiden, hauen' (vgl. REW 2, 505; Sadnik–Aitzetmüller 1955, S. 115; Diels 1963, Bd. 2, S. 101).

19. Zu Spandin und Spandau, von Schall (1964), S. 135–137) baltisch, zuvor jedoch von Brückner und Vasmer slawisch erklärt, vgl. Witkowski 1969, S. 481.

20. Sie enthält keinen einzigen Wortstamm, der in den obengenannten Namen vorliegen könnte.

21. Zu dieser Problematik vgl. auch Witkowski 1966, S. 264 f., 269; Witkowski 1969, S. 477 f.

22. Zur Problematik des Alteuropäischen vgl. zuletzt Schmid 1968.

Literatur

Brachmann 1969 = Brachmann, Hans-Jürgen, *Zur Geschichte der Slawen des Mittelelb-Saale-Gebieteas im 6. bis 10. Jahrhundert (auf Grund archäologischer Quellen)*, Philos. Diss. Halle (Maschinenschrift).

CDB A = *Novus Codex diplomaticus Brandenburgensis ...*, bearb. von Adolph Friedrich Riedel, 1. Hauptteil, Berlin 1838 ff.

Coblenz 1960 = Coblenz, Werner, ,,Zur Situation der archäologischen Slawenforschung in Sachsen", *Siedlung und Verfassung der Slawen zwischen Elbe, Saale und Oder*, hsg. von Herbert Ludat, Gießen, S. 1–14.

Diels 1963 = Diels, Paul, *Altkirchenslavische Grammatik*, I–II, Heidelberg[2].

Eichler–Walther Daleminze = Ernst Eichler – Hans Walther, *Die Ortsnamen im Gau Daleminze*, 2 Bände, Berlin 1966/67.

EO = Trautmann, Reinhold, *Die elb- und ostseeslavischen Ortsnamen*, 2 Teile, Berlin 1948/49; Teil III: Register (auch zu MH), bearbeitet von Hermann Schall, Berlin 1956.

Fischer 1967 = Fischer, Reinhard E., *Die Ortsnamen der Zauche*, Weimar (Brandenburgisches Namenbuch I).

Gimbutas 1963 = Gimbutas, Marija, ,,Die Indoeuropäer", *Archäologische Probleme*, 1963. Zitiert nach: *Die Urheimat der Indogermanen*, hsg. von Anton Scherer, Darmstadt 1968, 538–571.

Herrmann 1968 = Herrmann, Joachim, *Siedlung, Wirtschaft und gesellschaftliche Verhältnisse der slawischen Stämme zwischen Oder/Neiße und Elbe*, Berlin.

Herrmann 1968a = Herrmann, Joachim, ,,Slawen und Deutsche", *Germanen–Slawen–Deutsche. Forschungen zu ihrer Ethnogese*, Berlin, 21–29.

Jażdżewski 1961 = Jażdżewski, Konrad, ,,Bałtowie", *SSS* I, 73 f.

Knorr 1958 = Knorr, Heinz A., ,,Der Steigbügel von Pritzerbe Kr. Brandenburg", *Ausgrabungen und Funde* III, 111–113.

Krahe 1943 = Krahe, Hans, ,,Baltische Ortsnamen westlich der Weichsel", *Alt-Preußen* VIII, 43 f.

Krogmann 1937 = Krogmann, Willy, *Berliner Sprachproben aus sieben Jahrhunderten*, Berlin.

Lorentz 1966 = Lorentz, Friedrich, ,,Preußische Ortsnamen und Appellative in Namen im Raum links der unteren Weichsel, mit Anmerkungen von F. Hinze", *ZfSl* XI, 243–250.

Machek 1957 = Machek, Václav, *Etymologický slovník jazyka českého a slovenského*, Praha.

MH = Reinhold Trautmann, *Die slavischen Ortsnamen Mecklenburgs und Holsteins*, Berlin,[2] 1950.

MUB = *Mecklenburgisches Urkundenbuch*, 25 Bände, Schwerin 1863–1936.

Otrębski 1964 = Otrębski, Jan, ,,Die baltische Philologie und ihre Bedeutung für die indogermanische Sprachwissenschaft", *KZ*, Neue Folge LXXIX, 69–88.

PUB = *Pommersches Urkundenbuch*, Stettin, später Köln–Graz 1868 ff.

REW = Max Vasmer, *Russisches etymologisches Wörterbuch*, 3 Bände, Heidelberg 1953–1958.

Sadnik–Aitzetmüller 1955 = Linda Sadnik – Rudolf Aitzetmüller, *Handwörterbuch zu den altkirchenslavischen Texten*, Heidelberg-s'Gravenhage.

Schall 1962 = Schall, Hermann, ,,Baltische Sprachreste zwischen Elbe und Weichsel", *Forschungen und Fortschritte* XXXVI, 56–61.

Schall 1963 = Schall, Hermann, ,,Berlin — ein slawobaltischer Flurname", *KZ*, Neue Folge LXXVIII, 126–146.

Schall 1963a = Schall, Hermann, ,,Die baltisch-slavische Sprachgemeinschaft zwischen Elbe und Weichsel", *VII Congresso Internationale di Scienze Onomastiche*, Firenze — 4–8. Aprile 1961. Atti e Memorie, II, Firenze 1963, 386–404.

572

Schall 1964 = Schall, Hermann, ,,Baltische Dialekte im Namengut Nordwestslawiens'',
KZ, Neue Folge LXXIX, 123–170.

Schall 1966 = Schall, Hermann, ,,Kurisch-selische Elemente im Nordwestslawischen'',
Proceedings of the Eighth International Congress of Onomastic Sciences, ed. by D. P.
Blok, The Hague–Paris, 450–464.

Schall 1966 a = Schall, Hermann, ,,Baltische Gewässernamen im Flußsystem 'Obere
Havel''', *Baltistica* II, 7–42.

Schmid 1968 = Schmid, Wolfgang P., *Alteuropäisch und Indogermanisch*, Wiesbaden.

Schmidt 1961 = Schmidt, Johanna, ,,Das Problem des Namens Berlin'', *VI. Internationaler Kongress für Namenforschung*, München, 24.–28. August 1958, Kongress-
berichte. Hsg. von Gerhard Rohlfs und Karl Puchner, III, München, 672–679.

SRNG = Словарь русских народных говоров. Составил Ф. П. Филин, Moskva–
Leningrad, 1965 ff.

SSS = *Słownik starożytności słowiańskich*, pod redakcją Władysława Kowalenki,
Gerarda Labudy i Tadeusza Lehra-Spławińskiego, Wrocław–Warszawa–Kraków
1961 ff.

Stang 1966 = Stang, Chr. S., Vergleichende Grammatik der Baltischen Sprachen,
Oslo–Bergen–Tromsö.

Toporov 1966 = Toporov, V. N., ,,К вопросу о топонимических соответствиях
на балттийских территориях к эападу от Вислы'', *Baltistica I*, 103–111.

Toporov 1966 a = Toporov, V. N., "О балтийских элементах в гидронимии и
топонимии к эападу от Вислы'', *Slavica Pragensia* VIII, 255–263.

Tupikov 1903 = Н. М. Тупиков, "Словарь древне-русскихъ личныхъ именъ'',
Записки отдѣленія русской и славянской археологии Императорскаго
Русскаго Археологическаго Общества VIII (SPb), 58–913.

Unverzagt–Hermann 1958 = Wilhelm Unverzagt –Joachim Herrmann, ,,Das slavische
Brandgräberfeld von Prützke Kr. Eberswalde'' (Druckfehler, soll heißen: Kr. Brandenburg; T. W.), *Ausgrabungen und Funde III*, 107–110.

Vasmer 1947 = Vasmer, Max, ,,Zur Orts- und Flußnamenforschung'', *ZfslPh* XIX,
316–321.

Wauer 1963 = Wauer, Sophie, *Die Ortsnamen des Kreises Schönebeck*, phil. Diss.
Berlin (Maschinenschrift)

Witkowski 1965 = Witkowski, T(eodolius), (Rezension von) ,,VI. Internationaler
Kongress für Namenforschung. München: 24.–28. August 1958, Hsg. von Gerhard
Rohlfs und Karl Puchner, 3 Bände, München 1960–61'', *ZfSl* X, 582–588.

Witkowski 1966 = Witkowski, Teodolius, ,,Berlin — ein baltischer Name?'' *KZ* LXXX,
262–270.

Witkowski 1969 = Witkowski, Teodolius, ,,Die Bedeutung des Baltischen für die
slawische Namenforschung in Deutschland'', *Proceedings of the Ninth International
Congress of Onomastic Sciences*. Compiled and prepared for press by J. McN. Dodgson
and A. D. Mills, ed. by H. Draye, Louvain, 474–486.

Baltic Place-Names west of the Oder?

In the last ten years some onomastic articles have been published affirming
that there is a stratum of Baltic place-names in the territory west of the river

Oder. The author shows that many of these so-called "Baltic" place-names may without difficulty be explained as Slavic, German or common Indo-european names (*Alkun, Arkona, Berlin, Dargow, Peene, Rehse, Warnow,* etc.). There is no historical evidence of Balts west of the Oder. Archaeologists have found only two objects which seem to be connected with the mediaeval trade-route from Magdeburg to the Baltic countries. By contrast, however, there is much historical evidence about Slavs in this territory, and there are also more than 4 000 places where Slavonic archaelogical material has been found (villages, cemeteries, earthworks, pottery, implements, etc.). There is, therefore, no reason to believe in the existence of a stratum of Baltic place-names. Of course, there is also no reason to think that Slavs descend from Balts. If some place-names had to be explained by the aid of Baltic language this would arise from the fact that the Baltic and Slavonic languages are closely related, and that these names may contain words or affixes not existing in Slavonic languages as appellatives, but as relics in Slavonic names. In any case, the study of Baltic languages and the comparison of names west of the Oder with Baltic names or languages are very useful to onomastics.

VILMOS VOIGT

Hungaro-Baltica

1. In many respects, the Hungarian people and their language have been isolated for more than a millennium. As a result, a number of linguistic, folkloristic and biological characteristics have been preserved within their culture, which can throw light upon historical relationships of ancient European peoples. Accordingly, it is possible to imagine comparative philological research on Balto-Hungarian linguistic contacts. No such studies have been conducted to date. The aim of this paper is to contribute some pertinent material to such studies.

Balto-Hungarian relationships may be divided into two historical periods: a) the time prior to the arrival of the Hungarians in the Carpathian Basin (before 896 A.D.), when culture contact between the Baltic and Hungarian groups may be placed in the central part of Eastern Europe; b) the Middle Ages—and primarily via Polish mediation (approximately from Prince Gediminas to the end of the 16th century). During this period, in 1386 Jagello married Queen Jadwiga of Poland (in Hungarian Hedvig, the daughter of Lajos I, King of Hungary) and one of their sons, Władysław III, ruled both Poland and Hungary from 1400 to 1444 (under the Hungarian names of Ulászló or Lengyel ['Polish'] László). Between 1575 and 1586 the Hungarian István Báthory accepted the Polish throne and that way became the Grand Duke of Lithuania—the latter as a result of the Union of Lublin—and founded the University of Vilnius.

Mention of all the above is well justified, especially if we consider the lack of scholarly interest toward linguistic and other cultural relationships between the Balts and Hungarians, an inertia experienced on both sides.

2. Within period a) a relationship may possibly be established through the Baltic and Hungarian equivalents of the word 'amber'. This problem has already been touched upon by Baltic linguists (unfortunately without adequate historical and linguistic data on the Hungarian word) as well as Hungarian etymologists and language historians (who, in turn, ignored the results of the Baltologists). For this reason some pertinent material will be examined in greater detail below.

2.1. As is known, the Lithuanian *giñtaras* and the Latvian *dzintars* have no Baltic etymologies. Independently of J. Mikkola[1], recently B. A. Larin suggested that possible affinities might exist between these and the Hungarian word *gyanta ~ gyantár* 'amber'. His etymology[2]—held in high esteem by Soviet linguists[3]—depicts the following evolutionary sequence. The word 'amber' belonged to the language of the Pre-Finno-Ugric and Pre-Indo-European "northern peoples" who lived along the sea shore, and as a result of geographic proximity, trade and certain bilingual relationships was transmitted to the ancestors of the Hungarians (i.e. to a Finno-Ugric group). These, in turn, passed it to the ancestors of the early Balts by trade or perhaps by direct contact. As to the place and time of this transmission, Larin suggests that at the time the ancestors of the later Baltic tribes lived considerably farther east than the Baltic language area reaches today, without extending all the way to either the Baltic or the White Sea.

The Early Hungarians (or any other Finno-Ugric group) could have been anywhere in the area north or east of the Carpathian Mountains during the second and third millennia B.C. Larin's opinion is that the word later passed from Lithuanian to Latvian, and from there to the north-western Russian dialects, but not before the 9th or 10th centuries, and finally, considerably later and by Russian transmission, to the other Slavic languages.

Recent archaeological and historical results[4] both support and weaken this hypothesis. Increasing evidence suggests a Hungarian-Baltic tribal contact from 4000 B.C. on, in the area between the Vistula, Daugava and Dnieper rivers. On the other hand, it is conceivable that the Balts were already a "sea-shore" people at the time of their first contact with the Early Hungarians. In this case, the etymology of the word 'amber' becomes more problematic.

2.2. The etymology of the Hungarian word *gyanta ~ gyantár* is practically unknown. It seems to be an ancient loan-word from a hitherto obscure source. The following historical, semantic and morphological data are available on it[5].

I. Forms without final -r

[a]-stem:*gyanta** 1. 'succinum, electrum, amber' from about 1550 to about 1850, but no longer used; 2. 'resina, resin' continuously from 1585 to the present; 3. 'glissum, gypsum, glaze' from 1576 to about 1800, but no longer in use; 4. 'spirit, brandy' twentieth century, in jocular form: *hegedü-*

---

* In all Hungarian words the [a] is always labialized and the letter *gy* always denotes [ď].

gyanta 'colophony, rosin' > *torok-gyanta* 'throat rosin' = 'spirit' with a contemporary usage. MORPHOLOGICAL VARIANTS: *gyánta* documented 1611–1808, *jánta* 1685, *jánto* dialect word from the end of the 19th century. *Derivatives: gyantás* adjective from 'gyanta 1., 2., 3.' from 1585 to the present; *gyántás* adjective from 'gyanta 2. or 3.' once mentioned, in 1748; *gyantáz* verb 'supplies with gyanta 3.' continuous use from 1604 to the present.

[e]-stem: *gyenta* 1. 'amber' two data from around 1500 and 1519/1523 respectively; 2. 'resin' in current use in dialects.

[o]-stem: *gyonta* 'amber' three data, one from 1533 and twice in the same source from 1577.

II. Final -r forms

[a]-stem: *gyantár* 1. 'resin' from 1539 to at least 1800; 2. 'glaze' since 1576, and still found in dialects, especially in Eastern Hungarian (mainly in Transylvania). MORPHOLOGICAL VARIANTS: *gyántár* 1745. *Derivatives*: *gyantáros* adjective 1. 'electrinus, succineus' once mentioned in 1621; 2. 'resinosus' from 1590 to at least 1767; 3. 'gypsatus' both the dialectal and historical data mostly from Eastern Hungarian (especially from Transylvania), used from 1616 on, occurring in current dialects; *gyantároz* verb 1. 'supplies with gyantár' documented between 1611 and 1767; 2. 'supplies with resin' dialect word not restricted to Transylvania, current; *gyantározás* noun 'supplying with gyantár' documented between 1708 and 1767, but could have had a longer existence.

[e]-stem: *gyentár* 1. 'resin' around 1660; 2. 'glaze' from 1567 but out of use today. *Derivatives*: *gyentáros* adjective 'gypsatus' 1542.

[o]-stem: *gyontár* 1. 'amber' mentioned once in 1598, today unknown; 2. 'resin' dialect word, known in the past century, used mostly in Eastern Hungarian (especially in Transylvania). *Derivatives*: *gyontáros* adjective 1. 'resinosus' documented since 1662; 2. 'gypsatus' from 1636; used in contemporary dialects, especially in Transylvania, in both meanings, one of further morphological variants: *gyóntáros*.

[u]-stem: *gyuntár* 'resin' twice mentioned in one source, from around 1525. The correct spelling (originally written as "*Gijwnthar*") is not consistent. The letter *w* could very well be used as an *o* (and not as a *u*) phonetically.

2.3. The following phonetic and semantic conclusions may be drawn from the above. *Aa*) the forms without -r have been in use from 1500 to the present. *Ab*) of these, the relative sequence in time of the three stem variants [a], [e] and [o] cannot be ascertained. *Ac*) semantically, in all of these three variants the meaning 'amber' occurs, but not the other meanings. *Ad*) a possible development of the various meanings in relation to one another is the following: 'amber' > 'resin resembling amber' > 'glaze resembling amber' > other semantic derivations. *Ba*) the final *-r* forms have been used since 1525 and are current today in their derivatives, or as dialect words. *Bb*) here, too, it is impossible to decide the relative order of development of the stem variants [a], [e] and [o]. *Bc*) semantically, the most important meaning is 'resin', but 'amber' and 'glaze' also occur occasionally. *Bd*) their relative development suggests that a shift in meaning 'resin' > 'glaze' was already widely known by the middle of the 16th century. *Be*) nevertheless, the 'amber' form cannot be ascertained or dated by itself.

2.4. In order to draw further conclusions, additional facts must be introduced here. In Hungarian the first phoneme of the mentioned words is usually *gy-*, but not always. One historical datum from 1685 [*jánta*] and another dialect word from the end of the last century [*jánto*] indicate an initial *j-* [*j*]. Four other sources [1519–1523: *gentha*, 1533: *gonta*, 1542: *gentharos*, 1567: *genthar*] contain initial *g-* [*g*]. However, it is possible that in these cases the form variants are due to orthographic practices and that all these forms are to be pronounced as *gy-* [*d'*]. This would be supported by the fact that in the pronounciation of Medieval Latin in Hungary, when a *g* is preceded by an *e* or *i*, it is to be pronounced as *gy* [*d'*]. In any case, phonological alternations *j* ~ *gy* and *g* ~ *gy* are a well known characteristic of the Hungarian language during the Middle Ages.

Thus, the etymology of 'amber' in Hungarian may derive from a word with initial [*d'*]. The phoneme [*d'*] in Hungarian as the first sound in a word goes back prior to 896 A.D. According to different etymological postulations, this phoneme came either from the Finno-Ugric **j-* or the Turkic **ǰ-*. There are a large number of Hungarian words of unknown etymology with initial *gy-*[6], presumably loan words from an extinct language. Of 90 such words having the widest recent distribution, 60 may be considered to be loan words or derivatives: of these 25 are possibly Turkic, two Latin, two German and five Finno-Ugric in origin, and 30 have been generated by processes within Hungarian, but 26 of these words in Hungarian with initial *gy-* are of totally unknown origin. These are loan words most likely too, but despite their everyday use in the history of the Hungarian language we do not know where they came from[7]. Phonologically the words *gyanta* ~ *gyantár* belong to this group.

The other conspicuous phenomenon is the final *-r* itself, and its relationship with forms without such ending. Prof. G. Bárczi's opinion[8] is that the

longer form is the original, since this can be related to the Baltic words (and/
or to its Medieval Latin counterpart *gentarum*), whereas the shorter Hungarian form has no external parallel. The shorter form evolved within the
Hungarian language as a result of simplification through pronunciation
[*gyantár* > *gyantározni* verb > *gyantároztam* past tense > *gyantáztam* idem >
from this by abstraction:*gyanta-* > then finally *gyanta* noun]. A proper
linguistic antecedent to the Hungarian word *gyantár*—according to him—is
the Latin *gentarum*. This view is also shared by the late Hungarian Slavist,
Prof. I. Kniezsa[9]. In a similar vein, Prof. L. Hadrovics more recently dealt
with the relationship of these two forms. In his opinion the *-r* may have been
elided because it was considered to be a suffix[10]. (His examples, however,
are too far from the cognate words of *gyantár*.) The new Hungarian Histori-
cal-Etymological Dictionary follows the above principle: it postulates a
Medieval Latin source and accepts the phonological change *-r* > $\emptyset$.[11] The
only difference is that according to the Dictionary this change did not take
place in the conjugation, but in the cases: Nom. *gyantár* ~ Accus. *gyantárt* >
Accus. *gyantát* > Nom. *gyanta*.

2.5. Even though the above mentioned arguments seem sound enough, the
internal development of this Hungarian word is not completely understood.
Further important problems are dealt with below. *A*) If the shorter form,
postulated to be a later development, had a Hungarian usage around 1500, and
if in 1576 the same word has an additional meaning 'glaze', and, in addition,
the short forms are known in all three of their stem variants, when can we
place the adoption of *gentarum*, since the Latin word is a rather late derivative of its Baltic cognate words and not older than the Central Middle Ages?
(It should also be mentioned, that in the Hungarian Latin texts *gentarum*
never occurs; for 'amber' the forms *succinum* or *electrum* are used.) *B*) The
Hungarian stem variants [a], [o] and [e] are not without parallel in Medieval
Hungarian phonemic changes. If, on the other hand, we were to start out
with the Latin word, in the Hungarian the form *gyentár* ought to be placed
at the beginning of this process of phonetic change. *Gyentár*'s meaning of
'resin' since 1660, and its meaning of 'glaze' since 1567 are well known, but
no Hungarian evidence exists as to its meaning 'amber'. We would need a
much greater amount of time if we were to explain the presence of a form
gyanta by 1550, *gyonta* by 1533, and finally *gyenta* in 1500 [!]. (And, even more,
how and why is the meaning of all three forms at those dates already
'amber'?) Thus the search for a Medieval Latin origin of the Hungarian
word becomes difficult because of contradictions in the chronology. *C*) At
the same time, nor could the Hungarian word *gyanta* ~ *gyantár* have been

borrowed from other languages, because it has a significantly later occurrence in Slavic languages, and the Hungarian variant cannot be phonetically derived from them. The Rumanian *ghioántă* is known in its 'resin' meaning. However this is a direct borrowing from Hungarian, along with other, isolated borrowing of the Hungarian *gyontár ~ gyantár* forms in Rumanian dialects[12].

2.6. All this suggests that Larin's etymology may be the most acceptable in principle. The Baltic and Hungarian names of 'amber' indicate old affinities. We may postulate that Pre-Baltic and Pre-Finno-Ugric groups transmitted the word in the form of **dž.ntar* to the Baltic peoples, where it received a regular masculine *-s*; as well as to the Hungarians, where it changed to an initial *gy-* without any phonological difficulty[13]. In Hungarian three processes took place. First, the stems [a], [o] and [e] separated; secondly, the *-r* and *-Ø* forms split; and thirdly, the three main meanings, 'amber', 'resin', and 'glaze', became distinct from one another. All these had attained a well developed form by the beginning of the 16th century, and from the already plentiful linguistic data of this period it is clear that these phonetic and semantic changes required centuries.

Even though we may now consider the Hungarian *gyantár* a derivative prior to 896 A.D., in one respect more caution must be exercised than was by Larin. Although the Baltic [i] stem in place of the Hungarian [a], [o] and [e] makes it possible for us to derive such a distinction from an earlier date, it is precisely because of the popularity of this semiprecious stone during several millennia of trading activity that the word 'amber' must have been the object of linguistic migration and of unexpected linguistic survival without the need of any direct ethnic contact. Accordingly, it is not necessary to place its adoption within a time when the Balts and the Hungarians still lived in their original home. For its adoption by the Hungarians, the first millennium B.C. seems to be the most likely period.

3. Certain relationships of the Baltic *dainos*, the Rumanian *doină* and the Hungarian *dal* 'song' *dalol ~ danol* 'sings' may also be placed within this period. This question, however, requires closer investigation.

4. There is currently only one acceptable etymology reflecting medieval Hungaro-Baltic linguistic contact. During an analysis of the Lithuanian *lókšenos*, Fraenkel[14] submits that this word was originally Turkish, and was taken into Hungarian usage in the form *laksa ~ laska*, which, through Polish,

later became absorbed into Baltic. The number of similar examples of Hungaro-Polish-Baltic contacts could be multiplied, but only with more thorough research. This is also a problem which well deserves more attention.

Notes

1. J. Mikkola, in his paper "Einiges über den eurasischen Bernsteinhandel", *Senatne un Māksla*, I, 33–37, cites Prof. G. Gerullis's similar thesis. Cf. A. Spekke, *The Ancient Amber Routes and the Geographical Discovery of the Eastern Baltic*, Stockholm, 1957.

2. Б. А. Ларин, „О слове янтарь", *Rakstu krājums veltījums akadēmiķim profesoram Dr. Jānim Endzelīnam viņa 85 dzīves un 65 darba gadu atcerei*, Rīgā, 1959, 149–162.

3. Б. Л. Богородский, Л. С. Ковтун, Т. А. Лилич, „Борис Александрович Ларин [к юбилею учителя]", *Вопросы теории и истории языка. Сборник в честь профессора Б. А. Ларина*, Лениград, 1963, 8–9.

4. M. Gimbutas, *The Prehistory of Eastern Europe*. I, Cambridge, Mass.,1956; M. Gimbutas, *The Balts*, London, 1963; Gy. László, *Östörténetünk legkorábbi szakaszai. A finnugor östörténet régészeti emlékei a szovjet földön*, Budapest, 1961; *Hunor és Magyar nyomában*, Budapest, 1967. From the more recent general literature: A. Bartha, *A IX–X. századi magyar társadalom*, Budapest, 1968; K. Czeglédy, *Nomád népek vándorlása Napkelettől Napnyugatig*, Budapest, 1969. Here bibliography on pp. 122–134.

5. The historical data by: L. Benkő ed., *A Magyar Nyelv Történeti-Etimológiai Szótára*, I, Budapest, 1967, p. 1120, and the works mentioned therein.

6. E. Moór, "Die Ausbildung des uralischen Konsonantismus", *Acta Linguistica Academiae Scientiarum Hungaricae* II, 430–432; G. Bárczi, *Magyar hangtörténet*, Budapest, 1958, 120.

7. For example: *gyanu* 'suspicion', *gyapot* 'cotton', *gyarapodik* 'increases', *gyatra* 'sorry, miserable', *gyáva* 'coward', *gyenge* 'weak', *gyep* 'grass, lawn, green', *gyere* 'come' *gyermek* 'child', *gyík* 'lizard', *gyilkos* 'murderer', *gyors* 'quick', *győz* 'gains victory', *gyújt* 'lights fire', *gyűlöl* 'hates'.

8. G. Bárczi, "Gyanta", *Magyar Nyelv*, XLV, 185–187.

9. I. Kniezsa, *A magyar nyelv szláv jövevényszavai*, I/2., Budapest, 1955, 833.

10. L. Hadrovics, *Jövevényszó-vizsgálatok*, Budapest, 1965, 51–52, esp. 66.

11. See above note 5.

12. L. Tamás, *Etymologisch-historisches Wörterbuch der ungarischen Elemente im Rumänischen. (Unter Berücksichtigung der Mundartwörter)*, Budapest, 1966, 380.

13. G. Bárczi, *Magyar hangtörténet*, Budapest, 1958, 119. — G. Bárczi, *Hangtörténet*, In: G. Bárczi – L. Benkő – J. Berrár ed., *A magyar nyelv története*, Budapest, 111–112.

14. E. Fraenkel, *Litauisches etymologisches Wörterbuch*, Heidelberg, 1955–1965, 385.

TADEUSZ ZDANCEWICZ

Рельефные и топонимические названия с балтийской основой *plei- (и родственными с ней) на Сувальщине в северо-восточной Польше

I

Сувальщиной или Сувалкским поозерьем принято называть территорию приблизительно трех повятов (районов) на северо-востоке Белостоцкого воеводства (области): Сувалкского, Сейнского и Августовского. С исторической точки зрения эта территория является ятвяжской, которая от 1422 г. до 1795 г. принадлежала великому княжеству Литовскому и почти целиком входила в состав Троцкого воеводства, представляя собой три лесничества: Перстуньское, Пшеломское и Мерецкое[1]. Через Сувальщину проходит часть современной этнической границы между балтийцами и славянами, потому что в этом районе в пределах Польской Народной Республики находится, как известно, энклав литовского населения. Это население занимает приграничную полосу с Советским Союзом (Литовской ССР) на протяжении около 30 км и шириной от 10 до 15 км в восточной части Сувалкского и на северном востоке Сейнского повятов. В языковом отношении почти все литовцы, проживающие на Сувальщине, относятся к дзуковским диалектам и лишь только на севере на маленькой территории — к капсам[2].

Вследсвие национального положения, которое отличается сосуществованием двух своеобразных этнических групп, принадлежащих к двум разным индоевропейским языковым ветвям, ономастика Сувальщины также является неоднородной, балтийской и славянской. Это наблюдается как в рельефных, так и топонимических названиях. Однако характерной приметой является то, что распространение балтийских и славянских географических названий не совпадает с современной этнической границей. Особенно в ономастике на современной польской этнической территории исследуемого района сравнительно часто выступают со славистской точки зрения непонятные наименования. Из-за непосредственной близости территории, заселённой литовцами, и из-за балтийского характера данного района в прошлом их можно интерпретировать как слова балтийского происхождения. Заметим, что хотя в меньшей степени, но и славянская ономастика проникает на этнически литовскую территорию.

На исследуемой нами территории ономастическим исследованиям в более широком масштабе положил начало проф. Кнут-Олоф Фальк[3]. С исторической точки зрения много ценного в эти исследования внес доц. Ежи Висьневски. За последнее время появились интересные работы, написанные доц. Ежим Налепой и доц. Тамарой Бух, а также работы проф. Владимира Н. Топорова и проф. Антонины Обрембской-Яблоньской, посвященные балтийской ономастике на территории Подлясья, примыкающей к Сувальщине с юга. Вопросов, связанных с Сувальщиной, посредственно касаются также работы проф. Яна Отрембского, проф. Яна Сафаревича и др. о литовской ономастике и работы проф. Галины Сафаревич, доц. Губерта Гурновича и др., трактующих о славянской ономастике на соседних территориях и предлагающих решение некоторых общих проблем либо объясняющих отдельные сувалкские названия. Однако, несмотря на накапливающуюся приблизительно от 30 лет ономастическую литературу на тему Сувальщины, в лингвистической проблематике этого района есть еще ряд нерешенных вопросов.

Вопросы ономастики Сувальщины были затронуты автором настоящей статьи в докладе на I конференции исторических наук в Белостоке в 1961 г.[4] и в статье «Gwary powiatu sejneńskiego na tle procesów osadniczych»[5]. Однако с рельефными названиями и топонимами Сувалкского поозерья обстоятельно ознакомился лишь в 1963—1967 гг. В это время по поручению Кафедры белорусской филологии Варшавского университета в трех вышеуказанных повятах на польской и переходной польско-белорусской территориях собрал весь доступный в то время ономастический материал сам, а на литовской — вместе с доц. Тамарой Бух. Согласно с территориальной основой прежних наших исследований нас интересовали в основном ономастические данные на славянском ареале, зато собранный материал на этнически литовской территории должна была исследовать доц. Тамара Бух. Так как соответствующая работа доц. Тамары Бух не появилась и тем самым нет возможности сослаться на нее, при иллюстрации и интерпретации ниже исследуемых нами названий на славянской территории мы должны будем сами привести материал из литовского ареала.

II

Настоящая статья посвящена исследованию отдельной, со славистской точки зрения неопределенной группы названий рельефов и топонимов, которые близки по значению и этимологически родственны. Преимущественно (в 44 случаях) они являются названиями физиографических объектов и только в двух случаях — топонимами. Как видно из прилагаемой к статье карты, определенное количество их выступает на польской части Сувалкского поозерья, примыкающей к литовской территории, и в приграничной полосе бывших пшеломского и мерецкого лесничеств (последнее было заселено в основном литовским населением) достигает даже до Пшеросля[6]. Однако они концентрируются прежде всего на этнически литовской территории. Эти названия предлагаем считать балтийскими по происхождению.

На этнически польском ареале (вверх от 22 пункта[7]) нами отмечены как названия рельефов, так и топонимы. Первую группу составляют 10 следующих названий физиографических объектов: *Plíńa*, род. п. *Plíńi* — болото, заросли (47), — луг, болото (49), *Plínuća*, род. п. *Plínući* — луг (26), *Plínuta*, род. п. *Plínuty* — болото, луг (22), *Plíńove Baǧna*, род. п. *Plíńoveh Baǧen* — болото, заросли (30), *Plíńova Gura*, род. п. *Plíńovei̯ Gury* — холм, поле (30); *Poplinske Bagno*, род. п. *Poplinskego Bagna* — болото, заросли (25), *Paplínćova Gurka*, род. п. *Paplínćovei̯ Gurki* — холм (57); *Plíḱi*, род. п. *Plíḱof* — лесная поляна (25), *Plíkuv́izna*, род. п. *Plíkuv́izny* — поле (23).

Топонимы представлены следующими двумя примерами: *Plíńa*, род. п. *Plíńi* — часть деревни Романовцы (47) и *Poplin*, род. п. *Poplina* — деревня (24). На этнически польской территории вместе с названиями рельефов они составляют 12 примеров.

III

Как видно уже на первый взгляд, все приведенные наименования трудно объяснить вообще или толково (напр. *Plíḱi*) на славянской основе. Зато выше указанные географические условия, т. е. почти сплошное наличие этих названий только в той части Сувальщины, которая примыкает к литовской территории, указывают, что решения вопроса их происхождения следует искать на балтийской почве.

Именно на этнически литовской территории (пункты 1–21) исследуемые нами названия отмечени в 34 (!) случаях при наименовании физиографических объектов. К ним относятся следующие примеры: *Plýnė*[8] — луг, болото (1), — болото, заросли (2), — болото (3), — пастбище (4), — луг (5), — болото (9, 11), — луг (12), — луг, болото (13), — болото (14 — два раза), — луг (15, 16); *Raudóna Plýnė* — луг (5), *Kėžaplynė* — болото (6), *Liéptaplynė* — болото (6), *Plýnės* — луг (17), — болото, луг (19), — болота (20)[9], *Plýnabalė* — болото (18), *Plýnių̨ Salà* — луг (21), *Plynēlė* — луг (8), — болото (14 — два раза), *Beržų̨ Plynēlė* — болото (11), *Plynēlė* — болото (7, 11), — болото, луг (18), *Plynaĭtė* — луг (18), *Plynùkė* — луг (10); *Paplyny̆s* — болото, заросли (1), — болото (14); *Plùkė* — болото,

Территориальное распространение балтийских и славянских
географических названий с преобладающим значением
„дикий безлесный луг, болото"

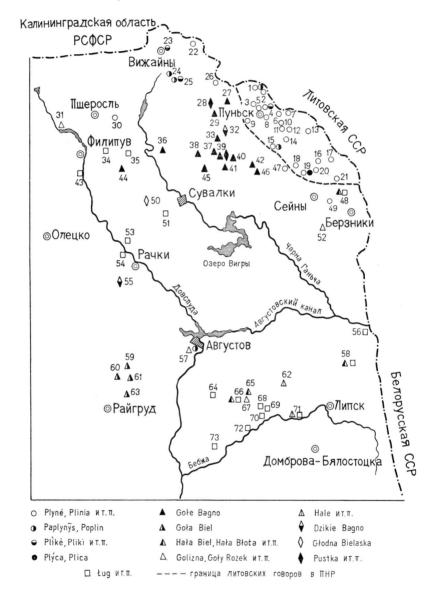

O   Plyné, Plinia и т.п.   ▲ Gołe Bagno   △ Hale и т.п.

◐ Paplynỹs, Poplin   ▲ Goła Biel   ◆ Dzikie Bagno

◓ Plìkė, Pliki и т.п.   ▲ Hała Biel, Hała Błota и т.п.   ◇ Głodna Bielaska

● Plýca, Plica   △ Golizna, Goły Rożek и т.п.   ◆ Pustka и т.п.

□ Ług и т.п.   - - - граница литовских говоров в ПНР ямы после торфоразработки (4); *Plýca* — луг (19)[10]. Следует подчеркнуть, что интересующих нас названий отмечено почти в три раза больше на этнической литовской территории, чем на польской.

Легко можно убедиться, что такие названия выступают часто также в более отдаленных частях литовской территории. Например, в словаре-справочнике Lietuvos TSR upių ir ežerų vardynas, Vilnius 1963 (на стр. 118 и 126) отмечается: *Plỹnas* — озеро (Kuktiškes), *Plýnupis* (K. Naumiestis), *Plýnupelis* (Gražiškiai); *Paplynė* (Vilkija); *Plikių ežerùkai* — два озера (Kintai), *Plìkupelis* (Šeduva). Также Słownik geograficzny[11] (в томах: VII, стр. 849, VIII, стр. 262–264 и 792, XV ч. II, стр. 457–458 и 495) фиксирует около 50 названий на современной или исторически балтийской территории, которые являются преимущественно топонимами и репрезентируют все соответствующие сувалкские ономастические типы.

Зарегистрированные же в данном словаре (том VII, стр. 849, 937, 944 и 949) названия со славянской территории, которых эвентуально можно бы подозревать в связи с сувалкскими, ограничены лишь следующими: *Peplin* alias *Pelplin*[12] — деревня (повят Старогардский), *Peplin* — поместье (повят Хойницкий), *Pepliner Aussendeich* (нем.) — имущество (повят Мальборский); *Paplin* — деревня, фольварк и поселок (повят Скерневицкий), *Paplin* — деревня и фольварк (повят Венгровский), *Paplińska Wólka* — деревня (повят Венгровский); *Paplińce* alias *Poplińce* — деревня (повят Литынский на западе Украины).

Среди этих нескольких названий только *Paplin* и *Paplińska Wólka* имеют достаточную славянскую мотивацию. Славянское же происхождение остальных не является бесспорным. Например, без более подробных исследований и без учета исторических данных нельзя решить вопроса о славянском или возможном балтийском характере названия *Paplińce* с его вариантом *Poplińce*. Дискуссионными являются также названия на Поморье, которые выступают в приграничной полосе древнепрусской территории. С одной стороны, с некоторыми трудностями М. Рудницки[13] высказывается за лехическим происхождением названия *Peplin* и его параллельных форм. С другой же стороны, новейшие исследования Г. Шалля[14] и В. Н. Топорова[15], по-видимому, обнаруживают, что к западу от Вислы через Поморье, Мекленбург Шлезвиг-Гольштейн балтийские названия достигают даже за Эльбу. Следовательно, название *Peplin* с его вариантами надо бы подробно рассмотреть в аспекте его отношения к балтийской ономастике.

Несмотря на этого рода еще не решенную сомнительность относительно отдельных названий на славянских территориях и независимо от результатов ее разрешения, уже теперь только на основании материала, не вызывающего никаких сомнений, можно считать, что в области географии как пространственные отношения, так и количественное расположение названий решающим образом свидетельствуют о литовском происхождении исследуемой группы сувалкских рельефных и топонимических названий.

IV

Неслучайно естественный образ мышления подсказал нам выдвинуть географические факторы на первый план. Они нуждались в привлечении материала из этнически литовской части Сувальщины, а это в свою очередь дает возможность осуществить семантический анализ исследуемых названий и предложить их этимологию на более широком материале. В данном случае особенно важным является факт, что на сувалкской этнически литовской территории довольно четко сохранилось апеллятивное значение группы рельефных названий типа *Plýnė* и его производных. Именно так жители данного района называют болото или дикий, неурожайный луг[16]. Такое же апеллятивное значение регистрирует Litauisches etymologisches Wörterbuch E. Френкеля[17], в котором (т. I, стр. 611) под заглавным словом *pleĩnė 1.* 'weit ausgedehnte, baumlose Fläche' отмечаются следующие интересующие нас нарицательные слова: *plýnė, plýnia* 'offene, baumlose, unbebaute Ebene, flaches, unbewaldetes Land, Einöde, Moor, Sumpfboden, Moorboden' и связываются с ними топонимические названия — древнепрусское *Plylawken* из **Plynlawken* и литовское *Plynlaukiai* и также литовское рельефное название *Plynės* (название болота).

Апеллятивное значение, выступающее в вышеуказанных литовских нарицательных именах, обнаруживают почти все сувалкские рельефные (топонимические также — об этом ниже) названия данной группы, ибо почти без исключений как на литовской, так и на примыкающей польской территориях названия *Plýnė, Plína* и их родственные употребляются по отношению к болотам или лугам (1–3, 5–21; 22, 25, 26, 30, 46, 49). Отступления наблюдаются лишь в небольшом количестве случаев, когда названия этой группы относятся к другим (не к лугу или болоту) рельефам, таким как: пастбище (быть может включающее также и болото) (4), холм и поле (вторично названные ввиду расположения рядом с болотом) (30) и холм[18] (57).

Весьма вероятно, что первоначально вся данная группа названий относилась только к болотам и к неурожайным лугам, непоросшим притом деревьями. В настоящее время это первоначальное положение,

основанное на соответствии значения названия с характером наименованного рельефа, во многих случаях подверглось существенным изменениям, потому что в результате мелиорации и освоения большинство
ранее неурожайных торфяников превратилось в высокоуражайные
луга. После осушения некоторые болота также поросли деревьями
(1, 2, 25, 30, 47). Однако эти изменения, вызванные человеческой деятельностью и самой природой, не повлияли на существующую ономастику,
в результате чего это приводило к противоречию между апеллятивным
значением названия и характером определяемого рельефа. Несомненно,
что на польской территории эти противоречия чувствуются только в
тех немногочисленных деревнях, в которых наблюдается двуязычие,
тогда как в ощущении поляков, не знающих литовского языка, указанные названия не имеют апеллятивного значения.

Кроме рельефных названий, принимая во внимание апеллятивное
значение и происхождение, к этой семантической группе относятся
также сувалкские топонимы *Plíńa* (47) и *Poplin* (24). Они являются
первичными названиями рельефов, перенесенными потом к топонимам.
Об этом неопровержимо свидетельствует существование соответствующих физиографических объектов в 47 пункте[19] и рядом с 24 пунктом:
Plíńa — болото, заросли (47) и *Poplinske Bagno* — болото, заросли (25).

Учитывая только что выясненное и выступающее в определенном
количестве названий, нарушение в отношении их апеллятивного значения к характеру названных рельефов, думается, что семантическая
связь вышеуказанной группы как рельефных, так их топонимических
названий с литовскими нарицательными существительными *plýnė*,
plýnia не подлежит сомнению.

Рельефные названия типа *Plìkė*, *Plíki* и их родственные связаны с
нарицательными словами *plìkė* 'Glatze, kahle Stelle, Blösse, kahle Wiese,
unfruchtbarer Acker'; *plykē* 'kahle Stelle im Getreidefeld', которые зафиксированы в словаре Е. Френкеля (т. I, стр. 623) под заглавным словом *plìkas* 'kahl, nackt, entblösst, mittellos, arm'. Значения и апеллятивного эквивалента для названия *Plýca* нам не удалось установить. В
словаре Е. Френкеля (т. I, стр. 612) под заглавным словом *pleĩnė 1.*
древнепрусское название *Plica Bartha* сопоставляется с древнепрусским
Plixlawken и литовским *Pliklaukiai* т. е. с названиями, связанными по
значению с литовским *plìkas*.

Рельефы Сувальщины, обозначенные этой группой названий, как
на польской, так и на литовской территориях являются менее однородными, чем в предыдущей группе. Наименования *Plìkė*, *Plíki* и родственные относятся к болоту (4), полю (23) и лесной поляне (25); на

именование *Plýca* — к лугу (19). Однако во всех этих случаях имеется в виду открытое, не поросшее деревьями пространство, т. е. соответствует значению литовского слова *plìkas*.

Обе указанные группы названий и апеллятивных слов, являющихся основой для названий, в указанном словаре (т. I, стр. 611) Е. Френкель считает родственными, излагая это следующим образом под заглавным словом *pleĩnė 1.*: «Lit. *pleĩnė, plýnas* und ihre Entsprechungen beruhen auf einer Basis **plei-*. Sollte die Grundbedeutung 'baumlose Fläche' bzw. 'baumlos' sein, so sind sie mit lit. *plìkas*, lett. *pliks* 'kahl, nackt' und deren Verwandten zu vergleichen (s. s. v. v. *plìkas, pleikanà, plaikstýti, pleĩkė, pliẽksti*), die von der idg. Wurzel **(s)p(h)el-* 'abreissen, spalten' (s. auch s. v. *pélti*) abgeleitet sind. Für diese Deutung würden sprechen einerseits lit. *pléinėti 1.* 'sich (ab)schuppen (von der Gesichtshaut)', andererseits die neben preuss. *Plylawken*, lit. *Plynlaukiai, Plynės* begegnenden preuss. ON *Plixlawken, Plica Bartha*, lit. ON *Pliklaukiai*.»

Таким образом в свете семантического и этимологического анализов балтийское происхождение исследованных рельефных и топонимических названий на Сувальщине кажется нам бесспорным.

V

Необходимо еще немного задержаться на вопросе об изменениях, которым подверглись интересующие нас названия в процессе славянизации. К сожалению, полное освещение этого вопроса (вместе со словообразовательными проблемами) будет нами представлено в другой работе. В настоящей статье это сделать невозможно как из-за отсутствия места, так и из-за того, что всестороннее и исчерпывающее истолкование этого вопроса возможно только на основании всего, подозреваемого в балтийском происхождении, ономастического материала из Сувальщины, а не на его лишь выборочной части, которая является объектом наших наблюдений в настоящей работе. Итак, ограничимся несколькими замечаниями относительно двух названий, которые по сравнению их с балтийскими первообразами в процессе славянизации подверглись трудно объяснимым преображениям. Такими названиями являются: *Paplińćova Gurka* — холм (57) и *Plikuvízna* — поле (23). Кроме того затрагиваем вопрос, связанный со всеми исследуемыми нами названиями, о так называемой трансляционной славянизации.

Название *Paplińćova Gurka* не является вполне определенным относительно его балтийского происхождения[20]. Однако, если принять ее балтийское происхождение, то допустимы две возможности интерпретации изменений, которым она подверглась в процессе славянизации.

Оно может быть вторичным от названия другого рельефа (как, например, в 30 пункте *Plińova Gura* от рельефа *Plińove Bagna*), название которого, сохраненное в сочетании *Plińova Gura — Plińove Bagna*, в данном случае (*Paplińćova Gurka*) утратилось. Оно может быть также притяжательным названием, образованным от названия владельца, которое в свою очередь произведено от названия местности, из которой данный владелец прибыл. В обоих случаях славянизированную структуру производящей основы названия *Paplińćova Gurka* мы должны восстановить как *Paplińćes и отнести его к балтийскому названию типа *Paplynỹs*. Относительно названия рельефа, то в процессе славянизации произошло замещение славянским аффиксом -*ес* балтийского -*ỹs*[21]. В случае личного имени по местности вероятным больше всего является присоединение славянского суффикса -*ес*, с помощью которого на этой территории образуются наименования жителей по местности[22], к топониму, славянизированному благодаря отсечению балтийского суффикса -*ỹs*[23], т. е. присоединился к форме *Paplin* или *Poplin*. Неисключена здесь также непосредственная субституция балтийского суффикса, образующего наименования жителей по местности, славянским -*ес*.

Название *Plikuvizna* принадлежит к сравнительно многочисленной группе рельефных и топонимических наименований с суффиксом -*izna* на Сувальщине[24]. По-видимому, оно связано с литовским названием типа *Plikių Laukas. Процесс славянизации последнего наименования протекал, по всей вероятности, через посредственную фазу *Plikove Pole как, например, название *Plińove Bagna* (30). На этом этапе в составной отличительной части названия произошла замена литовского род. п. мн. числа именительным ед. числа притяжательного прилагательного, образованного от балтийской основы с помощью славянского суффикса -*ov*- и совершился полный перевод его определяемого члена. Следующим этапом славянизации была семантическая конденсация определяемого члена *Pole* и субстантивация определяющего компонента при помощи суффикса -*izna* (ср. ниже приводимое название *Golizna*).

В связи с выше указанным названием мы коснулись явления славянизации путем перевода, т. е. так называемой трансляционной славянизации[25]. Балтийское происхождение так славянизированного названия легко установить, когда переводится, как например, в названии *Plikuvizna*, только часть названия. Но намного труднее это определить, когда имеем дело с полным переводом.

Так как Сувалкское поозерье, как указывает уже само название, в отношении рельефа местности сравнительно однородное, то физиографические объекты, названия которых являются объектом наших исследований в настоящей статье, выступают на всей его (как балтийской, так и славянской) территории. В связи с этим возникает еще один очередной вопрос; не славянизировались ли интересующие нас названия соответствующих рельефов путем полного перевода на польских и переходных польско-белорусских территориях данного поозерья? Чтобы ответить на этот вопрос, надо установить, как называются соответствующие объекты, т. е. не поросшие деревьями болота, неурожайные луга и, смотря по обстоятельствам, неурожайные поля на всей славянской территории Сувальщины и определить географическое расположение этих названий.

Для такого рода рельефов нами отмечены следующие названия: *Gołe Bagno* — болото, заросли (27), — болото (29), — болото, заросли (33), — болото, трясина (36), — болото, заросли (37, 38, 39), — болото (40), *Gołe Bagna* — болото, трясина (41), *Gołobagnove Gury* — холмы (41), *Gołe Bagno* — болото (42), *Pastevńig Goły* — болота, поля (44), *Gołe Bagno* — болото (45, 46), *Goły Rożek* — полуостров на озере (52); *Goła Beł* — луг (59, 60, 61), — луг, заросли (63), *Hała Beł* — болото, лес (48), *Hał'e Błota* — болото (58), *Hała Błota* — луг (65), — луга, заросли (66), *Hałi* — луга (62), *Hałe* — болота (71); *Gołizna* — полуостров на озере (31), — пастбище (67), *Goła Zośka* — полуостров на озере, поляна (57); *Łyse Murǵi* — поле, хутора[26] (71); *Žike Bagno* — болото (32, 55); *Głodna Bełaska* — луг (50); *Pustka* — луга, поле (28), *Pustki* — болото, заросли (39); *Łuk* — болото (34), — луг, пруд, долина (35), — луг (43), *Žabi Łuk* — котловина, лес (48), *Łuǵi* — поле, малый пруд (51), *Łuk* — болото, пруд (53), *Łuǵi* — болото, луг (54), *Šymkove Łuški* — болотце (56), *Łuǵi* — болото (58), *Lisa Łuk* — луг, лес (58), *Łuk* — болото, поле, холм (64), *Łuǵi* — лес (66), *Łuk* — пастбище (68), — болота, пастбище (69), *Łuǵi* — пастбище (70), *Łużek* — поле, перелесок, хутор (71), *Łusk'e* — луга, поле, хутора (72), *Adamkof Łuk* — луг, поле, хутора (72), *Łuk* — болото (73).

Исследуя процитированный славянский материал, особенно интересным снова оказалось рассмотрение его с географической точки зрения. Прежде всего обращают на себя внимание названия с прилагательным *goły*. Итак, как нетрудно заметить на карте, названия типа *Gołe Bagno* образуют тесную группу только на севере и вообще отсутствуют в остальных частях исследуемого района. Наибольшее сгущение их наблюдается в непосредственной близости с этнической литовской территорией. Также на территории, непосредственно примыкающей от юга к литовской, отмечено название *Hała Beł* с прилагательным в белорусской форме. Следующие четыре названия типа *Goła Beł* составляют также скопление на тесной территории между Августовом и Райгродом, правду говоря, более отдаленной от литовской, но на которой балтийские названия сохранились до нашего времени[27]. Кроме того названия *Pustka*, *Pustki* выступают лишь в пределах ареала, занятого наименованием *Gołe Bagno*, а следовательно, в приграничной литовской полосе. На основании такого географического расположения, по всей вероятности, можно принять, что по крайней мере в некоторых случаях данные славянские названия являются переводами соответствующих балтийских.

Не безразличным также для вопроса о трансляционной славянизации является географическое расположение славянского названия *Ług*, хотя оно почти отсутствует[28] на территории между Чарной Ганьчей и современной этнической литовской границей (бывшие Пшеломская и Мерецкая пущи). Выступает же оно в основном на юге Сувальщины на переходной польско-белорусской территории и еще на территории к западу от линии Чарной Ганьчи (бывшая Перстуньская пуща), т. е. на территориях, сравнительно отдаленных от приграничной литовской полосы. По-видимому, такое его географическое расположение является отражением пределов древнейшего польского и русского осадничества по побережьям реки Довспуды[29]. Одновременно это указывает на относительно недалекое прошлое славянской ономастики на территории к востоку от Чарной Ганьчи. Следовательно, подтверждается возможность частой славянизации балтийских названий в частности путем перевода.

Перечень местностей, условно обозначенных номерами в тексте и на карте

А. Этнически литовская территория:

1. Трамполе, 2. Гелуйше, 3. Калиново, 4. Крейвяны, 5. Пуньск (деревня), 6. Волыньце, 7. Бураки, 8. Тракишки, 9. Шолтаны, 10. Компоте, 11. Огурки, 12. Пелэле, 13. Буда Завидугерска, 14. Дзедзюле, 15. Рейштокеме, 16. Бубэле, 17. Радзюте, 18. Клейвы, 19. Лумбе, 20. Бержине, 21. Жегары.

Б. Этнически польская и переходная польско-белорусская территории:

22. Эйшерышки, 23. Вижайны, 24. Поплин, 25. Бондишки, 26. Купово, 27. Котёлки, 28. Кшывулька около Шиплишек, 29. Рыбальня, 30. Бленда, 31. Чарнэ, 32. Ситковизна, 33. Липово, 34. Мотуле Старэ, 35. Сметюхувка, 36. Червонэ Багно, 37. Глембоки Рув, 38. Рыхтын, 39. Клёнорейсть, 40. Калетник, 41. Дембово, 42. Орлинек, 43. Гарбас,

44. Аграфинувка, 45. Венгельня, 46. Еглювек около Краснополя, 47. Романовце, 48. Дворчиско, 49. Потькуны, 50. Тштянэ, 51. Зелёнэ Камедульске, 52. Посейнеле, 53. Сидоры около Рачек, 54. Малэ Рачки, 55. Витувка, 56. Рудавка, 57. Августов (город), 58. Рубцово, 59. Лабентник, 60. Попово, 61. Помяны, 62. Груске, 63. Солиступка, 64. Комашувка, 65. Длуге, 66. Колёния Тисув, 67. Крылатка, 68. Стёкла, 69. Красныбур, 70. Есёново около Красныбора, 71. Острове, 72. Красноборки, 73. Ямины.

Примечания

1. Ср. J. Wiśniewski, «Dzieje osadnictwa w powiecie sejneńskim od XV do XIX wieku», *Materiały do dziejów ziemi sejneńskiej*, Białystok, 1963, 34–38; T. Zdancewicz, «Gwary powiatu sejneńskiego na tle procesów osadniczych», *Materiały do dziejów ziemi sejneńskiej*, Białystok, 1963, 232–235.

2. Ср. T. Buch, «Litewskie nazwy miejscowe w powiatach Sejny i Suwałki», *Onomastica*, VII, 1–2, Kraków, 1961, 221.

3. Из-за ограниченных рамок настоящей статьи указываются лишь фамилии исследователей без цитирования соответствующих работ.

4. T. Zdancewicz, «Wpływy litewskie i wschodniosłowiańskie w polskich gwarach pod Sejnami», *Acta Baltico-Slavica*, I, Białystok, 1964, 232–233 (надо заметить, что на стр. 232 во второй строке снизу в корректе пропущено название *Šaryńis*).

5. T. Zdancewicz, *Gwary powiatu sejneńskiego* ..., 236–237.

6. Исключением является название холма *Paplinćova Gurka* (57), которое отмечено в пределах города Августова, сравнительно более отдаленного от этнически литовской территории. Несмотря на это балтийское происхождение данного названия не исключено, потому что еще дальше в западном направлении от Августова на расстоянии 10 км нами записано название болота *Trokele*, которое является несомненно балтийским. Надо также помнить, что Августов лежит на древнем пути сообщения Литвы с Пруссией и с Польшей, который использовался уже крестоносцами (ср. «Wegeberichte», *Scriptores Rerum Prussicarum*, II, Leipzig, 1863, 691–692). Этот путь, названный потом варшавско-ковенским, перестал играть важную роль только после постройки железной дороги в XIX веке. Вдоль его в эпоху великого княжества Литовского должны были существовать литовские селения.

7. В тексте и на карте цифры указывают деревни, в которых отмечено данное название. Перечень деревень приводится в конце статьи.

8. Во время исследовательской поездки на этнически литовской территории от информаторов-литовцев записи делала Тамара Бух.

9. В 19 и 20 пунктах записано также от информаторов-поляков: *Plińi*, род. п. *Plińof* — болото, луг (19), *Plińe*, род. п. *Pliń* — болота (20).

10. Также от информатора-поляка: *Plica*, род. п. *Plicy* — луг (19).

11. *Słownik geograficzny Królestwa Polskiego i innych krajów słowiańskich pod redakcją Bronisława Chlebowskiego*, I–XV, Warszawa, 1880–1902.

12. *Słownik geograficzny* (VII, 944–945) указывает, что в живой речи жителей данное название произносится только как *Peplin*, даже зачастую

Paplin, но никогда как *Pelplin*; в документах между прочим: *Polplin, Polpnin, Poplin, Pelplyn, Poelplinum.*

13. M. Rudnicki, «Nazwy geograficzne (Pomorza)», *Pamiętnik Instytutu Bałtyckiego, Seria B, Z. 1, Polskie Pomorze, I. Ziemia i ludzie*, Toruń, 1929, 271–308.

14. H. Schall, «Die baltisch-slawische Sprachgemeinschaft zwischen Elbe und Weichsel», *Atti e memorie del VII Congresso intern. di scienze onomastische*, II, Firenze, 1963. Его же: «Baltische Dialekte im Namengut Nordwestslawiens», KZ, LXXIX, 1964. Его же: «Baltische Gewässernamen im Flußsystem «Obere Havel» (Südost-Mecklenburg)», *Baltistica* II, 2, стр. 7–42.

15. В. Н. Топоров, „К вопросу о топонимических соответствиях на балтийских территориях и к западу от Вислы, *Baltistica*, I, 2, Vilnius 1966, стр. 103–111. Его же: „О балтийских элементах в гидронимии и топонимии к западу от Вислы", *Slavica Pragensia* VIII, 255–263.

16. В ощущении населения эти названия носят ярко выраженную обесценивающую окраску. Об этом свидетельствует добавочно записанная в 4 пункте информация об употреблении термина *plýnė* как бранного слова в адрес ленивых и бесполезных девушек.

17. E. Fraenkel, *Litauisches Etymologisches Wörterbuch*, I–II, Heidelberg-Göttingen, 1962–1965.

18. Название его не совсем ясное. Быть может оно вторично по отношению к рельефу, наименование которого не сохранилось, или возможно по отношению к владельцу. Ср. также стр. 583, сноску 6 и стр. 588–589.

19. О вторичном характере топонимического названия *Plińa* относительно 47 пункта свидетельствует также записанная там добавочная информация: *nazyvaįo Plińa, bo ońi i ṁeškaįo tam ƒ Plińi, v bagńe.*

20. Ср. стр. 583, сноску 6 и стр. 586, сноску 18.

21. K. O. Falk, «Ze studiów nad slawizacją litewskich nazw miejscowych i osobowych, 1. O wtórnej funkcji sufiksu -ec; o nazwach miejscowych na -ańce, *Scando-Slavica*, IX, 95. Его же: «O metodach slawizacji litewskich nazw osobowych i miejscowych. O genezie i rozpowszechnieniu nazw na -ańce.» *Språkliga Bidrag*, XII, 7.

22. K. O. Falk, «Ze studiów ...», 87; T. Zdancewicz, «Gwary ludowe powiatu augustowskiego jako wynik procesów osadniczych», *Studia i materiały do dziejów Pojezierza Augustowskiego*, Białystok, 1967, 315.

23. K. O. Falk, «Ze studiów ...», 88–89. Его же: «O metodach ...», 3–5. (См. также рецензию Т. Зданцевича на две вышеуказанные работы К. О. Фалька, *Acta Baltico-Slavica*, V, 434–440.)

24. Ср. H. Safarewiczowa, *Nazwy miejscowe typu Mroczkowizna, Klimontowszczyzna*, Wrocław, 1956, карта.

25. K. O. Falk, "Ze studiów ..", 88–90. Его же: "O metodach ..", 7–9.

26. Кроме этого примера, прилагательное *łysy* выступило (в 21 случае) только в названиях холмов типа *Łysa Góra.*

27. Ср. стр. 583, сноску 6.

28. Кроме единичного примера *Žabi Łuk* в пункте 48.

29. Ср. J. Wiśniewski, «Kilka uwag o osadnictwie południowych puszcz pojaćwieskich od XV do XVII wieku», *Rocznik Białostocki*, I, Białystok, 1961, 305–309 и карта XII.

Local and Place Names with Baltic Root *plei-
(and Cognates) in the Region of Suwalszczyzna, North-East Poland

The author examines 44 local names and 2 place names—obscure from the Slavic point of view—in the region of Suwalszczyzna (i.e., the Suwalki Lake District) in north-east Poland. In the past, Suwalszczyzna was largely a Baltic territory (it is an old Yatving territory, the north-eastern part of which was later colonized by Lithuanians, who live to-day in an enclave in the eastern part of Suwalszczyzna), and we may therefore suspect that these names are of Baltic origin.

In the Polish part of Suwalszczyzna 12 names have been recorded, e.g., *Plíña, Plíki* (and cognates); in the Lithuanian part 34 names, e.g., *Plýnė, Plìkė* (and cognates). From the semantic point of view the local names have reference mainly to swamps, barren land and sometimes to open fields. These local names were later transferred to place names.

Examination of the above onomastic material from the geographical point of view shows that in the region of Suwalszczyzna these names appear throughout the ethnically Lithuanian territory. On the ethnically Slavic territory they appear only in that part which is directly continuous to the Lithuanian territory. These names can be found throughout modern or historical Baltic territory. Thus, the geographical evidence speaks clearly for the Baltic origin of the names under consideration.

Moreover, the semantic and etymological analyses of the discussed names allow us to connect them with mutually related Lithuanian appellatives, e.g. *plýnė, plýnia* and *plìkė, plykẽ*, and thus explain their Baltic origin.

The onomastic material from the whole Slavic territory of Suwalszczyzna which relates to the above-mentioned physiographical objects is examined in the article. The areals compared with the ethnically Lithuanian territory permits the hypothesis that Polish local names in the Suwalki Lake District, such as *Gole Bagno, Gola Bel*, and *Pustka*, may be slavized loan translations of Lithuanian names.

Z. ZINKEVIČIUS

Dėl vienos rytų aukštaičių dviskaitos galūnės

Rytų Lietuvoje ē kamieno daiktavardžiai, turintieji prieš kamiengalį -ė-priebalsį l (avēlė, , kiaŭlė, pelē ...), vietoj laukiamos dviskaitos vardininko-galininko galūnės -i, pvz., dvì avelì, kiaulì, pelì, daug kur turi galūnę -ъι: dvì avelъι, kiaulъι, pelъι. Tokia galūnė pastebėta vietomis apie Pàmpėnus (Pùm-pėnus), Pãnevėžį, Taujėnus, Panemunēlį, Ùkmergę. Matyt, ji turima ir daug kur kitur rytų aukštaičių plote, tačiau tai ištirti sunku, nes moteriško-sios giminės daiktavardžių dviskaitos formos rytų Lietuvoje labai retai vartojamos ir baigia išnykti. Kiti ē kamieno daiktavardžiai (su -ė- ne po l) čia turi galūnę, -i, pvz., dvì katì, mergì.

Galūnė -ъι negali būti atsiradusi iš -i(< *-ie) dėl priebalsio l kietinimo, kadangi skiemuo li (lie) tarmėje nevirsta *lъι (*lъιe). Vadinasi, čia turime dvi skirtingas ē kamieno daiktavardžių galūnes (-ъι ir -i), kurių pirmąją gauna tik tie žodžiai, kurių po -ė- yra priebalsis l, antrąją — kurių bet koks kitas priebalsis.

D. Gargasaitė galūnę -ъι linkusi kildinti iš -u[1], plg. dvì avelù, pelù. Pasta-roji galūnė iš tikrųjų tarmėje daug kur vartojama. Ji užfiksuota, pavyz-džiui, apie Kar̃sakiškį, Síesikus, Pãpilį, Panemunēlį, Rõkiškį, Keřnavę. Šiaurės panevėžiškių plote balsis u galūnėje virtęs murmamuoju (žymima apostrofu), pvz., d'vė̇ av̇èl'. Tačiau liaudies dainose jis, matyt, dar ištariamas, bent jį užrašė A. Niemis ir A. Sabaliauskas[2]. Galūnę -u (šiaurės pane-vėžiškių -') turi ne tik daiktavardžiai su l prieš kamiengalį, bet ir visi kiti tiek ē, tiek ir kitų kamienų moteriškosios giminės vardažodžiai, pvz., dvì gerù šakù (š. pan. d'vė̇ ġèr' šàk'). Ji sutampa su vyriškosios giminės atitinkama daiktavardžių galūne, plg. dù ratù (š. pan. dọ̀ ràt'). P. Arumaa mano, kad galūnę -u moteriškosios giminės vardažodžiai galėjo gauti dėl dviskaitos formos sutapimo su pronominalinio linksniavimo daugiskaitos vardininku[3]. Iš tikrųjų, nykstant dviskaitai, dubletų dù gerù (vaikù) ‖ dù gerì (vaikaĩ) pavyzdžiu šalia dvì gerì (vištì) nesunkiai galėjo būti pasidarytas variantas dvì gerù (vištù). Tačiau galūnės -ъι, sekant D. Gargasaite, fonetiškai kildinti iš -u mums neleidžia gretiminių formų buvimas toje pačioje šnektoje, pvz., dvì pelъι ‖ pelù Panemunēlis. Be to, tokio kildinimo atveju būtų nesuprantama, kodėl galūnę -ы turi tik ē kamieno daiktavardžiai su l prieš kamiengalį, o ne visi kiti moteriškosios giminės vardažodžiai. Pagaliau, nesuprantamas ir pats balsio u virtimas ы, kadangi daugiau tokio virtimo pavyzdžių tarmėje nėra. Taigi, tokį aiškinimą tenka atmesti.

Tarmės ē kamieno daiktavardžių paradigmos analizė rodo, kad galūnei -ы atsirasti sąlygas sudarė *dviskaitos vardininko-galininko ir vienaskaitos įnagininko formų sutapimas*. Rytų Lietuvoje sakoma, pavyzdžiui, *pamačiaū dvì katì* ir *šuõ nubė́go su katì* 'su kate'. Tų ē kamieno daiktavardžių, kurie prieš kamiengalį turi priebalsį l, vienaskaitos įnagininko tarminė galūnė yra -ы (< *-ę̇), pvz., (su) *pel·ù* '(su) pele'. Formų instr. sing. *katì* ir nom.–acc. du. (dvì) *katì* pavyzdžiu ir šalia instr. sing. *pel·ù* lengvai galėjo būti pasidaryta nom.–acc. du. forma (dvì) *pel·ù* vietoj fonetiškai taisyklingos (dvì) *pelì*.

Kad ē kamieno daiktavardžių su -ė- po l ir po kitų priebalsių tarminės paradigmos viena kitą stipriai veikia, rodo kupiškėnų acc. sing. *dró·bы*. 'drobę' ir *pã.l'i*. 'pelę' (galūnės -i. antrinę kilmę išduoda šaknies balsis å̃.), su tarminėmis galūnėmis -ы. ir -i., kurių pirmoji gauta iš tokių fonetiškai taisyklingų formų, kaip *pã.lы*. 'pelę', antroji iš *š̃š.k̃i*. 'šakę' tipo formų (prieš kamiengalį turinčių tarmėje stipriai minkštinamus priebalsius k, g, š, ž). Taip čia elgiamasi ir su instr. sing. galūnėmis, pvz., *dró·bы* 'drobe', *sául'i* 'saule' su -u, -i pagal tokius pavyzdžius, kaip *sáulu* 'saule' (-u iš ā kamieno), *šakì* 'šake'. Analogiška sąveika pastebima ir kitose paradigmose, plg. rytų Lietuvoje plačiai vartojamą voc. sing. formą *méšl'e* (pagal *vaĩk̃e*, vietoj *méšla*), dubletus loc. sing. *stal·ù* ‖ *stalì* 'stale', nom. sing. m. *púolы·s* (*púolыs*) ‖ *púol'i·s* (*púol'is*) 'puolęs', nom. pl. m. *púolы·* ‖ *púol'i·* 'puolę' ir kt.[4]

Kad vieno iš homoniminę galūnę turinčių linksnių gretiminės formos pavyzdžiu gali būti padaroma tokia pati forma ir kitam linksniui reikšti, rodo Pándėlio šnektos (į)u kamieno daiktavardžių dat. sing. forma *sūnũm* 'sūnui' (galūnę -um gauna tik u ir įu kamienų daiktavardžiai!), atsiradusi vietoj tarminės *sū́nu* 'sūnui' (plg. *viĩku* 'vilkui'), nusižiūrėjus į instr. sing. *sūnũm* 'sūnumi' šalia gretiminio varianto su o kamieno galūne *sū́nu* 'sūnumi' pavyzdį[5]. Analogiškai atsirado Bìržų šnektos loc. sing. f. *baltái* 'baltoje' su galūne -ai, įsivesta iš dat. sing. f. *baltái* 'báltai' dėl dat. sing. ir loc. sing. formų sutapimo baritonų paradigmoje, plg. *ruñkɛ* 'rankai' ir 'rankoje' (ɛ iš ai nekirčiuotoje galūnėje; loc. sing. -āje > -aj > -ai). Rytų Lietuvoje plačiai vartojamai įvardžiuotinių būdvardžių instr. sing. f. formai *baltúoju* 'baltąja' pradžią davė abiejų giminių neįvardžiuotinio atitikmens fonetinis sutapimas, plg. *su báltu* 'su baltu' ir 'su balta'. Čia sakoma ir instr. sing. f. *su túo* 'su ta', plg. *su kitù* 'su kitu' ir 'su kita'. Analogiškai šiaurės panevėžiškių

Clinical and Experimental Hypnosis

Clinical and
Experimental
HYPNOSIS

In Medicine, Dentistry, and Psychology

William S. Kroger, M.D.

Clinical Professor of Anesthesiology, University of California, Los Angeles School of Medicine; Teaching Consultant, Department of Psychiatry, Cedars-Sinai Medical Center, Los Angeles; Consulting Psychiatrist, Department of Neurology, City of Hope Medical Center, Duarte, California; Board of Directors, Morton Prince Center for Hypnotherapy, New York; Member, American Psychiatric Association; Executive Director, Institute for Comprehensive Medicine, Beverly Hills, California; Past President, Academy of Psychosomatic Medicine; Past Vice President and Co-founder, American Society of Clinical Hypnosis; Co-founder, Society of Clinical and Experimental Hypnosis; Advisory Editor, International Journal of Clinical and Experimental Hypnosis, Journal of Sex Research.

SECOND EDITION

J.B. Lippincott Company
Philadelphia

Second Edition

Copyright © 1977, by J. B. Lippincott Company

Copyright © 1963, by J. B. Lippincott Company

ISBN 0-397-50377-6
Library of Congress Catalog Card No. 77-10320

Library of Congress Cataloging in Publication Data

Kroger, William S.
  Clinical and experimental hypnosis in medicine,
dentistry, and psychology.

  Bibliography: p.
  Includes index.
  1. Hypnotism–Therapeutic use. 2. Hypnotism.
I. Title. [DNLM: 1. Hypnosis. WM415 K93c]
RC495.K75 1977   615'.8512   77–10320
ISBN 0–397–50377–6

Printed in the United States of America

14 13 12 11 10

To Jimmy, Carol, Debbie, Lisa, and Billy,
who exert their own special kind of
hypnosis on the author

Psychiatric Foreword

The second edition of *Clinical and Experimental Hypnosis* is a welcome addition to the growing number of texts available to those interested in the theories and practice of hypnosis. New chapters on biofeedback, meditation, altered states of consciousness, acupuncture, and criminology have been added. The vast literature on hypnosis has been reviewed and brought up to date.

Dr. Kroger is one of the deans of American hypnotherapy. He has been practicing and teaching hypnosis over a period of four decades. His major contribution has been the development of the concept of hypnosis, so that it can be integrated with, and become part of, the science of behavior modification. His comprehensive text contains not only a complete description of almost every hypnotic technic and clinical entity, but a wealth of case studies as well. It also elucidates the relationship between general semantics, neurophysiology, cybernetics, and hypnotic theory and practice. Therefore, this book represents a major attempt to fit hypnosis into the framework of the behavioral sciences, where it belongs.

With the advent of the Freudian era, at the turn of the century, the dynamic unconscious soon became the acceptable theoretic concept. Within several decades it was discovered that when a patient finally uncovered an unconscious motive after an expenditure of much time, sweat, tears, and money, it did not follow that he spontaneously was "cured" merely because he knew the "reason" why he behaved in a certain manner. This clinical fact, now accepted by every experienced psychotherapist, has led to the surrender of the previous, obsessive, and futile search for traumatic infantile memories. Nevertheless, certain psychotherapists *always* report that their patients vividly experience sex relations, become involved in bizarre acting-out of symptoms, and express earlier hostilities and conflicts by sobbing and screaming. It has been my experience that these patients were "pleasing" their psychotherapists, who had repeatedly indicated to them that this was the *only* way to get well.

Repeated clinical observation has corroborated Dr. Kroger's thesis that symptom removal by the sophisticated and permissive technics described in this book is an effective method of treating many patients—*especially those who can endure living without* neurotic defenses. The author properly points out that the dangers of hypnosis have been greatly exaggerated. Most experts agree with Dr. Kroger that *neither one nor many hypnotic sessions can precipitate a psychosis unless a psychotic process already is present.* I agree with Dr. Kroger that the removal of a symptom by appropriate hypnotic technics does not produce a substitute symptom except in *very* disturbed individuals who need their neurotic encumbrances.

The author stresses that hypnosis is a particular kind of interpersonal relationship in which the patient permits increasing restrictions on his sensory intake and excludes all extraneous stimuli except those that the therapist brings to his attention. What is important is not the depth of the "trance" but the degree of rapport and emotional participation by the patient in the therapeutic relationship. Dr. Kroger repeatedly indicates that the therapist only "sets the stage," but that ultimately it is the patient who permits the hypnotic relationship to develop by selective attention.

The history of hypnosis contains descriptions of many patients who have improved and recovered without any psychodynamic "insight." What may be just as significant as "insight" is the patient's expectation in regard to the type of therapeutic procedure to which he can and would like to respond. The basic ingredients are the trust of the patient in the therapist and the conviction of both that the therapeutic modality elected is the best possible one for this particular patient. This helps to explain why a "therapy" can be effective in one era and a failure in another, when both patient and doctor no longer believe in the efficacy of the procedure. A patient is not hypnotized merely by concentrating and staring at a spot or at a revolving disk unless he *expects* this effect and complies mentally as well as physically. This was Braid's opinion in his latter years, and it is also Dr. Kroger's conclusion.

I am in complete agreement with the author that "cures" have been reported without searching for "causes." The common factor in these "transference" cures is the fostering of personal initiative and self-esteem (personal value) which is achieved by effective collaboration in the therapeutic situation.

Clinical and Experimental Hypnosis is a *tour de force* in the field of hypnosis—the best possible guide to the practice and the theory of modern hypnosis. The reader is taught from the very beginning that the "conviction of hypnosis leads to hypnosis," and that the important factors are motivation, belief, expectation, imagination, and the subsequent restructuring of the patient's reality percepts. This was also Bernheim's belief, and the author has transmitted the clinical wisdom of the past to a new generation of students of hypnosis.

The reader is fortunate to have available such an excellent text, and Dr. Kroger is to be congratulated for bringing to the attention of the medical, the dental, and the psychological professions the results of his many years of critical study and extensive clinical practice.

JACOB H. CONN, M.D.
*Assistant Professor of Psychiatry,
Johns Hopkins University Medical School;
Past President, American Board of Medical Hypnosis; Past President, Society for Clinical and Experimental Hypnosis*

Foreword

Dr. William Kroger's *Clinical and Experimental Hypnosis* has, since its publication during the modern resurgence of scientific hypnosis, served as a major text for physicians, psychologists, research investigators, and students in the mental health professions and behavioral sciences.

This new revised edition appears during a period of remarkable growth and productivity in the field of hypnosis. A major text for more than a decade, *Clinical and Experimental Hypnosis* now encompasses vast new research from the areas of experimental hypnosis and the conceptually as well as technically highly developed therapeutic procedures of contemporary clinical practice.

Clinical hypnosis as an integral technique in psychotherapy has made significant contributions to the management of a wide range of psychological and medical problems. The diagnostic categories within which significant therapeutic applications have been reported include psychosomatic illness, the major neurotic disturbances, psychotic reactions, psycho-physiologic correlates of neurological disease and circumscribed problems of obesity, cigarette habituation and some drug abuse and dependency problems.

Hypnosis has emerged as a major modality in the management of pain with respect to both organic and psychogenic manifestations. Recent research and therapeutic applications in cases of cerebral palsy, multiple sclerosis and post-traumatic syndromes have opened new avenues of provocative investigation and treatment.

The incorporation of hypnosis into a broad spectrum of psychotherapies ranging from behavior modification to psychoanalysis reflects the growing recognition of the multiphasic value of hypnosis as a cognitive and affective alteration in behavior organization of the consciousness. Experimental investigations continue to contribute to an integrative conceptual model of hypnosis consistent with related studies in learning theory, ego psychology and psychoanalysis. Current advances in the use of hypnotic techniques in forensic psychology and psychiatry are indicative of the development of an exciting and productive use of a new interface between psychology and law.

Dr. Kroger, an outstanding pioneer in medical and psychological hypnosis, has with this revised edition of *Clinical and Experimental Hypnosis* made available to a new generation of physicians, psychologists, and behavioral scientists a classic text reflective of the latest concepts in theory and practice for all who are concerned with scientific hypnosis as a therapeutic and research modality. It will be a major teaching and reference work for many years to come.

MILTON V. KLINE, *Director*
The Institute for Research in Hypnosis
and the Morton Prince Center for Hypnotherapy
International Graduate University
and Florida Institute of Technology

New York, N.Y., and Lugano, Switzerland

July, 1977

Preface

During the past two decades there has been an intense renewal of interest in the clinical applications of hypnotherapy in all branches of medicine and in its ancillary disciplines. This has resulted from the investigations made by reputable scientists in the preceding half century. Much recent work is summarized in this book in order to furnish the student of hypnosis with a broad picture of the more important advances.

My objective is to offer to the beginner and sophisticated practitioner the most useful hypnotic technics for induction and management of problems encountered in the practice of medicine and of dentistry. The principles of suggestion, the phenomena of hypnosis, and the factors that influence hypnotizability are discussed as well as the indications, limitations, and precautions in the use of hypnotherapy in medicine, dentistry, and psychology. There is particular emphasis upon the hypnotherapeutic management of various clinical conditions in medicine and in dentistry.

Hypnotherapy is a tool directed to the patient's needs, rather than those of the therapist, and therefore can be employed with other types of psychotherapy. Because the author is convinced that hypnosis will play an ever-increasing role in medical education and practice, he has included discussion of experimental psychology, the psychophysiology of emotions, the relevance of semantics to communication, and the general principles which govern perception and cognition.

An attempt has been made to condense this material, some of which admittedly is controversial. The humanistic element in psychotherapy has not been overlooked. This is the chief factor in healing by all methods of psychotherapy, including hypnosis. Moreover, it is now recognized that the phenomena of hypnosis are only an extension of the mechanisms involved in normal behavior, as all hypnotic phenomena can occur at nonhypnotic levels. Hence, with this new approach, hypnosis can be taken from the realm of the esoteric and placed in the cognitive. Hypnosis can now be related to the principles of everyday behavior dynamics, rather than to the more traditional beliefs which unfortunately have retarded its clinical acceptance for more than 50 years.

All schools of psychotherapy yield approximately the same results; therefore, it appears that a placebo effect is present. Hence, the basis for successful psychotherapy depends to a large degree on the rapport or the strength of the interpersonal relationship between physician and patient. Suggestion at different levels of awareness is wittingly or unwittingly utilized in this relationship. Since no one knows where suggestion ends and hypnosis begins, the real basis for all forms of psychotherapy must be "suggestion" and/or "hypnosis in slow motion."

If suggestion plays an important role in psychotherapy, why not use the acme of scientifically applied suggestion—hypnosis? This is not to imply that hypnotherapy helps more patients than other forms of psychotherapy. It does not, but it is more rapid and less cumbersome. It can be used effectively for the "port of last call" patient. It can be employed by the non-psychiatrist who is capable of assessing its indications and contraindications for various medical conditions despite the continual concern about the theoretic but remote dangers of symptom removal that are associated with hypnotherapy.

Most of the clinical entities described herein were treated by patient-centered hypnotherapy instead of by a physician-directed approach. The specialized hypnotic technics described in this volume, when combined with autohypnosis, sensory-imagery conditioning, and behavior modification, are vastly different from the older, dramatic, and authoritarian types of hypnotic symptom removal. Moreover, an existential approach was directed to the present and the future, instead of dredging the past to search for "causative" factors.

The old concept of cause and effect to explain emotional illness has been replaced by allowing the patient to develop a healthy understanding of the *emotional needs that he has for a symptom.* Hypnotherapy, therefore, is directed not only to eliciting these needs, but also to enabling the individual to face his difficulties in a more mature and realistic manner. An individual is not treated *by* hypnosis, but rather *in* hypnosis! The greater relaxation, concentration, receptivity, and self-objectivity provide a better awareness of *what* the emotionally ill person experiences. This is less tedious than attempting to elicit unexplored factors behind *what he professes to believe or what he thinks he believes.*

My thesis, at the risk of oversimplification, is that emotional illness and health are conviction phenomena that are "programmed" into the neural circuits by negative, destructive, and harmful experiential conditioning; positive, constructive reconditioning results in adaptive behavior. Such reconditioning by hypnosis incisively mobilizes the "built-in" adaptive processes that already are present in the organism. This effects homeostatic adjustments and stimulates the recovery forces by raising the threshold to specific or nonspecific stressors.

Teaching contacts with many thousands of doctors have made clear the need for a work on hypnotherapy that would enable the professional to have access to the actual clinical setting. Many of the technics are verbatim transcripts recorded at the author's office, hospital, or classroom.

I am grateful to the many patients described in this book, who enabled me to develop more insight into the interrelationships of hypnosis to that magnificent "computer"—the brain. I am indebted as well to the numerous doctors attending my workshops in hypnosis, who pointed out those areas of instruction and knowledge that are particularly germane for the practice of clinical hypnotherapy.

It is hoped that this book will stimulate the reader to test the methodologies discussed and to further his knowledge by studying the references listed at the end of the various chapters. It should be emphasized that an extensive literature has accumulated during the last decade. It is patently impossible to include more than a fraction of the contributions presented both in this country and abroad. In addition to the didactic material presented in this book, a practical introduction to the fundamentals of hypnosis at any one of the recognized medical school training centers is recommended. With training, the physician who already has the clinical judgment, the experience, the intuition, and the diagnostic acumen to practice medicine can employ hypnotherapy. It can be "prescribed" as a medicine because it is in reality the "art of medicine."

Finally, to quote Hippocrates, "Nothing should be omitted in an art which interests the whole world, one which may be beneficial to suffering humanity and which does not risk human life or comfort."

WILLIAM S. KROGER, M.D.

Acknowledgments

It would be impossible to write a book of this magnitude without the dedicated help of friends and the courtesies of my colleagues and publishers, who granted me permission to quote from their works.

I am particularly indebted to Drs. William D. Fezler, Bernard Saltzberg, Anthony Sances, Jr., J. Wesley Edel, J.H. Conn, and Martin Orne for help in assembling special material in the sections on learning theory and behavior modification, cybernetics, radiology, the emotional needs, and criminology respectively. Dr. Aaron Moss contributed the chapter on dentistry, and the late Dr. Meyer A. Perlstein collaborated on the chapter on Hypnotherapy in Physical Rehabilitation of Neuromuscular Diseases.

I am also obligated to Rabbi Samuel Glassner, Ph.D., for quotations from his publications on "Allusions to Hypnosis in the Bible and Talmud."

I wish to extend a note of appreciation to the many students whom I have taught at the undergraduate and postgraduate levels. They have helped me to understand the pertinent areas of concern and thus have assisted me in converting my thoughts and experiences into a textbook that would interest the elementary and advanced student as well as the researcher and clinician.

To Dr. Milton V. Kline go my sincere thanks for having been kind enough to read the entire manuscript with a critical eye.

I am deeply grateful to Stuart Freeman and Fred Zeller, of the J.B. Lippincott Company, for their patience and valuable advice in the preparation of this book.

Last but certainly not least, I wish to express my eternal gratitude to my loyal and loving wife, Jimmy Louise, and my daughter Lisa, whose editorial assistance facilitated revision of the entire manuscript.

WILLIAM S. KROGER, M.D.

Contents

1
History of Hypnosis

The history of hypnosis, going back to antiquity, has been reviewed by many writers.[5, 9, 29, 34] Hypnosis has been practiced under numerous labels in different places since time immemorial. Tribal medicine men, witch doctors, and religious leaders have employed it in various forms to heal the sick. The cures usually were ascribed to miracles performed by the gods. The Ebers papyrus, over 3,000 years old, describes how Egyptian soothsayers used hypnotic procedures similar to those practiced today. Centuries ago, the Greek oracles, the Persian magi, the Hindu fakirs, and the Indian yogi used hypnosis without realizing it. The earliest medical records describe miraculous healing by priests or demigods who induced a sleeplike state by ceremonial rites in the Aesculapian temples.

There are many allusions in the Talmud and in the Bible[1, 5] to the laying on of hands and to other quasi-hypnotic technics. Later, several religions introduced healing through touch and prayer. For many centuries, and especially during the Middle Ages, kings and princes were said to have the power of healing through the "Royal Touch." From the time of Clovis (466?–511), French monarchs were held to possess this remarkable power. After falling into ridicule with the fall of Louis XVI, its use was actually revived at the coronation of Charles X in 1824, with Dupuytren and Alibert in attendance. In England, Edward the Confessor was said to have cured scrofula by the "Royal Touch" in 1066. Though defended by the Stuarts, the practice was lampooned by William III, at the beginning of the eighteenth century, when he replied to his well-wishers, "May God give you better health and common sense."

The seventeenth century spawned healers such as Valentine Greatrakes (1628–1666), the "great Irish stroaker," who attracted a huge following. At the same time, Francisco Bagnone was operating in Italy in a similar manner and with equal success. He had only to touch the sick with his hands, or with a relic, to accomplish astonishing cures. Hardly less famous than these two was Johann Gassner (1727–1779), a Catholic priest, who believed that most diseases were caused by evil spirits and could be exorcised by conjuration and prayer.

Paracelsus (1493–1541) was among the first to point out the healing effect of the astral bodies and the magnet. His views on animal magnetism were shared by Glocenius, Burgrove, Helnotius, Fludd, Kircher, van Helmont, Balthazar Gracían, Porta, and Maxwell. All propagated the same doctrine: the magnet could cure most diseases. Writing in 1679, William Maxwell, a Scottish physician, assumed that a universal and vital spirit affected all humans. However, he recognized the influence of the imagination and of suggestion. F. A. Pattie's[28] extensive research reveals how Franz Anton Mesmer (1734–1815), an Austrian physician with little scientific insight, plagiarized the writings of the brilliant English physician Richard Mead (1673–1754), who was inspired by the research of his patient, Sir Isaac Newton. His attempt to explain living systems by natural laws led Mesmer to develop the "universal fluid" idea.

About 1771, Maximilian Hell, a Viennese Jesuit, became famous for magnetic cures obtained by applying steel plates to the naked body. Mesmer also borrowed these ideas from Father Hell's

1

work and Maxwell's doctrine, but applied them by means of contact and passes. The "new" method, which he called animal magnetism, attracted a large following during the latter part of the eighteenth century. Later, to treat the huge crowds that sought treatment by his methods, he developed a *baquet,* or large tub, filled with iron filings. Patients grasped the iron rods attached to this contraption to receive the "magnetic" flow. Thirty or more persons also were connected with each other by cords and were magnetized as Mesmer touched each person with a glass rod; many developed seizures or crises similar to those observed among some religious sects. At first he contended that the magnetism emanated from the astral bodies, and later that it was transferred from himself to the patient by his magnetic wand. His theories and practices showed little or no originality. He attracted followers and as a result his "genius" was recognized. Arnold M. Ludwig[23] provides a fascinating account of the early roots of mesmerism, including allusions to the potent effect of the imagination as it affects the healer and supplicant. F. J. MacHovec[24] describes how hypnosis flourished several thousand years before Mesmer.

A commission exposed Mesmer in 1784, stating that the cures were due to the imagination, not to magnetism. Charles d'Eslon,[10] a pupil of Mesmer, had already remarked, "If the medicine of imagination is best, why should we not practice the medicine of imagination." This aphorism has been neglected for almost 200 years. However, Mesmer unwittingly laid the cornerstone for present-day group psychotherapy, and such strange bedfellows as spiritualistic healing, imagery conditioning, and psychoanalysis. His later disciples were Petètin, the discoverer of catalepsy; the Marquis de Puységur, who first described artificial somnambulism, and Barbarin, who magnetized without paraphernalia and whose followers called themselves Barbarinists. In Sweden and Germany, the latter group were called Spiritualists; the mesmeric cures were acts of God. Those who followed Puységur were called Experimentalists, and they considered themselves the disciples of the Paracelsus-Mesmer fluidism theory. Mesmerism soon spread all over the world. Excellent treatises on Mesmer have been written by

Ann Jenson and Mary L. Watkins,[21] and by Arnold M. Ludwig.[23]

The next phase was ushered in by Abbé Faria, who came to Paris from India and gave public exhibitions, in 1814 and 1815, without manipulations or a *baquet.* He induced over 5,000 persons, and expressed the opinion, still valid today, that the cures were not due to magnetism but *to the expectancy and cooperation of the patient.* Following Faria, Bertrand and Noizet paved the way for James Braid's doctrine of suggestion. Mesmerism flourished for a time in Germany, but by 1840 it was on the wane.

The first recorded uses of hypnoanesthesia were in 1821, by Récamier, who performed operations on patients under mesmeric coma. Hippolyte Cloquet performed a breast operation before the French Academy of Medicine in 1829, using mesmerism. At about the same time, in the United States, Wheeler did a nasal polypectomy employing mesmerism, its first reported use in this country.

Through the influence of Dupotet in 1837, John Elliotson, one of the ablest physicians in England, and the first professor of medicine at the newly founded college hospital attached to the University of London, became an enthusiastic advocate of the little-known science of mesmerism. Elliotson, afraid of neither innovations nor criticism, was severely censured by editorials in *The Lancet* for alleged charlatanism. Though he had introduced the stethoscope to England, he was called a quack and an impostor. Subsequently, the university banned the use of mesmerism. The Church also opposed its use. Elliotson, a dedicated and fearless scientist, promptly resigned. For many years he published the *Zoist,* a journal in which numerous painless operations and other mesmeric phenomena were reported.

However, mesmerism grew and attracted many other disciples. Among them was James Esdaile, a Scottish surgeon practicing in India, who reported hundreds of painless operations between 1840 and 1850. In 1849, Crawford Long, who pioneered the use of ether in America, stated that many reputable physicians were recommending mesmerism for pain relief during surgery.

James Braid, a Scottish physician who merits

the title "Father of Modern Hypnotism," became interested in mesmerism in 1841 when he attended a demonstration in Manchester by La Fontaine, the Swiss magnetizer. Braid scoffed at the ideas of the mesmerists. He contended that the degree of expectation increased the subject's susceptibility to suggestion. He eschewed the occult and the mysterious and instead emphasized clinical observation and experiment. Unfortunately, he coined the terms "hypnotism" and "hypnosis" from the Greek word *hypnos*, meaning sleep. Later, he recognized that hypnosis was not sleep, but the term had gained common currency. He also made the basic discovery, ignored for over a century, that hypnosis could be induced without a formalistic induction.

In a brief résumé, it is impossible to mention the many contributions and contributors of this period. However, some stand out, such as Ambroise-Auguste Liébeault of Nancy, whose book *Le sommeil provoqué* was published in 1889. He has been called the real founder of suggestive therapeutics. Though a poverty-stricken country doctor, Liébeault, to avoid being branded a charlatan, said to his poor patients, "If you wish to be treated by drugs, you will have to pay my fee; if, however, you allow me to treat you by hypnotism, I will do it free of charge!" His integrity, selflessness, devotion to the needy, and success with hypnosis attracted the attention of Hippolyte-Marie Bernheim (1840–1919), a renowned neurologist from Nancy, who, at first skeptical, later became an ardent proponent of hypnosis. Together they developed Braid's theories, and without the theatrical legerdemain of Jean-Martin Charcot, treated over 12,000 patients! Bernheim and Liébeault, the legitimate innovators of modern psychotherapy, considered hypnosis a function of normal behavior and introduced the concept of suggestion and suggestibility. They also believed that symptom-removal was effective and harmless. They triumphed over the views of Charcot, who stoutly maintained that hypnosis was a form of hysteria and that it was dangerous!

Charcot's theories, based on working repeatedly with only a dozen hysterical patients at the Salpêtrière, an insane asylum, were completely discredited. However, because of his great scientific standing, his interest in hypnosis helped to make it respectable. Charcot, like many eminent scientists today, did not realize that some degree of hypnotizability could be induced in nearly everyone. Also, he did not recognize that hypnotic responses were a part of everyday subjective happenings and were not the kind of dramatic occurrences that he took great delight in demonstrating. Nor did he appreciate the broad therapeutic potentialities that Liébeault and Bernheim achieved in their impressive series of cases.

Although slowly accepted, hypnosis was emerging as a science by 1884, when Bernheim published his book *De la suggestion dans l'état hypnotique et dans l'état de veille.* He recognized, as did Braid, that suggestion was the basis for hypnosis. His unimpeachable reputation spurred the growth of the science. Hypnotherapy came into its own, and many respected scientists such as Bramwell, Tuckey, and Wingfield in England; Janet, Bérillon, and Pitres in France; Moll, Dessoir, and Vogt in Germany; Forel in Switzerland; Van Renterghem in Holland; and Morsell in Italy became interested in its clinical applications. Later, Heidenhain, Broca, Pavlov, Babinski, Krafft-Ebing, and Prince and Sidis in the United States, accepted its validity.

Sigmund Freud and Joseph Breuer also became interested in hypnosis. Freud had studied with Charcot and Bernheim; however, he *avoided* hypnosis for several reasons. First, he was concerned because he could not hypnotize many patients to a sufficient depth; second, the cures were temporary, inasmuch as the post-hypnotic suggestions could not be maintained, and he could not elicit buried traumatic material because of the patient's resistances. He also felt that hypnosis stripped the patient of his defenses. Freud's abandonment of hypnosis did not discredit its validity as a valuable psychological tool, but rather indicated his inability to incorporate hypnosis into his own hypnotherapeutic approach. Whether or not hypnosis is too authoritative a technic and covers up the resistances is open to question. A modern reassessment by Milton V. Kline[22] refutes many of Freud's subjective reasons for sidestepping hypnosis. These reasons will be discussed more fully in Chapter 51.

In contradistinction to Freud, Sidis, Prince, and Janet demonstrated that hypnosis could be utilized for intensive exploration of the personality. They did not believe that deeply repressed emotional forces were obscured by hypnotic suggestions. The failure of hypnotherapy was due largely to emotionally conditioned blind adherence to outmoded tenets rather than to critical evaluation. Leon Chertok[7] has reviewed the critical period from Liébeault to Freud.

Further criticism generally comes from those who naively regard hypnosis as belonging to a specific school of psychotherapy. They do not realize that the meaningful involvement of the patient with the therapist results in readier acceptance of suggestions. Contrarily, the hypnosis which was rightfully criticized was the dramatic symptom-removal type used at the turn of the century, which was essentially commanding and authoritative. Today, however, hypnotherapy is vastly different from the primitive hypnosis that Freud reluctantly abandoned.

The history of hypnoanesthesia and its relationship to the inhalation anesthetic drugs is an interesting one. Both were used by the street-corner "professors" and the tent-show exhibitors of chemical and psychic phenomena. Induction of hypnosis and lectures on the wonders of chemistry were favorite amusements, which often ended with the entertainer's demonstrating the effect of nitrous oxide or "laughing gas."

It is of historical importance that one of these showmen, Gardner Q. Colton, gave such a performance in Hartford, Connecticut, on December 11, 1844. Horace Wells, a dentist, who was in the audience, saw one of Colton's subjects, who had inhaled the gas, stumble against a chair and badly bruise his legs. When the young man sat down, Wells asked if he had hurt himself. He answered that he had not and was astonished that his legs were bloody. He stated that he felt no pain until the effect of the gas wore off. Wells immediately thought of using nitrous oxide for dental extractions, and the next day Dr. Riggs, a colleague, extracted one of Wells's own teeth after Colton had administered the gas. On regaining consciousness, Wells exclaimed, "It is the greatest discovery ever made. I did not feel so much as the prick of a pin!"

Thus, when hypnosis was commonplace, anesthesia was a curiosity. Now, after more than a 100 years, anesthesia is the vogue and hypnosis is the anomaly. Pierre Janet,[20] the great French psychologist who at first opposed hypnosis and later advocated its use after his epochal investigations on relaxation, stated: "If my work is not accepted today, it will be tomorrow when there will be a new turn in fashion's wheel which will bring back hypnotism as surely as our grandmother's styles." That his prophecy, made at the turn of the century, is now being fulfilled is evidenced by the expanding literature on the medical, dental and psychological applications of hypnosis.

The need for rapid treatment of battle neuroses during World Wars I and II and the Korean war led to a tremendous interest in hypnotherapy. The merger of hypnotic technics with psychiatry was one of the important advances to come out of these conflicts. Since the pioneering work of Pavlov and his disciples in the Soviet Union, and Clark Hull's[19] classic experiments at Yale, a spate of books has been published on the subject, chiefly by psychologists[15, 18] and physicians. More reports are appearing in scientific publications exclusively devoted to hypnosis all over the world in nearly every discipline, indicating the increased interest in this age-old science.

From a historical viewpoint, it is interesting that many nostrums and other medical fads have passed into the limbo of discredited procedures, but hypnosis has survived, and, at present, scientific interest is stronger than ever. This salient point alone indicates the indispensable value of hypnosis. Its powers, medically applied, to cure and to relieve pain have been greatly underestimated or ignored by the medical profession because of irrational prejudice. This is not surprising, since *prejudice is ignorance educated,* and it is difficult for any individual, in any given era, to see through the "smoke screen" of his own culture.

Clinical and experimental investigations into the scientific applications and the limitations of hypnosis are being conducted by well-trained investigators in nearly all the medical, psychological, and ancillary disciplines. Hypnosis is being taught at an ever-growing number of universities and medical schools. In addition, many thousands of physicians, dentists, and psychologists in the United States have received training in the introductory workshops on hypnosis conducted by leaders in the field.

The British Medical Association, on April 23, 1955, reported its approval of hypnosis for treatment of the psychoneuroses, and of hypnoanesthesia for relief of pain in childbirth and surgery. The report also advised that all physicians and medical students receive fundamental training in hypnosis. The Council on Mental Health of the American Medical Association, on September 13, 1958, recommended that, in view of our increasing knowledge, instruction in hypnosis be included in the curricula of medical schools and postgraduate training centers. The use of hypnosis for entertainment purposes was vigorously condemned. In a subsequent report in 1961, the A.M.A. Council on Mental Health recommended that 144 hours of training be given over a 9- to 12-month period at the undergraduate and postgraduate levels. To date, this has not been done except at a few medical schools. However, clinical and experimental investigations into hypnosis are being conducted by numerous workers in many countries. They are gathering data which should shed further light on the nature and clinical applications of hypnosis. It is unfortunate that, throughout the long history of hypnosis, it has been the favorite whipping boy of those who espouse the value of psychological and placebo therapy while denying the obvious correlation with hypnosis. However, it is true that hypnosis has been hurt more by the extravagant claims of its ardent proponents than by its opponents. The American Society for Clinical Hypnosis and the International Society of Clinical and Experimental Hypnosis have established sections in many countries throughout the world to maintain high ethical and training standards and to prevent the abuses that caused hypnosis to fall into oblivion twice during the past century and a half.

In the course of its tortuous history, and in spite of the many obstacles confronting those intrepid enough to risk hearing their thoughts called absurd, hypnosis has emerged as a valuable adjunctive psychotherapeutic tool to medicine. At last its therapeutic and psychological value is being recognized by many reputable scientists. The author believes that the links forged by Paracelsus, Mesmer, Bernheim, and Liébeault, which led to Freud, ultimately will be joined with those contributed by the behavioral scientists to make hypnosis a well-understood and fully accepted modality.

REFERENCES

1. Bowers, M., and Glasner, S.: Auto-hypnotic aspects of the Jewish cabbalistic concept of Kavanah. J. Clin. Exp. Hypn., *6*:50, 1958.
2. Braid, J.: Neuropnology. (Revised as Braid on Hypnotism, 1889.) New York, Julian Press, 1956.
3. Bramwell, J.M.: Hypnotism: Its History, Practice and Theory. New York, Julian Press, 1956.
4. Breuer, J., and Freud, S.: Studies in Hysteria. New York, Nerv. Ment. Dis. Pub. Co., 1936.
5. Bromberg, W.: Man Above Humanity. Philadelphia, J.B. Lippincott, 1954.
6. Chertok, L.: Hypnosis. New York, Pergamon Press, 1965.
7. Chertok, L.: From Liébeault to Freud: historical notes. Am. J. Psychotherapy, *22*:96, 1968.
8. Conn, J.: On the history of hypnosis. In Introductory Lectures on Medical Hypnosis. The Institute of Research in Hypnosis, 80–89, 1958.
9. Cutten, G. B.: Three Thousand Years of Mental Healing. New York, Scribner, 1911.
10. D'Eslon, C.: Observations sur le magnetisme animal. P.Fr. Didot, Paris, Lejeune, 1780.
11. Dessoir, M.: Bibliographie der modernen Hypnotismus. Berlin, C. Dunker Verlag, 1887.
12. Ellenberger, H.F.: The Discovery of the Unconscious. New York, Basic Books, 1970.
13. Glasner, S.: A note on allusions to hypnosis in the Bible and Talmud. J. Clin. Exp. Hypn., *3*:34, 1955.
14. Gordon, J.E.: Handbook of Clinical and Experimental Hypnosis. New York, Macmillan, 1967.
15. Hilgard, E.R.: Personality and Hypnosis. Chicago, University of Chicago Press, 1970.
16. _____: Hypnosis. Annual Review of Psychology, 1965.
17. _____: Hypnosis. Annual Review of Psychology, 1975.
18. Hilgard, E.R., and Shor, R.E.: Hypnosis: Research Developments and Perspectives. Chicago, Aldine-Atherton, 1972.
19. Hull, C. L.: Hypnosis and Suggestibility: An Experimental Approach. New York, Appleton-Century-Crofts, 1933.
20. Janet, P.: Psychological Healing. (2 vols.) London, Allen & Unwin, 1925.

21. Jenson, A., and Watkins, M.L.: Franz Anton Mesmer: Physician Extraordinaire. New York, Garrett-Helix, 1967.

22. Kline, M.V.: Freud and Hypnosis. New York, Julian Press, 1950.

23. Ludwig, A.M.: A historical survey of the early roots of Mesmerism. Int. J. Clin. Exp. Hypn., *12:* 205, 1964.

24. MacHovec, F.J.: Hypnosis before Mesmer, Am. J. Clin. Hypn., *17:*215, 1975.

25. Marcuse, F.L. (ed.): Hypnosis Throughout the World. Springfield, Ill., Charles C Thomas, 1964.

26. McDougall, W.: Outlines of Abnormal Psychology. New York, Scribner, 1926.

27. Moll, A.: The Study of Hypnosis. New York, Julian Press, 1958.

28. Pattie, F.A.: Mesmer's medical dissertation and its debt to Mead's De Imperio Solis ac Lunae. J. Med. Allied Science, *11:*275, 1956.

29. Rosen, G.: History of medical hypnosis. *In* Hypnosis in Modern Medicine. Springfield, Ill., Charles C Thomas, 1959.

30. Shor, R.E., and Orne, M.T.: The Nature of Hypnosis: Selected Basic Readings. New York, Holt, Rinehart & Winston, 1965.

31. Tinterow, M.M.: Foundations of Hypnosis: From Mesmer to Freud. Springfield, Ill., Charles C Thomas, 1970.

32. Watkins, J.G.: Hypnotherapy of War Neuroses. New York, Ronald Press, 1949.

33. Weitzenhoffer, A.: An Objective Study in Suggestibility. New York, Wiley, 1963.

34. Wolberg, L.: Medical Hypnosis. New York, Grune & Stratton, 1951.

2

Phenomena of Suggestion and Hypnosis

TYPES OF SUGGESTION

Suggestion can be defined as the uncritical acceptance of an idea. It is the process by which sensory impressions are conveyed in a meaningful manner to evoke altered psychophysiologic responses. One cannot necessarily equate suggestion with hypnosis unless the latter is accompanied by diversion. However, the acceptance of ideas by suggestion must be differentiated from logical persuasion. *Persuasion is not suggestion, and suggestion is not persuasion!*

Suggestion provides sensorial data input or information to the higher centers. All sensory input routes continually receive data from verbal, nonverbal, intraverbal, or extraverbal communications. This is done not only via the five senses, but through other sources (e.g., temperature and pressure sensations, and kinesthesia). *Verbal,* which includes preverbal, communication refers to information transmission by sounds and words. *Nonverbal* communication refers to gestures and grimaces. *Intraverbal* communication is concerned with modulation of the voice. An orator, for example, with emphatic vocal inflections holds his audience's attention more readily than one who speaks in a monotone. *Extraverbal* communication deals with the implications of words or phrases which are more apt to reduce criticalness. Thus the harsh command "stand up" is likely to produce resistance to carrying out a suggested act. Contrarily, if one softly asks, "Are you *not tired* of sitting down?" the chances are that the person will stand up, especially if the request is accompanied by a nonverbal gesture symbolic of the desired act. Thus the whole complex of mannerism, inflection of voice, and im-

plied meaning of the words employed plays an important role in facilitating perception, cognition, and response. Aristotle's maxim—"Nothing is in the mind that did not pass through the senses"—is literally true.

THE NATURE OF SUGGESTIBILITY IN HYPNOSIS

Nearly all subjects believe that their responses are produced by the hypnotist. In reality, it is the subject who initiates the acts in response to an appropriate expectant attitude. Where criticalness is reduced, a suggested act usually is automatically carried out without the individual's logical processes participating in the response. And when one suggestion after another is accepted in ascending order of importance—task motivated suggestions—more difficult ones are accepted, particularly if the sensory spiral of belief is compounded from the outset. This is called abstract conditioning and, in part, helps to explain the role that suggestibility plays in the production of hypnotic phenomena.

Suggestibility is further enhanced by a favorable attitude or mental set that establishes proper motivation. This depends not only on the technic utilized to produce it, but also and to a greater extent on the quality of the relationship—the rapport—established between operator and subject. Thus mere suggestibility *per se* does not account for hypnotizability, but rather increased suggestibility is a constant feature of hypnosis. However, the concept of increased suggestibility does not explain the complexity of the phenomena that occur during hypnotic behavior.

There is an extensive literature on the nature of suggestibility in hypnosis. Some investigations reveal that with a male operator suggestibility is slightly greater in females than in males.[47, 110, 112] Other data indicate that the sex of the hypnotist shows no appreciable differences.[48] However, since hypnotic suggestibility largely depends on motivation, it varies from person to person and even changes in the same person, depending on his needs and drives. Therefore, though it cannot be correlated significantly with sex, there are some changes with age.[76] Children are more hypnotizable than adults, peaking out between ages 9 and 12. However, the relationship of hypnotic susceptibility to personality in children remains to be clarified.[72] Adult responsivity levels are established about age 16, and diminish in middle and old age.[11] The degree of suggestibility also is determined by the way an individual reacted to suggestions from others in the past, either by the structuring or the setting or by the prestige of the person who gave the suggestions, and by the way the suggestions were interpreted. A subject may be highly suggestible to stimuli affecting his health, yet he may be nonsuggestible to persuasive salesmanship. In the latter area, his critical faculties are aroused. Yet the same person may be very suggestible to political and religious persuasion, especially if the exhortations seem to fit in with his cultural and value systems. Of course, suggestibility always must be differentiated from gullibility, which implies the use of deception.

Often the degree of suggestibility cannot be evaluated because of the extent of neurotic involvement. It is believed that psychoneurotics are more suggestible than emotionally healthy persons,[107] and that even psychotics are susceptible to suggestion.[1, 12, 38, 44, 53, 65, 69] Another investigator notes that normal subjects are more susceptible than neurotics and psychotics.[48] However, exhibitionists who submit to hypnosis for entertainment purposes are very suggestible because of their expectancies and also because they have no symptoms to lose. Of particular interest is the paradoxical reactor, who believes he is not susceptible to suggestion, but who, because of his innate stubbornness, reacts with positive suggestibility.

Hypnotizability is not related to intelligence. It often depends more on the manner in which subjects utilize their attention span,[43, 66] their ability to respond to vivid imagery,[95] and their creativity.[16] The way individuals become involved in imaginative experiences apparently has some correlation with the depth of hypnosis.[50, 97, 104] It has been observed in a landmark study that simulating subjects and subjects told "simply" to use their imaginations to experience suggestive phenomena did not differ in their overt responses from those subjects who were actually hypnotized.[80] However, the differences found between hypnotized and simulating subjects seems to be subjective. The hypnotized subject clearly sees the state as somehow different from normal waking consciousness. Hypnotized persons are more likely to describe the imaginal suggestions as real and vivid. This is contrary to the simulator's experiences, inasmuch as he has not been conditioned.

Conditioning theorists are aware that whenever a suggestion is repeated over and over again, this usually leads to a quasi-conditioned reflex, which, in turn, is dependent upon previously established associative processes. The effects of reflex conditioning have much in common with hypnotic conditioning.[19] Conditioning by suggestion or hypnosis has masqueraded under a multiplicity of healing terms from time immemorial and relies heavily on "misdirection of attention."

Misdirection of attention, as it relates to hypnosis, is merely a diversionary maneuver or "smoke screen" to obscure the fact that suggestion in one guise or another is used to influence an individual. A formal hypnotic induction procedure is a ritual which makes full use of misdirection; the operator "slips in" suggestions when the subject is least expecting them. During induction, for instance, the subject's attention is fixed upon his eyelids by the remark, "Your eyes are getting very, very heavy." If his eyes actually become very heavy, then he is ready to believe other suggestions that he attributes to the operator's "powers." The subject does not realize that the heaviness of his eyelids actually was induced by the constant and fatiguing position of the eyes, staring upward at the ceiling. He believes that his eye fatigue resulted from the operator's suggestions of heaviness.

EVERYDAY ASPECTS OF SUGGESTION AND HYPNOSIS

Suggestion by misdirection of attention accounts for the success of many types of "therapy." Whenever a patient with a psychogenic complaint develops a favorable mental set that a particular type of therapy will help, he is aided *not* so much by the therapeutic modality as *by his inner conviction or faith that he will be helped.* The effects are greater if he has been referred to the doctor by a person who has obtained results from similar "treatments." Here misdirection in the form of a placebo effect brings about the favorable mental set so essential for enhancing the subject's expectation of success.

One of the most important ingredients for hypnotic suggestibility is the expectation of help from one who is in a prestigious position. If convinced of the truth of this person's words, the subject *behaves differently* because he *thinks* and *believes differently.* From time immemorial, all healing by suggestion or hypnosis has been based on this mechanism. If the idea is accepted that increased suggestibility is produced by a favorable mind-set or attitude, catalyzed by the imagination, then hypnotic responses fall into the realm of conviction phenomena. As such, they are *subjective* mechanisms which are inherently present, to a degree, in all individuals. They result from the subject's imagination compounding the sensory spiral of belief until conviction occurs. Hence, "It is indeed a wise hypnotist who knows who is hypnotizing whom!"[67]

An extreme degree of suggestibility is illustrated by medical students who, owing to their imagination, develop the signs and symptoms of many of the diseases they study. The role of the imagination in the production of symptoms is generally admitted, and therefore it seems reasonable to infer that what is caused by the imaginative processes may be reversed by counterconditioning the imaginative processes.

Suggestibility also can affect the hypnotist. There is increasing evidence that the therapist has to be considered an integral part of the therapeutic setting.[14] It is important to study the hypnotist's response to the patient he is hypnotizing. The influence of the patient on the hypnotist also requires more evaluation.[14, 19, 42] Pertinent here is the patient who makes the therapist feel omnipotent because he thinks he cured the patient with his methods.

Altered states of consciousness, reverie, meditation, and sleep or wakefulness, which are fluctuating states of attention or awareness, are poorly understood at present. Is a mother who can sleep through a thunderstorm and yet hear the cry of her baby *really* asleep? In meditation or reverie, or a daydream, one often may not hear even though ostensibly "awake." Everyone has had the experience of "listening" attentively to another person and yet not hearing a word. For all practical purposes, we were "asleep" at the time. Data indicate that discussions that take place while a patient is anesthetized can be recovered postoperatively through hypnotic recall.[19] Sensory impressions noted subliminally can be reproduced; a song heard over and over again eventually can be hummed without our being aware of how it was "learned." Repetitive stimulation of any of the sensory input organs can induce a state of increased receptivity to suggestion. Therefore, if a stimulus is sufficiently maintained, the desired response eventually will be produced.

It is obvious that suggestions leading to hypnosis in its broadest sense occur as a part of everyday existence. This begins during our formative years—when a child hurts his hand, his mother's kiss usually relieves the pain. And, as an adult, he responds more readily to attentive suggestions whenever he is placed in a situation that contains some or all of the elements that were present during his conditioning as a child.[49, 100]

The capacity to be hypnotized is probably "programmed" into the central nervous system as the result of a million or more years of genetic endowment. One portion of the brain, the neocortex, deals with reality. During hypnosis there is a special kind of awareness, characterized by the ability of the phylogenetically older brain—the subcortex—to respond to ideas, images, and feelings which may or may not be related to reality. In a dream, for example, one can float out of the window and land on the roof. Here, distortion of reality occurs because of complete lack of discrimination or cortical inhibition. It is likely, therefore, that when cortical functioning is selectively inhibited, as it is apparently during hypnosis, the altered perceptions can be organized into a wide variety of thought patterns wholly unrelated to reality.

There is a wide field in which to maneuver when one uses hypnotic suggestions to "tap" the brain's capacities. According to neurophysiologists, the human brain has about 10 to 15 billion neurons in which to process and store information.[108] Each neuron, in turn, has the capacity to store a tremendous number of "bits" of information or memories. Furthermore, a single neuron has one or more synapses or "switches." The sum total of these limitless possibilities, associations, or potential interactions for memories, feelings, ideas, and attitudes simply staggers the imagination!

It is estimated that by the age of 50 the brain contains some 70 trillion "bits" of information or memories as part of what is referred to as the imagination or experiential background. This gives us some idea of the magnitude of the field that is capable of responding to the proper inputs. No wonder the brain has been referred to as an "enchanted loom"!

PHYSIOLOGICAL CHANGES DURING HYPNOSIS

The extensive literature bearing upon the physiological changes supposedly associated with hypnosis has been reviewed by several investigators.[21, 24] It has been proposed that such physiological changes might be due to "neutral hypnosis" (i.e., the hypnotic state before any type of suggestion is given for specific changes).[24] An increase in oral temperature was noted in neutral hypnosis with corresponding rise in temperature in other portions of the body.[87] The rise was attributed to the associated anxiety,[106] but other investigators observed that changes did not differ appreciably from those associated with relaxation.[85] Corroborative studies on electrodermal responses,[32] and on blood chemistries[55] showed no differences in hypnotized subjects as against the nonhypnotized. Identical physiological changes in simulators as in hypnotized subjects have been noted.[26] Crasilneck and Hall reviewed the pros and cons of this fascinating area.[25] They quote other investigators who observed an increase in venous flow during hypnosis.[107] Still other researchers noted reduced blood flow in the eye and increased tissue vulnerability.[18, 102] The interested reader would do well to consult Leon Chertok's fascinating treatise on the psychophysiological mechanisms of hypnosis.[21]

THE HYPNOIDAL "STATE"

The hypnoidal "state" refers to a precursor of hypnosis, usually induced by nonformalistic technics. Through fixation of attention, for example, the monotonous stimulus of a white line on a highway induces a tiring effect upon the driver. This eventually leads to some degree of dissociation that can produce a hypnoidal effect, and this, in turn, can merge with true sleep. Depending upon the degree of dissociation, it resembles hypnosis. The hypnoidal "state" is characterized by some detachment as well as by physical and mental relaxation. The attention span fluctuates more toward abstractional states. Since critical thinking is reduced, enhanced suggestibility results.

Our lives are full of hypnoidal contacts and relationships that are referred to by psychologists as "waking hypnosis." Repetitive radio and television commercials, advertising propaganda, and good orators or actors heighten the attention span in a meaningful manner and enhance our suggestibility. When watching an interesting motion picture, our attention is focused on the screen, and we soon enter into a hypnoidal "state." Varying degrees of emotion are registered as we identify with the action in the film. *Reality is made out of unreality.* Whenever the necessity for reality thinking is obviated, a type of waking hypnosis occurs. After walking out of the theater, we usually blink our eyes for a moment to orient ourselves. Without realizing it, we were in a hypnoidal "state" and on the way to being effectively "hypnotized." Waking hypnosis here occurs as the result of utilizing ordinary experiences.

The frequency of naturally occurring quasi-hypnotic experiences has been described,[96] but no correlation was found between a high incidence of such experiments and increased hypnotizability. The experience of so-called trance has also been analyzed in meticulous detail, indicating that it can occur spontaneously. Obviously, it is the result of a wide variety of stimuli, whereas hypnosis requires the interaction of another person who presumably induces the trance. However, as already mentioned, hypnosis is not simulation.[83]

Mass suggestion, mass hypnosis, subliminal projection, brainwashing, propaganda, and evangelistic appeals leading to altered behavior are also produced by nonformalistic hypnotic technics. Thus a knowledge of the everyday aspects of scientifically applied suggestion—hypnosis—has profound implications for an understanding of all mental functioning.

ANIMAL HYPNOSIS

Animal hypnosis is discussed in this section because of its relevance to understanding human hypnosis. Though different, animal "hypnosis," or immobility reflex (I.R.), displays some of the phenomena noted in humans.[41, 58, 59, 60] A chicken placed in a horizontal position develops a tonic immobility characterized by an extensor rigidity of the limbs—catalepsy—when a line is drawn from the eye that is closer to the ground. The immobility may be due, in part, to restriction of activity. Other illustrations of seemingly hypnotic phenomena are seen throughout the animal kingdom. The female spider, which is much larger than the male and ordinarily kills him, is rendered immobile by stroking her belly just before copulation. A snake is "hypnotized" or charmed by the to-and-fro movements of the flutist; and the bird that sings the most sweetly attracts the most potential mates.

The older literature posits a similarity between animal hypnosis and a hypnoidal stage, the latter being a primitive type of resting stage noted in animals. The more primitive the animal, the more apparently hypnoidal is its sleep state.[98] From a phylogenetic standpoint, sleep and hypnosis may have evolved from primitive hypnoidal mechanisms. However, it should be stressed once again that the capacity of a human to enter into hypnosis is due primarily to the social or interpersonal

relationships induced by the symbolic or experiential meaning of words and other stimuli. In animals, on the other hand, hypnosis is produced chiefly by physical manipulations, such as restraint which leads to fear, torpor, and regressive behavior. Thus animal hypnosis is not the same as human hypnosis.[20, 21] Klemm has reviewed the rather extensive literature on animal hypnosis and has had a wide experience in this area.[60] He states, "I am by no means certain that the two states are comparable, but animal hypnosis does seem to be characterized by heightened attention (or by less distraction), and as a result they learn conditioned reflexes more effectively than controls." Other investigators believe that animal hypnosis can be used as an experimental model for a better understanding of human hypnosis, at least in terms of its biological aspects.[52]

AUTOHYPNOSIS

Autohypnosis, or self-hypnosis, usually is produced by *previous posthypnotic suggestions* made by the operator. Every autosuggestion was originally a heterosuggestion. Varying degrees of autosuggestion and autohypnosis account in no small measure for the success of the metaphysical "sciences" and religious spiritual-healing movements.

Suggestions have a much greater chance of being followed when they appear to originate from the self rather than being instituted by another person.[77] If the patient feels that he can facilitate recovery by such therapy, he develops more motivation. The resultant self-pride in this achievement strengthens the confidence essential for recovery. Autohypnosis also makes available a tremendous reservoir of unrecognized potential strength—the "forgotten assets." Diligent practice, however, generally is necessary to obtain a satisfactory depth; lesser degrees are attained more readily.

It has been suggested that autohypnosis is the primary phenomenon, and that heterohypnosis is in effect guided self-hypnosis.[89] These findings contradict a stereotype of hypnosis based on heterohypnosis of a passive subject by an active hypnotist.

RAPPORT

Rapport has been defined as a harmonious relationship between two persons. In hypnosis, it results from restricted attention to some or all stimuli residing in the field of awareness.[34] Thus rapport, as it relates to the hypersuggestibility produced by the hypnotic situation, is a special kind of relationship in which the operator's suggestions are followed more readily. This is due to the greater belief and confidence established in him.

When greater attention is paid to the words of the operator, a subject usually responds with almost a pinpoint literalness or specificity to suggestions, especially if they are in accord with his wishes and needs. Thus, wherever a "pipeline of communication" is established between a sender and a receiver, a suggestion or "message" will be understood if there is no interference, "noise," or static on the circuits (garbling or unintelligibility of the signal).

Some subjects in good rapport even will respond to an operator's posthypnotic suggestions as a printed or written order, such as "Go into a state of deep relaxation." Even blind persons and deaf mutes can be hypnotized through other sensory modalities if there is good rapport. Others respond to the voice of the operator over the telephone, provided they have been appropriately "cued" for this posthypnotic suggestion beforehand. Even an associate without prior knowledge of hypnotic technics, upon a prearranged signal, can readily produce deep hypnosis in a willing subject.

It has been contended that the rapport in hypnosis is due to emotional dependency on the operator. However, there is no more dependency in the hypnotic situation than in any other psychotherapeutic relationship. When autohypnosis is incorporated into therapy, whatever dependency exists is minimized or eliminated. The success of all psychotherapy is based on a good interpersonal relationship, which is essentially a shared experience. Because of the intense and close interpersonal relationship produced by the hypnotic state, both operator and patient enter into good rapport, since it provides each with an emotional satisfaction that otherwise could not be obtained.[71] More research should be directed toward one of the most essential psychological phenomena of hypnosis—the shared qualities of rapport.

One can conclude from the above that patient rapport denotes the ability and willingness of the patient and the operator to enter into an intensified emotional relationship with each other. As a result, the subject is motivated to accept the beliefs that are so necessary for the establishment of conviction. These are the special requisites for hypnotic induction, utilization of the hypnotic state for production of behavioral responses, and subsequent behavioral changes.

CATALEPSY

Catalepsy, an interesting phenomenon of hypnosis, is characterized by a peculiar involuntary tonicity of the muscles. The limbs remain in almost any position in which they are placed; the waxy molding of the fingers and the extremeties is known as *flexibilitas cerea.* During eyeball catalepsy, the eyes do not move when the head is turned slowly—they remain "frozen" or "fixed" when the head moves. At nonhypnotic levels, there generally is a quick darting of the eyes, which is associated with a time lag or an economy of motion.

Catalepsy usually denotes that a light or a medium stage of hypnosis has been achieved, and its presence enables the operator to determine the depth at which he is working. Very few psychophysiologic investigations have been made of this common hypnotic phenomenon.

IDEOSENSORY ACTIVITIES

Ideosensory activity refers to the capacity of the brain to develop sensory images, which may be kinesthetic, olfactory, visual, auditory, tactile, or gustatory. A common example of ideosensory activity is looking at a fire and "seeing" the "face" of one's beloved. During negative ideosensory activity, there is a denial of actual sensory experiences, such as *not* seeing or hearing something that actually is present (e.g., looking for one's pencil and finding it in front of one). A typical example is the complete absorption in an interesting book that produces a selective type of "deafness" to irrelevant stimuli. Imagining the "smell" of a certain odor that does not actually exist is an example of a positive ideosensory activity.

Ideosensory activities are used as misdirection to obtain a somatic response. The subject must be involved in as many ideosensory experiences as possible, as this facilitates hypnotic conditioning. The subject must think of these in terms of his own memories, ideas, and sensations, that is, those that he has already experienced. When, for example, the author wishes to induce hypnoanesthesia, he has found the following suggestion to be helpful, "Your hand is getting just as numb as if it were frozen, or as if you had been sitting or sleeping on it." Nearly everyone has experienced this sensation. Naturally, to elicit ideosensory activities, the posthypnotic suggestions must revive responses previously experienced by an individual—his experiential background. The mention of a specific food to a hungry individual, for instance, is likely to produce salivation only if he has experienced the taste of that particular food.

The section on technics will illustrate how ideosensory activities are employed to effect somatic responses. Comprehension of the nature of ideosensory processes is necessary to understand the *modus operandi* of hypnosis.

IDEOMOTOR ACTIVITIES

Ideomotor activity is one of the phenomena used to facilitate suggestibility. It refers to the involuntary capacity of muscles to respond instantaneously to thoughts, feelings, and ideas. These built-in responses are necessary for survival. An example of ideomotor activity is seen when a mother puts a spoonful of food up to a baby's mouth and her own mouth opens. Leaning in the direction of the ball carrier on a favorite football team and the backseat driver's stepping on the brake of a careening car are other ideomotor activities spontaneously produced without the awareness of the individual.

All induction technics depend on the subject's being unaware that he has made such physical responses to suggestion. He does not realize that they are the result of his own thoughts. In the section on induction technics, it will be shown how ideomotor activities are utilized to invoke the subject's belief and thus lead to the expectation of hypnosis.

Chevreul's pendulum test (described in Chapter 5), the operation of the Ouija board, oil- and water-witching, clairvoyance, and even extrasensory perception to a degree, depend upon the involuntary or ideomotor muscular responses associated with the ideosensory processes of the individual. Subcortical mechanisms are responsible for the primary or inherited responses, manifested as involuntary reflexes. These are not learned, and include blinking, pupillary dilatation or contraction, endocrine responses, peristalsis, breathing, and cardiac functioning. Even though breathing and blinking can be controlled volitionally, most of the vital functions are under autonomic control.

It is possible, however, to "build in" other reflexes upon those that are involuntary and to make these increasingly subject to volitional control. Biofeedback has demonstrated that the autonomic nervous system is *not* as autonomic as we have been led to believe. The greater control of autonomic functioning accounts for the feats of Yoga and the transcendence of normal voluntary capacity achieved by posthypnotic suggestions.

It has been pointed out that highly motivated subjects can perform to the same degree at nonhypnotic levels.[7] One investigator contends that it is possible to obtain an increase in the range of behavior,[81] and according to another writer, subjects will oblige the hypnotist if the experimental setting is conducive to the expected response.[114]

At nonhypnotic levels, the autonomic nervous system attempts to act in response to all new situations, and it is corrected by awareness of reality. In the case of the back-seat driver, the discriminatory portion of the cortex appraises reality and returns the conviction that he is *not* in danger. Without such awareness, *he would produce responses as if he were the driver,* as happens in dreams, hallucinations, and psychoses.

Reality results whenever incoming information in the form of sensory perceptions can be validated with previously stored data; this results in automatic behavior and response. During hypnosis, however, the operator's suggestions are accepted as reality because of selective cortical inhibition; the incoming information does not have access to the stored data; therefore it cannot be validated. Thus the increased suggestibility, leading to production of hypnotic phenomena, is brought about by the interplay of two forces—automatic activity (ideomotor and ideosensory) and selective cortical inhibition. Stated simply, when ideas that lead to "ideoid" (idea-like) actions are interpreted as reality, the resultant convictions lead to hypnosis!

POSTHYPNOTIC SUGGESTIONS AND CONDITIONING

Acts carried out after the termination of hypnosis in response to specific suggestion are called posthypnotic phenomena.[111] A suggestion given during hypnosis serves as the stimulus, and the act becomes the response. A posthypnotic suggestion and a conditioned reflex serve a similar purpose except that the former is not established by repetitive trial and learning in the classic sense. Rather, a posthypnotic act is a complex task because it is related to some degree with the hypnotic induction. It is often carried out as the result of a single session of "learning." Moreover, it is not as rapidly extinguished as a conditioned reflex.

The posthypnotic act, even though carried out long after it is suggested, is probably a spontaneously self-induced replica of the original hypnotic situation. A posthypnotic suggestion may last for minutes to years.[33, 34, 37, 45, 56] It is agreed, however, that it may remain effective for several months.[57, 84] During this period, decrement occurs in the quality of the posthypnotic performance. Periodic reinforcement, however, tends to increase its effectiveness; repeated elicitation does not weaken it.

Posthypnotic suggestions usually are followed irrespective of the depth of the hypnosis. Completion depends more upon the nature and the difficulty of the suggested task than upon the depth of the hypnosis.[110] Internal or external factors, of one type or another, can prevent fulfillment. When this happens, profound anxiety may be produced. Therefore, a posthypnotic suggestion should not be of a bizarre nature, but in keeping with the subject's needs and goals.

Some subjects develop a complete amnesia for the posthypnotic act and yet readily follow the original suggestion. Others can be aware of the original suggestion as they carry it out. Still others remember the suggestion only after the completion of the act. Response to posthypnotic suggestions might be compared with the compulsive behavior noted in all of us at times. We know what we are doing, but do not know *why!* If the setting in which the posthypnotic suggestion occurs is altered, or if the expectant attitudes change between the time of the suggestion and the time when it is about to be carried out, then deeply hypnotized persons can cancel even the original suggestion.[36]

Unless the subject is a volunteer for a stage hypnotist, ridiculous suggestions usually are rejected. Most of these volunteers are exhibitionists and seldom mind carrying out suggestions that are compatible with their usual or desired behavior. Whether or not a suggestion is carried out also depends upon the wishes and the intentions of the subject.[13, 70] The type and the quality of the operator's communication also affect the response. When working with a subject in hypnosis, an extraverbal approach such as, "You wouldn't mind opening the window after you come out of this relaxed state, would you?" minimizes resistance. If the posthypnotic suggestion is not followed, a remark such as, "It's stuffy inside. I wonder how we can get some fresh air in the room?" is usually effective. A cue of this type often reinforces a posthypnotic suggestion given during hypnosis.

When a posthypnotic suggestion that is not fully in accord with the subject's desires is carried out, he usually rationalizes the unusual behavior. Purposeless posthypnotic suggestions are as readily forgotten as other instructions given at nonhypnotic levels.[93] The greater tenacity of posthypnotic suggestions stems from the graded effects of previously invoked beliefs such as lid heaviness and limb catalepsy, which, when compounded by ideosensory responses, lead to automatic conviction. Since the subject felt the operator's initial suggestions, he naturally believes and follows other and more complex posthypnotic suggestions. The subject, just as during the induction, is wholly unaware that his own ideomotor and ideosensory responses initiated the posthypnotic response.

The complex mechanisms involved in the fulfillment of a posthypnotic suggestion are the result of a series of conditioned sensory impressions and muscular activities. The subject develops a belief in the reality of a subjective experience and response following a posthypnotic suggestion. He accepts its reality as readily as any belief associated with dreaming, thinking, and perceptual reorganization. One investigator thinks that there is no *essential* difference between behavior in the "hypnotic" and "posthypnotic" periods; in other words, that all phenomena elicited by means of posthypnotic suggestions are seen during hypnosis.[4] However, the reverse is not always true, and there is a difference between a posthypnotic and waking suggestion in carrying out a task performance.

AMNESIA

Amnesia may or may not occur spontaneously during hypnosis. It is not a reliable criterion of the hypnotic state.[105] It may be conceptualized as a mechanism that interferes with the retrieval of information; the subject appears unable to bring the forgotten material into awareness.[78] More often it is produced through posthypnotic suggestions. When it has occurred, there is a selective loss of memory following dehypnotization. The subject is "unaware" of what has occurred during hypnotically produced amnesia; however, the recollections are only held in abeyance. Most good subjects, when rehypnotized, can remember nearly everything that happened during the hypnotic session; others gradually forget some or all of their experiences. Still others, even though deeply hypnotized, have an inordinate need to maintain control and will not develop amnesia. Intensive studies have been made to determine whether the consequences of amnesia derive directly from the specific content of posthypnotic suggestions.[15, 82, 101, 105]

The phenomenon of amnesia occurs as an everyday experience. The name of an old friend, for example, can be forgotten temporarily when an introduction is being made. Either spontaneous or suggested amnesia can be used for evaluating the depth of hypnosis; the former generally is indicative of deep hypnosis (i.e., somnambulism). Here loss of memory for whole segments of an individual's life is produced; the dissociation is analogous to the fugue states noted in amnesia victims. Suggested hypnotic amnesia is somewhat comparable with the everyday experience of repressing painful experiences. The duration of the amnesia is not predictable. The reader interested in all aspects of posthypnotic amnesia is directed to an excellent symposium on the subject, published in 1966.[103]

Amnesia can often be obtained by means of the following instructions: "You may find it very convenient to forget everything that I suggested. Imagine that your mind is like a blackboard that has just had everything erased." Another method is to say, "After you open your eyes, you will have no recollection of what I said to you while you were in a relaxed state. However, all the suggestions I gave you will be effectively carried out as specified."

DISSOCIATION

Dissociation is somewhat similar to hypnotic amnesia. It refers to the inherent ability of a hypnotized subject to "detach" himself from his immediate environment. This phenomenon occurs at nonhypnotic levels, as in reverie states. An individual may be completely dissociated and yet retain his capacity to function adequately. This dissociated state is similar to dreaming, when one "sees" himself performing many activities. Nearly all situations produced in dreams can be attained in the dissociated state by appropriate posthypnotic suggestions.

A well-conditioned subject can "step out" of himself and see himself sitting on the other side of the room. Dissociation frequently is used to induce hypnoanesthesia. The following remark to a deeply hypnotized patient in a dentist's chair automatically will raise the pain threshold: "You would not mind going out to the ball park, would you? It is such a nice day for a baseball game, isn't it?"

A portion of the body, such as a limb, can be "anesthetized" through dissociation; the person does not feel the "separated" part. This can be produced as follows: "You can feel and see both arms in your lap, can't you?" This suggestion may be given while the subject has his arm extended in rigid catalepsy. Obviously, if a positive visual and tactile hallucination is produced by the suggestion to "see" *both* arms resting comfortably in his lap, then *the extended cataleptic limb becomes the dissociated* arm, and it *automatically becomes impervious to pain* without any mention of anesthesia! It has been clearly demonstrated that during amnesia tasks of some complexity could be carried out simultaneously, even though some of them are out of awareness.[64]

DEPERSONALIZATION

Depersonalization can be induced readily in a good subject through posthypnotic suggestions. He can be told to forget his own identity and assume that he is another person. This is accomplished most easily by asking him, "Who is your favorite person?" The operator then suggests that *he* is that person. Depersonalization can be used for psychotherapeutic purposes that are similar to those mentioned under dissociation.

HYPERMNESIA OR MEMORY RECALL

Hypermnesia refers to the retrieval of information or an increase in memory recall greater than that achieved at volitional or nonhypnotic levels. This phenomenon, too, is seen in some degree as a part of everyday life. How often, when walking along a certain street, one thinks: "Whatever happened to my old buddy, Jim? I can remember when we used to play on this very block." All memories, no matter how trivial, are stored in the brain and leave an indelible impression. Most of these can be recovered when the proper pathways of association are stimulated.

Under hypnosis, a good subject apparently can recall memories long since forgotten. One investigator believes that the magnitude of recall or retrieval of information obtained under hypnosis is increased only slightly,[79] whereas another thinks it is much greater than at nonhypnotic levels.[93] One researcher reports increment in memory skills and an increased ability to forget or repress,[35] but this was not corroborated by others.[109]

The information recalled may be inaccurate, however, and one must realize that hypnotic subjects can fabricate material readily. Hypermnesia must be differentiated from revivification, which is essentially an actual reliving of an incident at the time at which it occurred. Memory recall is obtained by posthypnotic suggestions such as, "Perhaps you might like to tell me all about your graduation from grammar school, and what did you say *was* the name of your school?" The emphasis here is on the past tense, whereas in revivification the question would be asked in the present tense.

The author has used hypermnesia for recall of pertinent information that has helped to solve crimes and legal problems. In one instance involving a large sum of money, a subject remembered where he had been on a specific date 8 years prior to the hypnotization. In this instance, recall of the facts was verified.

Hypnotic recall has been used to pierce an amnesia for the cause of an air crash. The investigator induced a dissociation of the personality in which the "observing ego" watches what the "experiencing ego" is doing to cause the accident.[86] As a result of his fascinating work, the Civil Aeronautics Board (C.A.B.) decided that hypnosis would be the method of choice to bring to light hidden details of an air crash.

Working with the Federal Bureau of Investigation, the author has been involved in the use of hypnosis in getting witnesses to crimes to recall them in greater detail, thus providing useful investigative leads (see Chap. 23).

REVIVIFICATION AND AGE REGRESSION

Revivification must be differentiated from age regression. In revivification, the hypnotized person actually relives earlier events of his life; all memories following the age to which the subject is regressed are eliminated. On the other hand, in age regression, the subject plays a role; there is a simulated pattern of acting out of past events in the framework of the present.[88] This type of age regression is called pseudorevivification.

The phenomenon of revivification is produced by posthypnotic suggestions directed toward progressively suggesting disorientation as to the year, the month, and the day; then, by appropriate suggestions, an earlier age level is reached. Some investigators believe that long-forgotten memories are not reactivated but rather are simulated, and that nonregressive elements are present.[79] However, it has been demonstrated frequently that in revivification the subjects exhibit many of the personality traits of earlier periods in their lives. Intellectual functioning, for example, which is indicated by the manner of speaking and the choice of words, is childlike; the handwriting changes, and there are other objective manifestations that corroborate the validity of the revivification.

It is possible, however that much of the descriptive material revealed during revivification is due to role-playing or "screen memories." This "misremembering" can occur in response to a prior suggestion that a specific act took place; later the act is reinstated as if it were an original memory. It appears that recall is not improved for unimportant mnemonic material but is improved greatly under hypnosis when strong emotional elements are associated with the memories.[29] The meanings and the motivations associated with spontaneous revivification during hypnotherapy have been described.[22]

The best way to obtain revivification is for the operator to identify himself with a surrogate figure that the subject once knew. If, for example, the operator plays the role of a friendly person, he can remark: "You are now in the fourth grade. I happened to be talking to your teacher, and she told me how well you are doing in school." Some subjects will respond with genuine affection and warmth.

Though this has been challenged, psychophysiologic revivification is authentic if the Babinski reflex is elicited.[40] A spontaneous Babinski reflex may also appear whenever the subject's perceptions and sensations are compatible with the regressed chronologic age.[62] However, neither of these investigations used naive subjects—a crucial point. Revivification is not valid if the subject's vocabulary is incompatible with his present chronologic age level. Other observations at non-hypnotic levels indicate that revivification in the form of complex somatic changes can occur during drug-facilitated abreactions.[75] However, here too, the reliability of the results is open to serious question.

There are various degrees of revivification and regression that can occur simultaneously, depending on the depth of hypnosis. This accounts for the diversity of opinions as to their distinguishing features. Nevertheless, the effects of either revivification or regression can produce what seem like meaningful emotional experiences that are compatible with earlier age levels.[92] It seems that most spontaneous age regressions contain some facet of revivification as well as regression.[62] This has been referred to as retrogression[61] or dynamic regression.[91]

An interesting example of simulation once occurred while a female patient was being regressed to a very early age level. She imitated a neonatal position, became mute, and appeared to be sucking the breast. Fortunately, this patient had been given two sets of cues for dehypnotization: (1) she could terminate it herself, or (2) she could respond to the shoulder signal (a touch on the left shoulder). Both sets of signals should be given to all patients who are being regressed to ensure that the situation can be controlled if communication at the verbal level is lost. This should be done even if simulation or role-playing is suspected. It is possible that hypnotic age regression may function to produce those experiences which are retrievable. For those that are not, the individual may provide the best substitute possible by enacting the appropriate role.[99]

To obtain revivification, the subject is told that, upon a given signal, "You are soon going to be 10 years of age, and you can see yourself clearly at that age and everything that is happening." (A few minutes are allowed to elapse to allow sufficient time for the reorientation to take place.) The signal is now given. The subject is asked, "What is the date today? How old are you today? What are you doing? Who are some of the people around you?" Additional conversation in the past tense will help to establish the regression more firmly.

How the handwriting changes in a good hypnotic subject who has achieved revivification is illustrated by the examples given on page 18.

AGE PROGRESSION

It is believed that both hypnotic age regression and "age progression" are forms of psychological activity that involve disorientation for the subject and a reorganization of his perceptual equilibrium and control mechanisms, with particular reference to time-space perception.[61] The term "age progression" refers to the artificially induced disorientation of a hypnotized subject who hallucinates living in the future but who still retains his present chronologic age. It does not refer to reversing a regression (making a person return to his present chronologic age), as when a regressed subject is told during hypnosis, "You are now growing older: 10; 12 years of age; and now you are 14 years old."

Research concerned with "age progression" into future periods has been reported.[54] It is difficult to accept the data on age progression without checking the subject's ability to simulate advancing years at nonhypnotic levels. Moreover, the possibility of role-playing has not been ruled out. It is hard, too, to understand how an individual can relate material for which he has no inputs.

The fact that an individual can be regressed to a previous age by no means indicates that the opposite, namely, age progression, can be achieved. However, a form of "age progression" (i.e., pseudo-orientation in time) can be of great clinical value in understanding how a hypnotized subject might react in the future to stressful situations that are suggested at his present chronologic age.[23]

Good examples of pseudo-orientation in time from the author's clinical practice are cases of apprehensive and tense individuals who came for consultation for the advisability of having vasectomies.[68] In deep hypnosis, one subject was told that the actual surgery had been performed 5 years ago; an amnesia for the posthypnotic suggestion was given. He was then asked, "How have you been feeling since you were sterilized?" He replied, "Oh, Doctor! I haven't had a good night's sleep since my operation. It's made me very tense and nervous." After dehypnotization and removal of the hallucinatory experience, he was advised to postpone surgery until meaningful material could be worked through. By such measures he eventually was able to accept the conse-

(Age 7)

(Age 10)

(Age 47)

quences of the proposed surgery and ultimately achieved better personality integration.

HYPNOTIC ANALGESIA AND ANESTHESIA

Analgesia, or the first stage of anesthesia, is characterized by a lack of startle reaction, facial flinch, and grimaces. Although insensitivity to pain can be simulated readily, hypnotized persons seem to withstand more discomfort and pain than would otherwise be possible. Hypnoanalgesia usually is more effective than "biting the bullet" or voluntary control of pain. Soothing verbalizations suggesting insensitivity often can result in analgesia and occasionally in anesthesia. Hysterical anesthesia is obviously the "other side of the coin" of hypnoanesthesia.

Anesthesia refers to a complete lack of awareness of pain. The question arises as to whether hypnoanesthesia is due to amnesia, or whether the sensory threshold is increased due to role-playing. The latter was negated by recent studies which showed that increased stability of arousal was present and that evoked responses occurred during hypnosis in subjects who could control organic pain hypnotically.[2] Electromyographic studies indicate that in hypnosis the pain is present in the tissues, but there is no awareness of it. This has been validated in a brilliant presentation using automatic writing; the dissociated hand indicated on a scale that pain was being experienced while the subject consciously denied it.[51] Theories of pain transmission have been revised on the basis of comparison between relief of pain by lobotomy, opiates, placebos, and hypnosis.[3]

Since the physiologic reactions to painful stimuli, such as increased heart rate, respiration, and galvanic skin reflexes, are diminished, hypnoanesthesia apparently is genuine.[31, 94] Moreover, perceptual adaptation to prism displacement, which requires the presence of normal sensations and proprioceptive feedback, did not occur in hypnotic anesthesia.[39] It has been shown further that there is a positive relationship between the depth of hypnosis and the degree of induced anesthesia.[113]

HYPERESTHESIA

Hyperesthesia refers to increased sensitivity to touch. It is noted commonly in hysterics. That there is a wide variability in pain perception indicates that subjective interpretation of pain is not a reliable indicator of hyperesthesia or, for that matter, of anesthesia. Hyperesthesia may be due to a lowered threshold to discomfort.[3]

Hyperesthesia is produced hypnotically by means of the following suggestions: "Imagine that you are in your own bathroom. Would you mind describing the location and the color of your bathtub?" ("It is next to the toilet, and it is a white one.") "Now you will turn the hot water faucet on. Which one is it?" ("It is the left one.") "Notice the steaming *hot* water filling up the tub." (The patient nods.) "Now will you place your toes in the water to see how *hot* it is?" A good patient will grimace with discomfort. If he states, "I didn't feel the heat," one can use a posthypnotic suggestion such as, "You will feel a sensation of warmth when you are able to imagine your foot in the tub of hot water. Perhaps it will be at the next session."

Cutaneous hyperesthesia usually is induced readily in emotionally disturbed individuals. Those who have organic pain syndromes are more sensitive to hypnotically suggested discomfort. Thus it can be hypothesized that pain is not necessarily a fixed response to a hurtful stimulus, but rather that its perception is modified by our past experiences and expectations, and more subtly by our cultural attitudes. Hence pain is synthesized out of present thoughts, fears, and motivations. In support of these views, it has been noted that placebos are more effective in persons whose stress and anxiety are greatly intensified.[10] Their effectiveness is due largely to reducing the anxiety component associated with pain.

POSTHYPNOTIC HALLUCINATIONS

Negative and positive hallucinations involving any one of the senses can be produced, as in dreams, by appropriate suggestions. In deep somnambulism, the eyes may be opened without affecting the depth of the hypnosis. A good subject can be made to "see" a person, to "hear" a voice, or to be "deaf" to spoken words, as discussed on page 12.

During deep hypnosis, there is a hyperacuity of all the senses, at least for the suggestions of the operator. As a result, there apparently is an increase in vision, hearing, touch, and smell, which is greater than can be demonstrated at nonhypnotic levels.[30] Color-blindness, tubular vision, scotomata, and even "total blindness" have been induced. "Deafness," in varying degrees, involving one or both ears, has been described.[63, 73] Similarly, taste and smell have been altered.

Many of the hallucinations are difficult to distinguish from those produced by everyday experiences and distortions. It is contended that the hallucinations are due to elicitation of organic reaction patterns or, in some instances, to simulation[5] or role-playing.[28] Since various brain formations, such as the temperature center, may be influenced by posthypnotic suggestions involving hallucinatory experiences of coldness, the first explanation may be correct.

Posthypnotic hallucinations are produced with the following suggestions: "Perhaps you might enjoy opening your eyes and still remain in a deep, relaxed state. You will see everything that is suggested to you. At first everything will be blurry, and then the various things I suggest will get much clearer." It is a good idea to begin first with simple hallucinations of objects which fit into the immediate environment, such as an imaginary ashtray or desk.

One can first suggest, while the subject still has his eyes closed, that he "see" the ashtray on the operator's desk (it is vividly described), and he is to indicate when he sees it. It is then suggested: "After you open your eyes, you will see the ashtray on my desk just as I described it. Also, you will be able to walk around and look at it, pick it up, examine it, and describe it."

SOMNAMBULISM

Somnambulism is one of the deepest stages of hypnosis. It also is observed in sleepwalkers who have no recollection of their nocturnal experiences. Nearly everyone has had a roommate who talked in his sleep. A conversation can be carried on for some time without any recollection on the part of the sleeper. He can even respond to posthypnotic suggestions. It is surprising how many such individuals will perform various acts later without ever realizing how they were suggested. Most of these individuals are "natural" somnambulists who exhibit many hypnotic phenomena *without* going through formalistic hypnotic induction. These persons can develop spontaneous analgesia and anesthesia, dissociation, and depersonalization. Some are classified erroneously as multiple personalities.

Somnambulism generally is associated with amnesia; acts are performed without subsequent recollection. The subject appears to be in a dreamlike state; however, somnambulism is not sleep. Recognition of the objective signs of the somnambulistic stage are described below. The somnambulist still retains generalized memory but cannot remember the events that occurred during hypnosis. Hypnotically inserted suggestions automatically become convictions in the somnambule. Because of the extensive cortical inhibition, the subject has no knowledge of how the convictions were established. As a result, the hypnotically induced convictions prevent incoming sensory information from being tested against reality! This inability of the subject to appraise the operator's suggestions, together with the amnesia, furnishes an explanation for somnambulism.

The first thing to do when developing somnambulism is to get the subject to open his eyes without affecting the depth of hypnosis. The method for effecting this was described above. An amnesia must then be produced, if it has not occurred spontaneously. Finally, the subject must be cued to respond to a specific posthypnotic suggestion.

The nature of the cue can vary, depending upon whether hetero- or autohypnosis is utilized. In the former, a touch on the right shoulder can be the signal to reinduce somnambulism at the next session. Frequently, without saying a single word, the author makes use of a cue such as merely lifting the subject's arm. If it becomes cataleptic (the arm-drop test), deep hypnosis has been induced. The subject can use a count-down method from 100 to zero; as the numbers decrease, the hypnosis will get deeper and deeper until somnambulism is reached. Somnambulism often can be transformed into sleep, and vice versa.

AUTOMATIC WRITING

Automatic writing, too, occurs at nonhypnotic levels. "Doodling" while conversing on the telephone is a common manifestation of this phenomenon. The material produced by a good subject's automatic writing has considerable meaningfulness to the hypnotized patient. The hypnotherapist can make good use of its symbolic meaning, especially when working with those who cannot express themselves.

Specifically, the subject is told that the dissociated hand holding the pencil will write even while he is engaged in conversation. It will do so without any attempt on his part to control its movements. He is also instructed that he will have no knowledge of what is being written, that after being dehypnotized, he will understand that the significance of the material appears nonsensical or cryptic, and that it can be interpreted by the subject in a subsequent session.

The actual verbalization for establishing dissociated handwriting is as follows: "Your hand will get numb and cold; it is losing all feeling, all sensation, and all movement. You do not feel your hand as I rub it—it is getting very numb, and the hand no longer feels attached to your wrist. Now, as you raise your arm, it will feel as if the hand is no longer attached to your wrist. Now, as you raise your arm, it will feel as if the hand is no longer attached to your arm. You no longer have any control over your hand. However, your hand can remember everything about you. If you cannot remember something in particular about yourself, your hand will be able to remember it and write out the answer. If it is too painful for you to face or talk about it, your hand will write it. If you do not tell the truth, your hand will write the correct answer without your controlling it. Nor will you know what the hand is writing. However, after the relaxed state is terminated, you will easily recognize what you have written."

TIME DISTORTION

Time distortion is one of the most interesting and clinically valuable phenomena of hypnosis. It refers to the remarkable capacity of the human brain to appreciate time, condense time, or expand time.

Everyone has a "clock" in his brain that is capable of judging time with extraordinary accuracy. All of us have had the experience of arising at a much earlier hour than usual to do something we enjoy, and often we can wake up within several minutes of the designated hour. This indicates, of course, that many of us can estimate time at nonhypnotic levels with great precision.

Time can drag while one is waiting for a cab on a cold, rainy day, even though it is due in 2 minutes. In this instance, 2 minutes can seem like 20 minutes (time expansion). Contrarily, when one is pleasantly engaged in conversation with an old friend while waiting for a cab, 20 minutes can pass as if they were only 2 minutes (time condensation or contraction). It is maintained that a drowning man recapitulates whole segments of his life in a few split seconds. Thus the brain obviously has the capacity to condense a considerable amount of memorial data even at nonhypnotic levels.

In a good subject, time distortion can be induced readily through posthypnotic suggestions. Briefly, 1 minute of subjective or experiential time can be equated with 10 minutes of clock time (time lengthening). On the other hand, 10 minutes of clock time can be condensed to 1 minute of subjective or experiential time (time contraction). The phenomenon of time distortion utilized in hypnotherapy has been described by Cooper and Erickson.[23]

Posthypnotic suggestions to induce time distortion are given as follows: "Every minute of actual time will *seem* like 10 minutes to you. Time will go by very, very slowly; it will seem like an eternity. Every 5 minutes that you remain in this deep and relaxed state *seem* almost as long as an hour. If you wish, in less than 10 minutes, you can see almost an entire motion picture again, and *really* see it better than when you actually saw it."

The degree to which these phenomena can be elicited, however, often depends on the depth of hypnosis attained. Less than 20 percent of subjects readily manifest many of the phenomena, and the remainder share the experiences to varying degrees. One must keep in mind that the results are not as dramatic as some uninformed sources lead one to expect. This view has been supported by others.[7, 32] With reference to the validity of age regression, it has been posited that the idea that there is an "ablation" of all subsequent memories is too extreme to be supported by acceptable studies.[48] Nevertheless, the sensory alterations, when they appear in good subjects, have high validity.

SUMMARY

The important phenomena associated with hypnosis have been discussed briefly. Since they also occur at so-called nonhypnotic levels, hypnotic phenomena follow the natural laws of thought and behavior. Current and past literature is replete with many ingenious methodologies for obtaining hypnotic phenomena. Their fundamental characteristics have been discussed. These phenomena are elicited in various combinations, depending upon the therapeutic or experimental situation, the personality, and the motivations of the subject, and also, of course, upon the skill, the empathy, and the personality of the operator.

REFERENCES

1. Abrams, S.: The use of hypnotic techniques with psychotics: a critical review. Am. J. Psychotherapy, *18:*79, 1964.
2. Amadeo, M., and Yanovski, A.: Evoked potentials and selective attention in subjects capable of hypnotic analgesia. Int. J. Clin. Exp. Hypn., *23:*200, 1975.
3. Barber, T. X.: Toward a theory of pain: relief of chronic pain by prefrontal leucotomy, opiates, placebos and hypnosis, Psychol. Bull., *56:*430, 1951.
4. _____: Hypnosis as perceptual—cognitive restructuring: II. Post-hypnotic behavior. J. Clin. Exp. Hypn., *6:*10, 1958.
5. _____: The good hypnotic subject. Science Digest, *43:*36, 1958.
6. _____: The after images of "hallucinated" and "imagined" colors. J. Abnorm. Social Psychol., *59:* 136, 1959.
7. _____: Toward a theory of hypnotic behavior: an experimental study of "hypnotic time distortion." Arch. Gen. Psychiat., *10:*209, 1964.
8. _____: Hypnotism: Imagination and Human Potentialities. New York, Pergamon Press, 1974.
9. Barber, T.X., and Calverley, D.S.: "Hypnotic behavior" as a function of task motivation. J. Psychol., *54:*363, 1962.
10. Beecher, H. K.: Role of stress in placebo and drug effectiveness. Science, *132:*91, 1960.
11. Berg, S., and Melin, E.: Hypnotic susceptibility in old age: some data from residential homes for old people. Int. J. Clin. & Exp. Hypn., *23:*184, 1975.
12. Biddle, W.E.: Hypnosis in the Psychoses. Springfield, Ill., Charles C Thomas, 1967.
13. Birenbaum: Den Vergessen einer Vornahme; Isolierte seelische Systeme und dynamische Gesamtbereiche. Psychol. Forsch., *13:*218, 1930.
14. Blatt, S.: Is the hypnotist also being hypnotized? Int. J. Clin. Exp. Hypn., *17:*160, 1969.
15. Bowers, K.: Hypnotic behavior: the differentiation of trance and demand characteristic variables. J. Abnorm. Psychol., *71:*42, 1966.
16. Bowers, K.S., and Bowers, P.G.: Hypnosis and creativity: a theoretical and empirical rapprochement. *In* Fromm, E., and Shor, R.E. (eds.): Hypnosis Research and Perspectives. Chicago, Aldine-Atherton, 1972.
17. Brown, H.A., and Krasner, L.: The role of subject expectancies. Int. J. Clin. Exp. Hypn., *17:*180, 1969.
18. Chapman, L.F., Goodell, H., and Wolff, N.G.: Tissue vulnerability, inflammation, and the nervous system. Am. J. Clin. Hypn., 172, 1960.
19. Cheek, D.B.: Unconscious perception of meaningful sounds during surgical anesthesia as revealed under hypnosis. J. Am. Soc. Clin. Hypn. *1:*101, 1959.
20. Chertok, L.: Hypnosis. New York, Pergamon Press, 1966.
21. _____: Psychophysiological Mechanisms of Hypnosis. New York, Springer-Verlag, 1967.
22. Conn, J. H.: Meanings and motivations associated with spontaneous hypnotic regression, J. Clin. Exp. Hypn., *1:*21, 1958.
23. Cooper, L. F., and Erickson, M. H.: Time Distortion in Hypnosis. Baltimore, Williams & Wilkins, 1954.
24. Crasilneck, H.B., and Hall, J.A.: Physiological changes associated with hypnosis: a review of the literature since 1948. Int. J. Clin. Exp. Hypn., *7:*9, 1959.

25. _____: Clinical Hypnosis: Principles and Applications. New York, Grune & Stratton, 1975.

26. Damacer, E.F., Shor, R.E., and Orne, M.T.: Physiological effects during hypnotically requested emotions. Psychom. Med., *25:*334, 1963.

27. Dittborn, J.: Expectation as a factor of sleep suggestibility. J. Clin. Exp. Hypn., *6:*164, 1958.

28. Dorcus, R. M.: Modification by suggestion of some vestibular and visual responses. Am. J. Psychol., *49:*82, 1937.

29. _____: Recall under hypnosis of amnestic events, International J. Clin. Exp. Hypn., *7:*57, 1960.

30. Doupe, J., *et al.:* Vasomotor reactions in the hypnotic state. J. Neurol. Psychiat., *2:*97, 1939.

31. Dynes, J. B.: An experimental study in hypnotic anesthesia. J. Abnorm. Social Psychol., *27:*79, 1932.

32. Edmonston, W.E., and Erbeck, J.R.: Hypnotic time distortion: a note. Am. J. Clin. Hypn., *79,* 1967.

33. Edwards, G.: Duration of posthypnotic effect. Br. J. Psychiat., *109:*259, 1963.

34. Erickson, M. H., and Erickson, E. M.: Concerning the nature and character of posthypnotic behavior. J. Gen. Psychol., *24:*95, 1941.

35. Evans, F.J.: Recent trends in experimental hypnosis. Behavioral Sci., *13:*477, 1968.

36. Fisher, S.: The role of expectancy in the performance of posthypnotic behavior, J. Abnorm. Social Psychol., *49:*503, 1954.

37. Fontan, J., and Segard, C.: Eléments de Médecine suggestive, Hypnotisme, et Suggestion: Faits Cliniques. Paris, C. Douin, 1887.

38. Friedman, J., and Kleep, W.: Hypnotizability of newly admitted psychotic patients. Psychosomatics, *4:*95, 1963.

39. Garrett, J.B., and Wallace, B.: A novel test of hypnotic anesthesia. Int. J. Clin. Exp. Hypn., *23:*139, 1975.

40. Gidro-Frank, L., and Bowers Buch, M. K.: A study of the plantar response in hypnotic age regression. J. Nerv. Ment. Dis., *107:*443, 1948.

41. Gilman, T.T., and Marcuse, F.L.: Animal hypnosis. Psychol. Bull., *46:*151, 1949.

42. Gordon, J.E. (ed.): Handbook of Clinical and Experimental Hypnosis. New York, Macmillan, 1967.

43. Graham, C.: Hypnosis and attention. Paper presented at the Sixth International Congress for Hypnosis. Uppsala, Sweden, July, 1973.

44. Greene, J.T.: Hypnotizability of hospitalized psychotics. Int. J. Clin. Exp. Hypn., *17:*103, 1969.

45. Gurney, E.: Peculiarities of certain posthypnotic states. Proc. Psych. Res. Soc. London, *4:*268, 1886–7.

46. Guze, H.: The involvement of the hypnotist in the hypnotic session. J. Clin. Exp. Hypn., *4:*61, 1956.

47. Hilgard, E. R., *et al.:* Individual differences in susceptibility to hypnosis. Proc. Nat. Acad. Sci., *44:*125, 1958.

48. Hilgard, E.R.: Hypnotic Susceptibility. New York, Harcourt, Brace & World, 1965.

49. Hilgard, J.R.: Personality and Hypnosis. Chicago, University of Chicago Press, 1970.

50. _____: Imaginative involvement: some characteristics of the highly hypnotizable and the non-hypnotizable. Int. J. Clin. Exp. Hypn., *22:*138, 1974.

51. Hilgard, E.R., and Hilgard, J.R.: Hypnosis in Relief of Pain. Los Altos, Cal., William Kaufman, 1975.

52. Hoskovec, J., and Svorad, D.: The relationship between human and animal hypnosis. Am. J. Clin. Hypn., *180:*180, 1969.

53. Ihalainen, O., and Rosberg, G.: Relaxing and encouraging suggestions given to hospitalized chronic schizophrenics. Int. J. Clin. Exp. Hypn., *24:*228, 1976.

54. Israeli, N.: Experimental study of hypnotic imagination and dreams of projection in time: I. Outlook upon the remote future extending through the quintillionth year. J. Clin. Exp. Hypn., *1:*49, 1953.

55. Jana, H., and Pattie, S.: Biochemical changes in blood during hypnotic trance. Ind. J. Med. Res., *53:*1000, 1965.

56. Janet, P.: L'Automatisme Psychologique. Paris, F. Alcan, 1889.

57. Kellogg, E. R.: Duration and effects of posthypnotic suggestion. J. Exp. Psychol., *12:*502, 1929.

58. _____: Potentiation of animal "hypnosis" with low levels of electric current. Animal Behavior, *13:*571, 1965.

59. Klemm, W.R.: Physiological studies of the mobility reflex ("animal hypnosis"). J. Neurosci. Res. *4:*165, 1971.

60. _____: Identity of sensory and motor systems that are critical to the immobility reflex ("animal hypnosis") in neuropharmacological studies. Pharm. Biochem. Behavior, *4:*85, 1976.

61. Kline, M. V.: Hypnotic retrogression: a neuropsychologic theory of regression and progression. J. Clin. Exp. Hypn., *1:*21, 1953.

62. _____: Hypnotic age regression and psychotherapy: clinical and theoretical observations. Int. J. Clin. Exp. Hypn., *8:*117, 1960.

63. Kline, M. V., *et al.:* An experimental study of the nature of hypnotic deafness: effects of delayed speech feedback. J. Clin. Exp. Hypn., *2:*145, 1954.

64. Knox, V.J., *et al.:* The nature of task interference

in hypnotic dissociation: an investigation of hypnotic behavior. Int. J. Clin. Exp. Hypn., *23:*305, 1975.

65. Kramer, E.: Group induction of hypnosis with institutionalized patients. Int. J. Clin. Exp. Hypn., *14:*243, 1966.

66. Krippner, S., and Bindler, P.R.: Hypnosis and attention: a review. Am. J. Clin. Hypn., *16:*166, 1974.

67. Kroger, W.S.: It is a wise hypnotist who knows who is hypnotizing whom. West. J. Surg. Obstet. Gynecol., *69:*132, 1961.

68. _____: Hypnotic pseudo-orientation in time as a means of determining the psychological effects of surgical sterilization in the male and female. J. Fertil. Steril., *14:*535, 1963.

69. Lavoie, G., *et al.:* Hypnotizability as a function of adaptive regression among chronic psychotic patients. Int. J. Clin. Exp. Hypn., *3:*238, 1976.

70. Lewin, K., *et al.:* Mit Vorbemerkungen über die psychische Kräfte und Energien und die Struktur der Seele. Psychol. Forsch., *7:*294, 1938.

71. Lindner, H.: The shared neurosis, hypnotist and subject. Int. J. Clin. Exp. Hypn., *7:*61, 1960.

72. London, P.: Child hypnosis and personality. Am. J. Clin. Hypn., *8:*161, 1966.

73. Malmo, R. B., *et al.:* Electromyographic study of hypnotic deafness. J. Clin. Exp. Hypn., *2:*305, 1954.

74. Marcuse, F. L.: Hypnosis: Fact and Fiction. Baltimore, Penguin, 1959.

75. Moody, R. L.: Bodily changes during abreaction. Lancet, 254, 1948.

76. Morgan, A.H., and Hilgard, E.R.: Age differences in susceptibility to hypnosis. Int. J. Clin. Exp. Hypn., *21:*78, 1973.

77. Moss, C. S.: Therapeutic suggestion and autosuggestion. J. Clin. Exp. Hypn., *6:*19, 1958.

78. Nace, E.P., Orne, M.T., and Hammer, A.G.: Posthypnotic amnesia as an active psychic process: the reversibility of amnesia. Arch. Gen. Psychiat., *31:*259, 1974.

79. Orne, M. T.: The mechanism of age regression: an experimental study. J. Abnorm. Social Psychol., *46:*213, 1951.

80. _____: The nature of hypnosis: artifact and essence. J. Abnorm. Social Psychol., *58:*277, 1959.

81. _____: Hypnosis, motivation and compliance. Am. J. Psychiat., *122:*171, 1966.

82. _____: On the mechanisms of posthypnotic amnesia. Int. J. Clin. Exp. Hypn., *14:*121, 1966.

83. _____: The simulation of hypnosis: why, how and what it means. Int. J. Clin. Exp. Hypn., *4:*183, 1971.

84. Patten, E.F.: The duration of posthypnotic suggestions. J. Abnorm. Social Psychol., *25:*319, 1930.

85. Peters, J.E., and Stern, R.M.: Peripheral skin temperature and vasomotor response during hypnotic induction. Int. J. Clin. Exp. Hypn., *21:*102, 1973.

86. Raginsky, B.B.: Hypnotic recall of air crash cause. Int. J. Clin. Exp. Hypn., *17:*1, 1969.

87. Reid, A., and Curtsinger, G.: Physiological changes associated with hypnosis: the effect of hypnosis on temperature. J. Clin. Exp. Hypn., *16:*111, 1968.

88. Rubenstein, R., and Newman, R.: The living out of "future experiences" under hypnosis. Science, *119:*472, 1954.

89. Ruch, J.C.: Self-hypnosis: the result of heterophypnosis or vice versa? Int. J. Clin. Exp. Hypn., *23:*282, 1975.

90. Sakala, K.I., and Anderson, J.P.: The effects of posthypnotic suggestion on test performance. Int. J. Clin. Exp. Hypn., *18:*61, 1970.

91. Schneck, J. M.: Dynamic hypnotic regression. Am. J. Psychiat., *113:*178, 1956.

92. _____: Special aspects of hypnotic regression and revivification. Int. J. Clin. Exp. Hypn., *8:*37, 1960.

93. Sears, A. B.: A comparison of hypnotic and waking recall. J. Clin. Exp. Hypn., *2:*296, 1954.

94. Sears, R. R.: An experimental study of hypnotic anesthesia. J. Exp. Psychol., *15:*1, 1932.

95. Sheehan, P.W.: Hypnosis and the manifestations of the "imagination." *In* Fromm, E., and Shor, R.E. (eds.): Hypnosis Research and Perspectives. Chicago, Aldine-Atherton, 1972.

96. Shor, R.E.: The frequency of naturally occurring "hypnotic-like" experiences in a normal college population. Int. J. Clin. Exp. Hypn., *8:*151, 1960.

97. Shor, R.E., Orne, M.T., and O'Connell, D.N.: Psychological correlates of plateau hypnotizability in a special volunteer sample. J. Personality Social Psychol., *3:*80, 1966.

98. Sidis, B.: The value of the method of hypnoidization in the diagnosis and treatment of psychopathic disorders. Med. Times, *47:*245, 1919.

99. Solomon, D., and Goodson, D.F.: Hypnotic age regression evaluated against a criterion of prior performance. Int. J. Clin. Exp. Hypn., *19:*243, 1971.

100. Solovey, G., and Milechnin, A.: Hypnosis in everyday life. Dis. Nerv. System, *28:*1, 1957.

101. Stewart, C.G., and Dunlop, W.P.: Functional isolation of associations during suggested posthypnotic amnesia. Int. J. Clin. Exp. Hypn., *24:*426, 1976.

102. Strossberg, I.M., Irwen, M., and Vics, I.I.: Physiologic changes in the eye during hypnosis. Am. J. Clin. Hypn., *4:*264, 1962.

103. Symposium on amnesia. Int. J. Clin. Exp. Hypn., *14:*89, 1966.

104. Tellegren, A., and Atkinson, G.: Openness to absorbing and self-altering experiences ("absorption"), a trait related to hypnotic susceptibility. J. Abnorm. Psychol., *83:*268, 1974.

105. Thorne, D.E.: Amnesia and hypnosis. Int. J. Clin. Exp. Hypn., *17:*225, 1969.

106. Timney, B.N., and Barber, T.X.: Hypnotic induction and oral temperature. Int. J. Clin. Exp. Hypn., *17:*121, 1969.

107. Vanderhoof, E., and Clancy, J.: Effect of emotion on blood flow. J. Appl. Physiol., *17:*67, 1962.

108. Von Neumann, J.: The Computer and the Brain. New Haven, Yale University Press, 1958.

109. Wall, P.D., and Lieberman, L.R.: Effects of task motivation and hypnotic induction on hypermnesia. Am. J. Clin. Hypn., *18:*250, 1976.

110. Weitzenhoffer, A.: A note on the persistence of hypnotic suggestion. J. Abnorm. Social Psychol., *45:* 160, 1950.

111. _____: Posthypnotic behavior and the recall of the hypnotic suggestion. J. Clin. Exp. Hypn., *5:*41, 1957.

112. Weitzenhoffer, A. M., and Weitzenhoffer, G. B.: Personality and hypnotic susceptibility. Am. J. Clin. Hypn, *1:*79, 1958.

113. West, L. J., Niell, K. C., and Hardy, J. D.: Effects of hypnotic suggestion on pain perception and galvanic skin response. Arch. Neurol. Psychiat., *68:* 549, 1952.

114. Zamansky, H.S., Sharf, B., and Brightbill, R.: The effect of expectancy for hypnosis on prehypnotic performance. J. Personality, *32:*236, 1964.

ADDITIONAL READINGS

As, A., and Lauer, L. W.: A factor-analytic study of hypnotizability and related personal experiences. Int. J. Clin. Exp. Hypn., *10:*169, 1962.

Barber, T. X.: The concept of "hypnosis." J. Psychol., *45:*115, 1958.

_____: Hypnotic age regression: a critical review. Psychosom. Med., *24:*286, 1962.

Christenson, J.: An operational approach to hypnosis. J. Clin. Exp. Hypn., *4:*89, 1956.

Friedman, H., *et al.:* Direct current potentials in hypnoanalgesia. Arch. Gen. Psychiat., *7:*193, 1962.

Gebhard, J. W.: Hypnotic age-regression: a review. Am. J. Clin. Hypn., *3:*139, 1961.

Lerner, M.: Comparative aspects of human and animal hypnosis. Am. J. Clin. Hypn., *5:*52, 1962.

McCord, H.: The "image" of the trance. Int. J. Clin. Exp. Hypn., *9:*305, 1961.

Solovey, G., and Milechnin, A.: Concerning the nature of hypnotic phenomena. J. Clin. Exp. Hypn., *5:*67, 1957.

Weitzenhoffer, A. M.: Some speculations regarding the nature and character of hypnotic behavior. Am. J. Clin. Hypn., *4:*69, 1961.

3

Theories on Hypnosis

Even though hypnosis has always been an enigma, it is still one of the seven wonders of psychology. As in the fable of the elephant touched in different places by the four blind men, each investigator has formulated a different theory. Therefore there are as many definitions of hypnosis as there are definers. Like the nature of human behavior, there will be different theories about hypnosis since all hypnotic phenomena have their counterpart in the various aspects of human behavior. Inasmuch as the latter is poorly understood, it is no wonder that hypnosis is difficult to understand. However, we shall try to explain hypnosis as objectively as possible.

Unfortunately, nearly all theories on hypnosis mistakenly attempt to explain the induction procedure, the interactions produced by the emotions, and the resultant hypnotic responses together. This is patently impossible, since they are separate and distinct entities which involve the hypnotist's and patient's subjective reporting. Not to recognize its dual nature is like including a surgical procedure and an anesthetic induction in a unified theory. The following review briefly covers the older and more recent theories on hypnosis.

ATAVISTIC HYPOTHESIS: IMMOBILIZATION THEORIES

Hypnosis has been considered to be an atavism that at one time may have been necessary in humans as a protective defense mechanism to ward off fear or danger.[50] This theory was based on Pavlov's observation that an animal's only chance of survival is to remain *immobile* in order to escape detection.[68] His theory is discussed more fully below. The atavistic hypothesis was reinstituted by Meares.[62]

As emphasized in the last chapter, hypnosis has been compared with the immobility reflex (I.R.) noted in animals when subjected to fear-producing conditions.[45] Though induced differently in animals, the I.R. is produced chiefly by physical and instinctual factors. In humans it results from the interaction of these factors with the experiential meaning of symbols and words. Moreover, human and animal hypnoses are dissimilar in that repetitive induction in the animal decreases hypnotic susceptibility, whereas in humans it increases it.

In general, any powerful stimulus, such as fright, causes certain animals and humans to "freeze up." This concept led to the "death-feint" theory of hypnosis.[77] However, this theory does not explain how hypnosis occurs in humans. Similarly, hypnosis has been defined as "a state of readiness for emotional action increasingly subordinated to cortical influence as one ascends phylogeny, but nonetheless consistently present in animal organisms in a variety of forms."[33]

HYPNOSIS AS A STATE OF HYSTERIA

At one time, hypnosis was considered to be a symptom of hysteria; only hysterical individuals were believed to be hypnotizable.[13] This conclusion was drawn by Charcot on the basis of only a few cases in a pathologic setting. Such an hypothesis is untenable, inasmuch as susceptibility to hypnosis is not pathogonomonic of neurosis: normal individuals, in fact, are readily hypnotizable.[10] Although hysterics are more suggestible than normal individuals, it does not necessarily follow that increased suggestibility is a sign of hysteria.

PSYCHOPHYSIOLOGICAL THEORIES

Some investigators implicate the reticular formation,[1, 16, 73] the hippocampus,[15] and subcortical structures mediating communication.[7] Others give similar explanations.[8, 75, 100] Still other theories involve inhibition of the ganglion cells of the brain,[35] inhibition and excitation of neurons,[103] a focus of central excitation with surrounding areas of non-excitation,[52] cerebral anemia,[34] shift of nervous energies of the central nervous system to the vasomotor system,[60] and vasomotor decerebration involving anemia of the frontal lobes.[93] "Synaptic ablation," wherein neural impulses are directed into a smaller number of channels (selective attention), has also been considered.[21]

Psychophysiologic data are lacking to substantiate any of these theories, particularly those that posit that anemia of the brain or a shift of nervous impulses accounts for hypnosis. If hypnosis is due to a shift of one set of neural functions, what produces it? If it is due to anemia, then anemic individuals should be readily hypnotizable. Finally, if the cerebral blood flow is decreased during hypnosis, fainting rather than somnambulism should be produced.[61] More speculative formulations contend that hypnosis is due to psychophysiologic factors,[75, 100] psychokinetic field forces, and oscillating electromagnetic fields.[64]

HYPNOSIS AS A CONDITIONED PROCESS LEADING TO SLEEP

Pavlov believed that hypnosis was a "partial sleep."[68, 71] In his classification, those stimuli directly affecting the sense organs constitute the primary signaling system of both men and animals. Symbols or words belong to the secondary signaling system and are characteristic for man alone. They exert their conditioned effects via the primary signaling system. Thus words act as conditioned stimuli, which may in turn produce physiologic reactions.[17] A word (signal or cue) becomes the stimulus for conditioned reflexes which become involuntary for life. Pavlov observed that various gradations of hypnosis hardly differed physiologically from the wakeful state and that the fluctuating nature of hypnosis depended on insignificant variations of environmental stimuli. He hinted prophetically that lower brain stem mechanisms were involved in hypnotic conditioning. Some modern researchers continue to subscribe to the Pavlovian theory.[41, 47, 94] However, most authorities do not believe that there is any similarity between sleep and hypnosis. If there were, it would be better to start an induction procedure with the individual asleep! Even though some investigators have been able to convert light sleep to hypnosis,[8] this does not prove that the two are identical. Hypnosis is not a transitional state between sleeping and waking. Experimental data show a rapid decrement in motor response and reflexes during sleep. During deep sleep, conditioned reflexes or physiologic responses to a repeatedly given stimulus cannot be established, whereas in hypnosis the learning of conditioned reflexes is enhanced over and above that of the nonhypnotic state.

During normal sleep, suggestibility is decreased markedly, rapport is lost, and memories are eliminated. The whole concept of sleep, when applied to hypnosis, obscures rather than clarifies the issues. The subject appears to be asleep because eye closure usually is part of the induction procedure. Moreover, there is a considerable body of literaature on blood pressure, reflexes, and physiochemical and EEG studies which indicates that hypnosis more closely resembles complete wakefulness.[17, 53, 58]

A hypnotized person is more alert to his environment than when he is asleep.[46] However, if the operator uses a technic which emphasizes sleep, then the individual, because he responds experientially to the word "sleep," is apt to enter into a sleeplike state. Thus, in such persons, the EEG findings might resemble those associated with sleep.[81] On the other hand, for the same reasons, an entirely different result is obtained when the word "sleep" is not used. This was borne out by recent studies which showed that the behavioral characteristics which resemble sleep are not intrinsic phenomena of the hypnotic state.[48]

IDEOMOTOR ACTIVITY AND INHIBITION THEORY

It is contended by several authors that the effects of suggestibility are the result of ideomotor action and inhibition,[2, 26] and that suggestibility is merely an experience of imagining that which is actualized through ideomotor activities.[2] Although this theory accounts, to a degree, for physical reactions and even for some of the psychological reactions noted during hypnosis, it fails to explain the complex psychological reactions elicited during hypnosis.

THE DISSOCIATION AND NEODISSOCIATION THEORIES

For many years it was contended that the hypnotized individual was in a dissociated state: certain areas of behavior were split off from the main stream of awareness.[72] Accordingly, hypnosis abolished volitional control, and, as a result, the individual responded only with autonomic behavior on a reflex level. If the dissociation theory were valid, then amnesia could not be removed by the suggestions of the operator. Furthermore, the amnesia would always occur spontaneously.

Hypnosis has been described as "dissociation of awareness from the majority of sensory and even strictly neural events taking place."[96] While this is partially true, it does not help us to understand the actual nature of hypnosis. Dissociation characterizes not only hypnosis, but also many other altered states of consciousness, such as dreams, hypnagogic states, "highway hypnosis," reverie states, the detachment or depersonalization seen in many types of religious worship, and many other mental phenomena.

This older theory fell into disrepute when it was demonstrated that more often, instead of amnesia or dissociation, there was a hyperacuity and a better coordination of all the senses during hypnosis. Thus, although some degree of dissociation occurs when amnesia is present, it by no means indicates that dissociation produces hypnosis or is similar to it.

Hilgard found Janet's dissociation theory interesting, and postulated the neodissociation theory.[38] Although the theory is not finalized, Hilgard points out that the normal ego controls that take care of our needs allow socially acceptable behaviors and sensible choices. However, he notes that other processes are carried on outside of such normal controls, which, on occasion, can function simultaneously with them.

ALTERED STATE OF CONSCIOUSNESS THEORY

More recently, numerous writers have attempted to explain hypnosis by an altered state of consciousness (A.S.C.) paradigm which borrows heavily from Eastern philosophy.[56, 90, 95] Unquestionably, all such altered states are related, particularly the various types of meditative states such as transcendental meditation (T.M.) and the relaxation response, to be discussed in Chapter 27. These states allow greater preoccupation with internal sensations or mental processes. The relevance of A.S.C. for experiencing hypnosis independently and voluntarily sheds little light on what constitutes the hypnotic state. However, because a considerable body of literature exists, these shall be discussed in Chapter 27.

HYPNOSIS AS A STATE

Several authorities lean toward the idea of hypnosis as a state or "trance."[22, 37, 67] Most investigators, including the author, acknowledge the existence of an hypnotic state. Hypnosis has been related to an "ability component" or a "trait of hypnotic responsiveness," wherein its its fluctuating responsiveness is recognized.[37]

To separate responsiveness to the hypnotist's demands from the kinds of behavior clearly associated with the state of hypnosis, Orne ingeniously compared a group of highly responsive subjects ("reals") with a group of insusceptible subjects instructed to behave as they thought a deeply hypnotized subject would ("instructed simulators").[67] The "reals" demonstrated higher tolerance to pain, performed posthypnotic acts more readily, and were dehypnotized more slowly. Evans and Orne also showed that "reals" came out slowly, whereas the "instructed simulators" terminated rapidly after it was suggested that a "power failure" had occurred in the building.[25] Sheehan had noted similar differences between hypnotic and simulating subjects.[82] It has been argued that the relationship of simulator model to attribution theory (i.e., the subject's awareness of situational influences on his behavior) shows that hypnosis is a definitive state.[12]

In an earlier and elegant study, Orne differentiated the genuinely hypnotized subject from the hypnotic simulator by the phenomenon of "trance logic"—a unique, subjective experience characterized by a logical incongruity where the deeply hypnotized subject "buys things that do not add up." Moreover, he observed that hypnotized persons have no difficulty seeing a hallucinated person and the real person simultaneously, whereas the simulator does not "buy" this incongruity; either the real image or the hallucination disappears. These observations were recently replicated.[59] Thus it is highly presumptive to assume that hypnosis is a distinct state.

Orne also believes that sociocultural factors and the kind of experimental procedures employed play an important role in the behavior of the hypnotized subject.[66] He contends that subjects receive precise though indirect cues on how to behave in the presence of environmental expectations that a specific behavior will or will not occur. Every situation shapes expected responses and makes contrary responses more improbable. Orne has named these aspects of an experimental situation its "demand characteristics." In exploring these, he has not only shed light on the theoretical basis of hypnosis, but also on the social psychology of the psychological experiment. Orne's view is that if we are to identify the essential core of the psychotherapeutic process, we must isolate it from sociocultural aspects and "demand characteristics."

THE ROLE-PLAYING AND NON-STATE THEORIES

One theory holds that hypnosis is due to goal-oriented striving at an unconscious level.[101] Before Hilgard formulated his neodissociation theory, he postulated a developmental-interactive one.[36] His thesis was that the subject's ability to assume a role and relinquish reality orientation depends on the way he interacts on an interpersonal level with the therapist. Here one would have to consider the importance of rapport. Some theories of hypnotic behavior stress social and interpersonal relationships, while others maintain that the subject plays a role, that is, he acts in the manner in which he believes a hypnotized person would act.[77, 78, 79, 83]

Esdaile, who had such remarkable success with hypnoanesthesia, once made these particularly cogent remarks in relation to simulation and role-playing:[20]

I see two ways only of accounting for it. My patients, on returning home, either say to their friends, similarly afflicted, 'what a soft man the doctor is! He cut me to pieces for 20 minutes and I made him believe that I did not feel it. Isn't it a capital joke? Do go and play him the same trick,' or they may say to their brother sufferers, 'Look at me; I have got rid of my burden'—20,-30,40,50,60 or 80 lb., as it may be (scrotal tumors)—'I am restored to the use of my body and can work for my bread. This, I assure you, the doctor did when I was asleep, and I knew nothing about it.'

Thompson states that she finds it difficult to believe that a simulator could undergo an abdominal operation without an anesthetic.[88] Pearson holds similar views.[69] The author emphatically agrees on the basis of a large number of surgical and obstetrical operations which he performed on hypnotized patients.

Barber, a non-state theorist, raises serious doubts about the conceptual usefulness of hypnosis.[5] He argues that hypnosis is not a "state" or a "trance" and is not produced as the result of "suggestion," but rather, that it is based upon a number of overlapping antecedent, intervening, and dependent variables. Barber also stresses an interpersonal relationship [belief and faith] in which the operator restructures the "perceptions" and the "conceptions" [imagination] of the subject, because the subject is relatively inattentive to his environment [misdirection of attention]. This results because the subject [due to an expectant attitude] is ready, willing, and able literally to think as the operator wants him to think. Such "perceptual-cognitive restructuring," rather than "suggestion," is the essential element responsible for hypnosis.

The role-playing theorists are not denying that

hypnosis exists, but rather that all hypnotic behavior can be accounted for by the aforementioned variables, particularly the importance of motivation and the goal-directed imagination.[6] They also claim that what can be done in hypnosis can be achieved by "training in human potentials.[6] This has been refuted by others.[14, 23, 24, 39] Hypnosis adds more than suggestibility *per se,* even though the state may involve some degree of role-playing. The author believes that it is the conviction that an altered state has been produced which results in some transcendence of normal capacities.

If hypnosis were due solely to role-playing, then psychoneurotics would ordinarily make the best subjects. Multiple personalities, who are not actors, readily switch from one role to another. The greatest thespian would be ashamed by the facility with which this is accomplished during hypnosis.

THE REGRESSION THEORY: PSYCHOANALYTIC CONCEPTS

A synthesis between psychoanalytical and Pavlovian physiological theories was attempted by Kubie and Margolin.[52] These investigators felt that the subject undergoes an infantile regression, with the hypnotist fulfilling the role formerly played by the parents.[27] Gill and Brenman have utilized this hypothesis, contending that "hypnosis was a regression in the service of the ego."[29] For Gill and Brenman, transference (the transfer by the patient to the operator of emotions felt for some other person) is an important element of hypnosis. For Kubie, it is only a secondary phenomenon which may or may not be present.[51] To him there is no specific psychophysiological setting in which the hypnotic process takes place. Kubie believes motivation to be more significant than the regression concept in understanding hypnotic response. Hodge stresses the contractual aspects of hypnosis.[40] As an illustration of the concept of greater compliance, experimental data derived from volunteers, especially college students, differ from those obtained from clinical patients; the latter are more highly motivated.

An ego-psychological theory of hypnosis is seen as a special type of self-excluding function of the ego. A change occurs from conscious perception to preconscious functioning, akin to the performance of routine activities, and this is regarded as a "topological regression."[9] This hypothesis presaged the notions that subcortical functions played the important role in production of hypnotic phenomena. Fromm speaks of ego passivity or ego activity to describe various states induced during hypnosis.[28] Each is differentiated from its external behavioral counterpart.

Hypnosis has been attributed to the patient's nonrational submission and relative abandonment of executive control to a more or less regressed, dissociated state.[88] Ostensibly, the hypnotist shapes the regressed state to make it easier to achieve desired goals. These assumptions, however, have not been borne out by recent observations.[54]

A logical theory has been proposed by Gindes, wherein the proper motivation induces a favorable mental set (elimination or reduction of irrelevant stimuli) or readiness to comply.[30] When this is combined with relaxation, concentration, belief, and expectation—all catalyzed by the imagination—hypnosis ensues. The sensory changes or the phenomena become effective through distortion of the imaginative processes. Such a theory makes the "Svengali-Rasputin" trance concept of hypnosis untenable. More psychoanalysts would use hypnosis if this concept of the omnipotent hypnotist were invalidated.

Theoretically, the child who had a domineering father should be hypnotized easily by an authoritarian approach. Proponents of these theories are unable to correlate either the depth or successful incidence of hypnotic induction with the supposed parent-child relationship. Furthermore, if these things were valid, men would be much better hypnotists than women. Experimental data indicate little difference;[98] a good subject is hypnotizable by either a male or a female operator. Moreover, the regression and transference theories cannot account for autohypnosis and those spontaneous alterations in awareness which simulate hypnosis.

However, even though hypnosis in certain instances might involve transference phenomena, they are very likely only incidental to it. Shor added the concept of transference to his dual factor theory, in which role-taking and generalized reality orientation fade into nonfunctional unawareness.[84] Transference, when it occurs, is the result and not the cause of the hypnotic state.[52] It is probably facilitated by the intense interpersonal relationship or rapport, rather than by a "plunge" into regression and dissociation.[86, 88] This concept may apply to the somnambulistic state but certainly not to light and medium stages. A more likely interpretation would involve the concept of a "transference readiness."[57, 63]

There are many combinations of the transference theories that have just been described. Some stress fascination or sensual attraction as an important factor; others consider that hypnosis is due to erotic elements in the doctor-patient relationship. If there is anything to these theories, then a necessary prerequisite for successful hypnosis would be fascination or sensual attraction. If it were true, all lovers would swoon into mutual hypnosis! The sensual attraction theory thus cannot serve as a generalization for the hypnotic state or hypnotic relationship.[57]

THE HYPERSUGGESTIBILITY THEORY

The theory of hypersuggestibility has enjoyed a certain popularity.[3, 43] According to its proponents, the subject's attention span is narrowed to the words of the hypnotist, and the latter's voice takes over the inner voice of the subject. This only explains the phenomenon and not how hypersuggestibility actually occurs. It does not explain the spontaneous occurrence of amnesia or other bizarre, nonsuggested symptoms such as hallucinations. The hypersuggestibility theory, by inference, also implies that only gullible people are suggestible. This is not the case. As proof, the influence of demagogues on mob psychology and the persuasive effect of orators and salesmen have been compared with hypnosis. Although strong persuasion is one factor for successful salesmanship, salesmen do not produce somnambulism, actual hallucinations, or anesthesia.

PSYCHOSOMATIC THEORIES

An elaborate theory hypothesizes that suggestibility is ideomotor action, which, in itself, is a form of abstract conditioning.[96] Other investigators do not concur with the concepts of "abstract conditioning,"[31] and the idea of stimulus-response notions as an explanation for hypnotic behavior has received little support.[18]

Weitzenhoffer[97] notes that Wolpe's reciprocal inhibition is similar to a hypnotic induction technic: the desensitization procedures used in behavior modification are closely related to the "reconditioning" proposed by Wolberg.[102]

INFORMATIONAL THEORY

It is possible to advance a speculative hypothesis based on "brain-computer" analogies. Pursuant to this idea, it is important to note that the manner in which the central nervous system utilizes sensory processing and control of information can be studied in three ways: (1) by attempting to observe physiological events, such as electrical and chemical reactions, or other information-conveying mechanisms and energy conversions that are involved in nervous system dynamics; (2) by studying behavior as it occurs spontaneously or during experimentally designed situations; and (3) by attempting to develop physical models which retain certain essential characteristics of sensory processing of information and control at nonhypnotic and hypnotic levels. These three approaches may be labeled microscopic (the examination of detailed events in the CNS), macroscopic (the examination of behavior), and physical (the correlation with physical models of CNS control processes).

Since the first two approaches have been extensively described in relation to information processing, the emphasis of this discussion will be on the third approach—the physical model. This model is not to be confused with mathematical analogues of neurobehavioral functioning. Rather, it compares the evolutionary neurophysiologic development of the complex controls built into the human system design for self-regulation of homeostatic or adaptive mechanisms with those utilized by systems engineers for electronic high-speed "thinking machines."[49]

Engineers are well aware that whenever a system adjusts its feedback networks to increase the signal to noise ratio, it is functioning optimally—in dynamic equilibrium or negative feedback. This "steady state" has been called everything from hypnosis, Nirvana, Zazen, and exaltation to union with God.

The processing, storage, and retrieval of information in hypnosis can be understood better from the study of brain-machine (computer) analogies. This is not to imply that the brain is a computer, but rather that scientists must conceptualize that the brain functions according to the same principles set down by the physical sciences for the design of communication equipment. Thus greater receptivity in a receptor (the subject) enables messages (sensory inputs or percepts), to be received clearly from a transmitter (the operator) with a minimal degree of interference (noise), either in the external environmental communication pathways (channel), or in the internal receptors of the subject. This enhances the transmission of reception of signals. For a more complete exposition of the informational hypothesis on how hypnosis represents a "regression" from functioning like a general purpose computer (G.P.C.) to that of a special purpose computer (S.P.C.), the reader can refer to Chapter 32.

SUMMARY

Most of the foregoing theories, even though inadequate in many respects, contain some facet of truth. However, hypnosis cannot be explained by any single factor (e.g., cortical inhibition, hypersuggestibility, atavism, regression, death-feint, dissociation, drive, goal-striving, role-playing, regression, or transference) because, like any behavioral process, it cross-fertilizes with many areas of human thinking. A complete theory of hypnosis is not available to gain wide acceptance. Moreover, many psychological and physical factors, acting reciprocally through the imaginative processes, induce the perceptual response called hypnosis.

Hypnosis cannot be produced with greater frequency in individuals with passive, infantile needs; nor does a regression of the personality necessarily occur from the hypnosis *per se*. The dependency relationship is no more an essential feature of hypnosis than that present in all doctor-patient relationships, even at nonhypnotic levels.

Hypnosis, then, is not a sharply delineated state, but a process along the broad, fluctuating continuum of what is loosely referred to as awareness, depending, as it does, upon the degree of arousal or perceptivity. What is referred to as the hypnotic state must be differentiated from the hypnotic interpersonal relationship, even though the latter developed from the hypnosis. The capacity to enter into hypnosis is as natural a phenomenon as sleep, both presumably developed as phylogenetic adaptive response mechanisms.

During hypnosis, the excitatory cortical areas can be conditioned to remain selectively "awake" to specific sensory percepts (selective attention), while other cortical areas which are partially or completely inhibited prevent access to the stored or experiential data (selective inattention). In the presence of the proper mind-set, new conditioned responses can be "built in" the organism on the basis of new convictions compounded upon previously invoked beliefs (the ideomotor and ideosensory responses). Under these conditions, "unreality becomes reality," and the "conviction of hypnosis leads to hypnosis," as there is no other way to think.

The brain apparently functions similarly to a data processing apparatus, which, when unable to validate incoming information (sensory percepts) against stored data (memories, impressions), causes unreality to be interpreted as reality. More attention should be paid to the manner in which physical scientists describe events in the central nervous system. Perhaps a better model of what constitutes hypnosis will thereby be formulated.

REFERENCES

1. Akstein, D.: The induction of hypnosis in the light of reflexology. Am. J. Clin. Hypn., *7:* 281, 1965.
2. Arnold, M. B.: On the mechanism of suggestion and hypnosis, J. Abnorm. Social Psychol., *41:* 107, 1946.
3. Barber, T.X.: The concept of hypnosis, J. Psychol., *45:* 115, 1958.

4. _____: Hypnotizability, suggestibility and personality. A critical review of research findings. Psychol. Rep., *14:* 229, 1964.

5. _____: Suggested "hypnotic" behavior—the trance paradigm versus an alternate paradigm. *In* Fromm, E., and Shor, R.E. (eds.): Hypnosis: Research Developments and Perspectives. Chicago, Aldine-Atherton, 1972.

6. Barber, T.X., Spanos, N.P., and Chaves, J.F.: Hypnotism: Imagination, and Human Potentialities. Elmsford, N.Y., Pergamon Press, 1974.

7. Bartlett, E.E.: Hypnosis and communications. J. Am. Med. Wom. Assoc., *21:* 662, 1966.

8. Bechterew, W. V.: What is hypnosis? J. Abnorm. Social Psychol., *1:* 18, 1906.

9. Bellak, L.: An ego-psychological theory of hypnosis. Int. J. Psychoanal., *36*(Part 6), 1955.

10. Bernheim, H.: Suggestive Therapeutics. New York, Putnam, 1902.

11. Bigelow, N., Cameron, G.H., and Koroljow, S.A.: Two cases of deep hypnotic sleep investigated by the strain gauge plethysmograph. J. Clin. Exp. Hypn., *4:*160, 1956.

12. Bowers, K.: Hypnosis, attribution, and demand characteristics. Int. J. Clin. Exp. Hypn., *21:*226, 1973.

13. Charcot, J. M.: Lectures on Diseases of the Nervous System. London, New Sydenham Society, 1889.

14. Conners, J., and Sheehan, P.: Analysis of the cue characteristics of task motivational instructions. Int. J. Clin. Exp. Hypn., *24:* 287, 1976.

15. Crasilneck, H.B., McCranie, E.J., and Jenkins, M.T.: Special indications for hypnosis as a method of anesthesia. J.A.M.A., *162:* 1606, 1956.

16. De Moraes Passos, A.S.: Reflections on hypnosis and the reticular system of the brain stem. *In* Hypnosis and Psychosomatic Medicine. New York, Springer-Verlag, 1967, pp. 228–232.

17. Dittborn, J.M., and O'Connell, D.N.: Behavioral sleep, physiological sleep and hypnotizability. Int. J. Clin. Exp. Hypn., *15:* 181, 1967.

18. Edmonston, W.E.: Stimulus-response theory of hypnosis. *In* Gordon, J.E. (ed.): Handbook of Clinical and Experimental Hypnosis. New York, Macmillan, 1967, pp. 345–387.

19. Edmonston, W.E.: Hypnosis and electrodermal responses. Am. J. Clin. Hypn., *11:* 16, 1968.

20. Esdaile, J.: Mesmerism in India. Hartford, England, S. Andrus & Son, 1850.

21. Estabrook, G.H.: Hypnotism. New York, Dutton, 1943.

22. Erickson, M.H.: Advanced Techniques of Hypnosis and Therapy. New York, Grune & Stratton, 1967.

23. Evans, F.J.: Recent trends in experimental hypnosis. Behav. Sci., *13:* 477, 1968.

24. Evans, F.J.: Suggestibility in the normal working state. Psychol. Bull., *67:* 114, 1967.

25. Evans, F.J., and Orne, M.T.: The disappearing hypnotist: the use of simulating subjects to evaluate how subjects perceive experimental procedures. Int. J. Clin. Exp. Hypn., *19:* 277, 1971.

26. Eysenck, H.J.: Dimensions of Personality. London, Kegan Paul, 1947.

27. Ferenczi, S.: Introjektion und Uebertragung. Jb. Psychoanalyse, *1:* 422, 1909.

28. Fromm, E.: Ego activity and ego passivity in hypnosis. Int. J. Clin. Exp. Hypn., *20:* 238, 1972.

29. Gill, M.M., and Brenman, M.: Hypnosis and Related States: Psychoanalytic Studies in Regression. New York, International Universities Press, 1959.

30. Gindes, B.C.: New Concepts of Hypnosis. New York, Julian Press, 1951.

31. Gladfelter, J.H., and Hall, J.A.: The relationship of hypnotic phenomena to conditioning. Tex. Rep. Biol. Med., *20:* 53, 1962.

32. Granone, F.: Tratti di Ipnosi (Sofrologia). [Treatise of Hypnosis (Sophrology).] Turin, Boringhieri, 1972.

33. Guze, H.: The phylogeny of hypnosis. J. Clin. Exp. Hypn., *1:* 41, 1953.

34. Hart, E.: Hypnotism and Humbug. Nineteenth Century, January, 1882.

35. Heidenhain, R.: Hypnotism or Animal Magnetism. London, Kegan Paul, Trench, Trubner, 1906.

36. Hilgard, E.R.: Hypnotic Susceptibility. New York, Harcourt, Brace & World, 1965.

37. Hilgard, E.R., and Hilgard, J.R.: Hypnosis in the Relief of Pain. Los Altos, Cal., William Kaufman, 1975.

38. _____: Hypnosis in Relief of Pain (ed. 2), 1976, p. 185.

39. Hilgard, J.R.: Personality and Hypnosis. A Study of Imaginative Involvement. Chicago, University of Chicago Press, 1970.

40. Hodge, J.R.: Contractual aspects of hypnosis. Int. J. Clin. & Exp. Hypn., *24:*391, 1976.

41. Hoskovec, J.: A review of some major works in Soviet hypnotherapy. Int. J. Clin. Exp. Hypn., *15:*1, 1967.

42. Howarth, E.: Postscript to a new theory of hypnosis. J. Clin. Exp. Hypn., *2:*91, 1954.

43. Hull, C.L.: Hypnosis and Suggestibility—An Experimental Approach. New York, Appleton, 1933.

44. Janet, P.: Major Symptoms of Hysteria, New York, Macmillan, 1920.

45. Klemm, W.R.: Identity of sensory and motor systems that are critical to the immobility reflex ("animal hypnosis"). J. Neurosci., *2:*57, 1976.

46. Kline, M. V.: Freud and Hypnosis. New York, Julian Press, 1958.

47. Kraines, S.H.: Hypnosis: physiologic inhibition and excitation. Psychosomatics, *10:*36, 1969.

48. Kratochvil, S.: Sleep, hypnosis and waking hypnosis. Int. J. Clin. Exp. Hypn., *18:*20, 1970.

49. Kroger, W.S.: Sensory Information Processing and Control in Higher Nervous System Functioning and Behavior. Milwaukee, Marquette University Press Abstracts, 1966.

50. Kroger, W.S., and Freed, S. C.: Psychosomatic Gynecology; Including Problems of Obstetrical Care. Chicago, Free Press, 1956, (reprinted, Los Angeles, Wilshire Book Company, 1962).

51. Kubie, L.S.: A focus for physiological and psychoanalytical investigations. Arch. Gen. Psychiat., *4:*50, 1961.

52. Kubie, L.S., and Margolin, S.: The process of hypnotism and the nature of the hypnotic state. Am. J. Psychiat., *100:* 613, 1944.

53. Lerner, M.: Electroencefalograma e hipnosis. Acta Hipno. Latinoamer., *4:*35, 1963.

54. Levin, L.A., and Harrison, R.H.: Hypnosis and regression in the service of the ego. Int. J. Clin. Exp. Hypn., *24:*400, 1976.

55. Levitt, E.E., and Brady, J.P.: Psychophysiology of hypnosis. *In* Schneck, J.M. (ed.): Hypnosis in Modern Medicine (ed. 3). Springfield, Ill., Charles C Thomas, 1963, pp. 314–362.

56. Ludwig, A.M.: Altered states of consciousness. Arch. Gen. Psychiat., *15:*225, 1966.

57. Macalpine, I.: The development of the transference. Psychoanal. Q., *19:*501, 1959.

58. McCrane, E.J., Crasilneck, H.B., and Tetter, H.R.: The electroencephalogram in hypnotic age regression. Psychiatr. Q., *29:*85, 1955.

59. McDonald, R.D., and Smith, J.R.: Trance logic in tranceable and simulating subjects. Int. J. Clin. Exp. Hypn., *23:*80, 1975.

60. McDougall, W.: Outline of Abnormal Psychology. New York, Scribner, 1926.

61. Marcuse, F. L.: Hypnosis: Fact and Fiction. Baltimore, Penguin, 1959.

62. Meares, A.: A System of Medical Hypnosis. Philadelphia, W. B. Saunders, 1960.

63. Miller, G.A., Galanter, E., and Pribram, K.: Plans and the Structure of Behavior. New York, Holt, 1960.

64. Muftic, M.D.: A contribution to the psychokinetic theory of hypnotism, Br. J. Med. Hypnosis, *10:*24, 1959.

65. Orne, M.T.: The nature of hypnosis: artifact and essence. J. Abnorm. Social Psychol., *58:*277, 1959.

66. _____: Implications for psychotherapy derived from current research on the nature of hypnosis. Am. J. Psychiat., *118:*1097, 1962.

67. _____: On the simulating subjects as a quasi-control group in hypnosis research: what, why and how. *In* Fromm, E., and Shor, R.E. (eds.): Hypnosis: Research, Development, and Perspectives. Chicago, Aldine-Atherton, 1972.

68. Pavlov, I. P.: Experimental Psychology. New York, Philosophical Library, 1957.

69. Pearson, R.E.: Clinical and experimental trance: what's the difference? Am. J. Clin. Hypn., *13:*1, 1970.

70. Peters, J.E., and Stern, R.M.: Peripheral skin temperature and vasomotor response during hypnotic induction. Int. J. Clin. Exp. Hypn., *21:*102, 1973.

71. Platonov, K. I.: The Word as a Psychological and Physiological Factor. Moscow, Foreign Languages Publishing House, 1959.

72. Prince, M.: Dissociations of a Personality. New York, Longmans, Green, 1905.

73. Raikov, V.L.: Theoretical substantiation of deep hypnosis. Am. J. Clin. Hypn., *18:*23, 1975.

74. Reid, A., and Curtsinger, G.: Physiological changes associated with hypnosis: the affect of hypnosis on temperature. J. Clin. Exp. Hypn., *16:*111, 1968.

75. Roberts, D. R.: An electrophysiologic theory of hypnosis. Int. J. Clin. Exp. Hypn., *8:*43, 1960.

76. Sarbin, T.R.: Contributions to role-taking theory. I. Hypnotic behavior. Psychol. Rev., *57:*255, 1950.

77. _____: Some evidence in support of the role-taking hypothesis in hypnosis. Int. J. Clin. Exp. Hypn., *11:*98, 1963.

78. Sarbin, T.R., and Anderson, M.L.: Role-theoretical analysis of hypnotic behavior. *In* Gordon, J.E. (ed.): Handbook of Clinical and Experimental Hypnosis. New York, Macmillan, 1967, pp. 319–344.

79. Sarbin, T.R., and Coe, W.C.: Hypnosis: A Social Psychological Analysis of Influence Communication. New York, Holt, Rinehart & Winston, 1972.

80. Schneck, J. M.: A theory of hypnosis. J. Clin. Exp. Hypn., *1:*16, 1953.

81. Schwartz, B.E., Bickford, R.G., and Rasmussen, W.C.: Hypnotic phenomena, including hypnotically activated seizures, studied with the electroencephalogram. J. Nerv. Ment. Dis., *122:*564, 1955.

82. Sheehan, P.W.: A methodological analysis of the

simulating techniques. Int. J. Clin. Exp. Hypn., *19:*83, 1971.

83. Shor, R.E.: Hypnosis and the concept of the generalized reality-orientation. Am. J. Psychother., *13:*582, 1959.

84. _____: Three dimensions of hypnotic depth. Int. J. Clin. Exp. Hypn., *10:*23, 1962.

85. Shor, R.E., and Orne, M.T.: The Nature of Hypnosis: Selected Basic Readings. New York, Holt, Rinehart & Winston, 1965.

86. Spiegel, H.: Hypnosis in transference. Arch. Gen. Psychiat., *1:*96, 1958.

87. _____: Hypnosis and transference: a theoretical formulation. Arch. Gen. Psychiat., *1:*634, 1959.

88. _____: Hypnosis: An adjunct to psychotherapy. *In* Friedman, A.M., and Kaplan, H.I. (eds.): Comprehensive Textbook of Psychiatry. Baltimore, Williams & Wilkins, 1967.

89. Strosberg, I.M., Irwen, M., and Vics, I.I.: Physiologic changes in the eye during hypnosis. Am. J. Clin. Hypn., *4:*264, 1962.

90. Tart, C.T.: Altered States of Consciousness: A Book of Readings. New York, Wiley, 1969.

91. Thompson, K.F.: Clinical and experimental trance: yes, there is a difference, Am. J. Clin. Hypn., *13:*1, 1970.

92. Timney, B.N., and Barber, T.X.: Hypnotic induction and oral temperature. Int. J. Clin. Exp. Hypn., *17:*121, 1969.

93. Vanderhoof, E., and Clancy, J.: Effect of emotion on blood flow. J. Appl. Physiol., *17:*67, 1962.

94. Volgyesi, F.: Menschen- und Tierhypnose. Leipzig, Füssli, 1938.

95. Walrath, L.C., and Hamilton, D.W.: Autonomic correlates of meditation and hypnosis. Am. J. Clin. Hypn., *17:*190, 1975.

96. Weitzenhoffer, A. M.: Hypnotism—An Objective Study in Suggestibility. New York, Wiley, 1953.

97. _____: Behavior therapeutic technique and hypnotherapeutic methods. Am. J. Clin. Hypn., *15:*71, 1972.

98. Weitzenhoffer, A. M., and Weitzenhoffer, G. B.: Sex, transference and susceptibility to hypnosis. Am. J. Clin. Hypn., *1:*15, 1958.

99. Wells, W. R.: Experiments in waking hypnosis for instructional purposes. J. Abnorm. Social Psychol., *18:*389, 1924.

100. West, J.L.: Psychophysiology of hypnosis. J.A.M.A., *172:*672, 1960.

101. White, R. W.: A preface to the theory of hypnotism. J. Abnorm. Social Psychol., *36:*477, 1941.

102. Wolberg, L. R.: Medical Hypnosis. Vol. I. The Principles of Hypnotherapy. New York, Grune & Stratton, 1948.

103. Young, P. C.: Experimental hypnotism: a review. Psychol. Bull., *38:*92, 1941.

4

Misconceptions About Hypnosis

LOSS OF CONSCIOUSNESS

It is imperative to remove *all* the most popular misconceptions about hypnosis before attempting an induction procedure. The most common of these is that the subject is asleep, unconscious, or in a "knocked-out" state. The stage hypnotist has contributed to the widely held notion that hypnosis is a "trance," or a "sleeplike" or "out-of-this-world" state.

Apprehensive patients should be informed that they will not necessarily lose awareness or fall asleep. Rather, they will be more awake! One should explain carefully that all levels of hypnosis, including the deeper stages, are characterized by *increased attention* to the operator's suggestions, that this concentration facilitates receptivity to suggestions, and that the profound concentration achieved is one of the principal reasons for the use of hypnosis.

Actually, hypnosis has little resemblance to true sleep. Most ideas equating sleep with hypnosis stem from motion pictures that portray the hypnotized individual with his eyes closed. An explanation that the eyes are closed to facilitate concentration can be amplified by the following remarks: "Have you ever noted how a music lover at a concert often has his eyes closed while he is listening appreciatively to the performance? Even though he *looks relaxed and asleep,* he is *more alert; he can even follow a single theme through many variations.*" This analogy is useful for differentiating sleep and hypnosis.

The author seldom uses the term "sleep" in his verbalization technic to induce hypnosis, as it only creates confusion. However, many good operators use the word "sleep" as part of their induction technic. Most subjects are intuitively aware, nevertheless, that they are not expected to fall asleep. If, during the induction technic, the term "sleep" is used inadvertently, it can be qualified by stating, "You will feel as if you could go to sleep, or as if you are about to fall asleep."

Frequently, even after it has been emphasized repeatedly that the hypnotized individual does not fall asleep, patients state, "Doctor, I know I wasn't hypnotized. I heard everything you said." I often remark, "That's right. I wanted you to hear everything that was said. If you heard 100 per cent of what I suggested, you then have a 100 per cent chance of absorbing these suggestions, and if you absorbed *all* of these suggestions, there is a much better chance that you will follow these suggestions." This statement, when made in an affirmative manner, clears up any misconception that sleep and hypnosis are synonymous.

SURRENDER OF WILL

Another misconception is that the subject "surrenders his will" to the all-powerful hypnotist. Unfortunately, the "Svengali-Trilby" novel, comic strips, and television programs have perpetuated this myth. Since the capacity to be hypnotized is a *subjective* experience, nothing could be further from the truth. Many patients state, "I always thought that under hypnosis I could be made to do anything against my wishes." It is helpful to emphasize that subjects are not dominated by the will of the hypnotist; they are fully capable of making decisions at all times.

Those who fear that hypnosis can weaken their

moral code or permanently change their attitudes can be informed that strong persuasion, mass psychology, and propaganda (subtle forms of suggestion) are thoroughly capable, especially during wartime, of changing attitudes and behavior. However, it is conceivable that an unscrupulous hypnotist, by producing a total amnesia and establishing a valid motive, could get an individual, already predisposed to lie, steal, or kill, to commit a criminal or antisocial act. Naturally, such circumstances do not exist in the doctor-patient relationship. This will be discussed in more detail in Chapter 19.

WEAKMINDEDNESS

Some still believe that morons, imbeciles, and weakminded persons make the best hypnotic subjects. This, too, is a misconception. Rather, it appears that people of above average intelligence, who are capable of concentrating, usually make the best subjects. Motivation can be increased by stating, "If you are readily hypnotizable, this indicates that you are above average in intelligence."

In this connection, constant hypnotic induction does not weaken the mind or make an individual more suggestible. Thousands of subjects have been hypnotized hundreds of times without the slightest demonstrable harm.

REVELATION OF SECRETS

Few patients reach the deeper stages of hypnosis if they think that intimate secrets will be revealed, as might occur under anesthesia or "truth serum." They should be informed that they will be *aware of everything* while hypnotized and afterward, unless a specific amnesia is suggested. As a result, guilt-laden subjects relax and become more amenable to hypnosis.

FEAR OF NOT BEING DEHYPNOTIZED

Some subjects fear that they will not be "brought out of it." A common question is, "Doctor, what happens if you can't get me out of this?" Another is, "What happens if you should drop dead while I am hypnotized?" These fears

can disrupt the interpersonal relationship, and may cause a real resistance to being hypnotized. As has been mentioned, the patient actually induces the hypnosis through his own convictions. Therefore, he can readily dehypnotize himself in a split second, if necessary. The author points out that, when posthypnotic suggestions contrary to the wishes of the patient are given, invariably spontaneous dehypnotization occurs and breaks the rapport. One must remember that hypnosis is an *interpersonal* relationship between the therapist and the patient and that it is an *intrapersonal* one for the patient. Often, if the operator merely leaves the room, this causes deeply hypnotized subjects to dehypnotize themselves. Because many patients are now taught autohypnosis, they can terminate it at any time. Emphasizing this fact allays their fears, anxieties, and tensions.

CONFUSION BETWEEN HYPNOTIZABILITY AND GULLIBILITY

Some persons believe that, if they are hypnotizable, this indicates that they are gullible and believe everything told to them. The difference between the two states has already been explained. Mental discrimination is not impaired with regard to stimuli which threaten the integrity of the organism.

DOMINANT PERSONALITY REQUIRED

Another widely held misconception is that one has to have a strong personality to be a hypnotist and that males, having supposedly dominant personalities, are better hypnotists than females. This is not true, as a male hypnotist also can be an excellent subject for a female hypnotist.

SUMMARY

All misconceptions should be removed by adequate explanations during the initial visit. This discussion should be conducted at the level of the patient's intelligence. Readily understood examples should be used for illustrative purposes. Although this is timeconsuming, the results are rewarding. Mentioning that the phenomena of hypnosis occur as a part of everyday life is helpful in the removal of the commoner misconceptions.

The author finds that it is particularly helpful to have all new candidates observe an induction procedure in a well-conditioned subject. A few minutes of observation will save hours of explanation. A well-conducted induction also corrects the false impressions derived from stage hypnosis. The fallacious ideas about hypnosis, originating from uninformed sources, have to be removed.

As has been stressed repeatedly, hypnosis is not a "sleep" state, a "trance," or a state of unconsciousness. Rather, it closely resembles the waking state. The following points bear reemphasis in the interests of dispelling persistent miscon-

ceptions about hypnosis: (1) intelligent individuals usually make the best subjects; (2) the subject's will is not surrendered; (3) a hypnotized person does not lose control or reveal intimate material unless he wishes to do so; (4) susceptibility to hypnosis is not related to gullibility or submissiveness; and (5) hypnosis can be terminated readily by either the subject or the operator. Many other misconceptions, such as being helpless to resist undesirable posthypnotic suggestions, stem from outmoded and wholly unscientific tenets. Removal of all doubts and misconceptions helps to establish a closer rapport and the motivation necessary for successful hypnotic induction and therapy.

5

Suggestibility Tests

There are tests that presumptively can determine the degree of susceptibility to suggestion. Evidence has been presented that a hypnotic induction profile (HIP) has value in predicting hypnotic susceptibility.[2, 3] Sophisticated hypnotherapists seldom use these, however, as they are time-consuming. Nevertheless, it is a good idea for the beginner to use any one of the following suggestibility tests. If he doubts his ability to hypnotize a patient, under the pretext of testing, he can proceed immediately with an induction technic instead. If hypnosis is obtained, one can say, "I started to test you, but I recognized that you would be an excellent subject. Therefore, I continued hypnotizing you." Contrarily, this can be a welcome face-saving device for the novice in case hypnosis is not obtained.

THE HANDCLASP TEST

The handclasp test is excellent for quickly selecting suitable volunteers when using group hypnosis. Patients can be either in a standing or a sitting position and are instructed to clasp their hands firmly together, either above their heads or at eye-level. Before beginning, the operator clasps his own hands in the desired manner, explaining where the subjects' hands should be placed. Then they are asked to close their eyes tightly.

The following verbalization is used to determine which subjects will, in all probability, be hypersuggestible: "Please lock your hands tightly together. Press your fingers *tighter* and *tighter* together. Imagine, if you will, that your hands are glued together; that they are *sticking tighter* and *tighter* together . . . and the *tighter* they stick

together, the better you will respond to all suggestions. I am going to count slowly from 1 to 10, and with each number that I count, and with each breath that you take, you will find your fingers sticking *tighter* and *tighter* together. When I reach the count of 10, if you *really* wish to follow all other suggestions, you will feel your hands sticking *tighter* and *tighter* together. The *tighter* you can imagine that your hands are sticking together, the better you will be able to follow all other suggestions. Your fingers are locked so *tightly* that it would be difficult to pull your hands apart." (Here there is a pause of a second or two.) "Now, your hands are tightly locked together." If a subject has difficulty in unclasping his hands, this indicates a high degree of suggestibility.

There are modifications of this test, one of which is to have the subject place his hands above his head with the fingers interlocked and the palms facing outward. Either of these methods will test the subject's ability to concentrate, as well as his capacity to respond to suggestion. A direct authoritarian approach or a permissive one can be used. The latter is preferred.

THE BACKWARD POSTURAL SWAY TEST

In the postural sway test, the subject is asked to stand erect with his feet together, his hands at his sides, and his eyes closed. The operator stands behind the subject with the palms of his hands resting lightly on the subject's shoulders. "I am going to count from 1 to 10, and you will feel yourself falling backward, backward. One, you are falling backward, backward. Two, your body is getting rigid from your head to your toes. Three, you are falling backward! Your body feels stiff and rigid. Four, as I relax my hands on your shoulders, you will feel yourself being pulled backward . . . b-a-c-k-w-a-r-d. Five, you are f-a-l-l-i-n-g . . . f-a-l-l-i-n-g. . . ." The hands now can be drawn backward; at this point the subject usually begins to sway backward and, as this occurs, the tempo of the suggestions is increased. "You are falling backward, backward. You are beginning to lose your balance. You're beginning to fall! I will catch you. That's right. Let yourself go." Naturally, one must be ready to catch the patient as he falls backward. Before beginning the test, have the subject fall backward 2 or 3 times for assurance that he will be caught.

The ease and the manner in which he falls indicates whether or not the subject is trying to resist the operator's suggestions. A good subject will fall backward without any difficulty. By placing his hands lightly on the subject's shoulders, the operator can detect readily the slightest sway of the body. If the subject sways forward when the command to fall backward is given, or vice versa, this indicates either that the subject is not cooperating or that he has much involuntary resistance.

A variation of this test is for the operator to extend his arms, with his fingertips in front of the patient's face, as he stands directly behind the patient. As mention of falling backward is made, the hands are moved forward slowly, producing the illusion in the patient that *he is actually falling backward*. This modification is especially valuable for resistant subjects.

THE FORWARD POSTURAL SWAY TEST

Like its counterpart, the forward postural sway test is useful for "crossing up" the resistant subject. The verbalization is as follows: "Close your eyes and listen to my voice. If you really wish to go into a nice, deep, soothing, pleasant state of relaxation, you will notice yourself *falling, falling* forward, forward, forward." Any slight forward sway indicates positive suggestibility, provided that the movements are not voluntary on the part of the subject. If there is resistance, he will sway backward. At this point, to circumvent patient negativism, one can "reverse the field" and say, "You are falling backward." If he starts to sway backward, then the operator can remark, "See, you are falling backward." This increases the subject's suggestibility and also utilizes his resistance to achieve positive suggestibility.

THE EYEBALL-SET TEST

The eyeball-set test is not only a suggestibility test but also an important one for rapid establishment of belief in the operator's "power" or suggestions. The subject is asked to look at a spot directly above his forehead. He is told to stare intently at this spot. The following verbalization is used: "Your eyes are getting *heavier* and *heavier,* and the *heavier* you can *think, feel,* and *imagine* your eyes getting, the sooner you will close your eyes. The more *relaxed* your eyes get, the more deeply relaxed you will become. Your lids are getting *heavier* and *heavier.*" If the patient begins to blink, one should say, "Your eyes are blinking, blinking. That is a good sign. It shows that your are beginning to relax. Your eyes are blinking still more, as you relax deeper and d-e-e-p-e-r. I will now count from 1 to 3. Promptly, precisely, and exactly at the count of 3, if you really wish to learn how to relax deeply, you will close your eyes tightly together. . . . One, your eyes feel as though they are closing. Two, your eyes are closing . . . c-l-o-s-i-n-g. Three, shut your eyes together and let your eyeballs roll up into the back of your head for just a few seconds." Then the following is said all in one sentence: "You can feel your lids sticking *tighter* and *tighter* together, and the *tighter* they stick together, the better you will be able to *relax* and follow my suggestions. You can feel your lids sticking *tighter* and *tighter* together. See, the suggestions are beginning to work! Your lids are really stuck tightly together."

This test is actually based upon physiologic factors rather than psychological ones. The patient does not realize that it is extremely difficult to open the lids with the eyeballs rolled back into the head; he thinks that the effect is due to the operator's suggestions. This initiates the compounding of belief into conviction.

Another variation of this test is to have the subject turn his eyeballs upward as far as possible and close his eyes tightly. One can lightly press the forefinger of each hand on the subject's forehead just above the eyes and instruct him to "Look up at the spot where my fingers are placed." While he is doing this, one suggests, "Keep looking at this spot. You will find that it is extremely difficult to open your eyes now." Simultaneously, several downward passes over the closed eyes by the open palm reinforce lid closure. If the individual is unable to open his eyes, this generally indicates that he will be an excellent subject. This, in part, together with hand levitation, constitutes the essence of Spiegel's hypnotic induction profile (HIP).[3]

THE HAND LEVITATION TEST

The hand levitation test can be used not only as a means of determining whether or not an individual will make a good hypnotic subject, but also for the indirect or permissive type of induction of hypnosis by hand levitation. The subject is told: "Place your hands in your lap. Would you mind looking steadily at one or the other of your hands? And as you keep looking at them, you will soon feel some type of sensation in one hand or the other. Perhaps at first it might be a prickly sensation, or a numb feeling, or perhaps one of your fingers will begin to move or separate. Or perhaps one of the fingers may begin to twitch. Do not interfere in any way with the movements of your fingers but simply observe *any* and *every* sensation that occurs." One might remark, "You can speculate about the texture of the cloth of your trousers. Perhaps, as you keep pressing down, you can feel the warmth of your skin. As you keep pressing down and building up tension in your fingers, you may even begin to notice that one of your fingers will move." Call the subject's attention to even the slightest movement of his fingers. Invariably, some movement of one of the fingers will occur in time. Naturally, the subject does not realize this. To facilitate levitation, one can explain that the finger is beginning to move because it wishes to respond, and that the opposite of tension is relaxation (a perfectly logical remark). "As your finger gets more relaxed, it will begin to rise up into the air" (another logical remark). "As your finger begins to *lift,* it will get *lighter* and *lighter*—so light, in fact, that the other fingers will also get *lighter* and *lighter.* See? Your fingers are beginning to lift up, up, up . . . *lighter* and *highter,* Your hand now is getting *lighter* and *lighter,* and pretty soon the arm will begin to get *lighter* and *lighter.* And, as the arm gets *lighter* and *lighter,* it will lift higher and higher." The operator continues to suggest lightness, rising, or floating sensations. Then he suggests that the hand will continue to lift until it touches the face. Perhaps the subject might be willing to accept the suggestion that, when any portion of his hand touches any part of his face, this will be a signal that he will drop into a deep state of relaxation. If the rising of the hand is slow, smooth, and steady, this usually indicates that the subject is cooperating. If the hand and the arm are lifted rapidly, or if the movements are spasmodic or jerky, it usually indicates resistance. One should always attempt to correlate the lifting of the arm with the subject's breathing and state: "As your arm lifts *higher* and *higher,* your breathing becomes slower, deeper, more regular . . . slower, deeper, more regular." If the subject carries out these suggestions and his arm drops back into his lap with a thud after it has touched his face, one can be reasonably certain that the individual will be an excellent subject.

THE HAND-DROP TEST

The hand-drop test is an excellent method of choosing likely subjects from a group. The following instructions are given: "Would you all put your arms out in front of you? Now, close your eyes and visualize in your "mind's eye" or imagine that you have a 10-pound bag of sugar on the back of the palm of your right hand. Now, you can feel it getting *very, very heavy.* It is so *heavy* that your right hand is beginning to fall, beginning to get *heavier* and *heavier* as the heavy bag of sugar is getting *heavier* and *heavier, very, very heavy.* Your right arm is getting very, very tired because it is so difficult to support this heavy weight." (Positive suggestibility is indicated by the right arm's being well below the other.) "Now open your eyes. See, there is a difference of at least a foot between the right and the left arm."

THE THERMAL TEST

Even the heat- or the cold-illusion test can be used to predict the degree of suggestibility. An ordinary block of wet wood such as a child's wet alphabet block will suffice for this test. The subject is asked to close his eyes and extend his hand forward, palm down. The block is placed on the back of the palm and, in a confident tone of voice, the operator remarks, "I am placing this ice cube on the back of your hand. It is getting colder and colder. You can feel the chilling, paralyzing numbness of the ice cube as it begins to melt. You can feel your skin getting numb." The block is then removed. If the individual is convinced that this was an ice cube, he has a high degree of susceptibility.

In order to produce the illusion of heat, one can strike a match and tell the subject, while his eyes are closed, that a quarter or a half dollar is being heated. After a few seconds, the coin is placed on the back of the subject's hand, while his eyes are shut tight. If he winces or withdraws his hand, one can be fairly certain that the subject is susceptible.

This test can also be performed in another manner. The subject is given a coin to hold in his clenched fist. Remark, "The coin is getting warmer and warmer. It is now getting *hotter* and *hotter,* and the longer you hold it, the hotter it will get. It is getting hotter all the time. It is actually getting very, very hot. Don't hold it too long as it is apt to burn you. If it gets too hot, let the coin drop to the floor." If this happens, the subject is obviously a good one. The test can be made more plausible by explaining that the heat of the metal is produced by the sweat of the hand.

THE OLFACTORY TEST

The olfactory test also is an excellent one for choosing good subjects out of a group. For this test, a stoppered perfume bottle, filled with colored water, is used. The operator holds the perfume bottle up so that everybody can see it and,

as he takes the stopper out, he says, "The odor of this perfume is drifting toward the back of the room. It is beginning to become more and more pronounced. Will those who smell this odor please raise their hands?" As a rule, those who do so make excellent candidates for hypnosis.

THE KOHNSTAMM "TEST"

The Kohnstamm "test" is actually a maneuver, which produces a favorable mind-set. It involves physiologic muscular mechanisms rather than suggestion *per se.* It is very convincing and enables the subject to understand the mechanism of arm levitation. The subject is instructed to press the back of his tightly clenched fist against the side of a wall, with his entire arm held very stiff. He is informed that he should try to push against the wall only with his arm and not with his body. After several minutes he is asked to step away from the wall and allow his arm to hang freely at his side. The arm will begin to rise spontaneously until it reaches a horizontal position. It will feel weightless as it is rising. This is known as the Kohnstamm phenomenon. The subject does not know that contraction of the muscles of the arm naturally follows relaxation. He believes that the arm lifts because of the operator's suggestions; this heightens his susceptibility to further suggestions. This is a good technic to employ as a precursor to induction of hypnosis by an arm-levitation technic.

CHEVREUL'S PENDULUM TEST

To perform Chevreul's pendulum test, one must have a heavy ring or a glass ball on a string, which the patient holds in his hand, arm outstretched, over a piece of paper upon which is drawn a circle about 8 or 10 inches in diameter with a cross inside. The subject is told not to make any conscious attempt to help or hinder the movements of the ball (or ring), but that the ball will move spontaneously by just thinking about it. He is informed that the mere concentration upon the ball's moving from left to right, forward or backward, clockwise or counterclockwise, will cause it to swing in accordance with his thoughts.

The subject is instructed to let his eyes travel

around the circle, or up and down the cross, or from one side to the other of the horizontal line. It is again suggested that he will not be able to control the swing of the ball. If the ball follows the operator's suggestions, this indicates a positive suggestibility. When the swing is well developed, the subject is asked to concentrate on the ball's swinging in a clockwise direction. After this has been accomplished, it is suggested that it might swing in a counterclockwise direction or up and down. Individuals who are extremely susceptible to suggestion react in full accordance with the suggestions because of involuntary ideosensory activities. This is also the principle of the Ouija board. However, it should be emphasized that, regardless of the degree of his reaction to the suggestions, the subject's suggestibility can be enhanced by remarking convincingly, "Your reaction definitely shows that you will make an excellent subject. I know that you can be hypnotized."

DISGUISED TESTS

For patients who remark, "I doubt if anyone can hypnotize me," there is one disguised test that is particularly suitable for the physician's use. If the outcome of the "test" is successful, a favorable mind-set leading to positive suggestibility is produced. This ordinarily facilitates induction.

This disguised test is based on prestige suggestion. When the patient comes into the office, he is immediately given a placebo with the casual remarks: "This drug facilitates hypnotic induction. It takes exactly 30 minutes to act. Let me see, it is now 11 A.M. If you will wait in my reception room for one half hour, you will be ready to go easily into a nice relaxed state at that time." This, of course, generally produces an expectant attitude, withsubsequent hypersuggestibility. In about half an hour, the patient, who in the meantime has been sitting in the reception room building up his expectancy level, comes into the office. Then the right or the left eye is inspected in the following manner: The operator places his thumb just below the outer canthus of the eye to evert the lower lid. With the patient either sitting or standing, he carefully scrutinizes the conjunctiva in a professional manner. After

looking intently at the eye for several seconds, he nods his head approvingly and exclaims confidently, "Yes, it's beginning to work. You will be an excellent subject." The patient naturally does not understand how this conclusion was reached; yet he cannot fail to be impressed by the operator's self-assurance and confident demeanor.

One can use other disguised tests to determine susceptibility to hypnosis. The following one makes use of ideomotor and ideosensory activities. One places the bloodpressure cuff around the patient's arm and remarks, "Now as I relax the pressure and as you hear the air escaping, you will go *deeper* and *deeper* relaxed. You will go *deeper* and *deeper* relaxed." (The subject closes his eyes.) "That's wonderful. You are going *deeper* and *deeper relaxed!* That's fine." Now, as the cuff loosens and the air escapes simultaneously, the ideomotor effect of the deflated cuff and the sound of the escaping air (ideosensory) are conducive to even deeper relaxation. Usually, as the pressure falls, a good subject will relax readily. The effects of this test are dramatic.

This test can also be extended into an induction technic: "Now that's fine. I want you to relax still more; you are going deeper and deeper relaxed. As the pressure drops and as the cuff loosens still more on your arm, you are going *deeper* and *deeper* relaxed." Here, one can test for arm catalepsy.

Meares has described an interesting disguised method that is based on the repeated elicitation of the tendon reflexes which, in itself, aids in relaxation.[1] The method has the advantage not only of estimating suggestibility, but also of acting as a reliable guide to the best technic for the induction of hypnosis. The patient is unaware that he is being tested for hypnosis. If he proves to be unsuitable, the subject of hypnosis need not be discussed. The patient is not disappointed, nor does the therapist lose face. Since the rapport is not broken, the therapist is free to use another method. The association of the reflex movement of the limb with the verbal suggestions of movement accustoms the patient to the involuntary motions of his limbs in response to suggestion, and so paves the way for hypnotic suggestibility.

SUMMARY

The fact that subjects respond positively to suggestibility tests does not imply that every one of them will enter the hypnotic state. However, where there is no response, this is presumptive evidence of negative suggestibility. Most of these tests depend on elicitation of ideomotor and ideosensory activities and, since hypnosis is contingent on other factors, such as confidence and expectation, all tests have certain deficiencies.

Furthermore, they do not indicate what method will enable the subject to be hypnotized effectively. Also, they give little information as to what may be the deterrent factors contributing to negative suggestibility. Various modifications of most of the above tests have been described by others.[1, 2, 3]

If all tests are unfavorable, this naturally interferes with the rapport. Often there is a distinct disadvantage in using tests to determine the subject's degree of susceptibility, because many subjects might have been hypnotized readily without them. However, irrespective of the subject's reactions to the tests, he always should be informed that he responded favorably, and that he will do much better the next time!

Finally, the best test is a trial induction of hypnosis. The preinduction talk, described in Chapter 12, establishes good rapport, particularly if the commonly held misconceptions are removed. Then, too, the suggestibility tests are influenced by the prestige, expertise, confidence, and skill of the operator.

REFERENCES

1. Meares, A.: The clinical estimation of suggestibility. J. Clin. Exp. Hypn., 2:106, 1954.
2. Spiegel, H.: Manual for Hypnotic Induction Profile: Eye-roll Levitation Method. (rev. ed.) New York, Soni Media, 1976.
3. Spiegel, H., *et al.:* Psychometric analysis of the hypnotic induction profile. Int. J. Clin. Exp. Hypn., *24:* 300, 1976.

6

Factors That Influence Susceptibility to Hypnosis

Generally, highly motivated, intelligent individuals are the best hypnotic subjects because of their ability to concentrate;[5] exhibitionists, with the exception of those who use resistance as an attention-getting device, are easy to hypnotize. Imbeciles, morons, senile persons, certain types of psychotics, and children under 6 years of age, who are incapable of concentrating, are difficult or impossible to hypnotize. However, the ability to concentrate, though necessary for hypnotic susceptibility, is not in itself a sufficient condition since some subjects who show good concentration are relatively unsusceptible.[13]

Casually mentioning that persons of low mentality seldom are good hypnotic subjects increases motivation. Even though this statement is not strictly true, all patients wish to be regarded as above average in intelligence. Therefore, the remarks, by inference, increase their susceptibility. However, individuals with a real intellectual deficiency usually are insusceptible and tax the ingenuity of the operator.[1] Scientifically minded individuals are often poor subjects because of internal "noise"—self-analysis of their emotions.

Misdirection, by getting the subject's attention diverted to his own ideosensory or ideomotor responses, increases susceptibility to the operator's suggestions. The misdirection can be employed during the induction procedure as follows: "Would you mind shifting your attention to your toes and feet? As you do this, notice how very, very heavy your shoes are getting. Your shoes are getting heavier and heavier." (The subject invariably becomes aware of the heaviness, and this begins to build up his conviction that the operator's suggestions are producing changes within his own body.) After a pause, the operator remarks, "You are now becoming aware of the watch on your left wrist. It, too, is getting heavier and heavier . . . very heavy! Notice that you are no longer aware of the pressure of the shoes; is that not true?" (The subject nods.) "You now can feel the watch, can you not?" (He nods again.) "So, you see, you can either be aware of, or ignore, sensations that are constantly present within your own body." As has been mentioned, if the subject experiences one sensation after another, the conviction that other suggestions will be followed is enhanced.

Psychotherapists know that neurotics seldom relinquish the symptoms used to get attention. Such mechanisms are pleasurable. Naturally, this is vehemently denied. Instead, they ardently protest that they wish to be cured of their symptoms. However, once rapport has been established, they tend to be more suggestible than "normal" individuals.[6, 7, 14] On the other hand, as just mentioned, exhibitionists are easily hypnotized by the professional entertainer. The hypnosis is not produced by him, but, rather, because the subject expects it to happen. The stage hypnotist likes to give the impression that his passes, staring eyes, and verbalizations produce the hypnosis. He is very anxious to make his audience believe that he is an all-powerful person, so he uses the usual gesticulations and the "mumbo jumbo" to heighten this illusion. Such "window dressing" merely obscures the fact that the hypnosis occurred as a result of the subject's expectation and imagination! The stage hypnotist relies on the subjects to please not only him, but the audience as well.[11]

Another factor which determines the degree of susceptibility to hypnosis is the subject's ability to restrict his attention span to a given idea. Braid tried to change the name of hypnosis to *monoideism*—the ability of a person to concentrate on one idea at a time to the exclusion of others.

Cultural factors often determine the depth of, and the susceptibility to, hypnosis.[8, 12] The feelings and temperament of the operator also determine the outcome of the hypnotic induction; intuitive subjects respond in a positive manner to the operator's empathy and self-confidence. If they develop a good mind-set, they effectively concentrate on his suggestions; if not, they are refractory to all suggestions. If, for instance, the operator is absorbed in personal problems during the induction procedure, this adversely affects the intraverbal and meaningful aspects of his communications. Frankel has provided an excellent review of the characteristics of hypnotic responsivity.[4]

Susceptibility is definitely enhanced by motivation.[10] Though poorly motivated subjects are invariably insusceptible, this does not imply that they cannot be hypnotized. Frequently, the person who is not highly motivated may have an inordinate need for hypnosis. Even though such an individual uses the lack of motivation as a defense, he, too, is often very susceptible to suggestion. Rapport that is established quickly is conducive to greater motivation. It should be impressed upon all subjects that their full cooperation is essential, that they must be willing to respond to suitable suggestions, and that coercion will not be used. This also helps to increase motivation.

The specific technic for handling poorly motivated subjects is similar to the "misdirection of attention" approach described for extremely introspective or analytic persons. Moreover, saying "Even if your mind wanders, you will still hear my suggestions—this will help you to relax" is more effective than saying "Just make your mind a blank." Many subjects have been told that it is necessary to concentrate intensively in order to be hypnotized. Since some doubt their ability to do so, they should be informed that only ordinary concentration is required.

The factors which determine susceptibility depend on the capacity to be imaginatively involved, perhaps a genetic factor, and on the manner in which previously invoked beliefs are processed into convictions. These influence susceptibility to hypnosis more than any other factor.[5] Diamond does not believe that behavioral-situational factors or observational learning procedures enhance susceptibility to hypnosis.[3] This has not been the author's experience. However, he recognizes that certain technics enhance susceptibility to specific suggestions as conditions vary from subject to subject. This is in accord with other researchers, who were unable to relate hypnotizability to sex, age, psychiatric diagnosis, and various personality traits.[2]

REFERENCES

1. Beigel, H. G.: Some signs and causes of unsusceptibility. Br. J. Med. Hypn., *4:*34, 1952.
2. Deckert, G.H., and West, J.L.: The problem of hypnotizability: a review. Int. J. Clin. Exp. Hypn., *11:*205, 1963.
3. Diamond, M.J.: Modification of hypnotizability: a review. Psychol. Bull., *81:*180, 1974.
4. Frankel, F.H.: Hypnosis: Trance as a Coping Mechanism. New York, Plenum, 1976.
5. Hilgard, J.R.: Imaginative involvement: some characteristics of the highly hypnotizable and the nonhypnotizable. Int. J. Clin. Exp. Hypn., *22:*138, 1974.
6. Ingham, J.G.: Body sway suggestibility and neurosis. J. Ment. Sci., *100:*432, 1954.
7. ———: Psychoneurosis and suggestibility. J. Abnorm. Social Psychol., *51:*600, 1955.
8. Kline, M. V.: Toward a theoretical understanding of the nature of resistance to the induction of hypnosis and depth of hypnosis. J. Clin. Exp. Hypn., *1:*32, 1953.
9. Martin, R. M., and Marcuse, F. L.: Characteristics of volunteers and nonvolunteers for hypnosis. J. Clin. Exp. Hypn., *5:*176, 1957.
10. Meares, A.: A note on the motivation for hypnosis. J. Clin. Exp. Hypn., *3:*222, 1955.

11. Schneck, J. M.: Relationships between hypnotist-audience and hypnotist-subject interaction. J. Clin. Exp. Hypn., *6:*171, 1958.

12. Secter, I. I.: Considerations in resistances to initial induction of hypnosis. J. Clin. Exp. Hypn., *5:*77, 1957.

13. Van Nuys, D.: Meditation, attention and hypnotic susceptibility: a correlational study. Int. J. Clin. Exp. Hypn., *21:*59, 1973.

14. Weitzenhoffer, A. M.: A note concerning hypnotic susceptibility and maladjustment. J. Clin. Exp. Hypn., *6:*182, 1958.

7
Laws of Suggestion

THE LAW OF CONCENTRATED ATTENTION

There are several important principles or "laws" that should be followed when employing hypnotic suggestion.[2] The first is the *law of concentrated attention:* whenever attention is concentrated on an idea over and over again, it spontaneously tends to realize itself. Repetitive radio and television commercials that cause people to buy the advertised products are typical examples of this law. In many commercials, the listener's attention is gained without his knowledge through subliminal stimulation. This is even more effective than persuasion, as critical faculties are reduced.

THE LAW OF REVERSED EFFECT

The second is the law of reversed effect: the harder one tries to do something, the less chance one has of success. Trying to recall someone's name, for instance, often can be a difficult task. Regardless of how hard he wills himself to remember the name, he cannot. It seems that, whenever the imagination and the will are utilized, the imagination supersedes the will.

This law applies to the insomniac who tries to go to sleep, and to the food, drug, or alcohol addict who cannot stop by making an appeal or inner "speech" to his will. These respond more readily to imagination power than to will power! The sophisticated hypnotherapist employs technics which make full use of the principles embodied in the law of reverse effect.

It is difficult to negate the effects of the imagination, which comprises all an individual's past associations, feelings, and ideas. A typical illustration is the individual who lacks confidence in public speaking. When in bed at night, he "sees" himself walking up to the rostrum and "hears" himself delivering his address. The mere thought of the future talk causes palpitation, sighing, holding of the breath, and a panicky feeling. Thus the imagination produces the same effects *as if* the speaker were in front of the audience. This process is referred to as sensory imagery. If his imagination is negatively "programmed" in this manner, time after time, night after night, it is only natural that he will develop anxiety when he gets up to speak. Continually thinking negative, harmful, and destructive thoughts eventually leads to their realization *because of expectation and belief that they will happen.* Having an idea of an action often results in that action.

Therefore, one never resorts to the will to attain desired physiologic changes! The organism will not respond as well to direct authoritative commands as it will to permissive manipulation of the experiential background via the individual's imagination. When one is trying to develop glove anesthesia, for instance, it is incorrect to suggest, "I want your hand to get numb." Rather, one must use a descriptive sensory imagery type of verbalization, such as: "Imagine that you are putting your hand in a pitcher of very cold ice water. As soon as you can visualize this, you will feel you hand developing a numb, heavy, wooden feeling, the same as if you had been sitting on it, or the same as if you had had an anesthetic injected into it." Stimulating the imagination in this manner is more likely to produce the desired response.

THE LAW OF DOMINANT EFFECT

The law of dominant effect also plays an important role in enabling suggestions to be received in a more meaningful manner. It is based on the axiom that a strong emotion tends to replace a weaker one. Attaching a strong emotion to a suggestion tends to make the suggestion more effective. Thus, when a person is having a pleasurable emotional experience and danger is imminent, the stronger emotion of danger displaces the former, which disappears instantly if the danger is pronounced.

Another illustration of this law is the use of a strong physiologic effect to reinforce a psychological suggestion. Suggestions of relaxation are increased by massage or gentle stroking. The effect of this principle is noted when a child slams the door on his finger and his mother remarks, "Oh I'll just kiss it and the pain will go away." Here the mere touch of her lips becomes the more dominant suggestion and makes the finger feel better. Thus, at an early age, we become responsive to this fundamental principle or law.

Emile Coué popularized these laws.[1] He also made a point of suggesting only the end result. He avoided details of how recovery should be accomplished and emphasized that a general, nonspecific suggestion was best, since it would be received uncritically. He became famous for a phrase he urged his patients to say to themselves several times a day, "Everyday, in every way, I am getting better and better." He was specific, however, as to the end result, but he omitted the details involved in improvement. Such ego strengthening is now advocated by Hartland, who utilizes this approach with direct symptom removal without the need to ascertain the reasons for the symptoms.[3, 4]

REFERENCES

1. Coué, E.: How To Practice Suggestion and Auto-suggestion. New York, American Library Service, 1923.
2. Davis, L. W., and Husband, R. W.: A study of hypnotic susceptibility in relation to personality traits. J. Abnorm. Social Psychol., *26:*175, 1931.
3. Hartland, J.: The value of "ego-strengthening" procedures prior to direct symptom removal under hypnosis. Am. J. Clin. Hypn., *8:*89, 1965.
4. _____: Medical and Dental Hypnosis. Baltimore, Williams & Wilkins, 1971.

8

Recognition of the Depth of the Hypnotic State

As early as 1930, R.W. White made use of specific responses to suggestions given during hypnosis as a means of determining a score.[19] The Davis and Husband classification, published in 1931, depends on a point-scoring system and was the rating scale most commonly referred to in the older literature.[4] In 1947, LeCron and Bordeaux introduced a more involved scoring chart separated into six divisions instead of five, the last being a deeper stage which is seldom seen—the plenary or hypnotic coma state.[9]

On the basis of objective and subjective clinical signs, the first part of the light stage is characterized by a pleasant state of restfulness. The subject hears surrounding sounds, is well able to control his thoughts, and experiences no impairment of the senses. After spontaneous eye closure, muscle tension is slightly decreased and motor activities of the limbs are easily carried out. This is followed by drowsiness and lassitude; the carefully lifted arm drops limply. There is some difficulty in opening the eyes or moving the limbs. It has been noted, however, that subjects entering into hypnosis do not have the undulatory eyeball movements that characterize a person falling asleep.[20]

As the hypnosis deepens and the so-called medium stage is reached, the relaxation becomes more marked; the respirations become deeper and regular; some loss of motor activity occurs; the lifted arm remains upright but slowly falls (light catalepsy), and there is a loss of interest in extraneous environmental sounds. As this stage deepens, catalepsy of the limbs is more marked; spontaneous analgesia can be augmented by appropriate suggestions; the subject's thoughts begin to wander, and he now concentrates more on the words of the operator. Inability to move the limbs is noted at this stage, and the automatic movements become more pronounced.

In the deep stage, negative and positive hallucinations can be produced readily; partial or complete amnesia is present, and suggestions of active and passive motor reactions are easily affected. As this stage deepens, positive and negative hallucinations of all types can occur with the eyes open, and these can be maintained posthypnotically; total amnesia is generally present as are age regression, revivification, and other phenomena characteristic of the somnambulistic state. In several thousand patients, Crasilneck and Hall have noted that an area of pallor about the lips, just beyond the mucocutaneous border, is often indicative of somnambulism.[3] Noting this phenomenon obviates the need for challenging the patient to open his eyes or resorting to anesthesia. Another indicator is the Friedlander-Sarbin scale,[6] from which Weitzenhoffer and Hilgard developed their scales.[16, 17, 18] These are described below.

It is difficult to measure objectively the depth of hypnosis. We do not know whether characteristic hypnotic behavior is due to the approach used or whether the various depths are the result of the expectations of the hypnotist and subject. The various rating scales are used primarily for experimental work and are only of limited value to the experienced clinician. All rating scales are, at best, arbitrary divisions. Sometimes it is difficult to state with certainty that the subject is in a light or a medium stage of hypnosis. An experienced operator, however, can often make a close approximation.

In line with this, Spiegel has constructed a Hypnotic Induction Profile (HIP).[14] The two primary components of the HIP are eye roll and arm levitation. Each is given a score of 0 to 4; the average of the two is the profile score. An entire profile is complete when the patient has similar eye-roll and arm levitation scores. It is a rapidly administered test lasting 5 to 10 minutes and includes an assessment of the eye roll and two other hypnotic phenomena, namely, the ideomotor and posthypnotic responses. Amnesia for the signal that terminates the posthypnotic suggestion increases the rating. Sometimes only the eye-roll is given. The amount of sclera showing as the patient closes the eyes presumably indicates the subject's responsiveness to hypnosis. The HIP will be described in more detail in Chapter 9.

The Stanford Hypnotic Clinical Scale (SHCH) was introduced recently by Hilgard and Hilgard.[8] Here too, however, the items in the scale are not a constant. A subject in light hypnosis may experience some of the phenomena of deep hypnosis.[5] The final score is not always a reliable indicator of hypnotic responsivity. The profile scales, however, might be helpful in learning more about an individual's special capabilities.

For teaching purposes, five divisions of the various stages of hypnotic susceptibility are satisfactory, with three of these being sufficient for clinical purposes:

1. Insusceptible;
2. Hypnoidal (precursor to hypnotic state—no symptoms);
3. Light stage;
4. Medium stage;
5. Deep stage.

Other noteworthy scales include the Stanford Hypnotic Susceptibility Scales (SHSS:A, SHSS:B, and SHSS:C) of Weitzenhoffer and Hilgard;[16, 17] the Stanford Profile Scale of Hypnotic Susceptibility (SPS), with two forms;[18] and derivatives of these, such as Shor and Orne's Harvard Group Scale of Hypnotic Susceptibility[13] and London's scale for children, the Children's

Hypnotic Susceptibility Scale (CHSS).[10] Susceptibility is defined as the depth of hypnosis achieved under standard conditions of induction.

In the development of these scales, the standard procedures for construction of psychometric tests have been carefully followed. Samples of hypnotic phenomena were sought, a standardized induction procedure was worked out, and norms were obtained by testing more than 300 subjects. Reliability of the scales was studied by the test-retest method, with alternate forms and different hypnotists being used. Satisfactory coefficients were obtained. Validity was assessed by correlating scores on each item with the total score for the scale (minus the score for the particular item). Only one item proposed for inclusion, passive arm catalepsy, was discarded; it was found not to correlate positively with other measures of susceptibility.

Certain differences should be noted in the three Stanford Hypnotic Susceptibility Scales. Items in the SHSS:C are arranged in an ascending order of difficulty, and it contains more items of a cognitive nature (e.g., positive and negative hallucinations, dreaming, and age regression) than are found in the SHSS:A and SHSS:B.

The Stanford Profile Scales were devised in order to provide separate scores on six subscales: agnosia and cognitive distortion, positive hallucinations, negative hallucinations, dreams and regressions, amnesia and posthypnotic suggestions, and loss of motor control. These items are difficult to assay, and the SPS is intended only for those subjects who score 4 or more points on the SHSS:A or SHSS:B (the mean of SHSS:A is 5.62). A full diagnostic use requires the administration of both forms, each of which contains nine items and includes the scores from SHSS:A. The Stanford group has constructed an indispensable set of tools for many, if not most, kinds of scientific research in hypnosis. It follows the accepted technics of test construction.

To assay the hypnotizability of a group, Shor and Orne developed the Harvard Group Scale (HGSHS:A).[13] With this scale it is possible to test a whole class in one session. Barber and his associates have developed the Barber Susceptibility Scale (BSS) to test quasi-hypnotic behavior without prior induction of formal hypnosis.[1, 2] Both the BSS and the SHSS:A are satisfactory for preliminary subject selection but limited as criteria for the range of hypnotic responsiveness.[12] The Harvard Group Scale of Hypnotic Susceptibility, form A (HGSHS:A) has been assayed and found to possess adequate reliability.[11]

Although the author does not utilize these scales clinically, researchers have found them valuable for establishing standard criteria for assessing hypnotic depth.[15] Ernest Hilgard has reviewed the early and more recent quantitative susceptibility scales and, together with his wife, Josephine, has devised a series of scales with much practical value for the clinician. This series has been named the Stanford Hypnotic Clinical Scales (SHCS). Some of these score the effectiveness of posthypnotic suggestion, amnesia, age regression, and special abilities, such as the availability of imagery conditions. The interested reader is referred to the exhaustive studies of the Hilgards in these areas.[8]

The Harvard Group Scale and the Stanford Hypnotic Susceptibility Scales are the tests most widely used by experimenters. For details, the reader is referred to the original descriptions, the items to look for, and their correlation with the responses.

REFERENCES

1. Barber, T.X., and Calverly, D.S.: "Hypnotic behavior" as a function of task motivation. J. Psychol., *54:* 363, 1962.
2. Barber, T.X., and Glass, L.B.: Significant factors in hypnotic behavior. J. Abnorm. Social Psychol., *64:* 222, 1962.
3. Crasilneck, H.B., and Hall, J.A.: Clinical Hypnosis: Principles and Applications. New York, Grune & Stratton, 1975.
4. Davis, L.S., and Husband, R.W.: A study of hypnotic susceptibility in relation to personality traits. J. Abnorm. Social Psychol., *26:*175, 1931.
5. Evans, F.J.: Recent trends in experimental hypnosis. Behav. Sci., *13:*477, 1968.
6. Friedlander, J.W., and Sarbin, T.R.: The depth of hypnosis. J. Abnorm. Social Psychol., *33:*453, 1938.
7. Hilgard, E.R.: Hypnotic Susceptibility. New York, Harcourt, Brace & World, 1965.
8. Hilgard, E.R., and Hilgard, J.R.: Hypnosis in the Relief of Pain. Los Altos, Cal., William Kaufman, 1976, pp. 209–221.
9. LeCron, L.M., and Bordeaux, J.: Hypnotism Today. New York, Grune & Stratton, 1947.
10. London, P.: The Children's Hypnotic Susceptibility Scale. Palo Alto, Cal., Consulting Psychologists Press, 1963.
11. Peters, J.E.: A factor analytic investigation of the Harvard group scale of hypnotic susceptibility, form A. Int. J. Clin. Exp. Hypn., *22:*377, 1974.
12. Ruch, J.C., *et al.:* Measuring hypnotic responsiveness: a comparison of the Barber Scale and the Stanford Hypnotic Susceptibility Scale, form A. Int. J. Clin. Exp. Hypn., *22:*365, 376, 1974.
13. Shor, R.E., and Orne, E.C.: The Harvard Group Scale of Hypnotic Susceptibility, Form A. Palo Alto, Cal., Consulting Psychologists Press, 1962.
14. Spiegel, H.: Eye-roll Levitation Method. Manual For Hypnotic Induction Profile. New York, Soni Media, 1974.
15. Tart, C.T.: Self-report scales of hypnotic depth. Int. J. Clin. Exp. Hypn., *18:*105, 1970.
16. Weitzenhoffer, A.M., and Hilgard, E.R.: Stanford Hypnotic Susceptibility Scale, Forms A and B. Palo Alto, Cal., Consulting Psychologists Press, 1959.
17. _____: Stanford Hypnotic Susceptibility Scale, Form C. Palo Alto, Cal., Consulting Psychologists Press, 1962.
18. _____: Stanford Profile Scale of Hypnotic Susceptibility, Forms I and II. Palo Alto, Cal., Consulting Psychologists Press, 1963.
19. White, R.W.: The physical and mental traits of individuals susceptible to hypnosis. J. Abnorm. Social Psychol., *25:*293, 1930.
20. Zikmund, V.: Some physiological characteristics of natural and hypnotic sleep in man. Physiol. Bahemoslav, *13:*196, 1964.

9

Clinical Observations and Management
of Various Depths of Hypnosis

From the clinical aspect, the experienced operator can observe the signs and symptoms characterizing the progress of an induction. As belief is compounded into conviction, there is, in good subjects, a steady progression toward more obvious relaxation and alertness to the operator's suggestions.

EYE CHANGES

First, during the initial stages of the induction, the responsive subject generally closes his eyes promptly upon command. If there is a momentary lid lag or delay in eye closure, this often indicates resistance, poor motivation, and possible failure. The next objective is to produce a catalepsy of the smallest muscles of the body—those of the eyelids. The eyelid muscles are the easiest to catalepse. All suggestions are directed toward this objective in the manner described earlier.

After lid catalepsy has been achieved, the operator can assume that the subject will follow all the remaining suggestions, because it has already been emphasized that the final result will depend on how well he cooperates. Later the individual is asked to count backward from 100 to zero; this is one of the elementary suggestions. One can remark, "I have no way of knowing whether or not you are going to count backward and, if you do not count in this fashion or do *not* follow these simple suggestions as they are given, then, of course, you will not enter into hypnosis. The responsibility, then, for not entering the hypnotic

state is due to your failure to follow my suggestions in a specific manner." Thus the onus for entering hypnosis is placed on the subject rather than on the operator.

Other signs indicative of increasing depth are the blinking and the involuntary drooping of the eyelids. The trembling of the eyelids after closure usually indicates further deepening, contrary to the belief of inexperienced operators. After the suggestions are made that the lids are getting heavier and heavier, one notices some blinking and tiring of the lids. The subject, as mentioned earlier, does not know that the lids tire because of the upward position in which the eyes are held. The operator utilizes this blinking, saying, "The blinking indicates that your lids are *really* getting *heavy,* getting *heavier* and *heavier.*" The next step is based on the operator's judgment, experience and intuition. When there is an increased amount of blinking and fatigue, it is suggested in the following manner that the subject can close the eyes: "At the count of 3, if you *really* wish to go into a *deep,* deep state of relaxation, all you have to do is just let your lids close and let them close *tight,* very *tight.* That's right, closing, closing, closed. You will close your eyes not because you *have* to, but because you *want* to do this. Now, let your eyeballs roll comfortably up into the back of your head for a few moments so that you are 'looking' at your own hair. That's right. I can see your eyeballs moving up beneath your lids." The next suggestion is given in a casual manner: "If you *really* wish to go into a nice, deep, pleasant, soothing state of relaxation, it is

53

really so easy. All you have to do is just close your eyes and let your eyeballs roll up into the back of your head." This is much more effective than saying, "I want you to close your eyes promptly and exactly at the count of 3." (This peremptory command mobilizes a critical attitude. So does, "No matter how hard you try, you *cannot* open your eyes." Here you are challenging the subject; with the intonation of your voice or the intraverbal aspects of your communication, you arouse antagonism.)

One can evert the upper lid and, if the eyeballs are rolled upward, be sure that a considerable depth has been reached. If there is no lid reflex when the eyelashes are lightly touched by the tip of the finger, this is indicative of a good response —at least a medium stage of hypnosis has been reached. The production of lid catalepsy is described below.

Spiegel has evaluated over 4,000 cases by means of the Hypnotic Induction Profile (HIP).[9] Grades 4 and 5 are identified as highly hypnotizable. They have a typical group of personality traits which can help to formulate appropriate treatment strategies. The features of the grade 5 syndrome are: (1) the high eye-roll sign; (2) the high intact HIP score; (3) readiness to trust relative suspension of critical judgment; (4) an ease of affiliation with new experiences; (5) a telescoped time sense; (6) an easy acceptance of logical incongruities; (7) an excellent memory and a capacity for intense concentration; (8) an overall tractibility; and (9) paradoxically, a rigid core of private beliefs. Some investigators point out that the demand characteristics influence how a person responds to a hypnotic induction,[7] and another researcher, though agreeing that the HIP may possibly be a rapid method for screening, cautions that a more variegated procedure may be more effective in clinical situations.[2] This depends on the total interpersonal relationship between the patient and clinician.

Wheeler and co-workers on the other hand, found no evidence for the hypothesized relationship between eye-roll and hypnotic susceptibility. He used two widely accepted and validated measures of susceptibility. Eye-roll might be related to trance as gauged by the HIP, but these investigators feel that experimenter bias

and selective elimination of subjects must be considered before such a relationship can be accepted.

MOVEMENTS OF HEAD

If the head of the subject spontaneously rolls sideways or forward, the hypnotic depth is increasing. When this occurs, the operator should support the head, as a strained posture usually results in spasm, which can prevent the hypnosis from becoming deeper. Some individuals, however, do not seem to mind the abnormal position and sink deeper and deeper into relaxation. If the jaws relax limply, this, too, is significant of increasing depth.

CHARACTER OF BREATHING

Shallow, diaphragmatic breathing usually is associated with lighter stages, while slow, deep, regular, abdominal breathing generally is characteristic of deeper stages of hypnotism. One can remark, "You will go *deeper* and *deeper* with each breath you take. Your breathing is getting lower, deeper, and more regular." The second phase can be correlated with the rhythmicity of the breathing. To heighten the effect of this suggestion, the operator can breathe deeply in unison with the subject.

If the eyes have not closed, one should say, "Your lids are beginning to close and, as they close, they are closing *tighter* and *tighter;* getting *very, very* heavy; *getting heavier* and *heavier*" (ideosensory activity). The more ideomotor and ideosensory activities the individual is involved in, the more readily will he enter into hypnosis— another illustration of misdirection of attention.

LIMPNESS OF LIMBS

While hypnosis is being induced, an arm or a leg can be lifted to see how it falls. If the limb falls slowly, it indicates voluntary control and that not too great a depth has been reached. The test for depth is made by gently clasping the wrist of the patient between the forefinger and the thumb and slowly lifting the arm. If the arm is allowed to fall, and it falls with a thud to the side or the lap, this denotes optimal relaxation and at least a medium stage of hypnosis.

To achieve heaviness of the lower extremities, one remarks: "Your toes are getting *very, very heavy.* If you really wish to go *deeper and deeper* relaxed, you can feel a numb, heavy, woodenlike feeling moving up, up, up to your feet, and then to your legs, and then to your thighs. Just imagine, if you will, that you are sitting on your legs, crosslegged. Your legs, beginning with your toes and feet, are really getting heavier and heavier. Your legs are *relaxing* more and more from your toes, up, up, up to your feet, up, up, up to your legs, and up, up, up to your thighs. And you can, if you *really* wish to go deeper, tell yourself that your legs from your toes to your thighs are really relaxed!"

LID CATALEPSY

Inability to open the eyes may occur in either light or deep stages. It indicates that the subject can become deeply relaxed. To induce lid catalepsy, one can remark (when the lids are closed), "Your lids are locked *tight, tighter* and *tighter.*" At the very second that the eyeballs roll upward, one can remark emphatically, "Your lids are closed tight. Roll your eyeballs up into the back of your head." This is the eyeball-set. The subject is unaware that it is difficult to open the lids with the eyeballs rolled upward. He attributes this to the operator's suggestions, and this is another instance of misdirection of attention. These nuances of induction technics are picked up only with experience.

This important maneuver can also be accomplished in this way: "At the count of 3, you will close your eyes, not because you have to, but because *you want* to close your eyes. Do you not? And *after* you close your eyes, if you *really* wish to go into a nice, deep, soothing state of relaxation, you will do so. You can now, if you wish, close your eyes tightly—1 . . . 2 . . . 3. . . . Now, roll your eyeballs up into the back of your head. Very good. You're doing fine." It is always a good idea to praise the patient's efforts because most subjects wonder if they are responding adequately to the suggestions.

At this point, the individual may attempt to open his eyes. If the suggestions have been given properly, he will not be able to open them. This difficulty is evidenced by the furrows on the brow. If there is any doubt, one says, "If you really wish to go deeper and deeper, just imagine that the harder you try to open your eyes, the less chance you have of opening the eyes." Motivation is being established each step of the way to coax the patient to go deeper by telling him that, if he really wishes to benefit from future suggestions, he must follow the preliminary suggestions. In other words, one must motivate the subject or use "bait" each step of the way. By the use of such measures, the desire and the responsibility for achieving hypnosis are put on the patient.

ARM CATALEPSY

Arm catalepsy is manifested by the extension of the arm straight up, with the fingers outstretched. The entire arm appears to be drawn up as far as it can stretch. A cataleptic limb resists counterpressure involuntarily and is usually indicative of a medium to deep hypnosis.

The individual is asked to raise his arm slowly. He is told that, if he wishes to relax still more, with each motion of the arm upward, he is to think and to imagine that "with each motion of my arm upward, I am going deeper and deeper relaxed." By means of this suggestion, the subject associates the idea of relaxation with the resultant ideomotor activity. The following remark is helpful: "With each motion that the arm moves upward, if you think, imagine, and feel that you are *really* going deeper and deeper relaxed, you will indeed go *deeper* and *deeper* relaxed." This makes full use of ideosensory and ideomotor activities and invariably results in arm catalepsy.

Catalepsy is characterized by an increased tonicity of all the muscles of the arm from the fingertips down to the wrist and from the elbow to the shoulder. The whole body can be made cataleptic. The muscles are balanced against each other, and certain muscles become very rigid *without the subject's knowledge.* The fingers remain for long intervals in any position in which they are placed. There is an associated waxy flexibility—*flexibilitas cerea.*

FOLLOWING POSTHYPNOTIC SUGGESTIONS

A good test for medium hypnosis involves telling the subject that, after being dehypnotized, he cannot count the even numbers from 1 to 10. Some subjects will remember that the suggestion was given and can still count, but without omitting the alternate numbers. This indicates that no more than a light stage has been reached. Ways to induce the patient to follow post-hypnotic suggestions are given in Chapter 2.

DEVELOPMENT OF GLOVE ANESTHESIA

Although an objective finding associated with the medium stages, glove anesthesia is often characteristic of deep hypnosis. The entire hand can be made insensitive in a circumscribed area from the fingertips to the wrist. This area of the hand will be numb, woodenlike, and "anesthetic." It will feel just as completely "numb" as if an anesthetic had been injected. As proof, a large-bore needle can be placed through the skin without a facial flinch or grimace on the part of the patient. The technic for its production also is described in the obstetric section in Chapter 33.

FOLLOWING POSITIVE AND NEGATIVE HALLUCINATIONS

When patients accept the validity of hallucinatory suggestions, it indicates that a profound hypnotic depth has been achieved. A negative hallucination, as described in Chapter 2, is produced by making suggestions that an object that is present cannot be perceived (through any of the senses). A positive hallucination is produced when a suggestion is made that something is there that is not present.

SOMNAMBULISM

In somnambulism, patients can walk, talk, and engage in all types of activities with their eyes open, while in a deep stage of hypnosis. Due to the spontaneous amnesia, patients seldom recall what occurred during somnambulism. Anesthe-sia, hyperesthesia, and dissociation are readily induced.

Somnambulism is one of the deepest stages of hypnosis, easily recognized by the immobility of the features, the staring eyes, the widened palpebral fissures, the flattened nasolabial folds, the masklike countenance, and the dreamy look. There is also an economy of motion or a time lag between the giving of a suggestion and the following of it. The speech is slow and slurred, and there is loss of the startle reflex. The individual is in a state of fixed attention, and there is also a concomitant absorption in his own physiologic processes.

Somnambulism occurs at the nonhypnotic level, too, as in the sleepwalker, or in the individual who spontaneously develops a fuguelike state, without having undergone a formalized hypnotic procedure. During somnambulism, the subject generally responds automatically to nearly all suggestions.

A large body of research indicates that the degree of hypnotizability remains relatively constant and that the various depths cannot be altered by different behavioral-situational factors.[14] Gur could not obtain deep degrees of hypnosis using operant conditioning.[3] He believes that hypnotizability is largely determined by factors other than situational variables.

Even though all children are not deeply hypnotizable, they are more so than adults.[5] This predisposition may, in part, be genetic. Morgan tested 140 pairs of twins and found a significant correlation to support a genetic component.[6] He also found that parent hypnotizability was also present, and posited that the child's hypnotizability was environmentally influenced, either through social learning or identification.

REFERENCES

1. Diamond, M.J.: Modification of hypnotizability: a review. Psychol. Bull., *81:* 180, 1974.
2. Eliseo, T.S.: The hypnotic induction profile and hypnotic susceptibility. Int. J. Clin. Exp. Hypn., *22:* 320, 1974.
3. Gur, R.C.: An attention-controlled operant procedure for enhancing hypnotic susceptibility. J. Abnorm. Psychol., *83:*644, 1974.

4. Hilgard, E.R.: Hypnotic Susceptibility. New York, Harcourt, Brace & World, 1965.

5. London, P., and Cooper, L.M.: Norms of hypnotic susceptibility in children. Dev. Psychol., *1:*113, 1969.

6. Morgan, A.H.: The heritability of hypnotic susceptibility in twins. J. Abnorm. Psychol., *82:*55, 1973.

7. Orne, M.T.: On the social psychology of the psychological experiment with particular reference to demand characteristics and their implications. Am. Psychol., *17:*776, 1962.

8. Spiegel, H.: An eye-roll test for hypnotization. Am. J. Clin. Exp. Hypn., *15:*25, 1972.

9. _____: The grade 5 syndrome: the highly hypnotizable person. Int. J. Clin. Exp. Hypn., *22:*303, 1974.

10. Wheeler, L., *et al.:* Eye-role and hypnotic susceptibility. Int. J. Clin. Exp. Hypn., *22:*327, 1974.

10

Hindrances to Hypnotic Induction

One of the most important hindrances to hypnotic induction is the therapist who has neurotic problems. He may talk too much about his abilities or his successful cases. The various problem areas in which the hypnotherapist may have unrecognized countertransference reactions to the patient have been identified.[2] Orne cautions against the indiscriminate use of hypnosis by therapists, and especially by those who enjoy the self-aggrandizement afforded by being able to hypnotize and who are not concerned with its therapeutic effectiveness. He points out other problem areas as well, such as looking upon hypnosis as a test of wills or utilizing hypnosis in the seduction of attractive patients.

The emotional status of the subject may also be a hindrance to hypnotic induction. It was mentioned previously that a skeptical or an analytic attitude toward hypnosis is not conducive to the establishment of hypnosis. In others, over-cooperation often may be a defense against being hypnotized. Some subjects are merely curious or are unable to concentrate because of the fear of being hypnotized. All these factors decrease rapport and the ability to be hypnotized. Trivia, such as the pipe or cigar which the doctor is smoking, may be objectionable. These and other factors can produce resentment and interfere with successful induction.

Apprehensive individuals also show other elements of conflict, such as excessive giggling or laughing, sweating and trembling, weeping or crying; these are indicative of profound tension and anxiety. Unless the operator is experienced, induction should not be continued in such emotionally disturbed individuals, because chagrin, a sense of failure, and other depressive reactions can be brought to the surface. Although induction of hypnosis depends, to a degree, on the strength of the interpersonal relationship, it must be emphasized again that it is a subjective and intensely *intrapersonal* problem for the subject.

Hypnotic response usually is facilitated by making the subject comfortable and eliminating all distracting influences; freedom from interruption helps to promote relaxation. However, many therapists do not have soundproof offices; some have consultation rooms that overlook busy intersections. Often certain types of distractions can be utilized to facilitate a hypnotic induction. The monotonous traffic hum or other sounds can be incorporated in the induction technic as follows: "With every car that goes by, you will go deeper and deeper relaxed." If a secretary's typing is audible, one says: "With each click, click, click of the machine, you will go *deeper and deeper relaxed.*"

An office near the author's was being remodeled, and the hammering was continual. Several patients were hypnotized by using this distraction, as follows: "With each *beat, beat, beat* of that hammer, you will go *deeper and deeper relaxed.* With each pounding of that hammer, you will feel that *you are being pounded into a deeper and deeper relaxed state.*" Thus the operator must use what he sees and see what to use! He must utilize anything and everything that the patient manifests to build up his confidence and reduce his resistance to hypnosis.

The room must not be too hot or too cold. Even a draft will be uncomfortable enough to interfere with the induction procedure. The posture of the subject is important. If he prefers a chair, his feet should be flat on the floor and his hands on his lap. The back of the head should be well supported, as neck strain becomes unbearable and interferes with induction. If the subject lies down, he should assume his usual position for sleeping. Some subjects much prefer to lie on their sides.

Noises such as those made by a chiming clock should be eliminated from the room. Naturally, all outside noises, such as loud talking, should be discouraged. Subjects with a severe cough or a head cold should not be induced for the first time, as they often are disturbed by sneezing, coughing, or the need to clear their throats. Others may have a postnasal drip, and this can be a distinct hindrance to induction. All disturbing situations should be under control before any type of induction procedure is attempted with any individual.

REFERENCES

1. Orne, M.T.: Can a hypnotized subject be compelled to carry out otherwise unacceptable behavior? Int. J. Clin. Exp. Hypn., *20:*107, 1972.
2. Stein, C.: Some old-fashioned uncovering techniques in psychotherapy. Am. J. Clin. Hypn., *9:*140, 1966.

11

Practical Hints for Hypnotic Induction

Before beginning an induction procedure, the operator should describe as simply as possible what he is going to do, what the subject is supposed to feel, and what is expected of him—this raises the expectancy level. The operator must stress that the more attention the subject directs to his suggestions, the more successful the induction will be. Needless to say, all misconceptions regarding surrender of the will, loss of consciousness, inability to "wake up," and revelation of secrets must be removed. Rapport can be increased by mentioning that only suggestions compatible with the subject's wishes will be followed. It is axiomatic that induction is more successful in the presence of good rapport and motivation,[2, 6, 7] particularly if relief is really desired for the presenting complaint.[5]

Confidence is essential, since most subjects, on the basis of subliminal cues, pick up the operator's insecurities and hesitancies. Therefore, the operator must approach every induction with the expectation of success. The experienced operator is readily recognized, and there cannot be even a modicum of success in the absence of the conviction of success on his part.[1]

Modern technics seldom require challenges. Unsophisticated operators generally use them and, when subjects defy the challenges, the operator "loses face." This can be avoided by not giving the patient the impression that the suggestion will be acted upon. Rather, he should be given a wide latitude of choices to follow.

All suggestions should be made on the basis of logic and common sense rather than by deception. Subjects should be controlled, not fooled.

Failures during induction often are due to ina-bility to understand the full meaning of the operator's suggestions. Hence, clarity and simplicity in the verbalizations are mandatory.

The operator must never appeal to the will, but must stress that *willingness* to cooperate and to use the imagination induces hypnosis. Maximal effects are achieved if the patient's own ideational activities are utilized to the utmost. This depends on the subject's involvement in as many ideomotor and ideosensory activities as possible. An individual must be kept so busy thinking about the heaviness of his lids, his toes, his legs, and his thighs, while counting backward with each breath he takes in order to relax, that he figures he might as well escape all this intense mental work and enter instead into hypnosis.

When an individual is deliberately switched from one type of ideomotor and ideosensory activity to another, the resultant misdirection is conducive to induction of hypnosis. This approach works on analytic or overly introspective subjects. It also is of distinct value for the over-curious and over-cooperative patient; these are resistances against being hypnotized. Changing the suggestions or switching to a different technic minimizes the resistance. That is one reason why all skillful hypnotherapists must be conversant with a variety of technics. These must be adapted to the needs and the personality of the subject and the operator.

The following ten practical hints have proved useful in achieving successful hypnotic induction:

1. Make sure that the subject is absolutely comfortable. When an individual is sitting in an uncomfortable position, he may interrupt the induction by saying, "My neck hurts. Can't you stop

talking until it relaxes?" This distraction is "noise," and such interference prevents the subject from focusing his attention on your suggestions. If your "message" does not come through, failure in the induction is inevitable. The room should be free from distracting influences, and, if this is impossible, one can use the distractions as reinforcement (see p. 58).

2. It is helpful to remark, "If you follow the simple ABC suggestions, such as looking at a spot above your eyes, counting to yourself, *imagining, thinking,* and *feeling* that your legs are getting heavier and heavier, you will follow other and more complex suggestions."

3. Another effective instruction is as follows: "The ability to achieve hypnosis is within you. I do not hynotize you. You do! I cannot force you into hypnosis. However, if you *really* wish to be hypnotized at your own pace and by your own effort, all you have to do is to follow the ABC suggestions. If you follow these in sequence, you should readily develop a nice, pleasant state of relaxation, provided that you really wish to reach the ultimate goal of very, very *deep* relaxation."

4. Monotonous, repetitive stressing of key words, such as "heavy" and "relaxed," increases relaxation.

5. Sequentially building up ideosensory and ideomotor responses first by simple suggestions, then by more complicated ones, helps to limit voluntary movements and is conducive to hypnotic relaxation. For instance: "With every breath (ideomotor) you take and every number you count backward (ideosensory), *you will go deeper and deeper relaxed."* (The author never uses the word "sleep" in his induction technics for reasons discussed on p. 36.)

6. Reinforcing a psychological suggestion (ideosensory) by a physiologic effect, such as lightly stroking a limb (ideomotor), facilitates acceptance of suggestions.

7. Suggestions must be given slowly, with sufficient time allowed for their assimilation and response.

8. Never tell the subject that he is difficult to induce. Using positive conditioning such as, "You did very well considering that it was the first time; you will do better the next time," facilitates future inductions.

9. Fearful subjects never should be traumatized by too early testing for anesthesia; be certain that this phenomenon has been obtained.

10. Never blame the patient for his inability to enter hypnosis, as this only mobilizes resistances. Fear over failure to enter hypnosis, and subsequent anxiety, can be allayed by a confident, sympathetic, and reassuring approach, rather than by a condemnatory one.

The skillful operator closely observes his subject's responses to use every voluntary or involuntary manifestation to reinforce the subject's expectancy and belief that hypnosis will be induced. Here, too, the dictum bears repeating: *One must use what he sees and see what to use.* If the subject's eyelids tremble involuntarily during the induction, it is helpful to remark: "Trembling of your lids is a good sign that you are becoming deeper relaxed." If the patient voluntarily swallows, say, "You just swallowed. That's good; it shows you are relaxing!" Every inconsequential movement, even the uncrossing of the patient's legs, *is a good sign.* Constant reassurances, if made convincingly, especially during the initial phases of induction, are helpful to unsophisticated subjects. These promote relaxation in subjects who doubt the effectiveness of the suggestions.

If a suggestion is not followed, the experienced operator should use another one so that the subject thinks that he is progressing nicely. If the subject refuses to close his lids, one can suggest: "The harder you try to keep your eyes open, the deeper relaxed you become." Always emphasize that better results are obtained if the sequence of the suggestions is not broken.

This author finds that it is helpful (whenever possible) to have a new patient observe an induction procedure on a well-conditioned subject—a few minutes of observation are worth hours of discussion. Through identification with patients who successfully enter hypnosis, the subject now knows what to expect; this helps to overcome resistances due to misconceptions. Most patients have little or no reluctance when asked, "Would you mind allowing me to demonstrate the technic of hypnotic induction? After my new patient has seen you induced, he will leave the room." Since this was the way he was introduced to hypnosis, the old patient does not mind showing the uninformed one how easy it is to attain hypnosis. He also feels a sense of achievement by collaborating. And it must be remembered that many individuals are retreating from the world because they feel inadequate, insecure, frustrated, and lonely. This gives the unhappy and disturbed individual the feeling that he is finally being noticed and is capable of helping a fellow sufferer. Furthermore, this saves valuable time that would be lost in talking to uninformed and skeptical patients.

It should be emphasized that successful induction depends upon the subject's needs and his expectations of the way in which the hypnotic relationship will fulfill them. Thus it is up to the operator to instill in the subject a positive attitude *that he will be hypnotized.*

Some hypnotherapists are not concerned about the hypnotic induction procedure. This author feels that the initial induction procedure is a means of initiating the foundation for successful psychotherapy. If the patient feels that the suggestions of the operator are effective, there is greater likelihood that the desired changes will occur. A deeper degree of hypnotizability is attained if the goals that the patient is seeking are interspersed and paired with the induction procedures. If, for example, the individual is desirous of breaking the smoking habit, he can be told, "If you really wish to stop smoking, you will feel your lids getting *heavier* and *heavier.*" As one's experience increases, these goal-oriented suggestions can be integrated into a sophisticated induction technic. Moreover, the all important motivational factors are increased when the subject realizes that specific changes did indeed occur! It has been noted that if suggestions are given in a more positive manner, the depth of the hypnosis increases.[3] This, too, is the author's experiences.

A novel concept has been advanced to convince the subject that he will be hypnotized.[4] The patient, while in hypnosis, is instructed to produce muscle fasciculations (i.e., tiny, tic-like movements or twitches of small muscles with larger muscles). When these occur without additional control, they provide credible evidence for subject and hypnotist that a bona fide hypnotic state has been achieved. This establishes an expectancy and favorable mind-set that facilitates acceptance of additional suggestions.

REFERENCES

1. Blumenthal, L.S.: Confidence—the keystone of the physician-patient relationship: how hypnosis is based on this confidence. Am. J. Clin. Hypn., *1:*169, 1959.
2. Estabrooks, G.H., and May, J.R.: Hypnosis in integrative motivation. Am. J. Clin. Hypn., *7:*346, 1965.
3. Hartland, J.: The general principles of suggestion. Am. J. Clin. Hypn., *9:*211, 1967
4. Overglade, D.C.: The production of fasciculations by suggestions. Am. J. Clin. Hypn., *19:*50, 1976.
5. Podolnick, E.E., and Field, P.B.: Emotional involvement, oral anxiety, and hypnosis. Int. J. Clin. Exp. Hypn., *18:*194, 1970.
6. Von Dedenroth, T.E.A.: Trance depths: An independent variable in therapeutic results. Am. J. Clin. Hypn., *4:*174, 1962.
7. Wagner, F.: A dynamic approach to the problem of hypnotic induction. J. Clin. Exp. Hypn., *4:*93, 1956.

12

Preinduction Talk

It is advisable in nearly every instance to have a preinduction discussion, especially with the skeptical or apprehensive patient. The set of remarks to follow should prove a helpful guide in achieving a favorable mind-set.

"Physicians, dentists, and clinical psychologists are becoming seriously interested in medical hypnosis, which is not a state of 'trance,' 'sleep,' or 'unconsciousness.' Rather, it is an exaggerated state of being awake! More simply, it is *selective attention* to my words, with *selective inattention* to distracting noise and everything else around you. Now, if you wish to relax, imagine and feel all of my suggestions. Do not try too hard. Just try to concentrate on my suggestions to the best of your ability. Don't press, just relax! Remember that if you do this you will relax, and then, the better you relax, the better you will concentrate on what I am saying. As a result, you will respond more effectively to those suggestions which are for your benefit.

"Medical hypnosis is different from entertainment hypnosis. The entertainer-hypnotist makes you think that he hypnotizes you because he is a powerful person. Physician-hypnotists know that hypnosis is effective because of the patient's desire and expectant attitude. The physician uses this tool with respect, realizing that every patient is an individual personality who should be treated with dignity both in and out of hypnosis.

"I really do not hypnotize you, and I have never hypnotized a single human being in my life! However, many individuals have entered into deep hypnosis *because they really wanted to do so.* I cannot make you close your eyes by suggesting eye closure unless you *wish* to close your eyes. I cannot make you count to yourself if you *do not wish* to count. And I have no way of knowing whether or not you are counting to yourself. I cannot make you lift your arm, if you do not care to lift it. Our relationship, therefore, is a cooperative one and *not* a mental 'tug of war.' For instance, you will raise your arm, not because you have to, but *because you want to.* Also, if I suggest that you drop your arm limp, relaxed, that is the way it will drop—limp." (The operator can lift the arm and let it slip from his fingers. If the arm is relaxed, he can remark, "That's just the way you will relax.")

"Hypnosis is a learning process and, of course, as in any other learning procedure, one begins with very simple suggestions. Isn't that logical? And if you follow the simple suggestions, then naturally you will follow complicated ones. May I repeat, you will not really be in a trance, even though we refer to it as such for want of a better term.

"Actually, we are being hypnotized continually as a part of everyday life. When I sit in a rowboat, fishing, the monotonous ripples relax me and time passes by rapidly. The first thing I am apt to say is, 'Have I been here for 6 hours?' It seemed like 3 hours, because a part of that time I was in reverie. Or how many times have you been in a theater, engrossed in a movie? As you looked at that screen, you became fixated on the movie and registered all types of emotions just as if it was real. You forgot who was sitting on your left and who was sitting on your right. Because you identified with the picture on the screen, you may even have forgotten what city you were in at the time. Next time you are at the theater, turn around and notice the 'glassy' stare in everyone's eyes. Of course, after it was over, you realized that what made you cry and laugh was not reality. Yet, for an hour and a half, you reacted to what you saw and heard as if it was real—yet it was an illusion. In other words, you were 'entranced,' but you did not think of this as hypnosis. However, is this any different from what happens when a stage hypnotist tells you that you will itch because 'ants' are crawling all over your body?

"Attainment of deep relaxation is easy, if you follow my suggestions. The capacity to be deeply relaxed is already present within you. I merely bring it to the surface, and only act as a guide. Is that clear?"

In addition, it should be emphasized, "You will do nothing to violate your moral code; you will not reveal information of a personal nature unless you wish to do so; you will be completely aware of what is said; and you will not act contrary to your wishes. Finally, every suggestion will be for your benefit."

With this preliminary talk, the operator can remove the apprehension, fear, anxiety, and tension that are naturally present in all individuals undergoing a hypnotic induction for the first time.

Crasilneck and Hall describe their "screening" interview as a prelude to hypnotic induction.[1] This excludes those for whom hypnosis is contraindicated and helps to assess the possible symbolic meanings of the presenting complaint. They also use the initial interview for ascertaining why the patient has presented himself for therapy: Did he decide to come in on his own? Is he sufficiently motivated to yield the symptom, or is the symptom utilized to manipulate others? The introduc-

tory talk also is utilized to assay the patient's frustration tolerance, to obtain a good psychiatric history, and to ascertain his prior experience with hypnosis. This establishes a positive mind-set, diminishes fears, and corrects misconceptions. The screening is also used to emphasize that medical hypnosis and the showmanship of the stage hypnotist are different entities.

Despite the advances of serious hypnotherapy, many patients continue to harbor preconceived notions fostered by the stage hypnotist. To dispel the idea of sleep, unconsciousness, or trance, I state: "A hypnotized person is super-alert." I ask: "Do you think you are awake?" Invariably, the patient says "Yes." I then say: "I am going to ask you two questions to see if you are really as awake as a hypnotized person would be. The first is: Would you mind telling me your father's first name?" Nine out of ten times the patient will give the first name. Then I ask: "*What* is your father's first name?" The patient nearly always repeats the first name. I go on to ask: "What was the first question?" Most patients reply, "You asked what is your father's first name," to which I reply: "See, you forgot the first question entirely and did not even hear it." This has a potent influence on the patient, as he now understands in no uncertain terms that a person in hypnosis hears better and as a result responds with a literalness or pinpoint specificity to words. He will not say after being hypnotized, "I heard everything you said."

REFERENCE

1. Crasilneck, H.B., and Hall, J.A.: Clinical Hypnosis. Principles and Applications. New York, Grune & Stratton, 1975.

13

Authoritarian or Direct
Technics of Hypnosis

In general, even though variants are used, the methods most commonly employed for inducing formal hypnosis are: (1) direct or authoritarian; (2) indirect or permissive, with or without arm levitation; (3) confusion technics; and (4) mechanical technics. All technics utilize ideosensory and ideomotor conditioning. The formalistic technics described in this chapter make full use of ritual and expectancy of success. Hence, the technic which the patient expects to be hypnotized by is the most satisfactory one. Since one of the principal features of hypnosis is a regression to a primitive level of mental functioning, it can be initiated best by relaxation.[2] Therefore, it is imperative to establish belief that relaxation will occur during the initial portion of the induction. The simplest and best method for establishing this belief is to induce the feeling of lid heaviness or catalepsy that results from eye fixation. All direct induction methods—and there are innumerable combinations—depend on eye fixation with resultant fatigue and relaxation of various muscle groups, first small, then large. The following technic, which the author prefers, is illustrative.

MOTIVATIONAL TECHNIC UTILIZING PROGRESSIVE RELAXATION

The verbalization for the motivational technic, in which progressive relaxation is induced, is as follows: "Now get as comfortable as possible. Rest your head on the back of the chair. Fix your eyes directly above your forehead. Keep looking directly above your hairline at one spot on the ceiling. Notice now that your eyes are getting very, very *heavy;* your *lids* are getting very, very, very *tired.* Your lids are getting *heavier* and *heavier,* and the heavier that your lids get now, the better you will relax your lids. The better you relax your eyelids, the better you will follow all subsequent suggestions." (Note the motivation for eye closure implied here.) "Your lids are getting *heavier* and *heavier.* They are getting *very, very tired.* Your lids are getting *very, very heavy.* Your eyelids are blinking. That is a good sign that the lids are getting *heavier* and *heavier.* Your lids are blinking a little more. That is right. If you really wish to go into a deeper state of relaxation, all you have to do is to let your lids close *tightly,* very tightly, at the count of 3. You will close your eyes not because you have to, but because you really wish to go deeper and deeper relaxed. One —your eyelids are getting *heavier* and *heavier.* Two—getting much heavier. Your lids are blinking still more." The following must be said as if it were all one sentence: "Three—now, *close your eyes tight* and let your eyeballs roll up into the back of your head. As your eyeballs roll up into the back of your head, notice how your lids are sticking tighter and tighter together. You feel the tightness, do you not?" (Subject nods head.) "This shows that it's really beginning to work. And your lids continue to stick tighter and tighter together. And as your eyeballs are rolled up toward your forehead for a few moments longer, you will go deeper and deeper relaxed. And if you *really* wish to go deeper, all you have to do is to slowly count backward from 100 to zero. With each number that you count backward [ideosensory activity] and with each breath that you take [ideomotor activity], you will go *deeper and deeper relaxed.*" (More motivation is provided to relax.) "And if you wish to go *deeper,* just think of a numb, heavy, woodenlike feeling that is beginning in your toes. Just imagine, in your 'mind's eye,' if you will, that you are sitting on your legs in tailor fashion or cross-legged; or think, if you will, of the heavy, numb feeling that you may have had when you fell asleep on your arm; or think of a numb, heavy, stiff feeling similar to that which occurs when your dentist injects procaine into your gums." (Such suggestions really tap the subject's experiential background.) "The numb, heavy feeling is moving *up, up, up* from your toes, up to your feet, up to your legs, up to your thighs. With every breath, you will go *deeper* and *deeper* relaxed. Now, it is *your* privilege to go into as deep a state of relaxation as you wish. It's really so easy to let yourself go *deeper* and *deeper relaxed.* You will do so only *after* you raise your arm straight toward the ceiling. So if you *really* wish to go deeper, at the count of 3, slowly raise either your right arm or your left arm, whichever arm you choose." (Motivation for raising of arm.) "It is very important to concentrate on the idea that as you raise your arm you say, think, and imagine with each motion of your arm upward, 'I am falling deeper and deeper relaxed.' So, at the count of 3, you will slowly raise either the right arm or the left arm. You can now decide, 'Which arm am I going to raise *slowly* straight toward the ceiling?'" (Arm begins to rise.) "1 . . . 2 . . . 3. . . . Now slowly raise your arm, slowly, just a half inch or so at a time. And with each movement of the arm upward, just think to yourself that 'I am going *deeper* and *deeper* relaxed.' And if you really wish to go deeper after your arm has reached a perpendicular position, you will notice that you will go into a nice, deep, pleasant state of relaxation. The stiffer your fingers become, and the stiffer your arm becomes from the wrist down to the elbow, the deeper relaxed you will get. You will now feel

yourself going deeper and deeper relaxed, and *you just can't wait* until your arm is stretched straight toward the ceiling. That's right, straight as an arrow, just as stiff and rigid as an iron bar! *After* your arm is raised straight toward the ceiling, you will go deeper and deeper relaxed!" (Motivation is provided for limb catalepsy.) "That's fine. Now straighten out your fingers *stiff, stiffer. Spread them apart! Stiff* and *rigid, stiff,* and *rigid.* And now, as I stroke the arm, if you really wish to go deeper, the arm becomes *stiffer* and *more rigid, stiffer* and *more rigid, stiffer* and *more rigid.* Now straighten out your arm, straighten out the fingers. That's right! Just say to yourself, 'I cannot bend my arm. My arm is *stiff* and *rigid.*' You are not asleep, unconscious, or in a trance, but are completely awake! Thus you will derive more benefit from my suggestions because they will 'sink' in more readily." (Thus far there is no need for challenges. These often can handicap the inexperienced operator because, if the subject succeeds in meeting the challenge, the rapport is broken.)

The technic is deepened as follows: "Now, if you really wish to go deeper, all you have to do is *slowly,* and I do mean *slowly,* allow your arm to fall a half inch or an inch at a time. At the count of 3, perhaps, you might say to yourself, 'I am going deeper and deeper relaxed with each motion of my arm downward. I will go *deeper* and *deeper* relaxed.' Now, at the count of 3, let your arm fall. 1 . . . 2 . . . 3. . . . And as your arm falls, you too will fall into a *deeper* and *deeper* state of relaxation. As your arm falls, you will fall *deeper* and *deeper* relaxed. And now, perhaps, you might be willing to give yourself a suggestion, providing you really wish to relax deeper, that the moment your arm or any portion of your hand touches any portion of your body, you will go *deeper* and *deeper relaxed* (more motivation is given). You might be willing to accept this suggestion as a cue that every muscle and every fiber in your body will relax completely. Every muscle will relax. You are going to relax completely. Now, as I lift your arm, it is just as *heavy* as lead. And when I drop your arm, you are going to drop *deeper and deeper relaxed.* Your eyelids will remain *tightly* closed and you will feel yourself going *deeper* and *deeper* into a nice, pleasant, soothing state of relaxation. As I lift your arm, you are going to *relax* still *deeper.*" When the arm is slowly lifted, it is gently clasped at the wrist by the thumb and the forefinger of the operator. He lifts the arm gently and remarks: "As I lift your arm, it is getting *heavier* and *heavier.* It is going to get *heavier* and *heavier,* and it is going to slip out of my grasp. When it drops to your thigh, it will drop with a resounding *thud,* just like a towel heavy with water, and then you will drop even *deeper relaxed.* At the count of 3, I will drop your arm. 1 . . . 2 . . . 3 . . . deeper, way down!" Here, too, a psychological suggestion reinforces a physiologic effect. Some subjects drop the arm slowly. This indicates resistance. The subject may be only in a hypnoidal state—a precursor to actual hypnosis. If catalepsy has been obtained or if there is a waxy flexibility of the fingers *(flexibilitas cerea),* a somnambulistic state may have been achieved. In this state, subjects are very alert. They characteristically respond with pinpoint precision or literalness.

This technic continually motivates the subject. You are in reality, always in a "one-up position," but he seldom realizes this fact. The subject is always given an opportunity to cooperate, and, if he agrees to follow the suggestions, he will go deeper. The lid closure was our primary objective. Because some motivation was used every step of the way, the subject had to follow the suggestions. When I said, "If you really wish to go deeper, you will close your eyes," I was really saying, "If you don't want to cooperate, you don't have to close your eyes, and you won't enter into hypnosis." I generally preface my remarks by stating emphatically, "This is not a case of 'mind over matter.' It is your wish to enter into hypnosis, not mine. Now, if you wish to go still deeper, it's up to you."

TECHNIC FOR POSTHYPNOTIC SUGGESTIONS

If you wish to give your subject posthypnotic suggestions, the following remarks are conducive to their retention: "Everything that you wish to remember will be retained with remarkable ease.

It will *all* be remembered as if it has been indelibly etched on your mind; just as if a carbon copy had been made and imprinted on your mind! Because you are going to store all this information, you will be able to recall it more readily. Perhaps you won't remember all of it today or tomorrow, but you certainly will during the next week, month, or year. None of it ever will be forgotten! You are going to retain more than you would ordinarily.

"At this time, may I give you a posthypnotic suggestion that you will always remember? At any time that you wish to have hypnosis induced, and remember it will occur only with your permission, I shall touch you on the *right* shoulder. This will be a cue for you to drop promptly into a deep state of relaxation. Simultaneously, you will close your eyes, let your eyeballs roll up into the back of your head, and experience this exact state of complete muscular relaxation. I will repeat the suggestion. At any time in the future that I touch you on your right shoulder, you will relax completely, and this will occur only if and when you wish to relax. I can't induce hypnosis unless you desire it. Remember, a touch on your *right* shoulder will be a prearranged signal to close your eyes, let your eyeballs roll up into the back of your head, and promptly fall into a deep state of relaxation. Remember, you will not go to sleep, be unconscious, or even be in a trance. Also, you will hear everything, actually more than usual. A touch on the *left* shoulder will be the signal for dehypnotization. You will open your eyes, feel wonderful, very refreshed, relaxed and aware of everything that happened." It is very important to give suggestions conductive to the patient's well-being. Many subjects develop a headache as a result of the intense mental concentration.

Before bringing a subject out of hypnosis, always compliment him on how well he cooperated and then say: "Now, I am going to touch you on the *left* shoulder. You feel fine! You will open your eyes, feeling *perfectly wonderful.* Open your eyes wide. That's right."

Also, always compliment the subject after the hypnosis is terminated: "Thank you for being such a wonderful subject." Expressing your gratitude at both the hypnotic and the nonhypnotic level motivates the subject for the next session.

EYE FIXATION TECHNIC WITH SLEEP SUGGESTIONS

The eye fixation technic is a favorite of many operators who use the words "sleep" or "asleep." The following sequential instructions should be given:

1. "In gazing at that spot you will *relax quickly* and *deeply.*" (Pause 10 seconds.)

2. "Your legs will grow *heavy—very heavy.*" (Pause 10 seconds.)

3. "Your arms will grow *heavy—very heavy.*" (Pause 10 seconds.)

4. "Your entire body will grow *heavy—very heavy.*" (Pause 10 seconds.)

5. "And now your legs are *heavy,* your arms are *heavy,* and your entire body is *heavy.* You are deeply relaxed. You are relaxing *more* and *more* all the time." (Pause 10 seconds.)

6. "You are so *deeply* relaxed that your eyes are now growing *heavy,* and they are becoming *tired,* very *tired.* You will want to close your eyes. As you close your eyes, you will enjoy perfect relaxation." (Pause 10 seconds.) It is very important at this point, or at any point previous to this, to note and observe carefully the movement and the condition of the patient's eyes. Failure to do this may result in "loss of patient." (If the patient's eyes close at this time, or at any time previous to this, skip step 7 and proceed with step 8. **This is very important.**)

7. "Your eyes are growing *heavier* all the time. They are closing—closing—closing. They are so *very heavy* and *tired,* you cannot keep them open—closing—closing—closing." At this point the eyes will close in about 70 per cent of the subjects. If the eyes do not close, repeat these words for another minute or two. Then, if they still have not closed, direct the patient to close them by saying, "Close your eyes, please," which he will do presently. In rare instances, the patient may already be in a hypnotic trance at this point, and the operator should gently place a finger on each eyelid to close his eyes. Regardless of whether the eyes close spontaneously as suggested, or as instructed, it is important to proceed precisely at the moment that the eyes close, quickly and emphatically, without a second's delay.

8. "*Deep, deep asleep.*" This phrase is uttered in a decisive and emphatic voice, forcefully and yet not too loudly, instead of in the previous lulling and soothing tone. Repeat the phrase "deep, deep, asleep" 4 or 5 times every 2 or 3 seconds. This will tend to narrow down consciousness to only one idea, namely, *"deep, deep, asleep"*—as in fact the patient will be at this point in one of the several stages of hypnosis.

HANDCLASP TECHNIC

In performing the handclasp technic, ask the subject to sit in a comfortable position and proceed with the following instructions: "Close your eyes. Now clasp your hands together and make them as tight as you can." There is constant repetition to utilize sensory-imagery conditioning, as follows: "Think to yourself, 'I should like to make my hands stick tightly together.'" This is interspersed with the remarks: "Keep your eyes closed until I ask you to open them. Imagine how nice it would be to develop self-relaxation." When the hands tighten, the operator adds, "Now you feel the pressure in your fingers as your hands tighten and *tighten* still more!" The operator watches the hands; if they do not tighten, he waits, as this is indicative of resistance. If the hands are tightly stuck together, he continues: "Your fingertips are getting numb, very numb! Your hands are sticking tighter and tighter together, and you feel a pleasant sensation in your thumbs as they press down tightly upon one another." When the hands appear to be tightening from pressure, he proceeds: "Your hands are now so tightly stuck together that you cannot tell your left fingers from your right. Your hands feel as if they are a solid piece of wood. They are now sticking together without any effort. You have no desire to take them apart. *You don't want to take your hands apart.*" From here on, if the patient does not separate his hands, he is deepened in the usual manner.

THE COIN TECHNIC WITH EYES CLOSED

The coin technic is performed upon a subject with eyes closed in the following manner: "If you will follow my instructions exactly as I give them to you, you will go into a deep, deep state of relaxation. Take this coin in the palm of your hand and close your eyes tightly together. Now clasp your fingers tightly together so that the coin will not fall out of your fist. Place your arm in front of you. Keep your fingers tightly closed on the coin until I tell you to drop it.

"Notice, now, how the coin is grasped tightly between your fingers. I am going to count from 1 to 10. As you feel the fingers around the coin, you will notice your fingers relaxing. They will relax and open so that the coin will fall to the floor at the count of 10.

"Now close your eyes. Your eyes are closed very tight, tighter and tighter. When the coin drops to the floor at the count of 10, you will straighten out your hand and arm. The sound of the coin hitting the floor will seal your eyes still tighter. 1. Your fingers are opening. Your fingers are relaxing, and your eyes are tighter and tighter. 2. Your fingers are opening a little more, and your eyes are closing tighter and tighter. Your eyes are stuck so tightly together, it feels as if they are glued shut. And the tighter they stick together, the more comfortable and relaxed you will go. 3. You are doing fine. Your fingers are opening a little more and I notice that one of your fingers is beginning to open still more. That is fine. First one and then another. 4. All the fingers are beginning to open, just a little more, as you go deeper and deeper relaxed. 5. With each breath you take, your fingers are opening a little more. Remember that when the coin hits the floor, that will be the signal that your eyes will be closed tightly together. 6. Also remember that when the coin hits the floor, you will straighten out your fingers, stiff and rigid. Your right arm will get stiff and rigid from the fingers to the wrist, from the elbow to the shoulder. 7. Your fingers are opening still more, and the coin is about to drop to the floor. 8. Just a little more. You are going deeper and deeper relaxed. With every breath you take, you will go deeper and

deeper relaxed. 9. Remember that when the coin hits the floor, your right arm will become just as rigid as an iron bar, and your eyes will be stuck tightly together. 10. Open your fingers. Your arm is as stiff as an iron bar from your fingers up to your wrist to your shoulders." At this point, a deft stroking of the arm from the fingers up to the shoulder is sufficient to induce catalepsy.

This aspect of the coin technic can be made part of a deepening procedure, as follows: "At the count of 3, you will let your arm fall, and with each inch that it falls, you will fall deeper and deeper relaxed. 1 . . . 2 . . . 3. . . . Your arm is falling—slowly. That's right. And as your arm falls, you fall deeper and deeper relaxed. And when your arm returns to your lap, every muscle, every fiber in your body will be completely relaxed." (Patient's arm falls to his lap.) "I am going to pick it up and, as I let it fall, you will fall even deeper relaxed."

HANDLING RESISTANCE IN THE COIN TECHNIC

If resistance is encountered, the following instructions to the subject may be helpful: "As your arm remains outstretched, just tell yourself, 'I can't bend my arm to the right and I can't bend it to the left. I can't raise it and I can't drop it.' It just remains out there as you go deeper and deeper relaxed. Now it seems like it's lifting, lifting, higher and higher. And as it keeps lifting, the palm of your hand gets lighter and lighter. That's right." (The arm remains in the same position.) "Remember, if your arm falls, you will fall deeper and deeper relaxed." (The patient does not realize that the arm is bound to fall eventually.)

If resistance is still present, the following is helpful: Rapidly suggest different and contradictory sensory changes—that the right arm is getting lighter, the left arm is getting heavier, the right arm is getting heavier, the left arm is getting lighter. Similar suggestions referable to the lower limbs are made, interspersed with suggestions that the subject can move the arm upward if he wishes to remain "awake," or move it downward if he wishes to go deeper, or that one arm will spontaneously lift if his "subconscious" wishes to resist, or will fall if he wishes to go deeper. In addition, attention is called to the pressure produced by the shoes or by other objects such as a wrist watch, a ring or a tight collar. I have the subject count backward but I instruct him to use only even numbers from 100 to 70 and odd numbers from 75 to 45. Finally, from sheer mental exhaustion or in desperation, the subject "escapes" from the myriad suggestions and accepts the suggestions to be hypnotized.

STARE TECHNIC WITH SLEEP SUGGESTIONS

Many physicians object to using the direct stare—looking directly into the eyes of the subject—because it is associated with the stage performer who makes full use of dominance, submission, and seductiveness. In our culture, the "evil eye" is taboo. However, it often is effective when all other methods fail.[3] It is simply ridiculous to outlaw this method merely because of irrational prejudice. The stage technic with eye stare is a very powerful authoritarian technic which is effective on those who expect to be hypnotized by such a method. Staring has been shown to fix attention by controlling sensory input.[3]

The stare technic generally involves the following instructions: "Look into my eyes, and do not take your eyes off mine. . . . Keep looking at me. Let yourself go. That's right, look at me. Think of nothing but sleep. Your eyes are beginning to feel *heavy;* your eyes are closing . . . closing . . . closing. Close your eyes!" At this point the patient's eyes will close if they haven't already done so. (It is important that the operator does not return his gaze to the patient's eyes but fixes his gaze at the base of the nose between the eyes. The patient will not know the difference.) Then the operator continues: "Your eyes are now closed; they are heavy; you are going to sleep. Your arms are heavy, your legs are heavy, your entire body is heavy. You are going deeper into sleep all the time." The operator continues now with a deepening procedure. If the patient does not close his eyes at the point mentioned previously, the operator continues: "Your eyes are growing heavier all the time. Your vision is getting more and more blurry. You will go to sleep; you cannot do otherwise. You cannot feel anything; your body is growing heavy and numb."

And then he adds, in a commanding tone, *"Sleep, deep sleep."* This usually turns the balance, and the eyes close; the patient goes into a hypnotic state. If, on the other hand, the patient does not shut his eyes, it may be because of rigid fixation. The operator slowly closes the patient's eyes and continues with suggestions of sleep and heaviness. The operator removes his fingers from the patient's eyes after a minute or so and then makes his test for catalepsy.

REPETITIVE TECHNIC FOR HANDLING THE RESISTANT PATIENT

Meares has described an excellent technic for dealing with resistance in direct induction procedures.[4] The patient who resists pulls his arm backward when a forward movement is suggested. He is asked to close his eyes and move his arms to and fro, with the elbow supported on a table or couch. This is maintained until a rhythmic motion is well established. There is a gradual withdrawal of contact after the arm movements become automatic. The subject is then asked to open his eyes and to try to stop the repetitive movement. At the same time, the suggestion, "Your arm goes to and fro, to and fro," is kept up, only now the suggestion is really synchronized with the movements, whereas at first it was at variance with the movements of the arm.

There are several variations of this technic, such as, "Your arm is stiff as a board as it goes round and round, round and round."

These technics illustrate an interesting point, namely, that the resistant patient is resistant only to the second idea if two different ideas are suggested simultaneously. The first idea is uncritically accepted because the subject is thrown off guard by the second idea. In this variation of the method of repetitive movement, the first idea is the rigidity of the arm. The second idea is the movement of the arm. For a while many patients resist the suggestion of movement, but the fact that they have accepted the suggestion of rigidity of the arm means that they are well on the way to satisfactory hypnosis. Others resist if highly charged emotional material is elicited.[1]

REFERENCES

1. Gravitz, M.A.: Psychodynamics of resistance to hypnotic induction. Psychother. Theory Res. Practice, *8:*185, 1971.
2. Kroger, W.S.: Techniques of hypnosis. J.A.M.A., *172:*675, 1960.
3. MacHovec, F.J.: The evil eye: superstition or hypnotic phenomenon? Am. J. Clin. Hypn., *19:*74, 1976.
4. Meares, A.: A System of Medical Hypnosis. Philadelphia, W.B. Saunders, 1960.

14
Permissive or Indirect Technics

In this chapter, arm levitation and miscellaneous technics of various types are described. These may be used in conjunction with sensory imagery or picture visualization technics. The levitation technics are best adapted to emotionally disturbed individuals who require more permissive approaches. As was mentioned earlier, the psychoneurotic has resistances to yielding his symptoms and therefore is often refractory to an authoritarian approach.

All levitation technics make use of the subject's ideomotor and sensory activities. The author's technic differs from those herein described[2, 14, 16] in that the patient is motivated each step of the way. Moreover, the term "sleep" is never employed. The subject never realizes that he is being controlled at all times by carefully graded suggestions to deepen slowly the hypnotic state.

Levitation technics are initially time-consuming, but any posthypnotic suggestion or cue to reinduce hypnosis obviates the need for reinduction. Glove anesthesia is induced more readily than states requiring authoritarian technics. Watkins' progressive anesthesia technic, when combined with arm levitation, is excellent for those patients who for some reason must have anesthesia.[14]

THE ARM LEVITATION TECHNIC

The advantages of the author's modification of this technic are that the subject is not rushed, and he is convinced that the responses result from the operator's suggestions. It is time-consuming and frequently taxes the patience of the operator.

The verbalization is as follows: "Would you mind placing your hands on your thighs, and, if you please, just look down at your fingers, at your hands as they rest lightly on your knees. Perhaps you wouldn't mind pressing down real *hard;* if you will, just *press down hard,* just as *hard* as you *can,* as if you are pushing your knees and feet through the floor. Of course, this is impossible! Perhaps you can press a little harder and still harder. And, as you press harder and harder, become aware, if you will, that you are building up a great amount of tension in your fingers. Notice the tension building up in your fingers as you *press harder* and *harder.* Just keep pressing *harder* and *harder.* And, perhaps, you can feel an increased sensitivity in your fingertips. And notice, if you will, please, the texture of the cloth of your trousers. And maybe, as you keep pressing, you will notice the warmth of your body as it comes through the cloth of your trousers. And keep pressing, *harder* and *harder.* And, of course, you know that the opposite of the tension that you are building in your fingers is relaxation. So, any time that you might wish to relax, it is really so simple; all you have to do is just close your eyes and visualize, if you will, that one of the fingers on either the left hand or the right hand is getting lighter than all the others. Remember, the opposite of tension is relaxation; I am sure that you will agree to that. And if you *really* want to relax, one of the fingers on *either* the *left* hand or the *right* hand is getting lighter than all the others. And as it gets lighter than all the others, perhaps one of the fingers will begin to lift up in the air. And one of the fingers will begin to move on either the left hand or the right hand. Which finger will it be? Maybe it will be the little finger of the left hand, or perhaps it will be the ring finger of the right hand. It might even be the forefinger of the left hand. And I notice the forefinger of the right hand is beginning to lift. And it's *lifting, lifting, lifting.* And as it gets lighter than all of the other fingers, the other fingers of that hand can begin to lift. And very soon, if you wish, you are going to notice the most wonderful sensation—a floating, soothing sensation. The right hand is lifting in the direction of your face. Lifting, lifting, lifting. And perhaps you might be willing to give yourself the suggestions that 'With each motion that my arm lifts upward, I will go deeper and deeper relaxed; my arm is lifting not because it has to, but because it wants to. I will soon reach a *deep* state, a *deep state of relaxation.'* The right hand is now lifting, lifting, lifting, lifting, lifting! And perhaps you can visualize a balloon tied around your wrist, and now another balloon, three, four balloons are tugging at your wrist. And then you can visualize still another balloon. A red balloon, a blue balloon, and the arm is now *lifting, lifting, lifting, lifting!* And as soon as it touches your face, you might be willing to give yourself a suggestion that the moment any portion of your hand touches any portion of your face, that will be a signal, perhaps, for you to be willing to drop into an *even deeper* state of relaxation. As your arm lifts, you are going *deeper* and *deeper relaxed.* That's fine. You are doing just fine. You are really willing to learn, are you not? Hypnosis is a learning process. And if you learn these simple, elementary ABC suggestions, then you can learn other suggestions that are so necessary for complete mental and physical relaxation. And as the hand draws closer and closer to the face, just think of that wonderful feeling of relaxation that is going to come over your body." (The subject touches his nose with the back of his palm; the arm drops limply into his lap as his head falls forward.) "You drop even deeper relaxed, way down, deeper and deeper . . . complete relaxation. That's right. And now I am going to lift this arm and you will go even *deeper* and *deeper.* And if you wish to go really deeper, just let it *plop* right in your lap with a resounding thud. Now I will let it go at the count of 3. Can't wait. 1 . . . 2 . . . 3 . . . plop." (His arm drops to his lap.) "That's fine. Now, as long as your arms

and hands remain in that position, you will go deeper and deeper relaxed. And as I raise your arm, it will get stiff and rigid." (Catalepsy is induced by a deft stroke.) *"Stiff* and rigid; your arm is just as *stiff* and *rigid* as a bar of steel. Now it's *rigid.* And now, if you wish to go deeper, you may go still deeper by letting your arm drop even more relaxed into your lap. That's fine."

MODIFIED ARM LEVITATION

Christenson uses a levitation technic with *sleep suggestions.*[2] He informs the subject that relaxation will deepen with each number he counts. Simultaneously, the more relaxed he becomes, the more his hand will lift; the degree of lifting will determine the degree of relaxation. The lifting, the relaxing, and the counting are all cleverly tied in, one with the other, and their interdependence is stressed. He cues the touching of the hand to the face to complete hypnotic relaxation. He also uses sleep suggestions. Wolberg's modification of Christenson's technic uses a more permissive approach.[16]

HANDLING OF RESISTANCE IN LEVITATION TECHNICS

It bears reemphasis that when resistance is encountered, one should switch technics. If what started to be a permissive technic, with arm levitation, seems not to be successful, say, "That's fine. You have done your part very well. Now you will raise your arm directly overhead." Few patients will realize that the switch has been made. Because the ultimate goal is limb catalepsy, it is important to get the arm raised to the position where this phenomenon can be induced quickly. Expectation leads to hypnosis and, if that expectation is not instantaneously fulfilled, both the operator and the subject will be concerned. The time to switch to a different technic is before the patient senses that failure is inevitable. Thus the rapport is maintained.

Enlightened patients understand that a rather high order of concentration is necessary to achieve hypnosis and that it also requires more than a moderate degree of intelligence. Thus, if the operator emphasizes this point at some time during the induction, it becomes quite apparent to the subject that he is not utilizing his concentration to its fullest capacity. Some resistant patients may say, in the midst of an arm levitation induction, "I guess I'm no good, Doctor. My arm wouldn't go up. I just don't have what it takes." Here, reassurance that the subject is intelligent and can concentrate is helpful. The operator can remark, "Perhaps you are trying too hard; I am sure that if you try again you will relax."

When a subject's arm does not levitate, the operator can remark, "And as your arm remains comfortably in your lap, you can feel yourself going *deeper* and *deeper* relaxed with every breath you take. *Deeper* and *deeper* relaxed. Now I will raise your arm straight upward, and as it moves upward, you will become more relaxed." (The arm is moved slowly to an upright position.) "Now, straighten the fingers, spread them apart. That's right. Spread them apart. That's fine. And now the entire right arm will continue to get *stiff* and *rigid!* Like a bar of steel! *Stiff* and *rigid.* Like a bar of steel. *Stiffer* and more *rigid. Straighten* out the fingers. *Stiff* and *rigid.*" (The arm is lightly stroked from the fingertips down to the shoulder.) "And now, if you wish to go deeper, just say to yourself, 'I can't make a fist,' and the more you really believe that you can't make a fist, the *deeper* relaxed you will go. And I notice that now you swallowed. That is a very good sign that you will reach a *deep, deep* state of relaxation. Go *deeper* and *deeper.* Real deep. Deeper and deeper. Way down. *Deeper and deeper* relaxed. That's right. Just close your eyes and let your eyeballs roll up into the back of your head."

Resistance is often manifested by the subject's raising his arm too quickly. Here again, the operator must not be disturbed but, rather, should remark, "That's right. Your hand has reached your face. Now you can slowly allow your arm to fall toward your lap and, as it falls, you will go deeper and deeper. . . . "

Frequently, subjects do not close their eyes but keep them in a fixed and staring position. These individuals are in a somnambulistic state. The sophisticated hypnotherapist recognizes this immediately and proceeds with appropriate posthypnotic suggestions.

Another technic for handling resistance in the negatively suggestible subject is as follows:

"This hand is going to get increasingly light, but I am going to put my hand on it and hold your hand down. I will not allow your hand to come up. It keeps on getting lighter and lighter, but I force it down. You can sense the lightness as it is pushing up against my hand. I am in great difficulty trying to hold it down. In fact, it seems ultimately as if it would force my hand up in spite of my efforts to hold it down. You will prevail over me. I cannot keep your hand from rising into the air, and I cannot prevent you from *relaxing.* You go into a *very deep relaxed* state in spite of my efforts to stop you."[15] In this case the motivation to oppose the doctor is used in the actual hypnotic induction.

Often the arm may lift halfway and remain in a horizontal position. If this should happen, the following suggestions are valuable: "Your arm is now extended straight in front of you. You can move it upward, downward, or you can move it from side to side." This confuses most individuals; they do not realize that there is no other direction in which the arm can move. If they still resist, invariably they will move the arm in one direction: up, down, or sideward. If so, quickly remark, "That's right, you are moving it in the right direction, just as I suggested. Now all you have to do is to move it upward [if that is the direction] until it is extended straight toward the ceiling." If the arm moves downward, similar suggestions are made, ending with, "Return it to your lap or side" (where it inevitably must go).

COMBINATIONS OF TECHNICS

The sensory-imagery technics, with or without arm levitation, are excellent for the establishment of deeper hypnotic states. The principle of nearly all of them is to involve the subject in as many ideosensory activities as possible. Through this type of misdirection of attention, the suggestions of the operator are accepted more readily.

The technics of eye opening and closing, progressive relaxation, and tension and relaxation stress ideomotor activity, although ideosensory involvement is an essential feature of all these methods. Most technics of this type are ideal for the induction of children and also for handling the refractory individuals who state, "I doubt if you can hypnotize me because I have a strong mind." "Playing a game" appeals to the former group, and the latter group is caught "off guard." Nearly all of the technics can be used in various combinations, and the verbalization described can be altered to fit the needs of the subject and the operator.

The technics for tension and relaxation, hyperventilation, and catalepsy are dependent largely on physiologic effects to reinforce the psychological suggestions (the law of dominant effect).

The disguised technics are too numerous to mention. Many methods, such as transcendental meditation, the relaxation response, progressive relaxation, psychoprophylactic relaxation and natural childbirth, are disguised technics employing "waking hypnosis" or the alterations of awareness characteristic of hypnoidal states.

VISUAL IMAGERY TECHNICS

THE BLACKBOARD TECHNIC

The blackboard technic appeals primarily to the subject's imagination and is an excellent method for developing amnesia.[12] The individual is asked to see how well he can concentrate on all instructions. The following is the verbalization:

"Just visualize in your 'mind's eye' a blackboard in one of your high school classrooms. You are beginning to see it, are you not? When you do, nod your head to indicate that you see the blackboard." (The subject nods his head.) "Now you may imagine that you are walking over to the blackboard. You are picking up a piece of chalk. Write the numbers from 1 to 10. You will see each number on the blackboard. After you have done this, you will let me know by nodding your head." (The subject nods his head.) "Now, erase all of the even numbers. You see a smudge between each of the odd numbers. You do see it, do you not? All of the even numbers from 1 to 10 are now dropping out of your mind, are they not? You can see only the odd numbers, can you not?" (The patient nods his head, indicating that he is responding.) "You will remember now that when you are requested to count you will *not* be able to remember any even numbers. You are going *deeper* and *deeper relaxed. Deeper* and *deeper relaxed* with every breath you take, and with

each breath that you take, all the even numbers are dropping out of your mind. And now, since all the even numbers have dropped out of your mind, you may find it difficult to count out loud." (If the patient does not block, he may or may not be hypnotized. If he blocks but has not forgotten the even numbers, he may be in a light hypnotic state. Of course, if he is not able to remember the even numbers and merely counts "1, 3, 5, 7, 9," then you can be fairly certain that he is in a deep state of hypnosis and is capable of developing posthypnotic amnesia as well as of following other suggestions.)

THE TELEVISION TECHNIC

The television technic is a form of the picture-visualization technic that is excellent for the induction of children. They close their eyes and visualize a favorite television program. As soon as they say they have "turned on the TV" and are seeing the scenes changing, the operator remarks:

"You will pay more and more attention to the television screen. Keep looking at it. As you are looking at it, you will notice that your right arm will begin to lift up into the air by itself. That's right. It is beginning to lift. It is lifting, lifting, lifting. Higher and higher. Just keep looking at the picture. Your arm is lifting still higher. Listen to everything that is said and, as you keep looking at the screen, you are getting *very, very tired.* And now your arm is raised straight toward the ceiling. If you wish, you can go deeper relaxed. Just say to yourself, think to yourself, 'My arm is getting *stiffer* and *stiffer.* Rigid!' And, if you wish to go *deeper,* slowly allow your arm to fall, and as it falls, you too will go deeper and deeper." (The same deepening procedure is used as in the blackboard technic.)

THE EYE OPENING AND CLOSING TECHNIC

In performing the technic of eye opening and closing, the following verbalization is used:

"Would you mind fixing your eyes on a spot directly above your forehead? Keep looking at a spot directly above your forehead. As you keep looking at that spot, perhaps you would not mind opening and closing your eyes." (The eyes open and close.) "That is right. The more you open and close your eyes, the more you will be able to relax." When the lids begin to droop, the operator suggests: "Your lids are very tired now. If you keep them closed, you will relax. You may now let your eyeballs roll up into the back of your head and, as your eyeballs remain in this position for a few seconds, notice how your lids are sticking tighter and tighter together." If the subject is unable to open his eyes, this indicates success—manifested by furrowing of the brows and trembling of the lids. The lid catalepsy can be made more complete by saying, "If you really wish to go deeper and deeper relaxed, you will notice that your lids are *really* stuck tightly together. Your eyes can only be opened with difficulty." This does not leave the operator "out on a limb" and, in fact, he has not challenged the subject. The rest of the verbalization follows a standardized direct technic.

For resistant individuals who keep their eyes open, I rmark: "You see, your eyes remain open; you *cannot close your eyes.* If you do close your eyes, you will certainly go deeper and deeper relaxed." Most subjects do not realize that eventually they must close their eyes; when this occurs, they attribute it to hypnosis instead of fatigue of the eyelids.

THE PROGRESSIVE RELAXATION TECHNIC UTILIZING THE HANDCLASP AND THE POSTURAL SWAY

When handclasp and postural sway methods are to be employed in the performance of the progressive relaxation technic, the subject is asked to close his eyes tightly; a light touch on the lids is usually sufficient to give the impression that they are sealed tight, especially if the operator remarks, simultaneously, "Your eyes are locked tight, glued together, tightly, very tight." The operator now takes the subject's hands and clasps them together, saying, "If you really wish to go deeper relaxed, you will think, 'I cannot open my eyes and I cannot unclasp my hands no matter how hard I try.' " Simultaneously, he is gently swayed around and around, and it is suggested, "If you really wish to go still deeper, just imagine that you are on a boat, and the waves are

rocking you deeper and deeper relaxed." The operator can easily discern the degree of relaxation by the ease with which the subject sways. At this point, he remarks, "Your body is relaxing still more and you feel as if you could go into a deep, deep sleeplike state, almost like nighttime sleep. If I ask you to open your eyes, you will see everything that I suggest nothing else." This is accomplished by slipping from ideomotor to ideosensory suggestions. Since belief is invoked with each suggestion, as the result of conviction, sensory reality becomes unreality. Because he is convinced that the relaxation, the eye closure, and the inability to open the fingers were due to the operator's suggestions, the subject will readily develop sensory hallucinations. This is a good technic for developing somnambulists.

THE HYPERVENTILATION TECHNIC

In the hyperventilation technic, the subject is asked to close his eyes. He can be rocked to and fro as in the postural sway technic, with his eyes tightly closed. The following verbalization is used:

"Your eyes are tightly closed together. Take a deep breath and hold it. Hold it as long as you can. Take another deep breath and hold it! Now inhale deeply. Let all the air out of your lungs. Do it again. That is right. With each deep breath you take, you will notice that your head will get lighter and lighter. You are getting very light-headed. The longer you hold your breath, the more light-headed you get." This is kept up, together with suggestions that he will continually go deeper and deeper as he gets more and more light-headed. Naturally, the subject is not aware that he is getting light-headed because of the hyperventilation. He thinks that all the sensations are due to the operator's suggestions.

Light to medium hypnosis usually appears, even if no other suggestions are given. As long as the regular and deep breathing is maintained, the subject will remain relaxed and hypersuggestible. The operator must be on guard for syncope produced by hyperventilation. Usually hypnosis is achieved before signs of this occur. The literalness with which such suggestions as

"Breathe deeper and more rapidly" are followed is indicative of relaxation; a person in syncope develops shallow respirations and is unaffected by any type of suggestion. If fainting should occur, the hyperventilation is terminated automatically. The associated carpopedal spasm and muscular twitching are more awesome than serious. However, they are a good indication against further use of this technic. Catalepsy and deepening are produced as with other conventional technics.

THE DISGUISED TECHNIC

A disguised technic, which can also be used as an induction procedure, is performed in the following manner: If a small child or an adult with an extensive laceration of the thigh is seen and you wish to induce a hypnotic state without having anyone, especially the subject, know it, just place a towel over the subject's eyes and say: "Now close your eyes and keep them tightly closed! If you *really* wish to go into a nice state of relaxation so that you won't feel any discomfort, justrelax. You will go *deeper* and *deeper* with each breath you take. The more you relax, the less it is going to hurt you. Now, here comes the first stitch." (Gently place the needle on the edge of the wound without pressure.) Now you say, "See, stitch number 1 didn't hurt, did it? Stitch number 1 is a 'hallucinated' stitch." (This is misdirection.) "You are going deeper and deeper relaxed. Here comes stitch number 2. That's fine. You are relaxing wonderfully. You are going into a deeper and more pleasant state of relaxation. The more you relax, the less discomfort you will have. There, I just put in stitch number 2." (Again there is only light pressure against the wound.) Stitches 3, 4 and 5 are "put in" in a like manner. When the patient develops rigidity or limb catalepsy, and the breathing gets slower, deeper, and more regular, you can be fairly certain that the hypnotic state has been induced. Now, stitch number 1 can be painlessly inserted. (This is a nice, naturalistic approach for induction of hypnosis.)

Evans obtains hypnotic phenomena merely by "teaching relaxation."[5] Hartland uses a similar technic.[6]

"BLOOD PRESSURE" METHOD

The author has used a blood pressure apparatus to induce hypnosis by a nonformalistic approach. The method is as follows: The cuff is placed around the arm and is inflated to produce a pressure sensation. Then, as it is slowly released, the operator remarks: "You feel yourself going deeper and deeper relaxed. You can hear the air escaping and feel the pressure relaxing around your arm as you become deeper and deeper relaxed. Now close your eyes. . . ."

MECHANICAL TECHNICS

Any steady, monotonous sound has a tendency to induce relaxation. Any regular sound, such as the ticking of a watch, a metronome, or a clock, the constant falling of drops of water, or even listening to the heartbeat (a stethoscope is placed in the subject's ears) will induce hypnorelaxation. The operator must explain how and why the sounds will induce relaxation. He can suggest that the eyes will be opened and closed alternately with every sound of the watch or beat of the metronome or the heart.

A small microphone can be used to amplify and conduct the subject's own heart and respiratory sounds to his ears.[10] The rhythm of the heartbeat acts as a monotonous fixation stimulus, and the monotonic effect of the breath sounds serves as a conditioned stimulus for sleep. A verbalization technic also can be employed with this method. Another variation is to use intermittent visual stimuli, such as is provided by a flashlight, which can go on and off in synchrony with the metronome. Counting backward or forward is also helpful with either of these technics.

Passes of the hands over the face and the body often fit the expectancy of the subject. Frequently they facilitate induction. A rotating mirror or a brightly colored fish lure can accomplish the same effects. All of these technics can be combined with appropriate suggestions for relaxation. There are many other devices, such as hypnodisks and tape and record players, which can induce some degree of hypnosis in susceptible individuals. Recordings are valueless unless rapport with the operator is established first. However, as yet there is no device *per se* that is 100 per cent effective in inducing hypnosis. Invariably a standard verbalization technic is necessary.

The author helped to assay the brain wave synchronizer, an electronic instrument designed to induce various levels of hypnosis, probably by photic stimulation of the brain waves. The instrument should always be used in conjunction with a tape recording or a verbal induction and dehypnotization technic. It definitely increases receptivity to suggestion and has been tested clinically on many subjects, including obstetrical patients attending group hypnosis prenatal training classes. The apparatus induced light to deep hypnotic levels in over 90 per cent of the subjects. Hypnotic response is more readily produced if a favorable "mind-set" is created. Therefore, to some extent, the expectant attitude created by the structured situation enhances the hypnotic response, but about 30 per cent of the subjects, who had received no explanation or verbalization and who had no knowledge of what the brain wave synchronizer would do, were hypnotized to various degrees ranging from light to deep stages. The apparatus has excellent potentialities for deepening a previously fixed hypnotic level and for facilitating and speeding up hypnotic induction, which often can be time-consuming, especially in refractory subjects. A distinct advantage is that no physical connections or attachments are placed on the patient. The author has noted that refractory subjects with whom little rapport exists often are easily induced by the apparatus.

All mechanical technics depend to a degree on expectancy and rapport. The prestige factor is very important. If a subject expects to be hypnotized by a device and has confidence in the person who controls the instrument, then hypnotic relaxation can be induced readily in a susceptible subject.

OTHER TECHNICS

Two other technics are mentioned only to be condemned. The *carotid sinus method,* which is achieved by pressure on the carotid artery, is dangerous, as it may stop the heart. In the *shock technic,* a subject is caught off guard by the command, "Go to sleep, deep, deep sleep," accompanied by a snap of the fingers and a very authoritarian approach. Both of these methods smack of the entertainer, who uses them because of their dramatic appeal.

A *"lullabye" technic,* in which a monotonic rhythm is employed, has been described.[8] Writing technics can be utilized to induce hypnoidal states.[3] Grunts and subverbal cues have been employed to induce hypnosis.[11] Pantomime induction has already been described.[4] There is a specific technic for deaf mutes through an interpreter.[1, 7] The author has on many occasions performed this technic in the course of seminars in foreign countries where there is a language barrier. Telephone hypnosis has been resorted to on patients when the author was never seen. One striking case was the cessation of intractable hiccups, achieved in a single telephone session.[9] The author has often demonstrated a technic whereby patients go into hypnosis without a spoken word. However, a positive mind-set and reward inducement must be established *a priori.* In teaching seminars, for instance, the suggestion can be made that those who wish to remember better what has been taught will do so if they go into hypnosis. The operator leaves the room and then merely raises the arm, which immediately becomes cataleptic. This illustrates that the capacity to enter into hypnosis is more a function of the subject and his willingness to have his perceptual responses altered. However, I have never used this technic in a clinical setting, as it is too dramatic and theatrical.

For a verbatim transcript of other excellent technics of all types, the reader is referred to the Syllabus on Hypnosis and the Handbook of Therapeutic Suggestions of the American Society for Clinical Hypnosis. A recent study by Myron Teitelbaum, replete with technics of hypnotic induction, is also recommended.[13]

DRUG HYPNOSIS

It has been the author's experience that a drug seldom induces hypnosis by itself. However, some of the tranquilizing agents, such as the phenothiazine derivatives, can be helpful in decreasing central autonomic reactivity while maintaining a good cortical arousal pattern. Meprobamate preparations and phenobarbital often relax and facilitate induction in patients with musculoskeletal tensions.

Patients who are insusceptible to hypnosis are seldom made more suggestible by narcotics. On numerous occasions, the author has used sodium amytal or pentobarbital intravenously, carbon dioxide and nitrous oxide, ether, scopolamine, and Trilene with equivocal results. This may be due to personal bias against drugs. It is difficult to assay the value of drugs for facilitating hypnosis with any degree of accuracy unless double-blind studies are utilized.

The success of all hypnotic technics depends upon the strength of the interpersonal relationship. When one operator cannot hypnotize a subject, a successful induction is not precluded by another one; his personality and approach may appeal to the patient or may fit in with the latter's need.

The nuances of induction technics are learned by experience. The manner in which the arm is slowly being lifted, for example, is often indicative of whether or not the individual is going into hypnosis. Frequently, light stroking or the deft touch which reinforces a psychological suggestion by a physiologic effect instantaneously facilitates catalepsy. One can feel muscles that develop rigidity as they are stroked; the increased tonicity often cannot be simulated.

An induction procedure can be initiated with the subect's eyes tightly shut. The only reason for initial eye fixation is that the heaviness heightens the belief that other "suggested" phenomena will result. No one aspect of induction is as important as the dictum "Belief of hypnosis leads to hypnosis." Therefore, one must never arouse a critical attitude or resistance by using "loaded" words such as, "You are going to lie there perfectly still as if dead." To a hypochondriac, this would interrupt the necessary concentration for achieving hypnosis.

From a practical standpoint, no one technic is superior to any other, but, rather, the technic used must fit the *needs* of the subject at that *particular* time, his personality, and, most importantly, the ongoing relationship manifested by his behavior. If the patient believes that you are going to hypnotize him, then nearly any approach, formal or nonformal, will be successful. As a matter of fact, nonformalistic technics, as utilized by spiritualistic healers, are extremely effective, inasmuch as criticalness is reduced. Moreover, any technic which uses breathing exercises and a religious-philosophic approach, such as Yoga and Buddhist meditation, is effective for similar reasons.

An extremely authoritarian type of induction is seldom as efficacious as the permissive approach. Use of the patient's total experiential background, with all his feelings, ideas, and attitudes, allows him to decide *what he wishes—not what you wish!* This places the onus or responsibility for achieving the phenomena of hypnosis upon the patient's shoulders.

When using hypnosis in a child, always talk to him at his own intellectual level. If possible, make the induction procedure a sort of game. Use his imagination to "look" at a TV program. Get him to play a role in it or have him resort to some type of daydreaming fantasy. Imagery technics are more effective if the ideas are incorporated into the child's imagination. Let him think that he controls the situation by having him decide if he wishes to play baseball while getting an injection; there will be less discomfort if he is engrossed in the ball game. Most children go into hypnotic states readily through such naturalistic technics, especially if ideomotor and ideosensory involvement is fully utilized.

REFERENCES

1. Alderete, J.F.: The induction of hypnosis through an interpreter. Am. J. Clin. Hypn., *10:*138, 1967.
2. Christenson, J.A.: Dynamics in hypnotic induction. Psychiatry, *12:*37, 1949.
3. Coulton, D.: Writing techniques in hypnotherapy. Am. J. Clin. Hypn., *8:*287, 1966.
4. Erickson, M.H.: Pantomime techniques and hypnosis and the implications. Am. J. Clin. Hypn., *7:*64, 1964.
5. Evans, F.J.: An experimental indirect technique for the induction of hypnosis without awareness. Int. J. Clin. Exp. Hypn., *15:*72, 1967.
6. Hartland, J.: The general principles of suggestion. Am. J. Clin. Hypn., *9:*211, 1967.
7. Isasi, A.: Dos casos de sofrosis en sordomedos. Rev. Lat. Am. Hypn. Clin., *3:*92, 1962.

8. Klemperer, E.: Techniques of hypnosis and hypnoanalysis. Int. J. Clin. Exp. Hypn., *17:*137, 1969.

9. Kroger, W.S.: Hypnotherapy for intractable post-surgical hiccups. Am. J. Clin. Hypn., *12:*1, 1969.

10. Kubie, L.A., and Margolin, S.: A Physiologic method for the induction of states of states of partial sleep, and securing free association and early memories in such states. Trans. Am. Neurol. Assoc., *10:* 136, 1942.

11. Meares, A.: A System of Medical Hypnosis. Philadelphia, W.B. Saunders, 1960.

12. Moss, A.A.: Hypnodontics—Hypnosis in Dentistry. Brooklyn, Dental Items of Interest, 1952.

13. Teitelbaum, M.: Hypnosis Induction Technics. Springfield, Ill., Charles C Thomas, 1969.

14. Watkins, J.G.: Hypnotherapy of War Neuroses. New York, Ronald Press, 1949.

15. _____: Introductory Lectures in Medical Hypnosis. New York, The Institute for Research in Hypnosis, 1957, pp. 40–41.

16. Wolberg, L.R.: Medical Hypnosis. vol. I. New York, Grune & Stratton, 1948.

ADDITIONAL READINGS

Hamner, A.G., and Arkins, W.J.: The role of photic stimulation in the induction of hypnotic trance. Int. J. Clin. Exp. Hypn., *12*:81, 1964.

Kroger, W.S., and Schneider, S.A.: An electronic aid for hypnotic induction: a preliminary report. Int. J. Clin. Exp. Hypn., *7*:93, 1959.

Sadove, M.S.: Hypnosis in anesthesiology. Ill. Med. J., *124*:39, 1963.

15
Deepening Technics

Deepening is achieved by establishing a definite goal for each step of the induction procedure by such phrases as, "As you raise your arm higher and higher, and with every motion of your arm upward, you will go deeper and deeper relaxed." Linking these suggestions with ongoing physiologic processes is helpful here, too, as, for example, by the remark, "With each beat, beat of your heart, you will go deeper and deeper relaxed."

It is relatively simple to incorporate a deepening procedure into an induction technic, as follows: "If you *really* wish to go deeper, you will slowly raise your arm. With each motion of your arm upward, you will say to yourself, 'I'm going deeper and deeper relaxed.' In this way you will learn to coordinate your bodily functioning [ideomotor] with your thoughts [ideosensory]." Such suggestions of self-mastery appeal to the patient and effectively motivate deepening of the hypnosis. Achievement of arm catalepsy also is indicative of greater cooperation.

Even before the arm is raised, or while it is being lifted, one can remark, "If you really wish to go deeper, your arm will become stiffer, and the stiffer your arm becomes, the deeper relaxed you will go." This obviously implies that the stiffer the arm, the deeper the hypnotic state. One can then say, casually, "All you have to do if you *really* wish to go deeper is to tell yourself that you are going deeper and deeper relaxed with each motion of your arm upward." If the suggestions are incorporated as the subject's own ideas, there is a better chance of obtaining catalepsy.

After the extended arm is cataleptic, the hypnosis can be deepened by the following verbalization: "If you wish to go deeper, all you have to do is to let your arm drop slowly to your lap, and with each motion that your arm makes toward your lap, if you will suggest to yourself that you will drop deeper and deeper relaxed, indeed you will drop deeper and deeper relaxed. Remember that with each movement that your arm falls downward, if you imagine that you are falling deeper and deeper, you *will* fall deeper and deeper relaxed. Perhaps you might be willing even to give yourself the suggestion that 'The moment my arm returns to my lap, this will be a signal that I will go even deeper and deeper relaxed. And with each breath that I take, I will go deeper and deeper relaxed.'" (The arm slowly drops toward the lap, about one half or one inch at a time.) "Now your hand has returned to your lap. That's good. I notice that your breathing is slower, deeper, and more regular. Slower, deeper, more regular. With each breath that you take, you will go deeper and deeper relaxed. Every muscle, every fiber in your body, is becoming completely relaxed." Here the operator's breathing is coordinated with the rhythmicity of the subject's breathing; this facilitates deepening.

In general, the procedure for deepening is first to suggest that the relaxation is becoming progressively deeper and deeper; second, to allow periods of silence in order to allow it to deepen spontaneously. Finally, having the subject follow a variety of responses associated with ideomotor and ideosensory activities is conducive to greater relaxation and depth.

With reference to this last point, the most practical suggestions are as follows: "If you really wish to go deeper, just think, feel, and imagine that with each breath you will go *deeper* and *deeper* relaxed." (There is a period of silence.) "As long as your arms rest comfortably at your side, and as long as they remain in a comfortable position, and with every breath that you take, you will go deeper and deeper." (Silence.) This bewildering array of ideomotor and ideosensory activities automatically deepens the hypnosis.

To achieve even greater depths of hypnosis, visual imagery suggestions are helpful, such as: "If you really wish to go still deeper, would you mind thinking of one of the most relaxing experiences that you have ever had? Perhaps it might be lying on a beach, nuzzling in the hot sand. Or perhaps you can recall, after a particularly hard day, when you crawled in between the sheets of your own bed. It felt so good to let every muscle in your body relax. You are s-o t-i-r-e-d. It will be s-o good to go d-e-e-p-e-r and d-e-e-p-e-r relaxed." Here, too, it is most helpful to tap the experiential background of the individual for other memories involving relaxing experiences. Do not use such phrases as "blacker and blacker" or "Your legs will feel as if they are paralyzed," because such phrases can be misinterpreted by psychoneurotics.

A method that is particularly useful for deepening the arm levitation technic is to suggest: "If you will imagine that each time you move your hand in the direction of your face you will go deeper and deeper, indeed, you will go *deeper* and *deeper* relaxed. And perhaps *you* might be willing to give yourself the suggestion that when any portion of your hand touches any portion of your face, you will go deeper and deeper relaxed."

WEITZENHOFFER'S TECHNIC

For many other modifications involving induction technics and deepening procedures, the reader is advised to refer to Weitzenhoffer's comprehensive presentation on this subject. He has described an excellent procedure, which utilizes suggestion of sleep and challenges.[1]

HAND ROTATION TECHNIC

Another method to effect deepening is to start the hands moving around and around one another. After the movements are well established, it is suggested, "As you move your hands around

and around, faster and faster, you go deeper and deeper." This technic is particularly effective if a person who has not been able to develop deep hypnosis observes another subject who is capable of deepening the hypnosis in this manner.

VOGT'S FRACTIONATION TECHNIC

Another deepening technic that can be utilized is Vogt's fractionation technic.[2] Before dehypnotization, the subject is asked to relate the thoughts, feelings, and sensations he experienced at the moment of his maximal relaxation. The individual is then dehypnotized by the shoulder cue. Then these sensations are fed back when rehypnotized. He is told that he will go deeper with *each* rehypnotization. If he states, for instance, "I felt that I was floating on fleecy white clouds," this is incorporated into the next induction procedure by stating, "You will go deeper and deeper as you feel yourself floating on fleecy white clouds." If he remarks, "I saw all kinds of colored flashes of light," tell him, "Now as soon as you see these colored flashes, you will relax deeper and deeper." The elicited subjective information is repetitively utilized for immediately deepening each phase of the induction until a deep state is attained. Vogt's fractionation technic simply depends on the subject's being dehypnotized, questioned, and then reinduced by feeding in those relaxing sensations which he has just described. This procedure is repeated again and again until a deep state of relaxation is achieved. This technic is effective because it obviates the possibility of suggesting sensations which may antagonize the subject. Another advantage is that the information used is conducive to deep hypnotization. The fractionation method can be used in conjunction with the hand levitation method for subsequent inductions.

ESCALATOR TECHNIC

This technic is used frequently as a deepening technic in conjunction with a direct or an indirect approach. The following verbalization is used after light hypnosis has been produced: "Visualize, if you will, that you are in an elevator on a high floor. Notice the number of the floor. Perhaps it is the sixteenth floor or the twentieth floor.

Notice the number on the landing. And now the elevator is beginning to fall, and as you feel it *falling,* you, too, will feel yourself *falling deeper and deeper relaxed.* As each number on the landing gets smaller and smaller, you will fall *deeper and deeper relaxed. Deeper* and *deeper relaxed.* When the elevator stops at the ground floor or the lobby, you will be in a *real deep, deep state of relaxation.* Not asleep, not unconscious, not in a trance, but just a deep, pleasant, soothing, refreshing state of relaxation, in which you will listen to every suggestion that you wish to follow." Here, as in the blackboard technic (p. 75), the hypnotic state can be deepened by lifting the arm and allowing it to fall to the subject's lap.

HELPFUL HINTS IN DEEPENING

Before deepening, the patient is informed that in case anything should happen to the operator, he will be able to dehypnotize himself upon a split-second's notice. This allays the anxieties of apprehensive patients who fear being left in hypnosis. The suggestions must be given slowly and deliberately so that ideas of deep relaxation influence the subject in a positive manner.

Watch the patient and time the suggestions to coincide with the patient's objective responses. Remarking that "Your breathing will get s-l-o-w-e-r and more r-e-g-u-l-a-r" with the rise and fall of the chest is most conducive to deep relaxation. Let the patient deepen the hypnosis at his own pace. Inform him: "You have the privilege of going just as deep as you wish to go and through your *own* efforts." This places the onus for deepening the hypnosis on the patient. An experienced operator can recognize the depth by the manner in which the arm falls. If it drops limply and with a "thud" into the lap, a fairly deep stage has been attained.

When only a light state has been attained, a kindly, noncondemnatory approach maintains good rapport for the next session. The successful operator knows that giving a post-hypnotic suggestion, "You will go deeper the next time," usually begins to work in the second, third, or fourth session. Respect must be maintained at all times. Thus, thanking the individual for cooperating, at both hypnotic and nonhypnotic levels, results in better motivation and no loss of rapport.

As was said before, to deepen hypnosis, one should establish a goal to motivate the subject each step of the way: "After your arm is extended straight toward the ceiling, only then will you go *deeper* and *deeper* relaxed. You will do so, as I stroke your arm from the fingers to the wrist, if you *really* want to go deeper and deeper." By tying up your suggestions with other physiologic effects—"With each breath you take, you will go *deeper* and *deeper*"—you make use of the dictum that a physiologic effect always reinforces a psychological suggestion. When stroking the arm to deepen the hypnosis, use a light, featherlike caress.

Counting forward and backward in multiples, as 2 or 4, has a deepening effect: "Each time I count, you will go deeper—2 . . . 4 . . . 8. . . . You are going deeper—8 . . . 12 . . . 16. . . . You are going still deeper relaxed. Now, going backward —12 . . . 8 . . . 4. . . . You are going deeper and deeper" often is effective.

It is also important, when deepening the hypnosis, to make full use of intraverbal suggestion (intonation of words) and to stress certain words. It has been said that if you wish to be a good Hamlet, you actually have to *believe that you are Hamlet!* Therefore, *one must fully and emotionally participate in* the hypnotic interpersonal relationship. Put yourself in the subject's place. If you say, "Your lids are getting very tired, *getting heavier and heavier," you really have to feel these sensations yourself.* If you say, "I want your eyes to get tired, or your lids to get heavy," this does not affect the patient. But, if you state emphatically, "You will feel a numb, heavy, woodenlike sensation, the same kind of a sensation you may have had when your gums were anesthetized, or the same sensation you had from freezing the side of your face when walking against an icy, cold wind"—these are meaningful suggestions to a subject.

IMPORTANCE OF CONFIDENCE ON THE PART OF THE OPERATOR

It has been glibly stated that anyone can learn easily how to induce hypnosis. This is not quite true, as some operators are better than others. However, it requires years of clinical training, good judgment, intuition, and experience to be an accomplished hypnotherapist. One cannot read the description of an induction technic in a book and expect always to hypnotize someone successfully: the intraverbal aspects of the communication process will not sound real. A hollow approach seldom inspires the belief, the faith, the confidence, and the expectant attitudes that are so necessary for successful deepening of hypnosis. Moreover, each patient reacts differently; therefore the deepening technic cannot be standardized.

Reproaching the patient because hypnosis was not deepened usually alienates him. Likewise, remarking, "Well, you didn't go deep enough today. Maybe it was my fault," only weakens the relationship. It is better to say, "You did very well! You were excellent. You cooperated very well. Next time you will go much deeper. I'm really satisfied with the depth you reached." Speak in the same confident tone of voice that you use when you are handing a prescription to a patient.

MAINTAINING DEEP HYPNOSIS

To maintain deep hypnosis, as was mentioned above, merely suggest, "As long as your arms remain comfortably relaxed at your sides, and with every breath you take, you will remain in this very, very deep state of relaxation." Ideosensory and ideomotor responses are reinforced by these suggestions. Every individual must, of necessity, continue breathing; as long as he keeps breathing, and as long as he keeps his arms in this nice, comfortable position, he will go deeper and deeper with each breath. This sounds perfectly natural to the subject. Thus, by *extraverbal measures,* one can imply that the subject should go deeper. This obviates saying, *"I want you to go*

deeper and deeper." The first way appeals even to a refractory subject.

Frequently hypnosis can be deepened by leaving the subject alone after making the following posthypnotic suggestions: "I shall return in a few minutes. As long as you continue breathing slowly, deeply, and more regularly, you will remain in a deep, deep, relaxed stage as each minute goes by. And with each breath that you take, you will find yourself becoming more deeply relaxed. Upon my return, you will be in a deep, deep state of relaxation." An absence of 10 minutes is usually adequate. Longer periods may break the rapport—apprehensive subjects usually dehypnotize themselves spontaneously. A metronome, a flashing light, and any other monotonic stimulus can be utilized in such a situation.

The foregoing observations have been instrumental in achieving deeper stages of hypnosis than ordinarily would have been obtained. Naturally, every experienced operator has to "play it by ear" and change his technics to suit the personality needs of his subject and the various situational factors as they arise.

REFERENCES

1. Weitzenhoffer, A. M.: General Techniques of Hypnotism. New York, Grune & Stratton, 1957, p. 213.
2. Vogt, O.: Zur Kenntnis des Wesens und der psychologischen Bedeutung des Hypnotismus. Zeitschrift für Hypnotismus, 1894–95: pp. 3, 277; 1896: pp. 4, 32, 122, 229.

ADDITIONAL READINGS

Erickson, M. H.: Naturalistic techniques of hypnosis. Am. J. Clin. Hypn., *1:*3, 1958.
Levitsky, A.: Some additional techniques of hypnosis. Am. J. Clin. Hypn., *3:*231, 1961.

16

Autohypnosis

Autohypnosis is a highly suggestible state wherein suggestions can be directed to the self. It is a powerful tool in any therapeutic process, and well-trained patients often can parallel the success of heterohypnosis through their own efforts. When judiciously used, it can alleviate many distressing symptoms, substitute strong behavioral responses for weaker ones, help overcome bad habits, and also promote relaxation, concentration, and self-confidence.

In achieving autohypnosis, self-control is not relinquished, as is commonly believed. Actually, *more* control is gained. Its effectiveness depends upon strong motivation, the intelligent application of the autosuggestions, and diligence: these are the essential prerequisites. The time necessary to achieve autohypnosis varies: some subjects learn it in a half hour and others require much longer periods.

One question often asked is: "If I am under hypnosis, how can I give myself suggestions?" The patient can be told: "You are always aware of what is going on, and, therefore, you can think, reason, act, criticize, suggest, or do whatever you imagine or believe you need. You can give yourself the suggestions aloud or mentally." Another frequent question is: "How do I bring myself out of the autohypnotic state?" The patient can be informed: "You can terminate autohypnosis immediately upon specific suggestions or a prearranged cue."

Although Coué and Baudouin once unwarrantably hailed autosuggestion and autohypnosis as cure-alls,[1, 2] these technics are not panaceas, even though they often account for the cultists' success in curing psychogenically based symptoms. Spiritual religious healing modalities combine autohypnosis with various types of self-reflection, breathing exercises, and muscular relaxation technics. However, autohypnosis is not a religion. Autoscience, positive thinking, self-affirmation—all are modifications of self-hypnotic technics. It is interesting that criticism is never leveled at autohypnosis when used in a religious framework; nor are there any objections when recovery ensues without the basic causes or underlying conflicts being resolved. No one can deny that many emotionally disturbed individuals are helped and live well-adjusted lives through various "do-it-yourself" or autosuggestive technics.

METHODOLOGY OF AUTOHYPNOSIS

Generally, autohypnosis is induced as a specific technic taught by the physician. A tape recording or record with the appropriate posthypnotic suggestions often is satisfactory for autohypnosis. Occasionally, some patients can induce autohypnosis without prior conditioning; this is the exception rather than the rule.

Autohypnosis chiefly depends upon the nature and type of posthypnotic suggestions given to the self. In this regard, all patients must be given specific instructions (see below).

DYNAMICS OF AUTOHYPNOSIS

Percepts which require reasoning and decision-making when tested against reality are seldom accepted uncritically. On the other hand, our imaginative processes, through fantasies, dreams, and wishful thinking, are often accepted as realities. In other words, as our ideational processes shift more toward imagery activity, our mental images become more variegated and potent as they can be formulated, controlled, and utilized for purposeful behavior.

Thus all purposeful behavior depends on a dynamic and reciprocal reaction between our reality perceptions and our innermost feelings, needs, and goals. The personality structure of an individual is determined, in part, by this behavior. Hence, if the inner feelings of an individual are stimulated in a beneficial manner, healthful reality factors allow the organism to become more responsive. Autohypnosis is most useful in precisely this area of personality functioning by effectively increasing the potentialities for modifying behavioral responses. Nothing could be simpler!

A well-conditioned patient can hypnotize himself by a prearranged cue. The cue acts as a stimulus for the conditioned response—the autohypnosis. After the subject has been properly conditioned, he usually can bring this stimulus-response mechanism into action rapidly. It appears that autohypnosis produces increased receptivity to ideas and the capacity to examine these ideas for their inherent values. This self-objectivity is one of the reasons why autohypnosis is used.

When a person suggests thoughts to himself, this is much more meaningful than when they are given to him by someone else. When a person imagines himself to be in love, he seldom listens to another person's advice, even if it is logical.

INSTRUCTIONS TO THE PHYSICIAN FOR AUTOHYPNOSIS

1. The signal or cue for inducing autohypnosis must be one that will work only with the patient's permission. This prevents him from inadvertently responding to a similar cue or signal from another person.

2. It must be emphasized that, if optimal conditions for the safety of the patient are not present, the cue will be ineffective.

3. The patient should be trained in the method of suggesting actions to himself. Explicit directions should also be given as to how the suggestions can be carried out both during and after the termination of autohypnosis. Suggestions must be of a positive nature and oriented toward his own welfare.

4. Time limitations on the duration of the autohypnosis can be specified beforehand. However, even if only the slightest possibility of danger exists, the patient must be assured that he will be able to terminate the autohypnosis instantaneously and react to any environmental threat as he would at nonhypnotic levels.

5. The time for subsequent autohypnotic induction can be shortened by time distortion (20 minutes can seem like 1 minute).

6. The spontaneous development of complete amnesia during autohypnosis is impossible. Partial amnesia, if it persists after dehypnotization, follows the usual laws for forgetting: one can forget or remember almost everything on the preceding page after reading it.

7. Autohypnosis is a learned conditioned response; therefore, one must try to practice as much as possible every day. Half a dozen sessions of 2 or 10 minutes each throughout the day are more practical than lengthier sessions. However, longer sessions may be required if deeper stages or hypnoanesthesia are desired.

8. A somewhat similar format must be followed to "stamp in" the learning. The best one is a progressive type: from smaller to larger groups of muscles (i.e., eyelids to limbs to body).

9. If specific relaxation of any part of the body cannot be developed, concentration on ideosensory responses in these areas should be singled out for additional practice.

10. When a specific idea is suggested, the patient should try reviving an association that once produced this idea (if one wishes to make the arms heavy, he can recollect how his arms felt after lying on them for several hours). Therefore, the patient must associate actual experiences with the desired responses as much as possible. The more vividly these are imagined, the better the effect.

11. The patient must be certain to end each session by stating that he will go into autohypnosis more readily with each practice session, that he will follow all the autosuggestions to the best

of his ability, and that he will terminate each session by suggesting that he will feel relaxed, motivated, and confident. This obviates any "hangover" feelings, such as headache, nervousness, and tension.

12. The patient may also suggest that autohypnosis can merge with actual sleep. If this happens before bedtime, he will awake in the morning feeling just as he would after a normal night's sleep—refreshed and alert.

If the above instructions are discussed in detail, and the patients are reasonably intelligent, there is little possibility that danger will ensue from the mere production of autohypnosis *per se.*

INSTRUCTIONS TO THE PATIENT FOR AUTOHYPNOSIS

The technic and verbalization the author uses for autohypnosis are as follows: "Confucius once stated that one picture is worth a thousand words. Picture images are much more important than words. For instance, if you say, 'I will be confident,' the words must be implemented by a picture of yourself as the confident person you want to be. If you keep fortifying this image with appropriate suggestions, eventually these mental impressions will give rise to the confident feelings that you seek.

"I know that this technic seems too simple, but if you keep implanting positive images into your mind, they will become a part of your personality. Do not expect immediate results when you begin to use autohypnosis and don't ask, 'What's wrong?' All you have to do to attain autohypnosis is to use what we call sensory- or visual-imagery conditioning. This is an old technic that has been the basis for many different types of prayers.

"Any one can learn and practice autohypnosis, but to achieve the best results you must carefully consider what you wish to accomplish. Through self-exploration you can establish reasonable goals for improvement. Don't think that you have to be 'out of this world' to be in autohypnosis. This idea is produced by novels, comic strips, and motion pictures. Actually, you only will be in a very deep state of relaxation and concentration. You may develop a feeling of detachment, you may experience a very pleasant sinking feeling, or

you may get a feeling of peace and serenity. At times you may not even feel a definite change: it may just seem as if you had your eyes closed and heard everything at all times. However, if you aim for a deeply relaxed state, you will reach it.

"After you are satisfied that you have achieved autohypnosis, you may give yourself further suggestions to deepen it if you wish. Also, remember that it is not too important to reach a deep state on your initial attempts. Just realize that you are trying to establish a conditioned response which will cause you to react instantly to any cue that you wish to use. Through frequent repetition, the cue will bring on the autohypnosis.

"During every attempt to achieve autohypnosis, visualize yourself going deeper and deeper. At first you may experience some difficulty, but as you stick to it, you will be able to picture yourself deeply relaxed. Always use the visual imagery technics, whether or not you think you are under hypnosis. The images will become clear as you constantly repeat the appropriate suggestions. As you continue to work with yourself, you will develop confidence in giving yourself suggestions. To be effective, they cannot be given in a hesitant manner. They must be given with enthusiasm and anticipation. If you follow these instructions, you will see tangible results of your suggestions and efforts.

"Begin by selecting a quiet place and arranging to spend an uninterrupted half hour a day practicing there. Seated in a comfortable chair with your hands resting in your lap and your feet on the floor, fix your eyes on a spot on the ceiling above the level of your eyes.

"Then begin counting to yourself slowly from 1 to 10. Direct your attention to your eyelids and, between numbers, tell yourself repeatedly that your eyelids are getting *very, very heavy* and that your eyes are getting *very, very tired.* Again and again say: 'My lids are getting *so heavy.* I feel as if I want to close my eyes at the count of three. My lids are getting *heavier* and *heavier.* I feel my lids getting so *heavy,* and the *heavier* they get, the *deeper relaxed* I will become and the better able I will be to follow all suggestions I give myself. Now my lids are getting *very heavy.* It's going to feel so good to close my eyes.'

"By the time you count to 2, think of enough

suggestions like the ones just mentioned so that you actually 'feel' the heaviness of your eyelids. When you are sure that your lids are indeed heavy, count to 3 and let your eyes roll up into the back of your head for a few seconds. Then say: 'My lids are now locked so tight that I doubt very much that I can open them. My lids shut tighter and tighter, and as my lids lock tight, I begin to feel a nice, calm, soothing, relaxed feeling beginning in my toes, moving into my legs and into my thighs—as I keep counting. It's the same feeling that I have in my jaws when my dentist injects procaine into them—the same feeling that I have when I fall asleep on my arm— the same feeling that I have when I sit too long in one position—the identical feeling that I would have in my legs if I sat cross-legged on them. A numb, woodenlike feeling starting in my toes is beginning to move up, up, up from my toes into my legs.'

"Next, count to 4 and say: 'By the time I have counted to 5, my legs from my toes to my thighs will be just as heavy as lead. I can feel my legs relaxing from my toes to my thighs. I can feel them getting *heavier* and *heavier* and *heavier*. 5. They are so *heavy* now that I don't think I can move them.' Then double back for purposeful repetition. 'My eyelids are locked tight, so tight that I don't believe I can open them. My legs from my toes to my thighs are completely relaxed.' Each time you retrace these autosuggestions, you stamp in the learned response pattern.

"You continue in this way: 'By the time I have counted to 6 and 7, my fingers, hands, and arms will be very, very heavy. I am beginning to feel that same numbness moving up from my fingers to my shoulders. A heavy, detached feeling is moving up from my fingers to my hand, to my wrist, past my elbows, up to my arm, to my shoulder. Both my arms, from my hands to my shoulders, are getting very numb—a heavy, woodenlike numbness. When I have counted to 7, my arms will be just as heavy and relaxed as my eyelids, and as numb as my legs are now. My arms feel just as if I have been sleeping on them.'

"Do not worry if you forget the exact words. They are far less important than the effect that you are trying to achieve—a feeling of numbness

all the way from the fingertips to the wrist, to the elbow, to the shoulder, to the neck. In practice, this may be a bit more difficult to accomplish in the first few sessions at home, but the feeling will come faster in subsequent attempts. It is most important that you never become discouraged and that you not tire yourself by spending more than the half hour a day in practice.

"When you finally reach the point where, by the count of 7, your limbs are sufficiently relaxed, you repeat again all the suggestions you have given yourself, adding: 'My legs are so heavy that I don't believe I can move them. My eyes are locked so tight that I doubt that I can open them. My arms are so heavy that I cannot lift them, and, by the time I have counted from 7 to 8, my trunk will be relaxed.'

"Now go back to the lids, legs, and arms. Then say: 'By the time I count from 8 to 9, my chest will have relaxed, too. With every breath I take, I can just feel myself going deeper and deeper into a relaxed state. My back and abdomen are getting very, very numb. I can feel the muscles in my chest relaxing. 8. My entire body, from my neck down, is relaxed. 9. I am completely relaxed . . . I can't open my eyes . . . I can't move my legs . . . I can't move my arms. I feel my whole body relaxed, thoroughly and deeply. It is so refreshing to remain in this deep, quiet state.

" 'I will now relax my neck and head, so that, at the count of 10, I will be completely relaxed from my head to my toes. I can feel that with every breath I take I am becoming calmer and deeper relaxed . . . deeper and deeper relaxed . . . into a calm, soothing, refreshing state. Everything is just getting more and more relaxed. I feel as if I am floating away . . . falling deeper and deeper . . . not asleep, but just thoroughly relaxed. 10. I am completely relaxed. My eyes and limbs are as heavy as lead. My entire body feels numb, heavy, woodenlike, as I go deeper and deeper.' "

DEEPENING THE AUTOHYPNOTIC STATE

The key to deepening autohypnosis lies in the use of visual imagery technics. The patient can be informed: "By picturing yourself deeply relaxed in your 'mind's eye,' you will go deeper. If you can imagine yourself in your own bed comfortably relaxed, this can be a stimulus for deepening the relaxation. If you think of this again and again, you set in motion a conditioned response mechanism that ultimately will allow you to achieve a profound state of relaxation.

"It is well to remember that you deepen the autohypnosis by your own efforts and that the depth depends largely on how well you follow the principles which you are going to learn. It also is most important to have the proper frame of mind if you wish to achieve effective autohypnosis. If you approach it with a 'prove-it-to-me' attitude, nothing will happen. To attain ultimate success, self-confidence, persistence, and systematic conditioning are necessary. (Instructions for autohypnosis, as well as deepening verbalization technics, have been described by Salter,[6] Rhodes,[4] Powers,[3] and Weitzenhoffer.[7] The escalator technic, described on page 83, is an excellent procedure for deepening autohypnosis). "Further relaxation can be obtained by giving yourself the suggestion that when you think of a color (soothing green, perhaps), you will instantly become relaxed. You may select any other color that relaxes you."

DEHYPNOTIZATION

During autohypnosis, all patients are actually more alert to internal and external stimuli than at nonhypnotic levels; except for sight, all sensory inputs are increased. When reassured that, if necessary, they can terminate even a deep introspective state in a split second and that no untoward effects will occur, the depth of autohypnosis usually can be increased.

The apprehensive individual's fears that he will not be dehypnotized can be further allayed by describing what it feels like to be in autohypnosis. Autohypnosis is often confused with sleep. Therefore, it is imperative to distinguish between it and sleep. It is helpful to remark: "If you are asleep, you will only remember some of your dreams instead of your suggestions. Actually, it feels as if you are about to fall asleep, and yet you know you are completely awake. Time may pass by rapidly or it

may drag. At times, you may feel as if you are observing your own behavior.

"If you should not be able to open your eyes, don't worry. Just repeat the suggestions again, and emphasize that at the count of 3 you will absolutely, positively be able to open your eyes very easily and will feel fine. Should you not be able to come out of it, keep calm and give yourself the dehypnotizing suggestions with more emphasis."

Failures in self-dehypnotization are rare. The author has never had a case. However, occasionally some patients become so relaxed that they wish to enjoy this pleasant sensation. When this occurs, the patient may go into real sleep and will eventually come out of it.

RECOGNITION OF AUTOHYPNOSIS

Some patients may have difficulty recognizing subjectively whether or not they have achieved autohypnosis. In good subjects there is extreme responsiveness to autosuggestions. Other subjects who, in reality, are able to produce autohypnosis vehemently protest that they "felt nothing"; they think that they have to be "knocked out." Still others, even though they initially think they are merely role-playing and going along with the autosuggestions, suddenly realize they are spontaneously executing specific and relevant autosuggestions.

Autohypnosis can fluctuate from reverielike states or alteration in the body image to the complete detachment of the Yoga state. When these sensations are subjectively experienced, this is sensorial proof of autohypnosis.

HANDLING OF RESISTANCE IN AUTOHYPNOSIS

The most commonly encountered resistance in autohypnosis is that of the patient who feels that it did not work for him. One can suggest: "Even if you were not under autohypnosis, if you practice again and again, eventually you *will* slip into autohypnosis. After this has been accomplished, it will become automatic."

Those who are unable to develop autohypnosis are seldom aware of the needs for their resistances. The therapist must find out the reasons. This might well be compared with the removal of a neurosis in a disturbed patient. He certainly wishes to get rid of his symptoms, yet, because of the secondary gain value of the symptoms (neurotic needs for the symptoms), he is unable to "let go" of them.

The best way to dissipate the resistances is to agree that attainment of autohypnosis is difficult for some persons. However, *some degree* of suggestibility must be present in every intelligent person. If the patient agrees to this, the therapist should resort to Chevreul's Pendulum Test (see p. 42). The highly resistant patient will remark, "I am sure I didn't make it move." Upon the successful accomplishment of this task, the therapist can say: "If the pendulum moves without volitional direction, you have successfully influenced your mind. Autohypnosis involves the same procedure. The goal is to cause voluntary and involuntary reactions. If the experience does not work with your eyes open, try it with your eyes closed for about 5 minutes. You will be pleasantly surprised with the results. Should you want to prove to yourself that you are suggestible with your eyes open, practice the technic every day for a week or two. The idea of the practice sessions is to reinforce and increase the response of the involuntary movements until you develop proficiency. If, after several weeks, you should still not be successful, use the role-playing technic. Consciously make the object revolve. After a while, it will move automatically whenever you attempt the experiment.

"When this happens, you will have proof of your suggestibility. It is highly improbable that you will not be successful. It would be a rare occurrence. By the same systematic efforts, I can assure you that you can achieve autohypnosis."

DANGERS IN AND CONTRAINDICATIONS TO AUTOHYPNOSIS

The author has taught autohypnosis to hundreds of *selected* patients by the technics given above. In these or, for that matter, any other

patients, he has yet to see any of the dangers described by Rosen (one of the few psychiatrists who repeatedly warns against the use of autohypnosis), who states:

The desire for self-hypnosis, whatever the rationalization advanced by its practitioner, when investigated frequently turns out to be a desire to further fantasy formation, to facilitate sinking deeper and deeper into a dream world of one's own, and to indulge in fantasied or actual "acting out" of a type not allowable to the individual and for which, as a result, he may posthypnotically be amnestic. While it may be used for constructive purposes, it may be utilized self-destructively.[5]

There are few carefully documented cases that one or many autohypnotic sessions *per se* can cause regressive and harmful acting-out tendencies. Thousands upon thousands of patients have been taught autohypnosis by many thousands of physicians, dentists, psychologists, and even pastoral and spiritual healers—all without dangerous sequelae. Autohypnosis merely is an intensification of the capacity of an individual to examine his own mental processes in order to make the best "bets" as to how he should act.

Those few who regard autohypnosis as dangerous fail to recognize that an individual is in an almost identical state during profound prayer. If autohypnosis is dangerous, then prayer, religious ecstasy, the meditative states taught by Buddhist priests, and Yoga are also dangerous. The only theoretic danger is in teaching autohypnosis to a person who is already detached or depersonalized. No physician would think of pushing an individual who is already "out of this world" into autohypnosis; nor would he allow an individual who spends a great deal of time in autistic thinking or introspection to learn all about the practice.

SUMMARY AND DISCUSSION

The rules for teaching autohypnosis are similar to those for heterohypnosis. The operator must give all patients accurate and specific instructions as to *where* and *how* the autohypnosis is to be practiced. Definitive suggestions for its termination also must be given with the utmost clarity. Naturally, just as the use of hypnosis is often contraindicated as a form of psychotherapy for emotionally disturbed individuals, so is the *teaching of autohypnosis to narcoleptic and schizoid patients by untrained lay or professional individuals to be strongly condemned.* The real danger is that the patient might coincidentally be entering an unrecognized psychotic state, and the hypnotherapist would be held culpable. The limitations of autohypnosis should be stressed; it is not a panacea. Rather, it is a means of developing sensory imagery conditioning. However, hypnotherapists should recognize the limitations of autohypnosis and not oversensationalize its clinical applications.

REFERENCES

1. Baudouin, C.: Suggestion and Autosuggestion. London, Allen, 1920.
2. Coué, E.: Self-mastery Through Conscious Autosuggestion. London, Allen, 1951.
3. Powers, M.: Practical Guide to Self-Hypnosis. Los Angeles, Wilshire Book Co., 1961.
4. Rhodes, R. H.: Therapy Through Hypnosis. New York, Citadel Press, 1952.
5. Rosen, H.: Hypnosis, mental hygiene, and the dental hypnotist. J. Clin. Exp. Hypn., *5:*121, 1957.
6. Salter, A.: Three techniques of autohypnosis. J. Gen. Psychol., *24:*423, 1941.
7. Weitzenhoffer, A. M.: General Techniques of Hypnotism. New York, Grune & Stratton, 1957, pp. 327–329.

17

Autogenic Training

Autogenic training was developed some 50 years ago in Berlin by Johannes Schultz.[6] He trained patients to go into self-induced hypnotic-like states. Autogenic training consists of a graduated series of mental exercises designed to produce a general psychobiologic reorganization. The resultant changes improve the individual's capacity for introspection and purposeful activity, which help to modify maladaptive behavior processes.

Schultz, as does Vogt, uses definitive bodily sensations reported by the subject during induction. Most subjects, for instance, develop an abnormally *heavy* sensation of the limbs and/or the body, or a *warmth* that diffuses through the organism, and *lightness* of the extremities. He suggests that the subject correlate the sensation of heaviness with muscular relaxation. Thus, the development of self-relaxation invariably produces a hypnoidal state similar to that described by Meares.[4] As a prerequisite, subjects must be motivated, cooperative and capable of a certain amount of self-direction and self-control. Introspection on ideomotor and ideosensory activities is enhanced while the subject is in a relaxed position. Distracting stimuli are reduced to a minimum, and monotonic auditory stimuli are used to facilitate self-concentration; as a result, psychophysiologic changes occur.

The posture is similar to that used for hypnotic induction. The subject leans backward in an armchair with his arms held limply at his sides or resting on his thighs; or he can slump forward or lie on his back. The eyes are closed at the start and the subject emphasizes at the very beginning, "I am very relaxed." Then it is suggested that the subject can relax still more if he associates the thought of deep relaxation with memories of when he was actually relaxed, as, for example, the experience of dozing while sunbathing. In this way, mere words such as "relaxed" become fused into meaningful experiences. This is identical to hypnotic sensory-imagery conditioning.

After the subject attains relaxation readily, he is taught, through suggested ideosensory and ideomotor activities, to concentrate on making one arm very, very *heavy*. Here, too, stroking the arm facilitates a feeling of heaviness, which automatically spreads by generalization to the other arm, the lower limbs and the rest of the body. The right arm is chosen because most people are righthanded.

Schultz advises that at first this should be performed for only 10, 20, or 30 seconds at a time. Subjects described their feelings as "sleepy," "detached," and "dizzy."

He terminates this relaxed state by having the subject take a deep breath, and flex and extend his arms several times in quick succession. The subject breathes deeply several times more, and then opens his eyes. The importance attached to posture, concentration, an expectant attitude, a favorable mind-set and the use of a ritualistic procedure shows that all are modifications of hypnotic technics. Systematic practice of the exercises invariably results in a graduated mastery of bodily functioning.

Autogenic training is a kind of mental gymnastics; its principles are similar to progressive relaxation,[6] Yoga, Buddhist and transcendental meditation, and other ritualized practices. Benson and his co-workers use the term "the relaxation response" [1,2] (see Chap. 24). The mental exercises are practiced two or three times a day. The relaxation spreads whether or not patients were informed that it would happen. Schultz's technics are rather elaborate, and the reader can study his excellent book, *Autogenic Training,* for the specific steps involved.[6]

The importance of autogenic training is that hypnotic phenomena are not a mere matter of heterosuggestion, that is, of one person suggesting certain things to another. As used clinically, hypnosis is structured around autosuggestion and heterosuggestion. Thus, when a person is in hypnosis, something happens to enable him to do a great many things which often are not suggested. One may not know what to suggest for a specific purpose. Yet some patients develop the capacity to meet their somatic needs in an autonomous fashion. With autogenic training, some people learn to develop complete anesthesia automatically without its being specifically suggested. One must remember, however, that 5 per cent or more of the population can develop some degree of anesthesia without autogenic or hypnotic training.

Schultz also demonstrated that many individuals could induce self-relaxation without the instructor's presence. As they learned to relax deeply, many became interested in sensory changes such as feelings of heaviness, coldness or warmth of the extremities. He cites data to prove that, if warmth was produced in the right arm, a rise of 1°C. occurred, as measured by a thermocouple. The other arm was unaffected. Eventually, he had subjects learn as many hypnotic phenomena as possible. When subjects were merely hypnotized, peripheral skin temperature responses to hot and cold did not vary. However, when given "method acting" instructions in another experimental session, peripheral temperature of the hand increased.[5]

The clinical applications of autogenic training have not been explored in this country. Schultz's method has proved to be a rational and practical psychotherapeutic modality in Europe. The method has been employed primarily as an adjunctive procedure for relief of a wide variety of psychosomatic conditions such as asthma, hypertension, ulcers, female disturbances, and numerous others. He does not claim that he can cure asthmatics simply by autogenic training. However, in conjunction with other therapeutic measures, it is indispensable in their cure.

Autogenic training is very useful in that it teaches the patient to be self-reliant and enables him to feel that *he* is now doing something helpful. This undoubtedly builds up the patient's self-esteem. As happens when autohypnosis is utilized, the dependency situation is minimized.

The author has been able to duplicate Schultz's results. Autogenic training has given some individuals the feeling that they have learned something with which they can externalize their tensions. It can be used not only for relaxation, but for rather involved and complicated psychotherapeutic procedures, such as relief of impotency, or as in surgery or acupunctural analgesia (see Chap. 35). Autogenic training indicates that hypnosis is more than mere suggestion. It also beautifully illustrates that hypnotic behavior is primarily *a subjective experience* based on the inner conviction and the expectant attitude induced by the hypnotic state. This capacity resides within every person.

Autogenic training is a rather interesting aspect of hypnotherapy, and Schultz's work is timely and provocative. For many years the author of this book had been using similar technics for autohypnosis without being aware that they were a modification of Schultz's methods. Many therapists, unfamiliar with autohypnotic technics, fail to realize that psychotherapeutic results often can be attained almost wholly as the result of the patient's own efforts. Sellers corroborated Schultz's findings, noting that the technic was useful with a wide variety of situations.[7]

Edmund Jacobson's[3] progressive relaxation is similar to Schultz's autogenic training, and Schultz points out the similarity. Even though the "misdirection" for these methodologies is different, sensory-imagery conditioning and motivational strivings are the principal features responsible for the recoveries. Yoga employed similar technics centuries ago. The relaxation, meditation, and self-absorption produce some degree of dissociation, and the resultant cortical inhibition, similar to that which occurs in prayer, narrows the attention span to the imaginative processes. The more one responds to his own healthy mental pictures, the more likely his healthy fantasies will become healthy realities!

REFERENCES

1. Benson, H.: The Relaxation Response. New York, Morrow, 1975.
2. Benson, H., *et al.:* The relaxation response. Psychiatry, *37*:37, 1974.
3. Jacobson, E.: Progressive Relaxation. Chicago, University of Chicago Press, 1938.
4. Meares, A.: A System of Medical Hypnosis. New York, Julian Press, 1960.
5. Peters, J.E., *et al.:* Peripheral skin temperature responses to hot and cold suggestions. Int. J. Clin. Exp. Hypn., *21*:205, 1973.
6. Schultz, J.H., and Luthe, W.: Autogenic Training. New York, Grune & Stratton, 1959.
7. Sellers, D.J.: Teaching self-initiated control technique to individuals and a group in college. Int. J. Clin. Exp. Hypn., *22*:39, 1974.

18

Group Hypnosis

Mass suggestion or mass hypnosis is relatively easy to establish in a group. The reasons for this are: (1) there is an "emotional contagion" that takes place with other members of the group; (2) persons identify with what they see; (3) the inherent competitiveness is mobilized; and (4) there is usually an intense desire to please the leader (father-figure) of the group.

The beginner should use a suggestibility test such as the handclasp method to find out which persons are likely to make the best subjects. Those whose hands stick together are asked to act as volunteers. It is also advantageous for an inexperienced operator first to induce hypnosis in one whom he has already hypnotized. This produces a favorable mind-set and is highly motivating to the rest of the group.

Following demonstration of successful hypnosis in a volunteer, the group can be hypnotized as a whole, or from six to ten persons can be taken at one time. A comfortable sitting position is preferred, as deeply hypnotized persons are likely to fall off their chairs if not carefully observed. The audience is invited to ask questions about hypnosis. This not only enlightens the individuals but also helps facilitate rapport for those who volunteer.

PRELIMINARY DISCUSSION FOR GROUP HYPNOSIS

The following is a verbatim transcript of the preliminary discussion with a group, and some of the typical questions asked of the medical hypnotist. The actual induction technic is not included, but one similar to the author's progressive relaxation technic is used. Also included is the author's technic for inducing autohypnosis.

"All of you know that hypnosis and autohypnosis are being used for group training for childbirth, obesity, and other psychotherapeutic medical conditions.

"First, understand that there are many misconceptions about hypnosis. (These, as well as everyday aspects of hypnosis, are discussed.) There are many different degrees of hypnosis. May I enlighten you to the best of my ability about these matters? Please ask any questions you have, regardless of how elementary they may seem to you."

Q. "In autohypnosis, do I get the impression that I am inducing myself? And in such a situation, can I bring myself out of it, or is it necessary for someone else to do so?"

A. "You will always bring yourself out of autohypnosis. If you can produce it yourself, you can readily come out of it."

Q. "What makes a person go into a hypnotic state?"

A. "It's your belief, your faith, your confidence, your willingness to cooperate with my suggestions and the attention that you pay to my words that produce the necessary susceptibility leading to hypnosis."

Q. "Doctor, could you make me do something contrary to my moral code?"

A. "I can't make you do a single thing against your wishes."

Q. "What do I have to do, Doctor, in order to be hypnotized? That is, besides being cooperative?"

A. "If I ask you to close your eyes, you close

95

your eyes—not because you have to, but because you want to. If I say to you, 'Raise your arm,' you do not have to do it, but you raise your arm under your own control because you want to raise it. Now, why do we have you go through these simple exercises? Because hypnosis is learned exactly as you learn your ABC's in school. First, you learn simple, elementary words. You start with A . . . B . . . C. If you learn A . . . B . . . C . . . , then you will learn X . . . Y . . . Z. It's as simple as that."

Q. "Are all people suggestible? Also, how does hypnosis help one to get better?"

A. "We are all suggestible. Haven't you had the experience of being told, 'Say, you are looking bad. Are you working too hard?' Or, if another person says, 'Are you losing weight?' and if a third person says, 'You look awfully pale; are you getting enough sleep?', you are apt to look at yourself in the mirror, be horrified by what you see, and then make an appointment with your doctor. Actually, you can be 'salestalked' into being healthy! And it's much better if you do it through autohypnosis—the really scientific 'power of positive thinking.' Here your own affirmations that you will get better are accepted uncritically, and also you can better explore the nature of your problems."

Q. "Doctor, do you also give us medication?"

A. "Yes. Usually, if indicated, I use a comprehensive approach. Hypnotic suggestion can be combined with drugs and medical procedures. A combined approach is better than either alone."

Q. "Once I'm hypnotized, will I know everything that is happening?"

A. "You are always in control. You will remember everything you say unless a loss of memory for specific events is produced."

Q. "What is the difference between entertainment and medical hypnosis?"

A. "The stage hypnotist makes it appear as if he induces the hypnosis. The medical hypnotherapist knows that the patient really induces the hypnosis. Also, medical hypnosis is used for serious purposes, so naturally you will not be made to bark like a dog or perform other 'shenanigans,' as in entertainment hypnosis."

Q. "Suppose you have a problem that requires the use of autohypnosis. Can I still perform my normal duties afterward?"

A. "Yes, an individual can perform his normal duties and often can carry them out more effectively after posthypnotic suggestions."

Q. "Why not use suggestion instead of hypnosis? What is the difference?"

A. "Performance can be enhanced by hypnosis. Sometimes it is difficult to determine where suggestion ends and hypnosis begins. Between halves, a good football coach gives a strong pep talk that inspires the players. This is a mild form of hypnosis. Hypnosis is the acme of scientifically applied suggestion. However, I can't promise you that hypnosis is going to change your attitudes toward a given problem, but let us assume that you are only 10 per cent better. This is still 10 per cent better than nothing, is it not?"

Q. "Does one go to sleep at all during hypnosis?"

A. "No, you do not. Under hypnosis, you are more alert and better able to follow all suggestions because you are concentrating."

Q. "Why is hypnosis more effective than ordinary persuasion?"

A. "The purpose of hypnosis is to get an individual to respond with a pinpoint literalness. If you can get another person's attention just as a good orator or entertainer does, then the other person can be influenced by what you say because he does not realize that he is being persuaded. Otherwise he would have his guard up. This is the technic of an effective salesman. He get his suggestions through without you realizing that you are being given a 'soft sell.' This is the reason why hypnosis is more effective than strong persuasion."

Q. "Could I not use my will power instead of hypnosis?"

A. "No. Hypnosis is better than will power; it uses the imagination. You can't *will* yourself into salivating or 'goose-pimpling,' but you can salivate or develop goosepimples if you can imagine the experiences or memories which once produced such responses. A fundamental law of hypnotism is that you can't beat the will. You can't will yourself into a sickness, but you can imagine yourself into or out of an emotional sickness! Hence, we always use the imagination."

Q. "How do you account for having chronic pains when my doctor tells me it's all in my head? How is hypnosis going to help that?"

A. "Once an idea is launched in the central nervous system, it becomes like a 'satellite' which 'orbits' around the nerve pathways of the brain. Just as the rocket site for launching a rocket loses its importance and is forgotten, so is the original cause forgotten. Often a chronic discomfort is due to what is referred to as a conditioned pain pattern. The painful event which originated the response is no longer present, but its aftermath remains as a reflex. Often hypnosis can break up the chronic pain pattern by reversing or interrupting what we call a conditioned reflex."

TECHNIC FOR GROUP HYPNOSIS

The direct technic is the best for group hypnotherapy. The levitation technic is impractical because varied responses occur with each patient. Furthermore, one might have to wait 35 or 45 minutes for the arm to levitate.

VERBALIZATION FOR GROUP AUTOHYPNOSIS

"If you all are interested in going into a nice, deep state of relaxation, get as comfortable as you can.

"Now I want you all to listen to me because I am going to show you how hypnosis can be readily induced in all who wish to follow my suggestions. (The author's progressive relaxation technic for autohypnosis, described on pages 96 and 97, is employed.)

"Now, what is the purpose of going into this state of relaxation or meditation, self-reflection, contemplation, or absorption? It is to give yourself positive, healthy, constructive suggestions in order to neutralize negative, harmful, and destructive suggestions.

"In the case of the young lady who wishes to have a delivery under hypnosis, she can imagine, 'I'm going to look forward to having my baby with a feeling of joy and happiness. I will not have the slightest dread or fearful anticipation. It's going to be a wonderful, wonderful experience and I need not have any more discomfort than I

am willing to bear. Pain-killing drugs, too, will be available if I should need them. I will not hesitate to ask my doctor for these drugs. I am not going to feel guilty in asking for them. If the hypnosis does not work, I may have to have drugs. However, I will relax and, the more I relax, the less tension I will have. And the less tension I will have, the less discomfort I will have.' And really, childbirth is not a terrifying procedure unless you make it that way in your imagination. You can look forward to its being a beautiful experience in your imagination. It's as simple as that.

"And all of you can give yourselves positive suggestions for your own benefit. Now one more thing. While you are in this state of relaxation, it's remarkable with how much clarity and with how much precision you can think. It's almost like praying in church. It's almost like concentrating on your studying before an examination in a sound-proof room. As a result of this 'retreat into yourselves' right now, whatever you are thinking about is going to stick. And since you are planting ideas in your mind, you can rest assured that these eventually will become positive and constructive suggestions.

"Now, how are you going to bring yourself out of this? It's very simple. All you have to do is to count to 3. At number 1, you will say to yourself, 'I am going to go deeper the next time that I try this.' Number 2, 'I am going to try to the best of my ability to follow all suggestions.' Now in this state of introspection, reflection, meditation or contemplation (it doesn't make a bit of difference what you call it), these suggestions really stick. This is more effective than when suggestions are given while there is noise and distraction around you. When you are concentrating, tell yourself, 'I'm going to follow suggestions to the best of my ability.' And the third thing that you will think is, 'I will open my eyes and feel perfectly wonderful, free from all tensions, completely relaxed.'

"There are also two other suggestions you might like to follow. And that is, when your doctor wishes to rehypnotize you, he will touch you on the right shoulder—and this will happen only with your permission—it will be your cue for re-entering hypnosis. Remember, you are always in charge. When he touches you on the right shoulder, that will be a cue for you to drop into a deep stage of relaxation. At first you will close your eyes, then let your eyeballs roll up into the back of your head, and then you will feel a real, deep state of relaxation coming over you. Not sleep, but deep relaxation or hypnosis. A touch on the left shoulder will be the signal to open your eyes. So now you have two ways to enter into hypnosis; one in which the doctor can induce it and the other in which you do it yourself. That is all there is to it."

The author's methods of handling large groups for prenatal training are described in Chapter 36.

Invariably, one-third of those who are observing the volunteers being hypnotized will be hypnotized in varying degrees themselves. They will all dehypnotize themselves when the signal is given.

Group hypnosis has been employed effectively for stutterers, alcoholics, and those afflicted with headaches. However, group hypnosis reaches its greatest potential in relieving pain in obstetric patients and in the therapy of obesity. There is no reason why it could not be utilized in dermatology and anesthesiology, especially if conducted in a hospital setting.

19

Antisocial Aspects of Hypnosis

Considerable controversy exists as to whether or not a hypnotized individual will commit an antisocial act following posthypnotic suggestions. The situational context in which a request is made to carry out an antisocial act is important. Orne and Evans demonstrated that nonhypnotized persons manifested the same antisocial behavior as hypnotized subjects.[25] This indicates that the experimental control was recognized by the subjects as legitimate behavior. Many investigators believe it is possible,[1, 4, 17, 20, 21, 28, 29, 30, 32] whereas others do not think the evidence warrants such assumptions.[3, 5, 7, 14, 16, 24, 33] Kline denies the relationship,[16] Orne stresses that the patient always has control,[24] and Coe and associates emphasize that it is extremely difficult to perform a convincing study on antisocial behavior in a laboratory context.[5] This view has been supported by others.[2, 8, 24] Still other researchers take a position between the two camps.[5, 13, 27] Most of the experiments to show that antisocial behavior can be induced have not been carefully structured; the experimental setting suffers from a "pseudoreality" situation. More recently, other experienced investigators have concluded that it is possible to tip the scales toward criminal impulses and get antisocial behavior.[19] It has been posited that if a person harbors an antisocial impulse, he can act it out under hypnosis.[5] Even though it may not be a coercive force, it may be a facilitating agent, and in the applied sense, it can be responsible for behavior.

Evans notes there has not been a single case of a crime committed "under the influence of hypnosis" in which there had not been a long-standing personal relationship between the victim and the accused.[10] There is no concrete evidence that hypnosis *per se* enhances the degree of coercive control. Conn calls coercion through hypnosis a "myth" that belongs in the realm of demonology and folklore.[6] When a hypnotized person does antisocial things, it is not because the hypnotist has special powers, but because a *folie à deux* exists. Hypnosis can be used as an alibi, a rationalization, or a legitimation of behavior. Furthermore, since only a relatively few cases have been studied, more controlled clinical data is needed. Erickson, who believes that the possibilities for antisocial behavior are nonexistent, says that there are people "who will discount the theoretical possibility of hypnosis, yet will insistently attribute miraculous, effective, antisocial powers to even a single hypnotic suggestion."[7]

Soldier volunteers in a military setting have performed antisocial acts through post-hypnotic suggestions.[29] It has been pointed out that such subjects were strongly motivated to act in this manner because of the "demand characteristics" of the situation; they intuitively or subliminally knew what the experimenter was trying to prove. They also felt that the hypnotist, usually a superior officer, would ensure the safety of all involved, irrespective of their actions.

In similar experiments, a college professor in a psychology class has asked a student to shoot a supposedly loaded gun. The student, on more than one occasion, pulled the trigger and thought he was "shooting" the professor. However, the subject recognized the surroundings and the professor's voice. No professor has handed a student a loaded gun and put a bullet-proof vest on himself and said, "Shoot me." To evaluate the contradictory data that antisocial behavior can occur under hypnosis, one must consider many other factors such as motivation, role-playing and exhibitionism, as well as the needs of the hypnotist.

There is a well-documented case in which a person ostensibly committed murder as well as other criminal acts at the behest of a hypnotist.[9] This crime obviously was perpetrated because the subject, over a long interval, had developed a close emotional attachment to a mentally unbalanced hypnotist. In another case, a prisoner of war committed criminal acts through a posthypnotic suggestion.[26] Judging from his relationship to the hypnotist and the nature of the subject's acts, however, it seems possible that the antisocial behavior could have been performed just as easily through strong persuasion without the use of hypnosis. The consensus of opinion is that the antisocial behavior induced in an unwilling subject is primarily dependent upon the hypnotist and the extent to which he participates in the act himself. The subject is but a part of the newly created, structured hypnotic relationship.[15]

Because only three documented cases of actual criminal behavior involving hypnotic suggestion have been reported in the last 25 years, Orne does not think that a cunning hypnotist could force another individual to do his criminal bidding purely by hypnotic suggestion.[23] When a subject develops a strong personal attachment toward a hypnotist, as in the above-mentioned cases, it is not extraordinary for such a subject to become involved in an antisocial act which might benefit another individual. Orne concludes that "An explanation which purports to account for such behavior by singling out one aspect of the relationship, i.e., hypnosis, must be viewed with skepticism."

The explanations that characterize virtually all the experimental studies on antisocial behavior to date have been summarized as follows: The subjects believed that protective measures had been taken, since they knew it was only an experiment; they trusted the hypnotist either because they had confidence in him or because there were legitimate reasons for the hypnotist's requests; or the subjects had latent criminal tendencies. After studying all the available data, it is concluded that "hypnosis alone is incapable of causing antisocial behavior; that criminal behavior can be induced only if perceptual alterations are produced so that the act is not considered antisocial.[31] After an extensive review of the pros and cons of whether or not an antisocial act can be committed through hypnosis, Conn answers with an emphatic *No!*[6]

DANGERS FROM STAGE HYPNOSIS

Considering the thousands of people hypnotized daily by entertainers, there are remarkably few documented cases of harm. The author, however, is unalterably opposed to the entertainer-hypnotist's using hypnosis in any manner. Irrespective of his technical proficiency in inducing hypnosis, *he does not know the emotional makeup of the person he is hypnotizing.* Without this knowledge, he invites trouble for himself and his subject. Often the person hypnotized by the entertainer may have an emotional upset after he suffers embarrassment while on the stage. Frequently, some members of the audience will be hypnotized inadvertently. However, these are only temporary reactions.

Stage hypnotists supposedly have induced depressive reactions in some subjects. However, in most instances they failed to remove the suggestions which upset the subject. Typical is the following: "You will cry and feel sad because your husband is very sick." Inexperienced entertainer-hypnotists also fail to recognize that some subjects will *overreact physiologically* to psychological suggestions. If, for instance, a deeply hypnotized subject is asked to imagine that he is hanging from a 10-story window ledge, and that his strength is ebbing, it is possible that he could easily develop a cardiac collapse if he has a bad heart. Entertainers are going to give medical hypnosis a "black eye" until pending legislation prohibits them from using it for amusement purposes. The various bills in the state legislatures for these purposes have been reviewed. Harding contends that hypnosis is damaging not only to hypnotized subjects, but also to the audience.[11] The amateur operator often may encounter violent hysteric outbursts which he is poorly equipped to handle. Naturally, when this occurs, the hypnosis should be terminated immediately. Prompt removal of the subject from the stage, together with strong reassurance, will invariably remedy this difficulty. Heavy sedation may be necessary for those who overreact.

Age regression in the hands of the inept hypnotist is potentially the most dangerous of all hypnotic phenomena; here, deeply buried traumatic memories can erupt and result in panic reactions. If the resulting acting-out behavior is not handled properly, or if the regression cannot be removed, the hypnotist can identify with someone that the subject liked at an earlier age level. In the role of a benevolent surrogate figure, he can request the subject to return to his present chronologic age. It should be suggested that the subject will feel none the worse for his experience after dehypnotization.

Entertainer-hypnotists are not familiar with such technics, nor are they competent to handle conflictual material as it emerges. Therefore, the entertainer has no right to meddle with raw human emotions. Then, too, there are many amateur hypnotists and a few entertainer-hypnotists who treat a wide variety of medical conditions in which hypnosis is not indicated. Their inability to make a diagnosis can cause delay in effective medical assistance.

For over 40 years, the author has requested the American Medical Association and the federal authorities to ban hypnosis by the stage hypnotist because, as long as it is identified with entertainment, professional men will hesitate to employ hypnotherapy. This is particularly true where the physician must practice medicine according to the dictates of public policy.

Unfortunately, irrational prejudices about hypnosis are still held by the layman. It is sincerely hoped that healthier public attitudes toward hypnosis and appropriate legislation will eventually make it an exclusive medical tool. Yet it is regrettable that many serious-minded scientists who use hypnotherapy have to fight a two-front war—on the one hand, against the mountebanks who are promising quick cures with hypnosis and, on the other, against those colleagues who utterly disbelieve in its utility.

REFERENCES

1. Bernheim, H.: Suggestive Therapeutics. New York, Putnam, 1902.
2. Blatt, S.J., *et al.:* Is the hypnotist also being hypnotized. Int. J. Clin. Exp. Hypn., *17:*160, 1969.
3. Bramwell, M. J.: Hypnosis, Its History, Practice and Theory. Philadelphia, J. B. Lippincott, 1930.
4. Brenman, M.: Experiments in the hypnotic production of anti-social and self-injurious behavior. Psychiatry, *5:*49, 1942.
5. Coe, W.C., *et al.:* An approach toward isolating factors that influence antisocial conduct in hypnosis. Int. J. Clin. Exp. Hypn., *20:*118, 1972.
6. Conn, J.H.: Is hypnosis really dangerous? Int. J. Clin. Exp. Hypn., *20:*153, 1972.
7. Erickson, M. H.: An experimental investigation of the possible anti-social uses of hypnosis. Psychiatry, *2:*391, 1939.
8. _____: Observations concerning alterations in hypnosis of visual perceptions. Am. J. Clin. Hypn., *5:*131, 1962.
9. Estabrook, G. H.: Colgate University Symposium on Hypnosis, April 2, 1960.
10. Evans, F.J.: Behavioral compliance, coercial behavior, and the social context of hypnotic experience (paper read at the annual meeting of the Society for Clinical and Experimental Hypnosis, Philadelphia, 1976).
11. Harding, H.G.: Clin. Psychiat. News, *4:*17, 1976.
12. Heron, W. T.: Hypnosis as a factor in the production of crime. Br. J. Med. Hypn., *3:*15, 1952.
13. Hollander, B.: Methods and Uses of Hypnosis and Self-Hypnosis. New York, Macmillan, 1928.
14. Hull, C. L.: Hypnosis and Suggestibility—An Experimental Approach. New York, Appleton, 1933.
15. Kline, M. V.: The dynamics of hypnotically induced anti-social behavior. J. Psychol., *45:*239, 1958.
16. _____: The production of antisocial behavior through hypnosis: new clinical data. Int. J. Clin. Exp. Hypn., *20:*80, 1972.
17. Kost, P.: Dangers of hypnosis. Int. J. Clin. Exp. Hypn., *13:*220, 1965.
18. Levitt, E.E.: Can hypnotist coerce subject to commit a repugnant act? Clin. Psychiat. News, *4:*39, 1976.
19. Levitt, E. E., *et al.:* Testing the coercive power of hypnosis: committing objectionable acts. Int. J. Clin. Exp. Hypn., *23:*59, 1975.
20. Levendula, D.: Hypnosis in criminal investigation. Forensic Med., *31:*24, 1962.
21. Marcuse, F. L.: Anti-social behavior and hypnosis. J. Clin. Exp. Hypn., *1:*18, 1953.

22. Newsletter of the Society for Clinical and Experimental Hypnosis, *4:*9, May 1961.

23. Orne, M.T.: Book review of Reiter, P.J.: Antisocial or Criminal Acts and Hypnosis. Int. J. Clin. Exp. Hypn., *7:*133, 1960.

24. _____: Can a hypnotized subject be compelled to carry out otherwise unacceptable behavior? Int. J. Clin. & Exp. Hypn., *20:*101, 1972.

25. Orne, M.T., and Evans, F.J.: Social control in the psychological experiment: antisocial behavior and hypnosis. J. Personality Social Psychol., *1:*189, 1965.

26. Reiter, P. J.: Antisocial or Criminal Acts and Hypnosis. Springfield, Ill., Charles C. Thomas, 1959.

27. Schilder, P., and Kauder, O.: Hypnosis. Nerv. Ment. Dis. Monogr. Ser. No. 46, 1927.

28. Schneck, J.M.: A military offense induced by hypnosis. J. Nerv. Ment. Dis., *106:*63, 102, 1941.

29. Watkins, J. G.: Anti-social compulsions induced under hypnotic trance. J. Abnorm. Social Psychol., *42:*256, 1947.

30. Watkins, J.G.: Antisocial behavior under hypnosis: possible or impossible? Int. J. Clin. Exp. Hypn, *20:*95, 1972.

31. Weitzenhoffer, A. M.: Hypnotism: An Objective Study in Hypnotizability. New York, Wiley, 1953.

32. Wells, W. R.: Experiments in the Hypnotic production of crimes. J. Psychol., *11:*63, 1941.

33. Young, P. C.: Is rapport an essential characteristic of hypnosis? J. Abnorm. Social Psychol., *22:*130, 1937.

20

Dangers from Hypnosis

A wise man once stated, "It is much easier to ignore the obvious than to renounce the traditional." Thus thousands upon thousands of persons all over the world are hypnotized daily without harm and yet the method is considered dangerous simply because the "Svengali-Trilby" myth has been perpetuated for years.

However, an infinitesimally small number of dangerous sequelae following hypnotherapy have been reported. These isolated cases have been brought to the attention of the layman and the profession chiefly because of the ill-advised and promiscuous use of hypnosis by untrained and unqualified lay and medical hypnotists.[13, 14]

This situation is certainly deplorable, and adequate precautions to avoid the misuse of hypnosis are indicated. Yet a sober and objective evaluation of these cases shows that it is *not* the hypnoses, but many other variables, such as psychotherapeutic mismanagement of the relationship and misdiagnosis, that are etiogenic. The lack of documentation, personal bias, operator attitude, and hearsay evidence, together with the necessary warnings against the unwarranted current use of hypnosis—all contribute to exaggerated claims that hypnosis is dangerous. It is safe to say that hypnosis is the safest of all psychotherapies. Deaths and considerable permanent damage have been reported with shock therapy, steroid administration, narcosynthesis, and hallucinogenic agents. Yet no one has ever died from hypnosis!

Another issue is made of the proper criteria for selection of patients on whom hypnosis can be used safely. This author firmly believes that the only real criteria are the training, the judgment, and the experience of the operator, and the motivation and the willingness of the patient to be hypnotized, provided there is, of course, a specific indication.

The British Medical Association has reported:

The dangers of hypnotism have been exaggerated in some quarters. The subcommittee is convinced, however, that they do exist, especially when it is used without proper consideration on persons predisposed constitutionally or by the effects of disease, to severe psychoneurotic reactions or antisocial behavior.[2]

The initial approval by the Council on Mental Health of the American Medical Association stated:

The surgeon, obstetrician, anesthesiologist, internist and general practitioner may legitimately utilize these technics within the framework of their own particular field of competence.[1]

Whereas the report stresses that all who use hypnosis should be cognizant of its complex nature, it points out that controversy exists as to the hazards of hypnosis. There were few dissenting voices to contend that hypnosis was a dangerous medical tool. Yet the American Psychiatric Association report,[15] and the "Report on Training" issued by the Mental Health Council of the A.M.A.,[12] while making many worthwhile recommendations on training, indicate that the minority opinion of the original 1958 A.M.A. report has been accepted. The reader is also referred an article on this subject, written by the author.[9]

The A.M.A. was queried about their stand. The question "Has the A.M.A. Committee on Hypnosis ever published officially any statement defining or implying the dangers in the use of hypnosis by physicians?" elicited the answer that it had not done so, nor had it authorized one, and that a member of the committee who states this is "expressing his own personal opinions."

Platonov, an associate of Pavlov, who used hypnosis for over 50 years in over 50,000 cases, reported as follows in one of the most remarkable books written on hypnosis.

We have never observed any harmful influence on the patient which could be ascribed to the method of hypnosuggestive therapy, presumably leading to the development of an "unstable personality," "slavish subordination," weakening of the will, increase in suggestibility, pathological urge for hypnosis, etc.[11]

The author is in accord with Cheek, who has had a vast experience, when he states:

The mechanisms by which hypnosis can do harm are not different from the tools which Lady Macbeth used on her husband, which Cassius used on the honorable Brutus, which Iago used on Othello. We can do more harm with ignorance of hypnosis than we can by intelligently using the forces of suggestion.[3]

Julius Grinker long ago stated:

The so-called dangers from hypnotism are imaginary. Although I have hypnotized hundreds of times I have never seen any ill effects from its use. Bernheim, Liébeault, Ford, Wetterstrand, and a host of others who have practiced suggestive methods in thousands of instances have had similar experiences.[7]

Similarly, Pierre Janet, who at first opposed hypnosis and later became an ardent advocate, stated: "The only danger to hypnosis is that it is not dangerous enough."

Words can be more devastating than bacteria. During a physical examination, for instance, symptoms can be produced by merely placing a stethoscope over a patient's heart and carelessly saying, "Humph." The frightened and apprehensive patient is apt to ask, "What's the matter, Doctor, is there something wrong with my heart?" No amount of persuasion can convince this patient that his heart is perfectly normal. One would not indict the stethoscope or the physical examination as being responsible for the iatrogenic condition produced. But what was said and how it was done could be held culpable.

THEORETIC DANGERS FROM MEDICAL HYPNOTHERAPY

Seldom considered also is the fact that disturbed subjects can fabricate material as well as "acting-out" behavior in and out of hypnosis if they desire either to please or displease the experimenter. This can lead to dangerous conclusions on the part of the therapist. Moreover, it is not so easy to change behavior by hypnosis. If it were, a team of hypnotherapists could be sent into our penal institutions to hypnotize every hardened criminal into becoming a law-abiding citizen. This just could not be done. Thus, if wanted changes are difficult to obtain by hypnosis, certainly unwanted changes are not going to occur.

Not to belabor this point, in the usual doctor-patient hypnotherapy relationship, it is extremely difficult to hypnotize a patient without his consent or to induce untoward behavior in a subject from hypnosis *per se*. It is conceivable, however, that an unscrupulous physician, under the guise of giving vitamin B injections, could make an addict out of a patient by repeatedly giving him morphine and telling him that it was vitamin B. Likewise, through very devious and circuitous routes, it is theoretically possible to engraft an experimental conflict, covered over by an amnesia, in a somnambulist, and to give him posthypnotic suggestions to commit an amoral act. This "contrived" situation admittedly does not apply, however, in the doctor-patient relationship.

Wolberg states:

Employed by a reasonably trained professional, within the context of a structured therapeutic program, with proper awareness of limits of its application and with appropriate timing . . . the dangers inherent in its use are few or nonexistent, if it is skillfully employed by a responsible operator.[18]

Weitzenhoffer believes that there is no foundation for the belief that hypnosis weakens the will, leads to overdependency or causes neuroticism.[16] This author is in complete accord with this statement. The incontrovertible fact is that it is doubtful if, when properly used, there is another modality *less* dangerous in medicine than hypnosis. Yet there is no medical technic which makes a better "whipping boy" than hypnosis!

The supposed dangers from hypnosis can occur with therapy at nonhypnotic levels. Already emphasized is the sense of omnipotence and grandiosity that some therapists feel after obtaining spectacular results. Some of these therapists have psychopathological problems or oversell the method, and this leads to dissillusionment.[17] Motives on the part of the physician using hypnosis should be evaluated.[10] There are no dangers unique to hypnosis.[6,4] However, Crasilneck and Hall theorize that organic pain may be suppressed, thus obscuring the diagnostic picture.[5] In dealing with hundreds of patients, the author has never encountered this complication. Admittedly, it is possible to overlook a dangerous organic deficit, but this too occurs at nonhypnotic levels. A fuller explanation of complications and precautions in the use of hypnosis is given in Chapter 21.

REFERENCES

1. A.M.A. Council on Mental Health—Committee on Hypnosis: Training in Medical Hypnosis. Report approved by Council on Mental Health, February, 1960.
2. British Medical Association: Medical Use of Hypnotism: Report of Subcommittee Appointed by Psychological Medicine Committee, British Medical Association. Br. Med. J., *1:*1019, 1955.
3. Cheek, D. B.: Hypnosis: an additional tool in human reorientation to stress. Northwest Med., *6:* 177, 1958.
4. Conn, J.H.: Is hypnosis really dangerous? Int. J. Clin. Exp. Hypn., *20:*61, 1972.
5. Crasilneck, H.B., and Hall, J.A.: Clinical Hypnosis: Principles and Applications. New York, Grune & Stratton, 1975.
6. Friedman, J.J.: Psychodynamics in hypnosis failures. Psychosomatics, *2:*1, 1961.
7. Grinker, J.: Quoted in Quackenbos, J. D.: Hypnotic Therapeutics. New York, Harper, 1908, p. 109.
8. Janet, P.: Psychological Healing. London, Allen & Unwin, 1925.
9. Kroger, W.S.: It is a wise hypnotist who knows who is hypnotizing whom. West. J. Surg. Obstet. Gynecol., *69:*132, 1961.
10. Nesbitt, W.R.: The dangers of hypnotherapy. Med. Times, *7:*597, 1964.
11. Platonov, K.: The Word As a Physiological and Therapeutic Factor. Moscow, Foreign Languages Publishing House, 1959.
12. Plunkett, R. J.: Medical Use of Hypnosis. J.A.M.A., *168:*186, 1958.
13. Rosen, H.: Hypnosis and self-hypnosis in medical practice. Maryland Med. J., *6:*297, 1957.
14. Rosen, H., and Bartemeier, L.: Hypnosis in medical practice. J.A.M.A., *175:*128, 1961.
15. Ross, M.: Regarding Hypnosis: a Statement of Position by the American Psychiatric Association, February 15, 1961.
16. Weitzenhoffer, A. M.: General Techniques of Hypnotism. New York, Grune & Stratton, 1957, p. 424.
17. West, L. J., Deckert, G.: Dangers of hypnosis. J.A.M.A., *192:*9, 1965.
18. Wolberg, L.H.: Hypnoanalysis. New York, Grune & Stratton, 1945.

21

Precautions in the Use of Hypnosis

CONTRAINDICATIONS

The two most important contraindications to the use of hypnosis by the nonpsychiatrist are the queerly acting or unstable "crackpot" and the psychotic. The prepsychotic is difficult to recognize. He usually can be discerned by the intensity of his mood swings. The psychotic, especially the withdrawn, apathetic type, whose thinking is unreal, will be a liability for anyone but the trained psychotherapist. Conn has observed: "Neither one nor many hypnotic sessions can precipitate psychoses if no psychotic process has been at work."[1] Of course, organic conditions amenable to medical therapy should be given a careful differential diagnosis and not treated exclusively by hypnosis.

DANGERS OF SYMPTOM REMOVAL

Conn believes that there is no danger in the removal of a symptom and that one symptom is not replaced by another except in very disturbed, unstable persons.[1] As Eysenck says, "let those who castigate symptom removal even get symptom removal with their approach."* It is best, however, to use permissive suggestions oriented around the needs of the patient when hypnotherapy is employed for symptom removal. Symptom substitution or "trading down" to a less disturbing one enables the well-established

*H. J. Eysenck: Personal communication.

symptom to be manipulated more readily, and this prevents other symptom equivalents from being substituted. Spiegel suggests that the therapist should not expect or tacitly suggest that a substitute symptom may occur.[5] He uses the term "symptom alteration," which refers to directing the attention away from the symptom while simultaneously reminding the patient that more resourceful means are available for coping with his problems. Hartland also feels that past fears about symptom removal have been excessive.[4] He uses ego-strengthening technics prior to removal of the symptom.

Even if hypnosis is used for direct symptom removal there is very little danger that the original symptom will recur. In a 5-year follow-up study of two groups of patients who had phantom limb pain and hiccoughs, respectively, Dorcus noted that *not a single one of these symptoms returned when hypnotherapy for symptomatic relief was employed.*[2]

The dangers attributed to hypnotic removal of symptoms are grossly exaggerated. Such reasoning is not applied to generalists at nonhypnotic levels when symptomatic therapy is used. Furthermore, since other symptoms often make their appearance concomitantly during any form of psychotherapy, how can a new symptom necessarily be related to the "symptom removal"? And is not the bulk of nonpsychiatric treatment directed toward symptom removal? Moreover, there are no accurately controlled data to prove that other symptoms replace those that have been removed by hypnosis, especially when autohypnosis and permissive technics are employed.

It is often stated that repeated hypnotization can lead to emotional instability. There is no reliable evidence to substantiate this statement. Individuals who have been hypnotized hundreds of times have exhibited absolutely no harmful effects.

DANGERS TO THE OPERATOR

There are certain dangers to the operator, such as a charge of unethical conduct. This can be obviated if a third party, such as a nurse, is present. Tape-recording each session is also helpful. Permission of parents should be obtained when employing hypnotherapy in children. The inexperienced therapist should have another individual present when hypnotizing a disturbed female, or a subject who one suspects might be hysteroid, psychopathic or psychotic; psychopathic personalities often resort to confabulations characterized by wishful thinking, deceit, or actual fabrications.

A female patient may develop a spontaneous hypnotic amnesia and claim that the physician had raped her (this unfortunate situation can also occur at nonhypnotic levels), and because of the oft-associated idea that hypnosis can overpower the will, the hapless operator may find himself charged with unethical conduct. Aware of such possibilities, many operators obtain a signed release if unable to have a third person present. Three malpractice cases stemming from hypnosis were reported in a recent survey.[3] In each, the defendant was accused of assault during a hypnotic session; each case was later dropped by the prosecution, and each patient was subsequently judged insane.

Fortunately, most malpractice insurance policies protect physicians and psychologists against such lawsuits (see Chap. 23).

DANGERS TO THE METHOD

To protect hypnotherapeutic methods from adverse criticism, the therapist should not promise more than can be accomplished, and a guarantee of cure should not be made. However, if there is a valid indication, one can state that everything will be done to help the patient recover. All patients should be informed that the results obtained in hypnosis are based wholly on the patient's cooperation and willingness to cooperate. The following remark is helpful: "You are *not* being treated *by* hypnosis but rather *in* hypnosis. Hypnosis merely facilitates the understandings so necessary in all successful therapy. You are the one who developed the condition that you wish removed; therefore, it can be accomplished only by reversing those faulty thinking patterns which produced the symptom. Naturally, this will require your utmost concentration, receptivity, self-objectivity and understanding."

Hypnosis should always be employed for definitive goals. The dictum that "Hypnosis should be used for the good of the patient, not to enhance the prestige of the operator" must be kept in mind. It should never be used for entertainment by a physician or a dentist. Otherwise, respect for the method and the operator is destroyed. Finally, as emphasized, the inexperienced operator must never attempt to elicit deeply repressed and traumatic material unless he has been trained to recognize it and to know what to do with it when it appears. Otherwise, the patient will develop what has been referred to as "traumatic insight."

REFERENCES

1. Conn, J. H.: Preparing for hypnosis in general practice. Roche Report, *3:*3, 1961.
2. Dorcus, R. M.: The treatment of symptoms with special reference to removal by hypnosis (paper read before the University of Kansas Symposium on Hyp-

nosis Research and Clinical Psychology, May 8, 1960).

3. Could you use hypnosis in your practice? Med. Economics, May 22, 1961.

4. Hartland, J.: The value of "ego-strengthening" procedures prior to direct-symptom removal under hypnosis. Am. J. Clin. Hypn., *8:*89, 1965.

5. Spiegel, H.: Is symptom removal dangerous? Am. J. Psychiat., *123:*10, 1967.

22

Precautions in Dehypnotization

PRECAUTIONS

There are certain precautions that one should use when dehypnotizing a patient. As the result of the increased amount of concentration required for successful hypnosis, many subjects state, upon termination of the hypnosis, "I have a terrible headache." Therefore, the operator should remark, "Your eyes will open at the count of 3; you will feel perfectly wonderful; you will be completely refreshed and relaxed."

Always give posthypnotic suggestions so that hypnosis can readily be reinduced. The touch on the right shoulder is a good one, because one can remember "right" to induce, and "left" for dehypnotization. The same standardized procedure for each patient should be used in order not to become confused.

All posthypnotic suggestions, as anesthesia or hyperesthesia induced over any part of the body, should be removed by the statement, "You are going to feel fine. All of the suggestions that I have given you except the ones you wish to retain will disappear." Even though a subject is in control, one also should suggest, "Nobody can ever induce hypnosis without your permission, and this includes myself." This pleases most individuals, as so many patients fear they will be hypnotized against their will. This procedure nullifies the unfounded criticism that hypnosis can be produced against a subject's wishes.

Be sure to say *over* and *over,* "Now, remember, you were *not* asleep, you were *not* unconscious, you were *not* in any kind of trance, and *you heard everything I said.*" In spite of these clear-cut suggestions, subjects who were deeply hypno-

tized, but who do not understand the nature of hypnosis, state, "Doctor, I know I wasn't hypnotized. I heard everything you said." On the other hand, those who are conversant with hypnosis remark afterward how alert they were and how everything was heard clearly. I assure patients that this hyperacuity is characteristic of hypnosis. Patients who confuse hypnosis with sleep should be informed: "I am using hypnosis because I want you to be *more* 'awake.' If you are paying full attention to me, I can get more meaningful suggestions across to you." Patients then understand more about the nature of hypnosis.

All patients can be dehypnotized readily. This author, in several thousand patients and lecture demonstrations, *has never had a patient who would not or could not come out of hypnosis.* However, there are several reports on difficulties of dehypnotization.[1, 2, 3] The author remembers a case in which an amateur hypnotist could not dehypnotize a patient because he neglected to remove a suggested anesthesia from a subject's arm. The patient, naturally, did not wish to have a part of the body anesthetized. It was only when he informed the hypnotist about the arm that he allowed himself to be dehypnotized. Therefore, one must be careful to recheck all suggestions whenever a patient cannot be dehypnotized.

There is also the rare possibility that a somnambulist, who has been deeply hypnotized for a long period, may spontaneously reenter hypnosis unless completely dehypnotized after the initial induction. Therefore, it is always wise to keep such patients in the office for an hour or more, especially if they have to drive. Failure to do this might invite a law suit if an accident occurred.

Even though it would be difficult to prove negligence, the situation could prove very troublesome. Often, too, subjects who are reacting to a posthypnotic suggestion are not fully dehypnotized; some look "sleepy." Therefore, here too, sufficient time must be allowed for the relaxing effects of the hypnosis to be dissipated.

The pattern of actual sleep and the ease of awakening may be related to the ease of dehypnotization; heavy sleepers theoretically dehypnotize slowly. The particular mood of the subject at the time of dehypnotization can determine the way he feels and acts after the induction is terminated. Some cry, while others laugh—either is dependent on the type of associations stimulated during the hypnosis. Often the specific personality needs of the hypnotized subject can be correlated with the manner in which dehypnotization occurs. This is affected by the ability of the subject to face reality—a person who has a difficult life situation to face may prefer to remain in hypnosis.

Williams has described the difficulties associated with dehypnotization.[2] He points out that some individuals are only partially dehypnotized and then can lapse into deep hypnosis spontaneously. He also cites[2] three cases in which dehypnotization was delayed by the subjects' refusal to terminate the hypnosis. One subject became belligerent but finally was dehypnotized; another, who had been given a posthypnotic suggestion to misspell his name, was dehypnotized only after he had carried out the suggested act. The third subject refused to be dehypnotized because some preservation of highly charged emotional material of the preinduction period persisted during the hypnosis.

Bramwell cites two cases in which the subjects were reluctant to terminate the hypnosis (in both, disagreeable posthypnotic suggestions had been given).[1] Williams discusses other cases in which the hypnotist attempted to reinstitute an aphasia while the patient was being treated for hysteric aphasia. One patient told the physician-hypnotist that, if he persisted, she would refuse to "wake up." Another wanted to see a hallucinated movie again. He told the hypnotist he intended to remain in the hypnotic state.

Williams reviewed 30 cases in which difficulty in dehypnotization had occurred. In some, carry-over of the preinduction mood, malingering, incompetency of the hypnotist and other factors were responsible. Only scant data are available as to the exact time required for dehypnotization, but the periods ranged from one to several hours, despite medical intervention.

One of the "psychological" factors responsible for difficult dehypnotization is that the subject often deliberately attempts to test the hypnotist's ability to dehypnotize him. Frequently there is collusion with friends merely to embarrass the hypnotist. Errors and ambiguities in instruction, as well as omission of a relevant detail which is disturbing to the subject, can be responsible, as, for instance, failure to remove a suggested paralysis of the limbs, as mentioned above. Other factors include aggression toward the therapist, reliving of highly charged emotional material, association with what happened on television or in the movies associated with hypnosis, and combat fatigue treated by hypnoanalysis.

When some psychoneurotics fail to dehypnotize, the responsible factors often can be those which are also behind their symptoms—the behavior in hypnosis fits in with their emotional needs. This is borne out by the cases just described: the subjects were in control and decided how they wished to react.

DEHYPNOTIZING THE DIFFICULT PATIENT

Treat every patient with respect, as hypnosis is a dignified procedure which should be used only for medical reasons. Understanding the emotional needs of the patient who is to be dehypnotized is imperative. If an individual refuses to be dehypnotized, one can do several things. One can suggest that the hypnosis will merge with true sleep and that the subject will awaken from it none the worse for the experience, or that he will come out of it spontaneously.

If these measures fail, one can use time distortion, as follows: the patient can be informed that 1 minute of subjective or experimental time will *seem* like half an hour of clock or chronologic time. If 1 minute is equated to a half hour, then if he remains in hypnosis for 10 minutes it will *seem* as if 5 hours have elapsed. Thus he will have had his full measure of revenge. Now he will dehypnotize himself, because he has proved his point. If these methods are of no avail, one can resort to mild electroshock or Metrazol.

The best method is to superinduce another hypnotic state and make every effort to recognize and understand the specific behavior involved in the subject's refusal to be dehypnotized. If the hypnosis still cannot be terminated, another hypnotist can deepen the hypnosis and then impose his own conditions for dehypnotization. Sometimes further psychotherapy must be promised to get disturbed individuals, who demand more attention from the therapist, out of hypnosis.

REFERENCES

1. Bramwell, J. M.: Hypnotism. London, Rider & Son, 1921.
2. Williams, G. W.: Difficulty in dehypnotizing. J. Clin. Exp. Hypn., *1:*3, 1953.
3. _____: The termination of the hypnotic state. *In* Introductory Lectures in Medical Hypnosis. New York, The Institute for Research in Hypnosis, 1958, pp. 62–69.

23

Medical Training, Legal and Ethical Aspects of Hypnosis

MEDICAL TRAINING

Guidelines for medical training in hypnosis have been established.[12, 14] Some reports consider hypnosis to be a technic that should be limited primarily to psychiatrists.[14, 17] Inasmuch as hypnosis, in one form or another, recognized or unrecognized, cross-fertilizes with all the healing arts, it is not clear which of the numerous schools of psychotherapy should teach it. Since clinical practice and applications encompass the broad field of suggestion and behavior dynamics, it simply cannot be broken down into psychiatric, obstetric, or psychological hypnosis. Therefore, hypnosis cannot be claimed by any medical specialty or school of psychotherapy. Have not suggestion and/or hypnosis been responsible for the placebo effect in medical and psychological therapy for years? Waking hypnosis, together with other factors, accounts for the success of most spiritual-religious healers and the human potential movements. Even though most of their leaders have had no medical training, can anyone deny their achievements?

The mature physician, successful in his practice of medicine, already has demonstrated his capacity to deal adequately with emotional disturbances. Since psychosomatic illness comprises the bulk of his practice, it is inexcusable for any physician, oriented or trained in hypnosis, *not* to be able to conduct adequate hypnotherapy when indicated. This should be done within the usual restrictions of his medical training, judgment, intuition, and experience. Hypnosis can be used like any drug, especially as an adjunct to supportive therapy of psychosomatic disorders.

Because of inadequate numbers of psychiatrists, physicians now are demanding a less time-consuming psychotherapy. This has led to the current worldwide interest in hypnotherapy as an adjunctive psychotherapeutic procedure for *selected* patients. It is hoped that the behavioral sciences will incorporate hypnosis in their teaching programs.

The A.M.A. Committee on Hypnosis has formulated a curriculum on hypnosis to be taught in medical school.[14] To be sure, this is the logical way to teach clinical hypnosis. The University of Los Angeles School of Medicine (Extension) and the College of Physicians and Surgeons of Columbia University, among others, are now offering courses. When other centers institute such programs, this should eventually bring hypnosis to its full medical acceptance. Until further clarification is provided, physicians are urged to seek training in medical schools and other recognized societies and teaching organizations. All of these adhere to recent British and A.M.A. reports on medical hypnosis.[1, 12]

HYPNOSIS AND THE LAW

Due to the striking character of hypnotic phenomena, serious questions for legal consideration may arise. The legal aspects of hypnosis have been discussed from three standpoints: (1) criminal law, (2) the law of evidence, and (3) regulations placed on its practice.[18]

Several criminal cases involving hypnosis have reached the courts, in which women have claimed to have been raped or seduced while hypnotized. Nearly all have been dismissed on the basis of insufficient evidence or fabrication. Commission of other crimes has been recorded, such as murder, robbery, and assault following posthypnotic suggestions. In practically every instance, hypnosis was used as an alibi. In Chapter 20, it was emphasized that in the ordinary doctor-patient relationship it would be extremely difficult to perpetrate a crime under hypnosis and that, if sufficient criminal intent was present, the act could be performed just as readily by strong persuasion. The number of such cases decided is small. Now, however, with growing medical acceptance and greater application of hypnosis, the law will be called upon more and more frequently to cope with the medical uses and abuses of hypnosis. In some instances, present legal principles are adequate; in other cases they are not.

The most important claim is that hypnosis can induce antisocial behavior. However, as discussed in Chapter 20, extreme suggestibility and/or hypnotizability exists in varying degrees in all humans. Thus, current notions regarding suggestibility and hypnotizability need considerable revision. Standardized statutes are therefore needed, based on enlightened court decisions dealing specifically with hypnotic suggestibility, its limitations, and contraindications. Some of these will be reviewed.

HYPNOSIS IN CRIMINAL INVESTIGATION

Hypnosis has three primary functions in criminal cases. It can be employed (1) as an analytical tool to help determine an individual's state of mind prior to, or at the time of, a crime; (2) as a defense of criminal cases;[21] or (3) as an aid for developing investigative leads from witnesses to crimes.[15]

An early case was *People* v. *Eubanks* (117 Cal. [49 P 1049], 1897). In that case, the court refused to admit the testimony of an alleged expert who interrogated the defendant under hypnosis and found him not guilty of murder. The California Supreme Court upheld the lower court's finding,

stating, "The law of the United States does not recognize hypnosis." Between 1915 and 1950, there was only one reported case dealing with the medicolegal aspects of hypnosis (25 Ohio, LJ 2–3). Here, too, evidence obtained under hypnosis was inadmissible. In 1950, *State* v. *Pusch* (N.D. 46, NW 2nd 508) held that a recording made of interrogation under hypnosis was not admissible in evidence since no case had been found permitting similar evidence to be introduced.

The first case leading to the admission of evidence obtained through hypnosis is that of *Cornell* v. *Superior Court of San Diego* (52 Cal. 2nd 99, May 1959). Richard Cornell, an attorney, petitioned the California Supreme Court to compel the Superior Court and the Sheriffs of San Diego to allow his client, Paul Le Clair Conrey, to employ Richard Mikesell, a lay hypnotist, in order to prepare an adequate defense against a murder charge. The issues involved the 6th and 14th Amendment rights and also Article 1, Section 1 of the California Constitution. The Supreme Court ruled in favor of Cornell. The defendant could provide no evidence upon which a defense could be based. Cornell contended that hypnosis would aid in breaking through an alcoholic amnesia, which was accomplished by age regression and automatic writing. The Attorney General stated that information given under hypnosis was not admissible. The Supreme Court ruled that hypnosis could be used as an aid in defense, in that it was recognized by the medical profession, and then cited supportive information in the *Encyclopedia Britannica* (Vol. 12, 1944, pp. 22–24). The Supreme Court further ruled that the defendant had the right of privacy in his examination under hypnosis and, therefore, ordered the Sheriff of San Diego to provide the proper accommodations for conducting the interrogation under hypnosis in private. This case will be discussed more fully below.

The precedent set in the Cornell case facilitated a court order, designated No. A-104699, to allow an accused murderer to be hypnotized. When regressed to the scene of the crime, the suspect vehemently exclaimed, "I don't know where it is! I have never been there! I am innocent!" Even though incarcerated for 9 months in prison, he was exonerated when a witness confessed that perjury had been committed. His statements (6 full hours were taped) were corroborated by another witness. A robbery suspect later was arrested, and he confessed that he and others had perpetrated the murder.

In *People* v. *Bush* (55 Cal. 2nd, 1961), the defendant was charged with sexual assault and murder of two female victims after seeing the motion picture *Psycho*. The accused took the last victim to the movie. He stated that he was motivated by the film to commit the assaults and murders. Hypnosis was used as an analytical tool in regard to this defendant's state of mind. However, the hypnosis expert in this case was Dr. William J. Bryan, Jr., whose testimony was excluded because the court did not consider him qualified as an expert witness.

People v. *Modesto* (59 Cal. 2nd, 722, June 1963) involved a burglary, rape, and murder of two girls, ages 9 and 12. The principal issue of this case was whether or not the defendant was in the necessary state of mind to commit the crimes. A psychiatrist examined the defendant under hypnosis and came to the opinion that there was a lack of intent. The Superior Court admitted the testimony and also the tape recordings as evidence. The Court said that the proper procedure would be to waive the probative value of the tapes made under hypnosis as part of the expert's opinion against the rest of the evidence. In this way the jury might place too much weight on the information obtained under hypnosis to exclusion of the overall evidence. This opinion indicates that hypnosis can be used as long as there is a balance and as long as it does not unduly influence or confuse. Several other opinions cited below emphasize that the ability to cross-examine is extremely important, as it does not favor the side using hypnosis.

In *State* v. *Harding* (5 Md., Appellate 230, 246A 2nd, 203, 311–312, 1968), a girl was shot and raped and could not recall the crime. Subsequently, under hypnosis she recalled the events. The court ruled the evidence admissible. The question at issue was not the admissibility of the recalled evidence, but how much weight the jury would give to it. In this case, the court emphasized the importance of the professional expertise of the psychologist who had laid the foundation

for testimony under hypnosis. The court ruled: "Modern medical science recognizes that hypnosis can aid in recall, though fancy may be mingled with fact." Noyes and Kolb,[8] Wolberg,[22] and Spiegel[19] were cited as authorities.

A landmark case was that of the *State* v. *Nebb* (39, 450 Ohio, May 1962). The defendant, charged with manslaughter, was hypnotized in the courtroom before testifying. This was the first time that testimony under hypnosis was permitted in a courtroom. As a result of this testimony, the prosecution was convinced that the defendant was telling the truth about the death and reduced the charges against him. Later it was adduced that care would have to be exercised during this kind of procedure. If, for instance, incriminating evidence was developed under hypnosis, it would have to be excluded because of self-incrimination.

In a more recent case, *Greenfield* v. *Commonwealth* (214 Va. 710, 1974), the Virginia Supreme Court affirmed that the trial court erred in refusing to allow a psychiatrist to hypnotize a defendant during a recess in order to "jog" his memory before giving testimony. The Virginia Supreme Court stated that it agreed with the "vast majority of authorities which had concluded that hypnotic evidence, whether in the form of the subject testifying in court under hypnosis or through another revelation of what the subject said under hypnosis, may not be admissible."

In a recent California case, *People* v. *Peters* (4th Criminal 5996, March 1974), a police officer was ambushed the night that the suspect was elected president of his motorcycle club. The officer had difficulty recalling details of the event because of the circumstances under which it occurred. He was later hypnotized by a psychiatrist to enhance his memory and then remembered significant details which eventually led to the apprehension of the suspect. In this case, although the court did not directly rule on the question of hypnosis, it presented pertinent dicta which, although perhaps not legally binding, set guidelines for other cases. One of the dicta was that California law considers hypnosis as a state of mind. If the proper foundation is laid, the evidence obtained may be admissible. The court did not give blanket approval in these dicta, but followed previous decisions that as long as there was cross-examination, the evidence could be weighed as to its probative value. Here too, the value of hypnosis as a means of discovery was acknowledged, as in the precedent-setting Cornell case. The possibility of misuse by the prosecution was also raised, because of the increased suggestibility of the subject. Thus there can be problems in the above-mentioned situations, unless one is careful not to suggest extraneous matters to a person. However, most law enforcement officers are familiar with these tenets in routine investigations.

This is a partial review of the pertinent law related to the use of hypnosis as an analytical and investigative tool. Other cases have been reported. More will be in the courts as hypnosis is used more widely. It is worth noting that there are three evidence code sections in California. Section 702, A and B, relates to the personal knowledge of the witness; the witness' personal knowledge is pertinent when using hypnosis. Section 720 pertains to the qualifications of an expert witness. Section 801 has to do with the opinion testimony of an expert witness. All of the sections should be consulted and taken into account in preparing a case in which hypnosis is used as evidence.

As a consultant to the Federal Bureau of Investigation, which at present has a feasibility study on hypnosis, the author recently has been involved in several interesting cases. On September 22, 1976, he was called as an expert witness before a Federal grand jury to render his opinion with respect to a prison homicide. The author had used hypnosis to break through a retrograde amnesia induced by panic. The patient was ordered by the defendant, the leader of the most powerful gang in the prison, to stab his best friend. The motive for the murder was the victim's failure to pay off on a narcotic smuggling deal. The patient complied by stabbing the victim twice and inflicting only superficial wounds. Terrified, the patient dropped the prison-made knife and fled the scene of the crime. Other unidentified inmates finished off the victim, inflicting an additional 13 stab wounds. As a result of the panic and fear, the patient was able to identify some, but not all, of the inmates present at the scene of the assassination. Hypnosis utilizing age regres-

sion, time distortion, and imagery conditioning enabled the patient to recall and identify all of those who participated in the fatal stabbing. The patient's taped recordings were heard by the Federal grand jury, and these, along with other evidence, led to indictments against the alleged killers.

In another major homicide investigation, the author hypnotized a 17½-year-old girl who purportedly was a witness to the murder of a 15-year-old girl. The latter was found in a creek, having died of multiple stab wounds. No clues were found. The older girl, who had a history of antisocial behavior, was interrogated, subjected to a polygraph, and cleared of any association. However, she felt that she might have been amnestic for the entire experience, inasmuch as she had been under the influence of liquor and narcotics. She voluntarily agreed to be hypnotized for her retrograde amnesia so that she could establish an alibi for her whereabouts. She was regressed to the day of the crime and was able to relive most of the events, hour by hour, up to the time of the crime. She related having an argument with the victim over a boyfriend and vividly described how each had pulled a knife on the other. She detailed incidents up to the fatal stabbing and even gave the approximate location of the disposal of the murder weapon. Some automatic writing was used, as well, for obtaining a few significant details. Subsequently, however, she recanted this testimony. Four witnesses, including her mother and father, accounted for her whereabouts on the night of the fatal stabbing; all successfully passed polygraphic examinations. Margolin and Sinoway, her attorneys, believed it was a "hypnotically induced confession to murder."[7] This interesting case illustrates how individuals can lie convincingly and glibly under hypnosis. One might ask, "What were the underlying dynamics for relating erroneous data if the girl was innocent? Why would she want to implicate herself? Was she role playing? If so, she duped the author and three experienced law enforcement officers. Finally, were the polygraph examinations, both of her initially and of the four witnesses, accurate? With regard to questions such as these, Orne offers the following view:

Hypnosis has not been found reliable in obtaining truth from a reluctant witness. Even if it were possible to induce hypnosis against one's will, it is well documented that the hypnotized individual still can willfully lie. It is of even greater concern that cooperative hypnotized subjects remember distorted versions of actual events and are themselves deceived. When recalled in hypnosis, such false memories are accompanied by strong subjective conviction and outward signs of conviction that are most compelling to almost any observer. Caution and independent verification are essential in such circumstances.[10]

It is the author's impression that the girl's account might have been an "uncorroborated voluntary confession."

Another case of national prominence in which the author served as a consultant to the F.B.I. was the kidnapping of a bus driver, who was abducted with 26 passengers in Chowchilla, California. Using revivification, time expansion, and scene visualization the bus driver was able to recall all but one digit on the license plate of the kidnappers' getaway van. This materially assisted in the apprehension of the perpetrators of the crime.

The author has taken part in numerous other investigations involving recall of license plate numbers and better descriptions of assailants, leading to more accurate composite pictures by police artists. He has had many amnesic victims, has often helped to recover lost property, and has "jogged" witness' memories to recall dates and pertinent events. However, some cases have proved to be unproductive, in part because of the inability of the subject to relax, maintain an appropriate attention span, or show sufficient motivation. By using structured relaxing imagery to neutralize anxiety in a classic Pavlovian paradigm, he believes that empirically his overall results have been improved.

Several investigators have used hypnosis in legal investigations.[5, 6] Crasilneck and Hall have employed it with the informed consent of the subject and with the understanding that the information had no more reliability than statements given at nonhypnotic levels.[3]

Brunn reported piercing a retrograde amnesia in a murder suspect.[2] The abreaction and affect seemed genuine and matched with known facts.

Recall, except for one piece of evidence, seemed complete. He, too, notes that hypnotized subjects can truthfully report fantasy experiences dramatically and with convincing sincerity. Erickson states that the courts are justified in not admitting such testimony for the protection of the rights of both society and the accused.[4]

Psychological testing was used to verify a diagnosis of paranoid schizophrenia in a medicolegal case involving a male accused of voyeurism. He denied his guilt after being arrested several times for the same offense. The testing was performed to aid a psychiatrist and an attorney. Since the results were inconclusive, hypnosis was used to explore his past, and this led to the diagnosis that a psychotic process was present.[9]

Dr. M. Reiser, who has a criminal investigation program for the Los Angeles Police Department (L.A.P.D.), has had some very interesting cases.[15] One involved an officer who was shot four times in the abdomen and chest with his own weapon when he and his partner stopped a suspect who was involved in another series of cases. The suspect grabbed the officer's gun and shot the partner as well as the officer, escaping with the latter's weapon. Though the wounded officer was on the critical list, he was able to give the police artist a description of the suspect. The artist also made a composite sketch from the wounded officer's partner. The artist felt that the picture could be improved if hypnosis were employed. More details were recalled, under hypnosis, particularly about facial features such as the eyes, the shape of the nose, and the cheeks. The gravely wounded officer, upon viewing the composite picture, suggested other specific corrections. While still under hypnosis, he opened his eyes and said as he looked at the picture, "My God, that's him." Several months later the suspect was apprehended and one of the arresting officers stated that "the suspect was a dead ringer for the composite picture that had been given under hypnosis." The two composites—one made without the use of hypnosis and the other utilizing hypnosis—showed that the version given under hypnosis was almost photographic in detail.

Another case described by Reiser was that of a woman, who, while shopping with her infant, recognized an acquaintance she had previously met in a hospital waiting room and asked her to watch her baby for a few minutes. Upon her return, the acquaintance and the infant had disappeared. The woman was hypnotized and she recalled some pertinent details of what was said in the waiting room. She particularly remembered a ring that the acquaintance was wearing at the time. Under hypnosis she also gave an excellent physical description, enabling the police artist to develop an accurate composite picture. As a result, the investigator checked the hospital records and located the abductor and infant.

Another recent case of the L.A.P.D. involved a young woman who was kidnapped and raped by three males. During her abduction there was considerable conversation. Under routine interrogation, her recall was limited because of the traumatic experiences she had undergone. Under hypnotic revivification, she remembered the names the rapists called one another during the course of the abduction and the places they had mentioned. She also recalled that one of them had been on a methadone program. Additional information developed about one of the rapists having recently been let out of prison, who spoke of knowing people in northern California. Under hypnosis descriptions of the abductors were given to the police artist. The individuals later were apprehended, and the accuracy of the composite pictures was amazing.

The L.A.P.D. program on hypnosis has obtained significant evidence in more than 50 per cent of the crimes assigned to it. It is directed *solely to obtaining information from witnesses,* not suspects. No attempt at coercion is used.

HYPNOSIS IN CIVIL INVESTIGATIONS

In a recent case, *Wyler* v. *Fairchild-Hiller Corporation* (503, 9th Circuit, 503F, Sept. 13, 1974), two persons were killed and one person was injured in a helicopter crash near Katchikan, Alaska. In the subsequent civil case, compensation was awarded to the plaintiffs. The helicopter manufacturer appealed because hypnosis had been used as a recall device to get details surrounding this crash. As a matter of fact, the hypnosis was used 4 years after the original crash on one of the survivors. He had limited recall of the events prior to the use of hypnosis. In this case a psychologist performed the hypnosis and testified that he was qualified as an aviation expert as well as an expert in psychology. He also fully described to the court the age regression technics that were used in this case. On appeal, the evidence obtained under hypnosis was contested. The Court of Appeals held that it was for the jury to determine the credibility of the evidence.

Another case, *Kline and Selby* v. *Ford Motor Company* (523, F 2nd 1067, 9th Circuit, Sept. 22, 1975), reversed and remanded a lower court's ruling that the survivor's recall of events of an accident by hypnosis was admissible as evidence. Dr. L. Olinger used hypnosis to break through a retrograde amnesia. The court held that "although the device by which recollection was refreshed is unusual, in legal effect his situation is not different from that of a witness who claims that his recollection of an event which he could not earlier remember was revived when he thereafter read a particular document."

Raginsky reported a fascinating case in which hypnosis revealed the cause of an air crash.[13] Under hypnosis, an airline pilot described how he had caused a major air crash. The crash had occurred several years before and had baffled investigative authorities. A tape recording of two sessions revealed that as the plane approached the airport, 600 ft. too low, it snapped off some trees and rolled on its side. Passengers and crewmen escaped from the wreckage a few moments before it burst into flames. While many were burned, all of the passengers miraculously lived.

Prior to the hypnotic sessions, the reason given by the authorities for the crash was "fatigue and lack of alertness on the part of the pilot." The real reason, as disclosed under hypnosis, was that the pilot actually did not understand the working of a new type of altimeter, even though he had been checked out by training officials 2 weeks before. The hypnotic sessions also disclosed that the pilot was unconsciously fearful of high altitudes. Raginsky suggested that the pilot ground himself. However, he took a job with a noncommercial airline that made transatlantic flights. Some months later, a chartered four-engine plane piloted by this individual and carrying about 80 passengers crashed over North America. He and all the others perished. In the months between the two crashes the pilot himself had sought help in trying to determine what had happened in the first accident. He had developed amnesia when trying to recall the moments before the crash. He consulted physicians and psychiatrists and subjected himself to "truth serum."

In the first session Raginsky was able to get the key information. The pilot veered off course when he became upset emotionally. Raginsky then conceived the idea of dissociating the pilot from himself, making him an observer of what "another pilot" was doing. Under dissociation or "splitting off from awareness," the pilot described his fear of heights. He also emphasized how he was baffled by the altimeter. He admitted that he was too proud to admit having trouble with it. The pilot said he had a "nightmare" while flying over Newfoundland.

These cases show the value of hypnosis in obtaining information through hypnotic age regression, revivification, time distortion, and other relaxing technics to allay anxiety. The Civilian Aeronautics Board was so impressed that it decided to use hypnosis in investigations of all future air crashes.

HYPNOSIS IN INTERROGATION

In an exhaustive treatise on the utility of hypnosis in interrogation procedures, Orne states that it is doubtful that hypnosis can be induced in resistant subjects.[10] He found that hypnosis was not a useful defense against interrogation, but that appropriate instructions and autogenic training might be helpful.

Orne makes the distinction between hypnosis *per se,* and the hypnotic situation. The latter could be used, as mentioned, quite effectively for interrogation purposes. The common belief that an individual in hypnosis is not responsible for his actions, though probably incorrect, could be exploited. By relieving the subject of responsibility for his actions, the hypnotic situation alleviates guilt and thus allows the prisoner to divulge information which he might not otherwise yield.

Methods by which such a situation could be exploited, according to Orne, include the use of drugs, the use of a "magic room" (filled with instruments to detect lying), and various psychological measures such as a reward. Other investigators are using remote sensing devices capable of noting subtle changes in psychological functioning. By such measures they can tell whether or not a subject is telling the truth.

HYPNOSIS IN THE DEFENSE OF CRIMINAL CASES

K. E. Warner has examined the four main areas of criminal law in which hypnosis can and does play an important role, in addition to the rules of evidence which apply in those areas.[21] The areas pertain to (1) the preliminary investigation states, (2) the pre-trial hearing, (3) the trial, and (4) sentencing. Attorneys and physicians interested in these areas will find much valuable information in his excellent presentation.

Warner feels that the forensic aspects of the use of hypnosis are only just emerging.[21] Responsibility for explaining its technics, values, and disadvantages rests with those skilled in hypnosis. The courts are looking for answers and, as Warner points out, the major hypnosis societies have not issued a clear statement of the uses and abuses of hypnosis in the legal process. Without such guidelines, the courts will render individual decisions based upon the experts who happen to appear. The courts have no other choice.

MALPRACTICE AND INSURANCE ASPECTS

Physicians using hypnosis, as well as other forms of psychotherapy, are naturally concerned about malpractice. Most state and county medical societies completely protect the physician who uses hypnosis.

In a 1959 statement by the legal department of the A.M.A., physicians were warned that they would be faced with malpractice suits over hypnotic treatment if they were unable to establish their competence; two malpractice suits have been filed.[16] One of the largest insurance companies handling malpractice for physicians and dentists states that it has no restrictions on the use of hypnosis, nor are any contemplated:

No additional premiums are being considered by the underwriters for those who use hypnosis in the practice of their profession. At a meeting of the Professional Liability Underwriters, none had encountered any malpractice claims predicated on the use of hypnosis by dentists or physicians who were not trained psychiatrists. Not a single one knew of any difficulties whatever, and all recognized that hypnosis was being used to a great degree in the practice of medicine and dentistry—and quite successfully.

In response to a query to the leading malpractice insurance company in Los Angeles, which has the highest number of malpractice claims in the nation, the following reply was received:

As far as we can determine . . . there has not been a physician in California sued for hypnosis, and as far as we are aware, there has only been one physician other than a psychiatrist sued for hypnosis in the United States.*

A similar reply was recently given verbally in 1977 by another leading carrier in Los Angeles.

The precautions needed to prevent malpractice claims apply to all branches of medicine, and hypnotherapy is no exception. A generalist certainly would not perform a brain tumor operation. Similarly, without special training in handling psychotics at nonhypnotic levels, the hypnotist-physician might find himself in a hazardous position. He might be blamed for complications wholly unrelated to the hypnotherapy. As emphasized, improper suggestions easily can upset and embarrass disturbed individuals. Therefore, the hypnotist-physician must at all times assume full responsibility for what he says to his subjects.

Some writers have suggested the presence of a third person in the room to act as reassurance that fantasies are not likely to be acted out and as a legal protection to the therapist. This author works alone and, like other psychotherapists, seldom uses a third party unless the patient requests it. An exception might be the use of conjoint therapy for frigidity where imagery conditioning is deliberately utilized to evoke sexual responses.

In summary, from the medicolegal standpoint, there are important precautions to be taken. Hyp-

*The Nettleship Company: Personal communication, May 16, 1961.

notherapy should be restricted to those qualified by experience and training for diagnosing and treating medical and psychological disorders. The physician should not exceed his competence, and even then hypnosis must be used only for *selected cases.* The operator should never promise more than can reasonably be expected from hypnotherapy and should emphasize that it is by no means a panacea. Sometimes it is advisable to obtain permission for hypnotization from zealots and potential troublemakers as well as from the parents of children to be hypnotized.

Unfortunately, some malcontents may blame the physician on any pretext when they fail to recover. Therefore, it should be emphasized that hypnosis is being used primarily as an adjunct to psychotherapy and medical therapy in relation to the patient's needs. Hence, the degree of recovery is wholly dependent upon the patient's own motivations and cooperation and the extent of his emotional involvement.

With reference to a developing psychosis in a severely disturbed person, it is extremely doubtful that this can be attributed to the hypnosis *per se.* The onset of a psychotic breakdown is more temporal than casual: an iatrogenic remark, either at hypnotic or nonhypnotic levels, can be disturbing to an apprehensive person, especially one on the verge of collapse. If such precautions are kept in mind, medicolegal difficulties will be reduced or eliminated.

ETHICAL ASPECTS

Since hypnosis is rapidly becoming a dignified medical tool, a physician should not employ it in the parlor for the purposes of entertainment or self-exaltation. Ethical codes have been adopted by the Society for Clinical and Experimental Hypnosis, the American Society of Clinical Hypnosis, and the American Board of Medical Hypnosis. The interested reader is advised to obtain their guidelines.

REFERENCES

1. British Medical Association: Medical use of hypnotism. Report of Subcommittee appointed by Psychological Medicine Group Committee of the Brit-

ish Medical Association. Brit. Med. J., *1:*1019, 1953.

2. Brunn, J.T.: Retrograde amnesia in a murder suspect. Am. J. Clin. Hypn., *10:*209, 1968.

3. Crasilneck, H.B., and Hall, J.A.: Clinical Hypnosis: Principles and Applications. New York, Grune & Stratton, 1975.

4. Erickson, M.H.: Discussion of Brunn, J.T.: Retrograde amnesia in a murder suspect. Am. J. Clin. Hypn., *10:*209, 1968.

5. Heaver, L.: Hypnosis in the investigation of crime (paper read at the 18th annual meeting of the American Society for Clinical Hypnosis, Seattle, 1975).

6. Johnstone, D.C.: Experience with the courts in Southern California (paper presented to the 27th annual meeting of the Society for Clinical and Experimental Hypnosis: Hypnosis and the legal process, 1975).

7. Margolin, E., and Sinoway, R.M.: Hypnotically induced false confession to murder: preliminary questions regarding consent, admissibility in evidence and other legal issues. Forum, *3:*1a, 1976.

8. Noyes, A.P., and Kolb, L.: Modern Clinical Psychiatry. ed. 5. Philadelphia, W. B. Saunders, 1959.

9. Olinger, L.B.: The use of hypnosis as an aid to psychodiagnosis. Am. J. Clin. Hypn., *10:*84, 1967.

10. Orne, M.T.: The potential uses of hypnosis in interrogation. *In* Biderman, A. D., and Zimmer, H. (eds.): The Manipulation of Human Behavior. New York, John Wiley & Sons, 1961. pp. 169-215.

11. Orne, M.T., and Hammer, A.G.: Hypnosis. *In* Encyclopedia Britannica. ed. 15., 1974.

12. Plunkett, R.J.: Medical use of hypnosis: Council on Mental Health Report. J.A.M.A., *168:*186, 1958.

13. Raginsky, B.B.: Hypnotic recall of air crash cause. Int. J. Clin. Exp. Hypn., *17:*1, 1969.

14. Regarding hypnosis: a statement of position by the American Psychiatric Association, February 15, 1961.

15. Reiser, M.: Hypnosis as an aid in homicide investigation. Am. J. Clin. Hypn., *17:*84, 1974.

16. Rosen, H.: A.M.A. News, June 29, 1959.

17. Rosen, H., and Bartemeier, L.H.: Hypnosis in medical practice. J.A.M.A., *175:*128, 1961.

18. Solomon, J.: Hypnotism, suggestibility and the law. Nebraska Law Rev., *31:*575, 1952.

19. Spiegel, H.: Hypnosis as an adjunct to psychiatry. *In* Freedman, A.M., and Kaplan, H.I. (eds.): Comprehensive Textbook of Psychiatry. Baltimore, Williams & Wilkins, 1967.

20. Training in medical hypnosis: A.M.A. Council on Mental Health, Committee on Hypnosis, Approved February 1960, by A.M.A. Council on Mental Health. J.A.M.A., *180:*693, 1962.

21. Warner, K.E.: The use of hypnosis in criminal defense cases (paper read at meeting of the International Society for Clinical and Experimental Hypnosis, Philadelphia, 1976).

22. Wolberg, L.R.: Medical Hypnosis. (2 vols.) New York, Grune & Stratton, 1948.

ADDITIONAL READINGS

Aarons, A.: Hypnosis in Criminal Investigation. Springfield, Ill., Charles C Thomas, 1962.

Bryan, W.J.: Legal Aspects of Hypnosis. Springfield, Ill., Charles C Thomas, 1962.

24

Religious Attitudes:
Comparative Evaluation With Hypnosis

The only major religious groups objecting to hypnosis are the Christian Scientists and the Seventh-day Adventists. The former deny that their system of healing was or is associated with hypnosis, while the latter defend their opposition to it on ethical and moral principles. However, the Seventh-day Adventists admit that hypnosis has medical value if performed by qualified practitioners.[33] Their objection is that it deprives humans of freedom of the will. Without getting involved in an epistemologic discussion on free will, several writers question whether man can be deprived of his will.[10, 19, 29, 32] P. W. Bridgman, a Nobel prize-winning physicist, asks if there is objective proof that we really are free.[9] B.F. Skinner asks a similar question, arguing that our traditional concepts of freedom must be revised.[39] He feels that explanations should be sought in an individual's personal history. And has not the nervous system before birth been subjected to an elaborate preconditioning?

There are also unwarranted misconceptions about the ethical and moral use of hypnosis by uninformed lay Roman Catholics as well as clergy and physicians, who remark, "I always thought that the Catholic Church was against hypnosis." Actually, there never has been a blanket condemnation of hypnosis by the Roman Catholic Church at any time. The historical attitude of the Church toward hypnosis will be summarized from a theological frame of reference.

ATTITUDE OF THE ROMAN CATHOLIC CHURCH TOWARD HYPNOSIS

The first proclamation of the Holy See on this subject was a decree of the Sacred Congregation of the Holy Office, July 28, 1847:

Having removed all misconceptions, foretelling of the future, explicit or implicit invocation of the devil, the use of animal magnetism [hypnosis] is indeed merely an act making use of physical media that are otherwise licit and hence *it is not morally forbidden,* provided that it does not tend toward an illicit end or toward anything depraved.[11]

Aertnys-Damen,[1] Jone[21] and Davis[14] are in essential agreement and are favorably disposed toward the medical use of hypnosis. The chief objection to hypnosis, according to these theologians, is that, if hypnosis is not used in accordance with a person's wishes, it may deprive him of his free use of reason. However, St. Thomas Aquinas specifically says,

"The loss of the use of reason is not a sin in itself *(secundem se)* but only by reason of the act *(secundem actum)* by which one is deprived of his use of reason; thus, if the act is inordinate concupiscence by the use of wine, there will be a sin of intemperance pertaining to gluttony. But if the act that deprives one of his use of reason is licit in itself and is done for a just cause, there is no sin; if no just cause is present, it must be considered a venial sin.[35]

121

Thus the use of hypnosis for a definitive reason is not a venial sin. In the light of the recent pronouncements of the Holy See given below and the opinions of other qualified moral theologians, a properly trained Roman Catholic physician can use hypnosis where it is indicated.

A Jesuit theologian, J. T. Mangan, investigated the subject of hypnosis with the intention of making a medicomoral evaluation.[28] He interviewed six leading Catholic and five non-Catholic psychiatrists. The author also participated in the preparation of the questionnaire material. Mangan noted that hypnosis is not a state induced by so-called "occult" practices and is not associated with witchcraft, black magic, spiritualistic séances or the like. Nor is it fakery, foolishness, a game, or a form of entertainment. After a careful review of the various authoritative directives issued by Catholic ecclesiastical authorities in Rome, Mangan concluded that they *condemn the abuse but not the legitimate use of medical hypnosis.*[29]

Pope Pius XII made two statements about hypnosis, the first in his address to an audience for obstetricians and gynecologists, on January 8, 1956.[22] The Pope referred to deep hypnosis in delivery and suggested that one danger might be "emotional indifference" of the mother toward her child. He was careful to add, however, that some doctors thought this indifference need not be attributed to the use of hypnosis. Moreover, the danger could be avoided. The manner in which the Holy Father spoke of hypnosis in this context showed that he considered this primarily a medical question and that the judgment of its morality would ultimately be based on sound medical opinion. The papal statements are in complete accord with the views of nonreligious leaders in the field of hypnosis.

The progressive attitude of the Roman Catholic Church has fostered considerable interest in hypnosis among Catholic physicians. Many prominent Catholic physicians and psychologists have made significant contributions to hypnosis in medicine, dentistry, and psychology.

COMPARATIVE EVALUATION OF OTHER RELIGIONS AND HYPNOTIC PHENOMENA

BUDDHISM

Buddhist meditation is another modification of autohypnosis. Siryananda, a psychiatrist who practices in Bangkok, points out that hundreds of Buddhist priests use a primitive form of psychotherapy that is similar to actual hypnosis. He states:

I believe that they obtain this method from Buddhist meditation. Most of them seem to believe this primitive method works through their supernatural powers or is a miracle cure.[38]

Buddhist priests treat neurotic patients and are regarded as family doctors in many villages.

Zen Buddhists practice a personal meditation that is said to lead to insight and wisdom, to self-realization and lasting peace. In autohypnosis as in Zen, the meditation leads to increased concentration and increasing receptivity to healthy ideas. As a result, the corrective emotional processes are speeded up. Viewing the self with greater objectivity (insight) allows an appraisal of one's needs, and this leads to deeper understanding (self-realization).[25, 37]

After meditation, a Zen Buddhist receives instruction wherein a series of paradoxical problems are presented to him. This series, called a *koan,* treats of difficult and universal questions. It sometimes takes years to master the 1,700 or more prepared questions. This approach contains the "misdirection of attention" which prevents Zen from being recognized as hypnosis. Ikemi, who uses hypnosis, has described the similarities between autogenic training and "instant Zen."[20] These methods of psychoconcentration can be mastered in a short time, as against the 3 to 5 years it often takes to follow the older, classical Zen approach.

YOGA

The fundamental principles of Yoga are, in many respects, similar to those of hypnosis. It probably originated between 700 and 500 B.C. Yoga is a Sanskrit word meaning yoking or union. Yoga is not considered a religion, but rather a "science" to achieve mastery of the mind and cure physical and emotional sickness. It can work for the followers of a religious philosophy or for an atheist. There are many systems to Yoga, but the central aim—union with God—is common to all of them and is the method by which it achieves cure. There are four principal steps which one must master sequentially: (1) a cognitive approach *(nirvanam)* for the person who merely seeks intellectual fulfillment, (2) a dynamic active approach *(pratyahara),* (3) a metaphysical approach *(samkhya),* and (4) a reflective or meditative approach *(samādhi).* Their similarity to hypnosis and its associated phenomena will be discussed later. Das describes the nature of Yoga and its deep state of concentration—*samādhi.*[13] He compares *samādhi* with hypnosis, and observes that although the two differ widely in ultimate objectives, they have many points of functional and methodological similarity. In *samādhi* and deep hypnosis, the subjects are alert. After studying the EEG patterns of Yoga and Zen disciples, Gastaut concluded that the observed alterations in awareness were autohypnotic states.[17]

The aims of Yoga appear to be similar to the goals achieved by Zen Buddhism. From an analysis of R.S. Mishra's authoritative book on Yoga,[30] his description of Yoga and its technics are compared with hypnosis. A comparison of his statements and my interpretations is given below, the latter based on my studies with Yogi masters in India.

Mishra	*Kroger*
Never doubt your ability to control your mind.	Autohypnosis.
Be positive that you have eternal existence, knowledge and bliss.	Positive, constructive, healthful conditioning.
Always observe silence, according to your leisure, and make powerful *dhāranā, dhyāna,* and *samādhi* (fixation, suggestion, and sensation).	Fixation of attention with narrowing of the perceptual fields to outside stimuli.
Follow the instructions given in each lesson.	Heterosuggestions.
Never become excited when you are in an unfavorable situation.	Relaxation and avoidance of negative attitudes.
Never say "I will try to concentrate my mind," but say, "I will control my mind. I will concentrate."	Concentration necessary for hypnotic induction.
Do not become discouraged in your failure. You will eventually be successful in your practice.	Confidence; set realistic goals.
Be sure that you can do anything and everything—whatever has been done by any liberated souls. Have full confidence in yourself.	Belief and faith.
Understand exactly the science and the psychology of Yoga to become successful.	Expectant attitude.
Make a firm determination to control your mind. This is the first step or *yama.*	Motivation.
Follow strict rules to accomplish your determination. This is the second step, or *niyama.*	Practice.
Place your body in a firm and steady posture. This is the third step, or *āsana.*	Posture to facilitate sensory-imagery conditioning.
Practice control of your breathing. This is the fourth step, or *prānāyāma.*	Ideomotor activity in the form of slow, deep, regular breathing to produce relaxation.
Withdraw your conscious energy from the external world and external contact and identify yourself with supreme consciousness. This is the fifth step, or *praty āhāra.*	Depersonalization.

Fix your mind for local concentration on particular chakras and limbs which you choose, and for general concentration on the entire body. This is the sixth step, or *dhārana* (fixation).	Narrowing the perceptual fields; fixation on ideomotor and ideosensory activities.
Send strong suggestion after fixation. The suggestion depends on your intention, whatever you want, such as anesthesia, cold like ice, hot like fire, and so forth and so on. This is the seventh step, or *dhyāna* (suggestion).	Ideosensory activities; the law of dominant effect.
Feel the sensation of your given order, whether your subconscious mind is able to follow your command or not. After due practice it will follow your order. This is the eighth step, or *samādhi* (sensation).	Sensory-imagery conditioning.

After carefully studying Mishra's technics, I have concluded that the last three steps—fixation, suggestion, and sensation—are analogous to the ideosensory and ideomotor responses during autohypnosis. The first five steps involve the creation of a favorable mind-set or attitude. This creates the expectancy so necessary for the imagination to catalyze the entire process. The misdirection of attention is obtained through the various postural and breathing exercises, the rhythmicity of the breathing being conductive to complete relaxation. The goal of ultimate reality or *nirvāna*—the state of complete liberation—is strikingly similar to depersonalization and to other dissociated states characteristic of hypnosis. Naturally, I have respect for all religious systems, whether or not they are so classified—but belief compounds belief! The faith or religion that helps is the one that the individual has been taught to believe in.

After an exhaustive survey of the various types of Yoga, Arthur Koestler concludes, in his book *The Lotus and the Robot,* that it is "neither more nor less miraculous than the blisters and stigmata, the anesthesias, catatonias and hallucinations produced under hypnosis. . . ." It should not be surprising that there are various types of Yoga when one considers that we have many spiritual healing religions, many of which are mentioned in this chapter.

I have observed Yoga as practiced in India.[26] Yogis readily attain a deep stage of hypnosis comparable to somnambulism and the plenary state. Deeply religious persons, with experience in meditation, and introverts make the best subjects be-

cause of their self-objectivity. The Y-state is discussed in Chapter 50.

Variations of Yoga were also used by Jewish priests and, in the next section, the similarities of Jewish ritual and prayer, Yoga, and autohypnosis will be discussed.

JUDAISM

Bowers and Glasner, the latter a rabbi-psychologist, have compared the Jewish cabbalistic state of *kavanah* with autohypnosis.[9] Glasner noted that the experiences during prayer were strikingly similar to the phenomena observed in his hypnotic subjects. The common element in all the successful Jewish worship experiences and other ritualistic practices seemed to be reminiscent of autohypnotic phenomena. Both are crystallized in the concept of *kavanah.*[11]

The word *kavanah* contains the suggestion of empathy, rapport, righteousness, and steadfastness; its verb root is found in the context of "a heart properly attuned."[16] However, in the Talmud, *kavanah* implies concentration—correct intention (motivation). In Jewish theology the efficacy of ritual or prayer is wholly dependent on achieving *kavanah.*[8] Maimonides declared that a prayer without *kavanah* is no prayer at all. *Kavanah* was used to induce a state of religious ecstasy and also a state of deeper understanding and experiencing of God in inner reality.

In *Major Trends in Jewish Mysticism,*[36] which gives the impression of a Judaized treatise on Yoga, G. G. Scholem describes how Abulafia, a cabbalistic philosopher and mystic, developed a method of concentration upon the magical and mystical properties of the Hebrew letters, arranging and rearranging them, starting with the tetragrammaton and developing 99 further names of God. Bowers and Glasner were impressed with the autohypnotic nature of Abulafia's experiences; the various letter combinations produced hypnotic fantasies which accounted for the new truths and insight achieved.[16]

The development of a proper emotional state in preparation for devout prayer or ritual *(kavanah)* is similar to Yoga, Buddhist meditation, and autohypnosis. In all, posture and breathing play an important role. Centuries before, the Chinese used similar technics to conjure the spirits of the departed. Here, too, posture and prolonged eye fixation on the navel produced ecstatic states, which were autohypnotic in nature.

Prayer, particularly in the Jewish and the Christian religions, has many similarities to hypnotic induction. There is the regular cadence and intonation in the prayers (chanting), a relaxing environment, and the fixation of attention on the altar or religious leader. In Judaism, there is a rhythmic rocking of the body back and forth in time to the chanting which is hypnagogic. Finally, the contemplation, the meditation, and the self-absorption characteristic of prayer are almost identical with autohypnosis.

The Old Testament prophets probably utilized both autohypnotic and mass-hypnotic technics.[18] Talmudic scholars note that *kavanah* was used to produce depersonalization so that the prophet could see himself elsewhere. At this early date, the hypnotically dissociated self was recognized as such and was not regarded as a miraculous revelation of God.[7] Bowers and Glasner also point out that earlier generations had to describe and explain many experiences which would be regarded as autohypnotic in character by modern descriptive terms. This is what might be expected, as the concept of hypnosis is a very recent one. On the basis of their findings, they state that hypnotic research could possibly provide us with an operational understanding of prayer and its effects. On a nonreligious basis, Rund has described how prayer may be used as a method of induction for dental analgesia.[34]

In studying the underlying tenets of all the major religions, the scholar oriented in the phenomenology of hypnosis as well as in theology cannot help being impressed by the observation that suggestion and/or hypnosis are being utilized at many different levels of awareness. One need not refer to the Bible, the Talmud, the Koran, or any other religious work to realize that hypnosis in one form or another is practiced in nearly all religions. Our daily newspapers carry announcements of religious worship conducted in churches of all the major faiths. There are literally hundreds of types of faithhealers—all use suggestion and/or hypnosis. The very fact that there are so many religions which cure emotional ailments indicates that they must have a common denominator. As proof, the religion that does the most good is the one in which sufficient evocation of prior belief and conviction has been established. A Buddhist is not going to be helped by Catholicism, and a Protestant is not going to be helped by Buddhist meditation.

The author is by no means trying to derogate religion, but wishes to illustrate that the *raison d'être* of all religions is positive, constructive conditioning. If one observes pilgrims expecting to be healed at a shrine, one is immediately impressed by the fact that the majority of these individuals, as they walk toward the shrine, are actually in a hypnotic state. Shrine-healing is extremely helpful in many cases; however, it is not the shrine that actually cures the individual with a psychogenic disorder but *his belief, faith and conviction that the shrine will be effective.* Therefore, such healing falls into the realm of conviction phenomena that are strikingly similar to those of hypnosis. There are about two thousand religions among the two billion people in this world, and the more one studies the various religions, from the most "primitive" to the most "civilized," the more one realizes that there is an astonishing relationship, involving suggestion and/or hypnosis as well as conditioning, between religious phenomena and hypnosis.[2]

Bowers has observed:

The religionist can no longer hide his head in the sand and claim ignorance of the science and art of the hypnotic discipline. . . . Whether he approves or disapproves, every effective religionist, in the usages of ritual, preaching and worship, unavoidably makes use of hypnotic techniques, and is therefore subject to the same responsibilities as known and acknowledged by the scientifically trained hypnotist.[2]

In religious and medical healing relationships, the deeper understandings that we refer to as faith influence the body processes. The recognition of these age-old forces in the healing arts demands an explanation. It is obvious that both prayer and hypnosis are intrapsychic phenomena involving either dissociation or depersonalization while one is in communication with one's self or with God.

The rise of Christian Science and other metaphysical religious healing movements attest to this fact. A review of the past and the current attitudes of Christian Science and those of its principal founder, Mary Baker Eddy, indicates that the sect was indissolubly linked with the spiritualist movement which began in Europe, through the influence of the Chevalier de Barbarin. Without paraphernalia, he successfully "magnetized" people during the latter part of the eighteenth century. His influence spread to Scandinavia, where Emanuel Swedenborg, the Swedish scientist-mystic, embraced his method. Phineas Quimby, whose manuscripts were recently published, practiced comparable methods in America.[15]

Another famous disciple of Quimby, in addition to Mary Baker Eddy, was W.F. Evans, a Swedenborgian clergyman, who visited him in 1863. Evans became a noted and voluminous writer on mental healing, whose views were incorporated into the New Thought movement. The principles of New Thought are that the mind has an influence on the body, that good thoughts have a salutary effect, and that bad thoughts are injurious. Such views are similar to those currently held by advocates of transcendental meditation (TM).

MEDITATIVE TECHNICS

For centuries, Zen, Buddhist, Tibetan, and Yogic methods have used a system of meditation and an altered state of consciousness similar to hypnosis. All involve either a chanted mantra or the focus of attention on an object; incense, soft music, and a dark room facilitate changes in reality orientation. Although the followers of the Maharishi Mahesh Yogi claim to use a different approach, their T.M. practices are in no sense original. Deep relaxation, self-reflection, and contemplation are used in all methods to autohypnosis. In the ancient sleep temples, repetitive sensory input involving sight, sound, smell, and touch augmented the ceremony, resulting in almost complete sensory awareness, to produce a relaxed, receptive, aroused attention similar to autohypnosis. MacHovec states that these meditative states may indeed be one and the same.[27] The author would include practices in Hinduism, Sufism, Shintoism, and Taoism in this category.

Dalal and Barber disagree, contending that Yoga and hypnosis are not altered states of consciousness and that the Yogi's feats are readily explained.[12] It is true that fire walking, live burial, stoppage of the heart, and lying on nails without mishap are tricks which are explainable. However, this does not negate the validity of increased autonomic control. By presenting convincing arguments that Yogic feats are due to deception, these authors reason syllogistically that hypnotic phenomena are artifacts. Kim, on the other hand, illustrates the prominent role of hypnosis in shamanism, the major religion in Korea.[23]

In recent years there has been more interest in scientific investigations into autonomic changes associated with meditation.[41] Studies have shown that this state is different from sleeping, dreaming, wakefulness, and hypnosis. A recent study compared the autonomic effects of meditation and autohypnosis.[43] These researchers showed that meditation and hypnosis do not differ markedly from each other or from a control group given merely instructed relaxation. Other studies indicated decreased autonomic responses in Zen[2] and Yoga.[3, 44] Similar effects were noted in T.M.[43] Later it was observed that relaxation *per se* with a "mental trick" similar to meditative methods resulted in a hypometabolic effect.[4] Benson and his co-workers contend that autosuggestion and hypnosis are different from the meditative state on the basis of only slight changes in central nervous system functioning.[5, 42] This finding needs to be confirmed because of failure to use proper control technics; it also is at variance with other observations.[27, 40] It is posited that autonomic response levels reflect hypnotic susceptibility.[31] It may be that anxiety reduction is the crucial variable rather than the technic *per se.*

The author is amazed that "old medicine in new bottles" is accepted as a new prescription. Perhaps, assimilating the non-materialistic aims of Yoga and Zen with their inner-directed thought is difficult to accomplish in a Judeo-Christian culture which is directed more to outward events.

Benson admits that the relaxation response may well be induced by other technics, such as hypnotically suggested deep relaxation, autogenic training, progressive relaxation, and various religious prayers.[6] Transcendental meditation, therefore, is only one method of eliciting the "relaxation response." In modern physiologic terms it is not clear just how this control takes place. We can speak of Yoga or transcendental meditation as practical disciplines, but efforts to translate them into terms of alpha waves, reciprocal inhibition, hypothalamic stimulation, biofeedback or other medical approaches are as yet far from successful. However, if the rituals can provide peace of mind and self-control, this is what is important.

REFERENCES

1. Aertnys-Damen: Theologia Moralis, Secundum Doctrinam Sancti Alfonsi de Ligurio. Doctoris Ecclesial, No. 432, vol. 1. Turin: Marietti Press, 1947, p. 360.
2. Akishige, Y.: Psychological Studies of Zen. Bulletin of the Faculty of Literature of Kyushu University, 1968.
3. Anand, B.K., *et al.*: Some aspects of EEG studies in Yogis. Electroencephalography and Neurophysiology, *13:*452, 1961.
4. Beary, J.F., and Benson, H.: A simple psychophysiologic technique which selects the hypometabolic changes of the relaxation response. Psychosom. Med., *36:*115, 1974.
5. Benson, H., *et al.:* The relaxation response. Psychiatry, *37:*46, 1974.
6. _____: The Relaxation Response. New York, Morrow, 1975.
7. Bowers, M.: Friend or traitor? Hypnosis in the service of religion. Int. J. Clin. Exp. Hypn., *7:*205, 1959.
8. Bowers, M., and Glasner, S.: Auto-hypnotic aspects of the Jewish cabbalistic concept of kavanah. J. Clin. Exp. Hypn.,*6:*50, 1958.
9. Bridgman, P. W.: The Way Things Are. Cambridge, Mass., Harvard University Press, 1959.
10. Budd, W. C.: Is free will really necessary? Am. Psychologist, *15:*217, 1960.
11. Collectanea Sanctae Congregationis de Propaganda Fide, No. 1018, editio anni 1907.
12. Dalal, A.S., and Barber, T.X.: Yoga, "Yogic feats," and hypnosis in the light of empirical research. Am. J. Clin. Hypn., *11:*155, 1969.
13. Das, J.P.: Yoga and hypnosis. Int. J. Clin. Exp. Hypn., *11:*31, 1963.
14. Davis, H.: Moral and Pastoral Theology. New York, Sheed & Ward, 1946.
15. Dresser, H.W.: The Quimby Manuscripts. New York, Julian Press, 1961.
16. Enelow, H. G.: Kavanah—the struggle for inwardness in Judaism. *In* Enelow, H. G.: Selected Works. vol. 6, pp. 252–288. Private printing, Kingsport, Tenn., 1935.
17. Gastaut, H.: Hypnosis and presleep patterns. *In* Chertok, L. (ed.): Psychophysiological Mechanisms of Hypnosis. New York, Springer-Verlag, 1969.
18. Glasner, S.: A note on allusions to hypnosis in the Bible and Talmud. J. Clin. Exp. Hypn., *3:*34, 1955.
19. Huxley, T.X.: Methods and Results. Chap. 24. New York, Macmillan, 1893.
20. Ikemi, Y.: Instant Zen. Clin. Psychiat. News, *4:*23, 1976.
21. Jone, H.: Moral Theology. Westminister, Maryland, Newman Press, 1948.
22. Kelley, G.: (Quoted) Hypnosis as anesthesia. *In* Medico-Moral Problems. Chap. 32. St. Louis, The Catholic Hospital Association of the U.S. and Canada, 1958, p. 289.
23. Kim, W.: A further study of Korean shamanism and hypnosis. Am. J. Clin. Hypn., *11:*183, 1969.
24. Kroger, W.S.: Clinical and Experimental Hypnosis. Philadelphia, J.B. Lippincott, 1963.
25. _____: Comparative evaluation of Zen, Yoga, Judaism with conditioning technics and psychotherapy. Excerpta Medica Foundation, *6:*175, 1966.
26. _____: Newer trends in psychosomatic medicine and hypnosis as related to yoga. *In* Yogendra, S. (ed.): Yoga in Modern Life. Bombay, Yoga Institute of Bombay, 1966.
27. MacHovec, F.J.: Hypnosis before Mesmer. Am. J. Clin. Hypn., *17:*215, 1975.

28. Magnan, J.T.: Hypnosis: a medico-moral evaluation, Linacre Q., *26:*39, 1959.

29. Maier, N.R.F.: Maier's law. Am. Psychologist, *15:* 208, 1960.

30. Mishra, R.S.: The Fundamentals of Yoga. New York, Julian Press, 1959.

31. Morgan, A.H., *et al.:* EEG alpha: Lateral asymmetry related to task and hypnotizability. Psychophysiology, *11:*275, 1974.

32. Nettler, G.: Cruelty, dignity, and determinism. Am. Sociol. Rev., *24:* 375, 1959.

33. Provonsha, J. W.: Ethical implications of medical hypnosis. Med. Arts *14*(4), 1960.

34. Rund, J.: Hypnosis and prayer. J. Hypn. Psychol. Dent., *1:*24, 1957.

35. St. Thomas Aquinas: Summa Theologica. 2, 2, qu. 153, Art. 4, ad 2.

36. Scholem, G. G.: Major Trends in Jewish Mysticism. (Revised ed.) New York, Schocken Books, 1941. pp. 133–134.

37. Shimano, E.T., *et al.:* On research in Zen. Am. J. Psychiat., *132:*1300, 1976.

38. Siryananda, C.: Medical hypnosis in Thailand. Br. J. Med. Hypn., *10:*41, 1948.

39. Skinner, B.F.: Beyond Freedom and Dignity. New York, Knopf, 1972.

40. Tart, C.T.: Hypnotic depth and basal skin resistance. Int. J. Clin. Exp. Hypn., *11:*81, 1963.

41. Wallace, R.K.: The physiological effects of transcendental meditation. Science, *167:*1751, 1970.

42. Wallace, R.K., and Benson, H.: The physiology of meditation. Sci. Am., *226:*85, 1972.

43. Walrath, L.C., and Hamilton, M.A.: Autonomic correlates of meditation and hypnosis. Am. J. Clin. Hypn., *17:*190, 1975.

44. Wenger, M., and Bagich, B.: Studies of autonomic function in practitioners of Yoga in India. Behav. Sci., *6:*312, 1961.

ADDITIONAL READING

Wittkofski, J.: The Pastoral Use of Hypnotic Technique. New York, Macmillan, 1961.

Smith, J.C.: Meditation as psychotherapy: a review of the literature. Psychol. Bull., *82:*558, 1975.

Morgan, J., *et al.:* Position statement on meditation. Task Force of the American Psychiatric Association, 134:720, June 1977.

25

Magic, Spiritualistic Faith-Healing, and Hypnosis

ROLE OF MAGIC IN HEALING

Magic is the professed art of performing wonders by using misdirection of attention. The use of magic and faith-healing from earliest recorded history to the development of modern psychotherapy from mesmerism and spiritualism has been reviewed.[1]

The history of medicine closely parallels the development of magical healing, which was practiced when no rational physical cause for disease could be demonstrated. The magical healing was produced by amulets, herbs, naturalistic forces, and exorcism. Over the last several thousand years, magical healing became the special province of priests and, to a degree, it still is practiced as faith-healing. Only during the latter half of the last century has science infiltrated into the healing arts.

Just as primitive man developed the expectation that some type of magical gesture would heal him, so has his descendent, modern man, searched for a miraculous cure to relieve his suffering. The modern physician's role often is similar to the one played by the tribal medicine man. The latter's prestige is enhanced by his costume and headdress and, likewise, the physician's, by his garb, or, if he is a psychotherapist, by his couch or consultation chamber. The physician's instruments, prescriptions, reputation, skill, and bedside manner—all often are essential ingredients for recovery. Cultural factors such as the psychosocial attitudes toward the latest fad, wonder drug, or psychotherapeutic procedure poten-

tiate healing; those methods of therapy that occupy the limelight seem to be the most effective. Therefore, as true scientists, we should determine the relationship between magical methods, suggestibility, and hypnosis.

We might also investigate if and how magical procedures can kill. *Susto* or *aspanto,* in which the victim falls "dead," and then is revived following ritualistic procedures by a magician, has been described among the half-castes of Guatemala. In that country, a susceptible individual can go into coma and be cured of it almost instantaneously by a magical system of faith-healing.

SPIRITUAL FAITH-HEALING

In all magical healing one must distinguish between faith-healing, carried out through the confidence of the healer in his secular power, and spiritual healing, in which the healer may act as an intermediary in a spiritual process initiated by a deity. The faith-healer believes that his power is akin to drugs, rational psychotherapy, and other measures; the spiritual healer believes that he is a divine instrument of God and therefore is capable of healing solely through a religious approach. Both types of faith-healing are related to suggestibility and hypnosis, as discussed on page 134.

Faith is a difficult parameter to measure as it affects man's health; yet it is perhaps the most curative power on earth. Every physician has witnessed its force, and he can ill afford to ignore this valuable ally in his therapeutic approach. Since almost every organic condition has a psychological component, faith-healing can be successful in certain psychosomatic entities. Ulcers, neurodermatitis, arthritis, and asthma are often helped by faith in a certain medicament or procedure. However, it is doubtful if organic ailments can be cured by faith-healers—this in spite of the testimonials invariably produced following an emotionally charged impact on the participant. Faith-healing is not in any sense miraculous healing, but rather a method involving known psychological forces. However, some have exploited faith-healing for their own selfish purposes, thus destroying the subject's belief in faith. This is not an indictment of religious faith, but of those charlatans who feed on human misery.

Nearly all religious denominations agree that, when a person is ill, scientific procedures should be utilized together with faith. The latter merely supplements the doctor's therapy. Lack of faith can lower the patient's morale and adversely influence the course of a disease. No one can deny the power of the mind in any type of healing and say that faith is not the best antidote for despair.

DEVELOPMENT OF FAITH-HEALING FROM HYPNOSIS

To understand the rise of faith-healing during the past century, it is necessary to amplify its historical development in Europe and America. As mentioned in Chapter 1, its modern history began in 1765 with Franz Mesmer, whose observations were discredited. Those who were interested in animal magnetism divided into two groups. One became interested in phrenology. The other led by physicians, Drs. Braid and Liébeault, began to pay more attention to the psychological aspects of healing and steadfastly adhered to the practice of hypnotism. They believed that the cures of their patients were obtained solely by suggestion. Later, many prominent neurologists and psychologists began to study hypnotism. The role of hypnosis in personality dissociation was elucidated by Janet, Prince, Sidis, and others.

RISE OF OTHER FAITH-HEALING MOVEMENTS

The other offspring of mesmerism in Europe, the phrenologists, were led by Franz Joseph Gall and his associate, Johann Caspar Spurzheim. The former was discredited and the latter came to America, where Stanley Grimes introduced the concept of phrenomagnetism in 1845. By pressing a skull protuberance which he assumed to be responsible for the mesmerizing "propensity," he was able to invoke mesmeric trances directly. The uniting of mesmerism with cerebral manifestations excited scientific investigators for many years, and then died. Nevertheless, many other pseudoscientific healers, who followed, employed magic, physical measures, and hypnosis to effect a cross-fertilization between medical science and psychic phenomena. Cures were obtained by mesmeric clairvoyance, telepathy, and spiritism.

Just as the newly honored sciences of astronomy and physics led to mesmerism and its various "scientific" faith-healers, who used a religious approach, so did metaphysical neoreligions provide the matrix for faith-healers with no scientific pretensions. Among these were the mind-curers or spiritualists, who seldom realized that their cures resulted from the imagination, as postulated by the medical hypnotists.

Spiritualism, together with slight deviations acquired from various oriental religions, became the background for the various sects devoted to mental- or faith-healing in America. All focused their attention on the psychical-religious side of healing through faith. This faith has not diminished materially, and, even today, there is an ethical and cooperative therapeutic effort between theologians and psychiatrists in the form of "pastoral psychology."

Pastoral psychology had its origin in the Emmanuel movement.[13] This was a sincere spiritual movement for psychotherapeutic purposes developed by a Boston minister, Elwood Worcester. In conjunction with S. Weir Mitchell, a famed neurologist, Worcester introduced the healing ministrations of Jesus through religio-suggestive procedures. The Emmanuel Church aimed to inculcate suggestions from the Scriptures on the basis that a temporary dissociation of the personality facilitated acceptance of faith-laden ideas.[21] The advocates of the Emmanuel movement admitted that suggestion and hypnosis were utilized. The Dubois method of persuasion was considered good psychotherapy, and to this they added the serenity afforded by "surrender to God."

Men like Emerson, the essayist, and William James, the psychologist,[10] who was cured of melancholia, believed that strenthening the will or educating it was the object of our existence. James emphasized that ideas and emotional excitement could "energize" a man and release inhibitions which habitually cut down his capacity for work and enjoyment.

This new alignment of Christian faith within a clinical atmosphere continued its growth. During the past three or four decades a spate of books has appeared emphasizing the effect of spiritual life on the mind of man. Many scientists became impatient with the attempts to make disguised hypnotism serve religion, and refused to be associated with the numerous neoreligious movements which were springing up. But hypnotism could not be stifled. That this modality has received the attention of healers, generation after generation, and is today stronger than ever, is one of the most interesting phenomena in the history of mental healing.

One of the first mental healers to use magnetism in the United States was Phineas Quimby, a clock-maker's apprentice, who had little schooling. In 1838, he was impressed by a lecture on mesmerism by Charles Poyen. After briefly studying with him, he began to experiment, in this new "science," and became a professional mesmerist in Portland, Maine, in 1859, giving public demonstrations and successfully treating disease by magnetization.

Soon Quimby dispensed with magnetization, convinced that the patient's mind could be influenced directly through persuasion. He reasoned that if disease is due merely to belief, it was only necessary to refute the idea that disease existed; all disease was a delusion. Though not an adherent of Christianity, he believed that his methods were similar to those by which Christ healed. At various times he referred to his doctrine as the "Science of Christ," "Christian Science," "Science of Health," or the "Science of Health and Happiness." He was the first of the mental healers to align mind and soul with Christ. Nearly all the later religious sciences which supposedly healed physical ailments originated from Quimby's remarkably perceptive formulations. He held that "Higher spirit . . . is God spirit and healing is Christ's method."[15] He stated:

I give no medicine and make no outward applications. I tell the patient his troubles, and what he thinks is his disease; and my explanation is the cure. If I succeed in correcting his errors—I establish the truth, or health.

The world will not remember Quimby for his writings—10 volumes written in long-hand—but rather for the indelible imprint he made on his pupils. One was the Rev. W. S. Evans, whose influence still persists among the adherents of the New Thought movement. Evans propounded the following idea: "Disease being in its root a wrong belief, change that belief and we cure the disease." Borrowing further from Buddhism, his disciples stated, "All that we are is the result of what we have thought." The characteristic feature of all the spiritualistic mind-cures was a happy mental outlook—an optimism found in the gospel of modern spiritualists—and a belief that all things work together for good through a perfect Divine Universal Spirit.

THE RISE OF CHRISTIAN SCIENCE

The other famous pupil of Quimby was Mary Baker Eddy, who transformed his "Science of Health" into a religion and a psychotherapy which have attained enormous proportions throughout the world.

The relationship between mesmerism and Christian Science has been fully documented.[11] Also on record is the history of Mary Baker Eddy's career from the time that she discovered that she possessed considerable ability as a spiritualist and took part in séances, occasionally going into trance states and receiving "spirit communications" from her deceased brother, Albert.[11] The various testimonies, the substance of a new philosophy espoused by Mary Baker Eddy, the characteristic defects and the nature of her psychic "explorations" have also been detailed.[10] Mary A. Morse Baker, afterward known as Mrs. Glover, Mrs. Patterson, and later as Mrs. Eddy, has been subjected to veneration by her disciples and to the cold objectivity of unsympathetic critics. Possessing strong drives and great organizing ability, she combined religious inspiration and mystical poesy into a movement that has influenced the lives of millions.

Mrs. Eddy (then Mrs. Patterson) first consulted Quimby in 1862 for the relief of a "spinal disease." She improved, and became so enthusiastic about his methods that she asked him to teach her his "science." For several years she taught from one of his manuscripts, and she praised him in a letter published in the *Portland* (Maine) *Courier* on November 7, 1862, explaining that he healed her neither by spiritualism nor by animal magnetism.[12]

The main tenet of Mary Baker Eddy's "divine" metaphysics, which date from 1862, posits the all-comprehensiveness of mind and the nonexistence of matter. If bodies do not exist, diseases cannot exist and must be only mental delusions. If the mind is freed of these delusions, the disease is gone. This was, in essence, Quimby's doctrine.

THE ATTITUDE OF CHRISTIAN SCIENCE TOWARD HYPNOSIS

Mrs. Eddy castigated all medical therapy and psychotherapy as hypnotism—these belonged to "mortal mind" and hence were inherently in "error." Hypnotism (magnetism) in particular earned Mrs. Eddy's condemnation. She found herself hampered by the passes and the manipulations included in the theories of Quimby.[9] Animal magnetism had no scientific basis; rather, it was criminal, subtle, ubiquitous, and enslaving, and must be dealt with as evil. She stated that the effect of animal magnetism, called hypnotism, was the effect of illusion.[6]

The ready acceptance of Mrs. Eddy's teachings was due to a half century of belief in the exaltation of the spiritual over the material, via faith-healing. Both were phases of the movement initiated by Mesmer. Mesmer's tragic mistake was

that he believed that the healing occurred as the result of *his* efforts. The spiritualists, as disciples of God, thought that they healed through *His* methods. Neither group realized that it was the favorable mind-set of the patient that raised the adaptive responses to produce the results.

Contrary to the practice of religious healers, however, physicians and other nonreligious healers do not treat organic conditions by suggestion. Rather, they will use suggestive procedures only after ruling out the presence of organic disease. It is the author's object in this chapter to show that no healers have a monopoly on the use of faith and spiritual forces, that faith is another valuable arrow in the therapist's quiver, and that susceptibility to hypnosis is based on faith, and is largely brought about by conviction. Although it is not a panacea, it is especially effective in the case of emotionally disturbed individuals—*those who wish to have faith.*

REFERENCES

1. Bromberg, W.: Man Above Humanity. Philadelphia, J. B. Lippincott, 1954.
2. *Op. cit.,* p. 131.
3. *Op. cit.,* p. 137.
4. Eddy, M. B.: Miscellaneous Writings, 1883–1896. Boston, Stewart, 1917, p. 284.
5. *Op. cit.,* p. 107.
6. ———: Science and Health with a Key to the Scriptures. Boston, Stewart, 1917.
7. *Op. cit.,* p. 107.
8. *Op. cit.,* p. 109.
9. ———: A Life-Size Portrait. New York, Macmillan, 1950, p. 109.
10. James, W.: The Energies of Men. New York, Holt, 1916.
11. Podmore, F.: Mesmerism and Christian Science: A Short History of Mental Healing. Philadelphia, Jacobs, 1909.
12. *Op. cit.,* p. 253.
13. Powell, L. P.: The Emmanuel Movement in a New England Town. New York, Putnam, 1909, p. 6.
14. Provonsha, J. W.: The Healing Christ. Current Medical Digest, 1958.
15. Quimby, P. P.: The Quimby Manuscripts, Showing the Discovery of Spiritual Healing and the Origin of Christian Science. New York, Julian Press, 1962, p. 31.

16. Shapiro, A.: Hypnosis, miraculous healing, and ostensibly supernatural phenomena. *In* Kline, M. (ed.): A Scientific Report on the Search for Bridey Murphy. New York, Julian Press, 1956, p. 148.

17. Stetson, A. E.: Reminiscences, Sermons and Correspondence. New York, Putnam, 1913.

18. Twain, M.: Christian Science. New York, Harper, 1907, p. 72.

19. Wilbur, S.: The Life of Mary Baker Eddy. ed. 4. Boston, Christian Science Publishing Society, 1938, p. 87.

20. *Op. cit.,* p. 95.

26

The Dynamics of Faith, Placebo Effect, and Hypnosis

FAITH IN RELIGION AND HYPNOSIS

When therapeutics began to divorce itself from magic and superstition, all mental healing split into religious and nonreligious movements. The latter group consisted primarily of physicians, who used suggestive procedures in one form or another to heal. The former group, however, maintained that all cures were due either to metaphysical factors or divine faith. "Faith" is a loaded word and difficult to define. However, because it plays a significant role in all forms of psychotherapy, the dynamics of faith and its relation to religious and hypnotic types of healing will be discussed.

All faith is built up by conviction and the imagination. d'Eslon, the successor to Mesmer, discerned that conviction and imagination were responsible for the curative effects of mesmerism. He asked, "But since the medicine of conviction and imagination cures, why do we not use it?" In spite of his cogent observations almost 200 years ago, healers, both medical and nonmedical, do not use it as such, but unwittingly stimulate the imagination by some type of misdirection in the form of a new approach or method over which the public becomes enthusiastic, especially if it is mysterious and fashionable.

Faith-healing also depends to a degree on psychosocial and cultural factors. The savage expects to be healed by the incantations of the shaman because he is *convinced that he will help him.* For similar reasons, the civilized person is aided by the belief and faith engendered by the rapport and prestige suggestions from the omniscient figure—the doctor.

When an emotionally disturbed individual sees a religious healer, his faith is strong because of a previous conviction that "God heals." In other words, his faith in a cure has been continually validated or computed by the already thought-out conviction that the clergyman-healer is an emissary of God. He recovers, often as the result of a single session, because *he expects to recover.*

When the average person consults a physician initially for psychotherapy, he comes in with *uncomputed* conviction because he does not have the powerful built-up faith in psychiatry that he has in religion. However, with successive visits, a positive rapport develops and eventually his uncomputed conviction becomes computed conviction leading to faith in the therapist. He recovers for the same reason as with the religious healer—expectant faith in a cure.

When a patient sees a physician-hypnotist healer, his *uncomputed convictions* or negative attitudes are generally increased. Not only does he have to establish confidence in the doctor, but he has to be "sold" on the hypnosis; it invariably connotes something "magical." His *uncomputed* convictions become *computed* convictions as the result of the hypnotic-induction procedure; he attributes the ideosensory and ideomotor responses, such as lid and limb heaviness and arm levitaton, to the hypnotherapists's suggestions.

134

After these convictions are established, then he readily believes other suggestions even though they may be at variance with reality. Thus hypnotic healing does not require faith in a cure but only faith in the fact *that he was hypnotized!*

The question as to whether religious or hypnotic faith-healing is more effective obviously relates to previous conditioning of the subject. There is no ideal method applicable to all persons, nor is there a preferential religious approach. All methods can heal—the specific one being the one for which the person has been "programmed."

Paracelsus shrewdly observed: "Whether the object of your faith is real or false, you will nevertheless obtain the same effects." It is amazing that there are relatively few scientific observations on the relationship between faith-healing and hypnosis. One would expect that a medium which has such a pronounced effect on human emotions, autonomic functioning, mood changes, mental associations, and sensory imagery would be worthy of further investigation.

On the basis of the observed data, all faith-healing makes use of suggestion by effecting a temporary dissociation produced by selective cortical inhibition—the attention is diverted through misdirection—and the favorable attitude or the mind-set resulting from previously invoked beliefs allows the acceptance of faith-laden ideas. The misdirection is obtained by the ritualism that accompanies all religious healing. This also occurs as well in hypnotic procedures, but differs as mentioned above.

When a headache is relieved by hypnosis, for instance, the conviction that hypnosis has been established causes the subject to accept the hypnotherapist's suggestions as *true statements.* Then he behaves differently because he *thinks and believes* differently through the alteration in his beliefs. The power of hypnosis is the power of belief! Thus hypnosis is merely a catalytic agent through which conviction phenomena can be established. As such, hypnotic behavior is a particular branch of faith phenomena.

Most faith-healers and even unsophisticated medical hypnotherapists have the tendency to "play God"; they usually are unaware that psychogenically based symptoms are removed by activation of the latent recovery forces.[18] The sick person usually has his own mental representation of the disease, of the recovery he hopes to achieve and, often, even of the psychotherapeutic procedure he desires.[13]

An attempt has been made to explain how most cases of miraculous faith-healing, which appear in the professional and the nonprofessional literature, follow the principles of faith described in this section. However, occasional cures of organic illnesses occur in which faith is only part of the rationale. At Lourdes, for instance, many of the countless "miracles" can be explained as the result of the subjects' expecting to be cured. However, 51 official miraculous cures have been recognized by the Catholic Church, a Canonical Commission, the Medical Bureau, and the International Medical Commission.

Shapiro states:

If they are indeed produced by faith, then they are certainly not dependent on the intensity of faith. The devout and saintly believer may remain unhealed while the skeptic who suffers the same disease may be miraculously cured.[24]

(When this happens, the skeptic usually becomes a devout believer.)

Shapiro continues:

But the time, the circumstances and the person who evaluates the miracle always modify the description of the nature of the event. One man's religion is another man's superstition, and one man's man's magic is another man's science.

The only scientific explanation of this type of faith-healing is that a nonformalistic technic of hypnosis by misdirection would tend to mobilize the recovery processes that are inherently present in every individual. Here too, a placebo action, described in the next section, would exert an influence.

The rise of pastoral psychiatry and the human potential movement is evidence of the ability of faith to help large numbers of mentally ill individuals because of their previously invoked beliefs in the religionist. As a result, some psychiatrists are working hand in hand with theologians and lay healers to utilize the latent capacity for faith that is inherently present in all humans. Both a religious and a psychiatric approach are appealing to blind faith rather than to logical reasoning or persuasion. If the latter were better for mentally sick people, then more people would be cured by appealing to logic and common sense. Every psychotherapist knows that this is not the case.

PLACEBO-EFFECT CONCEPT

There is a growing recognition that the placebo effect plays a key role in drug therapy,[4, 5, 15, 19, 26] and also applies to all forms of psychotherapy as well as hypnosis. In this section, emphasis will be placed on an explanation of the placebo effect of drugs and psychotherapy as these relate to suggestion and hypnosis. The clinical applications and ethics of the placebo effect will not be stressed. If one substitutes "placebo effect" for "faith," one finds that in many instances the cause of the physicians' dramatic cures of today is similar to the cause of the miraculous healing of yesteryear.

DRUGS AND THE PLACEBO EFFECT

Osler points out that doctors often are ignorant of their own faith cures when prescribing medications and are just a wee bit too sensitive about those performed outside their ranks.[20] This observation hints that most drugs have no more value than a placebo. This dynamic placebo force sustained the medical profession for centuries, even when drugs were physiologically detrimental. One cannot help being impressed by the fact that placebo action has been the one constant in medicine—by whatever term it was called. And it is certain that our present cure rate for many of the psychogenic entities would not differ appreciably from that of any other period.

Chiefly responsible for the physician's placebo effect is the enthusiasm and the faith inculcated by his approach. This is transmitted to the patient, who develops the necessary confidence and faith for recovery. Thus the physician himself is still the most important therapeutic agent. The expression "the art of medicine" means nothing more than the rapport that exists between the patient and the physician. If the common denominator in medicine is the placebo effect (faith), then its chief ally is the imagination, for without imagination there would be no placebo cures. Oliver Wendell Holmes was cognizant of this when he stated that the greatest benefit can accrue to patients "through the influence exerted on their imaginations." Voltaire once stated, "There is probably more cure in the doctor's words than in many of the drugs he prescribes."

Factors other than rapport which contribute to the "success" of the placebo are not only the suggestive effect of prescribing a drug but also the spontaneous recoveries which occur in any illness. Environmental factors and cultural attitudes toward new drugs and procedures also enhance the placebo effect. Another interesting factor recently postulated is that all placebos are more effective in the presence of stress or in pain due to organic causes. All these factors simply illustrate the power of words!

At present, enthusiastic physicians are prescribing "wonder drugs" in all fields of medicine; the patient often obtains the effect that he has been told to expect. This is not to imply that the author is a therapeutic nihilist; he is not. It has been noted that whenever a new drug loses its popularity, its effect is markedly reduced. Conn remarked:

This is what occurred after the introduction and initial wide acceptance of bromides, chloral hydrate and the barbiturates, each of which was hailed as a "wonder" drug, and it also will happen to the "tranquilizers."[8]

Trousseau[6] facetiously advised, "You should treat as many patients as possible with the new drugs while they still have the power to heal.[13]

One of the most difficult things for any individual, living in any period, is to be able to shake off the rigid dogmas of his own culture. Future historians may laugh at what we consider modern-day therapies. The author has often wondered, after each new "wonder" drug has been exploded, how and why the honest and conscientious investigators were misled. Obviously, these drugs, despite statistical validation, acted by virtue of their placebo effect. Usually such variables as the emotional relationship, the dosage, the choice of subject, the use of inadequate controls, an improper assay of the data, the operator's attitude or bias, and other factors influenced the results. One author significantly states, "The ability of inert compounds . . . to modify a variety of conditions . . . has begun to have a serious impact on medical thinking."[12] Others believe that much time and money would be saved if placebo effects were analyzed before it was assumed that a drug had value.

In an excellent review of the history of the placebo effect, Shapiro writes that until recently, there was virtual silence about the placebo effect in spite of the fact that this effect is the unwritten therapeutic agent in almost every prescription.[25] The effect of placebos can be very powerful and often permanently modifies physiologic functioning. These effects are not superficial or transient. Yet their everyday use has been neglected.

PLACEBO EFFECT IN PSYCHOTHERAPY

The fact that there are contradictory theories being employed with identical results in a wide variety of psychotherapies indicates that here, too, a placebo effect is in operation! Psychiatrists need to know more about placebo effects because their rapport with patients is great and, as a result, the placebo potential of their therapy is thereby enhanced. With every physician, this potential consists of the patient's confidence, faith, and belief, interacting with the therapist's personality. The hypnotic situation contains within it the mystery, the ritualism, the repetitive conditioning, and the other factors that lead to increased suggestibility.

Recently, several authors have noted that hope and faith on the part of the patient and suggestion and persuasion on the part of the therapist constitute some of the universal factors operative in mental healing.[11, 22] Curiously, however, hypnotic suggestion was not distinguished from persuasion, and hypnosis from classic conditioning.

Most authorities do not even mention the placebo effect in psychotherapy, and those that do seldom equate it with their cures. Bromberg, who discusses faith-healing and suggestibility, does not mention it as it applies to medication or psychotherapy, past or present.[7] Although there is a subtle placebo effect in many forms of psychotherapy, nothing has been done about it, despite the fact that more therapeutic methods have been introduced into psychiatry than ever before. Using more knowledge of the placebo effect, modern-day psychiatry could more objectively understand its failures and eliminate ineffective methods.

Rosenthal and Frank, who have studied the placebo effect in psychotherapy, believe that all forms of psychotherapy, including hypnosis, uniformly yield successful results in about 60 per cent of cases.[21] They stress the effects of the interpersonal relationship, and that psychotherapists fit their results into their theories and therapeutic rationale, indicating that "the efficacy of any particular set of therapeutic operations lies in their analogy to a placebo in that they enhance the therapist's and patient's conviction that something useful is being done."

A placebo effect accouts for psychotherapy by nonpsychiatrists as well as for intensive psychoanalysis.[2] In short, improvement does not prove the correctness of the theory on which the therapy was based, or the efficacy of a specific technic employed, unless the improvement is greater than that produced by the patient's faith in the efficacy of the therapist and his technic—"the placebo effect."

On this basis, the old family doctor was a good psychotherapist because of his humanistic approach and willingness to listen to a patient's story. An analysis of the placebo effects of "homespun" psychotherapy should help to elucidate the roles of suggestion, waking hypnosis, and hypnosis in all forms of psychotherapy.

HYPNOSIS AND THE PLACEBO EFFECT

The nature of the placebo effect as it operates in hypnotherapy has been described by several investigators.[7, 20] In the light of newer knowledge gained from the placebo effect, the nature of the therapeutic deficiencies of early concepts now can be understood. During the period when mesmerism and hypnosis reached their peak, emphasis was on a very authoritative approach directed toward symptom removal. Even today, authoritarian methods employing suggestion or hypnosis by an omniscient father-figure are successful in helping some patients, at least temporarily. It has been observed, "It is surprising how frequently these so-called 'transference cures' persist even if no further treatment is administered." Genuine recoveries have been observed in patients "without any psychodynamic insight into their condition.[13] There is no experimental study which indicates that therapeutic effects based on insights or perceptual reorganization are less superficial or less transitory.[21]

Although suggestion and hypnosis are related to the placebo effect and have much in common, they differ from each other in some ways. The difference is analogous to the comparison made between religious and hypnotic healing. Healing by hypnosis requires belief in the validity of the induction of hypnosis, that is, in the "power" of the hypnotist. Cortical inhibition produced by misdirection of attention is common in hypnosis but not in placebo administration. Faith in the placebo merely indicates faith achieved by previously invoked belief in all drugs as well as the prestige of the physician. Here there is a proper mind-set, based on a high degree of enthusiasm or motivation, belief, confidence, and an expectant attitude.

Wickramasekera has intimated that sensory restriction and anxiety reduction contribute to the role of hypnosis in heightening the patient's faith and hope in the therapist.[27] He also reviews an extensive literature on the placebo effect, urging that it should be used rather than eliminated in psychological treatment procedures.

An experiment was performed to test for a placebo factor in hypnosis.[17] A tourniquet-exercise ischemic test was employed. There were three groups: a normal control without hypnosis, one with hypnotic analgesia, and a placebo condition. The placebo effect was fairly pronounced for the nonhypnotizable, but not at all for the hyp-

notizable. Hypnotic analgesia was very effective for the highly hypnotizable, but for the nonhypnotizable it was equivalent only to the placebo. It can be concluded that for subjects insusceptible to hypnosis, pain reduction can be achieved by hypnotically suggested analgesia, but will be analogous to a reduction by a placebo. For highly susceptible hypnotic subjects, pain reduction through hypnotically suggested analgesia is far greater than the placebo; the average placebo response is practically nonexistent. Such work indicates that response in hypnosis and placebo response are not one and the same. In a clinical setting, where motivation is high, hypnosis might well prove to be the acme of the scientifically applied placebo effect!

We are safe in concluding that all human beings need motivation, self-esteem, and something to believe in so that they can face their everyday tensions. The emotionally ill patient's value systems have failed him. As a result, he is ready to accept the therapist's, especially if they are presented with confidence, and it appears that they have a chance of helping him. It is also surprising how, on the basis of conviction, the incorporation of the therapist's suggestions can help large numbers of patients.

It is a sad commentary that those who now subscribe wholeheartedly to the concept that psychotherapy operates through a placebo effect still avoid hypnotherapy. The cumulative effect of successive and successful suggestions often results in a conviction of cure that cannot be achieved as rapidly by other psychotherapeutic modalities, especially if the therapy is directed to establishing the need of a symptom in a patient's emotional economy. When indicated, every psychotherapist owes it to his patients to utilize his unquestioned placebo effect at the highest level—hypnosis. Although hypnotherapy cannot be successfully applied to all disturbed individuals, there are certain cases, which respond to hypnotherapy, that orthodox psychotherapy cannot treat.

Considerable attention has been given to the placebo effect in psychotherapy, religious healing, and drug therapy. Obviously, the most suggestible patients will be the best reactors. However, response will vary from individual to individual and will even change in the same individual from time to time. Some respond because of the "halo effect," in which patients expect to improve because of a self-fulfilling prophecy. Many psychiatrists are opposed to placebos because they feel they should never be substituted for psychotherapy, even though there is a placebo effect in the latter.[19]

Recently, the placebo effect of tranquilizers has been noted.[3] According to uncontrolled and subjective methods of evaluation, from 53 to 80 per cent of the patients benefited from the new "drugs" (both drugs given were placebos, but patients were informed that one was real and the other a placebo). The authors point up the dubious value of the studies, which do not employ double blind and other controlled procedures.[16]

The capacity to respond to what is believed and accepted as true is simply amazing and, as hypnotic phenomena attest, is very valuable. The success of charlatans in beguiling the public is an unfortunate by-product of the placebo. Yet this only indicates how powerful the placebo is in the use of drugs and psychotherapy. Our thesis is that if the placebo is effective, then hypnosis employed prudently by a competent physician for a valid indication will serve the patient's best interest.

REFERENCES

1. Alexander, F.: Discussion of Hoch, P. H.: Aims and limitations of psychotherapy. Am. J. Psychiat., *112:*321, 1955.
2. Appel, K. E., *et al.:* Long term psychotherapy. *In* Psychiatric Treatment (A.R.N.M.D. series), vol. 31. Baltimore, Williams & Wilkins, 1951.
3. Baker, A. A., and Thorpe, J. G.: Placebo response. Arch. Neurol. Psychiat., *78:*57, 1957.
4. Beecher, H. K.: The powerful placebo, J.A.M.A., *159:*1602, 1955.
5. Benson, H., and Epstein, M.D.: The placebo effect: a neglected asset in the care of patients. J.A.M.A., *232:*1225, 1975.
6. Bernheim, H.: Translation from Trousseau's Dictionnaire, 1833. Paris, Librairie de la Faculté de Médecine, 1889.
7. Bromberg, W.: Man Above Humanity: A History of Psychotherapy. Philadelphia, J. B. Lippincott, 1954.
8. Conn, J. H.: Cultural and clinical aspects of hypnosis, placebos, and suggestibility. Int. J. Clin. Exp. Hypn., *7:*179, 1959.
9. *Op. cit.,* pp. 181–182.
10. Feldman, P. E.: The personal elements in psychiatric research. Am. J. Psychiat., *113:*52, 1956.
11. Frank, J. D.: Persuasion and Healing: A Comparative Study of Psychotherapy. Baltimore, Johns Hopkins University Press, 1961.
12. Gliedman, L. H., *et al.:* Reduction of symptoms by pharmacologically inert substances and by short term psychotherapy. Arch. Neurol. Psychiat., *79:*345, 1958.
13. Hoch, P. H.: Aims and limitations of psychotherapy, Am. J. Psychiat., *112:*321, 1955.
14. Holmes, O. W.: Medical Essays, 1842, 1892. Cambridge, Mass., Riverside Press, 1891.
15. Lasagna, L.: Placebos. Sci. Am., *193:*68, 1956.
16. Loranger, A. W.: The Placebo Effect in Psychiatric Drug Research, J.A.M.A. *170:*920–925, 1961.
17. McGlashan, T. H., Evans, F. J., and Orne, M. T.: The nature of hypnotic analgesia and the placebo response to experimental pain. Psychosom. Med., *31:*227, 1969.
18. Milechnin, G. S., and Milechnin, A.: Concerning the criterion of recovery. J. Clin. Exp. Hypn., *6:*1, 1958.
19. Modell, W., and Houde, R. W.: Factors influencing clinical evaluation of drugs. J.A.M.A., *167:*2190, 1958.
20. Osler, W.: Medicine in the Nineteenth Century in Aequanimatas. Philadelphia, Blakiston, 1905.
21. Rosenthal, D., and Frank, J. D.: Psychotherapy and the placebo effect. Psychol. Bull., *55:*294, 1956.
22. Sargant, W.: Battle for the Mind. New York, Doubleday, 1957.
23. Shapiro, A. K.: Hypnosis, miraculous healing, and ostensibly supernatural phenomena. *In* Kline, M. (ed.): A Scientific Report on the Search for Bridey Murphy. New York, Julian Press, 1956, p. 133.
24. *Op. cit.,* p. 147.
25. ———: A contribution to a history of the placebo effect, Behav. Sci., *5:*109, 1959.
26. ———: Placebo effects in psychotherapy and psychoanalysis. J. Clin. Pharmacol., *10:*73, 1970.
27. Wickramasekera, I.: The effects of sensory restriction on susceptibility to hypnosis: a hypothesis, some preliminary data, and theoretical speculation. Int. J. Clin. Exp. Hypn., *17:*217, 1969.

ADDITIONAL READINGS

Barber, T. X.: Death by suggestion. Psychosom. Med., *23:*153, 1961.

_____: "Hypnosis," analgesia, and the placebo effect. J.A.M.A., *172:*680, 1960.

Bowers, M.: Hypnotic aspects of Haitian voodoo. Int. J. Clin. Exp. Hypn., *9:*269, 1961.

Glass, L. B., and Barber, T. X.: A note on hypnotic behavior, the definition of the situation and the placebo effect. J. Am. Ment. Dis., *132:*539, 1961.

27

Biofeedback, Meditation, and Altered States of Consciousness

Biofeedback is a recent addition to psychotherapy. The term feedback was derived from Norbert Weiner's concept of a method of controlling a system by reinstating into it the results of its past performance. These technics and the term biofeedback originated from laboratory research in which instrumentation was utilized to amplify a variety of physiological changes, such as blood pressure, muscle tension, skin temperature, and certain EEG patterns. The internal signal promptly initiates an external signal, such as a sound or light, that upon repetition enables the patient to identify the cues of his own internal state. Biofeedback theory and research assume that when the patient receives immediate information about his external changes, he might eventually control these processes without the continued utilization of instrumentation.

Kamiya noted that certain subjects could, on command, go into a kind of Zen meditation or hypnotic "trance" and alter physiological parameters.[11] By means of biofeedback training (B.F.T.) employing electronic devices, it was seriously considered possible to implement control of inner thought processes. Kamiya's subjects recognized, with remarkable accuracy, whether or not they were emitting alpha waves at a given second. They were also trained to maintain or repress alpha waves by an audio feedback tone, achieving control over ephemeral and altered states of consciousness (A.S.C.). He explained that there are four primary brain-wave patterns—delta, theta, alpha, and beta rhythms—all of which are contained within a total energy spectrum of about 0 to 40 cycles per second (C.P.S.). The alpha rate moves at 8 to 12 C.P.S.; it is the most prominent brain wave activity, since it is readily recorded by EEG. It appears that everyone slips in and out of alpha from 5 to 30 times a minute without ever knowing it.

Good subjects contended that the alpha state was associated with feelings of detachment and yet was accompanied by alertness. These serene feeling states are also characteristic of autohypnotic states and A.S.C. Some subjects even referred to it as an "alpha high." The latter state seemed to be accompanied by a lack of anxiety, suggesting that such beatific relaxation might be a useful substitute for tranquilizers, hypnotics, and soporific drugs. It was, however, doubted that the alpha state would ever be a substitute for relaxing drugs or meditation. Observations on Zen meditators and hypnotized persons indicate that alpha probably plays an important role, but is not the whole picture. Alpha training is probably nonspecific as far as neural processing is concerned. However, a broad neural system may be enhanced by its use.[20] Nevertheless, it was theorized that if persons could be trained with B.F.T., they might learn control of desired inner states in a relatively short period of time and thus facilitate any type of psychotherapy.

Brown hypothesizes that alpha can act as a feedback control for regulating gastric acidity and body temperature.[3] She believes that beta influences eye movements and that theta (4–7

C.P.S.) controls muscular activities, heart rate, and pulse pressure. She observed that when subjects learned to control their alpha, they became adept at controlling other bodily functions. The beta waves fall into a fast-paced 14 to 28 C.P.S. She also believes that theta, which is defined as that rhythmic EEG activity of from 4 to 7 C.P.S., may facilitate awareness, correlate with creative thinking and learning, and in general lead to an increased efficiency in mental functioning.

BIOFEEDBACK LEARNING PROCESSES

There seems to be no question that there is some validity to the biofeedback process *per se.* The instrumentation informs well-trained subjects of physiological changes occurring in the organism, who then temporarily can control those processes they have become aware of through feedback. However, it should be emphasized that a subject cannot be trained to produce alpha waves, but rather can be trained to produce the *subjective* state that is associated with alpha waves.[20] Since EEG waves do not have any sensory representation that can be recognized as such, the trained subject can only recognize and learn to manipulate the feeling that accompanies any one of the various EEG patterns. In other words, no physiological processes can be sensed *per se,* yet all can come under volitional control by B.F.T.

There is, however, a welter of confusion and mutually contradictory theories regarding B.F.T. Not only is there the question of the reliability of the instrumentation, but over half of the brain rhythms are lost before they reach the surface, and between 30 and 60 per cent of those registered depend on the individual's consciousness and "state of mind," as well as other factors. Deep brain activities simply cannot be assessed by surface potentials or EEG measurements. What the person is thinking, the amount of light involved, and whether eye closure is present or not can all affect EEG patterns. Relaxation is not needed to produce alpha, and some individuals do not even have alpha; the latter unfortunately have not been

studied to see whether they too can learn to control their internal processes.

CLINICAL APPLICATIONS OF BIOFEEDBACK TRAINING

Serious-minded researchers believe that B.F.T. can, by diminishing secretions, cure ulcers. Other claims are for asthma and pulmonary insufficiency, pain of migraine, cardiac arrhythmias, Raynaud's disease, physical rehabilitation of stroke, cerebral palsy, and multiple sclerosis victims. Feedback of finger temperature has been employed as a visual signal. It has been demonstrated that B.F.T. can increase temperature over a 10° F. range, while simultaneously and effectively decreasing skin temperature of the forehead; the latter prevents development of migraine headaches by regulating the vascular supply to the brain and hand areas.[10] Recently it has been observed that long-term retention was better for learning differential control of hand temperture when hypnosis was compared to a group receiving B.F.T.[7] Others found that the degree of hypnotizability did not matter in reference to hand-warming.[19]

Muscle biofeedback has been utilized to reduce the incidence of anxiety-produced headaches.[4] It has been observed that learning to control the difference in brain alpha wave activity between the two cerebral hemispheres has facilitated learning.[18] B.F.T. is thought to be useful in essential hypertension,[21] asthma, and other medical conditions. One investigator isolated a 12 to 14 C.P.S. high-voltage pattern which comes from the motor cortex.[22] Cats could be conditioned to produce this rhythm, which was named the sensorimotor rhythm (SMR). Sterman found SMR training has qualitatively and quantitatively brought about significant reduction in anxiety and depression, and reduced the seizures in epilepsy.

In spite of all the voluminous publications, the data in the above areas are still ambiguous and the early enthusiasm accorded B.F.T., like any other new modality, is now being tempered with caution and assessed more realistically.

CURRENT STATUS OF BIOFEEDBACK TRAINING

It is agreed that B.F.T. is of little or no value for organic disorders. It is no mere coincidence that it works for the same psychosomatic disorders that are responsive to hypnosis and the behavior therapies. When thoughts are turned inward, the patient develops more responsibility for his own recovery, and through reduction of tension he develops a "do it yourself relaxation"—like self-hypnosis—to neutralize anxiety.

Melzack and Perry studied B.F.T. for pain relief in three groups receiving alpha B.F.T. and hypnotic training, hypnotic training alone, and alpha B.F.T. alone.[13] Results indicated that the first group had less pain. Pain reduction was not due to alpha training *per se,* but it added something to the results either by distraction, reinforcing the idea that the pain would diminish, or by giving the sufferer the suggestion that he had the means to bring about anxiety reduction.

A more cautious attitude is now being taken. Miller, an ardent proponent of A.N.S. learning, states that B.F.T. "has not been rigorously proved by enough long term follow-up studies."[14] Recently it has been referred to as "a *furor therapeuticus.* "[20] Orne comments that it is interesting that B.F.T. researchers are now talking about the influence that suggestion, motivation, and emotions have on results.[16] He notes, "This is another instance where a new technique is introduced and found to be wanting, so it is combined with older proven therapies but is presented as a new package. . . ." More recently he added that alpha feedback "promises something for everybody, but it is a promissory note that is not likely to be delivered as written."[17] Brady warns that a placebo effect has not been ruled out.[2]

As B.F.T. researchers become interested in hypnosis, they will soon realize that demand characteristics, expectancies, and suggestions at various levels of awareness are the crucial variables chiefly responsible for the results of B.F.T. Thus we are dealing by and large with another suggestive approach. With further research, the combination of hypnosis and B.F.T. (hypno-biofeedback), together with behavioral technics, ultimately should prove to be a valuable therapeutic modality.

MEDITATION

The ancients employed magical rites and incantations to induce meditation by chanting, breathing exercises, and dancing. The Hebrews used fixation on the four letters of the tetragrammaton and developed other names for God.[1] Methodical meditation, breathing exercises, and ecstasy states are similar to the practices of Yoga, Zen Buddhism, Hinduism, Shintoism, Sufism,[8] and Christian meditation, including the repetitive prayers developed in the Byzantine Church[15] and the praying of the Rosary.

It is obvious that the cadence and intonations of prayer in a relaxing environment, posture, eye fixation on an altar or religious symbol, and rhythmic chanting are hypnagogic. Finally, the self-contemplation and self-absorption characterizing prayer and meditation are practically identical with modern-day autohypnosis. Meditation as a potent modality for changing behavior has certainly withstood the test of time. A modern version is transcendental meditation (T.M.).[24] Although the ritual for each differs, they are fundamentally the same and are based on similar principles of conditioning. A common EEG and neurophysiologic basis for mystical states of consciousness has been noted.[9] That hypnosis and Eastern methodologies such as T.M. are now being increasingly accepted indicates they are here to stay and are modalities that American psychotherapy must eventually incorporate. Hypnosis, behavior therapy, and T.M. have recently been employed for reducing severe anxiety states.[6]

ALTERED STATES OF CONSCIOUSNESS

The behavioral technics of imagery conditioning during hypnosis have also stimulated renewed interest in attaining A.S.C. for modifying behavior. Through use of more precise technics, finer sensory discriminations will be made so that these states can facilitate therapy. At present there is a burgeoning interest in guided affective imagery, fantasy encounter, and the use of standardized images.[12]

The subjective experience of some practitioners of T.M., Zen, or Yoga resembles, in many respects, the heightened sensory awareness and uniqueness of perceptual and cognitive experiences of many LSD users. Patients undergoing hypnotic sensory-imagery conditioning report similar experiences. It has been noted that in states of meditation, habituation of the orienting reflex is delayed or abolished. This suggests that in some way the lack of habituation of the alpha blocking by sensory input is a correlate of heightened perceptual sensitivity. Clearly, the subjects, in unusual degrees of reduction in the level or variety of external sensory inputs to the brain, can induce "ecstasy" or an A.S.C. by appropriate training.

These altered states of consciousness also show a remarkable parallel to rapid-eye-movement (REM) sleep and dreaming. Both involve a state of cortical and visceral arousal associated with inhibition of skeletal muscle tone in trunk and limbs. A loss of distinctiveness in spatial orientations and vivid perceptual imagery with condensation of imagined persons and events are correlates of both dreams and the ecstasy state. The deepest, or plenary, hypnotic state achieved through sensory-imagery conditioning shows the same parallel.[5] Skeletal muscle tone in trunk and limbs is inhibited. The time sense is distorted, expanded, or concentrated, and in some cases, abolished. Perceptual or sensory imagery is incredibly vivid. More study of the similarities between these altered states and hypnosis is needed, as is an examination of their relationship to anxiety reduction.

It is increasingly apparent that all altered states of consciousness have a common goal: the blocking out of the conscious mind to find the "No-Mind" of Zen, the "Immortal Self" of Yoga, the *Fana el Fana* (annihilation of the self) of Sufism. The early Judeo-Christian traditions taught that man must "empty" himself to hear God's voice, using fasting and meditation to attain that emptiness.

Ornstein believes that the objective study of A.S.C. may yield insights as to the capabilities for human self-regulation.[18] The latter term is nothing more or less than self-hypnosis. A lack of sophistication in the West has led to much confusion and has impeded the scientific study of volitional control. The A.N.S. is not as autonomic as was formerly believed. By appropriate training it can be put under volitional control through autogenic or enteroceptive feedback. A well-trained Yogi, for example, does not need an external signal or device to control autonomic functions.

SUMMARY

Although B.F.T. establishes control over normally involuntary processes, its long-term effectiveness has yet to be demonstrated. There are important differences between B.F.T. and hypnosis. In B.F.T. the patient learns to be acutely aware of physiological changes. In hypnosis *per se,* the patient suppresses what is happening within. As Hilgard and Hilgard point out, the two approaches may be complementary. For the patient who can temporarily direct his attention away from bodily processes, hypnosis might be preferred. For those whose reality ties are too strong to do this, biofeedback might be preferable.[10a]

Practitioners of B.F.T. who are not familiar with modern and sophisticated technics of hypnosis, which do not require an induction technic, will naturally not believe they are using task-motivated instruction in a hypnotic manner. Likewise, those using various forms of meditation and A.S.C. are seldom aware that they are resorting to self-hypnosis.

A new interdisciplinary approach is emerging which combines the instrumentation of the West with the principles of behavioristic psychology and the practices of traditional Eastern philosophy. Whether these will provide a better understanding of human capabilities for self-regulation remains to be established. However, there is no doubt that increasing personal motivation in this modality will certainly help those with psychosomatic disorders—just like hypnosis.

REFERENCES

1. Bokser, B.Z.: From the World of the Cabbalah. New York, Philosophical Library, 1954.
2. Brady, J.P.: Claims for biofeedback as a therapy method disputed. Clin. Psychiat. News, *3:*8, 1975.
3. Brown, B.B.: Recognition of aspects of consciousness through association with EEG alpha activity represented by a light signal. Psychophysiology, *6:* 442, 1970.
4. Budzynski, T., *et al.:* Feedback-induced muscle relaxation. *In* Barber, T., *et al.* (eds.): Biofeedback and Self-Control. Chicago, Aldine-Atherton, 1970, pp. 57–61.
5. Calloway, E.: Psychiatry today. West. J. Med., *122:* 349, 1975.
6. Daniels, L.K.: The treatment or psychophysiological disorders and severe anxiety by behavior therapy, hypnosis and transcendental meditation. Am. J. Clin. Hypn., *17:*26, 1975.
7. Engström, D.R.: Hypnosis vs. biofeedback among hypnotizable and unhypnotizable subjects. *In* Schwartz, G.E., and Shapiro, D. (eds.): Advances in Research. vol. 1. New York, Plenum Press, 1976.
8. Fujiawa, C.: Zen and Shinto. New York, Philosophical Library, 1959.
9. Gellhorn, E., and Kiely, W.F.: Mystical states of consciousness: neurophysiological and clinical aspects. J. Nerv. Ment. Dis., *154:*399, 1972.
10. Green, E., *et al.:* Voluntary control of internal states: psychological and physiological. J. Transpersonal Psychol., *1:*1, 1970.
10a. Hilgard, E.R., and Hilgard, J.R.: Hypnosis in the Relief of Pain. Los Altos, Cal. William Kaufman, 1976. p. 199.
11. Kamiya, J.: Operant control of the EEG alpha rhythm and some of its reported effects on consciousness. *In* Tart, C.T. (ed.): Altered States of Consciousness. New York, Wiley, 1969, pp. 507–517.
12. Kroger, W.S., and Fezler, W.D.: Hypnosis and Behavior Modification: Imagery Conditioning. Philadelphia, J. B. Lippincott, 1976.
13. Melzack, R., and Perry, C.: Self-regulation of pain: the use of alpha-feedback training for the control of chronic pain. Exp. Neurol., *46:*452, 1975.
14. Miller, N.E.: Biofeedback results said to be good but overpublicized. Clin. Psychiat. News, *4:*3, 1975.
15. Norwich, J.J., and Sitwell, R.: Mount Athos. New York, Harper & Row, 1966.
16. Orne, M.T.: Claims for biofeedback as a therapy method disputed. Clin. Psychiat. News, *3:*8, 1975.
17. _____: Clin. Psychiat. News, *4:*8, 1976.
18. Ornstein, R.E.: Selections from the psychology of consciousness. *In* Barber, T.X. (ed.): Advances in Altered States of Consciousness and Human Potentialities. New York, Psychological Dimensions, 1976.
19. Roberts, A.H., *et al.:* Voluntary control of skin temperature: unilateral changes using hypnosis and auditory feedback (paper presented at meeting of Biofeedback Research Society, 1972).
20. Segal, J.: Biofeedback as a medical treatment. J.A.M.A., *232:*179, 1975.
21. Shapiro, D., and Schwartz, G.E. (eds.): Biofeedback and Self-Control. Chicago, Aldine-Atherton, 1973.
22. Sterman, M.B., and Friar, L.: Suppression of seizures in an epileptic following sensorimotor EEG feedback training. Electroencephal. Clin. Neurophysiol., *33:*89–95, 1972.
23. Trimingham, J.S.: Sufi Orders in Islam. Oxford, Clarendon Press, 1971.
24. Wallace, R.K.: Physiological effects of transcendental meditation. Science, *167:*1751, 1970.

28

Neurophysiologic Mechanisms
in Mediation of Emotions at
Nonhypnotic and Hypnotic Levels

Little is known of the brain's dynamic properties and even less of the neuropsychological meaning of its anatomic structures. As a result, there are few studies to explain the precise nature of drives and other behavioral phenomena. Another reason for this lack is that the ideational processes, which distinguish humans from other living organisms, such as self-experience, imagery, and creativity, as yet cannot be measured and analyzed because it is difficult to understand what makes up an emotion or an idea. Only the physiologic effects of a stimulus, as it affects behavior, can be explored in terms of cause-and-effect or input-and-output relationships. Thus, vegetative reflexes, conditioned responses, learned behavior, and problem-solving can be measured to some extent. Before one can predict, however, what specific areas of the brain will do in response to a specific emotional stimulus, more must be known about the biologic roots of creativity processes initiating it. Microbiologists believe that what takes place, as new organizing activity or creativity, is in essence a reduplication and amplification of those biologic processes that take place at the microcellular level. More succinctly, "micro-events in the genes produce macro-events in those new activities which man imposes upon his environment."[12] The entire process at both biologic levels is based on codified information and is self-regulated by feedback control—a concept which plays an important role in the organization of adaptive responses and behavior of all living and nonliving systems.

In this presentation, brain structures have been separated into arbitrary divisions but, unfortunately, simple spatial separations into discrete centers, each representing a specific function, do not explain how similar stimuli from respective regions contribute to differences in psychological functioning. More importantly, what interplay of forces in the central nervous system accounts for "spontaneous" activity, and what happens in the time between the initiation of an ideational stimulus and its resultant response? Is the reflex monitored by the "control of feedback"? Where and why are the ideas or mental images which are responsible for the diversity of drives in the organism produced? How are they influenced by motivation or expectation, mood swings, and changing life situations? What produces such fluctuating degrees of attention as sleep, wakefulness, and hypnosis?

These and other questions, especially that of localization, which only answers the "where" of higher nervous activity, have to be worked out before we can thoroughly understand "how" and "why" the brain works at hypnotic (selective attention) and nonhypnotic (less selective attention) levels. Until newer research sheds light on the organization of behavior, we are handicapped in our full understanding of brain functioning. However, in this chapter, we shall, for descriptive purposes only, discuss the more important brain structures separately and what is known about their *neuropsychological* functioning.

There is virtual agreement among neurophysiologists that the vertical or two-brain "concept" of a core system surmounted by a cerebral mantle, in contrast to classic "horizontal" types, represents a major change toward clarification of neuropsychological and neurophysiologic mechanisms. Thus the two arbitrary divisions of the brain, the cortical and subcortical portions, are complementary and interdependent. This dynamic and reciprocal interaction helps to maintain the purposeful goals necessary for survival. In achieving this optimal state of equilibrium, some of the brain's structures tend to influence the function of others by regulating and dominating these. An integration of cerebral mechanisms subject to the regulation of one another and ultimately dominated by one of them is called a hierarchy. Self-regulation of the hierarchic functioning enables the brain to become not only more adaptive but also more discriminative in its behavior. In this respect, the brain can be compared with an efficient, automatically regulated machine.[3] However, brain functioning not only attempts to maintain self-regulation by feedback control but also to produce something new. Thus, its function is not only adaptive but also creative.

An attempt to reconcile the two speculative concepts—control of feedback and hierarchy—may provide a crude model for understanding the relation between behavior and higher neural organization. One significant drawback is that it is difficult to make definitive analogies to psychological processes. It is hoped that the development of modern computers and mathematical analog models will provide the tools required for simulating such brain processes as creativity and other poorly understood mechanisms.

At this point, the important brain structures involved in the mediation of emotional stimuli and their chief neurophysiologic functions at both hypnotic and nonhypnotic levels will be discussed.

ROLE OF THE CEREBRAL CORTEX

In man, the cerebral cortex has evolved to its highest neural level of integration. As a result, discriminatory thinking has been developed to a maximum with the ability to meet the present and anticipate the future in terms of past memory experiences stored as information. Though the biologic needs of an organism initiate behavior, behavioral patterns are integrated through higher neural levels and are also influenced by past learning.

The cerebral cortex represents a huge network of intricate and interlacing systems in which storage, comparison, and coding of impulses can occur to provide perception, memory, and learning. Wakefulness, sleep, hypnosis, and a wide variety of complex emotional affects depend upon varying degrees of arousal. These are a property of the midbrain or diencephalic level in which attention recently has been focused on the differences in organization and function of the ascending reticular activating system (A.R.A.S.) as it is involved in somatovisceral adjustments.[28]

These observations apparently confirm the existence in the upper brain stem of a network of interconnected neurons, the central reticular formation which acts as a sort of "mixing network" from widespread cortical areas. It is logical to conceive of such an integrating center here, because, within a few millimeters, one finds neurons with both ascending and descending connections to the frontal, temporal, parietal, and occipital lobes.

Also at this level, research has been concentrated on clarifying the functions of the thalamocortical and hypothalamic systems which connect with the A.R.A.S.[8, 16] Others have differentiated the functions of the medial and basal "limbic" formations of the forebrain from those of the more laterally located portions of the cerebral cortex.[22, 26, 29]

It seems likely that perceptual discrimination of stimuli, involving the cortex, operates in human and infrahuman animals to evoke arousal from sleep. In narcolepsy, where the EEG shows typically slow waves, loud noise accelerates the EEG momentarily, but the patient does not awaken. However, softly speaking the patient's name produces prompt awakening with concomitant changes of the EEG to an alert pattern. Thus the central reticular formation may act like a tunable two-way amplifier to modulate important signals at hypnotic and nonhypnotic levels. Sperry and his associates severed the corpus callosum surgically and observed that the two halves of the brain are essentially two brains, almost identical but differing in function.[46] In right-handed persons, the left hemisphere is primarily concerned with verbal behavior and analytic tasks. The right hemisphere is more involved with imagination, space perception, and music. The former acts like a stimulus-response digital computer. The latter acts like an analog computer—a "gestalt" brain. In left-handed persons, these relationships are reversed. The recognition that there are two cerebral hemispheres specialized to operate in different modes allows some understanding of the fundamental durability of what is referred to as consciousness or unconsciousness. Gur and Gur observed that a hemisphere preference correlates with measured hypnotizability.[11]

ROLE OF THE INTERPRETIVE CORTEX

Penfield has electrically stimulated certain areas of the temporal lobes of epileptics to activate memory sequences which may be classed as experiential and interpretive.[37] An experiential response occurs as a flashback to a seemingly random event in the subject's past; it ceases when the stimulus is removed. Such scanning or interpretive "signaling" is manifested by strange emotional reactions such as fear, loneliness, panic, and a false sense of familiarity or the *déjà vu* phenomenon.

These scanning mechanisms functioning reciprocally with other specific brain areas are unquestionably involved in age regression, revivification, amnesia, hyperamnesia, negative and positive sensory hallucinations, and other hypnotic phenomena.

Although access to the past is available from either temporal lobe, both the experiential and interpretative responses indicate the existence of a permanent ganglionic recording of the stream of consciousness that is formed and preserved in a constant pattern of electrical impulses projected from a hypothetical integrating system for thought in the upper brain stem—the centrencephalic system.[37] This pattern is a sort of neuronal record in which present experience is preserved for life by means of successive facilitation through the cells and synapses which constitute this pathway. It seems likely that some of this same record is used when recurring judgments are made in regard to familiarity with and the meaning of each new experience. The actual recording of the stream of consciousness may be utilized for the purpose of comparison long after it has been lost to voluntary control.

ROLE OF THE LIMBIC SYSTEM

Recent research on the neurophysiologic mediation of emotions has pointed more clearly to the importance of a series of older cortical structures given the name "Papez action circuit" or, more recently, the limbic system.[35] Structurally, this system constitutes the inner core of the brain concealed by the convolutions of the neocortex or the new brain. This ancient structure, the rhinencephalon, was the primitive "nose-brain." Experimental evidence indicates that it may serve as a nonspecific activator for the cortex, facilitating or inhibiting learning, memory, overt behavior, and internal feelings, even though it is under neocortical control.[13]

Thus the limbic system is to feeling states what the reticular system is to somatovisceral adjustments. The presumed primacy of the role of the limbic system in emotional behavior supports the assumption that it is here that the important neural mechanisms for "feeling drive" and "conceptual will" are located.[25] In this regard, the role of the limbic system, as it functions in the brain's hierarchic order, helps to elucidate the nature of hypnosis, hysteria, schizophrenia, and psychosomatic diseases.

Behavioristically, the limbic system gives expression to the visceral needs of the body rather than to its purely ideational functions. It interprets experience in terms of feeling rather than in terms of intellectualizing symbols. The latter type of interpretation is presumed to be predominantly under neocortical control. However, the modulating influence of the limbic system is not exclusively concerned with the mediation of subjective emotional expressions, but it also acts in correlating primitive motivational-emotional processes. Homeostatic and adaptive centers also are abundantly located around the third and fourth ventricles; these, too, react to neocortically directed activities in general, as for example, during voluntary physical work or intense intellectual concentration, or when we voluntarily induce ourselves to relax, or, as described below, to enter into hypnosis.

Since both the striated and the smooth muscular systems are under the influence of the limbic system, this helps to explain the close relationship between voluntary and involuntary control of visceral functions during hypnotic behavior. The involuntary system is not as involuntary as it is believed to be, and portions of the voluntary system can come under neocortical control with appropriate conditioning, such as in biofeedback, Yoga, or hypnosis.

The controls which the limbic system exercises are massive and diffuse, and, as a result, entire organ systems as well as the body image appear to be symbolically represented as a whole rather than specific muscles or movements. This is different from the sharply exercised controls in the neocortex.[19] Thus, because of the interconnections among the various structures of the limbic system, this subcortical region acts as a sort of "automatic pilot," and, together with the reticular formation, seems to provide a mechanism in which

. . . sensory afferents and symbolic representations of the outside world, and sensory afferents from the symbolic representations of the bodily structures plus all the autonomic components of experience can become integrated. It is here that a triple linkage may occur involving the "I" or self, the "non-I" or non-self, and the intermediate or communicating worlds.[10]

The amygdaloid complex, an important structure of the limbic system, together with the reticular formation and the intralaminar systems, is capable of exerting a diffuse regulatory influence on the cortex.[9] As evidence of the hierarchic relations, the electrical activity recorded from the amygdaloid complex changes when an animal is startled or when, as a result of conditioning, its "attention" is focused on some environmental event.

When the hippocampus—still another subdivision of the limbic system—is inhibited, the electrical activity from the amygdala changes whenever the animal touches, hears or sees any environmental event.[32] Hippocampal seizures result in catatoniclike states similar to catalepsy.[26] Alterations in hippocampal activity also reflect the presence of a mechanism by which limbic system structures contribute a "staying" quality to emotion and pain. One important function of the hippocampus is to keep the brain attentive to carrying out goal-directed behavior and to prevent it from being shunted haphazardly by every fluctuation in the environment.[6] Crasilneck and his co-workers have described how hypnosis terminated each time during brain surgery when the hippocampus was stimulated.[7] They suggest that the hippocampus mediates whatever neural circuits are involved in hypnosis.

EEG findings indicate that the cortex can be desynchronized during arousal. Simultaneously, the hippocampus changes its electrical pattern in a way that has generally been associated with sleep. Livingston[23] poses an interesting hypothesis to explain what appears to be a paradox. He thinks that the limbic system plays a trophic role to restore and conserve energy to maintain visceral well-being. In the presence of anxiety-evoking arousal in which energy is expended rapidly, the temporary "going to sleep" of the involved nervous structures may be protective to the organism. Might not this mechanism also explain the effectiveness of Pavlov's protective "sleep" inhibition therapy (hypnosis)? The limbic system apparently also can develop an odd type of memory loss. When large lesions of the limbic system are produced, execution of complex action sequences cannot be carried out. An interference with feeding, fighting, mating, and maternal behavior may occur as well.

Although many seemingly unrelated effects on behavior have been attributed to limbic system activity, it can be hypothesized on the basis of the above data that these systems comprise the substrate concerned with motivational and emotional behavior—primitive, instinctual and "visceral" reactions. The kind of effect obtained depends on which of the major divisions of the limbic systems are involved.[32]

In the course of performing lobotomies and related operations, Heath observed a consistent reduction in "emotional overflow from memories" following removal of a part of the prefrontal cortex connected with a rhinencephalic region below the corpus callosum (septal region).[13] Stimulation of this area speeds movement and alerts the animal, whereas stimulation of the caudate nucleus has an opposite effect. Most important, his data indicated that the same emotional response always accompanied stimulation of a specific region. Such findings lend general support to ideas expressed by Herrick,[14] Papez,[34] Klüver[17] and others who opened up this line of investigation.

The foregoing data indicate that ideational processes which occur as a function of neocortical and limbic lobe activity reach peripheral nervous pathways via the R.A.S. Heath's work may have some connection with the increased alertness, the vividness of sensory-imagery and the facilitation of ideomotor activity noted during hypnosis. How else can we explain the alert behavior of the person who is ostensibly "asleep" or detached while in hypnosis or the person who is "awake" while supposedly asleep? And what about dreaming when cortical activity is completely inhibited? Does the rhinencephalon act as a "watch dog" to protect the dreamer? Even though their functional significance is different, the similarity between schizophrenic symptoms and states of reverie, hypnosis and sleep is well known.

In this section we have attempted to show how limbic system activity relates primarily to the execution of complex goal-directed emotional activities, as well as *how* and *where* these goals originated in the brain. The decision to execute a sequence of operations undoubtedly begins by transfer of control from the posterior "association areas" to the frontal "association areas" which have been referred to as the "organ of civilization." These are intimately connected with the limbic system to "serve as a working memory" in which plans can be retained tempo-

rarily when they are being formed, transformed or executed.[32] Thus selecting a goal from memory is largely a function of the primitive portions of the brain. The subjective experiencing of associated emotional affects in turn requires mediation by cortical portions of the brain.

ROLE OF THE HYPOTHALAMUS

The hypothalamus receives a complex pattern of afferent connections from higher brain areas such as the limbic and reticular activating systems. There are also two-way neural pathways, reverberating circuits or feedback mechanisms that reciprocally connect the hypothalamus and cortex via limbic system structures.[8] It is generally accepted that the expression of emotions is mediated by the hypothalamus—not only the autonomic reactions, such as those which result in pallor, blushing, palpitation, elevation of blood pressure, sweating, and peristalsis, but also the responses involving striated muscle, such as the grimaces and trembling of rage. The hypothalamus mobilizes the body for emergencies—coordinating the necessary build-up of breathing and other autonomic functions. It also regulates hunger and sexual activities.

The emotional influence of both the A.R.A.S. and the limbic system is expressed in part by modulating the functions of the hypothalamus; all three systems overlap. Thus the thalamus and the hypothalamus occupy an important position in the maze of intricate connections between the neocortex and the subcortical structures.

ROLE OF THE RETICULAR ACTIVATING SYSTEM

The reticular formation is the central axial core of the brain stem, which acts as a neuron pool and seems to have an influence on almost all sensory inflow to the higher centers as well as their motor outflow. Besides participating in vital autonomic responses, it elicits generalized inhibition of movement. It also reduces, or may eliminate, incoming sensory impulses at the level of their entrance into the brain stem.

Magoun and co-workers found that sensory stimuli reach the cortex by two pathways: the classic lemniscal pathways to the primary receptive areas, and "a series of ascending relays coursing through the mesencephalic tegmentum, subthalamus, hypothalamus, and ventromedial thalamus to the internal capsule."[27] It is this collateral network that is referred to as the A.R.A.S.[23, 26, 27, 29]

Activation of the brain stem reticular formation may cause generalized cortical arousal; that is, it induces electrical and behavioral manifestations of alertness. For this reason, it has been called the reticular activating system (R.A.S.). Corticofugal projections of the cortex, acting through the ventromedial nucleus of the hypothalamus, have some measure of reciprocal control of the reticular formation by exerting an inhibiting or deactivating effect so that painful stimuli are diminished or eliminated. Thus the R.A.S. is able "to burn the nervous system's candle at both ends.[23]

Impulses also reach the R.A.S. from the cerebellum. The R.A.S. is activated by epinephrine and acetylcholine and by other adrenergic or cholinergic substances. It modifies muscle tone and movement and visceral regulatory mechanisms. Hence, stimulation, inhibition, arousal, and depression can be reciprocally exercised simultaneously in different areas by the A.R.A.S.[27] When the cortex is prevented from being stimulated by impulses from the R.A.S., the brain is quiescent. Wakefulness is then maintained by lower brain centers which are activated by incoming afferent stimuli. As more of the R.A.S. is eliminated, the electrocortical activity changes from a waking to a sleeplike state.

Operationally, the relative quiescence of the brain may be observed in the variations of electroencephalographic patterns that occur in the transition from sleep to wakefulness. The arousal function of the R.A.S. and the thalamus have *specific* activating influences on the cortex. This may have relevance for the phenomena of hypnosis—it maintains wakefulness while some degree of cortical inhibition occurs. Although no significant alterations in the wave patterns have been noted in hypnosis, there may be sufficient basis, depending on the degree of cortical excitation and inhibition, to posit that the A.R.A.S. is an important screening mechanism for a continuum of sleep, hypnosis, and wakefulness.[31]

NEUROPHYSIOLOGIC MECHANISMS IN THE MEDIATION OF EMOTIONS DURING HYPNOSIS

The preceding section stressed that one difficulty in assaying cerebral functioning at any level of awareness is that the simplest neural event becomes enormously complex. Another problem is that the neuronal correlates responsible for hypnotic behavior are not likely to be found in the action and interaction of systems, nor in the activity of single brain structures. The reason for this is that hypnosis is a part of everyday behavior dynamics. Like other instinctual defense mechanisms, it is a phylogenetically determined adaptive response.[18] The basis for this assumption is that the activity of an inherited network of neuronal synapses to produce altered states of awareness can be modified by experience through learning. There is evidence that inherited ingredients enter into every learning process, and that in turn an extensive modification of these inherited ingredients may occur through the process of learning and conditioning, so that these overlapping determinants constitute broad bands on a continuous spectrum.[21] The capacity to enter hypnosis is already built into the organism and is merely elicited on the basis of altering the subject's "perceptions" and interpretations of himself and his surroundings.[4]

There are several other recent studies which have tried to elucidate the neural mechanisms by which hypnosis affects human thinking and behavior.[2, 42, 46] Arnold believes that, when irrelevant action impulses are excluded, the subject develops a set or a state of expectancy to accept what the hypnotist is describing, with the result that the flow of sensory impressions is reduced.[2] On a neurophysiologic level, cortical inhibition occurs in which the "set to imagine" is mediated by the limbic system; more specifically, the hippocampal action circuit connected with the diffuse thalamic system. The latter, in turn, mediates the reduction or the intensification of neural conduction to the limbic cortex and the hippocampus and is instrumental in excluding sensory impressions. The resultant distortion or exclusion of sensory information may help to explain negative or positive sensory hallucinations.

It is contended by Arnold that suggestions given for complete neuromuscular relaxation (cataplexy),* even though characterized by full awareness, are mediated via the limbic system connecting with the premotor and the motor cortex, and represent motor imagination (ideomotor) transformed into action.[2] Suggested sensations (ideosensory) are mediated via the limbic system which connects with the frontal "association areas" and the primary sensory receiving areas. These represent projected memory images which are accepted as real because the impulse to appraise and evaluate has been excluded. Suggested goal-directed actions (posthypnotic suggestions) flow from the suggested situation (suggestions given during hypnosis) and are mediated via the limbic system just like any action carried out without hypnosis.[1]

However, Roberts questions the role of the diffuse projection of the thalamic reticular formation in the production of hypnotic phenomena, as it cannot be safely posited that this area could serve as a vehicle of perception.[39] The pronounced loss of sensory-motor activity which occurs during hypnosis is consistent with the theory that perception may occur through a secondary system. This system may be in the upper part of the brain stem, where a switching over to the cortex occurs—that is, in the A.R.A.S. and the surrounding areas of the dorsal hypothalamus. Psychic excitement radiates from this center and probably has something to do with a central "pacemaker" of the cerebrum, possibly the centrencephalic system.[37]

Because of the resultant inhibition produced by electrodynamic factors (selective activity of brain rhythms of delta frequency), Roberts postulates:

During hypnosis the central nervous system is immobilized because the activating system has been deprived of the data—sensory, somesthetic, sensorimotor, affective, intentive, mnemonic—requisite to the normal direction of psychic activity and response. However, the continued activity of the A.R.A.S. and elaborative and effector cortical areas maintains the

capacity for integration, higher elaboration and response.[42]

In accord with the principle of selective neural inhibition, he believes that the subject cannot check incoming information against the stored data because these have been blocked. As a result, the subject uncritically accepts the suggestions of the hypnotist.

Akstein implicates the A.R.A.S.,[1] and Reyher theorizes on corticolumbar areas involving excitation and inhibition.[41] West believes that recently observed bioelectric variations during the hypnotic state, as well as differing reactions of hypnotic subjects to drugs under various circumstances, are compatible with mediation by the A.R.A.S.[46]

Recently, neurophysiologists and behavioral scientists have attempted to understand hypnosis in terms of altered states of consciousness (A.S.C.). The author does not feel that the concept of A.S.C. will contribute materially to a better understanding of the mechanisms of hypnosis. Such notions merit consideration only if it can be shown that psychological processes are dominated by specialized cortical areas.[33] Cortical left-right asymmetry, as discussed above, is illustrative. It is hoped that modern advances in electrophysiology will provide help in understanding the mediation of emotion at hypnotic and nonhypnotic levels.

Miller and his co-workers have postulated the TOTE unit (test-operate-test-exit) to show the relation between the *Image* (the experiential background) and a *Plan* (a hierarchic process which controls the order in which a sequence of operations is to be performed).[32] The TOTE concept, which incorporates the important notion of feedback, is a fundamentally different explanation of behavior from that provided by the reflex arc. This author, however, cannot agree with their concept of hypnosis as a hypnotist-directed approach, because hypnosis is a subjective phenomenon. It is not true that a hypnotized person has stopped making his own Plans, and therefore, executes the hypnotist's version of the Plan, since this is the only one he has. However, the reader is strongly urged to read their excellent book, which helps to elucidate the neuropsychological

---

*The author's interpretations are given in parentheses.

mechanisms involved in thinking, memory, personality, motor skills, intention, instincts, problem-solving, and hypnosis.[32]

Ravitz attempts to explain the possible neural basis of hypnosis and its biologic significance as the result of electric force fields; he holds that hypnotic states can be "distinguished from sleep by the development of characteristic force-field shifts with preservation of a waking EEG configuration."[39, 40] He also reported changes in direct current potentials at the point of induction of hypnosis and at the point of termination of hypnosis.

In the next section, attempts will be made to clarify what determines the brain's acceptance of suggestions in a noncritical manner during hypnosis, and also why some individuals at nonhypnotic levels have little or no difficulty in accepting suggestions uncritically. It is no wonder that Kubie remarked: "Hypnosis is at the crossroads for all levels of physiological and psychological organization, and . . . the phenomenon which we call hypnotism when more fully understood will be one of our most important tools for the study of normal sleep, of normal alertness, and of continuous interplay among normal, neurotic and psychotic processes."[21] The next chapter includes a practical discussion of the methods used by the hypnotherapist to induce an attitude of belief in his subject to alter his psychological processes in a particular way.

DISCUSSION

The induced state of selectively altered sensory awareness called hypnosis is mediated by exteroceptors (external signals), interoceptors (signals from internal processes), and proprioceptors (position of the body). During hypnosis, certain signals are selected for focused arousal and amplification to exclusion of irrelevant ones. In essence, hypnosis selectively rearranges certain stimulus-response cues so that they do not produce undesirable autonomic reaction patterns. The principal site of interaction between the C.N.S. and A.N.S. is the hypothalamus which also marks the junction between the brain stem and the cerebral hemispheres with the pituitary. Thus the hypothalamus becomes a three-way junction that integrates and coordinates the function of the C.N.S., the A.N.S., and the hormonal system.

The core of the brain stem (R.A.S.) up to the hypothalamus functions as a preamplifier for sensory (awareness) and motor (responsive) areas of the cortex. The R.A.S. performs two significant functions in conscious awareness. First, the "constant-pulse signal" it generates keeps the cortex alerted for incoming impulses, both from cranial nerves and spinal tracts mediating incoming sensory stimuli. Second, the R.A.S. operates as a "tunable amplifier" for the cortex, which selectively facilitates or amplifies some incoming sensory impulses (important ones) while suppressing others (unimportant ones). The R.A.S. is the site of significant neuroelectrical activity changes during hypnosis.

The A.N.S. incorporates two separate but interactive neural networks. Thus it functions as a "two-phase governor," regulating expenditure and conservation of emotional energy. The first is the sympathetic system, which *energizes* the activities of the visceral system. The second is the parasympathetic system, which *relaxes* or tranquilizes various visceral reactions. Many sympathetic or altered states can be pleasurable and not necessarily related to avoidance responses. Not all parasympathetic or relaxed states are related to pleasurable effects; some can be perceived as unpleasant experiences in the form of depressive reactions.

Hypnosis or altered states of consciousness can connect or associate sensory or cognitive stimuli with either sympathetic or parasympathetic reactions and effects. The key factor is that hypnosis involves saturation of one or more of the primary exteroceptive systems (auditory, visual, or tactile) combined with a directed inhibition of normal proprioceptor sensations and interoceptor awareness of visceral activity.

In sleep, nearly all channels of sensory input are inhibited from cortical awareness by the R.A.S. In chemical sedation, sensory blocking is generalized (as in normal sleep), while most of the inhibition occurs at the cortical level. Like hypnosis, the tranquilizing agents act on the hypothalamus and R.A.S., diminishing anxiety and tension without depressing cortical activity.

However, under hypnosis, selective reconditioning is possible; posthypnotic suggestions are more readily followed. This cannot be attained with drugs.

The physiological basis for perceptual awareness is the result of the induced parasympathetic dominance of the visceral systems, resulting in generalized relaxation. As awareness becomes associated with heaviness and drowsiness, attention can be more readily focused on specific cognitive processes, all of which are essential to selective conditioning of the A.N.S.

REFERENCES

1. Akstein, D.: The induction of hypnosis in the light of reflexology. Am. J. Clin. Hypn., 7:281, 1965.
2. Arnold, M.B.: Brain function in hypnosis. Int. J. Clin. Exp. Hypn., 7:109, 1959.
3. Ashby, W.R.: Design for a Brain. New York, Wiley, 1954, p. 6.
4. Barber, T.X.: The concept of hypnosis. J. Psychol., 45:115, 1958.
5. Benson, H., et al.: The relaxation response. Psychiatry, 37:37, 1974.
6. Brazier, M.A.B. (ed.): Central nervous system and behavior. Transactions of the second conference of the J. Macy, Jr., Foundation, New York, February 22–25, 1959.
7. Crasilneck, H.B., et al: Special indications for hypnosis as a method of anesthesia. J.A.M.A., 162: 1606, 1956.
8. Fields, W.S.: Hypothalamic-Hypophyseal Interrelationships. Springfield, Ill., Charles C Thomas, 1956.
9. Feindel, W., and Gloor, P.: Comparison of electrographic effects of stimulation of the amygdala and brain stem reticular formation in cats. Electroencephal. Clin. Neurophysiol., 6:389, 1954.
10. Glaser, G.H.: Recent concepts of central neurophysiology. Psychosom. Med., 17:337, 1955.
11. Gur, R.E., and Gur, R.C.: Handedness, sex and eyedness as moderating variables in the relationship between hypnotic susceptibility and functional brain asymmetry. J. Abnorm. Psychol., 83: 635, 1974.
12. Gutman, H.: The biological roots of creativity. Genetic Psych. Monog., 64:417, 1961.
13. Heath, R.G.: Correlations between levels of psychological awareness and physiological activity in the central nervous system. Psychosom. Med., 12: 383, 1955.
14. Herrick, C.J.: The amphibian forebrain. VI. Necturus. J. Comp. Neurol., 58:1, 1933.
15. Hess, W.R.: Functional Organization of the Diencephalon. New York, Grune & Stratton, 1957.
16. Jasper, H.: Diffuse projection systems; the integrative action of the thalamic reticular system. Electroencephal. Clin. Neurophysiol., 1:405, 1949.
17. Klüver, H., and Bucy, P.C.: Preliminary analysis of functions of the temporal lobes in monkeys. Arch. Neurol. Psychiat., 42:979, 1939.
18. Kroger, W.S., and Freed, S.C.: Psychosomatic Gynecology. Chicago, Free Press, 1956 (reprinted, Los Angeles, Wilshire Book Company, 1962).
19. Kubie, L.S.: The central representation of the symbolic process in psychosomatic disorders. Psychosom. Med., 15:1, 1953.
20. ———: Appendix I: Body symbolization and development of language (reprinted from Psychoanal. Q., 3:430, 1934). Cybernetics. New York, Macy, 1951.
21. ———: Hypnotism: a focus for psychophysiological and psychoanalytical investigations, Arch. Gen. Psychiat., 4:53, 1961.
22. Lindsley, D. H.: Emotion. In Stevens, S. S. (ed.): Handbook of Experimental Psychology. New York, Wiley, 1951, pp. 473–516.
23. Livingston, R. B.: Some brain stem mechanisms relating to psychosomatic functions. Psychosom. Med., 17:347, 1955.
24. MacKay, D. M.: The epistemological problem for automata. In Shannon, C. E., and McCarthy, J. (eds.): Automata Studies. Princeton, Princeton University Press, 1956.
25. MacLean, P. D.: The limbic system and its hippocampal formation; studies in animals and their possible application to man. J. Neurosurg., 11:29, 1954.
26. ———: Limbic system ("visceral brain") in relation to central gray and reticulum of brain stem: evidence of interdependence in emotional processes. Psychosom. Med., 17:355, 1955.
27. Magoun, H. W.: The ascending reticular activating system. Res. Publ., J. Nerv. Ment. Dis., 30:480, 1952.
28. ———: An ascending reticular activating system in the brain stem. Arch. Neurol. Psychiat., 67:145, 1952.
29. ———: The ascending reticular system and wakefulness. In Delafresnaye, J. F. (ed.): Brain Mechanisms and Consciousness. Springfield, Ill., Charles C Thomas, 1954, pp. 1–15.

30. _____: Paper read at Third World Congress of Psychiatry, Montreal, June 10, 1961.

31. Marmer, M. J.: Hypnosis in Anesthesiology. Springfield, Ill., Charles C Thomas, 1959.

32. Miller, G. A., Galanter E., and Pribram, K. H.: Plans and the Structure of Behavior. New York, Holt, 1960.

33. Ornstein, R.E.: The Psychology of Consciousness. San Francisco, W.H. Freeman, 1972.

34. Papez, J. W.: A proposed mechanism of emotion. Arch. Neurol. Psychiat., *38:*725, 1937.

35. Pavlov, I. P.: Selected Works. Moscow, Foreign Languages Publishing House, 1955.

36. Penfield, W.: Memory mechanisms. Arch. Neurol. Psychiat., *67:*178, 1952.

37. _____: The interpretive cortex. Science, *129:*1719, 1959.

38. Pribram, K. H.: A review of theory in physiological psychology. *In* Annual Review of Psychology. Palo Alto, Cal., 1960, pp. 6–7.

39. Ravitz, L. J.: Application of the electrodynamic field theory in biology, psychiatry, medicine, and hypnosis. Am. J. Clin. Hypn., *1:*135, 1959.

40. _____: Electrometric correlates of the hypnotic state. Science, *112:*341, 1950.

41. Reyher, J.: Brain mechanisms, intrapsychic processes and behavior: a theory of hypnosis and psychopathology. Am. J. Clin. Hypn., *7:*107, 1964.

42. Roberts, D. R.: An electrophysiological theory of hypnosis. Int. J. Clin. Exp. Hypn., *8:*43, 1960.

43. Shaefer, H.: Physiology and psychosomatic medicine. Med. Arch. Gen. Psychiat., *3:*99, 1960.

44. Snezhnevsky, A. V.: Paper read at World Psychiatry meeting, Montreal, June, 1961.

45. Sperry, R.: Quoted in Gazzaniga, M.S.: The Bisected Brain. New York, Appleton-Century-Crofts, 1970.

46. West, L.J.: Psychophysiology of hypnosis. J.A.M.A., *172:*672, 1960.

29

Psychophysiologic Mechanisms in the Production of Hypnotic Phenomena: Relation to Belief and Conviction

REALITY AND PERCEPTUAL AWARENESS

The current psychiatric literature postulates that there are two "minds," the conscious and the unconscious (subconscious). "Consciousness" is defined as awareness of one's own existence, self, and actions. It requires effort and is invariably referred to as the part of the brain which maintains critical faculties. It accounts chiefly for the cognitive aspects of most mental functioning. "Consciousness" and its associated mental states all involve discriminatory activities and are, of necessity, dynamic functions heavily dependent on the cortex.

The other portion of the brain is "nonconscious" and, at its lowest levels, is devoid of awareness even though it is never inoperative, either during sleep or wakefulness. Thought influenced by the neural centers below the cortex is egocentric, dreamy, and wishful. Its functioning depends largely on the activity of subcortical structures, which, as already described, play a role of equal or even greater importance in cognitive functioning.[15]

However, subcortical structures are not in continual strife, at lower levels, with the cortex. Since these subcortical centers apparently lack discriminative ability, they initiate rather than attempt to control the goal-directed activities of the organism. This reciprocal and dynamic interaction of the two arbitrary divisions of the brain makes up the experiential background of the individual—past and present. Without the subcortical centers, the cortex could not receive memories or current percepts. On the other hand, without the cortex, the lower centers cannot receive the necessary information essential for validating reality.

When any one of the senses is stimulated, the information is first received in the lower centers and then forwarded to the cortex for correlation with data from the other senses. After the information has been validated as reality, the original percept is then filed as information in the subcortical centers. Later, when a similar percept is received, these centers transmit not only this information to the cortex for validation, but the memory of percepts related to the original reality situation. This forms the basis for convictions. Incoming percepts may differ, so as to require different convictions, but earlier convictions influence the current ones. As past convictions accumulate, they become available for consideration of current problems as these relate to reality.

Hence, thought is the association of new percepts with past data, and past convictions afford possible solutions to new situations. In other words, reality is based on sensorily received information, which of necessity has to be continually validated against previously stored memories. Convictions result from acceptance of reality and, unless new reality situations are introduced, the older sensory impressions cannot be changed.[12] One might say the brain is guided by reality as it perceives reality, but this freedom is limited by past and present realities.

Studies in perception indicate that awareness of reality *comes from within us,* not from our environment.[9] This would fit in with the operational definition that hypnosis is a subjective phenomenon processed out of previously invoked beliefs which create a *readiness to believe.* All perceptual awareness in hypnosis is altered by compounding of beliefs, and this leads to conviction independent of reality.

PSYCHOPHYSIOLOGIC MECHANISMS IN HYPNOTIC PHENOMENA

The phenomenon of posthypnotic amnesia depends upon the type and degree of cortical inhibition. During deep hypnosis, the cortex is not even "aware" that such memories are accessible. Posthypnotic amnesia does not actually eliminate the memories but merely prevents information processed out of what constitutes reality for the subject from reaching the mnemonic data in the higher sensorium. In other words, instead of *reality, there is unreality.* It must be emphasized, however, that any sensory distortion negates reality for only that particular posthypnotic suggestion, that is, the amnestic material. The conviction of amnesia is brought about first by the reality of hypnosis, and then this is followed by the belief that amnesia will occur.

Posthypnotic suggestions that are carried out successfully are those capable of instilling convictions at variance with the previously invoked beliefs. However, conviction can be accepted without question even at nonhypnotic levels; this is noted in religious faith-healing and in the blind trust of children. Such conviction, deduced through normal thought processes, is, of course, subject to change unless altered by other information.

Hence, the function of all ideational activities is to process sensory information for the most useful combinations possible out of our experiential background. The importance of understanding the psychophysiologic basis of hypnosis as a phenomenological experience is set not only by what information the brain contains, but also by

what it will receive in terms of awareness or "consciousness."* Kline states:

. . . when one studies hypnotism and when one works with it, he is working with an important element for controlling and determining aspects of consciousness.[10]

He believes that more than the element of suggestion is involved, and emphasizes that "one must not confuse the hypnotic state with hypnotic behavior and with the nature of neuropsychologic processes in the hypnotic state."

It has been emphasized previously that words have the power to produce associative conditioning, that belief is based on experiential conditioning, and when the sensory spiral of belief is cumulative, it leads to hypnotic conviction. As the author stated in a recent publication, "Conviction of hypnosis leads to hypnosis."[11]

Some psychosomatic disorders may be due to increased susceptibility of the cortex induced by partial cortical inhibition. This is brought about by the inability of the integrating centers to interpret correctly new sensory information or data. This can occur whenever repetitive destructive conditioning activates faulty associations or whenever the resultant harmful emotional responses ultimately lead to adverse somatization reactions based on *conviction.* In the former, the beliefs can be changed only by correcting the faulty information through reeducation; in the latter, deeply ingrained convictions can be reversed best by implanting constructive conditioning through meaningful suggestions. Such reconditioning to alter the disturbed cortical dynamics is more readily achieved under hypnosis.

RELATIONSHIP OF BELIEF AND CONVICTION TO HYPNOTIC PHENOMENA

After the production of hypnosis, the need for reality testing is obviated. West states:

When there occurs a marked narrowing of focus of awareness on a particular aspect of reality, to the exclusion of much of the rest (as in the initiation of a hypnotic trance), then sensory data (verbal suggestions)

---

*Chertok has edited an excellent book on the psychophysiological mechanisms of hypnosis.[5] The interested researcher should consult this important monograph.

taken in through an open channel (rapport) become effective because they are not subjected to ordinary reality testing.[17]

It is precisely for this reason that posthypnotic suggestions can be carried out. The degree of effectiveness of a posthypnotic suggestion is based on the degree of suspension of cortical discrimination. Arnold states:

The connection of the hippocampal action circuit (which seems to be the repository of neuronal mechanisms that preserve the stream of consciousness) which mediates recall of the memory image together with the diffuse thalamic system allows the inhibition of irrelevant impulses from the visual area and thus prevents a correction of the hallucinations by the visual impression—as long as the singleminded concentration lasts he is incapable of seeing any incongruity either in his actions or perceptions.

Thus, if a suggestion seems to be a certainty because of belief and conviction, it has the power to effect an appropriate response in the organism. Conviction consists of two types, one of which is based on pooling present and past information. In this type, the brain functions logically because the validation results from past and present circumstances *which are real.* The other type, hypnotic or nonvalidated conviction, requires no checking against stored information because the suggestions are accepted with a literalness *as if they are real.*

The degree of "conscious" response depends on the manner and the number of beliefs necessary to establish conviction. Hence, if we hear something long enough and strongly enough, we can build up conviction, as in religious faith, or a faith in brand names built up by advertisers! It is no wonder that conviction can be put to work in hypnotherapy so admirably.

It is known that, in the presence of the appropriate mind-set, thoughts based on conviction can heal or kill. Conviction of illness can lead just as readily to hypochondriasis or to sickness. No more forceful example can be found than that of voodoo death. Cannon describes how sorcery and witchcraft kill young, healthy people in spite of all modern medical care.[4] Conviction of death processed into the brain may invoke the sympatheticoadrenal sys-

tem, which supersedes volitional control and leads to death!

Voodoo "possession" bears an important relationship to hypnosis. The role of the priest or *hungan* is quite similar to that of the hypnotist. However, group dynamics and psychology of the individual play a larger role in voodoo than in a hypnotic setting.[14] Bowers has made similar observations.[3] Goodfriend and Wolpert recently reviewed the literature on death from fright.[7] They concluded that psychological stress can be a precipitant of sudden death where there is no obvious cause.

Whenever distortion of reality is slipped into awareness through hypnotically induced heterosuggestions, it takes precedence over reality-testing even in well-adjusted individuals. It is by such measures that conviction at hypnotic and often at nonhypnotic levels can occur without volitional participation. The reverse is undoubtedly the mechanism for paranoid trends. The aberrant behavior characterizing the psychoses and the psychoneuroses is due, in part, to distortion of reality by the patient's autosuggestions. The phenomena of hypnosis temporarily mimic, in almost pure culture, the manifestations of deranged thinking and behavior. This does not imply that hypnotic behavior *is* psychotic behavior, but rather that they are opposite sides of the same coin.

If we can comprehend the relationship of belief and conviction to hypnosis, we should be able to achieve better insight into the basic causations of irrational mental functioning. Posthypnotic suggestions afford a remarkable experimental tool for studying the ontogenesis of many different types of neurotic behavior. Just as hypnotically produced suggestions are difficult to resist if they are in keeping with the individual's desires or rationalizations, so are delusional tendencies well-nigh impossible to eradicate by appealing to volition.

The following material has been mentioned in other chapters; however, in this context it warrants repetition. One can produce physiologic effects only if the corresponding imaginative processes are used to invoke the necessary sensory data. The fundamental principle of the law of reverse effect here holds true, namely, that the imagination is more powerful than the will. In this regard, imagining a posthypnotically suggested sensation results in its being experienced, provided contradictory impulses are excluded. The positive gustatory hallucination of "eating a steak" results because the needed data are available in the cortex. However, human beings cannot imagine ideomotor and ideosensory responses that have not been previously experienced.

Ideomotor and ideosensory responses are the *sine qua non* for facilitation of hypnosis. These activities depend on past experiences, which endow the organism with automaticity and require little cortical discrimination. When conviction becomes reflexlike and when it is accepted at this level, the resultant conviction leads to uncritical acceptance of other suggestions.

Briefly, then, an induction procedure makes full use of cortical and subcortical mechanisms. The technic, regardless of the methodology, provides the validation necessary for acceptance of beliefs.

Hypnotic susceptibility also has a high content of thought-out conviction. For instance, if a person expects to be hypnotized by someone in a prestige position, his expectancy level is raised. Subjects who are analytical or who know a considerable amount about hypnosis are difficult to induce by any technic because the prestige factor so necessary for conviction is not present. Furthermore, the initiated anticipate the carefully contrived sensory illusions. Because they cannot exclude irrelevant thoughts, they cannot give their full and continuous attention to the operator. As a result, the necessary diminution of sensory reality never occurs.

In summary, the ability to achieve hypnosis is often based on a single "learned" response, and once it has been achieved it is easy to develop more complex responses. The induction of hypnosis results from conditions which preclude logical thinking. If an individual has the conviction that he has been hypnotized, then further beliefs wholly or partially unrelated to reality are accepted as convictions. Stated simply, acceptance of hypnosis allows acceptance of all that follows, provided that the beliefs do not mobilize critical attitudes. First, cortical awareness is required to establish the sensory meaningfulness of the stimuli leading to hypnosis. This, in turn, allows the summation of convictions to gain control over critical faculties. Now, with reality held in abeyance, information that cannot be checked can be directly implanted to produce appropriate responses.

RELATIONSHIP OF CONVICTION TO DEPTH OF HYPNOSIS

The various hypnotic depths, as has been mentioned, are at best only arbitrary delineations, and no two individuals respond in a similar fashion to identical suggestions because reality varies from person to person and even changes in the same person from time to time. This accounts for the variations in hypnotic response often noted in even well-conditioned subjects.

It was pointed out that, in some highly suggestible individuals, conviction often can be instilled without hypnosis. For these, the need for conviction of hypnosis is obviated. Hence, the concept of "trance" really has no basis in fact, because nearly all "trance" phenomena can be produced without the necessity for inducing a formalistic state of hypnosis!

LIGHT STAGE OF HYPNOSIS

The fundamental principle in achieving any degree of hypnotic depth is to get the subject to accept the validity of simple suggestions first, and then build up to more complex suggestions (see Chap. 15).

MEDIUM STAGE OF HYPNOSIS

After limb catalepsy is attained, further belief is established by the suggestion of deep relaxation. As the depth increases, subcortical centers take over, much as in sleep.

SOMNAMBULISM OR DEEP HYPNOSIS

Here conviction is complete and there is no need for reality testing. The operator's suggestions are received with a literalness because no modification or distortion of the incoming information occurs. Furthermore, the suggestions cannot be compared with previous data, so they are accepted as convictions even though they are at variance with reality. If it is not present, amnesia is produced by a command to forget.

Negative and positive sensory illusions or hallucinations are readily produced because the subject's beliefs grow with *conviction!* In short, the brain can screen impressions selectively from awareness, or inhibit and distort sensory impressions so as to produce visual, auditory and other sensory hallucinations. Often, as a result of these impressions, there is an increase in voluntary performance. Erickson studied over 750 somnambulists and concluded that they spontaneously apprehend the surrounding environment of realities differently than subjects at nonhypnotic levels.[6] He also observes that one type of reality apprehension does not preclude the other type.

DEHYPNOTIZATION

When good subjects are dehypnotized they usually follow most posthypnotic suggestions, since they cannot recall how or why the commands were issued to them in the first place because of the associated amnesia. If they are able to remember, they can resist because the suggestion is no longer a deeply implanted conviction. If they obey the posthypnotic suggestions, subjects offer innumerable rationalizations for their actions.

Not to belabor the point, the nature of posthypnotic suggestions is similar to that of compulsive acts. Like compulsive behavior, which does not follow logical or reality thinking, a posthypnotic suggestion will be resisted only and after recall that the command was given during hypnosis. Here the reality of the situation is recognized, thus negating the effects of the command. For an explanation of other posthypnotic phenomena, such as hypermnesia, age regression, or revivification, the reader is referred to Chapter 2. Not all posthypnotic suggestions will necessarily be followed if the subject's convictions are at variance with the reality of the situation. Also, every individual has different convictions as to what is right and what is wrong. Likewise, some of the different convictions that subjects report when hypnotized, and some of the differences observed by

experimenters, have been reviewed by several investigators.[2, 8, 16]

In conclusion, the phenomenology of hypnosis as well as the degree of hypnotizability depend more or less on how the brain has been "programmed" by previous beliefs and convictions. Thus induction of hypnosis is the induction of conviction.[12]

REFERENCES

1. Arnold, M.B.: Brain function in hypnosis. Int. J. Clin. Exp. Hypn., *7:*109, 1959.
2. Barber, T.X.: Hypnosis: A Scientific Approach. New York, Von Nostrand, Reinhold, 1969.
3. Bowers, M.K.: Hypnotic aspects of Haitian voodoo. Int. J. Clin. Exp. Hypn., *13:*157, 1965.
4. Cannon, W.B.: "Voodoo" death. Psychosom. Med., *19:*182, 1957.
5. Chertok, L.: Psychophysiological mechanisms of hypnosis. New York, Springer-Verlag, 1969.
6. Erickson, M.H.: Further experimental investigation of hypnosis: hypnotic and non-hypnotic realities. Am. J. Clin. Exp. Hypn., *10:*87, 1967.
7. Goodfriend, M., and Wolpert, E.A.: Death from fright: report of a case and literature review. Psychosom. Med., *38:*348, 1976.
8. Hilgard, E.R.: Hypnotic Susceptibility. New York, Harcourt Brace Jovanovich, 1965.
9. Kelley, E.C.: Education is communication. ETC: Rev. Gen. Semantics, *12:*248, 1955.
10. Kline, M.V.: Clinical and Experimental Hypnosis in Contemporary Behavioral Sciences. Introductory Lectures in Medical Hypnosis. New York, Institute for Research in Hypnosis, 1958, p. 1.
11. Kroger, W.S.: Techniques of hypnosis. J.A.M.A., *172:*675, 1960.
12. Lacey, H.: Beyond Hypnosis. Whittier, Cal., Independent Publishing Company, 1952.
13. Penfield, W.: Some mechanisms of consciousness discovered during electrical stimulation of the brain. Proc. Nat. Acad. Sci., *44:*51, 1958.
14. Ravenscroft, K.: Voodoo possession: a natural experiment in hypnosis. Int. J. Clin. Exp. Hypn., *13:*157, 1965.
15. Rowland, V.: Conditioning and brain waves. Sci. Am., *201:*89, 1959.
16. Shor, R.E., and Orne, M.T.: The nature of Hypnosis. Selected Basic Reading. New York, Rinehart & Winston, 1965.
17. West, L.J.: Psychophysiology of hypnosis. J.A.M.A., *172:*672, 1960.

ADDITIONAL READINGS

Anokhin, P. K.: Electroencephalographic analysis of cortico-subcortical relations in positive and negative conditioned reactions. Ann. N. Y. Acad. Sci., *92:* 899, 1961.

Arnold, M. B.: Emotion and Personality. New York, Columbia University Press, 1960.

Bailey, P., and von Bonin, G.: The Isocortex of Man. Urbana, Ill., University of Illinois Press, 1951.

Barber, T. X.: Physiological effects of "hypnosis." Psychol. Bull., *58:*390, 1961.

Brazier, M. A. B.: Brain and Behavior. Proceedings of the First Conference of the Brain Research Institute, University of California, Los Angeles. Washington, D. C., American Institute of Biological Sciences, 1961.

Crasilneck, H. B., and Hall, J. A.: Physiological changes associated with hypnosis: a review of the literature since 1948. Int. J. Clin. Exp. Hypn. *7:*9, 1959.

Diamant, J., *et al.:* An electroencephalographic study of the waking state and hypnosis with particular reference to subclinical manifestations of sleep activity. Int. J. Clin. Exp. Hypn. *8:*199, 1960.

Gorton, B. E.: Physiological aspects of hypnosis. *In* Schneck, J. M. (ed.): Hypnosis in Modern Medicine. Springfield, Ill., Charles C Thomas, 1953.

————: The physiology of hypnosis. *In* The Annual Review of Hypnosis Litrerature. New York, The Society for Clinical and Experimental Hypnosis, 1953.

Simon, A. (ed.), *et al.:* The Physiology of Emotions. Springfield, Ill., Charles C Thomas, 1961.

30

Relationship of Semantics, Communication, and Perception to Hypnosis

In this chapter there will be a brief description of how communication, the chief tool of the hypnotherapist, relates to semantics, perception, and learning, as well as of the contemporary developments that the behavioral and physical sciences have made in the comparative study of the messages of control and communication in man and machine—cybernetics. These disciplines regard man as a highly evolved and complex automaton or "servomechanism," regulated by the transmission of feedback data—that is, a process by which error-correcting information is fed back to maintain homeostasis. Cybernetics suggests new hypotheses for understanding neurophysiologic functioning and, perhaps, such behaviorial responses as hypnosis.

ROLE OF HYPNOSEMANTICS IN THERAPY

It has been stressed that words are important tools in the arsenal of the hypnotherapist. Responses during hypnosis are due to the manner in which words are interpreted by the subject. Most hypnotized persons respond with a literalness to the meaning of words. For instance, if a nonhypnotized person is told, "Raise your right hand," he usually *lifts the entire arm.* The hypnotized individual invariably *raises his hand because he responds exactly as suggested.*

The anxiety-ridden patient, however, is likely to attach a different connotation to certain words, particularly during the induction. Therefore, such phrases as "going down, down," "falling deeper and deeper," "you are in a sleeplike state" should be avoided, as they may be equated to sexual or death fantasies. Illustrative is the phrase, "Imagine that your body is like a 'dead weight.'" Those who regard hypnosis as a death-like or a "suspended animation" phenomenon will generally respond unfavorably, but proper orientation will negate this misconception.

Others, with a low threshold to anxiety, will overreact even to harmless words. The degree depends on previous associations. At the first sign of an untoward reaction to a word or a phrase, corrective measures must be instituted. Words that might shock the patient should be eliminated from the vocabulary of the hypnotherapist, especially in obstetrics. Instead of asking a hypnotized patient in labor, "How are your pains?" the word "contractions" should be substituted for "pains." In surgery, lack of "word-watchfulness" often can interfere with recovery. The calamitous effect of words in the production of hypochondriasis is well documented.

It is also easier to make a disturbed person sicker by words, or even grunts or gestures, than to make him well. It is not without reason that it has been said, "A word can make or break a man," and *it is this which accounts for most of the dangers attributed to hypnosis.*

162

Much difficulty can be obviated by the careful measurement of words. The science of measuring words is called semantics—the systematic study of the meaning of words. General semantics is the study and the improvement of human evaluative processes to language with special emphasis on their relationship to signs and symbols, including language.

The semantic significance of words for psychophysiology is that they constitute real, conditioned stimuli. Thus patients can be habituated to key words which will invariably evoke behavioral responses, as in hypnosis. Pavlov bound up speech, hypnosis, and the conditioned reflex in a statement which the years have done nothing to alter.[22] He said:

Speech, on account of the whole preceding life of the adult, is connected up with all the internal and external stimuli which can reach the cortex, signalling all of them and replacing all of them, and, therefore, it can call forth all those reactions of the organism which are ordinarily determined by the actual stimuli themselves. We can, therefore, regard "suggestion" as the most simple form of a conditioned reflex in man.

In other words, the mere mention of a word associated with a certain physiologic or psychological reaction elicits that reaction even though the original stimulus has been forgotten. Thus a word does not become meaningful until a conditioned reflex between it and some conditioned or unconditioned stimulus takes place in the cortex. In the child, for instance, the word "hurt" acquires a definite meaning only after it has been associated with real pain. After that, the appropriate conditioned reaction to the word "hurt" can be evoked to reproduce the exact conditioned response (pain reaction). Once a conditioned reflex is established, the person automatically reacts without thinking to the nongenuine stimulus that has become a part of the reflex. In the example just given this would be the word "hurt."

It even has been observed that a verbal stimulus alone provokes a stronger reaction in hypnotically conditioned subjects than an actual pinprick.[24] Pavlov's conditioning, in the classic manner, is somewhat analogous to the effects obtained by repetitive posthypnotic suggestions.

The only difference is that, in the latter, full use is made of the inborn feedback mechanisms—the ideomotor and ideosensory responses. These do not require learning.

During autohypnosis, the mere thought of a word or a phrase elicits the same responses that it ordinarily would following posthypnotic suggestions. In hypnotic sensory-imagery conditioning, the words act in the "mind's ear" as "inner speech," because subcortical structures cannot differentiate between a vividly imagined experience and a real one. The reason is that the only information available to the cortex for validation about a given situation is *what one believes to be true about it!*

Illustrative is the work of Hudgins, who conditioned the pupillary reflex to voluntary control.[14] When the verbal command "Contract" was given to a group of hypnotized subjects, together with a light (unconditioned stimulus) and a bell (conditioned stimulus), the pupils contracted without the light or the bell. In other subjects, pupillary contraction occurred at the *mere thought of the word!* This response remained as long as 2 months without reinforcement. The importance of this work indicates that conditioned responses achieved through posthypnotic suggestions have great durability and tenacity. Similar conditioning, achieved at nonhypnotic levels, is more rapidly extinguished.

Conditioning by certain words can also "ring bells" to produce other psychophysiologic changes; the suggestion of "ice" or "snow" causes shivering and often a temperature drop in susceptible subjects. Everyone apparently "possesses verbally conditioned bells waiting to be rung."[28] However, it must be emphasized that physiologic responses are not obtained by the meaning of the word *per se,* but rather by the image that is conjured up.

The importance of semantics for hypnosis is that words establish associational reflexes which automatically activate ideomotor and ideosensory responses. The more the subject is involved in one ideomotor and ideosensory response after another, the more he will respond, and, as a result, the more dissociation from reality occurs: every suggestion is now accepted as a belief. Thus the subject now accepts the hypnotist's words as reality, and unreality is readily transformed into reality.

ROLE OF COMMUNICATION IN PSYCHOTHERAPY

To achieve a better understanding of the roles of thinking and learning, one must know how communication of information occurs. A comparison between the electrical transmission of messages and the exchange of information between humans will be described in more detail in the next chapter. The former, developed by telecommunication engineers, may help us to understand the psychology of the cognitive processes, especially hypnosis. Communication in the ordinary sense, however, is particularly important in psychotherapy and will now be discussed.

Communication has been defined as any process that leads to an exchange of information.[27] It is not a technic but, rather, an attitude directed toward the sharing of information for a purpose.[3, 5, 12, 27, 30] Whenever there is an overlapping of experiences, as in the doctor-patient relationship, both understand, accept, and adjust to each other's communications more readily. Therefore, effective communication in psychotherapy makes full use of the patient's capacities to respond experientially to meaningful suggestions of the operator. Also, greater response occurs if the operator recognizes the patient's needs and motivations.

Yet few physicians exploit the communication processes to their maximal potential. Still fewer recognize that the hypnotic relationship affords a vehicle for effective communication of ideas and understandings which can unlock the hidden recovery forces present in the patient. Skilled hypnotherapists, who utilize the nuances of permissive yet directive communication, are aware that clarity and warmth in the semantics and the sounds of words distinctly benefit their patients. So essential is good physician-patient communication that an updated course in therapeutic semantics should be mandatory for students in medicine and psychology.

The semantic approach has corrected spurious identifications, mis-evaluations, and recently acquired harmful conditioned reflexes through strong persuasion based on Korzybskian principles.[15] Ruesch and Bateson point out that "communication is the link that connects psychiatry with all other sciences."[25] They note that "jamming of the networks" or overloading of the neural pathways leads to disruption (anxiety). Continual exposure to semantic confusion, along with other factors, may produce schizophrenia in predisposed persons.[2]

The objectives of psychotherapeutic communication can be accomplished at the interactional level by "either reducing the number of confusing messages or by prevention of jamming."[26] There are two major problems in any type of psychotherapeutic communication. First, the depth of one's feelings must be meaningfully conveyed so that they can be understood and accepted by the patient. Second, the doctor must listen attentively. The important notion of the feedback of information is relevant to both patient and therapist as it automatically answers the questions, "How am I doing?" and "To what extent will I permit myself to share with another?" The insecure, anxiety-ridden patient usually cannot share or express himself effectively because of his own inadequacy. Other disturbed persons, such as the affect-blocked individual, fear self-revelation and subsequent loss of respect. To obviate these, the therapist, on the basis of the information available, must put the patient at ease and build up the patient's self-confidence and self-esteem.

Whenever communication bogs down to superficialities, rapport is decreased. As an unintentional defensive mechanism, many patients stray from the subject. Thus, to obviate resistance, the discussion should be relevant to the patient's problems. It is in the handling of the disturbed patient that the physician's ability to communicate reaches its greatest potential. Since the hypnotic situation induces greater receptivity, more information is available for the understanding necessary for personality integration.

ROLE OF COMMUNICATION AS A CONTROL MECHANISM IN PSYCHOTHERAPY

Haley contends that the therapist and the patient try to control different areas of the psychotherapeutic relationship.[7] The therapist does this by *setting the rules* for therapy, thus being "one up" while, at the same time, denying his superior position; the patient attempts to defeat the therapist by his symptomatic behavior. However, the therapist always wins because he can impose a "double bind." This refers to a situation in which an individual is confronted by two contradictory messages which prevent him from successfully protesting or leaving the field.[8] In the struggle to circumscribe each other's behavior, the person imposing the symptomatic double bind must win. An example of a double bind is the wife who asks her husband to wash the dishes because she claims that she is dizzy. She, of course, denies controlling the behavior of her husband but blames it on her symptom.

In a typical double-bind maneuver during therapy, a patient's insistence that he cannot help himself is *accepted* rather than opposed. He is directed in such a way that he must stop behaving in the way he does or stop denying that he is behaving in that way. There is a similarity between symptomatic behavior of the patient and the tactics of the therapist. When the patient behaves in a symptomatic way and uses the double bind, he is met by an opposing double bind. The patient can quit, comment on a contradiction posed to him, or cease suffering double-bind maneuvers himself.[9] Whatever he does, he loses. If he leaves, he remains sick; if he comments, he is trying to control the therapist; and if he abandons his own double-bind maneuvers, he gives up his symptomatic behavior. From this point of view the patient is forced by the therapist to behave differently, whether he likes it or not, particularly when the therapist is most permissive.

Resistant maneuvers are dissipated by accepting them and redefining them as cooperation by double binds. Suggestions can be concealed or given in the form of a double bind so that the patient will not be aware of their implications.[10] For example, if a patient has a pain, he can be told, under hypnosis, "Any pain that can be increased can be decreased," and then asked, "You do wish to have less discomfort, do you not?" If the pain is increased, the patient is accepting the premise that the pain can be decreased. Phobic reactions can be relieved in a similar fashion. As Haley aptly put it, "Hypnosis might be defined as the art of getting someone to do what you tell him while indicating that he isn't doing it."[10]

Psychodynamicists contend that they do not employ a directive approach. Yet, according to Haley, communication on a nondirective basis is an impossibility, because the therapist, by continually redefining the therapeutic situation, maintains control of the relationship.[11] The "nondirective" therapist makes the patient communicate in an indirect way—much as the patient once used symptoms to control others (secondary gains). This also permits the therapist to deny that he is in control of the relationship. In addition, the patient always hands control over to the therapist when he hangs onto his every remark, and especially when he asks him to interpret his dreams, thoughts, and free associations. Also, he must change his maneuvering voluntarily, on the slightest indication of the therapist. On the other hand, he cannot use the therapist's maneuvers because he is always in a "one down" position.

HELPFUL HINTS ON HOW TO COMMUNICATE EFFECTIVELY IN PSYCHOTHERAPY

1. In handling resistance, ask questions such as, "You can see my point of view, can you not?" Or ask a question that either leaves a choice or is good for the therapist's position. Still another approach is, "Do you mean that this is so?" This makes the patient feel accepted, and he will usually elaborate on the query in another way.

2. Remember that words have more than one meaning; therefore, rephrase the patient's statements in order to get his meanings.

3. Realize that words represent only a few selected details of what the patient really perceived. Therefore, when listening to the description of an object, an event or another reality situation, or when describing something to the patient, remember that important particulars usually are omitted.

4. Never make dogmatic judgments on insufficient facts. However, a decision often must be risked from an incomplete collection of facts. Take such risks only when absolutely necessary.

5. Never think in terms of black and white only; shades of gray may exist. Always examine the middle ground between two opposing ideas, since there is more than one way of doing a thing.

The possibility of alternatives must always be kept in mind.

6. Think before speaking. An inadvertent remark *often* is a common cause of a communication breakdown.

7. Being too friendly when conveying therapeutic explanations inevitably will cause a loss of prestige.

8. Never give a patient carte blanche with a phrase like "You know what I mean?" The patient usually does not understand!

9. Be brief, and discuss one specific topic at a time. This avoids "scattering" or distraction.

10. Watch for the psychological moment or the proper timing for therapeutic interpretations. Then *get across* what you want to get across and what you *mean to get across.*

11. Discuss the patient's explanations, so that you can be sure that they convey his point of view.

12. Remember that actions speak louder than words; note the implications of nonverbal communications in both yourself and the patient.

13. Listen to what the patient is trying to say. Inattention is disturbing. Never intimate beforehand that you know everything that is going to be said.

14. Avoid dogmatism. Be flexible and reasonable when voicing your differences. A handy formula to prevent being considered opinionated is to use the phrase "it seems to me," rather than stating flatly, "it is a fact."

15. Never directly challenge what is patently a falsehood. Rather, if the issue is important, ask subtle questions to ascertain the truth.

ROLE OF PERCEPTION IN HYPNOSIS

The problem of perceptual discrimination is pertinent for learning theory, and particularly important for understanding the nature of hypnosis. Recently, several investigators have increased our understanding of the ways in which we learn to perceive.[6, 16, 27] However, no one ever perceives "all" of any situation, but only enough to deal with it. What is perceived is based on the "functional probabilities" or the "best bets," based on the individual's past experiences. Hence, two or more individuals' perceptions will be similar only

if their past experiences and motivations are alike. Thus differences in views, kinds and rapidity of environmental change, and cumulative effects of experience mold perception. Bridgman observes that, since no one can get away from himself, there are limitations on our understanding of perception and reality.[4] Hence some of the major paradoxes of modern science have arisen. Actually, there is no absolute free will and no absolute determinism. Absolutes are human concepts and have no basis in fact.

Some learning probably occurs through the process of redintegration, which may be defined as the "triggering" of imaginative identifying impressions representing specific situations of prior experiences. Thus the brain has the freedom to manipulate and to be *guided by reality as it perceives reality.* In hypnosis there is an increased capacity for redintegrative processes. This is the basis for hypnotic sensory-imagery conditioning. Neurophysiologic observations indicate that an original experience can be recalled, whether or not it was a fact, a dream, or a fantasy.[23]

Until recently, little was known about the psychological interrelationships within which hypnotic phenomena could be considered. We are indebted to Kline for his penetrating insights into these fruitful areas for research.[17] He believes that there is no such thing as a hypnotic state *per se,* but rather that it manifests itself as a fluctuating phase of awareness closer to hyperacuity than to sleep. To be sure, however, there are hypnotic phenomena and hypnotic relationships, and these do not require a formalistic induction procedure for their establishment.

Therefore, it is obvious that hypnosis cannot be explained in terms of such constructs as "consciousness," "unconsciousness," or "deep sleep." Kline thinks that consciousness, too, is an illusion, which, though very real, cannot be separated from physical happenings, as it merely reflects the meanings conceptualized within one's own sensory order, namely, with existence or reality. He contends that reality is determined by a number of impressions, principally arousal, which are converted into behavior and become meaningful through the associations, the experiences, and the involuntary reactions that characterize the nature of responsiveness.[17]

Since illusions constitute an important part of reality, they produce exceedingly complex reactions. This is demonstrated during a great dramatic moment in the theater when the entire audience is, in reality, "hypnotized." Here a meaningful illusion is created, and each person's change in reality perception occurs as the result of his own experiential reactions to himself and his environment. New meanings and associations are brought forth which cause a subject to *behave differently because he thinks and believes differently.*

PSYCHOPHYSIOLOGY OF PERCEPTION

The psychophysiologic mechanisms by which past and present impressions blend into perceptual realities are not too well understood. Suffice it to say that under the affective influence of a comparison of an imagined future with an experienced past, the brain attempts continuously to predict the goals that will help maintain equilibrium. As Kline notes:

All of this infers a dependency upon those stimulus-response modalities which go into the organization and creation of self-equilibrium. Equilibrium starting on a molecular basis rises to equilibrium on a molar (whole entity as contrasted with molecular), self-concept, body image basis.[18]

The temporal lobes are in the center of perceptual activities. These areas with their deeper limbic structures mediate the integration of instinctual, affective and autonomic processes. To this, the activities of the sensory and premotor cortex add the processes of perception, their apperceptive integration, and the fantasy formation which is built around the central core of the instinctual drives. Ostrow also suggests that temporal lobe afferents may mediate the controls which pleasurable affects exercise on psychic functions.[21] However, much more data must be obtained before these concepts can be validated.

The neural mechanisms capable of recognizing visual and auditory forms have been described by Pitts and McCulloch.[19] They postulate a system of impulses which sweep up and down over interlacing fibers in the cortex and thereby provide a scanning arrangement for the recognition of patterns of incoming sensory stimuli. The methods by which hypnosis utilizes these scanning mechanisms for maintaining increased perceptual awareness or selective attention are discussed in Chapter 32.

ROLE OF LEARNING IN HYPNOSIS

The interaction between perception and learning is called a microgenetic process.[1] The cognitive theories of learning assign an important place to perception. Motivation based on needs and drives of the individual, as well as exploration, reinforcement and trial-and-error learning play an important role for all goal-seeking organisms.[13]

Attempts to explain learning theory have developed into behavioral theories of varying degrees of complexity and sophistication, beginning with Pavlov's conditioned reflex theory and extending to Watson[31] and others who immediately followed him and who incorporated his principles into psychological theory. They failed to realize that they were dealing with simple and elemental units of behavior. In their desire to introduce scientific rigor into psychology, they created their image of man and involved few variables of behavior beyond the stimulus-response sequence. Other behavioral learning theories avoided hypothesizing what might occur within the organism.

Although important proponents of learning theory still maintain this parsimonious view, the mainstream of learning theory recognizes that there are intervening variables before and between the time a stimulus impinges and a response occurs.[20] It is becoming self-evident that the reflex arc is not representative of the elemental unit of behavior. Rather, the fundamental building block of the nervous system is the feedback loop which follows the laws of electrical activity and cybernetic principles. The relationship of these important concepts to physiologic psychology and hypnosis will be discussed in Chapter 32.

The relationship of learning theory, hypnosis, and behavior therapy is discussed in the next chapter. Here a graduated approach is used in order to make contact with the unadaptive learned behavior so that the patient can unlearn it and replace it with adaptive behavior. Hypnosis can help to simulate real-life situations and make therapy easier by relaxing the patient, providing scene visualization and imagery to help in reducing the associated anxiety and tension.

REFERENCES

1. Arieti, S.: The microgeny of thought and perception. Arch. Gen. Psychol., *6:*454, 1962.
2. Bateson, G., *et al.:* Toward a theory of schizophrenia. Behav. Sci., *1:*251, 1956.
3. Bois, J. S.: Explorations in Awareness. New York, Harper, 1957.
4. Bridgman, P. W.: The Way Things Are. Cambridge, Mass., Harvard University Press, 1959.
5. Dollard, J., and Miller, N. E.: Personality and Psychotherapy. New York, McGraw-Hill, 1950.
6. Gardner, R. W.: Cognitive control principles and perceptual behavior. Menn. Clin. Bull., *23:*241, 1959.
7. Haley, J.: Control in psychoanalytical psychotherapy. *In* Progress in Psychotherapy. vol. IV. New York, Grune & Stratton, 1959, pp. 48–65.
8. *Ibid.,* p. 50.
9. *Ibid.,* p. 64.
10. *Ibid.,* p. 55.
11. *Ibid.,* p. 61.
12. Hayakawa, S. I.: Language in Thought and Action. New York, Harcourt, Brace, 1940.
13. Hilgard, E. R.: Theories of Learning. New York, Appleton-Century-Crofts, 1956.
14. Hudgins, C. V.: Conditioning and the voluntary control of the pupillary light reflex. J. Gen. Psychol., *8:*3, 1933.
15. Kelley, E. C.: Education for What Is Real. New York, Harper, 1947.
16. Kilpatrick, F. P.: Perception theory and general semantics. ETC.: Rev. Gen. Semantics, *12:*257, 1955.
17. Kline, M. V.: Clinical and experimental hypnosis in contemporary behavioral sciences. *In* Introductory Lectures in Medical Hypnosis. New York, Institute of Research, 1958.
18. _____: Freud and Hypnosis. New York, Julian Press, 1961.
19. McCulloch, W. S., and Pitts, W.: A logical calculus of the ideas imminent in nervous activity. Bull. Math. Biophysics, *5:*115, 1953.
20. Miller, G. A., Galanter, E., and Pribram, K. H.: Plans and the Structure of Behavior. New York, Holt, 1960.
21. Ostow, M.: Psychic contents of brain processes. Psychosom. Med., *17:*396, 1955.
22. Pavlov, E. P.: Twenty Years of Objective Study of the Higher Nervous Activity Behavior of Animals. Moscow, Medzig Publishing House, 1951, p. 376.
23. Penfield, W.: Memory mechanisms. Arch. Neurol. Psychiat., *67:*178, 1952.
24. Platonov, K.: The World as a Physiological and Therapeutic Factor. Moscow, Foreign Languages Publishing House, 1959.
25. Ruesch, J., and Bateson, G.: Communication: The Social Matrix of Psychiatry. New York, Norton, 1951.
26. *Ibid.,* p. 19.
27. Ruesch, J., and Prestwood, A. R.: Communication and bodily disease. *In* Life Stress and Bodily Disease. Assoc. Res. Nerv. Ment. Dis. Proc., *29:*211, 1950.
28. Salter, A.: What Is Hypnosis? Studies in Conditioning. New York, Farrar, Straus, 1955.
29. Santos, J. R., and Murphy, G.: An odyssey in perceptual learning. Menn. Clin. Bull., *24:*6, 1960.
30. Sondel, B.: The Humanity of Words. Cleveland, World Press, 1958.
31. Watson, J. B.: Psychology from the Standpoint of a Behaviorist. Philadelphia, Lippincott, 1919.

ADDITIONAL READINGS

Chase, S.: The Tyranny of Words. New York, Harcourt, 1938.

Korzybski, A.: Science and Sanity. New York, Dutton, 1933.

Lee, I.: Language Habits in Human Affairs: An Introduction to General Semantics. New York, Harper, 1941.

Meyers, R.: The nervous system and general semantics. E.T.C.: Rev. Gen. Semantics, *5:*14, 1948.

Miller, G. A.: Language and Communication. New York, McGraw-Hill, 1951.

Rapoport, A.: Science and the Goals of Men. New York, Harper, 1950.

31

Learning Theory, Hypnosis, Behavior Modification, and Imagery Conditioning

William D. Fezler, Ph.D.

Hypnosis facilitates learning. Pavlov—and later, others—contended that maladaptive behavior and faulty conditioning are learned responses. The process by which such symptoms can be learned or unlearned is subsumed under the rubric of learning theory.[1] Behavior modification is a form of therapy in which the basic tenets of learning theory—the elementary principles of how learning occurs—are used to change behavior. Since hypnosis enhances the application of these principles, it can be used most effectively in all behavior modification technics.[31]

It is most important to make the distinction between "overt" *(in vivo)* and "covert" technics. Overt technics deal directly with the environment, while covert technics rely on imagery. While hypnosis has generally been used only with covert technics, it can also be used "on the spot" in dealing with the actual situations. The following are overt behavioral technics. All have covert analogues, and all can be improved with the aid of hypnosis.

OVERT BEHAVIORAL TECHNICS

SYSTEMATIC DESENSITIZATION

Systematic desensitization is the procedure most often associated with behavior modification. At first it was used to treat phobics, and a tremendous amount of research has been devoted to its clinical efficacy. It was once thought that the only

conditions which could be successfully treated by behavior modification were phobic reactions. Fortunately, many other technics and disorders are now being given close scrutiny by the behavior modifiers.

The procedure consists of *gradually* exposing the subject to a situation or object which he fears. Gradual exposure alone, however, is not enough. A response incompatible with fear or anxiety must also be present. An early case was reported by Mary Cover Jones in 1924. A child was afraid of a certain animal. The animal was brought closer and closer to the child while he was eating. Eating was the response incompatible with fear. The exposure had to be gradual lest the anxiety elicited by the feared object override the pleasure derived from eating.

There are four basic states considered to be incompatible with fear or anxiety: hunger, thirst, sexual arousal, and relaxation. Pairing them with a feared object leads to counterconditioning in which the positive feelings cancel out the negative ones. I recall a case in which a young man was so anxious in public urinals that he could not urinate, a condition sometimes known as the "pee-shy" syndrome. Treatment involved his taking a copy of *Playboy* magazine with him to the urinal and gradually becoming aware of the stimuli associated with the washroom. Pairing erotic feelings with the washroom cancelled out the negative feelings.

Systematic desensitization involves the construction of a hierarchy. The subject begins with an act which he can accomplish with ease and does things that are progressively more difficult until he accomplishes his goal. A person afflicted with herpetophobia, for example, may begin simply by standing outside the room in which a snake is caged. The steps that follow might be: enter the room, gradually approach the cage, place a gloved hand on the outside of the cage, hold the hand above the snake, touch the tail, the middle, the head, and finally lift the snake. The steps must be calibrated by the therapist to create as little anxiety as possible.

The most common form of incompatible response used in desensitization today is relaxation. Before approaching the feared object, the subject is often run through previously taught relaxation exercises, the most common of which is Jacobson's technic of progressive relaxation. However, it has been my experience that hypnosis produces a greater state of relaxation than do any of the other methods for inducing relaxation. Since a subject can perform any act under hypnosis, whether it be walking, writing, or having sexual intercourse, he can also go through a desensitization procedure under hypnosis. After hypnorelaxation has been induced, the subject goes through his hierarchy, gradually approaching the feared object. The hypnotic relaxation counterconditions the fear that would be produced by the phobic object, and desensitization occurs.

It has been mentioned that desensitization works not only with feared objects, but also with feared situations, such as speaking in public or meeting people socially. Again, a hierarchy is first constructed, leading from the easiest situations to the most difficult. Then while actually in these situations, the patient induces hypnosis and neutralizes his anxiety. Since hypnosis, once it is learned, can be induced rapidly, it is more effective in these situations than is a progressive relaxation technic, which may require as many as 30 minutes to accomplish.

SENSITIZATION OR AVERSION THERAPY

While desensitization deals with getting the patient to like or not be afraid of a certain stimulus, sensitization leads to his disliking a stimulus which he presently likes. Aversion therapy has commonly been used for cigarette smoking, alcoholism, obesity, and sexual deviations. Stimuli associated with undesirable behavior are paired with a painful or unpleasant stimulus, such as electric shock or drug-induced nausea. This results in suppression of the undesired behavior. The taste of a cigarette, for example, could be paired with a shock to the forearm so that the chronic smoker would experience anxiety or the anticipation of pain whenever he smelled or tasted a cigarette. This procedure can also be applied while the patient is hypnotized. Conditioning is more rapid under hypnosis, and all extraneous distraction is eliminated.

FLOODING AND IMPLOSION THERAPY

In flooding and implosion therapy, the situation most deeply dreaded by the patient is presented in *intense* forms without benefit of associated relaxation. Implosion therapy, unlike flooding, is based on several psychodynamic assumptions which are not within the scope of this chapter. Theoretically, the anxiety elicited by these technics is finally extinguished by the absence of the patient's usual reinforcement: escape avoidance. Experience of anxiety in the absence of any real aversive consequences leads to extinction. A person may be in a hypnotic state without experiencing relaxation. Hypnosis can be used to strengthen *any* feeling, including intense anxiety, which is necessary for flooding and implosion.

MASSED OR NEGATIVE PRACTICE

Massed or negative practice seeks to extinguish a habit by repetitious and exhausting maneuvers. A person, for example, who blushes excessively whenever he hears words with a homosexual connotation may be asked to repeat these words over and over again. The technic has been used most frequently in the treatment of tics. The same procedure may be applied while the patient is in hypnosis.

ROLE PLAYING OR BEHAVIORAL REHEARSAL

The therapist assumes the role of significant persons in the patient's life. A series of increasingly exacting scenes is enacted within the protective confines of the therapist's office. The therapist then gives the patient feedback as to how he could be more effective in dealing with others to get the responses he desires.

Since the situations to be role-played are often anxiety-provoking for the patient, it may be easier for him to enact the scenes while in a hypnotic state paired with relaxation. This form of behavioral rehearsal while in hypnosis leaves an indelible imprint as to the appropriate means of interaction to be recreated later in the actual situation.

ASSERTIVE TRAINING

Patients are taught to give appropriate and direct expression of ongoing feelings, both positive and negative. People who habitually fail to stand up for their rights as well as those who typically overreact with rage to real or imagined slights from others are appropriate candidates for assertive training.

Hypnosis should be used in the actual situations where assertive training is necessary. If the individual is shy and passive in social situations, the hypnosis will counter his fears. He will use hypnosis to induce relaxation. He cannot be afraid and relaxed at the same time. If, on the other hand, he is overly aggressive because of feelings of rage in social situations, the relaxation will counter this response as well. He cannot be angry and relaxed at the same time.

MODELING, IMITATION, OR OBSERVATIONAL LEARNING

Virtually all learning phenomena resulting from direct experiences can occur on a vicarious basis through observation of other persons' behavior and its consequences to them. The patient will imitate behavior which he sees rewarded and refrain from behavior which he sees is punished. Fear and avoidance behavior are extinguished vicariously through observation of modeled approach behavior toward feared objects without any adverse consequences accruing to the performer.

An impression made in hypnosis is more durable than one made at a nonhypnotic level. There is no "noise" in the channel to corrupt the signal. Witnessing a model performance while the subject is under hypnosis produces a more lasting impression.

TOKEN ECONOMIES AND OPERANT PRINCIPLES

All behavior can be changed or shaped by the appropriate system of reward and punishment. Token economies, work-payment incentive systems, have been used effectively to modify the behavior of institutionalized patients. Much of the research in the field of experimental psychology deals with the most effective ways of applying reward and punishment to influence behavior by means of schedules of reinforcement.

Positive reinforcement is used to develop and maintain appropriate behavior. ("I'll give you an apple if you stop shooting spit balls.") Punishment is used to discourage inappropriate behavior. ("If you shoot another spit ball, I'll slap your face.") Withholding positive reinforcement can be used to decrease the frequency of inappropriate behavior. ("If you shoot another spit ball, I'll take away your allowance.") Removal of punishment can be used to increase the frequency of appropriate behavior. ("You can come out of the corner if you promise not to shoot any more spit balls.") It is by various combinations of rewards and punishments that learning takes place. And again, the lesson is more complete if learned while in a hypnotic state.

COVERT BEHAVIORAL TECHNICS

All covert technics involve imagery. An image is defined as "a mental representation of an actual object." The stronger the image, the more it approximates the actual object and the more it will generalize to "reality." The remarkable thing about the image is that it is capable of producing the same response as the actual object. For example, hypnotically imagining a lemon will produce salivation. Imagining holding your hand in a bucket of ice will produce numbness. Imagining holding your hand over fire can actually produce a rise in temperature of the hand. The implications are monumental. However, for our purposes here, we will limit this discussion to how the power of imagery influences hypnotic and behavioral therapy.

Cautela based his work on the assumption that a stimulus presented in imagination can affect overt and covert behavior in a manner similar to a stimulus presented externally.[11-14] He developed a number of behavior modification procedures which require the manipulation of imaginal stimuli and responses in ways analogous to the manipulation of overt stimuli and responses. It will be seen from the description below that what this involves is the imagining, rather than the experiencing, of the behavioral technics described above.

COVERT DESENSITIZATION

Wolpe is usually given credit for developing the desensitization technic.[39] In covert desensitization the patient *imagines* going though the carefully constructed fear hierarchy while in a relaxed state, rather than actually going through it. The patient is asked to signal by lifting his finger if the specific scenes prove disturbing. When this occurs, they are immediately withdrawn and the relaxation is deepened. The distressing scene is presented repeatedly in small doses until the patient can picture it without experiencing anxiety.

Hypnosis is used in conjunction with the covert behavioral technics for the same reasons delineated in the description of the overt technics. However, in the case of the covert technics, hypnosis provides one tremendous additional advantage—it greatly facilitates the production of imagery. All current research bears out that the stronger the image, the more effective are the covert technics, and the more they generalize to reality. If a subject can only vaguely *imagine* approaching a snake without fear, it is doubtful that he will be able to approach a reptile in reality. However, if his image of approaching the snake is very real, it is quite probable that he will be able approach it in reality. The stronger the fantasy, the greater the probability that it will generalize to reality. A general rule in hypnotic therapy is always to have the subject imagine doing in hypnosis what he would like to be doing in reality.

Deiker and Pollock integrated Erickson's hypnotic "pseudo-orientation" technique into a covert desensitization technic in the treatment of a beach phobic.[18, 19] The female patient was told during hypnosis to picture herself a week in the future coming out of the therapy room after her final desensitization session without her former fears. This technic was responsible for a shorter treatment time and further corroborates the possibility that extinction can take place in fantasy (i.e., covert extinction).

COVERT SENSITIZATION (AVERSION THERAPY)

Covert sensitization was first described in detail by Cautela.[10, 11] The patient is to imagine a scene in which he is committing the act he wishes to eliminate. The imaginal performance of this act is paired with negative experiences which serve to decrease the frequency of the undesired behavior.

An overweight person, for example, may wish to stop eating chocolates. He imagines a plate of chocolates before him, picturing them vividly. He must experience the situation with all five senses. Hearing the noises in the room, seeing and smelling the chocolates, feeling them when he picks them up. As soon as he tastes the chocolates, he imagines a sense of nausea coming over him. He throws up all over the chocolates. The rancid smell of puke and vomit mix with the sight of chocolates. The image may go on for several minutes, pairing the aversive vomit with the chocolates. This is a sensitization or aversion procedure.

If the patient imagines actually eating the chocolate first and then throwing up, it is a punishment procedure. Here again the image must be clear and the results made as repugnant as possible. As soon as the patient imagines himself to be freed of the sight, taste, and smell of the chocolate, he is to feel better.

Evidence from the behavioral literature indicates covert sensitization to be effective in reducing maladaptive approach behaviors such as smoking,[37] alcoholism[4] and sexual deviation.[8, 15, 17] Hypnotherapists have also commonly used similar procedures in treating maladaptive approach behaviors including alcoholism,[20, 29, 38] obesity,[30] face picking,[22] and nail biting.[36]

COVERT FLOODING AND IMPLOSION THERAPY

In covert flooding and implosion therapy, the situation most deeply dreaded by the patient is imagined in intense forms. If he has a fear of snakes, he images being covered by them, in a pit of hissing reptiles, with no escape. Theoretically, when he experiences no actual aversive consequences, his anxiety should be extinguished. Flooding techniques are open to much controversy, however, and can produce a stronger phobic response if not adequately handled.

COVERT MASSED OR NEGATIVE PRACTICE

In covert massed or negative practice, a person *imagines* repeating a habit over and over until it is exhausted. The covert technic is preferred in cases where repeating the habit in a reality could lead to some form of damage. Such is the case in bruxism, where forcefully grinding the teeth as many as a thousand times in succession could cause harm.

COVERT MODELING

As mentioned earlier, modeling is a procedure in which a client is exposed to someone else (a model) who engages in the behavior the client wishes to develop. Typically, live or filmed models are employed.[7] However, Bandura has observed that modeling is not defined by the mode in which modeling stimuli are presented, but rather by the symbolic and representational processes which code the modeled material and subsequently guide behavior.[6] Cautela has suggested that representational processes can be altered "directly" by having subjects *imagine* a model engaging in various behaviors.[15] This idea has received further support from other researchers.[16, 25] Modeling based on imagery (i.e., covert modeling) does alter behavior.

Kazdin further developed the parameters involved in covert modeling.[26] He found that subjects (in this case herpetophobics) who imagined multiple models, as opposed to a single model, showed greater avoidance reduction. Subjects who imagined a single snake and those who imagined different snakes showed no difference in avoidance.

COVERT ASSERTIVE TRAINING

In covert assertive training, patients are told to *imagine* giving appropriate and direct expression of ongoing feelings. Another form of this technic is to imagine someone else engaging in effective assertive behavior (i.e., covert modeling).[28]

COVERT OPERANT PRINCIPLES

In employing covert operant principles, the behaviors and the rewards and punishments are imagined rather than actualized. A cigarette smoker may imagine resisting a cigarette and then being rewarded by seeing himself in Tahiti. In recent years this *covert positive reinforcement* technic has been applied in over two dozen clinical and experimental studies.[13] Several of the experimental studies have failed to replicate earlier effects,[24, 35, 40] or have challenged the simple operant conditioning paradigm of covert positive reinforcement.[9, 32] Bajtelsmit and Gershman confirm the effectiveness of covert positive reinforcement as a treatment procedure, but fail to support the operant conceptualization of covert positive reinforcement.[5]

In a *covert punishment* technic, the patient is asked to imagine himself indulging in an undesired behavior such as drinking liquor. Then he imagines throwing up, feeling embarrassed in front of friends, and waking up with a hangover (punishment).

The removal of a positive reinforcer can also be adapted to covert methods, although there is no particular name for it. Here, for example, the smoker can imagine sitting in a beautiful garden which smells sweet and fresh. He then lights up a cigarette, and the sight and smell of the garden are obliterated.

The imagined removal of punishers to increase the frequency of appropriate behavior is called *covert negative reinforcement*. This technic, developed by Cautela, rewards the patient for an appropriate response by allowing him to escape or terminate a very unpleasant situation.[13] The technic is especially useful for patients who claim that there is nothing reinforcing in their lives and are thus not amenable to covert reinforcement. Patients with a fear of heights, for example, may imagine being caught in a flood. Just as they are about to drown, they climb a ladder to a skylight and are saved. Climbing higher thus becomes an activity associated with terminating a very unpleasant situation, whereas before it was itself a frightening event.

The hypnotherapeutic use of covert negative reinforcement was demonstrated by Abraham in the treatment of hysterical paralysis of the legs.[1] The hypnotized patient was told to imagine sitting on a beach in uncomfortably cold water and that he could only escape the cold water (negative situation) by lifting his legs out of it.

If the assumptions of covert positive reinforcement are correct, then it follows that when the subject imagines a response (which is being maintained in reality by external reinforcement) without a favorable environmental contingency, then the probability of occurrence of the response should decrease. This procedure has been called *covert extinction* because it is analogous to the operant extinction paradigm (i.e., withholding the reinforcing stimulus after the emission of the instrumental response).

An example of covert extinction is to have an overweight patient imagine eating his favorite fattening foods without any flavor. The reward (good taste) for eating is absent, and the behavior (eating) should be extinguished. Ascher and Cautela support this procedure and conclude that covert extinction is an effective method in facilitating the course of extinction, whether or not the environment continues to provide reinforcement for the specific response.[3]

FURTHER APPLICATIONS OF IMAGERY

Lawful relationships between autonomic arousal and imagery parameters have not yet emerged from ongoing research. Haney and Euse studied the relationship of skin conductance and heart rate responses to neutral, positive, and negative imagery.[21] Both positive and negative imagery produced and sustained high levels of skin conductance over 1 minute. Positive imagery was rated as clearer than negative or neutral imagery.

Success shown in the use of "emotive imagery" procedures suggests that the elicitation of positive affective states by pleasant imagery does serve to counteract phobic reactions.[33] Hurley reports a case of a severe bridge and height phobia treated by modified systematic desensitization.[23] The patient imagined an irrelevant pleasurable image at the beginning and again at the end of each session. Ten scenes of crossing bridges and mastering heights were used, but not in hierarchical order. It is interesting that a pleasurable image at the beginning and end of each session was effective as the source of anxiety inhibition (muscle relaxation exercises were not needed) and that the fear stimuli were not visualized in hierarchical order.

Positive imagery is a potent force in the treatment of all mental disorders. Thoughts make us ill, and thoughts make us well. As was stated before, the stronger the image, the greater the probability that what we imagine will become or generalize to reality. For concrete verbalizations on how to develop stronger imagery in hypnosis, and a detailed discussion of the hypnobehavioral model, the reader is referred to the work of Kroger and Fezler on imagery conditioning.[31]

REFERENCES

1. Abraham, H.A.: Hypnosis used in the treatment of somatic manifestations of a psychiatric disorder. Am. J. Clin. Hypn., *10*:304, 1968.
2. Abrams, S.: Implications of learning theory in treatment of depression by employing hypnosis as an adjunctive technique. Am. J. Clin. Hypn., *6:*313, 1964.
3. Ascher, L.M., and Cautela, J.R.: An experimental study of covert extinction. J. Behav. Ther. Exp. Psychiat., *5:*233, 1974.
4. Ashem, B., and Donner, L: Covert sensitization with alcoholics: a controlled replication. Behav. Res. Ther., *6:*7, 1968.
5. Bajtelsmit, J.W., and Gershman, L. Covert positive reinforcement: efficacy and conceptualization. J. Behav. Ther. Exp. Psychiat, *7:*207, 1976.

6. Bandura, A.: Modeling theory. *In* Sahakian, W.S. (ed.): *Psychology of Learning: Systems, Models and Theories.* Chicago, Markham, 1970, pp. 350–367.

7. _____: Psychotherapy based upon modeling principles. *In* Bergin, A.E., and Garfield, S.L. (eds.): Handbook of Psychotherapy and Behavior Change. New York, Wiley, 1971, pp. 653–708.

8. Barlow, D.H., Leitenberg, H., and Agras, W.S.: Experimental control of sexual deviation through manipulation of the noxious scene in covert sensitization. J. Abnorm. Psychol., *74:*596, 1969.

9. Bernal, G., Wisocki, P.A., and Tennen, H.A.: Imagerial rehearsal reinforcement in a covert behavioral technique: a single subject experiment. (paper presented at the Eighth Annual Meeting of the Association for Advancement of Behavior Therapy, Chicago, 1975).

10. Cautela, J.R.: Treatment of compulsive behavior by covert sensitization. Psychol. Rec., *16:*33, 1966.

11. _____: Covert sensitization. Psychol. Rep., *20:* 459, 1967.

12. _____: Covert reinforcement. Behav. Ther., *1:*33, 1970.

13. _____: Covert negative reinforcement. J. Behav. Ther. Exp. Psychiat., *1:*273, 1970.

14. _____: Covert extinction. Behav. Ther., *2:*192, 1971.

15. Cautela, J.R., and Wisocki, P.A.: Covert sensitization for the treatment of sexual deviation. Psychol. Rec., *21:*37, 1971.

16. Cautela, J., Flannery, R., and Hanley, E.: Covert modeling: an experimental test. Behav. Ther., *5:*494, 1974.

17. Davison, G.C.: Elimination of a sadistic fantasy by a client-controlled counterconditioning technique: a case study. J. Abnorm. Psychol., *73:*84, 1968.

18. Deiker, T.E., and Pollock, D.H.,: Integration of hypnotic and systematic desensitization techniques in the treatment of phobias: a case report. Am. J. Clin. Hypn., *17:*170, 1975.

19. Erickson, M.H. Pseudo-orientation as a hypnotherapeutic procedure. J. Clin. Exp. Hypn., *2:*261, 1954.

20. Feamster, F., and Brown, J.E.: Hypnotic aversion to alcohol: three-year follow-up of one patient. Am. J. Clin. Hypn., *6:*164, 1963.

21. Haney, J.N., and Euse, F.J.: Skin conductance and heart rate responses to neutral, positive, and negative imagery: implications for covert behavior therapy procedures. Behav. Ther., *7:*494, 1976.

22. Hollander, M.B.: Excoriated acne controlled by post-hypnotic suggestion. Am. J. Clin. Hypn., *1:* 122, 1958.

23. Hurley, A.D.: Unsystematic desensitization using pleasurable images to inhibit anxiety. J. Behav. Ther. Exp. Psychiat., *7:*295, 1976.

24. Johnson, R.G., and Scheurer, W.E.: Covert reinforcement: a replication of an experimental test by Wish, Cautela and Steffan (paper presented at the Annual Meeting of the American Educational Research Association, Washington, D.C., 1975).

25. Kazdin, A.E.: Covert modeling and the reduction of avoidance behavior. J. Abnorm. Psychol, *81:*87, 1973.

26. _____: Comparative effects of some variations of covert modeling. J. Behav. Ther. Exp. Psychiat., *5:* 225, 1974.

27. _____: Covert modeling, imagery assessment, and assertive behavior. J. Consult. Clin. Psychol., *43:*716, 1975.

28. _____: Assessment of imagery during covert modeling of assertive behavior. J. Behav. Ther. Exp. Psychiat., *7:*213, 1976.

29. Kroger, W.S.: The conditioned reflex treatment of alcoholism. J.A.M.A., *120:*8, 1942.

30. _____: Systems approach for understanding obesity. Management by behavior modification through hypnosis. Psychiat. Opinion, *7:*7, 1970.

31. Kroger, W.S., and Fezler, W.D.: Hypnosis and Behavior Modification: Imagery Conditioning. Philadelphia, J. B. Lippincott, 1976.

32. Ladouceur, R.: An experimental test of the learning paradigm of covert reinforcement in deconditioning anxiety. J. Behav. Ther. Exp. Psychiat., *5:*3, 1974.

33. Lazarus, A., and Abramovitz, A. The use of "emotive imagery" in the treatment of children's phobias. J. Ment. Sci., *108:*109, 1962.

34. Rachman, S.: Clinical applications of observational learning, imitation, and modeling. Behav. Ther., *3:*379, 1972.

35. Ripstrata, C.C., *et al.:* Covert reinforcement: A partial replication (paper presented at the Annual Meeting of the American Educational Research Association, Chicago, 1974).

36. Secter, I.I.: Tongue thrust and nail biting simultaneously treated during hypnosis: a case report. Am. J. Clin. Hypn., *4:*51, 1961.

37. Wagner, M.K., and Bragg, R.A.: Comparing behavior modification approaches to habit decrement—smoking. J. Consult. Clin. Psychol., *34:* 258, 1970.

38. Wolberg, L.R.: Medical Hypnosis. 2 vols. New York, Grune & Stratton, 1948.
39. Wolpe, J.: Psychotherapy by Reciprocal Inhibition. Stanford, Cal., Stanford University Press, 1958.
40. Yager, G.G., Pace, D.G., and Tepper, N.G. Differential covert conditioning: a replication of a study by Epstein and Peterson (paper presented at the Annual Meeting of the American Education Research Association, Washington, D.C.).

32

Some Relationships of the Physical and Behavioral Sciences to Psychotherapy and Hypnosis

CYBERNETIC APPLICATIONS

The development of a more scientific psychology has increased the need for mathematical models or symbolic representations of the most recent learning theories. These are mechanistic in nature and are classified under the general concept of cybernetics, which attempts to describe control processes in precise mathematical terms. The term cybernetics comes from a Greek word, *Kybernetes,* which means pilot or governor. Much has been written on this discipline in relation to the study of control processes in machines, organisms, and social groups.

On a broader basis, cybernetics combines the views from different but related fields of knowledge, including engineering, mathematics, physiology, biology, and psychology. Cyberneticians contend also that principles of learning and purposeful behavior characteristic of machines apply to human functioning. The theory does *not* imply that electronic or mechanical analogues can adequately represent the functioning of the central nervous system, but, rather, that living organisms parallel the over-all stimulus-response behavior patterns of automatically controlled machines (servomechanisms).

The central principle, as defined in the last chapter, is that goal-directed organisms as well as machines utilize *error-correcting* information to achieve purposeful behavior or equilibrium. This indicates that the system is in *negative feedback.* If the information fed back in an automatically controlled machine or organism causes the error to *increase,* with a resultant instability or breakdown, the system is said to be in *positive feedback.*

These principles are similar to Bernard's and Cannon's views on homeostasis. However, what is new is that dynamic equilibrium involves a perpetual exchange of energy with the environment. What leaves the organism is called "output," and what goes into it, "input." Man, as an open control system, therefore, receives from his environment and makes his contribution to it—but input and output do not interact.

With this model in mind, it appears that the hypnotic interpersonal relationship, as well as the resultant hypnotic conditioning procedure, depends largely on the manner in which the subject is willing to have his perceptual mechanisms restructured. If the subject incorporates the therapist into this system, the type of feedback is altered in the control process. This concept allows us to understand some of the fundamentals of behavior. It is hoped that the life sciences will join forces with the behavioral sciences to reveal other hidden factors in the tangled areas of human behavior. Hypnosis, because of its discriminative ability, affords an experimental device for penetrating this bewildering maze.

From the rapid strides of the engineering and mathematical sciences, cybernetics is providing newer applications for the older concepts of self-maintenance or equilibrium. These applications should lead to a better understanding of higher nervous system functioning, especially in reference to hypnotic behavior. Also, it is more apparent that research possibilities and new insights into the psychology of learning and the processing of information (thinking) will ultimately be developed to understand the complex neuropsychologic mechanisms of human relationships, responses and behavior.

Critics of cybernetics believe that it, like behaviorism, is an excellent theory from the viewpoint of scientific methodology, but that, like most of the behavioristic theories, it is inadequate since it neglects the role of man's creativeness (something no machine yet possesses). Overlooked, too, is the role of the essential meaningfulness which underlies man's experiences, past and present.

CYBERNETIC MODELS OF LEARNING

There are several models for understanding the mechanisms involved in learning, especially as it applies to the communication of information in man and the machine. Outstanding among these are the feedback, information theory and probability theory models. The first two are related to the design of telecommunications equipment—all are concerned with goal-directed behavior, probability and decision making. The probability theory developed from the strategy of games and has been used in the prediction of behavior in several other fields. Already it is being suggested that, if human specifications can be recast into machine-compatible specifications, this "could give clarity and rigor to the language and concepts of psychology, and open the possibility of man-machine comparisons, cross-simulation studies, and substitution experiments."[32] Also, these experiments would make possible the scientific validation of hypotheses, and would be especially valuable if one wishes to use the machine to study any factor which is not accessible in people.[32]

The following hypotheses are presented with due regard to the dangers involved in contending that there might be a comparative relationship between the machine and man. Neverthe-

less, there seem to be no objections when engineers attempt to design better machines by studying the behavior of living organisms. This new science is known as *bionics*. The physical and behavioral sciences are now revising our notions of communication processes as they relate to signal detection theory, neural control, and self-regulating features of brain functioning. These disciplines are destined to play an ever-increasing role in medical education. It is for this reason that cybernetic principles are presented in this chapter.

THE FEEDBACK MODEL

The feedback principle, though not new, is a unique method for viewing things: it introduces a new model for *thinking about thinking.*[30] A good example of negative feedback is its use in walking. Kinesthetic and postural feedbacks from muscles, joints and tendons automatically make the corrective movements necessary for effective locomotion. The gait of an alcoholic or a tabetic is illustrative of disequilibrium or positive feedback. Here, some of the necessary feedbacks are missing, and this results in incoordinated muscular activities of an oscillatory rather than a purposeful character. The placing of the feet has to be controlled visually—a less satisfactory substitute feedback.

In learning and adaptive responses to everyday life situations, the feedback principle constantly "monitors" behavioral response; the success or the failure of the results modifies future behavior. In other words, learning is by trial and error—adaptive. For instance, we have emphasized that, during hypnotic induction, the motivated subject automatically makes full use of his own internal feedback mechanisms (the ideosensory and ideomotor activities) for achieving a goal (hypnotic relaxation). Also, in the hypnotic interrelationship, patient and therapist use feedback mutually to improve their respective reactions to one another's communication processes. As these aspects of feedback mechanisms and cybernetics become more applicable to behavior disorders, the fundamental role and technics of hypnotherapy may greatly expand in this respect.

THE INFORMATION THEORY MODEL

It is not possible in a book of this type to treat the mathematics of information theory and its quantitative applications to the problems of information transmission, storage or its retrieval. For a deeper understanding of the scope and the application of information theory, the classical work of Shannon and Weaver is recommended for those with mathematical training.[28] However, an understanding of the principles of information theory is valuable even though one lacks a knowledge of higher mathematics. The following discussion will, therefore, avoid abstract mathematics, and will be directed to those with little or no previous acquaintance with probability or information theory.

The relevance of information theory to psychiatry has been described.[6] In psychotherapy, particularly in hypnosis, we are interested in meaningful measures of the *subjective or semantic value* of the information conveyed to a patient or to a therapist. If such measures are available, there is a possibility that scientific methods can be applied to a field which must otherwise remain an art. Therefore, it might be instructive to compare the technics employed by physical scientists in measuring and studying information, in the hope that information theory, allied with other theoretic and experimental work, will in the near future help to explain human communication processes on a more scientific basis.

In the physical sciences, the information in a message is defined in a purely statistical way without any reference *to the importance of the message.* The amount of information gained from receipt of a message is measured in terms of the amount of uncertainty removed by the message.* The resultant information, which leads to a reduction of uncertainty, enables decision making based on knowledge rather than on guesses. These ideas are intuitively obvious, but, until they are translated into the exact language of mathe-

matics, it is not possible to formulate the concepts in other than loose verbal terms.

In engineering design, information theory answers some very basic questions as to the ability of a communication system to transfer information from sender to receiver in the presence of "noise"—defined as any type of interference. Even the clearest message can lose some of its meaningfulness before its reception. This is known as *entropy,* and some entropy occurs at all levels of human communication. However, the theory allows one to state explicitly how information is lost due to noise in the communication channel. Also it allows one to determine the extent to which the signal must be strengthened in order to transmit the desired amount of information in the presence of noise. This is a fundamental consideration in design of all communication or telemetry systems.

At the risk of oversimplification, these concepts seem particularly germane to the objectives of psychotherapeutic communication, especially during hypnosis. The hypnotherapist, acting as a transmitter, wishes to communicate or encode information to the patient as accurately and reliably as possible in the presence of noise. The noise may take the form of disturbing sounds in the environment or internal noise generated in the "receiver" (the patient) by virtue of his unreceptive attitudes or preoccupation with irrelevant thoughts. Understanding the technics used by the physical scientist to cope with the problems of noise may offer interesting possibilities for improving the two-way communication† during any interactional relationship.

The following simple illustrations show how the amount of information possessed (the ability to select from a large number of alternatives) allows correct predictions or decisions to be made. The unit of information is the binary digit or "bit." It represents the amount of information necessary to resolve two equally likely alternatives. Symbolically, these two alternatives may be represented as "yes" or "no," or "1" and "0." Using such a pair of symbols, it is possible to

---

*Information gained $= \log \dfrac{\text{Probability of knowing the state of a system } \textit{after} \text{ receipt of the message}}{\text{Probability of knowing the state of a system } \textit{before} \text{ receipt of the message}}$

†For example, correlation technics are very effective in reducing the deleterious consequences of noise in electronic communications equipment.

encode any message—a printed page, a symphony, a picture—with any desired degree of detail. For instance, a message which gives a person's sex contains one bit of information, since there are only two equally likely alternatives. To resolve 8 equally probable alternatives, a message containing 3 bits is required. The first bit reduces the alternatives from 8 to 4, the second bit from 4 to 2, and the third from 2 to 1. Thus, in general, each bit reduces the number of alternatives by one half.

It is believed that all of man's experiences, memory and thought are based on such simple particles of information. Every perception is a pattern of impulses—unique only in that certain nerve fibers "fire" digitally ("all," "yes," or "1"), while others do not ("none," "no," or "0").

McKay believes that general information theory may provide a mathematical description of the nature of human behavior, that is, a reduction of all communication processes to statistical data.[20] He further contends that the *thought processes of living organisms may soon be imitated by mechanical means.* Already it has been applied usefully to learning problems which involve discrimination, judgment and decision making.[19]

Our interest in this fascinating area is particularly relevant during hypnosis communication, in which the prime objective is to convey meaningful verbalizations in order to narrow the attention span to a given idea and, as a result, eliminate "noise" in the form of semantic confusion. This reduces *entropy* or the number of possible meanings or alternatives.

For example, messages which have a high specificity contain more bits of information than do generalities. Suggesting to a subject that he is not "asleep," "unconscious," or in a "trance" does not effectively convey information. On the other hand, telling the subject that *he is* in a state of relaxed attention identifies hypnosis as a positive state, and eliminates all alternatives. Hence the therapist must be *specific in saying what he means as well as meaning what he says!* One might say that the heightened perception or acuity characteristic of hypnosis acts as a filtering "device" similar to that used in machines for screening out irrelevant signals.

Communications systems which stress accuracy in the receipt of a message utilize a high level of redundancy (repetition of the same information). This applies particularly to hypnotic induction, in which, for instance, a phrase such as, "Your legs are getting heavier and heavier," is used again and again to obtain the correct ideosensory and ideomotor responses. Once these are identified as correct, the chances that the subject will make the same responses again will be greater than ever. With sufficient repetition, the correct responses will become a virtual certainty, that is, they will be learned automatically and become a "habit." It is by such "ideoid" phenomena that one's beliefs are processed into convictions.

This section has dealt primarily with some of the basic aspects of information theory. Very few comments have been made regarding semantic information, not because this subject is unimportant, but rather because there is at present no sound quantitative theory for treating semantic information. Statistical information theory, however, has relevance to semantics insofar as it tells us what confidence we can place in the information received as truly representing the information sent.

One might conclude that information theory provides insight for analyzing and improving storage and communication processes, but does not unravel the bewildering complexities associated with significance, meaning, or value judgments.

THE THEORY OF GAMES MODEL

Von Neumann's mathematical theory not only estimates the probabilities of outcome but makes decisions (best "bets") based upon a course of action which has the greatest *value* or *utility*.[33] Since both of these are involved in motivation, the theory may have relevance to the psychology of individual learning. It may help to treat, in meaningful quantitative fashion, the outcome of an action that is not *completely determined.*

This theory closely parallels the field approach used in cooperative engineering. The old concept of cause and effect has been abandoned. A phenomenon is seen not as an effect but as an event taking place in a field, and every force in it, whether active or not, has some relationship to it. In order to produce a change, it is desirable to *ascertain which of the forces can be altered or eliminated to bring about the desired effect.* The goal is not to find the "cause" but rather *to discover a means of intervention.*[7] The physical scientist considers that we do not know the meaning of a concept unless we can detail the specific operations used in applying the concept in a concrete situation. Any abstraction which cannot be duplicated in terms of what the scientist does is considered unscientific. Thus such abstractions as "the underlying psychodynamics" or "hypnosis is nothing but suggestion" would be ruled out as meaningless constructs.

This approach is the essence of a relatively new concept called "operational analysis." It has much in common with the probabilistic game theory. Although developed independently, both are applicable to all situations in which a large number of variables have to be considered for increasing efficiency. This is particularly significant for medicine, especially psychotherapy, which is essentially a two-person interactional "game." Since game theory has apparently developed an approach to give the results of outcomes with certain theoretic assumptions for an unlimited number of multivariant processes, it may be that the "probability theory" can help us to evaluate how imaginative processes build up a notion of probability, calculate the odds and learn which decisions are most favorable based on these odds.

If higher nervous activities are to perform the task of making continuous predictions under the affective influence of a comparison of an imagined future with an experienced past, the brain must have available "counters" or images as the data ("bits" in the computer) for its computations.[17] These represent the elements of behavior patterns.[8] The reader interested in a new era of brain research should read a stimulating article on the subject of brain-computer analogies.[15] Black and Walter have provided the first objective evidence, in the form of EEG patterns, on how the brain responds to hypnotic suggestions.[3] They postulated that the anterior cortex—the silent area of the brain—acts as a "contingency computer" to extract information from the environment by the assessment of probability.

Modern neurophysiologists ultimately must deal with brain function in terms of more sophisticated analogue models. However, the staggering complexities in a system comprised of 10 to 15 billion cells, each of which might be regarded as a hybrid microcomputer, make it difficult to prove that the brain is a computer, but nevertheless the concept at this point in time is a useful one. For instance, the brain seems to function like a highly sophisticated model of a digital-analogue computer. By way of explanation, the digital machine performs numerical computations with incredible speed when the problems can be reduced to conventional arithmetic operations. The digital computer loosely approximates those of brain processes concerned with awareness and those which involve autonomic or reflex activities. The analogue machine attempts to solve a problem by recreating within the machine the physical circumstances which give rise to the problem and thus determine its outcome. It is useful for handling relatively complex situations. The cerebral mechanisms for those psychological functions which we now call, for want of a better name, unconscious and certain preconscious functions, approximate more closely the digital type of computer in their functioning.

There are other similarities of the brain to the digital machine. Control of an organism by thought processes is largely mediated by discrete or different distinct levels of neural functioning (digital). The execution of the digital "commands" are carried out in analogue fashion. For instance, humoral and endocrine functioning resembles the continuous levels of activity characteristic of analogue computers. It has been postulated that Pavlov's distinction between a primary signal system concerned with directly perceived stimuli and a secondary signal system devoted to verbal elaborations seems to parallel the above distinction between digital and analogue computers.[29]

Because cybernetics has disregarded nonoperational and useless constructs, it is making rapid strides in explaining, not only how information is processed in the machine, but also how perception, learning and concept formation are processed in the nervous system. Therefore, brain-computer operational analogies will be discussed more fully in an attempt to explain the phenomenology of hypnosis—its evolution and function as an adaptive response mechanism not as a singular thing, but rather as a process basic and fundamental to the organism, which, like behavior, is multifaceted as well as fluctuating. The author fully realizes the speculative nature of these assumptions, but believes that they constitute a rational hypothesis that will help place the understanding of hypnosis on a more scientific basis.

ANALOGY BETWEEN COMPUTER AND BRAIN FUNCTION

As of now, machines are not capable of thinking. However, from a purely mechanistic standpoint, devices capable of a wide range of selective behavior based on evaluation of a large number of variables are being developed, but they are incapable, even remotely, of equaling the tremendous capacity of human recall, learning, and perception.

Those who embrace the present highly formalized schools of psychology may object to a mechanistic approach since humanistic elements are ignored. But to conclude that research on the simulation of human behavior with a machine is wrong is somewhat analogous to saying that research on the simulation of the human heart with an artificial one is wrong because the latter organ is not a living one.

Let us examine some of the properties of living organisms which machines are capable of simulating. One of the key features of the behavior of living organisms is adaptability. This property can be simulated on the machine. Such a device automatically changes its internal structure in accordance with the environmental stimuli (input information signals) to function in a purposeful manner. This same adaptive property enables the mechanism to change from a positive to a negative feedback system by sensing and correcting its own performance. In the human, this trial and error process of learning causes physiochemical changes in the structure of the feedback networks to enable the organism to respond normally to the class of stimuli to which it has become adapted.

THEORETIC EVALUATION OF HYPNOTIC RESPONSES AND CONTROLLED ADAPTIVE BEHAVIOR BASED ON COMPUTER ANALOGIES

In the past, vague and nontestable formulations have been advanced to explain the nature of hypnosis and hypnotic responses. The reasons are obvious—these are built-in mechanisms—the result of responses developed during our genetic endowment and continually refined to give the organism greater adaptability.

My hypothesis is that hypnotic response was at one time a primitive adaptive mechanism which was necessary for survival. Its evolutionary development can be descriptively equated with that of the origin and behavior of modern computers.

Modern electronic "thinking" machines were originally developed as *special purpose computers* (S.P.C.) for solving relatively simple problems. As the physical sciences developed, it became necessary to perfect a machine that would solve a large variety of complex problems. Since the S.P.C. was inadequate, it inevitably evolved into the present large and complex *general purpose computer* (G.P.C.). However, in achieving this flexibility, the G.P.C.'s capability far exceeded the demands of limited problems. Nevertheless, when the G.P.C. is committed to limited problems it can solve them with amazing speed—but at a high cost for this increased celerity.

Although one cannot as yet demonstrate that analogies exist between computers and cerebral neurophysiologic systems, the evolutionary development of this model of automatic control closely parallels the evolutionary development of brain function before it was capable of analytic thinking, a comparatively recently acquired function. Early man had a primitive mechanism—the "nose-brain"—for sensing the world around him. Its function was specialized to receive nonverbal signals or impressions only through olfactory sensations. This was the only sense which provided information for coping with his environmental problems. In this respect, the simple behavior of the primitive "nose-brain" mechanism might be compared with that of the S.P.C.

As man's brain continued to evolve, other sensory stimuli, in the form of subverbal or preverbal suggestions, helped to shape his mental processes before he had the ability to think analytically and to adapt with a greater degree of affective feeling to environmental changes. A stage of development comparable with this archaic level of functioning is the behavior of anencephalic monsters and decorticated humans and animals, who apparently, in a primitive way, see, hear, taste, smell, utter crude sounds, cry and smile, and react with pleasure or displeasure to pleasant and unpleasant stimuli.[5]

In this evolutionary process, as the cortex expanded from the ancient smell centers, the simple adaptive responses were integrated into the lower or the subcortical centers to provide an automatic system for maintaining vital functioning of the organism—homeostasis. One of the adaptive physiologic response mechanisms manifesting this "mechanical calming" of the organism was hypnosis, which has been known under various appellations from "nirvana" to "suggested sleep." The fact that spontaneous quasi-hypnotic behavior is noted, to a degree, in animals and humans strongly indicates that it is still largely dependent on autonomic functioning, and as such, therefore, is an inherited behavioral response mechanism in the human. It is also known that neural control of behavior, when it becomes more complex in the process of evolution, retains simpler mechanisms as higher centers are added.

In primitive man, before the development of analytic processes, simple ideas must have been accepted by primitive mechanisms. Suggestions must have been the process which fulfilled this function.[22] It is also at this psychophysiologically regressed level of mental functioning that suggestions are uncritically accepted and acted upon with precision by the human. Here, hypnotic response is strikingly similar to the limited-goal behavior of the S.P.C., that is, when arousal or perceptivity is high, and when the cognitive processes are directed toward a special purpose, a hypnotic subject behaves like an efficient S.P.C. This regression is in rather sharp contrast with the logical and highly analytic but generalized mental functioning characteristic of nonhypnotic states.

Therefore, it is plausible to conclude that when an organism can have its sensing apparatus respond selectively to specific inputs, with its *fullest*

cognitive capacities, as during hypnosis, such functioning is a reversion to a more primitive but more adaptive level. The evidence cited below points to hypnosis as being an atavistic state or psychophysiologic regression serving as a substratum for the latter development of more complex life experiences. The author was among the first of modern writers to postulate the atavism or regression hypothesis as an explanation for hypnotic behavior.[13] He stated:

The hypnotic state at one time may have been necessary in humans as a protective defense mechanism . . . the hypnotic state may be an *atavistic reversion* analogous to the inanimate state of catalepsy so commonly observed in frightened animals when they "freeze to the landscape" in order to escape detection, the difference being that the presence of fully developed cortex in the human now makes unnecessary various instinctive defense mechanisms.

Later, several theoretic concepts based on a phylogenetic core were proposed. The hypnotic state was visualized as a condition which represented the most primitive form of psychophysiologic awareness of individual environment differentiation attainable among living organisms; this capacity was to some degree retained in all biologic systems.[27] Guze states that hypnosis may be defined as "a state of readiness for emotional action increasingly subordinated to cortical influence as one ascends phylogeny but nonetheless consistently present in animal organisms in a variety of forms."[9]

The concept that suggestibility is an archaic mental function thus can be used to explain the nature of hypnosis. According to Meares, the regression is not at the *behavioral* level, but rather at the perceptual or *mental functioning* level.[22] It is not implied that primitive man lived in a constant state of hypnosis; rather, that in the phylogenetic development of the nervous system, higher functions retained the ability to control the more primitive functions to a greater or a lesser degree. Hypnosis was one of these autonomic primitive functions to maintain homeostasis or a "steady state" in the organism.

The ability of man to survive is due largely to these autonomic functions built into the lower brain centers for selectively handling incoming information. This frees the cortex for the more specialized complex problems of adaptation. Similarly, when hypnosis is used to increase adaptive cortical responses, a comparison can be made with the G.P.C. operating with its total capacity directed toward a specific problem. This, too, represents an operational alteration or purposeful reversal in computer operation, that is, a highly developed device (G.P.C.) being used instead of an S.P.C. to solve an elementary or primitive problem.

RELATIONSHIP OF NEUROPHYSIOLOGY TO PSYCHIC PROCESSES AND HYPNOSIS

Neurophysiologic data[16] which tend to confirm our hypothesis are as follows: The reticular activating system (R.A.S.), phylogenetically speaking, is an ancient brain structure. Before the full development of cortical structures, the R.A.S. played an even more important role in regulating behavior, probably that of maintaining greater arousal. However, in the modern brain, the ascending reticular activating system (A.R.A.S.) can now selectively filter incoming sensory stimuli not only for maintaining selective arousal but for integrating incoming sensory information with awareness. This is significant in regard to autonomic responses, movements and sensations.

With reference to adaptive ability, higher nervous activity is apparently Pavlovian in type. As proof, Anokhin showed that the A.R.A.S. specifically and selectively involved *only some* of the synaptic endings in the brain stem.[1] He demonstrated this by involving biologically opposite activities, as eating and defense, which could occur only through different functional systems. The importance of this observation is that all biologic activities consist of continuous formation of newly established conditional reflexes on the basis of unconditioned stimuli of different quality.

This implies that the A.R.A.S. and the limbic lobes, to some degree, in the brain's hierarchy of other structures, govern discriminatory functioning during hypnosis. This is obtained by maintaining arousal of the cortex (selective attention or excitation), while simultaneously excluding irrelevant stimuli from awareness (selective inattention or active, concentrated inhibition) (see Chap. 28).

The arousal results either when narrowing of the attention span occurs in response to monotonic stimuli, or when there is an input-overload. In the latter instance, the high degree of arousal induced by strong emotions or vigorous stimulation tends to prevent extraneous sensory stimuli from reaching cortical awareness. Here the law of dominant effect is followed; a strong stimulus displaces a weaker one.

It seems also that whenever the integrity of the organism is threatened by imminent danger, the A.R.A.S. allows such vital and important information to be forwarded to the cortex for discrimination and instantaneous arousal. It has been noted, for instance, that a sleeping person generally awakens in response to a strange sound such as a footstep, but is able to sleep through much louder noises such as routine traffic.

Likewise, in hypnosis, arousal is maintained by limiting the patient's attention-span to specific input information from the operator. The limiting process may be due to a summation effect reaching threshold levels or saturation of the A.R.A.S. Here there is full utilization of its pathways. West contends that feedback mechanisms limit "nearly all additional information regardless of its significance under ordinary circumstances of adaptation."[34]

However, it appears that a feedback process is not necessary to explain the functioning of the A.R.A.S. under such conditions. It may be that the saturation is analogous to what happens under similar circumstances in electronic systems which filter information at their input to exclude less important or unnecessary information. In short, the A.R.A.S. reduces the saturation threshold to zero for all sensory inputs except those selectively permitted to get through to higher centers. As a result, selective attention exists, as mentioned above, to the exclusion of reality (i.e., internal inhibition).

In Chapter 3, it also was pointed out that Pavlov was the first to note this neural mechanism—internal inhibition—as it related to the neurophysiology of hypnosis. He observed that hypnosis had an inhibitory character; that is, the cortical neurons became, as it were, weaker and less efficient, the maximum limit of their possible excitability diminished. This hypothesis, too, fits in with the saturation threshold hypothesis.

The inhibitory character of internal inhibition during hypnosis also has a *protective* feature similar to the nonspecific therapeutic effect of sleep and tranquilizers in emotionally disturbed individuals. This has been borne out by Russian experiments involving toposcopic examination.[31] In this procedure, oscilloscopic representations of the brain's electrical potentials make a bioelectric mosaic or pattern of different cortical areas. In well-adjusted persons, the resultant bioelectric mosaic shows continual and rapid changes in potential distributed at random over the cortex. In severely disturbed individuals, such as psychotics, the changes in the mosaic are greatly reduced. Tranquilizers, sleep (generalized inhibition), and hypnosis (partial inhibition) increased the activity of the bioelectric mosaic (converted it to a normal pattern).

Particularly interesting in this respect is the use of hypnotic suggestion to inhibit specific or nonspecific stressors, such as harmful words, thoughts, and memories. Hypnotic suggestion directed to elimination of conditioned and unconditioned stimuli results in their inhibition.[12] The stimulation excluded by the suggestion acquires the characteristics of conditioned inhibition (neutralization of a harmful conditioned or unconditioned stimulus).

The neurophysiologic data supports Pavlov's thesis that emotional disorders are brought about by increased excitation of neurons, and that hypnosis *(protective sleep inhibition)* or even actual sleep prevents exhaustion or destruction of neurons, with consequent improvement.

Leading neurophysiologists are now urging reconsideration of internal inhibition as the neural mechanism which can be utilized in psychotherapy. Magoun points out that "If the inferences drawn from these many contributions [Pavlovian concepts] are correct, this is a brain mechanism whose function psychiatry must ultimately incorporate into its conceptions of inhibitions in mental activity and, I urge it, in understanding of the wellness and illness of the mind."[21]

COMMENTS ON ADAPTIVE CONTROL SYSTEMS AS THEY MAY RELATE TO PSYCHOTHERAPY

In order to gain some insight into the complex processes which take place in psychotherapy, it is instructive to compare the subject's response in psychotherapy with the response characteristics of adaptive servomechanisms. Since some modern electronic systems have the ability to adapt to their environment, these comparisons are becoming more meaningful.

In comparing electronic and human systems, the environment consists of the signals (stimuli) as well as the electrical noise and interference (specific or nonspecific stress), which appear as inputs (afferent stimuli).

The internal structures of these systems are allowed to vary so that the systems can learn from previous experience how to process the input information ("think") in an optimal way (successful adaptation). For example, if the positive feedback or the noise input to the system in a given frequency range is excessive, the system will reject this noise by means of a rejection filter centered at the noise frequency (scanning mechanisms). The system does this at the risk of rejecting useful information which may be centered at the same frequency. However, the system design essentially is based on the decision that it is preferable to run the risk of losing useful signals in a given frequency range rather than to allow the system to be swamped by noise which would prevent it from accepting useful information at other frequencies. This is rather similar to the physiologic functioning of the A.R.A.S.

Thus these adaptive systems react to interfering signals (stress) in a manner much like that of physiologic systems. For example, if an interfering signal causes instability, the system detects its own unstable behavior and causes the adjustable components in the system to change values so that the instability is decreased. In other words, after the system has been exposed to the signal environment for a period of time, it has learned where to place its rejection filters and how to adjust its internal structure to prevent unstable modes of behavior.

Automatic control systems used in engineering, like many analogous physiologic control systems, are stable in behavior when the input signal or stimuli are of one type and unstable when these signals or stimuli are of another type. In the adaptive control system, the system is required to adapt so that its mode of behavior will be stable when subjected to either type of input signal. The significance for psychophysiology, in studying the engineering uses of adaptive systems, is that it now appears possible to attempt a quantitative study of adaptive psychophysiologic behavior with simulated physiologic control systems.

The communications which take place between the psychotherapist and the subject, irrespective of whether the approach is permissive or directive, may be looked upon as a rather complex form of directed adaptive behavior. The psychotherapist may be thought of as providing the input signal environment, while the subject may be considered as the adaptive system which adjusts its behavior parameters (psychophysiologic variables) to conform with the environmental stimuli (inputs). As in engineering systems, the ability of the subject to adapt is a strong function of his present state. Also, if the range of adjustment required to cause stable behavior is very large, the parameters of the system may be unable to change their values enough to achieve stability. In engineering systems, such a situation would necessitate revision of the adaptive system to allow its adjustment parameters to be varied over wider ranges. The speculative implications to be drawn from this in the case of psychotherapy suggest that those subjects who do not respond require another approach, perhaps a revision or a restructuring of the therapeutic design.

NEUROPHYSIOLOGIC THEORIES OF MEMORY

Older theories of memory and learning maintained that experiences left "etchings" on the brain as traces. Still others contend that memory traces depended upon decreased synaptic resistances, with the resultant establishment of well-grooved pathways. These have been invalidated by pavlovian "learning," which is not confined to the cortex. Nor is memory limited to the midbrain or the brain stem, although some storage of

information takes place in these areas. Localized memory traces apparently have been demonstrated also as a function of the temporal lobes.[24] However, the data are inconclusive as yet. Other theories are that "experiences establish perceptual patterns of potential gradients in cortical electrical fields" or "resonance patterns occur in neural loops to produce altered physiochemical changes."[14]

The recently developed complex general computer stores "bits" of information as electrical pulses, which continually revolve until needed for computation. Since these pulses are not specifically located, they are referred to as "functional" or random memory; changes are not stored in a definite manner. Recent neurophysiologic data also indicate that human memory is random in nature, because no special part of the brain stores it—a wise provision in case of accident.[30]

As further evidence that memory is random, it has been hypothesized that the two-way feedback or reverberating neuronal chains are capable of manipulating thought according to symbolic or mathematical logic.[18] Lashley's alternative theories are that memory is due to "potential gradients in electrical fields" or that "resonance patterns in neural loops" account for it.[14] Pringle postulates a model of closed chains of neurons which act as "loosely coupled oscillators," similar to those occurring in the brain.[25] Irrespective of the validity of the above theories involving reverberating neural loops, it is certain that physiochemical alteration takes place in the circulating neuron chains to preserve "memories." This is more in accord with the most recent theory that every incoming percept leaves its trace by alterations in the arrangement of the large protein molecules of the neuron.

Hyden has demonstrated that some stimuli alter the ribonucleic acid (RNA) molecules of the neurons which cause the synthesis of altered protein molecules that are stored as "bits" of information or memory traces.[10] It is believed that the frequency modulation set up in a neuron by a specific stimulus may prescribe the arrangement of the RNA components (and thus of proteins) which acts as a code to pass on information to other neurons. In this way, whole chains of neurons can be molecularly conditioned to react to the repetition of a stimulus. From a statistical viewpoint, the molecules furnish the required permutation possibilities for the storage of all the bits of information received in a lifetime. Thus the recall of past experiences as memories is made possible.

Other scientists favor a molecular "switch" theory, which suggests that specific synaptic proteins subserve selective interaction between pre- and postsynaptic elements, thereby serving as an engram. The structure of such proteins would be genetically predetermined.

The best clinical data on the recovery of memory traces is Penfield's[24] work, cited earlier. It is interesting that a single recollection was recalled, not a mixture of memories or a generalization, as in ordinary memory. The evoked reaction was an exact reproduction of what the patient saw, heard, felt, and understood.

It seems that the memory records of all experiences are recorded by patterns of previous passage of nerve impulses. The patterns of neuronal memories are duplicated in both hemispheres since the removal of most of one lobe does not interfere with recollection. It is believed that these records are located in the centrencephalic circuits in the higher brain stem. Every experience seems to have access to both temporal lobes and evidently remains unchanged with the passage of time.

As discussed in Chapters 29 and 30, this may be the explanation for age-regression, revivification, sensory-imagery conditioning and hypnotic self-exploration. Scanning mechanisms unite stored memories with selected ideas, former experiences, and relate them to the incoming sensory percepts. Since peculiar disorders of memory also occur with lesions around the third ventricle, there are two other areas involved in various types of memory in addition to the temporal lobes, namely, the upper brain stem and the periaqueductal region.

These memory mechanisms also operate during dream states, reverie, hypnosis, and other dissociated states, the degree depending on selective "filtering," mediated chiefly by the reticular activating system. Since hypnosis is a state of hyperacuity, one would infer that greater arousal is being maintained to a selected input than during ordinary attention. The only difference is that, in hypnosis, the discriminatory ability of the cortex is held in selective inhibition. Normally, the cortex does not accept incoming information without prior computation. If stored data are not available for computation, unreality is accepted as reality—hypnosis.

Raginsky described how syncope and temporary cardiac arrest were induced under hypnosis in a patient who had Stokes-Adams syndrome and who had, until the time of the experiment, remained free of such symptoms.[26] Since the memory was sequential (always moved forward) in this patient as well as in several others, it was felt that hypnotic recall closely parallels electrical stimulation. Hypnotic recall is purer or more accurate than the recalls elicited by psychotherapy, in which patients bring up generalized memories or those that have been modified by subsequent thinking or experiences (screen memories).

Blum and co-workers offer the hypothesis that when the chances for interference are effectively minimized, well-entrenched memories do remain virtually intact over very long time spans, even in the absence of rehearsal.[4] They showed that under hypnosis the spontaneous emergence of distant memories differed markedly from the extraordinary feats performed by memory "experts." The latter rely upon all kinds of cues, including several forms of synesthesia, in combinations with intense eidetic imagery, to achieve success.

IMPORTANCE OF PSYCHOCYBERNETICS TO THERAPY

It has been pointed out that what the learner does in successive trials is regulated by the results of his performance—feedback. Incorrect responses usually are replaced by successful responses and, when these are remembered and automatically reinforced, they become adaptive or maladaptive habit patterns. However, incorrect responses or failures usually are forgotten and replaced by successful ones. There are numerous examples of how feedback modifies faulty behavioral responses. For instance, constructive self-criticism can correct maladaptive behavior to bring about a desirable state or goal. However, too much criticism is disastrous and is synonymous with psychological inhibition.

Kline has demonstrated that a continual delayed-speech (positive) feedback at nonhypnotic levels, with the inability to defend oneself against this feedback, produces acute emotional disorganization and signs of stress and psychopathologic behavior.[11] These reactions to positive or excessive physical feedback can be inhibited by hypnosis.

Extreme carefulness or fear of error is a form of positive feedback. This dynamism is noted in the stutterer who, in the presence of increased fear, develops bad motor response patterns because of inhibition. By having the stutterer listen to his own voice, negative auditory feedback automatically monitors correction of the speech. In the section on stuttering in Chapter 43, it is suggested that the patient listen under hypnosis to the playback of a tape recording of his own voice, speaking *normally*. Faulty enunciation, tone and such other impediments as blocking are quickly discerned and therefore readily corrected. Optimal functioning is established more effectively under hypnosis because the learned responses make use of the built-in reflexes, and, as a result, are eventually utilized automatically in a more spontaneous manner. The only danger is that overcorrection makes the stutterer too self-conscious, and, as a result, he worsens (inhibition).

Autohypnosis and sensory-imagery conditioning can alter behavioral responses either positively or negatively. If positively, purposeful behavior is brought about by healthy autosuggestions (input), which result in proper physiologic responses (output), and then a part of these regulate further "input" to control the behavior of the system to achieve equilibrium.

In a previous chapter it was noted that the brain can only process sensory percepts and correlate them with stored impressions. If the resultant computations are perceived as harmful, then a negative self-image is produced. Everyone has special images of himself and the environment, and behaves as though the images were real rather than imagined. At the risk of oversimplification, if an individual can imagine himself sick, he also can imagine himself well. Under hypnotic sensory-imagery conditioning, many "dry runs" can be processed to implant healthy convictions based on the stored data. A new image of the self is achieved by replacing negatively stored images by positive ones. As a result, new reaction patterns are formed which become available for involuntary functioning to maintain healthy adjustments. This is, in part, the very basis for behavior modification therapy. The well-adapted individual no longer has to check his mental ("How am I doing?") feedbacks, but, rather, can be more concerned with goal-directed activities. In general, it is the purpose of positive hypnotherapeutic suggestions to make available the *healthy stored data* in order to inhibit harmful impressions (disinhibition). This allows the subject to perceive and cope with reality in a more effectual manner.

With the advent of recent cybernetic concepts, the capabilities ascribed solely to humans are being chipped away slowly. Computers designed to model human mental processes can now simulate problem-solving, learning and decision making. Computers are making possible a much more intensive search for factual observations of multivariant functional relationships. It is hoped that these developments not only will give us a theoretic explanation of corresponding human behavior, but will help also to explain memory mechanisms, the bridge between nerve impulses and thought, and the continuum of awareness ranging from hypnosis to sleep.

REFERENCES

1. Anokhin, P. K.: Paper delivered at the First Pavlovian Conference on Higher Nervous Activity, Med. News, November 9, 1960.
2. Ashby, W. R.: Design for a Brain. New York, Wiley, 1952.
3. Black, S., and Walter, W.G.: Effects on anterior brain responses of an expected association between stimuli. J. Psychosomat. Res., 9:33, 1965.
4. Blum, G.S.: Distinctive mental contexts in long-term memory. Int. J. Clin. Exp. Hypn., 19:117, 1971.
5. Cairns, H.: Disturbances of consciousness with lesions of the brain stem and diencephalon. Brain 75: 109, 1952.
6. Crider, D. B.: Cybernetics: a review of what it

means and some of its applications to psychiatry. Neuropsychiatry, *4:*35, 1956–57.

7. Dunbar, H. F.: Anxiety, stress and tuberculosis. *In* Sparer, P. J. (ed.): Personality, Stress and Tuberculosis. New York, International Universities Press, 1956, p. 211.

8. Glaser, G. H.: Panel Discussion: Recent concepts of central neurophysiology; their bearing on psychosomatic phenomena. Psychosom. Med., September-October, 1955.

9. Guze, H.: Hypnosis as emotional response. J. Psychol., *35:*313, 1953.

10. Hyden, H.: Paper read at symposium, Control of the Mind, University of California, Feb. 27, 1961.

11. Kline, M. V.: An experimental study of the nature of hypnotic deafness: effects of delayed speech feedback. J. Clin. Exp. Hypn., *2:*145, 1954.

12. Korofkin, I.I., and Suslova, M.M.: On the neural mechanisms of hypnosis. *In* Winn, R. B. (ed.): Psychotherapy in the Soviet Union. New York, Philosophical Library, 1961.

13. Kroger, W. S., and Freed, S. C.: Psychosomatic Gynecology. Philadelphia, W. B. Saunders, 1951; reprinted, Los Angeles, Wilshire Book Company, 1962.

14. Lashley, K. S.: In search of the engram. Society for Experimental Biology Symposia 4: Physiological Mechanisms in Animal Behavior. Cambridge, Cambridge University Press, 1950.

15. Lindgren, N.: To understand brain. I.E.E.E. Spectrum, 52–58, 1969.

16. Livingston, R. B.: Some brain stem mechanisms relating to psychosomatic functions. Psychosomatic Med., *17:*351, 1955.

17. Luria, A.R.: The Mind of Mnemonist. A Little Book About a Vast Memory. New York, Basic Books, 1968.

18. McCulloch, W. S., and Pitts, W.: A logical calculus of the ideas imminent in nervous activity. Bull. Math. Biophysics, vol. 5, 1953.

19. McGill, W.J.: Applications of information theory in experimental psychology. Bull. N. Y. Acad. Sci., *19:*343, 1957.

20. McKay, D. M.: In Search of Basic Symbols, Cybernetics, New York, J. Macy Foundation, 1951.

21. Magoun, H. W.: Discussion of Anokhin, P. K.: Paper delivered at the First Pavlovian Conference on Higher Nervous Activity. Med. News, November 9, 1960.

22. Meares, A.: A System of Medical Hypnosis. Philadelphia, W. B. Saunders, 1961.

23. Ostrow, M.: Psychic contents and processes of the brain, Psychosom. Med. *17:*396, 1955.

24. Penfield, W.: The role of the temporal cortex in certain psychical phenomena. J. Ment. Sci., *101:*451, 1955.

25. Pringle, J. W. S.: On the parallel between learning and evolution. Behavior, vol. 3, 1951.

26. Raginsky, B. B.: Temporary cardiac arrest induced under hypnosis. Int. J. Clin. Exp. Hypn., *7:* 53, 1959.

27. Schneck, J. M.: A theory of hypnosis. J. Clin. Exp. Hypn., *1:*16, 1953.

28. Shannon, C. E., and Weaver, W.: The Mathematical Theory of Communication. Urbana, University of Illinois Press, 1949.

29. Simon, B. (ed.): Psychology in the Soviet Union. Stanford, Cal., Stanford University Press, 1957.

30. Sluckin, W.: Minds and Machines. Harmondsworth, Middlesex, Pelican Books, 1954.

31. Snechnevsky, A. V.: Paper delivered at the First Conference on Higher Nervous Activity. Med. News, November 9, 1960.

32. Uhr, L., and Vossler, C.: Suggestions for self-adapting computer models of brain functions. Behav. Sci., *6:*91, 1961.

33. Von Neumann, J., and Morgenstern, O.: Theory of Games and Economic Behavior. Princeton, N.J., Princeton University Press, 1944.

34. West, L. J.: Psychophysiology of hypnosis. J.A.M.A., *172:*673, 1960.

35. Wiener, N.: Cybernetics. New York, Wiley, 1948.

ADDITIONAL READINGS

Blum, G. S.: A Model of the Mind. New York, Wiley, 1961.

Coburn, H. E.: The brain analogy. Psychol. Rev., vol. 58, 1951.

Craik, K. J. W.: The Nature of Explanation. Cambridge, Cambridge University Press, 1943.

Hebb, D. O.: The Organization of Behavior: A Neuropsychological Theory. New York, Wiley, 1949.

Hilgard, E. R.: Theories of Learning. New York, Appleton-Century-Crofts, 1948.

McCulloch, W. S.: The brain as a computing machine. Electrical Engineering, vol. 68, 1949.

MacKay, D. M.: Mentality in Machines, Proceedings of the Aristotelian Society, 1952.

Rashevsky, N.: The neural mechanism of logical thinking. Bull. Math. Biophysics, *8,* 1946.

Reiff, R., and Scheerer, M.: Memory and Hypnotic Age Regression: Developmental Aspects of Cognitive Function Explored Through Hypnosis. New York, International Universities Press, 1959.

Rosenblatt, F.: Principles of Neurodynamics. Perceptions of Neurodynamics. Perceptions and the Theory of Brain Mechanisms. Washington, D. C., Spartan Books, 1962.

Sheer, D. E. (ed.): Electrical Stimulation of the Brain: An Interdisciplinary Survey of Neurobehavioral Integrative Systems. Austin, University of Texas Press, 1961.

Thomson, R., and Sluckin, W.: Cybernetics and mental functioning. Br. J. Philos. Sci., vol. 3, 1953.

Walter, W. G.: Possible features of brain function and their imitation, Symposium on Information Theory, London, Ministry of Supply, 1950 (reprinted 1953).

Wisdom, J. O.: The hypothesis of cybernetics. Br. J. Philos. Sci., vol. 2, 1951.

33

Hypnosis in Internal Medicine

REASONS FOR USE

Suggestion (in its most potent form—hypnosis) establishes the capacity for conditioning and formation of habit patterns that exceeds those that are developed at ordinary levels. Thus, reassurance, reeducation, and deconditioning are more durable than when employed at nonhypnotic levels. When repetitive reinforcement through autohypnosis is utilized, healthy responses become autonomous. It is this self-sustaining feature of hypnotic conditioning that reverses faulty thinking processes and behavior patterns responsible for maintenance of stress associated with a wide variety of psychosomatic disorders. Hypnosis *per se* is not a therapeutic modality, but rather is a technic used within the total approach of an overall therapeutic regimen.

Thus, there is no reason why hypnotic conditioning cannot be combined with drugs when the latter are indicated as part of a comprehensive treatment program. For instance, hypnotic conditioning can reduce the fears and anxieties which exacerbate attacks in cardiacs to instill optimism and feelings of well being. This can mean the difference between life and death. Recognized, but not generally appreciated is that preoccupation with structural heart disease can spark a chain reaction leading to generalized anxiety and harmful sequelae.

However, even when hypnotic conditioning is used alone for symptomatic control, it can be employed *in the same judicious manner as a drug.* Is not the bulk of medical therapy directed toward symptom relief? And why should not psychogenically based symptoms removed by hypnosis respond similarly to those eliminated by physical and drug measures? There are no well-controlled studies to support the contention that other symptom-equivalents take the place of the original one.

For refractory cases, hypnotic conditioning can be incorporated with other types of psychotherapy, such as behavior therapy. It also can be employed by psychodynamically oriented physicians to provide an understanding of what the *symptom means to the patient* (secondary gain value); how much of it he wishes to yield; and, most important, how he can face his problems and life situations in a more realistic and mature manner rather than resorting to infantile methods of coping with them.

Hypnotic conditioning also modifies or ameliorates organic conditions having a large psychogenic component; this occurs irrespective of whether the latter produced the illness or is the result of an organic disease. Each case is different because of the individual peculiarities of man's adaptive responses, conditioned as he is by the complexity of life's experiences. Therefore, whenever possible, a detailed life history is necessary to disclose the degree of emotional involvement, the conditions under which the pathophysiologic processes developed, and the strengths and weaknesses of the personality. This helps determine the degree of emotional support that will best motivate the patient during the initial phases of therapy when progress is imperceptible. Such an approach also helps structure the therapeutic goals. A number of investigators have discussed the role of hypnosis to psychosomatic disorders.

Hypnotherapy should be used only in carefully evaluated cases that have been screened by a thorough physical examination to establish the diagnosis. However, it is *not* a panacea for the illnesses of mankind.

Hypnorelaxation generally expedites therapy by counterconditioning anxiety, particularly in those who are affect-blocked; the increased relaxation, concentration, and cooperation allow them to talk more freely about their problems. As a result, the greater self-objectivity provides new ideas and understandings of the nature of their symptoms. Where indicated, in suitable subjects, posthypnotic suggestions temporarily can suppress a symptom or "hold it on leash" until the inordinate need for the symptom is understood and ready to be relinquished.

Autohypnosis also can be employed for self-exploration—when the symptom is removed by the patient rather than by the therapist, this accomplishment leads to longer lasting results. Artificial, hypnotically induced conflicts, in amenable subjects, often help resistant individuals recognize the "how" and "why" of their emotionally based disorders. After this knowledge is obtained, appropriate posthypnotic suggestions can be used to channel the harmful drives produced by a symptom-complex into more constructive outlets. Often, "trading down" or substituting a more innocuous symptom is helpful in this regard (see Chap. 50).

A prime indication for hypnotherapy is the hypochondriasis induced by alarmist health columns, magazine articles or remarks of well-meaning friends. The doctor, too, by ill-considered statements, a "polypragmatic" approach, an inadequate history or a careless physical examination, can unwittingly generate anxiety.

Another distinct advantage of hypnotic conditioning is that firmly established rapport acts to "bind the anxiety-ridden patient in therapy" during the initial phases of any psychotherapeutic relationship. It is at this crucial period that most emotionally disturbed individuals, through one rationalization or another, defeat the therapist by prematurely breaking off treatment, with the result that they then can cling to their neurotic behavior patterns without guilt and tension.

PSYCHOSOMATIC CARDIOVASCULAR DISORDERS

ESSENTIAL HYPERTENSION

In essential hypertension, stress due to chronic and inhibited rage is considered *one* important factor. The symptom often represents the individual's "cold war with his environment," manifesting itself as a sympatheticoadrenal, salt-retaining, blood-pressure-raising response. Since relaxation, sedatives and tranquilizers temporarily reduce the blood pressure, a stress factor apparently is operative.

Posthypnotic suggestions, together with sensory-imagery conditioning under autohypnosis, potentiate drug therapy to reduce the blood pressure. This cannot lightly be dismissed "as nothing but suggestion," as, in this state, conditioning phenomena, as disturbed feedback mechanisms, faulty associative learning patterns, and harmful stimuli, can be significantly altered. Thus it can be understood why this type of hypnotherapy is more effective than directive hypnosis. This new approach also is far superior to the old bromides such as, "You must take it easy and learn to relax." Or, "Why don't you just quit worrying?" Individuals with other types of hypertension can be taught specifically how to relax and to develop a better comprehension of their problems as well as their capabilities to cope with their everyday tensions.

Often, a disarming façade of calm cooperativeness in hypertensives obscures their aggressive drives. Many are depressed, threatened and easily frustrated because of their hostile dependency needs. However, modification or correction of these needs is often a difficult task with almost any type of therapy; relapses are commonly noted. In cases in which physical rest has been prescribed, the psychic stress of merely being inactive often raises the blood pressure. Here, modified activity and mental rest by sensory-imagery conditioning and behavior therapy are an ideal combination for all types of hypertensives. Autohypnosis should be used for reinforcement. Naturally this regimen can and should be combined with appropriate medicaments.

PSYCHOGENIC CARDIAC DISORDERS

Arrhythmias, Effort Syndrome, and Palpitation

Paroxysmal tachycardia, extrasystoles, and arrythmias can be produced by spontaneous recall of traumatic memories. Doubt as to the integrity of the heart can result in alteration of the rate and rhythm. Fright, anxiety, and sudden shock are commonly associated with precordial pain. Spectacular results often accrue following removal of dispelling "heart disease" that never existed. It is a difficult task to convince the cardiophobic patient that his problems are psychogenic.

Deconditioning, consisting of pleasant associations under hypnosis, often can relieve functional chest pain and associated symptoms in tense and anxious patients. Reflex conditioning of the heart to produce a rise in blood pressure and tachycardia, or bradycardia, has been demonstrated (the Danini-Aschner phenomenon).[69]

Other functional disorders of the heart respond to hypnotic conditioning directed primarily to symptom removal.[52]

Hypnotic age regression has been successfully utilized to reexperience and relieve arrhythmias due to rheumatic fever in childhood.[88] When the symptoms are functional in origin, hypnotic symptom removal is particularly effective.[42]

If the arrhythmias can be related to specific situations, the results are excellent if the patient is conditioned not to overreact to strong emotional stimuli. This is not surprising, as cortical regulatory mechanisms acting through specific nuclei of the hypothalamus affect the rate and rhythm of the heart, and are responsible for premature beats and paroxysmal tachycardia.

Suggesting conflictual situations to hypnotized patients has resulted in either the production or the elimination of extrasystoles. Creation of serene feelings eliminated the extrasystoles. Revivification of a combat scene, which resulted in abreaction of an affect-charged experience, produced complete recovery in a case of psychogenic heart disease. These cases, as well as others discussed in this book, apparently confirm Pavlov's observations that *traces of past experiences are indelibly "etched" in the brain, and can be activated by the proper associational reflexes*. It also appears that when some degree of abreaction of highly charged emotional material is relived under hypnosis, the resultant deconditioning significantly aids recovery.

In many instances, doctor-patient rapport is as effective as most of the vasodilating drugs in relieving even the pain of angina pectoris.[11] The placebo effect of pharmacologic agents and even surgical procedures, such as the Vineberg operation in cardiac disorders, is well recognized. Therefore, if placebos are effective, then hypnotic inhibition of excitatory stimuli should afford even greater relief.

Hypnosis has been employed successfully to decrease anxiety and the likelihood of arrhythmias during cardiac catheterization.[13] It has helped, at least temporarily, to interrupt cardiovascular disorders of psychosomatic origin.[88]

Direct suggestions under hypnosis have relieved cases of chronic palpitation. Raginsky reinduced a stoppage of the heart in a patient who had been operated for a carotid sinus syndrome several years before.[71] The cardiac arrest had not occurred since the surgery. It was reproduced by posthypnotic suggestions to revivify the "attack," and it was reexperienced with all its original manifestations and intensity. In spite of the absence of the carotid bodies, the objective findings of cardiac arrest were demonstrable in the serial electrocardiograms!

CORONARY DISEASE

Raginsky performed an immediate "hypnotic leukotomy" on several patients with coronary occlusion.[71] In one case, a man developed a massive cardiac infarct while Raginsky was at the patient's home. Prompt hypnotization reduced the pain, anxiety, and shock, and the patient was rushed to the hospital. Subsequent electrocardiograms indicated definitive improvement. He attributed the successful outcome to the hypnotic relaxation, as no other measures were employed. Of course, recovery could have been due to coincidental factors.

Recent data indicate that acute or chronic stress is an important factor in the production of coronary disease, especially if obesity, hypertension, and hypercholesterolemia are present.[22, 28]

Emotional tension *per se* can elevate serum cholesterol up to 35 mg. in an hour. In some cases of coronary insufficiency, it is difficult to understand how a patient can do a large amount of physical work at times and yet be unable to walk up a flight of stairs. Some sufferers have attacks while performing light physical duties and yet have no difficulties during more strenuous tasks. Levine remarks, "There is much about all this that makes one think of a conditional reflex. The number of foot-pounds of work is not the whole story."[54] In this regard, Platonov describes how cardiac output can be improved by appropriate hypnotic conditioning.[70] In addition to physiological factors, angina pectoris is also determined by personality factors which have a bearing on an "angina threshold."

Particularly pertinent to coronary disease are studies made possible by hypnotic conditioning and sensory-imagery technics to indicate that induced depression, anger, and fear are associated with an increase in the free fatty acids in the blood stream. The emotions equaled those experienced as reality situations in the past. Here is proof positive that the ability to experience sensory distortion in hypnosis is correlated with the ability to respond physiologically to hypnotically suggested emotion.

Many heart sufferers can live out their life span if they recognize their limitations, learn how to relax, and develop new interests. To minimize acute anxiety produced by aggravating situations, positive hypnosuggestions can augment tranquilizers and sedatives. Hypnosis also mobilizes faith and the "will to live." Unfortunately, not every heart victim is susceptible to deep hypnosis. However, even light hypnosis potentiates narcotics and sedatives, and can help those who react poorly to these drugs. Unquestionably, thoughts of death and impending doom take their toll. Extreme mental anguish, by production of hyperventilation, interferes with blood oxygen tensions, increases norepinephrine output, and sets the stage for acute exacerbations. These can be reversed by hypnosis or the relaxation response. The latter probably works by diminishing excessive sympathetic activity.

POSTMYOCARDIAL INFARCTION SYNDROME

The author has had gratifying results in a selected number of patients with postmyocardial infarction syndrome. Strong reassurance and reeducation under hypnosis directed toward achieving better adjustment to their condition, together with development of glove anesthesia, relieved or reduced their fears and anxieties and thereby raised their pain threshold. Those whose symptoms were ameliorated were advised to live within their limitations. They were carefully informed that the onset of shortness of breath and anginal pains was a warning signal to be heeded. All were checked and kept on routine medication by their physicians. Dietary control as well as reduction of salt and other risk factors can be maintained by posthypnotic suggestions in those who are obese or who have diabetes or hypertension. Posthypnotic suggestions can be used for promoting exercise and abstaining from fats and cigarettes. It would be interesting to compare a group of acute coronary and postmyocardial infarction cases treated as above with those treated by standard medical procedures. It has been observed that hypnosis had a beneficial effect on the apprehension accompanying postmyocardial infarction.[64] Reassurance, reeducation, desensitization guidance, and other direct support technics to get the patient rehabilitated have been used. Ego strengthening hypnotic technics can be used for the patient apprehensive of the sequelae supposedly produced during sexual intercourse.

Though hypnosis was not employed, Dunbar demonstrated that postmyocardial infarction patients who had received some type of psychotherapy outlived those who had not.[20] This area offers a fertile field for investigation. Other researchers showed that hypnosis and exercise were of benefit following myocardial infarction.[41] The personality profile that predisposes one to myocardial infarction has been described.[28]

Congestive Heart Failure

In congestive heart failure, the attacks of dyspnea are more frequent during the night when the sensory threshold is lowered. Everyone advocates complete mental and physical rest, but no one teaches patients specifically how the former can be attained. During periods of increased emotional tension, patients with congestive failure have increased sodium and water retention. The sodium output may be 20 per cent less than normal, thereby leading to decreased cardiac reserve.

In these patients, hypnorelaxation decreases stress, hyperventilation, and electrolyte retention, and often can stimulate the recovery forces to their maximal potential.

PSYCHOSOMATIC GASTROINTESTINAL DISORDERS

Numerous investigations[20] indicate that psychic influences can produce spasms in the gastrointestinal tract. Inability to recognize and treat these influences accounts for failures in many patients with gastrointestinal dysfunctions. The combination of hypnotherapy with a medical regimen in properly prepared patients readily offsets noxious cortical influences, and thus ameliorates the disordered mood and resultant disturbed motility.

The imagination plays an important role in digestive upsets; for instance, merely hearing a description of a nauseating smell or even thinking about swallowing castor oil can induce vomiting in highly susceptible persons. Radiographically, it has been demonstrated that gastric activity of the stomach can be varied with emotional affects.[70] Physiologic correlates of emotions also have been induced by hypnotic conditioning. In all probability, such emotions exert their influence on the gastrointestinal tract by a combination of hormonal and neural routes which act reciprocally with a local tissue vulnerability to result in functional symptomatology.

Emotional influences are transmitted to the gastrointestinal tract by way of the anterior hypothalamus and the vagus nerves. Another route is by way of the posterior hypothalamus and the pituitary-adrenal axis. The cortex not only actively participates in all visceral and autonomic activity, but also maintains equilibrium between the parasympathetic and the sympathetic systems.

The more common gastrointestinal disorders with a large emotional overlay that are amenable to hypnorelaxation are peptic ulcer, spasms of the bowel, gastritis and duodenitis, mucous colitis, diarrhea, pylorospasm, spastic constipation, and biliary dyskinesia. Other associated conditions are glossitis and bizarre tastes in the oral cavity, globus, dysphagia, cardiospasm, dyspepsia, aerophagia, anorexia, ptyalism, nausea and vomiting, pyrosis, bloating, and flatulence; all of these have a high content of severe anxiety.

Patients with such symptoms usually state, "I have always had a nervous stomach." Repeated physical examinations seldom reveal the cause of their difficulties. Many have had some type of abdominal surgery, a long history of digestive upsets and/or food intolerance, as well as severe symptoms of chronic anxiety and tension.

Since vacations, hospitalization, and removing the patient from his family or business worries often bring about a sharp reduction in symptoms, psychic factors obviously play an important role. In addition to medication and dietary measures, hypnotherapy directed toward relaxation and correction of faulty behavior patterns is often successful. Reassuring the patient that an organic involvement does not exist improves gastric function in many chronic dyspeptics.

Refractory individuals generally require hypnotherapeutic measures directed toward a reduction of their anxieties and tensions, and then a discussion of their problems, such as that described below under peptic ulcer

PEPTIC ULCER

It has been well established that peptic ulcers occur following severe burns, shock, and anoxemia—thus stimuli mediated via the cortex and reticular formation apparently excite the adrenals, and the resultant corticotropin output increases the activity of the parietal cells in the stomach. Other diverse factors such as heredity, age, conditioning by previous exposure to stress, and the nutritional state can affect both the production of the adrenal hormones and their feedbacks to the higher centers, and thus affect the gastric mucosa.

Before instituting therapy, a careful history and physical examination should be made. Sev-

eral multi-evaluation sessions are required to select patients for hypnotherapy. Initially, therapy
should elicit the relationship between the character of the emotional upsets and the symptoms. If
the patient is seen during an attack, questioning
should be directed to the type of mood, thoughts,
or environmental stimuli that preceded the onset
of the symptom. In good hypnotic subjects, one
can "trigger" the symptoms by suggesting specific situations or thoughts that obviously are etiologic. In this manner, the subject obtains a
clearer understanding of the manner in which
stressful stimuli exacerbate and maintain the
chronicity of the symptom.

It is helpful initially to tell the patient: "There
are persons who can get rid of their angry feelings
and promptly forget about it. Others cannot do
this and develop a great deal of aggravation and
they get terribly upset. No wonder that their sto-
machs act up." The patient can be motivated for
hypnosis by being asked, "How would you like to
learn not only how to control your nerves, but to
relieve your stomach symptoms?"

The patient is asked to identify and enumerate
those emotional situations connected with his
symptoms in order of their importance. Under
hypnosis, reciprocal inhibition technics described
in Chapter 50 are used to "immunize" him
against their harmful influences. He is asked to
think and discuss the least aggravating conditions
first and the more serious ones later. He is also
advised that while under autohypnosis he can use
self-exploration to assay his needs for the symptom. Then a constructive plan that will enable
him to meet his future needs without frustration,
anxiety and tension is discussed with him. Also,
posthypnotic suggestions to associate pleasurable
reactions with partaking of foods that were formerly upsetting is helpful.

Since most ulcer patients crave love and affection in the form of recognition, hypnotherapy
must be directed toward building up these strong
emotional needs. After these, as well as those
necessary for healthy functioning of the personality have been dealt with, the patient can be made
relatively independent of the operator by training
him in autohypnosis and sensory-imagery conditioning. Moody,[60] using controls, noted improvement in 20 patients treated *only* by directive hyp-

nosuggestive procedures. The successful therapy
of an ulcer patient by hypnosis has been described.[59]

Hypnosis in the form of prolonged "sleep" is
excellent for some refractory ulcer patients. Wen-
nerstrand, the great Swedish hypnotherapist,
kept his patients almost continuously under hypnosis for several weeks. Andreev recently described how prolonged hypnotic "sleep" is more
conducive to relaxation than is continuous intravenous Amytal.[2] The only disadvantage is that
a trained person has to be in constant attendance.
The patient is dehypnotized only for evacuation
and feeding. In this way, the organism is maintained at complete physiologic rest. Stress is
eliminated, and the ulcer has a good chance to
heal. Long-term follow-up psychotherapy is necessary to prevent relapses.

The rapid mobilization of faith and confidence
by hypnosis, together with the establishment of
healthy emotional attitudes, and the meeting of
his needs—all play an important role in facilitating recovery. Most ulcer patients will respond to
relaxation, reassurance, reeducation and hypnosuggestions for symptom removal when this
approach is incorporated with a medical regimen.
Those who cannot be helped by any type of psychotherapy require environmental manipulation,
change of occupation, hospitalization and/or
surgery.

COLITIS

Emotional maladjustments are closely related
to colitis. Fear and tension usually aggravate
such bowel symptoms as pain, diarrhea, bloating,
and bleeding. These are often associated with depression, migraine-like headaches, irritability,
and anorexia. Most sufferers with colitis have
fears and unresolved anxieties; they are characteristically referred to as "having no guts." The
bowel, for reasons unknown, becomes the target
organ for displacement of unexpressed anxieties
and tensions.

Hypnorelaxation, with strong posthypnotic
suggestions involving reassurance, helps some colitis sufferers face their conflicts; these generally
involve social and occupational maladjustments.
However, the majority respond poorly to hyp-

notic conditioning as well as to other psycho-therapeutic procedures. They usually improve on any regimen, but relapse rapidly. The ideal approach consists of permissive hypnotic technics, sensory imagery, autohypnosis, a dietary regimen, and tranquilizing agents. Surgery should be recommended for unresponsive patients.

ULCERATIVE COLITIS

Nearly all investigators agree that psychogenic factors play an important role in the cause and the maintenance of ulcerative colitis, especially with reference to the exacerbations of the symptoms. The physical aspects of the disease are serious and should not be neglected. Here, too, as in the colitis sufferer, one must find out how and why the patient reacts to his deep-seated emotional problems with his gut. A combined medical and psychological approach is always indicated. Hypnotherapy includes sympathetic understanding of the patient's plight, strong reassurance, even stronger persuasion and encouragement, and a thorough discussion of the patient's problems. Many of these patients feel that their prognosis is hopeless, so the major objective is continually to reinforce their confidence and outlook toward life. They deteriorate rapidly unless intensive psychotherapy is instituted. Without controls, it is difficult to determine how much these patients are helped by any type of psychotherapy. A few have been arrested, probably temporarily. Others go rapidly downhill and require successive resections of the bowel. On the surface, these individuals wish to live, but the majority have unrealized death wishes. Many are caught in marital or occupational "traps." As a group they are easily frustrated, ambitious, and compulsive.

EMOTIONAL DIARRHEA

Nervous or emotional diarrhea responds to hypnotherapy. It generally occurs in sensitive and unstable persons. Episodes usually follow stress, tension, and anxiety. The urge to defecate immediately after eating or drinking suggests a triggerlike gastrocolic reflex mediated by cortical and subcortical centers.

In addition to dietary and medical measures,

hypnorelaxation is particularly beneficial in mild cases when it is combined with direct suggestions, anticholinergic drugs, and tranquilizers. Those refractory to this approach require correction of the autonomic imbalance. This is best achieved by supportive psychotherapy under hypnosis. Many of these individuals already have had deep probing of their personalities without affecting the chronicity of the symptom. Often refractory cases respond to intensive hypnotherapy when directed toward enabling the patient to face his problems.

POSTGASTRECTOMY SYNDROME

Following subtotal gastrectomy, some patients develop the dumping syndrome, consisting of anorexia, nausea, vomiting, vertigo, sweating, fatigue, and weight loss. Often these symptoms become chronic, especially if associated with anxiety and tension. Cases have been treated successfully by hypnoanalysis.[71]

Dorcus and Goodwin treated a small series of cases by direct posthypnotic suggestions centered on reducing tension, removing fear of the symptoms, and improving the olfactory appeal and consumption of the food itself.[19] *Despite the fact that only direct symptom removal was used, not a single case relapsed.* In another study on nutritional problems, directive hypnotic technics increased caloric intake, relieved certain food restrictions, allayed pain and helped remove the accompanying loss of appetite.[24]

Good results have been attained by group hypnotherapy.[53] The author treated several cases by sensory-imagery conditioning. Posthypnotic suggestions associated with pleasant memories, involving the sight, the taste, and the smell of all the foods which the patient enjoyed before his surgery, were utilized. Glove anesthesia, transferred to the epigastrium, relieved the nausea and the vomiting in susceptible patients.

CONSTIPATION

Obstinate constipation that does not respond to laxatives can be helped by posthypnotic suggestions and sensory-imagery conditioning. One cannot merely suggest under hypnosis that the patient will have a bowel movement at a certain time but, rather, that *all* the *subjective* sensations associated with a normal evacuation will be experienced; these are "rehearsed" during autohypnosis.

The rectal sphincter is under autonomic as well as volitional control, which provides this area with a "time sense." One usually develops the desire for defecation as the result of a well-established habit pattern. When this pattern is disturbed, constipation often results. Patients are first trained in hypnosis and autohypnosis. Then, during a self-induced hypnotic state, the patient describes in minute detail what a normal evacuation feels like to him. All relevant details such as the time and the nature of the "call to stool" signal, and the type of spasms or tenesmus at the rectal sphincter are elicited. It is now suggested that all these sensations will be experienced during the next few days. The exact time can be suggested.

BILIARY DYSKINESIA

Dysfunction of the gallbladder may result from disturbances of the sphincter mechanism that is regulated in part by autonomic impulses, or from functional derangements in other portions of the biliary tract. Symptoms arising from a normally functioning gallbladder without stones frequently indicate a psychosomatic involvement. Emotional factors often can upset the function of the biliary tract.

After reviewing the literature, Ivy concluded that the choledochoduodenal mechanism can contract with sufficient force to prevent the evacuation of the contracting gallbladder and to counteract the secretory pressure of bile.[38] An increase of intracholedochal pressure has been associated with intense emotional stress. Such a rise may be due to hypertonus of the duodenal sphincter. There is also a physiologic basis for emotional jaundice. A syndrome has been described, consisting of distention of the gallbladder secondary to spasms of the sphincter of Oddi. The contractions are mediated by vagal impulses of central origin, with symptoms of biliary colic and even jaundice. The syndrome has responded to environmental ma-

nipulation, psychotherapy, and some monoamine oxidase inhibitors.

Surgeons are aware that some patients with prolonged icterus, intense pruritus, negative parenchymal tests, and normal structures at laparotomy, promptly establish bile flow with relief of itching on drainage of the ducts. This must be a functional jaundice. Even if calculi are present in the bile ducts, this does not necessarily rule out the possibility of emotional factors.

Derangement in cortical dynamics, acting through limbic system activity, can trigger spasms of the duodenum and of the sphincter of Oddi. Either of these can produce distention of the gallbladder, colic, and jaundice, and the resultant stasis can contribute to stone formation. This author has seen a Yoga who under fluoroscopy could voluntarily contract the duodenal sphincter. Thus far there are no reports of emotional icterus or biliary dyskinesia treated by hypnosis. However, the syndrome has responded to change of environment, mental rest and sedation.

Glove anesthesia and opiates are the methods of choice for short-term relief of pain. In the presence of intermittent substernal pain, further search for such physical factors as reflex coronary spasm should be made.

SUMMARY

Psychosomatic gastrointestinal disorders are, in part, produced by emotional factors and visceral reactions to physical stressors. Therefore, an interdisciplinary therapeutic program directed toward the psychic and the somatic factors is indicated. Hypnotherapy, judiciously employed in selected patients, can potentiate the medical therapy of gastrointestinal complaints caused or aggravated by emotional stress.

Hypnotherapy, as described, has proved to be beneficial in many patients who were unable to respond to a wide variety of medical measures. This approach has afforded considerable relief of pain, spasms and other related disorders such as heartburn, nausea, pylorospasm, eructations, and other symptoms. Sensory-imagery conditioning and glove anesthesia are valuable adjunctive procedures.

Hypnosis relaxes many anxious and disturbed

patients, reduces their tension, helps relieve the irritability caused by a strict dietary program, and also increases the likelihood of cooperation with the medical regimen. The dual approach provides the physician trained in hypnotherapy with a comprehensive and definitive therapy for conditions many of which are refractory to general psychotherapy.

It is unfortunate that some of our cases could not be followed and that space does not permit a fuller description of the nuances of the interpersonal relationship which in any form of psychotherapy affords a bulwark of support to the emotionally disturbed patient. The reader should not get the impression that all our cases were helped or cured. We have failures and these are discussed in Chapter 52. In this book, we are presenting primarily our successful cases, realizing full well that a placebo effect exists in every psychotherapeutic relationship, including hypnosis!

OTHER PSYCHOSOMATIC DISORDERS

TUBERCULOSIS

Tuberculosis is, in part, a disease of maladaptation due to stress.[76] The importance of the psychologist and the psychiatrist in the therapeutic program is incalculable. Correction of human factors which defeat the ministrations of the physician is mandatory in this disease. Almost half the patients institutionalized do not take their medications, refuse surgical treatment, or leave the hospital before being discharged as cured.

It is believed that adrenocortical activity plays a role in resistance to tuberculosis and that the effects of stress on the course of the disease may be mediated in part by the adrenals.[36]

The relevance of personality factors to the cause of tuberculosis has been described by many investigators.[20] Many patients are insecure, rebellious, over-assertive, hard-driving, and conflict-harassed individuals. Thus, at present, the research is directed more toward the host than the bacteria. The combination of psychotherapy, energetic drug therapy, and well-timed surgery can increase the cure rate in chronic tuberculosis. With reference to surgery, the need for an adequate personality study in all patients requiring

thoracoplasty has been stressed. Preoperative hypnosis can be useful in raising the threshold to shock, especially in debilitated patients or in those who have a "will to die."

Hypnosis can facilitate relaxation and feelings of well-being in subjects who require complete bed rest for months.[1] It can also be employed to stimulate the appetite, promote sleep and rest, and change the patient's unhealthy attitudes.

The author has had very little personal experience with hypnotherapy in tuberculosis, but believes that this area affords another promising area for research. Osler once advised that when a physician sees a patient with tuberculosis, he should not treat his chest, but rather his head. The reader interested in one of the best interdisciplinary studies made on tuberculosis should read *Personality, Stress and Tuberculosis.*[76] The resigned attitudes of consumptives to the disease itself must be taken into consideration.

Hypnosis has been used individually and by group therapy for tuberculars in the Soviet Union to alter the patient's outlook toward his misfortune and to inculcate cheerfulness and confidence in his recovery. Specific posthypnotic suggestions are: "You will eat everything with relish because your full recovery depends on it, especially butter, milk and rich food. Recollection of your difficulties no longer troubles you as you will maintain your interest in life." Such encouragement can invariably stimulate the adaptive processes and help the tuberculosis patient in the successful struggle against his disease.

MIGRAINE HEADACHE

Etiology

Although the precise mechanisms responsible for migraine headache have not as yet been elucidated, there seems to be little doubt that emotional tensions are precipitating factors in most instances. Likewise, the existence of a "migraine personality" cannot be satisfactorily substantiated even though many migraine sufferers are compulsive, rigid, hostile, and perfectionistic.

Many causes have been suggested, such as vasoconstriction, vasodilatation of blood vessels, leading to a combination of distention and altered sensitivity which results in pain,[67, 68] heredity and allergy.[82] Miscellaneous factors that have been suggested are electrolyte imbalance, histamine sensitivity, elevated serotonin levels,[67] anoxia, vitamin and hormonal deficiencies, ocular malfunctions, and chronic intestinal disorders.[27]

The author wishes to advance a speculative hypothesis for the currently accepted vascular basis for migraine headache. He postulates that, when we once walked on all fours, the head or cephalad portion of the body was functionally significant, especially for feeling states involving fight and rage reactions (head lowered to charge at an opponent). During our evolutionary development, the somatic manifestations of emotions involving rage continued to be displaced cephalad. Thus this deeply repressed response may occur as an atavism in those unable to express rage. In such predisposed individuals, the blood rushes to the head, with chronic vasodilatation and subsequent vasoconstriction. The blood vessels become hard, tender, and rigid, and this produces a steady ache accompanied by spasm and pain of the neck muscles.

Treatment

The possibility of such physical factors as brain tumor, sinusitis and other organic conditions must be ruled out before instituting any type of therapy. The psychogenic factors involved in tension headache or migraine respond readily to hypnotherapy, particularly cluster headaches (atypical facial neuralgia). There are numerous reports on this approach.[1, 3, 4, 16, 29, 31, 34, 37, 46, 71, 84] The author has utilized directive hypnotherapy for menstrual migraine and for headaches associated with premenstrual tension. The literature on hypnosis and behavior modification has been fully described by Kroger and Fezler.[50]

The purpose of all treatment is to relieve tension and raise the pain threshold. Should analgesics or local methods of therapy fail, hypnosis is the method of choice, especially if it is combined with autohypnosis and glove anesthesia.

The generalist who is familiar with hypnotic technics is in an enviable position for treating such individuals, as he knows the longitudinal life history of his patients and has already established a good rapport. Rarely is formalized depth psychotherapy indicated in resistant cases of migraine, as the results are about the same as with directive hypnotherapy, which is less time-consuming and less expensive.

Hypnotic relaxation, supportive psychotherapy, education, and adjunctive pharmacotherapy can reduce the frequency and the intensity of tension headaches, especially if the patient is enabled to understand how he is reacting to his life situations and what he can do about facing his problems with more equanimity.

Many drugs recommended for migraine headache have little more than a placebo effect. Friedman states:

In treatment of headache it is well to remember that the efficiency of any drug depends upon many factors. The emotional factors influencing results of treatment depend upon the personality of the patient, the method in which the medicine is applied and the doctor-patient relationship. The personal influence of the physician is most important.[27]

Ostfeld sums up the current attitude toward therapy by stating; "Two out of three patients with migraine can be greatly helped by any physician who is interested in human problems and is willing to spend a minimum of time with a patient in reviewing them with him."[67]

Cedercreutz and co-workers utilized directive hypnotherapy in 155 skull-injured patients.[7] Posttraumatic headache and vertigo were completely relieved, after an average observation period of 22 months, in 50 to 58 per cent of the patients, and partially relieved in 20 per cent and 16 per cent respectively.

ARTHRITIS AND RHEUMATISM

There is a large body of literature on the psychosomatic factors in arthritis and rheumatism. A high percentage of patients who complain of pain have minimal radiologic findings; contrarily, those who show extensive damage often have little discomfort. Most drugs and procedures employed to treat these conditions have little more than a placebo effect.[80] Data indicate that aspirin and salicylates are as good as steroid medication even in rheumatoid arthritis. Hypnotic suggestion is often effective for symptom-relief and dramatically relieves the distress in the milder attacks. Hypnosis is of little value in osteo-arthritis.

Pain can be controlled by the production of glove anesthesia and sensory-imagery conditioning; these reduce narcotics, steroids and analgesic drugs. Hypnosis should always be directed toward relaxing the musculoskeletal "armoring" which characterizes many arthritics. Even at rest, their muscles are in a continual state of spasm. Autohypnosis to promote relaxation and mobility of joints can be most effective. Dissipating the discharge of strong emotions which maintain chronic muscular tension often can prevent an attack.

Even strong suggestion *per se* can help many chronic arthritis sufferers, especially those who have a large psychogenic component to their ailment. Shrines and faith healers cure many such individuals. The value of spa therapy is due to the relaxation produced by separation from adverse environmental factors plus a nonspecific placebo effect.

The author has had gratifying success in ameliorating discomfort in small groups of arthritics by merely teaching the patients glove anesthesia and how to relax by autohypnosis. Contributory conditions such as overweight and dietary indiscretions are controlled by appropriate hypnotic suggestions.

Raginsky points out that attacks of arthritis can be either relieved or reinduced through hypnosis when the proper stimulus is applied.[71] He states:

> The emotional stimulus appeared to be almost specific for the individual so that he would become embroiled in a conflict which resulted in symptom formation. What is of interest here is that once the attack of rheumatism or gout developed in these patients, the attack could be shortened immeasurably through hypnotherapy.

It must be emphasized that arthritis is a disease of unknown etiology with protean manifestations involving all systems of the body. The spontaneous remissions and unexplained exacerbations which characterize the course of the disease make it difficult to evaluate critically the results of hypnotherapeutic management of this condition.

HYPNOTHERAPY IN METABOLIC DISEASES

DIABETES MELLITUS

The emotional factors in diabetes were recognized in the seventeenth century when Thomas Willis, describing the sweet taste of diabetic urine, said that the disease was due to "prolonged sorrow." Recently, an extensive literature has pointed out that the effects of stressful life situations are a contributing cause of diabetes.[20, 35]

The relationship to diabetes of fear and other psychic factors in anxiety has long been recognized by numerous investigators. These may interfere with therapy or indirectly affect the disease. Thus emotional stimuli originating in the cortex affect the hypothalamus via the limbic system. As a result, overstimulation of the adrenals causes impairment of glucose tolerance, increased insulin resistance, and sometimes ketosis. The concept of islet cell deficiency of the pancreas as an etiological factor is no longer valid. Heredity, obesity, hormonal dysfunction, and genetics play an important role. Hyperglycemia might be compared to an alteration in hemoglobin—both are symptoms. Emotional factors can precipitate hyperglycemia, particularly in the presence of sustained conflict.

Hypnotherapy can be directed toward a reduction of the stress component by achieving relaxation. Also, it can be helpful indirectly by maintaining weight reduction in obese individuals. Posthypnotic suggestions or autosuggestions enable poorly motivated persons to limit their dietary intake to prescribed foods.

Much more can be done for the diabetic than just keeping his urine sugar-free by means of diet and insulin. An appreciation of the patient's personality makeup, his strivings and frustrations, his home environment and relationships as well as recognition of how to cope with current stresses, allows a wider scope for the physician in the treatment of this condition. In selected cases, the use of hypnotherapy can reduce the quantity of insulin needed to keep the urine sugar-free and also can reduce the frequency of the attacks of ketosis.

The author remembers several patients whose

diabetes improved after emotional adjustments to domestic and sexual difficulties had been made. In one, a 42-year-old male who developed impotency, hypnotherapy directed toward this condition modified the course of the disease. In another, a very sick diabetic, drastic weight reduction through hypnosis alleviated the disease. In still another, reestablishment of potency materially reduced the need for insulin.

In general, hypnotherapy finds its greatest utility in the treatment of the psychic factors contributing to the diabetes. From recent experimental evidence there are strong indications that diabetes is not limited to being a dysfunction of carbohydrate metabolism, but rather is a multifaceted disease. For instance, some patients are diabetics but have normal fasting blood sugar levels and their urine examinations consistently are aglycosuric. Hence, insulin deficiency need not be the only factor involved in the production of lesions characteristic of diabetes. It is logical to postulate from this that unknown endocrine or metabolic processes secondary to corticohypothalamic dysfunctions may be implicated. It is in such cases that attention to the psyche by hypnosuggestive procedures is indicated.

Particularly germane to this discussion is the influence of the cortex on carbohydrate metabolism studied under hypnosis. When a hypnotized subject is given a concentrated solution of sugar, and is told it is distilled water, the blood sugar does not increase but may sharply diminish. Obviously, under the influence of suggestions at the verbal level, a strong unconditioned stimulus loses its force or provokes an unusually distorted action. This paradoxical phenomenon is well known among Pavlovians and may be the "unknown factor" accounting for unrecognized diabetes as well as explaining the results obtained by hypnosis. Foa recently described how the mediation of psychic stimuli and regulation of endocrine function resulted in diabetes.[23]

OBESITY

Overweight is one of the common problems that are brought to the physician's attention. It accounts for a high percentage of degenerative diseases; therefore, its treatment by hypnosis will be discussed in detail. Numerous authors have discussed the importance of psychic factors in stimulating the drive to eat. This is particularly pronounced during the evening, and has been referred to as the "night-eating" syndrome.

PSYCHOLOGICAL FACTORS

It has been demonstrated that, in addition to the deeper psychological forces at work, the ordinary vicissitudes of daily living contribute to the desire to overeat and to the inability to diet. Thus domestic upsets, fatigue, sexual problems, economic worries, and many other such common sources of tension interfere with the reduction of food intake. The treatment of overweight is much easier if tensions are eliminated. It has been noted that most of the patients who feel well as a result of reduced tension and frustration achieve successful weight reduction.[25] Only those who are emotionally stable should undertake a drastic reducing regimen.[5]

As has been mentioned, tension and frustration often lead to excessive caloric intake and subsequent obesity. These reactions usually depend on early developmental patterns. For example, the hungry infant soon learns that frustration is relieved by the pleasurable experience of nursing, thumb-sucking, or playing with a rattle. Although these earlier tension-relieving mechanisms are repressed, the individual always "remembers" the route by which gratification was once afforded.

Other oral methods for the relief of tension are chain-smoking, chewing gum, and nailbiting. Insecure adults, when faced with frustration, resort to one or more of these tension-allaying outlets. This "return-to-the-breast" mechanism now involves the use of food to satisfy the oral cravings, since the bottle, the nipple and the thumb are no longer acceptable. Contrarily, many individuals lose weight following stress.

Excessive food intake can also result from other causes. For instance, in certain "food addicts," overeating is often a substitute for suppressed hostile impulses. Since they cannot express anger toward those around them, they take it out on food, which is smashed to pieces. In homes where food is hard to get, the children eat everything available today, for tomorrow there may be no food. Many parents warn against wasting food, and also praise their children for being good eaters. Even after becoming wealthy, such individuals must "always clean the plate." Parental attitudes and other psychosocial factors determine one's eating habits. Thus a child brought up on large, rich meals usually imitates the parents' eating habits. This tendency is more often responsible for obesity than hereditary factors.

Overeating due to tension may follow the death of a friend or a relative. Frequently, food is used as a substitute for love. For example, people who are alone and who feel unwanted and unloved, substitute the pleasure of eating for affection. Their attitude is: *As long as no one loves me, I will be good to myself.* Unwanted children often become obese. To relieve their guilt feelings, some mothers become overprotective and stuff the children with food as a proof of their "love." Then, being concerned about their children's weight, they seek the physician's help. They refuse psychotherapy, however, because of their own emotional problems.

Adult obesity is a sign of social prestige and a "badge of wealth" in many cultures, in which a child is overfed to make it fat, not only because "big babies are healthy babies," but also because a plump baby is highly esteemed.

An occupation sometimes is the primary cause of obesity. In high-strung individuals such as actors, singers, or executives, eating may be used for relaxation. Conversely, people who lead a dull life eat more often than usual to relieve the monotony. This is commonly noted in housewives who "raid the icebox" between meals to lessen the drudgery of their work. There are many women who remain obese because their spouses prefer them fat. Since these husbands may have an inferiority complex, they feel more secure with plump wives, who are considered less attractive in a "thin-oriented" society such as our own. Sterile women often use obesity as a symbol of the wish for pregnancy.

Persons with heightened sexual impulses often displace these drives by food intake and eat ravenously. Sooner or later this type of individual reacts toward eating with the same feelings as he or she had about sex—namely, shame, guilt, and anxiety—and then more food is required to alleviate the tension. Many emotionally insecure individuals unconsciously believe that a heavy layer of body fat is a protective armor against a hostile world. For instance, the young girl, guilty over her sex drives, often retreats behind the "wall of obesity." By doing this, she now has a ready-made alibi for not being attractive to men. She can safely say, "I am so fat, no wonder boys are not interested in me."

Many young athletes enjoy eating large quantities of good food, but they do not gain weight when they are physically active. As they grow older and their lives become more sedentary, their caloric intake exceeds their energy requirements, yet their level of satiation is raised because of their previous eating habits. This type loses weight with difficulty.

The rationalizations proffered for overeating are many. Some of these are: *It runs in my family; it's my glands; others eat twice as much as I do.* However, the actual causal factors are hostility, anxiety, guilt, self-pity, self-punishment and depression. These are usually found in combination and are often repressed from awareness.

Obviously, with psychological factors so frequently at the root of obesity, the difficulties of weight reduction cannot be overcome on the level of general practice unless pharmacologic agents can provide powerful assistance. Amphetamines are the most effective appetite depressants in current use. The action of the amphetamines can be negated by severe emotional tension, premenstrual tension, untreated menopause, impotency, and other symptoms.

In addition to those resistant to medication, there are the paradoxical reactors who require much larger doses of sedatives, amphetamines and other drugs than the average person to achieve any type of pharmacologic response. In these individuals, one can use hypnotherapy as an adjunctive procedure.

The preliminary discussion is usually conducted after the physical examination and before the induction of hypnosis. It is as follows: "Our approach is a threefold one. First, it is axiomatic that you cannot lose weight unless you take in fewer calories—this means that you will have to follow a diet. All diets are good, but they are only as good as the way they are followed. You will be helped to avoid fattening foods through various hypnotic technics. Please be assured that you will not be hungry and that you will be able to eat an adequate amount of nutritious and healthful foods. Diets, as you know, can actually refer to eating *more* food, but of the right type.

"The second approach consists of medication. However, all types of medications, as appetite-suppressing drugs, have their limitations. They are useful, nevertheless, until proficiency has been developed in following the posthypnotic suggestions. They are particularly advantageous to get you started and motivate you to continue with other procedures. In addition, drugs will help overcome many depressive feelings that cause you to overeat. These drugs seldom produce nervousness, sleeplessness and palpitation of the heart. If you should by any possibility develop any one of these reactions, report to me at once and you will be given other medications.

"The third or hypnotherapeutic portion of the treatment consists of training in hypnosis and autohypnosis, wherein you will give yourself appropriate autosuggestions. The degree of success will be in direct proportion to the amount of effort you put forth in the practice sessions. If you practice autohypnosis faithfully, you can expect better results. You additionally will be helped to understand what your *need to overeat* represents. You will also be taught how you can face your problems on a more adult level instead of putting food in your mouth to allay anxiety-provoking tensions in the same manner you once used a rattle, a nipple, or a bottle."

The verbalization after hypnotization that has been found applicable to most patients is: "If you really wish to lose weight, you will roll the food from the front of the tongue to the back of the tongue and from side to side in order to obtain the last ounce of satisfaction and the 'most mileage' out of each morsel and each drop that you eat. By doing this you will more readily satisfy the thousands of taste cells that are located all over your tongue (there is an appetite center located in the hypothalamus), and, as a result, less food will be required and your caloric intake will be immeasurably curtailed.

"Secondly, you will 'think thin,' that is, you will keep an image uppermost in your mind of how you once looked when you were thin. Perhaps you have a picture of yourself when you weighed less. If so, place this in a prominent position so that you will be continually reminded of the way you once looked. There is considerable basis for this suggestion. You undoubtedly are aware that if a woman imagines or thinks that she is pregnant, her body will develop the contour of a pregnant woman; her breasts will enlarge and she may, in many instances, stop menstruating. Also, you may have at one time experienced a great deal of inner turmoil and lost weight in spite of the fact that you ate excessively. Cannot a frustrated lover also 'pine away' for the beloved?

"Thirdly, you might like to think of the most horrible, nauseating, and repugnant smell that you have ever experienced. Perhaps it might be the vile odor of rotten eggs. In the future, whenever you desire to eat something that is not on your diet, you will immediately associate this disagreeable smell with it. Also, you might like to think of the most awful and disgusting taste that you may have had in the past. This, too, can be linked up with fattening foods even when you merely think of them.

"Finally, for this session, remember that you cannot will yourself to lose weight. The harder you try, the less chance you have to accomplish your aims. So relax—don't press. The imagination determines this struggle, so would you mind purchasing the most beautiful dress that you can afford? Hang it up in your bedroom where you can see it every morning and imagine yourself getting into it within a relatively short time. You can speculate how soon this will be. Now this is important! The dress that you buy should be at least one or two sizes too small for you."

The suggestions above are given after the operator is certain that hypnosis has been induced. Following dehypnotization, the rationale for these suggestions may be discussed if the patient is inquisitive about them: "There is no question that there is a close association between the thousands of taste buds and the impressions that they convey to the higher brain centers for interpretation."

The "think thin" suggestion makes use to a degree of the alteration in body image secondary to strong emotional stimuli. It is well recognized that emotions can alter metabolic and endocrine activities to produce weight gain. This has been illustrated vividly in phantom pregnancy or pseudocyesis. If the autonomic nervous system can "trick" endocrine activities and bodily processes into responding with a weight gain to expressed or unexpressed wishes regarding pregnancy, then it is conceivable that these same pathways can produce loss of weight.

The association of fattening foods with disagreeable tastes and odors to produce an aversion is based on classic conditioning methods. While the organs of taste and smell are distinct, the impulses from each reach the cortex by different pathways. However, the two senses are closely associated psychophysiologically. They should be designated as chemical senses because chemical rather than physical stimuli act on the receptors in the higher centers. The most important aspect of flavor is due to the sense of smell rather than of taste. Olfaction is sensitive to small changes because it is capable of ascertaining the location of the source. In addition to these chemical sensations, smoothness and roughness, temperature, and pressure sensations originating in the mouth contribute to taste impressions.

Some attempts have been made to explain how various tastes can give rise to nerve impulses, but there is still insufficient knowledge to formulate a working hypothesis. However, in man the sense of smell remains closely associated with the motivation of the individual to eat. As described in Chapter 32, the close association of the limbic system (cortical areas, nuclei, and fiber tracts phylogenetically associated with the sense of smell) with the emotions is now generally accepted. Perhaps no sense is more provocative of moods and memories than that of smell, and so the smell of food may enhance or diminish the appetite. The close association of taste and smell with feeling states is further reflected in the words that we use to express our reactions to things— we speak of a "sweet" girl, a "salty" character, and "sour" grapes. In particular, we use the idea of "taste" to express our feelings.

The fourth suggestion has a twofold meaning. First, it is highly motivating, as it stresses the value of a nice figure by indirection or extraverbal suggestions. This approach does not mobilize a critical attitude. It makes full use of the imagination. One must be careful to suggest that not all these affirmations or aids will be utilized immediately, but that continual repetition through autohypnosis eventually will enable the overweight person to respond to these autosuggestions.

If the subject has had some modicum of success, the following verbalization is used on subsequent visits: "You will, if you really wish to lose more weight, consider the following suggestions: Do not plan on more than a 6- to 8-pound weight loss per month, but set a deadline for this weight loss. You will try harder when you have to meet a deadline. Wonder whether you will reach your objective before or after the deadline date.

"The desire to eat results when the appetite center in the brain is stimulated, whereas hunger is brought on by contractions of the stomach. If you wish temporarily to delay eating your next meal for several hours, all you have to do is to employ glove anesthesia over the pit of the stomach in order to "knock out" the hunger contractions which are initiated in this area. Another suggestion that might appeal to you, especially if you are interested in having a trim figure, is to think of your ultimate goal in terms of the actual weight desired. Let us assume, for instance, that you would like to get down to 130. This will be what I call a 'food stamp' suggestion, that is, every time you even think of eating something you are not supposed to, you will see the number 130 in blue encircled by a blue ring, much as the price of an item is stamped on the food can in a grocery store. You will give yourself this suggestion particularly at night if you get extremely hungry before retiring.

"Finally, if you find that you have exceeded the required food intake and you are still hungry, you can place yourself in hypnosis and *imagine* that you are eating enough pleasurable food to satisfy yourself."

During future visits the patient is asked to repeat the affirmations until they are remembered, and also for purposes of reinforcement. New suggestions to reduce caloric intake can be incorporated with the old. These consist of strengthening the patient's desire for weight loss by stressing the health, the social and the beneficial appearance of a trim figure; these act to reinforce the patient's own specific reasons for losing weight. Posthypnotic suggestions may be given to eliminate "eating between meals," "nibbling," and munching on such items as peanuts while watching television. For those who have a full social life, suggestions can be given to resist inordinate demands for eating and drinking. Suggestions for a specific type of diet, such as one high in protein but low in fats, carbohydrates, sodium, and liquids, may be employed at hypnotic levels. Likewise, suggestions at hypnotic levels may be given to induce proper alimentary functions.

Some of the above suggestions have a psychophysiologic basis. There are hypothalamic centers mediating hunger and satiety. They not only have separate anatomic locations but also different behavioral consequences. Appropriate lesions made in these brain areas in experimental animals result in bulemia, and they eat ravenously. Recent clinical studies suggest that either a decreased satiability or an increased hunger drive accounts for obesity.[25]

It has been established that one of the principal physiologic centers for initiating hunger contractions is just below the xiphoid process in the region of the epigastrium. Many obese individuals are not hungry but eat because the hunger contractions are conditioned to a time schedule. It is recognized that following the old adage, "Tighten up your belt a notch," can assuage hunger.

The deadline suggestion is obviously only to increase further motivation. This applies also to the "food-stamp" suggestion. Many of the other suggestions are based upon the correlation between taste and the visual senses being stimulated. Visual senses develop appetite at the expense of taste and smell. The tongue and the connecting brain centers are continually stimulated by the reciprocal feedback connections. No wonder one unidentified wit observed, "One tongue may have three times as many taste buds as another and the empire of taste also has its blind men and deaf mutes."

Hypnoanalytic technics are generally required (Chap. 50) to discover the basis of the patient's need to overeat (Chap. 50). A strong rapport, a noncondemnatory attitude, and encouragement when failure occurs facilitate psychotherapy. When permissive technics are employed and it is emphasized that it is a "do-it-yourself program," undue dependency is avoided. Furthermore, as described above, hypnotherapy is used as part of a total approach consisting of a sensible diet and appropriate medications.

Other investigators have used hypnosis for obesity with varied success.[8, 65, 66, 77, 81, 83] It has been employed in a psychodynamic behavior modification model emphasizing the holistic approach.[43, 49] Tilker and Meyer have combined hypnosis and aversive conditioning.[79] Wick and co-workers used the constructs of hypnosis without hypnotic induction.[83] Crasilneck and Hall discuss hypnotic management of obesity and dietary problems in detail.[14] It has been noted that one group paying a fee got better results than a control group which did not pay. Both groups were hypnotized.[77]

Group hypnosis for obesity is even more rewarding than individual sessions.[32] The same factors apply as those described in group training for childbirth. The author sees four to five patients for 1 hour, at first weekly and then biweekly. After the patients have learned autohypnosis and how to modify their eating habits, medication is discontinued. The use of psychotherapy is helpful in maintaining the optimal weight after it is reached. About 40 per cent of patients relapse and require periodic reinforcement to prevent further weight gain.

HYPERTHYROIDISM

Stress plays an important role in altering thyroid function. Overelaboration of the thyroid-stimulating hormone (TSH) is often secondary to cortical-hypothalamic factors. Though the causes of this condition are multiple, emotional factors can modify thyroid function. Nearly all patients are easily upset, sensitive to their environments, and exceedingly intolerant. Hypnotherapy must be directed toward a reorganization of personality functioning. Not only can it implement medical therapy in order to achieve this, but strong hypnotic rapport can also alter the individual's reaction to fears and other environmental stresses.

Hypnorelaxation is particularly valuable in the pre- and postoperative emotional preparation of the patient who requires thyroid surgery. Anxious patients can be conditioned for thyroid surgery by a "rehearsal" or a "dry-run" of the proposed surgery (see Chap. 34). The combination of hypnorelaxation and medication after surgery is better than either one alone. Clinicians are aware that the treatment of hyperthyroidism only begins after the surgery is finished. When such individuals are taught to relax, face and understand their difficulties through hypnotherapeutic technics, they become more stabilized, with a better prognosis.

ANOREXIA NERVOSA

The chief symptoms of anorexia nervosa are the loss of appetite and weight, and amenorrhea. Untreated cases have a high mortality. The condition occurs in very highstrung individuals, chiefly women. It must be distinguished from pituitary dysfunction, in which pubic and axillary hair is lost.

Hypnotherapy can be used to keep the patient relaxed in bed, and the appetite can be increased through posthypnotic suggestions associating food with pleasant memories. Concomitantly, feelings of aggression, disgust, and hostility should be ventilated. Crasilneck and Hall cured 50 per cent of their 70 cases by means of hypnosis.

In two cases of anorexia nervosa recently seen by the author, one patient lived and one died. Posthypnotic suggestions of an increase in appetite were accepted by one patient, and there was a subsequent weight gain. This patient, who came in regularly, faced the problems contributing to her depressive reactions. The patient who died of malnutrition did not come in regularly. She had profound guilt feelings and remorse because she had driven her daughter away from home. The daughter became a prostitute, and the mother never forgave herself and masochistically developed an intense need to punish herself.

Bruch has reviewed the literature in this area, and written a monograph on anorexia nervosa.[6]

BRONCHIAL ASTHMA

There is extensive literature on the psychogenic aspects of asthma.[20, 26, 82] Characteristically, these patients suppress all intense emotions involving threats to their dependent relationships, deprivation, and insecurity induced by sexual conflicts. As children, they are anxiety-ridden, lack confidence and are dependent to an extreme degree. Developmental failures in the functioning of the reticular formation, exacerbated by repeated allergic reactions in the brain stem, have been implicated as an etiologic factor.

TREATMENT

There is no doubt that suggestion plays a powerful role in asthma. The "rose asthma" case is a classical one in which an asthmatic was exposed to a paper rose under glass, and it precipitated an attack. More recently the experiment was repeated with pulmonary measurements, and over 50 per cent showed a definite increase in airway resistance.

Numerous authors have treated asthma by hypnotherapy.[9, 12, 16, 21, 33, 51, 57, 58, 59, 62, 73, 78] Abreaction under hypnosis may reduce attacks of status asthmaticus. For chronic cases of asthma, autohypnosis together with steroids and evocation of conflicts is often helpful. Asthmatics who became "adrenalin-fast" have been relieved by hypnotherapy directed toward understanding the responsible psychogenic factors.[70]

In children afflicted with asthma, it has been reported that, in a control series, reassurance by psychotherapy was slower and less certain in its effects than hypnotherapy.[56] In both series, parents had to be treated concurrently. Reinforcement suggestions under hypnosis are usually necessary long after recovery has occurred. Parents can be taught to give suggestions to neutralize the anxiety-provoking situations. Sutton taught three patients to use autohypnosis, and all improved.[77] For adults, a superficial uncovering type of hypnotherapy often is successful. Prolonged "sleep" can alleviate some severe asthmatic attacks. The author uses relaxation to regulate the breathing, and trains all patients in sensory-imagery conditioning. About 60 per cent of carefully *selected* cases can be helped by these methods. The reader, however, should not infer that our results would be as dramatic in a random population sample.

MacLaren and Eisenberg studied a group of 50 carefully selected asthmatics who showed no response to medical therapy, and who had overt signs of emotional instability.[56] Hostile, skeptical individuals or those who had advanced lung disease were rejected. They noted that if suggestions directed toward the patient's breathing in unison with the operator's counting was followed, the breathing soon became slower and quieter. Strong suggestions of the chest's relaxing usually eliminated breathing difficulties. Sensory-imagery conditioning involving relaxing experiences were employed. Posthypnotic suggestions that the bronchial tubes were opening helped relax the breathing. Scene-visualization technics oriented around the patient's seeing himself in a protected and comfortable position were most effective.

Their results, however, showed a high number of relapses brought about by exposure to a strong antigen, or respiratory infection. In the emotionally disturbed asthmatics, stress precipitated severe attacks. They concluded that, for more lasting results, threats to the individual's emotional stability had to be uncovered or the person's fears of the threats had to be corrected by psychotherapy.

When fear of choking, which is commonly noted in these patients, was neutralized by reassurance and relaxed breathing exercises, 75 per cent of the relapsed patients improved. Others were asked to ventilate their emotions prior to the attacks. Using an abreactive technic, they had their patients relive anxiety-provoking situations, but without effects. One in eight could not be hypnotized readily, and one in three can be hypnotized but gets little if any benefit. Two out of three get relief, varying from temporary to sustained effects.

Many deaths occur with steroids, and this alone makes the assessment of the potentialities of hypnosis more rather than less urgent. Edwards reports that hypnosis worked by decreasing airways' resistance or by a psychological effect (decreased awareness of airways' resistance).[21] Another report extolled the effect of dramatically saving an elderly man's life by hypnosis for a severe case of status asthmaticus.[74]

One particular observation deserves mention: typical attacks of bronchial asthma were hypnotically produced, and the attacks thus provoked were immediately terminated by appropriate hypnotic suggestions.[70] This indicates that bronchial asthma results from a conditioned reflex to harmful external and internal stimulation. African natives, who have a high incidence of tuberculosis, almost never have asthma.

In part, bronchial asthma may be a "neurosis of the lungs." The expiratory phase in humans is particularly "overloaded" because it underlies the entire complex of speech; hence, breathing is the first manifestation of suffering. The involvement expresses itself as an alteration in the tonus of the smooth muscles of the bronchi.

There are numerous reports of asthma treated by short-term hypnotherapy and behavior modification.[50] Soviet scientists believe that the results achieved by hypnosis may be due to ". . . liberation of the functions of the physiologically lower divisions of the central nervous system and that this may be achieved by inhibition of the higher divisions which normally regulate their work."[70]

ALLERGY

Allergic reactions are frequently associated with stress.[30, 74] Urticaria can be precipitated by traumatic life situations. There are significant differences between acute and chronic urticaria; specific allergens are not present in the latter.[71]

Hypnosis has been employed to prevent asthmatic attacks in individuals susceptible to certain allergens, even though skin tests remained positive and attacks were produced when these patients were shown an artificial rose or a picture of this. Wheals resulting from a cutaneous reaction to eggs have been suppressed by hypnosis.[10] The suppression of allergic skin reactions by hypnosis has not been confirmed.[90] However, some researchers have concluded that hypnotic suggestion influences cutaneous allergic reactions.[18, 47, 69]

The above data indicate that the widespread use of injections may be because of a placebo effect. Lowell believes that the rationale for injection therapy has not been validated to exclude coincidental factors, chance or bias.[55] He states:

. . . we cannot rule out the possibility of a happy coincidence—the initiation of treatment in a year of less intense exposure to pollen, instruction in allergic cleanliness and in the intelligent use of drugs, the allaying of anxiety, the spontaneous lessening of the patient's level of clinical sensitivity and, last but by no means least, the suggestion that accompanies the ritual of injection therapy. These, individually or in combination, might explain many a success without invoking any specific therapeutic or prophylactic merit for the solution that we put into the syringe.

The author is not surprised at these remarks. When he first began his practice, several hay-fever victims had complete relief from placebo medications. He has seen patients with angioneurotic edema, hives, and urticarial reactions who responded to hypnotherapy.

RAYNAUD'S DISEASE

Crasilneck and Hall report a 60 percent remission or improvement rate in Raynaud's disease.[14] However, in the absence of controls and the variations due to emotional factors, these investigators caution against over optimism. Others have had similar results.[39, 63]

DISCUSSION

Once again, the author wishes to emphasize that those who benefited from hypnosis are being presented in this section. Failures do occur, and at times the handling of such cases taxes the patience of both patient and therapist. It has been noted that, in most allergic patients, the benefits from hypnosis are not proportionate to the effort involved. However, in tense and anxious asthmatics, hypnosis reduced fright reactions. However, pulmonary function tests should be used to record actual progress. The reader must realize that results in any condition depend on many variables in the physician and patient rapport. One man gets recoveries and results, while another using the same approach gets only failures.

REFERENCES

1. Anderson, J.A.D., *et al.:* Migraine and hypnotherapy. Int. J. Clin. Exp. Hypn., *23*:48, 1975.
2. Andreev, B.V.: Sleep Therapy in the Neuroses. New York, Consultant's Bureau, 1960.
3. Andreychuk, T., and Skriver, C.: Hypnosis and biofeedback in the treatment of migraine headache. Int. J. Clin. Exp. Hypn., *23*:172, 1975.
4. Blumenthal, L.S.: Hypnotherapy of headaches. Headache, *2*:197, 1963.
5. Bruch, H.: The Importance of Overweight. New York, Norton, 1957.
6. _____: Obesity, Anorexia Nervosa, and the Person Within. New York, Basic Books, 1973.
7. Cedercreutz, C., *et al.:* Hypnotic treatment of headache and vertigo in skull injured patients. Int. J. Clin. Exp. Hypn., *24:*195, 1976.
8. Cheek, D.B., and LeCron, L.M.: Clinical Hypnotherapy. New York, Grune & Stratton, 1968.
9. Chong, T.M.: Treatment of asthma by hypnotherapy. Med. J. Malaya, *18:*232, 1965.
10. Clarkson, A.K.: The nervous factor in juvenile asthma. Br. Med. J., *2:*845, 1937.
11. Cole, S.L., Kaye, H., and Griffith, G.C.: Assay of antianginal agents—the rapport period. J.A.M.A., *168:*75, 1958.
12. Collison, D.R.: Hypnotherapy in the management of asthma. Am. J. Clin. Hypn., *11:*6, 1968.
13. _____: Cardiological applications of the control of the autonomic nervous system by hypnosis. Am. J. Clin. Hypn., 12:*150,* 1970.
14. Crasilneck, H.B., and Hall, J.A.: Clinical Hypnosis: Principles and Practice. New York, Grune & Stratton, 1975.
15. Dengrove, E.: Behavior therapy of headache. J. Am. Soc. Psychosomat. Dent. Med., *15:*41, 1968.
16. Dennis, M., and Phillippus, M.J.: Hypnotic and non-hypnotic suggestion and skin response in atopic patients. Am. J. Clin. Hypn., *7:*342, 1965.
17. Dias, M.M.: Hypnosis in irritable colon. Rev. Brasil. Med., *20:*132, 1963.
18. Diehl, F., and Heinichen, W.: Beeinfussung allergischer Reaktionen. Munch. Med. Wochenschr. *78:*1008, 1931.
19. Dorcus, R.M., and Goodwin, P.: The treatment of patients with the dumping syndrome by hypnosis. J. Clin. Exp. Hypn., *3:*200, 1955.
20. Dunbar, H.F.: Emotions and Bodily Changes. ed. 3. New York, Columbia University Press, 1948.
21. Edwards, G.: Hypnotic treatment of asthma. Br. Med. J., *2:*492, 1960.
22. Eliot, R.S., and Forker, A.D.: Emotional cardiac disease. J.A.M.A., *236:*3325, 1976.
23. Foa, P.P.: The mediation of psychic stimuli and regulation of endocrine function. *In* Kroger, W.S. (ed.): Psychosomatic Obstetrics. Gynecology and Obstetrics, Springfield, Ill., Charles C Thomas, 1962.
24. Fogelman, M.J., and Crasilneck, H.B.: Food intake and hypnosis. J. Am. Dietetic Assoc., *32:*519, 1956.

25. Freed, S.C.: Psychic factors in the development and treatment of overweight. J.A.M.A., *133:*369, 1947.

26. French, T., and Alexander, F.: Psychogenic factors in bronchial asthma. Psychosom. Med. Monog. Ser., *2:*34, 1941.

27. Friedman, A.P.: Migraine and Other Common Headaches. World-Wide Abstracts, September 1959.

28. Friedman, M., and Rosenman, R.: Type A Behavior and Your Heart. New York, Knopf, 1974.

29. Graham, G.W.: Hypnotic treatment for migraine headache. Int. J. Clin. Exp. Hypn., *23:*165, 1975.

30. Grant, R.T., Bruce-Pearson, R.S., and Comeau, W.J.: Observations on urticaria provoked by emotions, by exercise and by warming the body. Clin. Sci., *2:*253, 1936.

31. Hanley, F.W.: Hypnotherapy of migraine. Can. Psychiat. Assoc. J., *9:*254, 1964.

32. _____: The treatment of obesity by individual and group hypnosis. Can. Psychiat. Assoc. J., *12:*549, 1967.

33. _____: Individualized hypnotherapy of asthma. Am. J. Clin. Hypn., *16:*275, 1974.

34. Harding, H.C.: Hypnosis and migraine or vice versa (paper read at the 11th Annual Scientific Meeting of the Society for Clinical and Experimental Hypnosis, San Francisco, August 1959).

35. Hinkle, L.E., Jr., *et al.:* Studies in diabetes mellitus: the relation of stressful life situations to the concentration of ketone bodies in the blood of diabetic and nondiabetic humans. J. Clin. Invest., *29:*754, 1950.

36. Holmes, T.H., *et al.:* Psychosocial and psychophysiologic studies of tuberculosis. Psychosom. Med., *19:*134, 1957.

37. Horan, J.S.: Hypnosis and recorded suggestions in the treatment of migraine. J. Clin. Exp. Hypn., *1:*7, 1953.

38. Ivy, A.C.: Motor dysfunction of biliary tract: analytical and critical consideration (Caldwell lecture 1946). Am. J. Roentgenol., *57:*1, 1947.

39. Jacobson, A.M., *et al.:* Raynaud's phenomenon: treatment with hypnotic and operant techniques. J.A.M.A., *225:*739, 1973.

40. Kavanaugh, T., *et al.:* Importance of physical activity in post-coronary rehabilitation. Am. J. Phys. Med., *52:*304, 1973.

41. _____: Hypnosis and exercise—a possible combined therapy following myocardial infarction. Am. J. Clin. Hypn., *16:*160, 1974.

42. Kline, M.V.: Situational cardiovascular symptomatology and hypnosis. Br. J. Med. Hypn., *1:*33, 1950.

43. Kroger, W.S.: New perspectives in obesity: An integrated approach. Int. Rec. Med., *172:*212, 1959.

44. _____: Psychologic features in obesity and anorexic drugs. Am. Pract., *10:*2169, 1959.

45. _____: A comparison of anorexic drugs in the treatment of the resistant obese patient. J. Psychosomatics, *8:*1, 1962.

46. _____: Hypnotherapeutic management of headache. Headache, 2:50, 1963.

47. _____: Current status of hypnosis in allergy. Ann. Allergy, *22:*123, 1964.

48. _____: Comprehensive management of obesity. Am. J. Clin. Hypn., *12:*165, 1970.

49. _____: Systems approach for understanding obesity: management by behavioral modification through hypnosis. Psychiat. Opin., *7:*7, 1970.

50. Kroger, W.S., and Fezler, W.D.: Hypnosis and Behavior Modification: Imagery Conditioning. Philadelphia, J. B. Lippincott, 1976.

51. Kusano, T., *et al.:* Use and abuse of hypnotherapy for bronchial asthma. Japan J. Hypn., *12:*33, 1969.

52. Kupfer, D.: Hypnotherapy in a case of functional heart disorder. J. Clin. Exp. Hypn., *2:*186, 1954.

53. Leonard, A.S., *et al.:* Treatment of post-gastrectomy dumping syndrome by hypnotic suggestion. J.A.M.A., *165:*1957, 1957.

54. Levine, S.A.: Some notes concerning angina pectoris. J.A.M.A., *171:*1838, 1840, 1959.

55. Lowell, F.C.: American Academy of Allergy: Presidential address. J. Allergy, *31:*185, 1960.

56. MacLaren, W.R., and Eisenberg, B.C.: Hypnosis in the treatment of asthma (paper read before the Pan American Medical Association, May 5, 1960).

57. Magonet, A.P.: Hypnosis and asthma. Int. J. Clin. Exp. Hypn., *8:*121, 1960.

58. Maher-Loughnan, G.P.: Hypnosis and autohypnosis for the treatment of asthma. Int. J. Clin. Exp. Hypn., *18:*1, 1970.

59. Maher-Loughnan, G.P., *et al.:* Controlled trial of hypnosis in the symptomatic treatment of asthma. Br. Med. J., *2:*371, 1962.

60. Moody, H.: An evaluation of hypnotically induced relaxation for the reduction of peptic ulcer symptoms. Br. J. Med. Hypn., *5:*23, 1953.

61. Moorefield, C.W.: The use of hypnosis and behavior therapy in asthma. Am. J. Clin. Hypn., *13:*162, 1971.

62. Morton, J.H.: Hypnosis and psychosomatic medicine. Am. J. Clin. Hypn., *3:*67, 1960.

63. Norris, A., and Huston, P.: Raynaud's disease studied by hypnosis. Dis. Nerv. Syst., *17:*163, 1956.

64. Nuland, W.: The use of hypnotherapy in the treatment of the post-myocardial infarction invalid. Int. J. Clin. Exp. Hypn., *16:*139, 1968.

65. _____: Hypnosis and weight control (presentation at annual meeting of the Society for Clinical and Experimental Hypnosis, Montreal, 1974).

66. Oakley, R.P.: Hypnosis with a positive approach in the management of "problem" obesity. J. Am. Soc. Psychosom. Dent. Med., *7:*28, 1960.

67. Ostfeld, A.M.: Migraine headache, J.A.M.A., 174:110–112, 1960.

68. Ostfeld, A.M., *et al.:* Studies in headache: a summary of evidence implicating a locally active chemical agent in migraine. Trans. Am. Neurol. Assoc., 81st meeting, 1956, p. 356.

69. Perloff, M.M., and Spiegelman, J.: Hypnosis in the treatment of a child's allergy to dogs. Am. J. Clin. Hypn., *15:*269, 1973.

70. Platonov, K.: The Word As a Physiological and Therapeutic Factor. Moscow, Foreign Languages Publishing House, 1955.

71. Raginsky, B.B.: *In* Schneck, J.M. (ed.): Hypnosis in Modern Medicine. Springfield, Ill., Charles C Thomas, 1959.

72. Robinson, W.D.: *In* Hollander, J.L. (ed.): Arthritis and Allied Conditions. Philadelphia, Lea & Febiger, 1966.

73. Rose, S.: A general practitioner approach to the asthmatic patient. Am. J. Clin. Hypn., *10:*30, 1967.

74. Saul, L.J., and Bernstein, G., Jr.: The emotional settings of some attacks of urticaria. Psychosom. Med., *3:*349, 1941.

75. Sinclair-Gieben, A.H.C.: Treatment of status asthmaticus by hypnosis. Br. Med. J., *2:*1651, 1960.

76. Sparer, P.J.: Personality, Stress and Tuberculosis. New York, International Universities Press, 1956.

77. Stanton, H.: Weight loss through hypnosis. Am. J. Clin. Hypn., *18:*34, 1975.

78. Sutton, P.H.: A trial of group hypnosis and autohypnosis in asthmatic children. Br. J. Clin. Hypn., *1:*1, 1969.

79. Tilker, H.A., and Meyer, R.G.: The use of covert sensitization and hypnotic procedures in the treatment of an overweight person: a case report. Am. J. Clin. Hypn., *15:*15, 1972.

80. Traut, E.F., and Passarelli, E.W.: Placebo and the treatment of rheumatoid arthritis and other rheumatoid conditions. Ann. Rheumat. Dis., *18:*21, 1957.

81. Tullis, I.F.: Rational diet construction for mild and grand obesity. J.A.M.A., *226:*70, 1973.

82. Vaughan, W.T.: Practice of Allergy. St. Louis, C.V. Mosby, 1939.

83. Wick, E., *et al.:* Hypnotherapy and therapeutic education in the treatment of obesity: differential treatment factors. Psychiat. Q. *45:*234, 1971.

84. Wolberg, L.R.: Medical Hypnosis. vol. 1. New York, Grune & Stratton, 1948.

85. Wolff, H.G.: Headache and Other Head Pain. New York, Oxford University Press, 1948.

86. Wollman, L.: Hypnosis and weight control. Am. J. Clin. Hypn., *4:*177, 1962.

87. Wright, M.E.: Hypnotherapy and psychosomatic hypotheses. Am. J. Clin. Hypn., *8:*245, 1966.

88. Yanovski, A.G.: The feasibility of alteration of cardiovascular manifestations in hypnosis. Am. J. Clin. Hypn., *5:*8, 1962.

89. Zane, M.D.: The hypnotic situation and changes in ulcer pain. Int. J. Clin. Exp. Hypn., *14:*292, 1966.

90. Zeller, M.: Influence of hypnosis on passive transfer and skin tests. Ann. Allergy, *2:*515, 1944.

34

Hypnosis in Surgery and Anesthesiology

HISTORY

In this section, the "newer" clinical applications of hypnosis in surgery will be presented. Voltaire once said, "What is new is old, and what is old is not new." No further proof of this adage is needed than the following:

I put a long knife in at the corner of his mouth, and brought the point out over the cheekbone, dividing the parts between; from this, I pushed it through the skin at the inner corner of the eye, and dissected the cheek back to the nose. The pressure of the tumor had caused the absorption of the anterior wall of the antrum, and on pressing my fingers between it and the bones, it burst, and a shocking gush of blood, and brain-like matter, followed. The tumor extended as far as my fingers could reach under the orbit and cheekbone, and passed into the gullet—having destroyed the bones and partition of the nose. No one touched the man, and I turned his head into any position I desired, without resistance, and there it remained till I wished to move it again: when the blood accumulated, I bent his head forward, and it ran from his mouth as if from a leaden spout. The man never moved, nor showed any signs of life, except an occasional indistinct moan; but when I threw back his head, and passed my fingers into his throat to detach the mass in that direction, the stream of blood was directed into his wind-pipe, and some instinctive effort became necessary for existence; he therefore coughed, and leaned forward, to get rid of the blood; and I suppose that he then awoke. The operation was by this time finished, and he was laid on the floor to have his face sewed up, and while this was doing, he for the first time opened his eyes.

Although it may come as a surprise to the reader, this formidable procedure was performed by James Esdaile in India before 1850![24]

To undergo the knife during this period was tantamount to signing one's death warrant. Fear of pain was just as strong as fear of a fatal error by the surgeon. Many preferred death to the excruciating agony experienced during surgery. Those willing to undergo the ordeal usually screamed and struggled, which frequently affected the outcome. Some cursed, prayed, wept, or fainted. The operation invariably produced severe shock, depressive reactions, and other sequelae which delayed convalescence and wound-healing. Most operations were also a frightening procedure even for the calloused surgeon. Pain dominated the scene. Dupuytren summed up the situation for this period: "Pain kills like hemorrhage."

Four out of every 10 people died. Yet Esdaile's mortality rate was less than 5 per cent in a total of several hundred operations, about 300 of which were major procedures. The latter were all performed under mesmeric coma (hypnoanesthesia) and included the amputation of limbs and breasts and the removal of huge scrotal tumors. Even more interesting is the fact that Esdaile noted that neurogenic shock was noticeably diminished. This is remarkable, as he was without the benefit of anesthesia, modern-day asepsis, refined surgical technics, blood transfusions, and antibiotics. The significance of his observations was not recognized until recently.

RECENT DEVELOPMENTS

Today, more than a century later, hypnosis has been accepted as a valuable therapeutic adjunct to potentiate chemo-anesthesia. However, modern-day hynotherapists have modified the technics developed by Esdaile, Elliotson, Parker, Cloquet, and other hardy pioneers of the past century. The most significant developments in this area include the use of autohypnosis, suggestions to improve the postoperative period, glove "anesthesia," and autogenic training. The last named technic, developed by Schultz, employs a rehearsal or a "dry run" of the intended surgery.[50] This type of conditioning protects the patient against surprise, fear, and apprehension: the pain threshold is automatically raised by "blocking" the neurophysiologic paths that transmit the painful afferent impulses. No doubt a similar mechanism explains the marked difference in pain perception between most primiparas and multiparas; if one knows what to expect, the fear of the unknown is removed, and painful impulses are to some degree decreased in intensity.

In this connection, it is interesting that one of our patients (Case 1) complained of pain only when the towel clips were placed on her abdomen, prior to the skin incision. This apparently minor detail was inadvertently left out of the rehearsal. Several other patients operated on under hypnoanesthesia had similar experiences, indicating how well perceptual awareness can be organized into a variety of reactions, depending on the range of the adaptive processes.

Hypnoanesthesia has been used successfully for many other major and minor surgical procedures.[12, 26, 30, 34, 40, 47, 54, 55, 56, 58] Field used taped instructions for dealing with the emotional stress of surgery.[25] The results were attributed to patients' satisfaction rather than improved response to surgery.

Despite its effectiveness in major surgery, hypnosis will never be a substitute for chemoanesthesia, since it can be utilized in less than 10 per cent of the cases, and these must be very *carefully selected*. This figure may be a little high for major surgical procedures, such as laparotomies and amputations, but it is a conservative estimate if minor surgical procedures are included. Then, too, a great many individuals using hypnosis, including the author, do not report their cases unless they are medical firsts. The author recently administered the hypnosis for a vaginal hysterectomy, and near the end analgesia was given. This "contaminated" the hypnoanesthesia, and the case was not reported. The greatest use of hypnoanesthesia is to reduce the need for preoperative medication and chemoanesthesia. It also has other pre- and postoperative advantages.[36, 37, 38]

Systematic self-relaxation and self-suggestion to mitigate the discomfort following open heart surgery has been described.[31] However, it has been demonstrated that encouragement and reassurance without hypnosis reduced postoperative pain.[23]

ADVANTAGES AND DISADVANTAGES

Since the use of hypnosis allays fear and tension, induction of inhalation anesthesia is facilitated, anoxemia is reduced, and, because of the profound relaxation, less analgesia and anesthesia are required. In some patients the traditional preoperative administration of morphine, meperdine hydrochloride (Demerol), and pentobarbital sodium often can be eliminated even in those who can enter only the light stage of hypnosis. It is believed that, even in minimal doses, most analgesic agents produce some degree of respiratory depression and lower the blood-oxygen volume. Beecher states, "Narcotics are not necessary for preanesthetic medication but their presence is actually harmful."[2] He found that in patients on placebo medication (0.6 mg. of atropine sulfate), experienced anesthesiologists could not differentiate between those who had received the narcotic and those who had received the placebo. Since this form of suggestion is so effective, obviously hypnoanesthesia would be more efficacious.

Postoperatively, hypnosis is of inestimable value when it is used in suitable patients. For instance, when surgical patients wake up, they usually are afraid to cough because of excessive pain, especially those having upper abdominal operations. In good subjects, trained to enter quickly into hypnosis, fear, and often pain, may be eradicated in a matter of seconds by posthypnotic suggestion.

Through specific posthypnotic suggestions also, the breathing and the cough reflex can be regulated readily. Because of the extreme relaxation, hypnosis also facilitates aspiration through the tracheobronchial passages; this prevents pneumonitis and atelectasis. Excessive postoperative retching usually can be decreased and, in good subjects, this annoying complication can be entirely prevented by posthypnotic suggestions.

The chief disadvantage of hypnosis is its unpredictability and its effectiveness; not every patient responds as expected. Moreover, in those that are hypnotizable, the muscular relaxation may be less than required. As emphasized in the section on dangers, it should not be employed in severely disturbed persons, zealots, or "crackpots."

Unless the hypnotic conditioning is performed in a group, the procedure can be time-consuming; several hours of preparation may be required. However, since hypnosis is seldom utilized as the anesthetic agent *per se,* the unpredictability is not a deterrent—even if only partially successful, its advantages outweigh its disadvantages.

INDICATIONS AND REVIEW OF THE LITERATURE

Pharmacologic analgesia and anesthesia, with their ease of administration and effectiveness, are the methods of choice over pure hypnoanesthesia for major surgery because of their reliability. However, where there is a definitive contraindication to all types of chemoanesthesia, hypnoanesthesia is indicated.

Hypnosis, in combination with anesthesia, also can be employed routinely for the poor surgical risk as well as for the debilitated and geriatric patient undergoing major surgery. It also encourages early ambulation, acceptance of surgical deformities, as, for instance, enteric stomas, maintenance of morale during a stormy convalescent period, alleviation of bizarre types of pain and earlier intake of fluids.

The combined approach has been used by Marmer for a thoracotomy for heart disease.[42] Another patient, a 42-year-old woman, underwent mitral commissurotomy after receiving only hexylcaine hydrochloride topically for endotracheal intubation and succinylcholine chloride intravenously for muscular relaxation. This patient required no postoperative narcotics or sedatives and manifested total operative amnesia. Marmer concluded that the reassurance induced by hypnosis allays fear, anxiety and tension more effectively than the tranquilizing drugs.

Doberneck and co-workers utilized hypnosis as a pre- and postoperative adjunct in the treatment of 99 surgical cases, including the post-gastrectomy or "dumping" syndrome, postoperative pain, obesity (treated before surgery to lessen the operative risk) and various bizarre forms of pain.[17] Striking improvement occurred in 94 per cent of the patients with the dumping syndrome; 26 out of 32 gained an average of 5.4 pounds over an average 14-month follow-up. Posthypnotic suggestions in 31 cases before surgery significantly decreased their postoperative narcotic requirements; the patients were more cooperative and cheerful and less complaining. The relief of various forms of bizarre pain was sometimes spectacular, even occurring several times in patients who had had one to three unsuccessful cordotomies. Hypnosis was particularly effective in unexplained low back pain and pain of metastatic cancer.

Hypnosis is particularly useful for phantom limb pain[9, 19] as well as for the dumping syndrome.[20] The gastric symptoms were present from 8 to 26 months. Two to nine hypnosis sessions were required for remission in four patients. Suggestions were directed toward reduction of tension, removing the fear of the illness, and increasing food and liquid consumption by improving the olfactory appeal of the food itself. Many investigators have used hypnosis in patients who had severe burns; the dressings could be changed without discomfort.[4, 27, 32, 42, 48, 52] Nutritional illnesses are generally helped by the increased caloric intake. Pain, flatulence, and anorexia often respond dramatically; skin grafting is facilitated.

Postoperative hiccoughs are often an annoying complication of surgery. Dorcus and Kirkner observed that hypnosis produced muscular relaxation and alleviated anxiety in a series of 18 cases that were refractory to all other therapies.[20] Fourteen patients were permanently relieved, three were not helped, and one benefited temporarily. The author cured two refractory cases of postoperative hiccoughs—one following removal of the gallbladder and the other following a transurethral resection—in one session of hypnosis. Postoperative urinary retention often responds to hypnosuggestive therapy.[11, 18]

Hypnosis is of value in plastic surgery and for dermabrasion.[21, 22, 53] Patients requiring extensive suturing of facial lacerations or intermaxillary wiring of fractures of the mandible and the max-illa do not have airway problems under hypnosis. In most of these cases, a general anesthetic would be hazardous. The apposition of two widely separated areas can be maintained through posthypnotic suggestions while a tissue graft is being transferred from one to the other. Kelsey and Barron secured fixation by these means instead of a plaster of Paris cast, which is uncomfortable, causes sores, immobilizes the joint, and produces a stiffness that may require weeks of physiotherapy. Some subjects under hypnosis can be placed in bizarre postures; their limbs remain fixed until suggestions are given for their release.

Kelsey and Barron described a patient whose right foot was to be repaired with a pedicle graft from the abdomen transported via the left forearm. Under hypnosis, the left arm was fixed in rigid catalepsy against the abdomen through posthypnotic suggestions. This was so effective that it could not be moved voluntarily, nor could it be moved by attendants until it was "unlocked" by later hypnotic suggestions. The position was maintained until released at the next operation 3 weeks later. It was astonishing that, from the moment of release, movement of the elbow and the shoulder joints was full, free, and painless. A similar procedure was adopted for the transfer of the pedicle from the wrist to the forepart of the foot. The arm and the wrist were again placed in the optimal position and locked there under hypnosis. This position was maintained for 28 days, during which the patient slept sitting up! At the end of this time, the arm was unlocked by appropriate posthypnotic suggestions. Immediately, the movements of all the joints, including those of the spine and the fingers, were once again full, free, and painless. Physiotherapists and nurses were trained to reinforce the hypnosis.

A similar and more extensive report describes 13 patients who had pedicle and flap graft surgery.[51] Improved morale and marked drug reduction was observed. The real value of hypnosis lies in the positive outlook developed by the patient. The associated relaxation neutralizes pains and aches; insomnia is reduced. Limb projection, if attainable, makes it possible for the patient to feel subjectively that his limbs are in a different position. This is of obvious value during the fixation period required during plastic surgery. A bilateral mammoplasty on a tense and fearful patient

has been reported.[44] It is believed that hypnosis is valuable for relieving the pain of injuries sustained in accidents.[10, 44] Hypnosis has been effective in the setting of fractures and the repair of lacerations.[44] Hypnosis has been used in disguised form, especially in children, to perform minor surgical procedures.[1, 5, 14, 33] With light analgesia and hypnoanesthesia, they also react better and have smoother recoveries. Vaughn has performed an amazing number of all types of major surgery under a combination of light anesthesia and hypnosis. Several amputations of limbs were included in his series.* Bowen has reported on a transurethral resection under self-hypnosis.[8] Cataract excision has been reported.[49]

Hypnosis is a very valuable adjunct for the relief of bizarre types of postoperative pain, such as unexplained backache and abdominal pain, and for controlling the intractable pain of the terminal cancer patient. Through posthypnotic suggestion, autohypnosis and glove anesthesia, the need for opiates is markedly reduced. More important, strong faith and the "will to live" can be exceedingly helpful.

Obstinate constipation following surgery often responds dramatically to appropriate posthypnotic suggestions. Here, too, the posthypnotic suggestions must be directed toward the subjective feelings associated with the act. Werbel[1] used posthypnotic suggestions to prevent posthemorrhoidectomy pain in a series of 11 patients.[57] Their course was compared with that of the same number of other patients who were not hypnotized and acted as a control group. The first group was advised that rectal pain would not be felt after the surgery, that they would have relaxed bowel movements. All were cued to enter hypnosis readily. Not a single person in the hypnotized group had severe pain, and eight claimed to have less discomfort than anticipated. Its use has been described in anorectal surgery.[15]

MECHANISM OF HYPNOANESTHESIA

Though the mechanism of hypnoanesthesia is as yet poorly understood, current research indicates that the pain, perceived in the tissues, does not reach the pain receptors in the higher

*Vaughn, V.: Personal communication.

brain centers during hypnosis. With the higher cortical centers inhibited during deep hypnosis, the reticular formation and other subcortical centers prevent the intrusion of painful impulses into awareness. This raises the adaptive responses of the organism to them (painful stimuli). Further psychophysiologic investigations are needed to elucidate the mechanisms by which hypnosis reduces neurogenic shock in surgery.

From an operational standpoint, a subject is relieved of pain when he becomes "relatively inattentive and unconcerned about all stimuli to which the hypnotist does not specifically direct his attention." If the readiness to respond is minimized, "the sensation of pain" is no longer "painful"; it is an isolated "sensation" unaccompanied by pain.

TECHNICS FOR SURGERY

In order to reduce the surgical candidate's apprehension, the author always has a preliminary discussion with the patient, which may be as follows: "I have taught you hypnotic relaxation. You have demonstrated that you can enter into a very deep state of relaxation and be completely oblivious to all discomfort. Remember you will relax deeper and deeper with each breath you take. You also were able to achieve glove anesthesia readily. Before being taken to the operating room, you will transfer this glove anesthesia to the right side of your abdomen (or wherever the surgical field may be). You will have no more discomfort than you are willing to bear. Should you have even the slightest amount of discomfort, an anesthetic will be available upon your request —either gas, spinal, or procaine. There is no need to have the slightest anticipation because either way you will have a very pleasant experience. You can look forward to your operation without dread or anxiety. I will be present during the entire surgical procedure and will do everything possible to make you comfortable and free from tension." When using surgical hypnoanesthesia, the patient must be watched carefully. If there is any sign of severe pain manifested by a facial flinch or a grimace, supplementary chemoanesthesia is necessary. Fewer than 10 per cent of

individuals can go through an entire major surgical procedure *without* chemoanalgesia or anesthesia. Therefore, pain relief should not be limited to hypnotic methods, but one must use the balanced approach—hypnoanesthesia together with chemoanesthesia.

With reference to conduction anesthesia, at least half the success of local infiltration is *vocal*. The ideal method is the joint use of hypnoanesthesia and local anesthesia. One must continually reassure the apprehensive patient in a calm, confident, reassuring voice. Each patient must be inculcated with the idea that the hypnoanesthesia is going to help alleviate his fear and anxiety. The patient picks up this confidence, and he relaxes even further.

REHEARSAL TECHNIC

During a typical rehearsal session for abdominal surgery the patient is told, "Now your skin is being sterilized." (At this time the abdomen is swabbed with an alcohol sponge.) "I am now stretching the skin and making the incision in the skin." (The line of incision is lightly stroked with a pencil.) "Now the tissues are being cut. Just relax. You feel nothing, absolutely nothing. Your breathing is getting slower, deeper and more regular. Each side of the incision is being separated by an instrument." (The skin and the muscles are pulled laterally from the midline.) "Now a blood vessel is being clamped." (A hemostat is clicked shut.) "You feel absolutely no discomfort. You are calm, quiet and relaxed. Your breathing is getting slower, deeper and more regular. Just relax! Now I am going deeper and entering the abdominal cavity." (For the peritoneum, suggestions of relaxation and assurances of complete pain relief are repeated several times.) "Just relax. You are getting deeper and deeper relaxed; your heartbeat is getting slower and more regular. Just relax. You feel nothing, absolutely nothing." The viscera are relatively insensitive to cutting—one does not have to worry about pain. However, the patient has to be prepared for the discomfort produced by pulling and torsion of the abdominal organs.

The steps for closure of the peritoneum, muscles, fascia and skin are also described in a similar manner. There are really only three times when pain can be expected: when the skin is incised, when the peritoneum is incised, and when one is tugging on the viscera.

MAINTENANCE OF HYPNOANESTHESIA DURING SURGERY

The following is a verbalization for maintaining hypnosis: "All the muscles in your body are relaxed, and, with every breath you take, you will find yourself going deeper and deeper relaxed. You are doing fine. Just relax all the muscles of your abdomen and chest. You are breathing slower, deeper, and more regular. That's right. In and out . . . in and out. Going deeper and deeper relaxed. You feel nothing except a little pressure. The more relaxed you are, the less tension you will have, and the less tension you have, the less discomfort you will have." Frequently there is a slight trembling of the eyelids. This often is indicative of deep hypnosis. One can use this objective sign to deepen the hypnosis, as follows: "I notice that your lids are now trembling. That's a good sign. And, as they continue to tremble, you will go deeper and deeper relaxed. You feel yourself falling, falling, deeper and deeper relaxed with every breath you take. Remember, if you want to open your eyes at any time, you may. Voices won't bother you."

Production of catalepsy by light stroking of the skin frequently minimizes capillary bleeding, probably as the result of vasospasm. Here the law of dominant effect is put to use: a psychological suggestion is enhanced by a physiologic effect. As the region that is going to be operated on is stroked lightly, I remark: "This area is getting very stiff, cold and numb. Think, feel and imagine that there is an ice cube on your skin. Now it is getting more numb and colder. Numb and cold. Very, very cold." This verbalization and the stroking are most advantageous where bleeding from the skin is expected.

If the hypnosis fails during surgery, one can easily switch to intravenous or inhalation anesthesia. It is always advisable to have these available for prompt use.

POSTOPERATIVE VERBALIZATION FOR DEHYPNOTIZATION

Patients are dehypnotized as follows: "You will feel just as if you have awakened from a deep sleep, but, of course, you know you were not asleep. You will be very, very relaxed. Any time in the future when I touch you on the right shoulder, if I have your permission, you will close your eyes and let your eyeballs roll up into the back of your head. Then you will count backward from 100 to zero slowly, and you will go deeper and deeper relaxed with every breath you take and every number you count. You will find that the period after your operation will be a very pleasant one. Should you have any discomfort in and around the wound, you may use the glove anesthesia which you learned to develop to 'knock it out.' You will be able to relax and sleep soundly. Should you require medication for sleep, it will make you very sleepy. You will not hesitate to eat the food given to you and, as a matter of fact, you will relish every bite. You will be very, very hungry. The more nutritious food you are able to consume, the faster your tissues will heal. I am going to count to five and you will open your eyes." Dehypnotization should be done slowly: "You will feel completely alert, refreshed, and wonderful after you open your eyes. One, you are feeling fine. Two, more alert. Three, still more alert. Four, sound in mind, sound in body, no headache. Five, open your eyes. You feel wonderful."

Marmer and other practitioners use posthypnotic suggestions to ensure a better postoperative recovery as the patient is emerging from the chemoanesthesia.[3, 43, 58] These are repeated again and again while the patient is in the recovery room to provide additional reenforcement.

When general anesthesia is used with hypnosis, the sense of hearing may be acute during the state of analgesia. All remarks should be guarded when in this stage, especially if heavy doses of muscle-relaxant drugs have been given with resultant controlled respiration. Some investigators believe that trauma which may adversely alter the postoperative state can be inflicted by careless remarks.

DISGUISED TECHNIC

The following disguised technic is excellent for patients requiring minor surgery. It makes use of misdirection of attention. First, a bandage or a towel is placed over the patient's eyes. I state: "You are now going to go into a deep state of relaxation. Just close your eyes. Start breathing. Breathe slowly and deeply. With each breath you take, you will feel yourself going deeper and deeper relaxed. And, if you wish to go deeper, all you have to do is start counting backward from 100 to zero. Breathe slowly, deeply and more regularly. And with each number that you count backward, and with every breath you take, you will feel yourself going deeper and deeper relaxed. Now I am inserting the first stitch." (The needle is gently placed on the edge of the wound; no pressure is employed.) "There, the first stitch is in. You did not feel any pain, did you?" (The patient shakes his head.) "Just relax deeper and deeper and deeper, and with each breath you take, you will feel nothing. Now, here is the second stitch." (Again one resorts to the same procedure—a hallucinated stitch.) If one maintains a steady flow of words, such as, "You are going deeper and deeper relaxed," the individual will enter into deep hypnosis without being aware that it is being employed. After rigid catalepsy is produced, anesthesia for the entire area can be suggested. Because belief has been compounded into conviction of anesthesia, it will now be produced automatically. On numerous occasions I have been able to sew up extensive lacerations without the patient's awareness that hypnosis had been induced—all without discomfort.

CASE REPORTS

The following case reports illustrate how hypnoanesthesia, *without the use of any type of analgesia or anesthesia,* can be employed for major and minor surgery. All the patients were prepared by autohypnosis, glove anesthesia, and the rehearsal technic. During the rehearsal method, every detail in the surgery was fully described while the patient was under deep hypnosis. It should be emphasized that there are few indications for pure hypnoanesthesia. Nor does

this author advocate an "all-or-none" approach. However, the following cases were performed under rigidly controlled conditions to demonstrate the authenticity of hypnoanesthesia. The patients, with the exception of Case 1, were selected carefully. This is an important point to consider, as it would be impossible to perform an abdominoperineal resection or lobectomy by hypnosis *per se.*

CASE 1

Mrs. E. W., aged 18, had an extensive excision biopsy for a benign tumor of her left breast. This unselected patient was used to demonstrate the possibilities of hypnoanesthesia before a closed circuit telecast at the annual meeting of the New York State Society of Anesthesiologists in December, 1956.

I saw this patient for the first time the night before surgery and explained the advantages of hypnoanesthesia. On the first attempt, in the presence of the hospital's chief of anesthesiology, Dr. Vincent Collins, she was placed in a deep somnambulistic trance. An indirect and permissive hypnotic technic was employed. The patient was instructed in the method of developing "glove anesthesia" in her right hand and transferring this anesthesia to her left breast. After she had demonstrated satisfactorily that she could do this with ease, a number 15 needle, about 6 or 7 inches in length, was readily passed completely through the breast from the lateral to the medial border. No sign of pain was manifested, nor was there any bleeding. The patient developed a spontaneous amnesia for the entire procedure.

The next day, the surgeon, Dr. W. Mitty, removed the tumor. The start and the finish of the surgery were shown over the telecast and in the presence of a distinguished panel of anesthesiologists. The surgeon noted the marked relaxation of the tissues, the decrease in bleeding, the complete immobility of the patient and the absence of pain or discomfort. He also stated that he could have performed more extensive surgery, adding, "I would not have believed it if I had not actually done and seen it."

Upon termination of the surgery, the patient was alerted and had absolutely no recollection of the operation. I asked her if she was ready to undergo the surgery, and she answered "Yes." On my telling her that the tumor had been removed, she evinced considerable surprise and incredulity. In this instance the posthypnotic amnesia was similar to Esdaile's mesmeric coma. The amnesia could have been removed; this is optional and depends on whether or not the patient wishes to remember any part of the surgical procedure. No preoperative or post-operative medication of any type was used for pain relief, and the patient made an uneventful recovery.

This case is particularly interesting because only one training session was needed, and the entire procedure and the surgery were conducted under extremely difficult conditions. On reflection, the successful outcome can be explained by the following facts: I needed a patient for the telecast demonstration of hypnosis in surgery; this was the only one available, and I just had to induce hypnoanesthesia. It was my determination and self-confidence that established the necessary rapport between the patient and myself and this increased her inherent susceptibility to hypnosis. All these factors contributed to Esdaile's successful use of mesmeric anesthesia.

CASE 2

Mrs. G. D., a 28-year-old Para II, gravida II, had an elective cesarean-hysterectomy performed at the Chicago Lying-in Hospital by Dr. S. T. DeLee, without analgesia or anesthesia. This is believed to be the first such case on record.[39]

The patient experienced no objective or subjective discomfort. She was fully conscious and able to watch the birth of her baby, and there was no discomfort when the baby was delivered by forceps or when the uterus was extirpated. The patient made an uneventful recovery.

CASE 3

Mrs. R. W., aged 27, had a subtotal thyroidectomy *under hypnotic anesthesia per se.* This, too, is believed to be the first such case reported. She was seen eight times; trained to enter a somnambulistic state; and exhibited all the phenomena of deep hypnosis, such as amnesia, age regression, catalepsy, disassociation, glove anesthesia and autohypnosis.

During the last training session, a complete "dry run" rehearsal of the "removal" of the thyroid was done while deeply hypnotized. That anesthesia could be produced by disassociation or glove anesthesia indicates that a subject, even in a hypnotic state, is not at all subservient to the will of the operator.

Through preoperative posthypnotic suggestions she slept for 8 hours. The next morning, the prearranged cue induced a deep hypnotic state. No trace of nervousness was discernible, although she had been extremely fearful and tense the week prior to surgery, so much so

that it was necessary to reassure her that she was "not going to die." Because of their extreme nervousness, hypnotic relaxation is particularly indicated in hyperthyroid and hypertensive individuals who require surgery.

The patient was taken to the operating room in a state characterized by profound neuromuscular relaxation. She transferred the glove anesthesia and produced complete insensibility of the neck. The entire procedure, the removal of both lobes of the thyroid, was performed without discomfort except for the period of traction on the trachea. Immediately after surgery, she sat up, talked and drank a glass of water! She was able to eat immediately and had no nausea or vomiting. The entire operation took about 70 minutes, and the patient stated, "I felt no pain at any time. I could feel only pressure and tugging at my throat. The scalpel felt like a feather being drawn across my neck." She made a completely uneventful recovery and was not confined to bed during the 5 days in the hospital. The hospital personnel were amazed at the patient's progress; no analgesic drugs were required.

In Cases 2 and 3, not a single bleeder had to be clamped in the skin, probably because of the local ischemia induced by the rigid catalepsy usually associated with deep hypnosis. There was no sign of neurogenic shock, nor did the blood pressure fluctuate appreciably in either case! However, it must be emphasized that these patients were somnambules, and constitute a small percentage of the population. But most individuals can be hypnotized to some degree, and for these hypnosis can potentiate chemoanesthesia.

Crasilneck and Hall discuss other uses of hypnosis in surgery.[13] They stress that hypnosis can decrease the need for inhalation anesthesia in the presence of pulmonary infection, that movement can be restricted during delicate surgery under local infiltration, and that patient response is a necessary factor, as in chemopallidectomy. They also describe how the electroencephalogram can be monitored during brain surgery.

Meares discusses the relief of pain of organic origin.[45] He uses hypnosis to dull the critical faculties and to countercondition anxiety. He uses dissociation by autohypnosis and an atavistic regression in passive hypnosis to dull alertness to pain. He allows the patient to experience the pain in its pure form, and then conditions the patient by exposing him to increasingly severe, painful stimuli until he develops greater regression and no longer experiences pain.

CONCLUSIONS

Since hypnosis is a multifaceted tool, its effectiveness can be enhanced when it is employed in conjunction with other medical procedures. All physician-hypnotists who use hypnoanesthesia should recognize the limitations of this modality and not try to operate on every patient without careful selection, preparation, and availability of chemoanesthesia. This should promote a healthier acceptance of hypnosis, especially if its advantages are utilized judiciously.

REFERENCES

1. Antich, J.L.: The use of hypnosis in pediatric anesthesia. J. Am. Soc. Psychosom. Dent. Med., *14:*70, 1967.
2. Beecher, H.K.: Preanesthetic medication. J.A.M.A., *157:*242, 1955.
3. Benson, V.: One hundred cases of post-anesthetic suggestion in the recovery room. Am. J. Clin. Hypn., *14:*9, 1971.
4. Bernstein, N.R. Observations on the use of hypnosis with burned children on a pediatric ward. Int. J. Clin. Exp. Hypn., *13:*1, 1965.
5. Betcher, A.M.: Hypno-induction techniques in pediatric anesthesia. Anesthesiology, *19:*279, 1958.
6. Bonello, K.B., *et al.:* Experience with hypnosis and surgical service. Milit. Med., *126:*364, 1961.
7. Bowen, D.E.: Transurethral resection under self-hypnosis. Am. J. Clin. Hypn., *16:*132, 1973.
8. Bowen, W.F.: Hypnosis: useful adjunct in surgery. Surg. Bull., *46:*8, 1966.
9. Cedercreutz, C.: Hypnosis in treatment of phantom limb pain. Finska Laksalls Hendl., *95:*170, 1952.
10. ———: Hypnosis in surgery, Int. J. Clin. Exp. Hypn., *9:*93, 1961.
11. Chiasson, S.W.: Hypnosis in postoperative urinary retention. Am. J. Clin. Hypn., *6:*366, 1964.
12. Crasilneck, H.B., and Hall, J.A.: Clinical hypnosis in problems of pain. Am. J. Clin. Hypn., *15:*153, 1973.
13. ———: Clinical Hypnosis: Principles and Applications. New York, Grune & Stratton, 1975.
14. Daniels, E.: The hypnotic approach in anesthesia for children. Am. J. Clin. Hypn., *4:*244, 1962.
15. Day, W.A.: Use of hypnosis in anorectal surgery. Dis. Colon Rectum, *7:*331, 1964.
16. Dias, M.M.: Hypnosis in surgery. Rev. Brasil Med., *20:*318, 1963.
17. Doberneck, R.C., *et al.:* Hypnosis as an adjunct to surgical therapy. Surgery, *46:*299, 1959.
18. ———: The prevention of postoperative urinary retention by hypnosis. Am. J. Clin. Hypn., *3:*235, 1962.
19. Dorcus, R.M., and Goodwin, P.: The treatment of patients with the dumping syndrome by hypnosis. J. Clin. Exp. Hypn., *3:*200, 1955.
20. Dorcus, R.M., and Kirkner, F.J.: The control of hiccoughs by hypnotic therapy. J. Clin. Exp. Hypn., *3:*104, 1955.
21. Ecker, H.A.: Medical hypnosis in maxillo-facial and plastic surgery. Am. J. Surg., *98:*826, 1959.
22. ———: Hypnosis aid in plastic surgery. Factor, *6:*7, January 1960.
23. Egbert, D.L., *et al.:* Reduction of postoperative pain by encouragement and instructions of patients. N. Engl. J. Med., *270:*825, 1964.
24. Esdaile, J.: Mesmerism in India and Its Practical Application in Surgery and Medicine. Hartford, England, Silus Andrus & Son, 1850.
25. Field, P.: Effects of tape-recorded hypnotic preparation for surgery. Int. J. Clin. Exp. Hypn., *22:*54, 1974.
26. Finer, B.: Experience with hypnosis in clinical anesthesiology. Särtrych Ur Opuscula Medica, *4:*1, 1966.
27. Fogelman, M.J., and Crasilneck, H.B.: Food intake and hypnosis. J. Am. Dietetic Assoc., *32:*519, 1956.
28. Gentry, R.W.: Hypnosis in surgery (paper delivered at Pan American Medical Association, May 10, 1960).
29. Goldie, L.: Hypnosis in the casualty department. Br. Med. J., *2:*1340, 1956.
30. Grant, G.: Suggestion and hypnosis in surgery. Aust. J. Clin. Hypn., *2:*6, 1974.
31. Gruen, W.: A successful application of systematic self-relaxation and self-suggestion about postoperative reactions in a case of cardiac surgery. Int. J. Clin. Exp. Hypn., *20:*143, 1972.
32. Hartley, R.B.: Hypnosis for alleviation of pain in treatment of burns. Arch. Phys. Med., *43:*39, 1968.
33. Hoffman, E.: Hypnosis in general surgery. Am. Surg., *25:*163, 1959.
34. Jones, C.G.: Associated uses of hypnosis in surgery. Am. J. Clin. Hypn., *4:*270, 1962.
35. Kelsey, J.H., and Barron, R.R.: Hypnosis in plastic surgery. Br. Med. J., *1:*756, 1958.
36. Kolough, F.T.: Role of suggestion in surgical convalescence. Arch. Surg., *85:*304, 1962.

37. _____: Hypnosis and surgical convalescence: a study of subjective factors in postoperative recovery. Am. J. Clin. Hypn., *7:*120, 1964.

38. _____: The frightened surgical patient. Am. J. Clin. Hypn., *10:*89, 1968.

39. Kroger, W.S., and DeLee, S.T.: Use of hypnoanesthesia for cesarean section and hysterectomy. J.A.M.A., *163:*442, 1957.

40. Lassner, J.: Hypnosis in Anesthesiology: An International Symposium. Berlin, Springer-Verlag, 1964.

41. Le Baw, W.L.: Adjunctive trance therapy with severely burned children. Int. J. Child Psychother., *2:*80, 1973.

42. Marmer, M.J.: Hypnoanalgesia and hypnoanesthesia for cardiac surgery. J.A.M.A., *171:*512, 1959.

43. _____: Hypnosis in Anesthesiology. Springfield, Ill., Charles C Thomas, 1960.

44. Mason, A.A.: Surgery under hypnosis. Anesthesia, *10:*295, 1955.

45. Meares, A.: A System of Medical Hypnosis. Philadelphia, W.B. Saunders, 1960.

46. Mun, C.T.: The use of hypnosis as an adjunct in surgery. Am. J. Clin. Hypn., *8:*178, 1966.

47. Nayyar, S.N., and Brady, J.P.: Elevation of depressed skull fracture under hypnosis. J.A.M.A., *181:*790, 1962.

48. Pellicone, A.J.: Hypnosis as adjunct to treatment of burns. Am. J. Clin. Hypn., *2:*153, 1960.

49. Ruiz, O.R.G., and Fernandez, A.: Hypnosis as an anesthetic in opthalmology. Am. J. Ophthalmol., *50:*163, 1960.

50. Schultz, J.H.: Some remarks about techniques of hypnosis as anesthetic, Br. J. Med. Hypn., *5:*23, 1954.

51. Scott, D.L.: Hypnosis in plastic surgery. Am. J. Clin. Hypn., *18:*98, 1975.

52. Schafer, D.W.: Hypnosis use on a burn unit. Int. J. Clin. Exp. Hypn., *23:*1, 1975.

53. Steffanoff, D.N.: Maxillofacial surgery and hypnosis in the emergency and operating room. J. Am. Assoc. Nurs. Anesth., February 1961.

54. Tietelbaum, M.: Hypnosis in surgery and anesthesiology. Anesth. Analg., *47:*509, 1967.

55. Tinterow, M.M.: The use of hypnotic anesthesia for major surgical procedures. Am. Surg., *26:*732, 1960.

56. Van Dyke, P.B.: Some uses of hypnosis in the management of the surgical patient. Am. J. Clin. Hypn., *12:*227, 1970

57. Werbel, E.W.: Experiences with frequent use of hypnosis in a general surgical practice. West. J. Surg. Obstet. Gynecol., *68:*190, 1960.

58. _____: Hypnosis in serious surgical problems. Am. J. Clin. Hypn., *10:*44, 1967.

ADDITIONAL READINGS

Cheek, D. B.: Use of preoperative hypnosis to protect patients from careless conversation. Am. J. Clin. Hypn., *3:*101, 1960.

_____: Unconscious perception of meaningful sounds during surgical anesthesia as revealed under hypnosis. Am. J. Clin. Hypn., *1:*101, 1959.

Mahren, F. J.: Hypnosis and the surgical patient. Am. J. Proctol. *11:*459, 1960.

35

Pain, Acupuncture, and Hypnosis

NATURE OF PAIN

The exact nature of pain as well as the various mechanisms underlying the modulation of pain sensation are extremely complex and, at present, inadequately explained. One investigator has stated that there is no such thing as a pain fiber or even a pain neuron in the peripheral nervous system.[4] Pain is not a primary sensory modality, like seeing or hearing, but rather is, in part, an emotionally charged percept influenced to an astonishing degree by psychological factors. Moreover, allowing for variations in responses in humans, the *pain threshold* is more dependent on physiological factors,[7] whereas *pain tolerance* is influenced largely by psychological ones.[30]

The author has described elsewhere in this book how the pain tolerance is raised by various types of suggestive and/or hypnotic procedures *per se* in major and minor surgical operations, obstetrical conditions, and other problems such as headache, backache and pelvic pain. Therefore, the thrust of this chapter will be to explain some of the common denominators for hypnoanesthesia and acupunctural analgesia (A.A.). It is no mere coincidence that both of these valuable technics are ancient methodologies which are as yet poorly understood. However, even if A.A. turns out to be another form of the nonspecific placebo response, it *does* work—particularly for the Chinese—for the reasons mentioned below.

REASONS FOR EFFECTIVENESS OF HYPNOSIS AND ACUPUNCTURE

Both hypnosis and A.A. may have a similar neural basis and, therefore, may be opposite sides of the same coin. Hypnoanesthesia, like A.A., can be produced by different sensory inputs. As is the case with hysterical analgesia, the anesthesized areas follow no known segmental nervous distribution.

Clinically, A.A. would be better understood if it were realized that objective signs of hypnosis and a formal induction procedure are not necessarily required to induce analgesia and anesthesia.[1] Furthermore, few American scientist-observers of A.A. have had training or exposure to disguised or covert hypnotic induction technics for production of anesthesia. One might speculate as to what the acceptance of A.A. might be if the method had not received so much ballyhoo in recent years.

Empirically, the reasons for the clinical effectiveness of acupuncture in medical disorders have been discussed in numerous publications. Dimond succinctly summed it up when he stated, "A great deal of it is plain psychotherapy for psychosomatic complaints."[6] Melzack and Wall, whose gate theory has been used to explain the effectiveness of acupuncture, recognized the role of emotions in the perception of pain.[23] They state that ". . . relaxants, tranquilizers, sedatives, suggestion, placebos, and hypnosis exert a profound influence on pain. . . . These methods deserve more attention than they have received."

Other methods whereby pain can be obtunded employ counterirritation, such as heat (ignipuncture or moxibustion); acupressure and cupping; and transcutaneous electrical stimulation (by needles, electrodes, or static electricity). These methods, based on the distraction principle, work by diverting the attention to a stimulus other than the pain. The anxiety that ordinarily accompanies pain also is minimized by A.A., thus reducing fear and tension to raise the pain tolerance automatically.[11]

OPIATE RECEPTOR SYSTEM: ROLE OF ENDORPHINS IN PAIN

Recently, a dramatic breakthrough was made that may help to explain how pain tolerance can be increased by hypnosis and A.A. It has been discovered that the rat brain is equipped with specific opiate receptors.[26] Two different peptides have been isolated from pig brains, which were named methionine enkephalin and leucine enkephalin, respectively.[10] Subsequently, a compound named a-endorphin was isolated.[9] Both the enkephalins and a-endorphin manifested morphine-like activity which could be reversed by naloxone hydrochloride. It was suggested that all the opiate substances be referred to as endorphins.[8] As a class, the endorphins are similar to fragments of the pituitary hormone beta-lipoprotein and, like morphine, act as an analgesic. Some of these compounds may be inhibitory neurotransmitters of specific neuronal systems involved in pain perception. Like other pituitary polypeptides, the endorphins also act as hormones on distant organs.

Pomeranz suspected a hormonal mechanism to explain acupuncture and hypnosis before the endorphins were known to exist.[27] He and his co-workers tested A.A. on mice and compared the responses of intact, hypophysectomized, and sham-operated mice. The hypophysectomized group showed no analgesic effect; the others did. Pain blockade persisted for more than an hour. These researchers found that the opiate antagonist naloxone completely blocked A.A. in mice; saline-injected controls responded normally. Other researchers have demonstrated that

naloxone does not block hypnotically induced analgesia in humans, suggesting that another mechanism was involved.[27] Pomeranz believes that "hypnosis is ruled out by our anesthetized cats and by sham acupuncture."[27] It was postulated that acupuncture was driving the pituitary to release its endorphins. Another acupuncture-endorphin link was suggested by Goldstein, who noted that when specific brain areas in the rat were stimulated, pain tolerance was rapidly induced, with concomitant release of endorphins from their storage site in the brain. Apparently, the brain appears to compensate for the increased demand by synthesizing more peptides than usual.

While these exciting studies sound convincing with reference to the acupuncture-hypnosis controversy, one must consider that it is extremely difficult to extrapolate results from animal experiments to humans; in the latter, pain, as mentioned above, is mediated by complex psychological factors.

NEUROPHYSIOLOGY OF PAIN IN HYPNOSIS

Wykert has discussed the relationship of pain and hypnosis.[34] He posits that the activity of the rostroreticular system is dampened by hypnosis. The principal site of action is the lower (caudal) part of the reticular formation. It is here that pain impulses are blocked at the periphery, so that there is no central reception of pain. This is similar to the saturation threshold hypothesis advanced in Chapter 28, and also is in accord with Pavlov's internal inhibition—the neural mechanism postulated for hypnosis.

EXPLANATION OF ACUPUNCTURE IN TERMS OF CONDITIONING THEORY

Despite the spate of articles on acupuncture, the author still adheres to his published explanations of A.A.[14, 19] He believes that A.A. can best be understood in terms of a conditioning theory paradigm which often includes the preoperative use of Schultz's rehearsal method,[29]* desensitization, and "waking hypnosis." A comprehensive explanation of how A.A. works in "natural surgery," which the author was among the first to propose, includes the following significant variables: (1) a 5,000-year-old belief system; (2) the suggestive effects of the impressive charts, mannikins, and models with their meridians and spots; (3) Mao's words and exhortations on the subject, accepted as gospel; (4) the ideological fervor and evangelical zeal of the masses, resulting in patriotic adherence to Maoist doctrine; and (5) the characteristic stoicism of the Chinese.

Additional variables include (1) strong rapport; (2) motivation; (3) the conviction that A.A. would work; (4) the idea that the doctor must serve the patient (therefore, because he is convinced of the efficacy of A.A., his suggestions, either by words or actions, tend to reinforce the patient's suggestibility); (5) the knowledge that the State has done so much for the people that it knows what is best for them (A.A., like hypnoanesthesia, is a praiseworthy method as it markedly reduces the need for analgesia and anesthesia); (6) the special selection of patients, and wherever possible the mock rehearsal, of the various steps of the operation before surgery, in and out of the operating room by the same surgical team; (7) the training of patients in groups, which induces an "emotional contagion" and desire to please the doctor or group leader; (8) the mobilization of competitiveness which takes place in a group; (9) the use of preoperative analgesic agents and Novocain, which are nearly always employed singly or in combination during surgery; (10) the ritualistic placement of the needles; (11) the twirling of the needles, which produces distraction and acts as a powerful diversion; and (12) the teaching of yogic breathing and other relaxing exercises, where possible, for induction of calmness.

Some of the above-mentioned variables, though known to hypnotherapists, were appar-

ently overlooked by the first Western scientists who reported on A.A. For instance, pricking the Ho-ku points results in soreness and heaviness of the hand, and often the arm. This convinces the patient that the acupuncturist has the ability to produce even greater effects.[25] Hypnotists achieve the same effects when they insert large needles through the skin—which can readily be done at nonhypnotic levels—to impress the patient and, as a result, achieve a favorable mind-set. This prior indoctrination maneuver, like the "needling test" in A.A., is important for a successful outcome.

Chavez and Barber have advanced a six-factor theory similar to the author's explanations of A.A.[3] As usual they avoid the term hypnosis as they feel there is no need to explain A.A. by a term which at present cannot be defined. MacIntosh has remarked, "If someone will explain hypnosis to me, I am confident that the secret of acupuncture will be revealed at the same time."[21] However, it has been noted that those who responded well to acupuncture were the same persons who were good hypnotic subjects.[12]

The author has performed numerous major and minor surgical procedures *without analgesia or anesthesia* simply by using the rehearsal technic and hypnosis.[18] For want of a better name, I called the method "hypnosis," albeit the term is a misnomer. The patients reacted and looked like those shown in the official films made in the People's Republic of China.

Many investigators contend that A.A. is *not* due to any kind of hypnosis, because A.A. is used on a variety of animals. Ignored is an extensive literature on the "immobility reflex" (or I.R.), erroneously called "animal hypnosis."[13] Many animals develop the I.R. when held in restraint; they can be operated upon relatively painlessly. Therefore, the argument that animals can undergo surgery under A.A. does not invalidate the hypnosis hypothesis.

Those who cite that infants respond to A.A. and, therefore, are not amenable to hypnosis or Maoist teachings are not aware that swaddling or restraint produces the "still reaction"[33]; this raises the pain threshold.

Observations by others largely support the author's formulations about A.A.[2, 12, 19, 31] More re-

---

*After first hearing about this technic at a lecture given by the author at the Massachusetts General Hospital on December 13, 1972, Dr. P. D. White observed: "Now I know what the surgeon meant when he said it was the patient who helped me."

cently, Mann stated that "suggestion may be integral to A.A."[21] He demonstrated that the patient's belief in the effectiveness of acupuncture is crucial to its success. Acupuncture failed to produce analgesia to deep pin pricks in 90 per cent of subjects who were *not* told that it would be effective. Lee and co-workers found that it did not matter whether the needles were placed in the traditional meridian locations or in arbitrary fixed points.[20] Melzack states "every culture on every continent has developed its own type of acupuncture."[23] Thus the explanation for the Chinese puzzle falls into the realm of conviction phenomena—a sort of "tribal medicine."

SUMMARY

This presentation is not intended as a criticism of A.A. In the environment in which it is being applied, it is obviously the method of choice and should not be denigrated. The author's purpose is solely to clarify its *modus operandi* and to reconcile the mutually contradictory theories and the variegated formulations in an attempt to explain its scientific rationale. It is no mere coincidence that A.A. works as the sole analgesic agent in approximately the same number of patients (about 10–20%) as hypnoanesthesia, and for similar surgical conditions. Moreover, the indications, contraindications, limitations, and advantages are identical. It appears that mesmerism, the precursor of hypnotism, has been replaced by "needleism"!

The following conclusions may be drawn: (1) very responsive subjects are selected for A.A.; (2) "waking responsiveness" to suggestions is higher in such persons than commonly assumed; (3) the prestige of the doctor and acupuncturist makes it clear to patients that a high degree of responsiveness is desired and expected; and (4) the cultural setting facilitates or enhances suggestibility. This last factor is the crucial variable, and, therefore, requires a fuller understanding. Thus we should evaluate the socio-cultural and demand characteristics (expectations, roles and subliminal cues) as they appear in a regimented society such as China with the demand characteristics as they exist in the Occidental world. This accounts not only for variations in hypnotic phenomena, but

also applies in relation to the broad spectrum of psychologic experiences which have to do not only with well-known placebo responses, but also with more basic aspects of psychobiologic functions, such as attention, concentration, and perceptual awareness.

In a regimented society, the demand characteristics function in such a way as to bring about compliant behavior *without* the necessity of overt cooperation or motivational involvement. In a nonregimented society, there is much less evidence that compliance will be obtained unless cooperative behavior is elicited via strong interpersonal relationships or reward inducements, as designated in Mao Tse Tung's *New Thought Directives*. Thus the whole concept of acupuncture relates not only to hypnosis, but also to the whole aspect of behavioral shaping, in keeping with some of Skinner's contributions for one, and decidedly within the realm of the forming and shaping of adaptive behavior.*

The Chinese philosopher Lao-tse wrote 2400 years ago, "When the water is muddy, who can settle things? Only wait, and it will become clear."

REFERENCES

1. Barber, T.X.: A Scientific Approach to Hypnosis. New York, Van Nostrand, 1969.
2. Buser, P., and Viala, G.: A study on hypnosis in the rabbit. *In* Chertok, L. (ed.): Psychophysiological Mechanisms of Hypnosis. New York, Springer-Verlag, 1969.
3. Chavez, J.F., and Barber, T.X.: Needles and knives. Human Behav., 2:19, September 1973.
4. Crue, B.J.: Pain: Research and Treatment. New York, Academic Press, 1975.
5. DeBakey, M.E.: A critical look at acupuncture. Reader's Digest, September 1973, pp. 137–140.
6. Dimond, E.G.: Medical education and care in the People's Republic of China. J.A.M.A., *218:*1552, 1971.
7. Gelfand, S.: The relationship of experimental pain tolerance to pain threshold. Can. J. Psychol., *18:*36, 1964.
8. Goldstein, A.: Opioid peptides (endorphins) in pituitary and brain. Science, *193:* 1801, 1976.

---

*The author is indebted to Dr. Milton V. Kline for this concept. (Personal communication)

9. Guillemin, R., et al.: Endorphins, peptides, d'origine hypothalamique et neurohypophysaire a activité morphineominetique: Isolement et structure moleculaire de l'a-endorphin. C.R. Acad. Sci., *282:* 783, 1976.

10. Hughes, J., et al.: Identification of two related pentapeptides from the brain with potent opiate agonist activity. Nature, *258:*577, 1973.

11. Kaada, B.: Acupuncture analgesia. T. Norske Laegeforen, *94:*419, 1974.

12. Katz, R.L.: Pain, acupuncture, hypnosis. *In* Bonica, J.J. (ed.): Advances in Neurology. New York, Raven Press, 1974.

13. Klemm, W.R.: Use of the immobility reflex ("animal hypnosis") in neuropharmacological studies. Pharm. Biochem. Behav., *4:*85, 1976.

14. Kroger, W.S.: More on hypnosis and acupuncture. Soc. Clin. Exp. Hypn. Newsletter, *13:*2, 1972.

15. _____: Hypnotism and acupuncture. J.A.M.A., *220:*1012, 1972.

16. _____: Acupunctural analgesia: its explanation by conditioning therapy, autogenic training and hypnosis. Am. J. Psych., *130:*855, 1973.

17. _____: A scientific rationale for acupunctural analgesia. J. Psychosom., *14:*191, 1973.

18. _____: Current status of acupuncture in surgery, obstetrics and gynecology. *In* Greenhill, J. P. (ed.): Year Book of Obstetrics and Gynecology. Chicago, Year Book Medical Publishers, 1974.

19. _____: Acupuncture, hypnosis and magic. Science, *180:*1002, 1972.

20. Lee, P.K., et al.: Treatment of chronic pain with acupuncture. J.A.M.A., *232:*1133, 1975.

21. MacIntosh, R.: Tests of acupuncture. Br. Med. J., *3:*454, 1973.

22. Mann, F.: Suggestion may be integral to acupuncture anesthesia. Med. Tribune, May 16, 1973.

23. Melzack, R.: Med. Tribune, Aug. 23, 1973.

24. Melzack, R., and Wall, P.D.: Psychophysiology of pain. Int. Anesth. Con., *8:*31, 1970.

25. Paul, G.L.: Physiological effects of relaxation training and hypnotic suggestion. J. Abnorm. Psychol., *74:*425, 1969.

26. Pert, C.B., and Snyder, S.H.: Opiate receptors: demonstration in nervous tissue. Science, *179:*1011, 1973.

27. Pomeranz, B.H.: Endorphins may explain acupuncture. Med. World News, October 18, 1976, p. 54.

28. Saltoun, D.: Seeking the truth about acupuncture. Med. World News, May 4, 1973.

29. Schultz, J.H.: Some remarks about technics of hypnosis as anesthesia. Br. J. Med. Hypn., *5:*23, 1954.

30. Sternbach, R.A.: Pain Patients, Treats and Treatments. New York, Academic Press, 1974.

31. Tarpale, V., and Tarpale, I.: Clinical psychiatry. Arch. Gen Psychiatry, *29:*315, 1973.

32. Volgyesi, F.A.: Hypnosis of Man and Animals. Baltimore, Williams & Wilkins, 1966.

33. Wall, P.: The eye on the needle. New Scientist, *53:* 130, 1972

34. Wykert, J. (quoting Spiegel, H.): Scientist suggests acupuncture-hypnosis link. Psychiat. News, June 21, 1972.

ADDITIONAL READINGS

Bonilca, J.J.: Acupuncture Anesthesia in the People's Republic of China. J.A.M.A., *229:*1317, 1974.

De Jong, R.H.: Acupuncture anesthesia: Pricking the balloon. J.A.M.A., *237:*2530, 1977.

36

Hypnosis in Obstetrics

The use of hypnosis in obstetrics and surgery is not new. More than a century ago, mesmerism or hypnosis was one of the principal technics of pain relief for delivery. It was unfortunate that the discovery of inhalation anesthesia, in the middle of the last century, relegated hypnosis to undeserved oblivion.

In recent years, there has been a resurgence of interest in hypnoanesthesia.[29, 31, 32, 50] However, as stressed throughout this book, it will never be a panacea, nor will it ever supplant chemoanesthesia in parturition. Nevertheless, as the late J. B. DeLee once stated: "The only anesthetic that is without danger is hypnotism . . . I am irked when I see my colleagues neglect to avail themselves of this harmless and potent remedy."[15] Obstetricians are finally becoming aware of the use of hypnosis for obstetrical anesthesia as an adjunctive technic, as evidenced by the increasing number of reports.[39, 51, 53, 54]

SUSCEPTIBILITY OF THE SUBJECT

Unfortunately, hypnoanesthesia *per se* is effective in less than 20 per cent of *selected* patients. However, in this group, episiotomy, forceps delivery, and repair can be performed *without* analgesia or anesthesia. Approximately 50 per cent more can be carried through labor and delivery by a combination of hypnosis and drugs, preferably regional block. Where hypnosis potentiates chemoanesthesia, the combined method is better for this group than either method alone, as it permits a reduction of from 50 to 75 per cent in chemoanesthesia.

Conventional procedures are used for relieving pain in the remaining group, who are failures as far as hypnoanesthesia is concerned. However, by virtue of their exposure to prenatal hypnotic training, the majority of these are more cooperative and usually more relaxed, and regard their delivery as a most gratifying experience. Tom, who believes that hypnosis has a limited use in labor, comments, "It is interesting to note that, regardless of the results, all but one of the [73] patients thought that hypnosis was worthwhile and a great help during labor, and all wanted to use hypnosis again for the next delivery."[51] The exception was a patient who had an improperly conducted labor. Thus, even when hypnoanesthesia is only partially effective, repeated suggestions with or without medications can mitigate the discomfort of labor. This is not surprising, as there are two routes for pain transmission—one physical, the other emotional. With chemoanesthesia, only the physical route for perception of painful stimuli is blocked. Strong suggestion and/or hypnosis effectively blocks the emotional pathway for apperception of painful stimuli.

PERSONALITY FACTORS IN SUGGESTIVE ANESTHESIA METHODS

Candidates for both hypnosis and the "natural childbirth" method have been studied.[44] The author includes the Velvoski or psychoprophylactic relaxation method,[6, 10] education for childbirth,[22] the Lamaze method,[33] and the hypnoreflexogenous method[47] in the same category as natural childbirth—all are based on similar principles directed toward reducing anxiety by counterconditioning it with relaxation. In addition, these methods include a form of systematic desensitization to mitigate the fear of childbirth. These patients often have similar personality profiles as well as an identical need for these procedures. They usually have a high degree of compulsiveness and a desire to please the father-figure (the obstetrician). Generally, their choice of these methods is based on multiple factors of which fear of childbirth is only a superficial aspect. Other reasons are fear of pain in general, fear of death while unconscious, fear of losing control of themselves and injuring the baby, fear of what might be said when they lose consciousness, curiosity as to the birth process, and fear of pain as a punishment in cases in which the pregnancy is unwanted.

It has been contended that an emotionally mature attitude toward pregnancy is generally dependent on healthy psychosexual development. When a female approaches menstruation, marriage, sex, and motherhood with fear, it is only natural to expect anxiety during pregnancy and labor. Also, women who have rejected the feminine role, either because of latent or overt homosexuality or fixation at earlier levels of personality development (the infantile adult), are more than likely to have inordinate need for pain relief during childbirth. Unfortunately, too few patients seek the suggestive methods which are the methods of choice for a safe labor—both physically and psychologically—for mother and child.

COMPARISON OF HYPNOSIS, "NATURAL CHILDBIRTH," PSYCHOPROPHYLACTIC RELAXATION, AND OTHER METHODS

There is no doubt that the expectation of pain and fear associated with labor can be effectively relieved by suggestion and/or hypnosis. Education for childbirth by the "natural childbirth" methods or the other procedures mentioned above are aimed at establishing healthy attitudes and have the same purpose as hypnosis but cannot achieve as deep a relaxation or reduce discomfort to the same degree as the latter. Even the most ardent enthusiast of natural childbirth or the Lamaze method would not advocate it for major surgery.

An experienced observer will recognize that successful natural childbirth patients have been hypnotized to a degree; some have reached at least a light stage, and others a medium stage of hypnosis. For the most part, this is achieved without their being aware of it and usually without the knowledge of the obstetrician. Grantly Dick-Read remarks that many of his patients appear as if in a trance during the latter part of the first stage.[16] Thus, when natural childbirth and hypnosis are compared, it is obvious that both employ suggestion to raise the patient's pain threshold. Optimal results are attained, however, when the educational aspects of natural childbirth are combined with hypnosis to raise the pain threshold.

Psychoprophylactic relaxation, as recently developed in the Soviet Union, is yet another method of training or conditioning for childbirth, based on the principles of hypnosis and group dynamics. Those who have observed these classes in the Soviet Union have stated that the patients become absorbed in the instructions of the doctor, that his voice and manner are those of an experienced hypnotist, and that the appearance of those in attendance resembles that of persons in various states of hypnosis.[5] The total picture is one of confidence and faith. Oxygen administered by inhalation also has a highly suggestive effect. Since every citizen in the Soviet Union has heard the name of Pavlov since childhood, the element of prestige is high in any indoctrination method proposed by this eminent scientist. At the very least, it affords a definitive approach to eliminate fear about labor and delivery.

In a similar manner, in thousands of women, the educational and training methods establish a "power of positive thinking" about childbirth— a favorable mind-set. The prestige factor, along with belief, faith, confidence, the mind-set, and expectant attitude, provides the very basis for a hypnotic relationship. In psychoprophylactic relaxation, natural childbirth, progressive relaxation, autogenic training, and hypnosis, misdirection is produced by the various exercises learned in the classes, and these help to raise the pain threshold. Hilgard and Hilgard caution that even though the natural childbirth methods and hypnosuggestive methods overlap, there may be differences.[26] They state that "It is quite possible that the Read exercises can be taught satisfactorily to women who, in a strict sense, are not hypnotizable, even if more hypnotizable women achieve a state indistinguishable from hypnosis." They further discuss eight characteristics of hypnotic procedures in childbirth: (1) employment of a rehearsal procedure, (2) relaxation for deepening the hypnotic involvement, (3) use of symptom substitution, (4) displacement of the pain elsewhere, (5) direct suggestion of symptom relief, (6) indirect suggestions as glove anesthesia, (7) imaginative separation of the painful uterine contractions via fantasy evocation, and (8) posthypnotic suggestions to instill confidence.

ADVANTAGES OF HYPNOSIS

The benefits and the advantages of hypnosis in obstetrics are legion:

1. Reduction or eradication of fear, tension, and pain before and during labor with a consequent rise in the pain threshold.

2. Reduction of chemoanalgesia and anesthesia or their complete elimination in good hypnotic subjects.

3. Complete control of painful uterine contractions; the mother can choose to experience the sensations of childbirth or not, as she sees fit.

4. Decreased shock and speedier recovery.

5. Lessened incidence of operative delivery since the responsive patient cooperates more fully, particularly during the expulsive stage. Relaxation and anesthesia of the perineum are produced by autohypnosis or by direct suggestion from the hypnotherapist; this eases delivery, episiotomy, and suturing of the perineum.

6. Lack of undesirable postoperative effects such as may be encountered with drug anesthesia; hypnoanesthesia is also more readily controlled.

7. Hypnosis shortens the first stage of labor by approximately 3 hours in primiparae and by more than 2 hours in multiparae.

8. Hypnosis raises the resistance to fatigue, thus minimizing maternal exhaustion.

9. Hypnosis can be used in debilitated individuals, in those who have ingested food shortly before delivery, and in those who are allergic to drugs. Also, it is indicated in premature delivery.

10. Hypnotic rapport can be transferred to an associate, an intern or a nurse, or to the husband, any one of whom, without previous training, can readily induce and maintain the hypnotic state by means of a prearranged cue (this can be accomplished only with the patient's permission).

11. No elaborate education or ritualistic exercises are needed to achieve the strong interpersonal relationship essential to the success of childbirth under hypnosis. These *are* required in such pain-relieving technics as natural childbirth and psychoprophylactic and progressive relaxation, which are merely modifications of the hypnotic method.

12. There is no possibility that harm will be done to the mother or the baby by hypnoanesthesia. On the other hand, the literature offers a considerable amount of evidence that when drugs are given for pain relief they may decrease the oxygen supply to the fetus. Combined with other asphyxial factors such as trauma or difficult delivery, this may produce fetal anoxia and, in its wake, severe brain damage. With hypnoanesthesia, the danger of fetal anoxia is markedly decreased.

13. Childbirth under hypnoanesthesia is an intensely gratifying emotional experience for well-adjusted mothers. Hearing the baby's first cry or seeing him immediately after birth are thrills that mothers can never feel if they are "knocked out."

14. Hypnosis can be life-saving for mother and baby in obstetrical emergencies. Its successful application has been reported in abruptio placenta with delivery of a live baby.[24]

If these advantages were more widely known, more mothers would have their babies by hypnosis. If the pain threshold can be lowered by the anticipation of pain, it can be raised by eliminating the expectation of pain through hypnotic suggestion.

For generations, women have been "hypnotized" into thinking that they must have severe pain in childbirth by older, sadistic females who relate their "harrowing" experiences to impressionable young girls. Women do have pain in childbirth but, through appropriate training, they can be "dehypnotized" of these notions to reduce or eliminate the fear-tension-pain syndrome. In this manner, childbirth becomes a joyous experience which fulfills many of their unrecognized and unformulated needs.

Moya and James recently reported on the clinical and biochemical studies of 21 infants born to mothers under hypnosis, and compared these infants with a group of babies born under various anesthetic technics.[39]

They stated:

Serial determination of the acid-base status after birth showed a significantly greater ability of the hypnosis group to readjust rapidly and to recover from the asphyxia of birth. . . . These data indicate a definite superiority of the hypnosis group in establishing and maintaining effective ventilation which was not revealed by careful clinical examination alone.

DISADVANTAGES AND CONTRAINDICATIONS

Hypnosis is not without limitations and contraindications:

1. Despite the high percentage of people susceptible to some type of hypnosis, maximal relief of pain and discomfort can be achieved in only one out of four patients. This limits the application of hypnosis as the sole anesthetic.

2. Hypnotic induction can be affected easily by psychological factors: well-prepared hypnotic subjects often "go to pieces" when exposed to other screaming women in various stages of labor; good subjects are often "talked out of it" by apparently well-meaning friends and neighbors.

3. The added time required to achieve the rapport and the depth of hypnosis necessary for operative procedures is a potential problem. It can be solved, however, as group training for hypnoanesthesia becomes more widespread and more trained personnel become available.

4. A trained hypnotherapist must be available throughout the entire labor unless the patient can induce autohypnosis.

5. The prevailing misconceptions about hypnosis held by the laity prevent many patients from being more susceptible to hypnotic suggestion.

6. Hypnosis is contraindicated in a deeply disturbed individual, either psychotic or borderline-psychotic, except when employed by a therapist trained in psychiatry. However, there is little possibility that hypnosis *per se* can precipitate a psychosis. Most psychotics are difficult, almost impossible to hypnotize, but if they prove susceptible, the dangers are minimal.

Tom mentions five patients in whom neurosis or psychosis was exacerbated or precipitated, *all stemming from the work of one doctor,* who had been emotionally ill.[51] These cases are not documented, and it is obvious that, if a doctor is sick, he should not practice medicine.

7. Inappropriate remarks made to a hypnotized individual or a faulty interpersonal relationship between the hypnotist and the subject can be damaging. However, these dangers can arise at nonhypnotic levels in similar circumstances and they are always to be avoided.

8. Some psychiatrists contend that hypnosis fosters extreme dependency. This may be true, but a strong bond of dependency exists in every doctor-patient relationship, especially in obstetrical practice. This dependency is only temporary, however, and can be used to advantage during the early prenatal period to establish greater confidence in the obstetrician. As the patient is taught autohypnosis, the dependency is more or less dissolved.

PREPARATION OF THE PATIENT

When a woman asks to have a baby under hypnosis, there are three things that the hypnotherapist must ascertain: her reasons for choosing this form of anesthesia; possible contraindications, depending on her personality type; and her responsiveness to hypnotic suggestion.

DETERMINING RESPONSIVENESS

Since some patients are not susceptible to hypnosis *per se,* it is important for the therapist to ascertain the degree of rapport he can achieve and to assess the potentialities for hypnosis. This can be accomplished by attempting to induce a hypnotic state and then offering a posthypnotic suggestion. If the suggestion is followed, hypnosis is established. Subsequent training for deep hypnosis is not time-consuming if a posthypnotic suggestion to go deeper the next time is made during the initial session.

Hypnosis cannot be induced in some patients, due to a lack of motivation or rapport between them and a particular therapist. Rapport may be strong with one therapist and weak with another. It may even vary with the same therapist.

Hypnosis should never be attempted until a preliminary discussion has been held to remove all misconceptions and to enlighten the patient about hypnotic childbirth. The patient should be told that hypnosis does not always work by itself; that if only 20 per cent are partially successful, this is 20 per cent better than nothing; that the degree of success depends on the motivation; and that autohypnosis and the production of glove anesthesia are phenomena achieved by the patient.

If patients are doubtful, I generally remark: "Why not come to one of my prenatal classes and see what it's all about? If you think you wish to have your baby under hypnosis, you can join a class. Naturally, the more sessions you attend, the more you will understand about hypnosis. Then you can decide if you wish to continue."

REASONS FOR CHOOSING HYPNOANESTHESIA

Often a pregnant woman's reasons for choosing hypnoanesthesia may not be apparent. Many emotionally well-adjusted women who have an ardent desire for motherhood are seeking hypnotic childbirth. The majority of these women have a strong wish to experience all the pleasant feelings associated with delivery such as hearing the baby's first cry. Others wish to be fully aware and cherish the memory of this climactic event. These are bona fide reasons for seeking this type of delivery.

On the other hand, there are some women who seek hypoanesthesia who should be rejected because they are overzealous. Such patients usually have deep-seated feelings of inadequacy which they hope to lose by undergoing hypnosis— which is in their eyes a unique and, therefore, an ego-building experience. When these women are unable to get through labor and delivery under hypnosis alone, they feel a sense of failure and may become severely depressed. This is not an indictment of hypnosis. It is just something that

every practitioner of hypnosis should keep in mind, so that he will be alert to underlying personality disorders in prospective subjects. In working up the obstetrical patient who desires hypnoanesthesia, personality appraisal should be as routine as pelvic measurement.

TRAINING IN HYPNOSIS

Training in hypnoanesthesia may be carried out in private office sessions or in group training classes. In either case, the patient does not have to read extensively, carry out elaborate exercises, or necessarily be educated in the mechanisms of labor. She must only attend a varying number of sessions with the doctor, during which her pain threshold is raised and her hopes for an easy and uneventful delievery are enhanced.

All patients should be informed that analgesia and anesthesia *will be available on request,* should they need it. Moreover, they should be advised *not* to feel guilty about asking for it. They should also be told that they do not have to go through the entire labor and delivery under hypnosis *per se* just to please the therapist who, it should be explained, will not feel "hurt" if they require help. It should be stressed again and again that the purpose of hypnosis is to minimize, not to eliminate drug requirements. Since fewer than one out of four will be able to do without drugs altogether, none should be made to feel that they have to "sign a pledge" against anesthesia.

Ideally, hypnotic conditioning should begin during the third or the fourth month of pregnancy. The patient is hypnotized two or three times a month until maximal hypnosis is achieved. Exactly how many visits a patient will require before one can feel confident of satisfactory anesthesia is uncertain. It may vary from one to 20 or more sessions. Usually, if anesthesia is not obtained after 10 visits, the outlook for success is poor. Patients should be informed in advance that numerous sessions may be required to obviate discouragement.

During the conditioning period, the patient is taught auto- or self-hypnosis and "glove anesthesia." At each session, posthypnotic suggestions emphasize that the patient *need have no more discomfort than she is willing to bear.* Repeated conditioning enables the patient to reach deeper states of hypnosis and raises her pain threshold. Suggestions are made that she will look forward to her confinement with a feeling of joy and happiness instead of dread and apprehension. The more these posthypnotic suggestions are repeated, the more effective they become. The patient is told repeatedly that when labor begins she will promptly fall into deep hypnosis in response to a given cue—usually the touch on the right shoulder. With adequate preparation, a patient can enter into deep hypnosis in a matter of seconds by the shoulder signal. Glove anesthesia is best achieved through autohypnosis, and the area to be desensitized is chosen by the patient. This permissive approach directed toward teaching the patient to be self-reliant should stop the criticism that hypnosis fosters extreme dependency on an authoritarian figure.

Response to posthypnotic suggestions and production of autohypnosis and glove anesthesia during the prenatal training period presumptively indicates that the patient is ready for all stages of labor. An Allis clamp or a sterile needle may be used for testing the degree of anesthesia present in the perineum or the abdomen. Complete anesthesia during parturition is often accompanied by disassociation and amnesia, the active use of which is optional. For example, amnesia for part or all of the labor can be induced or removed in good hypnotic subjects according to the previously expressed wishes of the patient.

Verbalization for Glove Anesthesia

Glove anesthesia is produced as follows: "And now you will go into a deep, hypnotic state, way down, deeper and deeper! You are going to produce glove anesthesia. As I stroke this hand, it is going to get numb, heavy, and woodenlike. When you are sure that this hand has become numb, just as your gums would be after your dentist has injected procaine, you will then transfer this numbness to your face. *With every movement of your hand toward your face,* it will get more numb and woodenlike." (The hand moves to the side of the face.) "When it touches your face, press the palm of your hand close to your face" (the hand lifts and is pressed to the face), "and when you are certain that that numbness has transferred from your hand to your face, drop your hand and your arm. You are going deeper and deeper relaxed with every breath you take. You can just feel that numbness being transferred from your hand to your face. That's fine. Just fine. Excellent. Now, after you are certain that the area on your face is numb, you can remove your hand and it will be normal but your face will be anesthetized."

The glove anesthesia can be transferred to the abdomen by one or both hands. A posthypnotic suggestion can be given that the anesthesia can be transferred to the perineum at the appropriate time. As each site is anesthetized, the sensory proof of anesthesia can be demonstrated to the patient. However, one should remark, "Remember, you will *know* what I am doing, but you *will feel no pain* as I test for the degree of anesthesia." This is consistent with what is known of the phylogenesis of the nervous system. Since pain is the most primitive of all sensations, it does not have as much cortical representation as the other senses. Discriminatory sensations such as touch, having been acquired later, have more representation in the cortex.

MANAGEMENT OF LABOR

When labor actually begins, the patient induces autohypnosis. The physician also can induce hypnosis over the phone, or through another physician to whom he has transferred the rapport. An assistant, such as a nurse, can do it by handing the patient a written order to go into a deep state of relaxation. How it is done depends on the kind of conditioning and the cues the patient received during her training program. If the patient has not mastered autohypnosis, the doctor's presence is necessary for maintaining the hypnosis. Suggestions are given for complete anesthesia of the abdomen, the perineum and other hypersensitive areas.

The following is an actual verbalization taken from a tape recorder for the conduct of labor: "Now, Mary, you have been able to enter a deep state of relaxation through autohypnosis. Also, you have demonstrated that you can produce glove anesthesia and transfer this numb, heavy, wooden feeling to either side of the face. Now that you are in active labor, you will be able to develop the same anesthesia in both hands and transfer this numb, heavy, wooden feeling to the abdomen, in order to cut down the discomfort produced by your contractions (the word 'pains' is never used). You will also develop anesthesia of any other area of the body that I pick out, such as the area between the vagina and the rectum. This area will be without any feeling for a considerable length of time. Each time you practice producing the glove anesthesia, you will be able to maintain it for long intervals. When labor starts, you first will feel an ache which will begin in the back and then it will move around to the side of your belly. At this time, you will be able to use the autohypnosis and place yourself in a deep state of relaxation. Remember, you need have no more discomfort than you are willing to bear. Your labor contractions will get stronger and longer, and that is a good sign that you are making progress. Even though you know that the labor contractions are there, you will not be able to feel them. If the glove anesthesia does not relieve your discomfort completely, please do not feel guilty about asking for drugs, which will be available."

Eliminating the discomfort of labor does not impair those sensations and experiences that are a healthy part of natural parturition. A well-trained and responsive patient, freed of pain and discomfort, can dehypnotize herself for as many contractions as she wishes. Although she appears relaxed and "asleep," she is actually fully aware during the labor and the delivery process, and participates emotionally in these; she can hear her baby's first cry, and see it immediately.

Subjectively, the contractions are felt as a tenseness of the abdomen and the bearing-down sensation as a slight perineal pressure. Spontaneous or operative delivery is often managed with the mother fully aware of what is going on, no matter whether the operative procedure is major or minor. Patients who are not so responsive naturally do not do so well during labor and delivery.

Hypnotic age progression has been used to hallucinate a pleasurable birth experience *a priori,* such as hearing the baby's first cry.[9] It was used in 100 parturients, emphasizing relaxation rather than analgesia.[1] The first and second stages were definitely shortened, and hypnosis and relaxation produced a more favorable result than relaxation *per se.* Relaxation provided a more pleasant experience than controls which did not have either one.[20] Displacement of the pain from the uterine contractions with concomitant tightening of the hand-clasp during each labor pain is recommended by August.[3] He also suggests imagery of past pleasant experiences, especially those involving long trips, gardening, fishing—any fantasy that will take the place of the actual painful contraction. In 1000 patients, 850 were successfully delivered by these technics.[3] The superiority of hypnosis over the Read method was demonstrated in 210 women.[14] Hypnosis worked better even if it was initiated during the initial stages of labor for the first time.[46] Nearly all past and current methods of antenatal training have been evaluated. It is concluded that it is not so much a matter of suggestions, relaxation training, and breathing exercises used, but rather that highly motivated parturients are taught how to behave during parturition and to expect less medication.[13]

With reference to hypnotic responsiveness and its relationship for determining its effects, the data are often contaminated by many factors. For instance, if the obstetrician is present during the labor, this often is the equivalent of a quarter gram of morphine. The degree of cervical relaxation, the size of the birth canal, and other anatomical factors, such as the position and molding of the presenting part (occiput or breech), are other imponderables. The author has discussed many of these factors in his numerous publications as well as in a film.*

Other practitioners have found hypnosis to be valuable in obtunding pain during delivery.[11, 12, 14, 27, 34, 35, 37, 38, 40, 41, 52] The emotional support parturients receive during the prepartum period also has been stressed.[50]

---

*Kroger, W.S.: Hypnosis in Obstetrics (1959). Wexler Film Company, 802 North Seward, Hollywood, California.

HELPFUL SUGGESTIONS DURING LABOR

It takes years of practice to become adept with forceps or to be a good vaginal operator. Likewise, the ability to be adept in producing, maintaining, and controlling the applications of hypnosis to obstetrics requires much practical experience. The most useful suggestions are given below.

Misdirection of attention is used to mitigate the forcefulness of the labor contractions, as follows: "I want you to breathe deeply in the same manner in which you were trained during the prenatal classes. You will count the number of deep breaths or pants that you take with each contraction. In other words, as soon as you feel the contraction, start panting and keep a record of the number of breaths required for each contraction. Perhaps it might be 28 for the first one. In about 10 minutes, you should have another contraction which may last for 30 or 40 seconds; this one may require 30 deep breaths or pants. Keep an average between the first and the second by adding the total and dividing by 2, which, in this case, would be 29. I want you to keep this average for all of your contractions. As they get closer and closer, you will notice that the average number of breaths will increase, indicating that labor is progressing nicely."

The idea is to keep the patient's attention so concentrated on the addition and the division that she doesn't have time to think of the painful uterine contractions. Such a procedure can potentiate the use of hypnosis. This preoccupation undoubtedly explains to a degree the success of the natural childbirth method in which the individual spends a considerable amount of time thinking about whether or not she is carrying out this or that exercise correctly. "Finally, when you are in the last stages of labor, you will push down when requested to do so. Naturally, the more you relax, the more effective each push will be. If you follow these suggestions you will get the most out of each contraction."

Another way to deepen the hypnosis is to employ the husband's participation and posthypnotic suggestions: "I am going to instruct your husband that each time you develop a contrac-tion, he will squeeze your wrist with his forefinger and thumb. And, as he squeezes your wrist, this will be a cue, or a signal, that you will drop deeper and deeper relaxed with each deep breath you take."

Backache in the sacral area causes considerable discomfort, especially if the fetus is in an occiput posterior position. Here, too, the husband's aid can be enlisted: "I want you to place the palm of your hand, with your fingers fanned out, over the small of your wife's back. You will press firmly over this area. You will start this at the beginning of each contraction and release the pressure only after the contraction has disappeared." This maneuver often helps patients who complain bitterly of low back pain.

"If you do have more discomfort than you are able to tolerate, do not feel embarrassed if you have to moan. It will help relieve some of the tension. Also, if you wish to open your eyes, you may do so without interfering with the relaxed state you are in. As soon as you close your eyes, you will drop even deeper relaxed. You will not be bothered by any noises or sounds around you. As a matter of fact, you will become more and more concerned with your breathing and counting, and, as you become more involved in these, the sounds around you will fade into the distance. As the head of your baby descends down the birth canal, you will notice more of a desire to push. I have taught you how to breathe. You can grunt and bear down. Every contraction will be a signal for you to bear down harder. And, because you will be completely relaxed, you will obtain the maximal effect from each contraction. You can go through the rest of your delivery without any trouble. Remember, if you should require an anesthetic agent, it will be given to you. And, even if this is necessary, you will find that having a baby will be an exhilarating experience, especially if you are deeply relaxed."

For the actual delivery, the patient can transfer the glove anesthesia to the perineum before it has been "prepped" or sterilized. She is instructed: "This area will remain completely numb and anesthetic. As you push down, with each deep breath you take this area will become more and more anesthetic." One can also produce anesthesia by commenting: "As I stroke this area with my fingers, it will become numb and anesthetic, completely numb and anesthetic, just as if this area had been injected with procaine. It will become just as numb and anesthetic as your jaws become after the dentist has blocked off a nerve. This area is getting very numb, heavy, and woodenlike."

One can enhance the anesthetic effects of the above methods, after the vagina has been sterilized and the patient is ready for delivery, by the following suggestions: "I am now freezing all the skin between my thumb and forefinger." (Considerable pressure is exerted at this time.) "Everywhere I touch my thumb and forefinger together, you will notice a numb, heavy, woodenlike sensation that will get more numb with each breath you take." This, together with the delivery of the head, produces a considerable amount of pressure anesthesia which, in some patients who have a high pain threshold, is sufficient for the performance of an episiotomy.

Approximately 5 per cent of patients have high sensory pain thresholds; the pressure anesthesia is especially effective for this group. About 10 to 15 per cent, which includes this group, can have an episiotomy performed without analgesia or anesthesia. The combination of a paracervical and transvaginal pudendal block with hypnosis is the ideal prescription for painless childbirth. It is almost 100 per cent safe and enables the mother to participate emotionally in the birth process.

HELPFUL SUGGESTIONS FOR THE POSTPARTUM PERIOD

The glove anesthesia technic can be effective during the postoperative period for relief of perineal pain in an episiotomy produced by swelling. In a multipara, autohypnosis and glove anesthesia can be most effective in relieving the pain of postpartum contractions. The same suggestions as described in Chapter 14 are given.

INDUCTION OF LABOR BY HYPNOSIS

Labor can be induced by appropriate posthypnotic suggestions given to selected patients.[7] The author has induced labor in the multipara capable of entering the somnambulistic state of hyp-

nosis.[32] The patient is regressed to her last labor and delivery. In this way it is possible to revivify all the subjective sensations associated with the onset of labor, thus "tricking" the autonomic nervous system into initiating the uterine contractions. It is difficult to do this in the primipara as she cannot imagine memories which she has never experienced. Reynolds has been able to correlate the amplitude of the uterine contractions with suggestions of relaxation or contraction during deep hypnosis.[45]

Often, premature labor can be prevented by strong reassurance and deep relaxation under hypnosis. The author used hypnosis to prevent premature labor in a case of abruptio placentae reported by Hartman and Rawlins.[24]

GROUP TRAINING

Group training in hypnoanesthesia is a time-saving procedure for the busy obstetrician. The classes can be conducted by a nurse or a doctor. Motivation is heightened by the emotional contagion that occurs as patients identify and empathize with each other and by the spirit of competition that is mobilized within the group. Also, most patients undergoing group training attempt to please the doctor, and this is an added motivational spur.

The author's patients attend group training classes twice a month for 2 hours in the evening with their husbands. The first half hour is devoted to questions and answers on pre- and postnatal care, labor, delivery, kinds of anesthesia, and hypnosis. Patients are instructed that all questions, except those of a personal nature, are to be asked in the class. This saves valuable office time for the physician. Then several patients who have recently been delivered are asked to relate their experiences during labor. Their forthright and sincere discussion is highly motivating to the rest of the group.

Following these "testimonials" and the question-and-answer period, four or five patients who are good hypnotic subjects volunteer to illustrate how readily hypnosis can be induced. After induction, they are asked to induce autohypnosis and glove anesthesia. The way in which autohypnosis and glove anesthesia are produced is explained to the group. Once the glove anesthesia is transferred to the side of the face, the abdomen or the other arm, the insensitivity to pain is demonstrated. All patients alert or "awake" themselves; then four or more unsophisticated patients are asked to volunteer. Since a few minutes of observation of hypnotic induction is worth hours of talking about it, the beginner's susceptibility is increased. About 75 per cent of this group usually are hypnotized readily.

Platonov, in the Soviet Union, employed individual and group hypnosis to prepare large numbers of women for painless childbirth.[42] He quotes numerous investigators who reported on the successful use of hypnosis with results similar to this author's. Among these are the enormous numbers of women delivered over the last 20 years in Leningrad by Vigdorovich, an obstetrician who supervised 15 "hypnotariums," which were under the jurisdiction of the Leningrad City Board of Health. Painless childbirth was effected in 4,575 cases with 91 per cent positive results; toxemias of pregnancy were relieved in 95 per cent of 400 cases, and 126 false pregnancies were treated in these hypnotariums. With this impressive array of evidence, why are obstetricians in the West still "dragging their feet"?

NAUSEA AND VOMITING

HYPNOTIC MANAGEMENT

The dictum to "treat the patient who has the vomiting rather than the vomiting" is important. Nausea and vomiting and even hyperemesis gravidarum are astonishingly susceptible to hypnosis.

The incidence of cure in over a hundred patients seen in the author's private and clinic practice for a period of almost 45 years is approximately 75 per cent. Some, in spite of medical aid, were extremely toxic, with high icteric indexes, and some were almost moribund. Over 75 per cent of those for whom therapeutic abortion was considered were cured by hypnosis.[30] Platonov treated 583 grave cases of hyperemesis gravidarum and cured over 84 per cent with an average of 7 hypnotic treatments.[43]

Psychogenic factors are chiefly responsible for the majority of cases. Hyperemesis gravidarum is unknown in some cultures, such as the Asian, but it develops in these peoples after assimilation into Western society.

In predisposed individuals, the gastrointestinal tract is symbolically utilized as a way of showing disgust—by vomiting. This is substantiated by the observation that the gut is a common site for the expression of disgust. Many of our vomiters had a strong aversion toward sex or an overdependent attachment to the mother; there was often a history of "rejection dyspepsia."

Nausea and vomiting of pregnancy usually cease by the fourth or the fifth month, at which time the fetal movements are felt. The mother now becomes aware that the fetus is a separate individual and can no longer be "thrown up." Thus, there is insufficient time for any uncovering psychotherapy. A differentiation between the "nervous" and the "toxic" type depends not only on the history but also on the laboratory findings.

Treatment should be directed primarily toward the patient as a whole, and not toward the symptom! The judicious use of hypnotherapy to establish the need for the symptom, combined with adequate medical management, is indicated for all cases of hyperemesis gravidarum. This often has obviated the need for therapeutic abortion. The author demonstrated this in a series of desperately ill women—the salvage rate was 85 per cent.[19, 30]

Hypnotic Management Technic

After a patient has been hypnotized and taught autohypnosis, the following verbalization can be used: "You will notice that as you relax yourself through autohypnosis, your nausea and vomiting will decrease. You can also suggest that you will find it extremely difficult even to become nauseated or to vomit upon arising. Perhaps you might like to imagine that you are eating a delightful meal without getting sick. How about 'eating' something you like right now? You can see the food, can you not?" (The patient nods her head.) "Imagine, if you will, that you are eating the food and thoroughly digesting it. You will find that your stomach will be very, very relaxed if you look forward to eating; that it will be extremely difficult to vomit. Perhaps you would like to believe that no matter how hard you try, you cannot vomit. After you have practiced 'eating' enough times and have imagined that the food is going to stay down, you will enjoy it. However, if you really have to be nauseated, why not permit yourself to develop this sensation for 15 minutes every morning, especially in the bathroom? Then each day you can suggest that the time will be cut down by 1 or 2 minutes, so that at the end of a week or two you will wean yourself from the 'need to vomit.' Or, perhaps, you can increase the vomiting. You realize that if you deliberately increase your sickness, you are controlling it, and anything you can increase, you can decrease!"

"Now there are many needs for your nausea and vomiting. Perhaps you might tell me of some of your fears, anxieties and tensions in regard to pregnancy, delivery or care of the child. If you think of any problems concerning your pregnancy and delivery, relate them to me on your next visit. Regardless of how silly or inconsequential these thoughts may seem to you, tell me all about these matters. Then you will notice that with each day you will have *less need* to get sick. You can then look forward to having your baby with a feeling of joy and happiness."

Glove anesthesia can be utilized as follows: "You have learned to develop an anesthesia of the palm of your hand. You are aware that you can transfer this sensation to any portion of your body. Every time you develop the slightest nausea, all you have to do to relieve it is to transfer this numb, woodenlike feeling to your stomach. Just press firmly on the pit of your stomach and the entire area will feel very, very relaxed."

It is really surprising how effective this type of placebo therapy—in the form of "laying on of the hands"—is in abolishing the nausea and the vomiting. The patient's confidence and self-esteem are increased when she realizes that the "power" to eradicate the symptom is hers, and that no dependency on drugs or the doctor is required.

There are cases in which the vomiting persists even after an abortion. Here, the vomiting pattern is fixed in the cortex. This is similar to the pain pattern of phantom limb pain, and indicates the importance of altering the deranged cortical dynamics. Such psychopathology is more amenable

to hypnosuggestive procedures because the vicious reflex can be broken up with more certainty.

EMOTIONAL SPONTANEOUS ABORTION

The emotional factors contributing to the "abortion habit" may be similar to those of the "accident habit" of certain self-destructive individuals. Thus the author and Freed postulated that the corticohypothalamic pathway can, through alternations in hormonal balance, alter the biochemical reactions in the rapidly growing placenta.[32] Moreover, there is anatomic evidence that strong emotions can contract the uterine musculature and thus cause placental separation. Data of a positive nature which implicate the emotions consist of the evidence that the uteri of habitual aborters are hypersensitive to emotional stimuli, that there is a certain personality profile, that domesticated animals abort under unfavorable emotional environment, and that reports from a number of workers indicate favorable results following psychotherapy. There is also a considerable body of unclassified data which points to the role of emotions in abortion in patients who have miscarried during shock, fright or dangerous episodes.

More recently, proliferative changes in the placentas of spontaneous aborters, which resemble those of the collagen diseases, have been found secondary to mental stress. Gray and his associates noted that antibodies similar to those found in the collagen diseases can be detected in the serum of aborters.[23] The fluctuations in 17-ketosteroids and 17-hydroxycorticoids secondary to stress, specific or nonspecific, may produce the pathologic changes in the placenta noted by Gray.

Platonov quotes Miloslavsky's recent systematic studies which showed that hypnosis could reduce uterine excitability, terminate bleeding and salvage a large number of fetuses.[42] This substantiates Kroger and Freed's observations made in 1951.[32]

Nearly all investigators agree that the favorable results obtained in the treatment of this condition are chiefly due to the "mental rest" and the reassurance derived from the physician-patient relationship. The relationship of dreams and other unconscious factors in the production of threatened abortion and premature labor has been studied.[8, 9] Utilization of ideomotor finger signaling to elicit hidden psychodynamic factors responsible for these entities has yielded some very interesting correlations.[8]

HEARTBURN OF PREGNANCY

Heartburn of pregnancy has been termed a "monosymptomatic neurosis." Here, too, the esophagus and the stomach are symbolically selected as the expression of the pregnant woman's inability to "swallow" or "stomach" the pregnancy because of deep-seated aversion to it. The esophageal spasm is noted in apprehensive women with lowered thresholds to sensory stimuli, especially in those who harbor latent guilt feelings over their overt or covert rejection of the child.

The therapy of heartburn of pregnancy due to psychogenic causes is directed toward the relief of the anxiety and the tension. As discussed in the section on nausea and vomiting, this may be accomplished by hypnotic exploration with a discussion and an explanation of the harmlessness of the symptom. In refractory cases, autohypnosis and glove anesthesia are beneficial.

LACTATION

Lactation often is influenced by emotional upsets.[9] Conflicts can suppress lactogenic hormonal output via the hypothalamus and interfere with successful mammary function. Whether the hormonal dysfunction is due to a lack of love for the baby, or whether absence of motherly feelings is a product of a general psychosomatic immaturity, has yet to be established.

The literature relative to the influence of psychic factors on lactation has been reviewed.[15] Mohr treated a patient who developed a sudden inability to nurse following psychic excitement.[36] Under hypnosis she was given a suggestion that on the way home she would feel milk flowing from her breasts. Within an hour she functioned normally, and there was no recurrence of her

trouble. The French school of hypnotists—Liébeault, Bernheim and others—made innumerable observations that the flow of milk could be stopped or increased by hypnosis. Heyer, in discussing the use of hypnosis during delivery, states: "Later it is very often possible to stimulate vigorously a decreasing flow of milk."[25] More recently, Goll has discussed the role of suggestion in the treatment of deficient lactation.[21]

The effective use of hypnosis has been demonstrated in stimulating milk production in 77 cases with over 95 per cent success.[42] The technics involve the use of sensory-imagery conditioning and posthypnotic and autohypnotic suggestions. The results depend on the manner in which the suggestions are given. Usually, direct suggestions are not as effective as those that paint "mental pictures" of the milk flow from a full breast.

LATE TOXEMIAS OF PREGNANCY: PREECLAMPSIA AND ECLAMPSIA

The etiologic factors in the toxemias of pregnancy, especially preeclampsia and eclampsia, still remain inadequately explained. The author and Freed pointed out that the psyche plays some role in the operative mechanism of this disorder.[32] However, it is acknowledged that this condition is largely a somatic one, from the clinical standpoint, with typical pathologic findings. One finds, however, in examining the reports made by students of this subject, the suggestion that psychological factors may be involved.[49] Dieckmann states that preeclampsia and its complications are limited to civilized and cultured races, and that relatively primitive societies suffer from this condition only after contact with more "sophisticated" peoples.[17] Pommerenke comments, "Dr. Dieckmann hints—with a voice that is perhaps too faint—that factors which some may regard as psychosomatic or sociologic may be operative in the etiology of eclampsia."[44]

The author and Freed stated that the most likely possibilities to be considered in postulating a psychosomatic factor for this disorder are (1) placental ischemia, (2) stimulation of the posterior pituitary, and (3) imbalance or excess of certain adrenal corticosteroids.[32] Thus psychosocial and other nonspecific factors potentially may lead to a disturbance of the cortical-hypothalamic-pituitary-adrenal axis, resulting in imbalance or excess of adrenal corticosteroids and/or a direct excitation or stimulation of the autonomic (pressor) nervous system, similarly mediated via a hypothalamic-pituitary-adrenal axis. Salerno recently supported these observations by clinical studies.[48]

Cheek and Le Cron state:

Hypnosis becomes a tool of life saving value in the presence of pyramiding fears due to prolonged labor, toxemia, hemorrhage, premature labor and overwhelming infection when medical attendants have become discouraged and frustrated with their failure to cure. With hypnosis we have a means to reestablish hope, diminish pain, stop fibrinolytic hemorrhage, reverse some of the effects of toxemia and improve resistance to infection.[9]

It has long been recognized that preeclamptics improve when hospitalized—environmental stresses are reduced. Hypno-relaxation can also raise the adaptive responses to stress. Autohypnosis is extremely helpful for recognizing anxiety-provoking tensions. Inducing the hypnotic state several times daily for relaxation, together with intelligent prenatal care, diet, sodium restriction and proper elimination, relieves many preeclamptics. Resistant individuals should be placed under medical management. However, hypnosis can be used prophylactically to decrease appetite and prevent weight gain. Naturally, the acute, fulminating phase of severe eclampsia cannot be helped by hypnosis.

DISCUSSION

As a result of the medical profession's interest in relaxation procedures for painless childbirth, a marked increase in the scientific applications of hypnosis has recently become apparent. It has been a belated but welcome recognition of the usefulness of hypnoanesthesia, either as an anesthetic agent or as an adjunct to chemoanesthesia.

Hypnoanesthesia for parturition is not a panacea, nor will it ever supplant chemoanesthetic agents, but its applications are growing daily and it is proving a powerful ally in alleviating other psychosomatic conditions in obstetrics.

Hypnosis is almost a specific for relief of the psychogenic component responsible for nausea and vomiting during early pregnancy. Hypnosis and/or strong suggestion are particularly valuable in the prevention of habitual abortion. Hypnosis can frequently diminish the strength and the frequency of the uterine contractions, and miscarriage can be prevented in properly *selected* patients if placental separation has not occurred. Experience indicates that placebos are as effective as vitamins and hormones in reducing the abortion rate; contradictory theories, the varied responses to edocrine therapy, and the frequent relapses with other types of therapy, all incriminate the psyche to some extent. Hypnosis can also be employed effectively in heartburn, to promote lactation, and to curb the "eating for two" syndrome often responsible for rapid weight gain and subsequent preeclampsia and toxemia.

The average physician can learn to induce hypnosis for anesthesia as readily as he learns to make an abdominal skin incision. However, to use this double-edged scalpel for intensive psychotherapy he must have the intuition, the knowledge and the judgment that characterize the skill of the surgeon who wields the scalpel.

It is hoped that the foregoing will stimulate more physicians to utilize hypnosis in childbirth and other obstetrical conditions. More active participation and public education in hypnotic methodology will help dispel misunderstanding and apprehension concerning hypnosis among the lay public. Since hypnosis is a very flexible agent, its utility in mitigating the pain of parturition could be broadened if it were used more often in conjunction with chemoanesthesia. Its use in this manner should have a salutary effect during pregnancy, labor, and delivery. Likewise, if the disadvantages and limitations enumerated above are taken into consideration, it will not be hailed as a panacea. Most physicians initially are enthusiastic about hypnotherapy in obstetrics, but disillusionment sets in after they find that it requires years of experience to use it intelligently and successfully.

REFERENCES

1. Abramson, M., and Heron, W.T.: An objective evaluation of hypnosis in obstetrics: preliminary report. Am. J. Obstet. Gynecol., *59:*1069, 1950.
2. August, R.V.: Obstetric hypnoanesthesia. Am. J. Obstet. Gynecol., *79:*1131, 1960.
3. _____: Hypnosis in Obstetrics. New York, McGraw-Hill, 1961.
4. _____: Hypnosis in Obstetrics: varying approaches. Am. J. Clin. Hypn., *8:*47, 1965.
5. Ball, T.H.: Obstetrics in the Soviet Union. Trans. N.Y. Acad. Sci., *22:*578, 1960.
6. Bronstein, I.: Psychoprophylactic Preparation for Painless Childbirth. New York, Grune & Stratton, 1958.
7. Carter, J.E.: Hypnotic induction of labor: a review and report of cases. Am. J. Clin. Hypn., *5:*322, 1963.
8. Cheek, D.B.: Some newer understandings of dreams in relation to threatened abortion and premature labor. Pacific Med. Surg., *73:*379, 1965.
9. Cheek, D.B., and Le Cron, L.: Clinical Hypnotherapy. New York, Grune & Stratton, 1968.
10. Chertok, L.: Psychoprophylaxis or obstetrical psychotherapy. Fortschr. Psychom. Med., *3:*134, 1963.
11. Coulton, D.: Hypnosis in obstetrical delivery. Am. J. Clin. Hypn., *2:*144, 1960.
12. _____: Prenatal and post-partum uses of hypnosis. Am. J. Clin. Hypn., *8:*192, 1966.
13. Davenport-Slack, B.: A comparative evaluation of obstetrical hypnosis and antenatal childbirth training. Int. J. Clin. Exp. Hypn., *12:*266, 1975.
14. Davidson, J.A.: Assessment of the value of hypnosis in pregnancy and labor. Br. Med. J., 2, *13:*951, 1962.
15. DeLee, J.B.: Year Book of Obstetrics and Gynecology. Chicago, Year Book Medical Publishers, 1939, p. 164.
16. Dick-Read, G.: Childbirth Without Fear. New York, Harper, 1953.
17. Dieckmann, W.J.: Toxemias of Pregnancy. St. Louis, C.V. Mosby, 1941.
18. Dunbar, F.: Emotions and Bodily Changes. New York, Columbia University Press, 1946, pp. 311–315.
19. Fuchs, K., *et al.:* quoted by Crasilneck, H.B., and Hall, J.A.: Clinical Hypnosis. New York, Grune & Stratton, 1975, p. 115.
20. Furneaux, W.D., and Chapple, P.A.L.: Some objective and subjective characteristics of labor influenced by personality, and their modification by hypnosis and relaxation. Proc. Roy. Soc. Med., *57:*261, 1964.
21. Goll, H.: Role of suggestion in hormonal therapy of hypogalactia. Munch. Med. Wochenschr., *89:*55, 1942.
22. Goodrich, F.W.: Natural Childbirth. Englewood Cliffs, N.J., Prentice-Hall, 1956.
23. Gray, J.D.: The problem of spontaneous abortion. Am. J. Obstet. Gynecol., *74:*111, 1957.
24. Hartman, W., and Rawlins, C.M.: Hypnosis in management of a case of abruptio placentae. Int. J. Clin. Exp. Hypn., *8:*103, 1960.
25. Heyer, G.R.: (quoted by Dunbar) Hypnose und Hypnotherapie in die psychischen Heilmethoden. Hrsg. von Karl Birnbaum. Leipzig, Georg Thieme, 1927, pp. 73–135.
26. Hilgard, E.R., and Hilgard, J.R.: Hypnosis in the Relief of Pain. Los Altos, Cal., William Kaufman, 1976.
27. Hoffman, G.L., Jr., and Kipenhauer, D.B.: Medical hypnosis and its use in obstetrics. Am. J. Med. Sci., *241:*788, 1961.
28. Kroger, W.S.: The psychosomatic treatment of hyperemesis gravidarum by hypnosis. Am. J. Obstet. Gynecol., *51:*544, 1946.
29. _____: Hypnoanesthesia in obstetrics. *In* Davis, C.H. (ed.): Gynecology and Obstetrics. Hagerstown, Md., Harper & Row, 1960, pp. 111–130.
30. _____: Natural childbirth. Med. Times, *80:*152, 1952.
31. Kroger, W.S., and DeLee, S.T.: The use of the hypnoidal state as an amnesic analgesic and anesthetic agent in obstetrics. Am. J. Obstet. Gynecol., *46:*655, 1943.
32. Kroger, W.S., and Freed, S.E.: Psychosomatic Gynecology: Including Problems of Obstetrical Care. Philadelphia, W.B. Saunders, 1951.
33. Lamaze, F.: Painless Childbirth. London, Burke, 1958.
34. Malyska, W., and Christensen, J.: Autohypnosis and the prenatal class. Am. J. Clin. Hypn., *9:*188, 1967.
35. Mellgren, A.: Practical experiences with a modified hypnosis-delivery. Psychotherap. Psychosomat., *14:*425, 1966.
36. Mohr, Fritz: (Quoted by Dunbar) Psychophysiche Behandlungsmethoden. Leipzig, Hirzel, 1925.
37. Mosconi, G.: Il metodo ipnotico per la preparazione al parto. Minerva Med. Suppl., *3:*2156, 1966.
38. Mosconi, G., and Starich, B.: Preparacion del parto con hipnosis. Rev. Lat. Am. Hypn. Clin., *2:*29, 1966.
39. Moya, F., and James, L.S.: Medical hypnosis for obstetrics. J.A.M.A., *174:*80, 1960.
40. Oystragh, P.: The use of hypnosis in general and obstetrical practice. Med. J. Aust., *2:*731, 1970.

41. Pascatto, R.D., and Mead, B.T.: The use of post-hypnotic suggestions in obstetrics. Am. J. Clin. Hypn., *9:*267, 1967.

42. Platonov, K.: The Word as a Physiological and Therapeutic Factor. Moscow, Foreign Languages Publishing House, 1955.

43. Platonov, M.V., *et al.:* quoted by Volgyesi, F.A.: The recent neuropsychiatric and biomorphologic justifications of hypnotherapeutic empiricism. Br. J. Med. Hypn., *2:*6, 1950.

44. Pommerenke, W.T.: Discussion of Dieckmann, W.J., *et al.:* Etiology of eclampsia. Am. J. Obstet. Gynecol., *58:*1014, 1949.

45. Reynolds, S.R.M.: Uterine contractility and cervical dilation. Proc. Roy. Soc. Med., *44:*695, 1951.

46. Rock, N., *et al.:* Hypnosis with untrained, non-volunteer patient in labor. Int. J. Clin. Exp. Hypn., *17:*25, 1969.

47. Roig-Garcia, S.: The hypno-reflexogenous method: a new procedure in obstetrical psychoanalgesia. Am. J. Clin. Hypn., *6:*15, 1961.

48. Salerno, L.J.: Psychophysiologic aspects of the toxemias of pregnancy. Am. J. Obstet. Gynecol., *76:*1268, 1958.

49. Soichet, S.: Emotional factors in toxemia of pregnancy. Am. J. Obstet. Gynecol., *77:*1065, 1959.

50. Spiegel, H.: Current perspectives on hypnosis in obstetrics. Act Psychotherap., *11:*412, 1963.

51. Tom, K.S.: Hypnosis in obstetrics and gynecology. Obstet. Gynecol., *16:*222, 1960.

52. Werner, W.E.: Hypnosis and acute uterine inversion. Am. J. Clin. Hypn., *7:*229, 1965.

53. Winklestein, L.B.: Routine hypnosis for obstetrical delivery. Am. J. Obstet. Gynecol., *76:*152, 1958.

54. Zuspan, F.P.: Hypnosis and the obstetrician-gynecologist. Obstet. Gynecol., *16:*740, 1960.

ADDITIONAL READINGS

Chertok, L.: Psychosomatic Methods in Painless Childbirth. New York, Pergamon Press, 1959.

DeLee, S. T.: Hypnotism in pregnancy and labor, J.A.M.A., *159:*750, 1955.

Kroger, S. W.: Hypnosis in obstetrics and gynecology. *In* Schneck, J. M. (ed.): Hypnosis in Modern Medicine. Springfield, Ill., Charles C Thomas, 1959.

Kroger, W. S., and Steinberg, J.: Childbirth With Hypnosis. New York, Doubleday, 1961.

37

Hypnosis in Gynecology

PSYCHOSOMATIC FACTORS

The female generative tract is extremely susceptible to the physiologic expression of emotions. Therefore, a high percentage of gynecologic symptoms have a psychosomatic or a psychogynecic basis. Appropriate hypnotherapy can allay the anxieties and the tensions responsible for the majority of psychogynecic symptoms by altering faulty attitudes concerning femininity and sexuality.

The gynecologist, if trained in hypnosis, can use this modality much as he employs drugs for symptom removal. Symptom removal by hypnotherapy is not harmful, contrary to the belief of some psychiatrists. To assume otherwise is rather ridiculous when one considers that the bulk of gynecologic therapy for functional disorders is directed toward symptom removal. This goal readily can be achieved without an understanding of "psychodynamics." The author, a psychiatrist and gynecologist, used the psychodynamic approach for years until he realized that his therapeutic results were due to an empathic relationship, reassurance, and reeducation rather than to the "insight" and interpretations.

Modern hypnotic technics employ autohypnosis and sensory-imagery conditioning as described in this chapter. These, together with the rapport, are utilized for most patients in preference to direct symptom removal by authoritarian hypnotic technics. Those for whom superficial therapy is inadequate require an understanding of their neurotic needs for their symptoms. Thus present- and future-oriented psychotherapy shortened by hypnosis is more feasible for most psychogynecic symptoms than searching for causes by uncovering the past through complex psychoanalytic technics. Our hypnotherapeutic technics now will be presented.

AMENORRHEA

Psychic factors[30, 32] can prevent the release of the proper gonadotrophic hormones to produce functional or "hypothalamic" amenorrhea.[40] This form of amenorrhea can be due to fear of pregnancy, guilt feelings over masturbation and other emotional factors. A prerequisite to hypnotherapy of functional amenorrhea is not only a physical examination but also a psychological evaluation of the attitudes toward menstruation and psychosexual functioning.

Amenorrhea has been treated effectively by hypnosis.[11, 16, 20] Dunbar points out:

In many cases amenorrhea can be cured by one hypnotic session. In a patient who had been suffering from amenorrhea for 2½ years, menses were induced by hypnosis, and regulated to occur on the first day of each month at 7:00 A.M. to last for 3 days.[11]

Heyer has observed:

Numerous authors report results from hypnotherapy in menstrual disturbances, which are beyond question, i.e., relief of pain as well as regulation of the cycle. As a matter of fact, the time of onset for menstruation can be determined in deep hypnosis to the day and hour, as, for example, one may say every 4 weeks or every first day of the month, etc. . . . In all uses of hypnosis, it is important to give not just colorless commands, but to suggest the whole experience of menstruation forcefully and vividly. Where doubts as to the efficiency of this procedure have risen, faulty technic is responsible.[15]

Although this method does not always work, the author has on several occasions, dramatically induced the menses by hypnosis.

As mentioned, bleeding seldom can be initiated by direct suggestion. Rather, the technic is to ask the following questions: "Do your breasts get hot and heavy just before you are due to have your period? Do you feel like jumping out of your skin at this time? Is there any pain connected with the onset of the flow? If so, where is it? What is the character of the pain? Do you have a backache, or a feeling of pressure in the pelvic region? Are there any other symptoms associatied with the onset of the flow?"

If the answers to the above questions are fed back to the hypnotized patient, one has an excellent chance of reestablishing the menses by this type of sensory-imagery conditioning. The verbalization used is as follows: "In about 2 weeks, you will find it most advantageous to feel all the sensations that you previously described and associated with your periods. Think of the exact place where you have discomfort and pressure. Perhaps you might even imagine how 'jumpy' and irritable you felt just before your flow." In this technic, a "dry run" or a rehearsal of the onset of menstruation under autohypnosis helps to reinforce the appropriate post-hypnotic suggestions.

Another technic is to utilize hypnotic age regression. The patient is regressed to her last period and asked to recall the specific sensations associated with it; if she wishes, she can choose the approximate date for the establishment of the menses. Suggestions must be made in a confident manner. However, the physician should never get himself "out on a limb" by guaranteeing that the menses will occur on a specific date. Rather, he can preface his remarks by saying, "If you are able to feel the sensations associated with your period, you have a good chance of having your period. Or, perhaps, you can begin to wonder whether it will be a day or two before the date you chose, or maybe the period will come on a week afterward."

Cheek and Le Cron assay attitudes toward menstruation and orient the patient back to the last normal period and then search for a stressful event that preceded the cessation of the menses.[7] The patient is informed that efforts will be directed only toward ascertaining if she is free of problems. Also, she will bleed only if she thinks it necessary. After searching for causative factors, the patient is asked if she would like to bleed for only 3 days. If the answer is "yes" with ideomotor finger signaling, she is then asked to select the date for her next period. This does not always work on the first attempt, but repetitive suggestions invariably result in regular menses. This technic is wholly permissive. Furthermore, the responsibility for resumption of her menses is placed upon the patient, and the expectancy level is mobilized in a extraverbal manner, thus providing greater likelihood of success. This fascinating approach should be validated by controlled studies.

PSEUDOCYESIS

Pseudocyesis, or phantom pregnancy, is characterized by some of the signs and symptoms of pregnancy, such as amenorrhea, enlargement of breasts, and change in the body contour. Psychotic states, or a persistent corpus cyst, must be considered when the "pregnancy" persists. This condition convincingly illustrates how psychic factors can influence the endocrine system. Cortical-hypothalamic pathways to the anterior pituitary are utilized, causing release of the corpus luteum hormones and suppression of the follicle-stimulating hormone (FSH).[37]

One should not forcefully confront the patient with her delusion, but she must be aware of the emotional *needs* for maintaining the "pregnancy." Such an individual has to be "unhypnotized" out of ideas that she has "hypnotized" herself into; therefore, permissive hypnotic technics are more likely to uncover the *need* for the pregnancy fantasy.

Pseudocyesis beautifully illustrates how subcortical structures mediate impulses from the higher sensorium and transmit these repressed emotional forces to appropriate target organs. It also illustrates the astonishing susceptibility of the endocrine apparatus to psychic stimuli. I have noted that the darkened linea alba and other signs of pregnancy often occur in multiparas. This may indicate that the indelible imprint of an "experience" is filed away but is subject to recall at "appropriate" times. Sensory-imagery conditioning under autohypnosis, involving recall of the entire menstrual experience, often can be a valuable adjunctive procedure in relieving pseudocyesis.

DYSFUNCTIONAL UTERINE BLEEDING

Psychic shock may cause profuse vaginal bleeding. Menstruation of a bride on her wedding night often can be a defense against intercourse, or a reflection of fear of pregnancy or responsibility. Irregular bleeding may be the somatic equivalent of the grief and the depression following the loss of a loved one.[15]

An increase in endogenous adrenalin can cause vasoconstriction of the endometrial blood vessels. Bleeding of psychological origin could conceivably be mediated through the midbrain to the hypophysis with a subsequent alteration in ovarian and adrenal function. Psychotics frequently manifest functional menstrual abnormalities; these are corrected after alleviation of their mental symptoms. Before treatment is instituted, an organic etiology should be ruled out. Hypnotherapy is purely an adjunctive procedure to endocrine and medical treatment of uterine bleeding. Superficial psychotherapy, consisting of education for the correction of faulty sexual attitudes and domestic and social maladjustments, and the utilization of common-sense suggestions for other anxiety-provoking tensions can often be accomplished more rapidly through hypnosis. A high percentage of cases can be helped by a psychotherapeutic approach.

Cheek and Le Cron discuss all the organic factors responsible for abnormal uterine bleeding.[7] They have a six-point program for psychotherapy of bleeding dysfunctions:

1. Set up ideomotor responses.
2. Orient to the moment before bleeding starts and ask the "yes" finger to lift.
3. Advance from this moment to some thought or feeling that might be related to the trouble. If the "no" finger lifts, ask what the thought means.
4. Ask: "In the light of what you have discov-

ered, do you think it might be possible to stop this heavy bleeding and return to a normal type of menstruation?"

5. At this point, and no sooner, ask: "Does the deep part of your mind feel that you have a serious or dangerous disease?" Then ask: "Have you identified yourself with any other person who has bleeding like this?"

6. Scanning the thoughts and dreams before the onset of the bleeding may yield significant clues if the questions are confined to daytime activities. Cheek is an experienced gynecologist and he wisely points out that a search for organic factors must be made; they do occur even in the presence of psychological disturbances.

FUNCTIONAL DYSMENORRHEA

Dysmenorrhea is a "disease of theories." Menstruation and "the curse" have been synonymous for centuries. The actual mechanism responsible for the discomfort may be due to a conditioned pain pattern in the cortex, similar to that seen in amputees who complain of phantom limb pain. The absence of gross lesions, the monthly variation in pain according to mood swings, and the frequent relapses in endocrine therapy mark it as a typical emotional disorder.[29]

It is a serious mistake to minimize pain even if it is emotionally based. Pain is pain, whether physical or emotional. One only mobilizes resentment by such bromidic statements as: "Your discomfort is all in your head. Why don't you relax? Stop worrying about it. It will go away!" In addition to sedation, analgesia, and hormonal therapy, hypnotherapy is a very valuable adjunct. Autohypnosis, glove anesthesia, and autosuggestions to produce a conditioned relaxation for the entire menstrual period definitely can raise the pain threshold.

Hypnosis acts to bind these patients in therapy. As discussed in Chapter 50, the strong dependency helps to overcome the initial resistances involved in yielding the symptom. Later, the dependency is lessened as the patient learns how to control the discomfort by autohypnosis. Whether one employs psychotherapy, hypnosis or just plain common sense in treating functional dysmenorrhea, one should avoid offering such "therapeutic" suggestions as "Get married," "Have a baby," or "Find a suitable lover." These are, at best, unscientific, and, at worst, extremely harmful.

Cheek and Le Cron have developed a unique approach for dysmenorrhea of psychogenic origin.[7] First, they train the patient in ideomotor finger signaling. This is used to elicit the factors responsible for the first painful period. Second, they have her relive the feelings associated with this period. Then they ask her to turn off the pain at a subconscious level and allow an ideomotor signal to indicate completion and have her state when she feels comfortable. Third, the hypnosis is deepened, and she is asked if she would like to have scantier periods, and with complete comfort. By asking her to feel like she does when not menstruating, the therapist is giving helpful suggestions in the form of a question. If the next period is painful, search is made for previously undiscovered organic or emotional factors. The patient is informed that if the dysmenorrhea recurs, she should ask herself what psychologic mechanisms are involved. This can remind her how to turn off pain. Direct suggestion has been employed in 17 cases and more complex methods in three with a 20 per cent failure rate.[32] These technics and results are astounding.

INFERTILITY

Many factors are responsible for psychosomatic infertility.[25, 30] The author evaluated a series of infertile patients by psychological tests.[19] Behind the outward desire to get pregnant was the deeply repressed wish not to get pregnant, on the basis of emotional immaturity associated with fear of motherhood or feelings of inadequacy. Such conflicting emotions, mediated through autonomic, somatic, behavioral, and endocrine mechanisms, often can affect the physiology of ovulation implantation and, perhaps, even the viscosity of the cervical mucus, to produce the so-called hostile cervix. Other factors are avoidance of coitus during ovulation, transitory or persistent tubal spasm, and conflicts in the male which may affect the fertilizing capacity of the sperm.

About 35 per cent of infertile women get pregnant soon after treatment is begun. Often the enthusiasm with which the infertile patient is investigated is therapeutic;[17] diminution of anxiety results in endogenous epinephrine suppression (an excessive amount causes infertility). A similar mechanism operates in women who conceive following the erroneous diagnosis of "blocked tubes." They stop worrying over their infertility, their tubes relax, and they conceive.

The neural pathways by which emotionally conditioned disharmonic impulses produce tubal spasm have been described.[13] As proof of the validity of this hypothesis, selective denervation of the proximal tubes and the cervix often cures this type of infertility. The fallopian tubes, the most "hysterical" portion of a woman's anatomy, also relax following sympathomimetic drugs and hypnosis. Most pharmacologic or psychotherapeutic modalities, including hypnosis, owe a large percentage of their success to the placebo effect. Since infertility often is dramatically alleviated when stress is reduced, it is not hard to see how much more effective specific suggestions would be in achieving relaxation through hypnosis.

Hypnosis can be a helpful adjunct in the treatment of infertility if the physician can understand the psychological conflicts of both partners. Posthypnotic suggestions and autohypnosis, by relaxation and healthful sensory-imagery conditioning, neutralize other anxieties and tensions. The diminution in psychosomatic factors frequently helps establish regular ovulatory cycles and probably a normal pH in the generative tract; the chemistry of the vaginal secretions can be dependent on psychogenic factors.[20] Wollman described successful treatment of infertility by hypnosis.[41] Increasing libido where there was very little coitus helped overcome several cases of infertility.

The author's technic is as follows: After the patient has been conditioned to enter into hypnosis, she is taught autohypnosis. Posthypnotic suggestions are utilized to induce profound relaxation immediately after coitus. Under hypnosis it is further suggested: "Do not deliberately try to get pregnant. The harder you try, the less chance you have. Just relax. Every time you have intercourse, assume that you cannot conceive." This type of suggestion, or the reciprocal inhibition therapy, follows the law of reverse effect. By such measures the patient relaxes; harmful endogenous factors are decreased; if tubal spasm is present, it may be alleviated. This reasoning may seem farfetched, but twice the author erroneously diagnosed "blocked tubes." This achieved relaxation, mental and physical. He was not surprised to find that the patients soon became pregnant. With fear removed, relaxation of the reproductive apparatus occurs. Posthypnotic directions also can be suggested to inculcate a feeling of motherliness and to seek intercourse during the fertile period and, most importantly, to eliminate worry and tensions.

Hypnosis may potentiate the effectiveness of artificial insemination.[9] There is no clear-cut explanation as to why it works. However, since the associated tubal spasm is usually anxiety-mediated, it is not surprising that hypnorelaxation procedures are effective.

FRIGIDITY

The physician should emphasize that proficiency and complete gratification are not achieved until "there is a union of one personality with the other," or until each of the partners is capable of "giving" instead of "getting." Sexual compatibility is based on mutual respect, liking, and gradually established confidence—the basis for mature *love.* Many females blame their sexual problems on physical symptoms, particularly those which bring them to the physician. Organic frigidity is rare. Pseudofrigidity due to male ineptness or ignorance of sexual matters can readily be treated by superficial psychotherapy, consisting of discussion and reeducation of the male. True frigidity, including dyspareunia due to vaginismus, is not a distinct clinical entity but a symptom of faulty conditioning during early psychosexual development.[18, 22, 23]

Many women feel guilty if they do not have a specific type of pleasure response in the vagina. Sexual satisfaction cannot be reduced to a mechanical response. Kinsey contended that "orgasm is orgasm" regardless of how it is achieved, whether by digital, penile, or lingual manipulation, but less superficial studies do not bear this out. Because some women can achieve an orgasm only after being beaten, it does not follow that this procedure is normal. Orgasm has little to do with the size of the penis, the position, or the posture. What is important is the element of love. This entity is poorly understood and is lacking in many marriages. Since the understanding of love and sex relationships is important to any therapeutic approach, a discussion of these is indicated.

The author has classified the varieties of love.[22] Actually, there are four types of love. There is the "I love I" type which is seen in the child. This is primary narcissism and is in reality self-love. The child says, "This is my toy; give me this." If he doesn't get it, he gets angry, hostile and frustrated, and cries or stamps off. There are adults who have never really emerged from this "I love I" period of their psychosexual development. They are totally incapable of giving in any type of sustaining relationship. Naturally, from the start, such a marriage is destined to failure.

The next type is projected self-love ("I love me —in you"). This, too, is "I love I," except that these people worship themselves in another person. Like infants, these people "love" only those who do things for them. It is all incoming, not outgoing.

The third type of love is characterized by romantic affection in which sex is paramount. It is the same type of unrealistic, romantic love that is portrayed in our movies, novels, and popular songs. After the initial thrill of the honeymoon, the chill sets in. The sexual ardor begins to wear off, the quarreling begins. Eventually these frustrated individuals discover that they have nothing in common except self-love. They are not willing to give to each other. Since neither gives, neither receives. The last type of love, by far the rarest, is noted in the old married couple celebrating their golden wedding anniversary. They are just as much in love as when they first met. They did not enter this relationship thinking of what they were going to get but, rather, what they were going to give to each other! Their sexual responses may have been weak at first, but increased in intensity as they sacrificed for one another. Briefly, sex is the passionate interest in another body, and love is the passionate interest in another personality! Just as whisky and soda are found together, so are love and sex found together, but they are separate ingredients!

When trying to get at the factors responsible for sexual coldness, one must inquire how the wife feels about her husband. Does she love him? Is she a warm, outgoing person, willing to give of herself to him? What reservations does she have about sex? Has sex been presented to her as wicked, sinful, and dirty? Does she think that only a fallen woman has sexual climaxes?

The following case illustrates my technics:

A couple who were projecting their squabbling over their sexual tensions onto their four children decided to commit suicide! The wife's ignorance and apathy toward sexual matters were pronounced. She was a member of a very devoutly religious sect which frowned upon sex and taught that it was only for reproduction, not for pleasure. Hypnosis and autohypnosis were used. Like most women of this type, she said, "I can get plenty of satisfaction before, during, or after the sex act if my husband plays with my clitoris. However, I feel very guilty about this."

Her guilt was alleviated by the assurance that any type of sex play precoitally is all right if it meets the approval of both partners and the sex act ends in genital union. (Foreplay exclusively without genital-to-genital union is considered a perversion.)

Sensory-imagery conditioning under hypnosis was then utilized to transfer the sensation of clitoral climax to the vagina. Through posthypnotic directions it was suggested, "You can transfer the pleasurable sensation in the clitoral area to wherever you wish to experience it." Through hallucinatory intercourse during autohypnosis, she imagined having the pleasant sensation associated with clitoral climaxes transferred to her lower pelvic region. After 3 weeks of intensive psychotherapy, often consisting of 3- or 4-hour sessions, and practice, it was suggested that she have intercourse. "Do not deliberately try to have a vaginal orgasm, but relax and don't press—it will occur eventually. The most important matter is to enjoy sex without guilt. You can wonder whether you will achieve the type of response you wish during the first month or the second month. Perhaps it may even occur earlier. Let me know. The exact pleasure responses which you experienced during the practice sessions will occur when you are least expecting them." In due time, this patient was having the type of orgasms she wished.

One can also employ time distortion[22] by suggesting, "For every minute of friction you receive during the sex act, it will *seem like 5 minutes!*"

Thus, if the female requires prolonged contact and her husband has premature ejaculation, time can be "lengthened" to give them each greater satisfaction. Naturally, this mechanical adjunct, as has already been mentioned, must be combined with the overall relationship and attitudes of mutual love.

HYPNOBEHAVIORAL THERAPY OF FRIGIDITY, VAGINISMUS AND DYSPAREUNIA

Kroger and Fezler review some of the newer concepts in treating nonorgasmic females (primary orgasmic dysfunction) by a hypnobehavioral model.[28] They discuss the various classifications of these types of sexual dysfunctions and point out the importance of the relationship between the partners. This is usually the crucial variable in any kind of therapy. They employ specific images for obtaining arousal and hypnorelaxation to neutralize the associated anxiety which is invariably present. The unadaptive or faulty behavioral responses are unlearned, and new healthy patterns of responding are facilitated by hypnosis. Systematic desensitization and counterconditioning are used under hypnosis not only for overcoming anorgasmia, but also for alleviation of dyspareunia and vaginismus. Fuchs and co-workers have reported on desensitization under hypnosis procedures for intractable vaginismus.[13] Their approach essentially involves the principles of deconditioning *in vivo* (actually using vaginal dilators of increasing size to penetrate) or *in vitro* (imagery or visualizations of penetration by the penis) under hypnotic relaxation. The latter induces a feeling of safety so that the patient can be confronted with the lowest item on a hierarchy of anxiety-evoking stimuli. Each item is presented until eventually even the strongest of the anxiety-evoking stimuli fails to produce any degree of anxiety in the patient. Visualization of the suggested material becomes more vivid and realistic under hypnosis. Improvement of frigidity has been obtained with hypnobehavioral therapy.[12] About 60 per cent of 100 women on follow-up were cured of primary and secondary orgasmic dysfunction.[6]

Other investigators have used hypnotic technics *per se* for vaginismus,[10, 40] uncovering the psychodynamic factors responsible for the orgasmic dysfunction.[1, 35, 36] The "allure of the forbidden" has been employed by having the female imagine herself engaging in intercourse with a partner with a white square (representing censorship) over his genitalia.[5] The number of orgasmic responses in women with secondary orgasmic dysfunctions has been tripled.[39] More sensation in patients having "sexual anesthesia" has been reported.[4] Psychodynamic therapy and hypnosis have been recommended for frigidity.[2] A search for key or imprint-like experiences in childhood or other inhibiting subconscious factors has been recommended.[7]

LOW BACK PAIN

This discussion will be limited to low back pain of psychosomatic origin. There is an "organ language" which the body uses to voice its protests, and the choice of the organ system is determined by the focal area in which the emotional conflict occurs. To some of these individuals, worry is "a pain in the back," and their back symptoms only express the language of the body, saying, "I am carrying a load on my back—I cannot carry on. Can't people see how I am suffering? Why doesn't someone help me?"

If these and other questions can be answered, the emotional basis for the backache can be determined readily. A personality appraisal is generally necessary in refractory patients. Naturally, the signs and the symptoms of organic disease must be ruled out.

Low back pain of emotional origin, if its function is determined, can be treated hypnotically by symptom-transformation—switching the symptom to another less incapacitating one—but this must be only with the patient's permission. Through the induction of an artificial conflict, another target organ can be suggested for an equivalent symptom to replace the original conversion reaction. For example, it can be suggested that the low back pain be transferred to the stomach. This is not done by direct suggestion but by suggesting a conflict associated with deprivation and fear. If the patient develops the new symptom, it is indicative that she is willing to yield the

old one. The fact that the symptom can be manipulated indicates a favorable prognosis. Of course, the newly acquired symptom can be removed, either by hypnosis or autohypnosis, more readily than the long-standing one. In order to use this approach one must be familiar with the hypnoanalytic technics described in Chapter 50.

PELVIC PAIN

The same factors described above apply to the diagnosis of pelvic pain. However, there can be no question of "real" versus "psychic" pain. The reproductive organs reflect the effects of emotions. Pelvic pain is treated in a manner similar to that described for backache. The cases below are typical. Many individuals with pelvic pain are "polysurgical addicts," who are making the rounds of physicians' offices seeking another operation.

Previous operations usually include an appendectomy, the removal of "ovarian cysts," "straightening of the womb," and the removal of "adhesions." Patients with polysurgical addiction are not aware of their deep-seated need for an operative assault. Such women have deep-seated guilt feelings for which the surgery serves as punishment, atonement and, finally, license to commit new offenses. As a rule, there is improvement for several months following such obtuse "therapy," after which the patient again produces symptoms and demands for further surgery.

The author discusses in detail the use of hypnosis for pelvic pain of functional origin.[26] The psychophysiologic mechanisms are explored, and the differential diagnosis and contraindications to hypnotherapy are described. He cites cases treated by brief hypnotherapy through symptom removal, symptom substitution, symptom transformation and amelioration, as well as other types of treatment, such as reciprocal inhibition therapy, the Y-state of Yoga, hypnosis, suggestive sleep, and hypnosynthesis. Direct symptom-eliminating suggestions are valuable. For example, telling the patient, "What you have suffered belongs to the past" represents an inhibitory conditioned mechanism directed toward suppression of excitatory "trigger zones" in the cortex. Extensive probing for traumatic events is never used, and often only a light state is necessary for post-hypnotic suggestions to provide pain relief. On the basis of the author's empirical observations, it seems that a high percentage of patients with pelvic pain can achieve symptom control by hypnotherapy. The technics should be adapted to the needs of the patient. Hypnosis may act by breaking up noxious and well-established pain reflexes through "synaptic ablation"—a sort of "psychological lobotomy."

PREMENSTRUAL TENSION

Women with premenstrual tension suffer from emotional symptoms such as irritability, proneness to domestic friction, crying, and depression. The symptoms of physical discomfort, such as backache, headache, and varying degrees of edema of the breasts, the abdomen, and the legs, are not as important as the emotional concomitants which often disturb the patient's interpersonal relationships. In some instances, compulsive behavior, suicide, and unpremeditated criminal acts are due to the breakdown of defenses and the resultant lowering of the general sensory threshold coincidental with the premenstrual phase.

Excessive estrogens, progesterone, and the overproduction of antidiuretic hormones have been held responsible for the excess sodium and water in the tissues. A lowered blood sugar, following the hyperinsulinism secondary to emotional factors, was thought to increase the irritability of the nervous system. However, the use of hormones or diuretics *per se* cannot correct the emotional factors contributing to the difficulties.

The lack of uniformity of opinion as to what constitutes premenstrual tension, the varied methods and results reported in regard to treatment, and the frequent relapses after "cure" all indicate that there is no single causative factor. Therefore, an interdisciplinary approach directed to psychosomatic factors is indicated. Failures result if therapy is directed to only one portion of the syndrome.

The multifaceted approach should consist of antidepressants to elevate the mood, analgesic agents for the discomfort, diuretics and ammonium chloride for the edema, and the correction of the electrolyte imbalance—specific therapy, however, depends on the symptomatology. Hypnosis can be used to potentiate all these approaches.

The noncritical attitude of the physician, his empathy, and his acceptance of the validity of the patient's complaints are other important factors which aid in helping to correct the psychological symptoms. Supportive psychotherapy, consisting of reeducation, reassurance, and the development of strong rapport, through hypnosis, will enable most patients to face their life problems and not succumb to real or fancied symptoms, which often are used for secondary gain purposes—to master the world around them in an immature manner. Experience indicates that the symptoms of premenstrual tension disappear to a significant degree when understanding of the need for the symptom is achieved.

MENOPAUSE

Menopausal symptoms are attributed by the majority of clinicians to estrogen deficiency. This is reflected by the large number of patients treated with estrogens and by the numerous papers reporting the success of this therapy. Severe menopausal symptoms are unknown in some cultures, and the clinical picture is confusing in our society. The cause of the flushing is a failure of the heat-regulating mechanism of the body to dissipate heat properly. There are no correlations between clinical findings and vaginal smears. Women who have the worst symptoms may have smears indicating adequate estrogen stimulation. Others, who have no symptoms, show a complete absence of vaginal cornification. Evidence exists that a "third gonad" in the adrenal gland functions long after the ovaries atrophy.

Good results have been obtained in treating numerous patients with supportive hypnotherapy, oral estrogens, and sedatives.[24] Substantial improvement occurs after the ventilation of personal problems. Eradication of popular fallacies by reeducation, together with reassurance and the judicious use of hormones and tranquilizers, will often prove helpful. Such a psychosomatic approach serves to eliminate the "buttock syndrome," making the patient less dependent on "shots" and less cancer prone.

MISCELLANEOUS PSYCHOGYNECIC CONDITIONS

The author frequently sees women who demand urethral and vaginal treatments for nonexistent diseases. These are masturbation equivalents, and sexual gratification is obtained in the guise of the physician's treatment, whereas self-manipulation of the genitals is taboo.

Retroversion of the uterus is frequently held responsible for pelvic pain. However, it has been said that the patient whose genital organs seem to be "wrong" is likely to be a patient whose psychological processes relating to sex are "wrong"![21] The latter can definitely influence the former.

PELVIC EXAMINATION

Frequently hypnosis may be of considerable value when a pelvic examination is necessary in an obese patient. Merely having the patient enter into hypnosis usually produces adequate relaxation.

MINOR GYNECOLOGIC SURGERY

Hypnosis may be used as an anesthetic agent in suitable patients for performing a dilatation and curettage, a biopsy of the cervix, or a culdoscopy. It can also be employed to reduce analgesia and anesthesia for major operative gynecologic procedures (see Chap. 34).

LAPAROSCOPY AND HYSTEROSALPINGOGRAPHY

Hypnosis can be used to relax a tubal spasm in an infertile patient when performing a diagnostic procedure such as a hysterosalpingography, a tubal insufflation, a hysterogram, or a laparoscopic examination.

PRURITUS VULVAE

Pruritus vulvae will be discussed in the next chapter.

STERILIZATION

Pseudo-orientation in time can be used on selected women requesting sterilization. Under hypnosis, the patient is projected "several years ahead" and asked how she feels now that her tubes were tied several years ago (the date suggested should be at least 2 years ahead). Any feelings of guilt, remorse, or self-recrimination indicate the need for further investigation. Many women develop emotional disorders after sterilization; these can be obviated by projecting the patient into the hallucinated future.

MAMMARY AUGMENTATION

Breast enlargement through visual imagery and hypnosis was recently reported by Williams.[43] He used age regression to the time the breasts were growing to recapture the feeling and sensation of the breasts enlarging. He also age progressed the subjects to a time when the breasts would be the size desired. Results indicated that at the end of 12 weekly sessions, 13 subjects averaged an increase in the circumference of the breasts of 2.11 inches. No follow-up data were reported to see if these gains were retained. Others[41] replicated these findings and noted that during the three months after the cessation of treatment, 81% of the gains were retained.

Willard,[42] using a taped cassette program, observed that 20 of 22 subjects were able to use visual imagery for breast enlargement. All had some increase in breast size. Eighty-five per cent were aware of a significant increase in breast size, and 46% required a larger brassiere size due to the enlargement which occurred.

Though these measures do not equal what can be done with surgical augmentation, further refinement of these procedures might equal the results obtained by surgical methods.

SUMMARY

Any physician trained in hypnotherapy who utilizes an interdisciplinary approach can obtain gratifying results in many difficult gynecologic cases. Naturally, hypnosis here, too, is not a cure-all; there are many failures and relapses. However, autohypnosis, sensory-imagery conditioning, and posthypnotic suggestions directed toward the patient's emotional needs speed up any type of psychotherapy.

Dependency is not fostered when autohypnosis is used. Since the patient, to a degree, controls the therapy, her self-esteem is enhanced. Motivation, rapport, and confidence are more readily established when permissive technics that are noncritical are employed.

Dramatic symptom removal by a doctor-directed approach is outmoded. Symptom substitution or symptom transformation, as discussed more fully in Chapter 50, are valuable for achieving relatively permanent results.

It is not necessary for the patient to understand the origin of the symptoms, but *how she reacts to them and how she deals with her emotional problems are of the utmost importance.* Greater therapeutic leverage can be obtained by revivification, posthypnotic suggestion, time distortion, and other hypnotic phenomena.

Hypnotherapy for psychogynecic conditions helps many emotionally disturbed females to face their problems on a more mature level by developing healthier behavior patterns. Thus anxiety-provoking tensions can be dealt with more realistically. Such psychotherapy usually should be combined with a medical approach for optimal results.

REFERENCES

1. Abraham, G.: Possibilities of hypnosis in the treatment of frigidity. Minerva Med., *63:*962, 1972.
2. Alexander, L.: Treatment of impotency and anorgasmia by psychotherapy aided by hypnosis. Am. J. Clin. Hypn., *17:*33, 1974.
3. August, R.V.: Hypnosis: an additional tool in the study of infertility. Fertil. Steril., *11:*118, 1960.
4. Beigel, H.G.: The use of hypnosis in female sexual anesthesia. J. Am. Soc. Psychosom. Dent. Med., *19:*4, 1972.
5. Brady, J.P.: Brevital relaxation treatment of frigidity. Behav. Res. Ther., *4:*71, 1966.
6. Cheek, D.B.: Short-term hypnotherapy for frigidity using exploration of early life attitudes. Am. J. Clin. Hypn., *19:*20, 1976.
7. Cheek, D. B., and Le Cron, L.M.: Clinical Hypnotherapy. New York, Grune & Stratton, 1968.
8. Chernenkoff, W.: A case of frigidity. Am. J. Clin. Hypn., *11:*195, 1969.
9. Crasilneck, H.B., and Hall, M.D.: Clinical Hypnosis: Principles and Applications. New York, Grune & Stratton, 1975.
10. Dolezal, A.: The role of hypnosis in the treatment of vaginismus. Ile. Clin. Gynecol. (Charles University, Prague), in Excerpta Medica, *25:*222, 1972.
11. Dunbar, F.: Emotions and Bodily Changes. New York, Columbia University Press, 1938, p. 335.
12. Fabbri, R.: Hypnosis and the treatment of sexual disorders (paper given at the 18th annual meeting of the American Society for Clinical Hypnosis, Seattle, 1975).
13. Friedgood, H. B.: Neuroendocrine and psychodynamic factors in sterility. West. J. Surg. *56:*391, 1948.
14. Fuchs, K., *et al.:* Hypno-desensitization therapy of vaginismus. Part I: "in vitro" method. Part II: "in vivo" method. Int. J. Clin. Exp. Hypn., *20:*144, 1973.
15. Heiman, M.: Psychosocial influences in functional uterine bleeding. Obstet. Gynecol., *7:*3, 1956.
16. Heyer, G.R.: Hypnose und Hypnotherapie in die psychischen Heilmethoden. Hrsg. von Karl Birnbaum. Leipzig, Georg Thieme, 1927, pp. 73–135.
17. Israel, S. L.: Discussion of Buxton, L.: A critical survey of present methods of diagnosis and therapy in human infertility. Am. J. Obstet. Gynecol., *70:*741, 1955.
18. Kroger, W. S.: Treatment of psychogynecic disorders by hypnoanalysis. Am. J. Obstet. Gynecol., *52:*409, 1946.
19. _____: Evaluation of personality factors in the treatment of infertility. Fertil. Steril., *3:*542, 1952.
20. _____: Hypnotherapy in obstetrics and gynecology. J. Clin. Exp. Hypn., *1:*61, 1953.
21. _____: Psychosomatic aspects of obstetrics and gynecology. Obstet. Gynecol., *3:*504, 1954.
22. _____: Psychosomatic aspects of frigidity and impotency. Int. Rec. Med., *171:*469, 1958.
23. _____: Psychosomatic aspects of frigidity. J.A.M.A., *143:*56, 1950.
24. _____: Hypnotherapy in obstetrics and gynecology, J. Arkansas Med. Soc., *55:*412, 1959.
25. _____: An integrated approach to infertility. J. Psychosomatics, *3:*1, 1962.
26. _____: Hypnosis for relief of pelvic pain. Clin. Obstet. Gynecol., *6:*763, 1963.
27. _____: Sexual frustration. Sexual Behav., *2:*41, 48, 1972.
28. Kroger, W.S., and Fezler, W.D.: Hypnosis and

Behavior Modification: Imagery Conditioning, Philadelphia, J.B. Lippincott, 1976.

29. Kroger, W.S., and Freed, S.C.: Psychosomatic treatment of functional dysmenorrhea by hypnosis. Am. J. Obstet. Gynecol., *46:*817, 1943.

30. _____: Psychosomatic aspects of sterility. Am. J. Obstet. Gynecol., *59:*867, 1950.

31. _____: Psychosomatic factors in functional amenorrhea. Am. J. Obstet. Gynecol., *59:*328, 1950.

32. _____: Psychosomatic Gynecology: Including Problems of Obstetrical Care. Philadelphia, W.B. Saunders, 1951.

33. Leckie, F.H.: Hypnotherapy in gynecological disorders. Int. J. Clin. Exp. Hypn., *12:*121, 1964.

34. _____: Further gynecological conditions treated by hypnotherapy. Int. J. Clin. Exp. Hypn., *13:*11, 1965.

35. Levit, H.I.: Marital crisis intervention: hypnosis in impotence/frigidity cases. Am. J. Clin. Hypn., *14:* 56, 1971.

36. Power, E.: Hypnosis as a diagnostic auxiliary medium in internal medicine, gynecology and obstetrics. Am. J. Clin. Hypn., *4:*127, 1961.

37. Rakoff, A.E., and Fried, P.: Pseudocyesis: a psychosomatic study in gynecology. J.A.M.A., *145:* 1329, 1951.

38. Reifenstein, E. C.: Hypothalamic amenorrhea, Med. Clin. North Am., *30:*1103, 1946.

39. Richardson, T.A.: Hypnotherapy in frigidity. Am. J. Clin. Hypn., *5:*194, 1963.

40. Schneck, J.M.: Hypnotherapy for vaginismus. Int. J. Clin. Exp. Hypn., *13:*92, 1965.

41. Staib, A.R., and Logan, D.R.: Hypnotic stimulation of breast growth. Am. J. Clin. Hypn., *19:*201, 1977.

42. Willard, R.D.: Breast enlargement through visual imagery and hypnosis. Am. J. Clin. Hypn., *19:*195, 1977.

43. Williams, J.E.: Stimulation of breast growth by hypnosis. J. Sex Research, *10:*316, 1974.

44. Wollman, Leo: The role of hypnosis in the treatment of infertility. Br. J. Med. Hypn., *2:*38, 1961.

38

Hypnosis in Dermatology

EMOTIONS AND SKIN

The effectiveness of hypnotherapy for alopecia areata, dermatitis, eczema, hyperhidrosis, neurodermatitis, psoriasis, pruritus, lichen planus, herpes simplex, pemphigus, verrucae, and other dermatologic disorders has been reviewed.[39] The psychosomatic etiology for many of these disorders is well established. The well-known phenomena of goose pimples, sweating, blanching, and temperature changes in the skin following psychological stimuli constitute further corroborative evidence.

The skin mirrors the inner self. It is richly endowed with emotional symbolism. Such expressions as "thick-skinned" and "thin-skinned" may mean "insensitive" and "sensitive" respectively. "To get under my skin" and "itching to do something" are common expressions; if one fails to act in response to these feelings, actual itching and scratching may result. The epidermis and the nervous system originate from the ectoderm and, since both are nurtured by a mesenchymal derivative composed of vascular connective tissue, it is only logical to assume that there is a "cross-fertilization" between the skin and the autonomic nervous system. Experiments in which radiant heat was applied equally to both forearms, one made "vulnerable" and the other "resistant" by hypnosis, resulted in rubor and edema in the former.[8] Other data on 57 subjects showed that skin pathology induced by conditioning was histologically identical to that produced by a noxious substance from lacquer trees.

Direct hypnotic suggestion has produced erythema, blisters,[31] wheals, urticaria, tumefaction, congestion, hemorrhage, and various sensory effects ranging from anesthesia to hyperesthesia, cold to hot, and itching to pain. However, after reviewing the literature, other researchers concluded that motivated nonhypnotized persons can produce or mimic the same physiological changes as deeply hypnotized persons.[36] Organic skin manifestations do not respond as well to mere suggestion *per se* but, rather, to hypnotic sensory-imagery conditioning. This enables the individual to react to a hallucinated stimulus as if to a reality perception. However, the ability to relieve organic changes varies from one individual to another, depending upon the degree of autonomic control induced by hypnotic conditioning.

The role of the autonomic nervous system in cutaneous physiopathology has been treated.[34, 42] The nervous system apparently is capable of directing repressed emotional forces to appropriate target organs; the site selected is determined by a local vulnerability of the skin as well as a correlation between the nature of the emotional stimulus and the type of the physiologic response. Why the skin lesions vary with the type of conflict, and from person to person, appearing and disappearing during the life-span of the same person is, at present, poorly understood. Skin reactions relating to previous experiences have been described.[45] Reddening of the skin was unrelieved until a mustard plaster was applied.[48]

HYPNOSIS IN DERMATOLOGICAL DISORDERS

There are studies which indicate that harmful reactions in the skin can be blocked by hypnosis. Posthypnotic suggestions of coldness neutralized reactivity to allergens and histamines.[13] Reduction in skin sensitivity after hypnosis alone has been reported.[18] The hypersensitivity response has been inhibited by direct hypnotic suggestion.[5, 6] The Prausnitz-Küstner reaction and the Mantoux tuberculin reaction also have been inhibited.[7] Inhibition of the Mantoux reactions has been demonstrated in Mantoux-positive patients on one arm with a normal reaction on the other.[28] However, some investigators were unable to effect the normal dermal response to mumps antigen, trypsin, or histamine.[3]

Hypnosis has relieved itching in refractory cases of intractable eczema,[19, 30, 38, 39] nevus, herpes zoster,[26] lichen planus, psoriasis,[17, 32, 40] hyperhidrosis,[16] and other skin disorders.[4, 9, 20] There are several favorable reports on its use in chronic ichthyosis.[23, 29, 37, 49] Acne has been cured by hypnosis merely by suggesting that thinking of the word "scar" would symbolize an ugly facial appearance; thus picking and spreading of the lesions were prevented.

The itching of generalized neurodermatitis has been relieved by hypnosis,[24, 35] probably through vasomotor alterations. Others have investigated the physiology of masochism in relation to itching. A typical personality profile has been postulated.

There is an extensive literature on the psychosomatic aspects of pruritus ani and pruritus vulvae. I have obtained gratifying success with hypnotherapy used for direct symptom removal in pruritus vulvae. The primitive pathways developed during infancy and childhood, when masturbation and other autoerotic tendencies were associated with guilt feelings, are often utilized during adulthood to express unrequited sexual tensions via the genitals. The pruritus occurred as often in virginal girls as in married women, and frigidity played an important role in the latter; "necking" and "heavy petting" resulted in genital tensions in the former. Some women rub their legs together to obtain relief—"onanistic pru-

rique"—from the itching. Tickling and itching, as pleasurable sensations, only emphasize the intimate connection between sexual feelings and the modification of skin sensibility. Hence, it is not surprising that masturbation equivalents are engrafted on an actual itching dermatosis. By such measures, the scratching obviates guilt.

Some people utilize their pruritus masochistically to express inward rage over their inability to obtain love and affection. By such measures, the dependency and the subsequent hostility are denied and masked by a façade of cooperation and submissiveness. The unrelieved frustration and hostility are then activated in overt symptoms such as irascibility, insomnia, fatigue, anorexia, bodily pains, and an attitude of "If I don't get some relief soon, I might just as well be dead." These typically depressive reactions only cover the real, underlying emotional difficulties.

Numerous investigators have found that 60 to 70 per cent of warts respond to suggestive therapy.[12, 14, 43] There have been many types of lay-healing, from "charming" away warts by bizarre and mysterious procedures to using prayers and incantations. Ullman, in excellent monographs on the subject, assayed the use of hypnosis—since it emulated lay-healing—for the treatment of warts.[46, 47] In eight out of 15 deeply hypnotized patients, a complete remission of the warts occurred in contrast with two cures in 47 patients who could not be deeply hypnotized. If a lay hypnotist had not been used, the results would have been better because the rapport would not have been divided. This work was recently corroborated in a series in which half of a group was treated and the other half was used as a control.[41] Cures were obtained in 10 out of a total of 15 patients on the treated side in from 5 weeks to 3 months. Unequivocally, directive hypnotherapy played a significant role in catalyzing the curative processes in certain patients with warts.

The author recently had a patient who had had surgical removal of a wart under the nail bed of her thumb on five occasions. While deeply hypnotized, the wart was sprayed with ethyl chloride. It was suggested that this application would freeze the wart away. The wart disappeared after three applications. The patient was a somnambulist. Follow-up 1 year later showed no recurrence.

However, other investigators could not get warts to disappear with either hypnotic or nonhypnotic suggestions.[43] The conflicting results reported may be attributed to studies that differed in design.[22] The responses depended largely on the degree of hypnotizability.[2]

Kroger and Fezler discuss the hypnobehavioral approach to skin disorders.[26] They stress imagery conditioning, reinforcement learning, and the production of artificial conflicts to produce a specific emotional attitude which might elicit the specific skin reaction desired. They advise the use of structured images calculated to produce alterations in body image. These are then directed toward condensation of the lesions. They report successful outcomes in cases of dermatitis factitia (picking at the skin) and trichotillomania (hair pulling) treated by hypnosis and behavior modification. Fabbri and Dy describe two cases of the latter condition successfully treated by hypnosis.[15]

HYPNOTHERAPEUTIC METHODS

The intensified hypnotherapeutic relationship, combined with the therapist's ability to release a sufficiently strong affect, often results in dramatic recovery. In dermatologic disorders, it appears that the greater the patient's conviction of cure, the less the physician's suggestive "power" is required, probably because of the lability of the skin to emotions. However, lack of conviction on the part of the therapist leads to poor results and frequently makes the anxious patient worse. Hypnotherapy also can potentiate x-ray therapy, ointments, and drugs.

Hypnonarcosis has been employed to relieve chronic itching dermatoses. Various types of dermatitis have been cured by prolonged hypnosis—6 or more days of continuous "hypnotic sleep." However, follow-up studies are meager. Prolonged hypnotic sleep has been used successfully for a wide variety of medical conditions.[1] The author has had no experience with this approach in skin diseases.

An extensive literature on the use of hypnosuggestive procedures, often combined with electrosleep and balneotherapy (usual resort or spa treatment), has been reviewed. This combination can prove to be more effective than hypnotherapy alone, particularly for neurodermatitis, eczema, and psoriasis.[21]

VERBALIZATIONS FOR AUTHORITARIAN HYPNOTIC TECHNICS

Direct hypnotic suggestion sometimes relieves itching and scratching. Here the physician must convincingly suggest, "Immediately upon coming out of the hypnotic state, your itching (or pain, pimples, rash) will disappear." More effective is the method of telling the hypnotized subject, "You are lying under an ultraviolet light" [or "in the hot sun"], and your face [if this is the area involved] is becoming very warm. This wonderful feeling will remain for several hours [or all day]; your skin will feel fine until your next visit."

When this older approach is used, it is advisable to enhance the psychological suggestions by the physiologic effect of touching the area with an instrument. Reinforcement is usually necessary.

PERMISSIVE HYPNOTIC TECHNICS FOR SYMPTOM REMOVAL

Regardless of the hypnotherapeutic approach, itching must be controlled to prevent further scratching and aggravation of a skin disorder. Invariably, medical measures must be supplemented by explanations of the underlying disorder and the *need* for the symptom. As emphasized throughout this book, most patients do not have to understand the origin of their symptoms, nor is symptom substitution likely, but *how they react to and face their problems in a realistic and mature manner is of the utmost importance!*

USE OF SENSORY-IMAGERY CONDITIONING

Permissive hypnotic technics which do not mobilize critical attitudes are employed to facilitate sensory-imagery conditioning. However, as mentioned above, correction of faulty attitudes and habit patterns is not obtained by fiat or conscious exhortations to use the will. A direct frontal attack to remove the skin disorder by an authoritative hypnotic approach often can overwhelm the patient and achieve only temporary results. Kroger and Fezler[26] and others[17, 24, 25] use such technics for psoriasis. These consist of imaginal basking in the sun—a procedure that in real life often helps to resolve this condition. With these technics, one first learns how to control a portion of the body, and then, in a manner similar to that of Yoga, control of more autonomic functioning is established.

USE OF GLOVE ANESTHESIA

Transfer of glove anesthesia (the self-induced palmar anesthesia) to the affected area often alleviates the itching and scratching. The busy dermatologist can save time by employing group hypnotherapy in a method similar to that used by obstetricians (see p. 230).

SYMPTOM SUBSTITUTION

Another successful hypnotic technic is to exaggerate the itching. If the itching can be increased, it can be decreased! A systematic attempt then is made to "wean" the patient from the *need* to itch and scratch by symptom substitution or by symptom transformation (i.e., by "trading down"). Through conditioning under autohypnosis, the itch can be displaced or transferred to another portion of the body. When successful, this indicates that the patient is willing to yield the symptom. The new symptom naturally is easier to remove than the long-standing one.

An interesting technic to relieve itching is to suggest a negative sensory hallucination. This can be accomplished by the misdirection of attention as follows: The patient is to imagine, while under hypnosis, that as he looks at his lesions he "sees" that the skin looks and feels as normal as any other area of the body devoid of lesions. Unfortunately, success with this approach requires a subject who is capable of entering the somnambulistic state or one closely allied to it. One can remark: "Look at your right wrist; you can begin to speculate on whether or not that area will look like your left wrist, which does not have any involvement. Now, keep looking at the left wrist; notice the texture of the skin—it also feels per-

fectly normal, does it not?" (The patient nods his head in agreement.) "Every time you look at this wrist, you will observe that this area on your right wrist is becoming as normal looking as your left wrist. You may also close your eyes, and in your 'mind's eye' see or imagine that the lesions have disappeared—the skin is normal in appearance. However, you may keep just as much of the itching on the involved area of the wrist as you wish to retain. You do not have to get rid of this itching all at once but, rather, allow it to disappear slowly." The patient is given another posthypnotic suggestion such as: "You might raise the question whether you wish this lesion (on the wrist) or that lesion (one near the elbow) to disappear first. Also, you might begin to consider the possibility of just when this will occur. Will it be tomorrow, a week from tomorrow, or several weeks from now? At any rate, the more you keep thinking about this under autohypnosis, the more likely the rash will go away." Thus the theoretic dangers attributed to symptom removal are obviated.

Motivation, belief, and confidence are readily established when permissive hypnotic technics, such as sensory-imagery conditioning, symptom substitution, or symptom transformation, are employed. This type of scientific hypnotherapy, through effective rapport, enables the physician to establish a beachhead on the periphery of the patient's disorder—but he helps the patient to cure himself! Dependency on the therapist is minimal when autohypnotic conditioning is used to raise the adaptive response. Thus the theoretic dangers attributed to symptom-removal therapy are obviated, the physician being merely a catalytic agent.

SPECIALIZED HYPNOTIC TECHNICS

Revivification, automatic writing, dream interpretation, and other projective technics are often effective in the dissolution of refractory skin disorders. The patient is asked to revivify the disturbing experiences that preceded the onset of his symptom. Discussion of feelings associated with these experiences can help resolve emotional conflicts. Abreaction, plus education and reassurance, generally obviates the need for further working-through of conflictual material.

Of particular value is engrafting of an artificial conflict, calculated to produce a given specific emotional attitude which might elicit a given skin reaction. Unfortunately, too few patients are amenable to these complex technics. When applicable and wisely used, such hypnotherapeutic technics can alter the prognosis of many refractory cases of psychosomatic dermatologic disorders.

REFERENCES

1. Andreev, B.V.: Sleep Therapy in the Neuroses. New York, Consultants Bureau, 1960.
2. Asher, R.: Respectable hypnosis. Br. Med. J., *1:* 309, 1956.
3. Beahrs, J.O., *et al.:* Failure to alter skin inflammation by hypnotic suggestion in five subjects with normal skin reactivity. Psychosom. Med., *32:* 627, 1970.
4. Biondo, R.: Hypnosis and dermatology (paper given the 18th annual meeting of the American Society for Clinical Hypnosis, Seattle, 1975).
5. Black, S.: Inhibition of immediate-type hypersensitivity response by direct suggestion under hypnosis. Br. Med. J., *14:*925, 1963.
6. _____: Shift in dose-response curve of Prausnitz-Küstner reaction by direct suggestion under hypnosis. Br. Med. J., *5346:*990, 1963.
7. Black, S., Humphrey, J.H., and Niven, J.S.F.: Inhibition of Mantoux reaction by direct suggestion under hypnosis. Br. Med. J., *5346:*1649, 1963.
8. Chapman, L.F., *et al.:* Changes in tissue vulnerability induced by hypnotic suggestion. Am. J. Clin. Hypn., *2:*172, 1960.
9. Cheek, D.B.: Possible uses of hypnosis in dermatology. Med. Times, January 1961.
10. Clawson, T.A., and Swade, R.H.: The hypnotic control of blood flow and pain: the cure of warts and the potential use of hypnosis in the treatment of cancer. Am. J. Clin. Hypn., *17:*160, 1975.
11. Cleveland, S.E., and Fisher, S.: Psychological factors in the neurodermatoses. Psychosom. Med., *18:* 209, 1956.
12. Crasilneck, H.B., and Hall, J.A.: Clinical Hypnosis: Principles and Applications. New York, Grune & Stratton, 1975.
13. Dennis, M., and Philippus, M.J.: Hypnotic and non-hypnotic suggestion and skin response in atopic patients. Am. J. Clin. Hypn., *7:*342, 1965.
14. Ewin, D.M.: Condyloma acuminata: successful treatment of four cases by hypnosis. Am. J. Clin. Hypn., *17:*73, 1974.
15. Fabbri, R., and Dy, A.J.: Hypnotic treatment of trichotillomania. Int. J. Clin. Exp. Hypn., *22:*210, 1974.
16. Fernandez, G.R.: Hypnotism in the treatment of the stress factor in dermatological conditions. Br. J. Med. Hypn., *7:*21, 1955–1956.
17. Frankel, F.H., and Misch, R.C.: Hypnosis in a case of long-standing psoriasis in a person with character problems. Int. J. Clin. Exp. Hypn., *21:*121, 1973.
18. Fry, L., *et al.:* Effects of hypnosis on allergic skin responses in asthma and hay fever. Br. Med. J., *1:* 1145, 1964.
19. Goodman, H.P.: Hypnosis in prolonged resistant eczema: a case report. Am. J. Clin. Hypn., *5:*144, 1962.
20. Hartland, J.: Hypnosis in dermatology. Br. J. Clin. Hypn., *1:*1, 1970.
21. Hoskovec, J.: Review of some major works in Soviet hypnotherapy. Int. J. Clin. Exp. Hypn., *15:*1, 1967.
22. Keller, R.: Psychotherapy in psychosomatic disorders. Arch. Gen. Psychiatry, *32:*1021, 1975.
23. Kidd, C.B.: Congenital ichthyosiform erythroderma treated by hypnosis. Br. J. Dermatol., *78:* 101, 1966.
24. Kline, M.V.: Delimited hypotherapy: the acceptance of resistance in the treatment of a long-standing neurodermatitis with a sensory-imagery technique. J. Clin. Exp. Hypn., *1:*18, 1953.
25. _____: Hypnodynamic Psychology. New York, Julian Press, 1955.
26. Kroger, W.S., and Fezler, W.D.: Hypnosis and Behavior Modification: Imagery Conditioning. Philadelphia, J. B. Lippincott, 1976.
27. McDowell, M.: Hypnosis in dermatology. *In* Schneck, J.M. (ed.): Hypnosis in Modern Medicine. Springfield, Ill. Charles C Thomas, 1959, pp. 101–115.
28. Mason, A.A.: Hypnotism for Medical and Dental Practitioners. London, Camelot Press, 1960.
29. _____: A case of congenital ichthyosiform erythrodermia of brocq treated by hypnosis. Br. Med. J., *2:*422, 1952.
30. Motoda, K.: A case report of the counter-conditioning treatment of an eczema patient by hypnosis. Jap. J. Hypn., *15:*46, 1971.
31. Muftic, M.K.: Fenomeno vesicatorio por hipnosis (Vesicular phenomenon produced by hypnosis). Rev. Lat. Am. Hypn. Clin., *2:*29, 1961.

32. Poissaint, A.F.: Emotional factors in psoriasis. Psychosomatics, *4:*199, 1963.

33. Portnoy, M.E.: Un caso de asma y eczema tratado con hipnoses (A case of asthma and eczema treated by hypnosis). Acta-hypnol Lat. Am., *1:*71, 76, 1961.

34. Rothman, S.: The role of the autonomic nervous system in cutaneous disorders. Psychosom. Med., *7:* 90, 1945.

35. Sacerdote, P.: Hypnotherapy in neurodermatitis: a case report. Am. J. Clin. Hypn., *7:*249, 1965.

36. Sarbin, T.R., and Slagle, R.W.: Hypnosis and psychophysical outcomes. *In* Fromm, E., and Shor, R.E. (eds.): Hypnosis: Research and Perspectives. Chicago, Aldine-Atherton, 1972..

37. Schneck, J.J.: Ichthyosis treated with hypnosis. Dis. Nerv. System, *15:*211, 1954.

38. Scott, M.J.: Hypnosis in Skin and Allergic Diseases. Springfield, Ill., Charles C Thomas, 1960.

39. _____: Hypnosis in dermatologic therapy. Psychosomatics, *5:*365, 1964.

40. Secter, I.I., and Barthelemy, C.G.: Angular cheilosis and psoriasis as psychosomatic manifestations. Am. J. Clin. Hypn., *7:*79, 1964.

41. Sinclair-Gieben, A.H.C., and Chalmers, C.: Evaluation of treatment of warts by hypnosis. Lancet, *2:* 48, 1959.

42. Sulzberger, M.B., and Zaidens, S.H.: Psychogenic factors in dermatologic disorders. Med. Clin. North Am., *32:*669, 1948.

43. Surman, O.S., *et al.:* Hypnotic treatment of a child with warts. Am. J. Clin. Hypn., *15:*12, 1972.

44. Tenzel, J.H., and Taylor, R.L.: An evaluation of hypnosis and suggestion as treatment of warts. Psychosomatics, *10:*252, 1969.

45. Ullman, M.: Herpes simplex and second degree burns induced under hypnosis. Am. J. Psychiatry, *103:*830, 1946.

46. _____: On the psyche and warts. I. Suggestion and warts: a review and comment. Psychosom. Med., *21:*473, 1959.

47. Ullman, M., and Dudek, S.: On the psyche and warts. II. Hypnotic suggestion and warts. Psychosom. Med., *22:*68, 1960.

48. Vasiliev, L.: Mysterious Phenomena of the Human Psyche. (Volochava, S., trans.) New York, University Books, 1965.

49. Wink, C.A.S.: Congenital ichthyosiform erythroderma treated by hypnosis. Br. Med. J., *2:*741, 1961.

39

Hypnotherapy in Physical Rehabilitation of Neuromuscular Disorders

The purpose of this chapter is to describe the use of hypnosis as a potentiating agent in the physical rehabilitation of patients with various neuromuscular disorders, including multiple sclerosis, poliomyelitis, Parkinson's disease, and cerebral palsy. Hypnosis also is applicable for differentiating psychogenically based neurological deficits from organic conditions. It can potentiate some return of function, even if full recovery is impossible, and by increasing motivation, it can enable patients to cope with discomfort and increase desires for rehabilitation.

EFFECTS OF PLACEBO THERAPY

It is well known that in some of the chronic neurologic disorders, particularly multiple sclerosis[10, 11, 30, 32, 38, 39] and parkinsonism,[21] exacerbations and remissions may occur, regardless of the management or the drugs employed. The beneficial effects that are often attributed to nonspecific physical measures may be due, in part, to the cause of the disease and to a placebo effect operating at many different levels of awareness. This nonspecific or psychological portions of the various physical rehabilitation therapies can be enhanced by hypnosis or other forms of suggestive therapy. Patients are seldom aware that a nonspecific or placebo type of therapy may be camouflaged through misdirection by drugs, massage, electrotherapy, and other physical measures.

Unfortunately, by omitting hypnotherapy, physicians are literally driving many patients with chronic neuromuscular disorders to cultists and faddists, who, through misdirection, employ various types of suggestive procedures, including hypnosis, often with astounding success. However, the unscientific application of suggestive procedures by lay and religious healers is to be condemned because they may cause the sufferer's hopes to be raised too high and because of their inability to make a differential diagnosis. Furthermore, specific therapy for an organically based malady may be overlooked.

EFFECTS OF MUSIC THERAPY

The application of music and rhythm therapy as an adjunct in physical rehabilitation is another example of a quasi-hypnotic procedure. It is well known that repetitive, monotonic auditory stimuli, if continued long enough, are capable of inducing relaxation and even hypnosis. Incantations of primitive tribal rituals, religious rites, and some musical compositions have a seemingly hypnotic effect. Musical therapy readily achieves relaxation by its rhythmic and soothing qualities and is particularly successful in the mentally retarded or the brain-damaged child unable to concentrate on a standard hypnotic verbalization technic. Such patients may have their attention span increased under a combination of musical therapy and hypnosis. Music, by misdirection, may also be used as a method of defocusing attention. As an example, motor aphasics may have no trouble in verbalizing in song. At times, loud, frenzied passages, isomodic with the mood of the hyperexcited, disturbed patients,[55] may be more relaxing than soft lullabies.

In relation to cerebral palsy, several investigators have noted that if the rhythm was sufficiently slow, so that there was no strain in "keeping up" with the tempo, rigid limbs relaxed and athetoid motions noticeably decreased.[14, 15, 41] Carlson used music therapy and corroborated Lord's findings.[14, 15] He states, "Low rhythmic music will obviate the difficulty, or anything else which will tend to reduce the sensorial input to a minimum will be helpful."[14] He also speaks of the influence that selective inhibition or misdirected sensory stimuli have on the patient's ability to control his muscles.[15]

A close parallel has been noted between music therapy and hypnotic conditioning.[20] Thus, whenever muscular activity is satisfactorily correlated with sensory (musical) concentration, muscles react automatically. Similarly, posthypnotic suggestions are effective in promoting relaxation by a series of conditioned speech and muscle acts—ideomotor activity. It has been observed that it is possible to increase or control the severity, the rate, and the stability of an athetoid tremor by means of sound (and visual) stimuli.[48]

PSYCHOSOMATIC FACTORS

The precipitating emotional triggers in many ailments are often more important than the disease itself. It is now widely recognized that, in rehabilitation centers, the combined approach, directed toward emotional adjustment of the patient, may be more important than the correction of his physical defects. Within this framework, hypnosis can be an important potentiating tool for establishing healthy motivation for recovery.

HYPNOTHERAPY IN PHYSICAL REHABILITATION

In many of the technics employed in physical rehabilitation programs, suggestion and/or hypnosis are unwittingly used. For instance, Sister Kenny employed hot packs and massage in muscles "mentally alienated" by poliomyelitis. The hot packs were of some benefit, but she also used ideosensory conditioning when she asked the victims to think that they were "moving" their paralyzed limbs. Though she denied any similarity to hypnosis, this conditioning may have been more

effective than the physical therapy *per se* in facilitating the recovery of nonfunctioning muscles. She also made use of the "law of dominant effect," namely, that whenever a psychological suggestion reinforces a physiologic effect, *supramaximal motor responses* may be obtained. It might be well to call attention here to the fact that in physiology one means by "maximal effort" the largest load that a specific muscle can carry under given conditions. Then the paradoxical term of "supramaximal" is used to indicate that the maximal effort was not really the greatest but only maximal without psychological synergy.

The author has observed that numerous patients with proven neurologic deficits respond supramaximally when hypnosis and imagery conditioning are employed. Other investigators have made similar observations.[8, 68, 69] Crasilneck and Hall, who have a vast experience in this area, believe that maximizing of function "can be conceptualized as a change in the balance of facilitating or inhibiting neural impulses."[19]

The author recalls an interesting case of a 59-year-old paraplegic who was a former jet pilot. During deep hypnosis while being given an image of descending rapidly in a plane, he moved his right arm involuntarily toward the "controls." He came out of hypnosis spontaneously and with tears in his eyes explained, "Why, I haven't moved my arm in 5 years." Another case was reported, in which, at autopsy, the patient was found to have had a tumor which had destroyed the entire motor and sensory cortex of the dominant left hemisphere. The investigators could not explain how hypnosis had prevented the usual paralytic progression that should have occurred.[64] Also, an organic paralysis of the right arm had cleared up. It is speculated that in deep hypnosis a rapid transfer of dominance of the cerebral hemisphere may occur.[58] The possibility that motor pathways exist in the frontal lobe, which occasionally act as a substitute motor cortex has been suggested.[67]

Essentially, the author's thesis is that if these simple types of suggestion often help, then hypnosis, the acme of scientifically applied suggestion, should be even more efficacious in enhancing psychological synergy. The fundamental basis for this hypothesis is that hypnotized individuals respond with a pinpoint literalness or specificity to suggestion, providing that these are in full accord with their wishes and do not mobilize critical attitudes. Kline points out that hypnotically motivated behavior is not due to mere acceptance of authority or to hypersuggestibility alone but is due to:

. . . the capacity to recognize and accept communication that centers directly into the perceptual system. This is what permits the alterations, the changes, and the reorganizations of behavior that may be observed at all levels of response, emotionally and physiologically.[33]

Pavlov showed that serial conditioning, culminating in a conditioned response, was similar to hypnotic conditioning, the difference being that often "learning" in the latter can be achieved in a single session (see Chap. 26).[52] More importantly, a posthypnotic conditioned response lasted longer and was more difficult to extinguish than a similar conditioning at nonhypnotic levels.

The clinical improvement that followed the giving of posthypnotic suggestions in patients with neuromuscular disorders was due to elicitation of supramaximal responses. The "forgotten assets" of patients with muscular dystrophy often are not mobilized because of "fear of failure."[44]

Most patients with organic neuromuscular involvements *believe* and *think* they can no longer carry out certain activities. Therefore, they do not try because they apparently have accepted a level of performance that is actually lower than their capabilities. Improvement results after increased performance occurs. Usually, they can accomplish these acts and repeat them for some time thereafter.

Utilization of "forgotten assets" is demonstrated when a frail girl, while in a cataleptic state, suspended between two chairs and supported only by her head and heels, supports considerably more weight than at nonhypnotic levels. Here, through suggestion, a transcendence of normal voluntary muscle capacity results in a feat many athletes could not accomplish. This indicates that a potential reservoir of supra-maximal strength exists in the human body and, if properly harnessed, can increase the performance of the physically disabled individual.

POLIOMYELITIS

The Delorme technic of muscle strengthening emphasizes the need for exercises by increasing gradations into the overload zone.[16] Inasmuch as a person performs at supramaximal rather than at maximal levels under hypnosis, a more rapid and effective strengthening of muscles can be expected. In addition, the increased motivation obtained by hypnosis can also increase the skill and coordination of all the affected muscles and limbs. There are three effective methods for eliciting supramaximal effort by hypnosis: (1) by actual exercises carried out following posthypnotic suggestions; (2) by sensory-imagery conditioning healthy past performances during autohypnosis; (3) by vividly imagining the *successful* effort to be made. A hypnotized person acts, feels, and performs in accordance with what he imagines to be *true*.

Several investigators have demonstrated that hypnosis can reactivate earlier and healthier response patterns by the use of sensory-imagery conditioning technics, by age regression and/or revivification.[22, 28, 54] Others, however, did not find supportive evidence that hypnotic age regression evokes true neurophysiological regression.[6, 46]

The following case history illustrates the revivification technic:

A 34-year-old female had a marked weakness in both gastrocnemii muscles due to poliomyelitis during girlhood. She had reached a plateau of improvement after a long term of treatment by the orthodox technics of physical therapy. Under hypnosis, she was told that she could "relive" all the athletic activities participated in prior to the onset of her symptoms. She used this type of sensory-imagery conditioning, together with daily resistive exercises, under autohypnosis. Within 10 weeks she was able to stand on the toes of the right leg alone, something she had been unable to do prior to hypnotherapy.

This patient did not have actual regeneration of muscle as a result of hypnosis but, rather, as a result of the paralysis or weakening of some of her muscle groups, she was failing to use even her remaining, unaffected muscle groups. This naturally resulted in atrophy of disuse as well as loss of voluntary control of a muscle. Hypnosis, in this case, was effective in motivating the patient to use muscles which were still functional but which were not being used for psychological or neurophysiologic reasons. Similar beneficial results, over and above those obtained from physical therapy alone, were also obtained on three additional patients who had had poliomyelitis.

PARKINSONISM

A wide variety of therapeutic medicaments have been employed in the treatment of parkinsonism, with equivocal results. Doshay states, "Probably in no other branch of medicine is psychotherapy as important or as effective as in paralysis agitans."[25] Five cases of paralysis agitans were covered in his report: three patients were improved, and the other two could not be taught to develop self-hypnosis.

In the other two patients, the improved status was not so prolonged. In a man of 57 years and a woman of 48 years, improvement lasted for 6 months and 1 year respectively, while they were being trained by hypnotherapy. However, in both of these patients the improvement ceased when hypnotherapy ceased, indicating that no carryover was maintained. Others noted some improvement in the tremors associated with paralysis agitans when hypnosis was employed.[7, 9, 13]

No one infers that parkinsonism can be remedied entirely by hypnosis, but rather that psychological factors may be paramount in aggravating the condition. In some patients, in whom the disease is organically progressive, one would expect to get either temporary improvement or none at all. In others, in whom the disease is slowly progressive, the hypnotherapeutic approach results in a clinical remission. The reader must not assume that drugs, chemopallidectomy and other procedures are only of secondary importance. Where indicated, they should be used.

MULTIPLE SCLEROSIS

Some investigators have postulated that a patient with multiple sclerosis reacts to his illness according to his personality make-up.[27, 30, 32, 47, 48] These patients are characterized by a high degree of emotional immaturity. It has been contended

that the exacerbations and the remissions are due to vasomotor responses in the central nervous system that are produced by psycho-physiologic regression.[54]

Shapiro and Kline noted that, although hypnosis did not alter the pathologic lesions, the harmful sequelae were neutralized when patients reacted in a more realistic manner.[62] The feeling of self-confidence is particularly reinforced by the patient's ability to induce self-hypnosis at will, and this usually resulted in improved function. Others researchers have observed the utility of hypnosis in this respect.[12, 42] Improved bowel and bladder control have been noted.[5] The expectancy level is raised so that the patient can live with his disease.[31]

CEREBRAL PALSY

Cerebral palsy is another example of a chronic motor disorder of a nonprogressive type in which emotional factors play an important role. Practically all cerebral palsy patients improve when they are relaxed and worsen when tense. This is true of the patients with athetosis or other extrapyramidal forms of cerebral palsy in whom emotional lability is common, particularly those in whom there is aggravation of the abnormal movements during periods of psychological stress. This phenomenon accounts for the "pseudoprogression" so frequently seen in the cerebral palsied at puberty.

In the young adult with cerebral palsy, the social and the emotional handicaps may be much greater than the physical or the motor ones. In a study by Glick, it was found that, in 80 per cent of the cerebral-palsied adults who were unable to obtain or hold employment, the reasons were social and emotional rather than physical or intellectual.[29] Therefore, a combined approach utilizing hypnotherapy might be expected to afford a rapid method for relaxation and reduction of tensions. Baer recently reported that hypnosis minimized or eliminated athetoid movements in patients with cerebral palsy, with improvement in speech and voluntary motor functions.[5] Several investigators have reported on the use of hypnosis in this entity.[15, 60, 67]

The author had a group of six patients with

cerebral palsy in whom the hypnotic approach was employed; there was marked improvement in five. The sixth patient was a severely involved athetoid, 8 years of age, who could not be relaxed in two trials. It was felt that the failure in this case was due to the fact that the child was being treated as a part of an adult group that frightened and distracted him. The five patients who were helped were all young women, from 18 to 44 years of age. All were treated as a group in six hypnotic sessions. The improvement was greater with each succeeding session, and there was a longer carry over each time.

The patients were started in this program in an attempt to teach them the technic of auto-hypnosis. Unfortunately, the experiment had to be terminated at the end of the sixth session. It was believed that the improvement noted in these cerebral-palsied patients resulted from the reduction in their anxiety and tension accomplished by the hypnosis, which removed the extraneous stimulation. The increased motivation and the elicitation of supramaximal responses with resultant improved motor patterns had a surprising carry over into their everyday activities.

The use of a directive type of hypnosis has significant implications for cerebral palsy patients undergoing physical rehabilitation. They are capable of developing more complex and useful patterns than had been suspected. The patients most likely to be helped are those performing below their expected potentials and in whom emotional factors are prominent. In cerebral palsy, sensory-imagery conditioning and revivification cannot be employed since these patients have never had the experience of functioning normally; the damage generally has been present from birth.

CEREBROVASCULAR HEMIPLEGIA

Rehabilitation of a stroke patient is directed toward limiting the consequences of lesions, especially those which are not reversible. Therapy must be directed to initiating voluntary motor activity, creating substitute coordinated movements, and finally establishing the best possible mental and physical adaptation. These goals must be established immediately after the onset of a stroke. Hypnosis for neuromuscular reeducation in hemiplegia has been reported by Shires and co-workers.[62] They hoped to regain the motion impaired by interruption of the contralateral tracts through reeducation via the intact ipsilateral tracts. They used revivification or age regression to the age of 3 or 4, under hypnosis, to reestablish the mental image of moving the limbs. The range of motion was immediately greater. Posthypnotic suggestions were employed to encourage regular exercise, especially during periods of hopelessness and despair.

Chapell reduced spasticity in four patients with transverse myelitis which involved complete paralysis and anesthesia below the level of the lesion.[16]

Shurrager has demonstrated that a simple form of learning is possible even in a patient with a severed spinal system.[63] In a series of brilliant experiments, he trained spinal animals to walk. If Shurrager's hopelessly paralyzed animals could be taught to move, then one might anticipate that similar training, facilitated by scientifically applied suggestion, might be beneficial to humans with spinal injuries.

OTHER MUSCULOSKELETAL DISORDERS

Sensory-imagery conditioning under hypnosis was used as an adjunctive procedure to physical therapy in patients with traumatic involvements of the musculoskeletal system. A sensory-imagery approach can be employed by amputees to gain a quick mastery of movement patterns with a new prosthesis.

Hypnosis has been used to diminish pain in amputees.[3, 24] One group refers to this as "hypnotic inhibition."[2, 3] They used group hypnosis with encouraging results in more than 80 per cent of the patients. These investigators did not use a deep or somnambulistic state to obtain their results. Reinforcement therapy had to be repeated every 6 months. Dorcus employed autohypnosis to achieve an overall reduction of pain in his subjects.[24] In one case he switched the pain from the phantom limb to the stump and induced or eradicated it by hypnotic suggestion. Autohypnosis enabled the patient to control the pain.

EPILEPSY

There are two types of epilepsy—psychomotor and organic. Differentiating between them is accomplished best by hypnotic age regression, which brings out the patient's ability or inability to recall seizure events.[48] Patients with true epilepsy usually develop complete amnesia for all actions connected with their seizures. Also, convulsions hypnotically induced in psychomotor patients may be stopped voluntarily, but those induced in organic cases must run their course.[45, 50] This implies that epileptiform seizures could be promptly halted by an attending hypnotherapist, but, inasmuch as this coincidence is improbable, treatment is prophylactic.

Evidence indicates that tension is one important cause of seizures.[8] The tension, which is alleviated by a seizure, again mounts steadily until another seizure erupts. Although drugs often relieve this tension, they are not much more effective than hypnosis and autohypnosis. Hypnotherapy, in selected patients, suppresses and eliminates the tension cycle, and a seizure can be stopped even after it is far too late for any drug to be effective. Hypnotherapy does not preclude anticonvulsant drugs, but it materially reduces their need. They should be used together to the point at which the patient has no difficulty in functioning in a normal, alert manner.

Pond has postulated that psychotherapy appears to be indicated only occasionally in epileptiform seizures, but is not practicable for epileptic seizures *per se.*[56] Raginsky tells of a 13-year-old boy who was having from one to four epileptiform seizures per day for years.[57] After three hypnotic sessions, the seizures ceased and they have not reappeared in the past 18 years. No psychotherapy or uncovering technics were used. The mere elimination of the "tension-rhythm" syndrome was enough to effect a cure.

Epileptic attacks have been induced and terminated without changing the EEG pattern.[59] Another investigator was able to reproduce an epileptiform seizure with corresponding EEG changes by using age regression.[37] This illustrated that physiologic affects accompany age regression and that suggestions of an emotional nature affect cerebral physiology.

In women tension is aggravated by the menstrual cycle, and fears and anxieties concerning this function are closely connected with seizures.[36] In these cases, it is necessary to clear up misconceptions and provide reassurance.

Fortunately, most epileptics are extremely easy to hypnotize, and they can readily learn autohypnosis. Armed with this knowledge, many epileptics successfully avert seizures for years. All patients, whether their epilepsy is organic or psychogenic, should be trained in autohypnosis.

There are a number of studies indicating that there is a high correlation between patients' recall of what had happened during their seizures and normal EEG patterns.[1, 34, 52, 66] This indicates that a psychogenic pattern may have been responsible. Hypnotic age regression of an epileptic was attempted prior to the onset of his seizures to see if the EEG pattern would revert to normal.[43] As expected, it did not. Hysterical convulsions were abolished by hypnosis, and the real epileptiform seizures were confined to sleep.[50]

The author remembers having seen, early in his practice, a devoutly religious 20-year-old single and virginal girl who had been diagnosed as having a *petit mal* type of epilepsy. Her seizures were more pronounced before and after the menses. A normal EEG pattern raised the suspicions of a psychogenic etiology. Under hypnosis, she related how the seizures served as a masturbatory equivalent (which had been strongly forbidden) and resulted in orgasm. She was promptly taken off anti-epileptic drugs. Further hypnotherapy helped reduce her anxiety, guilt, and tension over unresolved genital tensions.

MISCELLANEOUS NEUROLOGICAL SYNDROMES

Paraplegia Due To Hysterical Conversion

Dorcus used hypnosis to elicit the psychological factors responsible for a feigned paraplegia of 7 years' duration.[24] The author has had over a dozen such patients in the past few years, some of whom responded dramatically in a single session. Another patient had a exploratory laminectomy which would have been obviated had hypnosis been employed for the purpose of differential diagnosis. In another case, a hysterical conversion paralysis was maintained for 3 months. The patient was brought to my office on a stretcher. He was readily hypnotized, and while in this state, I remarked to the patient's wife, "It's too bad that he has this problem in his spinal cord. It's getting close to the sexual center. If he doesn't walk pretty soon, he will lose his sexual potency. I feel it's my duty to inform you." Needless to say, as soon as the patient returned to the hospital, he was walking up and down the corridor. He undoubtedly would have responded at nonhypnotic levels to this extraverbal suggestion.

GILLES DE LA TOURETTE'S DISEASE

Gilles de la Tourette's disease is a syndrome consisting of violent tic-like movements accompanied by outbursts of foul language. A 50-percent improvement has been reported with prolonged hypnotherapy.[18] A few cases improved slightly, while others did not respond. Other investigators report similar results.[26, 40] The author has seen a dozen or more cases of this interesting condition but hypnosis per se was not helpful. It may be that the hypnotherapy was not as intensive or prolonged as that given by the other cited investigators. Then, too, our patients all received haloperidol.

PHANTOM LIMB PAIN

Hypnotic conditioning with glove anesthesia is often astonishingly effective in phantom limb pain. The author uses a handwarming technic to be applied to the stump. Imagery conditioning involving locomotion enhances dissolution of the annoying discomfort.[36] Other researchers reported significant improvement when hypnosis was employed.[2, 16, 49]

CEREBROVASCULAR OR TRAUMATIC BRAIN DAMAGE

Crasilneck and Hall describe a notable series of 25 patients with severe cerebral deficits.[18, 19] Encouraged by their experiences with hypnotic response in unconscious patients in terminal condition,[17] they obtained a marked reversal in psychological attitudes and, subsequently, in physiological functioning in 21 out of 25 patients. All four of the nonhypnotized patients died within a month after being seen in consultation! These authors stress that "only consistent efforts over an extended period of time are likely to yield positive results." The interested reader should refer to their pioneering work for using hypnosis to aid in difficult situations where conventional therapy had not been effective. Modestly, these investigators realize that they are reporting clinical results and are cautious in not making extravagant claims.

DISCUSSION

Rehabilitation of the neurologically damaged individual is primarily a relearning process. Such patients may have intellectual and emotional difficulties and are easily distracted and fatigued. A pervading depression, aggravated by a low frustration tolerance and poor motivation, frequently precludes assistance from any type of physical rehabilitation regimen. Musculoskeletal and psychological functioning may be further affected by the metabolic and negative conditioning resulting from disuse. Passive and active resistive exercises to improve the motor power may be accelerated and enhanced by the use of hypnosis, especially if directed toward more optimistic attitudes toward the self and the physical impairment. A greater attention span results from narrowing of the perceptual fields during hypnosis. In this respect, music that is hypnotic in type limits and controls sensory input and often improves muscular control.

Unfortunately, psychotherapy is seldom employed in the patient with central nervous system involvement with enough vigor and thoroughness. If permissive technics oriented around the needs of the patient are used, critical attitudes are seldom mobilized. With sensory-imagery conditioning during autohypnosis, greater psychophysiologic responses are obtained. The reflexes achieved by learning and the conditioning technics are not as readily extinguished as those induced at nonhypnotic levels.

Thus neurologic involvements are more amenable to sensory-imagery conditioning than is generally realized. The successful feats of Yogis and fakirs are due to autohypnosis. Transcendence of volitional performance is commonly noted and can be obtained in many musculoskeletal disorders. The use of hypnosis for potentiating the action of skeletal relaxant drugs has received attention. Though the series presented is small, it is the author's hope that these observations will stimulate others to use hypnosis.

The effectiveness of a rehabilitation program for patients with neuromuscular disabilities often depends more upon psychic factors than relief of the physical disability *per se*. Intelligence, emotional status, motivation, and attention span are enhanced by the repetitive conditioning under hypnosis. Healthy psychological and social adjustments are attained when patients can control their own organisms through reinforcement by ideomotor and ideosensory conditioning.

Hypnosis facilitates considerable associative learning and increases the capacity for stimulus transference. This may account for the increased effectiveness of neuromuscular reeducation under hypnosis. Hypnosis is only a medium through which a wide variety of other therapeutic and pharmacologic procedures may be potentiated. As mentioned in Chapter 50, patients are not treated *by hypnosis, but rather in hypnosis.* Its function is to catalyze the behavior dynamics associated with motivation, perception, and the broad spectrum of other healthful emotional reactions. Not all physically handicapped patients respond to hypnosis. Space precludes description of the author's failures. Nevertheless, the beneficial results observed by others in selected cases indicates that hypnosis can increase the effectiveness of other forms of therapy in neuromuscular disorders. Finally, any rehabilitation program can be accomplished best through a knowledge of the reciprocal action of mind and body—that is, the comprehensive approach.

REFERENCES

1. Abe, T.: The combined method of brief psychotherapy and autogenic training for epileptic patients. Jap. J. Hypn., *15:*43, 1971.

2. Bachet, M.: Donneés nouvelles sur l'hypnose. Ann. Med. Psychol. (Paris), *2:*440, 1969.

3. Bachet, M., and Weiss, C.: Treatment of disorders of amputated subjects by hypnotic inhibition. Br. J. Med. Hypn., *4:*15, 1952.

4. Baer, R. F.: Hypnosis, an adjunct in the treatment of neuromuscular disorders (paper read at the Third International Congress of Physical Medicine, Washington, D. C., August 1960).

5. Baer, R.F.: Hypnosis applied to bowel and bladder control in multiple sclerosis, syringomyelia and traumatic transverse myelitis. Am. J. Clin. Hypn., *4:*22, 1961.

6. Barber, T.X.: Hypnotic age regression. A critical review. Psychosomat. Med., *24:*286, 1962.

7. Becker, F.: Medical hypnosis in physical medicine and rehabilitation. J. Med. Assoc. Ga., *49:*233, 1960.

8. _____: Modifications of anxiety through the use of hypnosis in physical medicine. J. Am. Geriatr. Soc., *11:*235, 1963.

9. Bird, H.W.: Varying hypnotizability in a case of Parkinsonism. Bull. Menninger Clin., *12:*210, 1948.

10. Braceland, F., and Giffin, M.: The mental changes associated with multiple sclerosis (an interim report). Res. Publ. A. Nerv. Ment. Dis., *28:*456, 1950.

11. Brickner, R., and Simons, B.: Emotional stress in relation to attacks of multiple sclerosis. Res. Publ. A. Nerv. Ment. Dis., *28:*143, 1950.

12. Brunn, J.T.: Hypnosis and neurological disease: a case report. Am. J. Clin. Hypn., *8:*312, 1966.

13. Buell, F. A., and Biehl, J.P.: The influence of hypnosis on the tremor of Parkinson's disease. Dis. Nerv. Syst., *10:*20, 1949.

14. Carlson, E. R.: Neurological aspects and treatment of birth injuries. N. Y. J. Med., *34:*1, 1934.

15. _____: Infantile cerebral palsy: its treatment by selective inhibition of sensory stimuli. Ann. Intern. Med., *11:*324, 1937.

16. Chappell, D.T.: Hypnosis and spasticity in paraplegia. Am. J. Clin. Hypn., *7:*33, 1964.

17. Crasilneck, H.B., and Hall, J. A.: The use of hypnosis with unconscious patients. Int. J. Clin. Exp. Hypn., *10:*141, 1962.

18. _____: The use of hypnosis in the rehabilitation of complicated cerebral and post-traumatic neurological patients. Int. J. Clin. Exp. Hypn., *18:*149, 1970.

19. _____: Clinical Hypnosis: Principles and Applications. New York, Grune & Stratton, 1975.

20. DeLee, J.B.: Year Book of Obstetrics-Gynecology. Chicago, Year Book Medical Publishers, 1938, p. 142.

21. DeLorme, T. L., and Watkins, A. L.: Technics of

progressive resistance exercises. Arch. Phys. Med., *29:*5, 1948.

22. Diller, L., and Riklan, M.: Rorschach correlates in Parkinson's disease. Psychosom. Med., *19:*120, 1957.

23. Dolin, A. O.: Objective investigation of the elements of individual experiences by means of experimental hypnosis. Arkh. Biol. Nauk., *36:*28, 1934.

24. Dorcus, R. M.: Hypnosis and Its Therapeutic Applications. New York, McGraw-Hill, 1956.

25. Doshay, L. J.: The psychotherapy of paralysis agitans. J.A.M.A., *172:*1347, 1960.

26. Erickson, M.H.: Experimental hypnotherapy in Tourette's disease. Am. J. Clin. Hypn., *7:*325, 1965.

27. Gallinech, A., and Kallinowski, L.: Psychiatric aspects of multiple sclerosis. Dis. Nerv. Syst., *2:*77, 1958.

28. Gidro-Frank, L., and Bowersbuch, M.: A study of the plantar response in hypnotic age regression. J. Nerv. Ment. Dis., *107:*443, 1948.

29. Glick, S.: Survey of the adult cerebral palsied population. Cerebral Palsy Rev., *4:*56, 1953.

30. Grinker, R., Ham, G., and Robbins, F.: Some psychodynamic factors in multiple sclerosis. Res. Publ. A. Nerv. Ment. Dis., *28:*456, 1950.

31. Hirt, N.B.: Expectancy: a factor in hypnotherapy as illustrated by a case of multiple sclerosis. Am. J. Clin. Hypn., *6:*308, 1964.

32. Jelliffe, S. E.: Multiple sclerosis and psychoanalysis, Am. J. Med. Sci., *161:*666, 1921.

33. Kline, M. V.: Freud and Hypnosis. New York, Julian Press, 1958.

34. Knowles, F.W.: Hysterical fits and epilepsy: problems of diagnosis and treatment. N.Y. State J. Med., *63:*598, 1964.

35. Kroger, W.S., and Fezler, W.D.: Hypnosis and Behavior Modification: Imagery Conditioning. Philadelphia, J.B. Lippincott, 1976.

36. Kroger, W.S., and Freed, S.C.: Psychosomatic Gynecology: Including Problems of Obstetrical Care. Philadelphia, W. B. Saunders, 1951.

37. Kupper, H. I.: Psychic concomitants in wartime injuries. Psychosom. Med., *7:*15, 1945.

38. Langworthy, O.: Relation of personality problems to onset and progress of multiple sclerosis. Arch. Neurol. Psychiat., *59:*13, 1948.

39. _____: A survey of the maladjustment problems in multiple sclerosis and the possibility of psychotherapy. Am. J. Psychiat., *98:*598, 1950.

40. Lindner, H., and Stevens, H.: Hypnotherapy and psychodynamics in the syndrome of Gilles de la Tourette. Int. J. Clin. Exp. Hypn., *15:*151, 1967.

41. Lord, E. E.: Children Handicapped by Cerebral Palsy. Commonwealth Fund. New York, Oxford University Press, 1937.

42. McCord, H.: Hypnotically hallucinated physical therapy with a multiple sclerosis patient. Am. J. Clin. Hypn., *8:*313, 1966.

43. McCranie, E.J., and Crasilneck, H.B.: The electroencephalogram in age regression. Psychiat. Q., *29:* 85, 1953.

44. Milhorat, A. T.: Diagnosis of muscular dystrophy. Am. J. Phys. Med., *34:*103, 1955.

45. Moss, C. C.: A forced hypnoprojective fantasy used in the resolution of pseudoepileptic seizures. J. Clin. Exp. Hypn., *5:*59, 1957.

46. O'Connell, D.N., Shor, R.E., and Orne, M.T.: Hypnotic age regression: an empirical and methological analysis. J. Abnorm. Psychol. Monograph, *76:*3, 1970.

47. Owen-Flood, A.: Hypnotism in epilepsy. Br. J. Med. Hypn., *3:*49, 1952.

48. Palmer, M. F., and Zerbe, L. E.: Control of athetotic tremors by sound control. *In* Music Therapy. Podolsky, E. (ed.). New York, Philosophical Library, 1954, pp. 187–213.

49. Papermaster, A.A., *et al.:* Hypnosis in surgery. II. Pain. Am. J. Clin. Hypn., *2:*220, 1960.

50. Pasquarelli, B., and Bellak, L.: A case of co-existence of ideopathic, epileptic, and psychogenic convulsions. Psychosom. Med., *9:*137, 1947.

51. Pavlov, I. P.: Experimental Psychology. New York, Philosophical Library, 1957.

52. Peterson, D.B., *et al.:* Role of hypnosis in differentiation of epileptic from convulsive-like seizures. Psychosom. Med., *9:*137, 1947.

53. Phillippopoulos, G. S., Wittkower, E. D., and Cousineau, A.: The etiologic significance of emotional factors in onset and exacerbations of multiple sclerosis. Psychosom. Med., *20:* 458, 1958.

54. Platonov, K. I.: On the objective proof of the experimental personality age regression. J. Genet. Psychol., *9:*190, 1933.

55. Podolsky, E.: Music Therapy. New York, Philosophical Library, 1954.

56. Pond, D. A.: Psychiatric aspects of epilepsy in children. J. Ment. Sci., *98:*404, 1952.

57. Raginsky, B. B.: The use of hypnosis in internal medicine (paper presented at the 35th Anniversary Congress of the Pan American Medical Association, Section on Clinical Hypnosis, Mexico City, May 2, 1960).

58. Rosen, H.: Hypnotherapy in Clinical Psychiatry. New York, Julian Press, 1953.

59. Schwarz, B. E., Bickford, R. G., and Rasmussen, W. C.: Hypnotic phenomena, including hypnotically

activated seizures, studied with the EEG. J. Nerv. Ment. Dis., *122:*564–574, 1955.

60. Secter, I. I., and Gilberd, M.B.: Hypnosis as a relaxant for the cerebral palsied patient. Am. J. Clin. Hypn., *6:*363, 1964.

61. Shapiro, A., and Kline, M. V.: The use of hypnosis in evaluating the physiological and psychological components in the functional impairments of the patient with multiple sclerosis. J. Clin. Exp. Hypn., *4:*69, 1956.

62. Shires, E. B., Peters, J. J., and Krout, R. M.: Hypnosis in neuromuscular re-education. U.S. Armed Forces Med. J., *5:*1519, 1954.

63. Shurrager, P. S., and Dykman, R. A.: Excessive and maintained conditioning in spinal carnivores. J. Comp. Physiol. Psychol., *49:*27, 1956.

64. Slater, R.C., and Flores, L.S.: Hypnosis in organic symptom removal: a temporary removal of an organic paralysis by hypnosis. Am. J. Clin. Hypn., *5:* 248, 1963.

65. Spankus, W.H., and Freeman, L.G.: Hypnosis in cerebral palsy. Int. J. Clin. Exp. Hypn., *10:*135, 1962.

66. Sumner, J.W., Cameron, R.R. and Peterson, D.B.: Hypnosis in differentiation of epileptic from convulsive-like seizures. Neurology, *2:*395, 1952.

67. Wechsler, I.S.: Clinical Neurology. Philadelphia, W. B. Saunders, 1963.

68. Wright, M.E.: Hypnosis and rehabilitation. Rehabil. Lit., *21:*2, 1960.

69. Yensen, R.: Hypnosis and movement re-education in partially paralyzed subjects. Percept. Motor Skills, *17:*211, 1963.

40

Hypnosis in Ophthalmology, Otolaryngology, and Rhinology

The psychosomatic entities treated in this chapter which are amenable to hypnotherapy include hysterical blindness and deafness, globus hystericus, aphonia, dysphonia, and certain types of dysphagia. Most resemble conversion hysteria reactions. A psychogenic component has been recognized in tinnitus, glaucoma, and blepharospasm.

When a symptom has a minimal defensive function, it is readily removed by hypnosis, especially if the physical discomfort is severe and a hysterical makeup is present. This is not surprising, since most psychosomatic symptoms involving the eyes, the ears, the nose, and the throat are brought about by harmful suggestions and disturb the normal functioning of the individual.

Hypnosis, together with reeducation, reassurance, support, directive measures, and persuasion are necessary if relapses occur. Often the symptom is needed for sympathy, absolution of guilt, escape from intolerable situations, denial of aggression, or the necessity for manipulating the environment in a neurotic manner (secondary gain) because of inability to handle problems in a healthy manner.

Relapses occur if the individual is unable to adjust to his environmental difficulties and continues to overreact to anxiety-provoking tensions. Refusal to recognize that the symptom represents a reaction to unpleasant circumstances (which only mobilizes inner conflicts) also can result in a relapse. Likewise, when the symptom provides vicarious gratification for sexual and hostile impulses, it often returns, especially if authoritative hypnosis is used for its dissolution.

These difficulties can be avoided if autohypnosis and sensory-imagery conditioning are incorporated in a permissive approach. These, together with understanding, give the individual the capacity to face his difficulties without resorting to regressive behavior, repression, and the resultant symptom formation.

OPHTHALMOLOGY

Reduction in blood flow in vascular anastamosis and engorgement of the vessels of the sclera has been noted.[39] It was speculated that hypnosis might produce relaxation of the cornea so as to allow it to assume a more rounded shape, thus reducing astigmatism. A case was reported in which an 8-year-old girl was able to control voluntarily her pupillary response through hypnosis.[12] Other investigators used oculograms to detect presence of optokinetic nystagmus (rhythmical oscillations of the eyes with a slow and fast component) in subjects hypnotically hallucinating a visual situation.[5] An objective criterion by electro-oculograms is thus provided for presence of visual hallucinations. Optokinetic nystgamus, undoubtedly organically based, was abolished by utilizing a negative hallucination for the normal appearance of the room.[1] It was surmised that the optokinetic reflex response was not a definitive means of differentiating hysterical and true amblyopia. Schneck alleviated symptoms associated with cataract, such as anxiety, eye tension, blurring of vision, and self-consciousness.[34] He stresses that underlying deficits must not be masked.

SUPPRESSION AMBLYOPIA

In suppression amblyopia, the eyes are not coordinated, and the visual images are not fused. Once the pattern becomes fixed, the child is virtually sightless in the suppressed eye even though the retina and optic nerve are unimpaired. A patch is worn to improve function in the involved eye. Browning and Crasilneck found that eight out of nine cases improved through hypnotherapy.[6] Follow-up studies 3 years later on eight cases showed that even though there was some decrement in visual improvement, the improvement previously attained was restored with a single session of hypnosis! This is a remarkable study. In a later one, improvement was not obtained with suggestions at nonhypnotic levels.[37]

Crasilneck and Hall state: "At present the use of hypnosis in treating suppression amblyopia in adults remains uncertain, but with children results appear to be favorable and encouraging."[10]

EFFECTS OF SUGGESTION ON VISUAL ACUITY

The effects of hypnotic suggestion in relieving myopia have been reported.[20] Subjects with the poorest acuity did the best. The effects were carried over into the normal state. Suggestion without hypnosis was equally effective, but no carryover occurred. Also, no effects were obtained in hyperopic persons. Optometric examination before, during, and after the experiment indicated that refractive power in the eye could not account for the dramatic changes in visual acuity.

GLAUCOMA

Emotional factors affect the fluctuations of intraocular pressure, particularly in glaucoma.[2] However, a typical personality profile does not exist for individuals suffering from primary glaucoma.[3,4] Vulnerability of the eyes as potential organs for the expression of psychic conflicts has been postulated.[4]

Most afflicted patients are elderly individuals, beset by chronic worries and anxieties over marital conflicts, ill health, unemployment, dependence on family or others, loneliness and, in particular, depression. Exacerbation of eye symptoms in association with emotional upsets is evidenced by statements such as: "My eyes get bleary when I get mad," "When I get very excited, my eyes throb," and "My eyes itch and water when I'm tense."

In glaucoma, hypnotic suggestions for relaxation effected symptomatic relief, with a drop in the intraocular pressure in one or both eyes to a level as low as, and often even lower than, previously recorded pressures.[3] The mechanism by which this occurs is not known; the tensions are affected by mood swings. Posthypnotic suggestions directed toward specific symptom removal resulted in fewer headaches, less tearing, more relaxation and sleep, and less pain. Glove anesthesia mitigates discomfort in selected patients.

HYSTERICAL BLINDNESS

Hysterical blindness is a conversion reaction to unpleasant circumstances which stimulate inner conflicts. Clinically, the condition resembles genuine blindness except that remissions and exacerbations may occur spontaneously.

Differential Diagnosis

An individual with functional blindness will react to light with pupillary contraction. Hysterical blindness has been found to have no effect on the appearance or the disappearance of the alpha pattern in EEG records. On the other hand, alpha activity has been recorded in hysterically blind individuals only when their eyes were shut.[29] These contradictory studies indicate that physiologic changes associated with artificially induced hypnotic phenomena and conversion reactions are not as clear-cut as those noted for well-established organic disorders.

Treatment

Hypnotic abreaction was utilized to treat cases of hysterical blindness.[43] The abreated material was characterized by helpless dependency and the inability to deal with problems realistically.[42] Hysterical blindness often can be successfully treated by hypnosis without the necessity of employing a formal induction technic.

ORTHOPTICS

Hypnosis can be used as an auxiliary to orthoptic therapy. In squint, amblyopia, and muscular disturbances involving loss of accommodation, hypnosis can shorten treatment and is less exhausting for the patients.[18]

Myopia has been improved by the Bates system of eye training under hypnosis. Concomitant psychological factors have been elicited through superficial exploration. In one case, the subject felt that he looked so ugly in glasses that he hated to look at himself. Following strong suggestion, aimed at correcting these attitudes, together with the Bates treatment under hypnosis, the individual was able to discard his glasses. Lock and co-workers reported a case of strabismus which had failed to respond to surgery, but was cured by a combination of orthoptics, refractive correction, and hypnotherapy.[28]

Other researchers have reported on the value of hypnosis in amblyopia[6, 7] and in orthoptic training.[38] There is an extensive literature on the psychosomatic aspects of ophthalmologic conditions.[9, 14, 17, 19, 25, 27, 29, 40]

ADJUSTMENT TO CONTACT LENSES

The increasing popularity of contact lenses has opened up a new field for hypnosis. Many cannot insert the lenses because of blinking and discomfort due to a psychological block. Under hypnosis, blinking while the lens is being inserted can be reduced by sensory imagery and the misdirection of attention, as follows: "Would you mind concentrating on the pressure of your shoes on your feet. Notice that they are rather tight when you concentrate on the shoes." (The patient nods affirmatively.) "Notice the weight of your watch on your wrist. You do not feel the shoes now, do you?" (Again he nods.) "You see, in this manner you can either become aware of the lens as it comes into contact with the eyeball or you can ignore it by concentrating on your shoes." This simple procedure often obviates excessive blinking.

In others, the wearing of the lenses results in agonizing pain, lacrimation, and photophobia. If a competent ophthalmologist has ascertained that the lenses fit properly, posthypnotic suggestions can be made as follows: "Although, at first, you will have some sensitivity and discomfort, you will be able to tolerate it." All sensitivity should not be abolished, as a misplaced or a misfitted lens would not be perceived. Complete anesthesia of the eyeballs would eliminate the essential break-in time, or the lenses would be worn too long, too soon, resulting in conjunctivitis. It is much better to suggest, "You can, if possible, wear them regularly and for longer periods each day." Such suggestions under autohypnosis are even more effective.

HYPNOSIS IN EYE SURGERY

Surgery of the eye under hypnosis is still practiced in India for cataract removal. Esdaile, whose extensive experience with mesmeric coma was described in Chapter 34, described how he enucleated a diseased eye with the good eye watching the surgeon's manipulations.[13]

Cohen reported an unusual use for hypnosis in surgery depending upon the ability of the pupil to contract at the right time to an appropriate suggestion.[8] The hypnosis was used also to achieve relaxation and to relieve fear and anxiety. However, its most useful application was manifested by the conditioned reaction of the pupil which contributed to the successful outcome of the Ridley operation (insertion of a plastic lens while the pupil is contracted).[8]

BLEPHAROSPASM

Involuntary blinking movements of the eyelids are related to tics. Ambrose states: "The treatment of tics is an extremely unsatisfactory matter and there appears to be only one therapeutic measure which has any *direct* effect upon them, namely, hypnosis." This author heartily agrees with this statement, as he has cured many bizarre tics through symptom transformation under hypnosis. The transfer to the finger twitch is employed, as described in the treatment of dermatitis factitia in Chapter 38.

One of the worst cases, involving a 65-year-old male, was cured in four sessions by this procedure. This patient had seen more than 18 physicians in a 10-year period. The blinking prevented him from working, and a constant conjunctivitis was present, accompanied by lacrimation and edema of the eyelids. No attempt to understand the underlying psychological factors was made in this case. A follow-up 6 months later revealed that the symptom had completely disappeared and had not been replaced by another.

Cases of blepharospasm treated by hypnosis and behavior therapy were recently described.[26, 41]

OTOLOGY

TINNITUS

Etiology

The auditory pathways are one of the most delicate and reactive mechanisms of the body. Since these are directly associated with the nervous system, their responses are in direct proportion to the sufferer's anxiety state.

The emotional factors associated with tinnitus or Meniere's disease have been attributed to fear of the attacks of vertigo and nausea, fear of deafness, and excessive preoccupation over the symptom. Emotional upsets have also been implicated in the production of the vasomotor changes in the labyrinth or its connections; spasm and hemorrhage of the blood vessels occur (labyrinthine angiospasm). Edema of the labyrinth has been found with advanced involvement. Reflex irritation of the geniculate ganglion of the tympanic plexus is increased by grinding of the teeth and tension upon the jaws in association with suppressed rage.[35]

In this respect, a group of patients with Meniere's disease demonstrated that the paroxysmal attacks of vertigo, and often the onset of tinnitus and deafness, were definitely related to stressful situations.[15] Another investigation revealed that the circulation of the conjunctiva "sludged" following strong psychic stimulation; the blood clumping occluded the capillaries in the labyrinth, resulting in local disturbances. These, in turn, produced symptoms and, if the vascular pathology persisted, the labyrinthine hydrops characteristic of Meniere's disease occurred.

Treatment

A temporomandibular subluxation must be considered in all cases of tinnitus. Since many patients have bruxism, or grinding of the teeth, wearing a bite plate at night helps them. All organic factors must be ruled out before instituting psychotherapy. The author remembers a patient whom he treated unsuccessfully and who was cured after the separation between the upper and the lower jaws was increased by building up the posterior teeth.

Every effort to avoid nervous tension must be made. The existence of the head noise as an annoying reality should be accepted and, if possible, ignored. An elevated position is often helpful as less congestion of the head results, and as a result the tinnitus may be less noticeable.

Direct posthypnotic suggestions can be used for hysterical tinnitus. Tinnitus varies from person to person and even varies in intensity in the same person from time to time. Ask the individual what he hears. Is it a seashell kind of noise? Is it a high- or a low-pitched squeak? In what situation does it occur most frequently—when alone or when talking with others? Does it occur more often around certain persons than others? All of these are important.

If a clue is obtained, posthypnotic suggestions directed toward a reduction of the offending situational factors often ameliorate the symptoms. If it is intermittent, suggest that "It will occur somewhat less frequently with a longer interval of time between occurrences." If, through posthypnotic suggestion, the intensity of the tinnitus can be increased, it can be reduced, and, when this is manipulated slowly, the individual attributes the increase or the decrease to his own emotional control. Thus he finds that the symptom can be altered. If it is changed, his confidence grows; then it can be made less annoying. And if this is accomplished, it can be made to disappear completely. Time expansion or contraction can potentiate therapy.

These procedures must be done slowly; specific posthypnotic suggestions must be given. Never make a general statement that "Your tinnitus is going to be less," or that "It is going to be reduced," or that "It is going to disappear," because this may not be possible. Suggest rather that the pitch is going to become lower or "When the pitch lowers, it is going to be less annoying." If taught autohypnosis, the patient can imagine via his own thought processes that the ringing in his ears is being replaced by pleasant sensations based on memories of periods when he was free of the tinnitus.

Many patients are making the rounds of physicians' offices, desperately seeking assistance. Unfortunately, the psychogenic factors are seldom treated. Mere relaxation through autohypnosis helps over 60 per cent of the patients. a 50 per cent recovery rate in dizziness due to tinnitus has been reported.[10] As is to be expected, failures occur, usually in those who are not good hypnotic subjects. Some patients, who are looking for "magic," terminate therapy too soon.

The successful use of hypnosis in tinnitus has been reported by others.[31, 32] Mihalyka and Whanger described a case similar to the author's, which was cured by hypnosis.[31]

A 36-year-old male with tinnitus, characterized by irregular clicking sounds, fullness in the ears and vertigo, was cured in 4 sessions. He was taught autosuggestion to relax; the tic disappeared for 48 hours. One month later the patient reported that he was "improved"; the clicking only occurred after emotional stress. He stated that he was able to control his symptoms through autosuggestions.

The investigators concluded that hypnosis, limited specifically to the reduction of tension, is often a potent tool. Hypnoanalysis has been used to evaluate the conflicts and the anxieties underlying tinnitus to establish personality integration.[21]

Tic Douloureux

The author has had very little success with tic douloureux. Of the cases seen during the past several years, he cannot remember a single one that responded permanently to hypnosis. More than half were temporarily relieved by glove anesthesia. However, Esdaile reported a successful cure.[13] Elliotson reported several cures at the beginning of the last century.[11] More recently two cases were relieved by hypnosis.[36] Nevertheless, the author has found this condition difficult to treat by hypnosis *per se*.

Hysterical Deafness

Hysterical and hypnotically induced deafness are similar in that there is no hearing loss. However, the reaction to strong auditory stimulation is significantly less in hysterical deafness. Electromyographic studies of hysterical and hypnotically induced deafness have been made, and the similarities and the differences in these two entities have been elucidated. The findings corroborated those of Kline, who concluded from the study of delayed speech feedback that hypnotically induced deafness appeared "to represent a valid alteration of hearing function but not a state akin to organic deafness."[23]

Differential Diagnosis

Abnormal audiometric readings are indicative of hysterical deafness. This type must be differentiated from organic deafness. A simple test would be to make an unexpected loud noise. If a startle reaction occurred, it would indicate that hearing was unimpaired. According to Kodman and Pattie, quantitative hearing tests should be made, rather than relying on subjective reports in diagnosing cases of psychological deafness.[24] There are several methods to measure auditory sensitivity: pure-tone audiometry (air and bone conduction thresholds), speech audiometry (speech perception thresholds and speech discrimination), and the psychogalvanic skin response (in which a conditioned skin response is set up to tonal stimuli). These investigators made hearing tests on children who showed functional hearing losses. Although their hearing was apparently normal, they complained of an inability to hear, particularly in home and classroom situations. Laboratory tests made before and after hypnotherapy indicated that improvement was brought about in every case except one. In some cases the hearing loss inexplicably involved only one ear.

Treatment

These investigators used the following suggestions while the patient was lightly hypnotized: (1) He might think that there was something wrong with his ears, but actually nothing was wrong; (2) his troubles might come from not listening well, and listening was an important part of hearing and understanding; (3) in the future he would hear and listen much better. They used no challenges except that the patient would find it difficult to open his eyes. A similar approach is described by Hurst, who used strong persuasion to make patients listen more attentively.[22]

Other researchers have described hypnotic technics which could be used to reeducate and improve hearing acuity.[30] It is concluded, from their clinical observations, that hypnotherapy can be effective for abnormal hearing difficulties which are believed to be psychogenic in origin. Symptom substitution was not utilized in any of the series. The hearing behavior improved in nearly all cases.

LARYNGOLOGY

Globus Hystericus

Globus commonly occurs in nervous individuals who are under severe stress. Since the mechanism is based on a conversion reaction, direct symptom removal by hypnosis is effective. When the patient recognizes the psychogenic basis for the symptom, the emphasis should be on present and future adjustment. Other symptom equivalents are not likely to return if permissive technics are utilized.

Hysterical Aphonia and Dysphonia

There are many kinds of speech and vocal conditions that are refractory to therapy, such as hysterical aphonia and dysphonia, and harsh, scratchy, rough voices that are very hard to treat. Nervous individuals who make their livings by using their voices are the ones generally affected. They know that they must sing or speak well; therefore they cannot become tense, or their vocal productions will be endangered. Many orators are nervous when they first start speaking, and the tension immediately shows itself in altered voice qualities. There may be harshness,

huskiness, tremolo, or perhaps either an elevation or a depression of pitch.

Platonov described how three or four hypnosuggestive sessions cured opera singers of "footlight neuroses."[33] Psychotherapy administered while the cortex is in a "lowered tone" made it possible to eliminate the neurosis completely.

Gagging

Hypnosis is used to control or eliminate the gag reflex. Generally a light stage is sufficient. Many individuals, on the basis of psychological factors, believe that they will gag. Several technics that are effective in a high per cent of cases will be discussed in Chapter 46.

RHINOLOGY

Epistaxis

Hypnosis has been used to control severe epistaxis.

There are innumerable reports from dentists who contend that bleeding can be stopped and started by hypnotic suggestion. The author believes that more accurately controlled data are needed before the conclusion is reached that bleeding can be stopped so readily by hypnosis.

Rhinitis

Vasomotor rhinitis is astonishingly susceptible to emotional factors in its production and its dissolution. The common cold often responds to hypnosis. The author sees many patients who, coincidental to their chief complaint, have the "sniffles." Susceptible persons under hypnosis can be told, "Imagine that you are walking home. It's a very hot day, and your nose and throat are very, very dry, *real dry!* Wouldn't you give anything for a nice, cold drink of water? Your mouth and nose are getting very dry, very dry, are they not?" Or, "Imagine you are in a steam bath and the hot vapor is going up your nose. You've been in this steam bath a long time and you're very parched. . . ."

As has been mentioned, physiologic effects can be obtained through hypnotic suggestion only by sensory-imagery conditioning and not by direct command. To suggest, "Your nose will stop running" is futile. Suggestions of generalized warmth can also alleviate the rhinitis. The author has often demonstrated how "goose-pimpling," sneezing, shivers, and a drop in body temperature can be induced by hypnotic suggestion to a good hypnotic subject.

The fact that the common cold responds to a wide variety of medicaments implicates emotional factors, even though a viral etiology has been postulated. It has been demonstrated that specific or nonspecific stress lowers the threshold to viral invasion.

REFERENCES

1. Backus, P.S.: An experimental note on hypnotic ablation of optokinetic nystigamus. Am. J. Clin. Hypn., *4:*184, 1962.
2. Berger, A. S., and Zamet, C. N.: Emotional factors in primary glaucoma. Psychosomat. Med., *22:*391, 1960.
3. Berger, A. S., and Zimet, C. N.: Effect of hypnosis on intraocular pressure in normal and glaucomatous subjects. Psychosom. Med., *20:*321, 1958.
4. _____: Personality features of patients with primary glaucoma. Psychosom. Med., *20:*389, 1959.
5. Brady, J.P., and Levitt, E.E.: Nystagmus as a criterion of hypnotically induced visual hallucinations. Science, *146:*85, 1964.
6. Browning, C. W., and Crasilneck, H. B.: The experimental use of hypnosis in supression amblyopia. Am. J. Ophthalmol., *44:*4; 468, 1957.
7. _____: The use of hypnosis in suppression amblyopia of children. Am. J. Ophthalmol., *46:*1, 53, 1958.
8. Cohen, M. H.: The use of hypnosis in the Ridley operation for cataract. J. Psychosomatics, *2:*184, 1961.
9. Crane, M.: Mental effort in orthoptic treatment. Br. Orthoptic J., *14:*91, 1957.
10. Crasilneck, H.B., and Hall, M.D.: Clinical Hypnosis: Principles and Applications. New York, Grune & Stratton, 1975.
11. Elliotson, J.: The Harveian Lecture, delivered before the Royal College of Physicians, London, June 27, 1846.
12. Erickson, M.H.: Acquired control of pupillary responses. Am. J. Clin. Hypn., *3:*207, 1965.
13. Esdaile, J.: Mesmerism in India (Hypnosis in Medicine and Surgery). New York, Julian Press, 1957.
14. Eyles, M. A.: Some psycho-physiological aspects of vision related to orthoptic procedure. Br. Orthoptic J., *13:*7, 1956.
15. Fowler, E. P., and Zechel, A.: Psychosomatic aspects of Meniere's disease. J.A.M.A., *148:*1265, 1952.
16. _____: Psychophysiological factors in Meniere's disease. Psychosom. Med., *15:*127, 1953.
17. Godtfredsen, E.: Psychosomatic opthalmology. Acta Psychotherap., *1:*211, 1953.
18. Goldberg, E. L., and Kliman, G.: Improved visual recognition during hypnosis. Arch. Gen. Psychiatry, *7:*155, 1962.
19. Gonzales, J.: Hypnosis in opthalmology. Rev. Bras. Oftalmol., *201:*271, 1961.
20. Graham, C., and Leibowitz, H.W.: The effect of suggestion on visual acuity. Int. J. Clin. Exp. Hypn., *20:*169, 1972.
21. Guild, J.: Hypnosis for tinnitus. Can. Med. Assoc. J., *78:*426, 1959.
22. Hurst, A.: (quoted by Guild, J.) Medical Diseases of War. ed. 3. Baltimore, Williams & Wilkins, 1943.
23. Kline, M. V., Guze, H., and Haggerty, A. D.: An experimental study of the nature of hypnotic deafness: effects of delayed speech feed-back. J. Clin. Exp. Hypn., *2:*145, 1954.
24. Kodman, F., and Pattie, F. A.: Hypnotherapy of psychogenic hearing loss in children. Am. J. Clin. Hypn., *1:*9, 1958.
25. Kraemer, R.: Psychotherapy of squint. Psychotherapie, *1:*93, 1956.
26. Kroger, W.S., and Fezler, W.D.: Hypnosis and Behavior Modification: Imagery Conditioning. Philadelphia, J. B. Lippincott, 1976.
27. Lichtenstein, L. C. S.: Hipnose em Ortoptica. Arq. Bras. Oftalmol., *22:*101, 1959.
28. Lock, Y.K., *et al:* Hypnotherapy in strabismus. Am. J. Clin. Hypn., *7:*335, 1965.
29. Loomis, A. L., Harvey, E. N., and Hobart, G. A.: Brain potentials during hypnosis. Science, *83:*239, 1936.
30. Malmo, R. B., Booz, T. J., and Raginsky, B. B.: Electromyographic study of hypnotic deafness. J. Clin. Exp. Hypn., *2:*305, 1954.
31. Mihalyka, E. E., and Whanger, A. D.: Objective tinnitus aurium hypnotically treated. Am. J. Clin. Hypn., *2:*85, 1959.
32. Pearson, M. M., and Barnes, L. J.: Objective tinnitus aurium: report of two cases with good results after hypnosis. J. Phila. Gen. Hosp., *1:*134, 1950.
33. Platonov, K. I.: The Word as a Physiological and

Therapeutic Factor. Moscow, Foreign Languages Publishing House, 1955.

34. Schneck, J.M.: Hypnotherapy for symptoms associated with cataract. Int. J. Clin. Exp. Hypn., *15:* 45, 1967.

35. Schneider, D. E.: Growth Concept of Integration. Nerv. Ment. Dis. Mono., *78:*42, 1949.

36. Shafer, T.A.: Hypnosis in the management and control of trigeminal neuralgia: two case reports. Am. J. Clin. Hypn., *5:*138, 1962.

37. Smith, G.C., Crasilneck, H.B., and Browning, C.W.: A follow-up study of suppression amblyopia in children previously subjected to hypnotherapy. Am. J. Ophthalmol., *52:*690, 1961.

38. Sowden, A. S.: The value of hypnosis in orthoptic training. Optician, *123:*619, 1952.

39. Strosberg, I.M., Irving, M., and Vics, I.I.: Physiologic changes in the eye during hypnosis. Am. J. Clin. Hypn., *4:*264, 1962.

40. Sukhakarn, K. V., *et al.:* A record of the discovery and investigation of how vision is attained through the cheek by the blind or blindfolded persons. Bangkok, The Training Center for Concentration and Memory, 1960.

41. Wickramaskera, I.: Hypnosis and broad spectrum behavior therapy for blepharospasm: a case study. Am. J. Clin. Hypn., *22:*201, 1974.

42. Wilkins, L.G., and Field, P.B.: Helpless under attack: hypnotic abreaction in hysterical loss of vision. Am. J. Clin. Hypn., *10:*271, 1968.

43. Wolberg, L. R.: Medical Hypnosis. vol. 1. New York, Grune & Stratton, 1948, p. 227.

41

Hypnosis in Genitourinary Conditions

Selective cases of postoperative retention of urine, premature ejaculation, impotency in the male, dysuria, ureteral spasm, and chronic bladder irritation respond to hypnotherapy. Pseudo-orientation in time can help emotional repercussions that might be expected with male or female sterilization. Hypnorelaxation indirectly may have an important bearing on female infertility, as the fertilizing capacity of the sperm is possibly affected by stress factors.

POSTOPERATIVE URINARY RETENTION

TREATMENT

Postoperative urinary retention, after pelvic or perineal surgery, often is completely relieved by posthypnotic suggestions.[3, 5, 8, 21, 25, 27] An authoritarian hypnotic approach, such as, "You will void in exactly 20 minutes," is seldom successful. Permissive technics together with sensory-imagery conditioning are more successful. Under hypnosis it is suggested, "Perhaps you may be able to remember in detail what it felt like the last time you urinated. Try to imagine the sensations you experienced the last time you emptied your bladder." When able to do this, the patient is asked to describe the subjective sensations associated with the act of micturition. These are fed back immediately or during subsequent sessions. No time limit for carrying out the act is mentioned.

After the patient is trained in autohypnosis, he is told, "If you imagine yourself urinating again and again, then you will have no trouble starting the stream. Try not to urinate until you have reexperienced urinating in your mind first." Asking the patient to carry or not to carry out the act places him in a position in which he cannot refuse or resist the operator's suggestions. Whether or not he urinates, he is being controlled without realizing it. Since the patient does not set the terms, there is no way for him to mobilize further fears that he will not urinate. As the result of the repeated rehearsals of "urinating" under autohypnosis, confidence replaces his irrational fears. Invariably these patients will urinate within several hours, especially if deeply hypnotized and taught autohypnosis during the initial sessions.

These technics are indicated where repeated catheterizations are required. Several publications fail to mention psychogenic factors in urine retention.[12, 21] This is surprising, as the contraction of the bladder muscle and the maintenance of urinary continence are cortically controlled. The concepts of "voluntary" and "involuntary" control of micturition need to be modified.

The author has seen a number of patients in consultation, many of whom were used for teaching purposes in a hospital setting. In those with highly resistant symptoms, hypnosis was successful in over 80 per cent of the cases. Direct symptom removal by command is seldom effective, as the fearful subject thinks his inability to urinate is "involuntary." The author recently saw a 60-year-old female who had not voided for 10 days after a hemorrhoidectomy. Utilizing the technics described above, urination occurred within 4 hours after her initial hypnotic induction.

HEMODIALYSIS

There is a growing body of literature on the psychological responses of hemodialysis patients. Of particular interest is the common occurrence of anxiety and apprehension, both before and during dialysis. Hypnosis effectively reduces the anxiety and enables patients to become more tractable to the procedure.[9]

CHRONIC BLADDER IRRITABILITY

Chronic and recurrent irritability of the vesical neck of the bladder, secondary to psychogenic factors, often is noted in women.[28] The predominant symptoms are discomfort, frequency, and dysuria; these respond to hypnotherapy. Many female patients use frequent micturition as a masturbatory equivalent, especially if frigid. One patient's dysuria cleared up only after correction of her husband's impotence. For another, a severe cardiac who was unable to have sexual intercourse, glove anesthesia under autohypnosis was used to relieve her bladder discomfort.

"PEE-SHY" PROBLEMS

Crasilneck and Hall describe a much-neglected syndrome—the "pee-shy" problem.[4] Persons so afflicted are unable to urinate in public toilets or when others are watching. These writers recommend that hypnosis be employed in a reassuring, calming way, with suggestions for ease and relaxation in the usually anxiety-filled situation. Patients also can respond to systematic desensitization wherein a hierarchy is set up, and then each step of the situation producing anxiety is treated by successive approximation or stepwise progression. Hypnosis would greatly facilitate this approach.

PREMATURE EJACULATION AND IMPOTENCE

Premature ejaculation and impotency are so widespread in our culture that they might well be called the "emotional plague." Impotency accounts for many gynecologic symptoms, such as the congestion-fibrosis-hyperemia syndrome. The vascular stasis is secondary to orgasmic dysfunction.

Organic or primary impotency can be established or ruled out by the history. Absence of erection, or premature ejaculation, is always noted, whether the situation is copulatory or masturbatory. No nocturnal emissions or morning erections occur. Heredity, physical factors, and age are predisposing factors to psychogenic or secondary impotency. Ejaculation occurs before or soon after penetration; the erection cannot be maintained.

The psychological causes may be due to anxieties produced by faulty attitudes toward sex as guilt, fear of failure brought on by intense mental activity, preoccupation, fatigue or repeated episodes of failure, hostility toward the spouse, and lack of affection. Abstinence also leads to impotency. The idea is common that sex is wicked, sinful, and not to be used to demean the mate, whom the patient may equate with his mother; moreover, he may be potent with other women (facultative impotency). Another common factor is a deep-seated need to fail in order to reject the mate for various reasons, which are usually unrecognized. Other factors, such as an overly aggressive or highly experienced sex partner, may intimidate the passive male, particularly if latent or overt homosexuality is present. Alcoholism and diabetes are entities often resulting in impotency. Traumatic experiences during childhood, unresolved oedipal conflicts, and feelings of organ inferiority contribute to secondary impotence. Often secondary impotence can be a conversion reaction to threatening life situations. The female who shows her revulsion for the sex act or has the desire to "get it over in a hurry" can render the male impotent. The psychophysiology of erection and ejaculation has been described.[15, 26]

TREATMENT

Such drugs as testosterone to increase the libido, anesthetic ointments to abolish sensitivity of the glans penis, and prostatic massage have only a placebo effect. Premature ejaculation is often refractory to all types of psychotherapy. Misconceptions and faulty attitudes toward sexual matters must be corrected by reeducation.

The male who is sometimes impotent requires only superficial psychotherapy. Most need better communication, particularly if boredom and monotony set in. Many men are totally incapable of love in a mature sense.

Strong reassurance under hypnosis often establishes confidence for the prematurist. Von Schrenck-Notzing reported many forms of impotence that were treated by suggestion and directive hypnotherapy. The first step is to demonstrate that the patient is capable of an erection. Recovery is initiated once self-confidence is strengthened and reinforced. The constant preoccupation with the symptom can be reduced if an indifferent attitude over failure is suggested. Forcing the sex act is harmful. The non-demand performance approach is often helpful.[20] Favorable results have been obtained by hypnobehavioral therapy.[11, 18]

Hypnotic treatment of impotence has been reported by several writers.[2, 6, 14, 19, 23] Anesthesia of the penis has been cured by hypnosis.[7] Others have utilized hypnosis for the homosexual component of the impotence.[1, 14] Four hundred cases of impotence treated by hypnosis and psychotherapy have been reported.[4]

More recently, technics have been developed utilizing revivification of previous satisfactory sexual contacts under autohypnosis. This effectively conditions the prematurist to perform adequately. In other cases, especially in those who have never had a satisfactory sex act, the premature ejaculation can be treated by reversing the fear of too rapid ejaculation. The following posthypnotic suggestion is illustrative: "You might consider the possibility of being very concerned over *not* being able to ejaculate, regardless of how hard you try. The more you try, the more difficult it will be to lose your erection."

Time distortion can be employed to prevent premature ejaculation in a good subject by making him think that he has maintained an erection for a relatively long time. During deep hypnosis it is suggested, "Thirty seconds of subjective or experiential time *will seem* like 2 minutes of clock time." Thus, if the prematurist maintains an erection for only 30 seconds, he will think that he had it for 2 minutes. This positive hallucination by which time is "expanded" can be reinforced through further posthypnotic suggestions; it rapidly helps to restore confidence in the patient's staying ability. The wife should be apprised of the situation and told to praise her husband's ability. Naturally, the husband is not made aware of this.

The above hypnotic technics are incorporated with supportive psychotherapy. If the patient feels accepted, he will wittingly or unwittingly reveal the basis for his fears and anxieties that are associated with his sexual inadequacy. Guidance directed toward breaking up the harmful reflex patterns enables the individual to react to his problem in a healthier manner. Extensive probing and attempting to exhume the past is fruitless, especially for the impotent male, who has never been erectively and ejaculatively potent. What should be emphasized is that the spiritual relationship between the partners influences the performance of the sex act.

Sensory-imagery conditioning under autohypnosis combined with behavior therapy are especially effective for refractory cases.

The most disheartening cases are those unfortunate individuals who contend that they are unable to develop an erection during the sex act. The author sees many of them. The majority of these feelings, too, are psychogenic in origin. It has been demonstrated recently that the midline and the anterior thalamic nuclei via the limbic system cortically control sexual functioning. A modification of autogenic training and desensitization therapy is helpful.

Over 60 per cent of individuals can be helped by behavior modification and reconditioning under autohypnosis. The results are relatively permanent, but the work is tedious and often heartbreaking for therapist and patient.

CYSTOSCOPY AND SURGICAL PROCEDURES

There are several reports on the use of hypnoanesthesia for cystoscopy,[3] with or without pyelography and other urologic procedures such as urethral dilation and catheterization. Posthypnotic suggestions of relaxation can prevent postinstrumental spasms.

Many different types of minor surgical procedures have been performed under hypnoanesthesia, such as amputation of the penis, circumcision, meatotomy, vas ligation, and fulguration of venereal warts. Many huge scrotal tumors, weighing up to 80 pounds, were removed by Esdaile under hypnosis *per se.*[10] He also performed circumcisions, removed testes, injected hydroceles, and did other similar surgery—*all without anesthesia* and all before 1850! Today there is no need to eliminate anesthesia, but hypnosis can reduce preoperative anxiety and tension, as well as neurogenic shock in seriously ill patients.

VASECTOMY

Pseudo-orientation in time or hallucinated age progression can be employed to ascertain possible contraindications for vasectomy.[16]

Since posthypnotic amnesia is always necessary, this procedure can be used only in good hypnotic subjects. Pseudo-orientation in time and abreaction under hypnosis do not necessarily prove that a vasectomy may produce serious psychological repercussions. However, it is better to err on the side of safety when highly charged material evoked without the subject's knowledge points toward a personality difficulty which might be aggravated years after the sterilization. Therefore, the motivation for vasectomy must always be evaluated carefully in terms of its psychological significance.

MALE INFERTILITY

The male is responsible for over 50 per cent of all barren marriages. Little is known about the relationship of disturbed emotions to semen quality and motility. These, rather than the total sperm count, are often important factors in the ease of conception. There is a growing awareness that emotional conflicts can alter the sperm's fertilizing capacity. It is well known that fatigue, shock, worry, and tension often produce infertility in both animals and humans.[16] This is due to overproduction of endogenous norepinephrine, secondary to specific or nonspecific stress. Hypnosis has not been able to increase the sperm count or influence sperm motility. However, adverse enzymatic changes can be produced in the sperm, secondary to autonomic imbalance, and

thus inactivate the sperm's ability to penetrate the ovum, even though the sperm appears morphologically normal and adequate in quantity.

FEMALE INFERTILITY

Posthypnotic suggestions directed toward relaxation, tranquility, and freedom from anxiety may behelpful for certain cases of infertility in the female that defy all types of therapy. Though the author has no adequately controlled data to present in this important and neglected entity, it offers a fruitful area for further research.

REFERENCES

1. Alexander, L.: Treatment of impotency and anorgasmia by psychotherapy. J. Am. Inst. Hypn., *12:* 165, 1971.
2. Biegel, H.G.: Therapeutic approaches of impotence in the male. II. The hypnotherapeutic approach to male impotence. J. Sex. Res., *7:*168, 1971.
3. Brown, T.B.: Hypnosis in genitourinary diseases. Am. J. Clin. Hypn., *1:*165, 1959.
4. Crasilneck, H.B., and Hall, J.A.: Clinical Hypnosis: Principles and Applications. New York, Grune & Stratton, 1975.
5. Cucinotta, S.: Acute urinary retention successfully treated with hypnosis. Am. J. Clin. Hypn., *3:*201, 1961.
6. Dittborn, J.: Hypnotherapy of sexual impotency. J. Clin. Exp. Hypn., *4:*181, 1957.
7. Doane, W.L.: Report of a case of anesthesia of the penis cured by hypnotherapy. J. Am. Inst. Hypn., *12:*165, 1971.
8. Doberneck, R.C., and McFee, A.S.: The prevention of postoperative urinary retention by hypnosis. Am. J. Clin. Hypn., *3:*235, 1961.
9. Dy, A.J., and Fabbri, R.: The use of hypnosis with the hemodialysis patient. Am. J. Clin. Hypn., *14:* 173, 1972.
10. Esdaile, J.: Hypnosis in Medicine and Surgery. New York, Julian Press, 1957.
11. Fabri, R.: Hypnosis and behavior therapy: a coordinated approach to the treatment of sexual disorders. Am. J. Clin. Hypn.,*19:*4, 1976.
12. Fleming, A.R.: The use of urecholine in the prevention of postpartum urinary retention. Am. J. Obstet. Gynecol., *74:*569, 1959.
13. Gonzaga, J.G.: Sophorological treatment of psychic impotence. Am. J. Clin. Hypn., *14:*206, 1972.
14. _____: Treatment of male homosexuality by

means of hypnosis. Am. J. Clin. Hypn., *14:*206, 1972.

15. Kroger, W.S.: Psychosomatic aspects of frigidity and impotency. Int. Rec. Med., *171:* 469, 1958.

16. _____: Hypnotic pseudo-orientation in time for determining psychologic effects of vasectomy and sterilization in the female. Fertil. Steril., *14:*535, 1963.

17. _____: Help the impotent male help himself. Consultant, *10:*37, 1972.

18. Kroger, W.S., and Fezler, W.D.: Hypnosis and Behavior Modification: Imagery Conditioning. Philadelphia, J.B. Lippincott, 1976.

19. Levit, H.I.: Marital crisis intervention: hypnosis in impotence/frigidity cases. Am. J. Clin. Hypn., *14:* 56, 1971.

20. Masters, W.H., and Johnson, V.E.: Human Sexual Inadequacy. Boston, Little, Brown, 1970.

21. Nourse, M.H.: Management of the patient who fails to void after operation. J.A.M.A., *171:*84, 1959.

22. Owen-Flood, A.: Hypnosis in anesthesiology. *In* J. M. Schneck (Ed.): Hypnosis in Modern Medicine. Springfield, Ill., Charles C Thomas, 1959. Pp. 88–100.

23. Schneck, J.M.: Psychogenic impotence with a hypnotherapy illustration. Psychosomatics, *11:*352, 1970.

24. Solovey, G., and Milechnin, A.: Concerning the treatment of enuresis. Am. J. Clin. Hypn., *2:*22, 1959.

25. Van Dyke, P.B.: The case of the recalcitrant bladder. Am. J. Clin. Hypn., *14:*256, 1972.

26. von Schrenck-Notzing, A.: The Use of Hypnosis in Psychopathia Sexualis. New York, Julian Press, 1956.

27. Werner, W.E.F.: Hypnosis in the prevention, control and therapy of urinary retention. Am. J. Clin. Hypn., *5:*64, 1962.

28. Williams, G.E., and Johnson, A.M.: Recurrent urinary retention due to emotional factors. Psychosom. Med., *18:*77, 1956.

42

Hypnosis in Oncology

EFFECT OF EMOTIONS

Undoubtedly, no single factor is responsible for cancer. Recently, however, psychological factors have been considered in the causation, pathogenesis, and prognosis of neoplasms.[40] In a Presidential address to the American Cancer Society in 1959, Pendergrass stated:

"I personally have observed cancer patients who have undergone successful treatment and were living and well for years. . . . There is solid evidence that the course of disease in general is affected by emotional distress. . . . We may learn how to influence general body systems and through them modify the neoplasm which resides within the body. . . . As we go forward . . . searching for new means of controlling growth both within the cell and through systematic influences . . . we can widen the quest to include the distinct possibility that within one's mind is a power capable of exerting forces which can either enhance or inhibit the progress of this disease.

It also has been observed that the empathic physician who establishes good rapport is an important factor; that patients treated by one physician tended to have a smoother course than those treated by another; and that patients seem to do better if informed of the nature of their condition.

PERSONALITY FACTORS AND EMOTIONAL REACTIONS

The author has reviewed the extensive literature on the effect of personality patterns on cancer growth, personality profiles, and psychometric evaluation of patients known to have cancer.[32] The effect of cancer, emotions, and mental illness have recently been studied by Surawicz and co-workers.[51] They analyzed the relationship between psychological factors and cancer, assaying the role of personality patterns and stress on development, site, and course of the cancer. Handling the psychiatric sequelae and awareness of death also are fully discussed.

Bahnson implicates despair, object loss, depression, and hopelessness as etiologic factors.[2] Other researchers have also studied personality patterns associated with cancer.[21, 23, 37, 44] Maladaptive coping mechanisms, such as denial and repression of the illness, have been assayed extensively.[3, 15, 25, 29, 30, 31] Unfortunately, the investigations and the findings are subject to rather generalized interpretations. The studies of withdrawn schizophrenics, for instance, show that the death rate for carcinoma is half that for the population at large; however, for paranoid schizophrenics with overt hostility, it is four times the normal rate. The personality patterns responsible for the development of cancer vary from grief over deprivation, inhibited rage, sexuality and masochism,[1] inability to tolerate emotional stress, constitutional inadequacy, and marital status (higher rate among widowed),[39] to overcompliance, sincerity, and dependability.

The investigative procedures used included anecdotal collations, interviews, sociologic and demographic analyses, and psychological testing. In spite of faulty design, inadequate controls, and statistical evaluation, there is a general consistency in the surveys (i.e., cancer patients are immature, depressed, fearful, full of self-recrimination, have suffered a loss of some type, are sexually maladjusted, and are incapable of expressing anger). Patients with rapidly growing tumors appear to be more defensive, anxious, and inhibited than those with slow-growing malignancies. Of course, many of the emotional reactions cited above are similar to those noted in psychoneurotics and are not specific for cancer. It may be an injustice to infer that patients develop cancer because of an immature personality development or that a real or symbolic loss precipitated their malignant illness. However, it may be that specific personality factors become operative in the presence of other variables—the correct combination resulting in carcinoma.

METHODOLOGICAL CONSIDERATIONS

On a related issue, any efforts made with correlational designs to distinguish psychological reactions from psychological predispositions to cancer were completely arbitrary. Virtually every study published had taken dependent measures from patients where carcinoma had already been detected. This procedure only allows for a post hoc personality assessment, hardly a suitable design for the valid measurement of causal factors. Granted, there are numerous practical and ethical problems involved when doing cancer research. It would hardly be defensible to create cancer in a group of individuals as a means of determining the cause of the disease. But too often researchers have made assumptions far beyond their collected data. Future researchers may develop solutions to these formidable obstacles.

PSYCHOPHYSIOLOGIC AND BIOCHEMICAL FACTORS

According to Potter, the key role in the formation of neoplasms may be played by the enzyme-forming systems controlled by the deoxyribonucleic acid (DNA) pattern and molecules in a metabolic pool. He states:

The successive mutations that produce cancer cells may be due to inherent errors in nucleic acid replication, to errors induced by carcinogens, or to loss by segregation of enzyme-forming systems that fail to replicate fast enough during cell division.[40]

This theory hypothesizes that "certain viruses might substitute for endogenously altered nucleoproteins." More specifically the DNA of the viruses may replace the mechanisms controlling the enzyme-forming systems, while the ribonucleic acid (RNA) of viruses would substitute for the enzyme-forming systems themselves. Certain protein molecules are remarkable in that they can reproduce like living things.

There is an assumption that there exists—in DNA to RNA to DNA information transfer—a process that can generate new nucleic acid sequences. It is posited that human cancer is a result of formation of the genes for neoplastic transformation by "misevolution of a normal cellular information transferring process.[53] Such misevolution is caused by chemicals, physical agents or viruses." It is hoped that recent advances in immunology will ultimately solve the baffling problem of cancer.[41] A recent review of this area now seems to confirm that the body does indeed have natural or immunocompetent defenses against cancer.[27] A speculative hypothesis has been advanced to the effect that psychological variables could interfere with the body's natural defenses and, in this way, affect the cancerous process. Current research has yielded interesting and significant data.[4, 50] In summing up this evidence, Bahnson concluded: "Thus, hard-nosed data from the neurological and endocrinological fields corroborate the notion that psychological events mediated by the nervous system may influence endocrine and immune reactions related to malignancies."[2]

The fascinating work of Black, though not involved with cancer, points up that direct suggestions under hypnosis (DSUH) have an effect on the immune system.[9] His formulations should be consulted by the reader interested in the control of the immune response by imagery conditioning (see p. 253). Barrios and Kroger state:

If such is the case then it seems a logical conclusion that if we had some effective tool for reversing these negative psychological factors, we should in turn revive the defense mechanisms. This, in turn, might lead to the body's natural rejection of the cancer. Thus, we should no longer fear proposing the hypothesis that one means of facilitating the cure of cancer may very well be through 'the mind.'[8]

The hormonal mechanisms implicated in the growth or arrest of certain tumors are those involving the breast[22, 41, 50, 55] and the prostate. These, in part, are dependent on the extent of hormonal activity and, to a degree, are mediated through corticohypothalamic impulses.

SPONTANEOUS REMISSION AND THE ADAPTIVE RESPONSES

As pertinent as the changes in the cell is the kind of person who has the cancer. Host resistance appears to be affected, in part, in those who have the "will to live." They often survive longer than otehrs with similar degrees of cancer involvement.[54] The phenomenon of "voodoo death" is illustrative. Stress has been held responsible for rapid metastases and recurrences of cancer after surgery.

Spontaneous remissions of neoplasms have been reported.[16, 20] Though rare, and inexplicable, the possibility of spontaneous regression of cancer may be of some psychotherapeutic value in offering hope to sufferers and relatives of patients with "incurable" cancer. Often, indeed, the mere thought that regression might possibly take place changes their attitude from complete despair to hopeful toleration.[10, 28, 47]

It has long been recognized that wart tumors, even though benign, are due to a viral involvement and often respond to suggestion and/or hypnosis (see Chap. 38).[32, 52] This noteworthy example of alteration in tissue pathology is pertinent to our discussion.

HYPNOTHERAPEUTIC MANAGEMENT OF THE CANCER PATIENT

There are several reports indicating that hypnosis diminishes the need for narcotic drugs,[11] lessens the ill effects of x-rays, and reduces discomfort following radiation therapy.[19] Together with empathy and positive reinforcing suggestions, it decreases the patient's shock upon learning that he has cancer. Improved mental attitudes, motivation, and relaxation in cancer patients have been attributed to hypnosis.[21] Successful management of pain and suffering often depends more on the rapport and reduction of

anxiety than on the hypnotic depth;[37] These factors raise the pain threshold. Other investigators have described effective use of hypnosis in relieving cancer pain.[8, 12, 13, 14, 17, 18, 24, 26, 35, 45] La Baw advises hypnosis in lieu of hospitalization for the terminal cancer patient.[41] He and his associates have also obtained good results using self-hypnosis in children with cancer.

The author has used hypnosis as an adjunct for the management of intractable pain in terminal cancer patients. Many were considering lobotomy, posterior rhizotomy, alcohol block, dorsal column stimulation, or chordotomy for pain relief. All were on high doses of opiates. After these patients learned how to induce glove anesthesia under autohypnosis, the dosage of narcotics was drastically decreased in over 60 per cent of them.

Hypnosis apparently blocks the perception of pain—it is a sort of "psychological" lobotomy. When it is used individually for direct symptom relief, the procedure is tedious and the results are often disappointing. One investigator has had only indifferent success with direct hypnosis.[37] Group hypnosis (1 hour per week) is preferable, as faith, hope, and confidence are mobilized more readily; susceptibility to posthypnotic suggestions is increased when the readiness to respond to painful stimuli is minimized by misdirection of attention.[5]

As a consultant to the City of Hope Medical Center and the Pain Clinic at U.C.L.A., the author has treated a number of cancer patients in various stages using hypnosis. He has noted that about 20 per cent can control their discomfort and another 40 per cent can drastically reduce the need for narcotic drugs. Another advantage is that narcotic drugs can be held in abeyance. Even when the disease progresses, there often is no need for addictive pain-killing drugs. Since the tolerance for such drugs has not been increased, smaller doses, if necessary, can be employed. Many patients can live in relative comfort and peace of mind until the disease becomes terminal.

In an excellent review of the control of cancer pain by hypnosis, Hilgard and Hilgard point out that ego-strength is provided, pain is reduced by relief of anxiety, insomnia is mitigated, interests are broadened, and the dependence on the hypnotherapist is diminished through self-hypnosis.[26] They also mention the various strategies that can be employed, such as symptom transference, glove anesthesia, time distortion, disassociation, age regression, and amnesia for the pain.

One of the first studies on the use of hypnosis in cancer was done by Hedge.[24] The shortcomings of Hedge's study have been noted by Barrios.[6] Hedge used only one standard hypnotic induction. More effective and varied hypnotic induction technics, such as those used by Hilgards, might have increased the effectiveness of the hypnotherapy. Moreover, Hedge did not make full use of the hypnosis. Often the success of hypnosis depends on how it is used. Apparently, Hedge used it primarily to instill a positive attitude regarding one's own ability to fight off the disease. This is *definitely* an important part of the therapy, but, in addition, the negative attitudes, beliefs, and habits that might be precipitating factors in causing the host's natural defenses to malfunction must be permanently eliminated. A holistic approach must be followed. One that will ensure more joy and happiness as opposed to despair and hopelessness.[56] A more recent and ongoing study seems to be proceeding in this direction.

Simonton's technics are used to improve mental attitudes in his radiation therapy patients.[48] In addition to pointing out to the patient, in a manner similar to Hedge, that the body has natural defenses against cancer, Simonton has also incorporated technics aimed at inculcating positive attitudes and bolstering the will to live. His basic tools are meditation or self-hypnosis exercises (suggesting relaxation to oneself with every breath exhaled), which give the patient greater control over the ability to relax. He also shows the patient how to use the meditative state for instilling positive suggestions via positive imagery. Thus far the results are quite encouraging. In a study involving 134 patients treated with meditation and visualization since 1972, 100 are still alive—and these survivors have lived longer than those similarly afflicted. Even the 34 who died lived longer than expected. Simonton concedes the importance of scientific proof to validate his approach. However, Simonton and Tatera found a strong correlation between positive mental atti-

tudes and progress of the disease.[49] Simonton maintains that the cancer patient should grasp the concept that he can influence the immune mechanisms and realize that the mind can powerfully alter the development and course of the disease.[48] The Simontons[47] report remissions in far-advanced metastatic cancers. However, they need 5-year follow-up data before publishing further results.

A major shortcoming of the Simonton approach, however, is how does one get the person really to believe in positive thinking? This shortcoming is similar to the one mentioned in regard to Hedge's study, namely, that only hypnotic relaxation was used. By using more varied technics, the physician or therapist can increase the belief factor which is so important if one wants one's words to have an effect.

SELF-PROGRAMMED CONTROL

Self-programmed control (SPC)[7, 8] has two major components: First there are the SPC technics—seven highly effective self-hypnosis* technics, which, in combination with the use of biofeedback as a reinforcer, give a person greater control over his involuntary functions (his habits, attitudes, emotions, and tensions) and make the possibility of a positive change really believable. This makes the patient receptive to the second component of the program—a positive philosophy which helps the individual to develop new attitudes toward life and himself, and often can provide the solutions to many personal problems plaguing the anxiety-ridden cancer patient.

The combination of these two components is effective for eliminating the negative psychological factors which have been posited as interfering with the natural defenses of the body. It is especially effective in eliminating the feeling of despair which has been felt by many to be the major culprit.

The program has many advantages. It is simply structured and easy to teach to physicians and paramedics, as well as to patients. As with most

---

*The term hypnosis is not generally used in connection with SPC because of the many misconceptions and negative connotations associated with the former.

forms of hypnotherapy, it takes considerably less time than conventional forms of therapy. It was designed specifically for working with groups, therby also cutting down on costs. And since the technics are aimed at self-control, much less dependency is created.

To test the hypothesis that such an approach can improve a person's ability to raise host resistance to cancer (it should be stressed that at the present time it is still just a hypothesis), the following initial study is proposed, using SPC in conjunction with any ongoing medical therapy (surgery, radiation therapy, chemotherapy, immunotherapy, etc.). As comparison controls, one could use statistical expectations or, if necessary, a matched control group. Tests for the immunological response[55] as well as measurement of mental attitudes could be run concurrently to test the hypothesis that these factors are all correlated with the course of the disease.

As pointed out by Sacerdote, it is important to convince anyone in contact with the patient of the feasibility of any program, especially attending physicians and nurses.[44] Negative attitudes can adversely affect or "contaminate" motivations of the patient. The study should not be limited to terminal cancer patients.

With ever-increasing reports of effectiveness, the author strongly feels that hypnosis should be the first method used to control pain in the cancer patient. It should not be used as a last resort, as is so often the case, particularly after surgery has been attempted for pain relief. Kroger and Fezler have combined hypnosis with operant conditioning, behavior modification, and imagery.[33] The specifically constructed images have a potent effect on pain relief and also inculcate motivation and faith to fight the disease. A physician using hypnosis in these kinds of cases can expect a high failure rate. However, he should realize that he is doing the best he can under the circumstances.

REFERENCES

1. Bacon, C.L., *et al.:* A psychosomatic survey of cancer of the breast. Psychosom. Med., *14:*453, 1952.
2. Bahnson, C.B.: Psychological complementarity in malignancies: past work and future vistas. Ann. N.Y. Acad. Sci., *164:*319, 1969.
3. Bahnson, C.B., and Bahnson, M.B.: Role of the ego defenses: Denial and repression in the etiology of malignant neoplasms. Ann. N.Y. Acad. Sci., *125:* 277, 1966.
4. Bahnson, C.B., and Kissen, D.M.: Psychophysiological aspects of cancer. Ann. N.Y. Acad. Sci., 125:826, 1966.
5. Barber, T.X.: Toward a theory of pain: relief of pain by prefrontal leucotomy, opiates, placebos and hypnosis. Psychol. Bull., *56:*430, 1959.
6. Barrios, A.A.: Hypnosis as a possible means of curing cancer. Unpublished manuscript, 1961.
7. _____: Hypnotherapy: a reappraisal. Psychother. Theory Res. Prac., *7:*2, 1970.
8. Barrios, A. A., and Kroger, W.S.: Hypnosis as a tool in the fight against cancer. J. Holistic Health, *1:*71, 1975–1976.
9. Black, S.: Some Physiological Mechanisms Amenable to Control by Direct Suggestion Under Hypnosis. *In* Chertok, L. (ed.): Psychophysicological Mechanisms of Hypnosis. New York, Springer-Verlag, 1969, pp. 10–19.
10. Bolen, J.S.: Meditation and psychotherapy in the treatment of cancer. Psychiatry, *6:*19, 1974.
11. Butler, B.: The use of hypnosis in the care of the cancer patient. Cancer, *7:*1, 1954.
12. Caricoppa, J.M.: Hypnosis in terminal cancer. Am. J. Clin. Hypn., *5:*205, 1963.
13. Chong, T.M.: The use of hypnosis in the management of patients with cancer. Singapore Med. J., *9:* 211, 1968.
14. Clawson, T.H.: The hypnotic control of blood flow and pain and the potential use of hypnosis in the treatment of cancer. Am. J. Clin. Hypn., *17:*160, 1975.
15. Cobb, B.: Emotional problems of adult cancer patients. J. Am. Geriat. Soc., *1:*274, 1959.
16. Cole, W.: Dissemination of Cancer: Prevention and Therapy. New York, Appleton-Century-Crofts, 1961.
17. Crasilneck, H.B., and Hall, J.A.: Clinical hypnosis in problems of pain. Am. J. Clin. Exp. Hypn., *15:* 153, 1973.
18. _____: Clinical Hypnosis: Principles and Applications. New York, Grune & Stratton, 1975.
19. Dempster, C.P., *et al.:* Supportive hypnotherapy during the radical treatment of malignancies. Int. J. Clin. Exp. Hypn., *24:*1, 1976.
20. Everson, T.C., and Cole, W.H.: Spontaneous regression of malignant disease. J.A.M.A., *169:*142, 1959.
21. Greene, W.A.: The psychosocial settings of the development of leukemia and lymphoma., Ann. N.Y. Acad. Sci., *125:* 794, 1966.
22. Greer, S., and Morris, T.: Psychological attitudes

of women who develop breast cancer: a controlled study. J. Psychosom. Res., *19:*147, 1976.

23. Hagnell, O.: The premorbid personality of persons who develop cancer in a total population investigated in 1947 and 1957. Ann. N. Y. Acad. Sci., *125:*846, 1966.

24. Hedge, A.R.: Hypnosis in cancer. Br. J. Med. Hypn., *12:*2, 1960.

25. Henderson, J.G.: Denial and repression as factors in the delay of patients with cancer presenting themselves to the physician. Ann. N.Y. Acad. Sci., *125:*856, 1966.

26. Hilgard, E.R., and Hilgard, J.R.: Hypnosis in the Relief of Pain. Los Altos, Cal., William Kaufman, 1975.

27. Holmes, E.C., et al.: Immuno-therapy of malignancy in humans. J.A.M.A., *232:*1052, 1975.

28. Ikemii, Y., et al.: Psychosomatic consideration of cancer patients who have made a narrow escape from death. Dynamische Psychiatrie, *8:*77, 1975.

29. Katz, J., et al.: Psychoendocrine consideration in cancer of the breast. Ann. N.Y. Acad. Sci., *164:*509, 1969.

30. Kissen, D.M.: The significance of personality in lung cancer in men. Ann. N.Y. Acad. Sci., *125:*826, 1966.

31. Kissen, D.M., et al.: A further report on personality and psychosocial factors in lung cancer. Ann. N.Y. Acad. Sci., *164:*534, 1969.

32. Kroger, W.S.: Clinical and Experimental Hypnosis. ed. 1. Philadelphia, J.B. Lippincott, 1963.

33. Kroger, W.S., and Fezler, W.D.: Hypnosis and Behavior Modification: Imagery Conditioning. Philadelphia, J.B. Lippincott, 1976.

34. Kroger, W.S., and Freed, S.C.: Psychosomatic Gynecology: Including Problems of Obstetrical Care. Philadelphia, W.B. Saunders, 1951.

35. La Baw, L.W.: Terminal hypnosis in lieu of terminal hospitalization. An effective alternate in a fortunate case, Gerontol. Clin., *11:*312–320, 1969.

36. La Baw, L.W., et al.: Use of self-hypnosis by children with cancer. Am. J. Clin. Hypn., *17:*233, 1975.

37. Lea, P.A., et al.: The hypnotic control of intractable pain. Am. J. Clin. Hypn., *3:*3, 1960.

38. Le Shan, L.: An emotional life history pattern associated with neoplastic disease. Ann. N.Y. Acad. Sci., *125:*780, 1966.

39. Le Shan, L., and Worthington, R.E.: Some psychologic correlates of neoplastic disease: a preliminary report. J. Clin. Exp. Psychopathol., *16:*281, 1955.

40. Meerlo, J.A.M.: Psychological implications of malignant growth: a survey of hypotheses. Br. J. Med. Psychol., *27:*210, 1954.

41. Mihich, E.: Immunity, Cancer and Chemotherapy. New York, Academic Press, 1967.

42. Potter, V.R.: Address to the Federation of the American Society for Experimental Biology, Philadelphia, April 28, 1958.

43. Sacerdote, P.: Additional contributions to the hypnotherapy of the advanced cancer patient. Am. J. Clin. Hypn., *7:*308, 1965.

44. ———: The uses of hypnosis in cancer patients. Ann. N.Y. Acad. Sci., *125:*1011, 1966.

45. ———: Theory and practice of pain control in malignancy and other protracted or recurring painful illnesses. Int. J. Clin. Exp. Hypn., *18:*160, 1970.

46. Schmale, A.H., and Iker, H.P.: The affect of hopelessness in the development of cancer. The prediction of uterine cervical cancer in women with atypical cytology. Psychosom. Med., *26:*634, 1964.

47. Simonton, O.C., and Simonton, S.S.: Belief systems and management of the emotional aspects of malignancy. J. Transpersonal Psychology, *7:*29, 1975.

48. ———: The role of the mind in cancer therapy. The dimensions of healing: a symposium. Acad. Parapsychol. and Med., *3:*139, 1973.

49. Simonton, O.C., and Tatera, B.S.: The role of increased fractionation and patient attitude in radiation therapy (unpublished report, Air Force Base Medical Center, Los Altos, California, 1973).

50. Solomon, G.F.: Emotions, stress, the central nervous system and immunity. Ann. N.Y. Acad. Sci., *164:*335, 1969.

51. Surawicz, F.G., et al.: Cancer, emotions and mental illness: the present state of understanding. Am. J. Psychol., *133:*1306, 1976.

52. Surman, O.S., et al.: Hypnosis in the treatment of warts. Arch. Gen. Psychiat., *28:*439, 1973.

53. Temin, H.M.: Med. Tribune, *15:*1, January 9, 1974.

54. Trunnell, J.B., Personality, Life Stress and Carcinoma. In Kroger, W.S. (ed): Psychosomatic Gynecology, Obstetrics and Endocrinology. Springfield, Ill., Charles C Thomas, 1962.

55. Twomey, P.L., et al.: Cellular immunity in cured cancer patients. Cancer, *33:*435, 1974.

56. Wittkower, E.D., and Lipowski, A.J.: Recent developments in psychosomatic medicine. Psychosom. Med., *28:*722, 1966.

43

Hypnosis in Pediatrics

Hypnotherapy is an effective and flexible tool for selective cases of enuresis, nail-biting, stammering, asthma, epilepsy, tics, and behavior problems associated with chronic tensions, stress, and environmental difficulties. Hypnotherapy is also useful for attacking the psychogenic components of minimal brain damage, mental retardation, neuromuscular involvements, and chronic debilitating ailments requiring prolonged bed rest.[16] Hypnosis can help those with learning problems[30, 36] and, according to Laquarte, can aid in correcting vocal difficulties.[34] Hypnoanesthesia also can be used for children as well as for adults to minimize fear reactions prior to surgery.

Children over 5 years of age have the necessary verbal understanding to be hypnotized. Their blind trust and vivid imaginations make them very susceptible to suggestions. Children have a short attention span, and the best induction procedures are those which continually involve them in fantasy experiences, such as those described under Picture Visualization Technics (p. 75).

Dentists who hypnotize children draw "Mickey Mouse" on their thumbnails and maintain interest by relating a series of humorous incidents built around him. Games appeal to children, and they are easily shifted from reality to unreality by such measures, often being dissociated without their knowledge. Thus fear reactions are minimal because criticalness is reduced.

Because of children's autistic tendencies, a light to medium stage is usually sufficient for hypnotherapy. Picture or scene visualization is employed to enable the child to "see" himself as a character on an imaginary television screen—this reinforces the artificial dissociation.

Further imagery manipulation is oriented around the child's rapidly developing emotional responses by utilizing his greater flexibility, overtness and curiosity, his intense desire to learn, and his eagerness to participate. However, since he has only a limited ability to understand the meaning of a suggestion, communication must be at his level. One should never use "baby talk," "speak over his head" or "talk down to him," as this angers the child. Also, there should be no sudden and unexpected change in tone or content, as this may disrupt the rapport. Wright has detailed the technics particularly applicable to children.[64] Gardner recommends an approach involving a great many specific images and emphasizes ego-strengthening technics and self-hypnosis for reinforcement.[16] Parental attitudes are also included in the total therapeutic setting.

If the child is told what actions to expect rather than be taken by surprise, rapport is enhanced. Startle reactions usually terminate the hypnosis and produce resistances. Asking the child to imagine himself relaxing in his bed or on a comfortable couch deepens hypnosis. The escalator technic is helpful for further deepening. The child, at all times, must be flattered and given the impression that the suggested ideas originated from his own feelings, thinking, and experience.

A reward for his efforts, such as a medal, a prize, or a treat, strengthens the interpersonal relationship, shows the therapist's appreciation, and increases motivation. If new ideas are presented in such a manner as to apprise him fully that therapy is a collaborative venture, cooperation is increased. An authoritative approach rarely succeeds with children. They require patience and understanding; it is easier to agree that a symptom is annoying than to argue a child out of it. This helps to establish further rapport. Children seldom respond to logical ideas but readily comprehend those dealing with their own experiences, especially those affording them the most satisfaction and achievement.

Thus, with an enuretic child, it is useless to suggest that "Only babies wet the bed." It is better to ask, "How do your playmates feel about this? How many of them do this?" If the answers indicate a desire for help, therapy can be instituted. If not, further interrogation should be made. Assuming a desire for treatment, the next statement is, "With your help, I think we can lick this problem together. Wouldn't you like to do this? If you really want to, I'll show you how it can be a 'do-it-yourself' treatment." Such statements invite the child's participation in helping to remove an undesirable habit pattern which he recognizes as his problem. They also build up self-esteem. All psychotherapy must be directed toward helping the child to cope with the emotional significance of his difficulties. Recently, the coping mechanisms of children have received considerable attention.[16, 17]

The use of hypnosis in child therapy has been discussed, varying from supportive treatment directed toward release of tension, reassurance, and reeducation to acting out and other complex hypnotherapeutic procedures.[3, 5, 9, 10, 14, 35, 39, 50, 64] Call emphasizes that symptomatic improvement should be reinforced by the total need-systems of child and family.[6] This view has been reiterated by Williams and Singh, who advocate using a total approach consisting of family and behavior therapy with hypnosis.[62] Unfortunately, space limitations preclude their detailed description. The reader is referred to an excellent bibliography on these aspects prepared by Weitzenhoffer.[60] Several of the commonest conditions that are amenable to hypnosis will now be discussed.

NOCTURNAL ENURESIS

ETIOLOGY

Bed-wetting is a difficult symptom to treat. The causes can be divided into two broad classifications: physical and psychogenic. Physical causes comprise spina bifida, congenital and mechanical factors, a small bladder capacity,[24, 57] neurogenic factors, cystitis, hypospadias, and other involvements. Psychogenic factors such as sibling rivalry, loss of a mother or a nurse, faulty attitudes toward masturbation, improper development of urinary control due to frequent micturition, inadequate toilet-training, poor hygiene, deep sleep, and emotional immaturity due to overprotection must be considered.

Often the symptom is a manifestation of a passive rebellious interplay between child and parents. Once the child realizes, following his initial bed-wetting, that he now possesses a weapon against the parents, he may maintain a conditioned pattern long after the original cause for his hostility is forgotten. When this reflex becomes firmly entrenched, the harder he tries *not* to wet the bed on a volitional level, the more likely he will be to lose control during sleep.

Even though it is used as an aggressive act, the child is ashamed of the bed-wetting. However, he is loath to give up the secondary gain value that the symptom of enuresis affords. The mother, unable to cope with the problem, resorts to nagging, which, in turn, makes the child more frustrated. She also becomes insecure, intolerant, and harsh, and displaces her own hostilities and tensions upon him, not realizing that he desperately needs sympathy and support. This further increases the child's tensions and insecurities so that he is unable to adjust to more mature levels of development. The chronic bed-wetter has never developed beyond the diaper stage! In dealing with the situation thus created, the parents must be treated concurrently with the child by family therapy.

TREATMENT

Before instituting therapy, the presence of physical problems such as kidney infections, bladder involvements, and diseases of the nervous system must be eliminated. Treatment is not simple, and various combinations of therapy, such as reeducation and psychotherapy, must be used together. Parents must not humiliate, punish, or use the child for the displacement of their own tensions. There are a number of well-controlled studies showing that imipramine is effective in nocturnal enuresis. Several other studies indicate that anticholinergic drugs are of little value. Hypnotherapy, as a potentiating agent, has been used successfully by numerous investigators.[1, 8, 18, 33, 35, 52, 59] The following scenario illustrates the author's approach:

The child usually is brought in for the initial visit against his will. Therefore, a friendly relationship must be established immediately. The following ruse is often effective: In mock anger, the mother is asked, "Why did you bring Johnny in on such a beautiful day?" Without waiting for her reply, I remark, "Isn't that right, Johnny?" Wide-eyed, he now sees in me a new-found friend. (The mother has been apprised of these tactics prior to the first appointment.) Then he is told, "Johnny, you have a perfect right to wet the bed as often as you please, and it is also your privilege to stop wetting the bed whenever you feel like it." After listening carefully to his views, one can ask him, "How would you like to play a little game where you can relax and imagine seeing your favorite television program?" Invariably, Johnny will agree, because of the good rapport that has been established. Visual-imagery technics are used to induce hypnosis.

After hypnosis is achieved, the child is asked, "Do you enjoy wetting the bed?" If a negative response is elicited, the following questions are asked: "How many of your classmates wet their bed?" (By indirection, this makes him feel unusual and helps to establish the motivation for a change.) "If you slept overnight at the house of a friend, who did not wet his bed, and had an accident, how would you feel?" If he agrees that this would be embarrassing, he is asked, "Would

you like to be helped to avoid this situation in the future?"

These questions focus his attention on the fact that he has a problem, and yet he has not been made to feel guilty. They also reveal his personality structure and, hence, the most appropriate therapeutic route. With an aggressive child, a permissive approach is used in order not to identify the therapist with the parents. The therapist can also point out, providing the child is mature enough, that he is harming himself more than his parents. If the child is passive and dependent, he can be encouraged to assert himself the way others of his age group do, by allowing him to vent his resentments on the therapist, and later, channel his aggression into more constructive outlets.

The usual posthypnotic suggestions for symptom removal are presented briefly as follows: "Would you try holding your water (urine) as long as possible during the day?" (This increases the bladder capacity.) "Also, perhaps you might be interested to see how well *you can start and stop* the passing of your water." (This invites his participation.) "Maybe you will gain better control than your friends. If you concentrate on what it *feels* like to pass your water during the day, you will have little or no trouble *feeling* this identical sensation even when you are sound asleep. And after you have gone to the toilet, you will return to your bed and immediately fall deep asleep." The child should be given positive suggestions that, when he gets out of bed to urinate during the night, the time intervals between trips to the toilet will be increased until he can sleep through the night without urinating.

Under hypnosis, he is taught how to contract the diaphragm and simultaneously relax the pubococcygeus muscles; the downward push on the vesical neck stimulates contraction of the detrusors and opens the internal sphincter, which leads to urination. Rehearsal of the act of urination should be repeated several times during each session. Under autohypnosis he can "rehearse" or have a "dry run" of all the accompanying sensations of micturition, and thus speed up bladder control.

The next step is to reverse the child's fears about the bed-wetting. The youngster is asked, while under hypnosis, "Would you be interested in how much of your bed can remain dry?" This shifts his attention from himself to the bed. It can be suggested that since *he* controls his own bladder functioning, he can have a *dry* bed if he wants it badly enough. The word "wet" is never used! The mother also is instructed always to speak in terms of a "dry bed." She can remark, "My goodness, your bed was three quarters dry!" or "Last night it was all dry!" If this positive approach is used over a period of time, the idea of a "dry bed" will be indelibly imprinted on the child's mind. Convincing the child that a dry bed is a sign of maturity is in itself often therapeutic.

Therapy is facilitated, in some instances, by establishing a time limit for when the bed will be dry. Most effective are posthypnotic suggestions such as, "Johnny, you can set a time when you will be able to have full bladder control." If he names a date, this goal can be strengthened by saying, "You can be very proud if you reach your goal beforehand." This, of course, implies that bladder control will be developed (extraverbal suggestion). A child can be hypnotically conditioned to derive pride in the achievement of establishing bladder control. These suggestions may be repeated as necessary to effect a conditioned response. Any reason for failure should be analyzed.

The urine also can be measured every morning, a larger amount indicating increased bladder capacity. It is very helpful, too, to give a reward for achieving a goal within a certain period. A calendar used to mark off the nights on which the bed was dry helps to add to the sense of achievement. Drugs to reduce the depth of sleep, tranquilizers, atropine, and such procedures as fluid restriction have only a placebo effect. However, if parents and child are convinced of their utility, they may be employed. Interrupting sleep is of little help and only increases tension. Devices which sound alarms when the bed is wet are seldom helpful.

The parents are instructed not to scold or chastise the child over a wet bed. Humiliation and ridicule only serve to compound the problem. The entire family should look upon the child's progress in overcoming his difficulty as an important event, and he should be praised for each small victory. He should likewise be encouraged to overcome a sense of defeat if the bed is wet on occasions. Often the problem is intensified if the child cannot communicate effectively with his parents. The insecurity, the inadequacy, and the tensions present in the mother, therefore, must be corrected. She can be advised to read a bedtime story in a soft and soothing manner and to emphasize her love for the child. Other members of the family who need help for their own tensions often must be treated as part of the total therapy. The following case illustrates the author's approach:

Simon B., a 12-year-old boy, was a chronic bed-wetter. In addition to poor grades in school, he had poor relationships with playmates, superiors, and relatives. The bed-wetting began soon after the adoption of a sister for him when he was 4.

He was hypnotized readily in the first session. During the second session, he was taught autohypnosis. It was also suggested that he practice inducing self-hypnosis frequently and that the more he practiced, the more proficient he would become. On the third visit, a week later, he readily induced self-hypnosis, and related how his mother continually "rode" him, that he was unwilling to accept any of his mother's suggestions because she favored his adopted sister. During subsequent sessions, he stated that he was looking for ways to get even with his parents and that perhaps the bed-wetting pattern was being maintained for this purpose.

At this time, Simon's mother was interviewed. She said that Simon had always wanted a baby sister; he knew that she was adopted. She thought that perhaps because of her own perfectionistic attitudes and demands she had pushed Simon too rapidly. In addition, she was not getting along too well with her husband and wondered if she might not be displacing her tensions to Simon. Simon and his sister were constantly fighting, and this, too, made her nervous. For some reason, she always protected the little girl. One day, in a fit of anger, Simon remarked, "Pretty smart girl we've got here." After this, she noted that Simon was becoming increasingly argumentative and sulky. During the next few sessions, other ambivalent attitudes toward his mother were brought out. He angrily remarked, "The tone of my mother's voice annoys me. She never even lets me finish what I have to say."

Other areas of insecurity were explored. During the next three sessions, at weekly intervals, he was given posthypnotic suggestions to maintain a full bladder until the last possible moment; to remember the sensations accompanying a full bladder, and to reexperience these sensations even during the deepest sleep. It was emphasized that all sensations accompanying a full bladder would be "telephoned" to his brain and would wake him up; that if he wished, he would then awaken and go to the toilet, empty his bladder, and promptly return to his bed and fall asleep.

Simon reported at the next session that during sleep his bladder "felt like a big balloon," and that he awakened, was able to pass his water and again immediately fall asleep. It was now suggested that under no circumstances would the symptom be given up until he was willing to yield it, and that this would occur through autohypnosis and in full accordance with his wishes. When autohypnosis is employed, there is little possibility that other symptom equivalents will be produced.

The mother was also instructed never to mention the word "wet" but always to speak in terms of a "dry bed." She was advised particularly to watch the tone of her voice when speaking to Simon. In several sessions, at nonhypnotic levels, it was made evident to her that she should love the boy for himself rather than for his intellectual accomplishments. She was advised not to vent her ire on him; this would curb his rebellious attitudes. Through the combined use of hypnosis, directed toward symptom removal, and psychotherapy for the mother, Simon overcame his bed-wetting pattern within 3 months from the time he began therapy.

NAIL-BITING

Nail-biting is generally indicative of insecurity and anxiety. Therefore, therapy must be directed to the causes of the child's tensions, which usually involve the parents. The latter must be cautioned against evincing displeasure over the habit, as this only mobilizes more guilt and frustration and serves to perpetuate the vicious circle.

Treatment

Hypnotherapy can be employed for direct symptom removal; at least, the conditioned pattern can be interrupted until the emotional needs are elicited, as the following case illustrates:

A child of 9, who had an older and a younger sister, began to bite her nails following the birth of the younger one. Utilizing the permissive technics described above, posthypnotic suggestions were employed as follows: "Would you like to stop biting your nails by your own efforts? Then, perhaps, you might be willing to bite *one nail* on each hand as often as you wish. Which one would *you* like to choose?" If the forefinger on each hand is chosen, one can remark,

"Let's make the nail-biting more interesting. Maybe you would like to start biting the nail on the left side of your mouth first, using one bite from each tooth in succession across the mouth, and then doubling back to the side where you started. You will find it fun to repeat this at least three times. If you still think you are not satisfied, turn the nail upside down and repeat the same procedure." This makes the nail-biting so complicated that it becomes a chore.

As soon as the other nails began to grow, the child was praised for following instructions: "Aren't you really proud that the other four nails on each hand are as good looking as your girl friends? Haven't any of your schoolmates noticed the other nice-looking nails?" Under hypnosis, it was suggested, "You can increase or decrease biting the nail you selected to the degree that you think necessary." Such a suggestion is designed to make the nail-biting a routine and boring task against which the patient will rebel just as she did against parental admonitions not to bite the nails. This reaction follows the law of reversed effect.

Four more sessions were required to "wean" the child from biting the one nail. During this period, the procedure was continually made more complex until the child's natural resistance to regimentation made the nail-biting nonrewarding in terms of her oral satisfactions. At this point, she described her jealousy of her parents' attention to her baby sister.

Therapy was now directed toward the emotional needs for the nail-biting. She was asked whether it was her desire to stop the habit or whether it was the wish of her parents that she do so. In order to determine how much of the habit the patient needs to maintain equilibrium, it is necessary to evaluate the strength of the desire to stop as opposed to the degree of oral satisfaction obtained. At a subsequent session, the child was asked to see herself as a little baby, and it was pointed out that it was perfectly natural for her at this earlier age to put a rattle or a thumb in her mouth. She readily agreed to this and stated, "I guess I was trying to be a little baby all the time, wasn't I?"

The parents were instructed to pay equal attention to all the children, to ignore the nail-biting and not to punish the girl if the habit returned. Further psychotherapy directed toward the parents, and permissive technics employed for reinforcement, enabled the patient to break the habit in several months.

Often, excessively dominating parents, or those who delegate the care of their youngsters to servants, need psychotherapy more than the child who is made insecure by such factors. Children who are unresponsive to permissive technics can be counterconditioned by a more direct approach: "Whenever you bite your nails, you will get a very bitter taste in your mouth; you will feel sick to your stomach." Weekly reinforcements under hypnosis are necessary to break the habit. In general, however, a permissive approach is more successful. Manicuring the nails weekly is also a valuable adjunct to hypnotherapy.

TICS OR HABIT SPASMS

Tics or habit spasms may involve all sorts of facial or bodily movements. They occur usually in hyperkinetic, sensitive, and nervous children. Other extenuating factors, such as familial traits and mannerisms, quarreling parents, an insecure mother who continually screams at the child, or physical defects, contribute to the child's unhappiness and tensions. Anxiety over poor grades, lack of interests, fright, and identification with children who display similar involvements are other causes. It is also believed that some tics are suggested.

A 13-year-old boy who was failing in school had had a blinking tic of the eyelids for 3 years. The constant blinking was accompanied by a severe conjunctivitis. He had been treated unsuccessfully by psychotherapy. His father was a physician and wanted the boy to follow in his footsteps. However, the boy was more interested in mechanical hobbies such as radio and electronic devices. It was apparent that the frustrated father was attempting to live out his life in the son.

Under hypnosis it was suggested, "Would you mind twitching the forefinger of your right hand several times a minute? This will take the tension off your lids." Four sessions were required for reinforcement of this suggestion under autohypnosis before the blinking tic of the lids was transferred to a finger-twitch. During the next six sessions, the finger-twitch was reduced in frequency until it, too, subsided. The father's faulty attitudes were discussed, and he decided not to push the boy.

Symptom transformation is usually successful because it is much easier to remove a recently acquired conditioned reflex than a long-standing one. When the new reflex is manifested, one can be fairly certain of a successful outcome. If psychological guidance is combined with conditioning under autohypnosis and proper posthypnotic suggestions, better results can be obtained. For refractory cases, the specialized technics discussed in Chapter 50 are indicated.

Lindner and Stevens discuss the hypnotherapeutic approach for a young male with Gilles de la Tourette syndrome.[37] These investigators felt that the underlying dynamics probably consisted in the compulsive tic's replacing a strong physical aggression to strike his mother. The author has had poor results in this syndrome when hypnosis *per se* was employed. My results are more in accord with Clement, who used hypnotherapy, haloperidol, and psychotherapy— each played an essential part in the apparent "cure."[7] (See page 264).

STUTTERING

Stuttering in young children, adolescents, or adults is often a very difficult problem. There are some interesting cases of the use of hypnosis in speech therapy and clinical audiology.[2, 15, 41, 53, 63]

TREATMENT

Stuttering is an enormously resistant symptom which cannot be removed by simple posthypnotic suggestions. Some cases, especially those of mild stutterers, do respond to this approach. However, a moderate or a severe stutterer ordinarily requires an intensive evaluation of what is taking place between himself and his hearers. Ordinarily, there is a great deal of repressed hostility, the expression of which is masked. The stutterer feels insecure around other persons, and is unable to express his feelings since he is always on guard. Stuttering is a compromise between the simultaneous desire to express an idea and to inhibit it.

In children, the anticipation of stuttering brings it about by setting up a conditioned pattern. The attempt to defeat this anticipation and to control it, and the resulting heightened tension, lead to further hesitation and disruption of speech. Thus the stutterer believes that he is going to stutter, and that he must not stutter. He is controlled by these two conflict-ridden thoughts, which have become entrenched through repeated enforcement in speech situations, often since he first started to talk. He now finds it impossible to eliminate them by will alone.

Most stutterers are, of course, very reluctant to deal with the symptom itself. The stutterer is so ashamed and overwrought about the symptom that he is unable to cope with it directly. Because stuttering is not a uniform phenomenon, its severity is more or less dependent upon the environmental situation.

Therefore, one must elicit situations that the individual fears or emotional expressions in relation to other people that he finds it impossible to make freely. Under hypnosis, the symptom is much more amenable to a direct attack, as he can rehearse speech situations particularly dreaded by him, especially in relation to those who upset him.

Hypnosis is an excellent method for investigating the particular situations and stimulus patterns that produced the stuttering. It enables the patient to understand the need for the avoidance reaction, to rehearse it and to work it through so as to help to release the specific tensions which arise in his oral musculature during the act of speaking. Exploration through hypnotic age regression in good subjects often helps to pinpoint specific episodes which brought about these inhibitory patterns. Orton contends that the critical periods are when speech and writing were first learned.[48]

The stutterer often develops auxiliary symptoms which are a misguided effort to overcome his speech defect. He blinks his eyes, stamps his foot, or pounds his fists in order to overcome the blocking. He develops these reactions to avoid becoming aware of certain words and sounds. He then substitutes other words or sounds in a vain attempt to hide his stuttering. These attempts invariably lead to more symptoms. The individual who starts out by stuttering and finds that, initially at least, he stutters less when he lifts his head, will begin to lift his head more and more until he develops a real spasm. And this spasm can often become more disabling than the initial stuttering symptom which he is trying to overcome by this mechanism.

Successful hypnotherapy must be directed to all the accompanying symptoms. The subject is shown that in the hypnotic state he can speak in a manner that is more satisfactory both to himself and to his listeners. Stutterers are surprised that they can speak without the involuntary head motions, the foot stamping, the finger snapping or whatever other muscular manifestation they employ.

The tape recorder can be used to good advantage with hypnotherapy. Stutterers are almost always free of symptoms when their ears are plugged, when they are reading from a prepared text, when they are speaking in unison with someone else, or when alone. It is helpful to have the individual speak into the tape recorder while he is by himself. Then he listens to himself while under hypnorelaxation, and reads the same passage in unison with his tape-recorded verbalization. The resulting good, fluent speech encourages him to identify with a person who obviously is able to speak normally.

This procedure is accomplished best by a permissive approach, judiciously utilizing posthypnotic suggestions. Suggesting that the subject is never going to stutter again is seldom effective, as this works for only a short time. As a result, the patient becomes disheartened and loses confidence not only in the therapist but also in hypnotherapy.

Posthypnotic suggestions and autohypnosis can be limited to specific situations; for example, comfort and ease can be induced in the child who dreads speaking in class by remarking, "Under self-hypnosis you will imagine that you feel relaxed and more comfortable in class, and if you can see yourself talking without difficulty in your imagination, you will find it easier to talk." If each situation is approached through sensory-imagery conditioning, there is a good chance that, to a degree, the vicious fear-reaction cycle in which the child has become enmeshed can ultimately be reversed. The following selected case is illustrative of the author's technic:

A 12-year-old child was taught hypnosis and autohypnosis in one 50-minute session. He was a hissing stutterer who took about half a minute to say one word. Yet, under hypnosis, he said, "Around the rugged rock the ragged rascal ran" and other tongue twisters, all in one breath, without any hesitation whatsoever. This indicated that a psychological approach would be helpful.

Since his speech difficulty began at age 2, it was patently impossible to elicit traumatic episodes that might have occurred prior to this age. He also had received intensive psychotherapy. It was decided that the best course was to break up the reflex at one level or another.

During the next session, he spoke under hypnosis into a tape recorder without difficulty. It was suggested: "If, under autohypnosis, you listen enough to yourself, you will become accustomed to the sound of your own voice speaking normally. After all, when we hear a tune played over and over again, do we not hum the tune exactly the way we heard it?" Such measures establish a healthy pattern, so that the stutterer has a firm foundation upon which to build a more natural and normal type of speech. At first, if he wishes, he can hum a tune, then sing words, and later speak short sentences. The first tapes can be compared with later ones; the resultant improvement instills confidence.

During the third hypnotic session, it was suggested that perhaps the blocking of the muscles involved in speaking might be transferred to another portion of the body. It was pointed out that the subject had no control over the gestures and the spasms that usually accompanied his stuttering; that Nature's first line of defense could be employed in a constructive manner by giving him something that he could control. A twitching of one of the fingers of either the right or the left hand was suggested. Under hypnosis, he was asked, "Which finger would you like to twitch; would it be the little finger on the left hand, or perhaps the little finger on the right hand, or even the thumb on the left hand?" The fact that he was given a choice led him to believe that he was acting under his own volition. A posthypnotic suggestion was given that "Each time you feel that you are going to stutter, you can control it by twitching your finger. And you can, if you feel embarrassed, do this with your hand closed. In this way no one will see it."

The transfer of the blocking from the muscles of the speech to the muscles of the finger is a "trading down" or an attempt to siphon off the energy with which the original symptom is invested. Furthermore, the finger twitch takes the place of stuttering in fulfilling the need for a symptom. Symptom transformation of this type does not remove the symptom all at once but, rather, substitutes a weak conditioned response for a noxious or well-entrenched one. In this case, the child made progressively more use of the finger twitch for several weeks. At this point, the twitch could be either increased or decreased. If it can be increased, obviously it can be decreased. The child was eventually weaned from the finger twitch by posthypnotic suggestions directed toward increasing and diminishing it. During this period, considerable improvement in his speech difficulty was manifested.

Under hypnosis, he was next taught "loose contact." Most stutterers have difficulty only with the first letter or two of any word on which they block. Therefore, it is advisable to reverse the emphasis by suggesting, "You are going to worry about the last syllables. For example, if you have trouble saying the word 'democratic' and you find yourself saying 'de-, de-, de-,' become more interested in the 'mo-cra-tic' portion, and you will notice that if you direct your attention to the bulk of the word, you will easily slide over the first two or three letters."

In the case just described, the child had considerable resentment toward the father, who was too busy to spend an appreciable amount of time with him. In another case, that of the son of a physician, a similar mechanism was elicited. In both instances the parents were interviewed and these problems were discussed. Both boys were completely cured of their stuttering after attending the author's group hypnosis speech-training program. In many instances, such patients must be prepared for a relapse. Rather than regarding this as a failure, they should be asked to describe the factors that produced the relapse. Patients are urged to return at monthly or bi-monthly intervals for reinforcement suggestions.

Other posthypnotic suggestions are commonly employed, such as, "If possible, try looking at the face of the person to whom you are speaking." Most stutterers look down or away in shame. It is emphasized that they should maintain a steady gaze at all times; that, just as they need not be ashamed of speaking rapidly, they likewise should not feel embarrassed if they speak slowly. Reading backward and forward again and again helps to slow rapid speech, and also favorably conditions the auditory centers to adopt normal speech patterns. Other posthypnotic suggestions are directed toward improvement in vocalization and articulation.

Another feasible approach, as described above, is via the use of sensory-imagery conditioning under autohypnosis. In this technic, the individual imagines that he is speaking normally. Just as we have a "mind's eye," we have a "mind's ear." In the hypnotic state, the subject is asked to "listen" to his own voice, and to "hear" himself talking on a wide variety of subjects, without hesitation, blocking, or difficulty of any type. After he begins to think that he can "speak" normally, he finds it much easier to speak at nonhypnotic levels.

It is easier to recognize the basic speech patterns than to direct treatment primarily to the cause of the speech disorder. As fluency improves, the stuttering will diminish, particularly if training is directed to sensory functions rather than to motor ones. The thinking processes involved in speech are more important than the talking process. Thus, as the ear-training establishes a good mental pattern of speech, talking becomes "thinking out loud." As a result, the autonomic portion of the brain transmits impulses to the mouth; the words "say themselves." Sensory-imagery conditioning was most efficacious in the case of a 16-year-old boy with hysterical aphonia who had not spoken for 2 years because of profound guilt over masturbation.

Another valuable approach is to suggest that the stutterer speak out loud as often as necessary when he is alone. A 15-minute session daily is suggested. Through post-hypnotic suggestions, the duration can be decreased by 1 minute daily, and then 1 minute every other day, every third day, etc., until he is weaned off the symptom. It is surprising that, when a stutterer deliberately tries to stutter, he is unable to do so. By reversing his fears, one can break up the reflex; through hearing his own voice speaking normally, especially when speaking into a mirror, the stutterer gains confidence in his ability.

Group hypnotherapy is ideal for the stutterer. The "emotional contagion" of the group operates with beneficial effects when stammering is being treated by hypnosis. Most stutterers feel that they are "all in the same boat" and do not hesitate to speak before other members of the group. It is surprising how quickly they pick up another individual's mistakes and make constructive suggestions for improved speech. This, of course, increases the stutterer's self-esteem and confidence and motivates him toward further therapy.

Faulty parental attitudes can arouse tensions in a child and lead to stuttering. Many parents are worriers and perfectionists. They react to their child's nonfluent speech with concern or impatience. By correcting him, they make the child conscious that his speech is unacceptable. He responds by talking less and less, with the growing fear of failure—until he is speaking with the fear and stress of a stutterer. Hence, parents should allow the child to develop at his own pace, and his speech should not be judged by adult standards.

Since stuttering often begins early, there is no use exhuming a great deal of memorial data; nor is it helpful to search for early traumata by questioning about events before the age of 4 or 5. Attempting this generally yields diminishing returns. Johnson states: "Considerable research to data provides no appreciable support for the hypothesis that stuttering is characteristically associated with or symptomatic of severe emotional disturbance or neuroses in a clinically significant sense."[26] In this regard, he states that speech training often does more harm than good, as it emphasizes the use of the will rather than the imagination. The stutterer becomes more conscious of his speech difficulty, and it thus becomes intensified.

According to Johnson, the symptom developed because the stutterer had too critical a listener during a crucial period of speech learning. It begins the day that a listener, usually the mother, begins to worry that perhaps her pre-school-age youngster is unduly repeating himself or hesitating in his speech. Once this notion enters her head, the stage is set for the child to become a stutterer.

If the mother would pay no attention to his hesitancy and repetitiveness—which is a natural part of speech development in a 3- to 4-year-old—there would be no stutterers in the world. Unfortunately, however, too many mothers judge a child's speech by adult standards. They make the child conscious of their own unfounded fears. They attempt to correct the child's speech, and the child, if he is desirous of pleasing the parents, will develop doubt and fear of his ability to express himself and stuttering begins.

If a child gets past the age of 3 or 4 years without being classified as a stutterer, the chances are that he will never stutter unless he runs into the same problem with listeners when he enters school. There are approximately two and a half times as many male stutterers as female. One possible explanation of this is that mothers are less likely to be critical of the speech of girls than of boys.

Marchesi cured 75 to 80 per cent of 98 cases of stammering by hypnotherapy directed toward symptom removal, even though antecedent emotional tensions and traumas apparently were causative factors.[47] Stammering developed as an imitative reflex; removal from the person who caused it is all that is necessary. The condition also may be due to an accident, with personal involvement or as a witness.

The specific treatment begins with a study of the vital capacity of the lungs, as breathing exercises are employed with hypnotherapy. The breathing is chosen as the starting-point because the arrhythmic respiration, upon which the stammering is based, is restored to a more normal rhythm. More important, as a result of the rhythmic breathing, the emotional aspect of the stammering is now separated from the association with the abnormal breathing. Hypnotherapy is continuously maintained—on the average, two sessions weekly for about one month. The breathing exercises are prescribed in the office for use during hypnorelaxation there as well as at home. Concentration is directed to the character of the breathing as well as to subjective thoughts. However, the patient is informed that he should not try to concentrate too hard, as failure is inevitable. At the beginning, he is apprised that progress will not be upward and that relapses can be expected.

Marchesi stresses a nondirective hypnotic approach which leads to very deep hypnotization because criticalness is not developed. This provides considerable self-satisfaction because the patient gets the impression that the operator needs his help. Objectivity and the self-realization that hypnosis produces psychophysiologic alterations enhances the expectancy level of the patient. By the second week, the patient is able to develop numbness and lightness of the extremities, and is able to breathe so that the rhythm is undisturbed by any type of noise. After this the breathing becomes smooth in type.

The stammering is attacked by asking the patient to spell out words which caused difficulty in the past. Success in doing this leads to a more positive attitude. The patient who does not respond is asked to speak under those emotional conditions which formerly caused the stammering. Attention is directed to spasmodic contractions of the diaphragm, the glottis, and the character of the breathing. Errors are pointed out, and under hypnosis he is asked to breathe as taught, to spell words without any hesitation, and to note the differences in speech when these functions are correctly performed. This, too, adds to his confidence.

In the failure group, 15 per cent did not respond, due to insufficient attention by the therapist. About 5 per cent did not have the necessary intelligence to participate in the program. Another method that often stops stuttering requires that patients interrupt their speech to take an exaggerated deep breath when they begin to stutter. This gives them time to relax their throat muscles when they begin to stutter, and thus they have time to think of what they are going to say. Hypnotherapy has been used by other investigators with moderate success.[10, 21, 22, 26, 49]

DYSLEXIA

Crasilneck and Hall report that over 75 per cent of children unable to recognize and read words normally can be helped by direct hypnotherapy.[10] During the initial sessions, the child pronounces new words very carefully, with attention to each syllable. Following hypnotherapy which includes positive suggestions for improving performance, pronunciation, and recognition seem to become much more rapid and automatic. These results are as good as those reported by the behavior modifiers.

MENTAL RETARDATION

McCord finds that mentally retarded children are readily hypnotized; good intelligence is not an important requisite for hypnotizability.[44, 55] Rather, these children are "uneducated" and really have never been taught how to learn; I.Q. tests are not indicative of their learning capacity;

and many generalizations about "intelligence" do not apply to the mentally retarded child.

Hypnosis, by increasing motivation, convinces the child that he can learn more than was anticipated; thus the child's self-concept is altered and healthier attitudes are developed. The author noted similar findings when he was working with spastic children, as described in Chapter 39; their learning capacity was improved after teaching them how to "tap their forgotten assets."

McCord reported on a series of "mongoloid-type" subjects with I.Q.'s under 40.[43] In addition to bringing about an increased motivation to learn, vocational motivation, and a lengthening of the attention span, hypnosis was believed to be of possible help in controlling perseverative excitement, including relaxation and relief of insomnia. McCord and Sherrell noted that altering the self-concept was an important motivational variable for improving learning when hypnosis was used.[45] Kroger and Fezler add time distortion to facilitate learning.[32]

Uhr's excellent review of the effects of hypnosis on learning indicates that the results are inconclusive.[58] However, the clinical observations overwhelmingly show definite and possibly striking improvements in learning. Other experiments indicated an improvement in learning of from 2 to 40 per cent when time distortion, specifically time condensation, was employed.

The consensus from Uhr's studies is that "suggestion" or "motivation" or "attention" may well prove to be the crucial variable, and that *hypnosis merely potentiates these factors.* This view is in keeping with what is known about hypnosis.

EXAMINATION ANXIETY AND READING

Several investigators have demonstrated that hypnosis improved performance in cases of examination anxiety.[10, 23, 38] Motor capacity, attention and perception, association, learning and memory, speed of reading, and comprehension were improved. Taped suggestions were more effective if given during hypnosis than during sleep.[33] Another investigator in this area found hypnosis more effective than a tranquilizer, and the latter better than ordinary waking suggestions.[20] These results through hypnosis could not be replicated by others.[13] With reference to reading skills, there are several studies which indicate that hypnotic subjects do better than nonhypnotic ones.[12, 15, 31] This has been the author's experience for a wide variety of children with reading disorders. It is self-evident that counterconditioning the associated anxiety must be of benefit.

THUMB-SUCKING

Most infants suck their thumbs, but the maneuver becomes more marked when a baby is weaned too soon. This results in an inner need for more sucking activities, and unless he gets more food, he may suck his thumb or even his whole hand. Not all children are alike, and the process of weaning cannot be governed by a timetable. Thumb-sucking at this early stage of development is not harmful even though it is done vigorously. The baby teeth may be distorted, but the effects are temporary, provided that the youngster discontinues the habit before the permanent set erupts.

Interference only intensifies the symptom and makes the child rebellious. Thumb-sucking usually is gradually stopped by the age of 4. Some children return to it as a consolation when bored, tired, sleepy, or hungry. Others revert when lonely, tense, or upset because a younger brother or sister is getting more attention. If the youngster is made to feel important, loved, and secure, the habit disappears completely.

But something must be done if the child persists in sucking his thumb after his fourth birthday. Elbow-splints, mitts, rings, and horrible-tasting concoctions are valueless. Little is accomplished through nagging, shaming, bribing, teasing, or punishing an already unhappy child. Parents should make it a point to fuss over the child, and it will help if other children in the family, relatives, and friends will do the same, or at least make *no* mention of the habit. Adequate rest and play outlets should be encouraged.

Eventually most children give up the habit, as by age 5 they are capable of self-discipline and can be taught to help themselves. But if the problem has been mishandled, the youngster may switch to nail-biting. Hypnotherapy can be very helpful in thumb-sucking and is employed in a fashion similar to that used for nail-biting.[35]

BEHAVIOR DISORDERS

The behavior pattern of the child is laid down from the first few weeks of life. Recently it was shown that, if newborn monkeys were taken away from their mothers and nursed on a wire surrogate "monkey," these monkeys, deprived of warmth, became asocial, detached, quarrelsome, nervous, and, in short, psychoneurotic adults. When a control group was nursed on a soft, cuddly, teddy bear "monkey," they grew up to be warm, gregarious, mature adults, normal in every respect. It was also found that leaving the monkeys on the wire "mother" for only a week and then transferring them to the teddy bear monkey did not reverse the harmful patterns that were laid down. This ingenious experiment indicates that personality is molded early in life.

The developing personality, in order to mature into a healthy one, as pointed out by Freud, must pass through the early emotional mileposts of infantile sexuality. If an individual is unable to adapt himself to a mature orientation, he will do one of two things: He will either retreat to a previous stage of development or remain at the latest one. This is analogous to the soldier who finds that the pillbox which he is attempting to attack is too heavily fortified, and so he retreats back to his slit trench where he once knew safety. Immature, frustrated individuals who are insecure hate to leave the "slit trench of childhood" and remain fixated at early levels of development.

To encourage growth of the personality, parents, particularly the mother, of necessity, have to "walk a tightrope"; they must give the child an equal amount of love and of discipline. However, children must not be reared as if they were mass-produced; each child needs to have his own particular needs, wishes, and feelings satisfied in his own particular manner. Therefore, mothers especially must make their children feel that they are loved for themselves and not for their accomplishments. If he is given a considerable amount of love, the child will be willing to abandon his hostility and reciprocate with compliance and the giving up of earlier patterns of behavior. "Smother love" is not "mother love," and mothers must be careful not to be oversolicitous toward the child. This will only make him more dependent and less likely to mature in a healthy fashion.

Parents should also remember that unruly behavior, rebellion, and delinquency of any type are often used as attention-getting devices—the child uses these mechanisms to invite interest on the part of the parents. This type of behavior is often seen in the chronically ill child, who uses complaints as a means of gaining sympathy and attention.

It is important to ascertain whether or not parents are taking out their own frustrations on a child as a means of acting out their own neurotic needs. Other parents live out their own thwarted ambitions through the child—the stage mother is a typical example. And still others make unreasonable demands that the child is unable to fulfill, and, as a result, he retreats to earlier levels of behavior and develops many of the sequelae described in this book.

A big problem in evaluating the emotional behavior of a child is that the same symptom may signify different levels of disturbance in different children. There are criteria for evaluating the seriousness of a child's behavioral difficulty that can be helpful in determining whether or not a child needs hypnotic treatment. Whether the conflicts are internalized or external is an important criterion. Problems created by the environment are much easier to deal with than internal conflicts.

Another criterion is whether the disturbance is limited or affects most aspects of the child's development. Does the child have difficulty getting along with his mother only, or does he have difficulty in other interpersonal relationships? Most normal adolescents are in a state of turmoil. In fact, the adolescent who is not struggling to conquer his impulses and to achieve independence is the one who may eventually need psychological care. However, the particular type of emotional disturbance which develops depends on the parental behavior, the degree of the child's exposure, and the response of the parents and others to his psychological disorder. The length of time that the disturbance has been present also is important. One present for a month will clear up more readily than a symptom present for years.

School phobia can be treated in the incipient stage by posthypnotic suggestions directed to increasing the child's interest in his studies. If this approach is not successful, arrangements can be made for the mother to sit in class with the child for gradually diminishing periods of time. If the classroom, schoolmates or teachers are disturbing factors, these should be discussed at either hypnotic or nonhypnotic levels.

Eating problems, appearing early in life, usually represent hostility toward parents. When eating becomes a means of expressing pleasure or displeasure, hunger ceases to dictate the amount of the food intake; a vicious cycle is established, the origin of which is eventually forgotten. In this situation, the mother needs greater confidence in her ability as a parent. She must recognize that the child's own physiology will ensure an adequate dietary intake as long as she does not fuss about his eating habits.

Dawdling is probably normal in preschool children and it, too, denotes resentment of the "nagging" parent. Fear of punishment or loss of love causes the child to choose this pattern rather than one of overt rebellion. Therapy should be directed against parental overreaction but, the longer dawdling has existed, the more time and support will be required to help parents guide their child through this phase of adjustment.

Rebellious behavior suggests that the child is angry and has such a poor relationship with his parents that he fears neither punishment nor loss of love. At other times, rebellion occurs when the child feels omnipotent as a result of lacking parental control. Thus the parents require guidance regarding the need for parental unity in providing realistic, consistent demands on the child, combined with continuing love and acceptance.

Sadistic and destructive behavior gives pleasure to most 2- or 3-year-old youngsters, as they seek and even enjoy punishment for their misdeeds. Parents should recognize this as an attention-getting device, and increase approval, and decrease rejection and punishment. If the syndrome is noted too late, psychotherapy will be required when the child is older.

Ambrose employed hypnotherapy in a child guidance clinic and reported cures or improvement in school phobias, nightmares, chronic anxiety states, and other psychosomatic disorders.[2, 3] Symptomatic cure was established in over 60 per cent of the cases. In investigations he demonstrated how hypnosis could speed up psychotherapy, as compared with more time-consuming methods.[3] Hypnotherapy was utilized primarily to relieve tension, and positive suggestions were stressed along with reeducation and supportive therapy for both parents and children. Symptom removal by direct authoritative suggestion is seldom effective.[52]

DRUG ABUSE

Addiction to drugs of all types, including narcotics, is increasing. Many drug abusers can be treated in the office rather than in a hospital setting. However, unless the entire family is treated and the environmental factors are altered, the results are poor. Children must be motivated to change. Hypnosis can countercondition the anxiety resulting from drug withdrawal, and it can also enhance motivation to "kick the habit." All children who use drugs invariably need supportive psychotherapy, either by insight therapy or behavior modification. Those who fear damage to their health do better than those who conceptualize their drug intake as harmless.[5] The author's results with hypnosis *per se* have been poor. However, when combined with behavior therapy and imagery conditioning, the results have improved.[32]

JUVENILE DELINQUENCY

Hypnotherapy has been employed effectively in juvenile delinquency.[18] Relaxation alone, under hypnosis, relieved the significant tensions.[18] Behavioral problems such as stealing, truancy, sex offenses, and lying were helped in patients who were followed for 1 to 6 years.

Ambrose and Newbold have an excellent chapter devoted exclusively to the use of hypnotherapy in delinquency.[4] They note that many anxious children have a need to provoke their parents into punishing them for their wrongdoings. The causes may be an overly strict upbringing, excessively high standards, parental hostility, or rejection. Hypnosis was used to allow children to vent their fears and, together with reeducation, helped a high percentage of delinquents. Parents were also treated to correct aggravating factors. When they saw the improvement in their children through hypnosis, the parents became even more cooperative. In some cases, abreaction, regression, and revivification were used to relieve actual traumatic episodes. The protective value of hypnosis, as well as its corrective features, is emphasized.

N. H. Mellor cured 13 of 14 hardened juvenile delinquents, who had resisted all types of therapy, in an average of 6 sessions. He made use of communication with the "unconscious" by technics involving finger or hand levitation to produce answers establishing the authenticity of traumatic or emotional causative factors. This technic (finger signalling) rapidly eliminated emotional blocks and avoided anger and defiance.

In several cases the benefits occurred during the first session. It is likely that the finger signalling here acts as a "magical gesture," fitting in with the subject's inordinate need for security, attention and love. This, together with a permissive and noncritical approach, could be of distinct value in the juvenile delinquent.

Weitzenhoffer recently questioned the validity of eliciting the "wisdom" of the "unconscious" by ideomotor finger signalling.[60] He believes that there is little justification for assuming that some sort of psychic entity, "the unconscious," has been communicated with, or is responsible for, the observed phenomena. Nevertheless, Mellor's brief pilot study indicates that the method established good motivation for self-improvement. Regression, revivification, and cathartic recall aided recognition and understanding of the underlying reasons for the tensions. Mellor thinks that, during hypnosis, subjects overcome their difficulties by developing insight and learning better ways of responding to their tensions.

ASTHMA

Numerous investigators have found hypnosis valuable for relieving asthma in children (see Chap. 33).[46, 51, 56] Some of these reports stress individual therapy, and others employ group hypnosis. Diamond reported the complete cure of 40 cases of asthma by eliciting the "causative" factors, emotional or environmental.[11] He stresses that hypnosis is never to be used for symptom suppression. Other researchers agree with this tenet.[4] La Scola has developed an ingenious hypnotic technic involving imagery, double-bind technics, and fantasy evocation.[35] He states: "The asthmatic child responds most dramatically to the hypnotic approach, and the cure is so gratifying that it seems incredible for any other method of treatment ever to be considered."

HYSTERICAL SYMPTOMS

Ambrose and Newbold have classified under hysterical reactions a group of bodily symptoms which had "purposive" aspects and symbolic significance.[4] Here hypnotherapy with reeducation was helpful.

MISCELLANEOUS CONDITIONS

Many of the other psychosomatic disorders described in the chapter on hypnotherapy in internal medicine have been treated effectively by hypnotherapeutically oriented pediatricians. Pain of physical origin often can be helped by hypnotherapy.[10, 35] Other conditions reputedly treated by hypnosuggestive procedures are the hyperkinesis of infectious chorea, hyperkinetic syndromes associated with encephalitis, and other neurologic conditions. The hypnosis was employed as a symptomatic auxiliary method to other forms of medical and psychological therapy, especially for encopresis,[35] anorexia nervosa, obesity, and nutritional problems.

REFERENCES

1. Aboulker, P., and Chertok, L.: Emotional factors in stress incontinence. Psychosomat. Med., *24:*507, 1962.
2. Ambrose, G.: Hypnotherapy for children. *In* Schneck, J.M. (ed.): Hypnosis in Modern Medicine. ed. 3. Springfield, Ill., Charles C Thomas, 1963.
3. ———: Hypnosis in the treatment of children. Am. J. Clin. Hypn., *11:*1, 1968.
4. Ambrose, G., and Newbold, G.: Handbook of Clinical Hypnosis. London, Bailliere, Tindall and Cox, 1956.
5. Bauman, F.: Hypnosis and the adolescent drug abuser. Am. J. Clin. Hypn., *13:*17, 1970.

6. Call, J.D.: Children, parents and hypnosis: a discussion. Int. J. Clin. Exp. Hypn., *24:*149, 1976.

7. Clements, R.O. Gilles de la Tourette's syndrome: an overview of development and treatment of a case, using hypnotherapy, haloperidal and psychotherapy. Am. J. Clin. Hypn., *14:*167, 1972.

8. Collison, D.R.: Hypnotherapy in the management of nocturnal enuresis. Med. J. Aust., *1:*52, 1970.

9. _____: Hypnotherapy with children, Aust. J. Clin. Hypn., *2:*106, 1974.

10. Crasilneck, H.B., and Hall, M.D.: Clinical Hypnosis: Principles and Applications. New York, Grune & Stratton, 1975.

11. Diamond, H.H.: Hypnosis in children: asthma. Am. J. Clin. Hypn., *1:*124, 1959.

12. Donk, L., *et al.:* Toward an increase in reading efficiency utilizing specific suggestions: a preliminary approach. Int. J. Clin. Exp. Hypn., *16:*101, 1968.

13. Egan, R.M., and Egan, W.P.: The effect of hypnosis on academic performance. Am. J. Clin. Hypn., *2:*30, 1968.

14. Erickson, M.H.: Pediatric hypnotherapy. Am. J. Clin. Hypn., *1:*25, 1958.

15. Falck, F.J.: Stuttering and hypnosis. Int. J. Clin. Exp. Hypn., *12:*67, 1964.

16. Gardner, G.G.: Hypnosis with children. Int. J. Clin. Exp. Hypn., *22:*20, 1974.

17. _____: Childhood, death and human dignity: hypnotherapy for David. Int. J. Clin. Exp. Hypn., *24:*122, 1976.

18. Gilbert, S.F.: Hypnotherapy in children. Br. J. Med. Hypn., *6:*36, 1954.

19. _____: Juvenile enuresis: hypnotherapy in children, Br. J. Med. Hypn., *8:*43, 1957.

20. Goldburgh, S.J.: Hypnotherapy, chemotherapy, and expressive-directive therapy in the treatment of examination anxiety. Am. J. Clin. Hypn., *11:*42, 1968.

21. Grable, R.H.: A refractory speech problem successfuly treated with hypnosis. Am. J. Clin. Hypn., *11:*125, 1968.

22. Granone, F.: Hypnotherapy in stuttering. Minerva Med. Suppl., *3:*2158, 1966.

23. Hammer, E.F.: Post-hypnotic suggestion and test performance. J. Clin. Exp. Hypn., *2:*178, 1954.

24. Higham, A.R.C.: An approach to the problem of simple enuresis. Proc. Roy. Soc. Med., *46:*889, 1953.

25. Hilgard, E.R.: Hypnotic phenomena: the struggle for scientific acceptance. Am. Sci., *59:*567, 1971.

26. Hubbard, O.E.: Hypnotherapy of a patient complaining of a speech defect. Am. J. Clin. Hypn., *5:*281, 1963.

27. Illovsky, J., and Fredman, N.: Group suggestion in learning disabilities of primary grade children: a feasibility study. Int. J. Clin. Exp. Hypn., *24:*87, 1976.

28. Johnson, W.: The Onset of Stuttering. Minneapolis, University of Minnesota Press, 1959.

29. _____: Problems of impaired speech and language. J.A.M.A., *170:*148, 1959.

30. Koster, S.: Hypnosis in children as a method of curing enuresis and related conditions. Br. J. Med. Hypn., *5:*32, 1954.

31. Krippner, S.: The use of hypnosis with elementary and secondary children in a summer reading clinic. Am. J. Clin. Hypn., *8:*261, 1966.

32. Kroger, W.S., and Fezler, W.D.: Hypnosis and Behavior Modification: Imagery Conditioning. Philadelphia, J.B. Lippincott, 1976.

33. Kulikov, V.N.: Obuchenie vo sne (sleep learning). Sov. Ped., *28:*51, 1964.

34. Laquarte, J.: The use of hypnosis with children with deviant voices, Int. J. Clin. Exper. Hypn., *24:* 98–104, 1976.

35. La Scola, R.L.: Hypnosis with children. *In* Cheek, D.B., and Le Cron, L.M. (eds.): Clinical Hypnotherapy. New York, Grune & Stratton, 1968.

36. Lawlor, E.D.: Hypnotic intervention with "school phobic" children. Int. J. Clin. Exp. Hypn., *24:*74, 1976.

37. Lindner, H.: Hypnotherapy and psychosomatics in the syndrome of Gilles de la Tourette. Int. J. Clin. Exp. Hypn., *15:*151, 1967.

38. Lodato, F.J.: Hypnosis: an adjunct to test performance. Am. J. Clin. Hypn., *2:*129, 1968.

39. London, P.: The Children's Hypnotic Susceptibility Scale. Palo Alto, Consulting Psychologists Press, 1963.

40. London, P., and Cooper, L.M.: Norms of hypnotic susceptibility in children. Dev. Psychol., *1:*113, 1969.

41. McCord, H.: Hypnotherapy and stuttering. J. Clin. Exp. Hypn., *3:*40, 1955.

42. _____: Hypnosis as an aid to the teaching of a severely mentally retarded teen-age boy. J. Clin. Exp. Hypn., *4:*21, 1956.

43. _____: The hypnotizability of the mongoloid-type child. J. Clin. Exp. Hypn., *4:*19, 1956.

44. _____: Hypnotizing the mentally retarded child. Br. J. Med. Hypn., *8:*17, 1956–57.

45. McCord, H., and Sherrell, C.I.: A note on increased ability to do calculus post-hypnotically. Am. J. Clin. Hypn., *4:*124, 1962.

46. Magonet, A.P.: Hypnosis and asthma. Int. J. Clin. Exp. Hypn., *8:*121, 1960.

47. Marchesi, C.: Hypnotic Treatment of Stammering

(paper read at Pan-American Medical Association meeting, May 5, 1960).

48. Orton, S.: Reading, Writing, and Speech Problems. New York, Norton, 1937.

49. Rousey, C.L.: Hypnosis in speech pathology and audiology. J. Speech Hear. Disord., *26:*258, 1961.

50. Schneck, J.M.: Hypnosis in Modern Medicine. Springfield, Ill., Charles C Thomas, 1959, pp. 329–332.

51. Smith, J.M., and Burns, C.L.: The treatment of asthmatic children by hypnotic suggestion. Br. J. Dis. Chest, *54:*78, 1960.

52. Solovey, G., and Milechnin, A.: Conduct problems in children and hypnosis. Dis. Nerv. Syst., *16:*249, 1955.

53. _____: Concerning the nature and treatment of stuttering, Brit. J. M. Hypn., *10:*2–9, 1959.

54. _____: Concerning the treatment of enuresis. Am. J. Clin. Hypn., *2:*22, 1959.

55. Sternlicht, M., and Wanderer, Z.W.: Hypnotic susceptibility and mental deficiency. Int. J. Clin. Exp. Hypn., *11:*104, 1963.

56. Sutton, P.H.: A trial of group hypnosis and autohypnosis in asthmatic children. Br. J. Clin. Hypn., *1:*11, 1969.

57. Troup, C.W., and Hodgson, N.B.: Nocturnal functional bladder capacity in enuretic children. J. Urol., *105:*129, 1971.

58. Uhr, L.: Learning under hypnosis: What do we know? What should we know? J. Clin. Exp. Hypn., *6:*121, 1958.

59. Van Pelt, S.J.: Hypnotism and the Power Within. London, Skeffington, 1950.

60. Weitzenhoffer, A.: A bibliography of hypnotism in pediatrics. Am. J. Clin. Hypn., *2:*92, 1959.

61. _____: Reflections upon certain specific and current "uses of the unconscious" in clinical hypnosis. Int. J. Clin. Exp. Hypn., *8:*165, 1960.

62. Williams, D.T., and Singh, M.: *Quoted in* Call, J.D.: Children, parents and hypnosis: a discussion. Int. J. Clin. Exp. Hypn., *24:*149, 1976.

63. Wolberg, L.: Medical Hypnosis. New York, Grune & Stratton, 1948.

64. Wright, M.E.: Hypnosis and child therapy. Am. J. Clin. Hypn., *2:*197, 1960.

44

Hypnosis in Orthopedics

Hypnosis can be an adjunct to psychotherapy for certain types of spasmodic torticollis, hysterical contractures, backache due to "vertebral neuroses," pain relief in traumatic emergencies, and the setting of fractures where analgesia or anesthesia are unavailable. It also can help to reduce neurogenic shock in debilitated or elderly individuals requiring extensive surgical procedures such as the nailing of hip fractures and spinal fusion. Rheumatism, fibrositis, and certain types of arthritis which have a psychogenic component are amenable to a combination of hypnotherapy and medical procedures.

TORTICOLLIS

Spasmodic torticollis or wry neck is due to a hysterical conversion reaction; the torsion often symbolizes deep-seated anxieties which are too difficult to face. This condition is extremely resistant to physical therapy and often requires resection of muscles and nerves. Hypnosis has proven effective in numerous cases of recent origin.[1, 7, 10]

Often hypnosis dramatically removes the torticollis in a single session, but invariably it returns; this indicates its functional significance. A case of torticollis cured by ideomotor finger signaling to ascertain the underlying psychodynamics has been described.[5] Using the concept of "organ language," guilty fears were elicited over an illicit relationship which caused a "turning away" from the problem. If the condition is of long enough duration and accompanied by muscle hypertrophy and scoliosis,

the prognosis is well-nigh hopeless. Where no anatomic involvement exists, there is a better response to hypnosis.

A 33-year-old male was seen with a torticollis of 14 months' duration. No gross anatomic changes were observable. Eight months before the onset of the torticollis, he had fainted while receiving an injection. Two months later he saw his mother fatally burned. Following this latter episode, he developed dizzy spells, and always "needed more air." One month later his wife suffered a nervous collapse which required shock therapy. Soon after, his neck started turning to the left. However, the torsion was relieved whenever he held a pencil in the right side of his mouth or whenever he touched the top of his head. Posthypnotic suggestions were directed toward increasing utilization of these two mechanisms, which inhibited the turning of the head. Through sensory-imagery conditioning, he imagined these acts to be associated with a normal alignment of his head and neck. The more he actually put the pencil in his mouth and touched the top of his head, the longer the torticollis disappeared, often for several hours. Posthypnotic suggestions were given that he could, if he wished, increase the intensity of the torsion. It was further explained that whenever one could increase the severity of a symptom, one could deliberately *decrease* it! An uncovering type of psychotherapy revealed considerable resentment over his wife's sexual coldness. He related that he had had considerable hostility toward his mother, "who was always cold and distant." After his wife had a "nervous breakdown," he was unable to look directly at the customers of his small-town drugstore because of his strong guilt feelings. Alleviation of his anxiety and feeling of guilt, together with hypnotic manipulation of the symptom, as described above, and a cathartic type of psychotherapy altered his attitudes toward his wife's sexual problems. These, together with the sensory-imagery conditioning, ultimately resulted in dissolution of the spasm and tic.

In another case, a 44-year-old woman developed a spasmodic torticollis, more marked when she had to talk before groups. Particularly significant in her history was her husband's demand for intercourse *almost every night* of their 25 years of marriage. She acquiesced in the act merely as a wifely duty. After having a mechanical-like coitus, her husband would fall asleep promptly. An interview with the husband revealed strong fears of impotence. Since the patient was Catholic, she was referred to her priest for consultation on the moral aspects of the intolerable situation. He advised psychotherapy for the husband, which was refused. Autohypnosis and the use of sensory-imagery conditioning directed toward imagining that she was speaking before groups without anxiety afforded some relief of the torticollis. However, she generally relapsed within several days. Posthypnotic suggestions to twitch the forefinger of the right hand helped to decrease the intensity of the spasm. She was advised to face and discuss the sexual situation with her husband, who finally agreed to decrease his inordinate demands. Soon after, the spasmodic tic of the neck cleared up. However, on a follow-up 6 months after the author had left the area, it was discovered that she had relapsed. Further psychotherapy for the husband, who eventually reverted to his former demands for intercourse, was strongly recommended.

HYSTERICAL CONTRACTURES

Recent hysterical contractures can be relieved in a few sessions by hypnosis. If active participation of the patient is enlisted by autohypnosis, the results are more permanent than when direct symptom removal is used. The hypnotherapeutic approach is similar to that described for the torticollis cases. When chronic joint fixation or fibrosynovitis are marked, the outlook is poor.

VERTEBRAL NEUROSES

Spasm of the neck and back muscles, and their etiology, differential diagnosis, and psychotherapeutic approach have been reviewed in detail by Kroger and Freed.[9] Backache may be a conversion reaction to the commonly observed physiologic expression of emotional tensions. They state:

It seems clear to us that "low back pain" in the neurotic personality may very well be a conversion reaction to (1) emotional insecurity, as an excessive need for attention and sympathy; (2) strong dependency attitudes, as inability to make decisions and pronounced inclination to lean on others; (3) antisocial feelings, resulting from a marked reaction to poverty or an intense opposition to existing social or moral codes; (4) deep-seated guilt, as "pangs of conscience" because of expressed or unexpressed hostility which was unacceptable to the patient.

When situations arise that are demanding, the physical complaints are aggravated, especially when the patients feel threatened by feelings of deep humiliation and worthlessness.

PSYCHOGENIC RHEUMATISM

Most cases of psychogenic rheumatism are conversion symptoms, usually hysterical in nature, in which the emotional conflict symbolically expresses itself in musculoskeletal disorders. Functional camptocormia, in which the patient assumes a position of extreme kyphosis after trauma, falls into this category. These patients are not malingerers but, rather, are exploiting the symptom for secondary gain purposes. Establishing the need for the symptom can be accomplished by hypnosis. This enables such individuals to face their life situations more realistically. Autohypnosis, glove anesthesia and sensory-imagery conditioning can be utilized to implement psychotherapy.

In infectious arthritis, traumatic synovitis, gout and rheumatoid arthritis, hypnosis potentiates medical and physical therapy. The clinical applications have been discussed in Chapter 33.

MISCELLANEOUS APPLICATIONS

Hypnosis helps to reduce the excruciating pain of traumatic emergency cases encountered in military and civilian settings. Although it is usually difficult to induce, hypnosis can relax an injured person and ease the discomfort when drugs are unavailable. Before attempting induction in such situations, the therapist must develop a rapid rapport. He can remark, "I know that you are in great discomfort, but if you wish to relax and have *less* discomfort, then follow my instructions." A direct authoritative approach is more effective in such instances.

Hypnoanesthesia minimizes neurogenic shock in amputations, in the setting of fractures, and in cases requiring extensive major surgery, such as spinal fusion and hip-pinning in elderly individuals. Hypnosis is particularly indicated for the setting of fractures and orthopedic surgery in children, as psychic trauma is minimized. Children from 3 to 8 years of age respond to nursery tales, cartoons and popular TV shows and to suggestions such as "You are very tired," accompanied by prodigious yawns on the part of the anesthesiologist. As has been mentioned, television provides almost inexhaustible material for hallucinatory or sensory-imagery conditioning in the 8- to 14-year-old group. These youngsters will even recite commercials along with the story plot when they imagine that they are watching their favorite show. Orthodox eye-fixation technics can be used on those over 14 years of age.

Bachet and Weiss used group hypnosis for pain relief in a series of patients who had undergone amputation of limbs.[2] They cured more than 80 per cent. Opiates and sedatives were drastically reduced. Phantom limb pain, spasm, and clonus were alleviated in many instances by hypnotic inhibition.

The author is frequently called in consultation for many bizarre types of pain syndromes associated with orthopedic conditions.

HICCOUGHS

Persistent hiccoughs are included in this section because the orthopedic specialist is often called in to resect the neck muscles and the nerves. Hiccoughs are due to involuntary spasms, which are caused by reflex action, and are usually unilateral. They occur with a wide variety of physiologic and functional disorders. The entire subject has been reviewed.[6] The usual therapy consists of interrupting the reflex action by pharmacologic measures and surgical intervention. From 1 to 10 hypnotic treatments were required

to relieve 14 of 18 patients who had not responded to other therapeutic procedures.[6] Hypnosis induced complete relaxation and relieved the spasm.

My experiences are similar to those reported by Dorcus and Kirkner[6]—about 75 per cent of the patients can be helped by a permissive hypnotic approach. Often a single session dramatically and permanently alleviates the most intractable cases. Psychological probing is seldom indicated because of the time factor. It is also of considerable interest that direct symptom suppression does not result in other symptom equivalents taking the place of hiccoughs.

Other investigators have employed hypnosis for relief of intractable hiccoughs.[4, 8, 11, 12] As was cited earlier, the author reported a case of intractable hiccoughs stopped in a single session of "telephone hypnosis."[8] The subject, who was unknown to the author, was entirely relieved within minutes. The induction was a life-saving procedure as the patient, a physician, was moribund.

REFERENCES

1. Ampato, J.L.: Hypnosis: a cure for torticollis. Am. J. Clin. Hypn., *18:*60, 1975.
2. Bachet, M., and Weiss, C.: Treatment of disorders of amputated subjects by hypnotic inhibitions. Br. J. Med. Hypn., *4:*15, 1952.
3. Bendersky, G., and Baren, M.: Hypnosis in the termination of hiccups unresponsive to conventional treatment. Arch. Intern. Med., *104:*417, 1959.
4. Bizzi, B.: On two cases of hysteric hiccough and hysterical sneezing treated with hypnosis. Rass. Stud. Psychiat., *53:*60, 1966.
5. Cheek, D.B., and Le Cron, L.M.: Clinical Hypnotherapy. New York, Grune & Stratton, 1968.
6. Dorcus, R.M., and Kirkner, F.J.: The control of hiccoughs by hypnotic treatment. J. Clin. Exp. Hypn., *3:*104, 1955.
7. Friedman, H.: Brief clinical report: hypnosis in the treatment of a case of torticollis. Am. J. Clin. Hypn., *8:*139, 1965.
8. Kroger, W.S.: Hypnotherapy for intractable postsurgical hiccups. Am. J. Clin. Hypn., *12:*1, 1969.
9. Kroger, W.S., and Freed, S.C.: Psychosomatic

Gynecology, Including Problems of Obstetrical Care. Philadelphia, W.B. Saunders, 1951.

10. Le Hew, J.L.: Use of hypnosis in the treatment of long standing spastic torticollis. Am. J. Clin. Hypn., *14:*124, 1971.

11. Smedley, W.P., and Barnes, W.T.: Postoperative use of hypnosis on a cardiovascular service: termination of persistent hiccups in a patient with an aortorenal graft. J.A.M.A., *197:*371, 1966.

12. Theohar, C., and McKegney, F.P.: Hiccups of psychogenic origin: a case report and review of the literature. Compr. Psychiatry, *11:*377, 1970.

45

Hypnosis in the Removal of Habit Patterns

ALCOHOLISM

Chronic alcoholism is a symptom of a deep-seated personality disorder usually selected to avoid intolerable life situations. There is no typical personality profile, but hostility, insecurity, and feelings of inadequacy are usually present. Alcoholics have a low frustration tolerance, increased sensitivity, and feelings of omnipotence characterized by the belief that "nothing can happen to me." Outwardly they present a diffident appearance, which is usually a façade for their deep-seated dependency needs.

Some have little or no concern about the trouble caused by the habit. For instance, a binge, with its days of misery and sickness, often results in a lost job, a ruined career, and a broken marriage. The alcoholic is an "injustice collector" for whom the overt self-punishment fulfills a pleasurable need, as well as a rationalization for the inability to face reality. Seldom is he aware of his masochistic needs to suffer.

Such individuals do not have the courage to commit suicide and are, in reality, slowly destroying themselves by the noxious habit. To allay their tensions they retreat to a childlike behavior pattern, with a need for attention, pity, and love. By becoming inebriated, the alcoholic develops a greater capacity to give and receive attention from others. This temporarily increases his self-esteem and well-being.

Many alcoholics have never emerged from adolescence—the undifferentiated period of their psychosexual development which is characterized by homosexual tendencies. The *esprit de corps* noted among gregarious drinkers at any bar illustrates the desire to be a "part of the gang" spirit. The homosexual manifestations are seldom overt, but merely represent a strong identification with an individual of the same sex. The alcoholism serves the purpose of fending off unrecognized homosexual drives (panic). Often, however, the drunkenness removes the inhibitions and allows these tendencies to emerge.

In the typical history of the alcoholic there is a compulsive pattern represented by repeated incidents involving self-debasement, various types of sexual involvements, and defiance of authoritarian and other surrogate figures. When the demands for sympathy and attention are not met, more frequent "binges" are usually necessary to provide a respite from the mounting tensions. Exhortations aimed either at shaming the individual into sobriety or pointing out the harmful medical sequelae are useless. Since the alcoholic seldom realizes the needs for his habit, he cannot control his drinking. Successful therapy requires that these needs must become self-evident to him. Intellectualizing or moralizing on the dire mental and physical dangers is utterly futile in the chronic alcoholic.

TREATMENT

The purpose of therapy is first to motivate the individual to stop drinking and then to teach him how to adapt to his difficult problems, rather than using regressive behavior patterns at the first sign of stress. Here a sympathetic, noncondemnatory attitude will make the patient feel that he is being treated like an adult, and this helps to establish healthy motivation. Chronic drinkers are seldom motivated if their immaturity and strong dependency preclude admitting that they have a drinking problem.

Since most alcoholics are generally passive and dependent, the hypnotic relationship initially helps the patient in therapy at a time when he is most resistant. Later this dependency is dissolved, and the needs for it and other reasons are worked through. Because of greater rapport with the therapist, the patient now is willing to trade his self-destructive tendencies and immature attitudes for healthier goals.

The chronic alcoholic who does not wish to be helped, or who is literally brought in by friends or relatives against his will, cannot be helped by any psychotherapeutic approach unless he is institutionalized for long-term psychotherapy. The prognosis is usually poor, as each recovery is only a "flight into health." His ardent protests that he is cured and his vows that he will never drink again are only rationalizations for the breaking off of therapy. Overcompliance merely follows the old adage, "If you can't fight them, join them." Follow-up studies indicate that severe cases are difficult to help, irrespective of the therapy employed.

Conditioned Reflex Treatment by Hypnosis

Conditioned reflex treatment has been successful for some patients. In this approach the individual is given a drink and an emetic is administered. An association between vomiting and drinking is produced by this method, but it is not helpful unless the patient is highly motivated or is seen immediately after a "hangover." Relatively permanent recovery in carefully selected patients is obtained by reinforcing this technic through posthypnotic suggestions to vomit at the sight, taste, or smell of liquor.[21] Under sensory-imagery conditioning, the patient recalls repeatedly the horrible nausea and the disgusting sensations produced by the emetic. Thus the unpleasant memory is seldom forgotten, and the constant revivification of a repugnant experience dissuades him from drinking.

If a healthy relationship exists between therapist and the patient, the recovery forces will be mobilized. The desire to abstain is reinforced by appropriate posthypnotic suggestions. Motiva-

tion is increased by such other posthypnotic suggestions as the setting of a deadline for the daily or the weekly decrease in the quantity consumed, the stressing of the health factor, and, above all, the effect of the patient's self-esteem that has been enhanced by the permissiveness of the therapeutic regimen.

The key points in the conditioned reflex treatment under hypnosis, outlined by Kroger,[21] Wolberg,[44] Miller,[30] and others,[22] are based on repeatedly emphasizing, under hypnosis, the deleterious effects of alcohol, the conditioned repugnance for alcoholic beverages, and the patient's ability to control his own behavior, and finally establishing the emotional needs for the symptoms. The self-destructive drives should be channeled into healthy outlets such as hobbies, sports, social activities, and other constructive endeavors.

Aversion Treatment

After hypnosis and autohypnosis have been instituted, strong suggestions are given, such as, "Each time that you even think of drinking, you will develop a horrible disgust and taste for the liquor by associating it with the most horrible, repugnant smell and taste that you have ever experienced. After you have said this to yourself again and again, you will *really* begin to believe that a drink will smell and taste awful." Such autosuggestions are repeated continuously for reinforcement purposes. After sobriety has been maintained, these can be made at longer intervals.

Wolberg has described a very interesting technic in which symptom substitution is utilized.[44] He informs the patient that "Every time you crave a drink you will reach for a malted milk tablet and this will give you a sense of pleasure and relaxation."

Another effective method is to open a bottle of whiskey while the patient is hypnotized and to assure him that the bottle has not been tampered with or opened. He is offered a drink, and requested to hold it in his mouth for several minutes to get the full taste. Naturally, a burning sensation on his tongue is created. After the patient has finally swallowed the drink, he is asked how he liked it. His usual reply is, "It tasted fine," whereupon the therapist informs the subject that he has been deceived. "You have not been given whiskey but a mixture of lemon juice and ammonia." If hypnotized, the subject will exhibit marked revulsion and disgust.

If this is unsuccessful, the procedure is repeated and the chances are that the next time he will react in the expected manner. Before concluding the hypnotic session, the patient should be given a posthypnotic suggestion that any time he is offered a drink, these reactions will certainly occur. Even the thought or the smell of a drink will induce profound distaste.

A substitute habit should be suggested to take the place of the drinking. For instance, drinking nonalcoholic beverages satisfies the oral cravings. Whenever a deeply ingrained habit pattern is changed, it should be replaced by a more innocuous substitute habit. Tranquilizers or amphetamines can be employed during the "weaning-off" period.

Before terminating every session, suggestions should be made that the patient will feel very relaxed. Immediately after dehypnotization, he can be offered a drink to see how much disgust is immediately produced. In selected subjects, this approach often produces a 60 to 70 per cent total abstinence. Social drinking is discouraged. Suggestions to bolster self-confidence and overcome feelings of inadequacy can be given during hypnosis.

It has been observed that alcoholics are good hypnotic subjects.[14, 26] An ego-building approach under hypnosis has been employed with frequent self-hypnosis sessions using reinforcement.[6] Other investigators noted equivocal results,[1, 9, 11, 12] and still another found hypnosis to be of little value.[8] Complete abstinence after cessation is usually emphasized,[24] whereas some authorities allow only moderate drinking in a social setting.[6] Switching to non-alcoholic beverages after one or two drinks has been recommended.[6] The author believes that many alcoholics have a lowered resistance to alcohol, and this approach should not be employed for the hard-core alcoholic who has been "cured"; one or two drinks are enough to send him on a binge.

Hypnotherapy is used with autogenic training, conditioned reflex therapy, work therapy, and other measures in the Soviet Union. Group hypnosis and classical aversive conditioning are also employed by Soviet researchers in response to an increasing national incidence of alcoholism.[16]

Group Therapy

The success of Alcoholics Anonymous (A.A.) depends upon the same factors described in Chapter 35. The powerful group identification factor, which makes the sufferer feel accepted, and his intense desire to please the leader of the group or the person assigned to him (his sponsor) are additional factors. The group situation mobilizes the inherent competitiveness present in every individual and, through the strong support given by other members, his weak personality structure is bolstered. Finally, as a result of healthy motivation established by the emotional contagion, and alliance with a power greater than himself, the recovery forces of the individual are unleashed. Faith in a beneficent power means the difference between success and failure. The alcoholic has little or no reason to take issue with this new parental figure or to challenge his omnipotence. Through further friendly exhortations from former alcoholics, he often renounces his drinking habit. The author has a high regard for A.A.

Individual Hypnotherapy

Most problem drinkers are looking for a magical gesture and, because of their strong dependency strivings, attempt to "crawl into the lap" of the therapist. From the initial visit, they must be informed that this is a "do-it-yourself" program and that results are in direct proportion to the desire for recovery and the willingness to perfect their sensory-imagery conditioning technics. By using such measures, the therapist cannot get "out on a limb" or "lose face" with the patient.

It also is stressed that if the symptom returns, it can be controlled by autohypnosis; resistances are diminished whenever suggestions are self-originated. The therapist must not be too authoritative.

To avoid criticalness, the author states, "You will stop drinking as soon as you desire to, will you not? And it will be because you really want to do so down deep inside. I am only a friend who wishes to guide you as long as you need me." This obviates the therapist's being placed in the role of a dominating parental figure.

Group Hypnotherapy

The author has found that the results in small groups are often better than with individual hypnotherapy. In addition to hypnosis, the technics include free discussion and expression of feelings, reeducation, reassurance, strong emotional support, and thorough explanations of the commonly encountered problems.

There are many rationalizations that alcoholics use to explain their drinking. They must recognize that dishonesty with themselves and with others, omnipotence, impulsiveness, guilt, shame, and the inability to establish durable relationships are related to the drinking. The manner in which tensions are displaced, self-abuse, the striving for perfection, and the need to manipulate others also should be pointed out.

When a permissive approach is employed that is directed toward these needs, guilt, anxiety, insecurity, and fear can be resolved, especially if the individual identifies with strong members of the group. The stronger the identification, the more will the alcoholic emulate those whom he admires. The important factor in group as well as in individual psychotherapy is giving the patient the feeling that the therapist really understands the patient's problems and is willing and able to help him. The greater ability to concentrate speeds up any type of psychotherapy. When group hypnotherapy is combined with decreasing doses of Antabuse medication, maximal improvement occurs. Wallerstein obtained 53 per cent improvement with Antabuse, 36 per cent with group hypnotherapy, 26 per cent with milieu therapy, and 24 per cent with conditioned-reflex treatment.[42]

Two-hour weekly sessions are held. Each one begins with a general discussion of alcoholism. Questions and answers pertaining to all aspects of drinking are dealt with in the first half hour. Then several former patients, who have been helped and who have returned to visit the group, cured, relate their experiences. They usually state that initially they could not believe that this kind of an approach would help them. Then, after observing improvement in other members, they were more motivated to obtain similar results. One or more grateful patients describe how they were taught hypnosis or autohypnosis and how through sensory-imagery conditioning they finally developed a profound disgust for alcohol (the technics outlined in the section below were used). In having a sufferer sincerely relate his feelings to the group, a considerable amount of hope rapidly develops, especially for the neophyte, the unsophisticated, or the disbeliever.

Those volunteers who are successfully hypnotized are given the appropriate suggestions for producing disgust and a strong aversion for drinking. Since a specific disgust to taste and smell will vary from patient to patient, it is wise to let each one pick these. In successive sessions, the technics of autohypnosis and sensory-imagery are inculcated into each person. The incidence of success is much higher where autohypnosis is employed. With this approach, the patient realizes that he must achieve the results through his own efforts. This is highly motivating and contributes to his self-esteem.

The medical management of the chronic alcoholic is not within the scope of this presentation. It involves a knowledge of the effects of long-term consumption of alcoholic beverages, including metabolic factors. The rehabilitation of the chronic alcoholic is tedious and requires painstaking attention, patience, and a mixture of empathy and firmness. At all costs, the therapist must not become too involved and must maintain a prestige position at all times.

Importance of Autohypnosis

It is not difficuilt for the alcoholic to practice autohypnosis. Frequently, however, he may procrastinate, saying, "I just can't find the time," or "I don't feel up to it." Here a careful step-by-step explanation should be given, stressing that the autosuggestions so necessary for his recovery should be under his control. This factor is of the utmost importance for establishing healthy motivation. Under autohypnosis, the patient can suggest when he thinks he will be able to substitute a soft beverage for the liquor. Through use of these measures, direct symptom removal is not employed. Instead, recovery is obtained by a weaning-off process in which the patient decides *how* and *when* to cut down on the number of drinks taken per day. It is also helpful to allow a choice of the type of beverage substitute that is to replace the liquor.

Importance of Posthypnotic Suggestions

Irrational fears of the patient that he will not be able to stop drinking can be reversed through posthypnotic suggestions directed to the possibility *that maybe he will stop too abruptly.* Other posthypnotic suggestions can be given to pick a date in the not-too-distant future when he will have reduced his drinks to one or two a day. It is suggested that he will be extremely worried as to whether he is going to be taking one drink a day or three drinks a day by the chosen date. Such extraverbal suggestions produce overreaction, with resultant improvement.

As in the treatment of obesity, posthypnotic suggestions are given that, if the patient is in doubt about taking a drink, he will imagine his therapist shaking his head in disapproval. When all these technics are employed with supportive psychotherapy consisting of rapport, ventilation of problems and skilful guidance, excellent results can be obtained in a high percentage of patients.

If a patient, who apparently is doing well, relapses or "falls off the wagon," he is never censured or criticized. However, the question can be raised with him as to *what* the particular situation was for doing this and *why* he had to take 10 drinks—perhaps he could have gotten by with four drinks, or two drinks, or perhaps one drink. Also, what was he thinking about before he began drinking? These and other problems are fully discussed. It is important to emphasize that, with most chronic alcoholics, the ultimate therapeutic goal is directed toward total abstinence.

With greater maturation and growth of the personality, the alcoholic thinks more like an adult and eventually realizes that he no longer has the need to utilize harmful tension-allaying mechanisms to meet his life problems. Even after the problems responsible for the need to drink are made self-revealing to the patient, they are frequently of such magnitude that he feels there is no solution. Here it is imperative that one of two things be done: either the individual must be given the knowledge to make the proper decision

as to what course he will adopt (and it should be emphasized that the decision must come from him and him alone), or, if he is unable to make a decision, he should walk away from the problem and stop using it for self-punishment.

The following verbalization is typical for the aversion treatment of alcoholism: "John, you are deeply relaxed. Listen to all my suggestions, as each one will be indelibly imprinted in your mind. You will not remember all these suggestions today, but eventually you *will* remember all of them. Each and every suggestion will be remembered over the coming weeks and months.

"If you really wish to stop drinking, think of the most disgusting, nauseating taste that you have ever had. Maybe a drink will taste like onions, rutabagas, parsnips, or whatever other food you dislike. That's right. You are beginning to taste something awful, are you not?" ("Yes.") "Did you say it's turnips; is that what you said?" ("Yes.") "Now, each time you even think of taking a drink, you are going to experience this taste of turnips . . . this vile, horrible taste of the turnips during the next few weeks and months. Each and every time you take a drink, you will associate it with the disgusting taste of turnips. Right now, this awful taste is getting more and more marked, is it not?" ("Yes.")

"Now, think of the most putrid smell that you've experienced. Take your time and try to think of the most horrible stench that you've ever smelled. . . . Rotten eggs? Well, that's a good one. All right, now each and every time you hold a drink in your hand and smell it, you will think of rotten eggs . . . the horrible, violent, disgusting smell of rotten eggs. And each and every time you even think of taking a drink now, you are not only going to get the terrible taste of turnips, but also the smell of rotten eggs. This may not make itself apparent until you have said this to yourself over and over again, perhaps 50 or 100 times, under autohypnosis. Eventually you will associate this smell with the odor of liquor until you are sure that you really hate the sight, taste, and smell of a drink (sensory-imagery conditioning).

"John, the next thing I'd like to have you do is to recollect how horrible you felt after you had a lot of drinks last Saturday night, just as if you were doing it all over again (age regression). Remember the terrible feeling that you had in your stomach, and how you had to vomit? Recollect, if you will, that sickening feeling you had and how you trembled and shook all over and how weak you were, and the headache and the dizziness and all the other symptoms associated with your hangover. Recall all the details of that hangover and, if you really think about it, you will really become disgusted with drinking. Each and every time you even think of taking a drink, all of these positively awful tastes and smells will be etched in your mind. You can reexperience all of these sensations in a few minutes, even though the hangover lasted for several hours.

"I'm going to show you how this can be done by condensing (distorting) time. You know how when you're waiting for a cab on a cold, wet, rainy day and the cab is due in 2 minutes . . . it seems like 20 minutes. Or, conversely, when you're chatting with an old friend and a cab is due in 20 minutes, it seems like 2 minutes. And so, during the next 2 minutes, you are going to be able to experience all of the unpleasant, disgusting sensations associated with a half hour of the hangover that you had last Sunday morning. Fifteen minutes of actual time will *seem* like 1 minute of time. So, therefore, in 2 minutes by the clock, you will be able to relive all of the disgusting feelings that you experienced in approximately one half hour." (Two minutes elapse, during which the individual screws up his mouth, begins to get sick, and has a tendency to vomit.) "Your time is now up. Wasn't that a horrible sensation? Now, each time when you have the desire to take a drink, you will reexperience the horrible sensations of that last hangover.

"Remember, this is your problem. If you wish to drink, it is your privilege. After all, as I mentioned, this is your mind and your body, and it's up to you to direct your own treatment. Over the next few weeks, you might raise the question as to exactly how much you have the *need* to drink. Do you need to drink 80 per cent of the time, or 50 per cent, or 10 per cent? Maybe 5 or 10 per cent will fulfill your needs. I'm sure that once you realize the need to drink, you should be able to recognize the deep-seated feelings responsible for the habit. Don't press or try to think of these reasons, but just rest assured that some of the

reasons will become apparent to you in the near future.

"Now, John, perhaps you can step out of yourself, much as you would in a dream (depersonalization). Look at yourself standing at a bar, uncertain, wobbling, making a fool of yourself. Take another good look at yourself. Are you not disgusted with the terrible smell of liquor on your breath? Observe the sloppiness of your clothes. When you are sober, you are always very neat. Are you not disappointed with what you see?" (depersonalization often can be very effective in creating a disgusting self-image).

"Picture yourself at one of the drunken brawls where everybody is making a fool of himself. Is it not disgusting to see someone you respect sink lower and lower into utter insensibility and helplessness? I am interested in all your problems, and I want you to remember that any time you feel you need my help, regardless of where you are, I want you to please call me. If this is not possible, and if you are in doubt as to whether or not you should take that second or third drink, you will really see me standing beside you, shaking my head in disapproval (introjection of therapist).

"And now you can come out of this very nice state of relaxation, which is not sleep or unconsciousness and is not a trance. You can slowly open your eyes in the following manner: Number 1, say to yourself, 'I will go deeper next time.' Number 2, 'I will follow all the suggestions that I am giving to *myself* to the best of my ability.' Note that I said, '*I am giving to myself,*' rather than 'those given by the doctor.' Three, 'I will open my eyes. I will feel supremely confident that I can lick my problems.'

"You will feel, John, that you were the one who did it. Remember that. You were the one who was able to *control your need to drink.* Remember, the degree of success you achieve will be in direct proportion to the amount of effort you put forth. Practice makes perfect! Think of a foul-smelling, evil-tasting sensation every time you crave a drink. If you do this again and again, *you will be able to break up this vicious habit.*

"You need not feel guilty if you 'fall off' at any particular time. Progress is never in a straight line. It is characterized by a series of ups and downs. However, the long-term trend will ever be upward.

"You have a very powerful tool that is only as good as you use it. Use it well, sharpen it, and it will cut to the core of your problem. The manner in which you use it can be very helpful in this regard. A tape of this discussion with you is being recorded. It would be a good idea if you played it on your tape recorder every night. Then these suggestions will be deeply implanted again and again into your mind until they achieve a conditioned response. Whenever we hear a suggestion again and again, we eventually carry out the suggested act. You do have a great deal of confidence in yourself and you know that you can lick this problem in your own particular fashion."

EXCESSIVE SMOKING

Excessive smoking is one of the commonest symptoms the hypnotherapist is asked to treat. Almost every chain smoker has at one time or another attempted to break the habit. Numerous authors have used hypnosis for smoking control.[3, 4, 5, 7, 13, 20, 23, 29, 31, 33, 37, 38, 41, 45] One writer reviewed the current literature on smoking and was disappointed with the results.[4] Spiegel utilized one 45-minute session, stressing an alert, self-renewing, vigilant sensitivity to new commitments, namely, that the patient stop injuring his body.[37] These commitments consist, in essence, of the following: "For your body smoking is a poison! You need your body to live! You owe your body this respect and protection!" His results showed a 20 percent effectiveness. Dengrove, commenting on Spiegel's approach, notes the motivating effect of the fee and the striking relationship to operant conditioning and behavior modification.[7] He also questions the value of the commitments requested by Spiegel. Another investigator noted that 90 of 121 of his patients resumed smoking within a month.[33] It is believed that, in part, the covert factors present in the Spiegel method are the strong desire to stop smoking in our health-oriented society.[45] Rose found that 50 per cent of his patients stopped smoking after a physical examination and three counseling sessions.[36] Transcendental meditation also has been found helpful in reducing tension.

Kline reported that a 12-hour group therapy session, utilizing hypnosis and other technics, was successful for 88 percent of the participants.[19] He contends that hypnosis, and particularly extended periods of hypnotherapy involving the reduction and control of deprivation behavior, offers a promise for relief of smoking habituation.

Nuland and Field,[33] and Crasilneck and Hall[5] obtained 60 and 82 per cent recovery rates respectively, using a personalized approach under hypnosis and follow-up by telephone. These results were not correlated with the depth of hypnosis. Kroger and Libbott advocated a holistic approach involving hypnosis, self-hypnosis, and treatment directed toward the patient who has the habit—understanding his emotional needs.[23] Relapses were frequent, and there were no long-term follow-ups.

Watkins describes a five-session approach based upon the study of the motivations of each client.[43] Specialized suggestions and tailored fantasies were directed toward removing rationalizations; reinforcement of the person's commitment to stop smoking was utilized. She used a number of technics combining a passive-concentration approach with behavior therapy. Those who did not stop appeared to be using smoking to control anger. Her results were excellent—67 per cent were not smoking at the end of 6 months. Kroger and Fezler have reviewed the behavior modification literature: in addition to aversive conditioning, desensitization, and self-control, a group of standardized images were added to increase motivation and unlearn the maladaptive smoking behavior.[22] They also used cassette instructions for the latter. Stimulus control, self-punishment, and other operant procedures were employed, but not too effectively. The long-term results were only equivocal. Careful study reveals that all methods after long-term evaluation yield about equal results. Group therapy is no better than the didactic methods.

The following suggestions can be added to my approach, as described below: (1) have patients switch brands in gradual steps toward lower nicotine content, (2) have them inhale rapidly every 6 seconds, (3) reinforce the aversive suggestions, (4) employ recitation of the rationalizations to return to smoking and then analysis of what is wrong with the rationalizations. Withdrawal symptoms are reduced if the therapist stresses that increased oxygen intake will neutralize them.

Regardless of the approach employed, the hypnotherapist's responsibility in smoking control is to present the facts about smoking, to relate these facts to current health problems, to give every smoker a firm admonition to stop smoking, and to reinforce these by posthypnotic suggestions repeated during subsequent visits or by taped instructions. Long-term follow-up reinforcement by visits or phone calls is a powerful incentive to comply.

It is apparent from all foregoing studies that motivation is of prime importance. Presence of premonitory symptoms of heart, lung, and peripheral vascular disease provides additional powerful motivation. For such individuals, forceful instructions can be effective. Unfortunately, those who do not stop smoking label themselves as failures even though many can be helped. Moreover, many persons who are interested in hypnosis are looking for a magical, mystical cure —these are destined to fail.

The following is a sample verbalization of the posthypnotic suggestions that the author has used successfully on many smokers: "Use your imagination to curb your desire rather than your will. Therefore, each time you even think of smoking a cigarette, associate the pleasurable aroma and taste of a cigarette with the most horrible and awful smell and taste that you have ever experienced. Under autohypnosis and sensory-imagery conditioning you can convert your craving for a cigarette into an aversion. This will not happen immediately but, after you have given yourself a sufficient number of autosuggestions in this regard, you will notice that slowly and surely you will have less and less desire for cigarettes.

"Next, if you really wish to stop smoking, every time you puff on a cigarette, associate the taste and aroma of a cigarette with the most repugnant taste and odor that you have ever experienced. The craving will be converted into an aversion with continuous practice.

"You will agree that the best results are obtained if one has a goal. Hence, suggest smoking half as much during the next 2 weeks. Then cut down half as much again for the following 2 weeks until you are able to wean yourself off the habit. You can set the goal and arbitrary number of cigarettes to be smoked daily according to your needs and at your own pace.

"Since you are right-handed, would you mind *holding the cigarette in your left hand* and, instead of placing the cigarette in the right side of your mouth, which is customary for you, would you mind using the left hand for putting the cigarette in the left side of your mouth? You will, I am sure, find that if you follow these suggestions, smoking will be a chore.

"Would you mind holding the cigarette first between your thumb and little finger, then your thumb and ring finger, middle finger, or other fingers. By utilizing different combinations, you will soon find that smoking becomes rather inconvenient.

"If you really are interested in giving up this habit, allow several cigarette butts to remain in the ash tray until they develop a very stale odor. Then sniff this odoriferous ash tray at least once every hour. If you do this, you will easily develop a distaste for cigarettes. May I suggest that another ash tray with stale butts be placed on your night stand beside your bed just before retiring. When you no longer can bear the obnoxious smell, place the ash tray out in the hall, but do not empty the ash tray, as you should repeat this procedure the next night until every fresh cigarette reminds you of a stale one.

"After your smoking is reduced, you might consider the possibility of trading down to a more innocuous habit. How about substituting a peppermint Lifesaver for each cigarette that you do not smoke? You will find that, whenever the tip of your tongue is put into the hole of the Lifesaver, the same satisfaction will be obtained as if you had smoked a cigarette. If this is not feasible, you can use chewing gum or a dummy cigarette instead. You can hold the latter between your lips and imagine it's real."

In addition to the above suggestions, one can stress the health and other beneficial factors related to abstinence. If the individual is a heavy smoker, he usually has his nails discolored by nicotine. One can, with tongue in cheek, point out that this discoloration occurs in the bronchial tubes, too; that the inside of the bronchial tubes actually "stinks" like the stale cigarettes. It is emphasized that all these suggestions, if given by the patient to himself, afford a distinct possibility that the habit can be broken because of his own efforts. Furthermore, it should be emphasized that all credit for breaking the habit belongs to him, since he really did it through his imagination. The posthypnotic suggestions are useful for symptom removal. About 40 per cent of the patients relapse. Therefore, it is advisable to reinforce the suggestions at least every week.

When the excessive chain smoking is a symptom of the underlying tension, the needs for the nervous tension must be eliminated. When hypnosis was used for symptom removal, the author has never seen the slightest harm. What is the difference between cessation of smoking through hypnosis and spontaneous remission? The author is not in accord with those who are continually pointing out the dangers of symptom removal. If these dangers are real, then proprietary products sold to stop smoking are also dangerous!

An ingenious method for smoking control has been described which uses a complicated, ritualistic 21-day approach.[19] The "will" is not utilized, but rather an appeal on physical, cosmetic, personal, and financial grounds. Medications, such as antihistamines and barbitals, are used to control "withdrawal" symptoms.

INSOMNIA

Hypnosis effects improvement in acute cases of insomnia. Often a single session is effective in restoring the sleep cycle, particularly if autohypnosis has been taught on the initial visit. It can be suggested that the autohypnosis will merge with real sleep. The following posthypnotic suggestions are efficacious: "After you have established a deep state of autohypnosis, with each breath you will find yourself going deeper and deeper relaxed. And as your breathing gets slower, deeper and more regular, you will find yourself going into a deeper and deeper state of relaxation. And as you relax deeper, you will find that you will become drowsier and drowsier until you get sleepier and sleepier."

Insomnia can take different forms and have many courses. Some insomniacs lay awake for hours before falling asleep. Others wake up and cannot fall asleep again. Early wakening with inability to fall asleep generally indicates the presence of a depressive reaction. None of these reactions poses a problem unless the individual is fatigued, tense, and anxious. If chronic, it can be debilitating, and the more the person worries about his sleeplessness, the more depressed he becomes. Pseudo-insomnia occurs in persons who think they do not sleep. This type responds to reassurance. Also, the older one gets, the less sleep one requires.

The physician should rule out brain disease and barbiturate addiction as causes for insomnia. Others have disturbances in their biological rhythms; they are nocturnal individuals. This type needs reprogramming to a more circadian rhythm. By far the most common type is the person who takes his worries to bed. Such individuals associate the bed with insomnia—a self-fulfilling prophecy. For these patients behavior therapy to recondition them to associate the bed with sleep often can be effective. Vigorous exercise, relaxation, meditation, and self-hypnosis are more effective than somnifacient drugs.

Chronic insomnia, however, is more difficult to treat. Many patients have deep-seated problems and the symptom cannot be alleviated unless the patient is able to recognize and deal objectively with these problems. When the tensions are decreased, the insomnia can be controlled. Here, too, the imagination plays an important role. Patients are instructed that the harder they try to fall asleep, the less chance they will have of doing so, and that lack of sleep seldom produces harm, but that worry wreaks more havoc than lack of sleep. Following the law of reverse effect, the posthypnotic suggestions must be directed *toward the need to keep awake!* The harder they try to remain awake, the more they will fall asleep. Adjunctive procedures such as regular hours for going to sleep, mild exercise to induce fatigue, hot drinks, and warm baths are helpful for promoting relaxation. Barbiturates and other drugs should not be removed at once but reduced gradually. Environmental factors such as noise must also be eradicated.

More specifically, hypnosis can be directed to symptom removal as follows: "At first you might consider the possibility of deliberately trying to keep awake; that is, do *not* try to fall asleep but, rather, imagine that you must stay awake as long as possible. Thus you can imagine that you are an airplane spotter and that it is necessary to screen all unusual sounds you hear. You will notice that it will become increasingly difficult to stay awake, and that sleep will gradually come over you.

"Next, sleep can be facilitated by 'stepping out of yourself.' In a dream you can see yourself performing all sorts of tasks, can you not? Thus, during hypnosis, you can also stand alongside the bed and see yourself there with your eyes closed. As you look at yourself, you can notice your breathing getting slower, deeper, and more regular, the rhythmic rise and fall of your chest, and the relaxed expression on your face. And as you keep looking at this image of yourself, you will become very, very relaxed. Very, very relaxed. As long as you keep your arms and legs in a nice, comfortable position, you will find that every muscle is relaxing more and more, and with every breath you will get very drowsy. And as you get very, very drowsy, you will find that even though your eyes remain tightly closed, you will get sleepier and sleepier."

In general, one must minimize the importance of sleep and reverse the patient's fears by suggesting that he remain *awake* and that the harder he tries to keep awake, the deeper he will get. Also, one can use strong suggestions that the hypnotic relaxation will merge with true sleep. Where hypnosis is not successful, intensive psychotherapy is indicated.

NARCOTIC ADDICTION

Drug addiction involves many of the psychological factors that account for chronic alcoholism and obesity. In general, there are three types. In the first, the addict attempts to meet stressful situations with more equanimity through the use of drugs. In the second, individuals use drugs to give them a "lift." In the third, the addict requires drugs to help to overcome depressive reactions due to characterologic disorders.

Regardless of the method of addiction, drugs are utilized to provide approval from others, security, and self-esteem. Initially, though physiologic gratification is all important, emotional satisfaction plays an even larger role. Eventually

physical cravings create a fear in the addict that he needs his drug in order to survive.

Addicts are usually unable to cope with or adjust to the demands of society. Many feel inadequate and inferior even though they present a facade of arrogance and confidence. They also manifest strong dependency strivings and succumb to peer pressures. Van Nuys posits a relationship between drug use and hypnotizability.[39] However, this is not a causal one. Rather, as Josephine Hilgard has theorized, there may be a connection between hypnotizability and those she classifies as "mental space travelers"—those who seek excitement through adventures of the mind.[15]

Therapy should be directed toward restoration of self-confidence, elimination of despondency, induction of well-being, and, in all instances, rehabilitation to prevent recidivism. Most methods of psychiatric rehabilitation yield poor results, since addicts generally return to their old environment.

On the whole, the results with hypnosis in narcotic addiction have been poor. Many addicts have well-established, conditioned pain-pattern syndromes, and it is difficult for such persons to give up the drug even temporarily. Therapy is more likely to achieve results, if employed in an institution where withdrawal symptoms can be handled and where the addict can be kept under strict supervision. Even then, however, many relapse after release and return to their drug habits. Sedatives, hypnotics, and narcotics help to control withdrawal symptoms. Long-term effects of methadone therapy (for "controlled" addicts) are ineffective; one habit is merely traded for another. Furthermore, withdrawal from methadone is more difficult than from heroin.

Autohypnosis is helpful for withstanding disagreeable sensations produced by withdrawal. Posthypnotic suggestions and deep relaxation help to countercondition anxiety and allay nervousness and insomnia. Other posthypnotic suggestions of an aversive nature can often reduce the craving for the drug. Narcotic addicts show increased susceptibility to suggestion.[40] However, lack of motivation, together with a weak personality structure, accounts for the poor results in most cases.

Behavior therapy and sensory-imagery conditioning in which the addict imagines that he is giving himself an injection or taking a drug by mouth while under autohypnosis often affords gratifying results.[22] When individuals can actually revivify the pleasurable effects afforded by the drug, withdrawal is accomplished more readily. In general, particular attention must be paid to the individual who has the addiction problem rather than to the symptom! Treatment by any method cannot be considered successful until craving has been abolished permanently. The methods for handling narcotic addicts by group psychotherapy under hypnosis have been described.[10] Ludwig and co-workers use a very authoritative approach with narcotic addicts.[28] Results of their study indicated that psychological factors played an important role in the narcotic drug experience and the drug abstinence state. A psychodynamic approach to understand the meaning of the symptom in the patient's psyche also has been stressed.[6]

Nelson and Nelson have described a method using three phases of therapy in drug detoxification:[30, 32]

1. The motivational phase requires that primary motivation exists.

2. During the "physical withdrawal" phase, therapists work around the clock for 3 days. This intensive approach is designed to lessen, but not to alleviate, the experienced pain.

3. The "personality reconstruction" phase begins after discharge from the hospital and consists of "reprogramming" the individual for reentry into society, including ego-strengthening, relief of tension, and counseling.

Other practitioners have treated heroin addiction with aversion therapy, relaxation training, and systematic desensitization.[27, 34, 35] A classical aversive conditioning procedure, employing electric shock and verbal imaginal stimuli, was used to extinguish the intense cravings resulting from heroin addiction. Progressive relaxation replaced drug-induced relaxation. The systematic desensitization approach counteracted the profound anxiety instituted by the consummatory response of heroin addiction.

The original concept of a biological drive in the heroin addict—"tissue dependency"—can no longer be equated with addiction. The former is a neurophysiological state which follows cessation of the drug and is self-limited; here the brief use of drugs is indicated. If, on the other hand, the addiction is due to behavioral disorders characterized by a compulsive and overwhelming preoccupation with using the drug, then the attitudes must be altered by a sophisticated therapeutic approach wherein hypnosis and behavior modification can change the behavior, provided the patients are highly motivated.

Management of heroin addiction by substitution therapy, such as methadone maintenance, has not been scientifically validated. The treatment program may foster an iatrogenic drug dependency which is very often worse than the initial addiction. Any benefit derived from methadone maintenance is not solely from its "blocking effect," but also from the interpersonal relationship and the potential for this human interaction to alter behavior. This applies to the abuse of drugs such as amphetamines, methaqualone, and barbiturates—these are more psychologically habituating than physically addicting. Success is increased if the tensions requiring the drug are identified and corrected.

Newton has used hypnorelaxation to relieve psychosomatic withdrawal symptoms in heroin addicts.* Three other procedures also were devised to deal directly with behavior relating to the use of drugs. One procedure consisted of having the hypnotized patient imagine himself using heroin and obtaining no effect from the fix. He was given posthypnotic suggestions to lead him to believe that the drug trip was of no value to him. Another posthypnotic suggestion was given that he remember this fantasied experience whenever the urge to have a fix occurred. A second procedure involved a hypnotic fantasy in which the patient's preparation for self-injection was paired with increasingly threatening stimuli, such as rats, spiders, and snakes. These aversive stimuli disappeared when the addict imagined himself completely rejecting the proposed drug experience. The final procedure dealt with hypnotically induced fantasies in which the addict imagined himself in situations that usually were resolved by injecting drugs. In these tenuous situations, the

---

*Newton, B.: Personal communication.

addicts imagined themselves declaring that they would not use heroin. This declaration during the imagery was immediately followed with a very rewarding and satisfying fantasy experience. The posthypnotic suggestion, in essence, was that whenever the patient found himself in these situations and had the urge to have a fix, he would imagine himself refusing the fix and then reward himself with the satisfying sequence.

The author firmly believes that no psychiatrist, regardless of his skill and experience and the particular therapy used, can manage a patient who takes drugs against the psychiatrist's prohibition and express orders. If the patient takes drugs which elevate or depress his moods, the problem becomes even more insoluble. Physicians who prescribe these drugs for other medical problems without obtaining a psychometric profile of the patient, or even determining if the patient is under psychiatric care, should be taken to task.

Every form of psychiatric help requires regular visits by the patient—to the degree that the psychiatrist determines and informs the patient. The willingness of the patient to cooperate can be determined by his meeting the schedule of appointments with the doctor. The psychiatrist attempting to help self-destructive patients often is faced with decisions which on one hand may have a short-term benefit and on the other may destroy the patient's trust in him, which is the essential ingredient necessary to continue therapy. The focus on a patient's rights has created a different perspective on consent to psychiatric hospitalization. Such a procedure often is difficult without the patient's informed consent.

Custodial care is not the end sought by psychiatrists. Such an objective suggests the elimination of hope for a functioning patient. We must accept the risks for allowing a patient who is functioning in his job or profession to continue to do so as an essential element in his road back to mental health.

REFERENCES

1. Abrams, S.: An evaluation of hypnosis in the treatment of alcoholics. Am. J. Psychiatry, *120:*1160, 1964.
2. Athanasou, T.A.: Smoking behavior and its modification through hypnosis: a review and evaluation. Aust. J. Med. Sophrol. Hypnother., *2:*4, 1974.
3. Bernstein, D.A.: Modification of smoking behavior: an evaluative review. Psychol. Bull., *71:*418, 1969.
4. Cohen, S.B.: Hypnosis and smoking. J.A.M.A., *208:*335, 1969.
5. Crasilneck, H.B., and Hall, J.A.: The use of hypnosis in controlling cigarette smoking. South. Med. J., *61:*999, 1968.
6. _____: Clinical Hypnosis: Principles and Applications. New York, Grune & Stratton, 1975.
7. Dengrove, E.: A single-treatment method to stop smoking using ancillary self-hypnosis: discussion. Int. J. Clin. Exp. Hypn., *18:*251, 1970.
8. Edwards, G.: Hypnosis in treatment of alcohol addiction: controlled trial, with an analysis of factors affecting outcome. Q.J. Stud. Alcohol, *27:*221, 1966.
9. Feamster, J.H., and Brown, J.E.: Hypnotic aversion to alcohol: three-year follow-up of one patient. Am. J. Clin. Hypn., *6:*164, 1963.
10. Fox, J.: The systematic use of hypnosis in individual and group psychotherapy. Int. J. Clin. Exp. Hypn., *8:*109, 1960.
11. Fox, R.: Psychiatric aspects of alcoholism. Am. J. Psychother., *19:*408, 1965.
12. Granone, F.: Hypnotism in the treatment of chronic alcoholism. J. Am. Inst. Hypn., *12:*32, 1971.
13. Hall, J.A. and Crasilneck, H.B.: Development of a hypnotic technique for treating chronic cigarette smoking. Int. J. Clin. Exp. Hypn., *18:*290, 1970.
14. Hartman, B.J.: Hypnotic susceptibility in chronic alcoholics. J. Natl. Med. Assoc., *58:*197, 1966.
15. Hilgard, J.R.: Personality and hypnotizability: inferences from case studies. *In* Hilgard, E.R. (ed): Hypnotic Susceptibility. New York, Harcourt, Brace and World, 1965.
16. Hoskovec, J.: A review of some major works on Soviet hypnotherapy. Int. J. Clin. Exp. Hypn., *15:*1, 1967.
17. Jackson, J.A.: Editorial. Aust. J. Med. Sophrol. Hypnother., *2:*2, 1974.
18. Johnston, E., and Donoghue, J.R.: Hypnosis and smoking: A review of the literature. Am. J. Clin. Hypn., *13:*265, 1971.
19. King, A.: The Cigarette Habit. New York, Doubleday, 1959.
20. Kline, M.V.: The use of extended group hypnotherapy sessions in controlling cigarette habituation. Int. J. Clin. Exp. Hypn., *18:*270, 1970.
21. Kroger, W.S.: The conditioned reflex treatment of alcoholism. J.A.M.A., *120:*714, 1942.
22. Kroger, W.S., and Fezler, W.D.: Hypnosis and

Behavior Modification. Philadelphia, J.B. Lippincott, 1976.

23. Kroger, W.S., and Libott, R.Y.: Thanks, Doctor, I've Stopped Smoking: A Modern Doctor-Patient Approach to Smoking Control. Springfield, Ill., Charles C Thomas, 1967.

24. Langen, D.: Modern hypnotic treatment of various forms of addiction, in particular, alcoholism. Br. J. Addict, *62:*77, 1967.

25. Lemere, F.: Psychotherapy of alcoholism. J.A.M.A., *171:*106, 1959.

26. Lenox, J.R., and Bonny, H.: The hypnotizability of chronic alcoholics. Int. J. Clin. Exp. Hypn., *24:* 419, 1976.

27. Liebson, I., and Bigelow, G.: A behavioral-pharmacological treatment of dually addicted patients. Behav. Res. Ther., *10:*403, 1972.

28. Ludwig, A.M., et al.: Group hypnotherapy techniques with drug addicts. Int. J. Clin. Exp. Hypn., *12:*53, 1964.

29. Miller, M.M.: Hypno-aversion treatment of nicotinism. J. Natl. Med. Assoc., *56:*480, 1965.

30. ———: Treatment of chronic alcoholism by hypnotic aversion. J.A.M.A., *171:*164, 1959.

31. Moses, F.M.: Treating the smoking habit by discussion and hypnosis. Dis. Nerv. Syst., *25:*185, 1964.

32. Nelson, G.R., and Nelson, M.: The psychology of hypnotic drug detoxification. J. Am. Soc. Psychosomat. Dent. Med., *22:*44, 1975.

33. Nuland, W., and Field, P.B.: Smoking and hypnosis: a systematic clinical approach. Int. J. Clin. Exp. Hypn., *18:*290, 1970.

34. O'Brien, J.S., et al: Treatment of heroin addiction with aversion therapy, relaxation training and systematic desensitization. Behav. Res. Ther., *10:*77, 1972.

35. Raymond, M.J.: The treatment of addiction by aversion conditioning with apomorphine. Behav. Res. Ther., *1:*287, 1964.

36. Rose, G.: Giving up smoking: how the various programs work. Med. World News, *17:*53, November 1, 1976.

37. Spiegel, H.: A single-treatment method to stop smoking using ancillary self-hypnosis. Int. J. Clin. Exp. Hypn., *18:*235, 1970.

38. Stein, C.A.: Displacement and reconditioning technique for compulsive smokers. Int. J. Clin. Exp. Hypn., *12:*230, 1964.

39. Van Nuys, D.W.: Drug use and hypnotic susceptibility. Int. J. Clin. Exp. Hypn., *20:*31, 1972.

40. Vogel, V.H.: Clinical studies of drug addiction: Suggestibility in narcotic addicts. Public Health Rep. Suppl., *127:*1, 1937.

41. Von Dedenroth, T.E.: The use of hypnosis in 1000 cases of "tobaccomaniacs." Am. J. Clin. Hypn., *3:* 194, 1968.

42. Wallerstein, R.S.: Hospital Treatment of Alcoholism. New York, Basic Books, 1958.

43. Watkins, H.H.: Hypnosis and smoking: a five session approach. Int. J. Clin. Exp. Hypn., *24:*381, 1976.

44. Wolberg, L.: Medical Hypnosis. vol. 1. New York, Grune & Stratton, 1948.

45. Wright, M.E.: A single-treatment method to stop smoking using ancillary self-hypnosis: discussion. Int. J. Clin. Exp. Hypn., *18:*261, 1970.

SUGGESTED READINGS

McCartney, J.L.: Hypnosis in treatment of narcotic addiction. Phi Chi Quart., *62:*140, 1965.

Vogel, V.H.: Narcotics and Narcotic Addiction. Ed. 4. Springfield, Ill., Charles C. Thomas, 1954.

Wikler, A.: Some implications of conditioning theory for problems of drug abuse. Behav. Sci., *16:*92, 1971.

46

Hypnodontics: Hypnosis in Dentistry

Aaron A. Moss, D.D.S., F.S.C.E.H.

As was mentioned in an earlier chapter, the hypnosis movement faded into oblivion for the third time as a result of Freud's abandonment of it. Two generations later, it was again "rediscovered," thus giving rise to the current resurgence, which is the fourth turn in the hypnosis cycle. At this time the United States is the world's center of activity in hypnosis. The impetus for the current resurgence is due to a few dentists, of whom the author is one, who banded together to teach the "gospel" of hypnosis at the end of World War II. Initially, only dentists were interested; later on, physicians and psychologists "joined the movement." This second wave now outnumbers the dental contingent. *However, credit is due the dentists for initiating the current widespread interest in hypnosis.*

The author coined the term hypnodontics in 1948, to signify the use of hypnosis in dentistry. This was to overcome the irrational prejudices of the lay public as well as in the dental and allied professions. The role dentists played in bringing hypnosis to the fore is as much a tribute to American dentistry as what they did in introducing general anesthesia one hundred years earlier, when Drs. Morton and Wells, both dentists, gave the first clinical demonstrations in general anesthesia. The latter, oddly enough, was introduced to nitrous oxide, or "laughing gas," during an exhibition of hypnosis in 1844 by G. Q. Colton, an itinerant chemist and hypnotist. Colton's claim to fame is that he was undoubtedly the world's first professional anesthetist. A little-known letter set forth clearly how hypnosis led to the development of anesthesia:

Colton Dental Association
19 Cooper Institute
New York, Feb. 2, 1891

Dr. I. C. Green

Dear Sir:

The only claim I have to the discovery of anesthesia is that I was the accessory of the discovery; and that I administered the nitrous oxide gas to Dr. Horace Wells of Hartford, Conn. on the 11th of December, 1844 for the first tooth that was ever extracted without pain. This was honor enough for me. The discovery was made at my exhibition (to facilitate hypnosis) of the gas the evening previous.

Yours very truly,
G. Q. Colton

DENTAL APPLICATIONS OF HYPNOSIS

What are the uses of hypnosis in dentistry? Although hypnosis can be a very dramatic way of producing anesthesia, that is notits primary or most prevalent use. If there were no other application, hypnodontics would be nothing more than a spectacular phenomenon, quite impractical for general dental application, since only a small percentage ofpeople are susceptible to complete hypnoanesthesia. Actually, there are several other areas in dentistry in which hypnosis can be applied. Space limitations permit the presentation of only a few of these applications. The uses of hypnodontics fall into two categories: therapeutic and operative.

The *therapeutic* uses of hypnodontics include:

1. Patient relaxation;
2. Elimination of the patient's tensions and anxieties, and his fears of pain and discomfort;
3. Removal of objections to necessary orthodontic or prosthetic appliances after the patient had agreed to accept them;
4. Maintenance of the patient's comfort during long, arduous periods of dental work;
5. Accustoming the patient to orthodontic or prosthetic appliances;
6. Modification of noxious dental habits.

The *operative* uses of hypnodontics include:
1. Reduction of anesthesia or analgesia;
2. Amnesia for unpleasant work;
3. Substitution for, or in combination with, premedication in general anesthesia;
4. Prevention of gagging and nausea;
5. Control of salivary flow;
6. Control of bleeding;
7. Postoperative anesthesia;
8. Reduction of postoperative shock.

TYPES OF SUGGESTION

Hypnodontics is that branch of dental science which deals with the applicatiion of controlled suggestion and/or hypnosis to the practice of dentistry.[24] Hypnodontics does not necessarily eliminate analgesia or anesthesia; rather, it is used as an adjunct to chemoanesthesia. Thus there is no danger of overemphasizing the use of hypnoanesthesia in hypnodontics.

Although the term hypnosis has been defined, the meaning of controlled suggestion needs some elaboration. The deliberate and careful feeding of a suggestion into the brain in order to accomplish a given effect is known as controlled suggestion. If the desired effect is accomplished, the suggestion is said to be realized. When a suggestion is realized, it effects the following changes:[13]

1. *Sensory change:* the hand (or any other part of the body) may feel colder or warmer, or have a tingling sensation;
2. *Motor change:* the arm may rise or float into the air; the leg may become rigid;
3. *Emotional change:* feelings of guilt, fear, or anger may be aroused;
4. *Change in ideas or beliefs:* confidence may be lost or enhanced (in the latter case, the patient develops a good rapport with his dentist).

Suggestion can be divided arbitrarily into two types: direct and indirect. A direct suggestion is one received during full awareness. It is used in the process of hypnotic induction. An indirect suggestion is one which bypasses awareness and, as a result, affects the perceptual processes subliminally; the subject is seldom aware of being exposed to the suggestion. Therefore, his responses are generally spontaneous. Since he is not aware of its origin, his defenses and resistance are not mobilized.

TESTS

Tests for hypnotic susceptibility, such as the falling back test or the handclasp test, are good examples of direct suggestion. The contagious effect of yawning after one has observed someone else doing it is an example of indirect suggestion. The individual concerned may be completely oblivious of his behavioral response to the suggestion.

HYPNODONTIC INDICATIONS AND APPLICATIONS

Does the hypnodontist apply his technics to every patient? Yes and no. This answer is contradictory and requires further explanation. For instance, hypnotic states are induced rarely and only when all other methods of dealing with the patient's problems have failed. They are used when drugs have failed to produce the desired anesthesia necessary for patient control and cooperation.[3, 5, 16, 25, 29, 31, 34]

Normally, the routine patient that comes to a hypnodontist's office is handled in only a slightly different manner from the one who goes into some other dentist's office. This slight difference consists in the routine application of hypnotic technics. The four levels or areas in which hypnodontics may be applied are controlled suggestion and light, deep, and waking hypnotic suggestion.

CONTROLLED SUGGESTION

In the dentist's office, controlled suggestion is applied constantly in both direct and indirect forms. In attempting to win a patient's confidence, the office personnel's choice of words is of the utmost importance. Mannerisms and the general office atmosphere constitute suggestions of prime significance.

The dentist's personality and appearance are also of tremendous importance in establishing the patient's confidence. For instance, the patient would doubt the dentist's ability to remove the decay from a tooth or the infection from a socket if he had dirty fingernails or soiled gown. Negative conditioning on the part of the dentist initiate powerful negative suggestions in the patient, making him mistrust the dentist. More often than not, the patient is not even aware of the fact that such indirect suggestions are affecting him. Thus he may reject the dentist's recommendations by rationalizing that the fees are too high.

Other less obvious but equally negative suggestions are not washing one's hands after answering the telephone; handling a soiled handkerchief, coughing into it or picking an object off the floor; being late for appointments; not properly organizing office routine; fumbling for instruments, charts, etc.

The application of hypnodontics to an office routine implies the administration of as many positive indirect suggestions as possible, such as instruction in proper toothbrushing technics and giving the patient a mirror to verify that all the decay has been removed from his tooth. These steps indicate to the patient that the dentist is interested in and concerned about his welfare.

Thus, by carefully controlled, positive indirect suggestion, confidence can be established and good rapport developed between dentist and patient. Persons interested in practice management and business administration can learn much from this phase of hypnodontics.

LIGHT HYPNOSIS

Another application of hypnodontics is the use of direct suggestion in producing light hypnosis to facilitate relaxation. In this state, the patient is amenable to suggestions directed to the lessening of tensions and the building of confidence. It takes only 5 or 10 minutes to achieve relaxation by means of direct suggestion. Since this type of hypnosis is not intended to produce anesthesia, conventional analgesic drugs may be used if necessary. This phase of hypnosis is used the most frequently.

There are several advantages to hypnorelaxation: it consumes relatively little time, it is successful in over 80 per cent of the cases, and the patient retains full awareness. Controlled relaxation, attained by the application of hypnotic technics, effectively influences the frightened dental patient whose pain threshold has been lowered as the result of negative emotions.

DEEP HYPNOSIS

Deep hypnosis is used when medication is contraindicated or when drugs alone or drugs in combination with light hypnosis are ineffectual. Generally the time element involved in producing a deep hypnotic state and the fact that less than 20 per cent of patients are susceptible make it impractical for use as a routine procedure. However, once somnambulism has been induced, it takes but a few minutes to reestablish it at the next appointment. Most dentists have the misconception that those who use hypnosis apply the deep state to every patient that comes to their offices.

Hypnotic or direct suggestion is used by some dentists to correct certain objectionable dental habits such as nail-biting, thumb-sucking, and bruxism (grinding of teeth). This involves psychotherapy and *should therefore be practiced only in conjunction with a psychotherapist or a physician.* Hypnodontics may also be used to condition patients to wear dentures that fit well but which cause gagging for psychological reasons. These cases are not very common, yet there are instances in which a light state is generally effective.

CONTRAINDICATIONS FOR HYPNODONTICS

The author would like to sound a strong warning to dentists using hypnosis: *Hypnodontics should not be abused by the dental profession.* The dentist using hypnosis has the means at his disposal of probing into the emotional problems of an individual. Even with limited experience, he can produce such characteristic phenomena of hypnosis as age regression, revivification, negative and positive sensory hallucinations, catalepsy, and automatic writing. These phenomena *lie in the highly specialized fields of either psychotherapy or experimental psychology,* and the training, the experience, and the background of a dentist *do not qualify* him for this work! This does not mean that the dentist should hesitate to use hypnosis in his work. Hypnosis can be a very valuable instrument in his hands as can a lancet, but having the legal and moral right to use it does not entitle him to remove an appendix with it. The dentist, as well as the physician, has an ethical and moral obligation to his patients to borrow knowledge from all fields of science to alleviate pain, suffering and discomfort, and to improve the general welfare of mankind. Because of this, the dentist should avail himself of hypnosis and apply it to his dental practice. Therefore, he should make judicious use of the lancet and the hypnotic technic, which, like anesthesia and drugs, are instruments that belong to the dentist's as well as to the physician's armamentarium.

LIMITATIONS OF HYPNODONTICS

The hypnodontist should understand enough basic psychology or psychiatry to realize the fact that he is dealing with a complex tool. He must avoid exceeding his competence in using hypnosis for medical or nondental purposes. For instance, he should not attempt to cure the smoking habit, which may be a manifestation of tension and serve as an outlet for the release of nervous energy. He must know that smoking, like thumb-sucking, constipation, headache, or inferiority feelings, is often the result of many hidden, powerful emotional forces. The removal of a habit, even by the trained psychotherapist, without "trading down" to a less noxious symptom, may throw the entire psyche of a deeply disturbed person into confusion and imbalance.

The untrained therapist may be satisfied with the dramatic and forceful removal of a symptom, but the sophisticated one knows that a permissive approach, preferably by autohypnosis, will prevent the appearance of other symptoms which

sometimes can constitute a powerful threat to the entire personality structure. Symptom removal by such measures does not have a traumatic effect and is in sharp contradistinction to the authoritative "bull in a china shop" hypnotic approach.

Psychodental therapy, however, is strictly within the province of dentistry. The elimination of fear and anxiety associated with drilling and surgery has been a constant problem for dentists. When necessary, the dentist has resorted to drugs such as sedatives, and to premedication. Hypnosis is an extremely useful substitute for these.

The elimination of fear and apprehension is difficult, owing to the deeply ingrained conviction that these are the concomitants of dental work. It is hard to convince a person that he will not have pain when all his life's experience tells him otherwise. Because the oral cavity is a very important erotogenic zone and all parts of it have great psychic importance, it may be that exposing these areas to the manipulation of another individual could have a highly disturbing emotional significance to many individuals. It is from these roots that fear and anxiety may spring. The extraction of teeth, for instance, may be associated with punishment, masochism, or even castration. The patient is not aware of this; however, the hypnodontist should be.

Because of these facts, one cannot possibly remove or even reduce fear in all patients, but it is possible to remove all fear in some people, and some fear in most people. More than one session may be required to accomplish this. Before dental work is started, perhaps two or three sessions should be devoted to hypnosis for the removal of fear. Severely emotionally disturbed individuals, particularly, require extra time and effort. As to the time factor, once fear and anxiety have been eliminated via hypnosis, or hypnoanesthesia has been produced, a hypnotic state can be induced almost instantaneously in all subsequent sessions.

HYPNODONTIC PROCEDURES

For didactic purposes, the hypnodontic procedure is divided into seven steps:
1. Mind-set (indoctrination);
2. Testing;
3. Induction;

4. Deepening;

5. Utilization (operation);

6. Posthypnotic suggestions;

7. Dehypnotization (termination).

1. *Mind-set.* Mind-set is the procedure used to accomplish a state of receptivity or cooperation on the part of the patient. This is done in several ways, as described in Chapter 11, but primarily via a preliminary conversation before the use of any hypnotic procedures. The object of this step is to correct the subject's previous misconceptions or inaccurate ideas about the hypnotic state. Only in this way can good cooperation and proper motivation be obtained.

2. *Testing.* Certain tests, already described in detail, are utilized to determine the patient's susceptibility to hypnosis. Frequently, these may constitute the first stage of induction into hypnosis. There are many who consider it unwise to make tests for susceptibility in actual clinical practice. It is the author's opinion that all patients should be considered susceptible unless actual experience proves otherwise.

3. *Induction.* There are many procedures used to induce hypnosis. Hypnotic mechanical aids may be employed, although, as a rule, verbal suggestions can accomplish the same results. Certain rotating spirals on a dental engine can be used as a hypnotic aid. The brain wave synchronizer is another aid. For a dentist, the ordinary pen light on the dental unit is as effective an aid as any, when used in conjunction with the *eye-fixation* technic. Induction may be *direct* or *indirect.* The direct method is used when the subject is aware that hypnosis is being employed. The indirect method implies the use of subterfuge; that is, the subject is prevented from becoming aware that hypnosis is being used. It is also known as a *hidden approach* in contrast with the *open approach,* in which direct hypnosis is used with the subject's awareness.

4. *Deepening.* Although it may take only a few minutes to induce a light hypnotic state, it may require several sessions to deepen it to the level at which it is compatible with the purpose for which hypnosis is being used. One of the commonest reasons for lack of success is failure to deepen the hypnotic state to one consistent with the requirements for Step 5. Step 4 requires training, patience, perseverance, and experienced judgment.

5. *Utilization.* The purposes for which hypnosis is to be used may vary widely. For example, the purpose for which the obstetrician uses it may be entirely different from that of the psychotherapist.

6. *Posthypnotic Suggestions.* Posthypnotic suggestions, in addition to making it easier and quicker to induce hypnosis at subsequent sittings, are used also for therapeutic dental purposes, as previously mentioned. At the final hypnotic session, the operator always gives the posthypnotic suggestion to the patient that in the future no one but a physician, a dentist, or a qualified psychologist will be able to place him in a hypnotic state. This procedure, called *locking the "unconscious,"* is a precaution against the patient's being exploited by a parlor or stage hypnotist for entertainment. The author is aware that some feel that this is not successful for the purpose intended; he takes issue with this view.

7. *Dehypnotization.* It is important that no patient be permitted to leave the office unless he is completely and fully coordinated. More about this will be said later in this chapter.

HYPNODONTIC TECHNICS

The following technic lends itself very adequately to producing relaxation prior to a dental operation. It is not dependent on somnambulism and, therefore, it has a wide range of success. It may be presented to the patient in such a manner that the words hypnosis, trance, and sleep are never mentioned.

The patient is seated comfortably, with eyes fixed on a given spot slightly forward and upward. There should be no strain on any part of the body; the hands are unclasped, resting comfortably in the lap. Instruct the patient to close his eyes when he feels like it and to keep them closed. The exact verbalization for *patient relaxation via hypnotic induction* is as follows (Step 1 and Step 2 are omitted):

I will teach you to relax. You will relax not only your body, but your mind as well. . . . When I pick up your right (or left) hand, let it fall limp. (Pick up one hand.) No, you've helped. Let your hand fall limp as though it were without any power or life, like the hand of a rag doll. Do not help or anticipate. (Try again and again until the hand and the arm are completely relaxed. This may take from 3 to 5 minutes, but it is absolutely necessary to accomplish complete relaxation before proceeding. Be patient and persevering. Then continue.) Breathe in deeply and relax your diaphragm. . . . Again. (This must be done five or six times in unison with the patient's breathing. Hyperventilation of the lungs will tend to relax mind and body.) Now, relax your feet and legs the same way as you did your hands. Make them very, very heavy. You'll probably find a very pleasant, tingling, relaxed feeling in your toes. It will travel through the soles of your feet, up your legs, to your abdomen and chest. (Pause.) Take another deep breath and relax your diaphragm still more. . . . Again. . . . Now relax your lower jaw . . . more . . . relax your cheeks. (By this time, the eyes are usually closed. If they are not, continue as follows.) Now your eyes are very tired and heavy. They are closing, closing, closing. (The eyes will then close.) Remove the wrinkles from your forehead and relax more. Let only my voice reach you. Drift pleasantly into a pleasing state of relaxation as you hear my voice. (Now give three suggestions, repeating each several times.)

1. You will remain relaxed as you are with eyes closed for 2 minutes. I'll inform you when the time is up.

2. When you open your eyes, you will be fully alert but completely relaxed and full of confidence for your dental appointment.

3. Each time, when you come back for your dental appointment, you will relax quickly and deeply with this method.

(After about 1½ minutes, dehypnotize the patient, using the following words:) When I count 3, you will open your eyes and be completely relaxed, feeling fine: 1 . . . 2 . . . 3. (If the patient does not open his eyes immediately, do not become alarmed, but repeat the above suggestions about 3 minutes later. Never show alarm or anxiety at slow dehypnotization.)

The above technic may be used routinely on all tense patients, provided, of course, that they will cooperate. It has some degree of success in over 80 per cent of cases. The technic is not spectacular, yet one will hear the following comment from the patient: "I feel very relaxed, but I was not hypnotized." The answer should be: "It was not the intent to hypnotize you but only to relax you." This should always be done prior to the operation, and the patient should be completely out of hypnosis before any dental work is attempted, the technic being intended for use as a substitution for or in conjunction with premedication.

HYPNODONTICS IN ADAPTATION TO PROSTHETIC DEVICES

Another use of dental hypnotherapy is in the conditioning of a patient to wear a prosthetic or orthodontic appliance. This is accomplished by giving him, while in hypnosis, positive, firm, posthypnotic suggestions that he will have no difficulty in becoming accustomed to the appliance. In this connection, there are times when it may be necessary to question the patient under hypnosis to get at the root of the problem. This is not recommended for the dentist, as he should realize that certain dental symptoms may ramify into the field of psychotherapy, and he should evaluate the advisability of using hypnosis accordingly. If direct suggestions are applied in several sessions, good results can frequently be obtained. But if the patient stubbornly persists in retaining his symptom, the case should be referred to a qualified psychotherapist.

HYPNODONTICS FOR BRUXISM

Most patients with chronic bruxism are under marked tension and loaded with inhibited rage and aggression. These areas must be alleviated by a psychologically trained individual. The symptom itself can be controlled by teaching the patient self-hypnosis. Each time he finds himself clenching his teeth during the night, he is to pair the clenching with a relaxing scene. The latter, with repetition and reinforcement, will eventually countercondition the bruxism. A case of bruxism has been reported that was reversed when she was regressed to a bus crash which precipitated her teeth-grinding.[14]

CONTROL OF BLEEDING

Dentists claim that bleeding can be controlled. However, the reports, though impressive, are anecdotal and poorly designed studies.[11, 14, 19, 27]

Crasilneck and Fogelman showed that there were not differences in the clotting time in hypnotized and nonhypnotized dental patients.[8] However, they admit that their experimental design did not measure the small capillaries. Hypnosis has been suggested as an ancillary measure in hemophilia —an approach that is certainly worth trying. Lucas and co-workers, and Lucas and Tocantins combined protective splints and packing of the sockets in 114 extractions in 24 hemophiliacs without the need for transfusions.[20, 21] La Baw has used hypnosis in hemophilia.[18] He notes the adverse effect of anxiety on blood coagulation and fibrinolytic activity. Bleeders are chronically anxious. Hypnosis reduces the anxiety and, as a result, the morbidity. Less blood was needed than in a control series. Fredericks reported two cases in which hypnosis was helpful.[12]

TONGUE THRUST AND SWALLOWING

Tongue thrust and swallowing often are refractory to all kinds of therapy; hypnosis has been recommended for control of these habit patterns.[9] Other investigators discuss swallowing difficulties and other psychophysiologic manifestations.[10] Many tongue thrusters are unable to be quiet while eating. Most have malocclusion. Barrett and von Dedenroth reported on 25 cases treated successfully with hypnosis in one to four sessions.[2]

HYPNODONTICS IN ANESTHESIA

The use of hypnosis in conjunction with, or as a substitute for, premedication prior to general anesthesia is quite a common practice today among medical anesthesiologists. Raginsky mentions that fear of anesthesia may be due to fear of loss of consciousness, or mutilation, of loss of life, or of the unknown.[28] He states that it results in change in blood pressure, heart rate, capillary permeability, urinary output, coronary flow, rate and depth of respiration, and carbon dioxide content of the blood. He writes:

He [the anesthesiologist] must learn the structure or normal personality, and see how and to what degree the patient to be anesthetized deviates from that of the normal. With this knowledge [hypnosis] he can quiet the patient more effectively, use much less of the anesthetic agent and have a smoother induction.

When this was written in 1948, the thought of offering hypnosis as part of the training and background of the anesthesiologist was far-fetched and remote. Today, this training has become routine for many anesthesiologists. If possible, the dentist, like the anesthesiologist, should see his patient several days before the scheduled operative procedure and begin the initial induction so that, by the time the patient reaches the office on the day of the operation, he may receive the full benefits of previous hypnotic conditioning. This brings about lessening of fear and anxiety, which results in less and easier anesthetic induction if it should be necessary. The element of safety is thus an outstanding feature in the use of hypnosis in conjunction with general anesthesia.

ELIMINATION OF GAG REFLEX

An important application of hypnosis is in eliminating the gag reflex which is so frequently a nuisance to the dentist. It is not necessary to place the patient under hypnosis for this purpose, because the elimination of gagging can be accomplished exceptionally well by *waking hypnotic suggestion.* The author and other dentists to whom he has taught this technic have had most gratifying results. The following technic is used for eliminating gagging reflex via waking hypnotic suggestion, for taking x-rays or impressions:

Stand in front of the patient and direct him to keep his gaze fixed continuously on your eyes during the entire procedure. Should his gaze wander, call this to his attention and start again from the beginning. Fix your own gaze on the bridge of the subject's nose. *Do not stare into his eyes.* Say:

1. "I am going to eliminate your gag reflex by instructing you in breathing exercises. You must keep your gaze fixed on my eyes at all times."

2. "Take a deep breath and hold it while I count to 5. 1, 2, 3, 4, 5. Now relax."

3. Repeat Step 2, never allowing the patient's gaze to wander.

4. "Now I have eliminated your gag reflex." Say firmly, with conviction, "You will not be able to gag. You may try as hard as you can *but you will not be able*

to gag." The patient's gaze must not be allowed to wander until the entire suggestion in Step 4 is completed.

5. "You may now relax, and *you will not gag* while I take your impressions (x-rays)."

6. The previous 5 steps should be repeated, after saying, "To make sure that you will not gag, I shall repeat the entire procedure once more." Continue Steps 1 through 5 and proceed to take the impressions (x-rays).

The success of this procedure is largely dependent on the strength of the operator's conviction. If it is weak and without firmness, the incidence of success diminishes.

This technic will be found quite adequate for taking roentgenograms or impressions; it will not be effective in eliminating gagging or nausea due to the wearing of dentures. The latter requires a more intensive approach. First and foremost, it must be ascertained that the dentures are well constructed and properly fitted. After this is ascertained, posthypnotic suggestions should be given which are aimed at helping the patient to use the dentures for twice the period that he was able to use them heretofore before gagging or nausea took place. For example, if the patient reported in his original interview that he could wear the denture for only 10 minutes, then the posthypnotic instruction should be, "You will find that upon coming out of hypnosis you will have no difficulty in keeping your denture comfortably in position for 20 minutes. You will repeat this on the hour daily, and report to me in 3 days." After the patient returns and is again hypnotized, the time is increased to 30 minutes, or perhaps 35. He is to repeat this every hour and a half. It will be found that, with this technic, at least 50 per cent of all denture gaggers either can be entirely improved or at least helped. It is important to take a very thorough history before using hypnosis.

It is inadvisable for the dentist who made the denture to treat the gagger. It is better to refer him to another "neutral" or disinterested dentist. When it is known that the patient is a gagger, dentures should not be constructed or even impressions made until after several therapeutic hypnotic sessions. These can save considerable time and trouble. In preventive hypnosis, however, it is acceptable for the dentist doing the prosthetic work also to perform the hypnosis. When failure to eliminate gagging via hypnosis occurs, it is advisable to refer the patient to a psychotherapist for further treatment. The symptom may be related to a deep-seated neurosis.

If the dentist uses hypnosis in this fashion for the treatment of gagging or of any other noxious habit, he is well within the limits of his field. Dangers are insignificant if the dentist does not resort to probing of the "unconscious." A clinical follow-up of failures referred to a psychotherapist has shown that half of the cases have successful outcomes. In other words, it may safely be said that with proper management, three out of every four patients can be safely cured of denture gagging or nausea (50% by the dentist and 25% by the psychotherapist).

Other practitioners have employed hypnosis to reduce the gag reflex with some modicum of success.[1, 4, 6, 30, 33] Often direct suggestions without hypnosis may be helpful. Ament used desensitization, reciprocal inhibition, operant conditioning, and time distortion on groups of patients with gagging due to dentures.[1]

CONTROL OF SALIVATION

Control of the flow of saliva can be achieved by hypnotic means,[17] since the autonomic nervous system is subject to volitional control. It is possible, in the experimental laboratory, to bring about (through hypnotic suggestion) vasoconstriction or vasodilation of peripheral blood vessels and to produce blushing or even blanching of a hand or a face. It is therefore not surprising that the flow of saliva can be affected in the same way. The advantages for the dentist are obvious. Fortunately, a patient need not be in very deep hypnosis to obtain this control. The salivary flow not only can be influenced during hypnosis but for a reasonable time thereafter by means of posthypnotic suggestion.

PREINDUCTION PROCEDURES

Because of the existing prejudices among the public, the method of suggesting hypnosis to the patient is of paramount importance. If the nature of the hypnotic phenomenon is not properly presented, the patient may refuse to undergo induction. Sometimes prejudices are so deeply rooted that, even with the proper approach, consent to hypnosis cannot be obtained. There are two ways of handling such resistance: the direct technic and the indirect (disguised) technic.

DIRECT TECHNIC

With the direct technic, the patient is told, either by the dentist himself or by his assistant, of the many advantages of hypnodontics. It may be helpful for him to observe another patient being operated on while in a hypnotic state. The role of the dental assistant is of great importance and, in many instances, by a careful approach, she can induce the patient to request hypnosis even without the dentist's having suggested it. Pamphlets or brochures on hypnosis may be placed carefully in the reception room. A patient should never be forced to accept hypnosis. Jacoby has used taped instructions on over 300 patients.[15]

INDIRECT TECHNIC

In the disguised approach, nothing is told to the patient which would make him aware that he is about to be hypnotized. He is told simply that he is being taught to relax and that he should make himself comfortable and let his arms and legs become loose and heavy. It is explained that in a relaxed state the threshold of pain is markedly raised, and also that fear and apprehension can be lessened if he remains completely relaxed physically and mentally. Through these means, using the technic previously described for waking relaxation, he is gradually brought into hypnosis. The patient is then unaware that he has been hypnotized. While such a method is usually successful, it must be understood that a patient might realize what is transpiring and become resentful. This can result in a bad relationship.

AUDIO-ANALGESIA TECHNIC

In discussing the disguised or indirect technic of hypnosis induction, it behooves the author to include two additional "non-hypnotic" technics of producing anesthesia and relaxation in dentistry. Reference has already been made to the first, namely, the use of nitrous oxide. The other technic, known as *audio-analgesia,* was in vogue some years ago. Although most advocates of the latter technic may be unaware of the underlying principle, namely, the state of hypnosis or suggestion, as the reason for its success, it is the opinion of the author that both these technics lean heavily on the disguised technic of hypnosis. This is not written with the intent of denying the strong analgesic or anesthetic action of the nitrous oxide gas. Rather, it is intended to point out that in many instances the anesthesia which might be attributed to the gas is due partly or solely to the effect of hypnosis or suggestion.

At a meeting of the American Analgesic Society in New York City, attended by about 100 dentists, the author, who was the clinician for the evening, asked for a show of hands of all those who had, at one time or another, obtained all the effects of nitrous oxide analgesia without actually administering the gas, either because of an oversight or deliberately. At least a third of those present raised their hands, indicating that they had obtained positive analgesic effects when the patient thought he was getting the nitrous oxide, while in reality he was inhaling only atmospheric air. The conclusions are quite obvious. The author has no doubt that the sounds coming through to the patient by means of the audio-analgesia set-up have the same psychological effects in producing anesthesia and relaxation in dental patients.

There is no question as to the efficaciousness of both nitrous oxide and audio-analgesia as hypnotic agents. In an article written by Cherry and Pollin in 1948,[7] a technic is described in which music is fed to the patient while nitrous oxide is being administered. The authors describe an elaborate set-up of earphones, connected to a phonograph with a microphone tie-in, and attached to the patient's ears, allowing the anesthetist to speak directly to the patient. Selected music, such as *Clair de Lune, Moonlight Sonata,* and *Evening Star,* was used. The authors conclude that ". . . in this method designed to reduce reflex irritability without resorting to depressing premedication, the nitrous oxide oxygen mixtures were maintained with a minimum of 24 per cent oxygen. Nausea, retching, excitement, jactitation, soft tissue obstruction, aspiration and swallowing have been *conspicuously absent.*"

HANDLING RESISTANT PATIENTS

Even though these technics are presented by the author as hypnotic aids or placebos, there are instances in which they are indicated in preference to outright hypnosis. For example, one encounters patients whose prejudices compel them to reject hypnosis. There are still other patients whose deepseated resistance to hypnosis makes them refractory to its use. But with the aid of nitrous oxide or audio-analgesia, the resistances, both conscious and unconscious, are not mobilized. Thus the patient can "let go" without having his self-esteem threatened.

"SEALING" THE PATIENT AGAINST HYPNOSIS

The hypnodontist should give the patient posthypnotic suggestions which will serve as a protection against the experimenting amateur or stage hypnotist. The wording of these suggestions might be: "In the future, no one will be able to hypnotize you except a dentist, a physician, or some other qualified person such as a psychologist. Unless you expressly desire to be hypnotized, no one can hypnotize you." It is important not to close out all future susceptibility, as the patient might later be a subject for therapeutic purposes.

DEHYPNOTIZATION

Before dismissing any patient who has been in a hypnotic state, it is imperative to observe two rules:

1. Remove any hypnotic suggestion that might continue to operate in the posthypnotic period.

2. Make certain that the patient is alert.

Any suggestions which might have been given, perhaps as tests, such as "paralysis" of a limb, should be removed. If a counter-suggestion is not made, there is a remote possibility that such a "paralysis" may continue to operate in the post-

hypnotic period. It is important to set a time limit to any analgesia or anesthesia in the posthypnotic period. If a negative or a positive sensory hallucination has been produced during hypnosis, it is important to remove it before dehypnotization. These are important considerations, whether the operator is a dentist, a psychologist, a psychiatrist, or an amateur hypnotist.

The hypnodontist, as well as the psychotherapist, is legally and morally responsible for a patient's condition and welfare at the time he leaves the office and after he has been in hypnosis. This is just as true for hypnosis as it is for general anesthesia. If a patient should meet with an automobile accident because of a partially depressed state owing to incomplete dehypnotization, the practitioner might be involved in legal complications. This is also the case with an ambulatory patient after the administration of a general anesthetic. It is wise to observe every patient for a short time and to converse with him before dismissing him to ascertain his complete recovery from the hypnotic state. This precaution is necessary only when a patient has been in a very deep state.

OPERATIVE HYPNODONTICS

The management of the operative dental technics after a patient is in a hypnotic state is known as *operative hypnodontics.* Through trial, error, and experimentation, a method of managing the patient has been established.

The following is the procedure which the author has developed and applied to hundreds of cases over the past several years:

Maintenance of Hypnotic Level. After inducting the patient and testing for depth, always end by assuring him that he will not awaken from the hypnotic state until you dehypnotize him. This will require several strong hypnotic suggestions such as, "You will remain deeply relaxed until I 'awaken' you. Nothing, absolutely nothing, will awaken you until I do!" This is the first step before attempting any work in the mouth.

Approach to Treatment in the Mouth. Sometimes, despite the above precaution, when the patient is asked to open his mouth, he may come out of hypnosis. Therefore, this second step is always applied with the following verbalization: "With eyes closed and without 'awakening,' open your mouth . . . wider!" Then massage the jaw muscles lightly on the outside of the face and continue, "Your jaw is becoming stiff, like a vise. It is now so stiff that you cannot close your mouth. You may try, *but you will find it impossible.* Stop trying! Deep, deep asleep. Your mouth will remain open until I tell you otherwise."

This step, known as muscle catalepsy, is taken not only to ensure an open mouth throughout the entire operation, but also to act as a test in determining the depth of hypnosis, and, finally, to deepen the hypnotic state. Whenever a test in the technics of hypnotic induction is made successfully, the suggestion of deep, deep "asleep" tends to deepen the hypnosis.

Production of Anesthesia. One should never assume that anesthesia is present, even though a patient may be in deep hypnosis. Always include this step to produce anesthesia first; then test before operating. The procedure is to take hold of the tooth to be treated between the index finger and the thumb, rocking it and at the same time depressing it in the socket, gently at first but gradually more firmly. While doing this, say: "As I press down on this tooth, you will find that it is getting numb and losing all its feeling. It is beginning to feel as though you've had an injection. You feel a tingling sensation . . . cold and numb. . . ." Then test for anesthesia.

Test for Anesthesia. Take a sharp explorer and gently press into the gingival area around the tooth, saying, "I am pricking your gum with this point, but, you see, you feel absolutely no discomfort." Stop, and say, "I shall do the same to the other side of your mouth, but you will feel a sharp pain there." Then prick the gingival tissues on the normal side very lightly. Almost always, the patient will react with a sudden start. Now go back to the first side and indicate the difference to the patient. If there is any doubt in the operator's mind, either the hypnosis should be deepened and the above words repeated, or the patient should be given procaine and further tests should be made.

Operative Procedure. The author always applies the following rules:

1. Never operate without an assistant.

2. Never attempt too much during the first visit.

3. Advise the patient to keep his eyes closed throughout the entire operation.

4. Keep the patient passive and do not disturb him by requesting that he spit or bend over. This can be avoided by the constant use of an aspirator by the assistant. The patient should be treated as though he were in a state of general anesthesia.

5. Never overheat the tooth. Work slowly and have a constant stream of water running on the tooth from any of the special water-cooling attachments on the market.

6. Complete the entire operation, including restoration, while the patient is in hypnosis. This is important because, in this way, it is possible to produce complete amnesia for the operative procedure and to avoid focusing of the normal waking attention on the operation in the posthypnotic period. Thus, it is necessary to place the matrix band, the wedges, and the restoration, and to remove the excess and carve the restoration while the patient is still in a hypnotic state.

Termination of Hypnosis. When terminating the hypnosis, always give the following posthypnotic suggestions:

1. There will be no recollection of any pain or discomfort.

2. If the patient is in a somnambulistic state, complete amnesia for the entire period of hypnosis may be suggested successfully. There are some who feel that amnesia is not desirable. The author often finds it useful.

3. The patient will feel normal, cheerful, and happy when he is dehypnotized.

4. He will enter hypnosis quickly and deeply each time in the future that it is suggested to him, provided, of course, that it is in accord with his wishes to be induced.

5. He will have no fear or anxiety about dental treatment at subsequent visits. Any other therapeutic suggestions might be given at this time.

After dehypnotization of a patient, never question him about discomfort. Always assume that it was diminished. Do not press a patient to exceed his threshold of response. Inform him of what you have done as though he knows nothing about it. Assure him that the procedure was entirely successful, as planned, and that he will do even better next time.

The author would like to emphasize that the above is a sketchy outline of the technic used. Certain factors had to be omitted, such as the importance of the attitude of the dentist as a determinant of success or failure; the practice of running a continuous commentary throughout the operative procedure to maintain a constant hypnotic depth and to prevent the patient from coming out of it; and the occasional need to stop treatment to deepen the hypnosis if signs of spontaneous dehypnotization appear. These and many other details must be excluded because of the necessary brevity of this chapter, but they are discussed elsewhere in this book.

PEDIADONTICS

Hypnosis has been found to be a useful adjunct in pediadontics.[32] It is particularly indicated in the control and the management of emotionally disturbed children who require dental work. The author, who specializes in dentistry for the emotionally disturbed and handicapped, has various means of coping with this class of patients. Among the technics in his armamentarium are all forms of drugs, such as local and general anesthetics, sedatives, tranquilizers, and analgesics. But hypnosis is always used as an attempt to eliminate or lessen the amounts used. In some instances, it is possible to avoid the use of general anesthesia in cases which had been scheduled for it.

DISADVANTAGES OF HYPNODONTICS

From the foregoing, it would appear that there is only good associated with the use of hypnosis in dentistry. Unfortunately, this is not the case. A disadvantage in using hypnosis is the time consumed in conditioning a patient. However, this can be obviated by group training (see Chap. 35). Busy dentists may find it impractical and undesirable to spend the required time on individual patients, in view of the uncertainty involved. Many practitioners also feel that the training and experience required for a high percentage of success is an obstacle. Insofar as time is concerned, it must

be pointed out that reinduction of hypnosis is only a matter of a few seconds or a few minutes, when proper posthypnotic suggestions to this effect have been given. There are times when a psychologist trained in hypnosis or a hypnodontic specialist may be called upon to condition a patient, either at his own office or at that of the dentist. Rapport can then be transferred to the dentist. There are more skilled psychologists capable of such work today than at any time in the past, owing to the growing use of and interest in hypnosis in fields other than dentistry.

ADVANTAGES OF HYPNODONTICS

Against the above disadvantages, there are a number of advantages which have been discussed throughout the text. Hypnosis is extremely useful in the relaxation of nervous and excitable patients, eliminating fear and tension, making long, arduous sittings more tolerable. The well-conditioned patient approaches the dental appointments with pleasant anticipation instead of dread and anxiety. There is a definite enhancement in the prestige of the hypnodontist because of his added interest, skill, and ability. It is the usual experience of hypnodontists that new patients seek appointments and request hypnosis when word-of-mouth information is spread by patients who have experienced hypnotic treatment. Many dentists, including the author, have found that with some patients it becomes unnecessary to continue the use of hypnosis after the initial sessions have overcome the fear and anxiety.

Although less than 20 years ago a dentist had to be a courageous pioneer in using hypnosis, this is not the case today. The company in which he travels, of those using hypnosis in disciplines other than dentistry, is both respected and substantial. The Boards in Hypnosis consist of three separate entities, of which the American Board of Dental Hypnosis is one. The others are in medicine and psychology. The fact that hypnosis is taught in at least a dozen dental colleges speaks for itself. It is hoped that those reading this chapter will view sympathetically the possibilities and the potentials of the use and the application of hypnodontics. Jacoby has provided practical suggestions for working with hypnodontics.[16]

CONCLUSIONS

1. The average dentist is capable of learning the technics of hypnodontics.

2. It is completely harmless in every way and from every point of view *when used by a dentist for dental purposes.*

3. There is no possibility of emotional or psychological trauma if no experimentation in psychiatric therapy is attempted. Stay within the limitations of dentistry. Do not attempt to practice psychiatry!

4. Susceptibility to hypnosis is not related to intelligence or to strong- or weak-mindedness.

5. It is a practice-builder, as it enhances the prestige of the dentist.

6. At present, it is relatively widely accepted by the medical, dental, and psychological professions, as compared with only 10 or 15 years ago.

7. There is a deep personal satisfaction in being able to render such a useful service to the patient.

8. Failures cannot be avoided, but practical experience, together with adequate postgraduate instruction, will minimize the incidence of failures.

REFERENCES

1. Ament, P.: Removal of gagging: a response to variable behavior patterns. Int. J. Clin. Exp. Hypn., *19:* 1, 1971.
2. Barrett, R.H., and von Dedenroth, T.E.A.: Problems of deglutition. Am. J. Clin. Hypn., *9:*161, 1967.
3. Bartlett, K.A.: Hypnotic treatment of Novocain allergy. Am. J. Clin. Hypn., *12:*222, 1970.
4. _____: Gagging: a case report. Am. J. Clin. Hypn., *14:*54, 1971.
5. Bodecker, C.F.: Hypnosis in dentistry. N.Y. State Dent. J., *22:*226, 1956.
6. Chastain, F.R.: A case of excessive gagging. Am. J. Clin. Hypn., *7:*257, 1965.
7. Cherry, H., and Pollin, L.M.: Music as a supplement in dental anesthesia. Dent. Digest, *10:*455, 1948.
8. Crasilneck, H.B., and Fogelman, M.J.: The effects of hypnosis on blood coagulation. Int. J. Clin. Exp. Hypn., *5:*132, 1957.
9. Crowder, H.M.: Hypnosis in the control of tongue thrust swallowing habit patterns. Am. J. Clin. Hypn., *8:*10, 1965.
10. Drewer, C.J., and Viljoen, P.T.: Abnormal swallowing habits. J. Dent. Assoc. South Africa, *16:*38, 1961.
11. Dufour, J.: Tooth extraction under hypnosis in a hemophiliac. Rev. Franc. odontostomat, *15:*955, 1968.
12. Fredericks, L.E.: The use of hypnosis in hemophilia. Am. J. Clin. Hypn., *10:*52, 1967.
13. Furneaux, W.D.: Experimental Hypnosis. New York, Macmillan, 1952.
14. Golan, H.: Further case reports from the Boston City Hospital. Am. J. Clin. Hypn., *18:*55, 1975.
15. Jacoby, J.D.: Statistical report on general practice hypnodontics: tape-recorder conditioning. Int. J. Clin. Exp. Hypn., *8:*115, 1960.
16. _____: Practical suggestions for dentists working with the patient in a trance. Am. J. Clin. Hypn., *10:* 39, 1967.
17. Koster, S.: Two cases of monosymptomatic ptyalism cured with hypnosis. Geneek Gids, *35:*305, 1957.
18. La Baw, W.L.: Regular use of suggestibility in pediatric bleedings. Haematologia, *4:*419, 1970.
19. Lucas, O.N.: Dental extractions in the hemophiliac: control of the emotional factors by hypnosis. Am. J. Clin. Hypn., *7:*301, 1965.
20. Lucas, O.N., and Tocantins, L.M.: Problems in hemostasis in hemophiliacs undergoing dental extraction. Ann. N.Y. Acad. Sci. *115:*470, 1964.
21. Lucas, O.N., *et al.:* Management of tooth extractions in hemophiliacs by the combined use of hypnotic suggestion, protective splint, and packing of sockets. J. Oral Surg. Anesth. Hosp. Dent. Serv., *20:* 488, 1962.
22. Marcus, H.W.: Psychophysiological considerations in dentistry. N.Y. State Dent. J., *32:*301, 1966.
23. Mintz, V.W.: The use of suggestive aids in denture gaggers. Dent. Surv., *27:*653, 1952.
24. _____: Hypnodontics, or Hypnosis in Dentistry. Brooklyn, Dental Items of Interest, 1952.
25. Moss, A.A.: Elimination of gagging by waking hypnotic suggestions. Dent. Surv., *26:*1958.
26. _____: Hypnosis for pain management in dentistry. J. Dent. Med., *18:*110, 1963.
27. Newman, M.: Hypnosis and hemophiliacs. J. Am. Dent. Assoc., *88:*273, 1974.
28. Raginsky, B.B.: Mental suggestion as an aid to anesthesia. Anesthesiology, Sept. 1948, p. 467.
29. Roston, G.D.: Workshop presentation. Society for Clinical and Experimental Hypnosis, 27th annual meeting, Chicago, 1975.
30. Secter, I.I.: Some notes on controlling the exaggerated gag reflex. Am. J. Clin. Hypn., *2:*149, 1960.

31. _____: Applied psychology in dentistry. Am. J. Clin. Hypn., *8:*122, 1965.

32. Smith, S.R.: The uses and limitations of hypnosis in children's dentistry. Br. Dent. J., *119:*499, 1965.

33. Stolzenberg, J.: Hypnosis in orthodontics. Am. J. Orthodont., *45:*508, 1959.

34. Thompson, K.F.: A rationale for suggestion in dentistry. Am. J. Clin. Hypn., *5:*181, 1963.

35. Webb, C.S.: Gagging: a method for positive control. Dent. Surv., *43:*54–55, 1967.

36. Weyandt, J.A.: Three case reports in dental hypnotherapy. Am. J. Clin. Hypn., *15:*49, 1972.

47

Miscellaneous Indications for Hypnosis

HYPNOSIS IN NONCONVULSIVE AND ELECTROCONVULSIVE THERAPY

Posthypnotic suggestions have been used to decrease apprehension in patients undergoing nonconvulsive and electroconvulsive shock therapy (E.C.T.).[43, 70] There is also a report of a disturbed patient treated successfully by simulated or "as-if" electroshock therapy under hypnosis.[57]

Hypnosis reputedly has helped to recover the loss of memory commonly noted after E.C.T. The few cases, however, in which the author attempted restoration of important memory gaps were not benefited by hypnotic age regression or revivification. Apparently, damage of the association pathways is irreversible. Bowers and Beckowitz contend, however, that if hypnosis were administered preceding E.C.T., some of its disturbing effects could be mitigated.[7]

IMPROVEMENT IN LEARNING AND PERCEPTION

Recent data indicate that both hypnotic and posthypnotic suggestions improve various task performances,[30] whereas, by comparison, waking suggestion is unsatisfactory.[55, 72] Swiercinsky and Coe contend that hypnosis does not facilitate learning in short-term experimental situations.[68] Other studies in this area have been made.[20, 42] Time distortion often facilitates recall in highly motivated persons.[13, 14] Those investigators who disagree with these findings, unfortunately, did not use time distortion, and *studied only the permanence of learning,* not its immediate effects.[16, 28, 67] Another report indicated that learning was increased in a group of students given special remedial learning sessions under hypnosis.[63] All of the students had tried the more conventional methods without success.[44] Reading speed and comprehension were significantly increased and maintained by hypnosis.[18] Stage fright and examination anxiety also have been eased hypnotically.[27, 47]

Posthypnotic suggestions directed to more favorable attitudes and moods facilitated problem-solving behavior.[17, 26] Thus favorable results can be expected when there is good motivation, hypnotic rapport, time distortion, and relaxation. Other investigators believe that the associated relaxation neutralizes the anxiety and thus increases learning. The degree of meaningfulness of the learned material is an important variable.[75]

Krippner showed that a group receiving hypnosis improved their reading capacity over a control group.[37] Others have demonstrated that creativity can be stimulated.[6, 53] In the Soviet Union, musicians, mathematicians, artists, and chess players have shown improvement.[53] In all cases, the subjects utilized images of being renowned leaders in their respective fields. Follow-up studies were made for 8 years, and the subjects invariably continued their improvement following hypnosis. Hoskovec quotes numerous Russian researchers who have found that hypnopedia (sleep-learning) is of benefit in selected subjects.[24, 34]

Erickson reports several hundred persons who had examination "jitters." On highly motivated persons he uses a technic in which the subject is instructed not to try for high grades, as this only reinforces panic states, but rather to try for pass-

335

ing grades. Oetting uses an "alert trance" to improve concentration.[51]

Some of the methods discussed above have been particularly suitable for actors, actresses, and musicians, as the following case reports show:

A famous singer always developed "mike fright" and usually required from six to ten retakes when she recorded an album. Using autohypnosis, sensory-imagery conditioning, and time distortion, she sang beautifully *without a single mistake* on her first attempt. Tape recordings, made by the author, were used in the presleep period to reinforce the posthypnotic suggestions. According to her severest critics, she performed better than at any other time in her entire career. Posthypnotic suggestions to really "live the song" and allay nervousness were important factors. Also, she was cued to enter hypnosis over the telephone. Several months later she was hypnotized during a long-distance telephone call to allay her opening night nervousness, and gave a very successful performance. This has been done for other prominent performers.

A well-known stage and screen star, who was an alcoholic and very undependable, always had trouble remembering his lines. Concurrently, while being treated for his alcoholism, he memorized an *entire script after it was read to him while he was in a somnambulistic state in a single 3-hour session.* Once, when he was regressed to the age of 5, he spoke in a foreign language. Upon dehypnotization, he emphatically stated that he had forgotten his native tongue, as he had emigrated to America when he was 6 years old. Although he never overcame his drinking, he gave many sterling film and stage performances and never again had trouble remembering his roles.

An actress had to learn a difficult role in 3 days. She was the star of a stage play and carried the bulk of the dialogue. She, too, was trained in autohypnosis, time distortion, and sensory-imagery conditioning. Suggestions were given that 1 hour of action dialogue, as measured by the clock, would be condensed into 5 minutes of subjective time. In other words, 1 hour of the play would be "seen" and "heard" in her mind's "eye" and "ear," respectively, in one twelfth of the actual time. In this way, she could have 12 "dry runs" or rehearsals for every hour that she spent rehearsing under hypnosis. According to the reviews, she gave one of the most magnificent performances ever seen on the American stage, and she received world-wide acclaim

not only for her marvelous performance, but also for the means through which it was accomplished!

The author has utilized the technics described above for concert violinists, pianists, and even writers who just "went stale." Rachmaninoff, who had been unproductive for several years, reportedly composed one of his famous concertos following posthypnotic suggestion.

These are only a few of many interesting cases. It is the author's impression that this increase in performance occurs not only because of attitudinal changes, but also because the inhibitory factors are reduced. The reader must not infer that all subjects respond as well as those just described; failures do occur. It may be that the confidence and enthusiasm of the operator and the creation of a proper mind-set were the responsible factors. Nevertheless, from an objective viewpoint, most patients were pleased with their increased self-confidence and greater ability to concentrate and learn.

PERCEPTION DURING ANESTHESIA

Cheek contends that much of what is said during surgery can later be recalled by age-regression technics.[9, 11, 68] Ideomotor signaling was employed under hypnosis to give "yes" or "no" answers as to the validity of the supposedly "heard" conversation. He admits that recollection of the operating-room experiences may have been colored by what one imagines goes on during surgery, or that the productions may have been an attempt to please the formulations of the investigator. However, the material obtained under hypnosis, when compared with the data obtained by a tape recorder set up in the operating room, showed some startling similarities.

Cheek's experiments were not rigidly controlled as to the depth of anesthesia and the evocation of irrelevant conversation. It is only natural to assume that "meaningful" data pertinent to the type of surgery readily could be fabricated by intelligent patients. "Talking to the subconscious," developed on the basis of ideomotor responses, is also open to question.[77]

Another one of Cheek's findings that should be explored is the distinct possibility of engrafting constructive posthypnotic suggestions on surgical and obstetrical patients who are coming out of anesthesia. During a light plane of anesthesia the sensory input channels are open and, where criticalness is reduced, constructive "programming" can be achieved. If Cheek's contentions are validated, all personnel must be careful about what is said and done in the operating room.

Another interesting speculation adduced by Cheek is that confidence can be instilled during anesthesia to improve the outlook for hopeless cancer patients. Suggestions inspiring faith and confidence are certainly helpful at all levels of awareness. However, in attributing all sorts of benefits to hypnosis, we must not, as serious-minded scientists, allow our enthusiasm to claim that hypnosis is going to solve all the ills and tribulations of mankind. However, the modern physician, with emphasis on pharmacologic therapies, laboratory investigations, and physical modalities, has grossly underestimated the "power of the mind." Figuratively, "faith can move mountains" and should not be neglected!

Several other investigators have shown that awareness occurs in the deeply hypnotized surgical patient.[10, 12, 41] Levinson has corrobrated Cheek's earlier observation that surgeons should be very careful about what they say when a patient is deeply anesthesized.[41] It is reported that various sequelae during and following the induction of hypnosis may have been related to earlier and unpleasant experiences with chemical anesthesia.[31, 33] Perception under anesthesia has been referred to as *parahypnosis,* a term originated by Van Dyke.[73]

RETROGRADE AMNESIA

Hypnotherapists frequently are asked to see cases of retrograde amnesia following trauma. Milos reported 20 cases of serious head injuries in which, after recovery, the anterograde and retrograde amnesias were explored by hypnosis. Seven cases cleared up. The duration of the post-traumatic coma did not seem to effect the outcome of the hypnotic exploration. Severe cases of amnesia have been helped.[36] The author has had about the same percentage of success.

HYPNOSIS IN RADIOLOGY*

Radiologists report that hypnotic relaxation in selected patients facilitates diagnostic procedures. In gastrointestinal work-ups on tense, anxiety-ridden patients, pathology often may be observed by bowel spasm, flatus, extreme alterations in motility, delayed or rapid emptying time, forceful evacuation of the barium enema, eructations, and vomiting of the barium meal, esophageal spasm, and aerophagia.

During fluoroscopy, reassuring suggestions improve patient cooperation. The following suggestions are even more effective when given under hypnosis: "Let your arms drop limply to your sides. Lean forward. Allow your chin to touch the front of your chest. Relax your abdomen and stick it out as far as you can. Now take a deep breath. Loosen up all over." Some apprehensive patients undergoing fluoroscopy are frightened by the darkness, the awesome sounds and the lights; therefore, any degree of physical and mental relaxation is worthwhile. All such patients should be hypnotized beforehand as it is virtually impossible to do it during the examination, especially if they are uncomfortable from the barium or have the desire to expel it. Hence, in order to ensure optimal relaxation, hypnotic conditioning must be established before fluoroscopy is performed.

Edel states:

During the initial interview, even if I am familiar with the symptoms, I have him discuss his present complaints and past history for the psychotherapeutic value. By evincing further interest, better rapport is established. I try to evaluate his present emotional status. If he appears tense, I ask if he is apprehensive about the examination. I always stress the importance of relaxation during the examination and ascertain if he would like to learn hypnorelaxation. If "yes," I then proceed with hypnotic induction and conditioning, stressing the advantages of relaxation. If induction fails, an antispasmodic and sedative are prescribed just before the next examination. This relaxes the patient so that hypnosis is readily induced just prior to the examination.

---

*I am indebted to Dr. J. W. Edel, of Baltimore, for most of the material in this section.

The technic for the initial induction depends on a number of factors; it should be informal, and one that effectively employs a posthypnotic suggestion for rapid reinduction. The shoulder cue is readily reproducible and easily remembered. Technics which involve sensory-imagery conditioning are the best for controlling involuntary functioning of the viscera. In accordance with the law of dominant effect, one must have the subject revivify a relaxing episode that actually happened. Therefore, specific suggestions for gastrointestinal relaxation will not work unless previous associational reflexes have been reactivated. Relaxation through autohypnosis is even more effective. Well-trained patients can enter a very satisfactory state of autohypnosis in a matter of seconds during the roentgenographic examination.

Edel states:

The use of more complex hypnotic technics as revivification and age regression depends on the discretion and training of the radiologist. This also depends on the evaluation of the personality and the relationship. If one feels insecure in the use of hypnosis and if one constantly seems to accentuate and amplify its dangers rather than its potentialities, it would be wise to resolve this insecurity before one proceeds further.

In properly conditioned patients, the characteristic patterns of gastrointestinal functioning can be observed during fluoroscopy. If the diagnosis is evident, no further procedures are necessary. When in doubt, the cue for hypnotic induction can be given, and, in the vast majority of cases, immediate relaxation of bowel spasm and diminution of intestinal peristalsis occur. During deep hypnosis, there is almost complete cessation of peristaltic activity, and all manifestations of spasm disappear. The gastrointestinal relaxation permits the examination to be made in half the time, and with less chance that hidden lesions might be overlooked. Hazards due to repeated examinations are obviated and there is no loss of prestige. During a barium enema examination, a patient who formerly squirmed, groaned, and evacuated on the table, experiences minimal discomfort when hypnotized. The patient should be dehypnotized slowly after the examination, and given the usual suggestions of well-being.

Other conditions in which the roentgenographic diagnosis can be facilitated by hypnotic relaxation are given below:

Respiratory:
1. Bronchography, whether by bronchoscopy, tracheal catheterization, or drip method;
2. Diagnostic pneumothorax;
3. Antral puncture and oil contrast studies.
Cardiovascular:
1. Arteriography;
2. Cardiac catheterization;
3. Angiocardiography;
4. Retrograde thoracic aortography.
Gastrointestinal:
1. G. I. series;
2. Esophagus, stomach, and duodenum;
3. Barium enema.
Genitourinary:
1. Retrograde urography;
2. Intravenous urography;
3. Rubin's test and other patency tests;
4. Hysterogram and pneumoperitoneum.
Neurologic:
1. Pneumoencephalography;
2. Ventriculography;
3. Cerebral angiography;
4. Myelography;
5. Diskography.

In these specialized examinations, hypnosis is used for anesthesia, analgesia, and relief of tension, anxiety, and fear. Psychogenic and allergic reactions secondary to injections can be controlled by hypnosis and drugs. During intravenous urography, the hypnotized patient is much more at ease and does not mind being strapped to the table with a pressure bag for 1 to 2 hours. There is a better concentration of dye, less gas to obscure film detail and, when hypnotic induction precedes injection, the reactions are minimal.

Heyer investigated digestive disturbances in women by means of hypnosis.[32] He observed gastrointestinal functioning at hypnotic and nonhypnotic levels. He remarks: "Most impressive were the disturbances in passage of the meal in patients who had in addition to their psychogenic disturbances organic complications such as adhesions."

Kroger and Freed noted that irritability of the

reproductive tract is a manifestation of autonomic disharmony and is the commonest cause for the erroneous diagnosis of tubal occlusion made by the radiologist.[39] However, spasm at the uterotubal or the isthmotubal portion of the fallopian tubes, which often is not relieved by sedation, can be relaxed during tubal insufflation in tense and anxious individuals by hypnosis; this can obviate mistaken diagnoses.

Hypnosis reduces the side reactions associated with radiation sickness and can decrease the pain of carcinoma in selected patients.[65] Radiologists trained in hypnosis can prepare such patients in groups. As more radiologists employ hypnosis for diagnostic procedures and report their results, it is certain that Edel's and Heyer's observations will be confirmed.

HYPNOSIS IN GERIATRICS

Posthypnotic suggestions, in responsive persons, can effectively raise the aged patient's confidence and help direct thoughts from himself to external events; this can minimize depressive reactions and hypochondriasis. The suggestions also can help establish closer interpersonal relationships; many are quarrelsome, hostile over their infirmities, and envious of younger and more agile persons.

Definitive suggestions potentiated by hypnosis can be directed to (1) taking an interest in the plans of younger persons (in this way the tragedy associated with the loss of friends or a mate is reduced); (2) developing avocational interests concerned with creativity, the acquisition of special motor skills, and cultural activities; (3) exercise, such as walking, as much as possible; (4) watching the diet and the weight; (5) correcting elimination; (6) overcoming insomnia; and (7) physical involvements, such as cardiac congestion, arthritis, and neuromuscular involvements.

HYPNOSIS IN SPORTS

Hypnosis can be an effective method for increasing athletic performance. In one form or another, it has been used to motivate athletes for many years. As Orne demonstrated, it is the motivation to perform well that has been increased;

this often can be done as well at nonhypnotic levels.

The author has used hypnosis for improving the ability of a considerable number of athletes competing in baseball, football, boxing, and golf. The results ranged from good to spectacular. The following case is illustrative:

A leading professional golfer was referred to the author for hypnorelaxation to improve his putting, especially during tournament play, when large crowds around the green caused him to become so nervous that his booming long drives and approaches were nullified by his miserable putting. He was taught self-hypnosis and sensory-imagery conditioning and within four sessions was able readily to enter a somnambulistic state. It was suggested that he could become completely oblivious to spectators any time he wished, and that, furthermore, he would "see" a dotted line between his ball and the cup. As further insurance of success, he was to suggest that the cup would appear from two to three times its normal size. He was also given suggestions that his self-confidence would not be shaken when he made a bad shot. Rather, he would imagine every stroke successful before it was played! To do this, he would "feel" the impact of the club and "see" the flight of the ball as if he had actually hit it.*

Although this golfer normally hit a long ball, it was suggested that he would have unusual driving power. Through this conditioning, both his putting and his driving improved greatly. A short time later he tied the course record in the National Open and missed winning only because of one bad hole when his ball hit a spectator and caromed into a trap. Several months later, he won a coveted championship. He attributed a good measure of his success to the hypnotic conditioning.

The daily press contains examples of basketball players who have scored a phenomenal number of points after hypnotic conditioning, boxers who have become veritable champions, and trackmen who have far surpassed their best previous records. There is no danger that an athlete will go beyond his physiologic limit. The built-in or involuntary reflexes protect the individual against danger at all levels.

One of the author's close personal friends is a

---

*Two popular books by Jack Heise, *How You Can Play Better Golf Using Self-Hypnosis* and *How You Can Bowl Better Using Self-Hypnosis* (published by Wilshire Book Company, Los Angeles), describe other excellent technics.

former track star, who, in college, participated unknowingly in experiments conducted by the psychology department of the University of Illinois. As a quarter-miler, he customarily ran just slightly faster than a teammate who was given a placebo pill and told that he would beat my friend that day. Beat him he did, and my friend recalls that he was really beaten from the time that his teammate took the pill. The following week my friend was given a pill and broke the "Big Ten" record, while the man who had beaten him the week before, minus his pill, finished exhausted and sick.

Were these performances the result of suggestion or hypnosis? Just one thing is certain: the cause of victory was the elimination of inhibiting psychological factors. There was nothing physiologic in the process.

Naruse describes the use of hypnosis in conjunction with autogenic training and progressive relaxation for relieving "stage fright" in 125 Japanese athletes participating in the 1960 Olympic games.[49, 62] Counterconditioning anxiety as well as "mental rehearsals" were employed. Additional encouragement and counseling were provided by a "psychological trainer." Gymnasts, volley ball and baseball players, and weight-lifters were among the champions who underwent psychological and physical training. Similar results were noted by Bankov.[3]

The Soviets have developed the practice of "psyching up" athletes for sports competition into a science. They, too, have used hypnosis, autogenic training, and other psychologic methods. These technics were first employed on the Soviet bicycling team with such great success that they won a gold medal at the 1972 Olympic games in Munich. The technics were especially valuable for those facing a competitor who had always beat them. An institute in Kharkhov holds regular classes for coaches who specialize in psychological technics to be used in preparing Soviet athletes for the 1980 Olympics. I cannot understand why more amateur and professional coaches do not use qualified, psychologically trained hypnotists to potentiate physical performance. The results speak for themselves.

In conclusion, it should be stated that there is no known reason why a competent hypnothera-

pist should not use his skill in helping an athlete to eliminate detracting psychological factors which prevent him from operating at his highest efficiency. There are no indications that he will drop dead "in the stretch," at least not from the effects of hypnosis.

HYPNOSIS IN SPACE TRAVEL

Physicians and psychologists are being called upon to utilize their knowledge in the rapidly expanding experimentation to make safe man's flight into space. Hypnosis is a seemingly neglected but potentially useful tool for learning more about man's ability to survive and function efficiently in space. For instance, in the interest of realism, hypnosis may be used to convince the space candidate that he is undergoing an actual, rather than a simulated, test.

Hypnotic relaxation can be utilized to reduce the metabolic rate and the oxygen consumption. Hypnosis would be of inestimable value in helping spacemen to maintain uncomfortable positions for long intervals. These conditions might be intolerable under normal circumstances. Hindu fakirs who allow themselves to be buried in a sealed coffin for several hours actually do so under autohypnosis. Since the number of cubic feet of air in the casket is known, the slowing down of respiration to 5 or 10 breaths per minute enables the individual to remain underground for what seems to be an incredible period of time. Thus suggestions of calmness and drowsiness slow down metabolic and oxygen requirements as well as digestive processes. The maintenance of "unbearable" positions under hypnosis was described in the section on plastic surgery. Moreover, it is known that hypnotic subjects can submit to tremendous amounts of physical stress without apparent reactions.

The nonspecific and the specific stress induced by weightlessness, cramped quarters, unnatural living conditions, and other psychophysiologic factors encountered by space travelers can be reduced. At least, their adaptive responses can be raised through conditioning under hypnosis.

Another potent tool to overcome boredom is the use of time condensation to speed up time. Although drugs can be employed for nearly all the above-mentioned purposes, subjects under their influence cannot awaken completely and respond or perform as effectively as they can under hypnosis. Well-trained subjects can be conditioned to enter into relaxed states for any desired period upon a designated signal. They also could be rapidly dehypnotized with a different signal.

These are only a few of the uses of hypnosis which can aid in testing space survival. The illusions of reality, the alteration of physiologic functioning, and other phenomena associated with hypnosis may play an important role in interplanetary travel. The author has acted in the capacity of consultant for these and other matters pertaining to utilization of hypnosis for space medicine. Halleck McCord, in a personal communication, has indicated his interest in the research possibilities of hypnosis in these areas.

HOMOSEXUALITY AND SEXUAL DEVIANCE

Homosexuality is no longer considered to be perverse behavior. The subject has been reviewed by Bergler and Kroger.[5] The hypnotic treatment of female homosexuality has been described by Kroger and Freed.[39] Kroger and Fezler have discussed the use of the hypnobehavioral approach for homosexuality and sexual deviance.[38] It is important to determine whether or not a feeling of guilt is present and if the patient really desires therapy. It is surprising how few homosexuals desire to change. There are two main types: the passive-feminine and the active-aggressive. Also, there are mixed types, as well as borderline cases who are bisexual. Every individual has latent homosexual tendencies which are more or less repressed and can be activated under conducive circumstances.

There are several reports on the use of hypnosis in the treatment of homosexuality.[1, 2, 45] Gilbert noted that the active-aggressive (male partner) was resistant to therapy.[25] The degree of success depends not only on the motivation, but also on the type of technic employed. An authoritarian approach is apt to be more successful with the passive-feminine type of homosexual, while a permissive approach is more effective with the active-aggressive type. Therefore, before instituting hypnotherapy or any other reconstructive therapy, the physician must ascertain the type and the degree of homosexual involvement. Some authors contend that latent homosexuality decreases susceptibility to hypnosis.[58, 59] This has not been the author's experience. It may be that those who have only a dim awareness of their homosexual tendencies will deny or resist recognizing the need for correcting these elements of their personalities.

Kroger and Fezler utilize erotic images, arranged in a hierarchy, under hypnosis to attain desired changes.[39] They also discuss similar technics of deconditioning for various types of sexual deviance, such as fetishism, voyeurism, and transvestism.

Unfortunately, those who evince a strong desire to change usually have deep-seated needs which prevent them from making heterosexual adjustments. Even though this type is readily hypnotizable, few permanently recover. Some make a temporary adjustment but quickly relapse.

Homosexuality should not be treated except by a psychiatrically oriented therapist. Homosexuals who are able to function adequately in their life situations without symptoms often are better off if they are not treated. For those malcontents who are continually involving themselves with the law, psychotherapy is indicated, rather than punishment.

The author has used a permissive hypnotherapeutic approach on selected homosexuals. However, rapid results are not obtained, as a considerable amount of time is necessary for psychobiologic reorganization of the personality. As the patient begins to show improvement, the sessions are further apart so that he can test his ability to face his problems and decide whether he really wishes to change. The goal of all psychotherapy in homosexuality is to enable successful adjustment to the opposite sex to take place. Posthypnotic suggestions to have intercourse with females are never successful.

The results depend on the therapist's ability to relieve guilt, anxiety and tensions and to guide the patient toward a mature orientation. The strong dependency created by the hypnotic relationship is advantageous and is deliberately fostered in order to keep the patient in therapy during the initial phases when resistances to change are marked. Later, the utilization of autohypnosis and sensory-imagery conditioning enables the patient to develop fantasies which ultimately will attract him to the opposite sex. By the time he makes the transition to the opposite sex, he is ready to be "weaned off" the therapist. The reasons for the dependency are made clear to him. Often it is the desire to please the therapist that enhances the motivation of the patient. One must continually bear in mind that a "flight into health" can and does occur with this approach; the homosexual has a flurry of heterosexual affairs but ultimately reverts to his previous patterns. Reinforcement hypnotic suggestions should be given at monthly intervals after the patient has been discharged from regular hypnotherapy.

MULTIPLE PERSONALITY

Dual and multiple personalities have been described from the earliest recorded history until modern times. They undoubtedly occur more frequently than is commonly supposed. Multiple personality must be distinguished from dissociation due to hypnosis, schizophrenia, hysteria, mediumistic trances, and simulation by spiritualists. Often multiple personalities are spontaneously or deliberately brought out by hypnosis.[48, 61] The induced personality then functions as the representative of the repressed facets of the individual's primary personality.

In true multiple personality, the other personalities usually have no knowledge of each other's existence: they are repressed from awareness. However, during hypnosis one or more of the personalities may have a complete or a fragmentary knowledge of the memories of the others, and the primary personality may interact with the repressed ones.

The production of multiple personalities by hypnosis has been discussed.[29, 74] Studies indicate that the induced personality takes on many of the characteristics of the subject's overt personality, as well as the ones hidden from awareness. Recently a case of multiple personality was reported which appeared to be bound up by a severely obsessive-compulsive defense, so that the "conscious personality" was constricted, rigid, and cold.[8] The Rorschach responses revealed that one of the personalities was schizophrenic. It was felt that studies of this type might be helpful in understanding psychotic development.

In an interesting series of 78 cases, Kampman found that 32 subjects were able, and 43 were unable, to create multiple personalities after being deeply hypnotized.[35] Oddly enough, those who could develop secondary personalities were clinically healthier as ascertained by psychiatric evaluation.

TREATMENT

Often trauma may be an etiologic factor, as in Prince's famous case of Miss Beauchamp, who had five personalities.[52] Therapy should ascertain the reasons for the dissociation. Integrating the various personalities into one is the goal of all successful therapy. Hypnosis speeds up this reintegration, and the secondary personality or personalities usually can readily be "directed" toward this end. Fortunately, most individuals with multiple personalities are good hypnotic subjects, but the therapy can be difficult in the absence of good rapport with all the hidden personalities.

Odencrants noted that one of the first indications of multiple personality is lapses of consciousness, which often cause confusion and concern to family and friends.[50] After hypnotherapy is initiated, the various personalities, be they one or more, must be identified. They may reveal themselves automatically, voluntarily, through automatic writing, and by posthypnotic suggestion. The record is held by a patient who displayed, at one time or another, 23 different personalities.[52]

Through hypnotic amnesia, the relationship of the various personalities to each other can be understood readily. The hypnotherapist should maintain an interested and sympathetic attitude with the various personalities at all times, or he may lose contact with them. Furthermore, he must not be impatient or surprised, as often the personalities which emerge may be wholly contrary to the patient's primary personality; petulance, immaturity, and sadistic tendencies make their unexpected appearance.

Through hypnosis, any one of the personalities which the therapist wishes to study can be summoned, and invariably the personality will reveal its name. From then on, it is really remarkable how quickly the various personalities can be made to appear and disappear. A now famous book, *Three Faces of Eve,* described how very dramatic situations arose as the patient switched from one personality to another.[69] At times, one personality will be amazingly well developed mentally, and at other times, childlike. Each of the personalities should be evaluated for simulation; chronologic time orientation may show considerable disparity. The therapist must be able to recognize the religious fanatics; they usually represent some departed soul and might be categorized as pseudo-multiple personalities.

Other investigators believe that the personality displayed can be viewed as a conglomerate of pseudoselves and need not be interpreted or analyzed. The therapy is based on restructuring of the family relationships, rather than on the interactions between therapist and patient.

HYPNOSIS IN AMNESIA AND FUGUE STATES

In hysterical amnesia, hypnosis invariably reverses the dissociative reaction. Amnesia serves as a protective defense against traumatic episodes, and, therefore, should be dispelled in a slow and permissive manner.[15] This may be true when the amnesia neutralizes severe psychic shock. However, in the amnesia victims the author has seen, especially in those following physical trauma, rapid dissolution of the amnesia has been a blessing.

In 1941, the author saw a case that received national notoriety. A young male had been amnestic for 45 days. He was readily hypnotized and, via scene visualization and age regression, he was told he was going home. A positive auditory hallucination was induced that he was hearing his name called when the front door was being

opened by a familiar person (his mother). Instantaneously, he remembered his name, city, and telephone number. Needless to say, his mother was overjoyed at hearing from her missing son, who developed the amnesia after being struck on the head by a piece of lumber while working as a carpenter. Without being aware, he got on a train and arrived in another city, where he was picked up by the police. The author made no attempt to uncover why the amnesia was produced. Other interesting cases of amnesia have been discussed by Schneck,[60] and Crasilneck and Hall.[15]

HYPNOSIS IN CRIMINOLOGY

Utilization of non-drug-induced altered states of consciousness (hypnorelaxation) combined with behavior therapy have lowered the recidivism rate to 5 per cent over a 30-month follow-up period in 49 borderline recidivists.[66] The study indicated that this approach may prove to be an effective means of treating these individuals.

Estabrooks has written on the use of hypnosis in criminalogy.[23] An interesting possibility is building up an informer service among trained subjects who have been criminals or who are willing to act as "stool pigeons." If the subject were a somnambulist, he would have no knowledge that he had been given a posthypnotic suggestion to "keep his ear to the ground." Authorities could plant such individuals in strategic places.

The ability of a hypnotized subject to control his responses to the polygraph has been studied. It can be concluded that a well-trained subject, who has committed a crime, can successfully pass the examination. Also, it has been observed that the apprehensive person may give false positives (see p. 113 for hypnosis in criminal investigation).

HYPNOSIS IN MILITARY MEDICAL PRACTICE

Hypnosis has been found to be of considerable value in the military setting. Its use in the treatment of acute traumatic neuroses in World Wars I and II has been well documented. Todorovic has reviewed some of the indications in military medical practice.[71] Some of these are the treatment of burns, injuries, mass hysteria, and other problems associated with nuclear warfare. He points out that hypnosis might be life-saving and could decrease suffering where there was an unavailability of medical supplies. It could be used, in those who are amenable, as an analgesic or anesthetic agent, as an adjunct to facilitate the healing of severe burns and, finally, in the treatment of shell shock and combat fatigue. With reference to group hypnotherapy, hypnosis could be used to make up for an acute shortage of psychiatrists. Hypnosis has been used with other types of psychotherapy for combat fatigue, hysterical conversion reactions, amnesias, "shellshock," and other conditions associated with warfare.

Hypnosis is assuming an ever-increasing role in the psychological aspects of warfare. For instance, a good subject can be hypnotized to deliver secret information. The memory of this message could be covered by an artificially induced amnesia. In the event that he should be captured, he naturally could not remember that he had ever been given the message. He would not remember the message. However, since he had been given a posthypnotic suggestion, the message would be subject to recall through a specific cue, this having been given to him in the form of a posthypnotic suggestion.

Hypnosis has also been used to extract information from prisoners. The best way is to talk to the subject while he is asleep and, when the conversation is carried out so that the subject will not be awakened by the talking, a great deal of important data can be revealed. Individuals who are lightly asleep can be readily hypnotized. Posthypnotic suggestions can be engrafted to steal faked military plans. The individuals are then allowed to escape. The consequences are obvious, as the enemy acts upon this information.

Estabrooks has an excellent chapter on other areas, such as the interrogation of prisoners, espionage and counterespionage, sabotage, and brainwashing.[23] The reader interested in this latter area is referred to Sargent's excellent book, *Battle For the Mind.*[56]

THE "PORT-OF-LAST-CALL" PATIENT

Hippocrates once stated, ". . . it is impossible to make all the sick well." This maxim applies to many chronic, emotionally ill persons. Many of these miserable "traveling case histories" have made the rounds of clinics, physicians, and quasi-medical healers without success, thus acquiring the sad designation of "port-of-last-call" patients. They constitute a high percentage of the author's practice.

All are desperate for aid and hopeful that the omniscient hypnotherapist can cure them by a "magical gesture." At the risk of raising false hopes, I must state that some respond surprisingly to hypnotherapy. It is admitted that we do not always know how the recovery forces are unleashed. Not infrequently, the dedicated therapist can provide the vital spark necessary to transform an apparently hopeless situation into one of renewed health. Years of suffering, hopeless resignation, and even suicide have been forestalled in the "port-of-last-call" patient. Often compassion constitutes competence; wisdom and interest are as effective as drugs.

The "will to get well" and the physician's use of his art to its fullest capacity are decisive factors in the alleviation of much misery due to illness. It is here that the hypnotherapist-physician rises to his greatest heights. Because of space limitations, illustrative cases will not be mentioned. Many cases of hysterical blindness, aphonia, amnesias, tics, and other conversion reactions have responded dramatically to symptom removal by hypnosis. Although more difficult to treat, obsessive compulsives of all types have responded to sensory-imagery conditioning and autohypnosis when conventional therapy had failed. Nearly all can be treated within the framework of any type of supportive psychotherapy.

REFERENCES

1. Abarbanst-Brandt, A.: Homosexuals in hypnotherapy. J. Sex Res., *2:*127, 1966.
2. Alexander, L.: Clinical experience with hypnosis in psychiatric treatment. Int. J. Neuropsychiatry, *3:* 118, 1967.
3. Bankov, M.: Autogenic training, hypnosis, revelation, and psychosomatic modeling and psycho-

therapeutic methods for athletes. Psychother. Psychosom., *21:*62, 1973.

4. Barmann, G. J.: Solving crime by hypnosis. Popular Mechanics, April 1960.

5. Bergler, E., and Kroger, W. S.: Kinsey's Myth of Female Sexuality. New York, Grune & Stratton, 1953.

6. Bowers, K.S., and van der Meullin S.J.: Effect of hypnotic susceptibility on creativity task performance. J. Pers. Social Psychol., *14:*247, 1970.

7. Bowers, M. K., and Beckowitz, B.: Clinical observations on the effects of electroconvulsive therapy in the hypnotic state. J. Nerv. Ment. Dis., *118:*355, 1953.

8. Bowers, M.K., and Brecher, S.: The emergence of multiple personalities in the course of hypnotic investigation. J. Clin. Exp. Hypn., *3:*188, 1955.

9. Cheek, D. B.: Unconscious perception of meaningful sounds during surgical anesthesia as revealed under hypnosis. Am. J. Clin. Hypn., *1:*101, 1959.

10. _____: Further evidence of persistence of hearing under chemoanesthesia. Am. J. Clin. Hypn., *7:*55, 1964.

11. _____: The meaning of continued hearing sense under chemo-anesthesia: a progress report and report of a case. Am. J. Clin. Hypn., *8:*275, 1966.

12. Cheek, D.B., and LeCron, L.M.: Clinical Hypnotherapy. New York, Grune & Stratton, 1968.

13. Cooper, L. F., and Rodgin, D. W.: Time distortion in hypnosis and non-motor learning. Science, *115:*500, 1952.

14. Cooper, L. F., and Tuthill, C. H.: Time distortion in hypnosis and motor learning. J. Psychol., *34:*67, 1952.

15. Crasilneck H.B., and Hall, J.A.: Clinical Hypnosis: Principles and Applications. New York, Grune & Stratton, 1975.

16. Dhanens, T.P., and Lundy, R.M.: Hypnotic and waking suggestions and recall. Int. J. Clin. Exp. Hypn., *23:*68, 1975.

17. Dickson, J. T.: Effects of hypnotically-induced emotional states, difficulty of task and anxiety on psychomotor behavior. Dissert. Abstr., *15:*149, 1955.

18. Donk, L.J., et al.: Toward an increase in reading efficiency utilizing specific suggestions: a preliminary approach. Int. J. Clin. Exp. Hypn., *16:*101, 1968.

19. Dorcus, R.M.: Recall under hypnosis of amnestic events. Int. J. Clin. Exp. Hypn., *8:*57, 1960.

20. Egan, R.M., and Egan, W.P.: The effect of hypnosis on academic performance. Am. J. Clin. Hypn., *11:*30, 1968.

21. Erickson, M.H.: Hypnosis in examination panics. Am. J. Clin. Hypn., *7:*356, 1965.

22. Estabrooks, G. H.: Hypnotism. New York, E. P. Dutton, 1943.

23. _____: Hypnotism. New York, E. P. Dutton, 1957.

24. Filatov, A.: Quoted in Hoskovec, J.: Hypnosis in the Soviet Union: a critical review of recent and major experiments. Int. J. Clin. Exp. Hypn., *14:*308, 1966.

25. Gilbert, S. F.: Homosexuality and hypnotherapy. Br. J. Med. Hypn., *5:*2, 1954.

26. Glasner, S.: Two experiments in the modification of attitude by the use of hypnotic and waking suggestion. J. Clin. Exp. Hypn., *1:*71, 1953.

27. Golburgh, S. J.: Hypnotherapy, chemotherapy, and expressive directive therapy in the treatment of examination anxiety. Am. J. Clin. Hypn., *11:*42, 1968.

28. Gray, W. H.: The effects of hypnosis on learning to spell. J. Educ. Psychol., *25:*471, 1934.

29. Gruenwald, D.: Hypnotic techniques without hypnosis in the treatment of dual personality. J. Nerv. Ment. Dis., *1:*153, 1971.

30. Hammer, E. F.: Post-hypnotic suggestion and test performance. J. Clin. Exp. Hypn., *2:*178, 1954.

31. Hartman, B.J.: Parahypnosis: unconscious perception under chemoanesthesia. J. Natl. Med. Assoc., *61:*246, 1969.

32. Heyer, G. R.: Psychogene Funktions-störungen des Verdauungstraktes. *In* Schwartz, O.: Psychogenese und Psychotherapie körperlicher Symptome. Vienna, Springer-Verlag, 1925, pp. 229–257, 464–466.

33. Hilgard, J.R., Hilgard, E.R., and Newman, M.: Sequelae to hypnotic induction with special reference to earlier chemical anesthesia. J. Nerv. Ment. Dis., *133:*461, 1961.

34. Hoskovec, J.: Hypnopedia in the Soviet Union: a critical review of recent and major experiments. Int. J. Clin. Exp. Hypn., *14:*308, 1966.

35. Kampman, R.: Hypnotically induced multiple personality: an experimental study. Int. J. Clin. Exp. Hypn., *24:*215, 1976.

36. Knowles, F.W.: Hypnosis an amnesic states. N.Z. Med. J., *63:*100, 1964.

37. Krippner, S.: The use of hypnosis with elementary and secondary school children in a summer reading clinic. Am. J. Clin. Hypn., *8:*261, 1966.

38. Kroger, W.S., and Fezler, W.D.: Hypnosis and Behavior Modification: Sensory Imagery Conditioning. Philadelphia, J.B. Lippincott, 1976.

39. Kroger, W.S., and Freed, S.C.: Psychosomatic

Gynecology; Including Problems of Obstetrical Care. Philadelphia, W.B. Saunders, 1951, p. 284.

40. Levin, M.: Hypnosis in the Law. Inst. Law. J., *14:* 97, 1964.

41. Levinson, B.W.: States of awareness during general anesthesia: preliminary communication. Br. J. Anesth., *37:*544, 1965.

42. Lieberman, L.R., *et al.:* Use of tape recorded suggestions as a aid to probationary students. Am. J. Clin. Hypn., *11:*35, 1968.

43. McCord, H., and Sherrell, C.I.: A note on increased ability to do calculus posthypnotically. Am. J. Clin. Hypn., *4:* 124, 1962.

44. Magonet, A.P.: The healing voice. Int. J. Clin. Exp. Hypn., *7:*229, 1959.

45. Maholick, L. T., and Warkenton, J.: Hypnosis in electric shock treatment. Am. J. Psychiat., *105:*623, 1949.

46. Milos, R: Hypnotic exploration of amnesia after cerebral injuries. Int. J. Clin. Exp. Hypn., *23:*103, 1975.

47. Mordey, T.: Conditioning of appropriate behavior to anxiety producing stimuli: hypnotherapy of a stage-fright case. Am. J. Clin. Hypn., *8:*117, 1965.

48. Morton, J.H., and Thoma, E.: A case of multiple personality. Am. J. Clin. Hypn., *2:*216, 1964.

49. Naruse, G.; The hypnotic treatment of stage fright in champion athletes. Int. J. Clin. Exp. Hypn., *13:* 63, 1965.

50. Odencrants, G.: Hypnosis and dissociative states. *In* LeCron, L.M. (ed.): Experimental Hypnosis. New York, Macmillan, 1954.

51. Oetting, E.R.: Hypnosis and concentration in study. Am. J. Clin. Hypn., *7:*148, 1965.

52. Prince, M.: The Dissociation of a Personality. New York, Longmans, 1925.

53. Raikov, V.L.: The possibility of creativity in the active stage of hypnosis. Int. J. Clin. Exp. Hypn., *24:* 258, 1976.

54. Rosenthal, B. G.: Hypnotic recall of material learned under anxiety and non-anxiety producing conditions. J. Exp. Psychol., *34:*369, 1944.

55. Salzberg, H. C.: The effects of hypnotic, post-hypnotic and waking suggestion on performance using tasks varied in complexity. Int. J. Clin. Exp. Hypn., *2:*251, 259, 1960.

56. Sargent, W.: Battle for the Mind. New York, Doubleday, 1957.

57. Schafer, D. W.: As-if electroshock therapy by hypnosis. Am. J. Clin. Hypn., *2:*225, 1960.

58. Schneck, J. M.: Notes on the homosexual component of the hypnotic transference. Br. J. Med. Hypn., *1:*24, 1950.

59. _____: Some aspects of homosexuality in relation to hypnosis. Psychoanal. Rev., *37:*351, 1950.

60. _____: Studies in Scientific Hypnosis. Baltimore, Williams & Wilkins, 1954.

61. _____: Hypnosis in Modern Medicine. Springfield, Ill., Charles C Thomas, 1959.

62. Schultz, J.H., and Naruse, G.: Autogenic Training and Self-Hypnosis. Tokyo, Seiskin, 1963.

63. Sears, A.B.: A comparison of hypnotic and waking learning of the International Morse Code. J. Clin. Exp. Hypn., *3:*215, 1955.

64. Simon, L.: Quoted in Todorovic, D.D.: Hypnosis in military medical practice. Milit. Med., August 1958.

65. Simonton, O.C.: The Role of Mind in Cancer Therapy. The Dimensions of Healing: A Symposium. Los Altos, Cal., Academy of Parapsychology and Medicine, 1973, pp. 139–145.

66. Spear, J.E.: The utilization of non-drug induced altered states of consciousness in borderline recividists. Am. J. Clin. Hypn., *18:*111, 1975.

67. Strickler, C. B.: A quantitative study of posthypnotic amnesia. J. Abnorm. Social Psychol., *24:*108, 1929.

68. Swiercinsky, D., and Coe, W.C.: The effect of "alert" hypnosis and reading responsiveness on reading comprehension. Int. J. Clin. Exp. Hypn., *19:* 146, 1971.

69. Thigpen, C. H., and Cleckley, H.: Three Faces of Eve. New York, McGraw-Hill, 1957.

70. Thoheld, F. H.: Nonconvulsive electrostimulation under narcotic hypnosis. J. Clin. Exp. Hypn., *2:*175, 1954.

71. Todorovic, D. D.: Hypnosis in military medical practice. Milit. Med., *23:*121, 1958.

72. Uhr, L.: Learning under hypnosis: What do we know? What should we know? J. Clin. Exp. Hypn., *6:*121, 1958.

73. Van Dyke, P.B.: Hypnosis in surgery. J. Abdom. Surg., *7:*1, 26–29, 1965.

74. Weitzenhoffer, A. M.: Hypnotism. New York, Wiley, 1953.

75. _____: The influence of hypnosis on the learning processes. J. Clin. Exp. Hypn., *3:*148, 1955.

76. _____: Unconscious or co-conscious? Reflections upon certain trends in medical hypnosis. Am. J. Clin. Hypn., *2:*177, 1960.

ADDITIONAL READINGS

Das, J. P.: Learning under conditions of hypnotically induced anxiety and non-anxiety. Int. J. Clin. Exp. Hypn., *9:*163, 1962.

Eitelberg, R.: Practical applications of hypnosis in space flight. Br. J. Med. Hypn., *13:*22, 1962.

Fowler, W.: Hypnosis and learning. Int. J. Clin. Exp. Hypn., *9:*223, 1961.

Kroger, W. S.: Psychotherapy of "port-of-last-call" patient (paper delivered at meeting of Academy of Psychosomatic Medicine, Minneapolis, November 1, 1962).

McCord, H., and Sherrill, C. I., III: A note on increased ability to do calculus post-hypnotically. Am. J. Clin. Hypn., *4:*124, 1961.

48

Practical Hints in Hypnodiagnosis

Although time exigencies because of patient overload make adequate history-taking more and more difficult, this unfortunate lack should be avoided at all costs in hypnotherapy. With physical diseases ruled out, preferably by a psychosomatically oriented internist, the alert hypnotherapist should first understand the methods by which patients deal with their anxiety-provoking tensions. He must realize, however, that his patients are only vaguely, if at all, aware of their emotional problems. Rather, physical discomfort and general anxiety are their chief concerns, and they seldom relate their symptoms to specific needs such as those described below.

Most individuals with these needs develop certain defensive behavior patterns in an attempt to allay their tensions. It is by such measures that they make a partial adjustment to difficult life situations. Some of the emotional manifestations of these disturbances, as hypochondriacal, addictive, hysterical, paranoid, depressive, obsessive-compulsive and phobic reactions do not always fall into clear-cut nosologic classifications. However, any of these reactions alone or in combination, through experiential conditioning, can symbolically be represented by physiologic complaints referable to the cardiovascular, respiratory, genitourinary, and gastrointestinal systems. These complaints are restlessness, diarrhea, palpitation, globus, vomiting, vague pains and discomforts, anorexia, headaches, lassitude, fatigability, profuse sweating, and even paralysis.

Nearly all such patients believe they are suffering from a physical malady and, when the therapist attempts to talk them out of this idea, he is apt to have a hostile ex-patient. Unfortunately,

too, our public educational program, which has attempted to make emotional illness as socially acceptable as physical involvements, has not been wholly effective. Therefore, most emotionally disturbed persons feel stigmatized and rationalize the diagnosis of "mental" illness until there is no other way to turn.

Mentioning that few persons in our culture escape being upset at one time or another is helpful in enabling patients to face their real difficulties. The therapist should discuss as simply as possible the "mind-body" interrelationships concerned with the bodily expression of emotional tensions by a simple explanation of how "nervous feelings," fears, and depression can interfere with the working of internal organs. He may cite the more commonly observed symptoms such as rapid heart action in response to excitement, "slowed" heart action caused by intense fear, and loss of appetite during periods of depression. The explanation should not involve the use of terms that imply mental disturbance, such as "psychoneurotic" or "psychotic," nor should terminology be employed that could give the patient the impression that his complaints are considered the result of an overactive imagination. To make light of the patient's suffering is a grave mistake and may damage the doctor-patient relationship irreparably. The therapist must let the patient know that he is aware that discomfort of psychological origin is always *real* to the person who feels it.

Actually, however, there is always a reciprocal and dynamic interaction between psychological and physical factors. Every emotion consists of a sequence of physical reverberations in the central nervous system. This aspect has been stressed throughout this book. Clinically, however, our knowledge is far from complete as to how and why specific organs are chosen for displacement of repressed emotional tensions. It cannot be said that any emotion can disturb the function of any organ, but, rather, that there is an intimate affinity between certain emotional states and certain vegetative functions; that emotional and physical factors in the production of symptoms vary in relative significance from individual to individual; and that typical emotional patterns in certain physical diseases also exist in persons with no physical symptoms.

CLINICAL MANIFESTATIONS OF ANXIETY

Anxiety is a universal human response due to hidden tension. It becomes pathologic when, without provocation or awareness, fears are experienced. When these fears cannot be handled, then even minor stresses lead to emotional disturbances. These will be discussed further in this book. These are chiefly insecurity, lack of self-esteem, inadequacy, inability to relate to others or to express pent-up feelings, and inordinate demands for attention. A typical example of an acute anxiety reaction is a person thrown into panic when some friend has suffered a heart attack or a nervous breakdown, or has developed cancer. Such symptoms can be corrected by adequate reassurance, wise counseling, and strong countersuggestions.

Repressed anxiety, on the other hand, is usually due to a painful emotion which cannot be expressed directly. Instead, the associations with the original conflict are blocked from awareness by a secondary or defensive symptom, which generally prevents further personality decompensation. These defensive symptoms constitute the bulk of the symptomatology.

There are roughly three types of anxiety reactions that are based on *indirect* expression. These can be classified as follows: *Physiologic conversions* are characterized by changes in smooth muscle, organ and glandular functions leading to psychophysiologic or psychosomatic illnesses, fatigue states, and debilitated conditions. These disorders have a logical evolution, their history can

be recalled, and they are subject to educational correction by psychotherapy including hypnosis.

The second type includes *hysterical reactions* such as the functional paralysis of a limb. The disorder has a logical development and an onset which can be recalled but cannot be corrected by reeducation *per se*. This symptom requires not only reeducation but reversal of the negative sensory spiral of belief which led to its development.

In hysterical conversions, the fright leads to expectation of anxiety in similar situations. The condition can be relieved only *after it is deconditioned or reexperienced without anxiety*. That is why the driver, following an automobile accident, should immediately get behind the wheel to prevent mobilization of fear and chronic anxiety; the lack of fear leads to the rebuilding of self-confidence. Hypnosis is almost specific in these disorders.

The third type is *psychological conversions*, in which the effects of anxiety are converted through many devious pathways into psychological symptoms and reactions. These include phobias, dissociation reactions, depressions, hypochondriasis, obsessions and compulsions, and certain character and personality disorders, as well as the regressive behavior and symptoms associated with the psychoses.

These last-named disorders might be termed "logic-proof"; their genesis cannot be recalled, their history is rationalized, and the symptoms cannot be educated away. They are relieved, but with difficulty, by reevaluation of the patient's needs and by positive conditioning. The second and the third types, to some degree, parallel the effects of posthypnotic suggestions. There are many combinations of these disorders. It is useless to elaborate on the specific characteristics of each one, as was stated, because of the overlapping mechanisms common to all.

DIFFERENTIAL DIAGNOSIS

Psychosomatic illness is one of the most insidious of all human afflictions and the end-product of an emotional illness which evolved so imperceptibly that no one, least of all the patient, recognizes it. To assume that the symptoms are functional without first being able to recognize and understand positive signs of the psychogenic disorder beclouds the issue, dulls the therapist's acumen, and exposes him to the dangers of committing serious clinical errors. Even the most severe psychoses which appear with dramatic suddenness have a long history of gradual development. The hypnotherapist will be better equipped to diagnose the manifestations of long-standing emotional difficulties if he has had training in the fundamental principles of psychiatry. Therefore, it cannot be emphasized too strongly again that *it is always necessary to rule out a physical basis* as follows: After a thorough physical examination, the need for certain laboratory tests can be suggested tactfully. The resultant discussion may reveal the fears, such as of heart trouble, cancer, and tuberculosis. Negative tests are of distinct psychotherapeutic value. The physical and the laboratory examinations thus help to establish rapport, as the patient now feels that he is a collaborator. If all the findings are negative, the patient can be informed that there is no sign of physical disease and that his presenting complaints are on a psychological basis.

The unsophisticated hypnotherapist, unfamiliar with psychiatric concepts and technics of history-taking, is quite likely to experience difficulty in obtaining the anamnesis necessary to understand the functioning of the personality. Patients who consult a hypnotherapist seldom recognize the inordinate needs for their symptoms. Some of the commonest of these are the need to exaggerate inadvertently the severity of their complaints as a means of getting more attention; to avoid the responsibilities of marriage or parenthood; to dominate their home environment in a neurotic manner to compensate for their complete inability to deal with their problems in a realistic and mature manner; and, finally, to use symptoms as a means of self-punishment for guilty fears.

Many such patients, even if aware of their needs, are unable to face their emotional problems. They resist psychological probing with puzzled silence or offer only vague replies when questioned. For such difficult cues, the skillful hypnotherapist may wish to devote several multi-evaluation sessions for formal history-taking. These diagnostic sessions will be more productive

if he proceeds in a casual manner to gather his data. If he is a generalist, he can start with the physical examination. It is here, during unguarded moments, that much valuable information can be gathered. After this, he can discuss the present illness, the pertinent facts that led up to it, and, more important, the patient's attitude toward these facts.

One need not follow a schematic outline. If the therapist knows what he is looking for, there is no need to be overly formal in his approach. Rather, he should let the information come freely and without pressure. He can gently guide the patient to tell his story if there is too much digression. The discussion of sexual and intimate information will be discussed below.

In the following section the material is presented in the first person singular to secure the greatest possible immediacy in description. I usually state, "Your organs are perfect, but you are emotionally upset. Please do not infer that I think you are mentally ill; rather, you seem to be deeply involved in your emotional problems. I think I can help you to help yourself."

Differentiation of the types of emotional disorders can be accomplished at either hypnotic or nonhypnotic levels as follows: Are the symptoms connected with, or aggravated by, emotional upsets? Is there any evidence of a previous personality disturbance? What was the patient's reaction to other environmental difficulties? How have acute or chronic illnesses interfered with sexual and social adjustments? Are the complaints compatible with the physical findings? Finally—and this is most important in females—does the woman really accept herself as a woman? A high percentage of the women seen by the generalist do not have "female trouble" but have "trouble being females"!

DIAGNOSIS FROM HISTORY-TAKING

When you are seeking answers to the above questions, control your intonation and choice of words so that you do not bias the patient's replies during the history-taking. Look for unintentional "slips of the tongue" or accidental remarks. Also, watch for frequent sighing, inordinate laughing, or crying. Are significant symptoms such as restlessness, insomnia, anorexia, and palpitation minimized? Conversely, are fleeting abdominal pains and headaches exaggerated? Look for flushing or blanching of the face, flickering or lowering of the eyes, tensing of the jaws or the fists and, most importantly, assess the quality of the patient's speech, particularly where blocking or silence occurs. If the patient stammers, it usually indicates that highly charged emotional material has been touched.

When a patient blocks or is silent for any length of time, I usually say, "Just take your time. Don't talk until you can do so without effort. You can act just as you actually feel, so keep your thoughts to yourself until you are ready to talk about them. After all, you are the one who controls things—not me." The anxiety-ridden patient is grateful for being helped, and usually the brief period of silence is followed by spontaneous expressions involving present needs and aspirations. As soon as the patient realizes that he has the freedom to choose when and what to say and to whom, he feels more secure in my presence, and then usually begins to reveal meaningful material.

I avoid rapid-fire questions, as this only invites glib answers. Remember also that two questions, asked simultaneously, enable the patient to dodge *one* question by focusing *entirely* on the other. *I never ask routine questions, because routine questions deserve only routine answers.* If I wish to understand the personality structure, I always take the history myself.

In interrogating disturbed patients, the following points are important:

1. The emotionally upset individual is extremely susceptible to chance remarks. Therefore, I seldom ask intimate questions or probe very deeply until good rapport is obtained. In general, the anxious patient should be handled with tact and consideration.

2. I find it helpful to be warm, sympathetic, and reassuring because as soon as the patient senses that I am interested in solving his troubles, he develops more confidence in me. Then he is likely to "open up" and tell me what is "really bothering him," especially if he is relaxed and certain that the room is soundproof and free from interruptions. If I can give the patient the feeling that I am going to try to understand what his frustrations, hopes, and suffering mean to him, then

greater faith and optimism for his recovery will be inspired.

3. It is a good idea, when taking the history, to make the patient feel accepted and, above all, to avoid a dictatorial or "know-it-all" attitude.

4. It is not good to make premature pronouncements such as, "You are going to be all right," especially if the diagnosis has not been made as yet.

5. It is prudent to keep within your psychotherapeutic limitations, and probing for deeply repressed material should be avoided unless you know what to do with it when it appears.

6. I always avoid such platitudinous remarks as, "A lot of people are worse off than you," or "Go home and forget about it." These are fighting words to the emotionally disturbed patient because now he *really* has to prove the validity of his complaints. He will also feel that I am giving him a "brush-off," and then he is apt to visit another physician and exaggerate his suffering in order to impress him with the gravity of his condition.

7. Before obtaining sexual information, be sure that you can discuss any type of sexual behavior objectively, *without* any overt signs of disgust and without social or moral evaluation. The skilled therapist will ask all questions relative to sex without hesitation or apology. Naturally, if patients sense that you are embarrassed over sexual matters you can usually expect incorrect or dishonest answers. Also, many are evasive about their sex life because of shame or have unformulated reasons for exaggerating or minimizing the facts. Likewise, many are confused or rationalize the *real* reasons for their complaints. Many who complain of pain and fatigue are using the symptoms as a façade for psychosexual difficulties.

8. If additional information is needed, it is very helpful to interview other members of the family. Referral to a clinical psychologist for the Rorschach or ink-blot test and other psychometric evaluations is a tremendous timesaver and affords a rapid survey of the personality. When patients question the rationale for these tests, I explain, "Just as laboratory tests and x-rays are useful for physical diagnosis, so are psychological tests valuable for uncovering the hidden personality factors responsible for many psychosomatic ailments."

It should be remembered that negative examinations should not contribute to the common error of diagnosing neurosis by exclusion. Here it should be reemphasized that it is just as important to obtain *positive evidence* on the diagnosis of neurosis as it is in any other pathologic condition; a valid diagnosis of neurosis is not made by exclusion of organic factors, but by positive signs that an emotional conflict exists, which the physician must recognize or learn to recognize. It is the emotionally disturbed patient who is not too sick who often presents the real diagnostic problem.

When taking the history, comparison of the adult personality with childhood behavior and reaction patterns is an excellent idea. It is also a good rule to accept nothing that seems significant at its face value. Patients are often confused about the nature of their illnesses, both past and present, and tend to exaggerate their importance or unnecessarily minimize them. Careful inquiry will usually reveal the reasons behind such attitudes. It should also be pointed out that the prominent personality features have their opposites in sharp contrast, such as amiability and hostility, dependence and independence, submissiveness and aggressiveness. Obviously these traits are contradictory, but the hypnotherapist should not be unduly surprised to find them coexisting. He must help the patient to understand these contradictions in his personality before he can help him to achieve an inner harmony.

After obtaining sufficient information, the physician may want to discuss the history material with a psychiatrist in order to understand its significance and to plan whatever therapy is indicated. Even the psychiatrically trained physician will at times seek this consultation, and certainly the physician-hypnotist who has not had psychiatric training will save himself much time and trouble if he recognizes the need for, and accepts, this type of help.

The author would like to stress that absence of anxiety may be pathologic; psychotics usually have diminished anxiety. Anxiety can also be an asset instead of a liability. For instance, Kroger

and Fezler point out that if anxiety is paired with a relaxing image in a classical Pavlovian conditioning paradigm, the anxiety can cue relaxation after a sufficient number of "dry runs."[5] Many different therapies are directed to the reduction or neutralization of anxiety-mediated symptoms. Often the mere removal of a single symptom results in improvement of the psychotherapy—the "ripple effect."[8] Hypnosis and psychotherapy have been found to be more effective than drugs in anxiety reduction.[3] Patients face their anxieties with greater calmness when these are counterconditioned by hypnosis.[1, 4, 6, 7]

By reducing anxiety, hypnosis is an invaluable tool in crisis intervention.[2]

REFERENCES

1. Armstrong, M.L.: The treatment of anxiety states by hypnotherapy. Aust. J. Med. Sophrol. Hypnother., *2:*21, 1974.
2. Frankel, F.H.: The use of hypnosis in crisis intervention. Int. J. Clin. Exp. Hypn., *22:*188, 1974.
3. Isham, A.C.: Hypnorelaxation: therapy for tension state. Am. J. Clin. Hypn., *5:*152, 1962.
4. Kalinowsky, I., and Lerner, M.: Medicina psicosomatica e hipnosis en a enfermedades carderiovasculares. Acta Hipn. Lat. Am., *1:*69, 1960.
5. Kroger, W.S., and Fezler, W.D.: Hypnosis and Behavior Modification: Imagery Conditioning. Philadelphia, J.B. Lippincott, 1976.
6. Moss, C.S.: Therapeutic suggestion and autosuggestion. J. Clin. Exp. Hypn., *6:*109, 1958.
7. Perin, C.T.: The use of substitute response signals in anxiety situations. Am. J. Clin. Hypn., *10:*207, 1968.
8. Spiegel, H., and Linn, L.: The "ripple effect" following adjunct hypnosis in analytic psychotherapy. Am. J. Psychol., *126:*53, 1969.

49

Practical Hints in Hypnotherapy

It is difficult to separate diagnosis from therapy, as the latter begins the moment the patient enters the office, if not before. This chapter will offer a practical, "how-to-do-it" approach for eliciting the emotional *needs and intentions* that many emotionally disturbed persons have for maintaining the chronicity of their symptoms. Naturally, the following suggestions for understanding most behavior disorders do not have to be followed literally. Rather, the therapeutic procedure needs to be varied from patient to patient and may even have to be changed as therapy progresses.

Highly complex hypnoanalytic procedures should be attempted only by the well-trained hypnotherapist. However, the mature physician, who has already proven his competence by successfully handling psychoneurotics in his practice, can use hypnotherapy as outlined below. The applications depend on the extent of his training and his ability to understand adequately the needs and values of symptoms.

Brief hypnotherapy for symptom removal, as distinguished from hypnoanalysis, can achieve relatively permanent results in psychosomatic disorders. Throughout this book it has been demonstrated that hypnosis is more than mere suggestion; it is a powerful vehicle for the communication of new ideas and understandings. Whenever a person relaxes, he can more effectively concentrate upon another's communications, and, as a result, he becomes more receptive, self-objective and, therefore, more capable of examining his needs. This leads to a better understanding of his difficulties and also establishes greater cooperation.

The following maxims should be reemphasized: that a patient is *not* treated by hypnosis, but in hypnosis; that hypnosis merely intensifies the rapport between therapist and patient; and, therefore, it merely extracts the patient's potentialities.

Hypnotic technics can be incorporated into any school of psychotherapy. The choice depends upon the nature and duration of the therapy and the experience of the therapist. Raginsky wisely states: "There is little scientific justification and limited value for a concept of hypnosis which remains isolated from the mainstream of psychological thinking and research."[3]

Assuming that the therapist finds out how and under what extenuating factors the symptoms occurred, and how they operate, he should then ask himself if he thinks he can modify and control these factors by hypnosis. There are no absolute rules for conducting hypnotherapy. What is necessary is common sense, clinical judgment and intuition, and a good knowledge of human behavior. All physicians, whatever their specialties, should be able to carry out hypnotherapy as skillfully as any other medical maneuver. Since psychosomatic problems constitute a large percentage of medical practice, it is inexcusable for any physician *not* to be able to use hypnotherapy, within the usual restrictions, as an adjunct to psychotherapy.

To be a successful hypnotherapist, one does not have to have a powerful personality. He does not have to sit behind the patient, or look for "complexes," or necessarily have to probe the "unconscious" in order to give "insight" into "causative" factors. Most patients accept logical and meaningful communications, especially if these help allay their tensions. The most successful communications include anything and everything that is part of a person—his hopes, his fears, his motivations, his attitudes toward right and wrong, and even his religious concepts and beliefs.

Modern-day hypnotherapy emphasizes the value of the present—the here and the now. Explaining human relatedness in terms of instinctual energies or libidinous drives, though helpful for understanding how a particular symptom developed, is not always necessary for attacking and removing symptoms. It is necessary, however, that emotional needs, satisfactions, and goals be understood rather than irrelevant minutiae of the entire life span. Hypnosis is more effective if the total life situation is viewed more in terms of current opportunities, successes, and reasons for past failures. It should never be forced on the patient.

The goal of hypnotherapy is to establish a willingness to accept those ideas that can enhance the patient's understandings. By such measures, the subject can recognize the need for symptoms used for secondary gain purposes. Through positive and constructive suggestions, he can neutralize harmful symptoms produced by destructive thoughts, feelings, and memories.

Under autohypnosis, one often can more readily explore the needs for a symptom. At least, the "how" and the "why" of a symptom are ordinarily more readily understood in a contemplative state of self-absorption. The unique receptivity or self-reflection which characterizes the autohypnotic state usually is conducive to greater understanding.

Many times a symptom which is maintaining a neurosis can be "kept on leash" by posthypnotic amnesia. By such measures, the therapist can be on the alert for possible symptom substitution. When trading down is successful, the patient can describe how he feels now that he no longer has to contend with the symptom.

Most disturbed patients suffer more from their inability to deal with their current problems than they do from hidden traumas. Therefore, they should be encouraged to express their feelings as to how they react to these and what they propose doing about them. This is of the utmost importance and is more valuable than merely telling a patient that he should "give love and affection" to replace hostility and aggression. These are, at best, ineffective intellectualizations. It is much better to teach him how to recognize and adjust to the everyday situations that affect his functioning.

Successful hypnotherapy, too, is in reality a collaborative and reciprocal effort between therapist and patient—each learning from the other. Thus it is not the type of therapy but the strength of the interpersonal relationship that is responsible for recovery.[2]

In some instances, an understanding of the role that the symptom complex plays in the patient's emotional economy is important. It is for such patients that hypnotherapy must be modified into an uncovering technic and adapted to a specific patient's needs. In this way, access to those aspects of the personality not accessible to psychotherapeutic technics at a nonhypnotic level can be gained. For such therapy to be effective, the therapist must give the patient an opportunity to gratify certain *basic needs* which are present in varying degrees in all psychosomatic processes.[3]

THE EMOTIONAL NEEDS*

THE NEED TO TALK

Talking is the best method for alleviation of tensions. The patient discharges pent-up feelings. A permissive attitude provides him with a sympathetic listener. Since the patient depends on the physician for understanding and guidance, therapy begins with the initial interview. Listening to what the patient states is really an art. The good clinician must pay particular attention to *everything* that is being heard. To the trained listener, the body "language" is as clear as a symphonic arrangement. There are no fixed rules which can be used for this phase of hypnotherapy. The following general principles, however, will be of assistance:

*The author is indebted to J.H. Conn, M.D., for much of this material.

1. It is wise to *let the patient talk,* especially during deep hypnosis since it is here that important facts are often revealed.

2. *Listen patiently* to what the patient is saying. Then he will feel that you are really interested in him and his problems.

3. Never interrupt when inconsequential material is being discussed. Keep in mind the old adage: "If one opens his mouth enough times, he will stick his foot into it." In a patient-physician interview, *the patient is expressing his feelings as well as talking about what he thinks are the facts.*

4. Always put yourself in the patient's position. Understand not only what he is saying, but *how* he is saying it, and *why* he says what he does at this particular moment. Does he need sympathy? Is he misinformed? Does he feel guilty and is he therefore seeking reassurance? Is he angry, afraid, or evasive as he talks about highly charged topics?

5. *Show empathy and personal warmth.* Ask for richer details, more complete examples, or amplifications of what he has stated. Ask, "Then what happened?" "So?" "And then?" Or, more pointedly, "Why?"

6. *Avoid criticism, argumentation, and condemnation.* Remember that emotionally disturbed individuals can accept only a part of what they know to be the whole truth. *Psychoneurotics deceive themselves over a long period of time;* seldom are they able to see themselves as objectively as others see them. *Therefore, never tell the patient that he is "seeking sympathy."*

Always encourage the patient to talk about himself and his attitudes toward work, marriage, recreation, and politics. Religious views should be brought into the conversation. Many deeply religious individuals misinterpret religious tenets and feel guilty.

A certain amount of time (30 to 50 minutes) should be allotted to each interview. The time interval can be *in keeping with the needs of the individual patient.* At times, 2 to 4 hours may be necessary for psychiatric emergency patients. Some patients need to talk of their childhood, their handling by parents, their attitudes toward school and work, and sexual experiences. The discussion should permit ventilation of the patient's true feelings, and this will indicate how faulty attitudes and sentiments have developed. Such questions as, "How did you *feel* when that happened?" or "What did you *feel like doing* when your father (or your husband or your mother-in-law) did or said that?" help to spur the patient to relate other significant experiences.

A detailed account of pertinent life situations which decreased or increased the patient's self-esteem, as well as those in which he experienced a sense of frustration and failure, is meaningful. Specific incidents at home, at work, and at play throw light on the *pattern of the personality,* with particular attention to faulty behavior or *attitudes.* These attitudes are brought to the fore by asking, "Why did you act in this particular way." "What purpose did it serve?" These questions may bring out that the patient needs to be independent and successful at all costs, that he feels resentful toward those whom he tries to please, or that he has a need for perfectionism to avoid criticism. Here hypnosis can be used in a supportive role, as it more readily permits the release of ideas and feelings which in themselves exaggerate conflictual situations associated with the presenting symptoms.

THE NEED TO BE TOLD WHAT TO DO

The patient comes to the doctor in need of support and guidance. He wants someone who can alleviate his sufferings. The value of an authoritarian approach may be attributed in part to being told what to do by a therapist who plays "God." The immature and emotionally disturbed individual *wants to be told what to do just as a child does.* Patients who look upon the therapist as an omnipotent father-confessor, and who expect a relatively paternal authoritative attitude in him, respond best to hypnotherapists who use such an approach. On the other hand, those who anticipate the most effective help from a therapist who is permissive do better with those who assume this role. A therapist must be flexible and, if critical attitudes are mobilized by an authoritative approach, he should be able to adapt his technic to the patient.

THE NEED TO BE ACCEPTED

The patient with psychosomatic complaints usually is tense, worried, and anxious. Often guilt is present because of hostile attitudes, depressed feelings, or the self-depreciation that makes him believe that he is "no good" or "a failure." Such a patient needs reassurance. (However, many an emotionally disturbed person is looking for *personal* reassurance rather than a "clean bill of health," that is, assurance that he is a *worthwhile* person.) The physician who makes a diagnosis of "no emotional disease," often will not help the emotionally inadequate person; he will be chagrined when such patients are not "cheered up" or pleased. Not infrequently, they may even feel worse—to the dismay of the well-meaning doctor.

However, if the physician shows that he is pleased with a cooperative patient's progress, he has given the patient what he really needs. When patients are told that they are cooperative ("You have done your best to help me") or are directly complimented ("That was an intelligent account of the development of your symptoms"), most of them begin to feel a sense of increased self-esteem. They generally respond with a desire to please the doctor who is so "understanding"! This is shown by an increased willingness to discuss personal topics and a readiness to accept the fact that they are immature, dependent, and inadequate; this is in contradistinction to previous patterns of blaming others for their troubles. With this approach, patients will feel complimented by your personal interest in their illnesses and encouraged to go on to discuss personal problems. I do not hesitate to prescribe medication that I deem is indicated.

THE NEED TO BE ONE'S REAL SELF

Therapy which allows ventilation relieves pent-up feelings; this often leads to emotional security. Thus patients are able to accept the responsibility for their behavior. In most discussions, patients reveal their dependence on the opinions of others, and they relate how they have avoided every opportunity to get away from the domination of their parents, or what they believed to be the demands of an employer, a husband, or a wife. Patients will now be encouraged to do what they *really want to do*. When a patient reports an incident of behavior, he is asked, "What did you *really* want to do? Why didn't you do it?" The patient, who already has accepted the doctor as an equal and a collaborator, begins to practice what he has been taught. He brings in reports showing how he has asserted himself in a life situation and is complimented on his progress. Gradually, he learns to speak up for himself and to please himself as well as others. He literally learns to think of himself and for himself for the first time; heretofore he had been apprehensive about the possibility of offending everyone with whom he came into contact. The patient becomes his true self and, with this change in behavior, there comes a sense of freedom of action and a feeling of well-being which he has not experienced for many years.

THE NEED TO EMANCIPATE ONESELF FROM THE INFLUENCE OF THE HYPNOTHERAPIST

Finally, there is the need the patient has to break off his dependency on the doctor. Any type of suggestion in the form of advice fosters dependency. I usually eliminate dependency through utilization of autohypnosis. Likewise, dependency is eradicated if I tell the patient, "You hypnotized yourself. I didn't. You were the one who developed the symptom, were you not? The same mechanisms by which you became anxiety-ridden can be used for dissolution of your problems if you yourself do it through autohypnosis." This takes hypnotherapy out of the realm of magic.

As hypnotherapy progresses, usually less regular interviews are necessary. Visits should be reduced and then discontinued as the reasons for the needs for the symptoms are clarified and recovery takes place. Patients who do not understand their problems should not be discharged, as not infrequently such patients will keep their neurotic symptoms. These will limit their activities and keep them semi-invalids, who become wholly dependent on the physician. This breaking up of the patient-physician relationship is of the utmost importance. It should be emphasized that the patient is not improved until he has completely dismissed his therapist, put aside his drugs and other routines, and progressed to the point where he feels free to act as a healthy, emotionally secure individual, in keeping with his own personal needs and interests.

REFERENCES

1. Conn, J. H.: Psychologic treatment of psychosomatic disorders (paper read before annual meeting of the Academy of Psychosomatic Medicine, October, 1957).
2. Kroger, W. S.: And psychotherapy is indicated. West. J. Surg., *68:*138, 196, 1960.
3. Raginsky, B. B.: The use of hypnosis in internal medicine. Int. J. Clin. Exp. Hypn., *8*:181, 1960.

50

Specialized Hypnotic Technics

There are specialized technics which the physician trained in hypnosis can employ in selected patients. Some of these can be used within the framework of other types of psychotherapy. These technics potentiate the patient's capacities to learn, react, and respond with supramaximal functioning to recognize the needs for an emotional disorder. It is this understanding which brings about recovery.

Depending on the patient's difficulties, there are some hypnotic technics which are better than others for tapping the "forgotten assets" of an individual and facilitating adjustment to reality situations. This often can be accomplished without tracing symptoms to their root causes. As mentioned in Chapter 52, causal relationships, established through "insight," can be based wholly upon the therapist's interpretations, which, in turn, often are in accordance with his insight.

The patient's self-esteem, self-assurance, and self-confidence should be raised by all available measures, such as wise counseling, encouragement of self-expression, and, most important where necessary, full acceptance of his acting-out behavior patterns; the latter usually obviates resistant maneuvers.

Many of the cases described in this chapter were treated successfully by brief hypnotherapy, consisting of symptom substitution, symptom transformation, symptom amelioration, and symptom utilization. These technics, pioneered by M. H. Erickson,[12] differ from authoritarian symptom removal. Since minimal resistances are created, there is greater therapeutic leverage.

Erickson notes that such an approach results "in increased receptivity, objectivity in viewing the self, and meeting neurotic needs ordinarily difficult to obtain by more formalized methods. This receptivity, unique to hypnosis, is characterized by an exact reception of ideas without an elaboration of them in terms of implied or associated meanings."[15] In this process of presenting ideas, understanding is accelerated and gives the patient the "capacity to examine ideas for their inherent values, rather than in terms of prejudgments, opinions, mistaken beliefs, or faulty attitudes." Gardner suggested that a sense of mastery may enhance the effectiveness of hypnosis, either by facilitating induction or strengthening hypnotherapeutic suggestions, or by maintaining hypnotherapeutic gains.[22]

Some of these highly specialized hypnotic technics borrow heavily from more ancient methods. For instance, the value of systematic training in self-objectivity during states of deep meditation was stressed centuries ago by the Tantric philosopher-psychologists of India, who espoused pure Yoga. This kind of Tantric training, according to Huxley, is simply being aware of the events going on inside or outside the organism.[31] He points out that, long ago, neuroses were not treated by dredging up traumatic experiences from the unconscious, but by "training the patient to live here and now in the world of reality experiences instead of in the world of emotionally charged symbols relevant only to events that took place long ago." How different is this from the currently popular existentialist approach?

BRIEF HYPNOTHERAPY BY SYMPTOM REMOVAL

Brief hypnotherapy for symptom control, consisting of from two to 30 or more sessions, is particularly applicable to individuals who have been frustrated by deep psychotherapy and those who ordinarily would terminate therapy prematurely. The latter often respond because deeper anxieties are not evoked by minimal probing. However, there are certain patients who are not amenable to this approach. These should be referred for other types of psychotherapy.

Brief hypnotherapy reaches its greatest potential and is indicated if desensitization or deconditioning is to be employed, especially the relaxation technics involving reciprocal inhibition psychotherapy, as proposed by Wolpe.[71] It makes full use of motivation, guidance, and suggestion by indirection. Frank notes that suggestion and persuasion constitute some of the universal factors operative in mental healing.[19]

If a patient can remember what it's like to experience relief from a specific symptom during hypnosis, then, after dehypnotization, such improvement can be reexperienced. Through appropriate sensory-imagery conditioning, autohypnosis, and sufficient reinforcement sessions, the results can be gratifying. Direct symptom-removal technics, however, are justified for sufferers from emphysema, bronchiectasis, tuberculosis, or peripheral vascular diseases because of the emergency nature of their conditions. Likewise, cardiacs and hypertensives endangered by overweight are legitimate candidates for this type of hypnotherapy. It can be life-saving in status asthmaticus, intractable hiccoughing, or continual sneezing; for these conditions there is little time to analyze personality functioning. Here, even temporary cessation of the symptom acts as an incentive to enhance the potentialities for recovery.

The following are typical examples of direct symptom removal combined with brief hypnotherapy:

A 56-year-old attorney had severe wheezing and coughing spells, preventing his working. During each of six sessions, the pulmonary spasm was alleviated by hypnotic relaxation. The coughing and wheezing were controlled for varying periods by sensory-imagery conditioning involving pleasant memories. He was instructed under hypnosis that he would have 5 or 10 minutes more relief each day. Concurrently, posthypnotic suggestions were directed toward developing a profound disgust toward cigarettes. The prompt and dramatic improvement in his breathing stimulated him to practice diligently the development of an aversion toward smoking. Within 8 weeks he could talk for long intervals without coughing. He also stopped smoking. He maintained improvement and soon resumed his legal occupation. A follow-up 6 months later showed that he still was able to function with a minimal need for medications.

An 18-year-old male somnambule with severe status asthmaticus was relieved in almost a similar fashion through the combined use of time distortion, autohypnosis, and sensory-imagery conditioning. He was trained to abort an attack as soon as he felt one coming on by "contracting" time (making 30 minutes seem like 1 minute). As a result, he could "telescope" an attack into 1 minute. The attacks became less frequent and finally disappeared.

The author saw a 42-year-old male who had been hiccoughing for several weeks following a prostatectomy. In two sessions, the symptom was controlled by suggesting that *it would occur only when he voluntarily held his breath.* The author left town for an extended visit and referred him to a colleague for further care. When he returned, he was surprised to discover that his colleague's attention had not been needed. This patient had never realized that all he had to do was to breathe normally.

HELPFUL HINTS IN BRIEF HYPNOTHERAPY

There is no rule of thumb for the use of brief hypnotherapy. Each case requires an individual approach, and this depends upon the sagacity and the skill of the therapist. As was mentioned, the therapist must restructure the patient's beliefs and then he behaves differently because he thinks differently. The patient is not overwhelmed or coerced into yielding the symptom. Rather, its dissolution occurs in accordance with his wishes and needs. A permissive approach sets the terms for each new and constructive change. Patients are not in a "one-down position" or subservient to the therapist at any time; they are not prodded, forced, or ordered to give up their symptoms. Thus the possibility that another symptom equivalent will take the place of the removed one is highly unlikely when such technics are utilized.

What the patient may expect from brief hypnotherapy should be discussed in a detailed and confident manner. Apprehensive patients often ask, "Doctor, do you think that I can respond to hypnosis?" Though the following is a gross oversimplification, the therapist can remark, "It is not a question of whether or not you can respond, but whether or not you wish to 'unhypnotize' yourself out of a symptom that you have actually hypnotized yourself into. After all, this is your mind, your body, and your problem; you are the one who developed the symptom and, therefore, you are the only one who can remove it. Would you believe it—not a single person has been cured by hypnosis, *but hundreds of individuals have learned how to help themselves* through hypnosis, especially when they *really* wanted to use it to better work through their problems.[26]

One also can raise the question of the need, and how much of his symptom the patient really wishes to keep. These contradictory suggestions, at one and the same time, suggest that the symptom can be removed and yet can be kept if it is still utilitarian in the patient's emotional economy. Such suggestions, as well as more general ones, are not a direct order to change and hence do not mobilize critical attitudes. The *sine qua non* of brief hypnotherapy always is to get the patient to realize that recovery is wholly dependent upon *his* efforts rather than upon those of the therapist. Most patients also feel that because of the need to practice autohypnosis and sensory-imagery conditioning, they now have "something to sink their teeth into," and that they can contribute to their recovery. Actually, "patients are helped to help themselves."

Such an approach is different than "pulling the rug" from under the patient's feet, and removing the symptoms. Spiegel refers to "symptom alteration" wherein guidance directs attention away from the symptom and directs the patient to more resourceful measures to cope with his problems.[63] Symptom alteration sometimes occurs with a few sessions, particularly if the symptom is needed in the patient's "emotional household." Often the symptom complex can be diminished or "held on leash" until the patient is willing to yield it. Hartland believes that the symptom will be abandoned when the patient is strong enough to function without it.[29]

Frankel utilizes hypnosis in crisis therapy.[20] He describes three patients whose trance-like clinical manifestations were used as maladaptive defenses against anxiety. He feels that milder degrees of trance capacity might contribute to the development of symptoms. The trust in the therapist encourages the development of regressive transference when the trance is induced in the therapeutic situation. Frankel's keen observation may help to explain hysterical psychosis.

HANDLING RESISTANT PATIENTS BY BRIEF HYPNOTHERAPY

In the presence of hostility, the reasons should be discussed immediately to prevent further resistances. Some resistant patients undermine the therapist by following the old adage, "If you can't fight them, join them."

Illustrative was an alcoholic who had defeated innumerable therapists by his disarming mannerisms. He attempted to "seduce" the author by gifts, invitations to his home, and other blandishments. It was pointed out that behind his ardent wish to stop drinking was his stronger wish to cling to his pleasurable neurosis. This was evidenced by his ingratiating gestures—all designed to defeat the therapist.

When successful, such persons boast that "No one can help me." They seldom realize that they maneuvered their defeat. Other resistant patients continually flatter the therapist. Here, too, "Beware of the smiling patient" is a wise aphorism to heed.

A noncondemnatory manner and being impervious to irritating remarks are conducive to the establishment of good motivation. Personal bias, blaming the patient for failure to recover, or discussions of wholly irrelevant matters arouse critical attitudes. Other resistances arise when the patient expects hypnotherapy to be an inordinately rapid method. The explanation that hypnotherapy is not the sole therapeutic agent, but that it merely facilitates recovery in the same way that an anesthetic agent expedites surgery, is helpful.

If the therapist pays strict attention to what the patient is saying, this minimizes the resistances. The grateful patient, because he realizes that the therapist is giving of himself, reacts in a healthier manner; each small victory paves the way for further therapeutic gains.

Some resistant persons, such as alcoholics, especially if seen after a "hang-over," should be hypnotized on the very first visit. At this time they are more highly motivated than later. If hypnosis is not induced, some feel rejected and will not return. However, the usual course with most patients is to take a good history and make a careful appraisal, remarking, "I do not use hypnosis until I have found out what your case is all about; then I can make plans as to how I shall treat you." Highly resistant and disturbed individuals are reassured by such remarks.

Haley reviewed the brilliant methods of handling resistances described by Erickson, the leading protagonist of the brief hypnotherapeutic approach.[24] The current functions of the symptom are explored, rather than childhood experiences. From the beginning, the patient's behavior is controlled by emphasizing, directly or indirectly, that he can either talk or be silent; this permissiveness usually enables him to ventilate his feelings readily. What he says and what he does not say are noted and, through specific instructions, he is asked to continue to do something that he is doing already, but to do it under the therapist's direction.

Rather than interpreting a woman's inability to speak as resistance, Haley describes how Erickson complimented her on being able to communicate, at least, by nodding and shaking her head. He asked her if she could write and, after she had nodded her head in the affirmative, he placed a pencil in her left hand. Since she was right-handed, he asked her, "How do you feel about that?" In this structured situation, since she could not write, she had to speak.

In Erickson's other cases, resistances are reduced and cooperation is obtained by always emphasizing the positive aspects of the patient's behavior. For instance, if a patient thinks that he is a failure, Erickson compliments him on whatever determination he shows; the passive person's ability to endure is stressed; the agility of the short person; the solidity and strength of the large individual. The patient cannot combat such obvious reasoning. Thus the positive aspects of the patient's behavior are accepted and utilized so that a change can be produced. Symptomatic behavior is encouraged, but always under direction of the therapist. For instance, a highly resistant, obese patient was instructed to *overeat* enough to maintain a weight of 260 pounds instead of her current 270 pounds. Thus her needs to overeat, to lose weight, and to rebel were satisfied at the same time.

Another resistant obese woman was deliberately instructed to *gain* from 15 to 25 pounds. While gaining, she was asked to speculate on how she would go about losing the weight. Despite her reluctance to gain more weight, he insisted that she gain 20 pounds. Then she was "permitted" to stop gaining weight, which subsequently led to a permanent loss. The acceptance of the need to gain weight is encouraged, and, as a result, the patient looks to the therapist for further direction. In general, the method involves the self-respect, the needs, and the desire of the patient to give up the symptom by committing him to "some activity which he does not like (but preferably feels he should accomplish) and persuading him to go through with the activity as directed.[26]

Often resistance can be circumvented by hypnotically directing attention to other activities rather than to the symptom itself. Erickson instructed an enuretic to walk when he wet the bed. This served a twofold purpose: the enuresis indirectly came under the control of the therapist; the walking was self-punishment. An insomniac was told to stay awake deliberately, but to polish the floor all night for self-punishment reasons. A migraine sufferer was told to remember what her headache felt like in order to alter it within a month. The hidden meaning implied is, "You might consider the possibility of skipping your headache for 3 weeks or a month.[25] Patients who are controlled without knowing it are usually unable to resist the directives (extraverbal suggestions). For instance, a casual comment arouses a patient's interest in a topic, and the later mentioning of another apparently unrelated topic "unconsciously" connects the two in his mind.

BRIEF HYPNOTHERAPY BY SYMPTOM SUBSTITUTION, TRANSFORMATION, AMELIORATION, AND UTILIZATION

Symptom Substitution

Erickson intentionally manipulates neurotic symptomatology in those who are inaccessible to a total psychotherapeutic approach.[12, 14] In these persons, direct symptom removal by hypnosis fails and usually results in resistance to further therapy; the neurotic manifestations are maintained continuously until satisfactory adjustments and needs are achieved.

Illustrative is a patient who desperately needed to keep his neurotic disability. Since the underlying maladjustments were impossible to correct, Erickson substituted another neurotic disability that was similar to the existing one, but nonincapacitating in character. Shifting attention from anxiety-provoking symptoms to less urgent problems makes the patient less preoccupied with his present difficulties. The substitutive symptom also satisfies the personality needs and, as a result, a healthy adjustment to reality occurs. Erickson concludes: "Regardless of how farcical, the above technic met his symptomatic needs."[12]

Symptom substitution should be used to "trade down" to a less handicapping symptom; the new substitute symptom is more readily removed. The poorly motivated individual, the "psychiatric veteran," or the geriatric patient responds well to symptom substitution; fortunately, deep hypnosis is seldom required.

Symptom substitution can be used with superficial therapy, as in the following case:

An extremely depressed and suicidal 60-year-old male complained bitterly of a pain in his left foot. He continually "cracked" the bones in one foot to relieve the pain. His trouble had been called "psychosomatic" by consultants; one physician told him that the cuboid bone in his foot was "slipping out of place." However, orthopedic evaluation was negative. He was told that the pain in his foot was real but was brought on by gout (he had a high uric acid level). Agreement that he had real pain established prompt rapport. Through posthypnotic suggestions, he was instructed to "crack" the knuckles of his left hand. The pain in his foot cleared up as soon as his attention was shifted to his hand. Further discussion revealed that he was envious of a younger and more successful brother on whom he depended for a livelihood. Multi-evaluation sessions of his problems made him realize that the incapacitating symptom not only accounted for his dependency but also served as a useful alibi for his deep, underlying sense of inadequacy. He made a partial recovery but never returned to work, since he was unwilling to face his difficult life situation.

This method took into consideration the patient's needs for independence and self-help. By "trading down," he made it much easier to give up the symptom. Though the underlying maladjustment was not corrected, the patient developed more self-esteem. He did not realize that he had received directive therapy which undoubtedly had prevented a possible psychotic break or suicide.

Autohypnosis and sensory-imagery conditioning can be combined with symptom substitution. A more effective response to suggestions occurs during autohypnosis, and this in turn depends upon the effort that the patient puts forth and how often and how well he practices. However, the therapist must never get himself "out on a limb" by raising the patient's hopes too high. Active participation in meditation, self-reflection, self-absorption, or whatever term one wishes to use when thoughts are subjectively turned inward, must be encouraged in all patients, especially in those who dislike being helped by another person. This approach works well in the patient who has an inordinate need for attention-getting symptoms.

The author was called in consultation to see a 57-year-old male who developed a paralysis of both arms following a "whiplash injury" incurred in a minor automobile collision. He had a bilateral hysterical paralysis of the legs sustained 28 years earlier, which had been diagnosed as astasia abasia, and which necessitated the use of crutches and braces on both legs. In the presence of the referring neuropsychiatrist, a pseudo-erudite discussion of a placebo diagnosis was conducted (while the patient was under hypnosis) as follows: "This is a typical case of a partial compression of the cervical vertebrae; several nerves are pinched, and this accounts for the paralysis of both arms. They usually *run a typical course* and clear up in 6 weeks. However, for some unknown reason, the little finger on each hand does not recover full motion. But, it, too, eventually clears up." It was suggested that the patient work on one arm first, and that he imagine under autohypnosis that he was able to move it up slowly—about an inch or two each day. He practiced faithfully, and at the end of almost 6 weeks he regained full function of both arms. He complained bitterly of the involvement of the little finger on each hand for some time. When it was suggested that he might be able eventually to walk without his crutches and braces, he stated, "I want to rest for a while before undergoing more therapy." Since the personality needs were met sufficiently to achieve a satisfying, constructive, personal success, it was decided to abide by his decision. As yet he has not returned for further therapy.

This patient had been in the limelight for many years as a well-known actor. When he no longer was noticed, he developed the "paralysis." It would have been useless to confront him with this or use logical persuasion. My discussion with his physicians concealed suggestions which were really directed toward him. Inasmuch as he was not aware that he was being influenced, his criticalness was decreased, and he was thus made much more receptive to the suggestions. The placebo diagnosis fitted in with his needs, and the statement that the paralysis would "run a typical course" placed the recovery *within him.* Most importantly, the "rug was not pulled from under his feet"; he was left with a temporary paralysis of the little finger. However, during therapy, he was "allowed" to remove this symptom—but, of course, not too rapidly. Orienting the therapy around the patient's accomplishing the results and taking full credit for these is the key to a successful outcome.

Symptom Removal by Symptom Transformation

It is generally the author's policy to teach the patient how to control specific ideomotor and ideosensory activities, such as thermal changes, alterations in size and shape of the limbs, arm-levitation, and breathing. When assured that he can produce these changes readily, the patient realizes that he can either remove or develop other somatization reactions through autohypnosis.

A middle-aged woman, because of an intense hostility toward her mother-in-law, developed a hysterical tic. She was treated by symptom transformation. She was instructed, under hypnosis, to transfer the twitching of the face to the little finger of her left hand; all her symptomatology could be "condensed" into the finger. She could, if she wished, choose the time of day that this would occur. After this occurred, permission was given to allow the twitching of the little finger to increase or decrease. In the meantime, the facial tic disappeared. She was then given a powerful but concealed posthypnotic suggestion: "You will gradually lose the twitching of your little finger. Perhaps it will be next week, next month or within the year. I am sure that when I see you, at any time during the next 5 or 10 months, you will be free from all involuntary movements."

In other words, there was no question that she would be relieved within a year, or sooner. When such individuals realize that they can transfer their difficulties to other areas, they realize that self-mastery over their symptom is now possible. A specific time limit is not set. Symptom transformation should never be attempted until the patient can follow posthypnotic suggestions readily and develop a posthypnotic amnesia. Attainment of these are "proof positive" that he will comply with suggested alterations in either sensory or motor areas.

Although this approach is seemingly similar to symptom substitution, the neurotic behavior is utilized by transformation of the symptom to a less noxious one *without changing the character of the symptom itself.* Erickson describes the following case:[12]

An adult enuretic who was about to be drafted was cured by transferring a bed-wetting anxiety to a lesser anxiety situation. Amnesia was engrafted for a complicated series of posthypnotic suggestions designed to transform his fears over the enuresis into anxieties about a forthcoming visit with relatives. After this was accomplished, his only anxiety was over his mother's adjustment to his being drafted into the service.

Recovery was accomplished by systematically utilizing the patient's anxiety through a process of redirecting and transforming it. He was deliberately confused and distracted by the complexity of the posthypnotic suggestions. Then his anxiety about his wet bed and home relationships was transformed into anxiety about relatives. The final transformation became that of his mother's anxiety about his military service. Thus some degree of anxiety was continually utilized and ultimately transformed (traded down) into a normal emotion which permitted a normal adjustment.

Symptom Amelioration

Symptom amelioration is indicated when the patient is inaccessible to most types of intensive psychotherapy.

A 15-year-old boy, who had been in therapy with several excellent psychiatrists, was referred with a hysterical reaction which involved the continual plucking of his eyelashes. Although he recognized that it was a masturbatory-equivalent symptom, it had gotten worse. Under hypnosis, it was suggested that he alternately increase and decrease the plucking. His symptom was ameliorated on the basis that whatever can be increased can be decreased.

However, not all cases respond as dramatically. Good rapport, motivation, and a warm, sympathetic approach are particularly indispensable in this approach.

Symptom Utilization

Symptom utilization consists in encouraging, accepting, and redefining behavior in order to control it. Typical was the uncooperative patient who continually paced the floor during the therapeutic sessions described below. By having his acting-out behavior shifted into more cooperative activity, the patient eventually follows other directions. These technics utilize the subject's own attitudes, thoughts, feelings, and behavior in a manner similar to that in which an induction procedure makes full use of the patient's own ideomotor and ideosensory responses. This differs from the more commonly used hypnotic technics for symptom removal. These are particularly applicable for stressful situations or for those not amenable to direct hypnotic symptom removal. The reader is referred to Erickson's excellent and extensive writings for a more detailed description of his technics.[12–17]

An agitated, suicidally depressed patient was seen in psychiatric consultation. As he walked up and down the office, gesticulating wildly, he stated, "No doctor can take care of me. My condition is hopeless." I asked him why he felt this way. He stated, "I must keep walking all the time, can't sit still, and I make every therapist nervous. They all gave me up as a bad job." I softly remarked, "You know, your walking is most refreshing to me. After all, *every* other patient either sits or lies down, and at least you are different." Taken aback, he said, "Do you really mean that?" I stated, "Of course I do. But there is one thing I must ask of you. Notice my pictures on the wall. They are all in line and not askew. Now you can walk as much as you wish, but please walk in a perfect square." Needless to say, he was readily hypnotized and eventually recovered.

An experience that happened to the therapist or to another person can be related, and a definitive idea to change can be included, which the patient recognizes as applicable to himself and defends himself against. However, while he is defending himself against the idea, other suggestions can encourage change by misdirection. There is seldom a need to work with resistances, as control of a symptom can be achieved by requesting that it be manifested at a different time than usual, or in a different context or purpose. When a relapse is inevitable, the conditions for its occurrence can be suggested so that it becomes part of a cooperative endeavor rather than resistance by the patient. Symptoms are encouraged to remain until there is no need for their utilization. If a resistant patient states that he is getting worse, Erickson negates this idea and accepts it by remarking, "Since you are worse, might it not be time for a change?"

Insight, transference interpretations, or connections between past and present are not employed. Erickson's fundamental purpose is to "bring about a change in the patient, not to focus on his mental or emotional structure." His ingenious structuring of the therapeutic situation is most rewarding.

Corrective Emotional Responses Obtained by Ideomotor Signaling

Time and effort are saved and unrecognized needs for acting-out behavior can be understood when repressed material is brought into awareness by hypnotic self-exploration. Deeply hypnotized patients are instructed to review material long since forgotten, and, after the material is verbalized, its significance is revealed to the patient. It has been observed that the ease with which understanding occurs is most impressive; often an apparently hopeless situation turns into an understandable, logical, and ready accomplishment.

In this technic, it is carefully impressed upon the subject that his "unconscious mind" will reveal information pertinent to his problem that was heretofore inaccessible. However, the information revealed is seldom in an immediately recognized form. To understand it, ideomotor signaling (finger responses that are involuntarily given to indicate "yes" or "no") is resorted to so that the "unconscious" can meaningfully answer questions that it cannot answer at the so-called conscious level. The chief protagonists of this interesting approach are Cheek and Le Cron. For a more detailed approach the reader should consult their book.[6]

Discussion of Rationale of Brief Hypnotherapeutic Methods

Direct suggestions to elicit physiologic responses are generally ineffective. Scene or picture visualization should be used. For instance, in treating the insomniac, posthypnotic suggestions should be that he "see" himself in a deep state of repose, that the "see" his chest moving up and down rhythmically, and, finally, that he "picture" himself deep asleep. This is more effective than the direct posthypnotic command, "You will get drowsy and fall asleep as soon as you lie down on your pillow."

When there is no apparent progress, the therapist should make full use of extraverbal suggestion irrespective of the degree of improvement. As an example, a patient can be asked to report when he slept one minute longer. When the patient concedes this, the groundwork is laid for further recovery by pointing out that, at least, he has taken a "turn for the better."

During symptom removal by brief hypnotherapy, continual reinforcement at monthly intervals is necessary for most cases. These sessions also can be used to follow the patient's progress and provide the necessary adjustments to changing conditions.

When therapist-centered hypnosis is used, the patient gives up the symptom to please him; it will disappear only as long as the patient has faith in the all-powerful therapist. Relapse occurs because the enforced dependency fosters ambivalence (the coexistence of love and hate) toward the therapist. As soon as the resentment gains the upper hand, the symptom returns. Therefore, all patients are informed as soon as they are taught autohypnosis, "You are now on your own, and each day you will have less dependency on me."

Janet, Freud, and many of the older hypnotists contended that, even though a temporary cessation could be achieved dramatically by hypnosis, symptom removal was not lasting. This was true because *of the way in which they used hypnosis.* They seldom made full use of autohypnosis, sensory-imagery conditioning and other sophisticated refinements. Had they been oriented in the technics of brief hypnotherapy described in this chapter, symptom removal would have been more permanent. Irrespective of the therapeutic goals, symptom removal by brief hypnotherapy provides many despondent patients with faith and hope.

PSYCHOBIOLOGIC HYPNOTHERAPY

Throughout this book, the author has espoused the dictum that "Anything and everything that helps the patient should be employed." In the psychobiologic approach, such medications as sedatives, tranquilizers, and other drugs can be used with hypnotization to induce a psychobiologic reorganization of the personality. Wolberg has described how healthy relationships based on guidance, reassurance, persuasion, reeducation, and reconditioning under hypnosis can raise the threshold to anxiety-provoking stimuli.[69] In an excellent presentation, Wolberg classified these as follows:

Guidance: The therapist assumes the role of a surrogate figure, and suggestions are in line with the psychological principles involved in guidance.

Reassurance: When suggestions are given by an omniscient authority they are more convincing.

Persuasion: Hypnosis reinforces persuasive arguments, and certain directions are followed more readily.

Reeducation: When individuals hold themselves

"out at arm's length for inspection," they become aware of their faulty behavior patterns, and a change occurs when the "sting" is taken out of these—densensitization.

Reconditioning: Conditioned reflexes are more readily engrafted when intensification of emotional stimuli occurs.

RECIPROCAL INHIBITION PSYCHOTHERAPY

Wolpe, has developed effective hypnotherapeutic technics which yield results of almost 90 per cent "apparently cured" and "much improved."[71] He contends that a habit can be eradicated by forming a new and antagonistic one toward the same stimulus situation. By deliberately opposing responses antagonistic to anxiety responses, neurotic anxiety response habits can be overcome—this is the reciprocal inhibition principle.

This principle was developed from the observations that only three kinds of processes can produce lasting changes in an organism's habit of response to a given stimulus situation. These are growth, lesions, and learning. Since neurotic behavior originates in learning, it can be eliminated only by "unlearning." Such other responses as relaxation and assertive sexual ones are capable of inhibiting anxiety. Breathing, conditioned-motor and conditioned-avoidance responses are employed in special situations. These conditions are always arranged in such a way that neurotic anxiety will be maximally inhibited by the antagonistic response selected.

Reciprocal inhibition therapy makes full use of progressive relaxation and hypnosis to counter the effects of anxiety-evoking stimuli. An "anxiety hierarchy" list is constructed, consisting of those stimuli to which the patient reacts with unadapted anxiety. The hypnotized patient is told to imagine the weakest item or the smallest "dose" of phobic stimulation on the list. If the relaxed state is not disturbed by this, a slightly stronger "dose" is presented at the next session from the next item on the list. The "dosage" is gradually increased from session to session, until at last the phobic stimulus can be presented at maximal intensity without impairing the depth of relaxation. This eventually prevents the patient from reacting with his previous anxiety to those situations that are associated with even the most intense phobic stimuli.

This systematic desensitization technic is applicable to most neuroses, as they are basically unadaptive conditioned-anxiety reactions. According to Wolpe, all psychotherapy is based on the reciprocal inhibition principle: emotional responses are evoked which have the capacity to inhibit anxiety. He recognizes that a nonspecific placebo effect (about 50%) is operative in all psychotherapeutic methods, ranging from traditional counseling to psychoanalysis. Thus, 50 per cent of his patients profit from this effect, but other factors must be considered, since his "cure" rate is almost 90 per cent.

SYSTEMATIC DESENSITIZATION

The patient first gets a "homework" task, wherein he is asked to make up a list of everything that frightens, disturbs, or embarrasses him. Systematic desensitization to increasing amounts of these anxiety-evoking stimuli is initiated under hypnosis. The basic assumption underlying this procedure is that the response to the imagined situation resembles that to the real situation. Experience bears out that individuals become anxious when they imagine stimuli that are fearful in reality. These will be used for desensitizing the patient.

In the first desensitization session, scene visualization is suggested by hypnosis. The least disturbing items from the bottom of the list are first presented at 2- or 3-second intervals. When tension is exhibited, the hand is raised as a signal and the ongoing scene is immediately "blacked out." After dehypnotization, the patient is asked if the scenes were clear and which ones were disturbing.

During the second desensitization session, those items that produced no disturbance are omitted and the next higher items are presented. If anxiety is manifested after the presentation of a weak scene, a weaker item must be substituted. Stimuli with a high anxiety-evoking potential must not be presented prematurely. If a major setback occurs, several hypnotic sessions should be devoted to deep relaxation without scene visualization. At subsequent sessions, subject matter far down the list from the items that produced the setback are introduced cautiously. Weaker reactions usually ensue when the same scene is presented several times during the session. When this occurs, therapy is accelerated.

With proper handling, most patients will report a progressive decrease of sensitivity in from 10 to 25 sessions. Progress also varies with hypnotic depth. Nonhypnotizable patients, however, ultimately do as well but are slower. A failure of about 50 per cent occurs in those who cannot imagine the suggested scenes. Progress is impeded when the disturbed reaction to the imagined scene is not experienced as reality. Here the relevant emotions can be aroused by having the patients *verbalize* the scenes; they then progress the same as the other patients do. Some patients, particularly those with hysterical conversion reactions, are treated by the repeated presentation of meaningful experiences under hypnosis. The reader is referred to Wolpe's excellent presentation describing desensitization sessions conducted during hypnosis. Illustrative case histories indicate that the method is useful regardless of the character of the neurotic responses; they disappear when the power of the stimuli to evoke anxiety is removed. He reports cures in ulcer, impotency, insomnia, migraine, paranoid obsessions, phobic reactions, and a wide variety of other psychosomatic conditions.

HYPNOBEHAVIORAL APPROACH

Wolpe's technics utilizing hypnosis have been modified by the behavior modifiers who prefer to use Jacobson's progressive relaxation or Schultz's autogenic training. This approach is most efficacious in phobic reactions. Kroger and Fezler have described the use of their hypnobehavioral model not only for phobias, but for obsessive compulsive, hypochondriacal, and depressive neuroses.[35] This approach can include the hypnoanalytic approach or concomitant psychopharmacologic therapy. The interested reader is referred to their chapters on conversion hysteria, depression, and an extensive section on schizophrenia and psychotic states. After reviewing a large body of literature in these areas, they conclude that psychotics are conditionable, trainable, and hypnotizable.

Polak and co-workers found that 16 out of 26 psychotic patients were hypnotizable in a single session.[49] However, they stress that hypnosis should be induced during periods of lucidness when patients can concentrate more effectively. Heath and co-workers hypnotized 9 out of 35 randomly selected psychotics.[30] The sample included deteriorated, lobotomized schizophrenics, some of whom were uncooperative. The investigators believe that with repeated inductions, the results would be better. Shibota and Motoda found that autogenic training benefited psychotics.[61] Others stress anxiety reduction and shaping appropriate behavior by reinforcement.[35]

Another hypnobehavioral but dynamically oriented approach for neurosis can be employed. It is a six-phase therapy consisting of (1) induction; (2) regression, interpretation, and insight therapy; (3) counterconditioning under hypnosis; (4) retraining *in vivo;* (5) self-hypnosis; and (6) ego-assertive training. This approach, when applied in a hypnoanalytic framework, is efficacious, particularly for phobic, hysterical neurosis, and psychosexual problems.

MISCELLANEOUS SPECIALIZED TECHNICS OF HYPNOTHERAPY

YOGA OR Y-STATE OF HYPNOSIS

According to Meares, the Yoga or Y-state of hypnosis is characterized by profound abstraction that is produced and maintained by an *active* effort of the will concentrated on a single idea.[44] It differs from sleep and ordinary hypnosis in that the cerebration is active and controlled and concerned primarily with subjective ideation. It is also particularly helpful for those who are unsuitable for hypnoanalysis and for certain types of introverts whose greater subjectivity facilitates the Y-state. Moreover, those who readily enter meditative, prayer, or reverie states appear to do better in the Y-state. Meares uses routine hypnosis for therapeutic suggestions and relaxation; here the patient remains utterly *passive.* The Y-state, on the other hand, is more suitable for auto-hypnotherapeutic technics.

RELIGIOUS HYPNOTHERAPY

Rodriquez makes full use of a religious approach in conjunction with hypnotherapy.[53] A constructive interpersonal relationship facilitates acceptance of the rationalizations.

Today, many clergymen, especially those who are also psychologists and psychiatrists, are employing hypnotherapy with astonishing success. Since they are already a sort of father-confessor to many of their parishioners, they are in an enviable position to help them because of well-established faith. Pastoral counseling has made rapid strides, and it is only a matter of time until there will be many more clergymen making use of hypnotherapy. The author has taught hypnotherapy to several clergymen who also were psychiatrists or psychologists. They report gratifying results when hypnosis is utilized within a religious framework.

SUGGESTIVE "SLEEP"

Platonov, in a psychophysiologic treatise on psychotherapy and hypnosis, describes how he used suggestive "sleep" over a period of 50 years for achieving positive therapeutic effects in thousands of patients. His beliefs are in line with Pavlov's, namely, that hypnosis affords curative protective inhibition (regenerative self-healing) of neurons disturbed by excitatory processes.

Platonov's hypnotherapy utilizes direct symptom-eliminating suggestions, as follows:

"What you have suffered belongs already to the past and does not trouble you any more. You have forgotten all your suffering, and when you remember it, it does not distress you." In treating a patient who has a fear of thunderstorms, he made the following suggestion, "You are no longer afraid of thunderstorms, and they do not disturb you."

According to orthodox Pavlovian doctrine, when the suggestion, "Your suffering belongs to the past and does not trouble you any more," is

repeated several times, an "inhibition of the point of concentrated excitation" is brought about. The words, "What you have suffered belongs to the past," represent an inhibitory conditioned reflex directed toward the suppression of the excitatory "trigger zone" in the cortex. In other words, the deranged regulatory activity of the cortex rather than the symptom is treated, and this is accomplished by the use of appropriate word stimuli.

Platonov's hypnosuggestive methods are combined with an eclectic psychotherapeutic approach. Therapy is begun with a series of interviews to ascertain how the symptom developed. Thus a careful history becomes an integral part of the psychotherapeutic approach to the patient as it establishes good rapport, especially in neurotics. Explanation and persuasion are used first, and this is followed by suggestion under hypnosis for the purpose of consolidating what has been said to the patient before the induction of hypnosis.

It is interesting that Platonov and his associates, who have hypnotized many thousands of persons in the Soviet Union for over half a century, remark:[48]

We have never observed any harmful influence on the patient which could be ascribed to the method of hypnosuggestive therapy. Presumably leading to the development of an 'unstable personality,' 'slavish subordination,' 'weakening of the will,' or an 'increase or pathological urge for hypnosis.'

It is also of considerable interest that he describes the important work done in 15 "hypnotariums" organized by the Leningrad City Board of Health over 20 years ago. Sparked by Pavlov's pioneering research in hypnosis, Soviet researchers have made some remarkable contributions.

ACTIVE COMPLEX PSYCHOTHERAPY

Another hypnotherapeutic approach based on the Pavlovian model is Volgyesi's active complex psychotherapy.[64a] In his book he describes how he treated over 56,500 patients by a combination of group psychotherapy, hypnosis, and supportive technics.

HYPNOSYNTHESIS

Conn calls his method hypnosynthesis.[9, 10] He utilizes hypnotherapy without extensive probing. The patient uses it as he sees fit, without being given any symptom-eliminating suggestions or being forced to remember unpleasant events, or being given preconceived interpretations or directions. With this method, in which no importance is attached to the depth of the hypnosis, Conn has obtained very satisfactory results in a wide variety of cases. In studying recovery under hypnosis, he remarks that "Much of the current interest in hypnotherapy is a rebellion against Freud's dictum that a patient can only get well at the price of sweat and tears and by an expenditure of much time and money."[9] His experience substantiates our contentions, namely that the hypnotist only "sets the stage"; it is the patient who induces the "trance by doing what is expected of him.[10] Solovey and Milechnin base their hypnotherapeutic approach on Conn's principles to achieve "emotional stabilization."[62]

TERPSICHORE TRANCE THERAPY

Akstein describes a new hypnopsychotherapeutic method called terpsichore trance therapy (TTT).[2] It is used by Afro-Brazilian spiritual sects. It is a trance obtained through movements of the body (mostly rotational) in a ritualistic dance. TTT is a special form of group psychotherapy in which tensions are released. It is similar to Conn's hypnosynthesis as the induction of the hypnotic state *per se* often is curative. However, in TTT, guidance and support prior to, and subsequent to, the sessions are employed, as are medications. TTT also involves sociotherapy as the therapy often is employed in small groups.

AUTOGENIC RELAXATION

Schultz's autogenic training has been discussed in Chapter 17, and its similarity to Yoga, Zen, T.M., and altered states of consciousness has been emphasized. It is valuable for hysterical conversion syndromes and the neuroses.

Patients learn to reach the autogen or "self-induced" state of consciousness quickly by practicing the exercises described in Chapter 17. The autogenic state supposedly brings the mechanisms of the right and left hemispheres of the brain into greater harmony. The state also has the EEG characteristics of R.E.M. sleep.

Vivid abreactions are produced which can elaborate descriptions and images that purportedly are more precise than dreams. The abreactions can be tape-recorded and played back to the patient. There then follows a process of "autogenic neutralization" in which the patient comments on their meanings, so that a "feedback to the patient's ego" occurs. Neutralization and integration are needed to assure meaningful insight.

Currently, Schultz's autogenic training is being used to augment the effects of biofeedback, and it has wide application in alleviation of pain problems through alpha autogenics.

HYPNOANALYSIS

Watkins contends that the hypnotic concept of "trance" and the psychoanalytic concept of "transference" are essentially identical.[66] When hypnoanalytic technics as automatic writing, projective technics, and crystal-gazing are employed, and the patient is required to talk, the patient inevitably shifts from deeper stages to lighter ones. For those hypnotherapists who wish to follow psychoanalytic technics, there is an extensive bibliography on the subject.[33, 37, 54, 59, 69]

When hypnosis is used with psychoanalytic procedures, the entire process can be speeded up, and there is no such undue dependency as compliance. Significant emotional participation occurs when deeply hidden material is released and, with appropriate technics, the meaningfulness of this data can be integrated into full awareness. If one wishes to work with resistances, these can be analyzed as in an orthodox analysis. Hypnoanalysis thus derives from hypnosis "a penetrative technical instrument that obviates many of the time-consuming elements which often render ordinary psychoanalysis objectionable and in some cases impossible."[38]

APPLICATIONS OF, CONTRAINDICATIONS, AND INDICATIONS FOR HYPNOANALYSIS

APPLICABILITY

Anyone who can be hypnotized can be hypnoanalyzed to a degree. Individuals who can attain deeper stages of hypnosis are the best subjects for hypnoanalysis. This limits the method to less than 20 per cent of the population.

CONTRAINDICATIONS FOR HYPNOANALYSIS

Those who can enter a sufficiently deep state and who are able to bring forth highly charged emotions require a competent and well-trained psychotherapist to deal with the material.

The fearful individual with weak and inadequate characterologic defenses, who is likely to be overwhelmed by the intensity of the therapy, and those who are too preoccupied with their negative fantasies, or those who fear an attack on their homosexual strivings should not be treated by this approach.

The manic-depressive, with wide mood swings, is seldom a good candidate for hypnoanalysis, as his disorganized mental state results in inadequate concentration. It is virtually impossible to treat detached schizophrenics, who are not in contact with reality, by this method. The lack of reality perception is a prime contraindication to hypnoanalysis.

Though the investigators did not use hypnoanalysis, Ihalainen and Rosberg noted that hypnotic suggestions can be employed with considerable benefit in chronic schizophrenic patients.[32] Greene has shown that psychotics enter hypnosis as readily as normals,[23] and Biddle recommended more regressive methods than mere relation.[3] Lavoie and co-workers review an extensive literature on clinical and experimental studies indicating that psychotics can achieve medium and deep hypnotic states.[36] Wolberg recommends hypnosis in certain cases.[70] However, Deckert and West found psychotics difficult to hypnotize,[11] and other researchers consider hypnosis as potentially dangerous.[39]

INDICATIONS FOR HYPNOANALYSIS

Hypnoanalysis is particularly indicated for psychoneurotics who do not respond to brief hypnotherapeutic procedures, or for those who already have had some type of unsuccessful psychotherapy. It is particularly suited for the poorly motivated patient such as the psychopath. Here utilization of posthypnotic suggestions to "bind" the patient in therapy is a distinct advantage until a healthy rapport is established. Though an extreme degree of dependency is fostered deliberately, it can be worked through and dissolved during later sessions.

Hypnoanalysis is both an investigative and a therapeutic technic in the refractory obese individual, the narcotic addict, and the alcoholic. This approach can lend support to the healthy aspects of the personality until the need for the symptom is worked through and controlled. Hypnoanalysis also has shown considerable promise in the treatment of phobias and compulsions.

Appropriate safeguards, such as enabling the patient to remove his own maladaptive responses through sensory-imagery conditioning and other technics, as a rule, prevent recurrence of the phobic or compulsive reaction. Rosen has described how age regression was hypnotherapeutically induced in several patients as an emergency measure to prevent suicide.[55]

METHODOLOGY OF HYPNOANALYSIS

Patients are first trained in hypnosis, autohypnosis, and other phenomena of the deep state. This may require 20 sessions or more. The number varies with the type of emotional involvement, the motivation of the patient, his inherent ability to achieve a deep state, and the effort he puts forth. At the end of the preliminary training period, the following criteria should be met: (1) the patient must be capable of entering a hypnotic state upon a given posthypnotic signal or through autohypnosis; (2) he should be able to follow posthypnotic suggestions readily, especially those which produce amnesia and age regression; and (3) through revivification he must be able to reexperience events long since forgotten.

Stillerman emphasizes that steps must be taken in the first few sessions to understand the patient's reaction to the therapeutic situation, that is, his anxieties, his reactions to the hypnotherapist, and why and how he is defending himself and thus resisting change and progress.[64] Before attempting induction, he questions the patient regarding his reactions either to observing or to experiencing hypnosis and how he feels about being hypnotized. Next, the subject's reactions to either physical or mental activities are closely observed, and he is immediately asked what he is thinking about. After the initial induction, the various emotional reactions experienced while entering hypnosis, being in it, or coming out of it are elicited. In subsequent sessions, dreams as well as verbal and nonverbal productions are included.

Following the training period, the analytic phase may be instituted. The resistances and the defenses are clarified by development of the transference neurosis. This phase of hypnoanalysis closely parallels the standard psychoanalytic procedure. The process utilizes free associations, dreams, analyses, and recollections, all of which are interpreted by the hypnoanalyst.

HANDLING RESISTANCES

Whenever marked resistances are encountered, the patient can be deeply hypnotized and the resistances in question undercut. The efficacy of hypnoanalysis, according to Lindner, is not reduced by undercutting resistances, nor is this merely superficial therapy.[37] All the resistances are not dispelled through hypnosis. As mentioned in the preceding chapter, the blocks are handled through discussion, interpretation, and evocation of the reasons for the various defensive mechanisms employed by the patient. This includes the more serious resistances which relate to the character structure, and the symptomatology of the patient, such as loss of memory for traumatic events and defense mechanisms, character malformation, and distortion through symptom formation.

HANDLING SYMPTOM FORMATION

Many hypnoanalysts believe that, for lasting therapeutic benefits, a protective amnesia for each hypnotic session must be induced in order to guarantee that the entire personality will participate in the therapeutic process. Lindner, the chief protagonist of this approach, has described how the imposition of posthypnotic amnesia is used in the recovery of lost, repressed, or rejected memories or in the disintegration of resistances.[39] He terms this the "interim phenomenon." Briefly, once repressed material has been divulged during hypnosis, the patient is slowly prepared to receive this information at nonhypnotic levels. Lindner states:

In other words, in the interim between the disclosure of significant but repressed memories or other resistance-forming material and waking free association, the ego is readied for the reception of what it had formerly rejected, for any one or a combination of possible reasons.[40]

Actually, this obviates the lengthy and controversial "analysis of resistances" which plagues so many psychoanalytic sessions. The saving in time is considerable, and the patient is prepared to accept what he formerly defended himself against.

A spontaneous flow of the material for which the amnesia was imposed filters up into awareness either after the termination of the hypnotic session or during a subsequent visit. Therefore, nothing of importance to therapy is lost and, more important, the patient participates with full awareness in the therapeutic processes. Finally, through posthypnotic suggestions, the patient can be instructed that some of the material which was too traumatic for him to face during the session can be the basis for a dream between now and the next visit. Thus, if there is a symbolic correlation between the revealed data and the dream, the validity of the exhumed material can be cross-checked via this approach.

When amnesia cannot be induced, posthypnotic suggestions can be utilized to have dreams that will indirectly elicit forgotten mnemonic data. Although these dreams may be rich in symbolism, they often can provide clues to significant repressed feeling states or situations. However, there is a difference between amnesia suggested by posthypnotic suggestions and the amnesia spontaneously noted during hypnosis. Spontaneous amnesia may indicate somnambulism, while the former may be a means whereby traumatic events may be artificially repressed.

Posthypnotic suggestions also can be used for reinforcement to help bolster the changes in the personality organization. Hence, adaptation to new and difficult situations becomes less painful and time-consuming. Hypnosis may also contribute to the dissolution of the transference relationship which is managed as in a routine analysis. The energies that were formerly of pathogenic significance and monopolized by the symptom can be redistributed along the line dictated by the entire course of the therapy.

Since the accord between patient and analyst is closer and more intense than in other forms of psychotherapy, the tools for therapy are sharper and more incisive. This undoubtedly accounts for the rapidity with which exploration of deeply repressed material can take place in hypnoanalysis. It is unfortunate that hypnoanalysis is too often ignored, as it is a valid therapy even though limited to those patients capable of entering deep hypnosis.

OTHER UNCOVERING HYPNOANALYTIC TECHNICS

HORIZONTAL EXPLORATION

Horizontal exploration of the personality structure can be utilized at various levels through hypermnesia.[65] Here the therapist identifies himself as a friend of the parents, or acts as one of the parents. The patient can be asked, "How did things go with you today?" Or, "What seems to be bothering you?" Or, after engrafting an amnesia for his own identity, the skillful therapist assumes the role of a sibling, a friend, a teacher, an employer, a lover, or a mate. In this situation, the patient's verbalization and behavior will reveal the way he felt toward significant persons in his life at different age levels.

VERTICAL EXPLORATION

Vertical exploration can also be used to trace the origin and the development of specific attitudes. Interweaving of the chronologic past with the present rapidly assesses earlier attitudes. This seems to be a function of the interpretative cortex, in which past events timelessly blend with current realities. Regression is attained by stating, "You are looking at a large calendar on the wall. Instead of numbers for each day and month, you will see numbers of the years. Whenever you wish, you may tear off each page. The first one is 1961. Now, 1960, 1959 . . ." (until the desired age is attained). The statements must be in the present tense, as, "It is now 1941. Do you know that today is your birthday? You are 8 years old *now*, are you not? What are you thinking of doing this afternoon?"

(*Top*) Normal handwriting at age 44. (*Center*) Sample of handwriting while regressed at age 8. (*Bottom*) Part of letter written to parents.

Other attitudes such as love, hate, fear, and sexual feelings can be traced by *age progression*. For instance, if a patient who has regressed to age 7 mentions that at age 5 he was extremely bitter toward his mother, he can be told, "You are no longer 5. With each breath you take, you are growing older: 5, 6, 7. Now you are 15 years old. How does it feel to be in high school?" If the answer is in the present tense and the person appears to talk and act in accordance with the suggested age, the age regression is valid. He is now asked, "Do you love your mother?" If the answer is affirmative, the hostility in all probability is deeply repressed, and it will require other and more complex methods, such as projective technics, to uncover the genesis of emotion. If the answer is negative, considerable light on the origin and the development of the hostility can be obtained.

Dissociated or Automatic Handwriting

This technic can be used to ascertain the reasons for a conflict. After the arm and the hand are dissociated, the patient, upon direct questioning, may give one answer while his hand is writing something else. This is because the dissociated hand is released from cortical control. The written material can be a clue for the cause of the patient's anxiety.

Illustrative is the case of a frigid 44-year-old woman who had an intense hostility toward her husband, who symbolized a father-figure whom she hated. The onset of this attitude was evinced by the following material, obtained under automatic writing.

When asked to explain the writing, after dehypnoti-

zation, she stated that she was very angry toward her father when she was 8 years old because he sent her to boarding school. The automatic writing reactivated a long-forgotten incident, and also revealed the cause of her hostile attitude toward her husband. She remarked, "My husband is just like Dad. He is always so bossy and opinionated. I just can't stand him."

Each patient should be "restored" to his present chronologic age and the hand "returned" to normal before dehypnotization. While still under hypnosis, the patient should be instructed to remember everything that was written. Protective amnesia can be instituted if the material is too traumatic to be faced at this time. An explanation of the written material, intelligible only to the patient, can be facilitated by posthypnotic suggestion, provided he really wants to explain it.

A controlled dissociation of the usual ego state has been found valuable for uncovering repressed material.[37] Repressed material must not be used to confront the patient if the defenses are inadequate. Mere elicitation of repressed material or buried mnemonic data by no means assures integration of the recovered memories.

Projective Hypnoanalysis

Such psychometric tests as the Rorschach, or other stimulating situations, are presented in the form of what seems to be nonsense material. Here, while not on guard, patients project significant conflicts. Variations such as the theater technic, crystal-gazing, or scene visualization obtained by gazing at a blank card, often reveal inner feelings which can be discussed after dehyp-

Age 10: angry with her father because he never took her with him when he went away. (Compare with the following samples.)

notization. However, as Watkins has mentioned, the more the situation is structured, the less significant will be the material which emerges.

Another useful technic is the Thematic Apperception Test (T.A.T.), which consists of the presentation of various pictures about which the hypnotized patient is asked to imagine a story or a theme suggested by them. In the Jung Association Test, the patient is requested to give the association evoked by the next stimulus word. Each response becomes the stimulus for the next. Regression can also be used. In an unreported series with Helen Sargent, the author has validated Watkins' contentions.

HYPNODRAMA

The methods introduced by those interested in psychodrama also can be employed while the patient is under hypnosis. The whole conflict situation can be dramatized, and the therapist or a professional actor can play one of the roles. While the patient is under hypnosis, a posthypnotic suggestion is given that he play the part of a specific character. The two then dramatize a situation in which the inner conflicts of the imaginary character with whom the patient has identified are portrayed.

The personality structure also can be split or dissociated for separate study: the patient can act out both roles. Naturally, the dissociation should be along the lines of the inferred conflict. In this way the patient actually reenacts his own inner conflicts. Regression, dissociated handwriting, and any of the projective technics can be used in conjunction with hypnodrama.

ABREACTION

An emotional reliving or reenacting of traumatic experiences, with a resultant release of energy, can be obtained in good hypnotic subjects. This approach is valuable for anxiety and hysterical reactions of recent origin, particularly those associated with war neuroses. The nature of repressed impulses can be studied to determine their purpose. Following release of the inhibited guilt, rage or fear impulses, intellectual as well as emotional reintegration can be accomplished.

Experience with these methods in a military setting indicates that, through enactment of the conflict, the original frustrating situations are brought to a more satisfactory and realistic solution. It is believed that:

An emotionally corrective experience is undergone which "completes" the unfinished strivings, which are

(*Top*) Age 16: son is born. (*Center*) Age 30: sample handwriting. (*Bottom*) Age 47: written in answer to the question "What is bothering you?" (Son's wife had divorced him; mother is worried about son.)

the repetitive core of the neurosis and relieves the need to continue its symptomatic manifestations.[66]

THE AFFECT-BRIDGE OR IN-AND-OUT METHOD

Watkins makes use of yet another interesting technic in which an emotion that is unpleasant in the present is intensified until it can act as a memory bridge to a previous traumatic event that involved the same condition.[68] The patient is moved experientially from the present to a past incident or an affect common to the two events, rather than through an overlapping "idea." The current affect is vivified and all other aspects of the present experience are hypnotically ablated. The patient is thus asked to return to some earlier experiences during which the affect was lived and to relive the associated event. Significant conflict material so secured can be "brought forward" to the present to receive "insight" and "working-through." The technic appears to achieve significant therapeutic changes in a comparatively short time.

INDUCTION OF DREAMS

Meares, in an excellent presentation, describes special procedures to facilitate hypnoanalysis.[42] He makes use of analysis of dreams produced through direct or indirect posthypnotic suggestions. This is a useful technic for cases in which regression and abreaction cannot be induced.

INDUCED HALLUCINATIONS

In a fashion similar to that in the technics described by Watkins, hallucinations are suggested without suggesting their nature. Conflicts ordinarily inaccessible to hypnoanalysis are revealed by this technic. The induced hallucinations are produced by suggesting that the subject visualize himself on a theater screen, or in a house in which he has been at one time, or that he "see" images which will appear in a crystal ball (crystal-gazing). The analysis of the content of the induced hallucination often throws considerable light on the repressed conflicts.

UNSTRUCTURED HALLUCINATIONS

Unstructured hallucinations are induced without structuring the therapeutic situation. Merely by asking the subject, while he is in deep hypnosis, to relate what is happening, significant material may be revealed, and spontaneous regression and abreaction often occur.

PRODUCTION OF EXPERIMENTAL CONFLICTS

An artificial situation which resembles the patient's conflict situation often can afford sufficient insight as to how and why he reacts to his own conflict. The patient is led to experience the appropriate emotion and he reacts to it with his own particular neurotic behavior. Posthypnotic suggestions are directed for recall of those experiences and feelings which the patient had while hypnotized. Thus, while observing the reaction to an imaginary conflict, insight is gained into the nature of his conflict situation. This approach should be used only by experienced hypnotherapists.

NARCOHYPNOANALYSIS OR NARCOSYNTHESIS

Skillful hypnotherapists seldom use drugs. However, occasionally a refractory patient may be given a small amount of Pentothal Sodium; this often allows the patient to talk more freely. The patient who benefits most by this approach is the one who states, "I doubt if I can be hypnotized." Other individuals, who associate hypnotizability with gullibility, respond well to various drugs, such as scopolamine. Such patients are merely looking for some excuse to respond to the suggestions of the therapist; they do not feel stigmatized by drug-induced "hypnosis."

HYPNOGRAPHY

Meares uses a form of graphic expression which has a much wider application than automatic writing in hypnoanalysis. Hypnography is integrated with verbal hypnoanalysis and waking psychotherapy. He has described hypnography as a "technique in hypnoanalysis in which the hypnotized patient projects psychic material in black and white painting." While under hypnosis, the patient associates to the painting. Meares feels that it is useful for patients who do not talk readily in hypnosis. He believes that graphic expression of conflicts has a greater therapeutic effect than verbal expressions of the same conflicts, as it speeds up hypnoanalysis. Suppressed and repressed material is disclosed more readily, and there is greater emotional participation of the patient in the treatment. The patient is less apt to defend himself from his emotions, and greater emotional participation usually leads to spontaneous regression and abreaction. This approach is particularly indicated for those who cannot adjust to current reality conflicts. The reason for this is that, when the patient is actually confronted with the problem which he expresses in hypnography, he develops a greater tolerance of the conflict. As a result, he is not so disturbed by it and makes a better adjustment to reality.

Often, however, when the elicited material is presented to the patient at nonhypnotic levels, it leads to anxiety manifestations. With somatic improvement, the patient slowly gains insight through the ventilation of traumatic material by hypnography. Often without any "waking psychotherapy," further symptomatic improvement results, which manifests itself by a change of the paintings. Partial amnesia often occurs after the sessions. Since conflicts are being expressed graphically and verbally by associations, hypnography facilitates hypnoanalysis. For a more complete account of hypnography, the reader is referred to Meares's excellent monograph on this subject.[41]

The dangers here are that the sudden and permanent recognition of the significance of the repressed material may result in an attack of acute anxiety. This necessitates a deeper stage of hypnosis. Meares points out that an unconscious misinterpretation of the therapist's behavior can result in the patient's not being able to be dehypnotized—a sort of defense reaction which calls for an elastic ("psychodynamic") handling of the hypnosis.

HYPNOPLASTY

This technic in hypnoanalysis resembles hypnography. The hypnotized patient uses clay to model whatever he wishes to make. The patient's conflicts find expression in plastic rather than graphic form. He is asked to associate to the model, and the disclosed material is used in his psychotherapeutic handling.

When the patient talks about the shapes which he has made, the specific meanings and the nature of the conflict which has motivated the making of a particular model are brought to light. Meares believes that this is an excellent approach for the resistant patient, and that hypnoplasty has a real place in hypnoanalysis. For a more complete account of hypnoplasty, the reader is referred to another fine monograph.[43] Raginsky's technics via sensory hypnoplasty have been among the most original and potentially fruitful extension of these technics to hypnosis.[50, 51, 52] Sacerdote has made use of sensory hypnoplasty and hypnography within a psychoanalytic frame of reference to obtain corrective emotional experiences.[56, 57] It is claimed that by means of hypnoplasty (1) dissociated material is tapped more effectively; (2) deconditioning is more dynamic; (3) spontaneous regression is facilitated and abreaction is intensified; (4) meaningful fantasy activity is increased; and (5) integration attitudes can be actively reinforced.*

REFERENCES

1. Abrams, S.: The effects of motivation upon the intellectual performance of schizophrenic patients. Am. J. Clin. Hypn., *8:*3743, 1965.
2. Akstein, D.: Terpsichore trance therapy: a new hypnopsychotherapeutic method. Int. J. Clin. Exp. Hypn., *21:*131, 1973.
3. Biddle, W.E.: Hypnosis in the Psychosis. Springfield, Ill., Charles C Thomas, 1967.
4. Brady, J.P., and Rosner, B.S.: Rapid eye movements in hypnotically induced dreams. J. Nerv. Ment. Dis., *143:*28, 1966.
5. Brenman, M., and Gill, M.M.: Hypnotherapy. New York, International Universities Press, 1947, pp. 121–134.

---

*Adkins, B.: Personal communication.

6. Cheek, D.B., and LeCron, L.M.: Clinical Hypnotherapy. New York, Grune & Stratton, 1968.

7. Conn, J.H.: Cultural and clinical hypnosis, placebos and aspects of suggestibility. Int. J. Clin. Exp. Hypn., *7:*175, 1959.

8. _____: Psychodynamics of recovery under hypnosis. J. Clin. Exp. Hypn., *8:*316, 1960.

9. _____: Hypnosynthesis: Psychobiologic principles in the practice of dynamic psychotherapy utilizing hypnotic procedures. Int. J. Clin. Exp. Hypn., *16:*1, 1968.

10. _____: Hypnosynthesis. Am. J. Clin. Hypn., *13:* 208, 1971.

11. Deckert, G.H., and West, J.L.: The problem of hypnotizability: a review. Int. J. Clin. Exp. Hypn., *11:*205, 1963.

12. Erickson, M. H.: Special techniques of brief hypnotherapy. J. Clin. Exp. Hypn., *2:*109, 1954.

13. _____: Self-exploration in the hypnotic state. J. Clin. Exp. Hypn., *3:*49, 1955.

14. _____: Further clinical techniques of hypnosis: utilization techniques, Am. J. Clin. Hypn. *2:*3, 1959.

15. _____: Certain principles in medical hypnosis (paper read before the Pan American Medical Association, May 5, 1960).

16. Erickson, M.H., and Rossi, E.L.: Two level communication and the microdynamics of trance and induction. Am. J. Clin. Hypn., *18:*153, 1976.

17. Erickson, M.H., *et al.*: Hypnotic Realities: The Induction of Hypnosis and The Indirect Forms of Suggestion. New York, Irving Publishers, Halsted-Wiley Press, 1976.

18. Evans, F.J.: Two types of posthypnotic amnesia: recall amnesia and source amnesia. Int. J. Clin. Exp. Hypn., *14:*162, 1966.

19. Frank, J. D.: Persuasion and Healing: A Comparative Study of Psychotherapy. Baltimore, Johns Hopkins University Press, 1961.

20. Frankel, F.H.: The use of hypnosis in crisis intervention. Int. J. Clin. Exp. Hypn., *22:*188, 1974.

21. Fromm, E.: Dissociative and integrative process in hypnoanalysis. Am. J. Clin. Hypn., *10:*174, 1968.

22. Gardner, G.G.: Hypnosis and mastery: clinical contributions and direction for research. Int. J. Clin. Exp. Hypn., *24:*202, 1976.

23. Greene, J.T.: Hypnotizability of hospitalized psychotics. Int. J. Clin. Exp. Hypn., *17:*103, 1969.

24. Haley, J.: Control in brief psychotherapy. Arch. Gen. Psychiatry, *4:*139, 1961.

25. *Ibid.,* p. 143.

26. *Ibid.,* p. 146.

27. _____: Advanced Techniques of Hypnosis and Therapy. New York, Grune & Stratton, 1967.

28. _____: Uncommon Therapy: The Psychiatric Techniques of Milton H. Erickson. New York, Norton, 1973.

29. Hartland, J.: The value of ego-strengthening procedures prior to direct symptom-removal under hypnosis. Am. J. Clin. Hypn., *8:*89, 1965.

30. Heath, R.G., *et al.*: Hypnotizability in state-hospitalized schizophrenics. Psychiat. Q., *4:*65, 1960.

31. Huxley, A.: Human potentialities. Menn. Clin. Bull., *25:*53, 1961.

32. Ihalainen, O., and Rosberg, G.: Relaxing and encouraging suggestions given to hospitalized chronic schizophrenics. Int. J. Clin. Exp. Hypn., *24:*228, 1976.

33. Kline, M.V.: Dynamic Psychology. New York, Julian Press, 1955.

34. _____: Hypnotic amnesia in psychotherapy. Int. J. Clin. Exp. Hypn., *14:*112, 1966.

35. Kroger, W.S., and Fezler, W.D.: Hypnosis and Behavior Modification: Imagery Conditioning. Philadelphia, J.B. Lippincott, 1976.

36. Lavoie, G., *et al.*: Hypnotic susceptibility, amnesia and I.Q. in chronic schizophrenia. Int. J. Clin. Exp. Hypn., *21:*157, 1973.

37. Lindner, R.M.: Hypnoanalysis as psychotherapy. Brit. J. Med. Hypn., *4:*34, 1952.

38. *Ibid.,* p. 35.

39. _____: Hypnoanalysis as a psychotherapeutic technique. *In* Bychowski, G., and Despert, J.L. (eds.): Specialized Techniques in Psychotherapy. New York, Basic Books, 1953.

40. *Ibid.,* p. 34.

41. Meares, A.: Hypnography. Springfield, Ill., Charles C Thomas, 1957.

42. _____: A System of Medical Hypnosis. Philadelphia, W.B. Saunders, 1960.

43. _____: Shapes of Sanity. Springfield, Ill., Charles C Thomas, 1960.

44. _____: The Y-State: an hypnotic variant. J. Clin. Exp. Hypn., *8:*237, 1960.

45. Moore, M.R.: Treatment of psychosis with hypnosis: report of a case (paper read at the annual meeting of the American Society for Clinical and Experimental Hypnosis, Seattle, 1975).

46. Orne, M.T.: On the mechanisms of posthypnotic amnesia. Int. J. Clin. Exp. Hypn., *14:*121, 1966.

47. Platonov, K.: The Word as a Physiological and Therapeutic Factor. Moscow, Foreign Languages Publishing House, 1959.

48. *Ibid.,* p. 424.

49. Polak, P.K.: Hypnotizability and prediction of hypnotizability in hospitalized psychiatric patients. Int. J. Clin. Exp. Hypn., *12:*252, 1964.

50. Raginsky, B.B.: The sensory use of plasticine in hypnoanalysis (sensory hypnoplasty), Int. J. Clin. Exp. Hypn., *9:*233, 1961.

51. _____: Sensory hypnoplasty with case illustration. Int. J. Clin. Exp. Hypn., *10:*205, 1962.

52. _____: Rapid regression through sensory hypnoplasty. *In* Lassner, J. (ed.): Hypnosis and Psychosomatic Medicine. Proceedings of the International Congress for Hypnosis and Psychosomatic Medicine, Paris, 1965. Berlin, Springer-Verlag, 1967.

53. Rodriguez, R.: Quoted in Solovey, G., and Milechnin, A.: Hypnosis as the substratum of many different psychotherapies. Am. J. Clin. Hypn., *3:*9, 1960.

54. Rosen, H.: Hypnosis in Psychiatry. New York, Julian Press, 1953.

55. _____: Regression hypnotherapeutically induced as an emergency measure in a suicidally depressed patient. J. Clin. Exp. Hypn., *3:*58, 1955.

56. Sacerdote, P.: Therapeutic use of induced dreams. Am. J. Clin. Hypn., *10:*1, 1967.

57. _____: Some individualized hypnotherapeutic technics. Int. J. Clin. Exp. Hypn., *20:*1, 1972.

58. Scagnelli, J.: Hypnotherapy with schizophrenic and borderline patients (paper read at the annual meeting of the American Society for Clinical and Experimental Hypnosis, Seattle, 1975).

59. Schneck, J.: Hypnosis and Modern Medicine. Springfield, Ill., Charles C Thomas, 1953.

60. Shibota, J.: Limits of autogenic training to schizophrenia and selection of patients. Am. J. Clin. Hypn., *11:*99, 1968.

61. Shibota, J., and Motoda, K.: The application of autogenic training to a group of schizophrenic patients. Am. J. Clin. Hypn., *10:*15, 1967.

62. Solovey, G., and Milechnin, A.: Hypnosis as the substratum of many different psychotherapies. Am. J. Clin. Hypn., *3:*9, 1960.

63. Spiegel, H.: Is symptom removal dangerous? Am. J. Psychiatry, *123:*1279, 1967.

64. Stillerman, B.: The management in analytic hypnotherapy of the psychodynamic reaction to the induction of hypnosis. J. Clin. Exp. Hypn., *5:*3, 1957.

64a. Volgyesi, F.A.: On the psychotherapeutic importance of hypnotic sleep and sleep protective inhibition. Br. J. Med. Hypnotism, *3:*2, 1951.

65. Watkins, J.: Hypnotherapy of War Neuroses. New York, Ronald Press, 1949.

66. *Ibid.,* p. 105.

67. _____: Trance and transference. J. Clin. Exp. Hypn., *2:*284, 1954.

68. _____: Psychodynamics of hypnotic induction and termination. *In* J.M. Schneck (ed.): Hypnosis in Modern Medicine. ed. 3. Springfield, Ill., Charles C Thomas, 1963.

69. Wolberg, L.R.: Hypnoanalysis. New York, Grune & Stratton, 1945.

70. _____: Medical Hypnosis. 2 vols. New York, Grune & Stratton, 1948.

71. Wolpe, J.: Psychotherapy by Reciprocal Inhibition. Stanford, Cal., Stanford University Press, 1958.

72. Worpell, D.F.: Hypnotherapy with a hallucinating schizophrenic. Am. J. Clin. Hypn., *16:*134, 1973.

ADDITIONAL READINGS

Estabrooks, G. H.: Hypnosis: Current Problems. New York, Harper, 1962.

Haley, J.: The control of fear with hypnosis. Am. J. Clin. Hypn., *2:*109, 1960.

McCartney, J. L.: Hypnoanalysis: combined use of hypnosis and analytic psychotherapy. Br. J. Med. Hypn. *13:*27–33, 1962.

Schneck, J. M.: Hypnoanalysis. Int. J. Clin. Exp. Hypn., *10:*1, 1962.

Watts, A. W.: Psychotherapy East and West. New York, Pantheon, 1961.

51

Comparative Evaluation and Criticisms of Hypnotherapy and Psychoanalysis

Fortunately, psychoanalysts and eclectic psychiatrists are now changing their views toward hypnosis. However, there are *valid* criticisms and limitations of hypnosis and psychoanalysis. The author hopes that the best features of these therapeutic methods will be synthesized and absorbed into the mainstream of American psychiatry.

DO WE KNOW HOW HYPNOSIS WORKS?

Critics of hypnotism often remark, "No one knows why it works." By the same token, no one knows the exact *modus operandi* of aspirin, yet we use it. Hypnotherapy in the presence of a strong *interpersonal* relationship between therapist and patient provides a meaningful *intrapersonal* experience for the patient which is particularly conducive to the establishment of expectations leading to convictions. In the presence of an expectant attitude, the imaginative processes unleash the inherent recovery forces.

Freud did not consider hypnosis as a subjective phenomenologic experience.[9, 15] Therefore, he did not think of it as even partial validation of his concepts. However, he correctly considered suggestion "as a nucleus of hypnosis and the key to its understanding. . . ."[14]

HYPNOTHERAPY IS NOT A PANACEA

Hypnosis must divorce itself from the unwarranted claims made by some of its ardent proponents. These persons often have done more harm than have its uninformed opponents. The latter,

however, while they deny its therapeutic efficacy, impute great harm to even a single posthypnotic suggestion. Even though hypnotherapy is no more curative than other psychotherapies, it is a relatively rapid method when compared with the more orthodox psychotherapies, and can reach certain disorders ordinarily refractory to conventional psychotherapy, such as chronic conversion reactions, phobias, compulsive disorders, addiction, and pain problems. It is unfortunate that many laymen and some uninformed therapists look upon hypnotherapy as a "magical gesture." It should not be oversold; otherwise it will soon be another nostrum.

DOES STRONG DEPENDENCY ON THE THERAPIST EXIST?

One criticism repeatedly stressed is that extreme dependency on the therapist is fostered because the hypnotic interpersonal relationship is "like that of parent and child."[7] Where dependency occurs, it may be due to the *manner in which the hypnotic interpersonal relationship was utilized!* One must consider the emotional needs of the therapist and the degree of neurotic involvement of the patient. Therefore, dependency is not produced because of the hypnotic situation, *but rather is due to the nature of the interactional processes between therapist and patient.* In psychoanalysis, undue dependency is analyzed, and this also can be done when it becomes a problem during hypnotherapy. Kubie states there is no dependency.[20] Not a single patient has become "addicted" to hypnotherapy.[39] Thus hypnotic dependency is a myth.

DOES HYPNOTHERAPY SEXUALIZE THE DOCTOR-PATIENT RELATIONSHIP?

One continually hears that in hypnotherapy the relationship has an erotic root. Sexual attraction between patient and therapist occurs in other therapeutic relationships and is not limited to hypnotherapy. It is highly unlikely that a subject in deep hypnosis will act out his sexual fantasies in a properly conducted hypnotic session. Sexual submission is a highly selective process, and, where it occurs, it is definitely the result of factors other than hypnosis.[5]

IS ANALYSIS OF THE TRANSFERENCE NECESSARY IN HYPNOTHERAPY?

The old concept of transference is no longer considered a blind repetition of childhood relationships. Freud took hypnotic rapport and called it transference. His remark that there was "something positively seductive in working with hypnosis,"[27] indicated that it is possible that his overemphasis on erotic elements in the therapeutic relationship was due to his own repressed sexual feelings (counter-transference).[18]

Watkins observes that the patient during analytic sessions is often in hypnosis without the analyst's awareness of it, and that during hypnosis the hypnotherapist's own attitudes are to a degree displaced to the patient without the former's recognition of it.[37] Transference is understood better in this sense than it is by assuming it to be a manifestation of child-parent relationships.

Freud denied the use of suggestion in his therapeutic approach. Despite this denial or lack of awareness, he stated:[15]

In psychoanalysis we work upon the transference itself, dissipate whatever stands in the way of it and manipulate the instrument which is to do the work. Thus, it becomes possible for us to derive entirely new benefits from the *power of suggestion; we are able to control it;* the patient alone no longer manages his suggestibility according to his own liking, but insofar as he is amenable to its influence at all, *we guide his suggestibility.* *

"Transference" for Freud became a wider concept than faith, and psychoanalysis made full use of reparation to obviate pain, anxiety, shame, and guilt.[18]

ARE FREE ASSOCIATIONS NECESSARY?

Freud used the technic taught to him by Liébeault and Bernheim. Later he discarded the "pressure method" and utilized what he called the "free association" method to recapture significant experiences and overcome resistances. It has been pointed out that free association often results in spontaneous hypnosis.[35]

Schmideberg asks:

Are free associations sufficiently standardized to permit comparable observations on different days and with different patients?[31]

If free associations and their interpretations resulted in a higher recovery rate than that of standard psychotherapy, it would have been a significant contribution. However, *deliberate* and *faulty* interpretations of free associations often lead to betterment.

DOES HYPNOTHERAPY OVERCOME RESISTANCES?

Freud thought hypnosis concealed the resistances.[13] Haley points out that there is often no need even to allow the resistances to develop during hypnotherapy: "A resistant maneuver is dissipated by having it accepted and redefined as cooperation."[17] He believes that "this type of interaction is central to winning control of a relationship; maneuvers to define the relationship are not opposed but 'taken over.' "

Freud referred to hypnosis as the "tyranny of suggestion."[10] Being a dedicated scientist, however, he was puzzled about hypnosis, and repeatedly tried to fit "the riddle of suggestion" into his theoretic formulations. Kline points out that Freud *avoided* rather than rejected hypnosis.[18] In the light of the historical development of

---

*The italics are the author's.

Freudian theory, perhaps "we need a psychoanalysis of current psychoanalytical resistance to the use of hypnosis."[22]

WHAT IS THE ROLE OF PSYCHODYNAMICS IN PSYCHOTHERAPY?

Psychodynamics has been defined as the motivational basis for human behavior. There have been numerous critics of psychodynamic psychiatry.[1, 4, 29] Bailey states:

The psychodynamicists must cease to teach their neophytes in terms of mythological pseudoscientific entities—that the system of explanation used by psychodynamics is really too simple to satisfy other than immature minds. It amounts to no more than a set of elaborate fictions.[1]

Conn adds:

It was becoming apparent that we had accepted a pseudoscientific system of metaphors and verbal traps that were primarily descriptive and could not serve as explanatory concepts.[4]

Eysenck, an outspoken critic of psychoanalysis, emphatically stated that it has no effect whatsoever.[6] Frank and his co-workers argued that it was difficult to demonstrate specific results from psychoanalysis.[8] Other authorities still believe that long-term therapy is an effective procedure.[2, 3, 21, 34]

Shortly before his death, Freud spoke very resignedly about the poor results of psychoanalysis in an article seldom mentioned by his loyal followers.[9] As Rado observed, "Digging into the past yields diminishing returns."[28] Others question the value of recapturing early fantasies and memories. This is not to imply that many of Freud's observations in human behavior will not be of enduring value. Contemporary technics in hypnoanalysis could not have developed had it not been for his penetrating insights.

Physical scientists currently are attempting to explain the many facets of behavior in terms of systems that can be evaluated statistically. This may provide a better understanding of behavior, particularly higher central nervous activities. In this regard, the open systems theory of von Bertalanffy,[36] the information-communication theory of Shannon and Weaver,[32] and the cybernetics of Wiener[38] should prove helpful (see Chap. 32).

ARE INTERPRETATIONS VALID?

When the therapist offers interpretations, is it not largely *what he thinks is going on,* and is not the patient being controlled without realizing it?[31] There is no reliably controlled evidence that interpretations are responsible for results. Before such contentions can be validated, there must be a control group in which the postulated cause produces similar symptoms. It is not the validity of the interpretations, but the faith in the therapist's methods, which leads to cure. Furthermore, any system using its own data to prove itself can only encounter a paradox (Gödel's theorem).

IS SYMPTOM REMOVAL DANGEROUS?

To Freud's everlasting credit, he noted that hypnosis had no deleterious effects, and that it was not a dangerous tool.[13] According to behavior therapists, the removal of psychological symptoms by hypnotherapy is more lasting.[40] Symptom removal by hypnosis "prevents the reinforcement of the inappropriate responses and new appropriate ways of handling the conflicts. As a result the appropriate responses are reinforced."

IS INSIGHT REALLY NECESSARY?

Hypnotherapy *without insight* is as effective in dealing with symptomatic behavior as those therapies which provide insight. If insight is necessary, then how do the various schools of psychotherapy explain the success of those groups that do not require insight?

Freud obtained recoveries in short analyses.[12] Brief psychotherapy, consisting of a few visits, has yielded good results. Most deep-seated conflicts are forgotten with the passing of time, and insight is never achieved.

Often "insight" is not the patient's insight, but the therapist's preconceived notion of what "insight" the patient should have. Usually the patient merely takes over the value systems, the faith, and the confidence of the therapist—this is actually what makes emotionally disturbed individuals better!

IS AUTOHYPNOSIS DANGEROUS?

Autohypnosis is employed in many spiritualistic religious-healing modalities. Therefore, it is difficult to see how autohypnosis can be dangerous when the very essence of prayer is based on the fundamental principles of autohypnosis.

CONCLUSIONS

It may safely be asserted that nearly all of the criticisms applied to contemporary hypnotherapy are untenable. Many justifiably are directed toward a type of hypnotherapy that was practiced in the last century. There is no proof of the superiority of any psychotherapeutic approach, as it is virtually impossible to eliminate the importance of the interpersonal relationship.[16] Well-trained psychotherapists, with considerable experience, cannot show a higher recovery rate than gifted neophytes with lesser training. However, there are limitations to hypnotherapy, and these are the same as those found in any other type of psychotherapy.

Current research in hypnosis does not substantiate a single reason for Freud's avoidance of hypnosis. The reader is referred to an excellent monograph on the subject, *Freud and Hypnosis*, for a detailed description of Freud's reasons for avoiding hypnosis.[18] Since scientific hypnosis was in its infancy in Freud's time, one can hardly blame him for adopting a negative attitude. However, there is no valid reason why Freud's successors should continue to use this embryonic period in the historical development of hypnosis to criticize contemporary hypnotherapy. Masserman recognized that hypnosis was the core that underlies all forms of psychotherapy when he recently spoke on "Hypnosis, the Misnamed Source of All Interpersonal Therapies."[23] Freud must have anticipated this when he prophetically wrote:

It is very probable too, that the application of our therapy to numbers will compel us to alloy the pure gold of analysis with the copper of direct suggestion; and even hypnotic influence might find a place in it again as it has in the treatment of war neuroses.[14]

All psychotherapists should at least become conversant with recently developed hypnotic technics, much as progressive physicians do with new drugs.

Orne has brilliantly traced the development and concepts of psychotherapy in contemporary America.[26] He describes how psychodynamic ideas were accepted because they were promulgated under medical and scientific auspices. He points out that the theory and practice of psychoanalysis (and no doubt behavior therapy as well) have met with an increasing lack of acceptance not only from the scientific community, but also from the public. Orne is a leader in hypnosis research and psychodynamic therapy. He sounds a clarion call for hard clinical and scientific data to prove that the insights derived from the dynamic view have, as he believes, a sound basis. He notes the difficulties in evaluating the effectiveness of any type of psychotherapy because of self-fulfilling prophecies,[24] experimenter-expectancy effects,[30] and demand characteristics.[25] More importantly, he warns against the plethora of irresponsible therapies that are springing up.

It is becoming increasingly obvious that American psychiatry is in the throes of an identity crisis. It is splintered by many movements, all of which seem to help to some degree. It is riding off madly in all directions. Powerful voices are now asking the psychotherapist to provide corroborative data of the efficacy of his particular school of therapy. This means that the recovery rate, as judged by empirical observations, can be meaningful only if it exceeds the 65 per cent cure rate—the placebo effect.

The author believes that hypnosis and behavior therapy (which is covert hypnosis) and some of the tenets so well enunciated by Freud, and which created a new discipline, will emerge as a practical therapeutic approach. Today, we are witnessing the impact of meditative states, the relaxation response, and other methodologies which grew out of opposition to traditional psychotherapies. That hypnosis and the Eastern methodologies, mentioned in

Chapter 24, have existed for several thousand years and now are being increasingly accepted indicates that they will play a meaningful role in psychotherapeutic processes. They are here to stay, and they are modalities that American psychotherapy must eventually incorporate.

No therapeutic modality is applicable to all problems. The skillful psychotherapist must be flexible and use a therapy that is adapted to the needs of the patient, rather than the patient to the method. However, much psychotherapy in the Western world has been applied as dogma. No therapist has any special curative remedies, yet each approach may serve a genuine purpose if used wisely and judiciously.

REFERENCES

1. Bailey, P.: Modern attitudes toward the relationship of the brain to behavior. Arch. Gen. Psychiatry, *2:*25, 1960.
2. Bergin, A.E.: The effects of psychotherapy: negative results revisited. J. Consult. Clin. Psychol., *10:*244, 1963.
3. Bergin, A.E., and Garfield, S.L. (eds.): Handbook of Psychotherapy and Behavior Change: Am Empirical Analysis. New York, Wiley, 1971.
4. Conn, J.H.: The decline of psychodynamics: the end of an era, or here we go again. J.A.M.A., *228:*711, 1972.
5. Eysenck, H.J.: Suggestibility and hysteria. J. Neurol. Psychiatry, *6:*22, 1943.
6. _____: The effects of psychotherapy: an evaluation. Consult. Clin. Psychol., *16:*319–323, 1952.
7. Ferenczi, S.: Introjection and transference. Jones, E., and Bedger, R.G. (trans.): Sex in Psychoanalysis. Boston, Gorham Press, 1916.
8. Frank, J.D.: Persuasion and Healing: A Comparative Study of Psychotherapy. Baltimore: Johns Hopkins University Press, 1961.
9. Freud, S.: Analyses terminable and interminable. Int. J. Psychoanal., *18,*373, 1937.
10. _____: Group Psychology and the Analysis of the Ego. (Strachey, J., trans.) London, Hogarth Press, 1948.
11. _____: Turnings in the ways of psychoanalysis. *In* Strachey, J. (trans.): Collected Papers. vol. 2. London, Hogarth Press, 1948, p. 392.
12. _____: The history of an infantile neurosis. *In* Strachey, J. (trans.): Collected Papers. vol. 3. London, Hogarth Press, 1949.
13. _____: The psychotherapy of hysteria. *In* Stra-

chey, J. (trans.): Collected Papers. vol. 5. London, Hogarth Press, 1950, p. 262.
14. _____: Complete Psychological Works. (Strachey, J., trans.) vol. 5. London, Hogarth Press, 1955, p. 11.
15. _____: A General Introduction to Psychoanalysis. (Riviere, J., ed.) New York, Perma Books, 1957, p. 459.
16. Grinker, R.R.: A philosophical appraisal of psychoanalysis. *In* Masserman, J. H. (ed.): Science and Psychoanalysis. Vol. 1, Integrative Studies. p. 126. New York, Grune & Stratton, 1958.
17. Haley, J.: Advanced Techniques of Hypnosis and Therapy: Selected papers of M.H. Erickson, M.D. New York, Grune & Stratton, 1967.
18. Kline, M.V.: Freud and Hypnosis. New York, Julian Press, 1958.
19. Kroger, W.S.: Comparative evaluation of Zen, Yoga, and Judaism with conditioning techniques and psychotherapy. Excerpta Medica, *119:*175, 1966.
20. Kubie, L.S.: Hypnotism: a focus for psychophysiological and psychoanalytic investigations. Arch. Gen. Psychiatry, *1:*77, 1961.
21. Luborsky, L.: Another reply to Eysenck. Psychol. Bull., *78:*406, 1972.
22. Marcuse, F.L.: Hypnosis, Fact and Fiction. Harmondsworth, Middlesex, Penguin Books, 1959.
23. Masserman, J.H.: Hypnosis, the misnamed source of all interpersonal therapies (address to the American Society for Clinical Hypnosis, October 13, 1971).
24. Merton, R.K.: The self-fulfilling prophecy. Antioch Rev., *8:*193, 1948.
25. Orne, M.T.: On the social psychology of the psychological experiment: with particular reference to demand characteristics and their implications. Am. Psychol., *17:*776, 1962.
26. _____: Psychotherapy in contemporary American: its development and context. *In* Friedman, D.X., and Dyrud, J.I. (eds.): Handbook of Psychiatry. ed. 2. New York, Basic Books, 1975, pp. 3–33.
27. Puner, H.W.: Freud, His Life and Mind. New York, Grosset & Dunlap, 1947.
28. Rado, S.: Recent advances of psychoanalytical therapy in psychiatric treatment. Proc. Assoc. Res. Nerv. Ment. Dis., *31:*57, 1953.
29. Rapoport, A.: Quoted in Locke, N.: Semantic psychotherapy: an exchange of views. E.T.C., *15:*37, 1957.
30. Rosenthal, R.: Experimenter Effects in Behavioral Research. New York, Appleton-Century-Crofts, 1966.

31. Schmideberg, M.: Goals and values in psychoanalysis. Psychiat. Q., *32:*233, 1958.
32. Shannon, C.E., and Weaver, W.: The Mathematical Theory of Communication. Urbana, University of Illinois Press, 1949.
33. Shapiro, A.K.: The placebo effect in the history of medical treatment: implications for psychiatry. Am. J. Psychiatry, *116:*73, 1959.
34. Strupp, H.H., and Bergin, A.E.: Research in Individual Psychotherapy: A Bibliography. Washington, National Institutes of Mental Health, 1969.
35. Tobey, H.S., and Vacchiano, R.B.: The similarities between hypnotic induction and Freud's free association techniques. Am. J. Clin. Hypn., *15:*86, 1972.
36. von Bertalanffy, L.: An Evaluation of Modern Biological Thought. New York, Wiley, 1952.
37. Watkins, J.: Trance and transference. J. Soc. Clin. Exp. Hypn., *2:*284, 1954.
38. Wiener, N.: Cybernetics, or, Control and Communication in the Animal and the Machine. Cambridge, Mass., M.I.T. Press, 1948.
39. Wolberg, L.R.: Medical Hypnosis. vol. 1. New York, Grune & Stratton, 1948.
40. Wolpe, J.: Psychotherapy by Reciprocal Inhibition. Stanford, Cal., Stanford University Press, 1958.

52

Failures in Hypnotherapy

In this book, many cases that have recovered following hypnotherapy have been described for illustrative purposes. However, just as there are dramatic successes, there are equally dramatic failures. These can be divided into problems during induction and problems during hypnotherapy.

FAILURES DURING INDUCTION

Fortunately, in the hands of a sophisticated hypnotherapist, failure to attain some degree of hypnosis is rare. This is especially true if the onus and the responsibility for going into hypnosis are carefully explained to the patient beforehand. Nearly all individuals can be hypnotized to some degree if the permissive and motivational technics described in this book are utilized. In the rare cases of those who cannot be hypnotized, one should be sure that certain misconceptions have been clarified. Some of these are described below.

FEAR OF SUBMISSION

The egocentric type of individual who fears being subordinated by the hypnotherapist's suggestions can be difficult to hypnotize. In spite of careful explanations to the contrary, many apparently willing individuals harbor this fear. Within this group are persons who have dominant personalities or who have a need to maintain a "one-up" position. To obviate this fear, which is a common cause for failure, the operator can casually remark during the initial phases of the induction, *"You need follow only those suggestions which are fully in accord with your needs and wishes."* It is really surprising how conducive to greater hypnotizability this statement is, if it is unobtrusively inserted during the verbalization technic. The following case is a good illustration:

A very successful insurance company executive, a chronic alcoholic, could not be hypnotized by several physician-therapists or by two lay hypnotists. During the author's initial discussion with him, it was obvious not only that he feared being relegated to a subservient role, but also that he was poorly motivated to relinquish the symptom. Because of his repeated failure to be hypnotized, he was emphatically assured before induction, "You will hypnotize yourself; I will only act as teacher. If you follow my instructions, and I cannot *force* you to follow these, you will develop a deep state of relaxation *at your own pace and in your own particular fashion.* You have actually hypnotized yourself to the point where, try as hard as you might, you cannot stop drinking. You are the one who developed the symptom, and you are the only one who can remove it." He agreed that all these assertions were logical and that he would do his best to follow all suggestions.

Five inductions were attempted over a period of 2 weeks. At no time did he appear to enter hypnosis, regardless of the technic employed. Following each session he triumphantly stated, "Doctor, I didn't feel a thing. I did everything you said. Guess I'm a hopeless case. You sure tried your best." Although it is easy to blame the patient, without doubt this individual was wholly unable to submit to another person's directions because of his inordinate need to maintain control. Furthermore, he was looking forward to defeating every therapist, and by such maneuvers he had a perfect alibi for maintaining the chronicity of his symptom.

LACK OF MOTIVATION

Those who have little or no desire to get well are poor subjects for hypnosis. It is almost impossible to induce hypnosis unless the patient is sufficiently motivated. Many patients, such as alcoholics, smokers, and overeaters, do not wish to yield their symptoms because they have a "pleasurable neurosis." The following is a typical example:

An extremely obese woman, who had seen numerous physicians, stated that she would like to try hypnosis for weight reduction, and that she would follow a diet, take her medication, and faithfully follow all directions. During her first visit she was informed, "Of course you mean every word you say, but behind your ardent protestations that you wish to lose weight are deeply unrecognized desires to cling to your symptom. We shall see how well you do." Hypnosis was attempted by a wide variety of technics during several intensive sessions. In all instances she stated, "I hear everything you say and I do follow all of your suggestions, but I just can't relax." She decided to break off therapy. Perhaps it would have been better if the nature of her resistances had been discussed and worked through before attempting hypnotic induction.

The hypnotherapist must recognize that, even though such failures will be encountered, there are other patients who, even though poorly motivated, can be helped by the establishment of healthy objectives. In cases such as the one just described, emphasizing the value of hypnosis as a powerful therapeutic adjunct in relationship to the cosmetic and health factors is highly motivating. The therapist must mobilize the patient's faith that he will be helped.

During the actual induction, many reluctant and poorly motivated individuals, especially those with habit patterns, can be induced by such suggestions as, "If you really wish to control your bodily functions (such as your appetite) and coordinate your thinking with your bodily processes, all you have to do is to slowly raise your arm about an inch at a time. With each inch that you raise your arm, tell yourself, 'I am going deeper and deeper with each movement of my arm up-

ward. I will indeed go deeper and deeper relaxed. In this way I will obtain greater mastery over such functions as my appetite.'" These suggestions are given just before arm levitation is suggested, and they can be repeated several times while the subject's arm is slowly being lifted to the perpendicular position.

To avoid failure, motivating the subject each step of the way usually ensures success, especially if the individual's attention is focused on one suggestion after another. If the suggestions are not clear to the patient, failure in induction can be expected. The commonest one is during eye closure or arm levitation. The patient will remark, "I thought my eyes (or arm) would close (or be raised) by itself."

RESISTANCES TO INDUCTION

The handling of resistances to induction has been discussed in Chapter 13. In general, those manifested during the induction procedure are utilized to defy the hypnotherapist. Many patients equate hypnotizability with imbecility; others are too analytic or know too much about the "misdirection of attention" that is involved in hypnotic induction. Still others, like the one just described, have an "I'll-bet-you-can't-hypnotize-me" attitude. Such individuals fear someone who they think is omnipotent. The explanation that no one hypnotizes another individual can eliminate this resistance. One can remark, "You are the only one who can hypnotize yourself; I really have very little to do with it. If you follow the simple suggestions, and I have no way of knowing whether or not you follow these, then you will follow the more complicated suggestions. However, if you break one link in the chain, then the entire sequence of suggestions will be interrupted. For instance, if I suggest that you count to yourself and you do not, since I have no way of knowing this, I cannot do very much about that, can I?" Such measures enlist the active cooperation and participation of the patient.

Other patients panic when they feel themselves entering into a hypnotic state:

A very well-known screen actor consulted me for his homosexuality. As he felt himself sinking deeper and deeper into the hypnotic state, he began to shake, perspire, and show other symptoms of inner turmoil. When asked why he was acting in this fashion, he stated that he had a mutual masturbatory fantasy which involved me. By such measures the patient was attempting to seduce me and yet at the same time he was attempting to comply. Since he had ambivalent feelings with reference to the acceptance or the rejection of my suggestions, he experienced panic when he felt that he was about to be hypnotized. Naturally, these feelings were worked through before further induction was attempted.

Other patients' resistances can be handled by asking them to discuss their feelings. It is generally a good idea to interrupt the hypnotic induction if the patient is not following the suggestions. For example, if the patient does not raise his arm when it is suggested, one can remark, "If you wish to continue, it's up to you. Your arm will *not* move up by itself. If you want to go into a deep, deep relaxed state, you will raise your arm at your own pace, and in your own particular fashion. Remember, you are in charge." If the arm does not rise, the hypnotic induction should be terminated. The therapist must not evince the slightest show of anger or blame the patient. Rather, it is much better to state, "Perhaps I did not make myself entirely clear in our preliminary discussion. You did very well, and next time I am certain that you will do much better."

Often, arrogant and skeptical patients cannot be hypnotized by the conventional approach. A disguised technic or giving a placebo under the guise of its facilitating hypnosis often increases the susceptibility of refractory subjects.

FAILURES DURING HYPNOTHERAPY

Disraeli once stated that there are three types of lies: little lies, big lies, and statistics. There are no accurate data available, comprising long-term follow-up studies, to evaluate the failure rate in selective cases treated by hypnosis. These probably do not exceed those treated by other psychotherapeutic methods. However, most of the cases of failure, as herein described, are in the therapy of symptoms of a bizarre nature which have exhausted other therapeutic approaches. Therefore, it is not surprising that a relatively high inci-

dence of failure will occur during hypnotherapy.

These failures are due to (1) difficulties in the patient; (2) difficulties in the hypnotherapeutic management; and (3) difficulties in the therapist management. All these, singly or in combination, are usually responsible for failures in patients, even if they readily can be hypnotized. One should, therefore, continually bear in mind the dictum, "One is not treated by hypnosis, but rather, in hypnosis."

DIFFICULTIES IN THE PATIENT

To avoid such failures in this group, patients should be carefully screened and selected.

A 42-year-old man was referred for hypnotherapy because he had a profound dislike for his facial appearance. Since childhood, he had been called "Hawky" because of his sharp, aquiline features, particularly his nose. In reality, he was a nice-looking, well-groomed individual of excellent body build. He had had three marriages, the first to a prostitute, the second to a burlesque dancer, and the third to a woman who had become pregnant by another man before he married her. His third wife, because of his "ugliness," insisted that she had the right to have sexual relations with another man. Otherwise, she threatened to divorce him. He never had been able to relate to women and had poor social relationships. He had no understanding of his deep-seated masochistic needs, evidenced by his neurotic attachments (all three of his wives browbeat him and were below his social and intellectual status). He stated that he had been in "therapy" for several years. Now he asked, "Can't you just hypnotize me into thinking that I am good-looking?"

It was obvious that he attributed all his troubles with women to his appearance, never realizing that he had a deep-seated personality problem. He was informed that it would be impossible to produce an amnesia by hypnosis for the feelings associated with his facial features. He mentioned that he was going to have plastic surgery for correction of his narrow nose. It was emphasized that this should be postponed until he understood the real *needs* for his emotional difficulties. Despite this advice, he insisted on being hypnotized. Naturally, this was refused. He went to another hypnotist-physician, who failed to help him for the obvious reasons given above. Fortunately, also, he could not get a plastic surgeon to operate on him.

If hypnotherapy is utilized as an adjunct in the framework of a psychotherapeutic approach based upon a good doctor-patient relationship, failures will be less frequent.

When hypnosis is indiscriminately employed, without careful patient selection, it is only logical to assume that a high incidence of failures will occur. Therefore, the therapist, on the basis of his judgment and clinical acumen, should understand the motivations behind the desire for hypnotherapy when it is requested. It is these motivations that can be the determining factor as to whether or not failure will ensue. All too often, patients are looking for the magical removal of symptoms and expect to be cured "in the third act." Failures are inevitable if patients are unwilling to recognize their unrealistic demands. The patient who is trying to "climb into the therapist's lap" is destined to be a failure.

A 44-year-old alcoholic woman requested that hypnosis be tried for the alleviation of drinking. She revealed that she was frigid with her husband but sexually responsive to another man with whom she had many clandestine meetings. She evinced considerable guilt over her extramarital relationships as therapy progressed, but refused to recognize the deep-seated need to suffer and atone, evidenced by her continual need to degrade herself in drunken debauches.

Though readily hypnotizable, she made little progress—she wished to maintain her relationship with her lover but could not face the realities of divorce. She had hoped that hypnosis would effectively suppress her drinking. It was pointed out that she could not have her cake and eat it, too; that if she wished to continue in therapy, she would have to decide whether or not she could make an adjustment to her husband, leave him, or "beat her head against a stone wall" by remaining in her present situation. She broke off therapy soon after, but returned at a later date—sadder but wiser—and began making an attempt to adjust to her husband.

DIFFICULTIES DUE TO HYPNOTHERAPY

Many individuals expect the impossible from hypnosis; namely, rapid relief from long-standing problems. Often they have had years of psychotherapy and yet, when they consult the hypnotherapist, they expect to be cured in several sessions. By far the commonest cause of failure with hypnotherapy is the termination of treatment because the progress is not as rapid as the patient had assumed it would be. It is also surprising how many physicians think that hypnosis is a rapid method. Although many cases involving severe disorders can be improved even in a few visits, the bulk of chronically disturbed patients require many visits and intensive therapy. Even so, this is more rapid than some of the more orthodox approaches.

The most difficult patient is the one who adopts a hopeless resignation about eventual recovery. It is here that the physician must give the subject greater self-confidence and inculcate a more optimistic outlook. Patients who do not develop the necessary mind-set, which is a prerequisite for the acceptance of posthypnotic suggestions, are destined to fail. Their prejudices, biases, and other negativistic attitudes militate against the full acceptance of hypnotherapy. Additional difficulties during hypnotherapy are due to the communication problem. Some therapists "talk down" to their patients; others may "talk over their heads." Still others show their indifference at nonverbal levels—they lack empathy and do not establish an effective rapport.

Many failures occur in hypnotherapy because the *needs* for the symptom are not made clear to the patient; this is a potent cause for failure. Psychoneurotics cling to their symptoms, as this provides them with a value system which often may act as a defense. It is, obvious, as well, that not all individuals can recover, as the very nature of their illness precludes recovery.

Many failures result when hypnosis is utilized indiscriminately, without definitive goals. The author remembers a writer who came in with a prepared list of suggestions, all of which involved concentration, creativity, enhancement of his ability, and following through on assignments. This patient expected hypnosis to remove his poor motivations. He had consulted several lay hypnotists without success. Such cases only point up the need to understand the nature of the complaints as they relate to the total character structure.

The following case of failure in hypnosis was tragic:

An exceptionally obese 48-year-old man was referred for weight loss. He had recently suffered a coronary attack. This individual was a successful, hard-driving businessman who was always looking for "angles." When the author stated his fee, the patient made a counterproposal that he would pay $10 for each pound that was lost. The patient thought that he was going to get the best of the bargain, but, much to his surprise, he lost 40 pounds in 2 months; thus he owed much more than he would have if he had come in at the regular fee. As a result, he broke off treatment and died several months later of another heart attack. A thorough evaluation of this man's incorporative needs was suggested during treatment but was refused. The characterologic difficulties should have been worked through before any type of therapy was instituted.

Another alcoholic woman made "a flight into health." She, too, had been in analysis and had been referred by her psychoanalyst for hypnotherapy. After four sessions she stopped drinking for 3 months, but then considered herself cured and refused to return either to the analyst or to myself. It was obvious that she used the referral as a means of escaping from the analysis, and the temporary improvement to avoid further therapy. Naturally, as expected, she resumed her drinking and she became very hostile for a slight pretext, namely, that I didn't talk to her long enough on the telephone when she called at 4 a.m. to announce that she had started drinking again. Her drinking was a defense against her intense anger toward an impotent, weak, and passive-feminine husband, who had her "caught in a trap." The defensive nature of her actions was pointed out.

To obviate difficulties due to hypnotherapy, it is important to outline therapeutic goals. Hypnosis can be directed either to a symptomatic approach or to a characterologic rehabilitation. Individuals who can be treated by symptom removal are those who have poor emotional resources, inadequate time, and poor motivation. For instance, hypnosis can be used for symptomatic relief of smoking in the patient who has a carcinoma of the lungs, or in the one who has a bronchiectasis, without working through the need for the symptom. On the other hand, relief of the symptoms of insomnia or alcoholism may be successful from one standpoint but still may be considered a failure because the individual is wholly unable to adjust to his life situation for other reasons.

In order to avoid these difficulties, it is best to enable the individual to function without the need for frustrations and tensions. Hypnotherapy can also be directed toward facing life problems, rather than retreating into childlike or regressive behavior. Such an approach facilitates a good work and relaxation record, unimpaired sexuality, and ability to adapt to life stresses. Some patients have to be taught how to accept a subordinate role without "boiling up inside." Others must understand that they can assume leadership, and still others must realize their limitations. In general, hypnotherapy will eliminate encountered difficulties, if the therapy is directed toward the establishment of confidence, self-assertiveness, and greater tolerance.

The use of autohypnosis usually enables the patient to use self-exploration to work out his problems more effectively. However, autohypnosis is seldom successful if the patient is not motivated to participate in the working-through processes.

Difficulties in hypnotherapy are noted in the individual whose emotional resources are inadequate to cope with his problems. Often it is permissible for the therapist to assume the role of a paternal figure and deliberately foster dependency. This is especially helpful for those who have had a recent bereavement. In others, who wish to cling to their symptoms, one can utilize symptom substitution, as described in other situations, to avoid therapeutic failure. In the case of the stutterer, for instance, anxiety was averted by teaching him to transfer his blocking to the twitching of one of his fingers. There are other individuals who never can completely recover. For these, partial improvement based on limited goals is not a failure. In the case of the passive-dependent alcoholic, who can be controlled for short periods and who makes only a partial adjustment, some modicum of success is achieved.

Other individuals rationalize their reasons for seeking hypnotherapy, and this results in failure. In one instance, a psychopathic male prostitute attempted to save his unhappy marriage through being hypnotized. At first he presented himself with symptoms of insomnia and nervousness. During the anamnesis the real reasons for seeking hypnosis were revealed. He was advised to seek marital counseling.

Another individual wished to learn autohypnosis, ostensibly to be able to concentrate on his work as a physicist. In reality, he felt wholly inadequate around women, and he had hoped that hypnosis would give him more self-reliance. He stated that he had been in psychotherapy for several years, but had heard that autohypnosis enabled individuals to overcome all sorts of psychological problems. A thorough personality evaluation was advised, together with a discussion of his various difficulties. It is important for the therapist to recognize that overcoming inadequacies and lack of confidence requires learning how to handle the reasons derived in therapy. This takes a considerable amount of time.

Difficulties occur when passive individuals, such as certain types of homosexuals, submit to hypnotherapy only to derive masochistic gratification from the all-powerful figure of the therapist. Unless these neurotic motivations are understood, improvement will be retarded. A case in point is a homosexual male schoolteacher who was unable to carry out his sexual needs for fear of apprehension. As the result of his frustration, he utilized the hypnotic situation to yield to and to fight against authority at one and the same time. Failure was averted when it was pointed out how he was fulfilling his passive needs and also reenacting the same conflict he had had with other surrogate figures. He ultimately made a satisfactory recovery.

To summarize, lack of motivation and inability to face life's problems are the commonest reasons for difficulties in hypnotherapy. Those who have no desire to make an adequate adjustment to their situations, because they develop anxiety reactions, fall into this group. Those who have poor inner resources and are unable to tolerate frustration and anxiety usually do not have sufficient strength to receive help from any type of hypnotherapy. Another common difficulty is the secondary gain value of the symptom to the psychoneurotic individual. All these difficulties have been discussed in this book.

DIFFICULTIES IN THE THERAPIST

In general, hypnotherapy should utilize the individual's own capacities to work out his problems. If the therapist assumes an authoritarian role, the patient will never become completely free from authority, nor will his character structure be changed. Therefore, throughout this volume, the use of autohypnosis and sensory-imagery conditioning has been stressed repeatedly. Every patient is informed that it is his problem, that he has "sales-talked himself into it, and, likewise, he can just as readily sales-talk himself out of his complaints." It is really remarkable how such a gross oversimplification can be highly motivating to the skeptical and resistant patient.

Often the therapist may set standards that are too high for the patient to fulfill; this only causes further depression and anxiety. By such an approach the therapist does not give the patient enough motivation to seek further assistance; this only mobilizes hostility and usually results in discontinuance of the therapy. Moreover, such a parental or authoritative approach never allows the individual to grow up and develop an acceptance of himself. He will remain dependent upon the therapist, requiring repeated reinforcement and support. If all these mechanisms are not understood, strong dependency always will be maintained.

It is surprising how minor factors may produce difficulties due to the therapist. The author recollects an interesting patient who had complained of menopausal symptoms of several years' duration. It is his custom after the third or fourth visit to call his patients by their first names. When this was done in her case, the patient broke off therapy, even though she was making good progress.

The commonest difficulty stemming from the therapist is his own countertransference feelings or the *way he feels about the patient and hypnotherapy.* If he feels some personal antagonism to the patient, he should not treat him. Or if he feels insecure with the method, he will, on the basis of subliminal cues, transmit his own insecurities to the patient. Such therapists will, as a result, see nothing but dangers, because hypnotherapy is, in reality, *dangerous for them!* Therefore, those therapists who think that hypnotherapy is fraught with dangers are undoubtedly transmitting their personal convictions.

In this chapter, the author has attempted to present briefly some of the reasons for failures with hypnotherapy. Usually, successful cases are stressed for teaching purposes. The hesitancy to present failures or unsuccessful cases is understandable, but these are equally valuable for instruction. Admission of failure is a sign of intellectual and emotional maturity. The author used to conduct a weekly class for postgraduate students which might well be called "My mistakes of the week clinic."

Hypnotherapy, while an ancient science, is still struggling against great handicaps because of irrational prejudice. The author has his share of failures and relapses following hypnotherapy. However, he generally attempts to analyze the reasons for them. He also is well aware that the placebo effect of any type of psychotherapy is over 60 per cent, and that many get better irrespective of the therapy. There are also spontaneous remissions. It is the author's hope that this chapter will contribute to a better understanding of the role that hypnosis plays in psychotherapy.

Also, it should be pointed out that one can overemphasize failures with hypnotherapy as well as sensationalize cures; neither should be told to patients. An increasing knowledge of its successful applications and the reasons for its failures eventually will accord this modality a secure position in medical practice and therapy.

In conclusion, it can be stated that the same measures may be utilized to avoid failures in hypnotherapy as in any other psychotherapeutic procedure. First, the nature of the patient's values as well as his motivation for recovery should be explored; next, the need for his symptoms in terms of their secondary gain value. Such information can usually be obtained in the one or more evaluation sessions before hypnotherapy is instituted or even attempted. To avoid failures, hypnosis should be used, in most instances, with reeducation, supportive and psychodynamic psychotherapy, behavior modification, group therapy, and other eclectic procedures, including drugs.

Index